Johann Peter Lange

The Gospel According To Mark

Johann Peter Lange

The Gospel According To Mark

ISBN/EAN: 9783741180774

Manufactured in Europe, USA, Canada, Australia, Japa

Cover: Foto ©Angelika Wolter / pixelio.de

Manufactured and distributed by brebook publishing software (www.brebook.com)

Johann Peter Lange

The Gospel According To Mark

THE GOSPEL

ACCORDING TO

MARK.

BY

JOHN PETER LANGE, D.D.,

PROFESSOR OF THEOLOGY AT THE UNIVERSITY OF BONN.

REVISED FROM THE EDINBURGH TRANSLATION, WITH ADDITIONS,

BY

WILLIAM G. T. SHEDD, D.D.,

PROFESSOR IN UNION THEOLOGICAL SEMINARY, NEW YORK.

FIRST EDITION.

NEW YORK:
CHARLES SCRIBNER & CO., 124 GRAND STREET.
1866.

ENTERED, according to Act of Congress, in the year 1866, by
CHARLES SCRIBNER,
In the Clerk's Office of the District Court of the United States for the Southern District of New York.

JOHN F. TROW & CO.
PRINTERS, STEREOTYPERS, AND ELECTROTYPERS,
50 Greene Street, New York.

II.

THE GOSPEL ACCORDING TO MARK;

BEING THAT OF THE NEW AND DIRECT MANIFESTATION OF CHRIST FROM HEAVEN, OF HIS ALL-CONQUERING DIVINE POWER, AND OF HIS DIVINE VICTORY.

(SYMBOLIZED BY THE LION.)

INTRODUCTION.

1. DISTINCTIVE CHARACTERISTICS OF THE SECOND GOSPEL.

THE Gospel by Mark, like that of Matthew, presents the *theocratic* side of the life and acts of Christ; while Luke and John bring out prominently their *universal bearing*, or application to mankind generally. On this common ground, however, it occupies a position distinct from that of Matthew. Matthew sets forth our Saviour as the New Testament King of the Jews, in whom the Old Testament has been completely and throughout fulfilled; Mark, on the other hand, exhibits Him in His independent Personality, as that new and absolute manifestation of the Deity in Israel which the whole Old Testament was designed only to pre-announce and make ready for. Matthew presents the history of the Lord as that of the true Prophet, Priest, and King, in His conflict with the spurious representations of these set up by traditionalism; while Mark shows how all the powers existing in the world, representing as they did the various phases of unbelief, rose in opposition to the Lord, and how all were vanquished by His absolute, victorious power. Hence, in the narrative of Matthew, the history of Jesus is presented as the summing up and culminating of the martyrdom of all the Old Testament worthies and prophets, as that deepest and fullest suffering which, through the Spirit of all grace, becomes and forms the expiatory service of the great High-Priest; in the Gospel of Mark, on the other hand, the element of victory and of triumph (Isa. ix.) appears, and is scarcely kept in the background, even amidst the scenes of intensest suffering. In the narrative of Matthew, Christ enters upon the scene in order to remove the conditions and limitations which had hitherto beset the course of history, and from His own infinite vantage-ground to transform it, and give it new direction; in the Gospel by Mark, the coming of Christ is presented as the absolute breaking up of the former state of things, by which the elements of the old broken world are reduced to subservient material out of which the new kingdom of salvation and of liberty is constructed. The first Evangelist delineates for us the life of Jesus in its theocratic aspect, and as bearing upon universal history; the second shows that, besides this human bearing, the life of Jesus, both in its nature and working, carries the direct impress of divinity. Thus the Gospel of history is followed by the history of the Gospel; the Gospel which details mighty suffering, by the Gospel which delineates mighty achievement; the Gospel which has appropriately been symbolized by the sacrificial bullock, by that to which even antiquity attached the symbol of the lion. (*See* the *Introduction to the New Testament*, p. 26.)

Hence, in tracing the Gospel history, Mark seems to have viewed his subject mainly in the light of that prophecy of the patriarch Jacob: "Judah is a young lion" (Gen. xlix. 9)—a prediction taken up once more by Hosea (xi. 10) and by Amos (i. 2), and swelling into a note of triumph in the last pages of Scripture (Rev. v. 8). Accordingly, although the great adversary of that Lion, even Satan himself, goeth about like a roaring lion (1 Pet. v. 8), he is not a lion in the genuine and spiritual sense. The simile applies only allegorically, in reference to his bold appearance in the open persecution of believers; in its higher symbolical meaning, that title belongs to the Lord Himself. In this respect, Peter has well described the agency of Christ (Acts x. 38) as "healing all that were oppressed of the devil." Mark delineates Christ as, from first to last, pre-eminently the victorious Conqueror of all Satanic powers. He has left us a record of the manifestation of Christ's power, when that great Lion seized upon the ancient world, and of His brief but decisive victory, after which only the ruins of the ancient world are left, which in turn furnish the materials for the new one.

This Gospel of the intrinsic power and life of Christ, in its original freshness, as it is reflected in the kindred soul of the Evangelist, possesses a great variety of distinguishing characteristics, both of a negative and positive kind. It is on the ground that it springs out into record from his own peculiar individual life, that we account for the conciseness of this the briefest of the Gospels, and not primarily on that of the historical occasion for its composition (Mark, one of Peter's Evangelists, relating the events of evangelical history by way of explaining his preaching). We can understand thus, why there is apparent in it no deliberate leisurely contemplation of things and events; why meditation gives place to rapid and picturesque description; why he omits the longer discourses of Jesus, and, when he does record any of His discourses, selects those burning words of controversy, denunciation, judgment, or triumph; why, occasionally, there is an indulgence in hasty, dashing expression (such as not to "put on two coats," ch. vi. 9); and towards the close he even breaks off abruptly and begins again (ch. xvi. 9); and why the arrangement of his material, though distinct, is so often obscured by the rapid succession of the great events described, that Papias suggested that Mark had not written in the order of succession, such as he conceived it to have been (οὐ τάξει, Euseb. iii. 39).

These negative traits owe their origin to the positive characteristics of this Gospel. The deeds of divine heroism which it describes, find, as it were, an appropriate body in peculiarities of expression, whether by an accumulation of strong negatives (οὐκέτι, οὐδείς) and by rapid transitions, or by rapid succession in the narrative. In fact, the word εὐθέως may be designated as the appropriate watch-word of our Gospel. While Matthew transports us gradually into the events of his time, as he relates what "came to pass in those days," the peculiar expression "immediately," "forthwith," "straightway," employed by Mark, hurries us from one event to another. So frequently, indeed, does the term occur, that ancient copyists not unfrequently questioned its authenticity, and in Codex D it is even omitted in several instances. (*See* CREDNER, *Introd.* i. p. 102.) It is this vividness of description also that leads to the frequent use of the present tense in the narrative (ch. i. 21, 40, &c.), and to the introduction of the very language used by individuals (ch. iv. 38, v. 8, &c.). On the same ground also, the identical Aramæan words are introduced which were employed in the actual occurrence (ch. iii. 17, 22, v. 41), and the new, customary, or popular expressions of the time are used (δηνάριον; κεντυρίων). But while the Evangelist rapidly sketches his great picture, he also greatly delights to dwell on those particular events which form its essential features. That enthusiasm and vividness of realization which account for the brevity, rapidity, and somewhat dramatic tone of the narrative, also explain the introduction of details which seem to give life to the scene. Thus we have certain graphic touches of description,—such as Christ being in the wilderness among wild beasts; the cursed fig-tree withering to the root; Jesus asleep on a pillow in the hinder part of the vessel while crossing the lake. Along with those lifelike touches of the historian's pencil, which appear in the delineation of that beautiful simile in ch. iv. 26, or in that of the gradual cure of the blind man in ch. viii. 22, we also find a freshness and accuracy of recollection, as in recalling, for example, the name of Bartimæus, the son of Timæus, the blind beggar on the road to Jericho, and a childlike affectionateness, leading to the frequent use of diminutive forms of expression, such as "little daughter," "little child," &c. Lastly, from the same causes there is a marked accuracy of details in reference to the persons introduced on the scene, the particulars of time and place, numbers, secondary circumstances, and other small points, more especially when the Evangelist describes the miraculous cures performed by the Lord. (*See* CREDNER, p. 103 *seq*.) Thus the second Gospel may be characterized as that of a rapt beholding of the Son of God manifesting His divine power by His divine working. The victorious work of Christ passes before us in a series of great life-pictures, rapidly succeeding each other. His mission of pardon and grace is accomplished in a few great stages, each the result of deepest energy and zeal, and the manifestation of His inmost life. It is as if the heavens were rent asunder, and were eternally pouring down their richest showers of blessing. Hence, also, both the attractive and the repelling influence of Christ are sharply and decisively set before us; the enmity of unbelievers rises immediately into mortal hatred, while the people, on the contrary, gather around Him in thronging crowds, bearing with them those who need His help. Sometimes there is not even room to stand, nor leisure so much as to eat. "Nay, His active love shines forth in such bright effulgence, and kindles such enthusiasm among the multitudes which surround Him, that on one occasion His kinsmen were about forcibly to remove Him from the throng, from an apprehension that He was beside Himself (ch. iii. 21). He produces the deepest impression on the people; they are filled with wonder, astonished beyond measure, and dismayed, wherever He makes His appearance to manifest His power and love." The effects produced correspond to the influence felt. "He healed many, insomuch that they rushed upon Him for to touch Him, as many as had plagues." Wherever His arrival is announced, the sick are brought from all the neighborhood, and laid in the street on their couches; and they beseech Him that they might touch if it were but the hem of His garment, "and as many as touched Him were made whole." Even His appearance among them causes the people to be greatly amazed, so that they tremble for joy and awe (ch. ix. 15). But every deed He performs is a victory over the hostile powers. Mark's Gospel is not so deeply pervaded by the anticipation of death as that of Matthew. Even of Christ's last words on the cross, only these are recorded: "My God, My God, why hast Thou forsaken Me?"—as if in this hour of agony, also, we were to hear only the Lion's cry of woe. In the same manner, in the history of the resurrection, only its astounding features are prominently brought forward. In their distress, the disciples believe not the tidings of His resurrection, whether from the lips of Mary Magdalene, or from those of the two disciples to whom He had appeared by the way. But as soon as Christ Himself appears among them, and upbraids them with their unbelief, they are completely changed; they are now ready to receive the commission to preach the Gospel to every creature. A continued manifestation of His power attends, after His resurrection and ascension, the messengers of Christ, and confirms the word. Thus characteristically closes the Gospel by Mark, even as, throughout his narrative, his eye was mainly fixed on those miraculous and healing manifestations of divine power by which the world was shaken and transformed. In this respect his narrative is unique; it exhibits the life of Christ as divine power pervading the world. Throughout, it presents the history of Christ as the working, manifestation, and influence of the God-man. From the pages of Mark we gather how, at the time, He touched every chord of feeling in the souls of the people—amazement, fear, confidence, hope, joy, and delight; and how He adapted His divine power to those varying states of emotion, whether by reproof, healing, or sanctification. The rapidity with which the Saviour achieved such immense results, the impetuous enthusiasm which characterizes that day's work in which He pervaded the world with the power and efficacy of His name, and the victorious strength with which He triumphed over the bondage of the world and the sorrows of the grave, and rose to His throne of glory, are here presented as the grand characteristics of the divine Redeemer, who accomplishes His work of redemption by a series of rapid victories. At the same time, this glorious life of work and victory is to serve as a symbol, in the light of which we are to view and to understand every deed wrought in the name of the Lord, every awakening and vivifying operation in hearts divinely moved, every triumph of christological power, every lion-like bound, shout, and victory of faith on earth,—in short, every outgoing of that eternal energy which proceeds from the throne of the Son of God. (*See* LANGE, *Life of Jesus*, i. p. 248.)

Another peculiarity of our Gospel deserves special mention. It will readily be noticed that the Evangelist lays emphasis on the periods of pause and rest which rhythmically intervene between the several great victories achieved by Christ. Each fresh advance, each new contest and victory, is preceded by a period of retirement. Thus, the Saviour, at the commencement of His work, leaves the obscure abode of His humiliation at Nazareth, that by humble submission to the baptism of John, He might insure His victorious progress. Thence He retires into the wilderness; again and again He repairs into the desert, to issue forth anew and to achieve ever larger conquests. Even His ascension is presented at the close of our Gospel under the peculiar aspect of Christ retiring in order to conquer, by His power and blessing, the whole world, through the instrumentality of His ambassadors. (*See* this feature fully brought out in Section 5.)

[To this sketching of LANGE may be added the remarks of a thoughtful English critic, which strikingly agree with it. "There are many, again, whose sympathies are entirely with the present, who delight in the activity and warmth of daily life, who are occupied with things around them, without looking far beyond their own age and circle. To them St. Mark addresses a brief and pregnant narrative of the ministry of Christ, unconnected with any special recital of His birth and preparation for His work, and unconnected, at least in its present shape, with the mysterious history of the Ascension. . . . It seems natural to find in St. Mark a characteristic fitness for his special work. One whose course appears to have been marked throughout by a restless and impetuous energy was not unsuited for tracing the life of the Lord, in the fresh vigor of its outward power. The friend alike of St. Paul and St. Peter, working in turn in each of the great centres of the Jewish world, at first timidly sensitive of danger, and afterwards a comforter of an imprisoned apostle, himself 'of the circumcision,' and yet writing to Gentiles, St. Mark stands out as one whom the facts of the Gospel had moved by their simple force to look over and beyond varieties of doctrine in the vivid realization of the actions of the 'Son of God.' For him teaching was subordinate to action; and every trait which St. Peter preserved in his narrative would find a faithful recorder in one equally suited to apprehend and to treasure it." WESTCOTT, *Study of the Gospels*, pp. 205, 213, 214.—*Ed.*]

§ 2. HISTORY OF MARK THE EVANGELIST.

In the Book of Acts, the writer of our Gospel is first designated as John Mark (ch. xii. 12, 25), then as John (ch. xiii. 5, 13), and lastly as Mark (ch. xv. 39). Comp. Col. iv. 10; 2 Tim. iv. 11; Philem. 24. Originally he seems to have borne the Jewish name of John; but it must not be imagined that on entering upon the duties of an Evangelist, he arbitrarily adopted the Roman name of Mark. His familiarity with the Latin, which may be gathered from the circumstance that he afterwards became "the interpreter of Peter" (his ἑρμηνευτής, according to Papias in Euseb. iii. 39, Iren. iii. 1 *et alia;* also Tertullian, Jerome), may have been due to some connection between his family and Italy. His father, or some other of his relatives, may have been a proselyte from Rome; or else a wealthy family like that of Mark may have had other reasons for giving him, along with the Hebrew, a Roman name. Certain it is that, in his capacity of companion to the Apostles, he is generally designated Mark, just as Saul took the name of Paul when engaged in his great work. Later ecclesiastical tradition has in the present, as in other instances, availed itself of this circumstance to transform our Evangelist into two or three saints. The Evangelist Mark was represented as being a different personage from John Mark; and again, these two as distinct from the relative of Barnabas (compare the art. *Mark* in WINER, *Real Encycl.*). Among later divines, Grotius, Calovius, and Schleiermacher (*Stud. u. Krit.* for 1832), and still more recently Kienlen (*Stud. u. Krit.* for 1843, p. 423), have endeavored, though unsuccessfully, to maintain the existence of two biblical personages of the name of

§ 2. HISTORY OF MARK THE EVANGELIST.

Mark,—the one a companion of Peter, the other of Paul. The fact that Mark acted as Evangelist alternately in connection with Paul and with Peter, is readily accounted for, both from the vitality and mobility of his temperament and character, and from the mutual understanding and accord between the two Apostles themselves. Nor is there more solid reason for including Mark among the seventy disciples,—upon the conjecture that he was one of those who were offended by the saying of Christ, about the necessity of eating His flesh and drinking His blood (John vi. 53, 60), but was afterwards restored through the admonitions of Peter. Stronger probability attaches to the supposition that Mark himself was the young man, of whom he relates in his Gospel (ch. xiv. 51), that on the night of the Lord's betrayal he followed Him clothed in a light night-dress, which he left in the hands of the officers when he fled from them (Comp. OLSHAUSEN, LANGE, *Life of Jesus*, i. p. 245, and our comment on this passage). From the Book of Acts, we gather that the mother of Mark was a wealthy proprietress; and the supposition does not appear far-fetched, that she may have owned a country-house in the valley of the Kidron, at the foot of the Mount of Olives,—perhaps even the garden of Gethsemane. At any rate, there is a striking resemblance between the character of that young man and the life of Mark, in whose quick and ardent, but mobile and inconstant disposition sin required to be specially met and conquered by sovereign grace. Thus we find that, while Mark boldly accompanied Paul on his first missionary journey, he suddenly forsook him, but afterwards again recovered himself, and offered his services in other expeditions of the same kind. For further particulars respecting the young man mentioned in ch. xiv. 51, *see* the Notes below.

As already noticed, Mark was the son of an influential Christian matron of Jerusalem, called Mary, in whose house the disciples were wont to meet for united worship, according to the custom of those days (Acts xii. 12). Mary had wholly devoted herself to the cause and service of Christ; for at a time when James the Elder had just fallen by the sword of Herod Agrippa, and Peter lay in prison awaiting a doom from which he was only delivered by a miracle, she risked her all by converting her house, so to speak, into the principal church of Jerusalem. Indeed, so well was this understood, that after his miraculous liberation from prison, Peter at once directed his steps to her house, as the great centre and meeting-place of the disciples. The son of such a woman—a worthy companion of the other heroic Maries of the Gospels—could not but be early acquainted with the blessed truths of Christianity. From the expression in 1 Pet. v. 13 (υἱός μου), it has been inferred that the Apostle Peter had been the instrument of his conversion. That his religious convictions, however, depended not on those of any man in particular, is evidenced by the fact, that his peculiar relation towards Peter did not prevent him from joining Paul and Barnabas on their return from Jerusalem to Antioch, probably with a view to that missionary tour on which he afterwards accompanied them in the capacity of an evangelist or minister (ὑπηρέτης, Acts xiii. 5). But this step was probably taken, mainly at the suggestion of his uncle Barnabas (Mark was ἀνεψιός to Barnabas, Col. iv. 10). We are not informed on what ground our Evangelist deserted the mission at Perga in Pamphylia, and returned to Jerusalem. Luke is silent on the point; although Paul regarded the conduct as so blameworthy, that when he and Barnabas resolved to undertake a second missionary tour (Acts xv. 36), he firmly refused to accept the proffered assistance of Mark (Acts xv. 38). Nay, of such importance did he deem the matter, that, when Barnabas insisted on allowing his nephew to accompany them, Paul, rather than yield, separated from his old companion, and that, too, although he was in many respects under considerable obligations to one who, under the influence of that love which thinketh no evil, had first introduced him to the Apostles at Jerusalem, and afterwards, with an unselfishness truly Christian, had brought him to Antioch, to share in the work going on in that city. We cannot doubt that Barnabas had spiritual grounds for his conduct in reference to Mark, beyond a mere natural feeling for his young relative, and that large-hearted charity of which he otherwise had given proof (*See* Acts iv. 36). Still, it may be supposed that the well-merited reproof administered by Paul, proved of greater use to Mark in after-life than the apology offered for him by Barnabas. It is just possible that, at the time, some of the views on which Paul acted in his missionary labors had appeared too liberal to the young convert from Jerusalem. Even Barnabas does not seem to have always felt equally confident on the subject (Gal. ii.). Suffice it that the presence of Mark was the occasion of "sharp contention" and separation between the two missionaries, who now took up different fields of labor. Paul went from Syria directly to Cilicia; while Barnabas took ship for Cyprus, his native island, where also, on his first journey, he had commenced a mission. It deserves special notice, that while Paul was in the habit of commencing a missionary tour by revisiting the place where on a former occasion he had first labored, he this time ceded it to Barnabas. It is on this occasion, that Luke for the first time designates our Evangelist simply by the name of Mark (Acts xv. 39). But the spirit of apostolic peace soon overcame the temporary misunderstanding and disagreement. Hence, we afterwards find Mark among the assistants of Paul during the time of his first captivity at Rome (Col. iv. 10; Philem. 24), *i. e.*, about the year 62. At a somewhat later period, however, he seems to have been with Peter at Babylon (1 Pet. v. 13), whence the Apostle, addressing the disciples in Asia Minor, sends salutations from Marcus his son. For we regard the following as settled points: First, that Babylon means the place of that name, and not Rome, as it could have served no rational purpose to conceal the name of a place under a mystical title, which might so readily be misunderstood; secondly, that the First Epistle of Peter bears evident marks of having been composed at the time when the persecution of Christians throughout the Roman Empire was just beginning, and the Jews were preparing for their last great war of nationality, *i. e.*, some time after the year 62. But as, during his second captivity, Paul charged Timothy (2 Tim. iv. 11) to bring Mark with him to Rome (probably from Asia Minor), the supposition is probable, that our Evangelist was at the time returning from Babylon. It is easily supposable, that in those great and portentous days—when, in rapid succession, the Epistle of James, that to the Hebrews, and the First Epistle of Peter were addressed to Jewish Christians, with the view of warning them against the danger of apostasy, and of entreating them to bear with patience the trials and sufferings which were approaching—Mark had been employed as the medium of special communication between Paul and Peter. At any rate, there is nothing strange in an interchange of service in the common work of the Lord, just as Silas was both a companion of Paul, and also engaged with Peter in the work of the Lord. Such special missions would be peculiarly in consonance with the bold and valiant character of Mark; and hence, we do not wonder to find him ranged by the side of the chief Apostles, like a young lion, at the most dangerous points of attack, now at Babylon, and now again at Rome. But from this commission of Paul to Timothy, it does not necessarily follow that the latter was in circumstances to obey it. In all probability, Peter arrived at Rome about the same time as Mark; as there is sufficient evidence of the fact, that Peter suffered martyrdom at Rome along with Paul, about the year 68. This fact, again, is the foundation for the other statements of antiquity (Papias in Euseb. iii. 39; Iren. iii. 1, and others), to the effect, that Mark acted as interpreter (ἑρμηνευτής) to Peter. Nor is it necessary to suppose, with Kuinoel, that, according to this statement, Mark translated into Greek what Peter spoke in Aramæan; nor, with Meyer (who quotes from Jerome a statement evidently marked with a dogmatic bias), that the expression Hermeneutes merely meant a secretary, whose duty it was to put on paper the oral communications of the Apostle (Comp. MEYER, *Introd. to the Gospel of Mark*, p. 2). It is evident that Mark, who was familiar with the manners and language of Rome, could render important assistance to Peter in Italy, as "interpreter" in the strictest sense, and that too, notwithstanding the apostolic gift of tongues. It is also sufficiently well attested (Euseb. vi. 14; Clemens Alex. *Hypot.* 6) that Mark was with Peter at Rome,—a statement wholly unconnected with the ecclesiastical hypothesis, according to which the Babylon of 1 Pet. v. 13 means the city of Rome (Euseb. ii. 15; Hieron. *Vir. Ill.* 8). The Gospel of Mark presents evidence of a protracted intercourse with Peter, as plainly as that of Luke shows that this Evangelist must have enjoyed continued intercourse with Paul. It is indeed true, that the New Testament idea of the kingdom of God is not so fully developed in the Gospel of Mark as in the Epistles of Peter; yet the narrative of the Evangelist presents Christ chiefly as the Lord of that kingdom, and as the conqueror of Satan and his legions,—and that in so marked a manner, as if the sacred historian had adopted for his motto the testimony of Peter, Acts x. 28. Similarly, also,

Irenæus (iii. 1; comp. Eusebius v. 8) records that, after the death of the Apostles Paul and Peter at Rome, Mark, as the disciple and interpreter of Peter, wrote down the statements of that Apostle. According to the testimony of Clemens Alexandrinus (*Hypot.* 6; *see* Euseb. vi. 14), Mark composed his Gospel during the lifetime of Peter, in accordance with the request of that Apostle's converts, and Peter, who was cognizant of the fact, did not interpose in the matter. (For other similar testimonies, *see* CREDNER, p. 113.) In that case, we must, of course, not confound the first draft with the final revision of the work. According to the unanimous testimony of antiquity, Mark went, after the death of Peter, to Alexandria, where he founded a Christian church (Euseb. iii. 39), became its first bishop, and suffered martyrdom (Epiphan. *Hæres.* li. 6; Euseb. ii. 16; Hieron. *Vir. Illust.* ii. 8, and others). The city of Venice, it is well known, has selected St. Mark as its patron-saint, and consecrated the renowned church of St. Mark to his name.

There is an entire correspondence between the character of Mark, and that of his Gospel. And this is another evidence of the fact, that the human form and aspect of a Gospel depended on the individuality of the Evangelist, and on the point of view which he took, deciding him in selecting, arranging, and presenting the historical material at his command. It may yet require some time before views like these will prevail in the schools, and the common error be discarded, that the auxiliaries and aids which the writer had enjoyed were the main thing, and the mental characteristics of the historian only secondary, if, indeed, at all to be taken into account. Mark the Evangelist, ardent and energetic (a kindred companion to Peter), kindly, warm-hearted, and affectionate (a nephew of Barnabas, in the spiritual sense also), liberal and original in his views (a friend of Paul), was called by the Lord to transmit unto the Church a Gospel, in which it is shown how the Lion of the tribe of Judah became the Lamb of God, and how all human heroism finds both its harmony and transfiguration in the glorious achievements and conquests of the God-man. Thus the Gospel of actual personal suffering, follows that of history and of historical suffering. [Lange's thought seems to be, that Mark represents the God-man in his concrete and actual personality, almighty both in his miracles and his passion, while Matthew presents him more as an object of prophecy.—*Ed.*]

§ 3. COMPOSITION AND INTEGRITY OF THE GOSPEL.

The oldest testimony as to the origin of the second Gospel is that of Papias, Bishop of Hierapolis, dating from the first half of the second century, and communicated by Eusebius (*Hist. Eccles.* iii. 39): "Mark, being the interpreter * of Peter, wrote down with great accuracy whatever he interpreted (in other words, what Peter stated), though he recorded not in the order (οὐ μέντοι τάξει) in which it was spoken or done by the Lord (*i. e.*, as Matthew, who arranged and combined together the sayings and the history of the Saviour); for he neither heard nor followed our Lord (as His disciple), but, as before said, he was afterwards the companion of Peter, who arranged his instructions as was necessary (for popular teaching *i. e.*), but did not give a history of our Lord's discourses (which was one of Matthew's main objects). Wherefore Mark has not erred in any way by writing some things as he remembered them. For he was careful of one thing, not to omit anything of what he had heard, or to falsify (or add) anything in these accounts." It appears to us, that in his excessive anxiety to vindicate the apostolic authority of this Gospel, Papias has represented the undoubted fact of a connection between Mark and Peter, as if the Evangelist had been merely the penman of the Apostle. Hence the other ancient testimony, derived by Clement of Alexandria from primitive tradition, and recorded in extracts from the Hypotyposes (in Euseb. vi. 14), must be regarded as supplementary of this account. According to the statement of Clement, a great number of those who had heard Peter proclaiming the word of God at Rome requested Mark, who had followed the Apostle for a long time, and well remembered what he had said, to reduce to writing what the Apostle had declared. It is added that Peter was cognizant of this, and

---

* [Lange translates by the word *gedolmetscht.* The original is ἑρμηνευτής, and denotes what Peter related from memory.—*Ed.*]

encouraged it (the work as a whole); while, at the same time, he abstained from all active interference, either in the way of directing or restraining (in its individual parts). We leave it to others to translate the passage so as to mean that he neither hindered nor encouraged (προτρεπτικῶς) the matter. His encouragement of the work as a whole (προτρεπτικῶς) consisted in this, that he did not find it necessary to omit anything from, or to add unto, its individual portions. It was the approbation of a work bearing evidence of independent authorship. This view of the passage agrees with the earlier account in Eusebius (ii. 15). In both cases, the ostensible reason assigned for the work is the same. We are told that Peter was cognizant of the fact that Mark had composed the Gospel by the revelation of the Holy Spirit, and that he rejoiced in the zeal of those who solicited the Gospel; finally, that he gave his authority to the work in order that it might be read in the churches. On these grounds the earlier Fathers were warranted in designating our Gospel as that of Peter, so far as its substance is concerned, without thereby invalidating the originality of Mark, so far as the style and arrangement of material are concerned. (Justin, c. Tryph.: τὰ ἀπομνημονεύματα Πέτρου; Tertull. c. Marc. 4, 5: "Marcus, quod edidit Evangelium Petri adfirmetur, cujus interpres Marcus"; Euseb. ii. 15; Hieronym. Vir. Ill. 8.)

A very slight examination will suffice to convince the student, that in the third Gospel the distinctive mental characteristics of Luke coincided with the views of the Apostle Paul, and exactly met the wants of well-educated Grecian inquirers and converts. Similarly, in our Gospel we note how the mental characteristics of Mark corresponded with the manner in which Peter presented the truth, while at the same time they also harmonized with the wants of Roman Christians, and were peculiarly suited to the popular mind in the capital. This fact, along with the special occasion for the composition of the Gospel, must be regarded as giving its tone to the narrative. But before proceeding to consider this factor, we must refer to, and refute, some of the more popular theories on the subject. These are: 1. Mark was merely a compiler, who derived his Gospel from those of Matthew and of Luke, if not from the former alone. 2. The Gospel of Mark was the original record from which the other two were copied. 3. The Gospel of Mark and those of the other two Evangelists were equally derived from a primitive Gospel or tradition. 4. The Gospel of Mark was written for a special purpose (*Tendenzschrift*). Lastly, 5. The special notion of those who carry their views of inspiration so far as to ignore throughout Scripture, and in our Gospel also, all human individuality.—The first of these views was propounded in its most extreme form,— viz., that Mark was merely the *pedisequus et breviator* of Matthew,— by Augustine, *De consensu Evang.* 1, 2, and after him by Euthym. Zigadenus and Michaelis. In a less extreme manner, Michaelis, Griesbach, Saunier (*On the sources of the Gospel of Mark*, 1825), Theile, Strauss, Von Ammon, and others, maintain that our Evangelist made use of Matthew and Luke. To this we reply, 1st, That Mark introduces a number of things not mentioned at all in the other Gospels (ch. iii. 20, 21, iv. 26-29, vii. 31-37, viii. 22-26, ix. 11-14, xiv. 51, 52, xvi. 9-11); and that he is marked by a peculiar way of presenting matter which he has in common with the others (ch. i. 42, v. 4, 5, vii. 3, 4, ix. 21-26, x. 24, 34, 49, xii. 32-34). 2. The Gospel of Mark commences and closes in an independent manner, and the material which it has in common with Matthew and Luke (39 sections), with Matthew alone (23 sections), or with Luke alone (18 sections), is presented in an independent form. Hence, these critics felt it necessary to modify the original hypothesis of Augustine as stated above.—The second hypothesis, that the Gospel of Mark contains the original and primitive record from which the other narratives were derived, was first propounded by Herder, and adopted by Storr, Wilke, Weisse, Reuss, and Ewald. Of late, critics have even gone further, and assigned to our Evangelist the authorship of the Book of Revelation (Hitzig, *On John Mark; or, which John was the author of the Book of Revelation?* Zürich, 1843). But it is evident that the other two Evangelists furnish too many details of their own—such as the history of Christ's infancy, the longer discourses of Jesus, &c.,— to warrant us in supposing that their narrative was derived from Mark. Add to this the consideration, that they also have their peculiar manner of presenting and arranging the evangelical history.—The third hypothesis, of the existence of some primitive Gospel, from which the canonical Gospels were derived, may now be regarded as finally discarded. The Aramæan Matthew, to which Papias refers, could not have been that primitive Gospel, as Corrodi and others suggest (*see* EBRARD, *Evangelien Kritik*, p. 5), since our first Gospel is itself a Greek version of it. The same objection applies to the Gospel of the Hebrews (Niemeyer and others), which was merely a Judæo-Christian and interpolated edition of Matthew; while the hypothesis of Herder and of Eichhorn, of an original Gospel now wholly lost, is evidently a baseless fiction. Greater importance attaches to the supposition of the existence of an original evangelical *oral tradition*, which, in some considerable degree, became fixed in a written form (Eckermann, Gieseler). Nor is it a sufficient objection to this hypothesis, that the Apostles at an early period became separated from each other; for each original witness told and retold the evangelical narrative of and by himself. There was a mutual and unceasing narration of the same history. Moreover, we gather from Luke i. 1, that at a very early period there existed individual sketches, memorabilia, relating to events in the history of our Lord. It will be readily understood how witnesses of such events would feel constrained to write down these glorious facts; nor is it improbable that such narratives may have been disseminated, until they were incorporated into, or superseded by, the four Gospels. But this hypothesis of an original Gospel must be modified in its application, in three respects: 1. The first, second, and fourth Gospels are evidently derived from the personal recollection of the Apostles; and the third Gospel, at least indirectly. 2. The unique style of the Gospels, their peculiar apostolic simplicity, could have been produced only by the continuous influence of the apostolic spirit. 3. So far as the form is concerned, the mental individuality of the Evangelists constituted a most important element in shaping the historical materials at their command.—In reply to the fourth hypothesis, defended by Baur, Schwegler, Köstlin, and others, that the Gospel of Mark was written with a special object, it is sufficient to say, that this has fallen to the ground along with the peculiar notions about Ebionism upon which it was reared. The main source whence the Gospel narratives were derived was the vivid recollection of the Apostles, deepened, strengthened, and purified by the Spirit of God. Thus Mark depended on the narrative of Peter, which shaped itself in accordance with the peculiar point from which that Apostle viewed the facts of the Gospel. As a secondary source of information, our Evangelist, no doubt, drew from that general evangelical tradition, which had in particular instances been chronicled by eye-witnesses. As to the origin of this tradition, it is of great importance to bear in mind, that both the evangelical narratives themselves, and the peculiar form in which they were couched, originated in evangelical faith and feeling, and that their integrity, affectionateness, and simplicity were due to the inspiration of these writers. Thus, our Evangelist drew his materials from subjective recollection (on the part of Peter), which in turn rested on the more general basis of objective recollection (in apostolic tradition). This material took form in agreement with his particular charisma; *i. e.*, objectively under the influence of inspiration by the Spirit, and subjectively under that of his mental idiosyncrasy.

According to the statement of Irenæus (iii. 1), Mark published his Gospel after the death of Peter and Paul (ἔξοδον, not their departure, as Mill, Grabe, Ebrard, and others render it). There is no contradiction between this and the statement of Clement of Alexandria, to the effect that this narrative had been composed during the lifetime of Peter, as Irenæus refers not to the commencement, but to the close of its composition. For the purpose of introducing the apocryphal story of the victory of Peter over Simon Magus at Rome, Eusebius has fixed the time of the Apostle's stay in the capital in the third year of the Emperor Claudius (A. D. 43), evidently post-dating it. The publication of Mark's Gospel must have taken place between the year 68 and 70. That it was written prior to the destruction of Jerusalem, we gather from the circumstance that in ch. xiii. the Evangelist relates the prediction of that event without referring to its fulfilment. Hence it must have been composed about the same time as that by Matthew and probably that by John; the Gospel of Luke having been published several years earlier.

According to the testimony of Clement, Eusebius, Jerome, and others, the Gospel of Mark was composed at Rome—a tradition which is credited by most modern theologians. Richard

Simon and others, on the strength of a statement by Chrysostom that Mark's Gospel was written at Alexandria, have conjectured that it existed in a twofold recension. A comparison of the notice in ch. xv. 21 with Acts xi. 20, led Storr to adopt the untenable hypothesis that it was composed in Antioch.

As our Gospel was, in the first place, intended for Roman-Christians, it naturally addressed itself mainly to such as had formerly been Gentiles. Still, it cannot be inferred, from the total absence of Old Testament proof passages (with one or two exceptions), that it was exclusively designed for Gentile Christians (Meyer). We have already seen that it is one of the characteristics of Mark, to evince Christ to be the Son of God by His immediate divine working. That Mark introduces no Judaizing elements (Köstlin), is a trait which he has in common with all the New Testament writers. On the other hand, it cannot be doubted that, when the ardent Evangelist found himself addressing Latin readers, this may have influenced his style, as in the choice of Latin expressions (ch. vi. 27, vii. 4, 8, xv. 39, 44), in giving explanation (ch. xii. 42, xv. 16), and in making certain additions (ch. x. 12, xv. 21).

There is the strongest historical evidence in favor of the genuineness of Mark. Besides the general ecclesiastical testimonies, commencing with Justin Martyr's Memorabilia and Tatian's Diatessaron, and those of Irenæus, Clement, and Tertullian, we have a sufficiently clear quotation in Justin and the primitive testimony of Papias in his favor, as in that of Matthew. But, just as the testimony of Papias in favor of Matthew has been turned against him by putting a peculiar meaning upon the words τὰ λόγια,* so in the present instance also it has been sought to invalidate the evidence in favor of our Gospel by an appeal to the expression οὐ τάξει, used by Papias. This view was first propounded by Schleiermacher in the *Studien und Kritiken* (1832), and for a time adopted by Credner, although that writer has since discarded this interpretation. The criticism of Schleiermacher was based on the ungrounded hypothesis, that Mark's Gospel was written in chronological order. Meyer refers the expression οὐ τάξει to the first outlines of notices which Mark had made after hearing the discourses of Peter, and which were afterwards revised and arranged. In our opinion, the language of Papias refers more particularly to the contrast between the Gospel of Mark and the careful arrangement adopted by Matthew (of whom he had previously spoken), especially in recording the Lord's discourses. Baur, as might be expected, supposes that the original Gospel of Mark was a work similar in character to the Clementines; Köstlin speaks of an original Gospel by Peter; while other writers indulge in similar fancies. In support of such freaks of critical imagination, each of these critics appeals to the οὐ τάξει of Papias, no matter whether it was originally well or ill founded, or is at present properly or improperly interpreted. Others, such as De Wette, have cast doubts upon the testimony of Papias, in order thus to invalidate the authenticity of Mark. According to Ewald, there were many recensions of Mark, which underwent different variations. All these suggestions are sufficiently refuted by a proper appreciation of the internal testimony of Mark's Gospel itself concerning its authorship.

The conclusion of ch. xvi. 9-20 has given rise to critical difficulties and doubts, which are better founded than any of those above referred to. Eusebius did not admit the authenticity of this passage (ad Marin. Quaestio I.), remarking, that in almost all manuscripts Mark's Gospel closed with a description of the flight of the women from the sepulchre. Jerome (though not uniformly), Gregory of Nyssa, and Euth. Zigabenus make the same statement. Besides, the passage is wanting in the Vatican codex B.; † and the Syriac Philoxeniana adds, that the close of the Gospel was different in other codices. Credner points out certain divergences in this paragraph from the ordinary modes of expression employed in this Gospel. He asserts that, while the distinctive characteristics of Mark are wanting in this passage, others not found throughout his Gospel may be traced there. Among the latter, are such expressions as πᾶσα κτίσις, γλώσσαις καιναῖς λαλεῖν, etc.

On the other hand, it should be noticed: 1. That Irenæus (adv. Hæres. iii. 10, 6) was acquainted with the present conclusion of our Gospel, as appears from the following passage:

---

* See LANGE, on *Matthew*, p. 42; [FISHER: *Essays on the Supernatural Origin of Christianity*. Scribner, New York, 1866.)
† [Also in *Codex Sinaiticus.—Ed.*]

§ 3. COMPOSITION AND INTEGRITY OF THE GOSPEL.

In fine autem Evangelii ait Marcus (xvi. 19): *Et quidem dominus Jesus, postquam locutus est eis, receptus est in cœlos et sedet ad dexteram Dei.* Considering how much older and more important the testimony of Irenæus is than that of Eusebius, we are naturally led to suppose it more likely that our present conclusion of the Gospel was originally found in all manuscripts, but was afterwards left out from ecclesiastical prejudices (because the Apostles were reproved in it, etc.), than that it was afterwards added. 2. In opposition to those codices in which this portion was wanting, we have the evidence of other codices in which it existed. 3. While the fact that minor characteristics of Mark—such as the expressions εὐθέως, πάλιν—are wanting in this section, is prominently brought forward by opponents, the leading features of the passage are overlooked. But these are quite characteristic of our Evangelist, and show the conclusion of his Gospel to be quite in unison with the total narrative itself. Among these we reckon the fundamental idea of the section, that the risen Saviour overcame the unbelief of His disciples, and the promise of the Lord, that those who believed on Him should triumph over devils and serpents, and over the powers of death. The form and contents of the section, also, correspond with the idea of the Gospel generally. The strong expression, "*Preach the Gospel to every creature*," is in keeping with the statement at the beginning of the Gospel, "*Jesus was with the wild beasts;*" as are also the closing words, "*The Lord confirming the word with signs following.*" Add to this, that the Gospel could not have closed with verse 8, without being fragmentary. Still, we cannot ignore the fact, that at an early period the Gospel of Mark seems to have existed in twofold recension or form. This we have, in another place (LANGE, *Leben Jesu*, i. 166) explained by the supposition that an incomplete work of the Evangelist may have circulated among the Christian public before our present and complete Gospel. A certain degree of probability attaches to this hypothesis from the circumstance, which the Fathers record, that the Roman Christians were very anxious to obtain Mark's Gospel. "This rapid compilation and publication, followed by delay and hesitation in view of new materials, and, lastly, the final completion of the work, are so many traits in accordance with the general character of Mark, as it is otherwise known to us." Nor should it be forgotten that, as hierarchical views gradually spread in the Church after the third century, the fragment in question may have excited greater interest from the fact that the Apostles had been presented by Mark in an unfavorable light in his narrative of the resurrection. Considerations like these may have weighed with such men as Eusebius. Thus, it would almost seem as if the very characteristics of the Evangelist, appearing in the passage, had given rise to the doubts about its authenticity. In this paragraph, as in his Gospel generally, Mark seems mainly bent upon presenting the risen Saviour in the full majesty of His power, as He transforms, by one stroke, the remaining unbelief of His followers into a faith that overcomes the world.—The authenticity of this section has been impugned by Michaelis, Griesbach, Credner, Ewald, Hitzig (who, however, ascribes its composition to Luke), and many others; among them Meyer, who designates the passage as an "apocryphal fragment." Its authenticity is defended by Richard Simon, Wolf, Bengel, Kuinoel, Hug, Guerike, and others.

In consequence of the supposition that Mark had composed his Gospel at Rome, and for Romans, the idea was broached in the Syrian Church, that he had originally written it in Latin. Hence the subscription of the old Syriac Peshito runs in these words: Completion of the Holy Gospel, the announcement of Mark; which he uttered and proclaimed at Rome. This view reappears in the Philoxeniana and some Greek manuscripts. Baronius availed himself of it in his Annals (ad ann. 45), for the purpose of adding to the authority of the Vulgate, and he was followed by others. Since the time of Richard Simon, however, the hypothesis has been abandoned, even by Romanist writers. A supposed Latin autograph of Mark's Gospel at Venice has been found to be a fragment of the Vulgate. The older Fathers partly imply, and partly expressly state, that Mark wrote in Greek.

§ 4. THEOLOGICAL AND HOMILETICAL WORKS ON THIS GOSPEL.

For those exegetical and homiletical works which treat of the Gospel of Mark along with other smaller or larger sections of the New Testament, we refer the reader to the General Introduction, and the remarks prefatory to the Gospel by Matthew.* To the writings there enumerated, we would add, the *Commentary on the Scriptures of the Old and New Testament*, by Drs. VAL. LOCH and W. REISCHL (Roman Catholic), Regensb., 1827; and *Luther's Exposition of the Gospels*, edited by EBERLE, Stuttg., 1857. Besides these, we would mention BESSER's *Bible-Hours* (*Bibel-Stunden*) HARMS' and JOSEPHSON's works on the *Sermon on the Mount*. For the older commentaries on the Gospel by Mark, *see* LILIENTHAL's *Evangelium secundum Marcum;* DANZ's *Universal-Wörterbuch*, Art. *Markus;* and WINER's *Handbuch*, i. 247. ROLLE, J. B. KOPPE, and WILKE, have written in defence of the originality of Mark's Gospel; while the opposite view, that he was dependent upon Matthew, has been maintained chiefly by GRIESBACH and H. SAUNIER. Compare also the works of KNOBEL, HITZIG, BAUR, and others. Of homiletical works, we specially mention those by SCHLEIERMACHER (Berlin, 1835), C. BRIEGER (Berlin, 1856), and W. L. BAUER (Dillenb. 1859).

§ 5. FUNDAMENTAL IDEA AND ARRANGEMENT OF THE GOSPEL ACCORDING TO MARK.

We find the motto of this Gospel in the declaration of Peter in Acts x. 38,—"Jesus of Nazareth, anointed by God with the Holy Ghost and with power, who went about doing good, and healing all that were oppressed of the devil, for God was with Him."

Jesus, the mighty God (אֵל גִּבּוֹר, Isa. ix. 6), who broke through all fetters and bonds, appeared as a Divine Person, both in His origin, mission and preparation, and as Prince of the kingdom of heaven engaging in warfare with, and achieving the victory over, Satan and his powers. Throughout, the narrative presents to view a continuous series of victorious onslaughts, like the leaps of a lion, followed by withdrawals on the part of Christ. Each victory is succeeded by a withdrawal with the acquired booty, which serves as preparation for fresh progress. The ascension of the Lord forms His last withdrawal, which is to be followed by His final onset and absolute victory.

Part First.

Grand preparation. Royal appearance of Jesus *by the side of* John the Baptist. First manifestation, when He quits the retirement of His humiliation at Nazareth, and first withdrawal.—In principle and germ all the succeeding contests are now decided. (Ch. i. 1-13.)

1st Section.—John (vers. 1-8).
2d Section.—Christ (vers. 9-13).

Part Second.

Royal appearance of Christ *after* the Baptist. His conflicts and victories in Galilee, in the old Jewish Church. (Ch. i. 14-ix. 50.)

1st Section.—Announcement of the kingdom of heaven (ch. i. 14, 15).
2d Section.—Conquest of the first disciples at Capernaum, victory over the demons in that city, and withdrawal into the wilderness (vers. 16-35).
3d Section.—Conquest of disciples in Galilee, victory over the demons in the country, and withdrawal into the wilderness (vers. 36-45).
4th Section.—Attracting and repelling influence of the Lord. The multitude filled with enthusiasm; the traditionalists offended. Conflicts with the powers of evil under the form of traditionalism. Hardening, and mortal hatred of the hostile party, and withdrawal of

---
* LANGE, on *Matthew*, pp. 19, 42, 43.

Jesus into a ship. (The preaching in synagogues gives place to that on the sea-shore.) (Ch. ii. 1–iii. 12.)

5th Section.—Conflict of Jesus with the unbelief of His countrymen, and withdrawal into the villages (ch. iii. 13–vi. 6).

6th Section.—Conflict between Jesus and the hostility of Herod. Calling and mission of the Apostles. Beheading of John, and withdrawal into the wilderness on the other side of the lake (vers. 7–45).

7th Section.—Contest between Jesus and the scribes of Jerusalem, and withdrawal into the Pagan country about Tyre, and into the region of Decapolis (ch. vi. 46–viii. 9).

8th Section.—Decisive conflict between Jesus and the Pharisees in Galilee, and withdrawal to the mountains east of the lake. The preparation for the new Church (ch. viii. 10–ix. 29).

9th Section.—Retirement of Jesus in Galilee, preparatory to His journey to Peræa and Jerusalem. Further preparation for the new Church (vers. 30–50).

Part Third.

Conflicts and victories of the Lord in Peræa. Transition from the old to the new Church. Withdrawal of the Lord for the purpose of collecting the disciples for His last journey. (Ch. x. 1–34.)

1st Section.—Carnal views of the Pharisees, and spiritual law of the Lord, concerning marriage.

2d Section.—Rabbinical notions of the disciples, and theocratic and New Testament arrangements of the Lord (vers. 13–16).

3d Section.—Temporal riches of the world, and poverty of believers (vers. 17–31).

4th Section.—Solemn gathering of the disciples on the road to impending sufferings (vers. 32–34).

Part Fourth.

Conflicts and victories of the Lord in Judæa. Christ founding the new Church. (Ch. x. 35–xv. 47.)

1st Section.—The departure and the triumphal entry of Jesus into Jerusalem (ch. x. 35–xi. 26).

2d Section.—Decisive conflict of Jesus with His enemies at Jerusalem, and withdrawal of the Saviour to the Mount of Olives (ch. xi. 27–xiii. 37).

3d Section.—The Saviour's conflict of suffering, and His rest in the grave. Withdrawal into the realm of the dead (ch. xiv. 1–xv. 47).

Part Fifth.

Resurrection of the Lord. The great victory, and appearance of the Victor in the midst of the Apostles for the purpose of completely establishing the new Church. Ascent to heaven (or last withdrawal), to achieve His victory throughout the whole world. (Ch. xvi.)

1st Section.—The risen Saviour victorious *for* the Church; or, preparation for belief in the resurrection. The three Easter messages: the angel, the woman, the two men (vers. 1–12).

2d Section.—The risen Saviour victorious *in* the Church, sweeping away the unbelief of the disciples, perfecting their faith, and giving them their glorious message and commission (vers. 13–18).

3d Section.—The risen Saviour ascending to heaven victorious *with* the Church, confirming the "word" and message of the disciples throughout the world (vers. 19, 20).

These periods of rest and withdrawal on the part of the Saviour, preparatory to fresh progress and victory, are also noticed by the other Evangelists, but not in so striking a manner as in Mark's Gospel. In two instances, indeed, they appear less clearly, showing that, while it was the leading idea of Mark to indicate these contrasts, his Gospel was nevertheless not strictly and uniformly constructed or arranged upon such a plan. We subjoin a brief survey of the Gospel, with the view of setting more clearly before the reader these contrasts of withdrawal and renewed progress.

The Prelude: John in the wilderness; John arousing the whole country.

Fundamental Fact: Jesus (the Son of God) concealed in Nazareth; glorified in consequence of His baptism in the river Jordan.

1. Sojourn of Jesus in the wilderness; His appearance in room and stead of John; conquest of Capernaum.

2. Retirement of the Saviour into the wilderness; evangelization of Galilee until the preliminary conflict with traditionalism, ch. i. 40, &c.

3. Retirement of Jesus into the wilderness (ch. i. 45); commencement and completion of the conflicts in Galilee.

4. Retirement (from intercourse with the synagogue) to the ship, and commencement of the open-air sermons (ch. iii. 7); and also, of the contest of the Saviour, in fellowship with His disciples, with the unbelief of the people.

5. Retirement to the villages in the mountains (ch. vi. 6); and reappearance of the Saviour, to enter, in fellowship with His disciples, into conflict with the enmity of Herod—in the way of healing and feeding the people.

6. Retirement into the wilderness on the other side of the Lake of Galilee (ch. vi. 30); and reappearance of the Saviour to enter into conflict with the scribes of Jerusalem. Preliminary separation from Judaism.

7. Retirement into the Gentile border-land of Tyre and Sidon, and to Decapolis (ch. vi. 24, &c.); and decisive conflict with Pharisaism in Galilee. Final separation from the hierarchical party.

8. Retirement to the mountains on the other side of the Lake of Galilee, and secret sojourn in Galilee (ch. viii. 13–ix. 50); journey to Peræa.

9. Gathering of the disciples on the journey to Jerusalem (ch. x. 32), triumphal entry into the city, and decisive conflict in Jerusalem. Separation from the temple and the ancient theocracy.

10. Retirement of Jesus to the Mount of Olives (ch. xiii. 1), and reappearance to enter on His conflict of suffering.

11. Rest and concealment of Jesus in the grave (ch. xv. 42), and reappearance in the personal victory and triumph of His resurrection. Victory over the realm of the dead.

12. Ascension of Jesus; being His personal retirement from this earth and His reappearance in the victories achieved by His Church. Victory over the world.

We conceive that there is scarcely any room for questioning the correctness of this arrangement, except perhaps so far as sections 5 and 9 are concerned. But section 5 certainly bears a special mark in the calling of the Twelve, which was preceded by solitude and prayer. And if it be objected that the theme of section 9 holds no very prominent place in Mark's Gospel, we reply that it occupies a highly prominent one in the Gospel of John, as the last sojourn of Jesus preparatory to His triumphal entry into Jerusalem (John xi. 54 etc.). And even in Mark's Gospel it is indicated with sufficient distinctness, provided we attach their full and proper meaning to those important words in ch. x. 32: "καὶ ἦν προάγων, etc., καὶ ἀκολουθοῦντες ἐφοβοῦντο," "καὶ παραλαβὼν πάλιν τοὺς δώδεκα," etc. Meyer rightly observes: "Hitherto the disciples had only partially and timidly followed Him; most of them, filled with consternation, had left Him by the way. But now the Saviour halted on His journey, and again called the Twelve around Him. This event marks the gathering of the disciples of Jesus in the wilderness of Ephraim for the solemn and avowed purpose of surrender to the final entry into Jerusalem, and all that it implied." In this progressive series of victorious conflicts, the four chosen Apostles form the first conquest of Jesus—the final subjection and possession of the whole world, His last triumph!

THE GOSPEL ACCORDING TO MARK.

PART FIRST.

GRAND Preparation. Christ's kingly appearing *by the side of* John the Baptist. First Victory and First Withdrawal. The virtual Decision of all subsequent Conflicts and Victories (CH. I. 1–13).

FIRST SECTION.

JOHN THE BAPTIST.

CHAPTER I. 1–8.

(Parallels: Matt. iii. 1–12; Luke iii. 1–20; John i. 19–28.)

1, 2   The beginning of the Gospel of Jesus Christ, the Son of God: As it is written in
   the prophets,[1] Behold, I send my messenger before thy face, which shall prepare thy
3 way before thee;[2] The [A] voice of one crying in the wilderness [desert], Prepare ye
4 the way of the Lord, make his paths straight.   John did baptize in the wilderness, and
5 preach the baptism of repentance for the remission of sins.   And there went out unto
   him all the land of Judea, and they of Jerusalem [the Jerusalemites], and were all[3] bap-
6 tized of [by] him in the river of Jordan, confessing their sins.   And John was clothed
   with camel's hair, and with a girdle of a skin about his loins; and he did eat locusts
7 and wild honey; And [he] preached, saying, There cometh one mightier than I after
8 me, the latchet of whose shoes I am not worthy to stoop down and unloose.   I indeed
   have baptized you with water: but he shall baptize you with the Holy Ghost.

[1] Ver. 2.—We regard the testimony of Irenæus and other fathers, with Codd. A., P., as sufficient to establish the reading ἐν τοῖς προφήταις, against the reading of Codd. B., D., L., and others, ἐν Ἡσαΐᾳ τῷ προφήτῃ, which Griesbach and most recent critics would prefer on their authority. That the text was changed into the form which it has in our reading is scarcely conceivable; on the other hand, the reading "in Esaias" might have been inserted from the second citation through an inexact reminiscence, especially as Mark is not elsewhere accustomed to quote minutely (ch. xi. 17; xii. 10; xiv. 27). If the reading "in Esaias the prophet" be preferred, the passage of Malachi must be regarded as a further development of the main passage in Isaiah, which is made prominent as the first announcement of the forerunner.
[2] Ver. 2.—Ἔμπροσθέν σου is not sufficiently supported.
[3] Ver. 5.—The πάντες belongs to the inhabitants of Jerusalem, according to the best MS., and does not come after ἐβαπτίζοντο.

EXEGETICAL AND CRITICAL.

Ver. 1. **The beginning of the Gospel.**—The superscription includes from vs. 1 to 3, closing with the words, "make his paths straight." The Evangelist designs by both passages (vs. 2 from "be- hold," etc., and vs. 3) to indicate the forerunnership of John. Hence the beginning goes on, according to Meyer, to vs. 8, and not, as Ewald says, to vs. 15. There is an analogous superscription in Matt. i. 1. When Mark points to John the Baptist as the beginning of the Gospel, he refers to its whole development, and this logically leads to and includes the narrative of the Infancy. But he does not include in his design generally, *processes* and *means:* hence John also must come upon the scene as the mature man. In this concise and sudden introduction, the Evangelist himself appears before us in all his own peculiarity. Indeed, this beginning of the Gospel was in the apostolical age the customary commencement of evangelical tradition, and as such always accompanied the apostolical preaching. It always started with the appearance of John the Baptist. The history of the Infancy and the doctrine of the Logos followed later for the initiated, the believers.—**Of Jesus Christ** (genitive of the object), **the Son of God.**—Matthew: The Son of David. In Mark, the theocratic relation of Jesus recedes, as he wrote especially for Gentile Christians.

Ver. 3. **In the wilderness.**—*See* on Matthew iv. 1. So also Luke iv. 1.—**The baptism of repentance.**—Baptism as not only obliging to change of mind (μετάνοια), but also exhibiting and symbolizing it.—**For the remission of sins.**—Meyer rightly: To be received from the Messiah; and not, as Hoffmann in the *Schriftbeweis* asserts, as assured by John's baptism. Thus it denotes the preparatory reference of John's baptism to Christ, or to the baptism of the Holy Ghost.

Ver. 5. **All the land of Judea, and (even) all they of Jerusalem.**—Peculiar to Mark, is this strong expression. But it is so far not hyperbolical, as the Baptist had at this crisis overpowered and led captive, not only the consciousness of the people, but that of the hierarchy also.

Ver. 6. **And John was clothed.**—*See* on Matthew iii. 4.

Ver. 7. **There cometh one mightier than I after me.**—Present. Decision and vigor of the Baptist, reflecting itself in the view of the Evangelist. Christ is already in the company.—**To stoop down.**—Pointing to his self-depreciation and humility. In this picturesqueness, peculiar to Mark.

Ver. 8. **With the Holy Ghost.**—As Mark does not record the severity of John's preaching, and his announcement of the judicial work of Jesus, he omits the clause "and with fire." Thus the omission proves nothing against the genuineness of the clause.

DOCTRINAL AND ETHICAL.

1. Jesus the Christ, and Christ the Son of God, in the full apostolical meaning. Thus the Gospel of the manifestation of the Mighty One of God is described and opened.

2. The Baptist is here, as in the Gospel of John, ch. i., the representative and final expression of the whole Old Testament. But the Old Testament itself, terminating in him, becomes one great forerunner, and the voice of the Spirit of God in the wilderness, which proclaims the manifestation of Christ; that is, it becomes a compendious introduction to the original New Testament, springing from heaven.

3. John appears here as at once summing up his office as forerunner: 1. Himself the preparer of the way; 2. and the voice summoning to prepare the way. For the prophecies of Isaiah and Malachi, see on *Matthew* iii. 3.

4. The great baptism of John: its seemingly slight, but yet great and decisive, results.

5. John in the desert as a hermit; John arousing the land: preludes of the Lord's self-humiliation and withdrawals, and of His victorious comings forth into the world.

HOMILETICAL AND PRACTICAL.

The beginning of the Gospel of Christ in the manifestation of the Baptist: 1. In his appearance, as described by the prophets; 2. in his vocation (preaching and baptism); 3. in his demeanor; 4. in his alarming influence; 5. in his reference to Christ.—The two Testaments, as they concurrently glorify Christ as the Lord.—How far the Lord will have a way prepared for Him, and how far He makes a path for Himself.—Repentance and faith a miraculous path through the wilderness.—The confession of sin, and its significance for piety: 1. Oftentimes, alas! nothing, or less than nothing; 2. oftentimes very much; 3. oftentimes everything.—John's great renunciation of the world, the silent condition of his great influence.—The hermit and the shaken land.—Collectedness in secret, victory in the world.—The two strong men, with whom the kingdom of heaven breaks into the world: 1. John, the strong man; and 2. Christ, the stronger than he.—The anointing of the Holy Ghost: the consummation of the baptism of Christ.—The greatness of John the Baptist, that he always, and in all things, points out of and beyond himself: 1. A preparer of the way, who summons his people to prepare their own way; 2. baptizing, and preaching the baptism of repentance; 3. the overcomer of the people, who predicts Christ as overcoming himself; 4. pointing from his own water-baptism to the baptism of the Spirit.—The baptism of water and the baptism of Spirit.—The heroic constancy and decision of John in his work, a symbol for all believers.

STARKE:—Thus the last messenger of the old covenant points to the first of the new. Thus truth agrees with truth.—The New Testament looks back to the Old.—The wilderness in which the Baptist appeared, a shadow of this world.—Word and sacrament the two essential elements of the preaching office.—Preachers furnished with the Spirit and power may have great concourse around them; but Israel soon becomes weary of the manna, John vi. 66.

GERLACH:—John's baptism as the conclusion, and consequently also the epitome, of all that the legal economy contained in itself.—It was not itself to communicate forgiveness of sins, but prepare the way for it.—Even Christians should not despise such preparations through the law for the Gospel.—In times of great declension in morals, the servants of the Lord appear with a special self-renunciation even in external things. So the ancient Elijah, 2 Kings i. 8.—GOSSNER:—A preacher should be only a messenger who proclaims the coming of the Lord and Saviour.—W. L. BAUER:—The man of humility, who aimed only to prepare the way.

SECOND SECTION.

CHRIST.

CHAPTER I. 9–13.

(Parallels: Matt. iii. 13–iv. 11; Luke iii. 21–iv. 13; John i. 29–42.)

9 And it came to pass in those days, that Jesus came from Nazareth of Galilee, and
10 was baptized of [by] John in Jordan. And straightway coming up out of [from, ἀπο¹]
the water, he saw the heavens opened [parted], and the Spirit, like a dove, descending
11 upon him. And there came a voice from heaven, *saying*, Thou art my beloved Son, in
12 whom² I am well pleased. And immediately the Spirit driveth him into the wilderness.
13 And he was there in the wilderness forty days tempted of Satan; and was with the
wild beasts; and the angels ministered unto him.

[¹ Ver. 10.—The reading of the Received Text is ἀπό, which is also adopted by Scholz, and agrees, moreover, with Matt. iii. 16. But Lachmann, Tischendorf, and Meyer, following D., D., L., and the Gothic Version, read ἐκ. Griesbach also favored this reading. The English Version "out of" accords with the latter reading, but not with the former. The use of the two prepositions is seen in Luke ii. 4: "And Joseph also went up from (ἀπό) Galilee, out of (ἐκ) the city of Nazareth," &c. "Beyond doubt," remarks Winer, "ἐκ indicates the closest connection; ὑπό, one less strict; παρά, and more especially ἀπό, one still more distant."—*Ed.*]
[² Ver. 11.—After D., D., &c., Lachmann and Tischendorf read ἐν σοί, "in Thee."]

EXEGETICAL AND CRITICAL.

Ver. 10. **Straightway,** εὐθέως.—Mark's watchword, constantly recurring from this time onwards. But here it means that Jesus only in a formal sense submitted to the act, and therefore did not linger in it. Much in the same way as Luke hastily passes over the circumcision of our Lord.—**He saw the heavens.**—Not John (as Erasmus and others), but Jesus is the subject of the seeing (Meyer): yet the concurrent and mediate beholding of the Baptist is not excluded; *see* John i. That the occurrence should not have been only an external one, but also an internal (*Leben Jesu*, ii. 1, S. 162), Meyer calls "fantasy." But it is certain that without the fantasy of theological spiritual insight we cannot penetrate the internal meaning of the text, and must fall now into mere dogmatism, and now into rationalistic perversions.

Ver. 12. **And immediately the Spirit driveth Him.**—Ἐκβάλλει is stronger than the ἀνήχθη of Matthew and the ἤγετο of Luke.

Ver. 13. **And He was there forty days tempted of Satan.**—According to Meyer and others, Mark (with Luke) is here out of harmony with Matthew. This difficulty springs from neglecting to distinguish, 1. between real difference and less exactitude, and 2. between the being tempted generally of Satan, and the being tempted in a specifically pregnant and decisive manner. But it is evident that Mark places the crisis of Christ's victory already in the baptism. That act of victory over sin, and humiliation under the baptism of John, had already assured Him the victory over the now impotent assaults of Satan.—**With the wild beasts.**—The older expositors find in this circumstance a counterpart of the serpent in paradise. Starke:—The wilderness was probably the great Arabian desert, and Satan attacked Him also through the beasts. Usteri and others:—Christ as the restorer of paradise, and conqueror of the beasts. De Wette:—This is a mere pictorial embellishment. Meyer:—He is threatened in a twofold manner: Satan tempts Him, and the beasts surround Him. But this is a misleading view. A threefold relation of Jesus is here depicted, 1. to Satan, 2. to the beasts, 3. to the angels; and it is arbitrary to separate the second from the third, and make it the antithesis of the first. There is nothing in the μετά to justify this.—**The angels.**—Not merely fortuitous individual angels. By the individuals which minister to Him, the angel-world is represented. Meyer:—By the ministering we are not to understand a serving with food, but a sustaining support against Satan and the beasts. This is more than fantasy.—The theory concerning the various forms of the history of the temptation, of which Mark is supposed to have used the earliest and simplest, we pass over, as flowing from the well-known scholastic misapprehension of this Evangelist's original view and exhibition of the Gospel.—*Ex ungue leonem!* This holds good of Christ, as He is introduced by Mark; and in another sense it holds good of the beginning of the Gospel itself. Remark the expressions: οἱ Ἱεροσολυμῖται πάντες—κύψας λῦσαι—εἶδε σχιζομένους τοὺς οὐρανούς, etc.

DOCTRINAL AND ETHICAL.

1. The self-denial and self-renunciation with which Christ, the Son of God, had lived in the seclusion of Nazareth, was the condition and source of that strength in which He subjected Himself to the baptism of John in the Jordan. This act of subjection sealed His submission under the law, His historical fellowship of suffering with His people, and His passion. The baptism of Christ was consequently the pledge of His perfect self-sacrifice. Hence it was in principle the decision of His conflict and His victory; and therefore it was crowned with His glorification. In this one act there was a consummation of His consciousness as God, of His consciousness as Redeemer, and His consciousness as Victor.

2. Christ really decided, in His baptism, His victory over Satan. He went into the wilderness and

made it a paradise. The serpent in this paradise assaults Him, but cannot hurt Him; the wild beasts sink peaceably under His majesty; and the angels of heaven surround and serve Him.

3. John is in the wilderness, and Satan tempts him not. Jesus is led up from the wilderness into the wilderness,—that is, into the deepest wildness of the wilderness (this being the residence of the demons, *see* Com. on Matthew iv.),—and Satan comes down to assault Him there. But the Evangelist deems it superfluous to remark that Jesus overcame Satan. After what had just preceded, this was self-understood. Moreover, it is in the casting-out of the devils, that Mark presents to us Christ's concrete victories over Satan. Yet this victory is intimated in the fact that He maintained His abode in the wilderness for forty days in spite of all the assaults of the devil, and that in that very wilderness the angels ministered to Him. The incarnate Son of God could hold His heavenly court in the place which Satan preëminently arrogated for himself. The Lord's relation to His surroundings is threefold. 1. It is a sovereign and inimical one towards Satan, whose temptations appear only as impotent assaults. 2. It is a sovereign and peaceful one towards the beasts: they dare not hurt the Lord of creation, nor do they flee before Him. Jesus takes away the curse also from the irrational creation (Rom. viii.). According to the same Mark, who places this circumstance at the outset of his Gospel, Jesus commanded at its close that His Gospel should be preached to every creature. *See* Daniel in the den of lions. Comp. GOETHE's *Das Kind und der Löwe*. 3. A sovereign and friendly one towards the angel-world. The world of the angels is subjected to the dominion of Christ: Eph. i. 21; Col. ii. 10; Heb. i.

HOMILETICAL AND PRACTICAL.

The abode of Jesus in Nazareth, or His self-humiliation, the foundation of all the Divine victories in His life, Phil. ii. 6 *seq*.—The greatness of Christ by the side of the greatness of John.—Even in humiliation Christ is above John, in that He *voluntarily* submits to his baptism.—With the submission of Christ to the baptism of John, and what it signified, the whole course of His life, and also His victory over Satan in the wilderness, were decided. Hence His tarrying in the wilderness was the festival before a new career.—The perfected unfolding of the consciousness of Christ at His baptism, in its eternal significance.—With the self-consciousness of Christ was perfected the consciousness of the Son of God and of the Son of man at one and the same time: Thus, 1. the consciousness of His eternity in His Godhead, and 2. of His redeeming vocation in His humanity.—The significance of perfect self-knowledge in self-consciousness: 1. Finding self, 2. gaining self, 3. deciding and dedicating self in God.—The kindredness and difference between the development of the Redeemer's consciousness and that of the sinner: 1. Kindredness: humiliation, exaltation. 2. Difference: *a*. Christ's humiliation under the judgment of His brethren; *b*. the sinner's under his own judgment;—*a*. Christ's exaltation through the contemplation of the communion of the Trinity; *b*. the sinner's exaltation through faith in the fellowship of the Redeemer.—As our consciousness, so our history: This holds good, *a*. of our true consciousness, *b*. of our false.—The abode of the Baptist and of the Lord in the wilderness, a token of the destruction of the satanic kingdom.—The inseparable connection between the divine dignity and the redeeming vocation of Christ: 1. He is Christ, and submits to John's baptism of repentance; 2. He sees the heavens open upon Him, and enters into the depths of the wilderness to contend with Satan.—The connection between the Lord's baptism and His temptation.—The connection between the humiliations and the exaltations of our Lord, an encouraging sign to all who are His.—The connection between the invigorations and the new conflicts of Jesus, an admonitory sign to all who are His.—Christ takes possession again of the wilderness (the world), without asking leave of Satan whose dwelling it is.—Christ in the wilderness Ruler of all: 1. Of the abyss, whose assaults He regards not; 2. of the earth, whose wild beasts and passions sink to rest at His feet; 3. of the heavenly world, whose angels minister to Him.—Wherefore the Lion of Judah, according to Mark, so often goes into the wilderness.—How the Holy Spirit opens, with the manifestation of Christ, the decisive conflict with the spirit of apostasy.—How the Holy Spirit, as the Spirit of might, drives the Lord into the decisive conflict. Even Christ did not go led by self into the contest.—Christ changing the wilderness, despite Satan, into a paradise.—Adam in paradise, and Christ among the beasts in the wilderness.

STARKE:—Humility the best adornment of teachers.—Jesus of Nazareth (despised): So little does the great God make Himself, and thus at the same time constructs a ladder by which we may go up.—Jesus sanctifies through His baptism the laver of regeneration in the word.—Rejoice, O soul, in that God is well pleased with His Son, and with thee also, who through Him art reconciled to God! But thou must in faith be made one with Him, Eph. i. 5, 6.—As soon as we become God's children, the Holy Ghost leads us; but the cross and temptation come forthwith.—What the first Adam lost among and under the beasts, the Second Adam has asserted and regained among the beasts.—A pious man has nothing to fear, among either wild beasts or bestial men.

GERLACH:—How infinitely high does Christ stand above all human teachers, even those inspired by God.—SCHLEIERMACHER:—The legal excitement which John occasioned, and the excitement which Jesus enkindled.—GOSSNER:—Solitude and the wilderness have their temptations equally with the world.—BAUR:—No one is near to celebrate this victory, yet God's angels are there to glorify Him.

PART SECOND.

ROYAL Appearance of Christ *after* the Baptist. His Conflicts and Victories in Galilee, in the Old Jewish Church (CH. I. 14—IX. 50).

FIRST SECTION.

ANNOUNCEMENT OF THE KINGDOM OF HEAVEN.

CHAPTER I. 14, 15.

(Parallels: Luke iv. 14, 15; Matt. iv. 12-17; John iv. 43 seq.)

14 Now, after that John was put in prison, Jesus came into Galilee, preaching the
15 Gospel of the kingdom of God, And saying, The time is fulfilled, and the kingdom of God is at hand: repent ye, and believe [in] the Gospel.

[1] Ver. 14.—Codd. D., L., and several cursive MSS. and versions, leave out τῆς βασιλείας. So Lachmann and Tischendorf. Meyer thinks it an exegetical addition. But what follows might also have caused the omission.

EXEGETICAL AND CRITICAL.

See on *Matthew*, ch. iv. 12–17.

Ver. 14. **Jesus came.**—Ewald: He would not let the Baptist's work fall to the ground. Meyer, on the contrary: that He might be safe; but see our Notes on Matthew in refutation of this. By the Baptist's imprisonment the Baptist community in Israel was broken up; Jesus therefore saw occasion first to receive to Himself the poor people in Gentile Galilee, and that as the representative of John. John was put in prison by the Galilean prince; Jesus summons the people of this prince to repentance, and to faith in the Gospel: this is the true political retaliation, and the sacred way to salvation and the restoration of right.

Ver. 15. **The time,** ὁ καιρός.—Not the period, but the *right* time; the great, fore-ordained, predicted and longed-for time of Messianic expectation; more closely defined by the following "the kingdom of God is at hand." (*See* Gal. iv. 4.) **Repent,** Μετανοεῖτε.—See the lexicon for the original meaning and the various significations of the word. [It includes the ideas of reflection, afterthought, and change of mind, *i. e.*, of judgment and of feeling, upon moral subjects, with particular reference to the character and conduct of the penitent himself. ALEXANDER *in loc.*—*Ed.*] **Believe the Gospel,** Πιστεύετε ἐν. Gal. iii. 26; Eph. i. 13.—By this expression faith is more strongly emphasized. Entering into the Gospel, we have decisive faith. The object of faith in this view is the manifestation of the kingdom of God.

DOCTRINAL AND ETHICAL.

1. From the still prayer of the wilderness, or from the new paradise in which Christ had conquered Satan, He has now come forth to endure all the individual conflicts of life for the founding of His eternal kingdom. Adam came from his paradise conquered, to endure in his descendants a constant succession of defeats.

2. As here, so everywhere, the economy of the Gospel takes the place of the economy of the law. The legal economy yields at last to the lawlessness of the world: the economy of faith and salvation triumphs over it even in yielding, and saves with itself also the ideality of the law.

3. An economy of the law which, in its tragical conflict with the spirit of the world, recognizes not the deliverance which is in the coming economy of salvation, like Elias (1 Kings xix. 13), is thereby converted into an economy of carnal precepts, which finally combines with the world against the economy of salvation. But, on the other hand, true evangelical faith knows how to give its due to the precursory office of the law, just as Christ gave honor to His forerunner, John the Baptist.

4. "Almost all the Jews of that time hoped for the kingdom of God; but it was a strange and unrecognized idea, that repentance and faith must be the entrance into it. Jesus begins with the promise, but immediately goes on to the conditions." Gerlach.

5. Mark, like Peter in his first and second Epistle, places the announcement of the kingdom of heaven at the head of his writing. The kingdom is his fundamental thought.

HOMILETICAL AND PRACTICAL.

Jesus, in the silent conflicts of the wilderness, prepares for the open conflicts of life—takes the place of John, delivered to death by the carnal mind. 1. The history: A testimony, *a.* that He honored the Baptist, *b.* that He did not fear the enemy, and *c.* that He was faithful to His people and His vocation. 2. The doctrine: *a.* The witnesses of the kingdom of God cannot be destroyed; *b.* after every seeming triumph of the kingdom of darkness, still stronger heroes of God come forward. 3. Christ is always Himself victorious at last in every scene.—Persecution the primitive furtherance of the kingdom of God.—The blood of the Church, the seed of the Church.—Where the law falls in the letter, it is re-established in the spirit.—The preaching of Christ: 1. It appears as the announcement of salvation in the place of danger and ruin. 2. What it announces: that the time is fulfilled, and that the kingdom of God is come. 3. What it requires: repentance (as change of mind, μετάνοια) and faith. 4. What it signifies: the saving presence of Christ Himself.—Christ and John as preachers: the might of their preaching itself. 1. John preaches in his whole life and manifestation; 2. Christ preaches out of the depth of His own divine life.—The seal of evangelical preaching the full harmony of the person and the word.

On the whole section (ch. i. 14–45).—The first victorious appearance of Christ the prelude of His whole path of victory; 1. In the announcement of His Gospel; 2. in His dominion over the hearts of the chosen; 3. in His victory of the kingdom of Satan; 4. in His miraculous removal of human misery; 5. in His salutary shaking of the world.—The glory of the Lord in its first actual exhibition: 1. A glory of grace (vs. 16–20), 2. of sacred judicial and redeeming power (vs. 21–28), 3. of healing mercy (vs. 29–39), 4. of purifying purity (vs. 40–44).—Christ proceeds from the wilderness of the earth into the wilderness of human life for the restoration of paradise.—Christ confirms His victory over Satan in the solitude of the desert by His victories over satanic powers among all the people.

STARKE:—Satan seeks to bind and to oppress Christ and His Gospel; but God's wisdom and power set at naught all his aggression.

GERLACH:—With the public appearance of Jesus, the end of John's work had come.—GOSSNER:—He who understands repentance to mean that he must first become pious and good, and then come to Jesus, and believe His Gospel, goes out at the door of grace instead of entering in. Repenting and believing the Gospel, or believing in Christ, must go together and be one.

SECOND SECTION.

CONQUEST OF THE FIRST DISCIPLES AT CAPERNAUM, VICTORY OVER THE DEMONS IN THAT CITY, AND WITHDRAWAL INTO THE WILDERNESS.

CHAPTER I. 16–35.

---

1. *The Authoritative Word of Jesus, which calls the four first and greatest Disciples.* VERS. 16–20.

(Parallels: Matt. iv. 18–22; Luke v. 1–11; comp. John i. 35–42.)

16 Now, as he walked[1] by the sea of Galilee, he saw Simon, and Andrew his brother,
17 casting a net into the sea: for they were fishers. And Jesus said unto them, Come ye
18 after me, and I will make you to become fishers of men. And straightway they forsook
19 their[2] nets, and followed him. And when he had gone a little farther thence,[3] he saw James the *son* of Zebedee, and John his brother, who also were in the ship mending
20 their nets. And straightway he called them: and they left their father Zebedee in the ship with the hired servants, and went after him.

[1] Ver. 16.—The expression παράγων is recommended by B., D., L., Lachmann, and Tischendorf. Instead of αὐτοῦ Lachmann and Tischendorf read Σίμωνος.
[2] Ver. 18.—Not "their" nets: αὐτῶν is wanting in B., C., L., Lachmann, Tischendorf.
[3] Ver. 19.—'Εκεῖθεν is wanting in B., D., L., Tischendorf; bracketed by Lachmann. It accords with Matt. iv. 21.

EXEGETICAL AND CRITICAL.

See on *Matthew*, iv. 18 *seq.*
Ver. 16. **As He walked by.**—The Evangelist would make prominent the apparently fortuitous character of this first vocation.
Ver. 19. **Who also were in the ship.**—Both pairs of brothers were called while in the earnest prosecution of their craft. The first two were throwing their nets into new positions in the water; the two others were mending them for new draughts.
Ver. 20. **With the hired servants.**—Why this addition? Paulus: It was to be made clear, how they could without impiety forsake their father. Meyer (after Grotius): It was only a proof that Zebedee did not follow his craft in a petty way, and that he probably was not without means. In any case, it also shows that Zebedee was not left helpless. That they forsook so thriving a business (Ewald), is indeed of less significance.

DOCTRINAL AND ETHICAL.

1. Christ Himself is the great Fisher of men. He catches the four elect ones as it were at one draught. These are the three (Mark ix. 2) and the four (Mark xiii. 3) confidential Apostles of after-

CHAP. I. 21-28.

times. Therefore there were first four fishermen called.

2. The power of Christ's word over these souls here appears direct and immediate. We learn the mediating circumstances of this vocation from John i. At the same time, this calling was something entirely new (see on *Matthew*, iv. 19), and their following so wonderful, that they at once forsook their calling, in the very act of pursuing it. The fishing life of these men was a preparation for their higher calling, as being fidelity in that which was least.

HOMILETICAL AND PRACTICAL.

The Lord knoweth His own.—The Lord and His elect quickly know each other.—The great increase of grace swiftly enters into our daily life.—Christ's walking by the sea apparently for relaxation, but at the same time the most noble work.—Christ's mark in this world the heart of man.—The great Fisher of men, and His art of making human fishers.—The calling of Jesus a call to become something new.—The mighty calling of the Lord: 1. Gentler than any human request; 2. mightier than any human command; 3. unique as the victorious wooing of heavenly love.—The calling of Jesus a calling at once to one thing and to many: 1. To one thing: into His discipleship and the fellowship of His Spirit, or to the Father; 2. to many: to discipleship and mastership, to coöperation, to fellowship in suffering, and community in triumph.—The greatness of the following of the four disciples was the effect of the great grace of their calling. They broke off suddenly in the midst of a new career of their labor, as a sign of the decision of their following.—The spiritual and the worldly vocation of Christians: 1. Opposition; 2. kindredness; 3. union.—The twofold earthly companionship of the disciples a foundation for the higher: 1. Companions in fishing,—companions in fishing for men; 2. brethren after the flesh,—spiritual brethren.—Leaving all for Christ's sake.—The Christian and ecclesiastical vocations in harmony with the sacred natural obligations of life.

STARKE:—Never be idle.—Pious handicraft acceptable to God.—The calling into Christianity binds us to faith and the following of Christ; how much more the vocation to spiritual office!—A true follower of Christ forgets everything earthly.—He who follows Christ loses nothing, though he may forsake all; for he finds in Him a full sufficiency, Matt. xix. 29.

LISCO:—The forsaking all must be experienced inwardly by every believer; and must be fulfilled outwardly also, in particular circumstances and occasions, Matt. xix. 27.—SCHLEIERMACHER:—The two tendencies in the life of the Redeemer: preaching to the multitude, and the separation of individuals to Himself.—GOSSNER:—The Lord's fishermen actually catch the fish; the world's fishermen swim with the fish.—BAUER:—One glance of the Lord, and He knows the heart under its rough garment.

---

2. *The Word of Authority, which delivers the Demoniacs and attracts the People.* VERS. 21–28.

(Parallel: Luke iv. 31–37.)

21 And they went into Capernaum; and straightway on the Sabbath-day he entered
22 into the synagogue, and taught. And they were astonished at his doctrine: for he
23 taught them as one that had authority, and not as the scribes. And there was in their
24 synagogue a man with an unclean spirit; and he cried out, Saying, Let *us* alone;[1] what have we to do with thee, thou Jesus of Nazareth? art thou come to destroy us? I
25 know thee who thou art, the Holy One of God. And Jesus rebuked him, saying, Hold
26 thy peace, and come out of him. And when the unclean spirit had torn him, and cried
27 with a loud voice, he came out of him. And they were all amazed, insomuch that they questioned among themselves, saying, What thing is this? what new doctrine *is* this?[2] for with authority commandeth he even the unclean spirits, and they do obey him.
28 And immediately his fame spread abroad[3] throughout all the region round about Galilee.

[1] Ver. 24.—'Ea is wanting, it is true, in B., D., and others; but it is as accordant with Mark as with Luke (ch. iv. 34).
[2] Ver. 27.—Lachmann, following B., L., Δ., &c.: τί ἐστι τοῦτο; διδαχὴ καινή· κατ', &c. Tischendorf connects διδαχῇ καινῇ κατ' ἐξουσίαν. Lachmann's is better. [Meyer accounts for the Received Text, by a comparison with Luke iv. 36.—ED.]
[3] Ver. 28.—Καὶ ἐξῆλθεν: "And the fame," &c.

EXEGETICAL AND CRITICAL.

The Evangelist, in harmony with his main point of view, proceeds at once to the act by which the Lord approved Himself the conqueror of the demons.

Ver. 22. **As one that had authority.**—See on Matt. vii. 29.

Ver. 23. **With an unclean spirit**, ἐν πνεύματι ἀκαθάρτῳ.—He was *in* the unclean spirit; that is, in his power, under his influence. Concerning the demoniac possession, see on *Matthew* iv. 24.

Ver. 24. **Art thou come to destroy us?**—The demonic consciousness still predominant on the part of the demon. Hence, "to destroy *us!*" Bengel: "*Communicm inter se causam habent dæmonia.*" The word involves also, 1. a testimony of the decided opposition between the demon empire and Christ; 2. a testimony of the perfect supremacy of Christ; 3. and a testimony of the beginning of the subversion of the satanic dominion.—**To destroy us.**—Meyer: By dismissing them to Hades. But even in Hades, Christ does not leave their empire to the demons. Thus it was by the destruction of their empire generally,

Certainly it was by dismissing them to the Gehenna of torment (according to which, the expression in Matt. (viii. 29), the Hades of torment, is to be explained).—**I know Thee who Thou art.**—The demoniac consciousness in its involuntary presentiment. See Acts xvi. 16. It feels already the influence of Jesus, who would draw it from the side of the demon to His side. The word is ambiguous, so far as it belongs to the demon and to the man.—**The Holy One of God.**—In the emphatic sense, and thus, according to John vi. 69, Rev. iii. 7 (comp. John x. 36), the concealed designation of the Messiah. ("So Origen:" Meyer.) As the typical Old Testament anointed ones represented the Messiah, so the typical saints, priests, prophets, and kings (Ps. xvi.) represented the Holy One $κατ'$ $ἐξοχήν$. The unclean spirit, however, describes Him by that opposite to himself which torments him, when he terms Him the Holy One of God.

Ver. 25. **Hold thy peace.**—This refers to the outcry of the demon. The Messiahship of Jesus was not to be prematurely spread abroad, least of all by demons. The kingdom of God and the invisible world scorns such precursors and coöperators. It bears testimony to itself by overcoming all these. Only after the decisive victory are such testimonies supplementarily, and in their own significance, admissible; then, when no intermingling is any longer possible.

Ver. 26. **Torn him.**—The decisive paroxysm with which the healing was declared; at the same time, a phenomenon exhibiting the knavish, spiteful, and degraded nature of the demons (ch. ix. 26; Luke ix. 42).

Ver. 27. **Questioned among themselves.**—The spirits are awake. They do not first ask the priests and Rabbis, but proceed to independent suppositions and conclusions.—**New Doctrine.**—From the appearance of a new power of delivering, they infer the appearance of a new revelation; for revelation and deliverance, miracle and prophecy, always to the Israelites were reciprocal in their influence. For various constructions and interpretations of this passage, see MEYER *in loc.*

Ver. 28. **Throughout all the region round about Galilee.**—That is, through all Galilee, and beyond into the neighboring districts everywhere.

DOCTRINAL AND ETHICAL.

1. The first miracle recorded by Matthew is the healing of the leper by a touch; for one main point of view with him was the opposition of Christ to the hierarchical theocracy and their ordinances. The first miracle which John records is the changing of water into wine; for his main point of view is the glorification of the old and darkened world into a world of spirit. The first miracle which Luke and Mark relate is this casting out of demons in the synagogue at Capernaum. But the points of view of the two latter in this matter are as different and characteristic as their respective Gospels. Luke, in harmony with his predominant object (the divine humanity of Christ), has in view preëminently the healed man. The demon threw him down, and departed from him, without hurting him at all. To Mark, on the other hand, the supremacy of Christ over the kingdom of the demons is the grand object, even as it declares and approves His doctrine to be a new one. Hence he makes it emphatic, that Christ commanded even the unclean spirits, and that they obeyed Him. This point of view runs through his whole Gospel, down to its concluding words.

2. To Mark belong the chief records of Christ's victory over the devils, while in the other Evangelists there is only a general reference to them. In John we do not find deliverances of this sort; on the other hand, he gives prominence to moral possession (John vi. 70, viii. 44, xiii. 27),—an idea which is found approximately among the other Evangelists as sevenfold possession. Further, here we must mark the relation of Christ and His kingdom to Satan and his kingdom, according to the New Testament teaching. Dogmatics must, more rigorously than heretofore, distinguish between the devil and this kind of demons, as well as between the children of the devil and those bound ones of Satan.

3. The synagogue cannot hinder a demoniac from entering it, nor that Satan should in it declare the victory of the kingdom of order and light. Christ cleanses the synagogue.

HOMILETICAL AND PRACTICAL.

Christ the Saviour of the synagogue and of the Church.—The adherence of Christ to the sanctuary of His people, legal and yet free.—By the perfect sanctification of the Sabbath and the synagogue, our Lord established the Sunday and the Church.—How the Child of the synagogue became the Prince of the Church.—Sabbath and synagogue; or, the holy time and the holy place in their symbolical meaning: 1. They signify rest from the toil of sin, and the temple; 2. the Christian Sunday and the Church; 3. the heavenly feast and the heavenly Church.—The demoniac in the synagogue; or, the daring incursion of Satan into the legitimate Church of God to be restrained only by the word of Christ.—How Christ always victoriously confronts the satanic power which insinuates itself into the Church.—Heavenly and hellish powers meet in the Church.—The healing of the possessed in the synagogue a decisive token of the redeeming empire of Christ: 1. Of His victory over the kingdom of Satan; 2. of His saving mercy to the wretched; 3. of His miraculous sealing of the Gospel; 4. of His awakening conquest of the world. —The consciousness of Christ a healing power for the consciousness disturbed by Satan.—The spiritually disturbed consciousness a figure of the curse of sin: 1. In its destruction and contradictions; 2. in its restraint; 3. in its despair; 4. but also in its dim feeling of its misery and of the coming of its Saviour. —The characteristics of the wicked: 1. Knowledge without love; 2. hatred to the Lord, and withal flattering acknowledgment; 3. pride even to madness, and yet impotent fear and flight. Or, 1. Darkness in its lie; 2. murder in its hatred; 3. death in its rending.—Christ immovably opposed to the flattery and hypocrisy, as well as to the threatening and pride, of Satan.—The antithesis of heaven and hell in the conflict of Christ with the demon: 1. Peace of soul and passion (the devil assaults first); 2. collectedness and distraction; 3. the spirit of mercy and the spirit of torment; 4. dignity and degradation; 5. victory and prostration.—Christ scorns the testimony of the demons, and obtains the praise of the people.—The glory of Christ, that He came into the world to destroy the works of the devil, 1 John iii. 8.

STARKE:—The public service of God not to be

neglected, Heb. x. 25.—Unclean spirits are found even in the Church, Jas. ii. 19.—Christ will have no testimony from the spirit of lies.—OSIANDER:—If the devil must give way, yet he rages fearfully: he must, however, give place to the Holy Spirit.—GOSSNER:—The devil knew Him as the Holy One of God, but not as the Saviour.—BRAUNE:—The possessed trembles before Him who is his Deliverer.

---

3. *Healing among the Disciples; Healings and casting out of Demons in Capernaum; the first Return of Christ after He had thus dealt with the susceptible in that city.* VERS. 29–35.

(Parallels: Matt. viii. 14–17; Luke iv. 38–41.)

29 And forthwith, when they were come out of the synagogue, they entered into the
30 house of Simon and Andrew, with James and John. But Simon's wife's mother lay
31 sick of a fever; and anon they tell him of her. And he came and took her by the hand, and lifted her up; and immediately the fever left her, and she ministered unto
32 them. And at even, when the sun did set, they brought unto him all that were dis-
33 eased, and them that were possessed with devils. And all the city was gathered to-
34 gether at the door. And he healed many that were sick of divers diseases, and cast
35 out many devils; and suffered not the devils to speak, because they knew him.[1] And in the morning, rising up a great while before day, he went out, and departed into a solitary place, and there prayed.

[1] Ver. 34.—Some Codd. add, "that He was Christ."

EXEGETICAL AND CRITICAL.

See on Matthew, viii. 14–17.

Ver. 29. **They entered into.**—Jesus, Peter, and Andrew are meant; the two latter as the ordinary occupants of the house, which Peter or both possessed in Capernaum (*see on Matthew*). In addition came James and John. Thus the Lord was with the collective four disciples who had been called.

Ver. 30. **And anon they tell him of her.**—Here also we have εὐθέως thrice in rapid succession. Immediately into the house, immediately to the matter in hand, immediately healed. Matthew transfers this miracle to a later period (*see on Matthew*). Starke for the sake of harmony: "It may have been that the mother-in-law of Peter twice had the fever, and that Christ healed her twice." (!)

Ver. 32. **At even, when the sun did set.**—The full close of the Sabbath. "*Judæos religio tenebat, quominus ante exitum Sabbati ægrotos suos afferrent.*" Wetstein.

Ver. 34. **Sick of divers diseases, and cast out many devils.**—The physically sick and the demoniacs clearly distinguished (ver. 34; Matt. viii. 16); just as they are in relation to the opposite charisms which were given with respect to them, 1 Cor. xii. 9, 10.—**And He healed many.**—Not as opposed to all who were brought to Him, but to describe the abundance and variety of the healings which took place so late in the evening.

Ver. 35. **Into a solitary place.**—To a secret place in the wilderness. It is to be noted that Jesus, according to Mark, thrice in quick succession, withdrew into the wilderness, vers. 12, 35, 45. Here we can understand only a solitude near Capernaum. That He thus took up His abode time after time in the wilderness, declared his supremacy over the demons of the wilderness. He made the desert place a temple of God by His prayers.

DOCTRINAL AND ETHICAL.

1. The succession of events marks the development of Christ's work: 1. The synagogue at home. 2. The house of Peter, as the hearth of the new community of disciples at its outset. 3. The whole town of Capernaum. 4. The entire land of Galilee.—The progression of the influence of our Lord's preaching: 1. His fame goes out through all Galilee. 2. The whole town of Capernaum presses for help at His door, yea, into His doors. 3. All seek Him after He had withdrawn. 4. Even in the wilderness they come to Him from all parts.

2. In order that they may punctiliously guard their own rest on the Sabbath, the people of Capernaum wait till evening with their sufferers, and rob the Lord of His rest in the night.

HOMILETICAL AND PRACTICAL.

Jesus the Saviour of the new as of the old community (Peter's house, the synagogue).—And they told Him of her: with faith waxes intercession.—Peter, as householder, a type of the ecclesiastic at home: 1. He is not hindered from his calling by domestic trouble (he also went into the synagogue); but, 2. he took his domestic trouble with him into his calling (he prayed the Lord for the sick).—The people at Capernaum seeking help; or, Christ the true Physician: 1. As the revealer of human misery; 2. as the marvellous deliverer from it.—An evening and a morning in the life of Jesus; or, His holy day's work: 1. Closed in the blessing of toil; 2. renewed in devotion.—The rapid diffusion of Christ's work and influence: 1. Through the believing house; 2. through the susceptible town; 3. through the amazed land.—New seclusion for new conflicts.—Private prayer the source of Christ's victories.—The Lord's early hours.—His morning devotion.—The significance of morning in the kingdom of God: 1. A festal

time in the life of Jesus; 2. an image of His whole life; 3. a blessed time in the life of Christians; 4. figure of their regeneration and their eternity.—How Christ sanctifies all times and all places.
STARKE:—QUESNEL:—The dwelling of a poor fisherman pleases Christ more than a great palace.—OSIANDER:—God is oftener in little huts than in rich palaces.—Christianity and household life agree well together.—Marriage unfits no man for the ministry.—Compassionate love suffers not the wretched long to wait, but thinks at once of help.—QUESNEL:—The love of Jesus is never weary.—There are always wretched ones in this vale of tears, who stand in need of the help of the Most High.—Christ the most approved Physician.—It does not become the man spiritually possessed of the devil to reveal Christ.—Early hours must be thought much of.—For prayer even sleep must be abridged.
GERLACH:—The gracious love of Christ amidst the household necessities of the poor and neglected.—LISCO:—Jesus connects together prayer and work, solitude and public life, in order to do good.—EUTH. ZIG.:—We must shun the praise of men, and thank God in silent secrecy.

THIRD SECTION.

CHAPTER I. 36–45.

1. *The Preaching and Healing of Jesus.* CH. I. 36–39.

(Parallel: Luke iv. 44.)

36, 37 And Simon, and they that were with him, followed after him. And when they had 38 found him, they said unto him, All *men* seek for thee. And he said unto them, Let us 39 go[1] into the next towns, that I may preach there also: for therefore came I forth. And he preached in their[2] synagogues throughout all Galilee, and cast out devils.

[1] Ver. 38.—The *Rec.* omits ἀλλαχοῦ after ἄγωμεν: it is supported by B., C., L., Copt., Tischendorf.
[2] Ver. 39.—"Into their:" εἰς τὰς in A., B., D., Griesbach, Lachmann, Tischendorf. The *Textus Receptus* reads ἐν ταῖς συναγωγαῖς,—an emendation, says Meyer.

EXEGETICAL AND CRITICAL.

Ver. 36. **And Simon, and they that were with him.**—Simon placed first, not on account of any superiority, but as the head of the house and the guide.

Ver. 38. **Into the next towns.**—The κωμοπόλεις only here in the New Testament. The primary object is to record the travelling through the Galilean hill-country, and its villages and towns.—**For therefore came I forth.**—The question is, whether the meaning be, "I am come from the Father to preach generally" (Bengel); or, "I have left the house (or Capernaum) in order to preach in the neighboring villages" (Meyer). We think that Christ lays stress upon preaching as His great vocation, in opposition to the pressure of individual applicants for help in Capernaum. The former of the two interpretations seems to be the better.

Ver. 39. **In their synagogues** (into).—The Accusative, twice occurring, makes it emphatic that he filled the synagogues and all Judea with a might of preaching that formed a contrast to the synagogue style.

DOCTRINAL AND ETHICAL.

1. Jesus prepared himself in the desert for His second great expedition. The spiritual awakening and conquest of the land of Galilee was now in question.

2. Here also Mark (like Luke) gives special emphasis to the casting out of devils, and to the command of silence, by which Jesus hindered the devils from uttering His name.

3. It is observed also that Jesus places preaching expressly above miraculous healings; this is seen in the use of the participle, δαιμόνια ἐκβάλλων. But the preaching has its root in the secret devotion: His public work sprang from His solitary prayer.

HOMILETICAL AND PRACTICAL.

How the Lord equipped himself anew for new labors.—Christ goes with His first four disciples into the land of Galilee: the small beginning of the universal mission.—How the Lord's preaching approves itself as the power of divine life: 1. As the spiritual word of His working; 2. as delivering power for the suffering; 3. as judicial power of victory over the demons.—Christ confronting the increasing pressure of the people: 1. How He restrains it (withdrawal into the wilderness); 2. how He regulates it (preaching on the individual miracles); 3. how He surrenders Himself to it (responding to every demand of help).—Christ does not shut up His activity within the walls of Capernaum, nor within the limits of any one people or any one confession.—The way of Christ among the surrounding villages: 1. Already to as many as possible; 2. one day to all.

STARKE:—We must have village preachers.—The Gospel of Jesus must sound out in all places.—Where Christ's kingdom is to be established, the devils must be abolished. So also in thee.—SCHLEIERMACHER:—The preaching of the kingdom of God was Christ's vocation: 1. Concerning Himself, as He who was come to save men; 2. concerning the true righteousness which avails before God; 3. concerning the worship of God in spirit and truth.—Within these limits it was His vocation to spread that kingdom as far as He could.—GOSSNER:—To this end am I come (He says) to save men.—Christ did not scorn the little towns and villages.

2. *The Touching of the Leper, and the Return into the Wilderness.* VERS. 40–45.

(Parallels: Matt. viii. 1–4; Luke v. 12–16.)

40 And there came a leper to him, beseeching him, and kneeling down to him,[1] and
41 saying unto him, If thou wilt, thou canst make me clean. And Jesus,[2] moved with compassion, put forth *his* hand, and touched him, and saith unto him, I will; be thou clean.
42 And as soon as he had spoken, immediately the leprosy departed from him, and he was
43, 44 cleansed. And he straitly charged him, and forthwith sent him away; And saith unto him, See thou say nothing to any man: but go thy way, show thyself to the priest, and offer for thy cleansing those things which Moses commanded, for a testimony
45 unto them. But he went out, and began to publish *it* much, and to blaze abroad the matter, insomuch that Jesus could no more openly enter into the city, but was without in desert places: and they came to him from every quarter.

[1] Ver. 40.—The omission of καὶ γονυπετῶν αὐτόν in B., D., and Lachmann and Tischendorf, is not sufficiently supported.
[2] Ver. 41.—Ὁ δὲ Ἰησοῦς omitted in B., D., &c. So Lachmann, Tischendorf. Meyer explains this omission, as also the dropping out of εἰπόντος αὐτοῦ, ver. 42, from an intention to conform the text with Matthew and Luke. So also with the μηδέν, ver. 44.

EXEGETICAL AND CRITICAL.

Respecting this narrative, and the leper, see on *Matthew*, viii. 1–13. The occurrence follows the Sermon on the Mount; and this is here intimated by the return of Jesus to Capernaum, ch. ii. 1.

Ver. 43. **And He straitly charged him.**—The ἐμβριμησάμενος is the opposite of the preceding σπλαγχνισθείς. Probably the leper had overstepped the limits of his discipline (lepers were not suffered to intrude into others' houses) and of the law, and had penetrated to the house where Jesus might have been tarrying in one of the towns. This Meyer reasonably infers from the ἐξέβαλεν—He forthwith sent him away. First of all, Jesus regarded the misery of the case, and, seized with compassion, healed the sick man. But then He proceeded to guard the legal obligation under which the sick man stood, and household rights and general order. Mark gives us a vivid view of the sending away of the healed man, and exhibits the scene in his own lively expressions.

Ver. 44. **To the priest.**—The Vulgate, romanizing, explains: *Principi sacerdotum*. But it only means the priest in general, whose function concerned the man.—**For a testimony unto them.**—The actual cleansing must be confirmed in a Levitically legal manner.

Ver. 45. **To blaze abroad the matter,** τὸν λόγον.—Fritzsche: The word of Jesus. De Wette: The matter. Meyer: The narrative of what had passed. There is implied, perhaps, a distinction between his narrative and the embellished report of the event which was spread abroad, and to which it gave occasion.—**Could no more openly enter.**—The reason of this withdrawal was not merely to obviate the increase of the crowd, but the fact that Jesus had touched the leper, which, according to the law, made a man unclean for a season. See *Leben Jesu*, ii. 2, 639. Moreover, this solitude imported a new withdrawal for a new advance.

DOCTRINAL AND ETHICAL.

See *Com.* on *Matthew, in loc.*

1. Wherefore does Mark close the delineation of Christ's first manifestation in public with the healing of the leper? This narrative is, first, a witness that Christ entered into the fellowship of sinners in order to suffer for them; and so far was a prelude of the end. Secondly, it marked His relation to traditionalism, the offence and assaults of which now follow.

2. The present withdrawal of Jesus took place under the presentiment of His conflicts with traditionalism, and as a preparation to meet them.

HOMILETICAL AND PRACTICAL.

The healing of the leper a testimony of the mightily cleansing purity of Christ.—Christ even in the influence of His purity the Lion of Judah.—Redemption, like creation, an omnipotent *Let there be!* (He speaks, and it is done: "I will, be thou clean.")—The need of deliverance breaking through the law. The leper presses into the house, like the paralytic through the roof, and the sinner into the Pharisee's house.—The leper a pattern of those who seek help, but not of those who give thanks: 1. His perfect trust and humble submission (If Thou wilt, etc.); 2. regardlessness of his friends, lack of docility towards the ceremonial law and of discipline.—Christ's interchange with the leper a symbol of His interchange with the sinner: He makes the leper clean, and contracts Levitical defilement. So Christ was made sin for us, that we might be made righteousness in Him.—The compassion of our Lord the source of our salvation.—The miraculous hand of Christ the instrument of all heavenly healing: 1. As delivering, 2. as distributing, 3. as consummating.—The disobedience of the leper; or, lack of ceremonial discipline in the reception of healing: 1. Excusable as far as it was the interchange of illegality and freedom; 2. blamable, because he constrained the Lord (even in His Church) to atone for transitory illegality by the legalities of prudence.—Christ in the wilderness and everywhere the centre of a wretched and needy world.—Christ, through His divine compassion, involved with human traditions.—A new collectedness of the spirit, a new blessing and victory.

Starke:—The spiritual leper.—Quesnel:—Prayer, humility, and faith as the source (the organs for the reception) of all righteousness.—We are directed to keep all right ordinances, etc. Abide by the public service of God.—Deliverance from misery demands its right and peculiar offerings of praise.—The more a servant of God withdraws himself from the world, the more highly does the world esteem him.

Gerlach:—The healed leper was like those who, out of thankfulness of heart indeed, but yet inconsiderately, neglect the inward commandment of the Holy Spirit, and make too much talk about the grace of God, to their own and others' hurt.—Schleiermacher:—The Redeemer by His touch took away the ban which sundered the leper from all human intercourse.—Likeness between leprosy and sin.—The one leper and the ten.—Bauer:—How Jesus respected the ordinances of His people.

FOURTH SECTION.

ATTRACTING AND REPELLING INFLUENCE OF THE LORD. THE ENTHUSIASTIC MULTITUDE AND THE OFFENDED TRADITIONALISTS. MORTAL HATRED OF THE HOSTILE PARTY, AND WITHDRAWAL OF JESUS INTO A SHIP. THE PREACHING IN SYNAGOGUES GIVES PLACE TO PREACHING ON THE SEA-SIDE.

Chapter II. 1—III. 12.

First Conflict.—The Paralytic, and the Power to forgive Sins. Vers. 1-12.

(Parallels: Matt. ix. 1-8; Luke v. 17-26.)

1 And again he entered into Capernaum after *some* days; and it was noised that he
2 was in the house.[1] And straightway many were gathered together, insomuch that there was no room to receive *them*, no, not so much as about the door: and he preached the
3 word unto them. And they come unto him, bringing one sick of the palsy, which was
4 borne of four. And when they could not come nigh unto him for the press, they uncovered the roof where he was: and when they had broken *it* up, they let down the
5 bed wherein the sick of the palsy lay. When Jesus saw their faith, he said unto the
6 sick of the palsy, Son, thy sins[2] be forgiven thee. But there were certain of the scribes
7 sitting there, and reasoning in their hearts, Why doth this *man* thus speak blasphemies?[3]
8 who can forgive sins but God only? And immediately, when Jesus perceived in his spirit that they[4] so reasoned within themselves, he said unto them, Why reason ye these
9 things in your hearts? Whether is it easier to say to the sick of the palsy, *Thy* sins
10 be forgiven thee; or to say, Arise, and take up thy bed, and walk? But that ye may know that the Son of man hath power on earth to forgive sins,[5] (he saith to the sick of
11 the palsy,) I say unto thee, Arise, and take up thy bed, and go thy way into thine
12 house. And immediately he arose, took up the bed, and went forth before them all; insomuch that they were all amazed, and glorified God, saying, We never saw it on this fashion.[6]

[1] Ver. 1.—Lachmann reads ἐν οἴκῳ, after B., D., L., —a gloss, says Meyer.
[2] Ver. 5.—Elzevir, Scholz, Lachmann read σοι αἱ ἁμαρτίαι; Griesbach, Fritzsche, Tischendorf, B., D., G. read σου αἱ ἁμαρτίαι. Lachmann, after B., reads ἀφίενται for ἀφέωνται.
[3] Ver. 7.—Lachmann and Tischendorf read λαλεῖ; βλασφημεῖ, after B., D., Vulgata.
[4] Ver. 8.—Αὐτοὶ before διαλογίζονται, after A., C., E., F., Syr. (utr.), Goth., Slav., Bengel, Matth., Griesbach, Fritzsche, Scholz, Tischendorf; οὕτως erased by Lachmann after B.
[5] Ver. 10.—Various order of the words: The ἐπὶ τῆς γῆς ἀφ. ἁμ. is given by Griesbach and Lachmann, after C., D., L., and others.
[6] Ver. 12.—Tischendorf reads οὕτως οὐδέποτε, after B., D., and L., &c.

EXEGETICAL AND CRITICAL.

See the exposition on Matthew, and on Luke. Mark introduces the conflicts of the Lord with traditionalism earlier than Matthew; Hence the earlier position of this narrative. Matthew, indeed, represents the chronological order, according to which the paralytic was healed after the journey to Gadara. The conclusion in Mark itself intimates that this must have been one of the later miracles.

Ver. 1. **That He was in the house,** εἰς οἶκόν ἐστι.—This means the house which Jesus occupied with His mother and His brethren, after His settlement there, ch. iii. 31. His adopted sisters probably remained, as married, in Nazareth (see ch. vi. 3), when the family of Joseph passed over with Him to Capernaum.

Ver. 3. **Bringing one sick of the palsy.**—See on *Matthew*, viii. 6. Κράββατος, a portable bed, used for mid-day sleep, and for the service of the sick.*—**Borne of four.**—Pictorial definiteness. So also the vivid description of the uncovering of the roof, or the breaking of a large opening through it. Luke tells us how they did it: *"through the tiling;"* thus they must have taken away the tilings themselves. MEYER:—We must suppose Jesus to have been in the upper room, ὑπερῷον, where the Rabbis frequently taught: LIGHTFOOT, *in loc.*; VITRINGA, *Syn.* 145. Meyer rightly rejects the view of Faber, Jahn, and others, that Jesus was in the court, and that nothing more is meant than a breaking up of the roof-awning. Certainly it is not improbable that the roof and the upper room were connected by a door; at least, the not improbable supposition of steps leading from the street to the roof suits that view. It is not at variance with the text to assume, with Lightfoot and Olshausen, an extension of the door-opening already there. Uncovering the roof can mean nothing else than actual uncovering, whether or not by means of an already existing opening. Strauss, after Wetstein, remarks, that the proceeding would have been too dangerous for those below. But *see* Hug's *Gutachten*, ii. p. 21. Moreover, a little danger would better suit the heroism of the act. It takes for granted the Oriental house with a flat roof, to which men might gain access either through the neighboring house, or by the steps on the outside.

Ver. 6. **Certain of the scribes.**—According to Meyer, who cites Mark ii. 16, Luke (ver. 17) introduces the Pharisees too soon at this place. But why may not the scribes have been mainly of the pharisaic party? These were so manifestly.—**The scribes:**—*See* on *Matthew*, ii. 4, and the article in WINER.

Ver. 7. **Why doth this man thus speak blasphemies?**—That is, *such a man* (scornfully), *such things* (such great words as are fit only for God, or for the priests in His name). MEYER rightly: "This man in this wise: emphatic juxtaposition." The idea of blasphemy, as expressed by Mark and Luke, is shown to be direct blasphemy: they cast that upon Him, because He was thought to have wickedly intruded into the rights of the Divine Majesty.

Ver. 8. **And immediately, when Jesus perceived in His spirit.**—The Searcher of hearts. In this lay already the proof that He could forgive sins. Matthew (ix. 4) here takes as it were the place of Mark: † *Jesus seeing* (ἰδὼν) *their thoughts.*

Ver. 10. **The Son of man hath power.**—Dan. vii. 13; comp. LANGE'S *Leben Jesu*, ii. 1, 235. Meyer asserts, without reason, against Ritzschl, that Christ by this expression declared undoubtedly, and even technically, His Messiahship. Certainly Daniel's Son of Man signified Christ; but the correct understanding of this expression does not seem to have been current in the Jewish schools at this time. Hence the choice of the expression here. They should know Him to be the Messiah, not according to their *false* Messiah-notions, but according to His *true* demonstrations of Messiahship; and the expression was meant to lead them to this.

---
* Oftentimes, however, the bed was a simple mattress or sheepskin.—*Ed.*
† In picturesque descriptiveness, *i. e.*—*Ed.*

Ver. 12. **We never saw it on this fashion.**—We must assume in εἴδομεν an object seen; and that can be no other than the essential phenomenon which corresponds to essential seeing, viz.: the appearance of the kingdom of God. But it is also included, that the omnipotent working of miracles had never been so manifest in Jesus before.

DOCTRINAL AND ETHICAL.

1. *See* on the parallels in Matthew and Luke. Quickly as the glory of Christ was manifested in His first works, so quickly did the contradiction of the pharisaic worldly mind develop itself. It is most significant that the evangelical forgiveness of sins was the first stumbling-block.

2. The healing of the palsied man gives us, in a certain sense, the key to all the miraculous works of our Lord; inasmuch, that is, as the healing of the members is here definitely based upon the healing of the heart, the forgiveness of sins, awakening and regeneration. Because Christ Himself was the new birth of man from heaven, He was the principle of regeneration to sinful man. That is, in other words, because He Himself was the absolute miracle—the new principle of life breaking into and through the old—therefore the miraculous energies for the renewal of life issued from Him as sudden and great vivifications, which, proceeding from the heart of the renewed, pervaded their whole life. The quickening of the heart was, therefore, always the soul of light in the miracle; the external miracle was its dawning manifestation, though not all such quickenings resulted in permanent bodily healing. Therefore, also, the kernel of the miracle has remained in the Church, and becomes more and more prominent, that is, regeneration. The dawn has retreated and vanished, since this sun of the inner life has come forth. Yet the dynamic unfolding of the heart's renewal in the renewal of the bodily members has in reality remained; only, now that Christianity has been incorporated with human nature, it develops itself only in gradual effect, until its full manifestation in the day of resurrection. The regenerating principle works in the regenerate gradually, and in almost invisible, leaven-like influence and transformation. But, as certainly as the regeneration of the heart is effected, so certainly is the germ of the renewal of the whole life present. Our scholastic notions have too carefully separated the external miracle from the internal, making it almost of itself a higher class of miracle. Luther, however, recognized regeneration as the great and abiding miracle, and had some feeling of its connection with the resurrection, as symbolized in the Supper of the Lord.—The power of Christ over the whole life, a demonstration of His power over the centre of life, the heart.

3. Christ the Searcher of the heart, knowing all things. In His messianic vocation, in His concrete sphere of life, He proved His Divine omniscience, and that too in the personal unity of the God-man. This concrete Divine-human knowledge He Himself distinguished from the universal omniscience of the Father. STARKE:—"Christ knoweth all things even according to His human nature; not, however, through the human, *tanquam per principium quo*, but through the divine." In a certain sense, also, through the human; through human sensibility to hostile dispositions, which assuredly had its source in the Divine nature.

HOMILETICAL AND PRACTICAL.

See on the parallels of Matthew and Luke.—How the Lord's redeeming power, breaking in, awakens the daring courage of faith.—Christ the restorer of victorious courage on earth.—Man inventive, above all in his faith.—The inventions of faith.—The boldness of faith, which leaps out of the anguish of a believing spirit.—How the miracle of Christ is appended to the word of Christ.—The miracle not without the previous word.—The return of Christ to His town; or, Christ does not willingly leave the place in which He has once settled.—And it was noised abroad that He was in the house,—when Christ is in a church, or in a house, it cannot be hid. —The courage of faith by which they uncovered the roof, in connection with the Divine courage in which Christ uncovered their hearts.—Great faith discovers and adopts wonderful plans.—Christ the Searcher of hearts: 1. This has a many-sided confirmation, 2. is full of comfort, 3. and full of terror.—The power of the forgiveness of sins a free and legitimate prerogative of Christ's rule: 1. A free exercise of His love; 2. a legitimate administration between free grace and free faith; 3. therefore the free prerogative of Christ. —The Divine love will not be restrained by man's narrow-heartedness.—God's grace is not bound to the ordinances of man.—The Gospel makes the Church, not the Church the Gospel.—The ordinance of absolution no monopoly of absolution.—The glorious and boundless blessings which result from the forgiveness of sins.—The paralytic more troubled about his sins than about his bodily suffering.— Christ the *fundamental* Healer.—As the paralytic had a new power of moving, so the witnesses had a new power of seeing.—Only he who has seen Christ has learned rightly to see.—Christ's miracles of grace always preachers of salvation, which prepare for new miracles.—All awakenings in order to regeneration are miracles of Christ, the subsequent influences of which must be manifest in the bodily life, though, it may be, in a very gradual manner.—The harder and the easier miracle: 1. The internal miracle was, in the Lord's judgment, greater and harder, inasmuch as it was the condition of the external. 2. The external miracle was greater and harder in the judgment of His opponents, as something impossible to the absolving priests. 3. Both were equally hard, in as far as both were impossible to man; and hence the external miracle was Christ's authentication in opposition to His enemies.—The limited blessing of healing a witness for the unlimited blessing of forgiveness of sins.

STARKE:—Moving to the house of God with the crowds.—The sick should come to Christ, the true Physician.—Benevolence, and still more, Christian love, demands that we should serve and help the sick in every possible manner.—He who would be a true Christian must strive to bring to Christ others who are weak and sinful, by prayer and all good offices, Jas. v. 16.—CANSTEIN:—We must somehow come to Christ, whether through the door or through the roof; that is, either in an ordinary or an extraordinary way.—True faith, working by love, breaks through all impediments.—Love makes all things good and decorous, though they may not externally seem so.—Those who are troubled we should not trouble more, but comfort, Ps. xxxii. 1; Isa. lxi. 2. —The ungodly change the best medicines into poison, and pervert the holiest truths.—MAJUS:—The slanderer's manner is, not to try to seek what meaning the speaker has, but to pervert at once and wrest his words.—That which is visible and before the eyes seems to men harder than the invisible; and they prefer what is bodily to what is spiritual.— QUESNEL:—Christ by His visible miracles taught men to understand His invisible miracles.—The priceless benefit of the forgiveness of sins worthy of all praise and thanksgiving.

SCHLEIERMACHER:—We have two things to mark in this whole narrative: first, that which passed between the Redeemer and this sufferer; and then, what referred to the thoughts of the scribes congregated around Him.—As sure as we are that the Redeemer knew what was in man, we must assume that the sufferer thought most of the spiritual gift of Christ, and its importance to himself.—The more powerful the might of love is, as being the energy of faith, the sooner vanish all lesser evils, losing their sting, which is the consciousness of sin.—Thus we see in miniature, in this history, the whole history of the kingdom of God upon earth.—BAUER:— We can thus, by our faith and our intercession, be helpful to the good of others.

Second Conflict.—The Eating with Publicans and Sinners. VERS. 13–17.

(Parallels: Matt. ix. 9–13; Luke v. 27–32.)

13 And he went forth again by the sea-side; and all the multitude resorted unto him,
14 and he taught them. And as he passed by, he saw Levi the son of Alpheus sitting at the receipt of custom, and said unto him, Follow me. And he arose and followed him.
15 And it came to pass, that, as Jesus sat [reclined] at meat in his house, many publicans and sinners sat [reclined] also together with Jesus and his disciples; for there were
16 many, and they followed him. And when the scribes and Pharisees saw him eat with publicans and sinners, they said unto his disciples, How is it that he eateth and drinketh
17 with publicans and sinners? When Jesus heard *it*, he saith unto them, They that are whole have no need of the physician, but they that are sick: I came not to call the righteous, but sinners to repentance.[1]

---

[1] Ver. 17.—The addition εἰς μετάνοιαν is found only in cursive MSS., after Luke v. 32.

EXEGETICAL AND CRITICAL.

See on the parallels of Matthew and Luke.—The narrative of Mark has here also its characteristic traits of vividness. A congregation of the people around Christ at the sea-side, and a discourse uttered there, form the introduction to the calling of Matthew. From ver. 15 we learn that many followed the Lord who belonged to the class of publicans and sinners (excommunicated persons). Meanwhile Matthew (ix. 13) alone has our Lord's appeal to the saying of Hosea (ch. vi. 6).

Ver. 13. **F'orth** (from the town), **again** (ch. i. 16) **by the sea-side.**—Setting plainly before us the position of Capernaum, connected probably with the sea by a suburb of fishers' huts and custom-houses.

Ver. 14. **Levi** (see the explanation in Matthew) **the son of Alpheus.**—Not to be confounded with Alpheus the father of James the Less.

Ver. 15. **In his house.**—Not in his own house, as Meyer thinks. See on *Matthew.* The ἠκολούθησαν must be understood of the spiritual following of the disciples, and not merely of outward accompanying.

Ver. 16. **When the Pharisees** (*see* on *Matthew*) **saw Him.**—Not coming into the house, which is improbable; but as observers of the feast, after which they came forward towards the disciples coming out.

DOCTRINAL AND ETHICAL.

1. *See* on the parallels of Matthew and Luke.
2. The offence taken at our Lord's table-fellowship with publicans and sinners has significance, first, in regard to Church principles as against Donatism and Novatianism; and, secondly, in relation to the true idea of communion as against Confessionalism; and, thirdly, in favor of Christian and social intercourse in opposition to the narrowness of Pietism.
3. The holy intercourse of Christ with sinners, the redemption of the world, is here represented in a concentrated image.

HOMILETICAL AND PRACTICAL.

1. *See* on *Matthew.*—The multitude of the needy people gave the Lord occasion to summon helpers to Himself.—Levi (Matthew) better than his reputation: a warning against all premature condemnation of our neighbor.—How different is the glance of our Lord's eyes into the world from that of the Pharisees' eyes!—Christ in the house of publicans and sinners an offence to the Pharisee; Christ in the house of the Pharisee was not strange and repulsive to sinners (the woman, Luke vii. 37); 1. Historical; 2. typical.—The feast in which Christ is a guest.—The feasts in which Christ was a guest all-saving and decisive for souls.—The slavish dread with which our Lord's enemies come to attack His disciples.—The attempt of His enemies to turn away His disciples from the Lord.—The narrative of the gradual boldness of our Lord's opponents: 1. The features of its development; 2. its symbolical character.—The mission of Christ a Gospel for sinners, who are in evil case: 1. For them with full assurance; 2. for them preëminently, and before those who think themselves sound; 3. for them in contradistinction to the others.—Jesus come for all, according to the law that He has come only for the sick.—The feast of Christ an expression of His Gospel.—The feast of a Christian an expression of his Christian vocation.—How this history stands in full harmony with Ps. i. 1.

STARKE, QUESNEL:—Grace draws Matthew from the love of gold, and makes of him an apostle; the love of gold drew Judas away from Christ and his apostleship.—HEDINGER:—As soon as God is revealed in thee, take no long counsel with flesh and blood.—Jesus receiveth sinners.—A converted man should bring all his acquaintance to God, and take care for their salvation.—Those are shameful enemies of the truth, who put on the guise of godliness but deny its power.—QUESNEL:—He who has not love cannot understand what another may do in care for his neighbor's salvation.—Be patient, and slow to judgment, 1 Cor. iv. 3.—That in which the children of God find their joy and blessedness is hateful to the wicked.—The more a man thinks himself righteous, the further does he remove himself from Christ.—Jesus calls to repentance.—We must bring into the pastoral work a heart filled with true sympathy with the wretched, and with Jesus the Physician.

GERLACH:—Every invitation to a feast was for Jesus an occasion for issuing His invitation to the heavenly feast.—LISCO:—Jesus the *one* Physician for *all.*—SCHLEIERMACHER:—The Pharisees a pure counterpart of the publicans.—The calling to repentance (that is, to change of mind) the essence of the work of Christ.—He describes them (the Pharisees) as they described themselves; but in such a manner that they could not but see that He thought quite differently concerning them (irony).—We should always, in our friendly social life, have spiritual things in view.

Third Conflict.—The Fasting of John's Disciples and of the Pharisees. VERS. 18–22.

(Parallels: Matt. ix. 11–17; Luke v. 33–39.)

18 And the disciples of John and [of] the Pharisees[1] used to fast: and they come and say unto him, Why do the disciples of John and of the Pharisees fast, but thy disciples
19 fast not? And Jesus said unto them, Can the children of the bride-chamber fast while the bridegroom is with them? as long as they have the bridegroom with them, they
20 cannot fast. But the days will come when the bridegroom shall be taken away from
21 them, and then shall they fast in those days.[2] No man also seweth a piece of new [unfulled] cloth on an old garment; else the new piece that filled it up taketh away from

22 the old,² and the rent is made worse. And no man putteth new wine into old [skin] bottles; else the new wine doth burst⁴ the [skin] bottles, and the wine is spilled, and the [skin] bottles will be marred: but now⁵ wine must be put into new [skin] bottles.

¹ Ver. 18.—The reading of the *Rec.*, οἱ τῶν Φαρισαίων, is not supported. Griesbach, Scholz, Lachmann, Tischendorf, Fritzsche read οἱ Φαρισαῖοι.
² Ver. 20.—*Rec.*: ἐν ἐκείναις ταῖς ἡμέραις, is an emendation. Griesbach, Lachmann, Scholz, Tischendorf read ἐκείνῃ τῇ ἡμέρᾳ.
³ Ver. 21.—We follow the reading: αἴρει ἀπ' αὐτοῦ τὸ πλήρωμα τὸ καινὸν τοῦ παλαιοῦ; adopted by Tischendorf and Meyer.
⁴ Ver. 22.—The Present is more vivid than Lachmann's Future, ῥήξει, found, also, in B., C., D., Vulgata.
⁵ Ver. 22.—The addition "now," ὁ νέος, is from Luke v. 37.

EXEGETICAL AND CRITICAL.

1. *See* on the parallels of Matt. and Luke.—The offence at Christ's meal with Levi, as it might represent similar meals, was twofold : 1. As an eating with publicans and sinners ; 2. as the opposite of fasting. In the former view the Pharisees took umbrage ; in the latter, the disciples of John,—the Pharisees also joining them. This offence was a point in which the legal Pharisees and the ascetic disciples of John, as spiritually related, might meet.

Ver. 18. **Used to fast:** ἦσαν νηστεύοντες.—Meyer: They were then in the act of fasting. It may be easily supposed that the imprisonment of John would give occasion to his disciples, and with them to many of the Pharisees, for an extraordinary fast (*see* art. "Fasten" in Winer). An ordinary legal season of fasting is not meant; for Christ and His disciples would not have neglected or outraged that. But if an extraordinary fast, occasioned by the Baptist's imprisonment or by any other cause, formed the primary reason of this question, yet we think that the particiciple is to be taken as emphatic, according to the parallels in Matthew (νηστεύουσι πολλά) and Luke (νηστεύουσι πυκνά).—**And they come.**—Of course only some, as representing the mind of all (Weisse) ; not necessarily all, as Meyer thinks. The combination of both parties on this point does not exclude the prominence of John's disciples, according to Matthew.

Ver. 20. **In those days.**—Emphatically, in those dark days.

Ver. 21. **Else the new piece that filled it up taketh away from the old, and the rent is made worse.**—The new piece is rent away from the old : the most approved reading is also the most expressive. The inappropriate and disproportionate is again made emphatic by the antithesis.

DOCTRINAL AND ETHICAL.

1. *See* on the parallels.
2. Compare the word concerning fasting, Matt. vi. 16. We may distinguish : 1. Legal-symbolical fasting (Lev. xvi. 20, xxiii. 27) ; 2. personal, real fasting—Moses (Ex. xxiv. 18), Elias (1 Kings xix. 8), Christ (Matt. iv.) ; 3. ascetic, penance fasting (the Baptist) ; 4. hypocritical fasting (Isa. lviii. 3, 4), which may easily combine with 1 and 3. Fasting generally is the ascetic symbolical exercise of real renunciation of the world, in which all true fasting is fulfilled.
3. Application of the two parables concerning old garments and old bottles to the history of Ebionitism, of the Interim * in the Reformation age, and of analogous incongruities in the present day.

* An ordinance of Charles V., "that all his Catholic

4. The meal of Christ everywhere a sacred, spiritual feast.

HOMILETICAL AND PRACTICAL.

How often do sincere legal souls suffer themselves to be led away by traditionalists into an assault upon the freedom of the Gospel !—The greatest danger of the *weak* brethren (Rom. xiv. 1, 15), that they fall under the bondage of *false* brethren (2 Cor. xi. 26 ; Gal. ii. 4), and thus become separated from the peace of the Gospel.— *Wrong* alliances of Christians in the Church lead to *wrong* alliances of ecclesiastical things, even in opposition to the *right* alliances of both.—Openness a characteristic of John's disciples as of their master: they apply themselves, as later the Baptist did, with their offence to Christ Himself.—Yet they are infected with the policy of the Pharisees ; for they ask, Why fast *Thy disciples* not ? (*see* on *Matthew*).—Christ at once the Physician and the Bridegroom : 1. The Bridegroom as the Physician ; 2. the Physician as the Bridegroom. Or, Christ is the supreme festal end, and the only means of salvation, in the kingdom of God : 1. He is the means of healing, while He calls souls to the participation of His blessedness ; 2. He is the Prince of the blessed kingdom in the midst of His redeemed.— We should think, on our feast-day, of our coming fast-day.—Even in the greatness of His fast, Christ with His disciples leaves far behind Him all the severe penitents of the old theocracy.—The secret fasting of Christians ; or, the great, silent, and festal renunciation of the world: 1. Its form ; 2. its reason, the reconciliation of the world ; 3. its goal, the glorification of the world.

STARKE :—It is a pharisaic and very common evil, that men are very much more troubled about setting others right in their living than about directing their own.—QUESNEL :—The busybody begins by talking about others, and comes afterwards to himself, but makes the best of his own case, 1 Tim. iv. 8.—CRAMER :—Fasting is good ; but to make a merit of it, or even to burden the conscience with it, is opposed to Christian freedom.—It is spiritual pride when, in matters which God has left to our freedom, people desire that others should regulate their piety by their rules.—The fasting of a penitent does not consist only in abstinence from food, but in abstinence also from all the pleasures and all the occasions of sin, Joel ii. 12.—Where Jesus is the Bridegroom of the soul, there is joy and refreshment ; where He is not, there is mourning and grief of heart.—CANSTEIN :—The right measures of pacification in religion are those in which truth and sincerity are consulted.—MAJUS :—The

dominions should, for the future, inviolably observe the customs, statutes, and ordinances of the universal church," etc. ; by which he endeavored to reëstablish Popery among the Protestants.—*Ed.*

nakedness of sin cannot be covered with old traditions. GERLACH:—Jesus terms Himself the Bridegroom of His Church.—Longing for the Bridegroom is the feeling of the Church, when He is away; bridal love and delight, when He is present again.—BRAUNE:—It is a special temptation to good-natured, well-meaning souls, not reconciled to Christ, His doctrine, His discipline, His life, His Church, when evil-minded cavillers fall in with them.—The disciples of Jesus a wedding company.—In all Christians there is more or less interchange of cheerful joy and gloomy sorrow, although the joyous temper when the Lord is near predominates.—New wine, new bottles.—SCHLEIERMACHER:—How Jesus would have us understand and treat the great new period which He came to bring in.—Thus the Redeemer compares Himself with John, Matt. xi. 18 seq.—"That day": the interval of uncertainty concerning the further course of the divine economy for man's salvation.—The old garment: He would thereby intimate that it was by no means lawful to cut up and divide the spiritual power with which He was furnished by God that He might communicate it to men, in order to repair and set in order again that which was obsolete and effete. —In our joyous fellowship with the Lord, let us preserve the happiness which He declares to be the prerogative of His people.—GOSSNER:—They have now once more discovered something. Envy looks at and judges only others, without caring about correcting itself. Another failing of the Pharisees was, that they required all pious people to measure according to their standard, and adopt their usages. The third error was, that they began to speak about others, in order that they might come to themselves, and exalt their own reputation at the expense of others.

Fourth Conflict.—The Ears of Corn on the Sabbath; the Son of Man also Lord of the Sabbath.
VERS. 23-28.

(Parallels: Matt. xii. 1-8; Luke vi. 1-5.)

23 And it came to pass, that he went through the corn-fields [*sowed-fields*] on the Sabbath-day; and his disciples began, as they went, to pluck the ears of corn [began to
24 make a way, by plucking off the ears: Meyer]. And the Pharisees said unto him, Be-
25 hold, why do they on the Sabbath-day that which is not lawful? And he said unto them, Have ye never read what David did, when he had need, and was an hungered,
26 he, and they that were with him? How he went into the house of God, in the days of Abiathar the high-priest,[1] and did eat the shew-bread, which is not lawful to eat but
27 for the priests, and gave also to them which were with him? And he said unto them,
28 The Sabbath was made for man, and not man for the Sabbath: Therefore the Son of man is Lord also of the Sabbath.

[1] Ver. 26.—"Under Abiathar the high-priest" is wanting in D.; omitted on account of the historical difficulty.

EXEGETICAL AND CRITICAL.

1. *See* on the parallels of Matthew and Luke.—In regard to the time, it is to be observed that this event belongs to a later section of the life of Jesus (after He had returned from the Feast of Purim * in 782), when persecution took a decided form against Him. The same remark holds good of the healing of the man with a withered hand. But the motive of Mark in inserting the matter here was evidently to connect appropriate facts. The first offence and the first conflict referred to the forgiveness of sins, which Christ pronounced, and which was alleged against Him as a blasphemous invasion of the rights of God, meaning especially the rights of the priests; the second offence was the intercourse of Christ with publicans and sinners; the third, the opposition of His festal, social companionship to the ascetic and pharisaic fasts,—on which then follows in our narrative the account of the offence taken at the freer position which He and His disciples assumed towards the Sabbath.

* A festival introduced by Mordecai, to commemorate the deliverance of the Jews from the designs of Haman. It was celebrated on the 14th or 15th day of Adar, or March, and was called Purim, from a Persian word which signifies *lot*; because Haman ascertained by lot the day on which the Jews were to be destroyed. Esther iii. 7; ix. 26.—*Ed.*

Ver. 23. **Went through the corn-fields.**—The παραπορεύεσθαι marks the circumstance that He opened His way right and left through the overhanging ears; whereas the disciples began to make their path by plucking and rubbing these ears. Thus does Meyer explain, and doubtless rightly, the ὁδὸν ποιεῖν τίλλοντες τοὺς στάχυας. It is true that Mark says nothing directly about eating; but that is to be taken for granted in any rational rubbing of the ears, and is further manifest from the Lord's justification of them, appealing to the fact of David having eaten the shew-bread. According to Meyer, the allusion to the history of David aimed only to vindicate the rubbing of the ears as an act of necessity; and he thinks that the unessential circumstance of the shew-bread having been eaten led to the insertion into the other Gospels of the tradition concerning eating the ears. This needs no refutation. It is impossible to make the rubbing corn in their hands, in order to clear the way, into an act of sheer necessity, such as eating the shew-bread was. In fact, Mark takes pleasure in presenting a vivid picture of everything. He here tells us how the disciples attained two objects by one and the same act. The less of the two, making a way, occupied his mind merely as the counterpart of Jesus' πορεύεσθαι in another manner; and the suggestion of plucking the ears was quite enough to denote synecdochically the eating them also.

Ver. 24. **Why do they on the Sabbath-day that which is not lawful?**—Meyer tries to establish this discrepancy between the other Evangelists and Mark, that he makes the Pharisees ask in this passage, Why do they on the Sabbath-day something that is forbidden in itself?* But in that case Jesus would have replied only to the first and less important part of their accusation. But if we regard their words as a question of surprise, abruptly asked, and as it were answered by themselves, the harmony of the accounts is sufficiently established. For the Sabbath traditions of the Rabbins, consult Braune. "It was not a journey, being only a walk through a by-path; 2,800 ells' distance from the town were permitted by the law."—"To pluck and rub with the hand ears from the field of a neighbor, was allowed; Moses forbade only the sickle (Deut. xxiii. 25). But the matter belonged to the thirty-nine chief classes (fathers), each of which had its subdivisions (daughters), in which the works forbidden on the Sabbath were enumerated. This was their hypocritical way, to make of trifling things matters of sin and vexation to the conscience.

Ver. 26. **In the days of Abiathar the high-priest.**—According to 1 Sam. xxi. 1, Ahimelech was the high-priest who gave David the shew-bread (Joseph. *Antiq.* vi. 12, 6). His son Abiathar succeeded him, who was David's friend (1 Sam. xxii. 20; 1 Kings i. 7). Moreover, in 2 Sam. viii. 17, Ahimelech is inversely called the son of Abiathar. So also in 1 Chron. xxiv. 6 and 31. Hence it was early supposed that the father and son had both names (Euth. Zig.), or that the son was the *vicarius* of his father (Grotius); while some have proposed to modify the meaning of the ἐπί (under Abiathar).† Later expositors, on the other hand, have assumed that the names have been mistakenly interchanged; but to insist, with Meyer, upon this view, appears to us hypercritical and arbitrary, when we remember that in Ex. ii. 18 the same father-in-law of Moses is once called Raguel and then Jethro, and especially that Jewish tradition was possessed of many supplements of the sacred narrative, as appears from the discourse of Stephen (Acts vii.), and the allusion to the Egyptian magicians, 2 Tim. iii. 8. Here the Old Testament itself gave occasion to supplementary tradition, and the scriptural knowledge of the time incorporated and used it. Moreover, it is to be assumed that the priest's son Abiathar stood in a nearer relation to David, which made the unusual proceeding more explicable. The tabernacle was then at Nob.

Ver. 28. **Therefore the Son of Man is Lord.** —The Son of Man, and not merely as man (Grotius); not, however, the Messiah in His official sense, but the Son of Man in His inviolable holiness, and in His mysterious dignity (intimated in Daniel) as the Holy Child and Head of humanity appearing in the name of God.—*Lord* over the Sabbath; that is, administrating and ruling over it in its New Testament fulfilment and freedom (comp. MEYER).

A clause is found appended to Luke vi. 5 in some Codd.: "The same day Jesus saw one working on the Sabbath, and said unto him, 'Man, if thou knowest what thou doest, thou art happy; if thou knowest not, thou art accursed.'" This historically questionable saying has been placed by some in the same traditional category with the words, "To give is more blessed than to receive," Acts xx. 35. *See* MEYER on *Luke*, and BRAUNE, *Evangelium*.

DOCTRINAL AND ETHICAL.

1. *See* on the parallels.—For the Jewish Sabbath and the Sabbath ordinances, consult the article in WINER. First, the opponents of Jesus thought that He sinned against sound doctrine; then they went further, and urged objections against His free treatment of discipline and pious usages; but now, finally, they would allege that He, in the person of His disciples, sinned against the decalogue, and against one of its most sacred commandments, that concerning the Sabbath. And if, at first, their exasperation against Him was only an internal matter, they now directly attack Him in the persons of His disciples, as appears without any disguise in the history that follows in the text.

2. Christ, even in the silent corn-field, is not safe from the plots of His enemies.—The different manner in which Jesus and His disciples made their respective ways through the field.

3. Abiathar = Ahimelech; or, the freer relation of the New Testament believers to the Old Testament. For the shew-bread, consult the article in WINER, as well as the various writings on Old Testament *Symbolism* of BÆHR, KURTZ, HENGSTENBERG, SARTORIUS, etc.

4. The Sabbath for man, not man for the Sabbath.—The spirit of traditionalism and fanaticism perfectly inverts the ordinances of the kingdom of God; making the means the end, and the end the means.

5. The Son of Man the Lord; or the roots of the supremacy and dignity of Christ which are found in the relation of His sacred human nature to mankind. The Son of Man, the Lord in all aspects and on all sides; therefore Lord of the Sabbath.—But the Lord is a ruler, administrator, and fulfiller of His ordinances; not the abolisher of them.

HOMILETICAL AND PRACTICAL.

The Lord's patience in making His way, and in abstaining, as contrasted with the conduct of His disciples.—Christ in the field among the ears of corn, a noble figure.—The blessing of nature and the blessing of grace in their unity.—The first tokens of the coming freedom of the disciples in its significance; or, Christian freedom a child of need and justification felt in the spirit of Christ.—The peculiar need of the moment pointing to the means of help for ever: 1. The failing way; the lacking bread; the idea that one need might be removed by the other. 2. The significance of this fact for the spiritual relations of the kingdom of God.—To make a way for the Lord the best means of nourishment for His disciples.—The Pharisees everywhere like a shadow of the free

---

* Meyer would find a discrepancy between Mark and Matthew with Luke, in the fact that the former says nothing about *eating* the grain, but only speaks of "making a path" through it. According to him, the Pharisees objected merely to the travelling or the Sabbath and the labor therein involved, and the story of the eating is an interpolation. But aside from the fact that ὁδὸν ποιεῖν may be rendered as in the Eng.ish version "to go," it seems improbable that the disciples should have taken pains merely to "make a path" through the yielding grain by pulling it up or plucking it off, when the simple stride would tread it down.—*Ed.*

† Wetstein and Scholz suggest that it stands for *coram*. —*Ed.*

Gospel.—Man himself the oldest Divine institution, and what follows from it : 1. Nothing in favor of the arbitrary treatment of Divine institutions ; 2. but much in favor of free dealing with human traditions. —The kingdom of heaven is preëminently a kingdom of personal life or of love.—The Sabbath for man ; that is, 1. its law is for the life of the soul, 2. its rest is for devotion, 3. the ordinance for salvation.—The Sabbath for man, and therefore for his eternal Sabbath ; and this also was made for man, as man for it.

STARKE :—QUESNEL :—Christ never performed miracles to feed Himself and His disciples in their hunger ; in order to teach them that they should never without necessity seek extraordinary ways, and that their neighbors' need should press on their hearts more than their own.—Jesus hungers, while His disciples eat; and thereby shows that a teacher, ruler, and leader should be more perfect than his disciples. —OSIANDER :—We should learn to suffer want with Christ, and to abound with Christ.—QUESNEL :—The pride of the Pharisaic nature drives a man to make himself a judge of others, and to demand of them an account of all they do.—CANSTEIN :—God's will is, that we should diligently read the books of the Old Testament, and set them before the people ; that we may derive thence teaching and example.—MAJUS :—All errors must be refuted out of Holy Writ.— QUESNEL :—The usages and ordinances of religion should have for their object the glory of God and the profit of men.—The true Sabbath festival.—Believers are with Christ and through Christ lords of the Sabbath, that they may use it for their own and their neighbors' necessities.

LISCO :—The highest end is man himself. The whole law was only the means for the education of men, whom God keeps thus under external discipline until the law is inwardly and spiritually apprehended and obeyed. But believers adapt themselves, in the spirit of love, to all outward ordinances (although, of course, in the spirit of the Lord),—Gerlach rightly adds : To all outward ordinances that assist the need of the Christian Church.—Every arbitrary violation of legal discipline, without the justification of the spirit of grace and love in Christ, is a heavy sin.— Only the spirit of adoption makes free from the yoke of the law.—BRAUNE :—As David was pitilessly persecuted by Saul, so were the disciples by the Pharisees.—Men are to find rest and refreshment in holy days, but not to suffer hunger and distress.—There is no law given to the righteous; and where the Spirit of the Lord is, there is liberty.—SCHLEIERMACHER :—The Redeemer might have more easily vindicated Himself had He referred to the words of the law, Deut. xxiii. 24, etc.; but He aimed at something higher, to show that all such laws were subjected to a higher spiritual law (the example of David).—The Son of Man Lord of the Sabbath ; the Redeemer is the measure of all ; the question must be, whether a thing is according to His mind and of advantage to His kingdom.—BAUER :—The Lord of the Sabbath has given to every believing mind a Sabbath-law, for its direction and not for its trouble : Thou shalt worship God in spirit and in truth.

Fifth Conflict.—Healing of the Withered Hand on the Sabbath. The Traditionalists hardened into purposes of Murder. Withdrawal of Jesus to the Sea. CH. III. 1–12.

(Parallels: Matt. xii. 9–21 ; Luke vi. 6–11 ; vers. 17–19.)

1 And he entered again into the synagogue ; and there was a man there which had a
2 withered hand. And they watched him, whether he would heal him on the Sabbath-
3 day; that they might accuse him. And he saith unto the man which had the withered
4 hand, Stand forth [up]. And he saith unto them, Is it lawful to do good on the Sabbath-
5 days, or to do evil ? to save life, or to kill ? But they held their peace. And when he had looked round about on them with anger, being grieved for the hardness of their hearts, he said unto the man, Stretch forth thine hand. And he stretched *it* out: and
6 his hand was restored [whole as the other].[1] And the Pharisees went forth, and straight-
7 way took counsel with the Herodians against him, how they might destroy him. But Jesus withdrew himself with his disciples to [εἰς, unto][2] the sea : and a great multitude
8 from Galilee followed him, and from Judea, And from Jerusalem, and from Idumea, and *from* beyond Jordan ; and they about Tyre and Sidon, a great multitude, when they
9 had heard what great things he did, came unto him. And he spake to his disciples, that a small ship should wait on him because of the multitude, lest they should throng
10 him. For he had healed many ; insomuch that they pressed upon him for to touch
11 him, as many as had plagues. And unclean spirits, when they saw him, fell down be-
12 fore him, and cried, saying, Thou art the Son of God. And he straitly charged them that they should not make him known.

[1] Ver. 5.—" Whole as the other " wanting in the most important Codd. Probably brought over from Matt. xii. 13.
Ver. 7.—Εἰς, after D., P., Lachmann, Tischendorf; stronger than the πρός.

EXEGETICAL AND CRITICAL.

See on the parallels.—The narrative of Mark is here particularly vivid and pictorial. He places the scene actually before us, giving his relation very much in the present tense. Like Matthew, he regards the incident in the light of an important turning-point. But he omits the parabolic word concerning the sheep fallen into a pit.

Ver. 1. **And He entered again.**—According to Luke, this occurred eight days later, on the Sabbath which immediately followed the Sabbath of the previous narrative. By the side of the reading εἰς τὴν συναγωγήν, Cod. D. [which Tischendorf follows] places the reading εἰς συν., into a synagogue: probably an exegetical hint that it was not the same synagogue as before. But the expression, "into *the* synagogue," does not designate of itself any definite synagogue. It has, however, this advantage, that it marks the fact of Jesus having gone into the synagogue again, in spite of all the machinations of the Pharisees and scribes.

Ver. 3. **Stand forth.**—Meyer: "Up! into the midst!"

Ver. 4. **To do good.**—The ἀγαθοποιῆσαι and κακοποιῆσαι may be taken generally, *to do good* and *to do evil;* or, more concretely, *to benefit* and *to injure.* Erasmus, De Wette, and others, take it in the latter sense; Meyer, in the former, and Matthew decides us for this. The question of Jesus, that is, was an answer to their question, May a man heal on the Sabbath? This question Jesus answers by an impregnable principle; as appears also from the words, It is lawful to do good, to perform a good act, on the Sabbath-day (καλῶς ποιεῖν).—**To save life.**—The antithesis of *doing good* and *doing evil* now receives its concrete force, to *benefit* or to *injure,* and thereby its application to the present case.

Ver. 5. **With anger.**—Mark gives vivid prominence to the indignation of Jesus. With a glance of displeasure and discomposure He looked round upon the assembly of men who were hardening their hearts before His eyes, as they could not refute His vindication of the right of healing, by reference to the design of the Sabbath.—**Grieved,** συλλυπούμενος.—The συν establishes Meyer's translation, "feeling compassion for."

Ver. 6. **With the Herodians.**—Comp. on *Matthew.* De Wette, without reason, thinks that the Herodians have been by error introduced here from Matt. xxii. 16. Tiberias in Galilee was a place of residence for the Herodians, that is, the Herodian political party; and the time had come when they began to take part in the persecution of the Lord. But it marks a great advance in the enmity of the Pharisees, that they, who had before leagued themselves with the disciples of John for the sake of gathering weight against Christ, now entered into fellowship with the Herodians, whom in reality they hated, in order to destroy Him whom they hated still more, by machinations behind his back.—**How they might destroy Him.**—Thus the Galilean conflicts had in rapid process reached their conclusion.

Ver. 7. **To the sea.**—Not merely to the coast. The life on the sea, in the ship which was now His chief place of instruction in opposition to the synagogue, and which more than once served Him for a transient retreat to the opposite bank, here had its commencement. Matthew also had made this turning-point prominent. But in Mark it is plainly enough characterized as a withdrawal of Christ from His customary work in the synagogue to the ship.—**And a great multitude.**—The great crowds who heard the ship-discourses of Jesus were formed of two main masses, who are distinguished by ἠκολούθησαν and ἦλθον πρὸς αὐτόν. Thus, after the words, "followed Him," we must, with Griesbach, and De Wette, and Meyer, place either a colon or a period. The Jews from Galilee followed Him. The strangers from other parts came to Him. The "following" does not merely indicate external following; it includes a moral element also. In the conflict between Jesus and the Pharisees, they held with Jesus. It was the beginning of a specific discipleship, from which indeed most afterwards receded, but from which the germ of the Galilean believers was afterwards developed. The remaining multitude testifies the extent of the fame of Jesus; but we must also take into account the Jewish traffic, and the commercial route through Capernaum, which attracted multitudes in that direction. The description of the crowd brings them from all parts.

Ver. 8. **They about Tyre and Sidon** are the Jews of that district. We quote the good remark of Meyer: "Observe the different position of πλῆθος in ver. 7 and ver. 8. In the one, the *greatness* of the mass of people is prominent; in the other, the idea of the mass itself is presented;" or rather their coming from all distances. With the followers, the most important thing was, that it was a great multitude; with the crowds coming, it was that they came from all parts, and from all distances. Comp. Luke vi. 17; Matt. xii. 15. Moreover, we must remark that the concourse of people round Jesus stood in a reciprocal relation to His excitement and His breach with the Pharisees. The time had now come when the people began to display an inclination to make a political party in His favor, and to exalt Him into a king. And on this account, also, He was constrained to withdraw from the people, now to this and now to the other side of the lake, in the ship that was provided. Comp. Mark iv. 1 *seq.;* John vi. 15. We must bear in mind the tendency of the rigorous and brave Galilean people to insurrection and uproar.—**And from Idumea.**—John Hyrcanus had brought the Idumeans by violence to embrace the Jewish faith. There were possibly some of that people by this time who voluntarily adhered to it, notwithstanding that unholy violence. But the words may refer to Jews who had been dispersed so far as Idumea and Arabia.—["This is the fullest statement to be found in any of the Gospels as to the extent of our Lord's personal influence and the composition of the multitudes who followed Him." ALEXANDER *in loc.—Ed.*]

Ver. 9. **A small ship should wait on Him.**—The immediate object was that the people should not throng Him. But this does not exclude the ulterior purpose, of having a freer position in the ship, and retreating often to the other shore.

Ver. 10. **Insomuch that they pressed upon Him.**—The cause of the thronging. It was not merely the pressure of a vast listening multitude towards the central speaker; it was rather the intenser earnestness of many who were urged by their desire to touch Him for their cure.

Ver. 11. **Unclean spirits.**—That is, demons, who identified themselves with these.

Ver. 12. **That they should not make Him known.**—That is, as the Messiah.

DOCTRINAL AND ETHICAL.

1. *See* on the parallels.—The Pharisees now seek to involve the Lord Himself in the charge of Sabbath desecration. The present case seemed to differ from the former in this, that the healing of the withered hand was a matter that might have been postponed. And it did not appear to be one of those urgent works of necessity which even the Pharisees permit-

ted themselves to do. On the other hand, the Lord declares the work of compassionate love, or doing good generally, to be of itself always urgent; and the thought is further involved, that sickness does not tarry at a stand, but that there is a continual sinking into deeper danger and need.

2. On the previous Sabbath a work of necessity was justified and established; on the present, the Lord justifies and establishes a work of love. The Christian glorification of the Sabbath into the Lord's day assumes two aspects: 1. The *ethical law* of the day of rest is, with the other laws of the decalogue, transformed into an *ethical principle* for the Christian social world, especially the State. 2. The divine law, and the human tradition, of the festival become now the Incarnate Lord's creation and institution of the Sunday. The Sabbath was the end of the old world, —a figure of its rest in death after its labor under the law. The Sunday was the beginning of the new world,—a figure of the rising to a new life, which began with the resurrection of Christ. The former was the close of a week of labor which had passed in restless activity, like the days' works of creation; the latter was the beginning of a festal week, the works of which should be performed in the joyful light of the Spirit and of love. On the historical and general relations of the day, consult Hengstenberg's treatise (Berlin, 1852). Comp. also the writings of Rücker, Liebetrut, Oschwald, Wilhelmi, and others.

3. Christ the personal fulfilment and manifestation of the law in glorified form, and thus also of the Sabbath. The source and the founder of the day: Himself the Sun of the Christian Sunday.

4. The Pharisees and the Herodians. "Hierarchs and despots are necessary to each other." F. v. Bander.

HOMILETICAL AND PRACTICAL.

See the parallels.—The Lord's Sabbath work: saving life and the soul; the traditionalists' Sabbath work: destroying life (that of the Messiah Himself). —The needy and wretched in the synagogue; or, the school of the law cannot save and heal.—The envious glance of the spy in the sanctuary; or, how carnal zeal does not look up to the Lord, but sideways at what others are doing.—Christ performs the glorious work of heaven in the midst of the dark contentions of those who harden themselves in unbelief: standing alone as Saviour with His faithful few.—The Lord's glance in the world is a looking *around* in indignation, or a looking *upon* in love.—The hardening of His enemies under the very eye of Christ.— Christ is to some a savor of life unto life; to others, a savor of death unto death.—As the paralytic, who could not move, took the boldest course through faith (over the roof); so the man with the withered hand learns by faith to come forward and stretch out his hand in spite of the mightiest enemies of faith.— As it was divinely great to work wonders in the midst of this envious circle of enemies, so it was humanly great to maintain faith in such a circle.— The old and new connection between need and the boldness of faith.—The leagues between carnal religious zeal and secular power against Christ (Pharisees and Herodians).—The transference of Christ's preaching from the synagogue to the ship, in its significance; or, God's word is not bound.—The thronging of the people round the Lord, in its various aspects: 1. A confused impulse to seek help, confused by a craving for the miraculous in that help; 2. an act of homage to the Prince of life: at Golgotha a band of deadly enemies, who cast Him out as if He had been the great enemy of man and destroyer of the people.—How men have ever sought to change the pastoral office, and preaching of the Gospel of Christ for the good of souls, into an office of external acts and helps (changing the spiritual Messiah into a worldly one).—Christ must often withdraw Himself, not only from His enemies, but also from His friends, in order to maintain the spirituality and freedom of His vocation.—It is beyond all important that we should accept Christ as the Physician of souls; for the redemption of the soul occurs now, the resurrection of the body at the last day.—The earthly mind would fain invert this order.—The ship* of the Church must save Christianity from intermingling with the politics of the world.—How often did Jesus retreat before the disposition of the people to proclaim Him as a Messiah in the carnal sense!—The crying demons mislead the people.—The infinitely discordant mixture of dispositions and characters in an excited mass of people.—The test of right-coming to Jesus: 1. A coming to Him alone, not only with, but also in spite of, the multitude; 2. a being alone with Him, whether among many or few; 3. a remaining alone with Him, and entering through Him into the fellowship of the saved.—The *confession* of the demons: how the Lord estimated its ambiguity and recoiled from it.—The demons were first in the confession that Jesus was the Messiah, but their confession was a slavish one.—The Lord had here to do not merely with the words of truth, but with the truth of the words.—The glance of Christ's anger a prelude of the judgment; yet it was qualified by compassion.—Christ, the gentlest friend of men, will one day be a most terrible personage to many.

Starke:—Majus:—The contradiction and slander of enemies should not restrain us from avowing the truth, but make us more courageous and joyful in our confession.—Quesnel:—A miser, an unfruitful Christian, a negligent ruler, a strong man that will not help, are all mere withered hands.—O avarice, how withered is thy hand!—To suck poison out of what is good, or to slander, is devilish.—Hypocrites are very urgent about ceremonies; but as it regards true discipline, they know nothing about it.— When we do what is right, we need not fear secret slanderers.—True love is not afraid of wicked men when it would do good to others.—Canstein:—The enemies of Christ are not sincere; they have seared consciences, and backbite in secret.—Quesnel:— There is much silence that proceeds from the Spirit of God, but there is also a devilish silence.—Here anger and love meet together; but the Socinians cannot, and will not, reconcile these.—The passions of Christ are a great mystery.—Majus:—Divine zeal against sin must be connected with love, with tender compassion towards the sinner.—Quesnel:—What a mystery is an envious heart! It poisons everything, and extracts poison from everything.—When Jesus is persecuted or forsaken of all, there is yet a little company of the faithful who follow Him.— Osiander:—The more fiercely the Gospel of Christ is persecuted, the more surely and widely it is diffused.—The hearing about Christ is not saving of itself; it must lead the soul to Himself.—Quesnel:—

---

* Perhaps there is an allusion here to the "nave" of the church edifice, which is derived from the Latin *navis*, from a supposed resemblance to the hull of a vessel.—*Ed.*

True love makes no difference among men, but does good to all, even to those who come with excitement and at an unseasonable time.—Christ would receive no testimony from lying spirits.

GERLACH:—The Sabbath was to remind us of, and introduce us into, that rest which God enjoyed when He contemplated the creatures happy in Himself after creation was finished, and that into which redeemed men shall again enter at the finishing of the new creation.—This rest is not the rest of death, but the highest life; and to spread abroad life and blessedness in the spirit of love, is the proper business of the Sabbath.—LISCO:—Herod's servants are his servile dependants. (This is true; for the dependants of an absolute despot can only be his servants.)—BRAUNE:—That the Sabbath would not tolerate what might be postponed, was a law to them: he that had the withered hand was not in deadly danger, and his cure might as well take place the next day. Jesus penetrated their thoughts.—Jesus established, that the not doing good was equivalent to the doing of evil; the sin of omission as bad as the sin of commission.—Their mouth was stopped, but their heart was not emptied of envy and malice.—Jesus' glance: the enemy of sin, the friend of the sinner.—The withered hand, 1 Kings xiii. 4.—Instead of joining the tempted Saviour, they made a compact with their deadliest enemies, the dependants of Herod; and instead of sanctifying the Sabbath by doing good and preserving life, they engaged in plans to put to death the Lord of the Sabbath and of life.—The hatred which Jesus encountered was already an earnest of His death; and the multitude of the people coming to Him from Gentile lands was already an earnest of the blessing of His death.—The praise of the Holy One cannot issue from unholy lips and an unclean spirit.—BEDA:—Jesus had victoriously defended His disciples from the charge of violating the Sabbath; but the Pharisees were all the more vehement in involving Him, the Master Himself, in the same condemnation.—CHRYSOSTOM: —Jesus places the unhappy man in the midst of the assembly, that his appearance might excite compassion, and his healing shame the wickedness of the enemies.—SCHLEIERMACHER:—What good thing we have to do, we must set about doing at once.—These Pharisees confederated with the officials of Herod against Him; those Pharisees in Jerusalem brought the affairs of the Redeemer before the Roman governor.—We see how one party stood in need of the other in order to accomplish that which was in each party a foul wrong, though there was something at the bottom like a dependence upon what they thought was the law of God.—How many examples of a similar kind in the history of the Christian Church!— (The withdrawal to the sea.) Here also He remained in the way of His vocation, and retreated from them without neglecting His mission.—(The cry of the demons.) The Redeemer would not that any faith in Him should arise which had not the right foundation.—GOSSNER:—The Saviour can be severe; but He is grieved that He must be angry.—BAUER:— The Pharisees were silent. The eye of the Lord rested upon them, but none of the Pharisees could stand that glance.—They kept angry silence, like that which precedes the storm.

FIFTH SECTION.

CONFLICT OF JESUS WITH THE UNBELIEF OF HIS GALILÆAN COUNTRYMEN, AND WITHDRAWAL INTO THE VILLAGES.

CHAPTERS III. 13–VI. 6.

Beginning of the Conflict. The Lord providing Himself Helpers, in the Calling of the Apostles.

VERS. 13–19.

(Parallels: Matt. x. 1-8; Luke vi. 12-16.)

13 And he goeth up into a [the] mountain, and calleth *unto him* whom he would: and
14 they came unto him. And he ordained twelve, that they should be with him, and that
15 he might send them forth to preach, And to have power to heal sicknesses,[1] and to cast
16, 17 out devils. And Simon he surnamed Peter; And James the *son* of Zebedee, and John the brother of James; and he surnamed them Boanerges, which is, The sons of
18 thunder; And Andrew, and Philip, and Bartholomew, and Matthew, and Thomas, and
19 James the *son* of Alpheus, and Thaddeus, and Simon the Canaanite,[2] And Judas Iscariot, which also betrayed him: and they went into a house.

[1] Ver 15.—"To heal sicknesses, and" wanting in B., L., Δ., Copt., and others. It is omitted by Tischendorf, and seems a supplement from Matt. x. 1. The omission of this makes all the more prominent the casting out of the demons, in Mark the main point.
[2] Ver. 18.—The reading καναναῖος here, as in Matt. x. 4, is best supported.

EXEGETICAL AND CRITICAL.

Ver. 13. *See* on the parallels.—**Into a mountain.**—Not "up into the mountain of that locality," for the locality was the margin of the sea; but it is used in accordance with the relations of the land in Palestine, and the phraseology concerning it: going up into a mountain, in contradistinction to abiding in the narrow vales or low strips of land. And it is to be observed that the expression is used to signify a withdrawal of the Lord, especially for solitary devotion.—**And calleth unto Him.**—The manner of the call is not defined, whether sending for them, or otherwise. The main point is the free choice of the Twelve out of the rest of the discipleship. Meyer supposes that Jesus made first a larger selection, and then in ver. 14 the narrower choice. But there is nothing to hinder our regarding ver. 14 as expressing the more specific end of the call, that is, the appointment and mission.

Ver. 16. **And Simon He surnamed Peter.**—Some cursive MSS. have πρῶτον Σίμωνα. According to De Wette, Mark passed over the statement of Peter's call, because the change of name was to him of special moment. But we may regard the statement of Peter's call as included in the ἐπέθηκε. Thus Christ added, not merely to his name but rather to his general vocation, the distinguishing name of Peter. On account of these distinguishing names, Andrew follows in the fourth rank, after the two sons of Zebedee. The solemn appendage of the name in this place does not contradict the preliminary naming of Simon, which had taken place before, John i. 42.

Ver. 17. **Boanerges:** בְּנֵי רֶגֶשׁ; in Aramæan, the sheva being equivalent to oa. The רֶגֶשׁ, in Hebrew meaning a threatening people (Ps. lv. 15), in Syriac meant *thunder.*—That the name refers to the event mentioned in Luke ix. 54 (according to Calmet, Heumann, etc.), is not contradicted by the supposition that it must have been a surname significant of praise, and not of blame. Comp. on this point the notes on Matthew. According to the ancients, the sons of Zebedee were so termed as μεγαλοκήρυκες καὶ θεολογικώτατοι (Theophylact, and others), because thunder is the ordinary symbol of solemn and profound utterances. We understand the expression to refer to the fiery, grand, sublime spirit, which found its utterance in correspondingly high, strong, and pregnant words. That the name was not habitually used, like the name Peter, may be explained by the fact that it was a collective one. It was distributed later, or merged in the several dignities of the first apostolical martyr, and the disciple who lay on the Lord's bosom, the last great Evangelist.

Ver. 18. **Canaanite.**—Though the form of the surname has in it something unusual, yet it is easily explicable by the term ζηλωτής in Luke, and the accompanying reading κανανίτης.

Ver. 19. **And they went into a house.**—For the chronology, Comp. the notes on Matthew. The Evangelist's arrangement here is not according to time, but regulated by a classification of the facts. For the circumstance described does not, as Meyer thinks, fall into the period after the return from the Sermon on the Mount, but into a later period, when Christ's work in Galilee was drawing to its close. According to Ewald, an original form of Mark might have introduced, before this return, the Sermon on the Mount, and the narrative of the nobleman in Capernaum. These, and similar suppositions of Hilgenfeld, we have sufficiently dealt with in our introductory account of this Evangelist. Finally, it does not follow from their coming into a house, that the ensuing discourse took place in that house.—["The true sense is most probably that given in the margin of the English Version, and long before by Wiclif, *they came home, i. e.,* returned to Capernaum again as their headquarters, and the centre of their operations. Comp. εἰς οἶκον in Mark ii. 1." ALEXANDER *in loc.—Ed.*]

DOCTRINAL AND ETHICAL.

1. Comp. on the parallels.—It is characteristic of Mark, that he gives prominence here to the sons of thunder. On the fiery zeal of John, comp. Gerlach, p. 118. "The peculiarity of John was pure simplicity, and also glowing, fiery zeal; this having been at first disturbed by impure passion (ch. ix. 38; Luke ix. 54), but sanctified afterwards by inward love to Christ. His epistles contain some of the sternest passages in the New Testament. See 1 John ii. 22, 23; iii. 8; 2 John 7-11. Comp. also the Seven Epistles in the Apocalypse. Church history also records many things concerning his sacred zeal." And then Gerlach introduces the narrative of John's hastily leaving the bath in which the heretic was found.

2. As it respects the calling of the Twelve, it must be observed that it falls into two separate crises, according to Mark, ch. iii. 13-19, and ch. vi. 7 *seq*. Only it is evident that the more precise characterization of the mission in ch. vi. 7 is identical with the mission in Matt. x. 1 *seq.*, and Luke vi. 12 *seq*. Hence, we assume that Mark here describes a selection of the Apostles preliminary to that mission, one that was a continuation and enlargement of the call of the four most select disciples at the Sea of Galilee, and intended primarily as a vocation to more decided discipleship and engagement in helping the Redeemer's work. Yet the more express apostolical vocation is kept in view even here, as is manifest from the very solemn account of Mark, in which he anticipates some features of the later vocation. It would appear, indeed, that the point of time to which Mark here carries us, was even later than the proper historical epoch of the more express vocation. The motive for placing it in this connection was the fact of the commencement of the great conflict of our Lord with the unbelief of the world, as it is exhibited in this section.

3. The names of the Apostles, or their call, introduced with respect to Christ by the appointment of the Father: mediate, and yet immediate.

4. Judas possessed a certain species of endowment; yet observe the doubtfulness of such kind of endowments in the affairs of Church and State, inasmuch as the superficial ability may easily outweigh the central character.

HOMILETICAL AND PRACTICAL.

See on the parallels.—The call of Christ's servants a call from the mountain: 1. Christ stands on the mountain; 2. those called go up the mountain to Him; 3. they come down from the mountain into the world of men. *See* Isa. lii. 7.—The place of Jesus' prayer the birthplace of apostolical and evangelical vocation.—Fellowships and collegiate bodies in the kingdom of God: 1. In their meaning: union of the divine and the human, even here. 2. Their design: mutual supplementing and strengthening, lessening of human one-sidedness, and increase of divine power.—Casting out of devils a main branch of ecclesiastical vocation.—The variety and differences of the disciples of Jesus are an unfolding of the riches of Christ and of His kingdom.—Judas

Iscariot among the Twelve an eternal sign, 1. Of the all-endeavoring love of Christ, 2. of the greatness of human depravity, 3. of the dangers of the spiritual office (or of a mere external connection with the Lord) without perfect fidelity in the spiritual life (an internal union with Him), 4. of the aim and end of the Church (not a community of perfect saints, but of redeemed men).—Degrees in the apostolical circle, notwithstanding their unity and equality.—Even the dark power which was displayed by the last of the Twelve testified of the spiritual abilities of this company, over which Jesus reigned in kindly majesty.—" Who betrayed Him : " the called Apostle a denounced traitor.

STARKE :—The choice of a pastor should be entered upon with prayer, Acts i. 24.—He who would be fit for the work of the Lord must first be much with the Lord.—QUESNEL :—Spiritual pastors make up, with Christ the chief Pastor, only one Priest; His priesthood in the preaching of the Gospel being continued, diffused, and perfected, 1 Pet. ii. 9.—The Lord gives the word along with the great host of the Evangelists. They who take their ease when they are placed in office, often become brethren of Judas.—It is a miserable delusion to repose in a legitimate call, while negligent of fidelity and diligence in discharging its functions.—Not all the names of Christians are written in heaven, though they may stand recorded in the books of the Church below.

GOSSNER :—He who would be a witness for Christ and His Gospel, must be much with Him, and by constant communion have learned to know Him.—How will they stand before Him, who learn what they have to say by heart, stand up, and only declaim, or read it off!—BAUER :—The death-roll of the Twelve Apostles itself a sermon.

---

1. *Conflict of Jesus with the* blaspheming *Unbelief of His Enemies, and His Triumph over Human Wisdom.* (CH. III. 20–30.)—2. *His Conflict with the well-meaning Unbelief of His Friends; Triumph over Devilish Malice and Human Policy.* (VERSS. 20, 21, and VERSS. 31–35.)

(Parallels : Matt. xii. 22–50; Luke viii. 19–21; xi. 14–26.)

20 And the multitude cometh together again, so that they could not so much as eat
21 bread. And when his friends heard *of it*, they went out to lay hold on him : for they
22 said, He is beside himself. And the scribes which came down from Jerusalem said,
23 He hath Beelzebub, and by the prince of the devils casteth he out devils. And he
 called them *unto him*, and said unto them in parables, How can Satan cast out Satan?
24, 25 And if a kingdom be divided against itself, that kingdom cannot stand. And if a
26 house be divided against itself, that house cannot stand. And if Satan rise up against
27 himself, and be divided, he cannot stand, but hath an end. No man can enter into a
 strong man's house, and spoil [plunder] his goods, except he will first bind the strong
28 man; and then he will spoil [plunder] his house. Verily I say unto you, All sins shall
 be forgiven unto the sons of men,[1] and blasphemies wherewith soever they shall blas-
29 pheme : But he that shall blaspheme against the Holy Ghost hath never forgiveness,
30 but is in danger of [liable to] eternal damnation :[2] Because they said, He hath an un-
31 clean spirit. There came then his brethren, and his mother, and, standing without,
32 sent unto him, calling him. And the multitude sat about him, and they said unto him,
33 Behold, thy mother and thy brethren[3] without seek for thee. And he answered them,
34 saying, Who is my mother, or my brethren?[4] And he looked round about on them
35 which sat about him, and said, Behold my mother and my brethren! For whosoever
 shall do the will of God, the same is my brother, and my sister, and mother.

[1] Ver. 28.—The words τοῖς υἱοῖς τῶν ἀνθρώπων precede τὰ ἁμαρτήματα in the best Codd.; and so they are placed in Griesbach, Lachmann, Tischendorf. B., D., G., Lachmann, and Tischendorf read ὅσα, instead of ὅσας.
[2] Ver. 29.—The reading ἔνοχός ἐστιν αἰωνίου ἁμαρτήματος, according to B., L., Δ., and others, is accepted by Griesbach, Lachmann, and Tischendorf. The readings κρίσεως and κολάσεως seem to have been explanatory paraphrases of this strong and pregnant expression.
[3] Ver. 32.—" His mother and His brethren " is the reading of B., C., D., G., Versions, Griesbach, Scholz, Lachmann; better established than the order in the *Recepta*, "His brethren and His mother," which is also adopted by Fritzsche and Tischendorf. Meyer holds to this last, thinking that the mother was afterwards put first on account of her rank, and in conformity with the parallels in Matthew and Luke. It may have been the purpose to make the mother less prominent, in a case of seeming error. An additional clause, καὶ αἱ ἀδελφαί σου, has A., D., E., &c., for it; B., C., L., and many Versions against it. Griesbach, Lachmann, Tischendorf accept it; so also De Wette and Meyer. We think the omission harder to account for than the insertion would be,—which probably had reference to ch. vi. 3.
[4] Ver. 33.—B., C., L., Versions, Lachmann, and Meyer read καὶ οἱ, instead of ἢ οἱ.
[5] Ver. 35.—The μου after ἀδελφή is omitted by Lachmann and Tischendorf, following preponderating authorities.

EXEGETICAL AND CRITICAL.

See on the parallels.

Ver. 21. **When His (friends).**—This very important feature in the evangelical narrative is peculiar to Mark. According to Baur, Mark here represents the mother of Jesus, with His brethren, as confederate with the Pharisees. Meyer, on the contrary, shows that their opinion, ὅτι ἐξέστη, was honest error (not wickedness), and that their design was to provide for Christ's safety. But if they really had thought Him beside Himself, their care for his safety would have taken the form of an attempt forcibly to seize and detain Him. We regard the step as having been the result of timid policy. At the crisis, when Christ's breach with the powerful party of the Pharisees was decided, they sought by a fiction to remove Him from publicity and a supposed extreme danger. We may regard the adoptive brethren of Jesus as the representatives of this idea; but it is evident that Mary also was drawn into this error of worldly policy (*see* the notes on *Matthew*). It is quite in keeping with the character of such a policy, that these brethren soon afterwards sought to thrust Him forward, John vii. 1 *seq.*—The household of Jesus did not come from Nazareth to Capernaum, as Meyer supposes, but from the house of their abode in Capernaum to the place where the crowds were thronging Him. That the Pharisees would here come against him with a public accusation would very well be known in Capernaum.—**For they said.**—Themselves, of course, the household of Jesus; and not, as Olshausen thinks, "it was said" by the malicious Pharisees, or by others generally (Ewald), or by messengers (Bengel).—**He is beside Himself.**—Not, as Luther says, "He will be beside Himself;" but not, with Meyer, "He is mad." It is designedly ambiguous, inasmuch as the ἐξέστη may mean, in a good sense, the being for a season rapt into ecstasy by religious enthusiasm (2 Cor. v. 13), as well as, in a bad sense, the being permanently insane. In His ecstasy, He is no longer master of Himself. The involuntary, religious μαίνεσθαι is, indeed, not an Old-Testament idea, but a Greek one: it was, however, current in the Jewish popular notion; and the more ambiguous it was, the better it would suit the aim of their policy. It must not be confounded, as Theophylact confounds it, with the allegation of Christ's opponents.* On the contrary, if His opponents should say that He was raging in demoniacal possession, the politic answer was at hand, "He is, indeed, beside Himself, but it is in a good demoniacal ecstasy." According to Meyer, this circumstance cannot be reconciled with the previous history of Mary in Matthew and Luke. The supposition of Olshausen (and Lange), that this was a moment of weakness in her life, he thinks very precarious. And Pius IX. would agree with him, though for a different reason. For the various interpretations of the passage, *see* Meyer. Euthym. Zigab.: "Some envious ones said so." Schöttgen and Wolf: "The disciples said that the people were mad." Grotius: "Report said that he had fainted." Kuinoel: "It was the message to come home to eat, for *maxime defatigatus est*," etc.

Ver. 30. **An unclean spirit.**—Characterization of Beelzebub, in opposition to the Holy Spirit.

Ver. 34. **And He looked round about.**—Mark often gives prominence to the Lord's glance around. Here it is in contrast with the indignant looking around of ch. iii. 5.

DOCTRINAL AND ETHICAL.

1. *See* on the parallels.—Mark omits, among other things, to give us the immediate occasion of the main matter of the section,—the healing of the demoniac. The reason that his friends came out to Him as they did seems to have lain in the thronging of the crowds, and in the fact that there was no room to eat. These facts, however, furnished them with a pretext for rescuing Him from the hands of His enemies, whose designs and power they well knew. John came not eating and drinking, and they said, *He hath a devil.* Spirit-like oblivion of the body and of its nourishment, they interpreted as involuntary demoniac enthusiasm. Thus did it seem to be with the Lord at this time; and using this representation, his family went out to gain their object.

2. The choice of the Twelve was soon followed by this erring conduct of His own friends towards Him, several of the Twelve being among them. These, therefore, mistook their vocation, in the same manner as Peter and the sons of Zebedee mistook theirs on another occasion. The new impulse given to the Lord's cause, and the new step it had taken, is followed by a new defeat and counter-stroke. As soon as He takes assistants to Himself, they aim to infuse earthly policy into His plans.

2. The worst manifestation of the kingdom of evil is the blasphemy with which hypocrites, unconsciously standing in the service of darkness, interpret the most glorious manifestations of the kingdom of heaven as works from below. The blasphemy against the Son of God, as approximating to the blasphemy against the Holy Spirit, is the most fearful display of the power of the arch-blasphemer.

4. While the pictorial vividness of the Evangelist is observable throughout the whole of the conflict which he depicts, he, however, omits the sign of Jonas, the statement concerning possession by seven devils, and the like.

5. *And looking round.*—Jesus, in His conflict with His enemies and the dark kingdom which they serve, does not trust to men, but does trust to His own influence on mankind; that is, he does not confide in His own friends, so far as they would dictate to Him with carnal policy as his natural family; but to His friends as they trustingly hang upon His lips as his spiritual family.

6. Christ's defence becomes immediately an attack. Earnest apologetics pass over into polemics.

HOMILETICAL AND PRACTICAL.

See on the parallels.—*No room to eat.* How often did the Lord, in the zeal of His vocation, forget eating and drinking and sleep!—The highest freedom of spirit and self-government are interpreted even by His people as bondage and being beside self.—How much to be reprobated is an ambiguous and feigned adoption of the notions of the enemies of truth, on the part of those who would represent the truth!—The concessions of carnal ecclesiastical policy to the unfriendly world always spring from evil.—The sound concession is the infinite forbearance with which Christ enters into the notions of His opponents to refute their assertions.—Christ exalted equally above the protection of His friends and the attacks of His foes.—Contrast between the Lord's great conflict with His opponents and his disciples' slight assistance: 1. Contrast in temper: heroic reliance in divine truth; petty trust in human cunning. 2. Contrast in the conflict itself: simple defence and simple attack; ambiguous apology and mediation. 3. Contrast in the result: high victory; deep humiliation.—The false and the true family of Jesus: 1. The one would watch over Him and His cause, the other will be watched over by Him; 2. the one would

---

* Namely, that he was in league with the demons.—*Ed.*

lead Him, the other will be led by Him; 3. the one would save Him, the other will be saved by Him; 4. the one would restrain and bring Him into danger, the other will be restrained and bound by His word and Spirit.—The Lord detects and cuts asunder the bands of perilous fellowship between His friends and His enemies: 1. He detects them: worldliness in religion, fear, cunning, and policy; 2. He cuts them asunder by the word of severance, by warning, and by blessing.—The divine dignity of our Lord in the decisive conflicts of His kingdom: 1. As opposed to His enemies, the instruments of darkness; 2. as opposed to His family, as they are confused by the apparent danger of His cause; 3. as opposed to His Church, which hangs upon His lips with child-like simplicity, not suspecting its danger.—Christ says to His people, in the days of apparent peril to religion: My thoughts are not your thoughts; neither are My ways your ways.—Christ's defence is, in its own nature, also a victorious attack.—Blasphemy against the Spirit is eternal guilt, and therefore exposed to eternal condemnation.—The calm declaration of Christ, that He wrought in the power of the Holy Spirit, in opposition to His blaspheming enemies, who charged him with being possessed by the spirit of darkness and working under his influence.—Maintenance of this opposition: 1. Divine repose against devilish excitement; 2. divine forbearance against devilish hatred; 3. divine illumination against devilish confusion.

STARKE:—CANSTEIN:—If Christ endures, the Christian Church endures.—ZEISIUS:—The devil never gives up the work that his name imports—slandering the good; nor do those who are on his side, John viii. 44.—QUESNEL:—We must strive to preserve our honorable name, so long as it is possible.—It is awful to ascribe to the devil that which comes from God. Thus God is made into Satan.—The Creator endures this blasphemy, in His patience and long-suffering, and men will endure nothing. We should be imitators of God.—Wolf does not eat wolf, nor does Satan drive out Satan.—Satan does not persecute Satan, yet Christians persecute Christians. O fearful wickedness!—Rebellion and insurrection are destructive and ruinous.—When once the devil is master of any heart, none but Jesus Christ can drive him out.—CRAMER:—Children must honor their parents; but in matters that pertain to office, and the things of God and conscience, they should not be overruled by any.—There is no carnal prerogative in the kingdom of God.—QUESNEL:—He who doeth the will of God to the end enters into an eternal alliance with God as his Father, with Jesus Christ as his brother, with the angels and saints as his sisters, and with the heavenly Jerusalem as his mother.—GERLACH: According to Mark, Jesus distinguishes general blasphemy against God from the particular blasphemy against the Holy Spirit; according to Matthew and Luke, He distinguishes from it also the blasphemy against the Son of Man: in both cases there is the contrast between a revelation which has been more external, and one which has seized the inner man with more convincing divine power.—"He that doeth the will of God:" He means thereby faith, which is the fount and beginning of all holy obedience.—BRAUNE: We must watch over zeal, as over fire in a house. But that cold moderation which the world loves so well is most offensive to Christ, who will spue the lukewarm out of His mouth, Rev. iii. 16. This is our Lord's official fidelity.—In the presence of this blaspheming malignity, the Redeemer exhibits a simplicity, a security, a freedom from all bitterness, which must have produced a sacred impression upon all who beheld, even as upon us now.—It is in the Spirit of God that Jesus overcomes Satan.—SCHLEIERMACHER (on the words, *He is beside Himself*):—So those have always been accounted whom God in hard times has chosen for His special instruments: it was in the time of the Church's Reformation, and it will always be so again when times of darkness shall return.—There have never been wanting such enemies of the truth, who have similarly sought to put another character upon that one only institute for human salvation which can never find a substitute. But, as in the text, their efforts are always vain.—How far blind and rash zeal may lead men!—"He that gathereth not with Me, scattereth."—"He that for My sake forsaketh not father and mother is not worthy of Me."—Christ on the cross: "Behold thy son! Behold thy Mother!"—There should be, then, no conflict between our natural and spiritual relationships. —All the household must be members of the one same family.

---

3. *Our Lord's Conflict with the carnal Unbelief of the People in the Delivery of His Parables, and His Triumph over Human Narrowness.* (CH. IV. 1–34.)

(Parallels: Matt. xiii. 1–23; vers. 31–35; Luke viii. 4–18.)

1 And he began again to teach by the sea-side: and there was gathered[1] unto him a great multitude, so that he entered into a [the] ship, and sat in the sea; and the whole
2 multitude was by the sea on the land. And he taught them many things by parables,
3 and said unto them in his doctrine, Hearken: behold, there went out a sower to sow:
4 And it came to pass, as he sowed, some fell by the way-side, and the fowls [birds] of
5 the air[2] came and devoured it up. And some[3] fell on stony ground, where it had not
6 much earth; and immediately it sprang up, because it had no depth of earth: But when
7 the sun was up,[4] it was scorched; and, because it had no root, it withered away. And some fell among thorns, and the thorns grew up and choked it, and it yielded no fruit.
8 And other fell on good ground, and did yield fruit that sprang up and increased, and
9 brought forth, some thirty, and some sixty, and some an hundred. And he said unto

10 them, He that hath ears to hear, let him hear. And when he was alone [apart], they
11 that were about him with the twelve asked of him the parable.⁵ And he said unto
them, Unto you it is given to know⁶ the mystery of the kingdom of God: but unto
12 them that are without, all *these* things are done in parables: That seeing they may see,
and not perceive; and hearing they may hear, and not understand; lest at any time
13 they should be converted, and *their* sins should be forgiven them. And he said unto
14 them, Know ye not this parable? and how then will ye know all parables? The sower
15 soweth the word. And these are they by the way-side, where the word is sown; but
[and] when they have heard, Satan cometh immediately, and taketh away the word
16 that was sown in their hearts. And these⁷ are they likewise which are sown on stony
ground; who, when they have heard the word, immediately receive it with gladness;
17 And have no [not] root in themselves, and so endure but for a time [but are transient]:
afterward, when affliction or persecution ariseth for the word's sake, immediately they
18 are offended. And these are they which are sown among thorns; such as hear the
19 word, And the cares of this⁸ world, and the deceitfulness of riches, and the lusts of other
20 [remaining] things entering in, choke the word, and it becometh unfruitful. And these⁹
are they which are sown on good ground; such as hear the word, and receive *it*, and
21 bring forth fruit, some thirty-fold, some sixty, and some an hundred. And he said
unto them, Is a candle [the lamp] brought to be put under a bushel [the measure],
22 or under a [the] bed? and not to be set on a candlestick [the lamp-stand]? For
there is nothing hid, which shall not¹⁰ be manifested; neither was anything kept secret,
23 but that it should come abroad. If any man have ears to hear, let him hear.
24 And he saith unto them, Take heed what ye hear: with what measure ye mete, it shall
25 be measured to you; and unto you that hear¹¹ shall more be given. For he that hath,
to him shall be given; and he that hath not, from him shall be taken even that which
26 he hath. And he said, So is the kingdom of God, as if a man should cast [the] seed
27 into [upon] the ground; And should sleep, and rise night and day, and the seed should
28 spring [sprout] and grow up [elongate], he knoweth not how. For¹² the earth bringeth
forth fruit of herself [automatically]; first the blade, then the ear, after that the full corn
29 in the ear. But when the fruit is brought forth [yields], immediately he putteth in the
30 sickle, because the harvest is [has] come. And he said, Whereunto shall we liken the
31 kingdom of God? or with what comparison shall we compare it?¹³ *It is* like a grain of
mustard-seed, which, when it is sown in the earth, is less than all the seeds that be in
32 the earth: But when it is sown, it groweth up, and becometh greater than all herbs, and
shooteth out [makes] great branches; so that the fowls [birds] of the air may lodge
33 under the shadow of it. And with many such parables spake he the word unto them,
34 as they were able to hear *it*. But without a parable spake he not unto them: and
when they were alone, he expounded all things to his disciples.

¹ Ver. 1.—Συνάγεται instead of συνήχθη: Lachmann, Tischendorf, after B., C., L.
² Ver. 4.—"Fowls of heaven." Τοῦ οὐρανοῦ has only D. of the uncial MSS. in its favor. Probably added from Luke viii. 5.
³ Ver. 5.—Καὶ ἄλλο instead of ἄλλο δέ: Lachmann and Tischendorf, after the best MSS.
⁴ Ver. 6.—Lachmann and Tischendorf, after B., C., D., L., Δ., Vulgate, read καὶ ὅτε ἀνέτειλεν ὁ ἥλιος, instead of ἡλίου δὲ ἀνατείλαντος.
⁵ Ver. 10.—Τὰς παραβολάς instead of τὴν παραβολήν: Tischendorf, after B., C., L., Δ. The parable just delivered gave them occasion to ask about the design of parables generally.
⁶ Ver. 11.—The γνῶναι is wanting in A., B., C.* So Lachmann, Tischendorf.
⁷ Ver. 16.—Καὶ ἄλλοι εἰσί instead of καὶ οὗτοί εἰσιν: Griesbach, Lachmann, Tischendorf, after B., C.*, D., Vulgate, &c.
⁸ Ver. 19.—Τούτου is wanting in the best MSS., and rejected by Griesbach, Fritzsche, Lachmann, and Tischendorf.
⁹ Ver. 20.—Ἐκεῖνοι instead of οὗτοι: Tischendorf, after B., C., L., Δ.
¹⁰ Ver. 22.—Ἐὰν μή, the most difficult and best authenticated reading (A., B., C., Tischendorf). [Meyer thinks that the δ is an addition, and would explain by comparison with Mark x. 30. He denies the assertion of Fritzsche and De Wette that ἐὰν μή is absurdly used here, and contends that it contains a logical analysis of the thought.—Ed.]
¹¹ Ver. 24.—Τοῖς ἀκούουσιν, omitted in Lachmann and Tischendorf, after B., C., D., G., L.
¹² Ver. 28.—Τὸ γάρ must be given up. Πλήρης σῖτος instead of πλήρη σῖτον: B., Lachmann, Tischendorf.
¹³ Ver. 30.—Πῶς instead of τίνι: Tischendorf, after B., C., L., Δ., Versions. Ἐν τίνι αὐτὴν παραβολῇ θῶμεν instead of ἐν ποίᾳ παραβολῇ παραβάλωμεν αὐτήν: Tischendorf, Lachmann, after B., C.*, L., Δ.
¹⁴ Ver. 31.—Κόκκῳ: Elzevir, Fritzsche, Tischendorf, Meyer; κόκκον: Griesbach, Scholz, Lachmann.

EXEGETICAL AND CRITICAL.

See on the parallels.—Matthew gives us a collection of seven parables; Mark, of three. Thus it is a round sacred number in both. Here also the individual parables are combined into one collective view of the kingdom of God. In Matthew, we see the *chronological* development of the kingdom of God in its historical periods; here, we have a picture of its development in space (statistically) according to its immanent principles of gradual expansion. The first parable depicts the kingdom of God in its universally difficult foundation; the second (a procious addition to the treasury of parables, in Mark alone), its certain and natural development; the third, its wonderful and glorious spread and consummation. It is probable that these three parables formed originally one single connected discourse; furnishing the basis of a later historical representation of the kingdom in the seven parables. The beginning of the parabolic discourses, however, had an earlier position than Mark indicates. His purpose is to connect them with the transference of Jesus' teaching to the sea-side; but he has also a motive arising out of the nature of the events for placing these parables here. They form a crisis in the conflict of Christ with unbelief in Galilee, and mark His conflict with the specially sensuous unbelief of the people. Hence, in ver. 12, he has the well-known strong ἵνα (βλέποντες βλέπωσι καὶ μὴ ἴδωσι); while Matthew has the ὅτι. He also quotes in a very suggestive manner, vers. 21-23, the words of Christ which we find in Matthew's Sermon on the Mount, ch. v. 15, and in the instructions to the Apostles, ch. x. 26, and which in Luke, ch. viii. 16, are connected with the parable of the sower. There is nothing improbable in the supposition that our Lord used these figures in various connections. Here the figure of the candle is designed to teach that the parables have it for their positive purpose to enlighten; that is, that the disciples should at the right season discover the spiritual meaning of the parables; and the figure of the measure, that the disciples were to measure out instruction liberally in hope.

Ver. 1. **And He began again to teach by the sea-side.**—Another emphatic reference to the contrast of this with His customary course of teaching; and as an expression of His decided breach with the Pharisees.

Ver. 2. **In His doctrine.**—In His doctrinal instructions. "Of the many things (πολλά), Mark makes some particular things prominent." Meyer.

Ver. 8. **Fruit that sprang up and increased.** —We understand the former, of strong and vigorous upward growth; but the latter, the αὐξανόμενον, of the seed-corn's spreading out into a number of stalks, as is the case with prosperous increase. Meyer also understands the καρπός as meaning the stalks in contradistinction to the grains, these not being mentioned till later: "some," etc. But the idea of the fruit is thus artificially weakened. The actual and excellent growth is described; but under the point of view of its fruit, this and the luxuriant stalk being embraced in one. It is better to understand the springing up and increasing of the fruit as meaning the springing up of the ears of grain with the stems.

Ver. 10. **They that were about Him, with the Twelve.**—The specific company of Christ's disciples, independent of and with the Twelve. Euthym. Zig.: The Seventy. But these were not distinguished from the rest until later.

Ver. 11. **Unto you is given to know the mystery.**—Significant; and to be explained in accordance with Matthew and Luke. The mystery is given through the knowledge of it.—*But unto them that are without*, οἱ ἔξω: in later phraseology, all non-Christians (1 Cor. v. 12); with the Talmudists, all who were not Jews; but also the uninstructed and uninitiated Jews. Here, however, it is doubtless a hint of the germ of the opposition between the old and the new community, which in the word ἐκκλησία Matt. xvi. 18) came somewhat later into full use.

Ver. 12. **They may see.**—The ἵνα is not to be softened, as if ἵνα *id*, as Rosenmüller and others assert. We must maintain that this hard utterance was based upon Isa. vi. 9 *seq.*, and therefore that it must be interpreted in the meaning of that passage: not as an absolute sentence, but as a *deserved*, *economical*, and *pedagogical* visitation. See on *Matthew*.

Ver. 13. **Know ye not this parable?**—The first parable of the kingdom is the basis of all the rest. If they understood not this, they could not understand any that followed. If they had the explanation of this, they had the key for the understanding of all others. According to De Wette, these are rebuking words; according to Meyer, they are a mere recurrence to the question of ver. 10. But it is certainly, at the same time, an intimation of the connection of all the parables in the idea of the kingdom of heaven; so that with the explanation of this one, all were explained.

Ver. 15. **These are they by the way-side, where the word is sown.**—Through the whole parable we must embrace in one view the field with the seed on it. In Luke, the idea of seed predominates; in Mark, the idea of ground sown over; in Matthew, there is an alternation. In the first instance, the view of the ground sown predominates; in the last, the view of the seed scattered.

Ver. 16. **Which are sown.**—Mark the change of tense in Mark: σπειρόμενοι, vers. 16 and 18, and σπαρέντες in ver. 20.

Ver. 18. **Who have heard the word.**—Hearers preëminently. Diligent hearers, but not doers; ἀκούσαντες instead of ἀκούοντες: B., C., D., L., Δ., Tischendorf. Mark gives the most vivid picture of them.

Ver. 21. **Is a candle brought to be put.**—Not an exhortation to virtue, as Theophylact and others thought, but a statement of the end for which He confided to them the mystery of the kingdom in parables. According to Erasmus: "Do not suppose that what I now commit to you in secret, I would have concealed for ever; the light is kindled by Me in you, that by your ministry it may disperse the darkness of the whole world."

Ver. 22. **For there is nothing hid.**—The concealed is in its very nature destined to be revealed in its time. A thing absolutely and forever concealed would not be concealed; it would as such have no meaning. There is this design in all the concealments of the kingdom of God. Thus the clause forms the complement of the ἵνα above, ver. 12.

Ver. 24. **With what measure ye mete.**—De Wette (after Euthym. Zig.): "According to the measure of your ability and diligence (as hearers, *see* the preceding verse), ye will receive instruction." But it seems more obvious, in the process of the thought, to say, According to the measure of your diligence in teaching will your Master add to your knowledge (*docendo discimus*, especially in the kingdom of God). For the mere hearing and receiving cannot well be described as a measuring out.

Ver. 25. **For he that hath.**—The proverb has, here, more reference to zeal in the teaching function. The living treasure of knowledge will always, by its own nature, go on increasing. We may compare the words concerning the spiritual life springing up within, John iv. 14; vii. 38; for living knowledge is never separable from internal spiritual life.

Vers. 26-29 are a continuation of the parabolic instruction addressed to the people. Meyer: Observe the Aorist βάλῃ, and then the following Presents: *has cast*, and then *does sleep*.

Ver. 29. **When the fruit is brought forth.**—But the παραδῷ is not intransitive: When the fruit shall have yielded itself. This relative spontaneousness of the fruit is as if it did not suffer premature cutting before its full ripeness.

Ver. 30. **Or with what comparison.**—Meyer: The hearers are now formally addressed in the discourse, as the omission of αὐτοῖς with ἔλεγεν shows.

Ver. 33. **And with many such parables.**—Manifestly, Mark knew of other parables of our Lord, which he passes over. **As they were able.**—This does not refer to their worthiness (Grotius), but to their ability to apprehend (Theophylact, De Wette). It also includes, however, their being able to bear without being offended. Thus it is not a mere literal ἀκούειν in the sense of being able to receive, as Meyer thinks.

DOCTRINAL AND ETHICAL.

1. *See* on the parallels.—On the ἵνα, ver. 12, see the notes above.
2. The parable of vers. 26–29 teaches, in the figure of the *relative* independence of nature in the regular development of the seed through an internal energy of growth (αὐτομάτη), the higher *relative* independence and regular development of the growth of the kingdom of God, or the establishment of Christianity and the Church in the world down to its consummation for the final manifestation of the kingdom of God. (The reapers: the angels, Matt. xiii. 39.) The proper point of comparison is the seed's impulse of growth from within outwardly, as if by an internal energy of its own, whence follow the apparent spontaneousness, regularity, gradualness, progressiveness, security, and perfection of the development. Thus the naturalness of nature, so to speak, the "metamorphosis of plants," becomes a symbol of the development of the divine life from the seed of the divine word or regeneration. The germinant energy of growth is here the actual freedom of the new divine-human (not abstractly human, but also not abstractly divine) energy of life in humanity; whether in the regeneration and sanctification of the believing community, or in that of the individual Christian. Here also the development proceeds from within, from the conscious internal being: independent or free (not from God, but in God), naturally and regularly legitimate, gradual, progressive, down to certain and decisive consummation. But it is assumed that human nature in its essence bears the same relation to the word of God, and has as much in common with it, as the earth to the seed-corn. And as the earth only by culture, and tillage, and sowing, overcomes its tendency to wildness, and the bringing forth of thorns and thistles, so also the human heart is set free from its wicked bias, and its thorns and thistles, only by the culture of grace and the seed of the word of God. Meyer: The spontaneousness here set forth does not negate the divine energies of grace; but the end of the parable is not to make the latter prominent, but the former. De Wette: The parable teaches patience, as that of the tares forbearance.—The period of the New Testament Church presents the natural development of the kingdom of God, yet not without the Lord's overruling, and not without the constant energy of His Spirit. The miraculous seed has become a new nature, from which at the Lord's appearance new fruits will grow.

HOMILETICAL AND PRACTICAL.

See on the parallels.—Christ teaching in the ship a parable itself of the kingdom of heaven: 1. A figure of the form of that kingdom: *a.* of the evangelical ministry, *b.* of the church, *c.* of missions; 2. a figure of its condition: *a.* small beginnings, *b.* poverty, *c.* mobility, freedom.—Christ in conflict with the *sensuous* unbelief of the world.—Christ the deliverer of the people from the bonds of ignorance, of carnal notions, and sensuous narrowness.—The teaching wisdom of Christ, as it speaks in parables, a seal of His divine power (of His love as of His wisdom). —He that hath ears to hear, let him hear!—The parables of Jesus as signs of the divine judgments: 1. Figuring the judicial concealments and symbols of truth in the spiritual life of mankind, *a.* in the Gentile world, *b.* in the people of Israel, *c.* in the Christian, specially the medieval Church; 2. figuring their scope and purpose, *a.* to spare, *b.* to instruct, and *c.* to discipline and educate the soul.—The interpretation of the parable of the sower a key to the interpretation of all the rest.—The three parables of our chapter combined, present a figure of the unfolding of the kingdom of heaven, as to its foundation, progress, and completion.—The parable of vers. 26–29. Nature, in its normal development from within, a representation of human freedom, and its development in the kingdom of grace.—The word of life in the figure of a grain of wheat: 1. Its internal energy of life; 2. its growth according to laws; 3. its gradualness; 4. its progressive stages; 5. the certainty of its development.—The work of grace, its normal unfolding, in the Church and in individuals.—In the kingdom of grace we must learn not to misapprehend even the immature forms of development (not counting the green stalk as common grass, etc.).—The seed of divine grace requires patient waiting for its maturity.—The human heart may become one with the word of God (in consequence of its original relation to it) through faith; and then there is unfolded in it a divine energy of new life.—For him who rightly cares for the seed, the fruit gradually ripens, although he himself may not know it.—Even in unconscious life, the divine word goes on maturing. (Narratives of the feeble-minded, in whom it gradually was developed. The action of the mind in going to sleep continues in sleep.)—Influences upon the seed of the kingdom of nature analogous to those of the kingdom of grace: the mysterious operation and movement of the Holy Spirit are the sunshine and rain in the kingdom of grace.—The seed, with all its certainty of development, under the necessary condition of sunshine and rain. Application of this to the work of divine grace in the soul of the believer.

STARKE:—QUESNEL:—An imperfect church, an unworthy pulpit, and poor hearers, may nevertheless form a true church, accepted of God.—CRAMER:—Jesus makes the little ship His pulpit: if we do not diligently hear and obey, He removes Himself with His little ship and pulpit.—CANSTEIN:—Tilling the land is the oldest work of men's hands, and the most pleasing to God; therefore Christ took His parables so willingly from that occupation.—God's word is a living seed, by which the spiritually dead hearts of men are made living and fruitful.—HEDINGER:—Unchanging seed, variable hearts.—OSIANDER:—If men did not harden themselves, they would not fall into the danger of reprobation.—HEDINGER:—We must not look at the mere shell, but at the kernel of Holy Scripture (on ver. 13).—QUESNEL:—The knowledge of divine mysteries is of God, and not of man.—The wisdom of God has not always remained secret, but at the right season has been made manifest to men, 1 Cor. ii. 7.—All things must come to light, whether after a longer or a shorter time.—Faithful pastors and diligent hearers obtain from day to day a larger measure of light and grace.—A faithful and diligent soul has a great treasure—its riches extend to eternity; but an idle soul becomes every day poorer, until at last it loses all.—Oh, how far should we have advanced in the way of salvation, if we had only always used aright the means of grace!—By the sleeping is signified an expectation of blessing, which leaves all care to God; as one may say, I sleep, but my heart wakes.—MAJUS:—God's servants should not be impatient when they do not at once see the fruits of their labors.—We must do our work sincerely, and commit to God the result; He will make His true servants rejoice in the day of harvest.—God conceals from His ministers some of the fruits of their diligence, to keep them in humility.—Hope in God, who will not neglect his work in thee.—Christians must aim high, and strive after perfection.—Where God's word is rightly sown and received, it is never long without fruits of salvation.—OSIANDER:—We must not expect at once perfect trees of righteousness in the paradise of the Christian Church; time is required for rooting, growing, and bringing forth fruit.

GERLACH:—The longer man retains and studies any one divine truth, the more manifest it becomes, and itself brings all others to light.—BRAUNE:—The unostentatious development of the divine word and the kingdom of God in the heart of man.—As the husbandman hardly distinguishes seeds, so is it with the results of the seed of the word. Learn patience.—SCHLEIERMACHER:—(He observes that Christ was not misled by the flocking of multitudes around Himself, but perfectly penetrated His whole auditory—four kinds of soils; but that at the same time He was not angered by this character of His auditory.) If the divine word is received and retained, it is changed into the life of the man; and then in a natural manner his acts are like his words, and become more and more the expression of thy divine word.—The fruit is that which is to be detached again from the plant, itself to be again sown, and from which new life is to arise.—The Redeemer says truly, that there is no other power be which the kingdom of God prospers than this power of the seed, this power of the divine word; that is, in relation to the office and work of the human sower.—The preparatory work, the tilling of the land, must be distinguished from the sowing.—GOSSNER:—On ver. 23. Him who made the ear, man will not hear.—If we mete out with the measure of Christ, it shall be meted to us again with the same.

---

4. *Conflict of Jesus with the* feeble-minded *Unbelief of the Disciples; the Stilling of the Storm; and His Triumph over Human Seafarers in their vocation.* (VERS. 35–41.)

(Parallels: Matt. viii. 18, 23–27; Luke viii. 22–25.)

35 And the same day, when the even was come, he saith unto them, Let us pass over
36 unto the other side. And when they had sent away the multitude, they took him even
37 as he was in the ship. And there were also with him other little ships. And there arose a great storm [squall] of wind, and the waves beat into the ship, so that it was
38 now full. And he was in the hinder part of the ship, asleep on a pillow [the boat-cushion]: and they awake him, and say unto him, Master, carest thou not that we
39 perish? And he arose, and rebuked the wind, and said unto the sea, Peace, be still.
40 And the wind ceased, and there was a great calm. And he said unto them, Why are
41 ye so fearful? how is it that ye have no faith? And they feared exceedingly, and said one to another, What manner of man is this, that even the wind and the sea obey him?

¹ Ver. 37.—Lachmann, Tischendorf, following B., C., D., L., &c., read ἤδη γεμίζεσθαι τὸ πλοῖον, instead of αὐτὸ ἤδη γεμίζεσθαι.
² Ver. 40.—The οὔπω is rejected by Lachmann, after B., D., L., Δ., Vulgate. Tischendorf defends it by important Codd. The insertion, indeed, is more easily explained than the omission. Griesbach, Lachmann read οὔπω, instead of πῶς οὐκ, in conformity with B., D., L., Vulgate, Itala, &c.

EXEGETICAL AND CRITICAL.

See on the parallels.—Pictorial vividness in the narrative of the voyage: evening, the sudden departure, the convoy of ships, the violence of the storm, the ship all but sinking, the image of Him who slept on the pillow, the reproach of the distressed men that Jesus cared not, the words of rebuke to the wind, the strong reproof of the disciples, their great fear, and its effect.

Ver. 35. Besides the arrangement according to matter, there is here a definite historical sequence to the preceding section.—**And the same day, He saith unto them.**—Thus it was before the stormy voyage that our Lord uttered the first parables concerning the kingdom of heaven.

Ver. 36. **Even as He was in the ship.**—That is, they proceeded at once, before they could make special preparation for the voyage. The evening voyage over the sea to the southeast coast was extended to several hours, and became a night voyage.

Ver. 37. **The waves beat into the ship.**—The ἐπέβαλλεν intransitive, referring to the waves.

Ver. 40. Meyer: The disciples' weakness in knowledge and faith is made more prominent by Mark than by the other Synoptics: comp. ch. vi. 52; vii. 18; viii. 17, 18, 33; ix. 6, 19, 32, 34; x. 24, 32, 35; xiv. 40.

DOCTRINAL AND ETHICAL.

1. *See* on the parallels.
2. Significance of the crisis of deep excitement: mutual reproaches. The disciples allege against the Lord, groundlessly and irreverently, the reproach of not caring for them; He on His side inflicts the well-founded reproof of despondency and lack of faith. They uttered their charge prematurely, before they had waited to see the Lord's manner of action; Christ did not utter his reproof (fully, comp. Matthew), until He had brought relief in the danger. This often recurs in the history of the Church's great tribulations, as well as in the private difficulties of the Christian life.
3. The personification of the wind and sea in Christ's address is most emphatic in the rebuking words of Christ, as found in Mark. But at the base of this personification there is a dogmatic element, to wit, that nature has acquired a character of apparently wild independence and anarchy since man became unfaithful to his destiny: Rule over it, and make it subject to you. But in this seeming anarchy, which is under the power of God, and is used by Him as a means of discipline and judgment, is reflected that real anarchy, that lack of obedience and faith in the human breast, which is at the same time felt as a lack of self-government and rule over the creature. Therefore we see confronting the unbelief of the disciples Jesus' confidence; His peace is opposed to their excitement, His self-possession to their distraction; His majestic supremacy over the winds and waves is opposed to their subjection to natural terrors. And the effect is, that his own disciples experience towards Him the same awe of reverence and fear which they had experienced before towards the frightful sublimity of nature. But now they are the subjects of a fear which passes over into the utterances of a rising and blessed faith.

HOMILETICAL AND PRACTICAL.

See on the parallels.—The voyage of the disciples of Jesus a night-voyage (according to Mark; *see* the notes) in the life of the disciples: 1. The history; 2. its significance.—The victory of the Lord over feeble-minded unbelief: 1. He leads little faith into danger; 2. He lets it wrestle with the peril to the utmost point; 3. He convicts, humbles, and heals it.—The fear of man before the terrors of nature, a sign that he is not consecrated through the terrors of the spirit.—The Lord's supremacy over human vocations (seafaring, fishing, government, learning).—Trial of the disciples in the danger of death.—The pride of the little apostolical crew, and its humiliation: a sign.—Jesus' sleeping and awaking: 1. His sleeping, the repose of His divine power, an exercise and test of the human; 2. His awaking, a new glorification of the saving divinity in humanity needing salvation.—Jesus the star of the sea (the anchor, the rudder, the lighthouse, the rescuer of the wrecked).—Danger to life always danger to the soul.—Divine help in our human life should be to us a sign for quickening and salvation.—How all fear of the creature should be changed by the awe of Christ's presence into peace.—To reverence the Son of God, and to obtain kingly power over the creaturely world, are one and the same—Perfect love casts out fear.—The wide wild world glorified by the Spirit of Christ into a blessed house of God.—Jesus Christ, the commander of wind and sea: 1. In nature; 2. in history; 3. in the fates of the Church.—What follows from His being obeyed by the winds and the waves,—as to Himself, as to the world, as to us?—Christ as the Ruler of nature, and Restorer of its paradisiacal peace.

STARKE:—The evening may be very different from the early morning.—Faithful servants of God may have some seasons of rest permitted them, lest they sink under their burden.—Going forth with Christ into a sea of tribulation.—If He be with us, we shall not sink and perish.—The little ship of the Church is often so beaten by the storms of tribulation and persecution, that it seems as if it must go down.—Distress teaches man to pray, although faith is never without prayer.—It is the error of men, that they take, at once, danger to be a mark that God takes no heed of them.—CANSTEIN:—A great storm followed by a great calm: so is it ever with God's consolations after trial.—QUESNEL:—God is so gracious and gentle, that He does not despise a slender faith, or reject an imperfect prayer, or cast out a fearful heart.—How profitable would Christians find it, if they would discourse in their social meetings about the wonders of God and the glory of Jesus Christ!

GERLACH:—It is always a blameable unbelief, when we fear to enter the ship with Christ.—BRAUNE: —The difference between Jonah's sleeping in the ship and that of Jesus.—He that is in us is greater than he that is in the world.—SCHLEIERMACHER:— That was their unbelief, He meant, that they thought He could sink at a time when He had not yet given them any commission; that they thought God could take so little care of His work, as that it should sink with them.—There is no one among us who can assure himself that the old man, however entirely he may seem to be buried into the death of Christ, will not rise up with his giant lusts, and involve the soul in storm and tempest.—But if we are members of His body, we should maintain the sure confidence, that in all times of severe trial and temptation, the bond of union between Him and us will not be severed.—As certainly as He could not sink with His disciples on that day, He will not suffer his disciples to sink in this.—GOSSNER:— When the help of man ceases, God's help begins; or, faith in the sure word.—When there is storm in the soul, and when thou art in great peril, thou knowest what it is for, and whither to fly.—What calmness in the soul, when the Lord arises and utters His voice!

THE GOSPEL ACCORDING TO MARK.

5. *Conflict of Jesus with the despairing Unbelief of the Demoniac, and the selfish Unbelief of the Gadarenes; Healing of the Demoniac, and Triumph over Human Devices for Security.* (CH. V. 1–20.)

(Parallels: Matt. viii. 28–34; Luke viii. 26–39.)

1, 2 And they came over unto the other side of the sea, into the country of the Gadarenes. And when he was come out of the ship, immediately there met him out of the
3 tombs a man with an unclean spirit, Who had *his* dwelling among the tombs; and no
4 man could bind him, no, not with chains: Because that he had been often bound with fetters and chains, and the chains had been plucked asunder by him, and the fetters
5 broken in pieces: neither could any *man* tame him. And always, night and day, he
6 was in the mountains, and in the tombs, crying, and cutting himself with stones. But
7 when he saw Jesus afar off, he ran and worshipped him, And cried with a loud voice, and said, What have I to do with thee, Jesus, *thou* Son of the most high God? I ad-
8 jure thee by God, that thou torment me not. (For he said unto him, Come out of the
9 man, *thou* unclean spirit.) And he asked him, What is thy name? And he answered
10 saying, My name *is* Legion: for we are many. And he besought him much that he
11 would not send them away out of the country. Now there was there, nigh unto the
12 mountains [mountain], a great herd of swine feeding. And all the devils besought
13 him, saying, Send us into the swine, that we may enter into them. And forthwith Jesus gave them leave. And the unclean spirits went out, and entered into the swine; and the herd ran violently down a steep place into the sea (they were about two thou-
14 sand), and were choked in the sea. And they that fed the swine fled, and told *it* in the city, and in the country. And they went out to see what it was that was done.
15 And they come to Jesus, and see him that was possessed with the devil, and had the
16 legion, sitting, and clothed, and in his right mind [sane]; and they were afraid. And they that saw *it* told them how it befell to him that was possessed with the devil, and
17 also concerning the swine. And they began to pray him to depart out of their coasts.
18 And when he was come into the ship, he that had been possessed with the devil prayed
19 him that he might be with him. Howbeit Jesus suffered him not; but saith unto him, Go home to thy friends, and tell them how great things the Lord hath done for thee,
20 and hath had compassion on thee. And he departed, and began to publish in Decapolis how great things Jesus had done for him: and all *men* did marvel.

[1] Ver. 1.—Many Codd. read ἦλθεν instead of ἦλθον. But this is not sufficiently authenticated: "probably from Matt. viii. 28." Lachmann and Tischendorf, after B., D., Vulgate, read Γερασηνῶν; L., Δ., &c., Γεργεσηνῶν; Cod. A., *Recepta*, Scholz. Meyer, Γαδαρηνῶν. Comp. the parallel in Matthew.
[2] Ver. 3.—Ἀλύσει, instead of ἀλύσεσιν, Lachmann, Tischendorf, after D., C., L. Οὐκέτι οὐδείς, Lachmann und Tischendorf, after B., C., D., L., Vulgate: strong negation.
[3] Ver. 5.—"In the tombs and upon the mountains," is the best attested order: Griesbach, Scholz, Lachmann, Tischendorf.
[4] Ver. 9.—Instead of ἀπεκρίθη λέγων (Elzevir), the better reading is λέγει αὐτῷ.
[5] Ver. 12.—Πάντες (Elzevir) is wanting in B., C., D., L., Versions; οἱ δαίμονες is wanting in B., C., L., Griesbach, Tischendorf.
[6] Ver. 13.—The ἦσαν δὲ is wanting in B., C.*, D., Syriac, Vulgate, Griesbach, and Tischendorf.
[7] Ver. 18.—A., B., D., Vulgate, Lachmann, Tischendorf, ἐμβαίνοντος.
[8] Ver. 19.—Καὶ οὐκ, A., B., C.; Elzevir reads ὁ δὲ Ἰησοῦς οὐκ.

EXEGETICAL AND CRITICAL.

Compare on the parallels.—Mark's vividness of realization here again appears in many characteristics: the untameableness of the demon, whom no man could bind, even with chains; his crying in the mountains, and the self-tormenting fury of his cutting himself with stones; his seeing Jesus afar off, running to Him, and crying with a loud voice at the first sight of the Lord; the adjuration of Jesus by God; the vehemence of his anxiety that He should not send him away out of that country (Luke: into the abyss); the number of the swine, two thousand; the contrast of the demoniac who was possessed by the legion, sitting clothed and in his right mind; the observation, that the healed man spread the report of the miracle through all Decapolis; and other similar traits. Luke, in his representation of the event, approximates to Mark. Matthew alone makes mention of two demoniacs, on which we may consult the parallels. As it respects the chronology, Mark goes back in the history, manifestly because his order is that of things and not of time. The voyage to Gadara fell in the first year of Christ's work, and preceded the healing of the paralytic and the controversies touching the Sabbath.

Ver. 4. **Fetters and chains.**—This distinction has been explained by referring the fetters to the hands, which Meyer rejects. Fetters are fetters, to whatever part of the body applied. However, these chains were ordinarily used for the hands.

Ver. 5. **Crying, and cutting himself with stones.**—Fearful picture of a demoniac terror,— having reached the extreme point of madness, down to rending his own flesh.

Ver. 6. **When he saw Jesus afar off.**—Vivid description of the wonderful influence of Christ upon the demoniac. Probably some intelligence concerning Jesus had reached his ears; but that he knew Him at once in this His appearance, can be explained only by an intensified spiritual presentiment. It is not probable that he was a heathen.

Ver. 7. **I adjure Thee by God.**—The daring misuse of the name of God in the mouth of the demoniac has nothing in it inconsistent, as Strauss and others have thought. The intermixture of praying and adjuring is characteristic of the demoniac, as under the influence of Christ.—**That Thou torment me not.**—Meyer: "The possessed man, identifying himself with his demon, dreads the pains and convulsions of the casting out." But if that had been meant, the possessed man would have distinguished himself from his demon, and not identified himself with him. In that identification he felt the nearness and the supremacy of Jesus itself a torment, and still more banishment into the abyss.

Ver. 8. **For He said** (had already said).— Compare Luke: παρήγγειλε γάρ, etc.—"If we rely on the exactitude of the sequence of the particulars in the narrative of Mark and Luke, we find here the remarkable circumstance, that the demoniac was not at once healed when the Lord spoke the decisive word. Christ had said to him, Come out of the man, thou unclean spirit! Now by this the demoniac consciousness in this man was shaken to its depths; but as he then felt himself to be possessed of a legion of evil spirits, the demoniac in him was not reached altogether by an address in the singular. Christ saw at once how the healing was to be perfected, and He asked him his name, etc." *Leben Jesu*, i. 296.

Ver. 9. **Legion.**—"The word occurs also in the rabbinical writings." Description of a psychical victim of all possible demoniac influences and possessions. At the same time, it gives a frightful picture of the unclean country in which so many impure spirits were congregated. At this crisis, however, it was partly a word of resisting pride, which sought by boasting to resist the influence; partly a word of silent complaint, in as far as the suffering consciousness of the possessed man coöperated. He does not give his own name, because he still identified his consciousness with that of the unclean spirits, and spoke through them. But when in this sense one calls himself Legion, he describes himself as their leader: as it were, the head of a whole regiment of demons. But the indistinctness and the error of the reply is characteristic of the condition of the man.

Ver. 10. **Not send them away out of the country,**—where they found themselves so much at home; especially, as Luke adds, into the hateful abyss of hell. The lawless nature of the country (where Jews lived mingled with Gentiles), which pleased the demons well, Mark denotes by the circumstance of the two thousand swine, emphasizing the greatness of the herd. If their owners were only in part Jews, who merely trafficked in these animals, still they were not justified before the law. Certainly we cannot regard this as exclusively a Gentile territory.

Ver. 14. **And in the country.**—In the villages and peasants' huts, where the swine-feeders partly lived. The whole scene derives from this circumstance a coloring in harmony with the country and the then state of things.

Ver. 15. **Him that was possessed, sitting.** —Beautiful and moving contrast.

Ver. 17. **They began to pray Him to depart.** —Gradually, after they had received intelligence of their loss, they took heart to desire Christ's departure, in the conflict of fear and anger, fawning and obstinacy.

Ver. 18. **That He might be with Him.**— According to Euthym. Zig., and others, fear of the demons conspired with other feelings in this request. Meyer thinks this could not have been the case, as the engulphing of the animals had already taken place; as if the man believed that, with the swine, the devils also had perished. But, doubtless, his present fearlessness stood on a surer foundation.

Ver. 19. **Jesus suffered him not.**—Wherefore? The healed man had friends at home. Probably he was now in danger of despising his own people. But Jesus appointed him to be a living memorial of His own saving manifestation for that entire dark district.

Ver. 20. **In Decapolis.**—*See* on *Matthew* iv. 25. "That Jesus did not *forbid*, but *commanded*, the promulgation of the matter, is explained by the locality (Peræa), where He was less known, and where there was not the same danger as in Galilee from uproar concerning His person." (Meyer.) We must also observe that Christ gave him notice of the things that he was to say. He was to announce to his friends how great things the Lord (the covenant God of Israel, the God of revelation) had done for him. This commission was enlarged by the man in two ways: he preached not only to his friends, but to the whole of Decapolis; and not only what the Lord had done to him (perfect), but also what Jesus (as the revelation of the Lord) had done to him, in that He had had mercy upon him (aorist: ἠλέησεν).

DOCTRINAL AND ETHICAL.

1. *See* on the parallels, and also the heading.— Christ the victor over despairing, as also over selfish, unbelief; and his elevation above human policy for safety, and care of the sick.
2. Demoniac faith, or the faith of fear (Jas. ii. 19), in all its characteristics: 1. Exalted presentiment and excited spiritualism, without the true spirit. 2. Contradiction and internal distraction: running, deprecating, confessing, denying, praying, adjuring. 3. Slavery: deliverance described as torment, and abandonment to a state of torment as deliverance. 4. Impure and destructive to the last breath (entering the swine and injuring the people).
3. Christ can change the demoniac faith of fear into a blessed and spiritual faith.
4. The entrance of Christ into the land of the Gadarenes a type of His victorious entrance into the kingdom of the dead: 1 Pet. iii. 20; iv. 6.
5. To a stupid and carnal people, under the power of demons without being fully aware of it, Christ discloses the terrors of the world of spirits, to give them a warning and arousing sign.

HOMILETICAL AND PRACTICAL.

See on *Matthew* and *Luke*.—The majestic entrance of our Lord into the district of Gadara: 1. The terror of the evil spirits in the land; 2. the deliverer of those who were bound by Satan; 3. the avenger of the law without legal tribunal; 4. a living condemnation of the earthly-minded in His going as in His coming; 5. the rejected one, who, after His rejection, leaves behind Him the preaching of the Gospel.—Christ annihilates, by the divine, awe-inspiring presence of His person, the horrors of darkness, even as the gentle light of day disperses the blackness of night.—Christ's stepping over the frontier, and its importance: 1. Over the border of a land, 2. over the threshold of a house, 3. and entrance into the heart.—The land of the Gadarenes a figure, 1. of sunk and darkened Judaism (lawlessness), 2. of degraded Christendom (estranged from the law of the Spirit, externalized), 3. degenerate Protestantism (indifferentism).—Image of a corrupt state of things in Church or State: 1. Perverted morals—swine cared for, men abandoned; 2. perverse policy—trade unlawful, the ways given up to madmen; 3. perverted legislation—demons tolerated legionfold, Christ rejected; 4. perverted religiousness—driving away Christ by prayers.—The true demons in the land mock at fetters and chains, but Christ rules them with a word.—The demons enter gladly into the swine; the devilish nature into the animal nature (the old serpent; half serpent, half swine).—Spiritual rebellion against God passes into the unbridled, animal nature.—To a besotted people the Lord preaches by grievous and terrific signs.—The towns and peasants of the Gadarenes; or, the hindrances which the kingdom of God meets with in the land.—Christ passes a milder judgment upon the common ignorance of spiritual sloth, than upon the false knowledge of the hardened; He leaves a preacher of salvation for the Gadarenes in the person of the healed demoniac.—The compassion of Christ in His final glance upon the land of Gadara.—Christ uttered no word concerning His rejection; His only answer was the appointment of this preacher.—The greatest demoniac of the New Testament narrative becomes a preacher of salvation to ten cities.—In the dark land of Gadara Christ leaves for a while a representative of Himself, since they cannot bear His personal presence.—All things in the kingdom of Christ have their time: He sometimes silences, and He sometimes stimulates, the witnesses of His miracles. —The rejections of Christ in their several and yet single character: 1. From Nazareth (through envy); 2. from Gadara (through selfishness and base fear); 3. from Samaria (through fanaticism); 4. from Galilee (through fanaticism and policy); 5. from Jerusalem (through obduracy).

Starke:—Majus:—Christ, the true light, shines in all places, and sends forth His beams even into the Gentile country.—Unrestrained rebellion.—Quesnel:—Hell is a tomb out of which the spirit of impurity proceeds, until God's judgment binds him in it for ever.—Cramer:—As the devil raged mightily at the time of Christ's first coming, so also will he at the time of Christ's second coming, knowing that his time is short, Rev. xii. 12.—Hedinger:—The delight of worldlings and slaves of sin, corruption, and the grave.—How tyrannically the devil deals with his slaves.—Canstein:—The devil has special delight in tombs.—The devil's love for mischief.—*Bibl. Wirt.*:—The ungodly do not love to consort with the godly.—It is a fiendish spirit to take it as torment when men receive benefits from Christ and His people.—O how many are in a spiritual sense possessed by a devil! so many ruling sins, so many unclean spirits.—That the devil desired to abide in that country, was, doubtless, because there were many Jews there who had fallen from their Judaism. (For, as Josephus tells us, this district was full ἑλληνιζόντων.) Eph. vi. 12; 1 Pet. v. 8.— The devil is in truth a poor spirit; he has nothing of his own, and is driven hither and thither by the glorious power of God.—Majus:—The children of God should have no fear of the devil, or of wizards, or of any other creatures of Satan.—If God be for us, who can be against us? Rom. viii. 31.—It is better that earthly creatures should perish, than that a child of God should be kept from salvation.— God's goodness may be discerned not only in manifest kindnesses, but also in misfortunes.—In rude and earthly hearts God's wonders excite only fear and flight.—Quesnel:—He who loves this world's goods will not have Christ long in his heart.—The converted soul longs to be with Jesus.—Canstein: —God uses every one as His wisdom sees will best subserve the interests of His kingdom.—Quesnel: —The grace of conversion is a talent which must be put out to interest, partly in spreading abroad God's grace and mercy, partly in edifying others in salvation.—Osiander:—God sends preachers for a season even to the unthankful.—Wonder the first step to faith in Jesus.

Gerlach:—The manifold misuse of the name of God among wicked men shows the falseness of the early notion that the devil could not utter it. (Yet this notion contains, in a mythical form, a secret truth, which appears in the declaration that no man can call Jesus Lord but by the Holy Spirit.)— Braune:—We see the same thing now in a certain sense: many there are who reject Christ or repel Him, in the secret consciousness or fear that if they obtain His help they will have to suffer much interruption of their ordinary habits of life, have to submit to many things unpalatable, and endure many severe sacrifices.—When the Christian spirit revives, there are many who would have it shut up only in the minds of others, or who would bind it in a dead letter, because they are concerned to save their unrighteous possessions, or their abused rights, or their licentious wickedness, or their cowardly idleness; not remembering the destruction which came upon those towns forty years after the rejection of Christ, and which always surely comes upon the same sin, and often in a much shorter time.—We must frankly and freely acknowledge the salvation of God and His grace in Christ.—Schleiermacher:—For all the perverse anxiety of men, who set not before them that goal of union with God which Jesus presents to us,—who indeed live under rule, but not that of the kingdom of God,—there is much of the same recoil from Christ as that of the demoniac; they are not in the way to reach the right end, any more than the miserable man in our Gospel. That which holds us firm to Him and His great design, is the immediate influence of the nearness of Christ the Redeemer, which holds our minds fast in a firm and established order, makes our steps sure in this changeable world, and directs them to that ultimate goal, to guide men to which He came into the world. Gossner:—He (the devil) marked that he was going to be hunted out, and therefore he cried. So is it with all hypocrites.—They saw Jesus, they saw the man, they saw the miracle on the man; but their swine they saw no longer, and that was their grief. —Bauer:—When the Lord comes to demand a sacrifice from them, how many are there in our own day who rather, that being the case, would send Him away altogether!

CHAP. V. 21-43.

6. *Conflict of Jesus with* desponding *Unbelief on the Sick-bed and Bed of Death; Healing of the Woman with the Issue of Blood; Restoration of Jairus' Daughter; and Triumph of Jesus over the Healing Art, and the World's Lamentations for the Dead.* VERS. 21-43.

(Parallels: Matt. ix. 1, 18-26; Luke viii. 40-56.)

21 And when Jesus was passed over again by ship unto the other side, much people
22 gathered unto him; and he was nigh unto the sea. And, behold,[1] there cometh one of the rulers of the synagogue, Jairus by name; and when he saw him, he fell at his feet,
23 And besought[2] him greatly, saying, My little daughter lieth at the point of death: *I pray thee*, come and lay thy hands on her, that she may be healed; and she shall live.
24 And *Jesus* went with him; and much people followed him, and thronged him.
25, 26 And a certain woman,[3] which had an issue of blood twelve years, And had suffered many things of many physicians, and had spent all that she had, and was nothing bet-
27 tered, but rather grew worse, When she had heard of Jesus, came in the press behind,
28 and touched his garment. For she said, If I may touch but his clothes, I shall be whole.
29 And straightway the fountain of her blood was dried up; and she felt in *her* body that
30 she was healed of that plague [scourge]. And Jesus, immediately knowing [having known] in himself that virtue had gone out of him, turned him about in the press, and
31 said, Who touched my clothes? And his disciples said unto him, Thou seest the multi-
32 tude thronging thee, and sayest thou, Who touched me? And he looked round about
33 to see her that had done this thing. But the woman, fearing and trembling, knowing what was done in[4] her, came and fell down before him, and told him all the truth.
34 And he said unto her, Daughter, thy faith hath made thee whole; go in peace, and be
35 whole of thy plague [scourge]. While he yet spake, there came from the ruler of the synagogue's *house certain* which said, Thy daughter is dead; why troublest thou the
36 Master any further? As soon as Jesus heard[5] the word that was spoken, he saith unto
37 the ruler of the synagogue, Be not afraid, only believe. And he suffered no man to
38 follow him, save Peter, and James, and John the brother of James. And he cometh[6] to the house of the ruler of the synagogue, and seeth the tumult, and them that wept
39 and wailed greatly. And when he was come in, he saith unto them, Why make ye
40 this ado, and weep? the damsel is not dead, but sleepeth. And they laughed him to scorn [jeered him]. But when he had put them all out, he taketh the father and the mother of the damsel, and them that were with him, and entereth in where the damsel
41 was lying.[7] And he took the damsel by the hand, and said unto her, Talitha cumi;
42 which is, being interpreted, Damsel, (I say unto thee,) arise. And straightway the damsel arose, and walked; for she was *of the age of* twelve years. And they were
43 astonished with a great astonishment. And he charged them straitly that no man should know it; and commanded that something should be given her to eat.

[1] Ver. 22.—The ἰδού not in B., D., L., Vulgate, Versions, Tischendorf, Meyer; bracketed by Lachmann.
[2] Ver. 23.—The Present παρακαλεῖ, Tischendorf, after A., C., L.
[3] Ver. 25.—Τις wanting in A., B., C., Vulgate, Versions, Lachmann, Meyer.
[4] Ver. 33.—Ἐπ' wanting in B., C., D., Syriac, Coptic, Tischendorf; bracketed by Lachmann.
[5] Ver. 36.—Παρακούσας, Tischendorf, after B., L., Δ.
[6] Ver. 38.—The Plural ἔρχονται has most support, viz.: A., B., C., D., F., Versions, Lachmann, Tischendorf.
[7] Ver. 40.—The ἀνακείμενον (Elzevir) is set aside by Tischendorf, after B., D., L., Versions; bracketed by Lachmann.

EXEGETICAL AND CRITICAL.

See on the parallels.—Mark connects the return from Gadara with the narrative of the first raising of the dead, in accordance with his own principle of arrangement. According to the more exact account of Matthew, we must place in the interval the healing of the paralytic, the calling of Matthew, and the offence taken by the Pharisees and John's disciples at Jesus' eating in the house of the publican. In his presentation of the events that now follow, we once more observe the exact delineation of Mark. Concerning his little daughter (θυγάτριον), the father here says ἐσχάτως ἔχει, and in an appeal which announces itself at once by an ὅτι. In the account of the woman with an issue, Mark makes it very prominent that she had suffered much from many physicians, which Luke, the physician, much more gently intimates. And the woman's healing is emphatically expressed: The fountain of her blood was dried up; she felt in her body (in her feeling of bodily vigor) that she was delivered from her plague (scourge). He does not (like Luke) expressly mention Peter as the one who replied to the Lord's question as to who touched Him, "Thou seest the multitude," etc.; but he records once more that Jesus turned and looked round to find out who had done this. We see how the woman comes forward trembling with fear, falls down before the Lord, and confesses all. We see Jesus separating Himself with Jairus and the three elect disciples from the multitude, in order to go into the house of death. The tumult of the lamentation for the dead is here vividly depicted. He defines accurately the group of those who enter; we hear the original Talitha cumi; we see the damsel at once, after her restoration, arising and walking, as she was able, being twelve years old; and hear how rigorously Jesus charged the people not to make much rumor about the miracle (which in itself could not be concealed); and finally, how He commanded that they should give the maiden food. Here and there Luke, and here and there Matthew, approximate to Mark's description.

Ver. 21. **He was nigh unto the sea.**—Meyer: "Here there is a discrepancy with Matthew's account, according to which Jairus entered the house of Jesus in Capernaum." But it was neither in Jesus' house, nor in that of the publican Matthew; for the transaction with the Pharisees and the disciples of John doubtless took place after the meal in a public place. Hence there is no discrepancy in the narratives.

Ver. 23. **My little daughter.**—(Tender expression of the troubled father).—**That Thou mayest come** (ἵνα ἐλθὼν ἐπιθῇς).—The ὅτι and the ἵνα give vivid reality to his urgent words; they are to be referred to the kneeling and cry for help (παρακαλεῖ). Hence there is nothing to be supplied in the text.

Ver. 26. **Had suffered many things from many physicians.**—"How various were the prescriptions of Jewish physicians for women in that case, and what experiments they were in the habit of making, see in LIGHTFOOT, p. 614." Meyer. Comp. also the article *Krankheiten* in WINER. "She probably suffered from a chronic hæmorrhage in the womb, and its long continuance endangered life." See also the article *Reinigkeit*. "Such a woman was, according to Lev. xv. 25, through the whole time unclean, and was required, after the evil had passed away, to bring on the eighth day an offering for purification." On the strong Oriental abhorrence of such persons, see the same article.

Ver. 28. **For she said,**—thinking in audible words.—**Touch but His clothes.**—That the more precise "hem of His garment," occurring in Matthew and Luke, is wanting in Mark, gives no warrant for conjectural emendation.

Ver. 29. **The fountain of her blood.**—Not euphemistic description of the womb, but vivid description of the cause of the evil; the blood being represented as flowing from a fountain.—**She felt in her body.**—Euth. Zig.: As her body was no longer moistened, etc. But here there is something greater signified: she experienced the healthy feeling of new life.

Ver. 30. **Virtue had gone out of Him.**—Meyer maintains that Jesus perceived the flowing of His virtue after it took place; a simultaneous knowledge of it being thought at variance with the words. But, on the contrary, it must be observed that the simultaneousness of the knowledge is declared in the ἐπιγνούς; first by the ἐπί, and then by the Aorist. The opposite explanation might be made to favor a magical interpretation of the event, and Strauss' criticism upon it. Yet Meyer himself refers with an emphatic note of exclamation to Calovius: "Calovius quoted the passage against the Calvinists: *vim divinam carni Christi derogantes.*"

Ver. 38. **Them that wept.**—A scene of Jewish ceremonial lamentation over the dead, in which Mark omits the minstrels (*see* Matthew), and lays less stress than Luke upon the weeping and bewailing, but only to give more prominence to the tumult and mechanical liturgical cries (by ἀλαλάζειν). On the Jewish lament for the dead, *see* GROTIUS on *Matthew*, and WINER's article *Trauer*.

Ver. 41. **Talitha cumi,** טְלִיתָא קוּמִי.—Similar original Aramaic words occur in Mark, ch. iii. 17; vii. 11, 34; xiv. 36.

Ver. 42. **She was of the age of twelve years.**—Reason for the statement that she arose and walked at once. Bengel: *Rediit ad statum, ætati congruentem.*

Ver. 43. **That no man should know it.**—That is, should know the occurrence in its precise characteristics, viz., the way and manner of the restoration of the dead. On the motive of this prohibition, *see* Meyer.*—**That something should be given her to eat.**—Theophylact: That the raising might not be regarded as only an appearance. Meyer: In order to show that the child was not merely delivered from death, but from sickness also. Chiefly, however, because she was in need of strengthening by food.

DOCTRINAL AND ETHICAL.

1. *See* on the parallels.—The touching of Christ's garment, and the conscious issuing of a divine virtue from Him as the result, are a testimony to the living unity and reciprocal influence of the divine and human natures in His personal consciousness; in which the human nature was not (as the old dogmatics taught) merely in a passive relation.

2. Two miracles of healing were wrought on diseased women. Otherwise, they are mainly male sufferers who are adduced as examples of His healing acts. Not that other instances were wanting; for the very first healing recorded by the Evangelists took place on a woman, Peter's wife's mother. Luke mentions some women who were dispossessed of devils, ch. viii. 2. But the deliverance of Mary Magdalene from seven devils we regard, after the analogy of Matt. xii. 45, as a symbolical expression of an essentially great conversion.—The woman with an issue of blood, the dead maiden; progression in the manifestation of suffering in the female sex. That the former had been afflicted twelve years and the latter was twelve years old, was a coincidence from which rash criticism has vainly sought to extract ground of suspicion.

3. We term this narrative a history of victory over *despairing* unbelief. This appears in the comfortless wail of the Jewish lament over the dead; in the circumstance that the people around the dead maiden laughed at the Lord, when He declared that she was not dead, but slept; but especially in the message which they sent to the ruler of the synagogue, Why troublest thou the Master any further? wherein there is an evident tone of bitter and almost ironical unbelief. The faith of Jairus itself appears, at first, as only a fruit of distress. Hence it was subjected to a severe test, that period of deep anxiety during Christ's delay while He cured the woman with the issue of blood. The weak germ of Jairus' faith was encompassed by desponding unbelief. Even the faith of the sick woman struggles with the despondency into which a long series of disappointed

---

* Meyer makes the motive to be, a desire on the part of Christ to repress the tendency to fanatical expectations and tumults concerning the Messiah, among the Jews.—*Ed.*

acts of trust in physicians had thrown her. She does not venture to bring her distress publicly before the Lord's notice; the rather as, being ceremonially unclean, she had in a forbidden manner mingled with the crowd, and as her malady was of such a kind as shame would not allow her to speak of. Hence her faith must be brought to maturity by a public confession, even as that of Jairus by a season of delay.

4. As Christ's work of salvation assumed a specific form in many acts of blessing in favor of the male sex, so also Christianity has wrought immeasurable specific benefits for the female. Here we see, first, a wretched sick woman, lost in the crowd; and Christ delivers her not only from her sickness, but also from the morbid dread and fear of her feminine consciousness. Even shame required redemption and sanctification by the Spirit of truth. And so the female sex has been redeemed from the reproach of inferiority, impurity, the rude contempt of man's prejudice, and the ban of self-depreciation.

5. Reischl: "The woman was afraid; partly ashamed on account of the nature of her malady, partly disturbed by the consciousness of impropriety, as having, while Levitically unclean, mingled with the people, and even touched the great Teacher Himself." In the last point she forms a contrast to the leper, whom the Lord Himself touched. Under the veil of diffidence, however, there was a touch of womanly boldness, which was excused by the faith that the touching of Christ would heal her.

6. "Daughter, be of good courage, thy faith hath saved thee: go in peace." Thus He blessed her in the same manner as He had blessed that palsied man. And in fact we must connect together these two petitioners for help, in order that we may see two characteristic forms of faith in the male and in the female contrasted. Both applicants pressed through with confidence, and seized their deliverance almost by force: the man did it in man's fashion, entering through the roof like a robber; the woman in woman's fashion, as it were, like a female thief. But both were recognised by the Lord, as showing the pure spirit of confidence." (LANGE's *Leben Jesu*, ii. 682.) But the faith of this woman had a superadded conflict to maintain with her timorous natural feeling confronting the fearful power of prejudice.

HOMILETICAL AND PRACTICAL.

See on the parallels.—The miracles of Christ a wonderful connected chain.—New life added to new life in the way of Christ, until the great word is fulfilled, Behold, I make all things new!—Christ at once ready to help the man who comes from the powerful party of His opponents.—The ruler of the synagogue at the feet of Jesus; or, the victory of the Gospel over party spirit.—The triumph of Christ over the whole domain of sickness and death, a sign also of His supremacy over all natural means of help and human skill in healing.—Christ the Physician of physicians (as the Preacher of preachers, the Teacher of teachers, the Judge of judges, the Prince of kings).—Christ's divine power the sign of salvation to all the despondency, little faith, and unbelief of man.—Christ in our history the conqueror of all hindrances to His own work and man's faith. —The woman with the issue, and the dead maiden; or, Christ the Helper in all suffering, whether secret or public.—Christ the Prince of salvation in the domain of secret sorrows and silent sighs.—Hearing and answering all the sighings of faith.—The test to which the faith of the ruler and of the woman was subjected: 1. The element common to both: they were wanting in the full surrender of trust. Both must be set free from fear and despondency. 2. The difference: the spiritual ruler must retire, wait, submit, despair of all signs for hope, and then in his despair learn to believe. He scarcely believed in the invigorator of the sick, and now He must believe in the awakener of the dead. He must, at the same time, in humility yield precedence to a poor unclean woman, and in the case of a seeming religious impropriety.—The woman must come forward and confess.—Even amidst the pressure of thousands the Lord perceives the silent and gentle touch of a single believer.—Internal union with Jesus high above the external.—The hastening and the delaying of Jesus sublime above the haste and delay of the world.— Christ purposed here to effect, not the healing of the sick, but the raising of the dead.—Twice (in the history of Lazarus too) He first yielded the point to death, that He might approve Himself afterwards his conqueror.—With the Lord the spiritual is everything, and the edification of the inner life the great concern.—The gradually progressive manifestation of Christ's power in raising the dead, a sign and symbol of the great and universal resurrection.

STARKE:—QUESNEL:—God has His own times and seasons; He delays and yet helps. Have patience, and walk in the way He marks.—HEDINGER: —Daring wins.—QUESNEL:—Men are slow to do for the healing of the soul what they are ready enough to do for the cure of the body.—CRAMER:— Medicines are not to be despised, Ecclus. xxxviii. 1; but God does not always see fit to prosper them.— To use them is not displeasing to God, but ungodly trusting in them is.—The humility of the woman.— CANSTEIN:—Shame and fear would keep us back from Christ, but faith presses near to Him with a right and laudable shamelessness.—OSIANDER:—In our sickness we should put our trust, not in medicine, but in God.—Faith is stronger than all earthly medicaments.—The Lord is not ignorant what benefits we have received from Him, and He will demand an account of all the good deeds He has done to us.— *Bibl. Wirt.*:—Tempted souls think that God takes no care of them, but He faithfully remembers their case; the deeper they are in misery, the more graciously does His compassionate eye rest upon them.— CANSTEIN:—To acknowledge our own weakness and God's power, is to speak the truth indeed.—What God has done for us in secret we should publicly speak of to His glory.—Go in peace.—HEDINGER:— Reason despairs at sight of death.—In perfect faith there is no fear.—QUESNEL:—Let us learn from Christ to confide only to a few elect ones the works of God which we have to do, that those works may not be thwarted.—To sorrow in secret over our dead is Christian, but to howl and cry is heathenish.—HEDINGER:—God's wonderful works must have devout and attentive witnesses: away with tumult !—*Nova Bibl. Tub.*:—Why do ye mourn, ye parents, over the departure of your children? Jesus will one day lay His mighty hand upon them, raise them, and give them back to you.

LISCO:—The question of our Lord was designed to free the woman from her false fear of man.—The delay of help, and the message, were severe tests of Jairus' faith; but the healing of the woman strengthened his faith again, as did the word of Jesus, ver.

36.—BRAUNE :—The urgency and continuance of her malady, the vanity of all human help, the lack of substance, were three steps which brought the sick woman to faith; and the feeblest cries of the believing heart were understood by her Lord.—The Jews received this custom of lamentation from the Romans [Qy.: see Jer. ix. 17]. This purchased grief was intended to make the occasion of death important, to distribute the impressions of sorrow over many, and lighten the grief of the friends. Thus it was mere heathenish vanity.—SCHLEIERMACHER :—The more mighty love is in those who can help others, and, on the other hand, the more longing and trust there is in those who need help, the more good will be the result in the particular case, though we may not be able to show how, and the beginnings of cause and effect may be concealed from us.—It is always the case that from those whom God has called to do good, many influences proceed which they themselves do not in the special cases know of. But how much more efficacious would charity be, if those from whom the influences proceed did not think so much about those which they themselves receive !—How important it is for the general order of the community that we should not neglect our own individual personal relations !—Christendom has now still to press through the world violently with its blessings.—Although the power of Christ is continually entering more and more into the order of nature, yet that which Christianity has wrought in the world from its beginning is the greatest miracle that we know ; but we must be careful to distinguish from it the internal miracle, which only those see who live in internal fellowship with the Redeemer.—BAUER :—Mark how He does not break the bruised reed, or quench the smoking flax !

---

7. *The Lord's Conflict with the envious Unbelief of His own City ; His Triumph over Human Prejudice ; His Return to the Mountain-Villages.* CH. VI. 1–6.

(Parallels: Matt. xiii. 54–58; Luke iv. 14–30.)

1 And he went out from thence, and came[1] into his own country; and his disciples
2 follow him. And when the sabbath day was come, he began to teach in the synagogue: and many hearing *him* were astonished, saying, From whence hath this *man* these things? and what wisdom is this which is given unto him, that even such mighty works
3 are wrought[2] by his hands? Is not this the carpenter, the son of Mary, the brother of James, and Joses,[3] and of Juda, and Simon? and are not his sisters here with us?
4 And they were offended at him. But Jesus said unto them, A prophet is not without
5 honour, but in his own country, and among his own kin, and in his own house. And he could there do no mighty work, save that he laid his hands upon a few sick folk,
6 and healed *them*. And he marvelled because of their unbelief. And he went round about the villages, teaching.

[1] Ver. 1.—Tischendorf, ἔρχεται, after B., C., L., Δ.
[2] Ver. 2.—Codd. C.*, D., K., ἵνα γίνωνται ; B., L., γινόμεναι, which Tischendorf adopts.
[3] Ver. 3.—Codd. B., D., L., Versions, Lachmann, Tischendorf, read Ἰωσῆτος ; the reading Ἰωσήφ occurs in some cursive MSS.

EXEGETICAL AND CRITICAL.

See the parallels on *Matthew* and *Luke*.—As to Nazareth, consult ROBINSON, iii. 419 ; WINER, *Realler.* ; my *Leben Jesu*, ii. 550. Mark's narrative is not only identical with Matt. xiii. 54 *seq.* but also in its leading features with Luke iv. 16, as is manifest from the recurrence of the question, " Is not this Joseph's son ?" and the saying, " A prophet," etc. Notwithstanding, the points of time are so diverse, and have such an interval between them, that we must, following Matthew and Mark, assume a second and later appearance in Nazareth ; one, however, which was only transitional and brief, inasmuch as the unbelief of the people of Nazareth remained the same. The special features of the narrative seem to belong mainly to the former of the two occasions. But how can a second visit of our Lord to Nazareth be conceivable, after he had been once rejected there? The first rejection had been no better than a tumult. This time He visits His own city in quietness, and for His own repose, after the decree to kill Him had gone forth from the Galilean Pharisees. But, experiencing the same utter lack of sympathy and regard on the part of His former fellow-citizens, He retreated back into the surrounding mountain-villages. It was the time (in the first year of His ministry) when He had accomplished the itineration of the mountains in the first Galilean journey, as also the second Galilean voyage over the sea to the farther bank ; and when He was on the point of travelling over the towns of the valley of Southern Galilee, in the direction of Jerusalem. As He would confirm and corroborate this third and last Galilean preaching-journey by sending out the Twelve, a retreat into the mountains, and especially to a particular mountain, was fixed upon to precede. And He most probably took this occasion of visiting the district of Nazareth.

Ver. 1. **And He went out from thence.**— Not merely, that is, " from the house of Jairus." From this time forward, He ceased to have His abiding residence in Capernaum, although He still assembled His disciples around Him there on passing occasions. After the first conflict in Nazareth, He went down to Capernaum ; He now designedly abandons again His permanent abode in Capernaum, without formally giving up His residence there.

Ver. 2. **He began to teach.**—This does not

mean His first entrance and its result; it rather refers to the interruption that soon followed.—That even such mighty works are wrought by His hands.—The ἵνα is characteristic. They regard the doctrine of Christ merely as a secret doctrine, which was intended to be the medium or instrument for the ultimate end of working miracles. And they enviously assume that this mysterious doctrine must have been entrusted to him by some one in a suspicious manner. Hence the emphasis laid upon the *hands* (laying on of hands, touching, etc.), as the method of performing the miracle. The working hands of the carpenter, they would say; as appears from what comes next.

Ver. 3. **Is not this the carpenter?**—According to the custom of the Jewish people, even the Rabbis learned some handicraft. We have the example of the Apostle Paul: *see* Lightfoot, Schöttgen. But Justin Martyr (contr. Tryph.) has the tradition, that Jesus made ploughs and the like. "Whether with an ideal allusion, so that they became in His hands symbols, as Lange (*Leben Jesu*, ii. p. 154) thinks, may very properly be left to fancy." Meyer. That Jesus regarded with a symbolizing mind and interpretation the toil of the fisherman, the fall of the sparrow from the housetop, the play of the children in the market-place—all this is not matter of mere fancy. But there is a kind of fancy, which men call inductive proof. It is represented, further, as a mere airy and baseless notion, to suppose that the brethren of Jesus would hardly have suffered Him to work much, because they saw in Him the glory of Israel. And yet it is not an airy and baseless notion, that His brethren early sought to deliver Him from the machinations of His enemies. What really deserves to be called fancy in the theological domain, is that aggregation of myth and anecdote which the scholastic learning of the present day so much abounds in.

No dogmatic importance can be attached (with Bauer and others) to the omission of "the carpenter's *son*," which Matthew has; since the expression, "the carpenter," is only a stronger declaration of the same thing. But the former expression would not occur to the people of Nazareth, since they spoke from recent observation or past remembrances. In this way, the position of Jesus was referred back to, or identified with, Joseph's. And it is obvious to suppose that Joseph had long before (between the twelfth year and the thirtieth of the Lord's life) gone off the scene. As τέκτων has primarily a general meaning, and signifies any artisan, some, following Justin, have thought it signified here a maker of carriages, etc.; while others have interpreted into "smith." But smith in the New Testament is ὁ χαλκεύς, and τέκτων is specifically a *faber lignarius*. Whether workmanship in wood was distributed into various kinds of handiwork, is a question not settled.—**The brother of James.**—As to the brethren of the Lord, comp. on Matthew. The apocryphal tradition adds to the four brethren, two sisters of our Lord: Esther and Tamar or Martha. Romanist expositors have, without reason, or for reasons well known, made these the sisters of His mother. These sisters seem to have been married in Nazareth; and therefore did not accompany the migration of Mary's family to Capernaum.

Ver. 4. **Among his own kin.**—Naturally, the immediate dependants and followers of Jesus stood related in manifold ways to the people of Nazareth. Christ does not say that His own house remained unbelieving, in the common sense of the term. But that there were restrictions of faith to be overcome even in this circle, springing from too great familiarity, is proved not only by the history of the Lord's brethren, but also by that of His mother.

DOCTRINAL AND ETHICAL.

1. *See* on *Matthew*.—This narrative exhibits to us the narrow, petty, bigoted, envious unbelief, which was unable to apprehend and understand the Divinely great in its human nearness and familiarity; and this makes the section a most striking example of unbelief, as it confronts and embarrasses the Lord. It is the unconscious self-condemnation and self-contempt of the spirit which, alienated from God, and sunk into the lowest level, cannot appreciate the prophet that has arisen in its own city. In our Lord's experience of this kind of unbelief,—to which a prophet is nowhere less esteemed than in his own country, and among his own kin,—we have fore-written for us a long chapter of the history of the world and of the Church. The history of Monophysitism, on the one hand, and of Nestorianism and Rationalism, on the other, may be referred to this principle. The prejudice of the base nature, that out of Nazareth, in the immediate neighborhood, from our own home, and finally out of humanity itself, nothing good can come, led to all those systems in succession which, on the one hand, *dehumanize* the God-man, and, on the other, *undeify* Him. But when we say that Christ celebrated His triumph over this unbelief of envious prejudice and of human self-depreciation, we do not thereby assert that He removed that unbelief in anything like a magical manner. He triumphed over it rather by leaving it alone, by going on His way, and by performing His miracles in the neighborhood around. He drew round the pestilent prejudice a circle of divine manifestations, like a besieger. The honor paid to the Divine, which from all sides reacts upon this centre of prejudice, and leads back the homeborn, with acclamation and celebrity on all hands, to his home again—that is His final triumph over Nazareth, over Judaism, over humanity.

2. *And He could there.*—This does not express inability in itself; but, as Theophylact rightly observed, it indicates the absence of the ethical conditions on which the miracles of Jesus depended. His miraculous power was not magical; but an ethical influence which required and presupposed faith. It is true that Christ also creates faith; but then that presupposes the felt need of faith. It is true that He excites that feeling also; but then that presupposes susceptibility, and the capacity of reception. And if this likewise is awakened by Him, it further presupposes sincerity, and a certain devotion which could not become hardened through evil motives into the always evil act of the heart of unbelief. The Evangelist further shows us that Jesus wrought miracles, even in this circle, according to the slender measure of faith there was; for he adds the observation, that He laid His hands upon a few sick folk, and healed them. Thus, he distinguishes from these lower miraculous works, the great manifestations of His wonder-working power; these latter could have and should have no demonstration under such circumstances. The condition on which the miraculous power of Christ was suspended was the reflection and copy of the conditions upon which the

divine omnipotence, in love wisdom and righteousness, deals with the freedom of the world of spirits.

3. *And He marvelled.*—Fritzsche: "ἐθαύμαζον (they wondered at Him, on account of their unbelief), following only two cursive MSS.; manifest error of copyist." Meyer: Stress has with great propriety been laid upon the contrast between the wondering of our Lord at the faith of the Gentile centurion, and His wondering at the unbelief of His own countrymen, who had so long been witnesses of His divine life. Jesus does not marvel at other human things generally; but He does marvel, on the one hand, at faith, when it overcomes in its grandeur all human traditional hindrances, and, on the other, at unbelief, when it can, in the face of multitudes of divine manifestations, and under the daily view of the opened heavens, harden itself into the pitiful acceptance of dead traditional prejudices. The former wondering might, humanly speaking, elevate and strengthen Himself; the latter, on the other hand, grieve and restrain His divine Spirit. He hastens away from the sphere of such spiritual evils, that He may in the distance unloose those spiritual breezes that shall dissipate them all. The Accusative (διὰ τήν), "on account of their unbelief," makes His astonishment all the more emphatic. It was hard for Him to reconcile Himself to this seemingly unconquerable dulness and limitation.

4. The history of Nazareth has been repeated on a large scale in the history of Israel. Israel, as a whole, also made the nearness of Jesus, His external "not being afar off," an occasion of unbelief and fall. This temptation, resulting from the constant beholding of the Holy One with common eyes, was pointed to in Deut. xxx. 14, according to Paul's interpretation of it in Rom. x. 8. It is the temptation which besets the intimates and fellow-citizens of chosen spirits and great geniuses; which besets theologians in the daily study and service of the truths of revelation, ministers in their commerce with the ordinances of grace, and all the lesser officers of the house of God in their habitual contact with the externals of divine things. It is the temptation also of ancient towns and churches, which have enjoyed exalted privileges, and indeed of the whole Church itself. "When the Son of man cometh, shall He find faith on the earth?"

HOMILETICAL AND PRACTICAL.

See on the parallel passages of Matthew and Luke.—Jesus was renounced by His own city, both at the beginning and at the end of His Galilean labors: or, the stiffneckedness of prejudice, which is bound to the lower and earthly sense by a thousand bonds (envy, cowardice, indolence, self-delusion, dissipation, slavish sympathies and antipathies, etc.). —How far was Jesus actually of Nazareth, how far not?—No man is altogether of the place where he was born or brought up: 1. He is so in his derivation, but not in his individuality; 2. he is so in his outward lot, but not in his personal endowments; 3. he is so in his external training, but not in his internal education; 4. he is so in his human relationship and acquaintance, but not in his highest relations; 5. he is so in the petty events of life, but not in his greater fortunes; 6. he is so in his immediate calling, not in his highest vocation and destiny.—Christ an alien, and yet at home, in His own city; both in an infinite measure: every man the same in his own degree.—The error of the men of Nazareth concerning the coming of Christ: 1. They forgot that He was of Bethlehem; 2. they did not know that He was from heaven.—The double origin and the double home of Christ: 1. An original contrast in Him; 2. an analogous contrast in every man's life below.— How Christ victoriously contends with the unbelief of prejudice among His own countrymen: 1. Prejudice everywhere opposes Him; and that, *a.* in an impure and gross apprehension of His dignity, as of a magical secret doctrine and art; *b.* in the reckoning up of all His earthly relationships, in order to urge them to the disparagement of His heavenly dignity; *c.* in a slavish community of envious and low judgment upon His life. 2. How the Lord lays hold of and overcomes this prejudice: *a.* He refers it all to a universal fact, which they might afterwards reflect upon (a prophet is not without honor, etc.); *b.* He does not forget, but heals, the few who needed and were susceptible of help among His scorners; *c.* He gathers up His influences, and withdraws; *d.* and He causes the light of His presence to shine brightly throughout the whole district around.—How the Lord surrounds the places which exhibit a corrupted prejudice against Him with the fiery circles of His divine deeds, in order to subdue them.—The Lord's not being able in Nazareth, an expression of the divine freedom as over against the abuse of human freedom.—The Lord's impotence a testimony to His perfect power and ability: 1. Of the divine power of His love (patience); 2. of the divine skill of His love (wisdom).—The sacred conditionality and free self-limiting power of Christ.—The omnipotence of God is not lessened, but glorified as spiritual power, by the fact that it conditions itself in love, wisdom, and righteousness.—To the man who had lost himself, and become to himself an object of contempt, the Lord brings back again his life.— Christ is both far off and nigh at hand, in order to overcome the stolid, careless minds of those who are bent on this world.—Christ's retirement among the villages; or, the loftiness of the Gospel in its humility.—Christ's own city, the old and the new: 1. Poor Nazareth, which rejects Him; 2. the great city of God in heaven and upon earth, in ten thousand places, which glorifies Him.—Nazareth a symbol of multitudes of streets and places rendered desolate by spiritual guilt.—How the Lord's love with holy tenderness encircles His poor land and people.

STARKE:—MAJUS:—The unreasonableness and wickedness of our countrymen should never restrain us in the performance of our duty, or cause us to forget any of our obligations to them.—*Nov. Bibl. Tub.*:—Birth, lineage, and descent are far from making a man a Christian; they often rather, on account of prejudices, are the greatest hindrances to Christianity.—QUESNEL:—Wicked men often admire and magnify gifted preachers; but they are never without some excuse or other for not obeying their instructions.—It is common enough for those who would defeat the force of a sermon, to exalt themselves above the preacher.—When we entertain ourselves with a thousand strange matters that have no connection with spiritual profit, the power of the divine word is lost.—CANSTEIN:—He who built heaven and earth became, in His humbled condition upon earth, a carpenter.—Christ honored and sanctified all honorable human employments and handiwork.— QUESNEL:—Christ's humiliation has been to many a stone of stumbling and an occasion of falling; while it was most essentially necessary to our external exaltation.—HEDINGER:—What is there that can grieve the Christian teacher beyond contempt and evil fruits?—Christ's example is a most mighty consolation.—*Nova Bibl. Tub.*:—Thou complainest that God saves thee not, and dost not reflect that thou thyself hast bound His hands.—QUESNEL:—The unbelief of a whole people does not hinder the mercy of God from extending to the small number of the righteous who are found amongst them.—BRAUNE:—Faith, which in its nature is *receptive* love, alone makes us partakers of the grace of God, which is *imparting* love.

SCHLEIERMACHER:—We find this (that a prophet is without honor in his own country) true among men, even as we sometimes find the contrary of it true. When any one is distinguished beyond others in any particular, his fellow-townsmen take pride in him, their vanity being flattered. Yet the contrary is not arbitrary, but usually dependent on the earlier or later period, and various spiritual or worldly influences. (The prophets killed, and the sepulchres of the prophets garnished.)—Much impressive truth is lost upon men, because they do not so much regard the matter as the source from which it comes. —Christ has as much cause to marvel at the unbelief of the present time, as He had to marvel in His own time.—GOSSNER, on ver. 4:—A warning to all preachers who do not like to leave their own home, kin, and country.—Nothing more outrages God's goodness than unbelief or rejection of it.

SIXTH SECTION.

CONFLICT OF JESUS WITH HEROD. THE CALL AND MISSION OF THE TWELVE APOSTLES. THE BEHEADING OF JOHN THE BAPTIST. THE WITHDRAWAL OF JESUS INTO THE WILDERNESS, AND THE MIRACULOUS FEEDING OF THE FIVE THOUSAND.

CHAPTER VI. 7–44.

---

1. *The Calling and Mission of the Twelve.* CH. VI. 7–13.

(Parallels: Matt. x. 1, 7, 9–11, 13; Luke ix. 1–6.)

7 And he called *unto him* the twelve, and began to send them forth by two and two;
8 and gave them power over unclean spirits; And commanded them that they should take nothing for *their* journey, save a staff only; no scrip, no bread, no money in *their*
9, 10 purse [girdle]: But *be* shod with sandals; and not put on[1] two coats. And he said unto them, In what place soever ye enter into an house, there abide till ye depart from
11 that place. And whosoever shall not receive you, nor hear you,[2] when ye depart thence, shake off the dust under your feet for a testimony against them. Verily I say unto you, It shall be more tolerable for Sodom and Gomorrha in the day of judgment than
12, 13 for that city. And they went out, and preached that men should repent. And they cast out many devils, and anointed with oil many that were sick, and healed *them*.

[1] Ver. 9.—The best reading is ἐνδύσησθε (A., C., D., E., &c.), which Griesbach, Lachmann, Tischendorf, and others adopt. The change in the construction, or the direct quotation of this command, makes it more emphatic.
[2] Ver. 11.—Tischendorf, after B., L., Δ., &c.; ὃς ἂν τόπος μὴ δέξηται μηδὲ ἀκούσωσιν ὑμῶν. Preferable in regard to importance of Codd., and is the more difficult reading. "Verily," &c., wanting in B., C., D., L., Δ. Probably taken from Matt. x. 15.

EXEGETICAL AND CRITICAL.

1. Compare on the parallel passages of Matt. x. and Luke ix.—It has been already observed, on Mark iii. 13–19, that he distinguishes the *separation* of the Twelve from their first *mission*: Luke does the same, while Matthew combines their call and mission in one. The two events are indeed one, as Matthew records them, in this respect, that the separation took place with reference to an appointment of duty which then immediately impended. But they are distinguished by this, that the election occurred in the solitude of the mountain-range (hence Mark and Luke place them on a mountain, the latter connecting with the event the Sermon on the Mount; while the mission, on the other hand, occurred at the beginning of the third preaching-journey, on which our Lord passed through the sea-towns of Galilee, as we are told by Matthew. But, since the calling of the Twelve, between the Sermon on the Mount and the passage to Gadara (the second Galilean journey), was only as yet a preparatory vocation, we must make a distinction between a general separation of the narrower circle of disciples and that calling of the Twelve on the mountain which briefly preceded their sending forth in the valley, during the first year of Christ's ministry. Now it is peculiar to Mark that he gives prominence only to the most essential points of the mission; that he records it as the beginning of the apostolical missions (ver. 7), and as a mission in pairs; that he lays emphasis exclusively upon the power given over unclean spirits (not that of healing the sick), in harmony with his fundamental point of view, and that to him this involved at the same time the preaching of the kingdom; that he most precisely gives the Lord's injunctions touching their staff, their shoes, and their clothing; and that he finally makes allusion to the anointing the sick with oil, in its relation to the work of the Apostles—here mentioning

the sick, who had been previously omitted. Mark's more limited account of the instructions given to the Apostles in comparison with that given by Matthew, is to be explained by the fact, that he has this first mission exclusively in view; while Matthew combines it with all subsequent missions, and consequently presents it in its ideal meaning.

Ver. 8. **Save a staff only.**—Meyer insists that there is here a discrepancy between Mark, on the one hand, and Matthew and Luke, on the other—to be explained, as it regards the two latter, by exaggeration. (Comp., on the contrary, EBRARD, p. 382; LANGE, *Leben Jesu*, ii. 2, p. 712.) They were to go forth with their staff, as they had it at the time; but they were not to seek one carefully, or make it a condition of their travelling. And thus it becomes no more in Mark than a rather more precise statement of the meaning of Matthew and Luke. The same may be said of the permission to take sandals, in opposition to the prohibition of the ὑποδήματα, or travelling shoes proper, in Matthew. So the injunction not to put on two coats (in change), is only another form of the injunction not to have two garments. The fundamental idea is this, that they were to go forth with the slightest provision, and in dependence upon being provided for by the way. Gfrörer and Baur see in Mark's expressions only intentional qualifications and softenings. We find in them no other than a more express view of their pilgrim-state, burdened with the least possible incumbrance, and as free as might be from all care.

Ver. 11. **For a testimony against them.**—As a symbolical, but to an Israelite perfectly intelligible, declaration, that they were excommunicated, —"no better than heathen."

Ver. 12. **Preached, that men should repent** (ἵνα).—They not only preached the doctrine of repentance, amongst other articles of doctrine; but their whole preaching had for its end the producing of penitence, and change of mind.

Ver. 13. **And anointed with oil.**—Oil was generally a very important medicament among the Orientals, according to Lightfoot and others. Here it is simply a symbolical medium of the miraculous work; just as the application of the spittle was (ch. viii. 23; John ix. 6), on the part of the Lord Himself. Meyer does well to contend against the supposition that the oil was applied as a natural means of cure (Baur, Weisse), or that it was used as a mere symbol (Theophylact, Beza, etc.),—not to mention other still less tenable notions. He is not right, however, in altogether detaching the symbolical significance from the medium. It is a fact, that the Old Testament anointing with oil preceded, as a symbol, the New Testament bestowment of the Spirit; and that it re-appears in the Catholic church, where the real impartation of the Spirit is wanting. Hence, it may be assumed that for the disciples, who could not like the Lord Himself awaken faith, it was appropriate to appoint such a medium for their miraculous power as would be at the same time a symbolical sign of the impartation of the Spirit, and the energy that awakens faith. Thus the anointing was a symbol of the bestowment of the Spirit as the preliminary condition of healing; consequently, not of the divine mercy (Theophylact), the healing virtue of which was symbolized by balsam, or of the divine regeneration (Euthym. Zigabenus), the symbol of which was water. The anointing with oil, which James prescribed to the elders in their ministry for the sick (ch. v. 14), appears, on the other hand, to have been a blending of the natural means of health with the saving energy of prayer as symbolized by it.

DOCTRINAL AND ETHICAL.

1. *See* on the parallel passages of Matthew and Luke.

2. *The sending of the Apostles by two and two.*—According to Grotius, with allusion to the Old Testament law concerning witnesses *ad plenam testimonii fidem*. But also for mutual complement, and encouragement, and strengthening. We have, accordingly, six special embassages: six was the number of labor and toil. The twelve missions of the individual Apostles were as yet only in the prospect.

3. We need only suggest here, that the New Testament anointing with oil—even that later one which James prescribed to the elders in their care of the sick—forms a perfect contrast to the extreme unction of the Romish Church. To us, this ecclesiastical anointing seems no other than an unconscious admission, on the part of the ceremonial church, that it had yet to bestow on its dying member the real communication of the Holy Spirit, whose type the oil was.

HOMILETICAL AND PRACTICAL.

The first sending of the Apostles abroad into the world may also be likened to the little seed-corn.—He began to send: the end of His sending is the end of the world.—The mission of the Apostles by two and two, in its significance for the Church: 1. As to ecclesiastical office, 2. as to the people.—The blessing of the mutual help of laborers in the kingdom of God.—The embarrassments, dangers, and disgraces which so often follow a too early isolation in office, and in the religious life generally.—Christianity in life and office is a discipline of unervying brotherly love.—The messengers and pilgrims of Christ not without needs, but without anxious needs. —The world loses, amidst its external equipments and means of resource, the internal end of life: the servants of the Gospel obtain, while they supremely regard the end, all the other equipments and resources.—The destruction of the kingdom of Satan, and the abolition of his power, is the great task of Christ's servants, under the example and in the strength of their Lord.—The shaking the dust from their feet is in its kind a Christian martyrdom to the disciples of Jesus (a testimony in suffering).—The anointing with oil; or, how the miracles of the kingdom of Christ have leaned upon the marvellous powers of the kingdom of nature.—The kingdom of the Son attaches itself to the kingdom of the Father in the great whole as well as in individual things.—Those bound by Satan, and the sick, are everlasting tokens of the need of Christ and His messengers.

STARKE:—This authorization a demonstration of the divinity of Christ.—The ministers of the Gospel should be one and united.—QUESNEL:—Ambition and avarice perilous things to the preacher and his work.—OSIANDER:—Ministers should be satisfied, though they do not at once have all advantages they could desire, and things at their will.—GERLACH:— On account of their weakness, the Lord does not send His disciples alone. Laborers in the Lord's harvest should look round for helpers in their work. —SCHLEIERMACHER:—The Lord's direction in regard to the equipments of the Apostles no literal rule [he refers to the cloak of Paul, 2 Tim. iv. 13], but a rule of wisdom.—If the provision of all these external things is so great as to rob us of a portion of our true strength, they are no real advantage, but tend rather to impair our usefulness and peace.—BAUER: —They were not to act as if they thought they might force men to hear.

2. *Beheading of John the Baptist.* VERS. 14–29.

(Parallels: Matt. xiv. 1-12; Luke ix. 7-9.)

14 And king Herod heard *of him;* (for his name was spread abroad;) and he said, That John the Baptist was risen from the dead, and therefore mighty works do show
15 forth themselves [miraculous powers work] in him. Others said, That it is Elias.
16 And others said, That it is a prophet, or as one of the prophets. But when Herod
17 heard *thereof*, he said, It is John, whom I beheaded:[1] he is risen from the dead. For Herod himself had sent forth and laid hold upon John, and bound him in prison for
18 Herodias' sake, his brother Philip's wife; for he had married her. For John had said
19 unto Herod, It is not lawful for thee to have thy brother's wife. Therefore Herodias
20 had a quarrel against him, and would have killed him; but she could not: For Herod feared John, knowing that he was a just man and an holy, and observed [protected]
21 him; and when he heard him, he did many things,[2] and heard him gladly. And when a convenient [favorable] day was come, that Herod, on his birth-day, made a supper to
22 his lords, high captains, and chief *estates* of Galilee: And when the daughter of the said Herodias came in, and danced, and pleased Herod,[3] and them that sat with him, the king said unto the damsel, Ask of me whatsoever thou wilt, and I will give *it* thee.
23 And he sware unto her, Whatsoever thou shalt ask of me, I will give *it* thee, unto the
24 half of my kingdom. And she went forth, and said unto her mother, What shall I
25 ask? And she said, The head of John the Baptist. And she came in straightway with haste unto the king, and asked, saying, I will that thou give me, by and by [im-
26 mediately] in a charger, the head of John the Baptist. And the king was exceeding sorry; *yet* for his oath's sake, and for their sakes which sat with him, he would not re-
27 ject her. And immediately the king sent an executioner, and commanded his head to
28 be brought: and he went and beheaded him in the prison, And brought his head in a
29 charger, and gave it to the damsel; and the damsel gave it to her mother. And when his disciples heard *of it*, they came and took up his corpse, and laid it in a tomb.

[1] Ver. 16.—The reading which drops ἐστιν, αὐτός (B., D., L., Δ., &c.), is strongly authenticated; but the omission is explained here by the similarity of οὗτος and αὐτός.—The omission of ἐκ νεκρῶν (Tischendorf, after B., D., L., Δ.) is not sufficiently supported.
[2] Ver. 20.—The reading πολλὰ ἠπόρει ("was often in doubt") has B., L. in its favor. So Ewald and Meyer. But it is probably a modification of the strong πολλὰ ἐποίει.
[3] Ver. 22.—Instead of the Participle καὶ ὀρεσάσης, the Codd. B., C.*, L., and others read ἤρεσεν, and afterwards εἶπε δὲ ὁ βασ. This construction loses the emphatic preparation of the words: "Then the king said unto the maiden." But the Greek construction of the *Recepta* may seem to be simply a softening of the text.

EXEGETICAL AND CRITICAL.

See on the parallel passages of Matthew and Luke.—The time of this occurrence was the return of Jesus from the Feast of Purim at Jerusalem, in the year 781; that is, in the second year of His ministry. On His return from this feast, the disciples were once more gathered round Him at the Sea of Galilee. It is peculiar to Mark, that he connects the suspicious observation of Herod Antipas (see Matthew) with the work of Christ as extended by the twelve Apostles. And this is quite natural; since the fame of Jesus was not only extraordinarily increased by their means, but also invested with the semblance of a political import. With regard to Herod's judgment of Jesus, Mark is more distinct than Luke; in exhibiting the relation in which Jesus stood to the Baptist, he is more distinct than Matthew. He is moreover very circumstantial in detailing the binding of John, the favorable crisis for Herodias, Herod's promise to the dancer, the scheme concerted between mother and daughter, the daring urgency of the latter, and other similar traits. But he omits the circumstance, that the disciples of John carried intelligence of the event to the Lord.

Ver. 14. **King Herod.**—The βασιλεύς in the ancient and wide sense. Matthew and Luke say more precisely, the tetrarch (here equivalent to prince). Starke: "Luke calls him, after the manner of the Romans, a tetrarch; Mark, after the manner of the Jews, a king.—**Heard.**—That is, that the disciples of Jesus preached and performed such miracles (Meyer), and that Jesus sent them forth. Hence what follows: *for His name was spread abroad.* Therefore, not (according to Grotius and others), he heard the name of Jesus.—**John the Baptist.**—'Ο βαπτίζων, substantively. Yet, perhaps, hinting an avoidance of the acknowledgment of his authority.* According to Luke, others declared that John was risen from the dead, and Herod was troubled at it. But the apparent contradiction is solved by our assuming that the idea was introduced by the courtiers, and that Herod, after slight hesitation, entered into their views with hypocritical superstitious policy (*Leben Jesu*, ii. 2). The expression might then be regarded as blending in itself a secret political meaning and a more popular one. According to the former it says, This new movement proceeds from the execution of John the Baptist; and if John was politically dangerous, the appearance of Jesus with His twelve Apostles is tenfold more so. Yet, at the same time, the expression might have been employed, in order to burden the conscience of the king and the people in reference to the execution of John.—**Therefore mighty works do show forth themselves in him.**—John had wrought no miracle; and the prince seems to have made this his excuse, the high legitimation of a prophet having been wanting to the Baptist. Now, in his new form, said the theologizing king, it is seen that he is actually a prophet; the miraculous powers at length manifest themselves in him.

Ver. 15. **As one of the prophets.**—That is, of the old prophets, even if not so great as Elias. It is manifest, first, that the opinions which then prevailed concerning the Person of Jesus, agreed in a certain acknowledgment of His higher mission; secondly, they differed in regard to the more specific definition of His dignity; thirdly, they presented a descending scale of lessening honor paid to Him, starting from a point below the primary recognition that He was the Messiah. And thus they mark the time when the persecution of Jesus was beginning, although the people generally were, in a narrower sense, entirely absorbed with His works and words. Matthew introduces this index of public opinion in connection with another event, which, however, falls within the same year of persecutions, ch. xvi. 14; and now this wavering judgment has become the popular cry.

Ver. 16. **Whom I beheaded.**—Meyer: "'Εγώ has the emphasis of a guilty conscience." "Mark the urgent expression of confident assurance which the terrified man utters: This is he; he is risen."

Ver. 20. **For Herod feared John.**—Seeming discrepancy when compared with Matthew, as Meyer here and always urges. Compare, on the contrary, EBRARD, p. 384; LANGE, *Leben Jesu*, ii. 2, p. 783. The θέλειν often indicates, in the New Testament, the natural willing in its weakness, the *fain would*, which, however, does not involve necessarily the full and perfect purpose of the will. Matthew, in his exhibition of the feeble, vacillating Herod, at the same time has in view his position on the side of Herodias as in opposition to the people; while Mark has in view his position on the side of the people in opposition to the thoroughly decided and resolute Herodias (*see* Macbeth).—**And observed him,** or *kept him.*—Not, *esteemed him highly* (as Erasmus and others, with De Wette, contend), but he protected him a long time against the attempts of Herodias (as Grotius and Meyer). And this, at the same time, reveals the vacillation of the man, since, as prince, Herod might have set John free. "Herodias was instigated partly by revenge, but partly by fear that her present husband might, in consequence of the

---
* He whom men call John the Baptist, *i. e.*—*Ed.*

exhortations of the Baptist, repent of his sin, and separate from her." Bede.

Ver. 21. **And when a convenient day was come;** that is, favorable for Herodias.—Grotius: "*Opportuna insidiatrici, quæ vino, amore et adulatorum conspiratione facile sperabat impelli posse nutantem mariti, animum.*"—**Lords, high captains, and chief estates.**—The first two classes are servants of the state, civil and military officials; the third includes the great men of the land generally.

Ver. 22. **The king said unto the damsel.**—The antithesis between "king and damsel" gives emphasis to his wicked folly.—**To the half of my kingdom.**—Starke: "This was a grand imitation of the great Ahasuerus; but in one without the supreme power, it was idle and boastful enough."

Ver. 23. **I will that thou give me, by and by.**—Strong emphasis, in the θέλω ἵνα. "Observe the *boldness* of the malignant girl." Meyer.

Ver. 26. **Would not reject her.**—'Αθετεῖν, to make anything an ἄθετον, illegal: therefore, to make invalid, or abolish, a decree, ordinance, covenant, or oath; and, in reference to persons, it means to deprive of a legal claim, or declare one unjustified: hence it involves the notion of humiliating, the *repudiare*. But the translation to "suffer her to ask in vain," is much too weak.

Ver. 27. **An executioner,** σπεκουλάτορα: one of his body-guard.—"To them was committed the execution of capital sentences (SENECA, *De Ira*, i. 16, Wetstein)." Meyer.

Ver. 28. **And the damsel gave it to her mother.**—Salome, the dancer, afterwards married her father's brother, the tetrarch Philip.

DOCTRINAL AND ETHICAL.

1. *See* on the parallel passages in *Matthew* and *Luke*.

2. The institution of the apostolate, and the mission of the Apostles, were like a revelation of avenging spirits to worldly policy and despotism, cowardly and superstitious, suspicious and fearful from the beginning.

3. Herod a forerunner and confederate of Pilate in this, that he acknowledged the innocence and dignity of John, and yet had not the courage to set him free. He is also like Pilate in the vacillation of his weak character.

4. The opinions of those who surrounded Herod were like the verdicts of the great world concerning Christianity.

5. Herodias a typical character: woman in the demoniac grandeur of wickedness—the opposite of Mary. The New Testament Jezebel, as Herod is the New Testament Ahab. Herodias, the murderess of the greatest prophet, with whom the old covenant ended; Mary, the mother of the Lord, in whom the new covenant is sealed.

6. The intriguing woman, the courtezan in the royal court, an historical symbol. So also the dancer, and the vain festivity, and the sympathies of pride and presumption.

7. One sample of the influences of Grecian habits, as introduced into Palestine and spread there by the Herodians. Doubtless this influence could not but serve to efface the limits between Judaism and heathenism; but the true reconciliation between Greece and the theocracy could be effected only by Christianity.

8. The oath, and the word of honor, and the honorable deeds of the worldly-minded great, as they often clash with the eternal laws of God. In the godless oath there is a real and essential nullity; for God cannot be the avenger of a broken vow which was in itself impious. "But the breach of an ungodly oath demands an open confession." Gerlach. "Herod should have said, *Thou askest of me more than my kingdom, for what shall it profit a man?*" etc.

9. Fearful contrasts, in which are reflected the satanic powers of wickedness: the head of the greatest preacher of repentance in the ancient world made a fee by an Israelite prince to a little Greek dancer at the court (a Jewess, who dances after the Greek fashion at the Israelite court); Christ, the Messiah of the Jews, betrayed by the kiss of a disciple to the hierarchy, condemned and given over to the Gentiles by the high-priests and the priesthood in Zion.

HOMILETICAL AND PRACTICAL.

See on the parallel passages in Matthew and Luke, and also the Reflections above.—Christ, with His twelve Apostles, described as John the Baptist risen from the dead: 1. How far this was a gross error, composed of a mixture of guilty conscience, superstition, policy, cunning, ignorance, and blindness; 2. how far, in another sense, a great truth, in which the living law of the kingdom of God found expression (ineffaceableness, growth, progress, consummation, "the blood of the martyrs, the seed of the Church").—The internal conflict of Herod and Pilate: 1. Similarities: impotent striving, long delay, critical suspense, shameful surrender. 2. Differences: a Jew, a Gentile; Herodias in the one case, the warning devout woman in the other; the people against the evil deed, the people in favor of it.—John the Baptist dignified and self-consistent as the great, heroic preacher of repentance: 1. Confronting the prince of the land, Herod; 2. in prison, and with the fear of death before his eyes.—The good impressions, which Herod had lost: therefore, 1. He continued in the sin; 2. in vacillation between the right and wrong; 3. in self-deception; 4. under the power of temptation.—The conflict between good living and living good.—The convenient season; or, the feasts and banquets of the world, and those of the kingdom of God.—The world's estimate of the value of things: the head of a prophet of less importance than a dance; a blasphemous, drunken oath more sacred than the eternal law of God.—How the weak and wavering characters, whilst they delay, are overcome by the bold and daring conduct of those who are resolute in their wickedness.—The judgment which followed the beheading of the Baptist: pierced conscience, further guilt touching Jesus, a death of misery.—The frightful abandonment by the Spirit, which, in the great world, may cloak itself under the disguise of brilliance and vigor of spirit.—The fidelity and troubles of the disciples of John figurative of the troubles of faith as held bound in legality: 1. The heroic courage with which they buried their master; 2. the lack of believing courage to attach themselves to Jesus.

STARKE:—Even the great of this world have always been excited and moved by the Gospel of Christ.—QUESNEL:—The sinner has no peace when he would seek it; because he rejected it when it was offered him by God.—HEDINGER:—The judgments of this world are always out of square when they deal with spiritual things; therefore, dear fellow-Christian, inquire not about them.—Public teachers should without fear rebuke the sins and blasphemies even of the great; they may rely, in doing so, on the Divine help.—LANGE:—O ye court-preachers, learn of John what your duty is: he was no court-preacher, and yet he bore fearless testimony to the truth.—HEDINGER:—Devotion is always honorable, even in the eyes of the most frenzied children of the world.—Carnality befouls the best thoughts.—QUESNEL:—The festivities of the world are the best appointed tables of sin.—ZEISIUS:—The poor have to give the rich their sweat and blood, and they riot in the proceeds, etc.—Vain swearing.—Promises made over the wine-cup.—OSIANDER:—At the court there are often heavy payments for ridiculous trifles.—A foolish promise brings repentance after it.—QUESNEL:—The oath is sinful, and therefore null, when it cannot be carried out but with sin and injustice.—LANGE:—No servant or official should let himself be made an instrument of injustice; rather should he let everything go.—Christians pay honor to the pious on their death, and carry them reverently to their tombs.—GERLACH:—Close connection between debauchery and cruelty.—GOSSNER:—Thus does the world deal with God's ambassadors.—BAUER:—See, what a marriage this was!

---

3. *Withdrawal of Jesus into the Wilderness on the other side of the Sea of Galilee, and the miraculous Feeding of the Five Thousand.* VERS. 30–44.

30 And the apostles gathered themselves together unto Jesus, and told him all things,
31 both[1] what they had done, and what they had taught. And he said unto them, Come ye yourselves apart into a desert place, and rest a while: for there were many coming
32 and going, and they had no leisure so much as to eat. And they departed into a desert
33 place by ship privately. And the people[2] saw them departing, and many knew him, and ran a-foot thither out of all cities, and outwent them, and came together unto him.
34 And Jesus, when he came out, saw much people, and was moved with compassion toward them, because they were as sheep not having a shepherd: and he began to teach
35 them many things. And when the day was now far spent, his disciples came unto him,

36 and said, This is a desert place, and now the time *is* far passed; Send them away, that they may go into the country round about, and into the villages, and buy themselves³
37 bread: for they have nothing to eat. He answered and said unto them, Give ye them to eat. And they say unto him, Shall we go and buy two hundred pennyworth of bread,
38 and give them to eat? He saith unto them, How many loaves have ye? go and⁴ see.
39 And when they knew, they say, Five, and two fishes. And he commanded them to
40 make all sit down by companies upon the green grass. And they sat down in ranks,
41 by hundreds, and by fifties. And when he had taken the five loaves and the two fishes, he looked up to heaven, and blessed, and brake the loaves, and gave *them* to his disci-
42 ples to set before them; and the two fishes divided he among them all. And they did
43 all eat, and were filled. And they took up twelve baskets⁵ full of the fragments, and
44 of the fishes. And they that did eat of the loaves were about five thousand men.

¹ Ver. 30.—The καί (ὅσα) of the *Recepta* has the weight of the Codd. against it.
² Ver. 33.—The οἱ ὄχλοι is an addition (from Matthew), and is wanting in A., B., D., Griesbach, Scholz, Lachmann. Lachmann and Tischendorf have συνέδραμον ἐκεῖ καὶ προῆλθον αὐτούς. The many variations are essentially the same in meaning.
³ Ver. 36.—Ἀγοράσωσιν ἑαυτοῖς, τί φάγωσι—Tischendorf, after B., L., Δ., &c.
⁴ Ver. 38.—Καί before ἴδετε wanting in B., D., L., Versions, Tischendorf.
⁵ Ver. 43.—Tischendorf and Meyer, following B. and cursive MSS., read κοφίνων πληρώματα.

EXEGETICAL AND CRITICAL.

See on the parallel passages of *Matthew, Luke*, and *John*.—The time is designated most clearly by John. Jesus has returned from the Feast of Purim (in the second year of His ministry) to Galilee; and the journey begins probably from the district of Tiberias. The time is evidently just before the Passover; as it is manifest, from Mark's mention of the green grass, that the spring was just beginning. According to Luke, it was, also, the time when the Apostles once more assembled around their Master, and when Herod began to take an interest in Him and in His doings. According to Matthew, finally, this miracle coincided with the time immediately after the execution of the Baptist, and the report brought concerning it. The peculiarities of Mark in this section are as follows: The disciples tell the Lord also what they had taught. They were to take a little rest in the desert place. As elsewhere there was no time for either the Lord or His disciples to eat, on account of the press of the people, so it was here. The fact also is mentioned, that the Lord's departure was made known to many, and that the crowds hastened to anticipate Him. We must add the allusion to these as sheep without a shepherd, and the vivid description of the people's dejected state.

Ver. 34. **When He came out.**—The crowds of people might seem to have rendered abortive the design of Jesus to withdraw for a season with His disciples; for, according to the most obvious connection, we should suppose that ἐξελθών must mean: "When He came forth from the ship." But as the Evangelist has mentioned the fixed purpose of Jesus to go into a desert place apart, we must retain the connection with this, and assume that the "coming out" refers to His leaving the wilderness again.— **And He began to teach them many things.**— This likewise confirms the previous explanation. Since a large portion of the day was gone, the time must have been drawing too near to the decline of day; and hence His discourse was interrupted by the suggestion of the disciples.

Ver. 37. **Two hundred pennyworth.**—See for the details in John,—"through whom this part of the scene, not recorded by Matthew and Luke, obtains the confirmation of authenticity." Grotius: "The amount that happened to be in the chest was two hundred denarii." Meyer: "This does not follow; it was the estimate made by the disciples of what the provision would cost." But they would doubtless make their estimate according to the condition of their treasury. The denarius, δηνάριον, was a Roman silver coin; it was used also at a later period among the Jews; somewhat lighter than the Attic drachma, but current at about the same value, being the customary hire of a day's labor, about sevenpence halfpenny. See particulars in WINER.

Ver. 39. **By companies,** συμπόσια συμπόσια.— A Hebraism, like the subsequent πρασιαὶ πρασιαί. Starke: "So that there were on each side 50, and 100 always together. Fifty such tables full made them just 5,000. Or, there were 50 seats in breadth, and 100 in length." But, why not simply companies of 100 and of 50, through which they might freely pass? A living town in the wilderness. Gerlach: "Two longer rows of 100, a shorter one of 50 persons. The fourth side remained, after the manner of the ancients' tables, empty and open."

Ver. 43. **And of the fishes.**—Reckoned among the relics which filled the twelve baskets. According to the account, these relics are distinguished from the κλάσματα, or broken pieces of bread.

DOCTRINAL AND ETHICAL.

See on the parallel passages in *Matthew, Luke*, and *John*.

HOMILETICAL AND PRACTICAL.

See on the parallel passage of *Matthew*.—The return of the Apostles, and the first resting-place provided for them by their Lord.—Come into a desert place apart, and rest a while: Christ's call to His overwrought, excited, and restless laborers.—This word of Christ perverted by many of His servants into a toleration of idleness: He says, *a while!*— Christ's rest, and His disciples' solemn prayer, in solitude.—The refreshments of the world, and the refreshments of Christ's disciples.—Into solitude, but with Christ.—How the Lord sacrificed for men both His solitude and His refreshment.—How He turned the seeming failure of His plan (touching solitude) into a higher realization of the same object.—How we should fashion the web of our life—our plans and the conjunctures of circumstances—into higher unity of godly action and suffering.—The miraculous festival which our Lord prepared for His disciples after their labors and journeys in the world.—How He continually comes forth in His mercy: 1. From the bosom of heaven; 2. from the darkness of Nazareth; 3. from the solemn season of prayer in the wilderness; 4. from the glory of the new life in the resurrection; 5. from the throne of heaven.—The school of Christ a free school in the highest sense.—With Christ, all that we have we have freely.—Christ was already King when they wanted to make Him king; but King: 1. In the kingdom of the Spirit; 2. in the kingdom of love; 3. and in the kingdom of divine blessing.—His earthly exaltation would have been the translation of His throne from the realm of the infinite into the realm of the finite and transitory.— Christ was constrained to repel the people with as much earnestness as that with which the mercy of His Shepherd-heart sought them.—Christ the breaker of bread, because He Himself is the Bread of life.— The riches of His kingdom.—Sufficiency with Christ is lavish abundance.

STARKE:—OSIANDER:—We should in such manner wait on our ministering as preachers of the Gospel, that we may be able to give in our account to the supreme Shepherd with joy.—It is good to rest after labor.—When we can separate ourselves from the tumult of the world, and send our spirits upwards to God, rest both of body and of soul is the result.— HEDINGER:—He who is in earnest to go to Christ, will let no trouble, labor, or expense hinder him.—OSIANDER:—Although we may have a certain amount of rest in this world, yet that is soon disturbed again by business. Here all is unrest; yonder is perfect repose.—The Church of God has indeed many shepherds; but since many of them are shamefully given to negligence, and many are busy with vain labor, it is reasonable to lament that the poor sheep have, after all, but few true shepherds.—QUESNEL:—The love of devout souls is indeed wise, but God's love is better in this than all.—Poor people cannot do better than hang upon God, &c.—HEDINGER:—Piety and faith never die of hunger.—What in men's eyes is impossible, may become possible through God's power.—As to the fragments, order and economy are in all things well-pleasing to God.—God is a God of order.—Take your food with prayer and thanksgiving, 1 Tim. iv. 4.—SCHLEIERMACHER:—Thus they came back with minds excited, and perhaps disturbed, by all these various opinions concerning Christ; and therefore it was very important that they should become composed, and readjust all their views in their original relation to the truth.—We should never find a contradiction between that which is our duty and the internal bias of our hearts.—Christ found between this will (to be alone with His disciples) and the great pressure of the people no contradiction: He knew how to reconcile one with the other, and by the other.—There is nothing more essential in the kingdom of God than what is incumbent upon us as duty, and what is the object of our wishes, should coalesce and coincide, the one upholding and preserving the other.—There is one entirely and purely simple wisdom.—To this nothing is so absolutely essential as simplicity of spirit.—The disciples were to be convinced (by the miraculous feeding), that if they applied themselves to the duties and obligations of the spiritual kingdom, their outward life would take no harm; whilst, on the other hand, everything would be interrupted if the Master should always act as they might think best.

SEVENTH SECTION.

CONTEST OF JESUS WITH THE ENMITY OF THE PHARISEES AND SCRIBES FROM JERUSALEM; HIS WITHDRAWAL INTO THE GENTILE BORDERS OF TYRE AND SIDON, AND INTO THE DISTRICT OF DECAPOLIS.

CHAPTER VI. 45—VIII. 9.

---

1. *The Return to Gennesaret; the Contrary Wind; Christ's Walking on the Sea; New Miracles on the Western Coast.* CH. VI. 45–56.

(Parallels: Matt. xiv. 22-36; John vi. 15-21.)

45 And straightway he constrained his disciples to get into the ship, and to go to the
46 other side before unto Bethsaida, while he sent away[1] the people. And when he had
47 sent them away, he departed into a [the] mountain to pray. And when even was
48 come, the ship was in the midst of the sea, and he alone on the land. And he saw[2] them toiling in rowing; for the wind was contrary unto them: and about the fourth watch of the night he cometh unto them, walking upon the sea, and would have passed
49 by them. But when they saw him walking upon the sea, they supposed it had been a
50 spirit [spectre], and cried out: For they all saw him, and were troubled. And immediately he talked with them, and saith unto them, Be of good cheer: it is I; be not
51 afraid. And he went up unto them into the ship; and the wind ceased: and they were

52 sore amazed in themselves beyond measure, and wondered.¹ For they considered not *the*
53 *miracle* of the loaves: for their heart was hardened. And when they had passed over,
54 they came into the land of Gennesaret, and drew to the shore. And when they were
55 come out of the ship, straightway they knew him,⁴ And ran through that whole region
round about, and began to carry about in beds those that were sick, where they heard
56 he was. And whithersoever he entered, into villages, or cities, or country, they laid
the sick in the streets, and besought him that they might touch if it were but the border of his garment: and as many as touched him were made whole.

¹ Ver. 45.—Ἀπολύει, after B., D., L., Δ. Tischendorf, Lachmann, Meyer.
[² Ver. 48.—B., D., L., Vulgate, Lachmann, Tischendorf, Meyer, read ἰδὼν instead of εἶδεν, and omit the following καὶ (B., L.), making a parenthesis of ἦν γὰρ ὁ, &c.—*Ed.*]
[³ Ver. 52.—B., L., Δ., Coptic, Vulgate, Tischendorf omit καὶ ἐθαύμαζον; rejected by Griesbach, bracketed by Lach-
mann, retained by Meyer.—*Ed.*]
[⁴ Ver. 54.—After αὐτὸν Lachmann inserts in brackets οἱ ἄνδρες τοῦ τόπου ἐκείνου, following A., G., Versions. Meyer
rightly regards it as a gloss.—*Ed.*]

EXEGETICAL AND CRITICAL.

See on the parallel passages of *Matthew* and *John*.—We owe to Mark the very important record, which sheds light upon the whole narrative, that the disciples were sent forward before the Lord in the direction of Bethsaida—that Bethsaida, namely, which lay on the eastern side of the sea. (*See* on *Matthew*.) Thus it was a passage across. Then his expression, ἀποταξάμενος, is an important parallel to the ἀνεχώρησε in John: it gave Him trouble to release Himself from the excited and enthusiastic people. Also, in the expression, ἤθελε παρελθεῖν, he coincides, in the meaning at least, with John, ver. 21, ἤθελον οὖν λαβεῖν αὐτὸν, κ.τ.λ. But while Mark omits the intervening incident connected with Peter—which that Apostle, whose Evangelist he was, would modestly pass over, as making himself prominent—he lays stress upon the fact that the dis-
ciples had not been brought to a true and living faith, even by the miracle of the feeding. But he has painted most copiously and vividly the tumultuous excitement of the people, as it was occasioned by the Lord's landing, and how they immediately knew Him and followed Him with their sick from place to place.

Ver. 45. **Unto Bethsaida.**—Meyer's notion, that this was the western Bethsaida, and not the eastern, appears entirely groundless. [Wieseler understands by it the eastern Bethesda. Alexander remarks that it was "not the city of Gaulonitis, at the north-
eastern end of the lake and eastward of the place where the Jordan enters it, in the desert tract south-
east of which the miracle had just been wrought (Luke ix. 10), but Bethsaida of Galilee, the birth-
place of Simon, Andrew, and Philip (John i. 45), elsewhere mentioned with Capernaum (Matt. xi. 21; Luke x. 13), and therefore probably not far from it, but at all events upon the lake-shore, as Eusebius expressly mentions."—*Ed.*]

Ver. 46. **Sent them away,** ἀποταξάμενος.—
Not merely, "bade them farewell," for which there would have been no necessity to send the disciples away first.

Ver. 48. **Would have passed by them.**—
They were to follow Him in a westerly direction: no longer fruitlessly rowing eastwards against the wind (*see* on *Matthew*). He went before them, as it were, to show the way. They had wished to take Him up on the eastern coast (John); He would go before them to the western coast (Mark): an intermediate course was the result in the end.

Ver. 51. **Were sore amazed in themselves**

beyond measure, and wondered.—The latter feeling found expression in exclamations; the whole strength of their internal amazement they did not express.

Ver. 52. **They considered not.**—They had not yet come to an understanding, οὐ συνῆκαν. They had not attained that living, self-developing apprehension of spirit, which would know how to draw the right consequences. Bengel: *debuerant a pane ad mare concludere*.

Ver. 53. **The land of Gennesaret.**—*See* on *Matthew*.

Ver. 55 **Began to carry about.**—Not merely in general, but some hither and others thither. It is also meant that they went with a sick man after Jesus from one place to another, when He had left the former.

DOCTRINAL AND ETHICAL.

1. *See* on the parallel passages of *Matthew* and *John*.

2. The first miraculous feeding marks precisely the moment when our Lord had most expressly to contend with the people's design to challenge Him as the Messiah, and make Him a king. In contrast with this design of the people, we must here take notice of the expression of Jesus' pity for the wretched multitude: so little can the attempt of a people to exalt Him prematurely, and in a worldly sense, exert any influence upon Him. In that very circumstance the misery of the people presented itself to His view most plainly. But even this earnest effort of our Lord to withdraw Himself from the people was successful only for a short period. Very soon afterwards He was obliged, in the synagogue at Capernaum (according to John vi.), to declare Himself most emphatically; and from that time onwards, that enthusiastic fanaticism among the people, which had before been prepared to take side with Him, even against Pharisaism the hierarchy and Herod, declined. From this time treachery began to ger-
minate in the soul of Judas.

3. The miracle of Christ's walking upon the sea was a manifestation of His divine power, not only over external objective nature, but also over His subjective nature, in the medium of His human equanimity. The mystery of this equanimity is the manifestation of the paradisaical, holy man in the midst of the nature subjected by the fall to vanity. (Meyer does not understand this: *see* Note on *Mark*.)

4. It is observable that the Evangelist Mark most expressly, and in the plainest manner, describes the state of the Apostles, down to the revelation of the

risen Lord among them, as a state of dulness, hardness, and unbelief. He does not thereby deny their fidelity as disciples. But the true and perfect faith did not, in his conception, exist until the new evangelical Spirit of life was given, that life which could approve itself in a personal spontaneous development. And the disciple of Peter approaches John in this, as in many other traits of his evangelical representation.

HOMILETICAL AND PRACTICAL.

See on the parallel passages in Matthew and John.—The temptability of the disciples of Jesus as over against the fanatical excitement of the people.—How Christ constrained them to take ship and go over the sea, in order to separate them from the people; and what significance this has for the Church and the ministers of Christ.—Christ (and Christianity) the guide on the sea.—The walking of Christ upon the waters.—How the phantoms and scarecrows of vain fear vanish before the glory of Christ, in sacred reverence of His divine power.—The climax of the enthusiasm of the Galilean people on behalf of Christ was also a turning-point.

STARKE:—QUESNEL:—Man is in the world like a little ship upon the stormy sea in the night; since he can neither counsel nor save himself. He who does not know danger, and does not pray, may soon perish.—Jesus sometimes leaves us alone, that we may know ourselves and our own weakness, and feel how deeply we are in need of Him; but He never leaves us out of His sight.—The wind of persecution is a useful wind; for it brings Christ to us, and us to land.—Christ is Lord also over all nature.—LUTHER:—By such an example (the feeding) they should have been made so strong in faith as not to have been terrified at an apparition.—SCHLEIERMACHER:—Thus, as the living consciousness of the Redeemer is awakened within us, our temper must be calmed into the true equanimity; and this will smooth and regulate all things external.—All the powers which God has given us we should put in motion to glorify the kingdom of God.—GOSSNER:—We are all still upon the sea of life.—But He never loses us out of His sight.—BAUER:—When they have rightly heard the Master's word, phantoms and night and storm are all forgotten.

---

2. *Contest with the Pharisees and Scribes from Jerusalem concerning Traditions respecting Eating.* CH. VII. 1–23.

(Parallel: Matt. xv. 1–20.)

1 Then came together unto him the Pharisees, and certain of the scribes, which came
2 from Jerusalem. And when they saw some of his disciples eat bread with defiled [com-
3 mon], that is to say, with unwashen hands, they found fault.¹ For the Pharisees, and all the Jews, except they wash *their* hands oft, eat not, holding the tradition of the
4 elders. And *when they come* from the market, except they wash, they eat not. And many other things there be, which they have received to hold, *as* the washing of cups,
5 and pots, brasen vessels, and of tables. Then² the Pharisees and scribes asked him, Why walk not thy disciples according to the tradition of the elders, but eat bread with
6 unwashen hands? He answered and said unto them, Well hath Esaias prophesied of you hypocrites, as it is written, This people honoureth me with *their* lips, but their heart
7 is far from me. Howbeit, in vain do they worship me, teaching *for* doctrines the com-
8 mandments of men. For, laying aside the commandment of God, ye hold the tradition of men, *as* the washing of pots and cups: and many other such like things ye do.³
9 And he said unto them, Full well ye reject the commandment of God, that ye may
10 keep your own tradition. For Moses said, Honour thy father and thy mother; and,
11 Whoso curseth [revileth] father or mother, let him die the death: But ye say, If a man shall say to his father or mother, *It is* Corban, that is to say, a gift, by whatsoever thou
12 mightest be profited by me; *he shall be free.* And⁴ ye suffer him no more to do aught
13 for his father or mother; Making the word of God of none effect through your tra-
14 dition, which ye have delivered: and many such like things do ye. And when he had called all the people *unto him*, he said unto them [again⁵], Hearken unto me every one
15 *of you*, and understand: There is nothing from without a man, that entering into him, can defile him: but the things which come out of him,⁶ those are they that defile the
16, 17 man. If any man have ears to hear, let him hear.⁷ And when he was entered into
18 the house from the people, his disciples asked him concerning the parable. And he saith unto them, Are ye so without understanding also? Do ye not perceive, that
19 whatsoever thing from without entereth into the man, it cannot defile him; Because it entereth not into his heart, but into the belly, and goeth out into the draught, purging⁸
20 all meats? And he said, That which cometh out of the man, that defileth the man.
21 For from within, out of the heart of men, proceed evil thoughts, adulteries, fornications,

22 murders, Thefts, covetousness, wickedness, deceit, lasciviousness, an evil eye, blasphemy,
23 pride, foolishness: All these evil things come from within, and defile the man.

¹ Ver. 2.—The addition ἐμέμψαντο (after ἄρτους) has slight support; and the κατέγνωσαν (after ἄρτους) of Cod. D. is equally weak. The former arose from undervaluing the emphatic συνάγονται, which itself suggests an act of the synagogue. Hence we cannot, with Tischendorf, take vers. 3 and 4 as a parenthesis, and ver. 5 as the conclusion.
² Ver. 5.—The ἔπειτα is a continuation of the former misunderstanding: Codd. B., D., L., Lachmann, Tischendorf, Meyer, &c., read καί.—The κοιναῖς, instead of ἀνίπτοις, is sanctioned by B., D., Versions.
³ Ver. 6.—Βαπτισμοὺς τὸ ποιεῖτε is wanting in B., L., Δ., &c. It is bracketed by Lachmann, struck out by Tischendorf. Meyer defends it.
⁴ Ver. 12.—The καί is omitted by Lachmann and Meyer, after D., D. It disturbs the connection of thought.
⁵ Ver. 14.—The reading πάλιν, recommended by Griesbach and adopted by Lachmann, Tischendorf, and Meyer, following B., D., L., Δ., is important. It shows, that is, that the previous incident must be regarded as an examination by the synagogue, in which Christ was separated from the people.
⁶ Ver. 15.—Τὰ ἐκ τοῦ ἀνθρώπου ἐκπορευόμενα, according to B., D., L., Δ., Lachmann, Tischendorf.
⁷ Ver. 16.—This verse is wanting in B., L. Omitted by Tischendorf, it is retained by Lachmann and Meyer. An interpolation here is not probable. The connection requires this point.
⁸ Ver. 19.—A., B., E., F., G., Δ., Chrysostom, Lachmann, Meyer, read καθαρίζων, not καθαρίζον; D. reads καθαρίζει.

EXEGETICAL AND CRITICAL.

Comp. the parallel place in Matthew. The occurrence before us took place in the summer of the year 782: in the midst of the year of persecutions. The combination of the Pharisees of Galilee and the Pharisees of Judea in their opposition to Jesus had already been concerted and entered upon. They had begun to institute against Him ecclesiastical proceedings in Galilee, and to watch His every step. The basis of the conspiracy consists of the preceding Galilean crisis, ch. ii. and iii., and the confederacy against Jesus at the Feast of Purim in Jerusalem, 782 (John v.). The progress and the conclusion of the scheme appear in ch. viii. 11. From the time of the Feast of Purim a common action and combination of the Sanhedrim in Jerusalem and the Galilean synagogue was inaugurated. The Sanhedrim were in constant connection and correspondence with the synagogues of the provinces, and even with those of foreign lands (see Acts ix. 2). Some, therefore, appointed by them, diligently visited the provinces; and watched especially those teachers whose doctrines declined from the principles of Pharisaism, at the head of which stood that of tradition (AMMON, Leben Jesu, ii. 264). There were two official transactions or interferences. And there were two retreats on the part of Jesus: the first time, as far as the borders of the Gentile territory; the second time, into the solitude of the mountain beyond the sea, and even to the borders of the other world (transfiguration);—and all for the preparation of the new Church. (See my Leben Jesu, ii. 2, 858.)—Between the narrative of the first feeding, the walking of Christ upon the sea, and our present narrative, there are many things to be interposed, which Mark has already communicated. Among these are the hereticatiou of Jesus in the cornfield; the healing the man with a withered hand; the allegation of the Galilean Pharisees, that the works of Christ were done in the power of Beelzebub, etc. (See the Table of Contents, Leben Jesu, ii. 2, 14.)—Peculiar to Mark is the expression, συνάγονται πρὸς αὐτόν, in which we cannot fail to see reference to an official interference of the Sanhedrim with our Lord. Also the exact account of the religious washings of the Jews; the detailed characterization of the conflict between the Pharisaic traditions and the commandment of God, including the Corban; the striking and profound sentence concerning the purging all meats; and the perfect description of those evil things which proceed out of the heart. Also, in the following section, which may be glanced at here, the design of Christ to remain concealed in a house (belonging to a friend) on the borders of Phœnicia, during the time of His sojourn there; and the Lord's return to the Sea of Galilee through the Sidonian territory and that of Decapolis. It is observable that Peter must have communicated the account of these remarkable travels, having faithfully preserved the individual details. On the other hand, this Evangelist omits the intercession of the disciples on behalf of the woman of Canaan, and the declaration of Christ that He was sent only to the lost sheep of the house of Israel.

Ver. 2. **And when they saw.**—Probably on the appearance of the disciples in Jerusalem at the Passover, which He did not attend in the year 782. The spiritual impulse of freedom which actuated the disciples might at that time have led them into the commission of certain acts of thoughtlessness.—**With common, that is to say, with unwashen hands.**—So Mark explains for Roman readers. We must particularly define the idea of unwashen hands by that of unwashen in the sense of a religious ceremony prescribed by tradition; and the idea of common by that of ecclesiastically profane, unclean, and defiling. Those who persisted in this uncleanness, which had for its result excommunication, must at last draw down upon themselves the decisive ban.

Ver. 3. **With the fist; oft.** [Margin of Eng. Ver. *diligently.*] Πυγμῇ.—Among the many explanatory translations which have missed the meaning of the difficult expression are these: Vulgate, *crebro;* Gothic, *ufta* (oft); Syriac, *diligenter.* See in De Wette and Meyer the various exegetical methods adopted. "Probably it was part of the rite, that the washing hand was shut; because it might have been thought that the open hand engaged in washing might make the other unclean, or be made unclean by it, after having itself been washed" (*Leben Jesu*, ii. 2, 858). The expression might mean a vigorous and thorough washing.

Ver. 4. **And from the market.**—Codex D. has the addition, ἐὰν ἔλθωσιν, *when they come;* which Meyer, De Wette, and others regard as a sound interpretation. According to this view the progression would be this: 1. Before every meal the washing of hands; 2. but, after the return from market, where there was so much danger of coming into contact with unclean men, the bath was used as a washing of the whole body; hence ἐὰν μὴ βαπτ. But that which follows—the βαπτισμοὶ ποτηρίων—requires still another degree in the progression, and proves that βαπτισμός here must be understood in a wider sense. Therefore we interpret it, with Paulus, Kuinoel, and Olshausen, of that which came from the market. De Wette, on the contrary, observes that this was everywhere customary. But it was not customary as a *religious* ceremony of washing, or as a kind of baptism, like that of the pots and cups, or the Romish baptism of bells. And, moreover, the same held good of the washing of hands; for the washing of hands before eating was generally customary amongst the Persians, Greeks, and Romans. Thus, in our view, there was a triple washing at meals: 1. That of the persons; 2. that of the victuals; 3. that of the vessels. — **Cups and pots.**— Made of wood, in contrast with those of brass, which follow; or, it may be, considered as earthen. ["Pots," ξεστῶν, perhaps from ξέω, to polish; or else from the Latin *sextus* or *sextarius*, denoting the sixth part of a larger measure.—*Ed.*] Meyer says, indeed, "Earthen vessels, when they were Levitically unclean, were broken to pieces, according to Lev. xv. 12." But the case supposed there was that of positive desecrations; and it is not to be supposed that the Jews, after or before every meal, broke all the earthen vessels which they used. [*Tables* (in the margin *beds*), *i. e.*, couches, anything on which men recline, whether for sleep, or, according to the later use of the ancients, to partake of food,—which accounts for the word used in the text of our Bible. That these couches were immersed in every instance of ceremonial washing, can be thought probable, or even possible, only by those who are under the necessity of holding that this Greek word not only means to dip or plunge, originally, but, unlike every other word transferred to a religious use, is always used in that exclusive and invariable sense, without modification or exception; to those who have no purpose to attain by such a paradox, the place before us will afford, if not conclusive evidence, at least a strong presumption, that beds (to say no more) might be baptized without immersion. ALEXANDER, *in loco.*—*Ed.*]

Ver. 9. **Full well,** καλῶς.—Ironically, as among ourselves. — **Your own tradition,** ἵνα. — Very strong and deep. At the bottom of all rigorous enforcement of traditional observances there is an unconscious or half-conscious repugnance to submit perfectly to the law of God. Bengel: *Vere accusantur, hanc suam esse intentionem.* "Not only unconsciously, but with the fullest purpose, the Rabbis exalted their precepts above the law of Moses." In the Talmud we read: "The words of the scribes are more noble than the words of the law; for the words of the law are both hard and easy, but the words of the scribes are all easy (to be understood)." —"He who deals with Scripture, it is said in the Bava Mezia, does a thing indifferent; he who reads the Mishna has a reward; but he who devotes himself to the Gemara is most meritorious of all." SEPP, *Leben Jesu,* ii. p. 345.

Ver. 11. **Corban.** — Comp. on Matthew xiv. 5; as also, for the ellipsis in ver. 11, Luther's marginal note: "Corban means an offering, and it was as much as to say, Dear father, I would willingly give it to thee, but it is Corban: I count it better to give it to God than to thee, and it will help thee better."

Ver. 14. **He said again.**—The significant πάλιν —the reading we adopt—throws light upon the whole preceding occurrence; and, together with the συνάγονται at the beginning, gives it the appearance of a judicial process of the synagogue.

Ver. 17. **His disciples asked Him.**— Comp. Matthew, where Peter is marked out as the questioner; and observe here, as elsewhere, his modest suppression of himself in the Gospel which sprang from himself. And here, again, there is emphatic prominence given to the disciples' want of developed spiritual vigor and insight of faith, and their slow advancement in knowledge.

Ver. 19. **Purging all meats.**—Meyer: καθαρίζον might be connected with the ἐκπορεύεται as an appositional expression. The apposition, however, would not be connected with the ἐκπορεύεται, but with its subject, that is, meat; and that could not be tolerated. Καθαρίζον is rather the substantival definition of ἀφεδρών, as being a general means of purification for all the external impurities of meats: the better supported reading καθαρίζων, on the other hand, expressed the same thought adjectivally.—The ἀφεδρών makes all meats clean, not because it simply takes away all impurities, but because the uncleanness or impurity of the object consists in its being out of its place, and therefore defiling something else. It is therefore a place of filth for all the house; a place of cleansing, on the contrary, for the great household of nature. Not without irony does Christ make prominent this ideal significance of the external means of cleansing for meats, addressing as He did the men of traditions, who strove to ensure a *prophylactic external* purity to their food.

Ver. 21. **Evil thoughts.** — In relation to the distribution here, we must notice the change between the plural and the singular forms; or, 1. predominant actions, and 2. dispositions. The acts in the plural are arranged under three categories: *a.* lust; *b.* hatred; *c.* covetousness. They then combine into wickednesses (πονηρίαι), by which the forms of evil dispositions are then introduced: *deceit* and *lasciviousness* indicate, in two contrasts, the concealed and the open wickedness of self-gratification; whilst the *evil eye* and *blasphemy* indicate concealed and open enmity (blasphemy against God and man). Pride or self-exaltation, and foolishness (נְבָלָה), are the internal and the external side of the one ungodly and wicked nature. "*The evil eye*" is notorious in the East; here it is the description of an envious look.

DOCTRINAL AND ETHICAL.

1. *See* the parallel passage in Matthew.
2. The Jews have fallen through their Sabbath or Rest-day traditions into eternal unrest, through their law of purification into moral defilement, through their many baptisms into an abiding lack of baptism, through their service of the letter into Talmudist fables, through their separation into dispersion all over the world, through their millenarian Messiahship into enmity to Christ, through their trifling with the blessing into the power of the curse. The irony of the Spirit, that He punishes extremes by extremes.
3. The prophecy of Isaiah (ch. xxix. 13) pronounces a condemnation, always in force, upon all dead and fanatical zeal, and upon all mere ceremonial worship and work.
4. Zeal for traditional observances in its abiding conflict with the eternal commandments of God and laws of humanity. The conflict between false ecclesiasticism and morality. The contradiction of fanaticism has for its foundation an evil bias towards externalizing the inner life. The worm of superstition is unbelief; the worm of fanaticism is religious death or atheism; the worm of hypocritical outside religion is impiety. For the conflict between human fanatical ecclesiasticism and the divine fundamental commandments of morality, *see* the history of Byzantism and Romanism.

5. Tradition and human ordinances identical. Tradition needs continual reform through the law of God; and human ordinances, through the living development of this law.

6. Contrast between external and internal fellowship; *i. e.*, between being excommunicated, and being out of the Church.

HOMILETICAL AND PRACTICAL.

See on Matthew.—Christ in judgment upon human tradition.—Christ the Deliverer of His disciples: 1. The Originator, 2. the Defender, 3. the Guardian, 4. the Director and Consummator, of their freedom.—Christ and Christianity a hundred times exposed to spiritual censure: 1. The censure of school-learning (theology); 2. of the tradition of the elders (clerical office); 3. of the synagogue (popular assembly).—Christ and tradition: 1. He is the foundation or kernel of all true internal tradition; 2. therefore He unites in one and renews all external tradition; 3. and He is the Judge of all externalized and impious tradition.—The conflict between the law and human ordinances, or between ecclesiasticism and morality. It is, 1. an unnatural conflict, for true ecclesiasticism and true morality can never come into collision. 2. It is a light conflict, when false morality contends with true ecclesiasticism. 3. It is a critical conflict, when false ecclesiasticism fights against true morality. 4. There is a frightful doom upon both, when false ecclesiasticism and false morality struggle with each other.—The old conflict between fanaticism and humanity. Ecclesiastical systems which bury piety (household relations, filial obligations, etc.) condemn themselves.—The indivisible unity of faith and love, of piety and duty.—The fearful perversion of the conflict between divine revelation and human sin into a contradiction between the divine and the human nature.—The triumph of human ordinance is always upon the ruins of the law of faith.—To enjoy with thankfulness, is the sanctification of enjoyment, 1 Tim. iv. 4.—In the place of the washing of hands before meat, has come in the folding of hands. Therefore we must mind the reality of the symbol, even in this latter case.—Isaiah, Christ, and the Reformation, agreeing in their judgment upon what is true and what is false worship of God.—The right process of a true reformation: 1. It distinguishes between spirit and flesh, between the internal and the external. 2. It fights against the false intermixtures of the two, in which the spirit is made subservient to the flesh, and the internal to the external. 3. It seeks to connect the two aright, so that the spirit may make the flesh its own and glorify it. 4. It therefore contends also against a false and unnatural separation between the two.—The purity and the purifying power of the great divine economy of nature.—Christianity has consecrated even natural infirmity; or, a beam of the glorification which shines upon the dark natural ways of men.—The decisive objection against human ordinances, that they vainly attempt to effect symbolically a purity which actual life better provides for: 1. Holy water, God's streams; 2. arbitrary penances, divine burdens; 3. ecclesiastical purgatory fires, God's salting fires.—The evil things which proceed from the heart and defile the man. *See Critical Notes* on ver. 21.

STARKE:—MAJUS:—As Christ and His disciples were not without their slanderers, so the devout are never without their accusers and rebukers, 1 Pet. ii. 12.—*Nova Bibl. Tub.:*—From Jerusalem hypocrisy went forth into all the land.—HEDINGER:—What is the dross to the pure gold? what the inventions of men to the truth of God? what superstition to faith?—QUESNEL:—As man may dishonor God by overmuch caring for beauty and external purity, Isa. iii. 16, so God is honored by the neglect of these things, when that neglect springs from humiliation of self and true mortification, Jonah iii. 6-10.—We must wash the heart after having been defiled by the world; that is, we must test ourselves and cleanse ourselves of sin, Job i. 5.—MAJUS:—With hypocrites, regard to man and human ordinances has more weight than the commandments of God.—The hypocrisy of hypocrites must be revealed.—CRAMER:—The enemies of the truth must be confounded by the word of God.—CANSTEIN:—The true worship of God is the union of the heart with Him.—Men commonly do willingly and cheerfully all things that do not set them about changing their own hearts.—Self-love, or the selfish mind, is so mad, that it prefers expending its care upon pots and cups rather than upon itself.—Many external ceremonies and human ordinances are not good in the Church of God; for, those who are bent upon rigidly observing them easily come to forget, or postpone to them, the true commandments of God.—QUESNEL:—The openly impious do not dishonor the truth of the divine law so much by their evil life, as those do who give themselves out to be lovers of the law of God, and yet falsely interpret it.—After God, our parents are most important; and them their children should honor as the channel of the first gifts of God—nature, life, nourishment, and education.—*Bibl. Wirt.:*—Christian children should learn well the fourth and fifth commandments.—QUESNEL:—Man may disguise his godlessness under the fairest show of piety, but God sees it nevertheless; and, as He condemns it now, He will hereafter make it manifest to all the world.—MAJUS:—Vows against the honor of God are sinful, and must not be paid.—*Bibl. Wirt.:*—He who departs from God's word in one point, and in that point prefers the ordinances of men, may become so thoroughly entangled as not again to escape, Tit. i. 15.—In the New Testament, the making distinctions of meats is classed among the works of the devil, 1 Tim. iv. 1-3.—CANSTEIN:—All depends upon the state of the heart: as that is, we are.—As the heart is the source of all evil, we should carefully watch its issues, Jer. xvii. 9.

SCHLEIERMACHER:—This was the sense in which the Lord Himself said that His yoke was easy and His burden light; for He contrasted Himself, and the fellowship which He would found upon His own name, with the yoke and the manifold external burdens which the elders were never weary of imposing upon the Jews.—Those who rest wholly on external things have always the same vain labor as the Pharisees; and this has its ground in a lack of confidence. It springs from the fact that man can never have so much firm assurance concerning that which is not the truth as he can concerning that which is the truth; and this unrest manifests itself in looking anxiously at the letter, and in seeking after external uniformity. The greater the number, the greater their hope of internal confidence: of that which is *strictly* internal they have nothing.—This also He would say, that whosoever contributes to confirm such notions in the minds of men, and make their notions of God's service purely external, leads them thereby away from the true worship of God in spirit and in truth, and seeks to give their ideas of God such a direction and such a form, that they no longer represent to themselves *that* God who will be worshipped in spirit and in truth, but an imaginary Being, such as the Gentiles frame in their imaginations.—The same feeling which leads to the honor of father and mother leads to the honor of our Father in heaven.—GOSSNER:— Manifestly, wicked human ordinances do not injure the divine doctrine so much as specious and seemingly holy superstitious inventions and false interpretations, which are received with confidence by the weak devout, and held fast with stubborn pertinacity.

3. *The Withdrawal of Jesus to the Gentile Borders of Tyre and Sidon, and to the District of Decapolis. The Woman of Canaan.* VERS. 24–31.

(Parallel: Matt. xv. 21–29.)

24 And from thence he arose, and went into the borders of Tyre and Sidon,[1] and entered into an house, and would have no man know *it:* but [and] he could not be hid.
25 For a *certain* woman, whose young daughter had an unclean spirit, heard of him,[2] and
26 came and fell at his feet; (The woman was a Greek, a Syrophenician by nation,) and
27 she besought him that he would cast forth the devil out of her daughter. But Jesus said[3] unto her, Let the children first be filled: for it is not meet to take the children's
28 bread, and to cast *it* unto the [little] dogs. And she answered and said unto him, Yes,
29 Lord: yet the [little] dogs under the table eat of the children's crumbs. And he said
30 unto her, For this saying go thy way; the devil is gone out of thy daughter. And when she was come to her house, she found the devil gone out, and her daughter laid
31 upon the bed.[4] And again, departing from the coasts of Tyre and Sidon, he came unto[5] the Sea of Galilee, through the midst of the coasts of Decapolis.

[1] Ver. 24.—Ὅρια: Lachmann, after B., D., L., Δ. Καὶ Σιδῶνος is wanting in B., L., Δ., &c. Tischendorf and Meyer omit it; taken from Matt. xv. 21.
[2] Ver. 25.—Tischendorf, after B., L., Δ., Versions: ἀλλ' εὐθὺς ἀκούσασα γυνή.
[3] Ver. 27.—Lachmann and Tischendorf: καὶ ἔλεγεν, after B., L., Δ., &c. (D.: καὶ λέγει; Vulgate: *qua dixit*). And this is more in keeping; for it is not a definitive utterance, like the ὁ δὲ Ἰησοῦς εἶπεν.
[4] Ver. 30.—See Meyer, concerning the inversions of this clause. (Lachmann and Tischendorf, after B., D., L., Δ., Versions, have adopted the transposition: τὸ παιδίον βεβλημένον ἐπὶ κλίνην καὶ τὸ δαιμόνιον ἐξεληλυθός. The Received Text is to be retained; the reading of Lachmann is accounted for from the fact, that the copyist passed immediately from the καί following ἐξεληλυθός to the καί in ver. 31, so that the clause, καὶ τὴν θυγατ. to κλίνης, was left out, and was afterwards inserted in the wrong, but what seemed to be the more fitting, place. Hence the clause, θυγατ. to κλίνης, and not the clause, τὸ δαιμόν. ἐξεληλ., is the omitted and restored one; so that all the variations in the readings are found in the former and not the latter. Meyer, *in loco.—Ed.*)
[5] Ver. 31.—Griesbach, Lachmann, Tischendorf, after weighty authorities, read εἰς instead of πρός (as in Mark iii. 7). Lachmann and Tischendorf, after B., D., L., Δ., Coptic, Ethiopian, Syriac, Vulgate, Saxon, Itala, read ἦλθε διὰ Σιδῶνος instead of καὶ Σιδῶνος ἦλθε.

EXEGETICAL AND CRITICAL.

See the parallel passage in Matthew, and the preliminary summary of the foregoing section, *Critical Notes*, p. 282.

Ver. 24. **And from thence He arose, and went.**—That His departure was at the same time a breaking away from the Pharisaic party, is emphatically shown both by Matthew and Mark. His travelling towards the borders of Tyre and Sidon was the prophetic and symbolic representation of the future progress of Christianity from the Jews to the Gentiles. So in ancient times Elijah travelled out of his own land into Phœnicia. Elijah was driven away by the ascendency of idolatry in Israel; Christ was driven away by ascendency of a hierarchy and of a traditionalism which in his eyes was apostasy from the law of God, and therefore idolatry. Yet Jesus did not yet separate from His unbelieving people; He did not actually go into Phœnicia, but only into the adjoining borders of Galilee (εἰς τὰ μεθόρια), that is, into the district of the tribe of Asher. But afterwards, during His travels among the mountains and on His return to the Galilean sea, He actually passed through the Sidonian region. On these travels, see on *Matthew*, xv. 21, *Critical Note*, p. 281.—**And entered into an house.**—Here also He had friends and dependants, as He had in the opposite direction, on the borders of Perea.

Ver. 26. **A Gentile,** or **Greek.**—Ἑλληνίς, according to the Jewish phraseology of the time, indicating a Gentile woman especially. This was not merely the result of the intercourse of the Jews with the Greeks specially; but it sprang from the fact that in the Greeks and in Greece they saw the most finished and predominant exhibition of this world's culture and glory. *Syrophenician,* as distinguished from the Λιβυφοίνικες, the Phœnicians of Africa, that is, Carthage (Strabo). The *Tex. Rec.* has Συροφοίνισσα; but the true reading wavers between Συροφοινίκισσα (Codd. A., K., &c., Lachmann) and Συρα-Φοινίκισσα (Tischendorf, after Codd. E., F., &c.). Thus she was a Phœnician-Syrian woman: most generally viewed, a Gentile; more specially, a Syrian; and still more specifically, a Phœnician. Phœnicia belonged to the province of Syria. But the word may also, more precisely still, describe the Syrian of Phœnicia, the Canaanite woman (Matthew).

Ver. 30. **And her daughter laid upon the bed.**—A sign of her perfectly tranquil condition:

the demon had previously driven her hither and thither. But there is also an intimation of her exhaustion after the last paroxysm; and this is one more instance of that gradual restoration which Mark loves to describe. The arrival of her mother, who was the subject of healing faith, perfected then her new life and vigor.

Ver. 31. **Through Sidon.**—Meyer thinks that the analogy of Τύρου requires us to understand the town of Sidon. But the coasts of Tyre do not refer to Tyre as a city, but to Tyre as a country. Thus we agree with Ewald, that only the travelling through the district of Sidon is settled. The direction of the journey was first northward towards Lebanon; thence from the foot of Lebanon northeasterly, and back through the district of Decapolis, that is, back through the region which lay to the east, or the farther side, of the sources of the Jordan, to the eastern bank of the Sea of Galilee. On Decapolis, comp. WINER, and the *Critical Notes* on Matthew xv. 21.

DOCTRINAL AND ETHICAL.

1. *See* on the parallel passage in *Matthew*.
2. The circumstance that Mark passes over the mediation of the disciples on behalf of the Gentile woman, is explained by the critics in various ways, after their favorite fashion of *external* comparison. Meyer thinks Matthew's the original account. But if we look at *internal* motives, this whole intervening occurrence, which would be very easily understood by the Jewish-Christian readers of Matthew, would not, without some commentary, be at all intelligible to the Gentile-Christian readers of Mark. Matthew gave prominence to the points which proved to the Jewish-Christian how strictly Christ remained, during His work in the flesh, within the limits of His calling; and that He received the Gentile woman into communion and fellowship of His healing works, only on account of her strong faith, attested by the Israelite witness of the disciples themselves. This motive had no force in Mark's account. Hence he might, in harmony with his own design, paraphrase the repelling word of the Lord, modifying it according to its inner meaning; and we need not, with Meyer, attribute it to the "softening down of later tradition."
3. As Christ, in the former narrative, let a ray of His transfiguring glory fall upon the low region of meats and the "draught," so here He casts one upon the poor dog. Under the light of the kingdom of heaven, everything common and natural obtains a higher meaning; it obtains a value in the economy of God, and as a figure of the relations of His kingdom. The place of daily corruption is a figure of the purifying grave and kingdom of the dead; the dog a figure of the Gentile world. Sin remains more than ever condemned, but only that it may be made subservient to the judgments and honor of God.
4. As the earnest coming of the Syrophenician woman evinced a strong susceptibility among the Phœnicians, humbled by many severe judgments, it was needful that Christ should for the present leave this country, in order that His Jewish people might not be alienated by his premature labors among the Gentiles. But He left the region with the glad anticipation that the prophecy of Ps. ii. 8 would one day be fulfilled.

HOMILETICAL AND PRACTICAL.

See on *Matthew.*—A solemn sign, when Jesus only seems to go forth.—The travels of Jesus towards west, north, east, south: also a sign.—Jesus has everywhere His hidden friends.—He could not remain hidden: that is, 1. He hid from Himself, in His humility, the consciousness of the great influence of His majesty; 2. He sacrificed His rest to the restlessness of passionate men; 3. He ever submitted His human will to the ruling will of His Father.—The work of the Son, under His Father's government, though free, yet conditioned: 1. In Nazareth, His own city, He could not reveal Himself; 2. in the dark boundary of heathenism, He could not be hidden.—The Gentile longing everywhere feels from afar and seeks after salvation, whilst the Jews reject it before their very eyes. (The nobleman at Capernaum; Cornelius, Acts x.; the Canaanitish woman; the symbolical man of Macedonia, Acts xvi. 9.)—The Gentiles likened to the dogs (house-dogs, not wild ones), not to awaken, but to humble a fanatical party spirit: 1. Unclean indeed, and without the natural gift to distinguish the pure from the impure; 2. but modest, tractable, docile, thankful table-companions of unthankful children.—Christ present with His fulness of help, wherever there is the slightest germ of faith.—"For this saying." Faith manifest in new and wonderful words: 1. Its source, words unspeakable (Rom. viii. 26); 2. its expression, new words of the Spirit, clear and joyful in confession, preaching, and prayer; 3. its glory, the speaking with new tongues.—The regeneration, sanctification, and glorification of speech.—Christ, the terror of evil spirits far beyond His own personal manifestation.—The great sign which the Lord gave His disciples, that the door of the Gentile world was open.—Even among a people of Moloch-worshippers, maternal love was not extinct.—Humility the test of faith.—Humility the deep ground into which all the streams of heavenly blessing are poured.—The Lord is high, and yet hath respect unto the lowly, Ps. cxiii. 5–7.—As Mary prophesied in her song of praise, such was Christ's rule.—The tarrying of Jesus in the mountain-range of Lebanon, a silent anticipation of His entrance into the heathen world; as the tarrying in the wilderness was an anticipation of His entrance into Israel.

STARKE:—CANSTEIN:—Christ's travels from one place to another.—QUESNEL:—A servant of Christ in the Gospel may indeed remain hidden, but it must be so as not to incur the shame of neglecting any duty owing to his neighbor.—CRAMER:—When we pursue honor in an unreasonable manner, it flies from us; when we fly from it, it pursues us.—QUESNEL:—Every sin is an unclean spirit which possesses the sinner; from Jesus we must in all humility, every man for himself, seek the only remedy.—Sufferings urge men to seek God: happy those who use them to that end.—Christ is still, and for ever, the Saviour of the Gentiles, Rom. iii. 29.—Parents should feel the utmost anxiety on account of their children, that they be delivered from the power of Satan and led back to God.—LANGE:—The sharper the test, the more blessing does it bring when believingly endured.—*Bibl. Wirt.*:—Faith in the heart permits no displacence against God's rule to arise in the soul. However God disposes, and whatever He says, must be best, 1 Pet. v. 5, 6.—HEDINGER:—Perseverance presses through, and a good warfare obtains the prize.—QUESNEL:—It is a great consolation to a Christian mother when God converts, in answer to her prayer, a daughter possessed by a worldly spirit. But how little prayer is urged for that blessing!—RIEGER:—A very little word, falling into a softened, broken, and humbled heart, works great things.—Faith derives greater advantage and strength from humble submission and willing acknowledgment of its unworthiness than from anything else.—BRAUNE:—Let every one limit himself to the field of labor which God has appointed to him: he will soon see whether or not God gives him a commission to go beyond it.—Let no one be offended if he is hemmed in by a narrow limit, according to God's will. Holy charity and heroic love are all in all.—SCHLEIERMACHER:—*For this word, go thy way.* It was not merely a word of faith, but such an answer, too, as fell in with our Saviour's design. Without abolishing the distinction between those who belonged to the people of the old covenant and those who were idolaters, it yet threw such a veil over the distinction that many demonstrations of love might seem proper to pass from the one to the other.—GOSSNER, on ver. 24:—Many might remain hidden enough, but they will not.—A seemingly great severity is often a preparation for great benefactions.—BAUER:—The first act of salvation in the Gentile world.—AHLFELD:—Persevering faith is sure to win its object. When a heavy cross weighs thee down, seek the light of Christ's countenance; hold on in faith, and doubt not; He will give at last all that thou needest.—THOMASIUS:—How the Lord awakens faith in the hearts of men.—GREILING:—The time of suffering is a time of test.—HARTOG:—The three stages of victorious faith: 1. It looks with longing at the divine Saviour; 2. it waits with all humility for help; 3. it holds fast its hope with firm confidence.—BÖDECKER:—Wherefore doth God delay His help?—C. G. HOFFMANN:—The mighty word of faith: I will not let Thee go.—DITTMAR:—Great faith in its three stages: 1. Its stage of distress; 2. its stage of sifting; 3. its stage of confirmation.

4: *The Healing of the Deaf and Dumb Man.* VERS. 32–37.

(Parallel: Matt. xv. 29–31.)

32 And they bring unto him one that was deaf,[1] and had an impediment in his speech
33 [a stammerer]; and they beseech him to put his hand upon him. And he took him aside from the multitude, and put his fingers into his ears, and he spit, and touched his
34 tongue: And, looking up to heaven, he sighed, and saith unto him, Ephphatha, that is,
35 Be opened. And straightway[2] his ears were opened, and the string of his tongue was
36 loosed, and he spake plain. And he charged them that they should tell no man: but
37 the more he[3] charged them, so much the more a great deal they published *it;* And were beyond measure astonished, saying, He hath done all things well: he maketh both the deaf to hear, and the dumb to speak.

[1 Ver. 32.—After κωφόν, Lachmann and Tischendorf, after B., D., Δ., Versions, have καί.—*Ed.*]
[2 Ver. 35.—Εὐθέως is wanting here in B., D., L., Δ., Versions, Lachmann, Tischendorf. Instead of διηνοίχθησαν, Lachmann and Tischendorf, after B., D., Δ., read ἠνοίγησαν.
[3 Ver. 36.—Αὐτός is wanting in A., B., L., Δ., Vulgate, Lachmann, Tischendorf.—*Ed.*]

EXEGETICAL AND CRITICAL.

See on *Matthew.*—The healing of the deaf and dumb man on the east side of the Jordan is a narrative peculiar to Mark. In regard to time it is closely connected with the two foregoing events: occurring at the termination of the Lord's travels towards Phœnicia and through Decapolis back to the eastern border of the Sea of Galilee (Gaulonitis). Mark shows, in his account of the miracles, a preference for those healings in which the gradual process of the cure, as connected with the instrument and the development of it, is vividly presented. Thus, in his account, the daughter of the Syrophenician woman lies exhausted upon her bed after her deliverance. Thus, he represents Jesus as commanding them to give the daughter of Jairus something to eat. And he alone records the healing of the blind man at Bethsaida—a process which was gradual, and performed in two stages. And here he alone communicates a narrative in which the miraculous act of the Lord is closely connected with the application of the saliva.

Ver. 32. **A deaf man, who could not well speak.**—Meyer opposes this translation: "κωφὸν μογιλάλον is wrongly translated, a deaf man difficult of speech (*see* Beza, Maldonatus, De Wette).—Μογιλάλος, although it seems in its formation to be *hard of speech*, corresponds in the Septuagint to the Hebrew אִלֵּם, dumb. *See* Isa. xxxv. 5, &c. Hence it is a deaf and dumb man (Vulgate, Luther, Calovius, Ewald), which is also confirmed by ἀλάλους." Since μογιλάλος does literally mean one who speaks with difficulty,—and it is said of this one, that after his cure he spoke ὀρθῶς (not simply *he spoke*),—the meaning of the words is sufficiently established. With deafness there is connected a disturbance of the organs of speech, or a general perversion of speech.

Ver. 33. **Aside from the multitude.**—Wherefore? 1. He would make no display (Theophylact); He would not nourish superstition (Reinhard); He would have an undisturbed relation between Himself and the sick man (Meyer). This last is the weakest reason; for we might for the same reason except the same thing elsewhere. Rather we may assume that the district of Decapolis was something like the region of Tyre and Sidon: it was not a purely Jewish land. Here it was necessary, especially in this time of crisis, that He should avoid a publicity which might bring together the Gentiles in crowds, excite superstition as much as faith, and create in the minds of the Jews a prejudice against Him. In an analogous manner the Lord acted in the case of the blind man of eastern Bethsaida: He led him altogether out of the village. In both cases, however, we must remember that it was a susceptibility of faith which was to be gradually awakened. *See* the *Doctrinal Reflections*.—**And put His fingers.**—A similar circumstantial procedure we have in the healing of the blind man, ch. viii. "But we are not to assume that Jesus desired in any sense to conceal the miraculous element in the cures (LANGE, *Leben Jesu*, ii. 1, p. 282), which would amount to untruth." Meyer. But, upon this principle, the disguise thrown over the evangelical truths of the Gospel through the employment of parables, would amount to untruthfulness.

And He spit.—Spitting, He touched His tongue. Meyer thinks that the touching was the direct spitting upon the tongue. But as the touching (ἅπτεσθαι) is elsewhere an application of the hand, it may be assumed that He moistened His finger and touched therewith the man's tongue. Saliva used in healing: here; ch. viii. 23; John ix. 6. De Wette: Saliva was in antiquity a remedy for the eyes (Plin. *H. N.* 28, 7; Tacit. *Hist.* 4, 21; Sueton. *Vesp.* Cp. 7; Tanchuma, f. 10, 2; Sauhed., f. 101, 1; Hieros. Sotah, f. 16, 4; Vajikra Rabba, f. 175, 2. Comp. WETSTEIN and LIGHTFOOT, *ad Joh.* ix. 6). Meyer: "The saliva is, like the oil (ch. vi. 13), to be regarded as a conductor of the miraculous power." Yet it was not applied in the cure of the ear, but only in the healing of the tongue here, as ch. viii. in the healing of the eyes. Wherefore then was this distinction? Probably because the saliva was better suited to be a symbolical medium for the awakening of faith, and it was never wont to be applied to the ear.

Ver. 34. **Looking up to heaven, He sighed.**—Manifestly the sighing of prayer. How much more easily He seemed to accomplish His healing on other occasions! Or was deafness, in its spiritual significance, much worse than blindness and possession; and did the Lord intend to signify that? We assume, 1. that in this half-heathen district, more imperfect and disturbed forms of faith presented themselves to Him, which made the healing on His part more of a conflict; and 2. that in this half-heathen district, where they generally believed in demigods and magic, He desired to make more definitely prominent His own dependence on God the Father. For the like reason—that is, because the Pharisees had blasphemed the source of His miraculous power—He accomplished the raising of Lazarus before the Jews from Jerusalem in connection with a loud prayer to the Father; and in healing the man born blind, John ix., He joined with Himself in the work the temple-fountain Siloam, the holy spring of the priests. 3. Since the Lord could not influence the deaf man by word, it was necessary that He should influence Him by a strongly speaking sign.—Mark everywhere sets a special mark on the sighing of the Lord, as also upon His manner of looking: comp. ch. viii. 12. Meyer remarks, and rightly, that this sigh was at the same time a sigh of painful sympathy.—**Ephphatha.**—An Aramæan word, in the Imperative: Be thou opened. Related, though not identical, is the Hebrew חתפ, in the Imper. Niphal.

Ver. 35. **And the string of His tongue was loosed.**—Thus he did not merely speak with difficulty on account of his being dumb, as Olshausen supposes.

Ver. 36. **But the more He charged them.**—The stronger His prohibition was, the more it enkindled a desire to spread the report of the miracle.

Ver. 37. **He hath done all things well;** that is, in the healing.—Thence they draw the conclusion: As well the deaf, He hath, &c.

DOCTRINAL AND ETHICAL.

1. Nothing is more instructive and full of significance than the prudence of our Lord in respect to the publication of His miracles, as soon as He had entered the borders of the land where there were closer relations with heathenism, and the people were more infected by heathen views:—the history of the woman of Canaan, the present narrative, and the healing of the blind man in eastern Bethsaida, all illustrate this. The reason was, that Christ would have a monotheistic faith, which traces all up to God the Father as the final source, and that He would not suffer His divine power of healing to be mingled and debased with superstitious and magical notions. This holy prudence will explain many and great restraints upon the full influence of Christianity in the heathen or heathen-Christian world, down to the present day.

2. We may compare the doxology of this people, ver. 37, with the doxologies of ch. i. 27; ii. 12; iii. 11, &c. Matthew explains: They glorified the God of Israel.

3. It must be particularly observed here also, that Jesus could affect this deaf and dumb man only through His glance, His immediate revelation, His signs, and manner of action. So far this instance stands alone; for the youth who was deaf and dumb through possession, ch. ix. 25, suffered not through the sealing up of his organs, but through the perversion and violence done to his soul. So also the possessed who was dumb, Matt. ix. 32; and the demoniac who was blind and dumb, Matt. xii. 22.

4. Our Christian institutions for the deaf and dumb are an abiding monument of that miraculous healing in the mountains: the natural development of the miraculous act of our Lord. The healing of the deaf and dumb by signs, was a type of the instruction of the deaf and dumb.

5. The Romish rite of baptism relies especially on this miraculous history, because it exhibits the use of several symbolical elements: 1. Separation from the multitude: dedication of Christ in baptism. 2. The baptizing priest touches, with an Ephphatha, the ears of the infant; 3. moistens its nostrils with saliva; 4. lays salt in its mouth. The Christian Church should do all this in a *real* manner; and not in a symbolical. As the symbol for it, and at the same time the reality of it, Christ instituted simple baptism.

HOMILETICAL AND PRACTICAL.

Sufferers to be brought to Jesus.—The healing of the deaf and dumb; or, the double disease and the double cure in their reciprocal connection. 1. The connection between deafness and the inability to speak: *a.* in physical things; *b.* in spiritual. 2. Right speaking conditioned by right hearing: in natural life, in spiritual things.—He who does not persevere to the end in hearing aright will surely cease by degrees to speak aright.—The true obedience is of eminently quick and sure hearing.—The education of the deaf and dumb man in faith: 1. He must yield himself up to be led by the strange Wonder-worker, who can only speak to him by looks, into the wilderness; 2. he must *see* His signs, especially the signs of His prayer and His sighing; 3. he must hear his word of power, that he may have his hearing and be able also to speak.—The holy care of the Lord in all His wonderful works, aiming ever at the glory of God's name.—How the wonder-working majesty of Jesus is concealed in His humility.—Christ, as He went on His way, opposed and avoided with the same decided earnestness the heathenism which deified men and the world, and the Judaism which deified the letter and ceremonial observances.—Christ had to struggle as well with superstition as with unbelief, to exalt both into faith.—All Christ's miracles were to the honor of God: 1. All His miracles were miracles of prayer, dependence on God, and strict union with His Father; 2. all His miracles were distinguished, not only in their reason and their end, but also in their form and manner, from the magical works of the heathen world.—Christ ever conceals the thousands of His miracles by the disguise of an unpretending medium.—Christ in His whole being full of saving power.—The sighing of Christ and of His Spirit (Rom. viii. 26) over the sin and the misery of humanity and the creature.—The sympathy of Christ. —Guilt and innocence in the popular proclamation of Christ's works.—The words of His astonished people: He hath done all things well : 1. In its human limitation ; 2. in its higher significance.—Concerning redemption as concerning the creation, the word holds good, The Lord hath done all things well (Gen. i. 31): 1. in the whole, 2. in the details.

STARKE:—Where Jesus goes in and out, there is nought but blessing.—CANSTEIN :—When we look at the deaf and dumb, it should make us reverence all the more the glorious gifts of hearing and speech, and determine to use both prudently to the glory of God.—ZEISIUS:—Most people can both hear and speak ; but how great and how common is spiritual deafness and dumbness !—LUTHER:—Christ begins His cure with the ears, and acts in accordance with nature ; since from hearing speaking comes: ἀκοή begets ὑπακοήν.—LANGE :—Let us seek silence.—A Christian should often sigh over spiritual and bodily misery.—The ears should be open for God, but shut to the devil and the world.—It is a sign that the tongue has been loosened by Christ, when the words become holy, and the new song is sung to His glory out of a new heart.—QUESNEL:—The humility of the benefactor, and the thankfulness of him who has received the benefit, may contend without damaging peace in the heart.—Wondering at God's works is well; but it should never end there.—*Nova Bibl. Tub.* :—God doeth all things well, not only in healing and binding up, but also in smiting and wounding.— ZEISIUS:—As Satan damages and ruins everything, so, on the contrary, Christ repairs all things.— BRAUNE:—The Lord guides all His own in various ways, every one in his own; but the goal for all is the great salvation longed for.—Jesus speaks the right language of signs to the deaf and dumb.— GERLACH:—The words, "He hath done all things well," seem to express an anticipation of the new creation.—Jesus finds His glory in the deaf ears of hardened sinners, and in the speechless or restrained tongues of unthankful, earthly-minded unbelievers. Even from among them He takes many into solitude with Him: His creating hand touches the sealed ear and the idle tongue, His high priestly intercession groans to the Father for them, and often His Ephphatha opens the ear and looses the bonds of their tongue, so that they may speak plainly.—LISCO :— The turning of the eyes of Jesus towards heaven should teach us to expect our help from thence, and thither to direct our thanksgivings.—SCHLEIERMACHER:—That love which could manifest itself so mightily in the Redeemer is among us in our benevolent institutions. But if we ask what has driven men to think upon this, we can say no more than that it is the selfsame Spirit of love who is for ever striving to meet and overcome all the woes and sufferings of humanity.—What a great and wonderful word is this " Be opened," which the Redeemer was ever speaking throughout His whole manifestation, and the influences of which have never ceased, but will go on until the whole race of mankind have come to the hearing and knowledge of His salvation, and their tongues shall be loosed to the praise of the Most High !—HEUBNER:—The significance of the healing of the deaf and dumb (in its spiritual application): 1. The person of the wretched one ; 2. the leading him to Jesus; 3. the action of our Lord; 4. His looking up to heaven and sighing ; 5. His work ; 6. His prohibition (the conversion of a sinner should not be boastfully trumpeted to the world ; it should exert its influence silently).—Christ the only Physician who can repair the mischiefs in God's creation. —How much knowledge of God may come through the senses.—BAUER:—How many are still deaf and dumb towards the kingdom of God !

KLEFEKER:—Even in the sufferings of His creature man, God finds His glory.—REINHARD:—How we, as Christians, should sanctify to our own good the defects, infirmities, and sicknesses of our bodies. —HUFFELL:—The Christian's look to heaven.— REINHARD:—The quiet unostentatious zeal with which Christians should do good.—THIESS:—The deaf and dumb man is a type of us.—COUARD:— He took him out of the crowd apart.—BOMHARD :— The Ephphatha of our Redeemer: 1. A word of omnipotence and grace ; 2. great and glorious in its effect ; 3. it is uttered to all of us; 4. it is vain for many ; 5. it proves its virtue on believers, ever more beautifully and abundantly ; 6. it will one day abolish for ever all our fetters.—RAUTENBERG:—He hath done all things well: 1. Praise of His perfection— wonder ; 2. praise of His benevolence—thanksgiving ; 3. praise of His glory—adoration.

5. The Miraculous Feeding of Four Thousand. Ch. VIII. 1–9.

(Parallel: Matt. xv. 32–39.)

1 In those days the multitude being very great,[1] and having nothing to eat, Jesus
2 called his disciples unto *him*, and saith unto them, I have compassion on the multitude,
3 because they have now been with me[2] three days, and have nothing to eat; And if I
send them away fasting to their own houses, they will faint by the way: for divers of
4 them came from far. And his disciples answered him, From whence can a man satisfy
5 these *men* with bread here in the wilderness? And he asked them, How many loaves
6 have ye? And they said, Seven. And he commanded[3] the people to sit down on the
ground: and he took the seven loaves, and gave thanks, and brake, and gave to his
7 disciples to set before *them*; and they did set *them* before the people. And they had
8 a few small fishes: and he blessed, and commanded to set them also before *them*.[4] So
they did eat, and were filled: and they took up of the broken *meat* that was left, seven
9 baskets. And they that had eaten[5] were about four thousand: and he sent them away.

[1] Ver. 1.—Instead of παμπόλλου, B., D., G., L., M., Δ., [Vulgate, Coptic, Gothic, Lachmann, Tischendorf,] read πάλιν πολλοῦ.—The ὁ Ἰησοῦς is probably an explanatory interpolation.
[2] Ver. 2.—Μοι is wanting in B., D., [Lachmann, Tischendorf, Meyer.]
[3] Ver. 6.—B., D., L., Δ., [Lachmann, Tischendorf, Meyer:] παραγγέλλει.
[4] Ver. 7.—Καὶ εὐλογήσας αὐτὰ εἶπεν καὶ ταῦτα παρατιθέναι. B., L., Δ., [Meyer.]
[5] Ver. 9.—The οἱ φαγόντες wanting in B., L., Δ., [Tischendorf, Meyer;] following ch. vi. 44.

EXEGETICAL AND CRITICAL.

See on the parallels in *Matthew*.—Mark's second miraculous feeding, with the following events, stands in the same connection as Matthew's with the mountain travels of our Lord. There is not in the slightest particular a difference between Matthew and Mark. The representations of the second feeding are more than ordinarily alike in both: the beginning and the end, especially, are essentially the same.

Ver. 7. **And he blessed and commanded to set them also.**—The Evangelist distinguishes the thanksgiving over the fish as a particular act, with the word εὐλογήσας, while concerning the bread he used εὐχαριστήσας. Both acts of devotion are to be regarded as benedictions of the food. But the prayer of praise (εὐλογεῖν) is related to the prayer of thanksgiving, as praise is related to thanks: it is the same thing carried to its higher pitch. That the thanksgiving becomes here blessing, characterizes the second act of the feeding, the festival anticipatory of the great feast; and it is all the more sublime as being pronounced over the ἰχθύδια ὀλίγα. The following Romanist distinction (Reischl) is without foundation: "Thanksgiving (eucharist) Jesus presents as man (and High-Priest) to the Father; but He Himself, as Lord and God, distributes the blessing of omnipotence."

Ver. 8. **Seven baskets.**—Comp. the explanations on *Matthew*.

Ver. 9. **About four thousand men.**—Matthew adds: *besides women and children*.

DOCTRINAL AND ETHICAL.

1. See on the parallel passage in *Matthew*.—The divine side of the second miraculous feeding is presented all the more expressly and clearly by the circumstance, that in the present instance the multitudes of the people were more alien, the scene of it was a place more desolate and remote from human habitation, the excitement of the people more intense; not to mention that Christ had just returned from an extended and fatiguing journey. As it respects the human side of the miracle, and its relation to the measure of faith, we cannot fail to observe the circumstance that a more abundant provision of food is made for a smaller number of the fed. As it regards the difference between the fragments gathered up in the two miracles respectively, we have to notice the distinction between σπυρίδες and κόφινοι: the former seem to have been vessels of larger capacity.

2. STARKE:—Σπλαγχνίζεσθαι means such a feeling of compassion as not only moves the mind, but causes a physical emotion—the rush of blood, yearning of the bowels, &c.—likewise. The word is used several times concerning our Saviour by the three Evangelists. The greater the love of Jesus was, the more susceptible was His sacred humanity of sympathy.

3. The first miraculous feeding took place when the malignity of Herod occasioned the Lord's departure from Galilee; the second, after He had retired from Galilee before the hierarchical and pharisaic party. Both times, as driven away, and as a refugee, He took upon Himself, forgetting His own sorrow, the needs of all the people.

HOMILETICAL AND PRACTICAL.

See on *Matthew*.—Christ's compassion towards the people was a compassion for their want of bread. —The Lord's resting-place after long travelling.— Christ does not let His people depart without food. —Where Christ is in the midst, the multitude never go away unfed.—The rebuke contained in the example of the people, who waited on Christ three days, though they had nothing given them to eat.—The impotence of the disciples, and the Lord's provident care.—Christ's thanksgiving becomes blessing, whilst the provision is diminishing.—Christ's royal law for the table.—The second miraculous feeding seemingly less, but in fact more, wonderful than the first. 1. Seemingly less; there was more provision, and a smaller number. 2. Really greater: *a*. in regard to the Lord (returning from long journey and much labor); b. in regard to the despondency of the disciples; c. in regard to the foreign elements of which the mass of this mountain-people was made up (probably in part Gentiles).—Wells are made, as by the Lord, so by the pilgrims of Zion, passing through the valley of banishment, Ps. lxxxiv.—The Lord's heavenly peace in His earthly need: He is Himself as a refugee in great straits, and yet feeds with compassion a host of thousands. 1. The peace of God in the forgetfulness of His own distress. 2. The self-renouncing love of others in this forgetfulness. —To-day He gives the people a feast; to-morrow all sorrows await Him.

STARKE:—True brotherly love does not look so much at the worthiness of the person as at his need and misery.—Believers may sometimes fall, even though Jesus be near, into temporal difficulties and need; but they do not and cannot come to harm or perish, Rom. viii. 35-39.—The Lord knows our need earlier and better than our complaints can tell Him. —OSIANDER:—How different from these people are some Christians amongst us, who can scarcely tarry one hour with Christ's servants, hearing the divine word!—Preachers should care not only for the souls, but also for the bodies, of their hearers.—*Nova Bibl. Tub.:*—When we truly love Jesus, we think little of the length or hardship of the way; we care nothing for want and weariness; but wait with Him, and prefer the kingdom of God to all other things.—Our unbelieving heart hangs on the means, and will believe nothing that it does not see, Matt. vi. 25-30. —We should thank God for everything, even for our scanty provision; He is bound to us for nothing.— (The breaking of bread.) When God puts anything into our hands, we should not keep it unbroken for ourselves alone, but break and dispense abundantly to others.—CANSTEIN:—Preachers should dispense the food of God's word among the people; but they should give to the multitude nothing which God has not first put in their mouth and in their heart.—The meek shall eat and be satisfied, Ps. xxii. 26.—The gifts of God only satisfy the *heart*.—In every fragment there is God's blessing: therefore it is right to gather up the fragments.—With God it is all the same whether there be little or much.—SCHLEIERMACHER: —He kept them near Him, and distributed spiritual gifts; nor did He remember their earthly need until He had found that they were filled with desires that extended much further. And this is the divine order, in this connection, between the spiritual and the temporal. All earthly things, so far as they go beyond necessity, have value only so far as they are connected with the spiritual.

HEUBNER:—Perseverance in hearing the word of God.—The design of Providence in letting us encounter earthly need.—Have we sought diligently, and first of all, heavenly things?—Trust in God when the season of scarcity comes.—The prevenient providence of God, and His anticipating care.—The Christian's attention to his neighbor's need.—God can bring help by small means.—Giving is better than receiving.—Christ's miracle as a figure of the miracle of divine sustentation.—Jesus as Householder.—The Christian householder after the pattern of Jesus: 1. Watchfulness, and attention to all needs; 2. love and sympathy for the distress of each; 3. trust in God when the question is, Whence shall we get? (Do the best: God will do the rest in His own way); 4. spiritual care of all who belong to Him.—How our partaking of food may be sanctified. —RAMBACH:—How may the Christian give God His honor in the enjoyment of his daily food?—MARHEINEKE:—The Christian should always see a higher significance in the means of his daily sustentation.— HARMS:—Instruction concerning table-worship.— DIETSCH:—The miracle in our nourishment.—HUFFELL:—The divine blessing on our food.—MEHLISS: —The glorifying of God in the care of His creatures. —REINHARD:—The connection between the necessity of nourishment in order to the sustentation of our bodies, and the growth and nourishment of our souls. —VALERIUS HERBERGER:—How should the guests at God's table comport themselves?—HEUBNER:— Jesus the people's holy Friend.—BURK:—Jesus Christ supplies all our need out of His riches in glory.—STIER:—The miraculous blessing of God's power, as shown, 1. in the domain of nature, and 2. in the kingdom of grace.—ULBER:—The meal blessed by prayer.—The compassionate heart of Jesus moaning over all our misery.—COUARD:—Reproof of the prevalent complaint over hard times.—REINHARD:—Christian benevolence at a time of general need.—BAUER:—When Christ's blessing rests on anything, it becomes infinitely more than it was in the hands of men.

EIGHTH SECTION.

THE DECISIVE CONFLICT OF JESUS WITH THE PHARISEES IN GALILEE, AND HIS RETURN TO THE EASTERN SIDE OF THE SEA. PREPARATIONS FOR THE NEW CHURCH.

CHAPTERS VIII. 10—IX. 29.

---

1. *Return to the Galilean Shore. Conflict; Return; the Leaven of the Pharisees and the Leaven of Herod.* CH. VIII. 10-21.

(Parallel: Matt. xvi. 1-12.)

10 And straightway he entered into a [the] ship with his disciples, and came into the
11 parts of Dalmanutha. And the Pharisees came forth, and began to question with him,
12 seeking of him a sign from heaven, tempting him. And he sighed deeply in his spirit,

and saith, Why doth this generation seek after a sign? Verily I say unto you, There
13 shall no sign be given unto this generation. And he left them, and entering into the
14 ship again,¹ departed to the other side. Now [And] *the disciples* had forgotten to take
15 bread, neither had they in the ship with them more than one loaf. And he charged
   them, saying, Take heed, beware of the leaven of the Pharisees, and *of* the leaven of
16 Herod. And they reasoned among themselves, saying,² *It is* because we have no bread.
17 And when Jesus knew *it*, he saith unto them, Why reason ye because ye have no
   bread? perceive ye not, neither understand? have ye your heart yet³ hardened?
18 Having eyes, see ye not? and having ears, hear ye not? and do ye not remember,
19 When I brake the five loaves among five thousand, how many baskets full of fragments
20 took ye up? They say unto him, Twelve. And when the seven among four thousand,
21 how many baskets full of fragments took ye up? And they said, Seven. And he said
   unto them, How⁴ is it that ye do not understand?

¹ Ver. 13.—The πάλιν precedes ἐμβάς, according to B., C., D., L., Δ. Εἰς τὸ πλοῖον (*Recepta*), or εἰς πλοῖον (Lachmann, after A., E., F.), wanting in B., C., L., D., and omitted by Tischendorf [and Meyer].
² Ver. 16.—The λέγοντες wanting in B., D., and Itala; and B., Itala read ἔχουσιν for ἔχομεν. So Lachmann and Tischendorf.
³ Ver. 17.—Ἔτι not in B., C., D., L., Δ., [Lachmann, Tischendorf, Meyer.]
⁴ Ver. 21.—Lachmann: πῶς οὔπω, according to A., D., M. Tischendorf merely οὔπω, according to C., L., D. So Meyer.

EXEGETICAL AND CRITICAL.

See on *Matthew*.—What follows is here closely and certainly connected with the preceding; and in this Matthew and Mark concur, as also in the essentials of the whole. Mark passes over the rebuke of Christ in relation to the Pharisees' knowledge of the weather, and also the sign of Jonas. On the other hand, he mentions the Lord's deep sighing. He notices the circumstance that the disciples had with them in the ship one loaf. Instead of the leaven of the Sadducees, he has the leaven of Herod; and he gives most keenly the Lord's rebuke of the unbelief of the disciples.

Ver. 10. **Dalmanutha** was a small place, not otherwise known; it lay probably in the district of Magdala, where, according to Matthew, Jesus landed. Robinson (iii. 514) leaves it undecided whether or not the present village of Delhemija is its modern representative. The specifications of locality by the two Evangelists, respectively, are not to be referred to any hypothesis of *earlier* and *later* accounts: Matthew's narrative has a more general cast, and Mark's a more special, in these respects. The landing was manifestly in a desert and unfrequented place; and the reason of this was, that the Galilean party of Pharisees were on the alert to seize Jesus, in order to bring Him under a judicial process; for this purpose having many spies abroad. The first illustration of this is found in Mark ii. 6; the second, ch. iii. 22; the third (in connection with ch. vi. 29–31), ch. vii. 1. That allegation touching neglect of purifyings, which the Pharisees, in connection with the scribes from Jerusalem, made against Him, is carried out here into its last issues.

Ver. 11. **And the Pharisees came forth.**—Meyer: "Out of their dwellings in that country." People generally come out of their dwellings; but these men came forth as spies out of a hiding-place; and their coming was proof that the most extreme care as to the circumstances of the landing of Jesus, in a quiet place and in the dead of night, could no longer protect the Lord from their eyes (see on *Matthew* and *Leben Jesu*, ii. 875). On the western side of the sea there might be, here and there, rich mansions, belonging to Herodian courtiers, which were well adapted to be loopholes of observance for the political and hierarchical party. According to Matt. xvi. 1, 2, the Sadducees were leagued with them. The act, therefore, was not merely an act of the Pharisaic school, but the act of the priests and politicians. Mark merges the Sadducees in the Pharisees; for they hypocritically played the Pharisee, inasmuch as they demanded a sign from heaven, although they believed in no such thing.—**And began.**—They had made their arrangements for a decisive contest, which began with the demand of the sign from heaven. For this sign, see on *Matthew*, p. 287.

Sighed deeply in His spirit.—Comp. ch. vii. 34. He sighed so deeply, not merely in general sorrow for the hardened unbelief of these men, but also in the feeling that the decisive crisis of severance from the predominant party had come. For the demand of a sign from heaven was a demand that He should, as the Messiah of their expectation, accredit Himself by a great miracle; thus it was fundamentally similar to the temptation in the wilderness, which He had repelled and overcome. But His deep sigh also signifies here the holding in of His judicial power, the silent resolution to enter upon the path of tribulation. Hence the refusal of the sign is immediate, and in the form of an affirmation most strongly uttered. It is to be observed that, the article being wanting, the nature of the sign from heaven is left free to Him: He was to perform *a* sign from heaven, which should be acknowledged as *the* sign from heaven.

Ver. 15. **And the leaven of Herod.**—See on *Matthew*; and for the combination of Pharisees and Herodians, compare the notes on Mark iii. 6. The one passage depends on the other; and it is observable how Mark both times gives marked prominence to this hypocritical and malignant combination of extreme parties. Meyer concludes from Matt. xiv. 2 that Herod was no Sadducee. But that passage must not be pressed too far. Herod certainly coincided with the anti-scriptural, anti-Messianic, Hellenizing universalism of the Sadducees, although he did not adhere to their party in its dogmatic views and coloring. Thus we have here only two aspects of the same idea. The Jewish dependence upon traditions and human ordinances, and the Jewish freethinking, form in their respective principles the two kinds of leaven which the disciples were to guard against. Compare on *Matthew*.

DOCTRINAL AND ETHICAL.

1. See on the parallel in *Matthew.*—The debasing effects of party spirit. The Sadducees must here submit to the Pharisees, and be merged in them. 2. As it regards the desired sign from heaven, it is to be observed further: 1. As they asked for a sign from heaven, they demanded the decisively attesting sign expected from heaven. 2. The consequence of this authentication would have been, that Christ must have come forward as a Messiah in their sense. Hence it is said that they tempted Him. The demand of a sign from heaven was like the temptation in the wilderness. The Lord had hitherto, since that time, escaped any such demand. If He now refused it, His death was certain. 3. The demand was so far not absolutely hostile, as they were still disposed to accept Christ, if He would adapt Himself to their views, and become a party instrument for their purposes. (*See* on *Matthew.*) 4. The sign from heaven which Christ denied to the Pharisees, stood in close relation with the sign of Jonas. The denial of the one was the announcement of the other. 5. What He denied to the Pharisees, He provided soon afterwards for the three chosen disciples on the Mount: the heavenly sign of His transfiguration.

3. The sighs of Jesus.—The Lord's sigh (ch. vii. 34) was the sigh of self-devoting mercy to the world; His deep sigh (ch. viii. 12) was the restraint and holding back of His judicial power over the world, under the holy resolution to suffer for it. The sigh of the Lion of Judah over the hardening of His enemies: the prophecy of His path of suffering, but also the prophecy of the world's judgment. The groaning of His spirit was, 1. a sighing from the depths of His being, 2. in the all-embracing glance of His consciousness over the path of His own suffering, and the path of the world's wretchedness.

4. *The return of Jesus.*—Not without a plan, but as the result of His last experience, Jesus now returns back to the eastern bank. It is clear to His consciousness that He must now go up to confront His death. He therefore needed solitude, that He might regulate the process of His departure. And to this there was necessary, 1. the confirmation of the disciples in faith for the establishment of the new Church, and 2. the provision that His death should take place at the right time and in the right way.

HOMILETICAL AND PRACTICAL.

See on *Matthew.*—The Pharisees perfect spies on all our Lord's ways.—The Lord cannot escape the Pharisees, and therefore the Pharisees cannot escape the Lord.—The demand of a sign from heaven: the tempting crisis that our Lord foresaw in the wilderness.—The confusion of the disciples, occasioned by this decisive conflict (and shown in the forgetting of bread, and anxiety about it), as opposed to the divine repose of the Lord: a prelude of their confusion on the eve of the Passion.—The great decisive No of the Lord.—The Lord's deep sigh in its great significance: 1. A silent and yet decisive sign of His conflict and of His victory; 2. an unuttered word, which contains a world of divine words; 3. a fulfilment of the primitive prophecy concerning the breach between the external and the spiritual Israel; 4. a prophecy which stretches forward to the cross and the final judgment.—The infinite meaning of this sigh of Christ: 1. As a breathing forth of the divine patience over the visible world (Omnipotence restraining itself in love and wisdom, when dealing with the enmity of the free will of the world); 2. a collective expression of all the sufferings and of all the patience of Christ; 3. a declaration of all the incarnate sorrow and endurance of the Lord in His Church.—The significance of sighs: 1. In the creature (Rom. viii. 22); 2. in humanity, and in the kingdom of God (Rom. viii. 23; 2 Cor. v. 2; Rev. vi. 10).—The return of Christ to the other bank: a sign of His return back to the other world.—How little the disciples understood that crisis.—The last loaf in the ship, the last loaf in the house (the last meal, the last piece of money, the last sheet-anchor).—In this matter, mark, 1. the disciples' spirit: they misinterpret the most sublime and the most spiritual things through their own over-anxiety; 2. the Lord's spirit: He makes provision for the testing of His disciples, especially now.—The displeasure of Christ at the lack of spiritual development among His own disciples.—True remembering, in its full import: 1. Christian wakefulness; 2. Christian life; 3. Christian progress.—The influence of the Holy Spirit, and life in the Spirit: bringing to remembrance (John xiv. 26; xvi. 13).—The retreat of Jesus in order to arrange His death.

STARKE:—Many desire new wonders; and when they have thought they have seen them, have not yet turned to God.—It is not becoming to prescribe to God the means by which we are to arrive at divine knowledge and blessedness.—HEDINGER:—Ingratitude drives Christ away.—QUESNEL:—It is a fearful judgment when the truth altogether forsakes men, and they are left to themselves.—Forgetfulness gives an opportunity for new instruction; and therefore even their failings should be turned to account by believers.—CRAMER:—Faithful teachers should, after the example of the Great Shepherd, diligently warn their sheep against false doctrine and false teachers (against every evil leaven to the right or left).—Out of one error many others gradually arise, so that the whole system of religion may become perverted. — QUESNEL: — Concerning the tendency to Sadduceism among courtiers.—The weaker our faith is, the more anxious and troubled we are about bodily need, and the more likely to make spiritual possessions of less account.—OSIANDER:—Ministers must be always ready to exhort their hearers with severity, and to rouse them out of the sleep of security.

BRAUNE:—When, after a joyful event, or the attainment of a great success, one is suddenly opposed by an obstinate contradiction, the result is often great disquietude or blank despondency. The Lord, whose case this was on the present occasion, knew very well what He would do, and did it without any restraint. Let all men learn this. They need the lesson in their family circles, and in their civil and political relations, whether more or less exalted.—Scarcely had Jesus ended with His enemies, when He must begin again with His friends.—Before His spirit rose the whole wickedness of His enemies' spirit, so perverse in itself, pervading with evil the whole of the people, and invading even His disciples. It had already seized and possessed the mind of Judas, 1 Cor. v. 7, 8.

SCHLEIERMACHER:—The Redeemer often uses the idea of leaven, as something of which only a little is needed in order to make the whole like itself.—In truth, He was the leaven, in the form of a servant indeed, destined to penetrate the whole mass of mankind and all human life by the divine power dwelling in Him.—If ye use only a little of the leaven of the Pharisees, ye will very soon be pervaded throughout with its influence.—The leaven of Herod: the family of Herod was a foreign one; they held to the law, and affected much devotion to ceremonial ordinances, in order to attach the people more firmly to themselves. The disciples must not use Christianity as something that might exert a good influence upon their external condition.—We must be pure disciples of the Master, and desire nothing but the pure kingdom of God.—GOSSNER (on ver. 19):—This is a test. They had the whole history in their head and memory, but they did not understand how to apply it.

2. *The Blind Man in Eastern Bethsaida.* VERS. 22–26.

22 And he cometh[1] to Bethsaida; and they bring a blind man unto him, and besought
23 him to touch him. And he took the blind man by the hand, and led him out of the town; and when he had spit on his eyes, and put his hands upon him, he asked him if
24 he saw aught. And he looked up, and said, I see [the] men as trees, walking.[2]
25 After that he put *his* hands again upon his eyes, and made him look up: and he was
26 restored, and saw[3] every man clearly. And he sent him away to his house [home], saying, Neither go into the town, nor tell *it* to any in the town.[4]

[1] Ver. 22.—The Plural, ἔρχονται, after B., C., D. Lachmann, Tischendorf, [Meyer.]
[2] Ver. 24.—The beautiful reading: βλέπω τοὺς ἀνθρώπους, ὅτι ὡς δένδρα ὁρῶ περιπατοῦντας is adopted by Meyer, Lachmann, Tischendorf, following [A., B., C.*, E., F., G., K., L., M., Δ., Gothic, Theophylact, Euthymius. (D. and most of the Versions have the Received Text).]
[3] Ver. 25.—Tischendorf, [Meyer,] διέβλεψεν, after B., C.*, L., Δ., &c.
[4] Ver. 26.—The Received Text and Lachmann follow Cod. A. Tischendorf, following B., L., Coptic, omits the clause μηδὲ εἰς . . . κώμῃ.

EXEGETICAL AND CRITICAL.

Mark alone records this history of Christ's healing miracles during the time of His final mountain-travels along the Gaulonite range, on the eastern side of the Jordan and the Sea of Galilee. The remembrances of Peter preserved for us these special treasures, belonging to a time so preëminently memorable to him and his spiritual development. But we have too often observed the peculiar feeling of Mark for the gradual, natural, progressive development of the kingdom of God (*see* his record of the parables, and the final miracles), not to perceive that this period of the ministry and work of Jesus would strongly rivet his attention.

Ver. 22. **To Bethsaida.**—It is evident that the Bethsaida of the western coast, in Galilee (John xii. 21), is not here meant, as Theophylact and others have supposed; but, as Grotius rightly perceived, it was Bethsaida Julias, which lay upon the north-eastern coast of the Sea of Tiberias. Reland was the first to indicate that there were two Bethsaidas. Josephus tells us (*Antiq.* 18, 2, 1), that the tetrarch Philip, who ruled only in the eastern part of Galilee, made the village of Bethsaida into a town, and named it Julias, after the daughter of Augustus. (*See* also *De Bell. Jud.* 11, 9, 1; and JEROME on Matthew xvi.) According to Pliny (*Hist. Nat.* v. 15), Julias was situated on the farther coast of the Sea of Galilee; according to Josephus, on the Jordan, 120 stadia above its junction with the sea. Pococke thought the ruins of Taluy, on the east side of the Jordan, marked the ancient Julias; Seetzen thought the same of a little village, Tellanihje; and Robinson, the ruins of Et-Tell. According to Luke ix. 10, the first miraculous feeding also took place in a desert place near this same Bethsaida. *See* VON RAUMER, *Palæstina*, p. 109. Bethsaida lay in the way from the sea towards Cæsarea-Philippi, in the higher mountain-range, a district to which Jesus subsequently returned.—**A blind man.**—What follows shows that he was not born blind, but had become so. He had evidently seen men and trees aforetime.

Ver. 23. **And led him out of the town.**—Here the separation from all others is still more effectual than in the case of the healing of the deaf and dumb man, ch. vii. 33. In addition to the motive already mentioned for performing His works as much as possible in retirement, viz., that He might insure His own decease in Jerusalem, we may assume that there was also a pædagogic element that influenced Him on the present occasion. The deaf and dumb man could not hear His voice, but only see His signs; this blind man could not see Him, he could only hear Him speak and feel His hand. Thus it was a test and a discipline of his faith, when he was led into solitude: a test and exercise which probably was still much needed by him.—**And when He had spit on his eyes.**—*See* the notes on ch. vii. 33 and John ix.

Ver. 24. **I see men.**—Expression of joy.—**As trees**; that is, I see men walking, large and unformed as trees. A distinct figure of an indistinct, twilight beholding. It was the first stage of healing. According to Euthymius Zigabenus, He healed the man by degrees, because his faith was weak, and the gradual experience of recovered sight would lead him to a higher degree of faith. In relation to this, we may observe the strikingly passive bearing of this blind man, as of the deaf and dumb man before: with this we may compare the passiveness of the impotent man at Bethesda, John v. According to Olshausen, a too rapid process of recovery might have been injurious, and the gradual cure had regard to the eyes themselves. But this and the preceding notion we leave to the reader's consideration; they may have a certain degree of force. But if we combine all the traits of this and the foregoing history, we see that Jesus designedly repressed the fame of

His miraculous works in a district where He was seeking an asylum of perfect retirement, in order to settle everything with His disciples; at a time, too, when, for their sake and His own, absolute solitude was essentially necessary with reference to the decision of the future. But the symbolical significance of these miraculous dealings—as bringing the divine power into gradual contact and contest with human nature—was more expressly brought out for the instruction of His disciples than in most of His miracles of healing.—The persons who appeared to the half-seeing man were probably his companions, and other sympathizing people, who looked on in restless motion.

Ver. 26. **To his house.**—He did not belong to Bethsaida, and he must go immediately from the place to his own home—not even to the village to which he had already come. Indeed, he was not to mention it to any one belonging to that village, and whom he might meet in the way. This explanation of the last expression ["any *in* the town"] is not, as Meyer terms it, an invention to meet the difficulty; it is the obvious and only natural meaning of the expression. Even the man's companions should find him recovered and seeing, only when they reached home; that is, if they were not permitted to be present at the healing.

DOCTRINAL AND ETHICAL.

1. Christ sought with His disciples the deepest solitude among the mountains. His feeling was that of an anticipation of His death, and all things in the signs of the times said, Set Thine house, Thy Church, in order! In this journey the people who brought the blind man interrupted Him, and there seemed danger of His way being embarrassed. It is true that this did not hinder His healing the man, but He healed him in the most undemonstrative and hidden manner. The secrecy of the performance was paralleled by the extraordinary care with which He sent the blind man to his own house, under a prohibition to speak to any man in the neighborhood concerning the miracle. The blind man, however, was not merely a means to an end; his own spiritual edification was in question also. Since his faith was weak, his spiritual state required the protection of solitude: only in the profoundest silence could the blessing of his experience ripen into perfection. But, thirdly, we must not forget the Lord's reference to those who surrounded the blind man. They asked that He would *touch* him. To this demand for an instant act, followed by an instant influence, the Lord opposed His own slow and circumstantial method of procedure. So also in the case of the deaf and dumb man of the same country: they asked Him that He would lay His hand upon the man. And if in this district of indistinct, half-heathen notions there was any idea arising of a magical influence on the part of Christ, His wisdom dispersed these foolish imaginations. He made prominent, 1. the religious aspect of the act; and 2. the struggle in His own spirit connected with its performance.

2. This present narrative illustrates how Christ performed His miracles in the most absolute self-renunciation (at the most unseasonable time); with the most profound humility (without any desire for honor among men); and with the most supreme wisdom and confidence.

3. The healing of the blind man at Bethsaida, like some other similar miracles, was especially fitted and intended to exhibit the harmony of miracle with nature, the natural elements in the miracle, the gradual entrance of the divine power into the old nature, and its issues in the new nature.

HOMILETICAL AND PRACTICAL.

The Lord, deeply occupied with thoughts of His cross and of His death, does not repel as an interruption the cry of the wretched.—The festal season of the Prophet's miracles is passing away, because the season of the high-priestly miraculous sufferings is drawing near.— The healing of the blind man at Bethsaida a testimony of the heavenly wisdom of the Lord: 1. In respect to Himself; 2. in respect to the blind man: he should not first see the multitudes of starers in the street, but the Lord in His solitary glory, and thus would he be taught more fully the lesson of faith; 3. in respect to the people around; 4. in respect to the disciples.—Abundant as was the inward life of Christ, His acts are equally abundant in their forms.—Christ, in performing His miracles, avoided a fixed and uniform manner, in order to obviate all the idle, superstitious notions of a magical influence.— How the mind, contemplating the same unchanging fundamental forms, has a tendency to become mechanical in its views.—As the wonder-working power of Christ's hand wrought in many fleeting forms of action, so also the fundamental forms of the ministerial work of the Church, in teaching, worship, and life, should be moulded, moved, and inspired by the life of the Divine Spirit.—The education of the blind man into faith.—The gradual return of the blind man's sight, a type of the gradual illumination of the soul.— Even the spiritually awakened see at first men as trees, unformed, without definite distinction.—I see men as trees. This represents, as it may be viewed, different conditions of the spiritual life: 1. It is a happy state, if it is the first stage towards clearly seeing in perfect knowledge; 2. it is a gloomy and uncertain state, if the Christian should remain in it; 3. worst of all, if through his own guilt he should return to this stage, falling into the new blindness of despair. — The blessed experience of the first believing look: a strengthening of faith, which becomes the transition to perfect sight. — Go not into the town: a solemn word concerning Bethsaida.—Bethsaida the modern city of the world, with an imperial name, and Bethsaida the town of the fishermen: the bright and the dark side.—How Jesus avoids the fame of His works, in order that He may seek in the shame of His sufferings His highest honor and glory.

STARKE:—Christ's gifts within us change with times.—CANSTEIN:—A weak and slight beginning is yet a beginning; and in God's methods a little is intended to become gradually greater.—QUESNEL:— The cure of spiritual blindness is only begun on earth; it will be fully accomplished only in heaven.—OSIANDER:— God often turns away our misfortune, and mends our unhappiness, by slow degrees: have patience! —Solitude and silence after conversion is much safer than much talk and running about.— We should let the truth take firm root in us, before we speak much about it.—The converted man must take care not to turn round again to the world.— CANSTEIN:—Fearful judgment, when God reckons a man, or a city, or a land, no longer worthy of the knowledge of His word and works.

GERLACH :—The gradualness of the operation is often our first inward assurance of the certainty of the change.—RIEGER :—Do not despise slight means [referring to the application of spittle].—BRAUNE :—Men must be ever known, not as trees, as perishable plants, but as rational creatures, called to eternal glory.—First of all, however, the blind man came to know Jesus aright: to know Him clearly is eternal life.

SCHLEIERMACHER :—The cure of the blind man in its resemblance to the next section : 1. The withdrawing to a place apart (special reasons for this in both cases respectively); 2. the gradual work (men as trees; obscure views concerning Christ); 3. the Redeemer's care as to what men say of Him ; 4. the sight restored, and the confession of Peter.

---

3. *The Opinions of the People, and Peter's Confession. Pre-announcement of His Sufferings. The Presumption of Peter. Christ's Teaching concerning Cross-bearing.* CH. VIII. 27—IX. 1.

(Parallels: Matt. xvi. 13-28; Luke ix. 18-27.)

27 And Jesus went out and his disciples into the towns of Cæsarea Philippi: and by
the way he asked his disciples, saying unto them, Whom do men say that I am?
28 And they answered,[1] John the Baptist: but some *say*, Elias; and others, One of the
29 prophets. And he said unto them,[2] But whom say ye that I am? And Peter answer-
30 eth and saith unto him, Thou art the Christ. And he charged them that they should
31 tell no man of [respecting] him. And he began to teach them, that the Son of man
must suffer many things, and be rejected of [by] the elders, and *of* the chief priests, and
32 scribes, and be killed, and after three days rise again. And he spake that saying
33 openly. And Peter took him, and began to rebuke him. But when he had turned
about, and looked on his disciples, he rebuked Peter, saying, Get thee behind me,
Satan: for thou savourest [mindest] not the things that be of God, but the things that
34 be of men. And when he had called the people *unto him* with his disciples also, he
said unto them, Whosoever[3] will come after me, let him deny himself, and take up his
35 cross, and follow me. For whosoever will save his life[4] shall lose it; but whosoever
36 shall lose his life for my sake and the Gospel's, the same shall save it.● For what shall
37 it profit a man, if he shall gain the whole world, and lose his own soul? Or what[5] shall
38 a man give in exchange [as a ransom] for his soul? ● Whosoever therefore shall be
ashamed of me, and of my words, in this adulterous and sinful generation, of him also
shall the Son of man be ashamed, when he cometh in the glory of his Father, with the
holy angels.
1 And he said unto them, Verily I say unto you, That there be some of them that
stand here, which shall not taste of death, till they have seen the kingdom of God come
with power.

[1] Ver. 28.—According to B., C.*, D., I., Δ., [Vulgate, Itala,] Lachmann, and Tischendorf add αὐτῷ λέγοντες. [Superfluous, and therefore more likely to be omitted than added. (Meyer.)]
[2] Ver. 29.—'Επηρώτα αὐτοὺς, instead of λέγει αὐτοῖς, after B., C., D., is the reading of Lachmann, Tischendorf, [and Meyer.]
[3] Ver. 34.—B., C.*, D., L., Δ., [Vulgate, Itala, Lachmann, Tischendorf,] read εἴ τις instead of ὅστις. A., B., Lachmann, Tischendorf have ἐλθεῖν instead of ἀκολουθεῖν.
[4] Ver. 35.—Τὴν ψυχὴν αὐτοῦ, Codd. A., D., Lachmann. (Τὴν ἑαυτοῦ ψυχήν, Griesbach, Scholz, Tischendorf.)
[5] Ver. 37.—Tischendorf, τί γάρ, instead of ἢ τί, after B., L., Δ.; he also omits δώσει ἄνθρωπος.

EXEGETICAL AND CRITICAL.

See on *Matthew* and *Luke.*—In respect to time, this is another section which stands in strict internal connection with the preceding crises. There are some important peculiarities in Mark. Matthew mentions the district of Cæsarea Philippi, Mark the villages which surrounded it, as the first goal at which our Lord aimed ; and the latter transfers the question to the way thither. Among the people's thoughts and verdicts concerning Jesus, he omits the mention of Jeremiah. It is observable that he leaves out the benediction of Peter, and the special prerogative assigned to him after his confession. Luke also omits these, while Matthew details them all in full. Here, as elsewhere, Peter, Mark's informant and voucher, omitted or kept in reserve points which tended to his own honor. On the other hand, Mark states prominently that the Lord's prediction of His passion was part of the instruction which He openly gave; he also quotes the Saviour's rebuking word to Peter, "Satan," without any of the definite explanatory particulars which Matthew gives, and without Christ's " Thou art to Me a σκάνδαλον." Mark speaks of the people as also called by Jesus to hear the statement of the universal law of suffering in the kingdom of God. He alone has the emphatic word, that he who is ashamed of the Lord is ashamed of Him (in a disgraceful manner) in an adulterous and sinful generation. In conclusion, Mark represents the coming of Christ more expressly than the other two Evangelists as a

CHAP. VIII. 27—IX. 1. 79

coming in power (majesty); while Luke speaks of His kingdom, and Matthew of His appearing in that kingdom.

Ver. 31. **After three days.**—General and popular way of speaking, instead of "on the third day," which afterwards is used as the more definite statement.

Ver. 34. **And when He had called the people unto Him.**—This scarcely requires us to understand great multitudes. But Christ makes the people who were present sharers in this part of His instruction, in order to impress it the more upon His disciples that the way of suffering was absolutely imperative, and in order to lay down the fundamental laws of self-denial and holy suffering in all their universality of application.

Ver. 37. **In exchange for: ransom-price.**—The ἀντάλλαγμα is the counter-price antithetic to the price, ἄλλαγμα. The price which the earthly-minded gives for the world, the ἄλλαγμα, is his soul. But, after having laid that down as the price, what has he for an ἀντάλλαγμα, to buy the soul back again?

Ch. ix. ver. 1. **There be some of them that stand here.**—See on *Matthew*.

DOCTRINAL AND ETHICAL.

1. See on the parallels of *Matthew* and *Luke*.
2. According to Mark, Jesus first called and collected the Twelve in the villages outside of Nazareth (ch. vi. 6, 7); then, in the villages of Cæsarea Philippi, again gathering them together and confirming them. Solitude and sequestered probation, a condition of establishment and confirmation in the spiritual office.
3. It is of great significance that Peter does not, in his own Gospel, once mention the word of Christ concerning *his* own personal priority among the Apostles, least of all as the institution of an official primacy.
4. So it is to be observed how strictly, according to Mark, the confession of Christ is conjoined with the announcement of His passion, and with the requirement of following Him in the way of the Cross.
5. *Let him take up his cross.*—An obscure intimation of His own approaching suffering upon the cross, which, even in its general terms, gave a definite meaning. Let him hold himself ready to follow Me, regarded as the vilest malefactor, and exposed to the deepest shame and the most cruel death. The cross of Christ, as such, is not a kind of suffering which is the natural consequence of sin, but which crosses the views of an ideal or newly awakened higher life.

HOMILETICAL AND PRACTICAL.

See on *Matthew;* and compare *Luke's* parallel.—The question of Christ: "Whom say the people that I am?" a means of exciting a definite Christian consciousness, in opposition to the uncertain notions of the world.—The answer of the disciples in all its significance: 1. No man says, and no man could say without madness, that Christ was nothing, or a person of no importance. 2. The scorners and slanderers of Christ are not regarded or alluded to. 3. The testimonies or opinions: *a.* John the Baptist (according to Herod, returned from the dead): thus Christianity was something ghostly and preternatural.

b. Elias (in the sense of Malachi): thus they were not able to distinguish Elias from Christ. Christianity seemed to them as a power exerted after the manner of Elias; thus in a spiritual sense as something legal. *c.* One of the prophets: something indefinite, a spiritual power, which none could clearly understand.—The question was not, what the people said concerning Christ, but what the Apostles said concerning Him.—Christ could be preached as the Christ of all the world, only after the fulfilment of His passion as the Crucified and the Risen. The confession of His people was to the Lord no sign that He would escape from suffering, but a certain sign that He would suffer.—What it means, that the Lord announces His sufferings to the disciples without any restraint: 1. In reference to Himself, 2. to the disciples, 3. to the world.—Only after we have known the person of our Lord in His word and work, can we understand and bear the knowledge of Christ's work in His passion. —The true confession of Christ must be confirmed by a readiness to follow Him.—The suffering of Christ is a divine sympathy: 1. As suffering through and for the world, it sprang from His sympathy with the world; 2. it establishes a divine sympathy in the world, as suffering on its own account and with Christ.—Self-renunciation of the believer is the soul of the confession of Christ.—The fundamentals of the Christian fellowship: 1. Its fundamental laws: 1. The true denier (of himself) is the true confessor; 2. the true cross-bearer is the true knight of the cross; 3. the true follower (after Christ in obedience) is the true conqueror. II. Its grounds: 1. He who will save his life in self-seeking, shall lose it; he who loses it in devotion to Christ, shall gain it. 2. He who lays down his soul to win the world, loses with his soul the world also; he who has gained his soul, has with his soul gained the world also. 3. To seek honor in the world while ashamed of Christ, leads to infamy before the throne of Christ; but shame in the world leads to honor with Him. 4. Readiness to die with Christ leads through death to the day of eternal glory.—It is in self-denial that we first find our true selves, recovering our personality again.—True self-denial is the raising of our buried personality out of the grave of self-deceptions.—The false and the true self.—How shameful to be ashamed of Christ in an adulterous and sinful generation: 1. As the deification of a vanishing honor, which is eternal shame; 2. as the refusal of a vanishing shame, which is eternal honor.—How Christ detects the thoughts of men in His communion.

STARKE:—CANSTEIN:—We may lawfully ask what others hold us for, if the question does not spring from pride, but from a desire to do ourselves or others good.—HEDINGER:—It is not wrong to be jealous of one's public repute. But Christ remains ever what He is, despite all the various opinions concerning Him.—QUESNEL:—The true knowledge of the secret mysteries of Christ is attained only by scholars of truth and light.—Here is a catechetical lesson given by Christ Himself.—All truths have a set time for their full revelation: we should be always careful that we do not prematurely speak, or anticipate that time, Eccles. iii. 7; we must suffer with willing heart, be rejected of the world, and be crucified with Christ, if we would be raised with Him, Rom. vi. 6–8.—The ungodly can do nothing against us but what the wise decree of God has already determined.—*Bibl. Wirt.:*—Flesh and blood always look rather at external danger and damage, than at the solemnity and claims of the call (Rom. viii. 6–8;

1 John ii. 15-17; 1 Pet. ii. 11, 20, 21; Gal. v. 21.)—You must not watch Christ, but follow Him; you must not boast about Him, but act like Him.—*Nova Bibl. Tub.*: — World gained, nothing gained; soul lost, all lost.—The greatest good is not to be met with in the transitory world, nor in the debauchery of the flesh: he whose soul is united with God has found it.— If thou art ashamed of Christ in His humble and lowly state, thou wilt have no part in His exalted and glorified state.— To die before one has seen the kingdom of God, is a wretched end.

Braune:—The kingdom of God is, in a certain sense, near at all times: there is no season when its beginnings are not manifest.— Genlach:—(Peter), rash and impetuous, spoke only, as he was wont to do, in the name of all the rest.

Gossner:—He who opposes himself to the cross of Christ and its doctrine, is a Satan, even though his name were Peter.— In the kingdom of God, all the world is inverted.—Losing is there called gaining, and gaining is there called losing.—Bauer, on ver. 35:—The beginning towards eternal life.

4. *The Transfiguration.* Vers. 2-13.

(Parallels: Matt. xvii. 1-13; Luke ix. 28-36.)

2 And after six days Jesus taketh *with him* Peter, and James, and John, and leadeth them up into an high mountain apart by themselves; and he was transfigured before
3 them. And his raiment became shining, exceeding white as snow;[1] so as no fuller on
4 earth can white them. And there appeared unto them Elias with Moses: and they
5 were talking with Jesus. And Peter answered and said to Jesus, Master, it is good for us to be here: and let us make three tabernacles [tents]; one for thee, and one for
6 Moses, and one for Elias. For he wist not what to say:[2] for they were sore afraid.
7 And there was a cloud that overshadowed them: and a voice came out of the cloud,
8 saying, This is my beloved Son: hear him. And suddenly, when they had looked
9 round about, they saw no man any more, save[3] Jesus only with themselves. And as they came down from the mountain, he charged them that they should tell no man
10 what things they had seen, till the Son of man were risen from the dead. And they kept that saying with themselves, questioning one with another what the rising from
11 the dead should mean. And they asked him, saying, Why say the scribes that Elias
12 must first come? And he answered[4] and told them, Elias verily cometh first, and restoreth all things [in the baptism of the people for the Messiah, and of the Messiah for the people]; and how it is written of the Son of man, that he must suffer many things,
13 and be set at nought.* But I say unto you, That Elias is indeed come, and they have done unto him whatsoever they listed, as it is written of him.

[1] Ver. 3.—The ὡς χιών is omitted by B., C., L., Δ., Tischendorf, probably on account of the strange comparison. [Meyer retains it, remarking that if it were an interpolation, it would be ὡς τὸ φῶς, in conformity with Matt. xvii. 2.]
[2] Ver. 6.—Most Codd. (A., D., E., F., G., H., K., Euthymius, Theophylact, Meyer) λαλήσει; other readings, λαλήσῃ (Elzevir, Fritzsche, Scholz, Lachmann), ἀποκριθῇ (B., C.*, L., Δ., Tischendorf).—B., C., D., L., Λ. have ἐγένοντο instead of ἦσαν.—B., C., L., Δ., Lachmann, Tischendorf, Meyer read ἐγένετο, with Luke ix. 35.
[3] Ver. 8.—B., D., Lachmann read εἰ μή instead of ἀλλά, with Matt. xvii. 8.
[4] Ver. 12.—Tischendorf and Meyer: ὁ δὲ ἔφη instead of ἀποκριθεὶς εἶπεν, after B., C., L., Δ., and Syriac, Coptic, Persian versions.
* [There are different modes of punctuation. According to Lachmann and Meyer the version would be: "And how is it written of the Son of man? that he must suffer," &c. According to another punctuation, followed by Hahn, the rendering would be: "And how is it written concerning the Son of man, that he must suffer many things, and be set at nought."—*Ed.*]

EXEGETICAL AND CRITICAL.

See on the parallel passages of *Matthew* and *Luke*.—This narrative stands in a definite historical connection with what precedes (ver. 1); as it does also in the accounts of Matthew and Luke. In regard to the locality, we may refer to our notes upon the scene in *Matthew*. The Tabor tradition is sufficiently accounted for by the manifestation of Christ upon the mountain in Galilee, Matt. xxviii. In describing the effect of the transfiguration, Mark uses the strongest illustrations ("white as snow," etc., "as no fuller," etc.). He, in common with Luke, records that Peter knew not what he was saying, or what he wanted to say. But he alone has the sudden vanishing of the heavenly visitors, and the inquiring look around on the part of the disciples. He joins Matthew in communicating the Lord's dealing with the disciples on coming down from the mountain. But he alone observes that the disciples questioned among themselves what the rising from the dead should mean. On the other hand, he omits, what Luke mentions, that Moses and Elias (ὀφθέντες ἐν δόξῃ) conversed with Jesus concerning His decease in Jerusalem. So only Luke has the delicate notices of the slumbrous and yet wakeful condition of the beholding disciples; while Matthew, on his part, alone applies the Lord's word concerning the Elias who had already appeared, to John the Baptist. Mark narrates the history of the transfiguration in his own characteristic manner, exhibiting its main traits in vivid and living touches.

Ver. 2. **After six days.**—*See* on *Matthew*.

Ver. 3. **No fuller on earth.**—The white glitter was supernatural. Gerlach: "In ancient times they wore but few colored garments. The fuller's business was to wash what was soiled, and to make it clean and glistening." Starke: "They used in the East to make linen garments so beautiful that they glittered with whiteness; but such as these the Lord's garments now outshone. The white color was that which the Romans called *candorem*, and which was so clear and so deep as to glisten splendidly. Materials prepared of such linen or other materials were, among the Jews, appropriated to priests and kings. Such garments also were in high estimation among other people, especially among the Romans. They were worn only by the highest personages, who were by such garments distinguished from those below them; hence, when they were seeking high offices of state, they distinguished themselves by such clothing, and were called *candidati*. And since among the Romans the glittering white upon their garments was refined to the highest lustre by art, and the Jews had been long in the habit of endeavoring to imitate it, we can understand the phrase, *That no fuller on earth could so whiten them*. That Solomon's magnificence was white, has been gathered from the fact that his array was likened to the lilies of the field (Matt. vi. 28, 29). What kind of glory was that of Herod's royal apparel, spoken of in Acts xii. 21, is shown in JOSEPHUS, *Antiq.* xix. 7.

Ver. 6. **For he wist not what to say** (or, **he would say**).—His words were an utterance of immediate feeling, expressing a state of perfect complacency, after the manner of dreams, ecstasies, and visions, in figure,—in figurative language which came to him he knew not whence.—**They were sore afraid.**—Matthew observes that *after* the sound was heard, they fell on their faces and were sore afraid. But there is no real difference. For their trepidation began naturally at the beginning, and continued increasing throughout. Matthew describes its climax; whilst Mark mentions the disciples' fear only for the sake of explaining the words of Peter.

Ver. 10. **And they kept that saying with themselves.**—Luke ix. 36. They concealed the fact which they had witnessed, after that command. Fritzsche: They obeyed the prohibition of Jesus. Meyer, on the contrary: They kept the words concerning the resurrection, and pondered them. The second, indeed, followed from the first. While they religiously kept their silence down to the day of His resurrection, they must have often asked when and how the bond of secrecy would be relaxed. Starke: "It requires much effort to overcome the tendency in beginners to prate. The word κρατεῖν shows it was not without trouble, and putting much restraint upon themselves, that the disciples kept this secret so long. The other disciples probably put questions," &c.—**The rising from the dead.**—That is, this express and particular resurrection from the dead which the Lord had predicted for Himself.

Ver. 12. **And restoreth all things.**—The way and manner in which Elias should do this (the idea is still indefinite, in the Present) is explained by what follows: *And how is it written of the Son of Man?*— What holds good of Him, that He must suffer many things, holds good also of His forerunner. This introduces the subsequent thought: Elias is come already. The punctuation given above, according to which the note of interrogation stands after "Son of Man" (Lachmann, Meyer), gives a clearer and more emphatic idea than the customary position of the note of interrogation after "be rejected." Instead of καί, one would in the latter case expect a particle of opposition; and the construction of ver. 13 should then have been different. Another construction is this: Elias cometh and restoreth all things. And how? It is written, &c.—**How it is written of the Son of Man.**—That is, his restoring all things proceeds, like the work of the Son of Man, through sufferings and death.—**That He must suffer many things.**— The ἵνα is here especially striking. Meyer says, that it sets before us the design of the γέγραπται. We take the sentence as a breviloquence, referring to what precedes—"Elias cometh first." And how is it written of the Son of Man, sc. that He cometh? In order that (ἵνα) He may suffer, &c.

Ver. 13. **As it is written of Him.**—That is, in regard to the persecution of the real Elias. See 1 Kings i. 19. (Grotius, Meyer.) That the unworthy treatment of the prophets accords (Kuinoel), is proved by the previous verse, where from the impending sufferings of the Messiah the conclusion is drawn that Elias-John must also suffer.

DOCTRINAL AND ETHICAL.

1. *See* on *Matthew*.
2. The transitory transformation of Christ a prelude of His abiding transformation. The transfiguration, as a transition into the second higher condition of human nature, was like the glorification. The transfiguration has the glorification for its result: the glorification is conditioned by the transfiguration. Into this condition the glorified Christ will raise His people also, 1 Cor. xv. But the glorification is the consummated, internal, spiritual power and glory, exalted above the changed, creaturely life, and manifested as the perfected light of life.
3. According to the privately communicated opinion of a respected Romanist theologian—personally unknown to me—the transfiguration upon the mountain was a night-scene. This was Schleiermacher's opinion also (see his *Sermons on the Gospel of Mark*). In favor of this supposition we may observe, 1. that the transfiguration of Jesus followed a solemn season of prayer; and we know that He commonly held these solemn seasons of prayer in the night; 2. that Luke mentioned their having gone down from the mountain on the day after that event. The transfiguration, by being considered as a night-scene, evidently has a peculiarly mysterious light thrown upon it.
4. As on the baptism of Christ His personal divine-human consciousness came to full maturity, so was here consummated the consciousness of His perfected prophetic work of word and deed. The goal of His prophetic work, in the narrower sense, was already reached. As Jesus, regarded in Himself, apart from His connection with sinful humanity, as the *personally* perfected God-man, might at His baptism have ascended into heaven, if He had willed to sever His destiny from that of mankind, so He might, as Prophet of the New Testament word of revelation, with the consummated consciousness of having done His prophetic work, have made the Mount of Transfiguration the Mount of Ascension. [But if Christ had ascended to heaven from the Mount of Transfiguration, He would have falsified the very prophecies alluded to; for these included His Passion and Crucifixion.—*Ed.*] The authority al-

ready referred to brings this out very excellently; and we also have alluded to it, in the *Leben Jesu*, ii. 908. "In fact, this was the moment (when the cloud received Jesus, and separated Him from the disciples) to teach them that He had power to retain His life, and that it was only free love that made Him leave the fellowship of the heavenly beings, and go down with His disciples into the valley of death."

5. Moses and Elias conversed with the Lord, according to Luke, concerning His departure in Jerusalem. The unknown Romanist expositor just alluded to thinks that these men appeared to the Lord as representatives from the kingdom of the dead, that they might add their argument to ensure His voluntary determination to encounter the sufferings of death, and thus redeem those who were held in the realm of death, or generally complete His work of redemption. The gratuitous and unwarranted idea of the intercession of the saints for the dead will not prevent our doing justice to the penetration of this view. But there are two things to be noticed: 1. According to Luke, Moses and Elias appear to the Lord in glory (ver. 31), not as supplicating intercessors; 2. Christ had already much earlier preannounced His passion: His baptism itself was, in this relation, decisive in its force as a preintimation. But that the kingdom of the dead had some interest in the voluntary determination of Christ to go on His way of suffering, Ebrard has well shown, and remarks: "In the transfiguration, Jesus had given the fathers of the ancient covenant the blessed intelligence of His perfect readiness to redeem them by His own death." Comp. my *Leben Jesu*, ii. 909.

6. *Let us make three tabernacles.*—A significant Future is added: for he knew not what he would say (λαλήσει). The man in ecstasy (as in a dream) brings the feeling or the thought; but the figure or form of the thought is imparted to him according to the secret laws that rule the figurative perception and language of the visionary condition. Thus came the figure to Peter: "build three tabernacles, one for Thee," etc., as an expression for his blessed feelings which he would utter.

HOMILETICAL AND PRACTICAL.

See on *Matthew.* So also *Luke.*—Between the confession and the transfiguration lies the week of temporal trials.— The mountain of prayer is the mountain of transfiguration.—The revelation of the life of Christ in His glorification here, a promise and sign for His people, 2 Cor. v.—The Lord's heavenly beauty.— Christ at the turning-point of His deeds and sufferings; by festal remembrance and sacrificial consecration glorified. — Consecration to the Lord changes man: 1. Internally: he is elevated into the spiritual world, and surrounded by blessed spirits. 2. Externally: he is renewed, adorned, transfigured.— The only true adornment of men: divine life of the Spirit.—Man upon the mountain: the first Sunday festival of the youthful Church of the Confession.— The transfiguration a sign and symbol 1. of the Sunday, 2. of the Ascension, 3. of the new Paradise.— The wish of Peter; or, the ideals of young Christians and the Lord's training: 1. Ideals of young Christians: that of retaining their early experiences, that of entire separation from the world, life of contemplation. 2. The Lord's guidance; further onward, deeper, higher.— All else comes and goes: Jesus alone abides.— Moses and Elias vanish from the disciples before His glory, and in the end they see Him alone.— The law and the prophets are merged in the glory of the Gospel.—The transfiguration of Christ upon the mountain: for Him, as for the three blest disciples, a preparation for Gethsemane.—The transfiguration of Jesus: 1. As a single central point in His life; 2. in its earlier types and symbols (Enoch, Abraham, Moses, Elijah, earlier crises in the life of Jesus Himself); 3. in its significance for the future, pointing to the resurrection, the ascension, the great manifestation of Christ, the glorification of believers.—The transfiguration of Christ the sure pledge of the renewing of the world, Rev. xx. 21, and of that new state of glory wherein the word is fulfilled, Behold, I make all things new!— The prophetic history of Christ's life and suffering, the history of the life and suffering of His people.— The Lord gives unasked to His disciples that sign from heaven which He had denied to the asking world.

STARKE:—OSIANDER:—God strengthens the faith of His people before trials come, that they may be able to endure them.—*Bibl. Wirt.:*—He who would be conversant with heavenly things must tear away his soul from earth, and soar towards God.— The heavenly glory is incomparable; greater and more excellent than all beauty and grace upon earth.— *Nova Bibl. Tub.:*—Moses and Elias still live: witnesses of eternity.—*Bibl. Wirt.:*—In Christ the law and the prophets attained their goal and fulfilment. Jesus is Lord of the dead and living; He has the keys of hell and of death, Rev. iii. 7; Ps. lxxxiv. 2, 3, 5.—LANGE:—God lets His people have, even in this world, extraordinary glances and views; but they are only of short duration, because their longer enjoyment would not be tolerable and profitable.— OSIANDER:—Human nature cannot bear the glory of eternal life; therefore our bodies will be glorified.— We must depend only and absolutely upon Jesus Christ.—QUESNEL:—Jesus Christ had His Elias who announced Him in the world; He will have more of them yet in times to come and before His last appearance.—One place of Scripture must not be opposed to another, but Scripture must be compared with Scripture.— The ungodly accomplish, against their own will, the holy will of God: they by their persecution not only create happiness for the saints, but make their own misery.—Marvel not that faithful ministers of Christ are cast out as evil, for it was clearly enough predicted in the Scripture.—RIEGER: Probably the disciples would desire, on going down, that they might communicate this vision to others; but the prohibition of Jesus forbade. The same holds good of us in many instances now.—SCHLEIERMACHER:—And that also was a spiritual glorification of the Lord when the disciples were taught that they had nothing more to do either with the one or the other (Moses and Elias), neither with the letter of the law nor with revolutionizing zeal. (Yet Moses and Elias were not set aside by Christ; but they were lifted up and lost in Him as their fulfilment.)— This spirit, which can only from within outwards renew our holy relation to God, and will spread abroad only through the energies of love the living knowledge of God among the children of men, will be to the end of time His glorification.

BRIEGER:—To glorify and transfigure, means to make perfectly clear and transparent (but of men, and especially of Christ, it means to exhibit the creaturely life in its spiritual glory). The eternal destiny of man was glorification.—Christ went on now to meet His sufferings. In order to obtain strength for the endurance of the extremest sorrows, He must have a foretaste of the glory which awaited Him.—But on account of His disciples too, it was needful that Christ should be glorified.—BAUER:—Peter would build tabernacles: for the heavenly beings who dwell above, skins and huts.

5. *The Healing of the Possessed Child after the Transfiguration.* VERS. 14–29.

(Parallels: Matt. xvii. 14–21; Luke ix. 37–43.)

14 And when he came to *his* disciples, he saw a great multitude about them, and the
15 scribes questioning with them. And straightway all the people, when they beheld him,
16 were greatly amazed, and, running to *him*, saluted him. And he asked the scribes
17 [them[1]], What question ye with them? And one[2] of the multitude answered and said,
18 Master, I have brought unto thee my son, which hath a dumb spirit; And wheresoever he taketh him, he teareth him; and he foameth, and gnasheth with his teeth, and pineth away; and I spake to thy disciples that they should cast him out, and they could not.
19 He answereth him,[3] and saith, O faithless generation, how long shall I be with you? how
20 long shall I suffer you? Bring him unto me. And they brought him unto him: and when he saw him, straightway the spirit tare [convulsed] him; and he fell on the
21 ground, and wallowed [rolled] foaming. And he asked his father, How long is it ago
22 since this came unto him? And he said, Of a child. And oft-times it hath cast him into the fire, and into the waters, to destroy him: but if thou canst[4] do anything, have
23 compassion on us, and help us. Jesus said unto him,[5] If thou canst believe, all things
24 *are* possible to him that believeth. And straightway the father of the child cried out,
25 and said with tears,[6] Lord, I believe; help thou mine unbelief. When Jesus saw that the people came running together, he rebuked the foul spirit, saying unto him, Thou dumb and deaf spirit, I charge [command] thee, come out of him, and enter no more
26 into him. And *the spirit* cried, and rent him sore [convulsed greatly], and came out of
27 him: and he was as one dead; insomuch that many said, He is dead. But Jesus took
28 him by the hand,[7] and lifted him up; and he arose. And when he was come into the
29 house, his disciples asked him privately, Why could not we cast him out? And he said unto them, This kind can come forth by nothing, but by prayer and fasting.[8]

[1] Ver. 16.—Αὐτούς, B., D., L., Δ., Vulgate, Coptic, Æth., instead of τοὺς γραμματεῖς (Elzevir, Scholz, Lachmann in margin).
[2] Ver. 17.—Αὐτῷ must be inserted after ἀπεκρίθη, according to B., C., D., L., Δ., Lachmann, Tischendorf, Meyer.
[3] Ver. 19.—Instead of αὐτῷ, it is preferable to read αὐτοῖς (A., B., D., L., Δ., Versions).
[4] Ver. 22.—Instead of δύνασαι here and ver. 23, Tischendorf and Lachmann read δύνῃ, according to B., D., L., Δ., Meyer. This form, in itself the Conjunctive, was used later even in the Indicative, instead of δύνασαι; but it lays stronger stress upon the question.
[5] Ver. 23.—The τὸ was omitted by many Codd. (D., K., M., U., Syriac, Persian) on account of its difficulty. Tischendorf omits the πιστεῦσαι, following B., C.*, L., D., and many Versions; Meyer says, it was an exegetical addition to the mere εἰ δύνῃ, not understood. But the clause, "If thou canst believe," may have been found still harder; and therefore corrected into "as it regards, If thou canst! All things are possible," &c.
[6] Ver. 24.—The μετὰ δακρύων is wanting in A.*, B., C.*, L., Δ., Versions, [Lachmann, Tischendorf, Meyer.] The κύριε is very doubtful; Meyer rejects it.
[7] Ver. 27.—Lachmann reads τῆς χειρὸς αὐτοῦ, after B., D., L., Δ., Vulgate; Meyer cites in comparison, Mark i. 31; v. 41; viii. 23.
[8] Ver. 29.—The omission of νηστείᾳ by D. (which Tischendorf follows) is not decisive.

EXEGETICAL AND CRITICAL.

See on the parallels of *Matthew* and *Luke.*—The immediate connection between this event and the transfiguration is affirmed by all three Evangelists. The time and the place are established, therefore, by the narrative of that event. In the communication of the incidents here before us, Mark is rich in individual traits, which place the scene in a much more vivid light. Jesus finds His nine other disciples at the foot of the mountain, not only surrounded by a multitude of people, but involved in controversy with the scribes, who have surprised them in a condition of entire impotence. The people are amazed, or are very much excited, when they see Jesus coming. They were probably in a profane and mocking state of mind, in consequence of the disciples' failure to work the miracle, and of the attack of the scribes; and were disposed to indulge this inclination, when the sudden and overpowering appearance of Christ smote their consciences. To this may have concurred better motives, which induced the multitude to run to Jesus as the real arbiter and the only helper in this strange case. Thus we find that our Saviour at the very outset reduced the scribes to silence by His question, Wherefore do ye contend with them? While Mark passes over Matthew's notice, that the demoniac youth was lunatic, and that of Luke, that he was the only son of his father, he gives the most vivid representation of his state of wretchedness: his dumb behaviour (he had a speechless spirit), his frightful sufferings (in his paroxysms foaming and grinding his teeth, and swooning away). In the Lord's rebuke he is content with the description, γενεὰ ἄπιστος: the explanatory διεστραμμένη he omits; on the other hand, he paints more vividly than Luke the scene in which the youth at once, on seeing Jesus, was overcome by the demoniac influence, fell down to the ground, and wallowed, foaming. But of priceless value is the passage between Jesus and the father of the youth, from ver. 21 to ver. 25. We see how the Lord, by His question as to how long the youth had thus suffered, pacified the excited feelings of all, especially of the father, and encouraged their faith. We hear the never-to-be-forgotten words, "If thou canst believe," and the cry, "Lord, I believe; help Thou mine unbelief." The words which expelled the demon, Mark recites in all their solemn emphasis; and in them the addition is remarkable, Enter no more into him. Mark alone describes the paroxysm under which the demon departed, and the important circumstance that the youth lay as one dead; that Jesus took him by the hand, and raised him to conscious life. Moreover, he makes prominent (as he often does the like) the entrance of Christ into the house, where the disciples put their confidential question to Him as to the reason why they could not cast out the demon. And he gives the answer of Jesus without Matthew's additional clause concerning the unbelief of the disciples, and without the words that liken faith to the grain of mustard-seed. Nor does he mention the circumstance, recorded by Luke, of the people's renewed astonishment and increasing excitement.

Ver. 15. **All the people were amazed.**— At what? Euth. Zigabenus: "Either on account of the singularly seasonable and sudden coming of Jesus, or at His glorious appearance." Of this latter we read nothing, and Meyer therefore thinks the former the sounder view: it was an astonishment of joyful surprise. But θάμβος betokens an astonishment which is related to fear, which sometimes passes over into amazement, and is sometimes called terror. Hence we explain the astonishment as the amazement of a crowd somewhat profanely disposed at the sudden interposition of a punitive event like this (see *Leben Jesu*, ii. 2, 317). "They sought to repair their error by running to Him with eager denials." And it is obvious to connect with that the supposition, that the reflection of the transfiguration glory still lingered on the Lord's countenance. *See* Ex. xxxiv. 29, 30.

Ver. 16. **And he asked them.**—Bengel refers this to the disciples; Griesbach, to the disciples and scribes; Fritzsche, with most others, to the scribes alone; Meyer, to the people, because the people were just before spoken of. But the context points simply to the scribes as the contending party; not excluding, however, the people, so far as they sympathized. — **What question ye with them?**— Concerning what? The scribes were dumb. But the father of the possessed child gave the answer as to what they were contending about, ver. 17. Evidently they had impugned the power of the disciples to work miracles, and the authority of Christ; therefore they were now silent, because they suspected that the Lord would by a miraculous act convict them.

Ver. 17. **Brought unto Thee my son.**— That was his purpose. He was seeking the Lord in the place where the disciples were. But as Jesus was absent, His disciples and the man became engaged together.

Ver. 18. **Wheresoever he taketh him.**— This does not hint at an intermitting possession, in favor of which Meyer, without reason, adduces Matt. xii. 44, but to the antithesis between a latent action (in which, however, the youth by his dumbness betrayed his possession) and frenzied paroxysms, in which the spirit seized the youth, in order, as it appeared, to destroy him; and, according to Matthew, these crises had a connection with the changes of the moon. The following μηκέτι εἰσέλθῃς, Meyer himself acknowledges, implies that the demon had continuous possession.— **He teareth him.**— Probably this manifested itself in convulsions, St. Vitus' dance, or the like. The fundamental form was epilepsy, or something of the kind. These circumstances depended partly on the change of the moon, partly on demoniac influences.

Ver. 22. **To destroy him.** — The father regarded the demon as a malicious enemy, who was bent upon the murder of his only son.—**If Thou canst do anything.**— Expression of doubt or infirm faith, which, having been at the beginning too weak, had become more and more weak in consequence of the failure of the disciples' attempt.

Ver. 23. **If thou canst believe.** — The difficulty in the reading of the *Text. Rec.*, together with the critical authorities in its favor, constrain us to retain it. The easiest solution explains the τό as a sign of quotation preceding the direct address (De Wette). For other explanations, *see* Meyer.* We take the sentence as a breviloquence: "the *if thou canst* means, *if thou canst believe.*" Τὸ εἰ δύνασαι = εἰ δύνασαι πιστεῦσαι. To be able, and to be able to *believe*, are with the Lord one and the same,—especially throughout Mark's Gospel. Hence the clause, "All things are possible to him that believeth," is an illustration of this fundamental law, this mathematical formula, so to speak, of the kingdom of God. The explanation of the passage on the other reading is indeed simpler: "As it respects *if thou canst*, all things are possible," etc. (Meyer); or, the first clause is a question: Dost thou ask, *If thou canst?* all things, etc. (Ewald).

Ver. 24. **Help Thou mine unbelief.**—Bengel: Help away mine unbelief. Meyer thinks to improve it: Do not deny me on account of my unbelief. Certainly the βοήθει, ver. 21, refers to the help of healing itself; but the man knew very well by this time that his son would be healed, if his unbelief was healed. And the faith which now sprang up in the man was the more spiritual, in that it was a belief that Jesus could strengthen the deficient faith into the ability perfectly to believe, and so by this means remove also his external distress.

Ver. 25. **When Jesus saw that the people came running together.**—His desire to preserve the secrecy of His journey tended now to hasten the

* [" After omitting πιστεῦσαι, the clause τὸ εἰ δύνῃ (δύνασαι) is to be regarded as Nominative Absolute: *The 'if thou canst,'*—*all things are possible to him that believeth, i. e.*, so far as concerns the words, '*if thou canst*,' which thou hast just spoken, everything depends upon *faith*; the believer can obtain *anything*. The article τό, belonging to εἰ δύνῃ as its substantive, takes up the words of the father, and with lively emphasis isolates them in the grammatical structure, in order to put them into relation to the faith that is required on his part. Griesbach, Tischendorf, and Ewald regard τὸ εἰ δύνῃ as a question, and πάντα δυν. τ. πιστ. as its answer: '*Tune dubitans si potes aiebas? Nihil non in ejus, qui confidat, gratiam fieri potest.*' But in case of a question we should expect τί τὸ εἰ δύνῃ." Meyer, *in loc.*—*Ed.*]

performance of the miracle.—**I charge (command) thee.**—"Emphatically, as in contrast with the disciples." Meyer.

Ver. 26. **The spirit cried.**—The crying out of the demoniac youth, seeming to be a work of the demon, though a shriek in inarticulate tones, was the first sign of cure: the youth had previously been dumb, whilst foaming and gnashing his teeth. See ver. 18.

DOCTRINAL AND ETHICAL.

1. See on the parallels in *Matthew* and *Luke.*
2. We have here not only the grand contrast between the heavenly glorification upon the mountain, and the demoniac degradation reminding of hell at the foot of it, but also the contrast between the sound spiritual ecstasy of the disciples, and the diseased physical possession of the youth. So also a contrast between the supreme festival and the severe toil of the Lord.
3. As the contemplation of the disciples upon the mountain had to contend with infirmity and sleep, so the premature activity of the disciples in the valley had to contend with impotence and vain endeavors. Christ is the Master upon the mountain and in the valley, in contemplation and in activity.
4. The heaviest burden which oppressed the Lord in His career upon earth, even amongst His disciples, was the burden of unbelief.
5. The colloquy of Jesus with the father of the child a school of faith.
6. Christ in this narrative may be compared to a general, who retrieves by his own presence a battle well-nigh lost by his army.
7. Through the faith of the father the son is healed (as in the history of the nobleman, and of the Canaanitish woman). These facts tell against the Baptists. Even the blessing upon the faith of sponsors is represented by the history of the centurion.
8. Reischle: "Over the life of the child the demon, despite his malignity, had no power. Later examples also show that possessed persons, falling from great heights, or into fire or water, are not easily killed or grievously hurt, while in their condition of unnatural paroxysms."

HOMILETICAL AND PRACTICAL.

See on the parallels of *Matthew* and *Luke.*—How the entrance of the living Christ into the community of the disciples changes its whole character: 1. The profane disposition of the people gives place to reverence; 2. the supremacy of the divine word takes the place of school controversy; 3. excitement is allayed by the spirit of His peace; 4. faith conquers unbelief; 5. His miraculous help and salvation follow their impotence and bewilderment.—The Lord comes at the right time for the help of His people.—Not only the demon of the abyss, but also the scribes, embarrass the company of the disciples not firmly standing in the power of faith.—The poor demoniac youth, and the world of poor, afflicted children (deaf and dumb, cretins, possessed, orphans, etc.).—The anguish of the father's heart could lead to faith, even as the anguish of the mother's heart (of the Canaanitish woman: but the mother's heart was the more brave).—The colloquy of the Lord with the father of the youth, a type of the way in which He guides the soul to faith. 1. The preparation: allaying of excitement, and clear view of the affliction. 2. Help: reference to the power of faith. 3. Support and consummation of faith.— The communication between Christ and the needy soul: 1. What is thy grief? 2. If Thou canst, help. 3. Thou canst, if thou canst believe. 4. I believe; help, etc.—Thou canst; that is, if thou canst believe.—The measure of faith, the measure of our ability.—Weak faith must, with the prayer, "Lord, help mine unbelief," stretch forward to its perfection.—The faith of parents is to the advantage of their children.—Prayer and tears the element of faith: 1. The expression of its ground, humility (prayer, the spiritual expression; tears, the bodily expression); 2. the voice of its need; 3. the nourishment of its strength.—The father's concurrence with the Lord in faith, severs the connection of the child with the evil spirit.—What are we taught by the final throes of the hostile spirit? 1. Redemption is attained by a decisive conflict, in which all the powers of evil are excited; 2. we must distinguish between the external manifestation and the internal strength of the evil one; 3. when the distress is greatest, the help is nearest.—The miracle of the Lord twofold: 1. Casting out demons with peril of life; 2. restoration of life, seemingly gone.—Unclean spirits must be cast out, even though life seems endangered.—If the soul is freed, the life is saved.—Many kinds of impotence, and the one divine power: 1. Inability: *a.* of the child—a miserable possession; *b.* of the people—a stupid prejudice; *c.* of the scribes—impotence of malice, disguised under wise phrases; *d.* of the disciples—occasioned by want of self-government and collectedness of spirit; *e.* of those who sought help—enabled to believe. 2. The almighty power of the Lord: punishing all the impotence of malignity, and confirming all the impotence of sincere infirmity.—The power of demons having its root in the weakness of men (like the vampire sucking the blood of the living, and nourished thereby), but sinking into nothing before the awaking power of faith, under the omnipotence of the grace of Christ.—The unclean spirit a murderer of man, and Christ the Saviour of man's life, here as everywhere.—Jesus puts compulsion upon the wicked spirit of envious, dumb, and murmuring misery.— He constrains him to cry out in his loudest utterance, and so expels him.

STARKE:—When a man has refreshed and strengthened himself in God, through prayer in secret, he must up and betake himself again to his calling.—CANSTEIN:—When the world thinks that Christ has departed from His people, it deems that a good opportunity for tempting them, and misleading them into evil.—QUESNEL:—The Lord Jesus sometimes suffers His people to be driven into a corner, that they may know how needful He is to them.—In their presence, the world shows itself respectful enough towards God's servants; but what passes behind their backs, He knows best who knows all things.—HEDINGER:—Children a precious gift of God.—Children may be a great joy, and also a great bitterness, to their parents.—QUESNEL:—The devil is as angry as ever when he sees that Christ will rob him of a soul.—We must not hold ourselves safe when we are disinclined to any particular sin. Satan knows how to vary his temptations; and to turn our thoughts now in one, and now in another, direction of evil.—CRAMER:—Unbelief is the greatest sin, hinders the greatest works of God, and plunges the soul in condemnation.—HEDINGER:—Faith is omnipotent (able for everything).—CANSTEIN:—He who implores faith with tears, has it already in his heart.—MAJUS:—Weak faith is nevertheless faith.—Amidst tears and prayers, we shall be delivered from unbelief, and attain unto true faith.—The humble Christian prays incessantly for the increase of his faith.—The devil must be rebuked, which he cannot bear; but he who would do it, must be armed with the power of the Holy Spirit.—QUESNEL:—Those who do not like to speak of God, or hear God spoken of, are possessed by a dumb spirit, from which Christ alone can free them.—OSIANDER:—Let those who are once delivered from Satan's power, take good heed that they be not entangled again in his snares.—Even if Satan, by God's permission, could inflict bodily death upon men, he cannot put their souls to death.—CANSTEIN:—When the Gospel has little fruit, its ministers should examine themselves how far they are the cause.—HEDINGER:—A submissive prayer.—OSIANDER:—Preachers should, beyond all others, be moderate and watchful.—RIEGER:—The future coming of Christ will inspire such terror as this into very many.—Men are not very willing to join cause with the poor disciples when they are in conflict, and at disadvantages. But when they see the Lord approaching, and have reason to think that He will utter His favorable and victorious voice concerning them, there is a great reaction in their favor.—BRAUNE:—The sharp rebuke of Jesus is general; but it touches the disciples most keenly.—Thou sayest to Me, "Canst Thou do anything?" but I must say unto thee, "Canst *thou* do anything, that is, canst thou believe? for then thou canst do all: faith can do everything."—There exists certainly between parents and children a deep, internal relation and sympathy.—This passage is most important in relation to the nature of faith.—It does not depend so much upon the theoretical consciousness of a truth, as upon the existence of a real and actual fellowship with God.—It was noble in the disciples so frankly and openly to test themselves in their Master's presence.—We should always act as they acted, when we fail of attaining what is the due of our office, and what our hearts are set upon.—REISCHLE:—Here also we find representative faith, as in Matt. viii. 5. (But connected with profound, living affinity between parent and child.)—LISCO:—(The people were amazed, and ran to greet Jesus.) Have you never found that, on occasion of special and mysterious interpositions of God, your neighbor's heart was more than ordinarily inclined towards you?—SCHLEIERMACHER:—(The disciples excited by disputation with the Jews.) There are only a few men who are able to contend peacefully, and without losing their calm and peaceful temper, even about such matters as do not affect their external prerogatives,—matters, for instance, of faith, which engender difference of opinion.—There can be no doubt that they were the scribes who, in consequence of the estimation in which they were held, moved and swayed the minds of the people on the present occasion; and those scribes were mainly and primarily the persons whom the Lord described as an unbelieving generation.—Ye were not able, because your minds were in so excited a state: ye could have accomplished it only in a tranquil, collected temper, in which alone can reside such spiritual power.—The kingdom of God is never advanced in a passionate temper of mind, even if the zeal is a zeal for good.—They must return into silence, and stillness, and rest (this, however, being attainable only on the condition of prayer and fasting; that is, devotion towards God, and self-denial towards the world).—GOSSNER:—If we do not abide in faith, we can do nothing.

NINTH SECTION.

THE RETIREMENT OF JESUS IN GALILEE PREPARATORY TO HIS JOURNEY TO PERÆA AND JERUSALEM. FURTHER PREPARATION FOR THE NEW CHURCH.

CHAPTER IX. 30–50.

---

1. *Christ's Prediction among His Galilæan Disciples of His Death.* VERS. 30–32.

(Parallels: Matt. xvii. 22, 23; Luke ix. 43–45.)

30 And they departed thence, and passed [passed by by-ways[1]] through Galilee; and
31 he would not that any man should know *it*. For he taught his disciples, and said unto them, The Son of man is delivered into the hands of men, and they shall kill him; and
32 after that he is killed, he shall rise the third day.[2] But they understood not that saying, and were afraid to ask him.

[1] Ver. 30.—Lachmann, ἐπορεύοντο, after B.*, D. Meyer: "The compound was given up as misunderstood."
[2] Ver. 31.—Lachmann and Tischendorf read, following B., C., D., L., Δ., Versions, μετὰ τρεῖς ἡμέρας, as in ch. viii. 31. But it is quite natural that the more definite expression should occur here.

EXEGETICAL AND CRITICAL.

See on *Matthew* and *Luke.*—It is plain that the return of Jesus to Galilee from Cæsarea Philippi is here described. As it regards the chronological relation to what follows, it is questionable whether this was the last residence of Jesus in Galilee before His departure to Jerusalem in the year of His death, or the last but one. The former is the opinion of

Lücke, Wieseler, Hofmann, and Ebrard. But on the other side is the fact, that Jesus now went through Galilee quite in secret; while His last journey from Galilee, through Samaria, was a very public one. (*See* Luke ix. 52; xv. 1.) This secret abode of Christ in Galilee coincides with the Lord's refusal, on the occasion of His brethren's challenge to Him to go up with them to the Feast of Tabernacles in Jerusalem, John vii. 1; and this took place before the penultimate and certainly concealed journey of Jesus to Jerusalem (*see Leben Jesu*, ii. 2, p. 28).—The Feast of Tabernacles fell in the autumn (on the fifteenth day of the seventh Jewish month, called Tisri). It began this year—the year of persecutions before the year of His death, 782 A.U.C.—according to Wieseler, on the twelfth of October. The present history, therefore, places us in the autumn of that year. (*See* on *Matthew*.) The proper and special characteristics of the present journey of Jesus through Galilee are found in the παρεπορεύοντο, ver. 30 (on which below), in the words, "He would not that any man should know," and in the particulars of the prediction concerning the Passion. Mark is here distinguished from Matthew by being more precise in his characterization. On the other hand, Luke gives prominence to a specific trait, Luke ix. 44—the Lord's reference to the contrast furnished by the praises which He received after the healing of the demoniac youth at Cæsarea Philippi. He also gives special emphasis, ver. 45, to the expression οἱ δὲ ἠγνόουν τὸ ῥῆμα.

Ver. 30. **And passed through Galilee.**—The παραπορεύομαι means a going aside or passing by. Meyer explains, "They were required to go rapidly through Galilee; that is, they so travelled as nowhere to tarry long." In Deut. ii. 4 the passing through the territory of the Edomites was a passing through their borders (not touching their central places). In Mark ii. 23 it means a passing through the cornfields, leaving the overhanging ears of corn. Hence Grotius (*Annott. in Marc.* p. 638: compare *Leben Jesu*, ii. 924; Sepp. ii. 418): they journeyed in by-ways and field-roads. But of a voyage by sea we read nothing. They travelled round the sea, through desert mountain-ways and woody paths; for Jesus desired uninterruptedly to prepare His disciples in Galilee for His approaching sufferings.

Ver. 31. **For He taught His disciples.**—We must understand by these only His disciples dispersed through Galilee; that discipleship out of which He at a later period, before His last journey, selected the Seventy, and from among whom a nucleus of more than five hundred brethren outlived the trial of the cross: 1 Cor. xv. 6; Matt. xxviii. 16. For the Lord had previously led the twelve Apostles to Gaulonitis, over the sea, in order to make them acquainted with the same great mystery. *See* ch. viii. 31.—**Is delivered,** παραδίδοται.—The future vividly exhibited as present.

Ver. 32. **But they understood not that saying.**—Compare especially the parallel passage in Luke. According to Matthew, they were exceedingly troubled. The saying concerning His violent death so contradicted their expectations, that they could not and would not think of it. Hence they would not ask for fuller explanation.

DOCTRINAL AND ETHICAL.

1. *See* on *Matthew* and *Luke*.
2. The whole passage is a psychological example that teaches us how difficult it is to enter into views which are opposed to our former views, and the tendency of our wills; how hard it is for the world, with its view of Christianity, and for Christians themselves, with their worldly views, to take a self-renouncing view of the mystery and doctrine of the cross. So every individual man of the world, and even the individual disciple of Christ, finds it ever.
3. Schleiermacher: "We see that the disciples had then as yet no conviction of the necessity of the death of Christ for the accomplishment of the work of redemption. They thought all was to be done without the intervention of the death of their Lord and Master, although not without many conflicts to befall both Him and them." We see, however, that for that stage their faith satisfied the Lord; but we see also how often He had again to rebuke their unbelief, until, after His crucifixion, resurrection, and ascension, they came to a perfect faith through the anointing of the Holy Spirit.

HOMILETICAL AND PRACTICAL.

See on *Matthew* and *Luke*.—The departure of Jesus from His asylum in the mountains on the other side of the sea.—The silent paths of the Lord in the dreary time of persecution (the ancient Christians in the Catacombs, the Waldenses, the Huguenots, Luther in the Wartburg, &c.).—The by-paths of Christ in contrast with the by-paths of the world.—The Lord's calm autumnal travelling: 1. It was autumn in the year; 2. autumn in His life; 3. autumn in the ancient world.—The Son of Man delivered into the hands of men; or, the heaven-wide difference and contrast between the Man and men: 1. Between the Son of Man and the hands of men; 2. between the new humanity and the old humanity.—The betrayal into the hands of men, the bitterest sting in the anticipation of His sufferings.—The displacency with which man hears the first solemn and fearful words concerning the cross.—Lack of the insight of faith, and lack of the obedience of faith, in their reciprocal influence.—The pains taken by our Lord with His people, before He brought them to believe in the great salvation wrought out in the great judgment. —We learn the meaning of Christ's death by the light of His life and suffering.

STARKE:—HEDINGER:—Christ's suffering was certain and prearranged, but to the natural reason incomprehensible: the flesh for ever hears of it with displacency.—MAJUS:—When the Church is in a prosperous condition, that is the time to remember what has been predicted in Holy Writ concerning the cross and sufferings of the faithful.

88 THE GOSPEL ACCORDING TO MARK.

2. *The Greatest among the Disciples and the Little Child. Zeal of John. Offences.* VERS. 33–50.

(Parallels: Matt. xviii. 1-0; Luke ix. 46-50.)

33 And he came¹ to Capernaum: and, being in the house, he asked them, What was it
34 that ye disputed among yourselves by [on] the way? But they held their peace: for
35 by [on] the way² they had disputed among themselves who *should be* the greatest. And
   he sat down, and called the twelve, and saith unto them, If any man desire to be first,
36 *the same* shall be last of all, and servant of all. And he took a child, and set him in
37 the midst of them: and when he had taken him in his arms, he said unto them, Whosoever shall receive one of such children in my name, receiveth me; and whosoever
38 shall receive me, receiveth not me, but him that sent me. And [But] John answered
   him,³ saying, Master, we saw one casting out devils in thy name, and he followeth not
39 us; and we forbade him, because he followeth not us. But Jesus said, Forbid him not:
   for there is no man which shall do a miracle in my name, that can lightly [readily]
40, 41 speak evil of me. For he that is not against us⁴ is on our part. For whosoever
   shall give you a cup of water to drink in my name,⁵ because ye belong to Christ, verily
42 I say unto you, he shall not lose his reward. And whosoever shall offend one of *these*
   little ones that believe in me, it is better for him that a millstone were hanged about
43 his neck, and he were cast into the sea. And if thy hand offend thee, cut it off: it is
   better for thee⁷ to enter into life maimed, than having [the] two hands to go into hell,
44 into the fire that never shall be quenched: Where their worm dieth not, and the fire is
45 not quenched. And if thy foot offend thee, cut it off: it is better for thee to enter halt
   into life, than having [the] two feet to be cast into hell, into the fire that never shall
46, 47 be quenched: Where their worm dieth not, and the fire is not quenched.⁸ And if
   thine eye offend thee, pluck it out: it is better for thee to enter into the kingdom of
48 God with one eye [one-eyed], than having two eyes to be cast into hell-fire⁹: Where
49 their worm dieth not, and the fire is not quenched. For every one shall be salted with
50 fire, and every sacrifice shall be salted with salt. Salt *is* good: but if the salt have
   lost his [its] saltness [have become saltless], wherewith will ye season it? Have salt
   in yourselves, and have peace one with another.

¹ Ver. 33.—Lachmann, Tischendorf, [after B., D., Vulgate]: ἦλθον Πρὸς ἑαυτοὺς is wanting in [B., C., D., Versions, Lachmann, Tischendorf, Meyer.]
² Ver. 34.—The omission of ἐν τῇ ὁδῷ in some Codd. [A., D.] is not important.
³ Ver. 38.—Tischendorf [and Meyer] read ἔφη αὐτῷ, [with the omission of λέγων,] after B., L., Δ., and Versions. Perhaps an explanation of the more difficult "John answered."—A. and others omit ἐν; D., D. retain it. The former seems more unusual and more correct.—*See* Meyer on the omissions of ὃς οὐκ and ὅτι οὐκ. [Ὅς οὐκ ἀκολουθεῖ ἡμῖν is wanting in D., C., L., Δ., while, on the contrary, this is found in D., X., Versions, Vulgate, Fritzsche, Tischendorf, but ὅτι οὐκ ἀκολ. ἡμῖν is wanting. Meyer retains both.]
⁴ Ver. 40.—A., D., E., F., Versions, read ὑμῶν.
⁵ Ver. 41.—Τῷ and μοῦ are omitted in A., B., C.
⁶ Ver. 42.—Τούτων is added by Tischendorf and Lachmann, after A., B., C.**; Meyer derives it from Matt. xviii. 6.—Lachmann: μύλος ὀνικός, after B., C., D. Meyer derives this also from Matthew.
⁷ Ver. 43.—Lachmann, Tischendorf, [Meyer]: καλόν ἐστίν σε, after B., C., L.
⁸ Ver. 45.—The omission of εἰς τὸ πῦρ ἄσβεστον [in D., C., L., Tischendorf, Meyer,] is to be explained by the fact of the repetition of the words concerning the worm; which only in ver. 48 is found in all the Codd. [In vers. 44, 46 it is wanting in B., C., L., Δ., and Tischendorf.]
⁹ Ver. 47.—Τοῦ πυρός is wanting in many Codd.

EXEGETICAL AND CRITICAL.

See on the parallel passages of *Matthew* and *Luke*.—As it respects the chronology, this residence of Jesus in Capernaum does not immediately follow the former section; but His appearance in Jerusalem at the Feast of Tabernacles must be interposed. According to John, our Lord went up to Jerusalem not only at the Feast of Tabernacles, but also at the Feast of Dedication. The former feast fell in the middle of the month of October; that of the Dedication in the second half of December (the 27th). The question arises, whether Jesus remained in Judæa during the interval between these two feasts, and then returned to Galilee and Capernaum for the last time; or whether this last journey homewards and the departure from Galilee fell within the interval of the two feasts. We assume that the latter is the true hypothesis, and for the following reasons:—1. The last journey of Jesus to Jerusalem led, according to the Synoptists, over Peræa. 2. According to John x. 40, Jesus went back, after the Feast of Dedication, to Peræa. Thus He must already have been once in Peræa; and this could have occurred only between the Feast of Tabernacles and the Feast of Dedication, that is, between October and December 782. Into this season falls His last abode in Capernaum, and His departure from Galilee (*see Notes on Matthew*). That between the secret travels of Jesus in the former section, and the position of things in the present, much must have intervened, is proved by the discussion going on among the disciples, which issued now in words, as to who should be the greatest among them. The glorious demonstration of Jesus at the Feast of Tabernacles, the healing of the blind man, the favourable feelings of the many, must have again enkindled within them the hopes of His speedy manifestation of the glory of His kingdom. This made them over more desirous to give His prophecy of His death a figurative meaning as referring to the sufferings of Messiah, the temporary obscuration of His name and of His cause. Thus they might come to the question as to who would have a fair prospect of the highest place under Him in His kingdom. Mark is more precise in his narrative here than either Matthew or Luke: first, in regard to the occasion of the act and the special circumstances; secondly, in the scene with the little child. The Lord had already spoken the decisive word, before He placed the child in the midst. Mark records that Jesus embraced the child. In the words of application that follow he is more copious than Matthew, somewhat less copious than Luke. Mark, on the contrary, communicates in the fullest manner the transaction between Jesus and John, which Luke has in brief; and, in the discourse touching the offending hand, &c., he is more solemnly detailed than the other Evangelists. The narrative about the stater, Mark seems to have passed over, as being a narrative which Peter omitted because it made himself prominent.

Ver. 33. **By the way.**—The fleeting journey through Galilee cannot here be meant, but the last return of Jesus from Jerusalem, when the disciples had recovered their tone of mind and their hopes.

Ver. 34. **Who should be the greatest.**—Obviously, only with reference to the Messiah's kingdom,—their hopes of the speedy establishment of which being now rekindled.

Ver. 35. **If any man desire to be first.**—Comp. Matt. xxiii. 12; xx. 27; xviii. 4. Our clause seems in one formula to include two rules: whosoever exalteth himself shall be abased; whosoever humbleth himself shall be exalted. Despotism makes man a slave; spiritual despotism makes him the lowest and most abject of all slaves, who must serve the most external and legal behests of a police for the internal kingdom of God. But voluntary service in the kingdom of love, and under the impulse of humility and self-denial, makes a man a spiritual power, and gives him an unconscious and blessed greatness in the kingdom of God, which does not complacently look at its own reflection. In this sense Christ came to minister unto all (symbol, the feet-washing), and has become Lord over all, Phil. ii. 5-11. But the emphasis falls here obviously upon the second rule.

Ver. 36. **When He had taken him in His arms.**—Peculiar to the vivid and pathetic style of Mark. Comp. ch. x. 16.

Ver. 37. **Whosoever shall receive one of such children.**—The natural child in the arms of Jesus is not only a symbol, but also identical in its susceptibility with the spiritual child; and it signifies, not a Christian ripe in humility, but a beginner in faith. The child baptized or blessed is in the catechumen state, like the thirty years' proselyte before baptism, or the beginner in faith. *See on Matthew*, p. 323.—**Not Me, but Him that.**—Meyer: "Not *non tamquam*, but with rhetorical emphasis the ἐμὲ δέχεται is absolutely denied." At the same time the rhetorical element must be strongly emphasized. It signifies a "much more," or "infinitely more;" with the idea that we receive Christ, with Christ we receive God, if the receiving is of the right kind.

Ver. 38. **And John answered Him.**—The ἀποκρίνεσθαι here, as often, in the wider sense: on a special occasion to begin the conversation. John had a fact in his mind which he must bring into the light of this act of Jesus. Meyer, following Schleiermacher: "The disciples had, to one who uttered the name of Jesus, done the opposite of receive." Or, rather, they had hindered one who in the name of Jesus was receiving the miserable, and doing works of mercy. John now hears that precisely to such an one the greatest promises are given.—**In Thy name.**—The τῷ ὀνόματί σου says less than ἐν τῷ, κ.τ.λ. Comp. Matt. vii. 22; Acts ix. 13. By means of uttering the name of Jesus. Meyer: "But our exorcist was not an impostor, he was a believer; yet not one belonging to the permanent company of Jesus." Had he been a deceiver, he would not have been able to cast out demons by the name of Jesus; for the name of Jesus wrought no magical effects: *see* Acts xix. 13. But if he had been a decided believer, John would have known him as such; for the ἀκολουθεῖν must be understood of actual and real following, and not necessarily of merely external discipleship. The passage therefore means, that there was in him a measure of trust in the name of Jesus, a germ of true faith. But we must not forget that the words are, "he followeth not with *us*," not, "he followeth not *Thee:*" this is certainly the utterance of an excited human party feeling. Gerlach and others suppose that the exorcist might have been a disciple of John the Baptist; but it is to be remembered that John himself did no miracle. All were indeed disciples of John, in the wider sense, who were hoping for the approaching kingdom, and had been baptized of John.—**We forbade him, because.**—We must regard John as the main agent in all this matter, though in perfect understanding and concert with the rest of the disciples. The "*because* he followeth not with us," &c., signifies that they desired of the man a decided following with them, or an abandonment of all working in the name of Jesus. Thus they did not deny that even an unregenerate man might do something by means of the name of Jesus; but they regarded him as not justified in so doing. Their watchword was: first a full conversion, and then the right and ability to work. It is strictly, "We interdicted him from that," or "hindered him." Easily might the prohibition of the disciples disturb his miracle-working confidence.

Ver. 39. **Forbid him not, for.**—Augustin: "*Distinguit inter neutralitatem epicuream et neutralitatem ex infirmitate.*" Such a man, the Lord tells them, would not immediately dishonor His name. His experience would prevent him from so soon turning round and going over to His enemies. And in this there was expressed, at the same time, the hope that he would earlier or later become an actual follower. Jesus, therefore, would impress it upon His disciples that they must honor and protect the isolated beginnings or germs of faith to be found in the world, without the circle of actual believers. We are not violently to constrain the men in whom such beginnings are seen, to adopt prematurely the party of faith: such a course might have a tendency to repel them, and drive them into the camp of the enemy. Moreover, it is contrary to the demands of a germ, and of gradual development; it is contrary to the rights of conscience, and the nature of the kingdom of God, whose kindled sparks of life fall far beyond the central hearth of the Church. But we must carefully distinguish here between forbidding and commanding. It is not permitted the disciples to forbid ; they should pay all respect to the unrestrained influence of Christ, and its results, even beyond the fold of the disciples. But it does not follow from this, that the Lord commands, outside the circle of discipleship also, a premature activity of the beginners in faith. It is wholesome and natural that every energy of faith, in every young Christian, should act and move, according to the measure of its development, under the condition of truth, sincerity, and supreme regard for its own internal growth and well-being. Meyer: "We gather, moreover, from this passage, how mightily the words and influence of Christ had wrought outside the sphere of His permanent dependants, exciting in individuals a degree of spiritual energy that performed miracles on others."

Ver. 40. **For he that is not against you.**—The reading ὑμῶν is better supported than the reading ἡμῶν, which the *Text. Rec.*, Fritzsche, and Tischendorf follow ; and thus the clause constitutes a formal antithesis to the word in Matt. xi. 42. (*See the Critical Notes* on that passage.) "And in order that they might not, in this sacred domain of tender beginnings, hurt any the least sapling, He converts His royal word, *He who is not for Me is against Me*, into a disciple-word for them to use, *He who is not against us is on our part*." (*Leben Jesu*, ii. 10–12 ; comp. Stier on the passage.)

Ver. 41. **Whosoever shall give you a cup of water** (see Matt. x. 42.) The third γάρ, *for :* a threefold significant establishment of the rule laid down by our Lord, *not to hinder beginnings*. First reason : Such a man will not soon become mine enemy. Second reason : If any one were against you, he would give assurance of the fact ; if he is not against you, it is to be assumed at the outset that he is for you. Third reason : The respect and love which is even outwardly shown you in the very slightest degree by men in the world, for Christ's sake, or in His name, proves that they stand in a certain spiritual connection with Him, which under His blessing may increase and become more strict. The smallest token of friendship you receive as disciples of Christ, is a token of friendship to your Master, which is rewarded by Him with the blessing of greater friendship. Thus : 1. The beginning of friendly feeling excludes the thought of a speedy enmity ; 2. so much so, that the cessation of enmity, in any instance, is to be regarded as friendship ; 3. because the slightest token of friendliness, which is understood by that cessation of enmity, is blessed and furthered until it has become decided love and friendship. From the external friendship which is manifested in external proofs of love, men go on to internal friendship : from the disciples of Christ, whom they acknowledge as such, they come to Christ Himself. Thus we must esteem holy all the roots, relations, and tendencies of good which Christianity finds in the world,—yet that Christianity which does not deny itself and the Lord (ἐν τῷ ὀνόματί μου). We assume that the three *fors* all directly refer to the "forbid him not," without disparaging the connection in which they stand to each other.

Ver. 42. **And whosoever shall offend one of these little ones.**—What follows is, down to the close, a strong utterance of our Lord against that fanatical ecclesiastical zealotry which is so much disposed to throw stumbling-blocks in the way of beginners in the faith, by imposing traditional dogmatic articles of faith. Saunier, De Wette, and others have lost the connection here. But it is evident enough when we bear in mind that the words of Christ, vers. 43–47, have here a reference altogether different from that which the related words of Matt. v. 29, 30 have. (Comp. *Leben Jesu*, ii. 2.)—Our passage forms a parallel with Matt. xviii. 6 *seq.* Matthew, however, did not adhere strictly to the place where the words were spoken ; Mark places the locality and circumstances very clearly before us. The sons of thunder had a series of their own particular crises to pass through, just as Peter had ; a series of crises for their fanatical and enthusiastic party zeal. The first is found here ; the second soon follows, on their departure from Galilee (Luke ix. 54); the third falls into a later period, before the final going up to Jerusalem, ch. x. 35.

Ver. 43. **And if thy hand offend thee.**—For the meaning of these words in this connection, *see* the notes on the parallel in *Matthew*. Offences of the hand, of the eye, and of the foot ; or, stumblingblocks of fanatical hierarchism, of heretical Gnosticism, and of political proselytism. In the formal shape which the word of our Lord assumes in Mark, "it may be regarded as an ideal formulary, which is designed to suggest to His Church the pious gentleness of the hand, the sacred spiritual clearness of the eye, and the peaceful and amiable apostolical movement of the foot." (*Leben Jesu*, ii. 2, 1016.)

Ver. 44. **Where their worm.**—Three times solemnly repeated. The reference to Isa. lxvi. 24 is manifest. It is a concrete expression for suffering in the fire of hell, Gehenna.

Ver. 45. **It is better for thee.**—Comp. on *Matthew*.

Ver. 49. **For every one shall be salted with fire.**—On this clause, which has no parallel (and which De Wette, Baur, and others, have so much doubted about), see Meyer, and the treatises referred to by him. Meyer, however, is wrong in interpreting this of the fire of hell mentioned previously. He explains : "πᾶς cannot mean every one generally ; but must, in harmony with the context, be restricted to those who in ver. 48 are described by αὐτῶν ; since afterwards another class is distinguished by πᾶσα θυσία from that which is meant by πᾶς, and its predicate is opposed to the predicate of the latter : πυρί and ἁλί are antitheses." They are indeed distinct points, but yet related to each other ; for otherwise we should not read "Every one must be salted with fire." We therefore thus understand the passage : Every (sinful) man must, according to the typical meaning of the burnt-offering, enter into the suffering of fire : either into the fire of Gehenna, which then in his case represents the salt which was wanting to him ; or as the burnt-offering of God into the fiery suffering of tribulation, those renunciations, namely and especially, which had just been mentioned—the sacrifice of the eye, the hand, and the foot—after he had been previously consecrated with the salt of the Spirit. This rule holds irreversibly good : those offending members which were not, as God's sacrifices, previously salted with salt, pass immediately into the fiery sufferings of punishment, which then represent and take the place of the salting. The καί in the clause, "*and* every sacrifice," does not therefore mean ὡς, καθώς ; but it marks the specific case in which the being salted precedes the suffering of fire, and in which it may perhaps (as in John's own later history) more or less supply the place of, and involve the fiery suffering of, *external* tribulations (1 Cor. iii. 13). Meyer's separation of the salt and fire, and his antithesis between them, with his exclusive reference of the fire to the punishment of the ungodly, are found in Grotius, Lightfoot, and others. On the other hand, both are referred to the good by Euthym. Zigabenus ("the fire of faith in God, the salt of love to man"), by Luther (the Gospel is a fire and a salt: the old man is crucified, renewed, salted), Calovius, Kuinoel, Schott.—Olshausen thus agrees with our interpretation: "On account of the universal sinfulness of the race, every one must be salted with fire; whether by his voluntarily entering upon a course of self-denial and earnest renunciation of his sins, or by his being involuntarily cast into the place of punishment." Similarly Ewald. The γάρ gives the reason of the exhortation which preceded. Sacrifice the hand, the foot, &c., in the self-renunciation of godliness, rather than fall with your whole being into the fire of judgment as a sacrifice of death. For this is a fundamental law for sinful humanity: all must enter the fire. But if the fire becomes to man a sacrificial fire, his sacrifice must be voluntarily prepared and seasoned with salt (made savory, like food); otherwise, the fire of Gehenna *supplies* the place of the salt and the sacrifice.

Ver. 50. **Salt is good.**—The καλόν is not exhausted by the word *good*. Something preëminently good in its kind and effect is intended. The better any product of nature is in itself, the worse it is in its corruption. Therein the salt is an image of man. Saltless salt is not to be saved; and so with the spiritless disciple, or Christian, or minister (without chrisma: without salt). *See* on Matt, v. 13.—**Have salt in yourselves, and have peace.**—The salt is figurative, not merely signifying wisdom, but the Spirit as *the Spirit of discipline;* and on that account it is the symbol of the covenant,—a blessing the preservation and assurance of which has peace for its result. The "have peace one with another" is therefore a consecutive exhortation. Have peace amongst yourselves, such peace as you must have if you have that salt. From this last application it follows that the Lord regarded the contention of the disciples, and their zeal against a beginner in faith not walking in their circle, under the same point of view. All undevout and unholy zealotry, whether towards those within or those without, He explains as resulting from one fundamental offence and fault, —the lack of salt and self-resignation, the want of the Spirit's discipline and of consecration to God.— Here, again, it is Mark who has given most prominence to words of the Lord which most strongly corrected and admonished His disciples.

DOCTRINAL AND ETHICAL.

1. *See* on the parallel places in *Matthew* and *Luke*.

2. Between a hierarchy and the true catechumen's nurture of the little ones in the Church, there is an essential repugnance. The latter seeks to train up the babes in faith to the full maturity of faith; the former would not only keep the babes in infancy, but would train up the adult to be dumb babes. The extreme adherents of hierarchy and the Baptist principle agree, in that the former ascribe no prerogative to baptism, but make the baptized laity a subordinate class of imperfect Christians; and the latter, with hierarchical exclusiveness, deal like a clerus with the little ones in faith.—The sign which Jesus gave to the Church by His repeated embracing (according to Mark) of the children, was directed the first time rather against the fanatical churchspirit of the hierarchy, and the last time (ch. x. 16) rather against the theological school-spirit of the Baptists. *Whosoever of you:* compare the history of the Papacy. Gregory the Great called himself the *servus servorum*, that he might be the first. The hierarchy has taken the ironical word of Christ's Spirit with unthinking and unintelligent literality; like the word of our Lord, on another occasion, concerning the two swords, Luke xxii. 38 (*see Leben Jesu*, ii. 3, 1345), and other similar expressions.

3. *But John answered Him.*—This history teaches us, in connection with ch. x. 35 and Luke ix. 54, how Christ dealt with and purified the zeal, noble but not yet free from fanatical excitement, of the disciples, and especially what may be called the idealistic fanatical zeal of the sons of thunder, as it formed a contrast to the realistic fanatical zeal of Peter. With every development of true faith there is interwoven, especially in its first stages, a certain measure of that other quality which stains its purity, and requires to be eliminated. But when its heart is sound, the flame is soon cleared of its bedimming smoke; the life of faith becomes ever more christianly human, wise, and gentle (*see* Jas. iii. 17, 18). But where the heart is evil, or becomes so through the influence of external things, the life of faith declines into fanaticism and perishes, as the history of Pharisaism and Judaism everywhere proves. Such a fanaticism lived indeed in the soul of Judas; he went on through enthusiasm and excitement to apostasy. The answer of John was a frank avowal, and revelation of himself or confession, before the Lord (*see Leben Jesu*, ii. 2).

4. *The connection of the beginnings of faith:*— pious work, ver. 38; its root in the devout mind, ver. 39; its nourishment in devout habits, humanity, ver. 41. Hence loving care for the disciples, leading to quiet recognition of their interests, and thence to active usefulness in the name of Jesus.

5. *The bigoted conduct of the disciples towards these beginnings of faith.*—In its issue and result an offence or injury to the little ones, and in a twofold sense: either as they are dishonored and wronged, or as they are offended and tempted to resistance and enmity. In its origin, it is an internal offence; offending self through the hand, or the foot, or the eye (*see Crit. Notes*, ver. 43, and on *Matthew*). In the Church, and for the Church, or in relation to the bride of Christ, that law of self-renunciation and self-sacrifice holds good which is the basis of the relations of marriage, Matt. v. 27 *seq.* We must be subject to the church, if we would edify it, Rom. xii. 3 *seq.*

6. That a millstone were hanged.—*See* on *Matthew*.

7. *Into hell, where the fire is not quenched.*— Concerning the difference between hell and Gehenna, and the kingdom of the dead or Sheol, *see* on *Matthew*. The additional clause, "where their worm dieth not," etc., points back, as it has been remarked, to the passage Isa. lxvi. 24, where the valley of Hinnom is expressly made a symbol of the punishment of the reprobate, and the Old Testament germ of the doctrine of future eternal punishment distinctly appears, as also it does in the earlier Cherem or death-sentence of the law, and in later passages, such as Ezek. xx. 47; Dan. xii. 2, and others. According to the passage in Isaiah, the bodies of those who were apostate from Jehovah lay without before the holy city, an abomination to all

flesh. The worm of corruption, which devoured them from within, died not; and the fire of judgment, which destroyed them from without, was not extinguished. And this manifestly presented a symbolical idea of eternal suffering; for, literally taken, the fire would be extinguished and consumed with the bodies and the worms. Eternal destruction within, eternal judgment without, and these in eternal reciprocal influence. On the doctrine of hell, compare dogmatic treatises.

8. *For every one must be salted with fire, and every sacrifice.*—Fire is the symbol of life in its renewing power, and especially of the judicial power and working of God, renewing by a divine energy: thus it is the presence and action of God in the full energy of His holy, penetrating nature: Gen. xv. 17; Ex. iii. 2; Mal. iii. 3; iv. 1. Hence it is for the sinful man generally a judicial visitation of God, the mercifully rebuking and correcting manifestation of His nature (Mal. iii. 3; iv. 1); for the penitent, believing man, it is the saving judgment of grace, the purifying fire, the fire of new quickening, transforming, glorification (Acts ii. 3); for the reprobate it is a fire of condemning judgment, Heb. x. 27; xii. 29.

9. This gives us the true meaning and significance of the sacrificial fire, of the fire of the altar. It forms a counterpart and contrast to the fire of hell. It is the fire of God, into which man voluntarily enters with his offering, in order that he may escape falling into the terror of the eternal fire. Thus, if we strictly judge ourselves, we shall not be judged. This absolute and inviolable law of the fire-alternative was symbolically exhibited by the Old Testament sacrifice: the Christian must have the reality of it accomplished in himself, whilst he makes himself, as it respects those members and their actions (hand, foot, eye) which might hurt his Christian life, a sacrifice upon the altar. This self-sacrifice is a burnt-offering, inasmuch as the Christian places himself daily at the Lord's disposal in pure self-dedication (Rom. xii.); it is a sin-offering, inasmuch as he actually renounces and rids himself of all those impulses and acts which are a hindrance. This applies, however, not only to sensual tendencies (Matt. v.), but also to those spiritual and ecclesiastical impulses of the self which are colored and disguised by religion (as it respects place and prerogative). Yet the sacrifice must not proceed from fear, but from loving obedience; it must not be an act of constrained dread, but voluntarily, an act of the spirit, of self-discipline. And that is signified by the salt (*see* the article *Salz* in WINER, BUCHNER, and the *Stuttgart Bibelwörterbuch*). The salt is the symbol of the Spirit, as the spirit of purifying and conserving discipline; even as oil is the symbol of the Spirit, as the Spirit of religious life and the living flame of devotion. Salt is the preserving, cleansing virtue of life: the Spirit who checks and kills sin germinating within. Fire is the transforming power of life: the Spirit who punishes the sin that is present, separating the sinner from sin as the judgment of grace, or destroying the sinner with his sin as the judgment of condemnation. Salt is discipline and conservation; fire is punishment, judgment, purification. Out of the fiery condemnation of Sodom a sea of salt flowed forth. The punishment of the doomed is a source of discipline and healing for those who still live. As fire and light are related to each other, and yet form a direct contrast, so it is with salt and light, Matt. v. 13, 14. Because the salt signified the spirit of discipline, it was needful (according to Ezek. xliii. 24, the testimony of this passage, and Jewish tradition) to every offering, and not only to the meat-offering (Lev. ii. 13); hence it was the proper symbol of the establishment and renewal of the covenant in the sacrifice. Hence, on the one hand, the salt is salt of the covenant (Lev. ii. 13), and, on the other, the covenant with Jehovah is a covenant of salt (Num. xviii. 19; 2 Chron. xiii. 5); while, in the common life of the Orientals, it was a sign of sacred covenant engagements and obligations. (*See* WINER, and BAHR, *Symbolik*.) To eat salt together, meant to make peace, and enter into covenant with each other (ROSENMULLER, *Morgenland*, ii. 150.) But as salt, or the spirit of discipline, was the fundamental condition of peace with God, so it was also the fundamental condition of peace in the Church, of the mutual peace of Christian people. Hence the word of our Lord: Have salt in yourselves, and peace one with another. The disciples were amongst themselves to *have* salt, but for the earth to *be* salt. In reference to the symbolism of the sacrifices, *see* the works on the subject by Bähr, Kurtz, and Hengstenberg.

10. In connection with the contrast, wide as heaven, between the salt and sacrificial fire on the one hand, and the unquenchable fire of Gehenna on the other, there must also be observed a certain relation, so far as, first, the salt is regarded as a symbol of the sacrificial fire; and, secondly, as the fire is regarded as a kind of salt: the Lord says that all must be salted with fire. The contrast between the two is this: the salt sustains and conserves; the fire, on the contrary, destroys and annihilates. But there is something more than a contrast; there is a strict relation. The salt preserves and sustains by an influence resembling that of fire: it is keen, biting, and pervasive; like a subtle flame, it penetrates all that is corruptible, separates that which is most corruptible and foul, whilst it fixes and quickens that which is sound. Thus it effects a kind of transformation or metamorphosis. So, on the other hand, the fire is a salt of higher potency: it destroys that which is perishable, and thereby establishes the imperishable in its purest perfection; it leads to new and more beautiful forms of being. Salt seems to petrify the object, fire seems to volatilize it; but the salt fixes it in its healthy normal condition, whilst the fire bears it upwards in its pure constituent elements to heaven. Thus the believer is first purified by the salt; but then by the fire of internal and external tribulation he is carried up to God. So it is with the whole world of mankind and the earth itself. First, it is purified and preserved by the salt of the apostolical Church (Matt. v. 13); then by the final fire at the end of the world it will be delivered from its condition of curse, and glorified: 2 Thess. i. 8; 2 Pet. iii. 10.

HOMILETICAL AND PRACTICAL.

See on the parallel passages in *Matthew* and *Luke*. —Despotism over fellow-disciples, and proselytizing those not disciples, spring from the same source: from the self-exaltation of a proud and unpurified zeal. —Spiritual pride is the common source of all hierarchical and fanatical movements.—The silence of the other disciples compared with John's answering: 1. In reference to the persons:—the more noble the disciple, the more free he is to make honest and open confession. 2. In reference to the matter:—

fanatical zeal in the Church is more readily confessed than the impulses of proud ambition and the lust of ecclesiastical dominion, because it is in its first motives much more noble and less guilty.—The question concerning the greater in the Church, is a question in the way to the judgment-seat of Christ. 1. It will not be resolved before: the primacy waits till then. 2. It will be resolved in the end by the Lord, as He resolved it at the beginning (the first, the last). —The simple image of the pure Church of Christ: 1. Christ sits upon His throne; 2. the preaching sounds out, Whosoever will be first, etc.; 3. the only image in the Church is a little child; 4. the prospect: revelation of the great God through the humble care of the little ones.—The Church of apostolical humility. It marks Christ's word, "Whosoever will be first," etc., 1. in its literal significance, a threatening word against all despotism in the external, legal Church; 2. in its spiritual meaning, a word of promise for humble, ministering love in the congregation of His Spirit.—The child and the Apostles: 1. The child their master; 2. the child their scholar; 3. the child their fellow.—How we may receive with the little child the highest life in the name of Jesus: 1. The Lord Christ himself; 2. God himself.—How we may receive with the little child the great God: 1. If the child is received in the name of Jesus; 2. if Jesus is received in the name of God.—The beautiful confession of John.—Christ the holy Master of all the sons of thunder in His Church: 1. How He represses the sons of thunder (or reduces to silence the thunder of carnal zeal); 2. how He arouses the sons of thunder (or lets the thunder of the Spirit resound, Rev. x. 4).—The prohibition of John, and the commandment of the Lord, in relation to free labor in the Church, and for the cause of Christ.—The law of fanatical zeal, and the law of the spirit of freedom in the Church.—Ecclesiastical party zeal in the light of the word and Spirit of Christ.—Christ the defender and guardian of all beginnings of faith, and of all germs of spiritual life: 1. Through His Scriptureword; 2. through His apostolical infant baptism; 3. through the evangelical rights of personal couscience. —The water-cups of mild, human customs, in their connection with the sacramental cup of the God-man. —The connection between false fire of zeal in the Church and the fire of hell.—The three great dangers of ecclesiastical zeal: 1. Dangers of the hand; 2. dangers of the foot; 3. dangers of the eye.—The law of sacred gentleness in the service of Christ.—The true sacrificial fire of self-denial and self-mortification, in relation to the fiery flame of hell: 1. The relation: all must be salted with fire. 2. The contrast: to be prepared for the fire by salt, or to be salted with fire.—We cannot escape the fire; but we have the choice between the fire of life and the fire of death.—Discipline of the Spirit: the fundamental condition of healthy life in the Church: 1. Of the right warfare, 2. of the right peace.—The zeal of Christ the purifying fire for the zeal of His people. —The thundering of men, and the Lord's thunder; or, the exaggeration of little strength, and the mildness of great strength: 1. In their origin: *a.* want of love, want of self-government; *b.* the zeal of love and divine moderation. 2. In their manifestation: *a.* thundering of the cannons, of the bulls, of the curses, scattering sudden and swift destruction; *b.* trumpet-calls to penitence, words of correcting love, alarming and yet not destroying. 3. In their effects: *a.* lost and ended in time; *b.* dispensing blessings for a time, and bringing salvation for eternity.—How Christ, with the anticipating grief of holy love, was inflamed with zeal against all covetous and party frenzy of zeal in His Church.—The alternative of the two fires of history: indifference must be burnt away, either, 1. in the fires of salvation, or, 2. in the fires of judgment.

STARKE:—Doubtless it is our duty to wrest from others their hurtful errors; but we are also bound to bear with them for a while, and give them time to come to a better apprehension.—QUESNEL:— Pride reigns in almost all conditions. Few are content to be placed beneath others; most people are intent only upon getting above their fellows, and mount aloft.—*Nova. Bibl. Tub.*:—Alas, how many will stand before Him with shame and fear, when Christ shall demand an account of all the useless and sinful contentions which they have mutually indulged in!—HEDINGER:—Pride, conceit, ambition, are all utterly out of harmony with the spirit of true Christianity.—LUTHER:—That man has a true nobility who is profoundly humble in heart.—True greatness consists in perfect lowliness.—QUESNEL:— Blessed is it to rest in the arms of the love of Jesus. —It is an honor to receive the great into our house; greater still to receive those who are lacking in all things but the spirit of Christ.—It is a holy work to do good to children, especially to poor and orphan children.—OSIANDER:—The most pious, devoted, and faithful ministers in the Church have their failings.—HEDINGER:—God has a marvellous method in the dispensation of His graces and gifts, and we must not be too ready to reject what is not as yet perfectly pure and flawless, Phil. i. 16.—QUESNEL:—We too often blend our own selves, our prejudices and notions, with the things of God; and our pride uses the honor of His name as a mere cloak.—OSIANDER: —Instead of envying and grudging, we should praise God for the wonderful variety of gifts which He bestows for the common good.—*Bibl. Wirt.*:—God's gifts are not bound to any particular person, or to any particular condition; but He distributes them Himself freely, if He will, to whom He will, and when He will.—CRAMER:—To deal with little children is a delicate matter; we may soon plant either what is good or what is evil in them.—That young people have offences so often thrown in their way is one reason why there is so much wickedness among the adult.—*Bibl. Wirt.*:—To give offence is, in those who hold the office of correction, a threefold sin: 1. They sin themselves; 2. they make others sin; 3. they cannot use their office.—To enter into life halt or lame: his fleshly lusts are as dear to man as one of his members.—CRAMER:—Who can doubt about hell, and the damnation of hell, when Christ has so often repeated and confirmed the truth?—Our foot offends us in two ways: 1. If it goes in evil ways; 2. if it stands still.—QUESNEL:—To be salted with the fire of hell, as an offering to the divine righteousness.—*Bibl. Wirt.*:—If God's word is falsified, or not with all solemnity and earnestness dealt with, there is no other salt for the sinful flesh: it breeds all kinds of corruption, and all kinds of sins have dominion.—CANSTEIN:—Faithful teachers must give all diligence to maintain the integrity of the sound doctrine of the gospel; yet they must avoid all contention, and approve themselves not only true, but also full of love and peace.

LISCO:—In earthly empires power rules; in the kingdom of heaven rules the power of devoted, self-sacrificing, and self-humbling love (ver. 38).—Secret pride was the reason why the disciples so acted.

But Jesus is displeased with their conduct; for He would have a love in them that should be ready to love heartily everything in others, wherever seen, that presented anything spiritually congenial.—Jesus rejects and condemns all casting off, shutting out, and repulsion, as unchildlike. The gnawing worm of the evil conscience, and the burning smart of divine wrath, are figures of the eternal destruction which will befall the seducers.—All things, that is, the whole of humanity, must be salted with fire.—GERLACH:—He who is not against you, is with you. Only in things merely external does Jesus include Himself with the disciples in the *we: We* go up to Jerusalem.—But, when internal relations are in question, He does not say *we* and *us*, any more than He says *Our Father*. And for this reason: 1. Because He distinguishes himself from them as sinners; 2. because He identifies himself with them as believers, —the branches united with the vine, John xv. 1.—He who is not with Me, etc. Both words must always be united; so that Christ's disciples must take equal care to instruct the ignorant and to bear with the weak, 1 Thess. v. 14.—BRAUNE:—They had indeed the feeling that this thought was not right in the sight of Christ. Therefore He asks them about it; He gives them opportunity to utter it aloud. And thus their Master makes them sensible how exceedingly improper that thought was.—Earthly, temporal relations, they carried over into their notions of the eternal kingdom of God.—There are indeed distinctions even in the kingdom of God (Peter, John, James); but that He termed Peter the Rock could not at that time have been misunderstood by the Apostles, as He was misunderstood by Catholic Christendom, especially by the whole of the Middle Ages. —At first they kept silence; and when they spoke, it was only through shame. And so it was right. It is not well to be put to shame at death; better is it to come forward and be exposed before God, and the Saviour and His people.—With the unpretending act of receiving a little child, He connects the greatest of all, the receiving God.—With perfect right the disciples of Jesus held their vocation high and precious. But that they supposed their vocation the only channel through which God could reveal His Son in men's hearts, was a great error.—We should be willing to trace and follow out all the threads in others which lead to Christ.—There is such a thing as an internal, though it may be weak, inclination towards Christ, without any external and full fellowship.—The Redeemer undoubtedly had in view those offences which are connected with the teaching office in the Church, when contentions arise, and love, humility, and regard for the little ones are discountenanced. We do not always perceive, or at least sufficiently consider, what great offence and damage may ensue from the neglect of heartfelt humility of poverty of heart and lowliness of spirit.—All that gives offence, and all that takes offence, must alike in the end be abolished and vanish away.—Jesus took no offence, and gave no offence; for God was in Him.—Happy are we if His spirit dwelleth in us.

SCHLEIERMACHER:—(With reference to Matt. xx. 28, and the ministering of Christ.)—He must in spirit descend into the unsaved depths of the human heart: it was needful that He should see how, and in what variety of ways, the most various tempers and spirits might be aided and saved—brought to sink into their own absolute nothingness, in order that they might attain to the new birth in Him.—That was His ministering; and in this sense He says that He—who is the first in the kingdom of heaven, who is all in all, He who is the One supreme over all and in all, He in whom all have all things—is at the same time the servant of all.—The greater the power of Christ in the disciple, and the more that power works through him for the well-being of others, the greater he is in the kingdom of heaven. —To receive God—what greater thing can be conceived!—(The transaction with John.) There is a condition under which the gradual influences of the Spirit best effect their work, and that is undisturbed self-concentration. The more men are excited in reference to external things, the more are their minds closed against higher influences; but when they are in perfect repose, the gentle inspirations of the Divine Spirit have their better effect.

BRIEGER:—Are we to understand the words to mean, that he who burns with desire to be the first should be the last, in order to compass that end? Would any such humility as that possess a value? The Lord could not possibly have intended to say that the being little was a means to becoming great. The "If any man will" is intended rather to show the way in which a man becomes great in the kingdom of God, without willing to be so.—This way is that of self-denial.—Because the Lord from heaven entered into the condition, or assumed the form, of a servant, His Church also must take the same form.—To receive is here indeed a high thing: to take up to Himself.—In reference to ourselves, we have to observe the word "He who is not with Me," etc. In reference to others, we have to observe the word "He that is not against you," etc., that we may judge them in the spirit of Jesus.

GOSSNER:—In the kingdom of humility there is no contention.—The more humble and simple we are, the nearer we are to the Saviour.—The holiest words, without anointing and salt, are good for nothing.—BAUER:—By their ruling we know the great ones of this world; by their serving we know the great ones of the kingdom of heaven.—Where love, the sacred regard for faith however little, is wounded, the retribution of the kingdom of heaven is severe.

PART THIRD.

THE Lord's Conflicts and Victories in Peræa. Transition from the Old Church to the New. The Disciples gathered together for the Passion.

FIRST SECTION.

CARNAL MARRIAGE LEGISLATION OF THE PHARISEES, AND THE SPIRITUAL MARRIAGE LEGISLATION OF THE LORD.

CHAPTER X. 1-12.

(Parallel: Matt. xix. 1-12.)

1 And he arose from thence, and cometh into the coasts of Judea, by [through] the farther side of Jordan: and the people resort unto him again; and, as he was wont, he
2 taught them again. And the Pharisees came to him, and asked him, Is it lawful for a
3 man to put away *his* wife? tempting him. And he answered and said unto them,
4 What did Moses command you? And they said, Moses suffered to write a bill of di-
5 vorcement, and to put *her* away. And Jesus answered and said unto them, For the
6 hardness of your heart he wrote you this precept: But from the beginning of the crea-
7 tion God made them male and female. For this cause shall a man leave his father and
8 mother, and cleave to his wife; And they twain shall be one flesh: so then they are no
9 more twain, but one flesh. What therefore God hath joined together, let not man put
10 asunder. And in the house his disciples asked him again of the same *matter*.
11 And he saith unto them, Whosoever shall put away his wife, and marry another, com-
12 mitteth adultery against her. And if a woman shall put away her husband, and be married to another, she committeth adultery.

[1] Ver. 1.—The reading of Cod. A, (διὰ τοῦ πέραν, &c.) must not be given up, with Lachmann and Tischendorf (who read καὶ πέραν), on account of B., C.*, L.
[2] Ver. 2.—Elzevir reads οἱ Φαρισαῖοι; but the article is not supported.
[3] Ver. 6.—The ὁ Θεός is wanting in B., C., L., Δ., &c., and omitted by Tischendorf [and Meyer, and bracketed by Lachmann].
[4] Ver. 10.—Περὶ τούτου. Lachmann, Tischendorf, Meyer, following A., B., C.
[5] Ver. 12.—Lachmann and Tischendorf read γαμήσῃ ἄλλον instead of γαμηθῇ ἄλλῳ, following B., C., D., L., Δ.

EXEGETICAL AND CRITICAL.

See the notes on the parallel in *Matthew*, xix.—Christ's abode in Peræa embraces three occurrences: the treatment of the subject of divorce, the bringing of the little children to Jesus, and the rich young man. These transactions all belong, doubtless, to the second abode of Christ in Peræa. We must, according to the connection of the evangelical narratives, assume two residences in Peræa; for we know that Jesus, after the Feast of Tabernacles in the year of persecution 782, returning into Galilee, assembled His disciples there; that with them He journeyed through the boundaries of Galilee and Samaria to Peræa (see Luke ix. 51–52, xvii. 11–19; comp. *Leben Jesu*, ii. 2, 1053), appeared then in Jerusalem at the Feast of the dedication, and afterwards returned back to Peræa, John x. 42. That the circumstances related by the Evangelists Matthew and Mark belong to the close of the second abode in Peræa, is manifest from the intimation that the rich young man came to Him as He was on the point of journeying; and the same applies to Matthew's account of the mothers bringing their children. But with this last transaction that concerning divorce was closely connected.—Concerning Peræa, *see* the *Critical Notes* on *Matthew*, as also concerning the *double* residence in Peræa, and the significance of the Peræan narrative in relation to the founding and preparation of the new congregation, the Christian Church.—Christian ecclesiastical regulations begin with regulations for the house; with the Christian legislation, 1. for marriage; 2. for children; 3. for property.

As to the relation of Mark to the Synoptists in the Peræan sections, he and Matthew alone record the matter concerning divorce. Mark states more precisely than Matthew that Jesus penetrated through Peræa to the borders of the land, ver. 1. In Matthew, on the other hand, there is a more definite account given of the first journey of Jesus to Peræa, accompanied by a great train. Matthew says that great multitudes followed Him, and He healed them there. Mark says that the people resorted to Him again (πάλιν, again in Peræa), and that, as He was wont, He taught them again. In the Lord's answer to the tempting question concerning divorce, Mark places first the reference to the Mosaic law of marriage, and brings in the paradisaical law afterwards: Matthew inverts that order. But it is in harmony with the character of Mark, that he introduces all by the piercing word of decision. The rebuke of the Pharisees is, moreover, made more keen by the fact that he assigns the saying concerning the Christian marriage law (vers. 10–12, compare Matthew ver. 9, ch. v. 32) *to the house* in which Jesus continued His discourse with the disciples on this question. Here also, as often elsewhere, Mark shows that the Lord, after His intercourse with the people, retreated to the house, that is, the inn, where He had been received, for the sake of confidentially continuing His words to the disciples. These are the lesser images of the Lord's greater retreats.—The words that follow were not for the Pharisees. Mark gives the addition, " If a woman shall put away her husband ; " but then he omits the conversation between the disciples and the Lord concerning the difficulty of true marriage, " If the case of the man," etc. (Matt. xix. 10–12). In the section about the children (which Luke also has), Mark alone makes it prominent that Jesus was displeased with the disciples. He records, in common with Luke, the saying about not receiving the kingdom of God as a little child. That Jesus here again took the children in His arms and embraced them, as He had done the child in Capernaum, Mark alone mentions. He also makes it more distinctly prominent than Mathew does, ver. 15, that the rich young man came to the Lord on the occasion of His leaving Peræa. Luke alone tells us that the young man was a ruler, probably a ruler of the synagogue. But Mark alone records that, after the declaration " All these have I kept from my youth up," Jesus looked upon him and loved him ; as he also later inserts the Lord's approbation of the questioning scribe, ch. xii. 28 *seq.* To him we owe the striking and vivid trait, that the rich young man put on a gloomy and fallen countenance (στυγνάσας) after the Lord's answer. The amazement of the disciples at the word, " How hardly shall the rich," etc., Mark exhibits as continued and increased, even after the Lord's explanation, " How hard is it for them that trust in riches." In the transaction that followed, between Peter and the Lord, Mark is more express than Luke in recording that Peter only *began* in his confusion to inquire about the reward, and that he did not give full expression to his words. He omits the clause, " What shall we have therefore ? " which Matthew inserts. It is very remarkable that Mark omits here again the saying of Jesus concerning the twelve thrones of the Apostles (Matt. ver. 28), even as he had omitted the special prerogatives of Peter. It is obvious to suggest on this point, that the saying about "judging the twelve tribes of Israel" was not so easily intelligible to Gentile Christians (although Luke also has it, ch. xxii. 30). On the other hand, Mark gives the broad and comprehensive promise of the Lord to the disciples who renounce all, and in the most full detail : ver. 30, there is the hundred-fold compensation, houses, and brethren, etc., already in the present life, although amidst persecutions.

Ver. 1. **And He arose from thence.**—In the wider sense, from Galilee ; in the narrower sense, from Capernaum, where He gathered together His disciples. — **By the farther side of Jordan.**— That Jesus did not merely come to Peræa, but travelled through Peræa to the borders of Judæa, that is, to the most eastern limits of Peræa, is plain even from the words of Matthew ; but is still more plainly declared in the expression here used by Mark. For the whole of Peræa could hardly be described as the borders of Judæa in the wider sense. A whole province of a land can never be merely regarded as its border. On the immediate occasion of this journey to Peræa, *see* on *Matthew, Critical Notes.*— **Again.**—The repeated πάλιν seems to have been employed in consequence of the distinct remembrance of a double abode of Jesus in Peræa. At any rate, the events that follow belong to the second residence.

Ver. 2. **Asked Him.** — Meyer: " Mark omits, what Matthew gives, the properly tempting element in the question, κατὰ πᾶσαν αἰτίαν." But, according to the explanation of Ewald (*see Critical Notes* on *Matthew*), the question was a critical and tempting one, even without that addition, because it was dangerous in the territory of Herod Antipas to say anything against divorce. De Wette supposes that the Pharisees may have been aware of the Saviour's earlier declaration concerning divorce. That may be true ; in any case they might very well guess that, on this question, His utterance would perfectly coincide with that of the Baptist. Either, thought they, He must in His answer touch Herod too closely, or the Baptist ; that is, He must fall under the condemnation either of worldly power, or of the pious.

Ver. 3. **What did Moses command you?** —The order of the main points is not the same in Mark as in Matthew. Matthew comes down from the paradisaical institute to the Mosaic ; Mark, on the contrary, rises from the latter to the former, and moreover makes Jesus Himself put the question concerning the law of Moses, and the tempter give the reply. This seems to have been the natural order. Elsewhere we have it as the first counter-question of Jesus : What is written in the law ? (*See* ver. 19, and Luke x. 26.)

Ver. 4. **Moses suffered to write** (see Deut. xxiv. 1).—In Matthew we read, Why then did Moses *command* to give a writing of divorcement, and to put her away? and the answer of Jesus : Moses, *because of the hardness of your hearts, suffered* you to put away your wives. And in Mark's account of the Pharisees' words, they give, as in Matthew, a distorted view of the Mosaic law. Moses had *suffered* to divorce, and *restrictingly commanded* that a letter of divorce be given in addition. In Matthew, it is true, the opposition between the design of the Pharisees and the mind of Moses is made more expressly prominent. But in Mark, the opposition is found in the emphatic statement, that Moses wrote this commandment on account of the hardness of their hearts ; that is, not in order to divorce, but, with the divorce, to give a *bill* of divorce therewith. The two accounts, in fact, are, as to their results, one and the same. The bill of divorce found divorce existing ; it was intended to limit and restrain it, and make it more moral. The man who put away his wife, required the services of a learned scribe in order to construct the bill of divorce ; it was necessary that he should give the grounds of the separation, and the ordinance of the lawgiver required those grounds never to be light or trivial. Moreover, there were two cases in which the marriage was indissoluble,— viz., when a man dishonoured a virgin, and when he slanderously denied the virginity of his young wife (Deut. xxii. 19, 29). In Mark, also, more weight is attached to the other point of opposition which our Lord brings out : His appealing to the paradisaical ordinance. We must also notice the expression, *wrote this precept*. It refers to a written, restricting law for hardness of heart, in contradistinction to the everlasting and original commandments of paradise: hence the written word is to be interpreted in harmony with these last.

Ver. 7. **For this cause shall a man.**—The words of Adam (Gen. ii. 24) are in Matthew words of God; in Mark, words of Christ. It is all the same; for Adam uttered those words prophetically as a paradisaical, divine, fundamental ordinance. They are words of God, as being eternally valid; and words of Christ, as rules for life to be reëstablished and sanctified. The Futures indicate the necessary realization of the original relation and condition of the sexes in marriage. As it *is* in reality and principle, it must *be* in development. *See Critical Notes on Matthew.*

Ver. 10. **And in the house His disciples asked Him.**—Here, as often elsewhere, our Lord, according to Mark's account, retreated, after a public transaction with the people, into the house, where He followed up His public teaching by more confidential instruction. Meyer: "The two Evangelists here differ, as it respects the place, the persons to whom our Lord speaks, and the substance of what He says." He then gives the account of Matthew the preference. But the thought of ver. 11 is already found in the words of ver. 9: What therefore God hath joined together, let not man put asunder. Divorce was by that word forbidden. It is an error to speak of any difference here; all we can say is, that Mark gave a more specific account. And this is strictly in harmony with the circumstances of the case; it was fit that Christ should give His fullest utterance concerning the New Testament law of marriage within the more confidential circle of His disciples.

Ver. 11. **Committeth adultery.**—The marriage contracted with the one is adultery towards the other. Meyer supposes that ἐπ' αὐτήν must mean, "in reference to her," that is, the forsaken woman. But, literally, ἐπ' αὐτήν refers back to the last mentioned. The great point is, that the adultery against the first woman is consummated by marriage with the second, and thus the second marriage is made into adultery. "The μὴ ἐπὶ πορνείᾳ (Matthew) is omitted by Mark. But it makes no difference, as this reason for divorce is self-understood." (Meyer.)

Ver. 12. **And if a woman.**—Meyer denies the genuineness of this added clause. Among the Greeks and Romans it certainly was customary for the woman to be the abandoned party; but not among the Jews, since the examples they furnish—Michal (1 Sam. xxv. 44), Herodias (Matt. xiv. 4), Salome (Joseph. Antiq. 15, 7, 10)—were preëminent enormities. But he overlooks the fact, that Jesus, according to Mark, here gives His disciples a confidential decree for His new Church, and appoints a new custom which, as did the primitive paradisaical ordinance, goes far beyond the good and ill customs of the Greeks and Romans. It is to be observed that the Herodians introduced amongst the Jewish people laxer customs as it respects woman.

3. **And in the house.**—Confidential household words of Jesus to His disciples, according to Mark: concerning the power of casting out demons, ch. ix. 28; the great in the kingdom of heaven, ch. ix. 33; and here concerning New Testament marriage. In other passages it is solitude generally, or solitude on a mountain, in which Jesus imparts to His disciples the confidential utterances that belong to the future of His new Church, ch. iv. 10, etc. On the other hand, the house of Jesus is often the centre of great assemblages of the people, ch. ii. 1, iii. 20; even the house which Jesus chose for His rest and retirement cannot continue hidden, ch. vii. 24. In the most important crises of His conflict, Jesus turns from official encounters with His opponents to a free exposition of His doctrine to the whole people. So in ch. vii. 14, xii. 36 *seq.* Thus the house of the Redeemer is, on the one hand, the most private, and on the other, the most public, place; always, however, in its most hidden privacy opened and known. And as the Lord, in His method of teaching, passes over from the general announcement of the word into confidential communications to His chosen disciples, so also we perceive that He passes over from dealing with the priests and the officials to a freer application of His words to all the people. In the former case He regulates His teaching according to their *being able to hear* His words; in the latter, according to their *being willing.* The doctrine of Christ is the most secret and the most public: the great and utterable mystery.

4. Not only does monogamy generally lie at the foundation of this passage, but also the idea of the true ideal monogamy, which is constituted not so much by the union of two human "exemplars" as rather by the blending of two human personalities (ἄρσεν καὶ θῆλυ), which are to each other similar to what (we do not say the same that) Adam and Eve were created to be to each other.

5. 1 Cor. vii.: The Pauline development of the Christian marriage-law with reference to mixed marriages.

HOMILETICAL AND PRACTICAL.

See on Matthew.—Jesus pressed on all sides to the limits of His land; or, Jesus within the limitations of His earthly vocation: 1. Sacredly observing the legal restrictions; 2. extending to them, touching them; 3. going beyond them in His spiritual life and work (endlessly towards north, east, south, west).—The Lord in Peræa provides beforehand for His Church: 1. He confirms and establishes that which is the fundamental condition of its establishment (the Christian household); 2. in this place He prepares a refuge and hiding-place for the future of His persecuted people.—Peræa the last refuge of the Redeemer; the first refuge of His Church.—The pilgrimages of Christians to Christ: 1. As they spring from impulse of heart, not human traditions; 2. the life of the Spirit, and not spiritual chains; 3. movements towards the true rest, and the true rest in movement (that is, on the one hand, not the running without an object, and, on the other hand, not frigid form).—How the Lord for ever refers the tempters to the word of God.—How He glorifies Moses: 1. As an expositor of the creation; 2. as a prophet of redemption.—How Christ confirms the unison between the old and the new covenants.—Moses wrote his law for sinners; or, the finite side of the written

DOCTRINAL AND ETHICAL.

1. *See on Matthew.*
2. *For the hardness of your heart.*—This word is in sharp contrast with the sentimental excuses made for breaches of the marriage-vow—such as rest upon the *softness* of the heart, the overpowering emotions of love, etc.

law of God in its changeableness, explained by the finite nature of the fallen child of God.—God, even in the external changeableness of His revelations, confirms His own unchangeable character. — The dignity of marriage measured by the dignity of filial piety (of the relation to father and mother).—In order to true marriage according to the mind of Christ, more than a man and a woman is wanting.— From the right of the husband follows necessarily the right of the wife; as from the obligation of the one follows the obligation of the other.—Concerning the contrast and the reconciliation between the laws of the State and the eternal, fundamental laws of the Church of Christ.—The reciprocal influence of the punishment of death and the divorce appointed in the Jewish law: 1. Ecclesiastically: an actual adultery is spiritual death, and death as to moral fellowship; 2. an inexorable prohibition of all divorce, on civil or ecclesiastical grounds, leads to death in many ways, even to the death of the higher moral family life (*see* the South American and other Catholic states); 3. the reference to spiritual death in adulterous sin must remove and heal the deadly influences of both lax and over-severe marriage ordinances.

The three sections together.—The Christian household 1. in relation to marriage, 2. the children, 3. the property, 4. the vocation of the members to walk according to God's will, and to deny themselves.

STARKE:—*Nova Bibl. Tub.*:—Envy is soon found in the track of a teacher who has a large body of dependants.—QUESNEL:—A true preacher is not soon weary.—Every age has its Pharisees, whom the devil often uses for the temptation of pastors, and whom God permits to test His people.—OSIANDER:—We must take care what answers we make when questions are put to us on doubtful matters; for many ask questions, not that they may learn, but that they may have something to blaspheme or except against. —QUESNEL:—The bond of marriage is a figure of the union of Christ with His bride, the Church; which He will never renounce, even as she will never be separated from Christ, Eph. v. 32.

SCHLEIERMACHER:—And thus we have here an example of the manner in which the Lord administered discipline in relation to the high and mighty ones of the earth. He was not moved by the fact that Herod was an example of the sin; nor did He present the matter in the slightest degree otherwise than it was, because a person was affected in whose land and in whose power He Himself then stood.— It was of the essence of the old covenant, if we go back to the legislation and lawgiver of the Jewish Church, that the divine law and the civil law were one and the same. The civil and political ordinances must be regulated by the condition of men at the time.—The civil law in relation to the actions of men, and the divine law, which utters the laws of conscience (in Christendom), distinguished. — The levity and impure motives which too often enter into marriage contracts.—Therefore we should regard it as a public evil, that such marriages are often contracted as should never be contracted.—Marriages are matters of public concernment.

BRIEGER:—Man must take his right place in the sight of God before he can take his right place in respect to his fellow-men, whether as husband, father, etc.— GOSSNER:—Alas! when we look round upon the condition of Christendom, and observe all the laws, usages, and customs which prevail, touching how many things must we say, *In the beginning it was not so!*—BAUER:—We may here again see how surely the man who stands firm to God's word shall escape the most cunning snares that his most cunning enemies may lay for him.

SECOND SECTION.

THE RABBINICAL (BAPTIST) HOUSEHOLD DISCIPLINE OF THE DISCIPLES; AND THE THEOCRATIC AND NEW TESTAMENT HOUSEHOLD DISCIPLINE OF THE LORD.

CHAPTER X. 13–16.

(Parallels: Matt. xix. 13–15; Luke xviii. 15–17.)

13 And they brought young children to him, that he should touch them; and *his* dis-
14 ciples rebuked those that brought *them*. But when Jesus saw *it*, he was much displeased, and said unto them, Suffer the little children to come unto me, and[1] forbid them
15 not: for of such is the kingdom of God. Verily I say unto you, Whosoever shall not
16 receive the kingdom of God as a little child, he shall not enter therein. And he took them up in his arms, and put *his* hands upon them, and blessed[2] them.

[1] Ver. 14.—*And* forbid them not. The καί is wanting in many documents.
[2] Ver. 16.—Κατευλόγει, Tischendorf, after B., C., L., Δ., and before τιθείς.

EXEGETICAL AND CRITICAL.

See on the parallels of *Matthew* and *Luke*.

Ver. 13. **That He should touch them.**— The modest form of request, as in Luke; not necessarily the expression of a superstitious notion of magical influence resulting from it. Matthew tells us that imposition of hands was what was meant.

Ver. 14. **He was displeased.**—This feature is peculiar to Mark. Displeasure against displeasure: the displeasure of the Master against the displeasure of the disciples; or, indeed, the displeasure of the Church, which believes in the blessing of children in Abraham and in Christ, against Separatism.

Ver. 15. **Whosoever shall not receive the kingdom of God.**—The same rebuking sentence in Luke: comp. Matt. xviii. 3. A man must first have received the kingdom of God into his heart if he would gain admission into the kingdom of God. See Matt. v. 3, 10; John iii. 3.—The kingdom of God, which a man may receive, is Christ as the personal kingdom of God, with His salvation in His word (hence Theophylact is right, in a certain qualified sense, when he explains it of the preaching of the Gospel); the kingdom of God, into which a man is received, is the heavenly society and Church of Christ's kingdom. The kingdom, as a principle in the heart, is unfolded and developed into the fellowship of the kingdom of Christ's manifestation.—**As a little child.**—In that spiritual condition which the child, in unconscious symbolism, represents by its disposition. And yet the Lord welcomes the little children not as mere figures of the poor in spirit and of simple believers. The symbol is inseparably connected with the reality: the child and the believer are one. In the childlikeness there is present the typical precondition of faith; that is, a germ of susceptibility which the word of God will fructify.

Ver. 16. **He took them up in his arms.**— Abundant answer to the prayers of pious mothers. He was expected only to touch them; He took them up in His arms, laid His hands upon them, and blessed them. Moreover, He made them a type to the disciples and adults.

DOCTRINAL AND ETHICAL.

1. See on the parallel passages of *Matthew* and *Luke*, as also the previous notes.
2. The blessings which Christ has brought into the world of little children. Jesus Himself is the proper Protector (patron and saint) of children: not the archangel Michael, not St. Nicolas, not St. Martin; although, as under the Lord, all angels and saints are appointed to love, guard, and minister to children.—We read twice of our Lord's taking to His arms or embracing: in both instances children were the objects.
3. The disciples, infected with the rabbinical zeal for inquiry concerning the laws of marriage, would not have the Lord interrupted by their coming. Jesus, on the other hand, regards the children themselves as the final word concerning the question of marriage.
4. We have no definite account of any ordination of the Apostles by the laying on of Christ's hands; but we do read of a laying on of hands upon children, and consequently of their ordination to the kingdom of heaven.

HOMILETICAL AND PRACTICAL.

See on *Matthew*.—How pious women here understood the Lord better than His apostolical disciples did; and why? 1. The fact. Similar examples: Mary in Bethany; the believing announcers of the Risen Lord. 2. Why? Because themselves nearer to children, and better acquainted with childhood and the childlike nature.—The disciples on the byeway of rabbinical ostentation called back by the Lord to true simplicity.—The sign of rising pedantry: offence at sound life in its most innocent and beautiful forms and expressions.—How often the high school in its pride has oppressed the true schools of life; especially, 1. the school of children, and 2. the school of childlikeness, or of simple faith.—What it signifies, that the Lord demanded childlikeness almost as often as repentance and faith, in order to entrance into the kingdom of heaven: 1. Repentance and faith must have the stamp of childlikeness; 2. true childlikeness is penitent and full of faith.—The cry of the Lord through all ages, Suffer the children to come unto Me, etc.—Jesus the Friend of children.—The great Friend of the little ones: the Founder of infant baptism, infant schools, infant catechising, and of all good institutions that care for children.—The Son of Man among the children of men: 1. As the heavenly new and fresh related to the earthly new and fresh; 2. as the humble One to the artless; 3. as the Prince of faith to the confiding ones; 4. as the great Warrior to the strivers; 5. as the great Hope to the hoping; 6. as the Blessed with the happy.—Christ embraced the children: 1. The fact: *a*. an act of God, *b*. an act of Christ, *c*. an act of holy humanity. 2. A sign of judgment: *a*. for the childhood-hating kingdom of darkness, *b*. for the children-despising proud world, *c*. for Christendom still too little childlike.

STARKE:—*Nova Bibl. Tub.*:—Alas! how many Christians are there who bring their children, not to Christ, but to the devil! who hinder them from entering the kingdom of heaven by their bad example, etc.!—QUESNEL:—Nothing is so precious to God as true simplicity.—All blessings come from the hand of the Lord Jesus.

BRAUNE:—The Lord, who is so gracious to the fruits (the children), is not less so to the tree (marriage).—Klopstock, in the "Messiah," brings many souls of children, before they are conducted by angels into human bodies, to the cross of Christ, in order that they may receive a deep impression of it, such as will fit them afterwards to receive the doctrine of the Crucified.—The source of our life lies beyond any investigation of ours.—Be only a child, that thou mayest be able to become a child of God. —Christ's embracing and laying on of His hands, and blessing, is a gracious figure of the love of God, which works upon us and for us long before we know anything about it.—GERLACH:—Children, to whom the feeling of helplessness and simplicity is rendered easier by their natural weakness and inexperience, enter most easily into the kingdom of God.—LISCO: —To us all, a regeneration for the kingdom of God is necessary.

SCHLEIERMACHER:—We should know that a future is coming after us, when the light of the Gospel will shine more clearly.—It is the proper nature of a child to live altogether and absolutely in the present. What the present moment brings, it receives with simplicity and joy; the past vanishes from its vision, of the future it knows nothing, and every passing instant suffices for the happiness of its innocent nature. —(Here simplicity merely is painted.)—GOSSNER:— The greatest condescends to the least. Oh, how dear to Christ is man!

THIRD SECTION.

THE WORLD'S RICHES, AND THE HOLY POVERTY OF BELIEVERS.

CHAPTER X. 17–31.

(Parallels: Matt. xix. 16—xx. 16; Luke xviii. 18-30.)

17 And when he was gone forth into the way [to Judea, *i. e.*], there came one running,
and kneeled to him, and asked him, Good Master, what shall I do that I may inherit
18 eternal life? And Jesus said unto him, Why callest thou me good? *there is* none good
19 but one, *that is*, God. Thou knowest the commandments, Do not commit adultery, Do
not kill, Do not steal, Do not bear false witness, Defraud not, Honour thy father and
20 mother. And he answered and said unto him, Master, all these have I observed from
21 my youth. Then Jesus, beholding him, loved him, and said unto him, One thing thou
lackest: go thy way, sell whatsoever thou hast, and give to the poor, and thou shalt
22 have treasure in heaven; and come, and take up the cross,[1] and follow me. And he
23 was sad at that saying, and went away grieved: for he had great possessions. And
Jesus looked round about, and saith unto his disciples, How hardly shall they that have
24 riches enter into the kingdom of God! And the disciples were astonished at his words.
But Jesus answereth again, and saith unto them, Children, how hard is it for them that
25 trust in riches to enter into the kingdom of God! It is easier for a camel to go through
26 the eye of a needle, than for a rich man to enter into the kingdom of God. And they
were astonished out of measure, saying among themselves, Who then can be saved?
27 And Jesus, looking upon them, saith, With men *it is* impossible, but not with God:
28 for with God all things are possible. Then Peter began to say unto him, Lo, we have
29 left all, and have followed thee. And Jesus answered and said, Verily I say unto you,
There is no man that hath left house, or brethren, or sisters, or father, or mother,[2] or
30 wife, or children, or lands, for my sake, and the gospel's, But he shall receive an hundred-fold now in this time, houses, and brethren, and sisters, and mothers,[3] and children,
31 and lands, with persecutions; and in the world to come eternal life. But many *that are*
first shall be last; and the last first.

[1] Ver. 21.—The omission of the words ἄρας τὸν σταυρόν in B., C., D., Δ., [Vulgate,] is not decisive.
[2] Ver. 20.—According to B., C., Δ., [Lachmann, Tischendorf,] the mother comes first. The transposition is explained by the fact of the more usual order. *See* Meyer.
[3] Ver. 30.—The Sing. μητέρα (Lachmann) is a correction. Fritzsche places first καὶ πατέρα, which is not sufficiently supported, and, like the καὶ γυναῖκα afterwards, came from ver. 23.

EXEGETICAL AND CRITICAL.

See the parallels on *Matthew* and *Luke*.
Ver. 17. **And when He was gone forth into the way.**—This can mean no other than the final departure from Perea to Jerusalem; and therefore, primarily, the journey to Bethany for the raising of Lazarus. It was the time between the last Feast of Dedication in the winter, when the Jews would have stoned Jesus, and the Passover in the spring (783). *See* John xi.—**There came one running, and kneeled to Him.**—The two words are the more emphatic, inasmuch as he who thus hastened and knelt was a distinguished man, and a head of the synagogue. These clear and realizing traits are peculiar to Mark.
Ver. 18. **Why callest thou Me good?**—As to the various acceptations of this expression, *see* on *Matthew* xix. 16, 17. According to the strongly supported reading of Matthew, Jesus leads the young man up to God, the source of all good, from the question, "What good thing shall I do?" but, according to Mark and Luke, from the appeal, "Good Master!" Both agree very well together. "Good Master, what good thing must I do?" runs the question; the answer is, "How divided and isolated seems to thee what is good! One is the good *Being,* and in this One is *good.*" Jesus does not decline the appellation "good;" He repels it only in the superficial sense of the questioner. The young man deals with good in its relative meaning; and in this sense he says "Good," that is, "Excellent" Master. Jesus teaches him to apprehend good in its absoluteness; and to that end he must understand the being good, which he ascribes to Christ, as being founded in God. Thus the answer is not to be explained deistically, but christologically: If thou wouldst call Me good, thou must apprehend My unity with God, and My divine nature. Meyer insists that it is the contrast between the divine perfection, and the human development in Jesus (which he confounds with limitation), that is meant, and he terms the explanation that has been current since Augustine, a dogmatic misinterpretation. That term may better be applied to his own notion of Christ's *relative* sinlessness, and his own confusion between development and limitation.
Ver. 19. **Defraud not,** μὴ ἀποστερήσῃς.—The ἀποστερεῖν may mean rob or defraud, and also withhold. De Wette translates it as the former, Meyer as the latter; but in both cases half the meaning is

lost. We have only to choose between several expressions: take advantage, withhold, defraud, do wrong. We prefer the last, because of its comprehensive and strong meaning; and hold that the ἀποστερεῖν comprises or comprehends all the preceding ten commandments (Beza), and at the same time explains the tenth (Bengel, Wetstein, Olshausen). Meyer thinks, on the contrary, that the specific commandment of Deut. xxiv. 14, οὐκ ἀποστερήσεις μισθὸν πένητος, is meant. But it is impossible that the Lord's summing up of the precepts should have issued in such a speciality, which moreover falls under the commandment, Thou shalt not steal. When taken in its comprehensive meaning, the words present a more concrete expression of the final sentence of Matthew, "Thou shalt love thy neighbor as thyself." Or, in other words, it signifies, Thou shalt not feel and act selfishly or egoistically (giving is better than receiving). In this case, the entire quotation of the commandments concurs with that of Matthew, only that in Mark the words, "Honor thy father and mother," are placed at the end. The last expression in Mark is keen, and comes at the end, because its pungent point was best adapted to touch the conscience of a rich man. Luke has omitted the parallel sayings—"Defraud not," and "Thou shalt love thy neighbor as thyself"—probably on account of the uncertainty of the tradition.

Ver. 20. **Master.**—This time not "Good Master."

Ver. 21. **Beholding him, loved him;** for He penetrated his inmost being and nature: exhibiting an honest striving, notwithstanding the self-righteousness in which he is involved. The ἠγάπησεν does not refer to His speaking to the young man in an affectionate manner, as Grotius and others thought. —**One thing thou lackest,** ἕν σοι ὑστερεῖ.—It is observable that in Matthew we find the word in a question of the man himself: τί ἔτι ὑστερῶ;—evidence that the Apostles drew freely from an abundant and never-ceasing fountain of objective original remembrances of their own, and traditions handed down to them.

Ver. 22. **And he was sad.**—Rather, he stood confounded, ὁ δὲ στυγνάσας. The verb occurs again only in the Septuagint of Ezekiel. In Ezek. xxvii. 35, it is the translation of בהל, to be astonished and confounded: properly, to stand in silent, amazed confusion. The expression at the same time denotes the being or appearing to be bewildered. It likewise denotes a sad and downcast state; and this is contained in the word στυγνάζειν.

Ver. 23. **And Jesus looked round about.**—The "looking upon" of Jesus, vers. 21 and 27, and His "looking round," ver. 23—both observable. Comp. ch. iii. 5; ver. 34; ch. viii. 33; Luke vi. 10; xxii. 61.—**They that have riches:** οἱ τὰ χρήματα ἔχοντες.

Ver. 24. **Children, how hard is it for them that trust in riches.**—Tranquillizing and explanatory. The whole discourse is of trusting in riches. But a severer word follows: *It is easier for a camel,* etc.; meaning, that it is infinitely hard to separate the trusting in riches from the possession of riches. The decisive explanation of the whole hard doctrine is found in ver. 27. A miracle of the grace of God can alone solve this dread mystery.

Ver. 28. **Then Peter began.**—It is evident that the "beginning" signifies a venturesome interruption, or taking up of the word (comp. ch. viii. 31, 32), followed by embarrassment. According to Mark, Peter himself seems here to have broken off in inward confusion, or at the suggestion of modesty.

Ver. 29. **There is no man that hath left.— Hath forsaken,** ἀφῆκεν. Meyer, correctly: "In case he shall not have received; that is, if the latter is not found the case, it is through the absence of the former. The hundredfold compensation is so certain, that its not having been received presupposes the not having forsaken. Precisely similar is the force and connection of the thought in Luke iv. 22." But it is at the same time positively declared that the ideal receiving of the new possessions in the kingdom of heaven is simultaneous with the renunciation of the old possessions; or even that it is the preparatory condition on which that forsaking depends.

Ver. 30. **Now in this time, and in the world to come.**—The compensating retribution in this world and the other definitely distinguished. So also in Luke. The number in hundredfold is manifestly symbolical, as the expression of an immeasurable advantage. The spiritual nature of the new connections is evident from this, that they do not include the father or the wife. The hospitable houses of friends, Christian brethren and sisters, spiritual mothers, spiritual children, lands, and fields, and ecclesiastical possessions.—**With persecutions.** —That is, not merely in the midst of persecutions and in spite of them: the persecutions are rather part of our best possessions. See Matt. v. 12; Rom. v. 3; Jas. i. 2, 4; 1 Pet. i. 6; Heb. xii. 6.—**Eternal life.**—The everlasting, all-embracing unity, consummation, fulness, and depth of all-compensating retribution.

DOCTRINAL AND ETHICAL.

1. See on the parallel of *Matthew.*

2. *Jesus looked upon him, and loved him.*—Even after so self-righteous a declaration. Evidently our Lord sees through the features of the self-righteous his inmost nature; and distinguishes that which is a mistaken effort of the soul from that which is a corrupt self-deception, that which is based upon ignorance from that which is based upon hypocrisy. But this man was not thoroughly self-righteous; for he had a lively conviction that something important was wanting to him; and he did not hesitate, disdaining all Jewish conventional notions of propriety and dignity, to cast himself at the Lord's feet, and utter the anxious question of his heart.

3. *Those who trust in riches.*—The explanatory word is peculiar to Mark. Because it is so hard to have riches without coming to regard them as the one thing; to possess much without being altogether possessed by the possession: therefore, with man it is, generally speaking, a thing impossible that the rich should be saved; but the grace of God makes it possible through the miracle of the new birth. Clemens Alexandrinus: τίς ὁ σωζόμενος πλούσιος;

4. It is very observable that Mark, and therefore also Peter, in quoting the words concerning spiritual compensation, speaks indeed of the substitution of spiritual mothers for an earthly mother, but does not set a spiritual father or spiritual fathers over against the earthly father. The reading which places the word *father* here before the word *mother,* has but little support, and is manifestly exegetical. The Singular *mother,* in opposition to the Plural *mothers,* is strongly authenticated, and should be preferred.

HOMILETICAL AND PRACTICAL.

See on *Matthew*.—The unsatisfactory encounter of the rich young man in its contrasts: 1. He runs to Jesus enthusiastically, he leaves Him in sorrow; 2. without reflecting, he throws himself at the Lord's feet, but he scorns reflectingly His advice; 3. he comes with the consciousness of his lack, but goes away with the consciousness of slavery and guilt.— How much depends upon the right use of words! —Christ sanctifies our greetings.—Truth is the salt of courtesy, which makes the difference between it and false compliment.—All commandments converge to the one saying: Thou shalt not covet (that is, thou shalt not deal selfishly or egotistically).—How the Lord entered into the legal notion of the rich young man, in order to lead him in the way of perfect knowledge of the law over into the way of evangelical repentance.—Jesus looked upon him and loved him: 1. A somewhat surprising fact (after he had made such a revelation of himself); 2. a very significant one (Jesus looks through the error and the confusion into the secret better impulse, the drawing of the Spirit); 3. a warning fact also (that we should not regard as the final judgment those humbling tests which the Lord applies to beginners).—The poverty of the rich, and the riches of the poor.—Trust in perishable possessions, the fundamental evil of the carnally-minded: 1. The vain image of a false blessedness; 2. the decisive hindrance to the attainment of true blessedness.—Only by a miracle of God can man be saved.—The hundredfold gain of a man who renounces for the sake of God this world's gain.— The persecution of a believer one of his best possessions in this life.—The simple gain of eternal life is infinitely greater than the hundredfold gain of the blessings of this life.—Persecutions are among the possessions of the kingdom of heaven: 1. A lessening of them; 2. an increase of them; 3. a consummating of them.—Christ the perfect example of the promise which He gave to the disciples: His people sacrificed, hundreds of peoples won; His life sacrificed, infinite life won; earth, etc., renounced, heaven with all its worlds won.—Paul also a very illustrious example.

STARKE:—QUESNEL:—Christ alone can show us the way to heaven, because He Himself is the way.— OSIANDER:—Men do not thoroughly know their own wicked and perverted nature; hence they fall into the folly of seeking to be saved by their works.— QUESNEL:—If we would pray aright, we must be perfectly convinced of our misery, and know that, because God is the perfect fulness of all that is good, we can only by Him be made good ourselves.—The law of God is the rule of our conduct.—HEDINGER: —The external in the law is the least matter: an honest heathen may make his boast on that point.— OSIANDER:—There are few to be found who really prefer heavenly to earthly treasures.—QUESNEL:— That we possess with undue satisfaction, which we cannot without smarting renounce. Let every one apply to himself this test.—Who can regard riches as an advantage, when they stand in the way of salvation?—To how many are these riches their greatest misfortune!—CANSTEIN:—Riches may be possessed without the possessor's trusting in them; and then they are neither sinful nor hurtful. Rich men, who rightly use their riches, may become very rich towards God.—The rules of Christianity make many things superfluous, but we must not qualify or alter them.—Salvation we must not regard as a matter so very simple and easy. Strive to enter in at the strait gate, etc.—To a sinner who experiences all his impotence, there is nothing more comforting than to know that God is greater than his heart, 1 John iii. 20.—Thou forsakest much, when thou not only forsakest all things in thy mind and spirit, but also forsakest the thought of any merit, and the hope of any reward.—QUESNEL:—It is a small thing to leave earthly possessions; for they are another's, and, strictly speaking, not our own. But we must forsake our own will and our own flesh, and sacrifice them unto God by crucifixion or mortification, Gal. v. 24.—CRAMER:—Hast thou at once done much and suffered much? Then do not exalt thyself, on that account, above others; for thou art bound to do and to suffer all this and more.—What they lost in Judaism as friends, they would find again among the converted Gentiles.—CANSTEIN:—Let go for Christ's sake what is taken from thee in persecution; and be fully assured that all will be abundantly given back to thee again. And at length thou hast the treasure of all treasures for thine own—eternal life. —CRAMER:—It is among true Christians as among racers for a prize: where one now goes in advance, then falls back, and then again goes forward. Let every one so run as to obtain, 1 Cor. ix. 24.

GERLACH:—The perpetual recurrence of wavering in the carnally-minded between the kingdom of heaven and the world. He feels himself, *a.* attracted by both, *b.* by both repelled.—He thinks, in his folly, that there must be some profound utterance beyond the commandments of God, which shall reconcile God and the world without. (Does not this last idea hold good, in a sacred sense, of the Gospel?) Nothing can be done without decision.—BRAUNE:—"What is good? That which makes itself common, communicates itself (or devotes itself to the life of others). Him we call a good man, who is common and useful. God is the most common and self-communicating of all: He gives himself to all things. Nothing created gives itself. The sun gives only its rays, but keeps back itself; but God gives himself in all His gifts. His Godhead hangs upon this, that He communicates himself to all things that are capable of receiving His goodness."—MASTER ECKHART:—In Christ, who is entirely for the use and benefit of all, God's Spirit is without measure.—Why does not Jesus suggest to the questioner the commandments of the first table? These all were contained in the words, God is good. And the duties to our neighbor were best fitted to aid the blinded mind in looking into his heart and life, Luke xii. 33; xiv. 33.— (Trusting in riches):—There are poor people also, who with difficulty enter into the kingdom of heaven, because they put too much trust in money. Thus it is the spirit and temper—relying too much upon this world's goods for happiness, whether possessing or not possessing much, whether rich or poor—that makes that entrance hard, Rom. viii. 17.—For Christ's sake, and the Gospel's, that must be given up which is given up; else it is not seed, and the promised harvest can therefore never be reaped.

SCHLEIERMACHER:—When thou askest what is really good, and what thou must do as being good, thou shouldst reflect that thou canst do absolutely nothing of thyself (and knowest nothing of thyself), and that God alone can give thee power to do or think anything good.—Why did the Redeemer love the young man? On account of unprejudiced and simple words, his earnest aim, and the fidelity with which he followed his conviction and views, albeit these were limited.—And if at this crisis he did not sustain the test, yet we see that the sympathy which the Lord manifested was so entirely without displeasure, that the young man must have been filled with hope, etc.—The heart should never hang upon worldly possessions, as sufficing to impart earthly satisfaction; but we should always regard them as one part of those gifts, for the use of which we must give a strict account.—It was a laudable purpose of the Apostle to clear up for himself and for others, by an express declaration of the Redeemer, the important matter of a reward for the good, and punishment for the evil:—it was not therefore the common desire for reward.—The nature of Christian love consists in this, that the spiritual bond assumes altogether the form of the natural (brothers, sisters).—So long as we find ourselves entangled in the endeavor to prove that there is any value in ourselves, we are liable to be put to the shame of experiencing that those who would be first become the last; and inversely we shall find that the Spirit of God often prepares for Himself His instruments in profound secrecy.— BRIEGER:—All the impediments must be removed, but following was the great thing.—GOSSNER:—When self-love breathes upon the mirror of the law, that mirror becomes obscured or falsified: instead of detecting his own ugliness there, a man finds himself beautiful.—The answer of Jesus was designed to reveal to him the depths of his own heart.—BAUER:— A man must give up, not only his riches, but also himself.

FOURTH SECTION.

THE ASSEMBLING OF THE DISCIPLES ON THE WAY TO THE CROSS.

CHAPTER X. 32–34.

(Parallels: Matt. xx. 17-19; Luke xviii. 31-34; John xi. 53-57.)

32 And they were in the way going up to Jerusalem; and Jesus went before them: and they were amazed; and as they followed,[1] they were afraid. And he took again
33 the twelve, and began to tell them what things should happen unto him, *Saying*, Behold, we go up to Jerusalem; and the Son of man shall be delivered unto the chief priests, and unto the scribes; and they shall condemn him to death, and shall deliver
34 him to the Gentiles; And they shall mock him, and shall scourge him, and shall spit upon him,[2] and shall kill him; and the third day he shall rise again.

[1] Ver. 32.—Meyer adopts the reading οἱ δὲ ἀκολοθοῦντες, after B. and others. So Ewald. Cod. C. reads καὶ οἱ, which identifies those "following" as the disciples.
[2] Ver. 34.—The spitting connected with the mocking in B., C., L., Δ., [Lachmann, Tischendorf,] may be explained by exegetical motives. B., C., L., Δ. read μετὰ τρεῖς ἡμέρας, Lachmann, Tischendorf. Probably this was introduced to conform it with ch. viii. 31, ix. 31.

EXEGETICAL AND CRITICAL.

See on the parallels of *Matthew* and *Luke*. Comp. also the observations in the Introduction to Mark.— Our Evangelist here brings into clear prominence a critical period in the history of our Lord, concerning which John has given us the most exact account. For there can be no doubt that the narrative has to do with the last retreat of the Redeemer into the town and desert of Ephraim, where He prepared Himself, and collected His disciples for the last journey to Jerusalem (*see* John xi. 53; *Leben Jesu*, ii. 2). We hear their tone of mind expressed on the occasion of the departure of Jesus from Perea in order to raise Lazarus. In the spring of the year 783 (P. U. C.), Jesus went from Perea to Bethany, and raised Lazarus from the dead; He then, because the Sanhedrim had laid Him under excommunication, and decreed that He should die, retreated back into the desert of Ephraim. That desert, eastwards from Bethel, extends towards the desert of Quarantania, between Jerusalem and Jericho. (*See* for particulars, ROBINSON, ii. 353.) The last abode of Jesus in the wilderness, His last retreat in this world, forms a counterpart and contrast to His abode in the wilderness after His baptism. In the former, it was necessary for Him to decide on going amongst the people as it were without a name, in order that He might avoid the *Messiahship*, as it had become an idea grossly perverted into a mere watchword of deception; but now He must decide to yield Himself up to the people, according to the true and purified idea of the Messiah, which He had in the whole tenor of His holy life re-established amongst them. This was the great task that He now contemplated; and Matthew himself points to it also. He took His disciples κατ' ἰδίαν ἐν τῷ ὁδῷ, and gave them the last and most express preannouncement of His passion. Luke gives the faintest record of the crisis: παραλαβὼν— ἰδοὺ, ἀναβαίνομεν. But Mark describes, first, the great confusion and terror with which the disciples regarded the final catastrophe, and how they followed their Master not without much fear. This expression, ἀκολουθοῦντες ἐφοβοῦντο, is stronger, in consequence of the seeming inversion of the participle and the Past tense. It indicates a wavering, and a danger of being scattered abroad, which Jesus prevented by the παραλαβὼν πάλιν. We therefore understand it thus, that this morbid depression, which the Lord contended against, was followed by a new and more mighty impulse of excitement, that found its expression in the immediately following appeal of the two sons of Zebedee. Mark is most copious in the prediction of the passion, and presents it to us in simple active propositions in the Future. Matthew lays the main stress on Jesus' being delivered over to the Gentiles: He is delivered up, betrayed to mockery, to scourging, and to crucifixion. Luke makes Christ's person the central-point, and records what He would suffer and encounter. Mark depicts the double betrayal in its vividly apprehended consequences; and the word of Matthew respecting the crucifixion he divides into two parts: they will spit upon Him, and they will kill Him. Luke gives prominence, moreover, to the fact, that Jesus declared at the beginning that the Scriptures must be fulfilled; and lays stress at the end on the circumstance, that the disciples could not and would not understand His prediction.

Ver. 32. **And as they followed, they were afraid.**—Meyer prefers the reading, οἱ δὲ ἀκολ. ἐφοβοῦντο, which would give this meaning: The greater number of the disciples held back in astonishment and confusion; those who followed Jesus, who advanced before them, followed Him only with great fear. We agree with Meyer so far as this, that the crisis was a very special one; but his reading makes it too emphatic. It is a reading not sufficiently supported; and, moreover, we have no sign in John that at that time many of the disciples left the Lord. If any are disposed to think that about this time the thought of betraying the Lord entered the soul of Judas as a germ, yet it must be remembered that there was no development of it until the subsequent feast in Bethany, and that it was not a fixed decision until the Passover. An express contrast between those who now left the Lord, and those who followed Him in fear, would have been expressed in stronger terms: as, for instance, at that earlier crisis, after the declaration of Jesus in the synagogue of Capernaum, John vi. 66. The fact that the sentence of death was now uttered against our Lord (John xi. 45), might indeed make some of those who reverenced Jesus waver and apostatize. But how decidedly His genuine disciples still put faith in Him and His cause, is proved by the subsequent palm-entry into Jerusalem, as well as by the circumstance, which Luke prominently mentions, that the disciples did not thoroughly lay to heart and believe the announcement which Jesus had made concerning His own death.—**And He took again the Twelve.**—See John's statement, ch. xi. 7 seq., and ver. 54.—**And began.**—The expression intimates that a series of new and decisive explanations took place (comp. ch. viii. 31, ix. 22). These consisted in, 1. The decision of the time. He had first declared that He must suffer death generally (ὅτι δεῖ), and that it was near at hand (μέλλει in Matthew and Luke; in Mark expressed by the Present παραδίδοται): He now declares more expressly that all this would take place at the coming journey to the feast (ἀναβαίνομεν, etc., καὶ ὁ υἱός). 2. In the more precise statement of the form of suffering: a. the being rejected generally (ch. viii. 31); b. the betrayal, and the delivering up by the Jews to the Gentiles (ch. ix. 12, 31); c. the great double betrayal,—the first betrayal, or the delivering up to the high priests, coming in our passage into marked prominence. 3. In the more precise definition of the critical elements of the passion, especially His execution by the hands of the Gentiles, Matthew expressly mentions the crucifixion, while in Mark and Luke it is plainly hinted at. Compare the *Critical Notes* on the parallel place in *Matthew*.

Ver. 34. **And they shall mock Him.**—The text does not require us, with Meyer, to limit this verb and that which follows to the Gentiles. Why should they be omitted who were the original movers of the whole, and who gave it their continual aid? Compare Matthew and Luke.

DOCTRINAL AND ETHICAL.

1. *See* on the parallel of *Matthew*.
2. Here again, as in many other passages, Mark goes beyond the other Synoptists, and decidedly approximates to John; and the account of the last Evangelist concerning the final abode of Jesus in the wilderness of Ephraim is made more plain by the circumstances given here by Mark. The amazement and hesitation of the Lord's disciples was occasioned especially by His heroic and decisive bearing as He went before them. They saw in His majestic, resolute, solemn, and fixed deportment, that a most important crisis was impending. Since the astonishment and wavering of His disciples precedes the definite prediction of Christ concerning His *now* approaching passion and death, it can only refer to the obscure and anxious foreboding with which the thought of something unknown, but critical and decisive and fearful, filled their minds (De Wette). For all this they were as yet but little prepared; hence the Lord collected them together, and strengthened them in solitude. He foretold to them His whole passion, so far as He could do so (that is, without a premature disclosure of the traitor, who had not yet decided on his treachery); He repeated to them all the comforting promises of His resurrection, and thus prepared them for all, while waiting for the Galilean-Peræan festival companies.
3. The abode of Jesus in the wilderness of Ephraim, in its connection with His abode in the wilderness of Quarantania, and in its contrast with that abode.

HOMILETICAL AND PRACTICAL.

See on *Matthew*.—Jesus as going before His disciples in the way of sufferings: 1. His heroic spirit; 2. their despondency; 3. their invigoration in His strength.—Follow Me, saith Christ our Leader and Champion.—Jesus, go before us!—Christ, the Captain of our salvation, Heb. ii. 10.—The Lord in the midst of His disciples, before the coming of the hours (or days) of great and solemn crisis and decision.—The shuddering presentiment of the disciples, contemplating the unknown future; excited by, 1. beholding the holy and joyful solemnity of the Lord; 2. the journey to Jerusalem; 3. the consideration of the people's disposition; 4. the consideration of their own frame of mind.—How the Lord seeks to deliver the disciples from an indefinite fear, by setting before them the clear idea of a fearful, but salutary and saving, certainty.—The trembling and wavering discipleship.—We must not tremble and be amazed in the uncertainty of the way of suffering, but be bold and dare in the certainty of it.—Morbid feelings must become cheerful; and feebleness must be invigorated by the thought of the glorious and final end.—The Lord's assembly in solitude for His great and decisive encounter with the world. (*See* running title.)—The importance of stillness for the kingdom of God: 1. Into stillness; 2. in stillness; 3. out of stillness.—How the Lord collects His disciples for the conflict of suffering: 1. Every one to Him (with Christ); 2. every one into himself (in the inner life); 3. every one singly (to his companions).—

The source of the suffering of Christ; or, the enmity of the world against Him.—The ever-recurring cry from heaven, in the prospect of all Christ's sufferings and His people's: and [the cry] on the third day.— The Lord deals with His disciples in the spirit of heavenly simplicity and fidelity.—The plain disparity between the temper of the disciples and the feeling of our Lord: 1. Its meaning; 2. its signs; 3. itself a sign of the betrayal, the denial, and the forsaking Him in the night of His passion.

STARKE:—Conversations in travelling should further us in the heavenly pilgrimage.—All the steps which are taken in suffering with Christ, are steps taken to glory, 2 Thess. iii. 5; 1 Pet. iv. 1; Heb. xii. 2, 3.—We should often remind ourselves of the cross.—Christ summons us to fellowship with Him, as often as we hear of His sufferings and death.— We should be of good heart (Luke xxiv. 26), remembering in our sufferings the resurrection, and expecting our redemption in patient hope.—LISCO:—They were amazed and affrighted at the way which Jesus so boldly took into the very presence and power of His enemies.—BRAUNE:—On account of their Master, they were amazed; for themselves, they feared.— Jesus going before them attracted them to follow.— A secret presentiment and longing of the spirit points to fellowship with Christ upon the cross; but the flesh grievously recoils.—We must train ourselves to endure sufferings.—GOSSNER:—All nature trembles when God leads man on the way of the cross.—BAUER: —The Master going before them, what remained but that they should follow?

PART FOURTH.

The Conflicts and Triumphs of the Lord in Judæa. Christ the Founder of the New Church.

FIRST SECTION.

THE TRIUMPHAL ENTRY INTO JERUSALEM.

CHAPTER X. 35—XI. 26.

---

1. *The Request of the Sons of Zebedee.* CH. X. 35–45.

(Parallel: Matt. xx. 20–28.)

35 And James and John, the sons of Zebedee, come unto him, saying, Master, we
36 would that thou shouldest do for us whatsoever we shall desire.¹ And he said unto
37 them, What would ye that I should do for you? They said unto him, Grant unto us that we may sit, one on thy right hand, and the other on thy left hand, in thy glory.
38 But Jesus said unto them, Ye know not what ye ask: can ye drink of the cup that I
39 drink of? and² be baptized with the baptism that I am baptized with? And they said unto him, We can. And Jesus said unto them, Ye shall indeed drink of the cup that
40 I drink of; and with the baptism that I am baptized withal shall ye be baptized: But to sit on my right hand and³ on my left hand is not mine to give; but *it shall be given to*
41 *them* for whom it is prepared. And when the ten heard *it*, they began to be much dis-
42 pleased with James and John. But Jesus called them to *him*,⁴ and saith unto them, Ye know that they which are accounted to rule over the Gentiles exercise lordship over
43 them; and their great ones exercise authority upon them. But so shall it not be⁵
44 among you: but whosoever will be great among you,⁶ shall be your minister: And
45 whosoever of you will be the chiefest, shall be servant of all. For even the Son of man came not to be ministered unto, but to minister, and to give his life a ransom for many.

---

¹ Ver. 35.—Lachmann, Tischendorf, [after A., B., C., D., Versions,] supply σε after αἰτήσωμεν.
² Ver. 38.—According to D., C.*, 1)., L., Δ., [Lachmann, Tischendorf, Meyer,] instead of καί read ἤ.
³ Ver. 40.—Instead of the καί here, also read ἤ. [after B., D., L., Δ., Lachmann, Tischendorf, Meyer.]
⁴ Ver. 42.—See the order in Tischendorf and Lachmann, [who read καὶ προσκαλεσάμενος αὐτοὺς ὁ Ἰησοῦς, after B., C., D., L., Syriac, Coptic.]
⁵ Ver. 43.—Instead of ἔσται here, ἔστιν is the reading of B., C.*, D., L., Δ. So Lachmann, Tischendorf.
⁶ Ver. 44.—Lachmann, after B., C., ἐν ὑμῖν εἶναι, instead of ὑμῶν γενέσθαι.

EXEGETICAL AND CRITICAL.

See on the parallel of *Matthew*, especially *Critical Note* on ver. 20.—Christ has prepared the Twelve for His final festival journey, and for its significance as a time of crisis. He has come forth from the wilderness of Ephraim; the first band of the Galilæan pilgrims to the feast — consisting probably of the most intimate friends and dependants of Jesus, who had come from Galilee through Samaria to Ephraim —had joined Him, purposing to go on with Him through Jericho to Jerusalem. This seems to be confirmed by the fact of the presence of Salome, and her participation in the request of her two sons. This request itself shows us how mighty had once more grown the joyful excitement of the disciples' hopes: in this respect, it makes the present section a perfect contrast to the previous one. Matthew alone accompanies Mark here; and he makes Salome prominent, putting the request into her lips. According to Mark, her sons present the petition to the Lord; but the records are evidently complementary to each other. Matthew's account makes Salome only the intercessor, and with marked accommodation to the spirit of Oriental court ceremony. Hence, even according to Matthew, Christ speaks immediately,—after the mother had proffered that request which, according to Mark, is the supplication of the sons,—to those sons themselves. Mark adds to the word concerning drinking of the cup, the word concerning the baptismal bath. Matthew says, "The sitting on My right hand and on My left is not mine to give, but for whom it is prepared of My Father;" Mark says briefly, "For whom it is prepared." He also says, in his manner, "The ten *began* to be displeased." The princes of the earth also he describes in his own peculiar way. For the rest, he agrees here with Matthew very closely; and down to trifling variations, such as between Matthew's "*your* servant," and Mark's "servant of *all*."

Ver. 35. **We would that Thou shouldst do for us.**—Strong importunity, θέλομεν, ἵνα.

Ver. 37. **In Thy glory.** According to Matthew, *in Thy kingdom.*—These are essentially the same. But we must reject the explanation, "in that glory which will surround us when we sit by Thee."

Ver. 38. **And with the baptism.**—Peculiar to Mark. On the double meaning of the expression, see *Matthew*, xx. 22.

Ver. 40. **For whom it is prepared.**—Matthew adds, "of My Father." In Mark the emphasis lies upon the fact that the matter of the honor was already decided.

Ver. 41. **They began.**—Here again follows at once a counter feeling: the appeasing word of our Lord.

Ver. 42. **Which are accounted to rule over the Gentiles,** οἱ δοκοῦντες ἄρχειν. — Meyer: The essence of Gentile government, the ruling ambition, is signified; not simply οἱ ἄρχοντες (Gataker and others) but *qui censentur imperare; i. e., quos gentes habent et agnoscunt, quorum imperio parcant* (Beza). He justly sets aside Fritzsche's exposition: "those who think they rule." But in Wetstein's interpretation,—*qui sibi regnare videntur, revera autem affectuum suorum servi sunt*,—there is an element worth noticing.

Ver. 43. **Whosoever will be great among you shall be your minister.**—Properly the "he *will* be" has the meaning of ἔστω, he should be, let him be; yet also with a hint of the thought that he will be such, either in the most internal sense or in the most external. Christ is the servant of all in the centre of the Church; the Pope, in the periphery of the Church, is the involuntary result of, and protest against, a too hasty development of the kingdom of God.

DOCTRINAL AND ETHICAL.

1. *See* on *Matthew*, especially the *Critical Notes*.
2. The last known instance of the Lord's apostolical training of the sons of Zebedee. The two preceding periods were Luke ix. 54, and Mark ix. 38. Thus there is an analogy and a contrast with the apostolical education of Peter. Our history throws light in many directions: 1. As the beginning of that enthusiastic Hosanna, which found its climax in the acclamations of the palm-entry into Jerusalem. Christ had predicted His sufferings on the cross. The sons of Zebedee declare, with glowing heroism, that they are willing to connect their fate with His in the strictest manner, and that they are fully resolved to go forward: they rather, however, hope for glory with Him, than fear the shame of His cross. 2. As the last outbreak of the high-toned, noble, natural pride of the sons of Zebedee. The mother and the sons are one. But John seems to interpose especially in favor of his brother James: he might, according to antecedents, have had some sort of claim to the right-hand place; but he now (as the younger) will take his place on the left hand. 3. As an unconscious request for martyrdom with Christ. 4. As a keen test of the heroism of Peter. 5. As an illustration of the stage of transition, through which the disciples were then passing. 6. As giving the Lord occasion to characterize the nature of earthly government, and to utter His protest against all ideas of a Christian hierarchy; as well as to distinguish expressly the economy of the Father, and the creation and preordination, from the economy of the Son and redemption; and still more expressly to mark out the royal road of humility as the appointed and only way to true and abiding Christian exaltation. Phil. ii. 6 *seq.*

HOMILETICAL AND PRACTICAL.

See on *Matthew.*—What was noble and what was evil in the request of the sons of Zebedee.—The bold petition of these disciples: 1. As a fault: with regard to the error and the sin in it,—*a.* they prayed for something which, *in the sense in which they prayed for it*, did not exist in the kingdom of Christ; *b.* for something which was *not yet* existing (not before the cross); *c.* for something about which decision had already been made: possibly in their favor, so that their request was superfluous; possibly not, and then their request was vain. 2. As a pious impulse of the Spirit, which was sanctified and abundantly gratified: it was an impulse, *a.* to remain always near Him; *b.* to share His lot and serve Him; 3. to work with self-devotement for His kingdom. One was the friend of Jesus, the other the first martyr.—The cup of Christ and His baptism: *a.* the tasting of all the bitternesses of the Messianic suffering; *b.* the experience of all the external trials, or the being baptized into the shame of the cross, the death, the sepulchre, the underworld. Or, *a.* His drinking (Gethsemane); *b.* His sinking (Calvary).—Cup and baptism in the kingdom of Christ: 1. The cup and the baptism; 2. the baptism and the cup.—As the Lord corrected Peter by rebuking lessons, so He corrects the sons of Zebedee by humbling lessons: 1. By making an express distinction between the suffering of Christ and His glory; 2. between martyr-fidelity with its reward, and the divine gift and its blessedness; 3. between the economy and work of the Father, and the economy and work of the Son; 4. between the eternal fundamental principles of the kingdom of God, and their realization in the work of man's free will; 5. between the earthly State and the spiritual Church.—The displeasure of the disciples at the error of the sons of Zebedee: 1. Probably a feeling on behalf of Peter's rights;[*] 2. not free from envy and strife; 3. but at the same time springing from a presentiment of a higher order of things.—Above and below in the Church of Christ: 1. An above which is below; 2. a below which is above (as oft-times the first is the last, and the last first).—Contrast between the appointments of the State and those of the Church: 1. Those are legal; these rest upon the fundamental principles of pure and free love. 2. Those are symbolical; these are actual powers in life.—The repeated testimonies of Christ against a primacy.—Christ servant of all and Lord of all, Phil. ii. 6 seq. Real and essential dignities in the kingdom of heaven: 1. Its names or titles are powers of life; 2. its powers of life are divine fruits; 3. its divine fruits are God's gifts.—Christ the Prince of peace among His people.

STARKE:—OSIANDER:—Ministers in the Church have their own failings.—Take good heed how thou prayest.—We should never look at anything high for ourselves.—QUESNEL:—Ambition is blind, and often knows not what it wants.—OSIANDER:—The cup of affliction is bitter enough to the flesh, but it is exceeding salutary. Take it in full confidence, and it will serve to the healing of the soul.—Christ does not say that He could not give the heavenly glory, but that He could not give it to any but those for whom it was prepared, 2 Tim. ii. 11, 12.—We must not trouble ourselves as to the place which we shall occupy in heaven, but see to it that we get there.—HEDINGER:—Christ does not disparage or overturn dignities, but their pride and vanity.—Variety of gifts in the Church: these should not exalt themselves, those should not envy, Rom. xii. 3; 1 Cor. xii. 15; Jas. i. 10.—In the kingdoms of the world, a man is called great when he rules; in the kingdom of grace, when he serves many.—LUTHER:—There is nothing which more adorns and dignifies the office of a true servant of Christ than genuine humility and simplicity.—BRAUNE:—There is ever a widening interval between seeking the applause of others and the cause itself (at first, he remarks, they coalesce, or are much more concurrent).—In the result, the ambitious man forgets the cause itself, and displays his own gifts and powers; from one false step he then proceeds to another.—If in their (Zebedee's sons') love to the Lord there was an admixture of ambition, this would tend to make their love impure: the kingdom of love could not and must not tolerate such a blending.—The displeasure of the ten was a proof that they were affected by the same fault.—The promises of Christ, Rev. ii. 10, 28; iii. 21. SCHLEIERMACHER:—Love to Christ is the measure for all the actions of men in His Church.—BRIEGER:—The kingdom of Christ is a kingdom of the cross.—Love teaches us to serve.—His serving should endear our service.—BAUER:—The whole life of the Son of Man was humble service.

[*] [The author here travels out of the record. There is not the slightest allusion to Peter in the narrative.—*Ed.*]

2. *The Passing through Jericho.* VERS. 46-52.

(Parallels: Matt. xx. 29–34; Luke xviii. 35–43; xix. 1-28.)

46 And they came to Jericho: and as he went out of Jericho with his disciples, and a great number of people, blind Bartimeus, the[1] son of Timeus, sat by the highway-side
47 begging. And when he heard that it was Jesus of Nazareth,[2] he began to cry out, and
48 say, Jesus, *thou* son of David, have mercy on me. And many charged him that he should hold his peace: but he cried the more a great deal, *Thou* son of David, have
49 mercy on me. And Jesus stood still, and commanded him to be called:[3] and they call
50 the blind man, saying unto him, Be of good comfort, rise; he calleth thee. And he,
51 casting away his garment, rose,[4] and came to Jesus. And Jesus answered and said unto him, What wilt thou that I should do unto thee? The blind man said unto him,
52 Lord, that I might receive my sight. And Jesus said unto him, Go thy way; thy faith hath made thee whole. And immediately he received his sight, and followed Jesus[5] in the way.

[1] Ver. 46.—We read, with A. and *Recepta*, υἱός without the Article, and ὁ τυφλός with the Article. [Lachmann, Tischendorf, and Meyer, following B., D., L., Δ., omit it.] So also προσαιτῶν, although important Codd., including B., L., Δ., Tischendorf, and Meyer, read προσαίτης. *See* the *Notes*.
[2] Ver. 47.—Ναζαρηνός, Lachmann, Tischendorf, Meyer.
[3] Ver. 49.—Εἶπεν · φωνήσατε αὐτόν : B., C., L., Δ., Tischendorf, Meyer.
[4] Ver. 50.—Instead of ἀναστάς, Lachmann and Tischendorf read ἀναπηδήσας, after B., L., D., Δ., Vulgate, &c.
[5] Ver. 52.—Αὐτῷ instead of τῷ Ἰησοῦ.

EXEGETICAL AND CRITICAL.

See on the parallels in *Matthew* and *Luke.*—From Ephraim and the desert, Jesus, with the Twelve and His trusted Galilæan dependents—who had joined Him at this point or before—turned to Jericho, where He united His company with that of the great Galilæan-Peræan band going up to the feast, which had come from Peræa over the Jordan. Upon the question of time, and Jericho itself, and the difference among the Synoptists in regard to the healing of the blind, consult the notes upon *Matthew.* Like that Evangelist, Mark passes over the narrative of Zacchæus, and gives instead all the more exact account of the healing of the blind man. The fundamental idea of Luke's Gospel demanded that the favor shown to the rich publican should not be omitted. Matthew and Mark are so intent upon depicting the great procession to the feast in its unity, that they cannot linger upon another episode, such as that of Zacchæus, in addition to the healing of the blind man. Matthew, indeed, might hesitate through modesty to record prominently so many instances of favor shown to the publicans; and Mark would probably prefer to omit a new remembrancer of the embittered hatred which subsisted between the Jews and the Romans—writing as he did so much for Roman Christians. Moreover, the occurrence with Zacchæus was not properly a miraculous history, such as both these Evangelists mainly record at this time.—Now, while Matthew gives an account merely of the departure from Jericho, Mark mentions also the entrance. In his account of the departure, he describes the great numbers that accompanied Jesus, and records the full name of the blind man, Bartimæus, the son of Timæus. Luke joins him in saying that this man was a beggar. Mark, again, has the specific note that he, Bartimæus, began to cry aloud. The words of the people to the blind man, "Be of good courage, rise; He calleth thee"—the conduct of Bartimæus generally, and his casting away his garment, and standing up, and coming—are all characteristic touches of painting which Mark alone gives. Only Matthew records the compassion of Jesus, and the fixing His eyes upon the man. Mark also omits "Receive thy sight." The word of healing is condensed, and the conclusion is briefer than Luke's, touching only the main points.

Ver. 46. **Bartimæus.**—The patronymic בַּר טִמָאִי is made into a proper name (after the analogy of Bartholomew and others); as it is explained by the additional clause, "son of Timæus." This last seems to place Timæus among the number of well-known Christians. Meyer: Probably a Christian who afterwards attained distinction. And this might be true, notwithstanding the fact that he had allowed his son, a blind man, to beg on the highway. But, if we read with Codex A. and the *Text. Rec.*, "a son of Timæus, Bartimæus the blind man, sat and begged," it is plain that this is an account of him more precise and consistently carried out, which however seemed too full and specific to most copyists. According to it, Bartimæus, the blind man, was himself a personage well known to Christians as a monument of the Lord's miracle, as was probably also Simon the Leper; and the designation "a son of Timæus" would distinguish him, not merely from the father, but also from other sons.

Ver. 47. **And when he heard.**—He therefore believed that Jesus of Nazareth was the son of David, that is, the expected Messiah. He thus bore testimony to the widely-scattered seed of faith, and especially to the renewed stimulus given to the Redeemer's cause, since the beginning of the festal journey, amongst the masses. But the blind man might also have heard on his hill-top of the recent resurrection of Lazarus, which took place in his own neighborhood; and this might have been matter of many silent night-ponderings in his blindness.

Ver. 49. **And Jesus stood still.**—We now have reached the great crisis. He now hears the loud cry of the people—Messiah! *See* on the parallel of *Matthew.*—**Be of good comfort.**—Meyer: θάρσει, ἔγειρε, φωνεῖ σε: most affecting *asyndeton.*

Ver. 51. **Rabboni,** רַבּוּנִי, *my* Master.—If the Yod is taken paragogically, it means merely "master" (*see* Meyer); but even then it has so emphatic a sense as to be almost equal in personal reverence. Bartimæus adhered from that time to the Lord. He followed Him, praising God, Luke says; he followed Him in the way, in the procession, says Mark. He immediately joined the festal company of Jesus' triumph. It was, indeed, the triumphal procession of the Prophet, and not yet that of the High Priest: this is formed by the living Church, even as the risen saints will be the triumphal procession of the King.

DOCTRINAL AND ETHICAL.

1. *See* on *Matthew* and the previous notes.

2. The contrast in the sentiments of the people round Christ: type of the contrast between the hierarchical and the evangelical Church. In the former, the poor and wretched are threatened, and bidden to keep silence, when they cry directly to Christ; in the latter it is, "Be of good comfort, rise; He calleth thee." It was natural that those who surrounded Christ should be led, by the thought that His kingdom was beginning, into conventional notions as to the value of courtly customs and hierarchical order; but it was also natural that the mercy of our Lord towards the wretched should scatter all such mists.

3. The casting his garment away was an expression of joyous boldness and zealous haste, and a removal of all impediments.

4. Mark intimates the dignity of the crisis in which the Lord now stands, by the circumstance that He heals the blind man simply by words: "Go thy way, thy faith," etc. We know from Matthew how they are to be explained in detail; nevertheless, it is observable that Mark, who earlier records the sighing, the anointing with spittle, etc., introduces here so few intervening circumstances.

5. The Lord declared, by act and deed, that He would have no courtly state in His kingdom, no intermediate personages between Him and His dependents; that He was come, not to rule, but to minister. And, so far as this goes, our history is an acted illustration of the former section.

HOMILETICAL AND PRACTICAL.

See on *Matthew.*—The beginning of the procession of Christ was the opening of blind eyes.—Light must be diffused in the world.—The fame of Bartimæus the best fame for all men; the best reputation for all Christians. (He was a blind man, a beggar; he believed and importuned; the Lord took pity upon him, and healed him.)—With the name of Christ the names of those whom He saved are immortalized.—The most beautiful homage with which Christ was publicly hailed as Messiah: Have mercy on me!—It is a pitiable thing when the cry, "Lord, have pity on me" (the κύριε ἐλέησον, to wit), becomes a dead formula in our poor Christendom.—How Jesus can transform the harsh threateners of the wretched into compassionate comforters and helpers.—The three words of true Christian sympathy and help for the wretched: Be of good comfort, rise ; He calleth thee.—Through the compassion of Jesus and nearness to Him, one is taught to preach the Gospel even unconsciously.—How the helping "Go thy way" of the Lord to Bartimæus and others becomes a glorious and encouraging announcement, "Come unto Me."—All the uncalled ceremonialists in the royal procession of Christ are unable to suppress the cry of faith sent forth to Him.—The ear of the King detects the lamenting cry of the blind beggar through all the tumult of the crowd.—Thus the royal procession is magnified by the cry of misery.—A blind beggar can arrest the course of it; a blind beggar, turned into a seeing disciple, can advance it and add to its dignity.—The true petitioners of God throw away for ever the beggar's array.—Mendicancy appears or vanishes as men are guided : 1. It appears in the ancient priestly and royal states of this world ; 2. it vanishes in the kingdom of Christ. Compare with this passage John ix. ; Acts iii. 2 ; iv. 34.—Men may at first hinder the beginnings of Christianity, and then agree afterwards further it prematurely and rashly. (The first three centuries, and the three following, are examples.)

STARKE :—LUTHER :—Blindness and poverty cause double distress : so it is in spiritual matters, when both are rightly felt and mourned over.—CANSTEIN : The preaching of the Gospel is a perpetual announcement that Jesus is near; and we should, knowing our misery, incessantly and confidently cry aloud to Him for His mercy.—LUTHER :—Sufferers oftenaces meet with scanty sympathy and poor intercession.—CRAMER :—It would be a sore thing if the good God were as easily wearied as men are with our praying and beseeching.—QUESNEL :—We should let no opportunity pass of getting good either to body or soul, for such opportunities do not always return.—HEDINGER :—In prayer we should let nothing interrupt or divert us.—The simplicity of faith in prayer holds fast and holds out.—LUTHER :—God's call is even in spiritual things the beginning of actual cure.—He who truly wants salvation must disencumber himself of all embarrassments and come to Christ.—HEDINGER :—He who would see, must acknowledge his blindness.—LUTHER :—Faith is counted of such high dignity that salvation is ascribed to it, although the work of God.—HEDINGER :—Christ is our Physician and our Light.—Faith is the best of all medicine.—CANSTEIN :—Those who receive gifts follow their benefactors. Ought we not then to follow Christ ?—He is indeed our greatest Benefactor.—RIEGER (with reference to those who murmured) :—Those who stand around are often unaware how much harm they may do by light words, and how easily a tender germ is trodden down and ruined.—The inward earnestness of the blind man broke through everything. Happy he who lets himself be restrained from faith and the cry of faith by nothing under the sun.—Things are continually occurring which might have a tendency to turn us in part or wholly away from Christ. What then ? So much the more does the blind cry out, and faith believe ; and the more it is hindered, the more it is helped.—The Lord was not always so willing to be followed by those who were healed ; but in this last journey to Jerusalem, an exception was admitted. Envy was not now to be excited ; it had reached its highest point. Praise, on the other hand, was now, by all the wonderful works of God, to demonstrate its power against " the enemy and the avenger."—GOSSNER :—The blind man runs to Jesus without seeing Him; so must we hasten to Him in faith, though we see Him not.

---

3. *The Triumphal Entrance of Jesus into Jerusalem.* CH. XI. 1-11.

(Parallels: Matt. xxi. 1-17; Luke xix. 29-46; John xii. 12-29.)

And when they came nigh to Jerusalem, unto Bethphage and Bethany, at the Mount of Olives, he sendeth forth two of his disciples, And saith unto them, Go your way into the village over against you: and as soon as ye be entered into it, ye shall find a colt tied, whereon never[1] man sat; loose him, and bring *him*. And if any man say unto you, Why do ye this? say ye that the Lord hath need of him; and straightway he will send[2] him hither. And they went their way, and found the colt tied by the door without, in a place where two ways met; and they loose him. And certain of them that stood there said unto them, What do ye, loosing the colt? And they said unto them even[3] as Jesus had commanded: and they let them go. And they brought[4] the colt to Jesus, and cast their garments on him; and he sat upon him. And many spread their garments in the way; and others cut down branches off the trees,[5] and strewed *them* in the way. And they that went before, and they that followed, cried, saying,[6] Hosanna; Blessed *is* he that cometh in the name of the Lord: Blessed *be* the kingdom of our father David, that cometh in the name of the Lord:[7] Hosanna in the highest. And Jesus[8] entered into Jerusalem, and into the temple: and when he had looked round about upon all things, and now the even-tide was come, he went out unto Bethany with the twelve.

¹ Ver. 2.—Lachmann reads οὐδεὶς οὔπω, after B., Origen, and others. [A. reads οὐδεὶς πώποτε.] Tischendorf and Meyer, after B., C., L., Δ. read λύσατε αὐτὸν καὶ φέρετε.
² Ver. 3.—In several Codd., B., C.*, D., L., Δ., &c., stands πάλιν. Thus the clause is made part of the answer of the disciples: The Lord will use the colt and send it back again.—Probably this was designed to soften the seeming violence of the transaction. [Elzevir and Fritzsche read ἀποστελεῖ.]
³ Ver. 6.—Καθὼς εἶπεν corresponding to the preceding εἶπον, according to B., C., L., Δ., Lachmann, Tischendorf, [Meyer].
⁴ Ver. 7.—B., L., Δ., Origen, Tischendorf, Meyer, read φέρουσιν instead of ἤγαγον. Ἐπιβάλλουσιν, emphatic Present, [B., C., D., L., Δ., Vulgate, Griesbach, Fritzsche, Lachmann, Tischendorf, Meyer].
⁵ Ver. 8.—Tischendorf's reading (recommended by Meyer), ἄλλοι δὲ στιβάδας, κόψαντες ἐκ τῶν ἀγρῶν, is not sufficiently supported. [Ἀγρῶν is found in B., C., L., Δ., Syriac (margin); Fritzsche, Lachmann, Tischendorf, and Meyer regard στιβάδας as the correct form.]
⁶ Ver. 9.—The λέγοντες is wanting in B., C., L., Δ., [Tischendorf; bracketed by Griesbach, Lachmann].
⁷ Ver. 10.—The reading, ἐν ὀνόματι κυρίου, has some important Codd. against it, but A. and others sustain it. It was probably corrected as being difficult; but the difficulty is obviated if we regard the expression "kingdom" (poetically brief, without the Article) as repeated in thought. [Meyer rejects it.]
⁸ Ver. 11.—Ὁ Ἰησοῦς is an explanatory addition. [Rejected by Griesbach, Fritzsche, Lachmann, Tischendorf, Meyer.]

EXEGETICAL AND CRITICAL.

See on the parallels in *Matthew* and *Luke*.—The Evangelist translates us at once into Palm-Sunday, as to time; and, as to place, into the region between Bethany and the Mount of Olives. The departure from Jericho took place on the Friday before the Passion-Week: it was the custom to spend the night in the district of the Mount of Olives, and to keep the Sabbath there. In Bethany, on the evening of Saturday, the meal took place in the house of Simon the Leper. On Sunday morning the journey from Bethany was continued. Now, in the accounts of the Synoptists, the beginning and the continuation of the festal journey are combined in one, because it is their object to describe the important palm-procession at once as a whole. Luke, indeed, informs us of the delay of the journey on Friday in Jericho, that is, through the Lord's entrance into the house of Zacchæus; and he adds the delivery of a parable which is connected with that entrance, and with the expectation of the people that He would at once found the Messianic kingdom in Jerusalem. But it is John alone who tells us that the tarrying in Bethany occupied an interval; and to him also we owe the most particular explanation of the procession, in the passage, ch. xii. 12–29. What is peculiar to Mark is this, that he places us by his minute specialities in the very midst of the scene. He writes in the present tense: "They come nigh; He sendeth." The sending of the two he relates somewhat more circumstantially; while, with Luke, he omits the mention of the older ass, and does not join Matthew and John in their allusion to Zech. ix. 9. He alone marks the fact, that the colt stood tied by the door of a house in a place where two ways met; and he also gives most vividly the particulars connected with the loosing of the ass. Then he again gives his record in the present tense: They bring the foal; they lay their garments thereon. In his description of the strewing of branches and garments in the way, as well as of the Hosanna, he agrees now with Matthew and now with Luke; yet he alone has the στοιβάδες, and the greeting to the kingdom of the Messiah, as well as to the King. Several traits which are found in Matthew, Luke, and John, he omits. Earnest and powerful is the final narrative. Jesus comes into the city, into the temple; takes all into His eye with silent, searching glance, and returns back to Bethany in the evening with the Twelve. For this distinction between the day of the entrance and the day of the cleansing of the temple, we are indebted to Mark alone.

Ver. 1. **Unto Bethphage and Bethany.**—They are approaching Jerusalem; and the approach is so ordered, that they arrive at Bethphage and Bethany. The intermediate stations are measured from Jerusalem, the goal; consequently, Bethphage comes first, and then Bethany, for they proceed from Bethany over Bethphage to the city. But how is it we read *towards Bethany*, when the departure was from that place? First, we must bear in mind that the Sunday procession from Bethany is blended into unity with the Friday procession from Jericho. Thus the passage means, that Jesus sent His disciples forth at once from Bethany. Moreover, it may be assumed that the Bethany of that time stretched wide into the country around, and that Jesus had found a lodgment in its eastern outskirts. The district of Bethany reached as far as to join the district of Bethphage. But Bethany they had not yet arrived at: the colt was sent for from thence. Concerning Jerusalem, Bethany, Bethphage, *see* on *Matthew*. Concerning the Mount of Olives, comp. Winer and the travellers.

Ver. 2. **Whereon never man sat.**—So also Luke. This circumstance is wanting in Matthew, but perfectly agrees with his account of the mother-ass. The foal had up to this time run with its mother. Meyer discerns in this notice "an appendage of reflective tradition, based on the sacred characteristic of the animal (for unused animals were put to sacred purposes, Num. xix. 2; Deut. xxi. 3; 1 Sam. vi. 7)."—Matthew did not note the circumstance, because it was self-understood that the foal was not yet used, so long as it was a foal running with the mother. *See* the notes on *Matthew*.

Ver. 3. **And if any man say unto you.**—That this significant interchange of sayings implies previous acquaintance and private watchwords, is proved by the use of the εἰπεῖν in Mark, and in Luke of the emphatic οὕτως ἐρεῖτε. So is it with the ordering of the Passover-feast by such a particular one: εἴπατε αὐτῷ. Luke has the equivalent ἐρεῖτε, with the addition, λέγει σοι ὁ διδάσκαλος.

Ver. 4. **Without, in a place where two ways met.**—The ἄμφοδον means primarily a way encompassing a block of houses; then the street, and even a quarter of the town. The animal being fastened to the door points to the open space before the house.

Ver. 8. **Branches.**—The word στοιβάδες is an error of the transcriber; the Codd. B. D., and others, read στιβάδες. The στιβάς is a scattering of straw, reed, branches, or twigs. The plural and the cutting down point to branches of trees. According to John xii. 13, palm-leaves were strewed (as the symbol of peace).

Ver. 10. **The kingdom of our father David.**—That is, the kingdom of the Messiah as the spiritual restoration of the kingdom of David, which had become, for the Jew, a type of the Messianic kingdom, as David was a type of the Messiah. "The Messiah

Himself was also called David, among the Rabbis (SCHÖTTGEN, *Hor.* ii.)." (Meyer.)

Ver. 11. **He went out unto Bethany.**—Meyer insists on it that there is here a discrepancy with Matthew. It is a discrepancy when the definite is opposed to the definite; but not when the definite is opposed to the indefinite. This well-founded canon of hermeneutics would demolish many of the discrepancies pointed out by school criticism. Matthew and Luke wrote no diaries. There is no difference here, any more than the blending of the parts of the palm-procession into the journey of one day makes the Synoptists and John disagree. Matthew and Luke connect the cleansing of the temple with the import of the palm entry; but this Mark does not. Christ, according to his account, takes a general survey, which in its silent observation betokened the cleansing which would take place on the morrow.

DOCTRINAL AND ETHICAL.

1. See on *Matthew* and *Luke*.
2. The expectation of the Messiah was the expectation of His kingdom; hence the salutation of the Messiah was the salutation of His kingdom. Christ and His kingdom are not to be separated; but the kingdom of His cross and the kingdom of His glory are to be distinguished, even as the glorified Christ is distinguished from the Christ in the form of a servant. Of this gulf between the kingdom here and the kingdom there, most of the jubilants had no idea; many rose not beyond it, but plunged below.
3. The Mount of Olives a symbol.
4. The palm-procession in Mark is brief, earnest, sublime. A swift progress to the city, and to the temple; ending in a wide and silent inspection of the temple until evening.

HOMILETICAL AND PRACTICAL.

See on *Matthew*, and the preceding reflections.—Christ's goal in His royal procession: to the temple.—The significance of Christ's coming to the temple: 1. The types and promises, Exod. xl. 34; 1 Kings viii.; 2 Chron. v.; Isa. ii.; lxvi. 20; Ezek. xliii.; Hagg. ii. 3, 9; Zech. xiv. 20; Mal. iii. 1. 2. The historical visits paid to it: the child Jesus in the temple, the visit when twelve years old, the feasts, Jesus as the public Messiah in the temple, the Pentecost, the burning of the temple in A. D. 70. 3. The spiritual visitations of the temple.—The history of the temple the history of the world; the history of the temple the history of the kingdom of God.—The palm-entry into the temple, according to its external and its internal form: 1. The great procession to the great cathedral; 2. Christ the judged, and Christ the Judge, conducted by a wretched people to the deserted house of God.—Christ comes to the temple, 1. from Galilee with the ecclesiastical devout, 2. from Jericho with the enthusiasts, 3. from Bethany with His friends and servants, 4. from the Mount of Olives alone with His Holy Spirit.—Christ in the temple as the Jesus of twelve years, and as the openly-proclaimed Messiah.—Christ in the beautiful new-built temple; or, the difference between an æsthetic and a spiritual inspection of the temple.—The fearfully silent glance of Christ in the temple until evening.—The Lord's visitation of His churches: 1. He knows and sees all; 2. He sees and looks through all; 3.

He looks through all, and keeps silence; 4. He keeps silence, thinking upon judgment and mercy.—Christ's entrance and exit at His temple visitation: 1. The entrance: through the city straight to the temple; 2. the exit: from the temple to Bethany.—The procession of the people with Christ to the temple.

STARKE:—Thus Jesus comes as the Lamb of God, and places Himself on the altar of sacrifice. Certainly this was not the act of a mere man, thus joyfully to come, to give Himself up to His enemies, and go to confront His death.—Comp. the foal, 1 Sam. vi. 7.—CANSTEIN:—The Lord needs not that we should give Him anything, for all is always His; yet He may require it for certain purposes.—QUESNEL:—All things must be cast under the feet of Jesus.—*Nova Bibl. Tub.*:—Where Jesus is, there is life, movement, praise, and joy.—How necessary is the visitation of the churches!—HEDINGER:—The eye and the heart may well take pleasure, as in nature, so also in art, her copy. (But all in its measure and in its time.)—GERLACH:—(The foal never yet used.) This trait points to the fact that Jesus made His entrance as Priest-King.—BRAUNE:—Believers gladly place their substance at the feet and disposal of Jesus, their Master.—In the way of obedience (which the disciples followed), light always arises upon light.—The Lord now came upon the animal of peace, not as one day upon the great white horse to judgment.—Thus they received with peaceful joy the Prince of peace.—Every festal pilgrim was received with the "Blessed is He that cometh in the name of the Lord;" but the greeting befitted Him in a peculiar and higher sense.

SCHLEIERMACHER:—We must confess that, though they may not have been the same men (who first cried *Hosannah!* then *Crucify* Him), yet that it was the same people.—The oneness and interdependence of the people makes the difference of the individuals disappear.—We cannot help regarding this gross fickleness and instability as the proper characteristic of the great mass.—(Christ keeping silence in the temple till even-tide.) The boundary between the old and the new covenant came nearer and nearer: the one was to find its end, and the other was to be erected on the ruins of the former.—What thoughts touching the past must have arisen, and how deep must His emotions have been, in the consciousness of what He came to do, when He compared the magnificence and glory of the old covenant with the spiritual life of the new covenant, which, far removed from all outward demonstration, unseen and unpretending, was creating for itself its own form in sweet and gentle silence; when He compared the magnificence and glory of the external temple with the spiritual temple built of living stones, in which His spirit should dwell, and where should be established for ever the worship of His heavenly Father in spirit and in truth!

BRIEGER:—The devotion of the garments to His service intimates something extraordinary. When Jehu in the camp was to be proclaimed as king, a throne of garments was erected for him. This, with the sound of trumpets, and the cry, "Jehu is king," made up the homage (2 Kings ix. 13). Here we have something similar, whereby homage is done to Jesus.—As a light before its final extinction blazes up once more, so Israel before their final fall lifted themselves up to Jehovah once more. But as at Sinai they were put to shame after professing obedience (Exod. xx. 19), through making the golden calf, so here they are put to more wretched shame, by so soon crying, Crucify Him! crucify Him!— Now does the Father set His Son as a King upon His holy hill of Zion, Ps. ii. 6.—Christ was a King from this hour. In all the parables from this point, His own Person is the centre. He speaks and acts as a king. (But we must distinguish between the time when the people heralded Him as king, and when God lifted Him up to His throne: between Palm Sunday and the Resurrection and Ascension.)

---

4. *The Withered Fig-tree, and the House of Prayer made a Den of Thieves. The Cleansing of the Temple.*
VERS. 12–26.

(Parallels : Matt. xxi. 12–22 ; Luke xix. 45, 46.)

12 And on the morrow, when they were come from Bethany, he was hungry.
13 And seeing a fig-tree afar off,[1] having leaves, he came, if haply he might find anything thereon: and when he came to it, he found nothing but leaves; for the time[2] of figs was
14 not yet. And Jesus[3] answered and said unto it, No man eat fruit of thee hereafter for
15 ever. And his disciples heard *it*. And they come to Jerusalem: and Jesus went into the temple, and began to cast out them that sold and bought in the temple, and over-
16 threw the tables of the money-changers, and the seats of them that sold doves; And
17 would not suffer that any man should carry *any* vessel through the temple. And he taught, saying unto them,[4] Is it not written, My house shall be called of [by] all nations
18 the house of prayer? but ye have made it a den of thieves. And the scribes and chief priests heard *it*, and sought how they might destroy him : for they feared him, because
19 all the people was astonished at his doctrine. And when even was come, he went out
20 of the city. And in the morning, as they passed by,[5] they saw the fig-tree dried up
21 from the roots. And Peter, calling to remembrance, saith unto him, Master, behold,
22 the fig-tree which thou cursedst is withered away. And Jesus answering, saith unto
23 them, Have faith in God. For[6] verily I say unto you, That whosoever shall say unto this mountain, Be thou removed, and be thou cast into the sea; and shall not doubt in his heart, but shall believe that those things which he saith shall come to pass; he shall
24 have whatsoever he saith. Therefore I say unto you, What things soever ye desire,
25 when ye pray,[7] believe that ye receive *them*,[8] and ye shall have *them*. And when ye stand praying, forgive, if ye have ought against any; that your Father also which is
26 in heaven may forgive you your trespasses.[9] But if ye do not forgive, neither will your Father which is in heaven forgive your trespasses.

[1] Ver. 13.—[Griesbach, Fritzsche, Scholz, Lachmann, Tischendorf, Meyer, after important MSS., read ἀπό before μακρόθεν.]
[2] Ver. 13.—Lachmann reads ὁ καιρός with the Article, following Origen and several Codd.; and thus the true meaning of the passage becomes more definite.
[3] Ver. 14.—'Ο Ἰησοῦς interpolated.
[4] Ver. 17.—Καὶ ἔλεγεν αὐτοῖς, according to C., L., Δ., &c. Πεποιήκατε, B., L., Δ., Origen, [Tischendorf, Meyer,] instead of ἐποιήσατε.
[5] Ver. 20.—The order of B., C., L., Δ., Lachmann, and Tischendorf is παραπορευόμ. πρωΐ.
[6] Ver. 23.—The γάρ (for) is wanting in B., D., Lachmann, Tischendorf. The additional clause, ὃ ἐὰν εἴπῃ, is wanting in B., C., D., L., Δ., Tischendorf.
[7] Ver. 24.—Lachmann, Tischendorf, Meyer, after B., C., L., Δ., read προσεύχεσθε καὶ αἰτεῖσθε: a more comprehensive promise.
[8] Ver. 24.—Codd. B., C., L., Δ., read ἐλάβετε, instead of λαμβάνετε: accepted by Lachmann, Tischendorf, and Meyer.
[9] Ver. 26.—This verse is wanting in B., L., S., Δ., and some others. Tischendorf gives it up, Lachmann and Meyer retain it, after C. and others. But it is an interpolation which some MSS., after ver. 26, add from Matt. vii. 7, 8.

EXEGETICAL AND CRITICAL.

See on the parallels in *Matthew* and *Luke*.—Notwithstanding Mark's conciseness in his record, we can yet distinguish three days of Jesus' abode in the temple; that is, of the Messianic residence there of the King. Sunday was the day of entrance and looking around, ch. xi. 1–11. Monday was the day on which the fig-tree was cursed, the temple was cleansed, and those festal works were done by Jesus in the temple which filled up the exasperation of His enemies, vers. 12–19. Then Tuesday was the day of His conflict in the temple with all the assaults of His enemies in their several divisions, and of His departure from the temple, ch. xi. 20; xiii. 37. On Wednesday Jesus remained in concealment, as we are positively assured by John (ch. xii. 37); and probably it was then that He completed His discourse of the last things by adding those eschatological parables which Matthew communicates: unless we may assume rather that they were uttered on the night between Tuesday and Wednesday within the circle of His most confidential disciples. The allusions to night might suit such a view, Matt. xxiv. 42, 43; xxv. 6, 30. The silent Wednesday of His concealment was then devoted to the preparation of His larger body of disciples, and to purposes of retired devotion.

The unity of this section lies in the narrative of

the fig-tree cursed. Mark makes it the starting-point of His account of Jesus' wonderful works in the temple during Monday. The individual particulars of these festal wonders are singled out prominently by Matthew, ch. xxi. 12–15. Therefore he brings into this second day the cursing of the fig-tree, with its withering up. Luke also indicates these festal hours, ch. xix. 47, 48. For the peculiar significance of the facts of the Greeks earnestly desiring to see Jesus, and the discourse which that occasioned, *see* the Notes on John xii. 20–36. But the Evangelist Mark takes the whole day into his view under its severe aspect. Hence he connects all this with the narrative of the fig-tree; and this section embraces the time from Monday morning to Tuesday morning. Thus, according to his account, the cursing of the fig-tree preceded the cleansing of the temple on Monday morning. With Matthew, who likewise has the narrative, it follows it; because Matthew purposed more strongly to stamp the contrast of the two temple-days—the day of peace and the day of contest. Concerning the fig-tree, Mark preliminarily remarks that it had leaves (which from afar might seem to be inviting). But in connection with the circumstance that Jesus found no figs upon it, he has the remarkable clause οὐ γὰρ ἦν, etc., the time was not yet (concerning which, *see* below). Matthew's word, "Let no fruit grow henceforth," he gives concretely: "Let no man eat," etc. He adds, that the disciples heard it. The cleansing of the temple he relates again with an ἤρξατο: He began. And he adds to the picture, that Jesus would not suffer any vessel to be carried through the temple. The explanatory word of Christ he introduces as instruction (ἐδίδασκε), and in vigorous interrogative form (οὐ γέγραπται). To the "house of prayer" he adds, "for all nations;" which Luke has not, and which reminds us of "every creature," ch. xvi. 15. The confusion of the Sanhedrim on this day, and their projects as to the manner in which they should kill Jesus—seeing that they feared the people, who did earnest homage to Jesus—he connects rightly with this day; while Luke records it more indefinitely (ch. xix. 47, 48), as also Matthew in somewhat similar manner (ch. xxi. 15, 16), and John also in another aspect of it (ch. xii. 17–19). Then follows, according to Mark, the departure of Jesus from the city. Matthew tells us that the fig-tree had straightway withered. Mark relates that it was early in the morning, as they passed by. Thus the withering had proceeded in the course of a day and night; and that, as he remarks, from the root. Matthew makes the disciples see, wonder, and speak; Mark records more precisely how Peter remembered the circumstance and spoke. The words themselves are more vivid here: Rabbi, behold, etc. Thereupon Jesus utters the word concerning the removing of mountains by faith: more concretely apprehended in Mark; more generally in Matthew. But Mark connects with this promise of Jesus the very important word concerning the hearing of prayer (ver. 24), and the condition of being reconciled with our brother (Matt. vi. 14).

Ver. 12. **And on the morrow.**—Therefore, on the Monday morning after the Sunday of the palms. —**He was hungry.**—Early departure, haste to enter the work of the day, and much else, lay at the foundation of this fact.

Ver. 13. **If haply,** εἰ ἄρα: that is, because it had leaves; since the leaves of the fig-tree appear after the fruit. Matt. xxi. 19.—**The time of figs was not yet.**—*See* the note on *Matthew*. As the tree had leaves, it promised fruit; for the harvest-time of figs, when it might have been stripped of its fruit, was not yet come. For the various explanations of this, *see* DE WETTE and MEYER. As καιρός signifies the full and perfect time, the meaning is clear enough. Between the period of leaf-formation and the time of fig-harvest, one might seek for figs from a tree standing exposed. But not till the καιρός had come could the tree be stripped. Thus the οὐ γὰρ is not an explanation of the circumstance that it had no figs, but of the Lord's coming and seeking, by which it appeared that the tree had only produced its leaves. The expression, "He found nothing but leaves only," signifies that He saw with displeasure that, as a worthless tree, it had nothing but leaves upon it. This He might conclude from the fact that the time of harvest had not yet come, and, therefore, that it was not already stripped of its fruit. According to Meyer, the meaning is, that the tree could not yet have borne fruit. "If it had been the time of figs, He would have found fruit besides the leaves."* But then a premature doom would have been pronounced on the tree. The early display of leaves was certainly irregular; but if it had been a certain sign of its dying, the Lord would not have sought fruit upon it. If it could put forth leaves, it must have been able previously to set its fruit.

Ver. 14. **And Jesus said unto it.**—Properly, answered and said. BENGEL: *arbori fructum neganti*.

Ver. 16. Concerning the temple, *see* on *Matthew*. —**And would not suffer that any man should,** ἵνα; the toleration of evil is the procurement of it.— **Any vessel.**—No man durst carry tools and implements through the sacred precincts of the temple, that is, through the fore-court. Was it intended to avoid a circuitous route, as in a great city profane passages may be made through holy places? But the temple space was not in the way of such passing. Many, however, might bring their implements of toil with them at their devotions, in order to have them conveniently at hand. The carrying them through was, therefore, not literally a passing through with them, but rather the having them at hand; and it is opposed to the business of money-changing and selling doves which was carried on within the temple itself. According to LIGHTFOOT and WETSTEIN, the Rabbins afterwards forbade the same thing.

Ver. 17. **Of all nations.**—The prediction of the prophets, that the temple should be a house of prayer for all nations, had a higher meaning (*see* Isa. ii. and other passages). There must be a distinction, however, between the Israelite bondsmen who brought their offerings (Lev. xvii. 8; xxii. 19; Ezra ii. 43; vii. 7), and the later proselytes of the gate; the relative recognition of these latter had given occasion to the symbol of the Court of the Gentiles. Therein lay the germ of the universality of the religion of promise. *See* on *Matthew*. That the additional clause occurs only in Mark, is not to be accounted for only on Gentile-Christian grounds; for it is wanting in Luke. It is peculiar to Mark that he everywhere lays stress upon the universality of the Gospel.†

* [" Οὐ γὰρ ἦν καιρὸς σύκων gives the reason why Jesus found nothing but leaves. If it had been the season for figs (viz., June, when the early fig, *Boccore*, ripens), he would have found fruit besides leaves, and would not have been deceived by the unseasonable (abnormal) leafage of the tree." MEYER, *in loc.*—*Ed.*]

† On the harmony here, Starke says: This was the third time that He thus cleansed the temple. The first time in

Ver. 18. **Sought how they might destroy Him.**—This was their counsel on Monday: that Jesus should die, had been already previously decided (John v. 16; vii. 32; x. 31; xi. 45). They now confusedly took counsel about the *how;* * since it seemed almost an impossibility, on account of the people, on this day of His wonderful ascendancy in the temple. Then again on Wednesday: "not on the feast-day," although Judas had preliminarily dealt with them on the Sunday concerning the matter. The Palm Sunday may have made Judas suspicious again, or brought his promise into doubt. Then he came on Thursday evening, after a new crisis had come (the departure of Jesus from the temple), and his exasperation had become complete.

Ver. 20. **They saw the fig-tree dried up from the roots.**—*See* on *Matthew*. Meyer naturally finds here another discrepancy with Matthew. Matthew is inexact in his record, only on account of a higher end that he contemplated in his narrative. Nor does Mark say that the withering had just then taken place, or been finished. The tree was now in a marvellous manner dried up; and that, as he adds, from the roots—from its diseased root upwards, throughout.

Ver. 22. **Faith in God.**—Trust towards God, πίστις Θεοῦ (Genitive of the object). More general view of faith, with reference to the personal source of miraculous power, the almighty God of the covenant: ch. ix. 23. Compare Matt. xvii. 20; Luke xvii. 6.

Ver. 24. **That ye receive them.**—That is, in the divine confidence of faith that is already received which in external reality has yet to come: Heb. xi. 1. The prayer of faith is heard: as prayer in the name of Jesus, John xiv. 13, 14; xvi. 23, 24, 26; or, as the prayer of a holy society, the Church, Matt. xviii. 19; or, as the prayer of the Holy Ghost, Rom. viii. 26–28.

Ver. 25. **When ye stand praying.**—Comp. Matt. v. 23, 24, and vi. 14, 15. As the word concerning the faith which moves mountains might have originally been uttered in more than one connection, so also that concerning the forgiveness of others, as the condition of all true offering of prayer, and its answer. But in this place, where Jesus connected this strongest assurance of the marvellous power of faith with the cursing of the fig-tree, it seems inevitable that He should declare how such a faith could not be sundered from a placable love; that it should never be used in the service of hate and fanaticism.

DOCTRINAL AND ETHICAL.

1. *See* on the parallel in *Matthew*, and also the previous notes.
2. The so-called cursing of the fig-tree is the rather to be regarded as a grand prophetic act, because Christ, as Christ, now stood at the climax of the palm festivity, and it was obvious that all Israel might now do Him homage. This symbolical act at such a crisis was a sure sign that He was perfectly conscious of the situation of things; as also was the

___
John ii.; the second time on the day before this, immediately after His entrance, Matt. xxi. 10, 12.
* [This would be indicated by the Future, ἀπολέσουσιν, of the Received Text; the Subjunctive, ἀπολέσωσιν, adopted by Lachmann and Tischendorf, would imply that the purpose itself to put Christ to death was now formed.—Ed.]

weeping over the city during the festal procession, according to Luke.
3. The cleansing of the temple at the beginning and at the end of Christ's pilgrimage, the earnest of a manifold cleansing of the Church from Gentile and Jewish perversions.
4. The declaration of the curse in its sacred form, a revelation to explain its real nature, and thereby to remove it; as contrasted with man's curse of evil wishing.

HOMILETICAL AND PRACTICAL.

See on *Matthew*.—The fig-tree a figure of Israel, and a warning sign to the Church: 1. As the fruitful fig-tree, which sets forth fruit sooner than leaves. So Israel. It had faith, and the works of faith, before it had the ceremonies of faith. So the early Church. 2. As the unfruitful fig-tree, which had an adornment of leaves, promising fruit deceitfully. So the Israel of the time of Jesus, and so the external Church of later times and the last.—The cursing of the fig-tree in its relation to the cleansing of the temple: 1. An indication of the morning thoughts of the Lord concerning Israel; 2. a prelude to the coming expurgation of the temple; 3. a prophetic token (for the hopeful disciples, concerning the coming solemn issue of things).—The judgment of Jesus upon the fig-tree, and His judgment upon the temple with its service.—Christ hungering on the morn of His greatest day of honor: or, the great sign of the spiritual purity and freedom of the kingdom of Christ.—The Lord's hunger on the temple-mountain, and His thirsting on Calvary.—How zeal for the Lord should keep itself pure from hatred against men.—Only in the spirit of reconciliation can the Christian execute the judicial office.—The flames of Christ's wrath a loving zeal, which is always one with the spirit of reconciliation.—We cannot help others in the way to heaven by the hateful and tormenting fury of fanaticism.

STARKE:—Christ knows what the feeling of the hungry is.—If we endure hunger, we should not murmur, remembering Him.—CANSTEIN:—Christ demands nothing of man, if he has not had time; nor does He come to seek till the time is up.—OSIANDER:—Hypocrites have a semblance of godliness, but no true fruits of faith; and so, if they repent not, they must perish.—HEDINGER:—We must rid the Church of every abuse, and spare no man.—QUESNEL:—Every believer is a temple of God, and must entertain the same zeal for his own soul's purity as Jesus displayed for the purity of the visible sanctuary.—OSIANDER:—The churches which celebrate a false worship of God are dens of thieves; they wrest for themselves the goods of simple people, and slay their souls.—Those who devote themselves to the correction of ecclesiastical abuses have commonly to encounter great opposition, their lives being sometimes laid in wait for.—An evil conscience must always tremble at itself, and is never bold in its work.—QUESNEL:—The truth everywhere makes a division among the people; some think to oppress it, while others hear it with wonder and faith.—GERLACH:—If you do not find that your believing prayer is granted, ask yourself what lies within that hinders your being heard.—BRAUNE:—Benevolent and like a Creator were all His miracles.—This is the only one which punishes and hurts, but it is performed on an inanimate object. It was designed to set luminously before us the reality of the divine punishments.—He pronounced here upon the tree that which, in the parable of the barren fig-tree, the vine-dresser had spoken of as in store for it.—Enmity to man suffers not the philanthropy of God to reach us.—Faith and reconcilableness go together.—SCHLEIERMACHER:—All that pertains to the community of Christian life and fellowship should be so ordered as to be free from all reference to the outward commerce of this world (on the cleansing of the temple).—GOSSNER:—Words, oral prayers, formularies, external exercises without the spirit, good wishes and mere resolutions, are mere leaves, if the Spirit of God does not invigorate them, and they bear no fruit.

SECOND SECTION.

THE DECISIVE CONFLICT OF JESUS WITH HIS ENEMIES IN JERUSALEM, AND HIS WITHDRAWAL TO THE MOUNT OF OLIVES.

CHAPTERS XI. 27—XIII. 37.

1. *The Attack of the Sanhedrim; or the Question concerning Christ's Authority, and His Counter-question concerning the Baptist's.* CH. XI. 27–33.

(Parallels: Matt. xxi. 23–27; Luke xx. 1–8.)

27 And they come again to Jerusalem: and as he was walking in the temple, there
28 come to him the chief priests, and the scribes, and the elders, And say¹ unto him, By what authority doest thou these things, and who gave thee this authority to do these
29 things? And Jesus answered and said unto them, I will also ask of you one question,
30 and answer me, and I will tell you by what authority I do these things. The baptism
31 of John, was *it* from heaven, or of men? answer me. And they reasoned with themselves, saying, If we shall say, From heaven; he will say, Why then² did ye not believe
32 him? But if³ we shall say, Of men; they feared the people: for all *men* counted John,
33 that he was a prophet indeed. And they answered and said unto Jesus, We cannot tell. And Jesus answering,⁴ saith unto them, Neither do I tell you by what authority I do these things.

¹ Ver. 28.—Tischendorf reads, with B., C., L., Δ., ἔλεγον, and ἢ for καὶ (τίς) with B., L., D.
² Ver. 31.—The οὖν is wanting in A., C.*, L., Versions, Lachmann, Tischendorf, Meyer.
³ Ver. 32.—The ἐὰν is wanting in the best Codd.; omitting it, the sentence takes a very characteristic interrogatory form.
⁴ Ver. 33.—The ἀποκριθείς is wanting in B., C., [L., Tischendorf, Meyer,] and elsewhere varies in its position.

EXEGETICAL AND CRITICAL.

See on the parallels of *Matthew* and *Luke*.—According to Mark's representation, this day of Christ's conflict falls on Tuesday of the Passion Week. But the conflict is subdivided into three parts: 1. The official demand as to Jesus' abode and supremacy in the temple, exhibited in the question of the Sanhedrim touching His authority; with its reply, as in our present section. 2. The ironical acknowledgment, on the side of the inimical party, of Christ's Messianic dignity, exhibited in a series of tempting questions and answers; with the great counter-question of Jesus. 3. The Lord's words to the people, and departure from the temple. Mark's account has in our text no prominent peculiarities; he agrees rather with Luke than with Matthew. His vivid style of delineation is seen in the trait that Jesus went round about the temple, while according to Matthew, He was in the act of teaching (though these are not inconsistent with each other); as also the second clause of the Sanhedrim's pondering—"But if we shall say." The Evangelist's choice of the expression λέγει αὐτοῖς, ver. 33, seems appropriate; while Matthew says ἔφη, and Luke εἶπεν. As the Sanhedrim refused Him a decisive declaration concerning John, who had prophetically authenticated Him as the Messiah, He also refused to them the decisive declaration they sought. This was, however, in itself decisive; but not in the form of an express statement.

Ver. 27. **Doest Thou these things?**—*See Matthew*. This meant, doubtless, the public appearance and work of Jesus in the temple under the Messiah-name which the people gave Him; amongst the rest, certainly, as an individual act, the cleansing of the temple also. The law ordained that prophets were to be tried, Deut. xiii. 1. The most essential requisite was agreement with the faith of the God of Israel; the accidental requirement was the performance of miracles. The latter was not valid without the former; but it was not said that the former without the latter was not valid. (Comp. Deut. xviii. 20; Ezek. xiii. 1). The Sanhedrim could hold themselves justified only in asking for the authority of Jesus. They could not deny that He had approved Himself by miracles. They were disposed, however, to make it a reproach, that He taught other gods, and a new religion. Hence they ask Him: 1. After the divine source of His power, prophetic inspiration; 2. after

His theocratic authentication. By the latter the former also was approved, and therefore Jesus appealed to John. John was the most recent monument of the truth and validity of the prophetic order in Israel. And this John had marked Him out as the Messiah. They had been compelled to allow his validity as a prophet, although they did not afterwards acknowledge him. They would entangle Jesus by making Him appeal to His divine dignity; but the word of Jesus entangled them and smote them at the same time. It was a reference to His theocratic legitimation, the bearer of which they durst not openly impeach; and at the same time a remembrancer that they themselves had, since the days of John, been falling deep into apostasy.

Ver. 31. **If we shall say.**—The abrupt form is expressive, and more significant than the full unfolding of it in Matthew and Luke, "We fear," which certainly declares the motive of their silence.

Indeed (of a truth).—According to the reading ὄντως ὅτι, which Tisch. adopts from B. C. L., Meyer translates "They were inwardly sure that John was a prophet." But A. D. and others form a counterpoise; as well as the consideration that this would attribute to the people altogether, and as a whole, the full and believing acceptance of John.

DOCTRINAL AND ETHICAL.

1. See on the parallels.
2. The counter-question of Jesus arose as the simple consequence of the question addressed to Him. That question was addressed to His theocratic authority. This was already involved in the authentication by John. If they acknowledged John, they must acknowledge also his witness to Jesus as the Messiah. If they did not acknowledge him, they were in a theocratic sense rebels; and Christ could, in the consciousness of His real, human-divine authority, transcending all theocratic authorization, refuse to give them an answer.
3. From heaven or of men.—Divine mission or human enthusiasm. The antithesis is here laid down, with reference to the contrast between the divine and the human in the human sphere, and does not prejudice the union of the divine and human in the Christological sphere.

HOMILETICAL AND PRACTICAL.

See *Matthew.*—Christ in His temple assaulted by the official rulers of the place.—Vainly would hierarchical official authority suppress the divine mission of Jesus.—The misuse of spiritual prerogatives against the rights of the Spirit of Christ a guilt which brings after it the severest punishments: 1. Misuse of dignity calls down the judgment of disgrace; 2. misuse of office calls down displacement and rejection from office.—The Spirit of Christ triumphs over the false spirituality of His enemies: 1. With His counter-question opposing their question; 2. with His counter-declarations against their declarations.—The authority of Christ to take possession of the temple of God, as opposed to the impotence of His foes: 1. The authority: *a.* His theocratic authority; *b.* His personal divine-human authority; *c.* the authority which rose out of His actual Passion-conflict. 2. The impotence of His foes: *a.* as rejecters of the God-sent Baptist, forsaken of human justice; *b.* as rejecters of Christ, forsaken of the Spirit; *c.* as enemies and murderers of Christ, forsaken of God in His government of the world.—The obedience of Christ as confronting the Jewish priesthood, an emblem of Christian faith confronting churchly office: 1. The Lord regards the office as under the condition of obedience to the revelation of God, because it issues from that revelation; 2. He regards Himself as under the obligation to obey the revelation of God, because He is the consummation of it. Or, 1. In His suffering a question; 2. in His declining to answer; 3. in His willingness to submit to officials, so long as their rejection is not complete.—The heavenly prudence of the Lord in its triumph over the human wisdom of His enemies.—How the spirit of the New Covenant confronts the false representatives of the Old Covenant in God's temple: 1. With the clear word of knowledge; 2. with the firm word of assurance; 3. with the sharp word of judgment; 4. with the abundant word of life and of freedom.

STARKE:—*Nova Bibl. Tub.:*—Zeal for God's house and for its purity is sure to awaken enemies.—Conscience bears witness against the worst of men: they are their own accusers, judges, condemners.—OSIANDER:—They who will not suffer the Church's amendment in rule and discipline must fall.—CANSTEIN:—When those in the teaching and ruling office are unfaithful to their calling, and God raises up others extraordinarily, the former take all pains to deny to the latter the power that God Himself has given them.—HEDINGER:—The good need prudence in their intercourse with cunning and wicked people, lest their simplicity and openness bring harm to them and their cause.—QUESNEL:—Miserable case when the men of light use their knowledge of the truth to oppose that truth.—How many will not in religious matters be sincere, and reveal the truth, lest they be assaulted and tried!—*Bibl. Wirt.:*—The scorners of the truth, God will in the end count not worthy of the truth they scorn; but, instead of it, will send them strong delusions, that they should believe a lie, 2 Thess. ii. 11, 12.

BRAUNE:—He might have appealed to many prophets (yet not in the same sense as to John). They would then have said: But that was in a former age. He takes the latest example (of a prophetic vocation).

---

2. *The Parable concerning the Counsel of the Sanhedrim against the Messiah.* Cu. XII. 1–12.

(Parallels: Matt. xxi. 33–46; Luke xx. 9–17.)

1   And he began to speak¹ unto them by parables. A *certain* man planted a vineyard, and set an hedge about *it*, and digged *a place for* the wine-fat, and built a tower, and
2 let it out to husbandmen, and went into a far country. And at the season he sent to

the husbandmen a servant, that he might receive from the husbandmen of the fruit of
3 the vineyard. And² they caught *him*, and beat him, and sent *him* away empty.
4 And again he sent unto them another servant: and at him they cast stones,³ and
5 wounded *him* in the head, and sent *him* away shamefully handled. And again⁴ he sent
another; and him they killed, and many others; beating some, and killing some.
6 Having yet therefore one son, his well-beloved, he sent him also last unto them, saying,
7 They will reverence my son. But those husbandmen said among themselves, This is
8 the heir; come, let us kill him, and the inheritance shall be ours. And they took him,
9 and killed *him*, and cast *him* out of the vineyard. What shall therefore the lord of the
vineyard do? He will come and destroy the husbandmen, and will give the vineyard
10 unto others. And have ye not read this scripture: The stone which the builders re-
11 jected is become the head of the corner: This was the Lord's doing [from the Lord],
12 and it is marvellous in our eyes? And they sought to lay hold on him, but feared the
people; for they knew that he had spoken the parable against them: and they left
him, and went their way.

¹ Ver. 1.—Lachmann, Tischendorf, [Meyer] read λαλεῖν instead of λέγειν, following B., G., L., Δ., [Syriac, Vulgate].
² Ver. 3.—Lachmann, Tischendorf read καί, after B., D., L., Δ. Meyer: from Matt. xxi. 35.
³ Ver. 4.—The reading of B., D., L., [Δ., Lachmann, Tischendorf, Meyer,] κἀκεῖνον ἐκεφαλαίωσαν καὶ ἠτίμησαν, does not seem thorough enough, as opposed to the climax supported by Cod. A. and others, viz., beating and sending empty—wounding in the head and sending home shamefully handled.
⁴ Ver. 5.—Codd. B., C., D., L., Δ. omit πάλιν.

EXEGETICAL AND CRITICAL.

See the parallel passages in *Matthew* and *Luke*.—Mark relates only the second of the three parables, which Christ, according to Matthew, connected with His rejection of the commission of the Sanhedrim, for the purpose of indicating to them what He awaited at their hands, and how they, as the murderers of the Messiah, should be subjected to the punishment of losing the Messianic kingdom. It is the very parable in which they are made to appear as the murderers of the Messiah in connection with the persecutors of the prophets. In the first verse, we obtain a hint from Mark that Jesus delivered several parables (ἐν παραβολαῖς λέγειν) before His opponents. Mark is, further, more exact than Matthew in the climax of the messages sent by the lord of the vineyard. According to him, the first servant is beaten upon the back, and sent empty away; the second is wounded in the head, insulted, and sent away covered with disgrace; the third is killed. This triple fate is then met by many others. In consequence of this conduct the lord of the vineyard despatches his son; and of him Mark observes that he was the only son. From Matthew we learn that servants were twice sent,—on the first occasion in smaller, on the second, in greater numbers; and their fate is to be beaten, killed, stoned. Luke records only an increased abuse of the several servants despatched. The actual ground-thought is in each case the same: repeated messages, increased injuries, and, as a consequence, augmented hardening of heart and rebellion. Then we have the opposition between the sending of the servants and the sending of the son,—between the generous hope of the lord, that pious fear and remorse would be manifested, and the flagitious design respecting the inheritance on the part of the vine-dressers. Christ, according to Matthew, makes His enemies pronounce judgment, and declare what would be the dealing of that lord with his servants; according to Mark, the condemnation is expressed by Christ Himself. The passage from the Psalms, Mark quotes in conclusion, as does Luke; the citation from Isaiah, introduced by Matthew, is not here given. And further, the μὴ γένοιτο, spoken by the opponents in Luke xx. 16, is wanting. Graphic narrative and a freshness of delineation are the characteristics of Mark in this passage, as in others.

Ver. 2. **Of the fruit.**—The stipulated portion of the product. For the agreement of Matthew with Mark in this passage, consult *Note* on *Matthew*.

Ver. 4. **And again he sent.**—We admit, there is undoubtedly a kind of periodic succession in the missions hinted at; but this is not to be settled in an external, petty way, of which an example is presented in Meyer.—**At him they cast stones.**—'Ἐκεφαλαίωσαν is to be explained in accordance with the difference between it and the simple ἔδειραν. Beating with sticks upon the back, casting stones at the head, marked the first gradation, to which the second pair corresponded,—being sent away empty, shamefully disfigured. As this word, in other collocations, means simply to recapitulate, to relate summarily, we must interpret here according to the context. Meyer says, Mark has confounded κεφαλαιόω with κεφαλίζω. But the latter would have been too strong; and it is possible that the verb before us might have recommended itself to him as capable of bearing two senses, and this double-force we have endeavored to indicate. Wakefield's interpretation, "They made short work of him," is too one-sided.

Ver. 9. **Killed him and cast him out.**—The order is reversed in Matthew and Luke. Grotius and De Wette make it a hysteron-proteron. Meyer says, it is only another description.

He will come and will.—Kuinoel, following Vatablus, makes this the reply of the Pharisees in Matt. xxi. 24. It is plain that Mark gives a more brief account of the matter. The Lord spoke the judgment which His parable forced from the lips of His enemies. *See Note* on *Matthew*.

Ver. 12. **For they knew that He had spoken against them.**—Meyer would make these words, as well as in Luke, apply to the people and not to the members of the Sanhedrim. He intends this explanation to account for the apparent want of the proper succession in words. According to some commentators, these words should follow κρατῆσαι. But the order presents no difficulty at all. They would have seized Christ at once very willingly, and yet they ventured not, etc. This is only a reflection; and our words present the key, the concluding explanation. Their common purpose, to put the Messiah to death upon the first favorable occasion, rose in these and similar moments of exasperation to such a pitch, that they would have gladly seized Him on the spot, and killed Him, if they had only dared to do so.

DOCTRINAL AND ETHICAL.

1. Upon the import of the parable, *see* the remarks upon the passage in *Matthew*. The planting of the vineyard is to be looked upon as the promise and the law, or generally as the covenant-word in its identity with believing hearts. The hedge is not the law in itself, but is to be interpreted as being that external institution by which Israel was separated from the other nations (Eph. ii. 14); the wine-press, or tank, considered in connection with the altar of sacrifice and the martyrdom of the prophets, indicates the inner side of the congregation; and hence we are led to consider the tower, typifying civil order, law, and protection, as the opposite of the wine-press. The wine-fat is sunk into the earth and hidden; the tower rises on high, apparent to every eye, the sign of the vineyard.

2. We must remark, further, that we have here pictured the gradual augmentation of selfishness, of hostility to, and revolt from, the Lord, on the part of the theocratic servants and vassals of God. This representation presents at the same time a type of the climax of injuries inflicted upon the prophets, and above all, of the climax of the Lord's magnanimity, as opposed to the disgraceful conduct of the servants. The struggle of divine grace with the obdurate unbelief of the administrators of His plan of mercy divides into two periods: 1. The period of long-suffering; and 2. the period of judgment. The first era has two chief periods: *a.* The Establishment, *b.* the Missions; which we may divide into, 1. The missions of servants, rising by a threefold climax; 2. the mission of the Son, in which, again, three points present themselves: A. The wicked proposal; B. the murder of the Son; and C. the casting of his corpse forth out of the vineyard. But, in the same manner, are three points to be observed in the Judgment: 1. The destruction of the evil-doers; 2. the entrusting of the vineyard to others; and 3. a donation of the vineyard to others, instead of a relation of vassalage.

3. The nature of the theocracy.—On the one side, it had a political, national end; on the other, a religious: and therefore the lord demands not all the fruit, but only a portion. The transformation of the theocracy into hierarchy: 1. The servants of God begin by converting His vineyard, which, under the condition of feudal service, He had let out to them, into a private possession. 2. They treat the prophets and reformers, who desire to call their condition of popendence back to their recollection, as enemies, and so treat mediately the Lord as an enemy. 3. They killed the son and heir, not in ignorance, but knowing him to be the heir, and actually because he was the heir: so evil-disposed were they.

4. The prospect, which the Lord presented, of the vineyard being handed over to strangers, to the Gentiles, must have exasperated the Sanhedrim almost more than the proclamation of their own downfall.

5. The parable before us is illustrated and expanded by the parables which Matthew makes precede and follow. If we examine the idea of this parable, we shall find that the germs of the two other parables are contained in the one before us.

6. Christ the beloved, the only Son, that is, the only-begotten Son of God; Christ, the last sent, is a mark of the revelation being perfected; Christ, the corner-stone, indicates the perfected Redeemer and Head of the Church.

HOMILETICAL AND PRACTICAL.

See the foregoing Reflections, and the *Commentary* on *Matthew.*—The mournful, historical fact, that the administrators of the sacred things of God fail so often to attain salvation; or, the *night side* of the priesthood.—The history of the priestly office under the old economy, a perpetual symbol of warning to the priestly (ministerial) office under the new.—The contest which the Lord, from the remotest ages, has been engaged in with the unfaithful servants of His word and His grace.—The immemorial contrast between unfaithful officers of God and faithful messengers from God.—How the gracious generosity of God strives with the obdurate unbelief of men up to the moment of final decision.—The final purpose of God (They will reverence My Son), and the last purpose of the rebellious servants (This is the heir; come, let us kill him, etc.).—The Lord in heaven is willing rather to have the appearance of folly in sending His Son, than that His grace should not be revealed to the uttermost.—Grace in highest glory appearing alone, or to the apparent neglect of wisdom, justice, and omnipotence, and yet, at that very moment, uniting in itself all the attributes of wisdom, justice, and omnipotence.—How all the perfections of God are comprehended in the glory of His grace: 1. By seeming to vanish in it; 2. by again appearing, glorified in it.—The last point by which God's grace seeks to obtain a hold, is pious fear in men.—Finally: Christ the last mission of God's grace to mankind, John iii. 16; Heb. x. 26, 27; xii. 18.—The contradiction in the words, This is the heir, let us kill him; or, the remnant of faith in unbelief, making unbelief damning.—To the exercise of long-suffering succeeds that of judgment.—The heir and the inheritance cannot be separated.—The murder of the heir converted into the glorification of the inheritance.—The parabolical statement of Christ's glorification, a supplement to the parable of His rejection.—The determination of God as to the wicked counsel of the opponents of Christ: 1. Their counsel allowed; 2. defeated; 3. turned to the service of God's design.—The theocracy as a building of God: 1. A completed building; 2. a preparation for a second building.—Christ, the great miracle of God.—The enmity manifested towards the Lord's word, enmity shown to the dazzling brightness with which the picture of His enemies was drawn.—The wicked shudder before the picture of their own life.—The impotency of Jesus' foes.—Jesus' address before the people; or, the fault of the priests, and the fault of the laity: 1. Difference; 2. connection.

HEDINGER:—God spares neither labor nor expense in sustaining and extending His Church.—Be fruitful in good works.—The fate of the servants sent into God's vineyard.—OSIANDER:—The more frequently the obdurate are called to repent, the more insane and senseless is the position assumed by them.—The riches of the goodness and long-suffering of God in sending faithful servants, who are zealous to the very death for His house.—The witnesses of the truth.—O that the pious would stir one another up to goodness with the same industry that the godless excite one another to wickedness!—CANSTEIN: —Sin is very frightful: it ceases not where it has begun; one sin springs from another.—QUESNEL:— So many deadly sins, so many murderous acts against Jesus Christ.—CANSTEIN:—The enemies of the truth can, no doubt, in some manner say such in itself is truth; yet their answer proceeds not from truth, because their hearts are not temples of truth.—*Nova Bibl. Tub.*:—God and His grace are bound to no people.—What the proud generation of Satan rejects, laughs to scorn, tramples under foot, that God raises in defiance of it, to the glory of Himself.—The world, despite its efforts, cannot execute its malice and wickedness sooner than God, from hidden reasons, permits.

LISCO:—That the only Son is sent, and sent the last, magnifies both the love of the Lord and the offence of the servants.—BRAUNE:—Official sins: The wine-press is the ministerial office, which should express the letters, the peel covering the divine word, which should expound the divine word, the fruit of the vine, and make wine from it to refresh the heart.

(Let it be remarked that this interpretation is not sufficient; comp. *Doctrinal Reflection,* 1.) Isa. v. 1, 2. Fates of prophets: Micaiah was scourged (1 Kings xxii. 24), and also Jeremiah (Jer. xxxvii. 15); Isaiah, Amos, and others were killed (1 Kings xviii. 13); Zechariah was stoned (2 Chron. xxiv. 21); and we find in Nehemiah (ix. 26) that the prophets of God had been slain: Acts vii. 52; Heb. xi. 36–38. —The judgment of Jesus in the Pharisees' mouths (The Lord will come, etc.), the first note of the fearful cry, His blood be on us, and on our children (Matt. xxvii. 25).—The world's salvation is, nevertheless, triumphant. From the Jews it passed to the Gentiles, from the benighted east to the clear west, from the enervated south to mighty north; and when yet farther?—Still God's kingdom remains.—They raged, but a hook had been put into their nose, and a bridle into their lips (Isa. xxxvii. 29).

SCHLEIERMACHER:—Truth we owe to men, yet we are ourselves bound by it according to our ability.— In every circumstance we must let love point out how we can render the best service to the truth in dealing with each individual.—BRIEGER:—Let us go forth, therefore, unto Him, etc.: Heb. xiii. 13 (referring to the heir being cast out of the vineyard); Isa. xxviii. 16.

---

3. *The Cunning Attack of the Pharisees and Herodians, and their Defeat.* VERS. 13–17.

(Parallels: Matt. xxii. 15–22; Luke xx. 20–24.)

13 And they send unto him certain of the Pharisees and of the Herodians, to catch
14 him in *his* words. And when they were come,[1] they say unto him, Master, we know that thou art true, and carest for no man: for thou regardest not the person of men, but
15 teachest the way of God in truth: Is it lawful to give tribute to Cesar, or not? Shall we give, or shall we not give? But he, knowing their hypocrisy, said unto them,
16 Why tempt ye me? bring me a penny, that I may see *it*. And they brought *it*. And he saith unto them, Whose *is* this image and superscription? And they said unto him,
17 Cesar's. And Jesus answering, said unto them, Render to Cesar the things that are Cesar's,[2] and to God the things that are God's. And they marvelled at him.

[1] Ver. 14.—Lachmann, Tischendorf, after B., C., L., Δ., read καὶ οἱ ἐλθόντες instead of οἱ δὲ ἐλθόντες.
[2] Ver. 17.—Lachmann, after A., D., reads ἀπόδοτε τὰ Καίσαρος Καίσαρι; Tischendorf and Meyer, after B., C., L., Syriac, read τὰ Καίσαρος ἀπόδοτε Καίσαρι.

EXEGETICAL AND CRITICAL.

Comp. the parallels in *Matthew* and *Luke*.—The turning-point here is the ironical acknowledgment of Jesus' Messianic dignity on the part of the Jewish rulers, after that they, in their attempt to overcome Jesus by the assertion of their authority in the presence of the people, had been covered with shame. It forms, consequently, the second section of our Lord's strife in the temple on the Tuesday of the Passion Week. In this history of the temptation, the object of which was to entangle the Lord, two chief attacks are specialized by Mark: the attack made by the Pharisees in connection with the Herodians, or the history of the tribute-penny; and the attack of the Sadducees. In the latter, however, the question of the scribes leaves no longer an impression of malicious temptation, but draws the transactions to a close with an example of the triumph of Christ over many minds among the scribes and Pharisees. It is, nevertheless, the same history, written more from the bright side, while Matthew pictures it from the darker side. This individual was better than his party who had despatched him to tempt Christ: he made no concealment of the effect which the wisdom of Christ made upon him. This history is allowed by Luke to pass unnoticed. The cunning shown in the temptation now under consideration, is distinctly emphasized by each of the three Evangelists, Matthew and Mark giving the additional fact of the union between the Pharisees and Herodians to effect their ends. Matthew states that those who were sent were *disciples* of the Pharisees, and consequently young persons; from Luke it appears they were worldlings, who could only feign scruples of conscience. At the outset, the lively addition characterizes Mark, "Shall we give, or shall we not give?" The rest of the narrative is quickly sketched, and remarkably graphic. In the conclusion he is shorter than Matthew and Luke.

Ver. 13. **And they send unto Him.**—Those mentioned in the preceding section, the Sanhedrim, are intended. But Matthew represents with propriety the Pharisees as the most active in the transaction.—To catch Him.—'Αγρεύειν refers primarily to the chase.

Ver. 15. Shall we give?—Important application of the question to their conduct. They appear, moreover, anxious to place the negation in His mouth.

Ver. 17. The things that are Cæsar's.—The order of the words in Mark is peculiar; the construction is more cautious, and yet more lively.—And they marvelled at Him.—The young aristocratic portion of the population of the capital had not, in its pride, expected such a blow from the Galilæan Rabbi. Matthew informs us that they felt themselves overcome: in Mark this is implied.

DOCTRINAL AND ETHICAL.

1. See Matthew.
2. The feigned alliance of hostile parties against Christ, a measure of the greatness of their hatred to Christ. Mark has already (ch. iii. 6) recorded the decision of the alliance. Compare the friendship of Pilate and Herod, as recorded in Luke.
3. Students and young nobles are often caught in the dangerous currents of their day. They are often, through their warm, generous feelings, misled and deceived.
4. Christ remains unmoved by the excitement; and what was confused, becomes, by a reference to manifest right, disentangled.
5. The word of Christ undermined, further, the alliance between the two allied hostile parties. The Pharisees were not willing to give to the Emperor what belonged to him; the Herodians gave not to God what was God's, not even in appearance.

HOMILETICAL AND PRACTICAL.

See the notes on Matthew.—Perfect rest and calmness is the perfect action and quickness of the spirit.—The spiritual presence of Christ fills the present with the might of eternity.—How a stream of light from Christ can become a piercing lightning-flash.—Hypocrisy, the original sin of an impure patriotism and feeling of false freedom.—The majesty with which Christ investigates the rights of Cæsar: 1. The free examination; 2. the just recognition; 3. the holy reservation.—Christ and the young nobility of Jerusalem: 1. How little they knew; 2. how royally He revealed Himself to them.—Students and earnest youths often the unconscious and deceived tools of impure endeavors.—Divine simplicity and integrity always triumphant over human and devilish cunning.—Speak the truth without seeking to please or to injure any one.—Amazement may form, particularly with youthful and deceived minds, the beginning of wisdom.

STARKE:—*Nova Bibl. Tub.*:—The meanest kind of persecutors betake themselves to the secular authority.—Truth must frequently find that hypocritical professors unite with worldlings against her.—HEDINGER:—Every station has its rights. Fear God. Honor the king: 1 Pet. ii. 17.—CANSTEIN:—The Pharisees flattered the Lord to destroy Him: He, however, put them to shame to bring them to salvation.—BRAUNE:—Those who, from their knowledge, should have been the friends of truth, are the first in enmity against the King of truth. (Pharisees and Herodians.) No one should allow himself to be employed to vex others: this is especially the duty of young persons towards noble, venerable men.—They thought He had within Him the spark of vanity, and that He would destroy Himself in His zeal for God's honor and His own personal dignity, which they presented in combination. So do men strive to entangle one another by praise.—See Braune's extract from CLAUDIUS' *Asmus*, p. 316.

SCHLEIERMACHER:—It were a different case if ye had never received the money, if ye had perilled blood and life for independence; but if ye have suffered the halter to be bound round your neck, and have not made any opposition, then bear the yoke.—Ye are giving your approval to the external regulations under which ye are living, as is sufficiently evident from your use of the money.—(God, what is God's.) He would remind them that they had other wealth, and were in undisturbed possession of the same.—They should distinguish between the tributary condition and the spiritual.—GOSSNER:—Out of hypocrisy they state the truth, in order to overthrow the truth.

---

4. *The Attack of the Sadducees, and their Overthrow.* VERS. 18–27.

(Parallels: Matt. xxii. 23–33; Luke xx. 27–40.)

18 Then come unto him the Sadducees, which say there is no resurrection; and they
19 asked him, saying, Master, Moses wrote unto us, If a man's brother die, and leave *his*[1]
    wife *behind him*, and leave no children, that his brother should take his wife, and raise
20 up seed unto his brother. Now there were seven[2] brethren: and the first took a wife,
21 and dying left no seed. And the second took her, and died, neither left he[3] any seed:
22 and the third likewise. And the seven had her, and left no seed:[4] last of all the wo-
23 man died also. In the resurrection therefore, when they shall rise, whose wife shall
24 she be of them? for the seven had her to wife. And Jesus answering, said unto them,
    Do ye not therefore err, because ye know not the scriptures, neither the power of God?
25 For when they shall rise[5] from the dead, they neither marry, nor are given in marriage;
26 but are as the angels which are in heaven. And as touching the dead, that they rise;
    have ye not read in the book of Moses, how in the bush God spake unto him, saying, I

27 am the God of Abraham, and the God of Isaac, and the God of Jacob? He is not the God of the dead, but the God[6] of the living: ye therefore do greatly err.

[1 Ver. 19.—The αὐτοῦ after γυναῖκα is omitted by B., C., L., Δ., Meyer.]
[2 Ver. 20.—After ἑπτά, Elzevir and Fritzsche have οὖν; it is not found in A., B., C., E., F., L.]
[3 Ver. 21.—Instead of καὶ οὐδὲ αὐτὸς ἀφῆκε, B., C., L., Tischendorf read μὴ καταλιπών.]
4 Ver. 22.—The reading, καὶ οἱ ἑπτὰ οὐκ ἀφῆκαν σπέρμα, [omitting ἔλαβον αὐτὴν and the second καί,] is strongly supported by B., C., L., Δ., [Tischendorf]; but the demands of the context go to strengthen the Codd. which give the other reading. That no seed was left by the seven, is in and for itself of no importance; it is merely the occasion of the seven taking the same woman to wife.
5 Ver. 23.—Ὅταν ἀναστῶσι is omitted by B., C., L., Δ. Lachmann puts it in parenthesis; Cod. A., &c., support it; and the consideration, that its omission is easier to account for than its insertion, is an additional argument in favor of this reading.
6 Ver. 27.—Θεός is wanting with ζώντων in A., B., C., D., Griesbach, Lachmann, and Tischendorf. [Tischendorf omits ὑμεῖς οὖν, after B., C., L., Δ.]

EXEGETICAL AND CRITICAL.

See *Matthew*, and the parallel in *Luke*.—In this section, Mark's individuality appears only in the more pictorial description of the seven successive marriages; in special supplemental strokes; in the more positive tracing of the error of the Sadducees up to a want of knowledge of the Scriptures and to unbelief; and in the final statement, Ye therefore do greatly err. While the immediate effect of Christ's word is not presented till the Evangelist comes to relate the next history.

Ver. 23. **When they shall rise.**—The immediate, special reference is to the seven. Perhaps doubt is also expressed.

Ver. 26. **How in the bush;** that is to say, in the appropriate passage, where the thorn-bush is spoken of—which ye will find something of a thorn-bush.

DOCTRINAL AND ETHICAL.

1. Comp. *Matthew*, and the conclusion of the Apostles' Creed, Resurrection of the body, etc. John v.; 1 Cor. xv.; 2 Cor. v.; Dan. xii., etc. Comp. the doctrine of the Scripture on the Resurrection, as unfolded in the works upon Biblical Theology, and the teaching of the Church as given in works on Dogmatics; the hopes of immortality cherished by the nations, recorded in histories of religion. Comp. the proofs of an immortality. The writings bearing on the topic from PLATO's *Phœdo* down.

2. Unbelief has always two springs: 1. The want of historic faith (Ye know not the Scriptures); 2. the want of personal faith (Ye know not the power of God).

3. Belief in immortality and belief in angels, or a world of spirits, are most intimately united: so also the respectively opposed elements of unbelief.

4. Unbelief is, on the one hand, united with rude sensuality ("marrying" in that world too); and, on the other, with a wild phantasy (indulging in phantasies upon the future state), and a carnal view of the uniformity obtaining throughout God's universe (*tout comme chez nous*).

5. Unbelief, which attacks one part of the truth, understands nothing of that part upon which it intends to support itself in attacking.

6. They tempted the Lord to the abandonment of the doctrine of the resurrection, or to the retaining of it, coupled with polygamy in the future as its consequence. They supposed, He must either state an absurdity, or be struck dumb by their supposed *deductio ad absurdum*. But they had political designs in addition. Comp. *Matthew*. They intended that, by a denial of the resurrection, He should deny His work, or should present Himself as an enthusiast, and yield up to the profane world the secret of His hope. Christ sent the especially "wise" home as the especially "foolish."

HOMILETICAL AND PRACTICAL.

Comp. *Matthew*.—The Sadducees constitute the historical counter-picture to the Pharisees.—The Sadducees, the deniers of immortality, are immortal.—They invented an improbable, indecent tale to deny a most trustworthy and glorious reality.—They find in the Bible a thorny bush indeed, but not the burning bush.—The sentimental expectations of a bodily sight and possession are not tenable: 1. Too great for the reason; 2. for faith too little; 3. for both preposterous.—The external revelation is not in itself weak through too strong faith, but through credulity springing from too little faith, which believes, 1. Many things, but not much; 2. the extraordinary, but not the miraculous; 3. the spectral, but not the spiritual; 4. the earthly in heavenly hue and dress, but not the heavenly as the glorification of the earthly.—The Sadducees and their faith: I. How they attack faith (while they propound the most improbable views), either, 1. with an improper explanation of Scripture and of the law, 2. with an improper picture of life, and 3. with an improper view of the world; or, 1. with improper reasoning, 2. with improper wit. II. How faith replies: with, 1. a deeper exposition of Scripture, 2. higher pictures of life, 3. a holier contemplation of the world in the light of God.—They say, our unbelief comes from our knowing: He says, it comes from your not knowing.—The belief in the angels makes the belief in the resurrection a necessity.—One truth of faith explains and strengthens another.—Unbelief in immortality a radical error: 1. A positive confusion; 2. a positive mistake.

QUESNEL:—The devil gives the Christian no rest. If one temptation does not entangle, another is tried; hence watchfulness is essential.—HEDINGER:—Preformed opinions constitute a hindrance to the truth.—Oh that there were none among Christians who doubt the resurrection! If they venture not to acknowledge their doubt, they manifest nevertheless by their deeds that they believe in no other life.—The thoughts of carnal men regarding the heavenly life are carnal and disreputable.—CANSTEIN:—Christians must stir themselves up, in thinking of the eternal life, to separate themselves ever more and more from the lusts of the body and fleshly-mindedness.

BRAUNE:—It was the extreme fleshly-minded (the Sadducees) who could not comprehend the reality and truth of the spiritual world.—The Gospel of the Risen One has brought forward more clearly for the spirit of man the kingdom of God and the hope of resurrection, of which we have frequent relations in the Acts of the Apostles, where the Sadducees repeatedly appear as foes.—The Saviour unites the Scriptures and the power of God. Hence comes Augustine's statement, The more we see of the Scripture, the more we die to the world; the more we live to the world, the less we see.—" Reason digs beside (Scripture), Frivolity stalks by, and Pride flies away over" (Zinzendorf). Many of the Rabbis dreamed of marriages according to passages in the prophets, as Isa. lxv. 20, 23, where we read of a new heaven and a new earth; and this was not once deemed base by the Pharisees.—Of marriage, accordingly, that alone remains which was spiritual, just as sex in regard to physical distinctions is lost, and that alone remains which had spiritually been developed; for the distinction between sexes, consisting in the development of what relates to spirit, and in that which lays hold of the mind's most inner nature, continues undoubtedly for ever.—Death breaks all bands, but destroys not existence.

Brieger:—He who has not in various ways experienced that God is the Living One, cannot from the heart believe in any resurrection. Is God called the God of Abraham? much more must He be called the God of Jesus Christ, John v. 29; 1 Cor. xv. 19; Rom. xiv. 8.

Gossner:—One sort of evil men after another come to Jesus to trouble Him, to tempt Him, instead of seeking their salvation from Him.

5. *The Scribe, first tempting, then half won.* Vers. 28–34.

(Parallels: Matt. xxii. 34–40; Luke xx. 39.)

28 And one of the scribes came, and having heard them reasoning together, and perceiving[1] that he had answered them well, asked him, Which is the first commandment
29 of all? And Jesus answered him, The first of all the commandments is,[2] Hear, O Israel;
30 The Lord our God is one Lord: And thou shalt love the Lord thy God with all thy heart, and with all thy soul, and with all thy mind,[3] and with all thy strength. This is
31 the first commandment.[4] And the second is like, namely this,[5] Thou shalt love thy
32 neighbour as thyself: there is none other commandment greater than these. And the scribe said unto him, Well, Master, thou hast said the truth: for there is one God;[6] and
33 there is none other but he: And to love him with all the heart, and with all the understanding, and with all the soul,[7] and with all the strength, and to love his neighbour as
34 himself, is more than all whole burnt-offerings and sacrifices. And when Jesus saw that he answered discreetly, he said unto him, Thou art not far from the kingdom of God. And no man after that durst ask him *any question.*

[1] Ver. 28.—Lachmann reads ἰδών for εἰδώς, after C., D., L.]
[2] Ver. 29.—Many variations. Tischendorf, adopting B., L., Δ., reads ὅτι πρώτη ἐστίν; Griesbach, ὅτι πρώτη πάντων ἐντολή, after A. and Minusculi.
[3] Ver. 30.—Tischendorf, following D. and some Minusculi and Versions, omits καὶ ἐξ ὅλης τῆς διανοίας.]
[4] Ver. 30.—Αὕτη πρώτη ἐντολή omitted by Tischendorf, following B., E., L., Δ.; retained by A., D., &c.
[5] Ver. 31.—Tischendorf reads simply δευτέρα αὕτη, and so B., L., Δ.; this means, "this is the second in importance." Lachmann, and the majority of the MSS., retain ὁμοία αὐτῇ.
[6] Ver. 32.—The best MSS. omit Θεός after ἐστι.]
[7] Ver. 33.—Tischendorf, following B., L., Δ., omits καὶ ἐξ ὅλης τῆς ψυχῆς. Meyer defends the reading.]

EXEGETICAL AND CRITICAL.

Comp. *Matthew.*—The peculiarities of Mark: Matthew causes the tempting Pharisees, who were for the moment influenced by friendly feelings towards the Lord because He had put the Sadducees to silence, to advance; while Mark brings forward into the light their representative, a well-meaning scribe, whom Matthew designates more specifically as a lawyer. Matthew emphasizes the temptation, Mark the questioning; and, in addition, the transaction is clothed in a much richer form than in the Gospel by Matthew. The statement of Jesus is first introduced, that the greatest commandment is to hear that God is one, as therefrom proceeds the unity of the commandment of love out of the unity or absolute simplicity of the entire inner life. To this succeeds the joyful assent of the scribe, and his well-nigh literal repetition of the Lord's words. And, lastly, the recognition by Christ that he had answered discreetly; to which the declaration is appended, that he was not far from the kingdom of God. The observation that the Jews dared not question further, forms the conclusion of this section in Mark. Luke appends this remark to the question of the Sadducees, Matthew to the counter-question of Christ. Considering the meaning, these three narratives form but one whole. For, after the Sadducees had been defeated, the hope to overcome Him was already destroyed. The temptation here narrated was only an ambiguous after-game, probably half devoted to the attempt of inducing Christ to allow Himself, in spite of all, to be won over as a partisan to the party of the Pharisees. But when Jesus had put His counter-question, to which no reply could be given, the mouths of His opponents were finally closed. Upon the allegation of Meyer, that a difference exists between Mark and Matthew, comp. *Note* to Matthew's account.

Ver. 28. **The first commandment of all.**—The first, and that in the sense of the chief importance. *See Note* upon *Matthew.* "The Jews enumerated six hundred and thirteen ordinances; three hundred and sixty-five prohibitions, according to the days of the year; two hundred and twenty-eight commandments, according to the parts of the body. The Pharisees distinguished between lesser and greater commandments." Braune.

Ver. 29. **Hear, O Israel; The Lord:** Deut. vi. 4, 5.—Jesus gives the introduction to the ten commandments as the first command itself, not in so far as it forms one of the commandments, but in so far as it is the principle of the commandments,— finding its full exposition in the words: And thou shalt love, etc. The inner idea of the introduction has been explained already in Deuteronomy, from which the citation is drawn. Directly in opposition to this *qualitative* conception, the modern Jews reckon, according to their division, the words: Hear, O Israel, etc., *quantitatively*, as the first commandment. Upon this division, as well as generally upon the various divisions of the decalogue, comp. GEFFKEN, *Ueber die verschiedene Eintheilung des Dekalogus*, Hamburgh, 1838, p. 9 seq. "This principle of all duties was termed specially, קריאת, or sometimes, after the initial word, שמע; and the words were usually recited daily, night and morning; see VITRINGA, *Synagoga Judaica*, 2, 3, 15; BUXTORF, *Syn.* 9." Meyer.

Ver. 30. **With all thy heart.**—The Hebrew text has the three following specifications: with all thy heart, and with all thy soul, and with all thy strength (מאד, a might which is at once the manifesting of strength, and employing of strength; Gesenius, *robur, vehementia*). Instead of the first word, heart, the Septuagint reads, διάνοια; the second is of the same tenor; and the third it properly renders δύναμις. Christ's quotation, as given by Matthew, follows the original text in the first and second word, heart, soul; but substitutes, with a fulness of meaning, for the third, διάνοια, the moral might of consciousness, of will. In Mark, the one word is expressed by two, διάνοια and ἰσχύς (= מאד). On the contrary, in Mark, the scribe divides the first conception (heart) into two, καρδία and σύνεσις; while the lawyer, in the narrative in Luke x. 27, where we have a similar, though not identical, interview, speaks as Jesus here does. Only ἰσχύς precedes διάνοια. From all this, it is evident that a freer mode of handling the Old Testament text prevailed in the apostolic circle; moreover, it is worthy of being noted that no Gospel contains the δύναμις of the Septuagint. Whether the differences are only "variations of the Greek tradition," occasioned by the habit of quoting from memory, or different points of view, is doubtful. In any case, it is noteworthy that the philosophizing Septuagint has explained καρδία by διάνοια; while, according to Matthew, Christ, spiritualizing ἰσχύς, gives its force as διάνοια, which is preceded by the heart and soul. Mark and Luke exegetically unite διάνοια and ἰσχύς. The lawyer, to indicate his legal stand-point, adds to καρδία, which the Septuagint had converted into διάνοια, the σύνεσις. Upon biblical psychology (upon which Roos, Beck, and Delitzsch have written), comp. *Note* upon *Matthew*.

Ver. 33. **With all thy understanding.**—Signification of the intelligence, as it develops into understanding.

Burnt offerings and sacrifices.—Ps. li.; 1 Sam. xv. 22; Hos. vi. 6. This very comparison proved that the lawyer was overcome by an emotion of courageous faith, the giving utterance to which might have easily caused offence to his companions. It was in this situation a testimony.

Ver. 34. **Discreetly, νουνεχῶς**: with knowledge and understanding.—Attic, νουνεχόντως; the opposite, ἀφρόνως.

DOCTRINAL AND ETHICAL.

1. *See* remarks upon *Matthew*.—From the unity and spiritual harmony of God proceeds the essential unity of His law in one principle—love. This principle has already been brought into view in Deuteronomy. The true covenant-God, as the one God and the one Lord over hearts and in them,—this makes one life-experience, one life-motive, love. So appears the royal law as given by James (ch. ii. 8) and Paul (Rom. xiii. 10). Upon the element of temptation in this question, comp. *Note* on *Matthew*. *In the passage before us, religion is declared to be the central, concentrated direction of the whole man, especially of his soul's powers, to the one God.*

2. The man, in whose inward parts the law of God has been by love inscribed, loves at first from the heart, in the very core of his being; next, notwithstanding the varying frames of his soul, in his soul likewise, in the disposition of his soul-life; and then in his practical intelligence or mode of thought, —in the practical resolutions and purposes of his life, with which all the powers of his life (as members and instruments of righteousness) enter into, and are spent in, the service of love.

3. BRAUNE:—These two commandments point to the two tables of the law. Upon the first are five laws, concerning God's glory, God's likeness, God's name, God's day, God's representatives; upon the second, five concerning person and life, marriage and household peace, goods and chattels, honor and right, and the heart of man. The two tables are one; containing the commandments of one, inseparable, heavenly law of love.

4. To be rational (discreet), the Lord here calls, not to be far from the kingdom of God. The reason, ideally conceived, is the faculty of understanding or perceiving the divine in its ideas. This faculty perceives the idea of love in the law. Discretion and subtilty mark the contrast between the true and false use of reason.

5. Thou art not far from the kingdom of God.— He who recognizes the law in its spiritual meaning, and in opposition to external forms and ceremonies (more than burnt-offerings and sacrifices), is on the road of the Spirit (rational in a moral sense), and on the way of return from self-righteousness and of turning back to self-knowledge, which conditions the entrance into the kingdom founded by Christ. Not far from, that is, near. What was still wanting was, the full surrender to his conviction, or the actual following of Jesus. This transaction is, accordingly, a sign and presage of Christ's victory in the centre of His enemy's camp.

HOMILETICAL AND PRACTICAL.

See Matthew.—The three unities in religion, a type of the Trinity of the one God: 1. The one God; 2. the one faith (giving heed to Christ's word); 3. the one commandment.—The unity of God is not mere individuality, nor singleness, but chiefly, His being alone and His being one, to which the unity of man in the simplicity of the faith must correspond. —Man is really a unity in obedience, when his inner life, in the trinity of heart (feeling), of soul (the will), and of reason or intelligence, is at one with itself and with God's word.—Unity and trinity, the secret of all spiritual life: 1. Of the highest life above us; 2. of the deepest life within us; 3. of the richest life around us.—In the true love of God and his neighbor, man would re-obtain his true self-love, and recover from his diseased self-love.—Thou art not far from the kingdom of God; or, the tempter transformed into the disciple. Or a meaning-fraught word,—1. of recognition, 2. of warning, 3. of encouragement.—Christ explained in the temple-court, in the circle of those who hated Him, the great law of love, as He upon the night of betrayal instituted the meal of love, and upon Golgotha overcame the curse of the entire world-hate, by His act, by His suffering, and by His sacrifice of love.

CANSTEIN:—Good men may be often so misled as to permit themselves to be employed against Christ: for such we must have compassion, pray for them, and endeavor to deliver them.—QUESNEL:—True religion consists in hearing, believing, and loving.—As thou lovest thyself, so act with thy neighbor.—HEDINGER:—Who can withstand the truth? Where but a little good-will is found, it pierces through. But ah! how hard the hearts that strive against her!—OSIANDER:—External ceremonies are no doubt good; but where they are found without love, they are only a mantle covering secret sin, and will be rejected by God.—*Bibl. Wirt.:*—Courage, ye teachers and preachers! God moves the heart of many a one, who has not known the fact, in a sermon, so that he goes forth better than he came in.—He who recognizes the worth of love, and what it is, is near the kingdom of God; but he who has experienced love, is in it.—HEDINGER:—Whosoever is, in the beginning, obedient and true to the divine leadings of grace, of him is there hope that he is won.—He who is near, is not therefore within the kingdom, Matt. vii. 13.—CANSTEIN:—Truth conquers.—QUESNEL:—A silence of contentedness and obedience is a wholesome silence; but that of rude ignorance and obstinacy is a damning silence.

RIEGER:—Upon the commandment of love to God and to our neighbor is all dependent; and yet God, on account of man's lost state, could not leave all to be dependent on this alone, but had to reveal many other, special, explicit commandments, and make us conscious of our captivity to sin by them. Not till that institution (these laws) has fulfilled its part, can we be brought by the grace of Christ under the law of the Spirit.

LISCO:—All external sacrifices are only weak types of the one perfect sacrifice, the perfect surrender of the heart to God.—With thy earnest moral striving, thou art upon the way by which the kingdom of God may be reached; for thou recognizest the existence of true piety, and deceivest thyself not with an external righteousness by works. The entrance is by faith alone in the Saviour, who is the Way, John xiv. 6.—GERLACH:—Through a living acquaintance with God's law, through heartfelt affection for its chief commandment, love, man comes *near* to the kingdom; but to come *into* the kingdom, he needs the knowledge of God, by which alone the conflict between pleasure in the law, and its constant transgression, can be stopped.—BRAUNE:—God is one, says Paul, Gal. iii. 20, to prove that law and promise are eternally one. So, too, says the Lord here, in that He calls to His support the fundamental doctrine of the law: Hear, Israel, etc. It is always the heart upon which God first looks.—The second command is the proof of the first. "If a man say, I love God," etc., 1 John iv. 20.—God says, No God beside Me; but man must say, Other men beside me.—On God's account we are bound to love our neighbor as ourselves.—Thou *shalt:* it is accordingly no merit if thou do so; but it is sin if thou neglect. Thou shalt *perfectly:* It is not a portion which suffices. This must drive us to Him who fulfilled this law, and helps us to fulfil.—The Master gives measured praise: of beautiful views and fine declarations He never makes too much, but recognizes these in all relations in such a way as to encourage to progress.—Let each take heed, that in his case the separation between knowing and doing, between the acknowledgment of the faith and the work of faith, become not fixed, and ever grow more terrible.

SCHLEIERMACHER:—See his *Sermons*, vol. iii. p. 765 ff.—BRIEGER:—To love God, who is the Love and the Life, is to live godly. But he who lives in and with God, or godly, loves also what God loves.—Love is the only self-sacrifice, and it is the only sacrifice that God wishes.—GOSSNER:—One God, one heart, one love.

---

6. *The decisive Counter-question put by the Lord to the Scribes.* VERS. 35–37.

(Parallels: Matt. xxii. 41–46; Luke xx. 41–44.)

35 And Jesus answered and said, while he taught in the temple, How say the scribes
36 that Christ is the son of David? For David himself said by the Holy Ghost, The Lord said[1] to my Lord, Sit thou on my right hand, till I make thine enemies thy footstool.
37 David therefore[2] himself calleth him Lord; and whence is he *then* his son? And the common people heard him gladly.

[[1] Ver. 36.—Some MSS. read λέγει ("the Lord said") instead of εἶπεν; Meyer asserts that εἶπεν comes from Matthew, Luke, and the cited passage in the Psalm.]
[[2] Ver. 37.—The οὖν is wanting in B., D., L., Δ., Syriac, Tischendorf; bracketed by Lachmann.]

EXEGETICAL AND CRITICAL.

See Matthew, and the parallels in *Luke.*—The great counter-question which Jesus, after all the tempting questions of His enemies, addressed to the Pharisees, is brought forward by Matthew in all its historic importance as the decisive, concluding interrogation put to the Pharisees. In Matthew, accordingly, this question has the form of a discussion or rabbinical disputation; and without doubt this is the original, historical form of the matter. Much of this external form has been rubbed away by Mark; yet he points out by the words, "Jesus answered," that the statement contained a reply to some question already put, with a view to try the Lord. Consequently the last is referred to. In this way, the preceding discussion also gains a new illustration; for which, consult the explanation of this last temptation. Mark, in allowing the form of the disputation to pass unnoticed, causes Christ's spiritual triumph to stand out all the more strongly to the view; just as he presented the preceding narrative likewise from its bright side.

Ver. 35. **While He taught in the temple.**—The last address Christ made to the Pharisees was a word intended for the whole people; and this is in Mark's mind the most weighty point: and from this view we see that His triumph, and the humbling of His enemies in the presence of the multitude, are implied as matters decided from the very outset.

Ver. 37. **And whence is He then his son?**—This question was intended to say to the Pharisees especially, that the Son of David, or the Messiah, as David's Lord, must, according to the Scriptures, be of divine dignity; while to the people especially it was intended to say, that He was not to be David's son in the sense that He had been appointed, as they expected, to found an external Messianic kingdom, after the nature of David's kingdom. But the one conception cannot be severed from the other.—He who brings in a divine kingdom must introduce one of a different nature from an earthly one; he who introduces one of another, higher nature, must introduce a divine.—**Heard Him gladly.**—Not merely in the common sense, but with special reference to His divine dignity as the Messiah, was it that they listened to Him. The people were in the best mood for doing, and were on the point of doing, homage to Him.

DOCTRINAL AND ETHICAL.

1. See *Matthew* and the foregoing remarks.
2. In their last question, the Pharisees gave the Lord to understand that if God be only One, He (Jesus) could not be God's Son, and desired in this way to force Him either to offend against monotheism, or to deny His own dignity. Christ, by His counter-question, lays down this proposition: Christ as David's son, and at the same time David's Lord, could not be man simply, though He is a real man. For David calls Him, not in a general way, his Lord; but Lord, *the* Lord, directly, and positively. At the same time, Jesus reveals to them mediately, by means of Ps. cx., that His kingdom is not of the same nature as David's, of a worldly character; that He should triumph over all His foes, and sit down upon the right hand of Majesty on high,—a declaration which comes distinctly and triumphantly forward in His trial before Caiaphas, ch. xiv. 62. See HAMANN's *Golgotha*, and *Scheblimini.*
3. Matthew marks chiefly the conviction which the last counter-question of Christ produced, made apparent by the silence of His opponents: Mark brings into prominence this presage of His victory over the rulers of the people, and the perfect spiritual might by which Jesus subdued His enemies. Hence, Mark notes this was a moment when Christ needed but to move His finger, and the whole hierarchy was overthrown, the people lay at His feet. And this was indeed no mere Galilæan triumphal entry, in which a few individual friends from Bethany and Jerusalem were mingled; but it was the Jewish people, who were assembled for the Paschal feast. It was the intensified repetition of the scene in Galilee, of which John gives the account, ch. vi. But Jesus wished to rule over the spirit, and through this rule establish a kingdom. The Israelitish authorities denied Him homage, in suppressed rage, in demoniacal silence. He retired, accordingly, now, in His full, decisive spirit-conquest over them, in secrecy, after He had finished His spiritual judgment in denunciations of woe, and in His decision regarding the gifts cast into the temple-treasury.

HOMILETICAL AND PRACTICAL.

The people heard Him gladly. One of the many beautiful, solemn moments which Israel lost, deceived principally on this matter by its priesthood. (Similarly upon the days of palms. The general repentance after the Feast of Pentecost, Acts v. The great moment in the life of Paul, Acts xxii. 22. A similar one in the life of James, according to HEGESIPPUS, in EUSEB. ii. 23.)—The mystery in the life of Jesus induces and allures unprejudiced minds to sink themselves into its depths.

STARKE:—The Holy Scriptures contain very deep mysteries.—If a true Christian is to be formed out of a Pharisee, the knowledge of Christ in His humanity and divinity must spring up within that man.—QUESNEL:—It is only faith which is able to unloose these knots (*i.e.*, unite divinity and humanity).

BRAUNE:—What think ye of Christ? This question is the sum of the law and the Gospel. He had *been questioned*, first, as to the tribute, from political motives; then regarding marriage and the resurrection, because of philosophical views; then concerning different commandments, on ethical grounds. He now *asks* the life-question of centuries (which springs from the centre of religion): Rom. ix. 5; 1 Cor. xv. 25; Acts ii. 34; Heb. i. 13.—Had Moses been superior to Christ, then had the chief question been, What is the chief command of the law? Because this is not the case, the question regarding the Saviour remains the chief and life-question. According to Christ's view of the case, however, that first query, conceived not according to the law, but according to the Gospel, belongs to this second.

SCHLEIERMACHER:—He does not say, If He is his son, how is He then his Lord? but reversed, If he himself names Him his Lord, how is He then his son? He consequently represents the first as the greater (and yet it is the latter which forms the concluding point, inasmuch as He wishes to call upon them to give up their conception of the Messiah for the Old Testament conception of Him, which His life had exemplified).

BRIEGER:—The Pharisees having interrogated Him as to His *power*, He interrogates them as to His *person* (for they knew, it is properly remarked, that the people considered Him the Messiah).—It was now recognition or rejection. By this question Jesus wishes to lead them to decide.—The throne of God, at the right hand of which the Anointed is to seat Himself, is the throne "high and lifted up," spoken of by Isaiah, ch. vi.,—the *heavenly* throne, Ps. ix. 7; lxviii. 18; xxix. 10. It is the symbol of His rule over heaven and earth, Ps. ciii. 19; Rev. iii. 12; 2 Tim. ii. 12.

7. The Lord's Public Admonition to beware of the Scribes. VERS. 38-40.

(Parallels: Matt. xxiii.; Luke xx. 45-47.)

38   And he said unto them in his doctrine, Beware of the scribes, which love to go in
39 long clothing, and *love* salutations in the market-places, And the chief seats in the syna-
40 gogues, and the uppermost rooms at feasts; Which devour widows' houses, and for a
pretence make long prayers: these shall receive greater damnation.

EXEGETICAL AND CRITICAL.

See *Matthew*, and the parallels in *Luke*.—Mark, like Luke, gives us, of the great denunciatory speech against the Pharisees and scribes which Matthew records, but a very brief warning against the scribes. And how exactly accordant with the intention of his Gospel! It was only the Jewish Christians, for whom Matthew wrote, who *could* at once, and at that time, be summoned to gaze upon the pharisaic Judaism in all the blackness of its sunken state; for young Gentile Christians, the great punitive speech was to a certain extent unintelligible, and was besides too strong food. Hence the picture of the scribes is briefly given in their three principal features: ambition, avarice, and hypocritical external piety. The address is made up of the introductory word of warning by the Lord against the Pharisees, and of the first woe denounced by Him against them. The expression in Matthew, "Do not ye after their works," is here, "Beware of them." The religious enlarging of the garments, as Matthew relates it, is here briefly given in the going about in long clothing. The seeking of greetings precedes the desire for the chief seats in the synagogue, and the civic seats of honor; while the anxious listening for the salutation of Rabbi is passed over. With these chief seats at festivals is admirably united the devouring of widows' houses, under pretence of long prayers, according to the first woe of Matthew. The address to the Pharisees, which we find in Matthew gradually passing into a direct, pointed attack, is here everywhere changed to the representation in the third person. Mark agrees almost verbally with Luke.

Ver. 38. **Which love,** θελόντων.—Meyer: "Demand, claim." But they did not first claim the walking about in long robes: they actually did this; and that, too, with pleasure, consciousness, and deliberation. They loved this, had pleasure in this.—**In long clothing.**—Gerlach: "Because they imitated the priests, who were the nobles of the Jewish people." But are not the priests themselves included? Braune: "Because they imitated the venerable matrons." Jewish Rabbis imitate women! The reference is undoubtedly to their wandering about the streets and public places with marks of distinction significant of religiousness, in long robes of office and rank; hence also in gowns and robes of various orders.

Ver. 40. **Which devour.**—Grotius, Bengel, [Lachmann], and others, make a new sentence begin with οἱ κατεσθίοντες. As administrators, guardians, representatives of unprotected widows (Theophylact); or also by embezzling the funds of the temple-foundations.—For the more lengthened denunciation, *see Matthew*.

DOCTRINAL AND ETHICAL.

1. *See Matthew.*—We have here three points of contrast: 1. Public appearance,—the proud walk in long trailing garments (devotion), the love of greetings (frivolity). 2. Demeanor in society,—love of the chief ecclesiastical seat, and at the same time of the places of honor at banquets and festive entertainments. 3. Personal and secret conduct,—the appropriation of the goods of the poor, under the veil and pretence of long prayers, and of supplications for the poor.

HOMILETICAL AND PRACTICAL.

Comp. *Matthew.*—The scribes distinguished as the worst of the Pharisees.—The false scribes are considered in three different ways, apart from the Scriptures:* 1. Upon the streets; 2. in business and at banquets; 3. as the appropriators of inheritances in families, and by secret means.—The veil of hypocrisy is a transparent covering: 1. The covering, *a.* the long robes, *b.* the long prayers; 2. the transparency of the covering, *a.* the walking about to be seen, *b.* the lust for the seats of honor, festive banquets, and unrighteous gain.—The hypocrite's terrible picture: 1. His public appearance contradicts his secret conduct; 2. his external importance, and desire to be important, is in contradiction to his internal emptiness and unworthiness.—The extent to which a hypocritical profession is carried, is the measure of approaching punishment.—Satan, who clothes himself as an angel of light, and plays the part of man's friend, is the archetype of all hypocrisy.

STARKE:—As sinners are distinguished, so are their punishments.—The confession of sin mitigates the judgment; to hide sin, under the pretence of God's service, makes the judgment heavier and more terrible, Prov. xxviii. 13.

BRAUNE (upon the long clothing):—Somewhat as formerly many clergymen were wont to seek especial dignity from the size of their wigs, and the monks from their cowls and rosaries.—STIER:—Satan was the first who exalted himself to be brought low (the opposite of Christ).

SCHLEIERMACHER:—They used their piety only for external profit.—BRIEGER:—It is to be remarked, that Jesus pictures forth not individual scribes, but the whole sect. There were not wanting a few in whom better tendencies were to be found; *see vers. 28–34.*—The warning has a twofold intention: first, we are not to allow ourselves to be deceived by them; second, we are not to imitate their conduct.

---
* [There is a play here upon words in the original: *Schriftgelehrten ausserhalb der Schrift.—Ed.*]

8. The Widow's Mite, and our Lord's view of the Piety and Good Works of the Jews. VERS. 41–44.

(Parallel: Luke xxi. 1–4.)

41 And Jesus¹ sat over against the treasury, and beheld how the people cast money
42 into the treasury: and many that were rich cast in much. And there came a certain
43 poor widow, and she threw in two mites, which make a farthing. And he called *unto him* his disciples, and saith unto them, Verily I say unto you, that this poor widow hath
44 cast more in than all they which have cast² into the treasury: For all they did cast in of their abundance: but she of her want did cast in all that she had, even all her living.

[¹ Ver. 41.—Ὁ Ἰησοῦς wanting in B., L., Δ., Tischendorf, Meyer; bracketed by Lachmann.]
[² Ver. 43.—Lachmann, after A., B., D., Origen, reads ἔβαλεν τῶν βαλλόντων.]

EXEGETICAL AND CRITICAL.

See the parallel passages in *Luke*.—This apparently trifling history is of inestimable importance. It shows how the Lord, in perfect quiet of spirit, can still seat Himself in the temple, after He had ended His great day's work in it, namely, after the silence of the Sanhedrim regarding His person, in which its rejection of Him lay,—after He had opened His mouth, and pronounced the great denunciations, and with these had, as theocratic King, whom the authorities of Israel rejected, taken His departure from the temple. In this He seems like a deposed king, who seats Himself, as he leaves, on the lowest step of his palace, not to weep on account of his fall, but to bless the poor child of a palace-domestic; or like one excommunicated, who is able, under the new burden of its fanatical ban, to judge with the greatest mildness, and freedom from prejudice, that religious society which cast him out. It is the divine manifestation of His freedom from all fanatic disposition and exasperation, with which He had fought through the great decisive epochs, made His denunciatory speech, and presented His great judgment-picture. In this sunlike clearness and purity, the old Catholic Christians did not in general leave the heathen temples, and but few of the old Protestants the temples of Roman Catholicism. This eternally figurative import is gained by our passage in consequence of its position. In itself, however, it shows us, in a most instructive narrative and act of our Lord, how His eye —and how, consequently, God's eye and the Spirit's —rests upon the treasury of the Lord, and marks the act and manner in which we give. Luke has recorded this circumstance likewise; but Mark presents it more picturesquely and more fully. The Lord's seating Himself opposite to the treasury, the statement of the worth of the mite, the summoning of the disciples to Himself, and the sublime elevation of tone characterizing the decision,—in all this we see plainly how important Mark deemed the history. It stands there to show that the Lord has His eye upon the offerings in His temple, and that, amid all the chaff of seeming religion, He finds out the noble grain of spirituality and truth.

Ver. 41. **The treasury,** γαζοφυλάκιον.—The sacrifice-fund is meant, which was distinguished from the proper temple-treasury, but yet, as belonging to it, was denoted by its name (JOSEPHUS, *Ant.* xix. 6, 1). The Rabbis tell us that this treasury consisted of thirteen **brazen chests** (שׁוֹפָרוֹת, "trumpets;" certainly not because the chests themselves were trumpet-shaped, but because the mouths through which the money was cast into the chests were wide at the top and narrow below). They stood in the outer court of the women. This offering-fund received also the voluntary gifts for the temple. LIGHTFOOT, *Hor.*: "Nine chests were for the appointed temple-tribute, and for the sacrifice-tribute (that is, money-gifts, instead of the sacrifices); four chests for freewill-offerings, for wood, incense, temple-decoration, and burnt-offerings." Before the Passover, freewill-offerings, in addition to the temple-tax, were generally presented. No one, we may easily suppose, entered the temple without putting something in. This is also the custom in the synagogue. The Church has taken an example from this habit.—**Many that were rich cast in much.**— They were not content to give only copper, which was the general offering, but presented silver. Or, perhaps, gave in copper, because a large gift in that metal was of greater bulk, and made more noise.

Ver. 42. **A certain poor widow.**—She is singled out from the whole crowd of donors.—**Two mites,** λεπτόν.—The very smallest copper coin. Two made one Roman quadrans, which was equal to the fourth of an as: ten or sixteen ases were equal to a denarius, which is equivalent to about five groschen, four pfennigs Prussian money (6½ *pence, nearly*). An as in Cicero's time was worth nearly four pfennigs (*or nearly a halfpenny*); hence the quadrans would be one pfennig (*one-tenth of a penny*,) and the mite half a pfennig. She gave two; and Bengel remarks, she could have kept one. "The rabbinic injunction, '*Non ponat homo* λεπτόν *in cistam eleemosynarum*,' is of no force here, because alms were not under consideration." Meyer. Nevertheless, the inference drawn by Schöttgen is by no means foreign; only it is probable this rabbinic habit became, at a later period, the matter of rabbinic legislation.

Ver. 43. **More in than all they.**—That is, in proportion to her means, as the Lord Himself immediately explains.

DOCTRINAL AND ETHICAL.

1. *See Exegetical Note.*

2. Jesus, to a certain degree as stranger, or observer of a religion now become foreign to Him, presents us with an ever-enduring example of the way in which one should, in the spirit of Christianity, look upon and judge all religious systems and associations. Such was the conduct of Paul at Athens, Acts. xvii. He found out the altar of the Unknown God.

3. The last object on which our Lord's eyes rested in the temple.—The widow's mite. It is not said that the gifts of the others were worthless. Many possessed, no doubt, no worth (Matt. vi. 1); others, a greater or a lesser. The greatest value, however, attached itself to the widow's mite.

4. And how much interest may that mite, in the course of the entire history of the Church, have accrued?

HOMILETICAL AND PRACTICAL.

See Doctrinal Reflections.—The Lord's sublime peace of soul in leaving the temple, where He had met no recognition.—The humble resting-place of the Lord at the temple-gate, after He had been refused the throne.—The backward glance of mildness which the Banished cast upon the Church system by which He had been banished.—Christ's example teaches the heaven-wide distinction between godly zeal and ungodly fanaticism.—The Lord's eyes are upon all offerings.—The mite of the widow as a gift: 1. The smallest gift; 2. The largest gift.—The freewill-offering of the heart, the real inner existence and life of the temple.—Christ observes with emotion the dying embers of the expiring fire of God in the temple.—The distinction between the treasury of the Lord in the law-church and Gospel-church (there, chiefly intended for symbolic temple necessities; here, chiefly for the poor. See the lame beggar at the Beautiful gate of the temple, whom Peter heals).—The ancient estimable institution of Church alms.—*Christo in pauperibus.*

STARKE:—CANSTEIN:—The Lord Jesus pays attention, without doubt, to men's alms; hence they should be willing to give, and take earnest heed how they give.—*Bibl. Wirt.*:—Christians must willingly deposit in God's treasury, and contribute to the support of God's service—churches, schools, the poor, 2 Cor. ix. 7.—J. HALL:—Where distribution is made to the poor, there Jesus pays attention, and takes pleasure therein.—O God, I have only two mites, a body and a soul.—CANSTEIN:—Christ remarks a compassionate and believing heart, when alms are being given.—*Nova. Bibl. Tub.*:—God's opinion regarding good works is infinitely different from that of men. Those who give the most, give often the least; and those who give the least, the most.—Servants must not exclude themselves from almsgiving.

BRAUNE:—He says, Verily I say unto you, because He wishes to make His judgment abide, as though it were a dogma and fundamental principle in His divine kingdom.—How she must have fixed her trust upon God, and not have cared for the morrow; since she did to-day, what to-day brought with it, Mal. i. 8; ver. 14.

SCHLEIERMACHER:—If there had only been many such to give as this poor widow, who was ready to contribute all that she could claim as her own, to the support of God's service, then might a purer zeal have developed itself, which had been far from degenerating into that tempest which destroyed the temple, and had contributed rather to prevent the downfall. This extreme tendency to externals on the part of the many was the first germ of destruction to that people.

---

9. *Jesus' Departure from the Temple. His Retirement to the Mount of Olives; and His Address concerning the Last Things.* CH. XIII. 1–37.

(Parallels: Matt. xxiv. and xxv.; Luke xxi. 5–38; Revelation.)

1 And as he went out of the temple, one of his disciples saith unto him, Master, see
2 what manner of stones and what buildings *are here!* And Jesus answering,[1] said unto him, Seest thou these great buildings? there shall not be left one stone upon another,
3 that shall not be thrown down. And as he sat upon the Mount of Olives, over against
4 the temple, Peter, and James, and John, and Andrew, asked him privately, Tell us, when shall these things be? and what *shall be* the sign when all these things shall be
5 fulfilled? And Jesus answering them, began to say, Take heed lest any *man* deceive
6 you: For many shall come in my name, saying, I am *Christ;* and shall deceive many.
7 And when ye shall hear of wars, and rumours of wars, be ye not troubled: for *such*
8 *things* must needs be; but the end *shall* not *be* yet. For nation shall rise against nation, and kingdom against kingdom; and there shall be earthquakes in *divers* places,
9 and there shall be famines and troubles:[2] these *are* the beginnings of sorrows. But take heed to yourselves: for they shall deliver you up to councils; and in the synagogues ye shall be beaten: and ye shall be brought before rulers and kings for my
10 sake, for a testimony against them. And the Gospel must first be published among all
11 nations. But when they shall lead *you*, and deliver you up, take no thought beforehand what ye shall speak, neither do ye premeditate;[3] but whatsoever shall be given you
12 in that hour, that speak ye: for it is not ye that speak, but the Holy Ghost. Now, the brother shall betray the brother to death, and the father the son; and children shall
13 rise up against *their* parents, and shall cause them to be put to death. And ye shall be hated of all *men* for my name's sake: but he that shall endure unto the end, the same
14 shall be saved. But when ye shall see the abomination of desolation, spoken of by

Daniel the prophet,⁴ standing where it ought not, (let him that readeth understand,)
15 then let them that be in Judea flee to the mountains: And let him that is on the housetop not go down into the house,⁵ neither enter *therein*, to take anything out of his
16 house: And let him that is in the field not turn back again for to take up his garment.
17 But woe to them that are with child, and to them that give suck, in those days!
18, 19 And pray ye that your flight be not in the winter. For *in* those days shall be affliction, such as was not from the beginning of the creation, which God created, unto
20 this time, neither shall be. And except that the Lord had shortened those days, no flesh should be saved: but for the elect's sake, whom he hath chosen, he hath shortened
21 the days. And then, if any man shall say to you, Lo, here *is* Christ; or, lo, *he is*
22 there; believe *him* not: For false Christs⁶ and false prophets shall rise, and shall show
23 signs and wonders, to seduce, if *it were* possible, even the elect. But take ye heed:
24 behold, I have foretold you all things. But in those days, after that tribulation, the
25 sun shall be darkened, and the moon shall not give her light. And the stars of heaven
26 shall fall,⁷ and the powers that are in heaven shall be shaken. And then shall they see
27 the Son of man coming in the clouds, with great power and glory. And then shall he send his angels, and shall gather together his elect from the four winds, from the
28 uttermost part of the earth to the uttermost part of heaven. Now learn a parable of the fig-tree; When her branch is yet tender, and putteth forth leaves, ye know⁸ that
29 [the] summer is near: So ye, in like manner, when ye shall see these things come to
30 pass, know that it is nigh, *even* at the doors. Verily I say unto you, That this genera-
31 tion shall not pass, till all these things be done. Heaven and earth shall pass away:
32 but my words shall not pass away. But of that day, and *that* hour, knoweth no man,
33 no, not the angels which are in heaven, neither the Son, but the Father. Take ye
34 heed, watch and pray:⁹ for ye know not when the time is. For the *Son of man is* as a man taking a far journey, who left his house, and gave authority to his servants, and to
35 every man his work; and commanded the porter to watch. Watch ye therefore: for ye know not when the master of the house cometh, at even, or at midnight, or at the
36 cock-crowing, or in the morning: Lest, coming suddenly, he find you sleeping.
37 And what I say unto you, I say unto all, Watch.

[¹ Ver. 2.—Ἀποκριθείς is wanting in B., L., Versions, Tischendorf, Meyer; found in A., K., Lachmann, Fritzsche; ὧδε before Λίθος supported by B., D.; received by Griesbach, Lachmann; omitted in A. and Tischendorf.]
² Ver. 8.—Lachmann and Tischendorf, on the authority of B., D., L., have omitted καὶ ταραχαί. Meyer would retain the words, and says, they have been left out by mistake; the scribe's eye running forward to the ἀρχαί following.
³ Ver. 11.—Μηδὲ μελετᾶτε, omitted by B., D., L., Tischendorf; Meyer would retain them.
⁴ Ver. 14.—Τὸ ῥηθὲν ὑπὸ Δανιὴλ τοῦ προφήτου, wanting in B., D., L., Coptic, &c. It is easy to see how they might be interpolated from Matthew; but their omission would be difficult to explain.
[⁵ Ver. 15.—D., L. omit εἰς τὴν οἰκίαν. Lachmann brackets it.]
⁶ Ver. 22.—Tischendorf omits, improperly, ψευδόχριστοι καί. So D.
⁷ Ver. 25.—A., B., C., &c., read, ἔσονται ἐκ τοῦ οὐρανοῦ πίπτοντες. Lachmann, Tischendorf.
⁸ Ver. 28.—A., B., D., L., Δ.: γινώσκεται.
⁹ Ver. 33.—B., D. omit καὶ προσεύχεσθε; Lachmann and Tischendorf follow.

EXEGETICAL AND CRITICAL.

See Matthew.—In our Gospel, the time and situation in which Christ delivered His great eschatological address present themselves, as is the case with Matthew. Upon Tuesday evening, immediately after His departure from the temple, the first introductory words were exchanged between Jesus and His disciples. Jesus declared Jerusalem's destruction. Thereupon He seats Himself in the circle of His most trusted followers upon the Mount of Olives, and reveals the eschatological import of Jerusalem's being destroyed. Hence it is exceedingly probable that this revelation by Jesus is a night-speech, or rather midnight address, succeeding the night-conversation which He had held upon His evening walk to Bethany, on the summit of Olivet, sitting opposite to the temple.

The three chief divisions of the address are, by all the Evangelists, distinctly enough marked: 1. The universal eschatological world-course to the end; 2.

the destruction of Jerusalem, with its succeeding days of trouble and contest, or the succeeding period of the Church of the Cross (the Christian Church), which period may be regarded also as a distinct division; 3. the indication and commencement of the world-end. The beginning of the first part is marked by Jesus' warning against being seduced by the pseudo-Christs (Mark, ver. 5); the end by the promise, "He who endureth," etc. (ver. 13). The beginning of the second part is indicated in Mark and Matthew by the reference to the abomination of desolation; in Luke by the investing of the city (Luke xxi. 20): the close is here shown by the words, "For in those days shall be," etc. (Mark, ver. 19); in Luke, ver. 23, the statement is—a time of wrath upon Israel. The interval between the destruction of Jerusalem and the end of the world, distinguished as the period of mitigated judgment, is brought forward in the words, "Except the Lord had shortened those days" (Mark, ver. 20): the close, according to Mark, is given in the exclamation, "Behold, I have foretold you all things;" according to Matthew, in the words, "Where the body is," etc. The chief point in this statement regarding the interval, in Mark and Matthew, is the warning against the false Christs; in Luke, the sufferings of the Jews, the treading under foot of Jerusalem, until the times of the Gentiles be fulfilled. The beginning of the section upon the world-end is brought most prominently forward by Mark—"In those days" (ver. 24); Matthew similarly; Luke, with a short καὶ ἔσται, a Future, which is connected with the Preterite of the fulfilment of the times of the Gentiles. All three Evangelists mark the end of this period as the deliverance of the faithful. The Son of Man, according to Matthew and Mark, appears and sends forth His angels to gather in His chosen. Luke makes this known in the words, Lift up your heads, for your salvation draweth nigh. To this succeeds the practical application of the speech in the parable of the fig-tree. The eschatological discourse of Mark's Gospel agrees most with Matthew; yet it is on the whole shorter, in particular points more circumstantial, and picturesque. Particularly strong is the call in Mark to foresight, to attention, and watchfulness, vers. 5, 9, 23, 33, 35, 37. The comparative characterization, however, will be most appropriately added to the consideration of the various sections. For the literature upon this portion, *see Matthew*. Worthy of special notice is EBRARD's tract: *Adversus erroneam nonnullorum opinionem, qua Christi discipuli existimasse perhibentur, fore, ut universale judicium ipsorum aetate superveniret*, Erlangen, 1842.

A. *The Occasion.* VERS. 1–4.

(Parallels: Matt. xxiv. 1–3; Luke xxi. 5–7.)

Mark brings before us a single speaker, who pointed out to the Lord the splendor of the temple; while Luke speaks of several, Matthew of the disciples in general. One might imagine it was Andrew who furnished in this manner the occasion, entering as he did this time into the circle of the intimate few. If it were not he, then it was most probably Peter. What the disciples bring before the Lord—interceding, so to speak, for the temple—is, according to Matthew, the building itself (the structure being perhaps, in some part, in process of reconstruction); according to Luke, the beautiful stones and the gifts; according to Mark, the greatness of the stones and structures. Braune: According to Josephus, the stones were, in part, twenty-five ells long, twelve broad, eight high. The thought that such a building should be destroyed, was too sad for them; and the precious stones alluded to by Luke, the consecration-presents of piety, upon the walls and in the courts, testified to a continued respect for the temple. The reply of the Lord is here very lively, Dost thou see these buildings? The seat upon the Mount of Olives is marked as a position *over against the temple*. Of the circle of the disciples who interrogate the Lord, we learn this only, that they are His trusted friends, and that Andrew was on this occasion present, in addition to Peter, James, and John. The two questions, regarding the destruction of Jerusalem, and the sign of the end of the world, given by Matthew, are likewise given by Mark, yet in a different form.

Ver. 2. **One stone upon the other.**—Meyer: "There would not be one stone left upon another, which should escape, in the further prosecution of the work of destruction, being torn down." But this is the depicting of a *regular* breaking down of a house, in which the chief thing is to separate one stone from another, down to the very last. Here, on the contrary, we have the picture of a violent destruction, in which many stones, as all know, remain lying upon one another, yet is each torn from his place and broken. In other words, καταλύεσθαι refers not merely to the mass of the temple, but also to the single stones: the temple should be so thoroughly destroyed, that each stone should be destroyed. Of course this strong expression is not to be pressed literally.

Ver. 3. **Over against the temple.**—The summit of Olivet made a *vis-à-vis* to the temple's pinnacle. *See* books of travel.—**And Andrew.**—*See Matthew.*

Ver. 4. **When shall these things be, and what**, etc.—The subject of the two distinct questions is here indicated in a twofold manner: ταῦτα and ταῦτα πάντα; ἔσται and μέλλῃ συντελεῖσθαι.—**When all these.**—Not once more the destruction of Jerusalem (Meyer). By Grotius and Bengel, πάντα ταῦτα is referred to the whole world. We understand it of all things which formed part of the Jewish regime, and which, according to the view of the disciples, were connected with the destruction of Jerusalem.

B. *The World's Course to the World's End in general. The Last Things of the Christian, or the Christian Signature of the End of the World.* VERS. 5–13.

(Parallels: Matt. xxiv. 4–14; Luke xxi. 8–19.)

Mark begins again with an ἤρξατο λέγειν. The warning against the pseudo-Christs is common to all the Synoptics. Luke alone has the addition, that the time draws near: the indication of the chiliastic (millenarian) element. The representation of the wars of the nations is in Mark the shortest. The signs of the world's development are given by Luke most complete: earthquakes, famines, pestilences, terrors, and signs in the heavens. Mark, with Matthew, omits the terrific things and signs in heaven, also the pestilences, and has instead ταραχαί, pointing out (from the Roman stand-point) chiefly the political condition of the world. After Mark has with Matthew denoted this as the beginning of sorrows, we have a second, Take heed unto yourselves, introduced. And now he depicts more fully than Matthew the persecutions of the Christians, giving, as does Luke, a view of those which had been already given by Matthew in the instructions to the Apostles, ch. x. 17, 18. These were very weighty words for the Roman Christians, at a time when the martyrdom of Peter and Paul, in Rome, was about to take place. Then, as early as the 10th verse, he gives the *concluding* statement of Matthew regarding the preaching of the Gospel in all the world; and appends the rules of conduct for the persecuted, which we find in Matt. x. 19. To this succeeds the presaging of fraternal hatred, and the detestation of the Christians, occurring Matt. x. 21. None the less does the concluding portion of that statement form here the conclusion: He who endureth, etc. Matthew has this final word once again in this passage; and this circumstance, as well as the connection between Mark and Luke, speaks for Mark's accuracy, and proves that all the various portions recorded by him have their proper place in this address. The words, Matt. xxiv. 10–12, are omitted by Mark, probably because they are implied in the statements already made.

Ver. 5. **Take heed lest**, etc.; **for many shall come.**—This warning against pseudo-Christs, pseudo-Christianities, false prophets, and false prophecies, being placed at the head, denotes that it is an essential point of view from which to contemplate Christian eschatology.

Ver. 7. **But the end shall not be yet.**—Meyer: "The end of the calamities, not of the world." But the end of the calamities is really the end of the world.

Ver. 8. **Troubles** (terrifying confusions), ταραχαί,—Mark alone gives this. The word denotes primarily a shock, or commotion (John v. 4); then a commotion of mind, overwhelming, a fright; and hence, with respect to political circumstances, public terrifying confusion, anarchical conditions of states, tumults, etc.

Ver. 9. **Ye shall be beaten.**—The question is, whether the construction be, Ye shall be delivered up to councils and synagogues, shall be beaten, etc. (Luther, Meyer), or as in the English text, with Bengel and others. Against this latter construction, Meyer says, the idea of motion lies not in δαρήσεσθε, but it does in εἰς. Meyer says, further, the scourging took place regularly in the synagogues. Then it is certainly a striking picture of fanatic maltreatment, if it had been already inflicted upon the way to the synagogues (Acts vi. 12; xxi. 30, 31). According to Meyer's construction, in councils and synagogues, we have a tautology. The view, however, is this: The trial and condemnation took place in the councils or ecclesiastical courts, which were annexed to the synagogues; and the condemned were then led into the synagogues, or congregations, to be beaten: fanaticism could not, however, restrain itself: they were scourged even on their way thither.—**For a testimony against them.**—*See Matthew.*

Ver. 10. **Among all nations.**—A result of the above-mentioned martyrdom. Through sufferings the Gospel was to be spread among all peoples. This is, accordingly, the end of their trials. Not till this be fulfilled does the *end* of the woes come, as distinguished from the ἀρχαί.

Ver. 11. **When they shall lead you.**—Rules for conduct. Above, it was **Take heed**; here, **Take no thought.**—Be on your guard against the seductions of the pseudo-Christs; be not anxious because of the threats of open foes. "Μελετᾶτε, the regular word for the committing to memory of a speech; see WETSTEIN; the opposite of extempore." Meyer. Comp. *Matthew*. Take no thought, *how or what*, as the more objective mode of Matthew puts it. Here equally a double prohibition in a more subjective form: Take no thought beforehand; do not trouble yourselves on account of it.—**For it is not ye that speak.**—*See Matthew.*

Ver. 13. **He that shall endure.**—Meyer explains by the context: In confessing My name. Compare the διὰ τὸ ὄνομά μου. Nevertheless, the endurance refers to the entire state of trial, which they should pass through faithfully; of course, confessing Christ. It is from sufferings that confession receives its name, as *the Confession.*

C. D. *The Destruction of Jerusalem, and the interval between this and the End of the World; or, the World's Course to the End from the predominating point of view of the Jewish Theocracy.* VERS. 14–20; VERS. 21–23.

(Parallels: Matt. xxiv. 15–21; 22–28; Luke xxi. 20–23; 24.)

The presage of the destruction of Jerusalem is given more briefly than by Matthew, still in biblical form; not as in Luke, who declares plainly the besieging and destruction of the city. The direction to flee is the same as in Matthew, only more exact. From the command, Pray that your flight be not in winter, he leaves out the additional statement of Matthew, Nor yet upon the Sabbath, as it was less easy to be comprehended by the Roman Christians. The description of this one great tribulation is expressed in a richer dress than by Matthew. In describing the appearance of the false Christs and prophets, he omits the details: If they say, Lo, he is in the wilderness, etc.; also the picture of the last judgment, the lightning, and the eagles. On the other hand, his conclusion is in the highest degree impressive: ὑμεῖς δὲ βλέπετε, ver. 23.

Ver. 14. **Where it ought not.**—*See Matthew.*

Ver. 19. **Shall be affliction.**—The very days themselves. Stronger expression: It will be the characteristic of those days that they are tribulation itself.—**From the beginning of the creation, which God created.**—This not a merely stronger emphasizing of the conception, Creation. The κτίσις which God created, forms an opposition to the κτίσις of men, the city Jerusalem and her hierarchy, which was now falling, while the former should endure. Similar is the expression regarding the elect: Whom God hath chosen,—who are, and shall remain, chosen. And just so we have a twofold reference to the shortening of the days: Although they are the days of vengeance, He has shortened them as such, and made them endurable. *See Matthew.*

Ver. 23. **But take ye heed.**—Ever-repeated emphasizing of the greatness of the temptation.

E. *The End of the Cosmos.* VERS. 24–27.

(Parallels: Matt. xxiv. 29–31; Luke xxi. 25–28.)

Mark, as well as Matthew, draws a very sharply defined distinction between the time of the destruction of Jerusalem, and the time when the sign of the end of the world shall appear. Mark: After that tribulation (the destruction of Jerusalem), in the period of the *shortened days*. Here he has omitted the εὐθέως of Matthew. The fall of the stars he expresses differently from Matthew. He passes over the picture of men's consternation at the appearance of the Son of Man, which Matthew gives; also the summons of the great trumpets. And the expression, "From one end of heaven to the other," runs, in his narrative, "From the uttermost part of the earth to the uttermost part of heaven."

Ver. 24. **After that tribulation.**—Meyer holds that, according to Mark, the appearing of the Son of Man should occur immediately after the destruction of Jerusalem. According to the text, however, after the destruction, follow only "those days," and these endurable. Between *those days* and *that day* is a great difference, which Meyer's exegesis has not noticed.

F. *The Parable of the sudden irruption of the Catastrophe, and the Exhortation to Watchfulness.* VERS. 28–37.

(Parallels: Matt. xxiv. 33–50; Luke xxi. 29–36.)

To the end of ver. 32, Mark writes to quite the same import as Matthew; then, however, a different statement comes in: Of that day and that hour know not the angels, neither the Son. At this point the three Synoptics separate and take different ways. Matthew represents the Lord as here pointing back to the days of Noah, as being symbols of the days of the world's end. The surprise of that day is depicted by him in a particular way. The parable of the midnight has its characteristic point in the coming thief; and, succeeding this, is another parable of the lord who, in coming home, surprises his servants. Mark has the exhortation, Watch, for ye know not, etc., which is found in Matthew. But then he adds a parable, peculiar to himself, of the lord going away upon a journey, appointing special duties to his trusted servants: and in this parable the chief person is the lowest servant, the porter, who must keep watch; while Matthew makes him the steward, who had charge of the house. It is evident that the parables are distinct. Matthew selected the steward, because watchful honesty seemed to him the chief thing; Mark selected the porter, because honest watchfulness seemed to him the chief thing. Matthew may have had before him, in his selection, the picture of the Jewish high-priest; and Mark, the picture of a porter attached to some noble Roman house. Mark notices the different hours in which the master may return, marking them out sharply by the statement of the divisions of the night. Luke brings prominently forward the common danger to man,—the heart must not be overcharged, etc.; the momentous day is compared by him to a snare (παγίς). Mark concludes with the word, Watch!

Ver. 28. **That the summer.**—"Τὸ θέρος, also in *Test.* xii. *Patr.*, is the symbol of the Messianic time." Meyer.

Ver. 30. **This generation.**—According to Meyer, the (then) present generation. *See Note on Matthew.* The generation which has these signs under observation. Had the generation of that time been meant, then the end of the time at least could have been specified; while Christ says, on the contrary, the day and the hour knoweth no man.

Ver. 32. **Neither the Son.**—An admission, which Meyer, in considering the human limitations in which the Son of Man moved on earth, places in its due position. Athanasius says, Jesus did not know as a human being; Augustine, He did not know it to impart to His disciples. For other interpretations, consult Meyer. Respecting our own interpretation, Meyer judges falsely or inaccurately. We assume that the Son, as God-man, knew not that day in His present daily consciousness, because He *willed* not to pass beyond the horizon of His daily task to reflect upon that day (*see* LANGE's *Leben Jesu*, ii. 3, p. 1280); because He preferred, accordingly, the limiting horizon of His holy, human observation and knowledge, which widened from day to day, to a discursive pedantic polyhistory, or preternatural pretension of knowing everything, the dim opposite of dynamic omniscience. *Self-*limitation in the knowledge of all chronological, geographical, and similar matters, is quite different from an absolute "limitation" of the theanthropic omniscience of Jesus. *See Matthew.*

Ver. 34. **As a man taking a far journey.**—According to Meyer, a part of a speech, "made up of the different rôles which formed the links between the several heads of the speech." Why not a special parable? Or, is a porter or a guard of a house formed by uniting the rôles of a house-proprietor and a house-steward? and out of a thief and a master of a house do we get, again, a master of a house? We assume, simply, a distinct, though connected, parable. In Matthew, the householder himself is first, then the steward, summoned to watch; in Mark, the house-watch or porter, to guard the house.—**As a man taking**, etc.—The anantapodoton [*i.e.*, the apodosis to be supplied] is found simply in the omitted ἐστί. It is as with a man who took a journey. The whole emphasis falls then upon the finite verb, in accordance with the participles following, viz., upon the injunction which the lord gave the porter to watch.—**Authority to his servants.**—A proof that we have here to do with another parable. The parable of the servant, to whom the highest authority was entrusted, is recorded by Matthew.—**And commanded the porter to watch.**—After he had given all the orders concerning the internal affairs, he gives finally, at the door, to the porter, the additional command to watch: this is the point of the parable. Contemplating them with reference to the Church this side of eternity, the porters are, of course, the Apostles of Christ, together with the body of Christians,—a different aspect from that in which the servant of Christ may be proëminently considered a steward.

Ver. 35. **At even, or at midnight.**—The four night-watches. See WINER, *Nachtwache* (Night-watch); the author's *Commentary on Matthew;* WIESELER, *Chronol. Synopse,* p. 406. The uniform thought is, The Lord comes in the night-season, in a dark, sad time; and it is not known in what stadium or moment of this time. He comes quite unexpected. From different stand-points, these periods (ὀψέ = 9 o'clock; μεσονύκτιον = 12; ἀλεκτοροφωνία = 3; πρωΐ = 6) may denote the same unexpectedness:—the evening, the evening of the old world (Matt. xx. 8); the midnight, the frame of mind of the slumbering Church (Matt. xxv. 6); the cock-crow, the voice of the watchers (Isa. xxi. 11); the morning, the dawn of Christ's appearing, the breaking into day of the new world (Mal. iv. 2).

DOCTRINAL AND ETHICAL.

1. Comp. the parallel in *Matthew*.—It is significant that Mark gives prominence to the *size and strength,* Luke *the beauty,* Matthew the restoration and *apparent theocratic rebuilding,* of the temple. All this could not save it.

2. The eschatological speech of the Lord, the germ of John's Apocalypse; the New Testament exposition and form of the Old Testament ideas and symbols; the opposite and corrective of all apocryphal Apocalypsism (Comp. LÜCKE, *Versuch einer vollständiger Einleitung in die Offenbarung des Johannes und in die apokalyptische Literatur überhaupt,* Bonn, 1848; AUBERLEN, *Der Prophet Daniel und die Offenbarung Johannes,* 2d ed. Basel, 1857.*) The eschatological hymns. Eschatology in dogmatic theology.

3. *Neither the Son.*—Comp. the topic Agnoetism in the History of Doctrine. Dogmatic theology has not reached the point of being able to do perfect justice to the œconomic and dynamic import of the Son's not knowing. In order to succeed in this, we must not carry the old human finiteness into the Logos, which men have deemed to be a further development of dogmatic theology; but we must do justice to the fact, that His divine nature transforms His human finiteness into the theanthropic condition and mode. Leo the Great says, "*Humana augens, divina non minuens.*" No safety can lie in the "*minuere divina.*" Not to know, and ignorance, are two entirely distinct things.

4. The strong emphasizing of Christ's exhortation, Watch!—According to this Petrine gospel, Christ's servants, above all Peter, should be the doorkeepers not so much of heaven as of the Church on earth, and should keep her awake, watching for the day of judgment.

5. Three is the number of the Spirit, four the number of the world. At the revelations of His personal spirit, Christ was attended by three trusted friends; at the unveiling of the world's fate He has four.

6. JOSEPHUS, *De Bello Jud.,* should be used with this passage; particularly his history of the destruction of Jerusalem. See VON RAUMER'S *Palästina;* also BRAUNE, p. 353.

* "Prophecies of Daniel and the Revelation of St. John, viewed in their mutual relationships," Edinburgh, T. & T. Clark.

HOMILETICAL AND PRACTICAL.

See *Matthew*.—*General thoughts upon the entire passage.*—Homily upon the Lord's speech concerning the end of the world, according to the preceding division.—The Judge has already announced Himself.—The last judgment in its presages: 1. The one great presage: the destruction of Jerusalem; 2. the continuous presages: the days of less terror in the New Testament seasons of trial; 3. the last presage, as signal.—The world's state and course between two great judgments, the destruction of Jerusalem (the symbolical end of the world), and the real end of the world in a place of judgment: 1. The picture of the state itself; 2. the misapprehension of the state. The world does not observe the forbearance, the administration, the approach of justice-dispensing righteousness.—The coming of Christ in our time with the baptism of the Spirit and of fire: 1. A true coming; 2. reminds us of His first coming; 3. an indication of His last coming.—The final words of Christ in His speech upon the end of the world: 1. Take heed unto yourselves; 2. Beware; 3. Watch.—The last day, a day which makes all things clear.—The day of the great revelation and the great appearance: 1. The great revelation of the old appearance (the phenomenal and visionary world); 2. the great appearance of the old revelation.

Upon A. Vers. 1–4.

See *Matthew*.—The exit of Jesus from the temple of His people: 1. A decisive step; 2. a melancholy farewell; 3. a decisive token; 4. the certain pledge of the rebuilding.—The prospect from the Mount of Olives of the temple and the city; or, the great difference between the sensuous (æsthetic) and a spiritual prospect from the Mount.—The Lord's repeated survey of the city from the Mount of Olives: 1. A look of a compassionate heart, during which the tears fall, Luke xix. 41; 2. a look of the solemnly earnest spirit in which the tears must disappear (here).—Jesus sitting in the circle of His four disciples upon the Mount of Olives; or, the night-conversation on the end of the world and the judgment, ever sad, yet solemnly joyous, because of its anticipations.—The great mystic discourse upon the last time: 1. Much overlooked; 2. much falsified; 3. ever of force; 4. ever efficacious; or, 1. in the world ever falsified and darkened; 2. in the Church continually illuminated and deepened.

STARKE:—*Bibl. Wirt.:*—Men's degeneracy, to be bewitched with the seeming reality of this world, and to forget, what they should necessarily consider, the statements of God's word.—*Nova Bibl. Tub.:*—If the wind of God's judgments storm around, there is nothing so firm, nothing so magnificent, as not to be torn down and destroyed. How many thousands of the fairest cities, of the most gorgeous palaces, of the most impregnable castles, have experienced this, lying now, because of their sins, in heaps!—Is this the city of which men say, It is the all-beauteous, on account of which the whole land rejoices, etc.? Lam. ii. 15 and 17.—CANSTEIN:—When we gaze upon great and glorious structures of this world, let us ever remember that a time will come when these shall be no more, and that nought is abiding but that which is not seen, 2 Cor. iv. 18.—At the house of God judgment must take its beginning, 1 Pet. iv. 17.—It is edifying to speak of the divine judgments, of the destruction of all that is splendid, yea, of the end, even, of this present world.

RIEGER:—In the minds of the disciples these two things [rather, these three, the destruction of the temple, Christ's future, and the world's end,] must have become confused, or they must at least not have been able to distinguish between them accurately [still in some measure. *See* above.] Just as now, in our belief of the future coming of the Lord to judge the quick and dead, many things also are united into one, which, nevertheless, the result itself might separate into distinguishable representations and periods.—The Lord Jesus, in His answer, has not explained it so fully, etc., because Jerusalem's judgment was such a famous symbol and earnest of the end of the world.

BRAUNE:—Comp., regarding the speedy coming of the Lord, Isa. xiii. 6; Ezek. xxx. 3; Joel ii. 1; Matt. xvi. 27; Phil. iv. 5; 1 Pet. iv. 7; 1 John ii. 18; Rev. i. 3; iii. 11. Quotation from Hamann's writings: "The death of every man is the time when the revelation of the Lord's coming is partly fulfilled to the soul. In this sense, it is literally true that the time of fulfilment is near." In the fragments of Jerusalem the last judgment is reflected.

SCHLEIERMACHER:—It was His object to represent all the institutions of the old covenant as something dedicated to destruction, in order to direct their attention by so much the more to the spiritual.—Hence we have to mark, that everything external in the Christian community is nothing else, and can and should be nothing else, than a shell, a covering in which the spiritual presents itself and works.—We find that the striving after externalism was soon renewed in the Christian Church.

BRIEGER:—The temple was the pride of the blinded people.—The destruction of Jerusalem is in a certain measure to be understood as a world-judgment. It befalls that people, namely, who for two thousand years had represented the human race. In the downfall of Jerusalem is depicted the downfall of the whole world (as in the exit of the Christians from Jerusalem is depicted the great deliverance of the believers in the last time).

Upon B. Vers. 5-13.

The foresight and fearlessness which the Lord enjoins upon His people in looking for His coming (or the end of the world): 1. Foresight in respect to the deceptive delusions of false Christs (spiritual delusions); fearlessness as to the threatening terrors of war and all the world-plagues (temporal terrors). 2. Foresight as to the enemies of the gospel, and as to their treachery; fearlessness as to the gift of tongues, and the power to reply. 3. Foresight as to temptations thrown in our way by our nearest relatives and the world; fearlessness as to the certain deliverance of the enduring Christians.—Take heed that no man deceive you; or, Antichrist comes before Christ comes, 2 Thess. ii.—The succession of signs: 1. False signs, and yet signs [false Christs, ver. 6]. 2. Weak signs, and yet sad signs [the wars; the end *not* yet, ver. 7]. 3. Stronger signs: national, political, terrestrial, physiological revolutions [the beginning of the woes, ver. 8]. 4. Striking signs [persecutions of Christians, ver. 9]. 5. The decisive sign [the gospel is preached among all people throughout the world].—The contradictory nature of the signs: 1. Signs which do not appear terrible, but enticing, and yet are to the utmost terrible; signs which appear to the utmost terrible, and yet are not so. 2. Saddening signs. 3. The great, joyful signs, ver. 10.—The great rules for our conduct, in looking forward to the last time, and in the midst of its signs: 1. Foresight; 2. fearlessness; 3. simplicity and a spiritual walk; 4. steadfastness.—The Lord's faithful admonitions. — There is an overcoming of these troubles.

STARKE:—In His teaching, Christ has regard not so much to what He knows, as to what is useful to, and necessary for, His hearers.—It does not behove us to know time and hour, but to observe the signs antecedent to the judgments of God.—*Nova Bibl. Tub.*:—Alas! how many good men has the pretence of Christ's name,—viz.: false hopes, outward show, seeming representations, fleshly accessories, etc.,—already misled, that they have fallen away into sad by-paths, and have been ruined!—The doctrine of the Last Things no useless doctrine.—QUESNEL:—He who properly understands this present world, how it is disposed and what end it shall meet, is always self-possessed regarding it, and is terrified by nothing.—Wilt thou save thyself from the awful judgments of God, then be not anxious regarding the judgments and wrath of man.—The gospel-trumpet must be blown before the archangel's trumpet is heard.—CRAMER:—God will not forsake His own people in the time of persecution.—In the defence of the truth, we must not look at our own weakness, nor the foes' might and strength, but we must consider the power of the truth and God's promise.—OSIANDER:—Imagine not thou art not bound to learn aught, etc.—QUESNEL:—Faith gives us as many fathers, brothers, and sisters, as there are Christians; unbelief changes those friends whom nature has given us into enemies, betrayers, and executioners.—The most dangerous temptation is that which comes from parents.—OSIANDER:—It is a mark of false religion that it is bloodthirsty.—The end crowns.—GERLACH:—No man can reckon more certainly upon the assistance of the Holy Spirit than those who confess Jesus' name in the time of their utmost peril.—STIER:—The end is patience, the saints' weapon (Rev. xiii. 10; xiv. 12), as the beginning is foresight (Matt. iv.).—BRAUNE: 2 Tim. iv. 16, 17.—The end comes not before the Gospel has finished its course. The nearer this completion approaches, the more certainly is the Lord's coming near.—SCHLEIERMACHER:—We should expect no other than Christ.—All may perish; we are sure that He and His kingdom will remain.—BRIEGER:—The Lord's communication includes in itself the nearest and the most remote; hence He speaks to those nearest, and to those farthest from Him.—As the hate of the world witnessed for Him, so does He witness for His own people.—The final winding-up is to be introduced by means of the Gospel.—The being saved is of the same import as being received to glory.—GOSSNER:—He who possesses the rights of a citizen of heaven, can remain unterrified though it should storm beneath heaven.

Upon C. D. Vers. 14-20, 21-23.

See *Matthew*.—Even in His great judgments is God's mercy revealed: 1. It warns of the judgments, and indicates the signs of their coming; 2. it opens a way of escape, and exhorts to use that way in flight; 3. it points to prayer as the means to mitigate

that judgment; 4. it has its eye fixed upon innocent sufferers; 5. it breaks the judgment off, and puts bounds to it, for the sake of the elect; 6. it warns against falling away to Antichrist, as the falling beneath the heaviest, the most fearful judgment.—The abomination of desolation, or the judgment inflicted on the holy place, a great admonitory sign: 1. The sign of the end of a now hoary period (and form of belief; or of a long series of judgments, which point forward to the last judgment); 2. the sign of a decisive separation between an old and new period; 3. the prognostic of a new period.—The prophet Daniel; or, the eternal spirit of the Lord in the old covenant, has foretold the end of the old covenant. (See Isa. lxvi. 3; Jer. xxxi. 31; Ezek. xxxvi. 26; comp. 2 Cor. iii. 13; Heb. viii. 7, 8).—The Spirit of the Permanent in the Church is the prophet of the downfall of her transitory forms (especially in the Middle Ages). —Whoso readeth, etc.: The old Scripture-word shows to all time the signs of the present and the future.— The flight to the mountains: The entire life of the Christians is a fleeing to the mountains.—In a season of distress, the saving of the trifling and the unessential (the clothes) has as its result the loss of the great and the essential (the life and soul): 1. *The fact* (in conflagrations, in times of war, in political convulsions, in times of religious crises). 2. *The reason:* because the small and trifling is the net which keeps men entangled in the old system and its judgment (Lot's wife, the Jews, the Middle Ages).— Woe to those with child, etc.: The Lord's compassion towards the special sufferers among mankind in the judgments inflicted on the specially sinful part of mankind.—The alleviations of the divine judgments which God has given to men: 1. Compassion (ver. 17); 2. prayer (ver. 18); 3. the steadfastness of the elect (ver. 20).—For the sake of the elect, *whom God has chosen,* God endures the world in sparing patience (*see* Rom. ix. 22).—The surest signs of the judgment which runs through the New Testament period of grace are the false Christs, the signs of the false Christs, and the hopes placed in them: 1. Among the Jews; 2. among Christians themselves.—The tendency to believe in false Christs is the most awful result of the rejection of Christ that is to be seen in the life of Israel, John v. 43.—The great temptations of the period which is hastening to its end: 1. Perceived beforehand; 2. declared beforehand; 3. overcome beforehand. — Foresight regarding the lying pseudo-Christian system, the salvation of Christianity in the last days.—Foresight the first and last means in preserving faithfulness during the last days.— Caution: 1. Regarding excited preachers who pretend to make Christ visible in themselves or in others, in this or that person or thing (See here or there); 2. regarding persons who will attest themselves as new saviours by means of deceptive signs and wonders (2 Thess. ii. 10, 11; Rev. xiii. 13).— The end of the world's history: unceasing self-confusion, self-blinding, and self-separation of the great majority from Christianity, and self-abandonment to pseudo-Christian systems.
STARKE:—CRAMER:—If we see even the greatest distress awaiting us, we should not allow ourselves by this to be turned aside from God and His love.— In public, national calamities, the majority think only of saving their goods and lives; few are anxious to make sure of their souls and salvation.—QUESNEL: —By far the most useful flight in the day of divine wrath is to flee the fleeting pleasures of the world, and escape from conformity to it, Ps. xc. 11.—*Nova Bibl. Tub.:*—God spares even this wicked world for the sake of His elect.
RIEGER:—Sad periods in the world's course are turned to their own benefit by false prophets.—LISCO: *Take heed unto yourselves ;*—an exhortation applicable to much more than the external danger of temptation, seduction, and falling away.—BRAUNE:—Luke, vers. 22, 23; Deut. xxviii. 15; Mal. iv. 1. *Lo, here is Christ,*—a voice which allures to itself; *or there,* —a voice which, unpartisan-like, points to others, and is accordingly still more dangerous—these voices are not to lead disciples astray.—Signs and troubles are no certain marks of Christ and His prophets: they are only indications of the connection of the individual with the spiritual world; they may be indications either of light and truth, or of darkness and lies.—Prove the spirits, whether they be of God.
SCHLEIERMACHER:—When we see how many imperfections have appeared in the Christian Church, one might be easily tempted to say, The light is not yet the right light. The true believer is, however, assured that the Christian faith has no share in all these imperfections; that it is the natural ruin of mankind alone which is the fountain of these, and this cannot all at once be removed.—God's kingdom is the spiritual temple of God, which needs not the external, and is raised above all external accidents, and which, where it has been once built, must endure to the end of days.
BRIEGER:—Not in the winter. It is well known that Jerusalem was destroyed in August.—The same sin, rejection of the Holy One, which brought Israel to its downfall, will cause the world's overthrow, so soon as *its* measure is filled.—The urging of precaution appears so much the less needful, inasmuch as He Himself says, it is impossible to deceive them. We may explain this in the following manner: God's acts do not *exclude* men's action, but *include* it (and that, too, not in the form of natural compulsion, but of the bond of love).—GOSSNER:—How must we ever fear to give our adherence to a false Christ!

Upon E. Vers. 24–27.

See Matthew.—The last day according to the Lord's announcement: 1. The great day of death, when the lights of heaven grow pale; 2. the judgment-day, when the Crucified appears in the glory of the world's Judge; 3. the great feast-day, when the Lord gathers His chosen by His angels from all ends of this and the other world.—Man's calamity completes itself at the end in the world's calamity.—As the sun was darkened at Christ's death, so will the entire starry world belonging to this earth grow dark in the death-hour of aged humanity.—The stars will fall from heaven. With mankind, not merely the earth, but also the planetary system which belongs to earth according to its old form, shall be dissolved, and assume a new shape.—When sun, moon, and stars shine no more, will Christ appear, and illuminate with His brightness the last day.—The last day the grand day of festival for perfected Christianity: 1. The creature-lights grow pale; the Lord appears as the festive light of His own day; 2. the impersonal being of the world disappears;* the glorified personality of Christ appears, and manifests His personal kingdom; 3. the wicked are shut out, and

---

* [Does this mean: The kingdom of materialism, or that "flesh and blood" which cannot inherit the kingdom of God?—*Ed.*]

have vanished; and all pure spirits are united; 4. Heaven's angels are the servants at the feast: all the elect shall be assembled who are upon the earth and in heaven.—The last day is, for the chosen of the Lord, the dawn of their blessed immortality, Job xix. 25.

STARKE:—QUESNEL:—O wished-for day of the elect! O long-desired purification, through which they shall be gathered by Jesus into the union of His body, His Spirit, and His glory!—OSIANDER:—Should we die in a strange land, yet shall we be assuredly gathered to Christ, our Head, at the last day, 2 Cor. v. 10.

BRAUNE:— Rev. i. 1; ch. xxii. 6 ["Shortly, quickly"]; Hagg. ii. 6–8 ["Yet once, it is a little while"]; Eccles. xii. 2; Isa. xiv. 12 ["How art thou fallen"]; Isa. xxxiv. 4 ["All the host of heaven shall be dissolved"].—The destruction of the creature will be an exodus into eternity.—STIER:—To the end of heaven. "Because earth and heaven now incline wonderfully to one another."

BRIEGER:—Ezek. xxxii. 7, 8; Joel ii. 3, 4; Dan. vii. 13; Acts i. 11; Heb. i. 14; Matt. xiii. 41, 42.— BAUER:—These violent things are only the heralds in the Lord's service.

Upon F. Vers. 28–37.

See Matthew.—The fig-tree with its late leaves is also a picture of the onward-hurrying judgment, upon the guilty Church (ch. xi. 12), upon the unrepentant Church (Luke xiii. 6), upon the fickle Israel (Hosea ix. 10).—The fig-tree according to its varied signification: 1. The early figs, the formation of fruit before the leaves shot forth: the early conversion of Israel and the elect. 2. The fig-tree unfruitful in the rich vineyard: a dying professing Church (and this is true of individuals) in the midst of the ever-living kingdom of God. 3. The fig-tree unfruitful, and yet pretentious with its leaves on the roadside; or, a church (congregation) without spiritual fruit, in the hypocritical covering of pious forms, fallen under judgment. 4. The blooming fig-tree, a prognostic of the summer's harvest; or, the theocratic, ecclesiastical, and cosmical indications of judgment as presages of the approach of the final judgment.—The holy certainty of believers respecting the day of the Lord strengthened and elevated through their ignorance of the time and hour: 1. The certainty, *a.* as to signs, *b.* as to His speedy coming, *c.* as to His unexpected coming, *d.* His coming during the life of a living Christian generation, *e.* in order to the destruction of the world, *f.* in order to fulfil His declaration respecting the necessity of watching. 2. Strengthened and increased through their ignorance: *a.* an ignorance regarding the day and the hour, to which He had voluntarily subjected Himself for their sakes; *b.* an ignorance regarding the time, to which He had subjected them for His own sake.—Christ's not knowing rests upon His knowing rightly [in a natural manner], or upon the holy *extension* of His range of vision. *—What Christ *may* not know, what angels *cannot* know, Christians should not *wish* to know.— The last day, the deep secret of the Father: Of the Father in His Creator-fulness, and in His gracious design; 2. of the Father in His preparing grace, and in His commands to the Son; 3. of the Father in the greatness of His patience, and the majesty of wrath. —The knowledge of Christ in itself exalted above the knowledge of men and of angels, is, on our behalf, a circle of holy self-limitation within the Father's omniscience.—Because He cannot deny anything to His own, He has denied Himself a knowledge of this.— The holy and useful uncertainty of the Church regarding the last day is to be compared with the holy useful uncertainty of individual men regarding the day of their death.—Through this holy uncertainty, we should be certain of our own salvation. Every day should for the Christian bear something like the appearance of the last day.—Christianity is a doorkeeper's office, as regards the future coming of the Lord.—Christ's alarm-call, or summons to all Christians for all time to watch!—Slumbering, in respect to the Lord's coming, is a danger fraught with death; while watchfulness is a fundamental condition of life. —Christianity is a constant living in the experience of judgment and redemption: 1. Judgment: *a.* a coming from judgment [Lange alludes, apparently, to the rise of Christianity at the time Judaism was subjected to judgment. Translator], *b.* an acting under judgment, *c.* a preparing for judgment. 2. Redemption: *a.* from the time onward, that the work of redemption was ended, *b.* proceeding under the cheering hope of redemption, *c.* looking forward to redemption.

STARKE:—Spring is a beautiful image: in the shrubs bursting into life, we are reminded of the coming of Christ, of the glorious judgment day, and the joyful resurrection from the dead.—QUESNEL:— Who is certain that he is not sooner to appear before God, his Judge, than summer is to come? If he meet not God to be condemned, the joyful everlasting summer will follow.—We have seen many things in our lives pass away: is that not a proof that all things fade away?—God has concealed from all creatures the time of His judgments; hence is many a one ruined in his calculation.—Beware of security! watch and pray!

BRAUNE:—Heaven and earth pass as leaves upon the world-stem in the harvest of the world-season: God's people are the sap, and God's word the power, which carries new life to all.—Jas. v. 7, 8: "I do not know." Will it be too hard for thee to say this? If so, Christ is not thy Lord.—The watching of the Christian must be also prayer (and *active watchfulness* will be at the same time prayer).— BRIEGER:—The kingdom of God, which will at last appear in power and glory, is to be compared with the joy-fraught summer.

---

* [Lange's thought seems to be, that the *voluntary* ignorance of Christ, which was a part of the voluntary humiliation to which the divine nature was subjected in its union with the human, was for the purpose of making possible a *gradual* growth in His theanthropic consciousness. For, had there been from the instant of the miraculous conception (the *punctum temporis* when the union of the two natures began) onward through infancy, childhood, and youth, the omniscient consciousness of the eternal Logos, of course it would have been contradictory to say that Christ, the God-man, "increased in wisdom" (Luke ii. 52), or that He did not know the time of the last judgment.—*Ed.*]

THIRD SECTION.

THE PASSION OF CHRIST, AND HIS REST IN THE GRAVE. THE RETIREMENT INTO THE STATE OF THE DEAD. THE LION OF THE TRIBE OF JUDAH AS THE PASCHAL LAMB.

Chapter XIV. 1—XV. 47.

---

1. *The Preparation for the great Passover. The Supper.*—The helpless impotency of wickedness in the old Church of God. The determined genius of wickedness in the new Christian Church. The Anointing of the Lord at the Feast preparatory to His Death; and the sale of the Anointed, or the Treachery, matured at the Feast-table. Ch. XIV. 1-11.

(Parallels: Matt. xxvi. 1-16; Luke xxii. 1-6; John xii. 1-8.)

A. *The weak Indecision of the Enemies.* Vers. 1, 2.

1 After two days was *the feast* of the passover, and of unleavened bread: and the chief priests and the scribes sought how they might take him by craft, and put *him* to
2 death. But¹ they said, Not on the feast-*day*, lest there be an uproar of the people.

B. *The holy Presentiment of the Female Disciple.* Vers. 3-5.

3 And being in Bethany, in the house of Simon the leper, as he sat at meat, there came a woman, having an alabaster-box of ointment of spikenard, very precious; and
4 she brake the box, and poured it² on his head. And there were some that had indignation within themselves, and said,³ Why was this waste [loss] of the ointment made?
5 For it might have been sold for more than three hundred pence, and have been given to the poor. And they murmured against her.

C. *The Lord's holy Decision.* Vers. 6-9.

6 And Jesus said, Let her alone; why trouble ye her? she hath wrought a good
7 work on me. For ye have the poor with you always, and whensoever ye will ye may
8 do them good: but me ye have not always. She hath done what she⁴ could: she is
9 come aforehand to anoint my body to the burying. Verily I say unto you, Wheresoever this⁵ gospel shall be preached throughout the whole world, *this* also that she hath done shall be spoken of for a memorial of her.'

D. *The Disciple's wicked Decision.* Vers. 10, 11.

10 And Judas Iscariot,⁶ one of the twelve, went unto the chief priests, to betray him
11 unto them. And when they heard *it*, they were glad, and promised to give him money. And he sought how he might conveniently betray him.

[¹ Ver. 2.—Lachmann, Tischendorf, after B., C.*, D., read γάρ instead of δέ.]
[² Ver. 3.—Lachmann, Tischendorf, B., C., L., Δ. omit κατά.]
[³ Ver. 4.—Codd. B., C.*, L. want καὶ λέγοντες; Cod. A. has it.]
[⁴ Ver. 8.—Codd. B., L. want αὔτη.]
[⁵ Ver. 9.—Codd. B., D., L. want τοῦτο; Lachmann brackets and Tischendorf omits.]
[⁶ Ver. 10.—Codd. B., C., D., Lachmann omit the article before Ἰούδας and Ἰσκαριώτης.]

EXEGETICAL AND CRITICAL.

Comp. the notes on *Matthew*.—The peculiarities of Mark in the history of the Passion generally are: life-like pictures, sharply-defined features, original statements of particulars. Peculiarities in this section. The two indications of Jesus' approaching death, namely, the indecisive deliberations of the Sanhedrim, and the anointing in Bethany, are found united in Mark, as in Matthew; yet he expresses himself regarding the decision of the leaders of the council much more briefly than Matthew,—more decidedly, however, than Luke. In the history of the anointing, he mentions, with John, a fact in addition to the statement as given by Matthew that Jesus sat at the table. Moreover, he describes the ointment more exactly. And, besides, to him we owe the fresh trait, that the woman broke the alabaster-box; according to several codices, the additional remark is made, that the ointment ran down from His head. In respect to diversity of statement, he assumes an intermediate position between John and

Matthew. John names Judas as the murmurer; Matthew, the disciples; Mark says, "some." With John, he declares the value to be three hundred denarii, and adds the strong word ἐνεβριμῶντο. To the words, Ye have the poor with you always, he appends,—And whensoever ye will, etc. To him again is the clause peculiar, She hath done what she could. The idea that this female disciple anticipates the anointing of Jesus for burial is here more clearly expressed. Peculiarly lively is the expression in regard to the preaching of the Gospel εἰς ὅλον τὸν κόσμον (Matthew, ἐν ὅλῳ, κ.τ.λ.). The treacherous visit of Judas to the high-priest is more briefly given than in Matthew. He does not name the traitor's question, neither the thirty pieces of silver; yet he emphasizes the joy of the chief priests.

Ver. 1. **The feast of the Passover, and of unleavened bread.**—A double feast-season. See *Matthew*. Comp. Luke's expression.—**After two days.**—Probably on Wednesday in the Passion Week, not on Tuesday (see *Matthew*). The anointing in Bethany was on the previous Saturday. The question is now, In what relation do the sitting of the council and the anointing stand to one another? We could imagine that the first history brings before us the chief priests, how undecided they still are; the second shows how Judas comes and gives advice. We must then assume that the thought of treachery had been brooded over by Judas from Saturday in the preceding week till at least Wednesday in the Passion Week, and came then first to maturity. The remark of Matthew, ver. 14, seems to speak against this, "Then Judas went unto." Judas had undoubtedly gone much earlier to the high priests. To this the statement points, "how they might take Him by craft." If they had just now decided, "Not on the feast-day," this is explained by the great triumphs which Jesus, on Palm Sunday, on Monday, and Tuesday, had celebrated over them; and with this, besides, the fact agrees well, that Judas had begun to hesitate during these days. The connection of the two recitals lies, accordingly, in the antithesis of the previous anticipation of the crucifixion on the part of the Lord and the strong presentiment of the female disciple, on the one side, and the much subsequent indecision and short-sightedness of His foes, on the other. But the second point of relation is this, that we see from the first narrative how far the foes had of themselves come; from the second, how Judas drove them to take their boldly wicked step, and succeeded in giving them the last impulse. They said, "Not on the feast-day;" Judas, on the contrary, bethought himself of the first, best opportunity.

Ver. 3. **Of spikenard, very precious.**—Upon πιστικῆς, comp. DE WETTE, MEYER, LÜCKE on *John*, vol. ii. p. 493. Not drinkable (πιστός), but veritable, real. Upon the nard, comp. *Matthew*.—**Brake the box** (bottle, or flask).—The narrow neck of the small flask. She did not wish to keep or hold back anything: offered up all, gave all away.

Ver. 4. **There were some.**—See *Matthew*. Mark presents, without a doubt, the most accurate historic picture, John defines most sharply the motive, Matthew gives the specially practical historic form.

Ver. 5. **And they murmured against her.**—De Wette: They scolded her. Meyer: They addressed her harshly. In ἐμβριμάομαι lies especially the expression of a passionate feeling which we strive to keep back in the utterance.

Ver. 8. **She is come aforehand.**—Προλαμβάνειν is the chief conception, not μυρίσαι; hence we see the error of Meyer's note, "A classic writer would have said, προλαβοῦσα ἐμύρισε."

Ver. 10. **One of the Twelve.**—Made prominent, as in Matthew. The tragic point lies not only in this, that one of the Twelve was false, but that he committed that most wicked act of treachery which was the particular sting in the sufferings of Christ. In a wider sense, he extended himself through the whole sufferings of Christ; for the treachery of the disciple who betrayed the Lord to the chief priests, led to the betrayal, on the part of the Sanhedrim, of Christ to the heathen power.

Ver. 11. **Were glad.**—They shuddered not, as the traitor laid before them his black design. They understood him. But Judas knew how to lead them still further into wickedness. He filled them with a satanic joy. And while they were still hesitating to take the last step, assuredly not from dread of the sin, but for fear of the people, Judas was watching for the first opportunity to accomplish his purpose.

DOCTRINAL AND ETHICAL.

1. See *Matthew*, and the parallel passages in *Luke*.
2. Judas the betrayer, because he had been most offended at the thought of the death and cross of Christ; Mary the commended disciple, because she was the first that was found possessing a self-sacrificing courage like His own in His way to death.
3. The treachery which springs up in the midst of the disciples of the Evangelical Church surpasses the wicked counsel of the hierarchies in the Middle Ages. The secret and open apostasies from the Evangelical Church to Romanism.

HOMILETICAL AND PRACTICAL.

Comp. *Matthew*.—The council in Jerusalem, and the supper in Bethany, in their relation to the central point of Christ's death; or, a picture of the uniting of all threads of ancient history in this death.—Not out of the camp of the foes, but out of the circle of the disciples, came the last decision regarding the death of Jesus.—Judas, the enslaved, and yet free, instrument of the deepest revelation of wickedness.—The faithless disciple of Jesus an instructor of the chief council in the way of destruction.—The unexpected turning-points in life, how they rise out of the depths of the spirit-world: 1. Out of the realm of light (Mary); 2. out of the realm of darkness (Judas); 3. out of the struggle between the two.—The ointment in the house at Bethany a savour of death unto death.—Greed in its demoniac greatness: 1. A child of perfected unbelief as to Christ, God, and mankind; 2. a father of treachery, which has often injured the saints; 3. a companion of avarice, envy, anguish, audacity, despair.—Judas determines to take the best opportunity he can to betray the Lord, i. e., in the sanctuary of His secret prayers.—Judas the calculator, and his miscalculation.—The estimation of Mary, and the estimation of Judas. The presentiment-filled spirit in its clear foresight as opposed to the selfish mind in its blindness.—The most multiplied purposes and projects, and over them the deep design of God.—Woman is here again before man, as is so often the case in the Gospel history.

STARKE:—HEDINGER:—Satan rests not till he has injured Christ and His cause in life, honor, and possessions.—At feast-seasons the devil generally excites the greatest uproar against Christians.—HEDINGER:—Nothing is wasted upon Christ. Miserable parsimony, when we refuse Him anything.—The prating of a fault-seeker can soon move others to join.—QUESNEL:—The pious must remain silent regarding the world's judgment. God will speak and conduct their affairs.—Behold, how the godless rejoice if they get an opportunity of fulfilling their wicked wish!—GERLACH:—The greatest praise ever spoken by Jesus regarding an act.—BRAUNE:—The Sanhedrim required him to point out Jesus' tarrying-place. And Judas is ready to do it.—BRIEGER:—Exactly what the enemies wished least of all to do, that must they.—To an uproar it came, only to the advantage of hell.—The greatest, most direct, most difficult, but the most blessed thing that ever a sinful being was able to do, namely, to receive the Lord's word in all simplicity and proceed to act, this did Mary; and this shall maintain her memory on earth till the end of time.—GOSSNER:—*She hath done what she could.* From this may every one take comfort, that nothing more than faithfulness is asked from them.—BAUER:—The deeds of love are often in the world turned into shame, because others turn them into an occasion to do evil.

---

2. *The Feast of the Passion, and of Victory.—The Paschal Lamb and the discovered Traitor. The Last Supper and the Lord's Triumph over the Traitor. The Prediction of the Disciples being offended, and of their denying Him.* VERS. 12–31.

(Parallels: Matt. xxvi. 17–35; Luke xxii. 7–38; John xiii.–xvii.)

A. *The Disciples' Passover-thought.—Unguardedness and Foresight; or, the Jewish Custom and Christ's Spirit.* VERS. 12–16.

12 And the first day of unleavened bread, when they killed the passover, his disciples said unto him, Where wilt thou that we go and prepare, that thou mayest eat the pass-
13 over? And he sendeth forth two of his disciples, and saith unto them, Go ye into the
14 city, and there shall meet you a man bearing a pitcher of water: follow him. And wheresoever he shall go in, say ye to the goodman of the house, The Master saith,
15 Where is the guest-chamber, where I shall eat the passover with my disciples? And he will show you a large upper room furnished *and* prepared: there make ready for us.
16 And his disciples went forth, and came into the city, and found as he had said unto them: and they made ready the passover.

B. *The Lord's Passover-thought.—The Passover, and the hardened and discovered Traitor in the circle of Disciples. The Lord's clear perception of the secret designs of the Traitor.* VERS. 17–21.

17, 18 And in the evening he cometh with the twelve. And as they sat and did eat, Jesus said, Verily I say unto you, One of you which eateth with me shall betray me.
19 And they began to be sorrowful, and to say unto him one by one, *Is* it I? and another
20 said, *Is* it I?[1] And he answered[2] and said unto them, *It is* one of the twelve, that dip-
21 peth with me[3] in the dish. The Son of man indeed goeth, as it is written of him: but woe to that man by whom the Son of man is betrayed! good were it for that man if he had never been born.

C. *The new Passover.—The Lord's fulness of Love on the night of the Betrayal.* VERS. 22–25.

22 And as they did eat, Jesus[4] took bread, and blessed, and brake *it*, and gave to them,
23 and said, Take, eat:[5] this is my body. And he took the cup, and when he had given
24 thanks, he gave *it* to them: and they all drank of it. And he said unto them, This is
25 my blood of the new[6] testament [covenant], which is shed for many. Verily I say unto you, I will drink no more of the fruit of the vine, until that day that I drink it new in the kingdom of God.

D. *A new Passover upon a new Night of Terror, and upon the Death of the First-born.* VERS. 26–31.

26 And when they had sung an hymn, they went out into the Mount of Olives.
27 And Jesus saith unto them, All ye shall be offended because of me this night:[7] for it is
28 written, I will smite the Shepherd, and the sheep shall be scattered. But after that I

29 am risen, I will go before you into Galilee. But Peter said unto him, Although all
30 shall be offended, yet *will* not I. And Jesus saith unto him, Verily I say unto thee,
That this day, *even* in this night, before the cock crow twice, thou shalt deny me thrice.
31 But he spake⁸ the more vehemently,⁹ If I should die with thee, I will not deny thee in
any wise. Likewise also said they all.

¹ Ver. 19.—Καὶ ἄλλος, μήτι ἐγώ; omitted by B., C., L., Versions, Vulgate, &c.; probably because the words were deemed superfluous, and that the construction was inadmissible. (We suppose εἰς to be supplied with the first μήτι ἐγώ.)
² Ver. 20.—The evidence against ἀποκριθείς is quite conclusive; [rejected by Lachmann, Tischendorf.]
[³ Ver. 20.—Lachmann, after A. and Versions, reads τὴν χεῖρα after ἐμοῦ.]
[⁴ Ver. 22.—Ὁ Ἰησοῦς is wanting in B., D., Versions; bracketed by Lachmann; rejected by Tischendorf.]
⁵ Ver. 22.—Φάγετε must be struck out, on the authority of A., B., C., &c.
⁶ Ver. 24.—Καινῆς is wanting in B., C., D., L., &c. Tischendorf rejects it, but it is retained by Lachmann. The uncertainty of the reading even in Matthew excites suspicion, that the Pauline tradition gave rise to it; for "the blood of the testament [covenant]" can mean nothing else than "of the *new* testament."
[⁷ Ver. 27.—Ἐν ἐμοὶ ἐν τῇ νυκτὶ ταύτῃ. B., C.*, D. want these words. A. has them. Lachmann retains ἐν ἐμοί, and brackets ἐν τῇ νυκτὶ ταύτῃ.]
[⁸ Ver. 31.—B., D., L., Lachmann, Tischendorf read ἐλάλει for ἔλεγε.]
[⁹ Ver. 31.—B., C., D., L. want μᾶλλον; Lachmann, Tischendorf omit it.]

EXEGETICAL AND CRITICAL.

Comp. *Matthew* and *Luke*.—The unity of these sections is to be found in the contrast between the disciples' unprepared state of mind, and the ever clear perception which the Lord had of what lay before Him. Next, we have the opposition between the Passover and the Supper, the great institution of love, and of treachery; finally, the contrast between the faithful care with which the Lord warned the disciples, and their presumptuous self-deception respecting the fact of their own weakness. Peculiarities of Mark:—Exact statement of the day, ver. 12, with Luke. He brings forward (what is passed over by Matthew) the sending of the two disciples, but does not name them, as Luke does; and this again is to be traced back to Peter's modesty, for Peter was one of those sent. The direction of Jesus also,—in Matthew, Go ye πρὸς τὸν δεῖνα,—is given here in a more expanded form, as also in Luke : the description of the man with the water-pitcher, who should meet them at the gate of the city, and the directions which they were to follow. He passes over, in his description of the Passover, the special narrations of Luke and John, and hastens forward with Matthew to the detection of the traitor. The indication of the betrayer has been already given : He who eateth with Me, ver. 18. The peculiar ἤρξαντο again, ver. 19. The audacious question of Judas, Is it I? which Matthew introduces, Mark omits, as he has previously omitted his words to the chief priests. In the celebration of the Supper, he agrees, excepting in a few trifling deviations, with Matthew. Peter has, through Mark, directed attention to the fact concerning the cup, "And they all drank of it." In recording, "Shed for many," Mark allows, "For the remission of sins," to fall out. The words concerning the new cup in the kingdom of God he causes to follow the words of the institution of the Supper, as is the case in Matthew, but more briefly expressed. The remark (recorded by John) to the disciples, "Ye cannot follow Me now," in Mark (and Matthew), runs, "All ye shall be offended because of Me." Peter's vow, "I will follow Thee," as given by John, is extended in Mark, "Although all shall be offended, yet will not I ;" shorter than in Matthew. The statement in John, "I will lay down my life for Thy sake," stands in Mark, "If I should die with Thee," etc., as in Matthew. The prediction that they would deny Him follows this asseveration in John, but precedes it in Mark and Matthew ; in this latter case, the asseveration was, of course, more presumptuous. Mark alone has the more definite signal, "Before the cock crow twice." The particular features which are introduced by Luke before this transaction, and which bring Peter still more prominently into view, are not related by Mark. He and Matthew present the strongest statement of the occurrence (an affirmation of faithfulness *after* the declaration of the denial).

Ver. 13. **Two of His disciples.**—Peter and John. Comp. *Luke*.—**And there shall meet you.**—The description is as mysterious as in the despatching of the disciples to bring the colt. So, again, is the prominence given to the talismanic word εἰπεῖν, to be noticed. Quite groundless is the view of Meyer (rationalizing), that we find in the wonderful manner in which the supper is ordered, as recorded by Mark and Luke, an evidence of the later origin of this account. In this passage Matthew has only hinted at what the other two have explicitly stated. *See Matthew*.—**A man.**—It is a very mistaken conclusion, if, from the fact that it was a slave's employment to carry water (Deut. xxix. 11 ; Josh. ix. 21), we conclude this man was a slave.

Ver. 14. **Guest-chamber,** τὸ κατάλυμά μου.—The reception-room, which is appointed for Me. With the word lodgings, the conception of a separate house is united. Much nearer the idea is, "My quarters."

Ver. 15. **A large upper room.**—The form ἀνάγαιον is best supported. Meyer : "In meaning, it is equivalent to ὑπερῷον, עֲלִיָּה, upper room, place for prayer, and assembling together." But, we must undoubtedly conceive of the "upper room" as being on the second floor: the Alijah, on the contrary, is a tower-like erection upon the flat house-roof (see 2 Kings iv. 10; comp. Acts x. 9). The learned Winer, too, has no clear idea of the Alijah. Comp. articles, "Houses, Roof." On the contrary, Gesenius : "עֲלִיָּה, *cubiculum superius, conclave, super tectum domus eminens ; ὑπερῷον ;*" and DE WETTE, *Archäol.* p. 146.—**Furnished** (provided with pillows).—That is, with pillow-beds laid around the table, as the custom of reclining at meals required.

Ver. 17. **With the Twelve.**—The two messengers have returned and announced that all is ready.

Ver. 18. **One of you which eateth with Me.**—The expression of grief. *See* John xiii. 18. Reference to Ps. xli. 10.

Ver. 20. **That dippeth with Me in the dish.** —Meyer: "He was one of those lying closest to Jesus, eating, namely, out of the same dish." Therefore, no very definite description. Yet the Passion meal was not the ordinary eating from a dish. The head of the family distributed the portions. The case is thus to be conceived: Jesus was about to hand Judas his portion. Now it is a psychological fact, that an evil conscience causes the hand to move with an uneasy motion, even at the moment when one succeeds in showing a hypocritical face full of innocence and calmness. The hand, in opposition to the steady countenance, makes a hypocritically tremulous motion. So, accordingly, does the traitorous hand of Judas, betraying him, hastily extend itself, it would appear, to meet the Lord's hand, as it is still in the dish, in order with feigned ease to receive the sop. The three statements—He who dippeth with Me in the dish (Matthew, and almost identically Mark); To whom I shall give the sop (John); and, The hand of My betrayer is with Me on the table (Luke),—agree, therefore, as regards the actual state of the case.

Ver. 24. **And He said unto them, This is My blood.**—That our Evangelist makes this expression follow the drinking creates no difference between Matthew, and Luke, and Mark. Because Mark, namely, wished to make this the prominent fact, that all the company in rotation drank of the cup, he represents the Lord as speaking these important words while the act of drinking was being performed; from which it is self-evident, that He speaks them while the cup was passing round.

Ver. 31. **Spake the more vehemently.**—We understand this not quantitatively,—he made regarding this many additional statements,—but qualitatively, of the increasing force in expressing himself, as the following sentence shows.

DOCTRINAL AND ETHICAL.

1. See *Matthew*.
2. As the first Old Testament Passover was celebrated before the actual exemption and deliverance of the Israelites in the Egyptian night of terror, in the believing certainty of their salvation, so was also the New Testament Passover, the Supper, celebrated in the certainty of actual preservation and deliverance, before the outward fact, the death and resurrection of Christ. Exactly thus, in the justification of the individual sinner, does the celebration of his salvation from condemnation precede the completion of his salvation in sanctification.
3. The way and manner in which Jesus unites with the celebration of the Supper the announcement that His disciples should be offended because of Him, and His solicitude for their preservation and restoration, brings before us the relation subsisting between this preservation and that of the first-born in Egypt, for whom atonement had been made. The disciples, too, must the destroying angel pass by. No doubt, because Christ, who is the First-born in an especial sense, presents Himself a sacrifice for them. But this First-born, too, wins back His life from death.
4. Three Passovers: The typical Passover of the typified deliverance; the actual Passover of the real deliverance, finished in principle, pointing to the completion in life; the coming Passover in the kingdom of God, the celebration of the perfected salvation.
5. The detection of Judas, and the announcement of the stumbling of the disciples after the Supper, is a sign that the Supper is appointed to exclude the apostate and the hypocritical, to strengthen, establish, and restore the weak.
6. The celebration of the Supper: 1. The external preparation, and the internal ("One of you"); 2. the celebration itself; 3. the practical improvement ("In this night").
7. The Lord changes the Passover into the Supper: Christ's disciples now make with great willingness a Passover out of the Supper, in various ways. A simply ecclesiastical meal of custom; a simply memorial meal; a dogma-teaching meal; a meal falsely alleged to be capable of removing guilt.

HOMILETICAL AND PRACTICAL.

See *Matthew*.—The pious recollection of the disciples, and the holy thought of the Lord (paschal lamb, the Last Supper).—The quiet, hidden friend of Christ in the city of His foes, and the concealed enemy of Christ in the disciple-band.—Both brought to view by Christ.—The Lord's Supper a celebration of salvation in the confidence of faith: 1. Outwardly, a pre-celebration; 2. inwardly, an after-celebration. —The holy appointment and efficacy of the Supper: 1. Revelation of hearts (acknowledgment of sins, and confession of faith); 2. the affrighting of sinful consciences; 3. the exclusion of the wicked; 4. the celebration of the pardon and the establishment of believers; 5. the determining of the future path; 6. the restoration of the erring.—The self-exaltation with which Peter goes forth after the Supper, is a sign that he had not yet properly understood it.— Peter, before and after the Supper, and during its progress; pointing to a mistaking of the Supper in its symbolic import.—The disciples forget too soon after Judas' departure how much they have in common with him.—The consciousness of success, with which the Lord looks to the coming season of the perfect reunion of His disciples and Himself, being fully assured that all their temptations and conflicts could not prevent this result.

HEDINGER:—At the approach of death, life-endangering perils, and other misfortunes, God's word and sacrament are the best anointing and refreshment. Happy is he who consecrates his room to Jesus as a household church, or entertains Him oft in His poor members.—If we hazard all to obey God, we shall find it as the Lord hath promised before.— OSIANDER:—Who serves, believes, and obeys Christ, shall be deceived in nothing.—CANSTEIN:—Whosoever receives the holy Supper aright, receives in it an assurance of the coming eternal glory.—OSIANDER:—In suffering and trouble look at redemption. —He will not break the bruised reed. So gracious is Jesus, that he promises consolation to, and addresses in the language of promise, even the stumbling disciples.—HEDINGER:—He who relies too much on self, is building on sand.—Whosoever in a deliberative assembly introduces anything evil, may easily (in a greater or less degree) bring all the others over to his own side, so that they all express the same views.

BRAUNE:—If amongst His friends there was a secret foe, there were many secret friends amongst His foes.—The traitor proceeds to complete his transgression, and Jesus proceeds to the institution of the sacrament of the Atonement.—IGNATIUS:— The Supper is a remedy bringing immortal life, an antidote to death.—Mark, who was most intimate with Peter, gives Jesus' words thus: Before the cock crow twice, thou wilt thrice deny Me. The third part of the night, from twelve to three, was called the cock-crowing: before this should end, Peter would have thrice denied the Lord.

BRIEGER:—In the Passover, Christ is shadowed forth from every side. According to the law, the paschal lamb must be set apart on the tenth day of the month Nisan. And upon the tenth of this month, upon the so-called Palm Sunday, Christ made His triumphal entry, etc. (Add to this, that Jesus died about the ninth hour, almost the time when the paschal lamb was usually slain; that all the people put Him to death, as every head of a family slew a lamb; that the roasting-spit for the lamb had the form of a cross; that no bone of the lamb should be broken.)—How precious the promise, that He, as the Risen One, should go before them into Galilee! But they have ears for nothing. They regard only that word which charges them so hardly, and so deeply wounds. The Apostles were now occupied so entirely with themselves, that they were unmoved by what was immediately to befall their Lord.—However, if they had not observed the statement that the sword should fall on Him, they could not have had regard to the promise of His resurrection.—GOSSNER: —Christ can raise the hymn of praise, although He knows His disciples are about to betray Him, etc. We must not be restrained from praising God because of anything.—BAUER:—His body, His blood; that is, receive His life.

---

3. *Gethsemane and the Betrayal; or, the Lord's sorrow of Soul.—The coming of the Traitor.* VERS. 32-42.—*The Betrayal and its Effect. The Arrest of the Lord. The Flight of the Disciples.* VERS. 43-52.

(Parallels: Matt. xxvi. 36-56; Luke xxii. 39-53; John xviii. 1-11.)

A. *Gethsemane.* VERS. 32-42.

32 And they came to a place which was named Gethsemane: and he saith to his dis-
33 ciples, Sit ye here, while I shall pray. And he taketh with him Peter, and James, and
34 John, and began to be sore amazed, and to be very heavy; And saith unto them, My
35 soul is exceeding sorrowful unto death: tarry ye here, and watch. And he went forward[1] a little, and fell on the ground, and prayed that, if it were possible, the hour
36 might pass from him. And he said, Abba, Father, all things *are* possible unto thee;
37 take away this cup from me: nevertheless not what I will, but what thou wilt. And
he cometh, and findeth them sleeping, and saith unto Peter, Simon, sleepest thou?
38 couldest not thou watch one hour? Watch ye, and pray, lest ye enter into temptation:
39 the spirit truly *is* ready, but the flesh *is* weak. And again he went away, and prayed,
40 and spake the same words. And when he returned, he found them asleep again; (for
41 their eyes were heavy;) neither wist they what to answer him. And he cometh the
third time, and saith unto them, Sleep on now, and take *your* rest: it is enough, the
42 hour is come; behold, the Son of man is betrayed into the hands of sinners. Rise up, let us go; lo, he that betrayeth me is at hand.

B. *The Betrayal.—The Arrest. The Flight of the Disciples.* VERS. 43-52.

43 And immediately, while he yet spake, cometh Judas,[2] one of the twelve, and with
him a great multitude, with swords and staves, from the chief priests, and the scribes,
44 and the elders. And he that betrayed him had given them a token, saying, Whomso-
45 ever I shall kiss, that same is he; take him, and lead *him* away safely. And as soon
as he was come, he goeth straightway to him, and saith, Master, Master;[3] and kissed
46, 47 him. And they laid their hands on him, and took him. And one of them that
stood by drew a sword, and smote a servant of the high priest, and cut off his ear.
48 And Jesus answered and said unto them, Are ye come out, as against a thief, with
49 swords and *with* staves to take me? I was daily with you in the temple teaching,
50 and ye took me not: but the Scriptures must be fulfilled. And they all forsook him,
51 and fled. And there followed him a certain young man, having a linen cloth cast about
52 *his* naked *body;* and the young men[4] laid hold on him: And he left the linen cloth, and fled from them naked.

[1] Ver. 35.—The remarkable difference between προσελθών and προελθών is found here, just as in Matthew. Most MSS. are in favor of the first; the sense favors the second. If we retain προσελθών, the *terminus ad quem* is wanting: unless there be a reference to drawing near to God in prayer, בָּרַךְ. Luke uses an expression denoting separation.

[2] Ver. 43.—After "Judas," A., D., K., Lachmann, Tischendorf read ὁ Ἰσκαριώτης.]
[3] Ver. 45.—The second ῥαββί omitted by Lachmann after B., C.*, D., L., Vulgate.]
[4] Ver. 51.—Lachmann, Tischendorf, after D., C.*, D., L., Syriac, Persian, Coptic, Itala, Vulgate, omit οἱ νεανίσκοι.]

EXEGETICAL AND CRITICAL.

1. See the parallel passages in *Matthew* and *Luke*. Peculiarities of Mark :—In narrating the sufferings of Christ in Gethsemane, Mark is the only Evangelist who gives the subject of Jesus' prayer,—that "the (dread) hour might pass from Him." The prayer, too, has with him a more earnest expression, with the "Abba," and "All things are possible unto Thee." In the passage recording the finding the three asleep, the reproof of Christ is directed especially to Peter, and Jesus calls him Simon, as He always does when He would remind him of his weakness and old nature. The modification of the first petition in the second, mentioned by Matthew, is omitted by him. Jesus prays, according to him, in the same words ; that is, Mark will emphasize the wrestling importunity in this petition likewise, while Matthew gives prominence to the stronger manifestation of the resignation of Jesus. The third prayer is not introduced by Mark, but is nevertheless implied in his recital. In the remark : "For their eyes were heavy," he employs, according to Codd. A., B., (Lachmann,) the stronger term, καταβαρυνόμενοι. He also has the noteworthy statement: "Neither wist they what to answer;" which recalls the similar expression in the history of the Transfiguration. Strikingly characteristic is the short phrase: "It is enough" (ἀπέχει); which is addressed by Jesus to the sleep-oppressed disciples. According to Mark's representation, Judas stands suddenly before our Lord, like some unearthly appearance. The traitor had given to the enemy a distinct, previously appointed signal (σύσσημον), and commanded them to seize the Master with all possible care, and to lead Him away. With a twofold salutation, Rabbi, Rabbi, the traitor here approaches Jesus eagerly and with feigned friendship. Jesus' address to Judas is here passed over. Of the sword-stroke of Peter he speaks in milder terms, saying he had cut off the ὠτάριον (diminutive) of the servant. The command of Jesus to Peter is also omitted. On the other hand, we are indebted to Mark for the remarkable episode of the youth who changed so quickly from a follower of Jesus to a deserter.

Ver. 33. **To be sore amazed, and to be very heavy;** ἤρξατο ἐκθαμβεῖσθαι καὶ ἀδημονεῖν.—Matthew has λυπεῖσθαι καὶ ἀδημονεῖν. Luke, instead of either expressions: γενόμενος ἐν ἀγωνίᾳ (in a dreadful struggle or agony). This agony has its two sides, which are described with about equal force in the phraseology of Matthew and Luke ; ἐκθαμβεῖσθαι is a stronger term than λυπεῖσθαι, and is given only by Mark ; indeed, the word is only found in the passages, ch. ix. 15 ; xvi. 5, 6. Upon this point consult the *Commentary on Matthew*, xxvi. 37. The traitorous, false, despairing world, represented in Judas, fills Christ with sorrow to amazement; He shudders before it, before the infernal powers lying behind it, and before the abyss of wickedness in his spiritual hell ; the impotent, poor, and lost world, which lay sleeping around Him, overcome with sorrow and devoid of all presentiment, as represented by the three sleeping disciples, gives Him the feeling of eternal abandonment, Isa. lxiii. 3. Comp. *Matthew*. Starke: ἐκθαμβεῖσθαι is used of fright at a peal of thunder, Acts ix. 3, 6 ; and before a phantom, Matt. xiv. 26 :* from this some conclude that the most frightful

* [In Matt. xiv. 26 the words employed are ἐταράχθησαν, and ἀπὸ τοῦ φόβου ἔκραξαν.—*Ed.*]

phantoms may have presented themselves to Christ, etc.

Ver. 35. **The hour might pass from Him.**—Not His suffering generally, but that hour. The whole feeling of suffering and judgment, to be so betrayed by the one half of the world, and to be so forsaken by the other half. *See Matthew.* [The "feeling" cannot be entirely accounted for by the desertion of the creature merely ; there was also to be the desertion of the Creator.—*Ed.*]

Ver. 36. **Abba.**—Most vivid narration. Citation of the actual words, as in the expression, *Talitha cumi*, and the exclamation on the cross. Meyer: "This address, among the Greek-speaking Christians, acquired the nature of a *nomen proprium*." Apart from the misunderstanding which would arise, the phrase *Talitha cumi*, and other expressions, speak against this opinion. Accordingly, ὁ πατήρ is certainly an explanatory addition. [Meyer remarks, *in loc.*, that the common view that ὁ πατήρ is a translation of *Abba*, is not congruous with the idea of earnest supplication ; and refers to Romans viii. 15.—*Ed.*] —**Nevertheless not.**—We supply: "But do not this, as I will, as My feelings would have." Meyer: "Let this not be which I will." Matthew indicates by πλὴν οὐχ ὡς. Luke uses appropriately τὸ θέλημα (inclination of the will), not θέλησις (act of will). Accordingly, ἀλλ᾽ οὐ τί is to be taken in rather a formal sense.

Ver. 40. **Found them asleep again.**—Luke: "For sorrow." Sorrow kept the Lord awake, but lulled the disciples to sleep.

Neither wist they what to answer.—Comp. ch. ix. 6.

Ver. 41. **Sleep on now, and take your rest.**—*See Note* upon *Matthew*. The ironical meaning, as conveyed by Matthew, is altered by Luke into a reproof: "Why sleep ye?" Mark presents an intermediate view ; first irony, then the call to wake.—**It is enough** (ἀπέχει).—This is the opposite of οὐδὲν ἀπέχει: nothing stands in the way, nothing hinders. The meaning accordingly is, It has failed ; it is no more of use, etc. "Meyer: "It is enough, = ἐξαρκεῖ." This is quite a derivative meaning, and an application of the word very remote indeed. (The Vulgate renders *sufficit*, &c.) Quite as untenable is another interpretation : "There is enough watching, ye have watched enough ;" or, "My anguish is past."

Ver. 45. **Master, Master.**—Not merely an exclamation of excitement, but also of hypocritical reverence carried to its greatest height.

Ver. 51. **A certain young man.**—This forms an episode as characteristic of Mark as the Emmaus disciples of Luke ; and given for similar reasons. That he was no apostle is evident from the designation : "A certain young man ;" from the circumstance that he had already the night-dress on ; and especially from the contrast he presents to the Apostles. He only presents himself after their flight, a youthful Joseph of Arimathea, and so a precursor of him. Some have without reason settled upon John as the person (Ambrose, Chrysostom, Gregory the Great) ; others have selected, equally without ground, James the Just (Epiph. *Hæres.* 87, 13). That the youth belonged to a family standing in a relation of friendship to the Lord, we may safely assume ; at least, he was himself an enthusiastic follower of Christ. On this account, it was natural to suppose a youth of the family where Jesus had eaten the Passover (Theophylact). In this case, however, we must assume that the young man had, on this occasion, been sleeping, or retiring to rest, in the house which belonged to the family, and which lay in the valley of the Cedron; for, that the young man had been startled from his sleep, or in preparing to retire to rest, in the neighborhood of Gethsemane (in some neighboring country-seat, says Grotius), is proved by his wearing the night-dress. Both circumstances might possibly be found united in Mark himself, whom we, with Olshausen, consider to be this "certain young man." (*See* Introduction.) Reasons: 1. The youth's picture agrees in every line with the character of Mark. 2. The circumstances of the youth agreed perfectly with those of Mark: the friend of the Lord, resting in this country-house for the night. 3. There is an analogical support of this view, in the fact that John also, by a mere hint, weaves himself and His mother into the Evangelical narrative (John i. 40, xix. 25); and probably Luke does the same thing (xxiv. 18). 4. The fact that this circumstance is related by Mark alone, which Meyer considers so very trifling, and Bauer holds to be a piquant addition.—**The young men.**—These certainly were not the temple-guards, nor yet the soldiery, but young persons who had of their own accord joined the company; partly from their interest in adventure. For this reason, they found themselves particularly tempted to make an attack upon this young man, their equal in years, in the nightdress, who wished to follow Jesus, clad in so ridiculous a manner.

Ver. 52. **And he left the linen cloth.**—The night-mantle, thrown about him, was easily loosed. Bengel: *pudorem vicit timor in magno periculo.* Whitefield has properly pointed out the action of this youth as the emblem of a late reception of Jesus, though others have praised it as the emblem of an early following of the Lord, as belief in youth. Both are to be found in it: a beautiful enthusiasm of belief, and a fanatical self-dependence and over-estimation of personal strength. Rather far-fetched is Guyon's allegory, that we must follow Jesus, stripping off all that is our own, and all that is false. This youth was a follower while he had the linen cloth; deprived of this, he became a deserter.

DOCTRINAL AND ETHICAL.

1. Comp. *Matthew.*
2. The suffering of Jesus in Gethsemane, and the treachery of Judas, stand in the most intimate relation to each other. The bringing about of His sufferings by means of the treachery which grew up in the midst of His disciples, and the spirit of worldliness, of worldly sorrow and worldly falseness, of self-disrespect and despair, manifested in this treachery, —this is, in the particular sense, the bitter cup which he had to drain; for it is the heaviest judgment of God, that sin itself must break forth in treachery proceeding out the disciple-circle; a fact, in which is revealed the full judgment of God upon the sin of the world in its faithlessness, and in its despair— upon the sin of that world which could break through the barriers separating the disciples of Christ from the world. In Christ's experience of this judgment, there are two points to be marked: the realization of His being perfectly deserted; the manifestation of the world's weakness, and of the imminent danger to which the wickedness of the world exposed Him even amid His disciples. That He must see Himself forsaken by His young Church, that He must grieve because of the apostasy in the midst of this Church: therein lies the bitter gall of His passion-cup, therein was judgment finished. He prayed that this hour might pass, if it were possible (ver. 35). And (ver. 41) it is said, The hour is come; behold, the Son of Man, etc. The betrayal marks and seals this hour.

3. The sleeping of the good disciples is contrasted with the watchfulness of the evil disciple. What was common to both parties, was the unspeakable sorrow. In the case of Judas, this has changed into absolute demoniacal distress, animosity, and rage; in the case of the Eleven, it is manifested in complete relaxation, cowardice, and indecision. On this account, Christ opposes to the sleep and indecision of the Eleven, the intensest agitation of soul and energy; to the fevered excitement of Judas, on the contrary, the most perfect quiet of soul.

4. The youth who follows the Lord in his nightgarb, and then flees, is a striking picture of the pious resolutions of Jesus' disciples, which are dissipated in the night-of great temptation.

HOMILETICAL AND PRACTICAL.

See Matthew.—The Lord's preparation as opposed to His enemies' preparation.—The unfathomable clearness of spirit in the agony of the Lord, and the unfathomable confusion of spirit in the agony of Judas.—The treachery of a disciple in Gethsemane, the Lord's secret place of prayer, forms a page black as midnight in the history of the world and of the Church.—God's providence has changed this terrific curse into a cup of blessing for the lost world, through Christ's obedience.—Jesus could pray twice or thrice almost the same words, yet make from them each time a new prayer (differently placed emphasis): 1. Take from Me this cup; 2. yet not what *I* will; 3. but what *Thou* wilt.—The chasm which opens between the Lord and His disciples, while He prays and they sleep: 1. Christ ever more wakeful, more calm, more sure of victory; 2. the disciples ever heavier with sleep, more confused, and undecided.—How the Lord Himself announces the hour of which He prayed that it might pass by: The hour is come; behold, the Son of Man is betrayed into the hands of sinful men.—Arise, let us go! lo, he that betrayeth Me is at hand.—Jesus' disciple as guide to the hostile band. —The kiss of Judas; or, here likewise is Antichrist concealed in the pseudo-Christ (a lying Christ).— Christ between the helpless assailants and the helpless defenders: 1. The assailants in their helplessness: *a.* the traitor, the soldiers; *b.* He grants them the might which they are allowed to have, according to the Holy Scriptures and God's providence, though it seems as if derived from human laws. 2. The defenders in their helplessness: *a.* the sword-stroke of Peter, the fleeing disciples, the fleeing youth; *b.* He grants them the might of His preserving grace.— There existed a natural relationship between this young man and the disciple Peter, as there existed a spiritual relationship between the Apostle Peter and the Evangelist Mark.—Christ betrayed and captured: 1. How all appears in this state of things to be lost; 2. how sin and Satan are thereby betrayed and captured.—By His bonds are we freed.

STARKE:—To pray is the best thing we can do in the hour of temptation.—QUESNEL:—God's will must be at all times dearer than our own, let it cost what it may to perfect it.—CANSTEIN:—Prayer is needed with watching, and watching with prayer. Both must go together.—Alas, if Israel's Shepherd should not be watchful, how evil would it be with us, from our lethargic security and sloth!—Judas sells Jesus. We should not consider the whole world a sufficient purchase-price for Jesus.—OSIANDER:—The wickedness of the world is so great, that the very persons who are appointed to administer justice persecute the just, and defend the unjust.—CANSTEIN:—Whosoever allures others into sin, sins himself, and loads himself with all the sin which the others commit.—OSIANDER: —Satan blinds men, that, when they do evil, they know not what will be its result.—CANSTEIN:—A good intention may lead to evil (the blow of the sword).— Hasty passions are dangerous; therefore, resist a blind zeal, which, the hotter it burns, displeases God the more.—HEDINGER:—Where the cross is, there is flight.

BRAUNE:—As Christ withdrew Himself, at the beginning of His public ministry, into the wilderness, so also now at the conclusion of His mission.—He addresses Himself to Peter at once, to do all that He could to bring him to see his weakness.—It is not the Scripture which makes the necessity of fulfilment: but the will of God, revealed in the prophets, causes the fulfilment of the Scriptures. The darkness, likewise, stands beneath God's light.—It is noticeable, that upon the spot where Jesus was seized by the band, Titus, the Roman commander, pitched his camp forty years after. The Turks, however, have walled the place where Judas kissed Christ, as an accursed spot.

BRIEGER:—Had Christ not been tempted as well from the side of terror as formerly from that of lust, the Scriptures could not say: He was tempted in all points.—Was that, perhaps, now fulfilled in His own person, which He prophesied of this time (Luke xxi. 26)? Then did that statement receive its accomplishment in Gethsemane: "I have trodden the winepress alone," Isa. lxiii. 3.—Rabbi, Rabbi. It was the last Rabbi his lips uttered.—The whole transaction (the arrest of Christ) presents itself as a drama arranged by the chief council. But all the pretence being destroyed, the leaders of the people stand before us as common criminals.—This terror could not have overmastered the disciples, had they not erred regarding the Lord. Being dissatisfied that Jesus did not deliver Himself from suffering, they held themselves bound to withdraw from danger.—GOSSNER, on ver. 27:—If thou canst not overcome sleep how wilt thou overcome death?—BAUER:—And these were the best of the disciples of Jesus!—Judas, accordingly, is there with his band already! He has been quick. Yes, sin runs a rapid race.

---

4. *Christ betrayed to the Jews, in the Palace of the High Priest, and before the Ecclesiastical Court. The False Witnesses. The Truthful Witness, and His sublime Testimony. The Sentence of Death. Peter's Denial.* VERS. 53–72.

(Parallels: Matt. xxvi. 57–75; Luke xxii. 54–71; John xviii. 12–27.)

A. Vers. 53–65.

53 And they led Jesus away to the high priest: and with him were assembled all
54 the chief priests, and the elders, and the scribes. And Peter followed him afar off, even into the palace of the high priest: and he sat with the servants, and warmed him-
55 self at the fire. And the chief priests and all the council sought for witness against
56 Jesus, to put him to death; and found none. For many bare false witness against him,
57 but their witness agreed not together. And there arose certain, and bare false witness
58 against him, saying, We heard him say, I will destroy this temple that is made with
59 hands, and within three days I will build another made without hands. But neither so
60 did their witness agree together. And the high priest stood up in the midst, and asked Jesus, saying, Answerest thou nothing? what *is it which* these witness against thee?
61 But he held his peace, and answered nothing. Again the high priest asked him, and
62 said unto him, Art thou the Christ, the Son of the Blessed? And Jesus said, I am: and ye shall see the Son of man sitting on the right hand of power, and coming in the
63 clouds of heaven. Then the high priest rent his clothes, and saith, What need we any
64 further witnesses? Ye have heard the blasphemy: what think ye? And they all con-
65 demned him to be guilty of death. And some began to spit on him, and to cover his face, and to buffet him, and to say unto him, Prophesy: and the servants did strike[1] him with the palms of their hands.

B. Vers. 66–72.

66 And as Peter was beneath in the palace, there cometh one of the maids of the high
67 priest: And when she saw Peter warming himself, she looked upon him, and said,
68 And thou also wast with Jesus of Nazareth. But he denied, saying, I know not, nei-

ther understand I² what thou sayest. And he went out into the porch; [and the cock
69 crew].³ And a [the] maid saw him again, and began to say* to them that stood by,
70 This is one of them. And he denied it again. And a little after, they that stood by said
again to Peter, Surely thou art one of them: for thou art a Galilean, and thy speech
71 agreeth thereto.⁴ But he began to curse and to swear, saying, I know not this man of
72 whom ye speak. And⁵ the second time the cock crew. And Peter called to mind
the word⁶ that Jesus said unto him, Before the cock crow twice, thou shalt deny me
thrice. And when he thought thereon, he wept.

[¹ Ver. 65.—Instead of ἔβαλλον, A., B., C., Lachmann, Tischendorf read ἔλαβον, "they took him" (away from the hall of judgment, into custody, i. e.).]
² Ver. 68.—We read, with Cod. A., &c., and the Recepta, οὐκ οἶδα, οὐδὲ ἐπίσταμαι. Certainly οὔτε, οὔτε is strongly attested by B., D., L., and is adopted by Tischendorf and Lachmann. We consider, however, this mode of expression too strong to be used in the circumstances. Matthew says, "I know not what thou sayest;" Luke, "I know Him not:" our reading, in what appears the original account, receives support from these two expressions.
³ Ver. 68.—Καὶ ἀλέκτωρ ἐφώνησε, wanting in B., L., Coptic, bracketed by Lachmann; probably interpolated from the parallel passage in Matthew.
⁴ Ver. 70.—Καὶ ἡ λαλιά σου ὁμοιάζει, omitted in B., C., D., L., &c., and in the texts of Tischendorf and Lachmann. It is interpolated probably from Matthew.
[⁵ Ver. 72.—Codd. D., D. have εὐθύς; A., C. have it not. Lachmann retains it; Tischendorf and Recepta reject it.]
⁶ Ver. 72.—Τὸ ῥῆμα ὡς, A., B., C., L., Δ., Lachmann, Tischendorf.
* [The Greek runs: "And the maid (that kept the porch, i. e.), seeing him, again began to say," &c.]

EXEGETICAL AND CRITICAL.

See *Matthew*, and the parallel in *Luke*.—Mark gives the same account of the false witnesses as Matthew; but he is the only one who mentions the reason why the chief council obtained no false witness, viz.: the witnesses did not corroborate one another. Matthew selects two witnesses as testifying to Jesus' statement respecting the destruction of the temple; Mark says, a few. Matthew had in mind the legal number which must be present; Mark, the smallness of the number. In Mark's account, the false testimony is strongest on the point, "I will destroy this temple," etc.; at the same time, he notices the contrast between the temple made with hands and that not made with hands. Again, he brings into view the conflicting nature of the testimony. Perhaps even in Matthew the divergent testimony is alluded to, under "I am able to destroy," etc. According to Mark, the high priest comes forward into the midst. The silence is strongly marked. The adjuration of Jesus by the high priest is only implied in the remark, he interrogated Him. The testimony of Jesus is more strongly expressed than in Matthew, ἐγώ εἰμι. On the contrary, he does not report literally the sentence of death, as does Matthew. But, again, he gives us the distinct view of how the servants—probably the prison-warders—take Christ to lead Him to a place of safe custody till the next morning. Then he says that Peter was below in the entrance-hall (of the palace); and gives us, thus, to understand that the trial had taken place in an upper story, or at least in an elevated hall. The maid of the high priest calls Jesus, The Nazarene. The first statement of Peter is characteristically ambiguous. The first cock-crow is mentioned by Mark alone (according to the exact remembrance of Peter). The second attack, Mark again appears to place, contrary to Matthew, in the mouth of the same maid; but it is, without doubt, the portress of the προαύλιον that is meant. The ἕτερος here, alluded to by Luke, belongs to the bystanders, of whom Mark here informs us. The portress did not address Peter himself, but denounced him to those about: upon this, one of them laid hold of Peter. Of the second denial, Mark gives a shorter, and thus milder account, than Matthew; there is here no mention of the oath. Upon the second denial, immediately follows the second crowing of the cock. At the end, he marks, with a brief, forcible expression, ἐπιβαλὼν ἔκλαιε, the repentance of Peter.

Ver. 53. **And with him** (αὐτῷ) **were assembled.**—Of course it is the high priest who is meant. The meaning given by Meyer is quite foreign to the passage: They come, that is, they meet Jesus there all at the same time. The words might, literally taken, bear this explanation; but the thought of their meeting there at the same time must have been expressed more precisely; not to mention, that according to Luke, several members of the Sanhedrim had joined themselves to the band, and had gone to meet the party. It was only because there was a council at the palace of the high priest that matters happened in this way, although, no doubt, the αὐτῷ which follows immediately must relate to Jesus.

Ver. 54. **At the fire,** πρὸς τὸ φῶς.—It is an open hearth which lights and heats the hall at the same time, at which they warm themselves. The designation is employed to explain the circumstance, that Peter was recognized in the light of the fire.

Ver. 56. **Agreed not.**—Two witnesses at least must agree, Deut. xvii. 6; xix. 15. In the main, however, the witnesses must not contradict one another.

Ver. 58. **We heard Him say, I will destroy this temple.**—The variations, as respects Matthew, constitute no difficulty in this passage; since, as is remarked by the Evangelist, the testimonies did not agree. In the contrast,—made with hands, made without hands,—we have probably one of the most false declarations. Meyer: From this it is evident that the one witness was not examined in the presence of the other. Let the conduct of the judges in the trial of Susanna be compared with this.

Ver. 61. **Of the Blessed.**—The εὐλογητός, or הַבְּרָכָה, in the absolute sense, is God. Undoubtedly this is a hypocritical expression of reverence in refraining from naming the name of God, intending to designate Christ's declaration blasphemy of God, of the Blessed. "The *Sanctus Benedictus* of the Rabbis is well known (SCHÖTTGEN ad Rom. 9, 5)." Meyer.

Ver. 63. **His clothes,** τοὺς χιτῶνας.—Comp. *Note* on Matt. xxvi. 65. He tore all his clothing, except that which was next his body. Winer: Persons of respectability, and travellers, sometimes wore two articles of underclothing.

Ver. 65. **And some began.**—Meyer: "The members of the Sanhedrim. The servants follow." Rather the temple attendants, who were surrounding the Lord in the hall (*see* John and Luke): those who afterwards took Jesus into custody, under the designation of servants, are prison-warders, as Matt. v. 25; hence servants in a special sense. Mark presents the scene of the mocking, which is given by Luke in detail, under the one aspect of abuse, which is in this way thrown out into stronger relief; and Matthew gives a similar view.

Ver. 66. **Beneath.**—This in opposition to the hall of trial, which was higher.

Ver. 68. **I know not;** or, it is unknown to me, not understood.—The double force in οὐκ οἶδα οὐδὲ, κ.τ.λ., is difficult to express. - If we translate, "I know not," this is too little; "I know Him not," this is too much; "I recognize not,"—then we have a phrase too decidedly unconnected. — **Into the porch,** or, according to Matthew, the entrance-hall. It is the same idea.

Ver. 69. **And a [the] maid.**—As soon as she noticed him. On the comparison between Matthew and Luke, and Mark, consult the introductory remarks to this section. **And began to say again.**—As the other had begun. The first πάλιν relates a repetition of the denunciation to the bystanders, the second πάλιν to the second denial of Peter in the same circumstances; the third πάλιν implies that those around had already once laid hands upon Christ, and in this way substantiates the recital of Luke, ver. 58.

Ver. 70. **For thou art a Galilean.**—Not meaning: As Jesus is also; but among the other proofs that thou art one of them, is this, that thou art a Galilean.

Ver. 72. **And Peter called to mind the word.** —A similar important thought or self-recollection of Peter is related in ch. xi. 21.

And when he thought thereon, he wept. —It is extremely difficult to bring out clearly what ἐπιβαλὼν ἔκλαιε imports. For the various explanations, compare BRETSCHNEIDER'S *Lexicon*, De Wette, Meyer, etc. Many consider it as the Vulgate, *copit flere;* but this is not grammatically correct. Others, he went out hastily (analogous to the phrases in Matthew and Luke); others, he threw a covering over his head; or, he cast his eyes upon the Lord; or, he continued to weep; or, according to Ewald, he interrupted with his weeping the sound of the crowing (that is, answering with loud sobbing the crowing of the cock); or, he took notice of that sound, bethought himself of the matter. (De Wette: 'Επιβαλὼν refers to the cock-crow; Meyer.) We find only three interpretations tenable: 1. He flung himself forth, that is, he involuntarily rushed out, as it were meeting the cock-crow as he hurried out, according to the narratives of Matthew and Luke. 2. Referring the phrase to the word of Jesus: he threw himself into it, under the condemnation of this word (took it to heart), and wept. Or, 3. making the cock-crowing to be as it were Christ's waking call; and thereupon he threw himself out of the place (as though Christ had called him; *Leben Jesu*, iii. 334), and wept. First a rushing forth, as if he had an external goal to reach, then a bitter sinking down into himself and weeping. The turning-point between the carnal and spiritual mode of viewing the life. He hastened forth at the call; on the outside, he found the call went inwards and upwards, and he stopped and wept.

DOCTRINAL AND ETHICAL.

1. Comp. *Matthew*.
2. Peter has not extenuated his **own** fault; for from him, through Mark, we are informed that the first crowing did not suffice to recall him to his duty, but a second was needed.
3. In the three words, καὶ ἐπιβαλὼν ἔκλαιε, we have given to us the perfect revolution in Peter's view of the world. As he rushes forth upon the call, as though in his remorse he sought some object exterior to himself, his world-view (his opinion of the world) is still an external one; when he begins to weep, it becomes an inner view. His whole outer world has fallen in ruins; he has no longer an external object of pursuit; he has been thrown back into himself, and comes through his inner self to the Lord, who has now become to him a new Christ in the light of the Spirit. Judas could not attain to this change and revolution: he rushed out—to the associates of his guilt, the chief priests—and they gave him, in his despair, the final blow. In the case of Peter it was: "Against Thee, Thee only, have I sinned."
4. The maid mentioned in this passage, and Herodias, are the only examples of female wickedness, or enmity on the part of woman to what was good, recorded in the Gospels.

HOMILETICAL AND PRACTICAL.

See the parallel passages in *Matthew*.—The true Shepherd betrayed by a faithless disciple at the tribunal of a false world: 1. By the treachery of the false one, He stands as the Faithful One at the bar; 2. by the false judgment, He passes forth as the Faithful.—The false judgment passed by the world upon the Lord: 1. The false judges, who seek false witness against Him; 2. the false witnesses, who contradict one another; 3. the false judgment, which stamps the true praise of God as blasphemy, and represents blasphemy of God to be the judgment of God; 4. the false servants of God, who abuse and make a mock of the prisoner entrusted to their guardianship.—As the sun bursts through mist and clouds, so breaks Christ triumphantly through all the false obscurations of His honor (by false judges, witnesses, judgments, guards).—So does God's truth, and work, break through all jugglerics, deceits, and time-serving judgments, of sin and lying.—Christ's true testimony and confession is the only star of salvation in the awful night of human destruction and judgment.—Self-contradiction, the everlasting self-judgment of Satan, of sin, and of Christ's foes.— Christ the confessor, and Peter the denier (Christ was the divinely faithful friend to men, Judas the betrayer; Christ was He who held His ground, the disciples were the runaways).—The great and marvellous spiritual combat: 1. One strove against all, and yet for all; 2. He suffered as a lamb, yet conquered like a lion; 3. He is overcome, and yet He is the victor.— Contrast the powerful opponents of Christ and the weak opponents of Peter.—The difference between the Christ's confession, and Peter's Galilean dialect. —Mark how the chasm which bursts apart between Christ and His disciples unites them for ever: 1. The chasm which opens: Christ, the denied confessor; Peter, the positive denier. 2. Peter, now an actually humbled sinner; Christ, in the fullest sense, now his Saviour and Comforter.—The Lord's great discourse in His deep silence.—Christ's sublime silence at the world's tribunal a prediction of His sublime speaking at the future judgment of the world.

STARKE:—QUESNEL:—Let the world say what it will, how entirely different are things to the eye of faith, from what they seem to the eye of the world! What is more distinguished than this assembly? There at the same time sanctity, rank, and wisdom appear to collect and unite together; and yet it is nothing but a company of murderers, and a godless assembly (except, indeed, that it possessed a historic right, which was destroyed at Christ's crucifixion).—He who audaciously flings himself into danger, will soon find that he sinks continually deeper, till finally he cannot free himself.—CANSTEIN:—It is dangerous to be in the company of the wicked.—Alas! how much injustice is found in law-processes and contentions!—Envy.—*Nova Bibl. Tub.*:—Is it not to be deplored that many strive in behalf of the stones of the temple, and yet pull down and destroy the temple of the living God!—QUESNEL:—The greatest truths, when ill-understood, are often considered blasphemies, and furnish occasions for rage and tumult, Heb. xii. 3.—Keep silent (before the godless world's accusations).—Reply (to those who exercise authority).—One may mislead many.—As is the shepherd, such are the sheep [said in reference to the high priest. But this is only partially applicable].—When the higher classes condemn Christ, those beneath them mock Him. This is the effect of evil example. Oh! what an account is to be rendered!—Sufferings generally come in troops.—PETRUS:—Lies of necessity are not to be excused.—The cock which still crows, when we deny Jesus, is the conscience of each; ah, would that we heard its voice!—*Bibl. Wirt.*:—God uses every means to bring men to repentance.

BRAUNE:—Death was pronounced upon Christ: in the sight of God, the haters of the divine love had no right so to act; it was merely the seeming appearance of right before the people.—We never hear that these false witnesses were punished.—The first Epistle of Peter shows how changed his views regarding suffering and the cross had become. This change of view dates from his repentance.—BRIEGER: —His sitting at the right hand of God they were soon to find to be true (the founding of the Church, the Apostles' acts, the destruction of Jerusalem, etc.)—Jesus, although awaiting condemnation and death, subdued Satan in His people.—This we recognize in the repentance of Peter.—GOSSNER:—Before Pentecost, the disciples fled from death; after Pentecost, they rejoiced in death.—BAUER:—A fearful assembly.—On ver. 72. Alas! how lonely, how isolated, does sin leave us in the world!

---

5. *Christ, betrayed to the Gentiles, standing before Pilate at the Tribunal of Temporal Authority: a. The Examination. Christ and the Accusers. The Confession, the Accusations, and the Lord's Silence. b. The Judge's attempt to deliver. Christ and Barabbas. The Outcry of the Enemy, the Silence of the Lord. The Surrender. The Mocking.* CH. XV. 1–15.

(Parallels: Matt. xxvii. 1–26; Luke xxiii. 1–25; John xviii. 1–16.)

1 And straightway in the morning[1] the chief priests held a consultation with the elders
2 and scribes, and the whole council, and bound Jesus, and carried *him* away, and delivered *him* to Pilate. And Pilate asked him, Art thou the King of the Jews? And he
3 answering, said unto him, Thou sayest *it*. And the chief priests accused him of many
4 things; but he answered nothing. And Pilate asked him again, saying, Answerest
5 thou nothing? behold how many things they witness against thee. But Jesus yet
6 answered nothing: so that Pilate marvelled. Now at *that* feast he released unto them
7 one prisoner, whomsoever they desired. And there was *one* named Barabbas, *which* lay bound with them that had made insurrection with him,[2] who had committed murder
8 in the insurrection. And the multitude, crying aloud,[3] began to desire *him to do* as he
9 had ever done unto them. But Pilate answered them, saying, Will ye that I release
10 unto you the King of the Jews? (For he knew that the chief priests had delivered
11 him for envy.) But the chief priests moved the people, that he should rather release
12 Barabbas unto them. And Pilate answered and said again unto them, What will ye
13 then that I shall do *unto him* whom ye call the King of the Jews? And they cried
14 out again, Crucify him. Then Pilate said unto them, Why, what evil hath he done?
15 And they cried out the more exceedingly, Crucify him. And so Pilate, willing to content the people, released Barabbas unto them, and delivered Jesus, when he had scourged *him*, to be crucified.

[1 Ver. 1.—Codd. B., C., D., Lachmann, Tischendorf read only πρωΐ.]
[2 Ver. 7.—Codd. B., C., D., Lachmann, Tischendorf read στασιαστῶν.]
[3 Ver. 8.—Codd. B., D., Lachmann, Tischendorf, ἀναβάς instead of ἀναβοήσας.]

EXEGETICAL AND CRITICAL.

Comp. the parallels in *Matthew* and *Luke*.—Mark, with Matthew, takes notice of the second formal council-meeting on the morning of the crucifixion: he, like Luke, brings more distinctly into view the circumstance that the whole Sanhedrim led Christ away to Pilate; and with him omits the end of Judas, recorded by Matthew, the dream of Pilate's wife, the

CHAP. XV. 1-15.

washing of the hands, and the cry—"His blood be on us," and our children." Again, Mark, like Matthew, passes over the fact that Jesus was sent to the bar of Herod, which Luke records; the full examination before Pilate, omitted by all the Synoptics, related by John; and, finally, the repeated hesitations of Pilate in condemning. Mark merely notices what John and Luke relate very fully, that many additional accusations were raised against Jesus, regarding which He maintained an unbroken silence. He limits himself, like Matthew, particularly to the two chief features in the humiliation of Jesus before Pilate: His confession of His Messiahship (King of the Jews), and His being placed side by side with Barabbas. The characterization of Barabbas he gives more accurately, in a manner similar to Luke. He marks the decision of Pilate in a peculiar way, ver. 15. It is worthy of note that he, along with Matthew, represents the scourging and mocking of the Lord in Pilate's prætorium (Luke, on the other hand, relates the putting to shame of Jesus in the palace of Herod) to be part of the crucifixion-agonies; consequently, the second unsuccessful attempt of Pilate to release Him, which, according to John, he sought to effect by bringing forth the scourged One to the people, is passed over unnoticed. The assembling of the populace before the prætorium, and the more exact designation of the prætorium, are peculiar to Mark.

Ver. 6. **He released unto them one prisoner.**—This was a voluntary custom of the procurator.

Ver. 7. **In the insurrection.**—In which he had been captured. One of the numberless Jewish insurrections; not known more exactly. "Paulus refers to JOSEPH. *Antiq.* 18, 4." Meyer.

Ver. 8. **That had gone up.***—The stream of the populace comes, namely, back from the palace of Herod, whither Pilate had sent the Lord. Meanwhile the priests have prepared their people, have instigated and instructed them.

When he had scourged Him, to be crucified.—John, viewing matters from the psychological stand-point, mentions the scourging among the acts of Pilate, as the final attempt to deliver Jesus; Mark and Matthew, viewing the events from the historical stand-point, judge from this act that all is decided, and they look accordingly upon the scourging as the opening act in the awful tragedy of the crucifixion, παρέδωκε φραγελλώσας. Both are equally correct points of view. The scourging should have moved the people; it only led them to obduracy. And, as the matter issued, the crucifixion had already begun. In relating this circumstance, Matthew emphasizes the fact that the scourging resulted in the yielding up of Christ to the Jews (φραγελλώσας παρέδωκεν); Mark points out that the scourging was the opening scene in the crucifixion, and took place in consequence of the surrender.

DOCTRINAL AND ETHICAL.

1. Comp. *Matthew.*
2. Christ before Pilate, beside Barabbas, amid the soldiers: a threefold climax in the world's judgment upon the Judge of the world.
3. Barabbas, the murderer, a representative of the first murderer, the father of lies, as Christ stood there in the name of His Father.—The people's choice between the two: 1. The miscalculated and improper juxtaposition caused by the political party, a self-condemnation of worldly polity; 2. the evil advice of the chief priests, a self-condemnation of the hierarchical guardianship of the people; 3. the horrifying choice, a self-condemnation of the self-destroying populace.

HOMILETICAL AND PRACTICAL.

See *Matthew.*—The world assembled to judge the Lord : 1. Jerusalem (the chief council) ; 2. Rome (Pilate); 3. the whole wide world (the soldiery).—Jesus condemned as Messiah, as the Christ of God. As Christ: 1. Condemned by the chief council ; 2. given over to judgment by Pilate; 3. mocked by the soldiery.—The surrender of the prisoner at the paschal festival (probably a Passover-drama to represent the atonement for the first-born of Israel) is here a judgment upon completed blindness.—Barabbas is made by the Jews to represent the first-born of Israel, Christ the first-born of Egypt.—Christ justified upon His trial by the hostile judges: 1. By the judge: he seeks to free Him ; 2. by the accusers and the people: their petition for the release of Barabbas reveals the bitterness of their hate ; 3. by the soldiers, who adorn Him with the symbols of His patience and His spiritual glory.—The very mockery of truth must witness, even by its caricatures, to the glorious original.

STARKE:—When superior judges act unjustly, they accumulate upon their heads much more guilt than the subordinate authorities; for in that case the oppressed have no further appeal.—QUESNEL:—The assembling of the magistrates is orderly and beautiful: but the more proper their appearance, the more sinful the abuse of their authority in the oppression of the innocent.—HEDINGER:—When innocence itself must appear and be accused before the judges, is it anything strange that Thou, precious Jesus, art persecuted by the devil, accused, slandered, and condemned ?—*Nova Bibl. Tub.*:—Liars' mouths can devise much; enough, if thou art guiltless.—Envy is hateful in every man, especially in ministers of the Gospel, who should content themselves in God.—QUESNEL:—What envy did here against Christ, the Chief Shepherd, that it does still to His servants, and will not cease to do till the world's end.—*Nova Bibl. Tub.*:—If the rulers among the people, who should put a stop to evil, themselves instigate and make the people sin, then must Christ be crucified.—HEDINGER:—In the last day the heathen will put many Christians to shame. — QUESNEL:—Love of honor and the fear of the world may lead a judge (who is not firmly settled in his love to justice) to many sins.—One single sinful passion makes slaves of men.—Natural honor a weak shield against temptation.—*Nova Bibl. Tub.*:—The King of glory wears a crown of thorns, in order that He may take the curse away from the earth, and gain for us the crown of holiness.—The crowns of princes, also, have their thorns. Should they wear these to the honor of the crowned Jesus, then will they discharge aright the duties of their difficult office.—Hypocrites and the godless still insult Christ, though they even bow the knee at His name.

BRAUNE:—The deeper He went down in suffering, the less He pleased them.—All that God did to perplex the enemies of Jesus in their acts, was in vain (Peter's tears, the acknowledgment of Judas, the silence of Herod on the chief point, the witness of

---
* [Lange adopts the reading ἀναβάς in his translation. Luther's version does the same.—*Ed.*]

Pilate, the dream of Procula; the comparison between the insurrectionist and murderer Barabbas, and Jesus in His majesty and tranquil greatness).—BRIEGER:—Pilate did not concede the truthfulness of the accusations of the Jews, yet condemned the Son of God to death. He thereby fulfilled in two respects the wisdom of God:—First, that the Lord should be crucified, and not stoned; second, that Jews and Gentiles should unite in His death.—BAUER:—Sad is the scene which here meets our eyes; as it ever is when goodness has to protect itself by the votes of the masses.

---

6. *Jesus on Golgotha.—His Death, and the Death-signs.* a. *The Mockings and the Lord's Silence.* b. *The Crucifixion; and Blasphemy against, and Silence of, the Lord.* c. *The World Darkened; the Anguish-cry, and the Silence of Victory; the Death-shriek, and the Death-silence of the Lord.* d. *The Rent in the Temple-vail, and the Silence of God upon the End of the Old Covenant.* VERS. 16-38.

(Parallels: Matt. xxvii. 27-53; Luke xxiii. 26-46; John xix. 17-30.)

A. Vers. 16-19.

16 And the soldiers led him away into the hall called Prætorium; and they call to-
17 gether the whole band. And they clothed him with purple, and platted a crown of
18 thorns, and put it about his *head*, And began to salute him, Hail, King of the Jews!
19 And they smote him on the head with a reed, and did spit upon him, and, bowing *their* knees, worshipped him.

B. Vers. 20-32.

20 And when they had mocked him, they took off the purple from him, and put his
21 own[1] clothes on him, and led him out to crucify him. And they compel one Simon a Cyrenian, who passed by, coming out of the country, the father of Alexander and
22 Rufus, to bear his cross. And they bring him unto the place Golgotha, which is, being
23 interpreted, The place of a skull. And they gave him to drink[2] wine mingled with
24 myrrh: but he received *it* not. And when they had crucified him, they parted his gar-
25 ments, casting lots upon them, what every man should take. And it was the third
26 hour; and they crucified him. And the superscription of his accusation was written
27 over, THE KING OF THE JEWS. And with him they crucify two thieves; the
28 one on his right hand, and the other on his left. And the scripture was fulfilled, which
29 saith, And he was numbered with the transgressors.[3] And they that passed by railed on him, wagging their heads, and saying, Ah, thou that destroyest the temple,
30 and buildest *it* in three days,[4] Save thyself, and come down[5] from the cross.
31 Likewise also the chief priests, mocking, said among themselves, with the scribes, He
32 saved others; himself he cannot save. Let Christ the King of Israel descend now from the cross, that we may see and believe. And they that were crucified with him reviled him.

C. Vers. 33-37.

33 And when the sixth hour was come, there was darkness over the whole land until
34 the ninth hour. And at the ninth hour Jesus cried with a loud voice, saying, Eloi, Eloi, lama sabachthani?[6] which is, being interpreted, My God, my God, why hast thou
35 forsaken me? And some of them that stood by, when they heard *it*, said, Behold,
36 he calleth Elias. And one ran and filled a spunge full of vinegar, and put *it* on a reed, and gave him to drink, saying, Let alone; let us see whether Elias will come to take
37 him down. And Jesus cried with a loud voice, and gave up the ghost.

D. Ver. 38.

38 And the vail of the temple was rent in twain from the top to the bottom.

[1 Ver. 20.—Codd. B., C., Lachmann, Tischendorf read αὐτοῦ instead of τὰ ἴδια (A., *Receptus*).]
[2 Ver. 23.—Codd. B., C.*, L., Tischendorf omit πιεῖν.]
[3 Ver. 28.—This verse is wanting in A., B., C., D., X.; and Griesbach and Tischendorf have decided against it. But it is found in P., in Origen, Eusebius, and the Versions. The verse has probably been omitted, because it was supposed to involve a discrepancy between Mark and Luke, as in Luke xxii. 37 the quotation is referred to the apprehension of Jesus.

(Lange might have added, as supporting his view, L., Δ., 1, 13, 69. Alford's remark, [which Meyer also makes,] that Mark rarely quotes from prophecy, however, is deserving of attention.—*Trs.*)
* Ver. 29.—The best MSS. read οἰκοδομῶν τρισὶν ἡμέραις.
[⁵ Ver. 30.—Codd. B., D., L., Δ., Lachmann, Tischendorf read καταβάς instead of κατάβα (*Receptus*).]
[⁶ Ver. 34.—The words ἐλωί, &c., are differently written in the MSS. Lachmann reads λεμὰ σαβαχθανί: Tischendorf, λεμὰ σαβακτανεί (ed. 1865); Fritzsche, λιμά; *Receptus*, λαμμα σαβαχθανί.]

EXEGETICAL AND CRITICAL.

Comp. the parallels in *Matthew* and *Luke*.—Mark points out more distinctly the ironical consciousness with which the cowardly Pilate yielded to the demands of the populace. With Matthew, he employs φραγελλώσας παρέδωκε, in which the thought is involved that the surrender was decided in the scourging. In describing the mocking, he omits, like John, the mention of the reed, which the soldiers, according to Matthew, forced into the Lord's hand, or sought to force, and with which they struck Him (probably because He let it fall). Mark designates Simon of Cyrene the most particularly: he is the father of Alexander and Rufus. The address of the Lord to the daughters of Jerusalem, as they were following, which Luke reports, is omitted by Mark, as well as by Matthew. The bitter wine he names myrrh-wine. He makes the crucifixion to begin at the third hour. The quotation of Jesus from Isa. liii. 12, which we consider genuine, is given by him alone. The address of Jesus to Mary and to John, beneath the cross, is passed over by him as by the other Synoptics; also the repentance of the thief, in which he agrees with Matthew. He describes more graphically than the other Evangelists the mockery of the passers-by, using the word οὐά for this purpose; the derision and irony of the priests is given in their own words. He records in the original Syriac, Eloi, Eloi, etc. Of the man who gave the Lord vinegar to drink, he says indefinitely, "A certain one," and that he called to the others, "Let alone." Of the seven sayings of the Crucified, he records, like Matthew, only the Eli, Eli, and the last loud, piercing cry of Christ, without stating what the Lord expressed in it.

Ver. 16. **Into the hall** (within, into the inner court).—Comp. *Note* on Matt. xxvii. 27. They conducted Him into the palace-court, which we may easily suppose was surrounded by the neighboring buildings of the governor's palace, forming a kind of barracks.

Ver. 17. A scarlet military mantle (*see* on Matt. xxvii. 28) was made to represent the imperial purple; hence the designation *a purple* (πυρφυραν), a purple robe, as Mark and John describe it. And because this is the symbolic import of the robe, there is no discrepancy. The scarlet military cloak no more required to be a real purple, than the crown of thorns required to be a real crown, or the reed a real sceptre; for the whole transaction was an ironical drama, and such a one, too, that the infamous abuse might be readily perceived through the pretended glorification. The staff must be a reed, the symbol of impotence; the crown must injure and pierce the brow; and so too must the purple present the symbol of miserable, pretended greatness: and this was done by its being an old camp-mantle.

Ver. 21. **And they compel.**—Upon the term ἀγγαρεύειν, comp. *Note* on Matt. v. 41.—**The father of Alexander and Rufus.**—These men must have been well-known persons in the then existing Church; and they testify to the personal, lively recollection and originality of Mark, as does his "Timæus, the son of Bartimæus." It is most natural to regard them as persons well known to the Church at Rome. On this account, Rufus, whom Paul greets, Rom. xvi. 13, may well be this Rufus. The Alexander, however, who is spoken of in the Acts of the Apostles, ch. xix. 33, appears not to have been a Christian, but to have belonged to the hostile Judaism. (LANGE'S *Apostol. Zeitalter*, ii. p. 275 f.) Whether he was the same person as Alexander the coppersmith, who was the enemy of Paul, cannot be positively made out. Meyer: "But how common were these names, and how many of the then well-known Christians are strangers to us. In '*Actis Andreæ et Petri*' both are mentioned as the companions of Peter in Rome." They are, of course, here brought forth from the treasures of the evangelical tradition.
—**Coming out of the country.**—Meyer will have it, that this fact, mentioned likewise by Luke, is a proof that Jesus was not crucified on the first day of the feast. But in this opinion, no attention is paid to the circumstances: 1. That the country, or the country-seat as it might be termed, from which Simon was coming, might have lain within an easy Sabbath-day's journey of Jerusalem (Meyer maintains,—If so, it must have been stated!); 2. that in case the Passover began with Friday, the *second* day, as Sabbath and Passover together, would be the chief festival-day; 3. that it is by no means historical to admit no contraventions of the Sabbath-law, and, furthermore, that it would be the very thing to turn the attention of the multitude to Simon, if there was anything remarkable, anything offensive, in his appearing at such a time. Such results are by no means uncommon in the similar instances of multitudes running together; so that the notice rather supports the view which adopts the first feast-day as the one. Jesus was crucified under the pretext that He was the great Sabbath-breaker. The people, in their witticism, might perhaps say, See, there comes another Sabbath-breaker from the country; let him suffer a little along with the other.

Ver. 22. **Golgotha.**—Meyer makes Golgotha genitive* (as if, Golgotha's place). Because the translation is κρανίου τόπος. But the question is, Has not τόπος in the first instance a more general import,—the place (Golgotha)? John retranslates κρανίου τόπος into Hebrew, Golgotha; Matthew also names the place, Golgotha; Luke simply, Skull. No doubt it is strange that Mark has τόπος following Golgotha. Probably the place was called sometimes Skull, and sometimes Place of a Skull, and Mark gives the more exact designation. *See* on Matt. xxvii. 33.

Ver. 23. **They gave Him**; that is, they offered Him myrrh-wine. This myrrh-wine cannot, from the different descriptions of Mark, be identical with the vinegar, or the wine-vinegar, of which a drink was at a later period given to Jesus. Most likely the wine was in each case the same, but the narcotic intermixture was omitted in the second instance.

Ver. 24. **Parted his garments.**—John gives the more exact description. The prevailing point of view among the first three Evangelists was the

* [Tischendorf (ed. 1865) reads ἐπὶ τὸν γολγοθᾶν.—*Ed.*]

making the division an occasion for gambling. Comp. *Note* on Matt. xxvii. 35. The form of the play is not closely described. Meyer: "We must leave unsettled the question, Whether the lot-casting was performed with dice, or the lots were shaken in some vessel (a helmet), and that which first fell out decided in favor of him to whom it belonged."

Ver. 25. **And it was the third hour.**—Upon the apparent discrepancy between this declaration of Mark and Matthew, and the statement of John, ch. xix. 14, comp. *Note* on Matt. xxvii. 45. We cannot avoid, however, drawing attention to the striking relation subsisting between the third and the sixth hour. At the third hour, by the crucifixion of Jesus, the endurance of the cross for His people was decided, as it meets us in the superscription, The King of the Jews, and is represented in the crucifixion of the thief (and the later deridings of the chief priests, etc.). But when the sixth hour came, and the darkness spread over the whole land —literally, over the whole world and earth—then was the judgment of the whole world decided. The third hour was the dying hour of Judaism: in the sixth hour, the dying hour of the old world was present to the view in typical signs. We have here, also, to carefully note the relation between the superscription, which according to Mark was decided upon about the third hour, and the declaration of John, that it was about the sixth hour: "And he saith to the Jews, Behold your King! But they cried out, Away with Him, away, crucify Him." When the third hour had come, and it was advancing to the sixth, then was the crucifixion of Jesus decided in His being scourged, in accordance with the judgment of the people and of Pilate; but in this was, also, the crucifixion of the Jewish people themselves determined, which was first made apparent in the crucifixion of the two thieves in company with Jesus. About the sixth hour, according to John, the judgment of the world was decided along with that of Judaism — the presage of the *dies iræ* prescnted itself; that is to say, John has made this sign of the third hour to be the decisive, universal symbol, and has, on this account, probably brought it into connection with the sixth hour.

Ver. 27. **And with Him they crucify.**—As to the alleged difference between the accounts of Mark and Luke, consult *Note* on Matt. xxvii. 38, 44.

Ver. 34. **Eloi.**—*See Note* on Matt. xxvii. 46.

Ver. 36. **Let alone; let us see.**—According to Meyer, this is contradictory to the account given by Matthew, xxvii. 49. But it is not to be overlooked, that there is no reason why, in this moment of the intensest excitement, two divisions might not make the same exclamation, and that, too, in different senses,—the one mocking, the other speaking more earnestly. (Comp. the scene in SHAKESPEARE's *Macbeth* after the murder.) If this sympathizer meant it humanely with his cry, "Let alone," perhaps the idea shot through him, that Elias might interpose in the last extremity.

DOCTRINAL AND ETHICAL.

1. **The death.**—The death of humanity in its life-germ is here completed in the death of Jesus. Considered in this light, Christ's death is prophetical of the great dissolution of the world, to ensue at the end of all things. The extinction of the primary life: Christ condemned, His rights unacknowledged; derided, and by this derision looked upon by the world as destroyed; led forth, robbed, crucified, and in this act rejected in His person, and with His work, as the curse of the world; blasphemed, and so made to pronounce sentence of death upon the obdurate; Christ dead upon the cross. Hence there is announced, in presages, the future extinction of the derivative life, (*i. e.*, the death of the world): The sun of the old world darkens at mid-day; the holy of holies of the divine ordinance in the old human world vanishes like a vision of the night, when the temple-vail rends asunder. All is now over with the old world; it has but to live out its remnant of life. It has judged itself; and in that self-condemnation lay God's condemnation,—a condemnation which nothing but the conquering love of Christ could turn into a blessing.

HOMILETICAL AND PRACTICAL.

See Matthew; also the preceding reflections.— Christ was, notwithstanding, the King of the Jews the whole crucifixion through. This is seen: 1. In the accusation of His enemies; 2. in the impression produced upon Pilate, and in his decision; 3. in the kingly ornaments which the soldiers placed upon Him; 4. in the train which bore Him forth with them out of Jerusalem; 5. in the superscription on the cross; 6. in the terror which breaks forth in the blasphemy of His foes; 7. in the miracles accompanying His death.—The great dying on Golgotha: 1. There dieth the King of the Jews; 2. there dieth the Son of God; 3. there dieth the old world; 4. there dieth old sin; 5. there dieth old death.—Simon of Cyrene and his sons; or, the everlasting memory of the crossbearers and their children.—Simon; or, how man becomes unconsciously separated from his commonplaceness, and involved in the great history of the cross.—The terrifying world-darkness at bright midday forms a symbol of the terrifying world-darkness spread over mankind by their blindness of heart.— Christ the clear light of the world in this night of the world.—His heart and His eye are fixed most earnestly on God during this world-judgment; and that preserves the world, which is lost in itself, from sinking into the abyss.—The unholy and the holy Golgotha: 1. The unholy: men of violence, drunkards, gamblers, thieves, blaspheming priests. 2. The holy: the great Sufferer, the temperate One in holy clearness of soul and knowledge, the Laborer, the Warrior of God, the Supplicant.—[The potion rejected and the potion accepted, or holy refreshment in the conflict of suffering enjoyed after the example of Christ: 1. As refreshment at the right time; 2. in the right place; 3. in the right measure; 4. in the right consecration.]—The despair in the seeming triumph, and the triumph in the seeming despair: 1. In the conduct and mockery of the enemies; 2. in the supplicatory cry of the Lord: My God, etc.—The signs of hellish madness in the blasphemies with which the chief priests end their work.—Let alone, let us see; or, how, at the life-flame of the dying Jesus, a new life has kindled in the dying world: 1. From the horrors of His death springs the horror of the world; 2. from His trust in God, the world's belief; 3. from His pity, the compassion of the world. —Let alone, let us see: or, this history is not yet completed; it is only beginning at the time when it seems to approach its completion.—The death-shriek of the Lord is the great waking call to a new life for the world of man.

STARKE :— QUESNEL :—Christ, by becoming the derision of His creatures, has atoned for the criminality of the creatures in mocking God and religion. —Many would willingly pass by the cross of Christ; but, before they are aware of it, they are laid hold of, and forced into companionship with Christ in suffering.—Participation with Jesus in the cross, is that which alone makes our name in truth eternally renowned, and prevents it from passing into forgetfulness.—At the end, the world is bitter as gall, but heaven is sweet.—HEDINGER :—View, O my soul, in faith this picture of martyrdom !—Christ has been reckoned with the transgressors; hence we may console ourselves, that we shall come to God's blessed companionship, and the company of the holy angels. —The understanding, in its wisdom, is offended at the cross of Christ.—He succeeds ill in the faith, who must *see* (John xx. 29), and who will believe when he pleases (John vi. 44).—Christ died for thee; be thou ready to die for Him.—When the true Lamb of God was offered, all the Levitical offerings found their completion.

BRAUNE :—They caught him, and cast him out of the vineyard, and slew him, Matt. xxi. 39.—God's wrath is heavier to bear than Christ's cross.—Isa.

liii. 12.—" My God," etc. Let us imitate Him in the employment of the Holy Scriptures; also, that, when in the anguish of our hearts we cannot pray any more in our own words, we may allow the Spirit, whose work the holy word is, to represent us with groanings that cannot be uttered.

BRIEGER :—*And they that passed by.* So thoroughly helpless was Jesus upon the cross, that this crowd easily persuaded themselves that all was deception that they had seen and heard of Jesus.— *The chief priests.* So spake Satan, too, in the wilderness : If Thou be the Son of God, command that these stones, etc. To self-help he there challenged the Holy One of God : here he does the same through his well-approved servants.—Ps. ii. 5.—*The darkness.* God must witness against these murderers.—In the destruction of the holy of holies, Jehovah destroyed the temple itself. The Most Holy was taken forth from the city of Jerusalem and laid outside the gate upon Golgotha. There, too, was a vail rent, even the flesh of Christ (Heb. x. 20).—GOSSNER, on ver. 30 :—Self-help.—One might often free oneself by a mere word. But if the truth and the honor of God suffer by that word, one may not speak it.—His death was the rising sun for the spirit-world ; and therefore the world's natural sunlight veiled itself before Him. (LAMPE :—The sun set over Christ, and rose for me.)

---

7. *The Descent of Jesus into the Realm of Death. His Death, and the Tokens of the New Life.* VERS. 39–47.

(Parallels: Matt. xxvii. 54–56; Luke xxiii. 39–56; John xix. 31–42.)

39 And when the centurion, which stood over against him, saw that he so cried out,[1]
40 and gave up the ghost, he said, Truly this man was the Son of God. There were also women looking on afar off: among whom was Mary Magdalene, and Mary the mother
41 of James the less and of Joses, and Salome ; (Who also, when he was in Galilee, followed him, and ministered unto him ;) and many other women which came up with
42 him unto Jerusalem. And now, when the even was come, (because it was the prepara-
43 tion, that is, the day before the sabbath,)[2] Joseph of Arimathea, an honourable counsellor, which also waited for the kingdom of God, came, and went in[3] boldly unto Pilate,
44 and craved the body of Jesus. And Pilate marvelled if he were already dead: and, calling *unto him* the centurion, he asked him whether he had been any while dead.
45 And when he knew *it* of the centurion, he gave the body[4] to Joseph. And he bought
46 fine linen, and took him down, and wrapped him in the linen, and laid[5] him in a sepulchre which was hewn out of a rock, and rolled a stone unto the door of the sepulchre.
47 And Mary Magdalene, and Mary *the mother* of Joses,[6] beheld where he was laid.[7]

[1 Ver. 39.—Codd. B., L., Tischendorf omit κράξας ; Lachmann retains it with *Receptus.*]
[2 Ver. 42.—A., B., Lachmann read πρὸς σάββατον (Meyer : only an error of the copyist); Tischendorf reads with the *Receptus* προσάββατον.]
[3 Ver. 43.—A., B., C., Lachmann, Tischendorf read εἰσῆλθεν instead of ἦλθεν.]
[4 Ver. 45.—D., D., L., Lachmann, Tischendorf read πτῶμα (corpse) instead of σῶμα.]
[5 Ver. 46.—D., D., L., Lachmann, Tischendorf read ἔθηκεν ; *Receptus*, κατέθηκεν ; Cod. A., κάθηκεν.]
[6 Ver. 47.—Cod. A. reads Ἰωσήφ ; B., Δ., Lachmann, Tischendorf read Ἰωσῆτος, which is merely the Greek form of Ἰωσῆ.
[7 Ver. 47.—A., B., C., Lachmann, Tischendorf read τέθειται ; *Receptus*, τίθεται.]

EXEGETICAL AND CRITICAL.

See *Matthew* and *Luke.*—In the account of the centurion's exclamation, Mark harmonizes with Matthew : the occasion of it he makes, characteristically, to have been the loud cry of the expiring Jesus. The three women beneath the cross, he mentions, like Matthew ; also Salome by name, adding many other women, whom he does not specialize. Still more generally and comprehensively is this sorrowing circle alluded to by Luke. Like the other two Synoptics, Mark is less full in his narration of the burial than John ; nevertheless he declares with exactness, as do John and Luke, the day to have been the παρασκευή. Nicodemus is missing here ; Joseph of

Arimathea is described as the disciple of Jesus in words different from Matthew, and more explicitly than Luke: "Who waited for the kingdom of God." In this, the Petrine idea of the kingdom appears. That the step of Joseph was a bold one; that Pilate called the centurion, and assured himself of the certainty of Jesus' death: these are features which are peculiar to Mark.

Ver. 39. **Said, Truly this man.**—Comp. *Note* upon *Matthew*.—The noticing of the motive of the centurion's cry, viz.: that he saw that Christ οὕτω κράξας ἐξέπνευσεν, is peculiar to Mark, and is strikingly characteristic of him. The Lion of Judah is, even in His departing, a dying lion. The expression of a wondrous power of life and spirit in the last sign of life, the triumphant shout in death, was to the warrior, who had learned to know death from a totally different side upon the battle-fields, a new revelation. Theophylact: οὕτω δεσποτικῶς ἐξέπνευσε. De Wette, following some others, gives but a weak conception: He saw in the speedier death of Jesus a favor from the gods. As to the monstrously gnostic explanation of the passage given by Baur, consult Meyer.

Ver. 40. **James the Less.**—Meyer makes this remark apply solely to the stature. Comp., on the contrary, Judges vi. 15. No doubt it points to a second James, rather than to James the disciple in the stricter sense, since James the son of Alpheus, as he is elsewhere termed, was not the brother of James the Greater. Comp. *Note* on *Matthew*. That this Mary the mother of James the Less and of Joses is identical with Mary the wife of Alpheus, is proved by John xix. 25.

Ver. 42. **And now, when the even was come, because.**—We cannot construe this passage: Because it was even, Joseph came. Reasons: 1. The Jews, indeed, who, according to John, prayed Pilate to remove the bodies, had no other ground for the request than that the next day was the Sabbath. Joseph, on the contrary, had quite a different motive. He wished to entomb the Lord's body with respect, and for this purpose could only employ the circumstance that the Jews themselves wished it removed. The connection of the words, ἐπεὶ ἦν, κ.τ.λ., with ἐλθὼν Ἰωσήφ, κ.τ.λ., would be, notwithstanding all that is said to the contrary, very clumsy; and the correction ἦλθεν, moreover, goes to prove this. 3. Then had Joseph in a legal sense come too late. He must come before the evening. Accordingly, we understand the passage thus: between ὀψία and ὀψία there was a difference (sunsetting and twilight); upon the evening preceding a feast, the earlier ὀψία was observed. About this time Joseph appeared upon Golgotha, and then he went to Pilate.—**Was the preparation, that is, the day before the Sabbath.**—See *Note* on *Matthew*. Meyer says: "Here, accordingly, there is not a trace that this Friday was itself a festival." The trace is given fully, ch. xiv. 12. If the day mentioned there was the 14th Nisan, then the following day must have been the 15th Nisan. Besides, we know that upon a Passover-feast, where the second day of the feast was at the same time a Sabbath, upon this day, according to the Jewish ideas of the Sabbath, the chief feast fell, as is distinctly shown in John xix. 31. See WIESELER, *Chron. Synop.* p. 386. By the Sabbath occurring upon the second day of the feast, the first feast-day became the preparation, the day before the Sabbath.

Ver. 43. **Came, and went in boldly.**—He had come; had seen what occurred as the bones of the crucified were broken; knew that Jesus was about to be taken down; and now he felt that there was no time to be lost, and hence he dared to ask.

Ver. 44. **Whether He had been any while (already long) dead,** πάλαι.—Before the return of the centurion. He wished to be sure as to what he did.

Ver. 45. **Gave the body.**—Joseph being known as a wealthy man, we might have expected, from the character of Pilate, that he would have extorted money, because the bodies were frequently sold (*see* the quotations in Meyer). This generosity was the mark of a strange state of mind. Probably he was glad to hear that Jesus was really dead, because the Saviour in His higher nature had grown awful to him.

Ver. 47. **Where He was laid:** ποῦ τέθειται.—From this time onward, there appears to have been a relation of confidence and friendship between the old disciples (the women), and the new disciples (Joseph and Nicodemus). In consequence of this new-born confidence and friendship, the Galilean women enter without hesitation the garden of the rich counsellor, and kneel down before the grave. According to Mark and Luke, their intention was at the same time to mark accurately the grave; already they were thinking of the anointing after the Sabbath. Bauer: It was not always the custom in Israel to employ a shroud in burying, and the shortness of time on this occasion did not admit of it.

DOCTRINAL AND ETHICAL.

1. See the parallel passages in *Matthew*.
2. The signs of the new life, which present themselves in the death of Jesus.
3. The Lord's death-cry, as expressing the might of His life and spirit, was the awakening of the heathen captain. Death is swallowed up in victory, 1 Cor. xv. The death of believers is henceforth a new death, the prospect of a new world, the presentation of a new world for contemplation.

HOMILETICAL AND PRACTICAL.

The last word of the Jewish priest: He was a blasphemer, is contradicted by the first word of the heathen soldier: He was the Son of God.—Golgotha becomes changed by the Lord's death: 1. The enemies, mockers, and blasphemers have vanished; 2. the friends, confessors, and worshippers appear.—The alternation of life and death in the dying hour of Christ: 1. While He still lived, all sank in death; 2. when He died, all awoke to a new life.—With Christ's death, the presentiments of His resurrection spring up in the minds of believers.—The miraculous workings of the death of Jesus upon those who come under its influence, so different and yet so uniform: 1. So different: the heathen, Roman warrior, the emblem of the Roman Empire shattered to its foundations; the timid Jewish women transformed into heroines; the honorable Jewish counsellor, a Christian grave-digger to the Lord; Pilate, the proud man of the world, himself overcome by the spirit of mildness. 2. So uniform: all agree in the self-forgetful manifestation of their homage, and in an expression of readiness to do or to suffer, evidencing the beginning of a new life.—The soft sleep of the Saviour, and His sacred watchers: two female disciples on Good Friday, two angels on Easter morning.—The little congregation at the grave of Jesus, the germ of all Christian congregations. — All Christian Churches are Churches of the Holy Sepulchre.

STARKE:—Christ is also the heathen's Saviour.—*Nova Bibl. Tub.*:—Even in the assembly of the wicked, and in a godless council, there may be a pious councillor; therefore beware of impious judgments.—QUESNEL:— God knows where to find persons who will carry out His plans, how dangerous soever they may be.—What appears to be destroyed, will turn out well at the end. Therefore despair not, dear Christian; believe and trust.—Whosoever hazards anything for the Lord, God will enable that venturer to succeed.—The counsel of the godless never succeeds; that of the righteous stands sure.— Look more to Christ's glory than to self-interest and personal praise.—It is a beautiful work of love when the rich bury the poor.—Let the grave be as deep and as well-guarded as it may, the omnipotence of God will open it, and bring forth the dead.— BRAUNE:—The Head, like the members, was carried to resurrection through the grave.

BRIEGER:—The pious confessors (the first, the penitent thief; the second, the captain) condemn the chief council and all the people, Isa. liii. 9. He was to have been buried, like other transgressors, on Golgotha. The heavenly Father had decreed otherwise.—BAUER:—From this time forward, God's witnesses for the crucified Jesus come forward into view.

PART FIFTH.

THE Resurrection of the Lord. The Great Victory, and the Appearance of the Victor in the Company of the Apostles, to bring to Completion the New Church. His Ascension (Last Withdrawal) to complete His Conquest of the World.

FIRST SECTION.

THE RISEN ONE AS CONQUEROR ON BEHALF OF THE CHURCH; OR, THE INTRODUCTION OF THE BELIEF IN THE RESURRECTION OF THE BODY. THREE EASTER MESSAGES: THE ANGEL, THE WOMAN, THE TWO MEN.

CHAPTER XVI. 1-13.

(Parallels: Matt. xxviii. 1-15; Luke xxiv. 1-35; John xx. 1-18.)

---

1. *The Resurrection. The Angelic Message, and the Women.* CH. XVI. 1-8.

1 And when the sabbath was past, Mary Magdalene, and Mary the *mother* of James,
2 and Salome, had bought sweet spices, that they might come and anoint him. And very early in the morning, the first *day* of the week, they came unto the sepulchre at
3 the rising of the sun. And they said among themselves, Who shall roll us away the
4 stone from[1] the door of the sepulchre? (And when they looked [up], they saw that the
5 stone was rolled away,) for it was very great. And, entering into the sepulchre, they saw a young man sitting on the right side, clothed in a long white garment; and they
6 were affrighted. And he saith unto them, Be not affrighted. Ye seek Jesus of Nazareth, which was crucified: he is risen; he is not here: behold the place where they
7 laid him. But go your way, tell his disciples and Peter that he goeth before you into
8 Galilee: there shall ye see him, as he said unto you. And they went out quickly, and fled from the sepulchre; for they trembled and were amazed [trembling and ecstasy held them]: neither said they anything to any *man;* for[2] they were afraid.

[1 Ver. 3.—Codd. A., B., Tischendorf read ἐκ; *i. e., upwards* from the descending entrance. With this corresponds the reading ἀνακεκύλισται in B., L., Tischendorf.]
[2 Ver. 8.—Codd. B., D., Lachmann, Tischendorf read γαρ instead of δε.]

EXEGETICAL AND CRITICAL.

See the parallel passages in *Matthew* and *Luke*.—This portion, considered in itself, is manifestly a fragment; for no treatise, especially no Gospel, can conclude with ἐφοβοῦντο γάρ. Upon the critical question, as to the authenticity of the following part, compare the Introduction. In this section, we have followed the remarkable division of the Pericope; but we would point out that this part might most properly be united with the following, under the common idea with which we have designated the section. Mark gives the day of the resurrection in such a way as to supplement the other Gospels. The early morning is termed by him the sunrising. He is the most accurate in the account of the women who came to anoint Christ's body, stating their number to be three, and giving their names. He agrees with Luke, in saying that the women came for the purpose of embalming the Lord's body. The representation of the moment of the resurrection, and the revelation to the women as they were returning from the grave, of which Matthew gives the details, is omitted by him; and we find here, moreover, but a brief notice of the meeting of the risen Lord with Mary Magdalene. He alone remarks upon the anxiety of the women, as to how the stone was to be rolled from the door of the sepulchre. Only *one* angel, according to his account, appears to the women; and the same is true of Matthew. This was the first appearance, whereas Luke and John relate a later appearance (*see Matthew*). In describing the return of the women from the grave, the Evangelists differ the most from one another. Matthew states: "And they departed quickly from the sepulchre with fear and great joy, and did run to bring His disciples word." Luke similarly. Mark, on the contrary: "And they said nothing to any man; for they were afraid." The circumstances, however, are different. These women who were afraid, are Mary the mother of James, and Salome, who had gone into the grave after Mary Magdalene had hurried forth on finding the grave empty. The women, however, who departed quickly with great joy to declare what had taken place to the disciples, form a larger group, composed of those who had been the first at the grave with the materials for embalming, and of those who had followed them. (*See Matthew*.) Mark omits this fact in order to introduce the separation of Mary Magdalene from the other two women. And yet he makes it appear that the first impression produced on the women was a mingling of fear and ἔκστασις.

Ver. 1. **And when the Sabbath was past.**—That is, on Saturday evening, after sunset. Luke says, xxiii. 56: After their return (when they came back), they prepared spices and ointments; and rested the Sabbath day, according to the commandment. It is not said, "and thereafter," but, "and of course rested;" so that it is intended as a special explanation of the preceding. We have no contradiction, accordingly, between Luke and Mark, as Meyer would make out. The antecedent embalming, John xix. 39, is not excluded by this. Neither is the fact excluded, that some of the women purchased the spices as early as Friday evening, before sundown; only the two Maries had remained too long at the grave to do so, and hence they could not make their purchases till the Sabbath had passed. (*See* LANGE's *Leben Jesu*, ii. 3, p. 1623.)—**Spices,** ἀρώματα.—"Aromatic herbs to mix with ointment." Meyer. The ἀρώματα are not necessarily dry substances. "The ointments were seldom *simplicia* (*e. g.*, the nard); they were generally composed of various substances (Job. xli. 22; Plin. 29, 8),—of olive oil (that much-praised product of Palestine), and various fragrant, especially foreign (Ezek. xxvii. 22), vegetable extracts,—namely, oils and resins, such as nard and myrrh. Such ointments were, in part, very expensive, and special articles of luxury. Amos vi. 6." Winer.

Ver. 2. **When the sun had begun to rise.**—We translate thus somewhat singularly, because De Wette (and, following him, again Meyer) maintains that ἀνατείλαντος τοῦ ἡλίου can only mean, when the sun *had risen*, not, as it *was rising*.* The words, "very early," immediately preceding, contradict this view. But between the beginning of the sunrise and its ending is a considerable interval, as between "eve" and "evening;" and according to this distinction has Mark conceived of the matter, as he previously distinguished the two evening seasons. The sunrise, accordingly, had begun: *oriente sole*. Meyer discovers in this passage not only a discrepancy between Mark and John, who indeed says it was still dark, but in a certain measure between the statements of the Evangelist Mark himself ("very early, when the sun had risen").—Beza's conjecture, οὐκέτι ἡλίου ἀνατ., is quite unfounded.

Vers. 3, 4. **From the door of the sepulchre... when they looked up... rolled away... it was very great.**—These are all accurate statements, which are characteristic of Mark's clear view of things. The stone was lying in the hollow cut deep into the rock, so as to form the door, and must accordingly be rolled forth from this recess outwards; hence "rolled-away." The rock-tomb, however, itself lay upon a height; hence the women saw the stone when they looked up. That upward glance, accordingly, does not form a mere contrast to the supposed circumstance, that before this "their eyes were cast down to the ground." And because the stone was very great, they could even from a great distance see it lying. This latter explanation of Meyer, respecting the stone, is to be preferred to the reference (by Cod. D., and Wessenberg) of the clause, "for it was very great," to the clause, "who shall roll us away the stone?"—although this conveys a natural meaning.

Ver. 5. **A young man.**—The angel is described in these terms, because of his external appearance. Similarly does Luke express himself: "Two men in shining garments." The facts, as they occurred in point of time, must be distinguished in the following way: First, the appearance of *one* angel *in* the tomb, who showed himself to the two Maries after Mary Magdalene had hurried forth to inform Peter and John (Mark); then, two angels who manifested themselves to her upon her return (John). These two appearances of the angels are given only generally by Luke, (they appeared "to the women which came with him from Galilee.") Finally, we have the appearance of the angels before the tomb upon the stone, which was seen by the larger group of women who assembled in the garden at a later period (Luke xxiv. 1: "And certain with them"). This construction commends itself, if we adopt the view that Luke's account is not designed to give an exact description. The first point then is, that there are three women who are witnesses: Mary Magdalene hastens back to

---

* [The English version agrees with Lange's: "At the rising of the sun."—*Ed*.]

tell the disciples, and the other two Maries see an angel in the sepulchre. The second point to be considered is, that the Magdalene sees two angels in the tomb, then the Lord, while the two Maries wait irresolutely for the other women, or go to meet them. The third point is, that the assembled women, among whom also is Johanna, first see the angel upon the stone (or two angels,—one of them in the sepulchre); then, as they are returning, the Lord Himself.

Ver. 6. **Be not affrighted.**—In the liveliness of the words, we find by asyndeton the copulatives omitted.

Ver. 7. **And Peter.**—Especially. Meyer (following De Wette): "Because of his superiority, not because Peter as denier required a mark of forgiveness (as is the common opinion)." But the superiority of Peter had ceased for a time. It must be first, according to John xxi., restored to him. So it is, accordingly, a gracious token to unfortunate Peter. —**He goeth before you.**—"Ὅτι introduces the message.—**As He said unto you.**—See ch. xiv. 28. Upon the apparent contradiction between this announcement, that Jesus would precede the disciples, and His appearing unto them so shortly after, consult the commentary on *Matthew.* The first message applied especially to the Galilean disciples in a body. They, as such, first saw the Lord in Galilee again. Secondly, it was in a more special sense a preparation of the disciples for the approaching appearance of the Lord, which was by no means excluded by the message. And thirdly, the return of the disciples to Galilee was delayed, contrary to the wish of the Lord: first, through their own unbelief; secondly, through the unbelief of Thomas. See *Leben Jesu*, ii. 3, pp. 1064–5–6.

Ver. 8. **They trembled and were amazed.**—The term εἶχε δέ is intended without doubt to express the idea, that, even when out of the sepulchre, their former feelings held fast possession of them. These feelings were the opposing sentiments of trembling and ἔκστασις, which latter cannot be possibly conceived of as horror. It is the parallel to the phrase in Matthew: With fear and great joy. The ecstasy indicates always, that one is not master of oneself; and here it indicates such a state of feeling, in opposition to the extreme measure of fear, τρόμος. It is a state of transition from trembling and amazement; and while this play of feeling continues, men find it impossible to act.—**Neither said they anything to any man.**—De Wette maintains that this is contradicted by Matthew and Luke. It certainly does not mean simply, that they said nothing to any one by the way (Grotius), nor yet to any man beyond the circle of the Apostles; but, nevertheless, there is no contradiction. The intention of Mark was to lay hold of the fact of their indecision, and to unite it to the two following manifestations of hesitating unbelief. The women did not act upon the message of the angels, the individual disciples did not act upon the women's message, the assembled Apostles did not act upon the message of the men and of the disciples who had been met upon the way to Emmaus. The intention of our history is this, to bring out prominently the barriers which unbelief throws up, by which the ever-increasing urgency of the pressing messages is repelled. In the first instance, the weak faith of the two Maries prevented them from fulfilling their mission. The Magdalene met them in this state, and they did not allow themselves to be cheered by her information till they had met the other women (*see Luke*), and with them had seen the Lord. Now, their message was naturally a new and different one. Meyer distinguishes thus: They *related* the message at a later period, but it is self-evident that they had not *fulfilled* it. We distinguish thus: They did not fulfil their original commission, but, at a later period, the related, along with the other women, the earlier and later occurrences in one united narrative.— **They were afraid.**—This can only mean: The occurrence was so new to them, great, unheard-of, that they ventured not in the full confidence of faith to publish it, and that they, still more, did not expect to find any faith among the disciples.

DOCTRINAL AND ETHICAL.

1. Consult the parallels in *Matthew.*
2. The entire chapter in its one central idea: Christ risen in perfect certainty and in the might of His resurrection, the destroyer of all unbelief in His people, and thereby the destroyer of the kingdom of darkness throughout the world; or, Christ appearing in His triumphal glory, able to redeem to the uttermost by that unlimited power which He acquired through His victory.
3. The three grand divisions of the chapter are —the Risen One as Conqueror *for* the Church, *in* the Church, *with* the Church.
4. The contrast in the chapter: The annunciations of the resurrection of the Lord to the Church, by the angels, by the women, by individual disciples, are not sufficient to overcome fully the unbelief of the disciples; *the circle of disciples becomes a believing Church only when Jesus Himself reveals Himself personally in their midst.* And this is, indeed, the thought underlying the entire Gospel of Mark, which is founded upon the mission of Peter—of that Peter whom man would and will make the head of a new Church in which, by the tradition of an Apostle, angel-voices, holy women, and visions to women, should be made to represent Christ Himself.

HOMILETICAL AND PRACTICAL.

Upon the whole chapter, consult the superscription and the *Doctrinal Reflections.*—*Upon the Section*, vers. 1–16: The Church has not arrived at the full belief in a risen Saviour by even the most glorious messages, but by the personal revelation of the Risen One Himself.—*Upon the Section up to* ver. 13: The three Easter-messages of Jesus to His Church in their progressive effect: 1. Through the angels to the women; 2. through the women to the amazed disciples; 3. through the two amazed disciples to the assembled company.—*Upon the Section before us:* The [Jewish] Sabbath is passed away, the [Christian] Sunday has appeared; or, a new arrangement of the periods of rest and labor has been made by Christ. Man proceeds no more to the holy day from his labor, but from the holy day to his labor. 1. So is it in the life of the glorified Christ: first sitting at the right hand of God, then ruling, then coming again. 2. So is it in the life of the Church: first Sunday, then the consecrated working-day.* 3. So in the life of the believer: first justification, then sanctification. Conclusion: In this form, Christianity is the beginning (the principle) of the glorified world.—Our conversa-

---

* *Sonntäglicher Werketag:* a secular day into which the spirit of Sunday is carried.

tion is in heaven.—The walk of the three women to the grave is a symbol of the separation between the old and the new world in the history of the Passover: 1. The three women with their solicitude [Mary Magdalene in the deepest emotion; the others, two mothers of five Apostles, two aunts of Jesus of Nazareth, calmer, quieter]; their unconsciously-entertained hopes of life, and their ointments for the dead corpse. 2. The rising sun, but the heavy stone of their anxiety. 3. The angel appears, but the Lord has disappeared. 4. The resurrection of Christ declared, in the distant prospect of His re-appearance, out of the mouth of the grave. 5. The delightful commission to proclaim these good tidings; but their souls are oppressed by the overmastering feelings of fear and joy. —"And Peter" [Peter could never forget this addition, and hence Mark records it].—How the sinner ever thinks of the word which shows that the Saviour thought of him.—The first Easter-message, a message from the Prince of Life given by angelic lips to the women who wished to anoint the dead.— This message is not carried to its destination; but in the contending feelings of the women, between their fear and joy, is left unfulfilled.—Why the female disciples, even now, do not come up to that evangelizing faith which the message enjoins: 1. They are not yet able to give themselves up to that obedience of faith, because the fact overcomes their feelings [could not believe for joy]. 2. They cannot yet give themselves up to the confidence of faith, because their feelings amid the signs of the fact are not yet stilled [they cannot believe for fear; they miss the Lord, whom they have not seen; and they are still afraid of finding among the disciples no faith to receive their great news]. 3. They cannot yet give themselves up to the peace of faith, because these conflicting feelings are contending in their hearts.—As Christ is elevated above the angels, so is the certainty of the resurrection elevated above the testimony of the angelic appearance.—Since Christ died, a new heavenly activity is demanded, which lies far above all the visions of the old economy.

STARKE:—*Nova Bibl. Tub.*:—What does not love do, when it is strong?—Through woman was life lost at first; by women must it be first sought, found, and revealed.—(The stone.) Hindrances in the way of salvation.—Men often make to themselves unnecessary anxieties: before they actually meet them, the Lord has helped them already.—If we look with believing eyes into Christ's grave, all our anxiety falls into it; for Christ's resurrection is our resurrection. —God will comfort the penitent, and will make their anguished hearts joyful again.—Christ's heart is as compassionate after, as before, His resurrection— God's promises pass certainly into fulfilment, and that too more gloriously and sooner than their mere form would lead one to expect.—OSIANDER:—Untimely fear often hinders from fulfilling one's office.

BRAUNE:—No shrine is made of the grave, and no worship from the contemplation of it; but the women are bidden to carry the good news and to awaken faith.—Weak sentimentalism avails nothing in the kingdom of God which has been established in the earth by the death of Jesus.—BRIEGER:—The resurrection, which is also a birth, is a mystery, like every birth. It is also an act of God's omnipotence, like every other birth.—If we are because of sin related to death, which is so foreign to our being, much more are we related to life.—HEUBNER:—The morning of the resurrection of Jesus: 1. Distinguished by heaven itself; 2. bringing a glorious reward to Jesus Himself; 3. fearfully condemnatory as regards His foes; 4. joyfully quickening as regards the disciples of Christ.—DIETZSCH:—The mingling of fear and hope which the thought of death and immortality is wont to awaken in us.—SCHULTZ:—The first witnesses of Christ's resurrection: 1. They were strong [their love is manifested in their going to the grave]; 2. they were weak [their sorrow, their fear].— THIESS:—The cross of Calvary illumined by the rays of the Easter-sun.—RAUTENBERG:—Easter at the graves: 1. The stone of the curse is rolled away; 2. angels inhabit them; 3. the dead are risen.

---

2. *Mary Magdalene and the Two Disciples.* VERS. 9–13.

(Parallels: Matt. xxviii. 9–15; Luke xxiv. 9–35; John xx. 11–19.)

9 Now, when *Jesus* was risen early, the first *day* of the week, he appeared first to
10 Mary Magdalene, out of whom he had cast seven devils. *And* she went and told them
11 that had been with him, as they mourned and wept. And they, when they had heard
12 that he was alive, and had been seen of her, believed not. After that he appeared in
13 another form unto two of them, as they walked, and went into the country. And they went and told *it* unto the residue: neither believed they them.

EXEGETICAL AND CRITICAL.

See *Matthew* and *Luke*.—According to Meyer, the apocryphal fragment of some other evangelical writing begins here. Compare the Introduction on this point.* The epithet apocryphal, would not be appropriate, even if the section were an addition taken from another Evangelist's narrative. The narrative contained in our Gospel comprehends within its very brief hints the detailed statement of John regarding the

They are in copies of the Old Latin, in the Vulgate, Curetonian Syriac, Peshito, Jerusalem Syriac, Memphitic, Gothic, and Æthiopic. 2. Irenæus (*Cont. Her.* iii. 10, 6) recognizes their existence; as do also Hippolytus, Cyril of Jerusalem, Ambrose, Augustine, Nestorius. Schole also claims that Clement of Rome, Justin Martyr, and Clement of Alexandria sanction the passage; but Tregelles regards this as an error. The chief argument against its genuineness of this section is found in the fact, that it was wanting in *some of*

---

* [The reasons for assuming that vers. 9–20 are an original portion of Mark's Gospel much outweigh those to the contrary. 1. They are found in the Uncial Codd. A., C., D., X., Δ., F., G., H., K., M., S., U., V.; as well as in 33, 69, and the rest of the Cursive MSS. which have been collated.

Easter-message of Mary Magdalene, and the still more detailed account by Luke of the Easter-message sent by the disciples met on the road to Emmaus. Mark groups both accounts under the single head of two duly-authorized embassies, which do not meet with full credence. The first and second halves of this chapter are, however, united into an inseparable unity in the one fundamental thought, that the risen Saviour is the absolute and universal conqueror of unbelief, which was already, even in the circle of disciples, throwing obstacles in the way of Jesus; and that Christ, as the subduer of this unbelief, stands raised above all the messages of men and angels.

Ver. 9. **Was risen early.**—The manifestation of the Risen One by the angels had been preceded by His own personal appearances. The first day of the week is again named, of course, for the purpose of bringing into prominence, even at that early period, the Christian day of rest. We would translate: Upon the **first** of the seven days (τὸ σάββατον indicating here, as frequently, the week, after the later and more extended custom of the Jewish language). Upon this day He appeared to the Magdalene, out of whom He had cast seven devils. Christ, as the Risen One, has sanctified the week as a holy period; and at the beginning of the holy week, He reveals Himself to one who was preëminently sanctified and susceptible, because He had cleansed her from seven demons. The Evangelist has, accordingly, not merely before him the contrast,—the risen Saviour revealing Himself to a poor woman,—but the spiritual relationship,—she who had been freed from seven devils stands especially near to the conqueror of demons on the morning of His great triumph, and she is peculiarly fitted in spirit to be the first to see Him, and to announce to the disciples His resurrection. Accordingly, in this revelation we have the activity of the Saviour, His conquest over devils, set over against the passivity of the pardon-seeking woman, who had been freed from the seven devils. Meyer considers this remark concerning Mary as not belonging to this passage. We view the expulsion of *seven* devils in connection with the sacred number seven, and regard the term symbolic of a glorious deliverance out of the great snares which Satan had prepared. (Comp. Matthew.) Mark is wont to employ ἐκβάλλειν in other passages to express strongly a glorious redemption. It is questionable whether the words, "early on the first day of the week," go back to ἀναστὰς δέ (Beza, Ewald, etc.), or are to be construed with ἐφάνη (Grotius and others). We prefer the first construction, because the second mention of the resurrection as having occurred upon the first day of the week appears to point at the sanctification of that period. In verse second, μία σαββάτων had reference to Jewish customs; but here the allusion is to the renewed week, the πρώτη σαββάτου.

Ver. 10. **And she went.**—That is, even she. It must be conceded that Mark employs πορεύεσθαι to express a solemn proclamation of the Gospel only in this place (ver. 15 excepted). By this, however, he reminds us of the mode of expression employed by his teacher, Peter: 1 Pet. iii. 19.*—**Them that had been with Him.**—This also is a peculiar expression to indicate the disciples in a wider sense. It indicates, however, their scattered condition, their present despairing state, as opposed to their former blessed communion with Him. The expression itself is not an unusual one with Mark; *see* ch. i. 36.—**As they mourned and wept.**—Comp. Luke vi. 25. This has undoubtedly a special reference to the sorrowful and weeping Peter. To bring prominently out that Jesus revealed Himself to Peter, after the message given to Mary, consists not with the matter-of-fact disposition of Mark.

Ver. 11. **And had been seen of her,** ἐθεάθη.—A strong expression. "That Θεᾶσθαι is not found elsewhere in the Gospel by Mark, considering how frequent is its use by others, is one of the marks of a strange hand." Meyer. Hermeneutics might, we think, have taught him: *new facts, new words.*

Ver. 12. **In another form.**—An explanation of the expression in Luke xxiv. 16, but by no means a condensation of Luke xxiv. 13–35, as Meyer would represent. Jesus' form was, on the one hand, changed: different clothes (John xx. 15), traces of the sufferings during the crucifixion: on the other hand, more sublime in its appearance, Jesus being in the transition-state from humiliation to glorification.

After that.—The three specifications, πρῶτον, μετὰ δὲ ταῦτα, ὕστερον, relate manifestly to one another. Hence it cannot be at all remarkable that μετὰ ταῦτα is not elsewhere to be found in Mark (comp. ch. xiii. 24).—**Of them**—of the unbelieving disciples in a wider sense.

Ver. 13. **Neither believed they them.**—Even they did not gain credence. Meyer: "A different tradition from that given in Luke xxiv. 34." It is certain that no interpolator would have allowed this manifest appearance of a discrepancy. But the Evangelist, who was writing from the stand-point of a special idea of the resurrection, was not afraid to employ it. And Luke gives the means of knowing what is meant. The Eleven knew for a certainty, in the evening, that Christ had appeared to *Simon*, and were consequently for the moment believing. Now the Emmaus disciples arrive, and declare that Jesus had revealed Himself unto *them*. Not being able to comprehend this new mode of existence on the part of Christ, that He now is here, and now there, new doubts fill them. The thought of a spiritual apparition occurs to them; and hence they are affrighted when Jesus at length appears in their midst, and imagine that a ghost is present. And now the Lord must convince them as to the truth of His new corporeality. The point brought forward by Mark testifies, accordingly, to an exceedingly accurate, and moreover, a perfectly independent, knowledge of the facts of the resurrection. The expression is, of course, explained by Luke xxvi. 34, without, however, referring to it (Schulthess). And so it is unnecessary to suppose, with Augustine, that the λέγοντες were certain believing disciples, to be distinguished from certain who did not believe; or to say, with Calvin, "At first they doubted, then they believed." The situation of affairs was of such a nature as to lead them into new difficulties on hearing the message of the Emmaus disciples, instead of strengthening them in their belief. Because, as yet they were not in possession of the idea of a glorified body; and hence

---

the early copies of Mark's Gospel. This is attested by Eusebius, Gregory Nyssa, Victor of Antioch, and Jerome. But this is certainly an insufficient reason for affirming its spuriousness in the face of the strong testimonies upon the other side. *See* TREGELLES on the Printed Text of the Greek Testament, p. 246 *seq.* Its genuineness is affirmed by Simon, Mill, Bengel, Matthæi, Eichorn, Kuinoel, Hug, Scholz, Guericke, Olshausen, Ebrard, Lachmann; is denied by Griesbach, Rosenmüller, Schulz, Fritzsche, Paulus, Wieseler, Ewald, Meyer, Tischendorf.—*Ed.*]

* [Lange seems to have in his eye the objection of Meyer (*in loc.*) to the genuineness of the section, drawn from the fact that the word πορεύω occurs three times in it.—*Ed.*]

they thought very naturally, that if the Lord had appeared to Simon in Jerusalem, He could not at the same time have appeared unto others at a distance from the city. Not to speak of this, that several of the Eleven might very reasonably have thought: Why should He reveal Himself to these two at Emmaus earlier than to us at Jerusalem?

DOCTRINAL AND ETHICAL.

1. See *Matthew* and the parallels in *Luke* and *John*: also the foregoing *Note* on ver. 13.

2. The Easter-embassy of the angelic world to the human world has been replaced by the message of the resurrection passing from man to man, at first from the female disciples to the male disciples, then the message passing between individual disciples and the disciple-band. The Risen One has destroyed, in His resurrection, the bands and bolts of the grave; He must now destroy, likewise, the doubts, the weak faith, the unbelief of His own, in order with them to destroy in like manner the unbelief of the world. The certainty of His resurrection presses gradually forward; but the Church comes only to perfect knowledge when He reveals Himself in her midst.

3. The appearing and disappearing of Jesus in the circle of disciples is a type of His appearance in, and of His disappearance from, the Church.

HOMILETICAL AND PRACTICAL.

See *Matthew*, and the parallel passages in *Luke* and *John*.—The risen Saviour presents Himself to be recognized by one who stood especially near to the kingdom of heaven and of the Unseen, because He has freed and cleansed her heart from seven devils.—Mary Magdalene, the much-forgiven sinner, sent as a comforter to the weeping Peter, to the sorrow-laden and mourning disciples.—The two Maries, who had remained with Jesus beside His grave, late into the night of His dying day, are to be the first to see Him on His resurrection morn.—The distinction made in the case of the two disciples going into the country: 1. Because they, like Magdalene and Peter, especially required consolation; 2. because they united in going before the Lord as two messengers and witnesses unto the Church.—The risen Saviour brings His own at once together again.—Jesus appearing in another and new form, as the Prince and Pledge of another, new world: 1. In the form of one who had passed through death; 2. with the glorified crucifixion-marks; 3. with the signs of the new life (even the Magdalene did not at once recognize Him).—The threefold form of the unbelief which departed not, even from the community of believers, without assistance: 1. They cannot conceive to themselves the mysterious majesty in which Christ caused an angel to represent Him; 2. they cannot conceive to themselves the greatness of the grace, in consequence of which He appears to Mary Magdalene first; 3. they cannot conceive to themselves the might of His exaltation, by reason of which He appears now here, now there.—Neither the angels, nor the women, nor the two Evangelists, satisfy their faith: they wish to be assured of His actual existence by His own appearance.—Not having yielded themselves to faith in His prediction, they find it difficult to believe in its fulfilment.

STARKE:—As the woman was the first to sin, so hath Christ, after finishing salvation, chosen to reveal Himself to a woman first.—The most despised in the opinion of the world are often the most precious in the eyes of God.—QUESNEL:—God delights in blessing those who have remained faithful to Him in persecution, and have not been ashamed of the cross.—Christ imparts His grace according to the need for it, Matt. v. 4.—Jesus ever, even upon our journeyings, with us.

BRAUNE:—The intelligence brought by Mary and the women concerning the resurrection of the Saviour is believed neither lightly nor superstitiously; and hence we see that their belief, and their testimony, is the more firmly founded, and the more trustworthy.

SECOND SECTION.

THE RISEN LORD AS VICTORIOUS IN THE CHURCH, DESTROYING UNBELIEF, PERFECTING FAITH, AND PREPARING THE CHURCH TO GO FORTH WITH THE GOSPEL MESSAGE.

CHAPTER XVI. 14–18.

(Parallels: Matt. xxviii. 9-20; Luke xxiv. 36-49; John xx. 19-21, 25.)

14 Afterward[1] he appeared unto the eleven as they sat at meat, and upbraided them with their unbelief and hardness of heart, because they believed not them which had
15 seen him after he was risen.[2] And he said unto them, Go ye into all the world, and
16 preach the Gospel to every creature. He that believeth, and is baptized, shall be saved;
17 but he that believeth not shall be damned. And these signs shall follow them that believe: In my name shall they cast out devils; they shall speak with new tongues;
18 They shall take up serpents; and if they drink any deadly thing, it shall not hurt them; they shall lay hands on the sick, and they shall recover.

---

[1] Ver. 14.—C., D. add δὲ to ὕστερον.
[2] Ver. 14.—'Ἐκ νεκρῶν, supported by A., C., X., Δ., 1, 33.

³ Ver. 17.—The omission of καιναῖς by C., L., Δ. is not decisive against it.
⁴ Ver. 18.—Codd. C., L., M.**, X., Δ., the Coptic, Armenian, and Syriac versions, read before ὄφεις, καὶ ἐν ταῖς χερσίν. But it is probably a mere explanatory addition.

EXEGETICAL AND CRITICAL.

See the parallel passages in *Matthew* and *Luke*.—The section before us is another of those peculiar passages which are so characteristic of Mark. The object sought in it is to show the full persuasion of the Apostles of the truth of the resurrection,—the complete subduing of their hard-heartedness, so often brought out by the Evangelist (ch. vi. 52; viii. 17), and of their unbelief. This is with him the decisive point; and hence he connects all further information with the manifestation made by Christ of Himself in the midst of the disciples upon the evening of the first day after the resurrection. In the account of this manifestation, contained in ver. 14, he agrees with Luke and John. But while Luke brings prominently forward the pains Jesus was at to free His disciples from all fear, through convincing proofs of His bodily presence, Mark gives prominence to the fact, that Christ blamed their unbelief; and also to the facts of the completion of the disciples' training, of their deliverance from hard-heartedness, and of their being brought at last to a full belief. Luke's account is not, however, wanting in the points which go to corroborate the Lord's reprimand, vers. 38, 44, and especially ver. 45. John relates this revelation of Jesus from the other side,—from the side of the solemn perfecting of the disciples' faith. Mark then brings forward in this connection, ver. 15, the apostolic commission, which Matthew represents to have been issued on the mountain in Galilee. As to this point, we have only to remark, that he connects the anticipatory re-installation of the Apostles upon the first Easter evening, of which we are informed by Luke and John, with the sending forth of the Apostles from Galilee, and gives to the whole the solemn expression of the latter commission. In doing this, he selects a stronger term than Matthew, "Preach the Gospel *to every creature ;*" this is the phrase corresponding to "Disciple all nations." Mark alone, in accordance with his energetic character, gives the alternative, "He who believeth and is baptized," etc.; and he combines in the brief expression, "and is baptized," both the words, "make disciples of," and the baptismal formula contained in Matthew. Very strong, and peculiar to him, is the promise given by the Lord to the Apostles; and it is a grand thought, that He gives it to the Apostles for all who believe, vers. 17 and 18. It is the full, the last unfolding of the *charisma*, which the Lord (according to ch. iii. 15; Matt. x.) has imparted to the Apostles; the wonderful proclamation through them of the forgiveness of sins, the institution of absolution recorded by Luke and John, and also the promise of Jesus given by Matthew, "Lo, I am with you alway."

Vers. 14. **Afterward.**—By ὕστερον we are, certainly not, to understand, lastly; still it marks here the later, the personal revelations of Christ in the circle of the disciples, which succeeded His former isolated manifestations, and which established the fact of His resurrection. The confusions, which Meyer discovers in the account now following, rest upon critical prejudices, and upon the absence of details in the narrative of the Evangelist, which last characteristic also appears in the final chapter of Luke.—**And upbraided them with their unbelief.**—Upbraiding, the original form which Christ's contest took with the weak faith, the doubting, and feeble yielding to the influences of the evil one. (*See Leben Jesu*, ii. 1. p. 295.) And these are the causes of Christ's last upbraiding among His disciples.—**And hardness of heart.**—Comp. ch. viii. 17 *seq*.

Ver. 15. **And He said unto them.**—Thus Mark, exactly as Luke xxiv. 45, passes over to a general conclusion.—**Preach the Gospel to every creature;** πάσῃ τῇ κτίσει, the entire creation.—We find no reason to limit, with De Wette, this phrase to the conception, "all men" ["literally, all creatures, that is, all men, as also the Jews use בְּרִיָּה: " Lightfoot, Wetstein]. Comp. Rom. viii. 21. Because the miraculous gifts of the Christians, here mentioned, point to a glorification of all nature through the Gospel. *See* Isa. xi. Still less is the phrase to be restricted, with Lightfoot and others, to the heathen, who were contemptuously termed by the Rabbins חבריהו; for, as Meyer remarks, this would be in opposition to vers. 16 and 20.

Ver. 16. **He that believeth.**—Expressed from the stand-point of Christ, as He who was one day to return in the capacity of the world's Saviour and Judge, for the purpose of giving the due recompense. Baptism is not named along with faith as in itself an indispensable matter, but as the natural, certainly, also, necessary consequence of faith; because baptism indicates the entering of the believer into the communion of the believing Church. There is no occasion for the distinction made by Meyer between the newly converted and the children of Christians, because the antithesis runs, ὁ δὲ ἀπιστήσας; and it is not self-evident that baptism was not dispensed to such children. It is manifest that Jesus, according to Mark, has made the damnation depend upon a positive, personal disbelief, or rejection of the Gospel. But the Gospel is to be proclaimed to every creature, without exception. In this we have a connection opened between this passage, and the passages 1 Pet. iii. 19; iv. 6.*

Ver. 17. **Signs.**—Σημεῖα is first brought forward, the term indicating that miracles of all kinds should accompany them, should make their testimony trustworthy; but these signs Christ will specify.—**That believe** (that have believed).—That is, who have become believers, have adopted the faith. This promise holds good not merely of the Apostles and the Seventy (Kuinoel), but also of all Christians, without exception. Meyer: "Finally, Jesus does not mean that each of these signs should manifest itself with each believer, but this miracle with one, that with another." In entire Christendom, however, all of them; and, apart from their original, miraculous form, these signs were always to be more and more glorious and potent in their action, as the forces which are transforming the world.—**Follow;** παρακολουθήσει.—Literally, to follow in company, to proceed along with. *See* the expression, Luke i. 3.—**In My name.**—The miraculous power by which they were to effect all the succeeding wonders. To the expulsion of demons corresponds speaking with new tongues, and to the taking up of serpents the drinking of anything deadly; and, finally, to the laying of hands upon the sick, their recovery. The first

* [These passages, however, speak only of *human* creatures.—*Ed.*]

division indicates, negatively, the overthrow and expulsion of ethical evil (the casting out of devils); positively, the new form taken by the ethical world in the life of believers (**speaking with new tongues**). The second division indicates, negatively, the destruction of what is physically injurious, and its transformation into what is beneficial for the world (to take up serpents); positively, the overcoming of all that is physically injurious, through the strengthening of the life of Christians. The third division (laying hands upon the sick) indicates, negatively, the removal of all ethico-physical sufferings from others; positively (they shall recover), the return of the perfect, natural feeling of health to those who believe. These six members represent a proclamation, by means of facts, of that Gospel which is designed for every creature, or better, for the whole creation.— **Cast out devils.**—Employed in the most extensive sense, and with the deepest meaning. Purification of the new, divine world from all evil spirits.— **Speak with new tongues.**—This statement is to be restricted neither to the form under which "the speaking with tongues" showed itself at Pentecost, nor to the more general form of the Corinthian gift of tongues, obtaining commonly among the new converts of the apostolic era (Acts x. 46; xix. 6). For the statement of Christ applies to Christians generally, and to all time. The germ of this promise, of speaking with new tongues, lies in the instructions to the Apostles, ch. xiii. 11; comp. Matt. x. The new form which the spiritual world assumes, under the teaching of the Spirit, is here revealed by means of a symbolic expression; and we have an indication of the miraculous development of that world when the apostolic gift of tongues appeared. Meyer declares that there is a reference in this passage to the Apostles speaking with tongues under the influence of ecstasy (a state as entirely different from the Montanist conception, as the free, ethical inspiration is from pathological somnambulism); that tradition has explained this "speaking," with reference to what occurred at Pentecost, as speaking in foreign tongues, —the fact being that Mark, influenced by traditions, conceived of the matter in a mythical way, and went far beyond Luke's idea. But, holding such opinions, Meyer is on the high road to a mythological explanation of the passage, and only obscures a statement which is to be received as an exalted expression, symbolical in character, but in meaning most fully accordant with the Bible.

Ver. 18. **Take up serpents.**—By αἴρειν may be understood destroy, drive forth (Luther), or exterminate (Theophylact). This explanation would give a good sense, and might find support from some other passages of the Scriptures (Luke x. 19): nevertheless, to express such an idea, no such peculiar expression would have been selected; and moreover the conception we obtain thus is too trifling, for Hercules had already proved himself able to exterminate serpents. The word may, however, have another meaning: throw into the air (and so mediately destroy the reptiles), as Paul did with a serpent (Acts xxviii. 5). But to express this idea, the term before us is not sufficiently clear. Or it may signify, to draw forth by means of some potent conjuration; an idea that savors too much of heathenish magic arts. Or, finally, it may mean, to set up on a pole, as a token of victory. Commentators have hitherto passed over unnoticed this signification of αἴρειν, to lift up, or elevate as a σημεῖον or signal upon some pole or staff, and yet it is a force properly belonging to the verb; and it leads our thoughts back to the lifting up of the brazen serpent in the wilderness as a symbol of victory. The expression ἱστάναι ἐπὶ σημείου, Num. xxi. 9, is of the same import as αἴρειν, for which John employs (ch. iii. 14) ὑψοῦν for a particular reason. The special reference of that brazen serpent was to Christ, who was elevated upon the cross in the character of a heretic and transgressor, rejected by the old world, and so formed a type of the arch-enemy, and yet was made by God Saviour of, and means of life to, all that looked up to Him. Still, the more general reference was this, that the deadly and horrible serpent was not only overcome, but that its image was made to be a standard of victory. And this is accordingly a type which has been fulfilled to the fullest extent in Christianity: serpents are not simply overcome, destroyed; they are lifted up on high as ensigns of victory, with healing efficacy. What was in itself injurious has been serviceable to the interests of God's kingdom, as we find represented in the Gothic cathedrals. And this occurs not merely in a typical manner, but with actual serpents,—of course according to their symbolic signification. The fact that Christ only represented a serpent (that is, represented a deceiver and destroyer of the people dying on the cross, by whom the world was delivered from ruin), does not prevent our adopting the more general explanation, according to which actual serpents, the signs of death in the world, are changed into signs of life. Meyer, in his remarks on this passage, far surpasses De Wette, when the latter says, "If Mark had before his mind the serpent-charmers so common in the East (Mich. *Mos. Recht*, § 255), the account is apocryphal." Meyer puts this view aside with the one hand, and with the other takes it back again, with many additions. This conversion of the symbolism of the Bible into obscure, mythical allusions is now altogether antiquated. [The simplest explanation is the most rational. The "taking up of serpents" is immediately connected with the "drinking of any deadly thing," and denotes that their lives would be preserved by the miraculous power of God, whenever the exertion of such power was needed. The extension of the statement to believers generally, in every age of the church, is not warranted by anything in the text, and introduces confusion. This was a promise to the Apostles, and the apostolic age.—ED.] **—And if they drink any deadly thing.—**This expresses symbolically the restoration of life to such a degree as to be actually inviolable. De Wette thinks that the apocryphal story of John having, without injury, drunk a poisoned cup, and the similar story regarding Barnabas, related by Eusebius, *Hist. Eccl.* iii. 39, gave origin to this passage. Meyer has good reasons for opposing this view; but he is somewhat inconsistent, since he considers this section to be an apocryphal addition. The remark has more force, that the custom of condemning a criminal to drink a cup of poison suggested the idea. And why should this custom not have occurred to Christ? yea, why may He not have thought of the condemnation of Socrates, and then have declared, "The poisoned cup shall not harm My people;" primarily, of course, in a symbolic sense (just as the cup of hemlock hurt not the soul of Socrates)? But also in a typical sense the life of believers should grow more and more able to overcome all injurious influences, and often *literally* to overcome these influences in a miraculous manner. The passage Matt. xx. 23 is the most general, the passage Matt. xxvi.

39 the most special, Christological conception of the similar thought in a symbolic form.—**Sick.**—Miraculous cures. Also a symbolical expression of the removal of sickness. — **They shall recover.** — Guided by the two preceding parallels, we consider this last sentence to refer to believers themselves. They are, on their side, to enjoy perfect well-being.

DOCTRINAL AND ETHICAL.

1. Comp. the parallel passages in *Matthew*, in *Luke*, and *John*.
2. By the first appearance of Jesus in the full assembly of the disciples, on the first evening after the resurrection, the certainty of His having risen is decided for the Church, and so mediately for the world. This first revelation of the risen Christ stands opposed to the last rising of the unbelief of the disciples. They have sinned, in respect to His resurrection, through unbelief; and hence His appearing is accompanied with an upbraiding of their want of faith, which wakens shame in them. The last remnant of unbelief is now actually driven forth by rebukes with this departing unbelief, the hardheartedness disappears, the spiritual life of the disciples becomes free and active; they can now yield themselves up to the perfect revelation of His glory, and all succeeding revelations of that glory, with full confidence, and with an ever-growing soul-life. This upbraiding of the unbelief, which passes over into a blessing, marks the perfected triumph of the Lion of the tribe of Judah, and so gives the concluding thought of Mark, through whose entire Gospel the contest of Christ against the unbelief and hardness of heart of His disciples is found running as the fundamental thought. Least of all could the Gospel by Mark conclude, as a Gospel of fear, with the little faith of the disciples. In the belief, however, of Christ's absolute glory through His victory, the spiritual glory of the Church is also declared. According to the Gospel of Peter, the Church of Christ must go on from one degree of faith to another, till it attains unto perfection. It cannot, like the Romish phantom of Peter, remain amazed for ever upon the first step of faith; it must advance with the almighty administration of Christ, must grow and work in the fulness of spiritual life, till the Gospel be preached to every creature.
3. *The Gospel to every creature.* — Out of the demon-polluted, the enslaved, the fear-ruled world, shall arise an evangelized, freed, glorified world of faith, of peace, of life. The glorification of the world through the Gospel is an idea and a promise which runs through the whole of Holy Writ (Deut. xxviii.; Song of Sol.; Isa. xi.; ch. lxv. 17; Rom. viii.; Rev. ii. 1): and Christ here makes this promise to take the form of an institution. What His resurrection is in fact,—a proclamation of the Gospel to every creature: this the apostolic preaching is to make known to the world, to bring about, and to seal by the sacraments. And every true, living, earnest preaching of the word is consequently a proclamation of that Gospel, the aim of which is to free all creatures from their subjection to vanity, a power conducing to that regeneration which the great *palingenesis* is to bring about, and which shall appear along with the world's end. This thought of the great regeneration of the world rests altogether upon views peculiar to Peter: Acts ii. 20; iii. 20, 21; 2 Pet. i. 4; ch. iii. 13.

4. *He that believeth.*—With the Gospel, accordingly, begins the great crisis, the separation, which comes to view at the end of the world. *See* John iii. 19, 36. Belief and unbelief form the grand distinction in the new history of the world; and they are operating to bring to its completion the separation of the eternal, divine world from the territory of death and of the devils' torment; and they will continue to act thus until judgment begins. That the believer, as such, is at once baptized, that is, enters under the sacramental seal of his faith into the communion of the believing Church, is a self-evident presupposition; therefore, whoso believeth and is baptized. The promise of salvation, of deliverance, is not annexed to baptism in itself, but to the faith which receives its completion in baptism. Hence, on the other hand, want of baptism is not followed by damnation, but the want of faith, which may undoubtedly evidence itself, even though baptism be lacking.

5. Upon the doctrine of baptism, consult the dogmatic systems.

6. *The accompanying miracles.*—The new birth of creation is completed in three stages: 1. The personal stage, preaching the Gospel: 2. the social stage, the sacrament; 3. the cosmical stage, the cures, as they enter into the natural life, and lead it on to its transformation, by working on the one hand to purify, on the other to liberate. Compare the preceding observations on the single miracles. Heubner: "Promise of miraculous powers. How far does it extend? Many commentators maintain that it extends to all time, and in a very wide sense; *e.g.*, Grotius. He says, we are to blame that the χαρίσματα have ceased (so also Lavater, Hess). But have, then, the later Christians,—*e. g.*, from the third century down, the most spiritual of the Christian Fathers, the Reformers,—had no faith, because they wrought no miracles? Augustine says: The miraculous gifts continued so long as they were needed, until firm ground was laid for the Church to rest upon; they could be dispensed with, when the Church became firmly established (comp. *De Civ. Dei.* x. 7)." According to Mark, however, this promise is given in as universal a form as the sending of the Gospel into all lands, for all times. The elder theology was wanting in the defined conception of the Church as an organic whole; otherwise, it would have seen that the miraculous signs continue, though the forms are not the same,—least of all, do the forms at the beginning correspond with those to obtain at the last end.

7. The festival of the Ascension.—It was from the first, undoubtedly, celebrated within the great Quinquagesima period, between Easter and Pentecost. After the fourth century, it assumed the form of a special festival, and was celebrated when the fifty days began to end.

HOMILETICAL AND PRACTICAL.

See Matthew, and the parallel passages in *Luke* and *John*.—*This section*, vers. 14–18. Not until after the personal appearance and presence of Christ in the Church, did the belief of the Church in the resurrection become perfect: 1. The personal revelation as opposed to the earlier, preparatory revelations; 2. the belief in the resurrection as opposed to those degrees of faith, at which the hardness of heart remained stationary.—With the personal announcement of Christ in the Church comes the Spirit and spiritual life, in which all hardness of heart ceases.—The last upbraiding of Christ in the circle of His disciples changes into a blessing.—Lo, the Lion of the tribe of Judah had prevailed!—The last death-cry of the Lord upon the cross, and His first life-word in the Church, in their great and ceaseless efficacy.—The Easter-period, the great turning-point at which the Church of the disciples became the Church of the Apostles.—The Lord's upbraiding in the Church; or, the seven thunders which from time to time resound in her (Rev. x.): voices of reformers, which affright the demons, and predict new summer-seasons.—The expulsion of unbelief from the hearts of the disciples is succeeded by their being sent into all the world.—The Gospel of faith: 1. From the faith; 2. in the faith; 3. for the faith.—The Gospel in its unlimited appointment: 1. To the end of the world—all creatures; 2. to the end of all time—blessed or damned; 3. appointed to work till all imperfection in the kingdom of God is ended [the miracles].—The Gospel in its threefold attestation: 1. By itself; 2. by the sacrament; 3. by miracles.—The miracles which accompany the Gospel: 1. In the world of spirit: a. the evil spirits expelled; b. the good spirits praise the Lord [new tongues]. 2. In the external world of nature: injurious things overcome, the evil in life made serviceable, life triumphing over death. 3. In the personal life, as soul and body: diseases removed, the restored rejoicing in a new existence.—Christianity remains a continuous miracle of curing and of life till the new, great signs of the world's glorification. — *The Lesson for Ascension Sunday,* vers. 14-20. *See* the following section.—The ascended and glorified Christ, in His perfect victory over the world's unbelief: 1. In the Church [vers. 14, 15]; 2. by the Church [vers. 16-18]; 3. above and along with the Church [vers. 19, 20].—The exaltation of Christ, how it was unfolded in the resurrection and ascension of the Lord: 1. The resurrection, the beginning of His ascension; 2. His ascension, the completion of His resurrection.—The last retreat of the Lord into concealment the ground of His victorious advance into, and progress through, the entire world: 1. He retires from view, in order to advance again into the light as the risen Lord; 2. He retires to heaven, in order to advance again as He who had been raised to the glory of heaven. — Preaching faith is an upbraiding of unbelief to the end of the world.—The upbraiding of unbelief in the Church and the world, the sweetest message of highest love and grace.—The Lord's glorious upbraiding: 1. Glorious in the storm and the thunder-peal; 2. glorious in the law; 3. still more glorious in the Gospel. Or, 1. Fearful only to devils, opposed only to them; 2. to all susceptible, pious hearts a greeting of peace.—Whosoever cannot rebuke in the spirit of Christ, can expel no demons.

STARKE:—*Bibl. Wirt.*:—We must willingly and pleasantly receive even the denunciatory statements of God's word. They proceed from the purest love, to effect our salvation.—LUTHER:—The words of Christ are words of majesty; for that may well be termed majesty, by virtue of which these poor beggars are commanded to go forth and preach this new truth, not in one city or country, but in all the world, in every principality and kingdom, and to open their mouths freely and confidently before all creatures, so that all the human race may hear this preaching. This was most assuredly stretching the arm far out, grasping on all sides, and lading itself with a great burden. This is a command so strong and powerful, that no injunction of earth has surpassed it.—Those alone can preach repentance who have repented, and are truly humble.—*Nova Bibl. Tub.*:—Lo, Jesus has instituted the ministerial office for the benefit of all the world. The portals of grace stand open to all: oh! let us enter, and not delay!—OSIANDER:—God will exclude no one from eternal blessedness, who does not obstinately oppose himself through unbelief.—Faith is enjoined upon all, but given only to those who do not obstinately oppose themselves. — *Nova Bibl. Tub.*:—Mark well, my soul, how blessed thou mayest be, and escape damnation! One way alone leads to heaven, faith; one way alone to hell, unbelief.—Unbelief is the sole ground of damnation.

GERLACH:—Although no man can be saved except through Christ, nevertheless Christ declares him alone damned who has refused the salvation offered to him.—All miracles which accompany the proclamation of the divine word are signs: they point to that internal wonder of salvation and the new birth which the word effects, and only in so far have they value.—LISCO:—He who is ashamed of such a confession of Christ [baptism] should think of Matt. x. 32, 33.—In the name of Jesus, in faith upon Him, empowered by His might, for the furtherance of His ends, were these signs to be wrought.

BRAUNE:—From Rieger: "Wonder not, although in thine own case faith is a constant overcoming of unbelief."—BRIEGER:—The command of Christ ["Go ye," etc.] given to the Church, which came into prominence at Pentecost.—The Gospel is for all. —The state of a Church may be seen in what it does for missions.—After the signs which accompanied belief have ceased, the ascension of the Son of God can be evidenced only in that which manifests itself as the life of faith [and this is the sign of the regeneration of the world; a sign, no doubt, manifesting itself ever under new forms, while the divine power remains ever the same].

The Lesson. HEUBNER (compare, in addition, Luther's explanation, Works ix. 2546-2747):—Unbelief is blameworthy, is dependent upon the heart, upon being willing or not willing. Were it otherwise, Christ could not rebuke.—The world is the theatre for the display of the Gospel.—Christianity is a matter for humanity.—It is a duty continually to spread the Gospel.—We must profess the faith we have in our hearts (baptism).—Faith is necessary for all without exception, would they be saved. To disbelieve is very different from not knowing the Gospel (unbelief and ignorance are two essentially distinct ideas): unbelief is rejecting an offered, an understood Gospel, which has to some degree influenced one. Unbelief is chargeable, when it is a positive, determined rejection. The heathen cannot be charged with (deliberate) unbelief.—The revelation of the glory of Jesus in the moment of His parting from His disciples.—The departure of Jesus from the earth: 1. The description itself; 2. how edifying for us.—The power of faith in the heavenly majesty of Jesus.

SCHLEIERMACHER (*Predigten*, Bd. ii., 1834, p. 204): The close of our Lord's appearance upon earth compared with its beginning.—GRUNEISEN (*Pred.* 1842, p. 280):—Upon the blessing of the exalted Redeemer.—HEIDENREICH:—The ascension of the Lord, contemplated from the stand-point of faith.—ILLGEN:—How heaven appears to us in the light of Christ's ascension: 1. As our eternal fatherland; 2. as the land of our spiritual perfection; 3. as the place of our highest blessedness.—VON KALM:—Let the entrance of Jesus into glory strengthen us during the period of probation; let it strengthen, 1. Our faith in heaven; 2. our longing for heaven; 3. our striving to attain heaven.—UHLE:—What Christ in His exaltation is to men upon the earth.—RAMBACH: —If we look into the hearts of the disciples of Jesus, upon His exaltation to heaven, we see the deepest reverence for His divine majesty, living faith in His promises, heart-longings after the better world, joyous zeal to fulfil His commission, courage undaunted by consequences.—REINHARD:—The connection between true Christians and the Church above.—RAMBACH:—Seek the things above.—The ascension of Jesus in its power to elevate the heart.—REINHARD: —Our unbroken communion with the perfected of our race.—KUMMICH:—Our Lord's ascension shows us the way to heaven.—HOSSBUCH:—Our Lord's ascension is the real completion of His work on earth. —HERBERGER:—The ascension, the last miracle; with it the Lord closed His visible sojourn on earth: a blessed termination of Christ's entire journey, as St. Bernard says.—KAPFF:—The ascension of Jesus shows us heaven now standing open.—DIETZ:—The ascension of Jesus contemplated as His entrance upon government as the King of God's earthly kingdom.—HARLESS:—The Gospel being preached to every creature is the best testimony of Christ being raised to the right hand of God.—BENGEL:—With the ascension, the kingdom begins to extend on all sides.—GENZEN:—The Lord ever continues to bless His Church.—AHLFELD:—The last expression of the will of our Lord Jesus Christ.—KEM:—Not till His ascension did He become properly our Saviour [*i. e.*, the most remote distance becomes the most immediate contiguity].—FLOREY:—The disciples' pain and consolation in the departure of the Lord.— BURK:—Consider how Jesus, by His ascension, has opened all that formerly was closed: 1. The human heart to faith; 2. the whole earth to the Gospel; 3. heaven for all to enter who believe on Him.

THIRD SECTION.

THE RISEN SAVIOUR IN HIS ASCENSION, AS CONQUEROR WITH THE CHURCH, GIVING POWER TO THE MESSAGE OF SALVATION THROUGHOUT THE ENTIRE EARTH.

CHAPTER XVI. 19, 20.

(Parallels: Luke xxiv. 50–53; Acts i. 4–12.)

19 So then, after the Lord[1] had spoken unto them, he was received up into heaven, and
20 sat on the right hand of God. And they went forth, and preached everywhere, the Lord working with *them*, and confirming the word with signs following. Amen.

[1] Ver. 19.—After κύριος stands Ἰησοῦς in Codd. C., K., L., Δ. Lachmann adopts this reading. (Lange renders literally: "The Lord Jesus, after he had spoken thus unto them, was raised," &c.— *Trs.*)

EXEGETICAL AND CRITICAL.

Comp. the parallels in *Luke* and *Acts*; also the comments upon the conclusion of *Matthew*.—Mark's account of the ascension possesses a noble simplicity; and so conveys to the mind a comprehensive idea of Christ's majesty and rule, which consists most fully with the character of this Gospel. The ascension, described accurately by Luke, is here briefly sketched: the exaltation of Christ in the words, "and sat on the right hand of God," implies the supreme rule of Christ, as related by Matthew; while the last verse is analogous to the end of the Gospel by John, and expresses in a word the essence of all contained in the Acts.

Ver. 19. **The Lord Jesus.**—Term of reverence.—**After He had spoken.**—Augustine and the majority of commentators understand this to refer to the forty days; but Meyer will not concede this. According to him, this account and the lapse of forty days are quite irreconcilable. It is only when the Gospels are treated as mere *chronicles*, in which an exact sequence of all events in time is expected, that it becomes impossible to reconcile them with each other.

He was received up.—Taken up. Meyer properly combats the representation given by Strauss and Bauer, that Christ ascended to heaven from the room where they had supped. Yet, if we must not interpret this passage literally regarding *the place*, Meyer has as little right to insist upon a literal view as to *the time*. The account of the ascension is in every point to be supplemented by that of Luke, with whom Mark stands in no contradiction.—**And sat on the right hand of God.**—An account, resting partly upon the direct vision of the disciples (Acts i. 19), partly upon a revelation (Acts i. 11), partly upon the words of Christ (John xiv. 3), and upon the lively inference of faith, especially from the events occurring at Pentecost, Acts ii. 33. The fact is itself, on the one hand, local—that is, the being seated upon that throne of glory where the self-revelations of God take place, and in the midst of that majesty whence the manifestations of His power proceed; and, upon the other hand, is symbolic of Christ's royal dominion, Phil. ii. 10.

Ver. 20. **Everywhere.**—As it is probable the Evangelist wrote in Rome, and had been in Babylon, he knew that the Gospel was extending over the earth.—**The Lord working with them.**—*See Matthew*, close; Eph. i. 19.—**With signs following.**—The previously-promised powers to work those signs have been conferred; the miracles have appeared in striking forms, and conveying their symbolic import in their more general working. We see here the Gospel's absolute power to conquer in the might of the Lord. From this we perceive how close the connection between the closing of this Gospel and its beginning, and its every statement. Each

Evangelist concludes in a manner peculiar to himself, but with each the common topic is the glory and the kingly rule of Christ. The view peculiar to Mark is the forthputting of Christ's power by His servants on earth, to free the world and remove all demoniacal powers by which the earth was polluted.

DOCTRINAL AND ETHICAL.

1. See the conclusion of *Matthew* and the parallels in *Luke*.—We find the explanation of the circumstance, that Mark has combined the ascension in his Gospel narrative, in the fundamental principle of his Gospel, viz.: Christ, the omnipotent conqueror bursting through all barriers, the Lion in His retreat and advance. On this principle he was led to briefly mention the last withdrawal of Christ, the ascension; but then, only as the basis for the last forthcoming of Christ in His people, in their preaching of the Gospel and their working of signs in all places. Matthew presents Christ as a spiritual, invisible, theocratic King, beneath whose jurisdiction the present and the future worlds both lie, and whose administration over His people is in this present world universal, and of a specially spiritual character. By John, the universality and the present manifestation of Christ's glory are still more strongly emphasized. The typal form of this administration of Jesus is to be seen in the activity of a John and a Peter; that is, in contemplation and profound meditation combined with earnest labor and constancy in faith. Respecting Christ Himself, it is only hinted by John that He goes and comes again. According to Mark and Luke, Christ is with equal distinctness characterized as King of both worlds; but He works individually and personally from the other world outwards: and hence both these Evangelists present the ascension as a link, connecting Christ's life on earth with His work in and from heaven. In addition to this, however, Mark, like Peter, makes the rule of the exalted Christ in and with His people to prevail, because it is a work of the exalted Jesus which success will certainly crown; while Luke, with Paul, makes this prevalence result from the exalted *state* of the working Jesus.

2. When we estimate the resurrection properly, and consider that it was not the return of Jesus to His old, His first life, but His exaltation to His second, His new life, we see at once that the ascension must be joined to the resurrection as its necessary consequence. Christ's last departure from His disciples must have therefore, in any case, been termed His ascension; nevertheless, it consisted with His glory, that His return home should be an imposing and sublime ascension.

3. The doubts of critical writers as to the history of the ascension rest upon a mistake, often alluded to, regarding the nature of the Gospels, which are held to be memorabilia collected from various sources, instead of being received as individual, graphic life-pictures and views, organic in form, and Christological in character. The doubts of writers upon dogmatics are to be connected with their doubts regarding the resurrection itself, the divine dignity of Christ, the eternal continuance of personality, and the reality of a future state in heaven. In each of these two points the Apostles agree, as witnesses of the ascension, in their testimony with one another.

4. The theologians of the Lutheran school have thrown as much obscurity around the historical ascension, as those of the Reformed school around Christ's descent into hell (the Heidelberg Catechism). The Reformed Church has gone too far in its teaching regarding the glorified Christ's spiritual, omnipresent working; and the Lutheran, in its views upon the distinct localization and extension of Christ, now exalted. (Luther upon the Supper.) But the descent into hell and ascent to heaven must not be separated; and the localization of the exalted Redeemer in heaven must be held, along with His omnipresent manifestation. "That He reveals Himself in one way only in heaven amid the blessed, and that He in some other sense is everywhere present, are not contradictory propositions." SPENER, *Katechismus-Predigten*, 2 Bd. p. 914.

5. When we represent the ascension as the triumph of Christ and His Church, let us not forget the sad, earnest side for the Church in her human weakness. But as death is swallowed up in victory, so human sorrow is swallowed up in divine joy.

6. For the accounts given in Church history, and for the various traditions regarding the apostolic labors in preaching the Gospel, see LANGE'S *Apost. Zeitalter*, 2 Bd. p. 401.

HOMILETICAL AND PRACTICAL.

See *Matthew* and *Luke*.—Christ's exaltation the great turning-point in His life and work.—The exaltation of Christ to heaven, a sign of the completion of His work on earth ("After the Lord," etc.).—The union of the Father and the Son seen in the ascension: as He had been *sent*, and yet *came* freely,—as He had *finished* the work *given Him* by the Father, and *unfolded His own secret life*, was *given up* to the death, and *resigned* His life,—as He *was raised* from the dead, and *rose* by His own power,—so *He is exalted* by the Father, and yet *ascends* by virtue of His own might.—The degrees of Christ's exaltation shadowed forth in the ascension: 1. It points back to His descent into hell, and His resurrection; 2. it points forward to His being seated upon the throne of glory at the right hand of God.—Christ's ascension: 1. A return home; 2. an exaltation; 3. a never-ending march of triumph.—The import of Christ's exaltation for His people. It settles, 1. the ascension of the members in Him, as the Head; 2. the ascension of the members after Him, in the spirit; 3. the final ascension of the members at the coming of the Lord. —Christ's seat at the right hand of God, the goal of His pilgrimage; or the point of rest between His two great careers: 1. His career through all the misery of the world; 2. His career through all the salvation of the world.—Because Christ is the highest above all heavens, He is the nearest to His people in all their depths: In their depth, *a*. of struggling, *b*. of suffering, *c*. of want, *d*. of death and the grave.—The Lord's rest causes the activity of Apostles, and of the members of Christ's body.—From the tranquil, rejoicing, divinely-human heart above, proceeds every pulsation of the new life throughout the entire world. —All Christ's Apostles are Apostles of His royal authority.—The blessed consciousness of Christ's glory, the motive power of the Gospel in the hearts of believers.—The preaching of Christ is a preaching for all places.—Human proclamation of salvation confirmed by the divine manifestations from the Lord.—The truth of the faith established by the signs of love.—The Lord was one with them in the power of the Spirit.—The ever-blessing and victorious efficacy of the Gospel, a witness for Christ's everlasting administration of blessing and conquest. —Christ above all; Christ here, too, in His people. —Lo, the Lion of the tribe of Judah hath prevailed! —Our faith is the victory which overcometh the world.—Christ's seat, His throne: 1. The unceasing rest and festival in heaven; 2. unceasing work on earth; 3. unceasing rule in both kingdoms.—At the right hand of God, working in concert with Him; or, the revelation of the Trinity in Christ's exaltation (as at His birth and baptism, in His death and resurrection).—Where the exalted Christ appears, there doth heaven appear: 1. Where He is throned, there *is* heaven; 2. where He works, thither heaven *comes* (the spiritual, glorified world; the inheritance incorruptible, undefiled, that fadeth not away, 1 Pet. i. 4; 2 Pet. i. 4, 11).—We are with Christ transferred to the heavenly state.

STARKE: —Let each see that he hold his confidential interview with Jesus, ere he leave the earth. —God is gone up with a shout, Ps. xlvii. 6.—The ascension of our Jesus is our after-ascension. Where the Head is, there are the members. "Where I am, there shall My servants be, that they may see My glory."—The heavens stand open: we are certain of our salvation. Even so come, Lord Jesus!—The presence of Christ in the earth has not ceased with His ascension; it is rather established, being combined with His session at the right hand of God.— HEDINGER:—Be faithful and industrious in thy calling; God will add His blessing and success.—If believers are not able to see Christ with their eyes, yet they feel His working in their hearts (proof sufficient that He is with and in them).—OSIANDER:—Jesus is to the present day with the preachers of the Gospel. —When the spiritually blind are enlightened, the spiritually dead quickened, the spiritually deaf and dumb made to hear devoutly and speak piously, the spiritually lame made to be righteously industrious and active, and the spiritually leprous are cleansed from sins, these are greater signs and wonders than physical changes.

LISCO:—He wished to depart from them in such a way that they, seeing whither He had gone, could not imagine that they had lost Him: rather should the thought that He lived and was in heaven be ever present to them, that they might testify courageously of Him, and labor for Him, as though they had Him by their side.—They should know Christ no more after the flesh (2 Cor. v. 16), but as the exalted Son of God, whose glorious elevation filled them with the most blessed hopes and opened to them the most blessed prospects.—BRAUNE:—A close of the activity of the visible, personal Redeemer, that corresponds perfectly with the beginning. Not more mysterious than the birth and resurrection of the Saviour is His ascension.—Christ, having conquered death, could not die, and so ascended to heaven.—BRIEGER:—Ps. lxviii. 19; Eph. iv. 8: Christ, to manifest His victory over the devil and his angels, returns as a conqueror to heaven, Col. iii. 1, 2; Heb. viii. 1.— We are the subjects of the Heavenly (the second Adam), who is transforming us more and more into His likeness.—BAUER:—Holy, holy, holy is the Lord of hosts, the whole earth is full of His glory.

A

COMMENTARY

ON THE

HOLY SCRIPTURES:

CRITICAL, DOCTRINAL, AND HOMILETICAL,

WITH SPECIAL REFERENCE TO MINISTERS AND STUDENTS.

BY

JOHN PETER LANGE, D.D.,

IN CONNECTION WITH A NUMBER OF EMINENT EUROPEAN DIVINES.

TRANSLATED FROM THE GERMAN, AND EDITED, WITH ADDITIONS ORIGINAL AND SELECTED,

BY

PHILIP SCHAFF, D.D.,

IN CONNECTION WITH AMERICAN DIVINES OF VARIOUS EVANGELICAL DENOMINATIONS.

VOL. II. OF THE NEW TESTAMENT: CONTAINING THE GOSPEL ACCORDING TO MARK, AND THE GOSPEL ACCORDING TO LUKE.

NEW YORK:
CHARLES SCRIBNER & CO., 124 GRAND STREET.
1866.

THE
GOSPEL
ACCORDING TO
L U K E.

BY

J. J. VAN OOSTERZEE, D.D.,

PROFESSOR OF THEOLOGY IN THE UNIVERSITY OF UTRECHT.

TRANSLATED FROM THE SECOND GERMAN EDITION, WITH ADDITIONS ORIGINAL AND SELECTED,

BY

PHILIP SCHAFF, D.D.,

AND

REV. CHARLES C. STARBUCK.

FIRST EDITION.

NEW YORK:
CHARLES SCRIBNER & CO., 124 GRAND STREET.
1866.

ENTERED, according to Act of Congress, in the year 1866, by
CHARLES SCRIBNER,
In the Clerk's Office of the District Court of the United States for the Southern District of New York.

JOHN F. TROW & CO.,
PRINTERS, STEREOTYPERS, AND ELECTROTYPERS,
50 Greene Street, New York.

PREFACE OF THE AMERICAN EDITOR.

It affords me great pleasure to introduce the author of this Commentary on the Gospel of St. Luke to the American Churches, well assured that his name will soon be esteemed and beloved wherever the Anglo-American edition of Dr. Lange's Commentary is known.

Dr. JOHN JAMES VAN OOSTERZEE was born at Rotterdam, Holland, in 1817, and brought up in the faith of the Reformed Church. He studied at the University of Utrecht, and commenced his theological career in 1840, with an able Latin dissertation *De Jesu e virgine Maria nato*, in defence of the gospel history against the mytho-poetical hypothesis of Strauss. He labored as pastor first at Eemnes, and at Alkmaar, and since 1844 in the principal church of Rotterdam, where he continued eighteen years.* In 1862 he was called to his alma mater, as Professor of Theology. He opened his lectures in Utrecht with an apologetic oration *De scepticismo hodiernis theologis caute vitando*, 1863.

Dr. van Oosterzee is generally considered as the ablest pulpit orator and divine of the evangelical school in Holland now living. He combines genius, learning, and piety. He is orthodox and conservative, yet liberal and progressive. He seems to be as fully at home in the modern theology of Germany, as in that of his native country. To his attainments in scientific theology he adds a general literary culture and fine poetical taste.

It is as pulpit orator that he first acquired a brilliant and solid fame. He has been compared to Adolph Monod, in his more calm and matured days, when he stood at the head of the Evangelical Protestant pulpit of Paris and of France. His sermons on Moses, on the seven churches of the Apocalypse, and other portions of Scripture passed through several editions and some of them have been translated into the German language. He was selected as the orator of the festival of the Independence of the Netherlands, where he delivered in the Willems Park at Hague, in the presence of the whole court, an eloquent and stirring discourse under the title *De eerste steen* (*The first stone*).

In midst of his labors as preacher and pastor, he prepared a number of learned works which gave him an equal prominence among his countrymen as a divine. His principal contributions to theological science are a *Life of Jesus*,† which is mainly historical and apolo-

---

* There I made his personal acquaintance in 1854, and kept up some literary correspondence with him since. I hope to see Dr. Oosterzee and Dr. Lange again during this summer.

† *Leven van Jesus*, first published in 1846-1851, in 3 vols.; second edition, 1863-1865.

getic; a *Christology*, or *Manual for Christians who desire to know in whom they believe*, which is exegetical and doctrinal;* and *Commentaries* on several books of the New Testament, of which we shall speak presently. These and other works involved him in controversies with Dr. Opzoomer and Professor Scholten of Leyden, which bear a part in the conflict now going on in Holland between supernaturalism and rationalism. He also founded and edited, in connection with Professor Doedes, the Dutch Annals of Scientific Theology from 1843-1856. His essays on Schiller and Goethe, and similar subjects, prove his varied culture and deep interest in the progress of general literature and art.

The merits of our author have secured him a place in several literary societies, and also the decoration of the order of the Dutch Lion, and the Swedish order of the Pole-star.

It was a happy idea of Dr. Lange to associate so distinguished a scholar with his comprehensive Commentary, at the very beginning of the enterprise in 1857. He could hardly have found, even in Germany, a co-laborer who combines in a higher degree all the necessary theoretical and practical qualifications for a theologico-homiletical exposition of the Word of God, and who could more fully enter into the peculiar spirit and aim of this work. Dr. van Oosterzee may be called the Lange of Holland. He is almost as genial, fresh, and suggestive as his German friend, in hearty sympathy with his christologico-theological standpoint, and philosophico-poetic tastes, and equally prepared by previous studies for the task of a commentator. If he is less original, profound, and fertile in ideas, he compensates for it by a greater degree of sobriety, which will make him all the more acceptable to the practical common-sense of the Anglo-American mind. His style is clear and natural, and makes the translation an easy and agreeable task, compared with the translation of Lange's poetic flights and transcendent speculations. The Dutch mind stands midway between the German and the Anglo-Saxon.

Dr. van Oosterzee has already contributed several parts to Dr. Lange's *Bibelwerk*, which are undoubtedly among the very best, viz., Commentaries on the *Gospel of Luke*, the *Pastoral Epistles*, the *Epistle to Philemon*, and the Doctrinal and Homiletical Sections to the Commentary on the *Epistle of James*.†

The first edition of the Commentary on the Gospel of Luke appeared in 1859, and was translated by Miss Sophia Taylor for Clark's *Foreign Theological Library* at Edinburgh, in two volumes, 1862-'63. The second, revised and improved, edition was published in 1861, and from this the present American translation was prepared, without change or omission, but with considerable additions original and selected, according to the plan which is laid down in the Preface to the first volume. I acknowledge my indebtedness to Miss Taylor for assistance derived from her translation to the close of the third chapter.

---

* *Christologie, een handboek voor Christenen die weten willen in wien zij geloven*, Rotterdam, 1855-1861, also in 3 volumes. The first part discusses the Christology of the Old Testament; the second that of the New; the third states the results and forms a complete work in itself, describing the Son of God before His incarnation, the Son of God in the flesh, and the Son of God in glory. The third part has been translated into the German by F. Meyering under the title: *Das Bild Christi nach der Schrift*. Hamburg, 1864. It is well worthy of an English translation. Dr. van Oosterzee wrote also a reply to Renan's *Vie de Jésus*, under the title: *History or Romance?* It was translated from the Dutch into the German and published at Hamburg, 1864, and republished by the Am. Tract Society, N. Y. 1865.

† The Pastoral Epistles in the Anglo-American edition of Lange's *Commentary* have been assigned to Prof. Dr. DAY, of Lane Theol. Seminary, Ohio (who knows Dr. van Oosterzee personally, and is acquainted with the Dutch language and literature); the Epistle to Philemon to Prof. Dr. HACKETT, of the Theol. Seminary at Newton Centre, Mass., and the Epistle of James to the Rev. J. MOMBERT, of Lancaster, Pa. All these translations will probably be finished during the present year or in 1866.—[P. S.—Owing to the removal of Prof. Day to Yale College, the Epistles to Timothy have since been assumed by the Rev. Dr. ED. A. WASHBURN, of New York.]

It was my intention to prepare the whole Gospel of Luke alone. But owing to pressing engagements, and a proposed voyage to Europe during this summer, I have secured the co-operation of a competent assistant, the Rev. CHARLES C. STARBUCK, of New York, who is vigorously engaged in the work, with the help of the same literary apparatus, and the same study in the valuable exegetical library of the American Bible Union.

For the Introduction and the first three chapters I am alone responsible.

The department of textual criticism—the most difficult and laborious, though perhaps the least grateful task of the American editor—is wholly new, and hence enclosed in brackets. As the esteemed author notices very few readings in the first three chapters, and never refers to the English version, it was deemed unnecessary to retain them separately and thus to multiply brackets and initials. In these additions, as in the volume on Matthew, full use has been made of the Sinaitic Manuscript, and the latest discoveries and researches in the department of Biblical criticism.

From the author's *Exegetical Notes* I have in several important instances freely and fully expressed my dissent, *e. g.*, from his solution of the census difficulty, ch. ii. 3 (pp. 30, 32), his exposition of the angelic hymn, ii. 14 (pp. 38, 39), and his view of the dove at the baptism of Christ, iii. 22 (p. 58).

But these differences of opinion do not affect the unity of faith or at all diminish my admiration of the author. His book is sound, evangelical, fresh and interesting as few commentaries are. He has a happy tact in steering at equal distance from learned pedantry and unscholarly popularity, from tedious prolixity and cursory brevity. In the homiletical sections he shows rare talent and experience as a pulpit orator, and very properly confines himself to brief hints or finger-boards to the inexhaustible mines of Scripture truth and comfort, leaving the reader to explore them and to work up the precious ore for practical use.

I cannot conclude without publicly expressing my profound gratitude for the hearty and even enthusiastic welcome with which the first volume of this Commentary has been greeted in all the evangelical churches of America. Dr. Lange also expressed himself highly gratified with the plan and outfit of the American edition. I take the liberty of translating an extract from a letter of March 9, 1865. "In your brilliant sketch," he wrote to me, "I could hardly recognize the aged worker whom you have so leniently described; nor could I identify your stately Matthew with the humble German original; excepting, of course, the faithfulness and reliableness of your reproduction of the original text, in which I knew from the start you would fully satisfy every reasonable demand. As an author, I am thankful for the honor thus conferred upon me ; as a Christian, I rejoice in the furtherance of a work which has been owned and blessed by the Lord."

This success, which far surpasses the expectations of the editor and his co-laborers, will only increase their zeal and energy in the prosecution of their noble work. It is their aim to prepare, on an evangelical catholic basis, the very best Commentary for practical use which the combined scholarship and piety of Europe and America can produce.

From God must come the strength, and to Him shall be the praise.

PHILIP SCHAFF.

BIBLE HOUSE, NEW YORK, *June* 10, 1865.

[SINCE the above was set in type, I spent some happy days of last summer and autumn with my esteemed friend, Dr. Lange, at Bonn, on the charming banks of the Rhine, in delightful spiritual communion, as also with several of his co-laborers in the *Bibelwerk*, and with his intelligent publisher, Mr. Klasing at Bielefeld, all of whom feel deeply interested in the English reproduction of their work for the American churches. I regret that I was unable to follow the urgent invitation of Dr. van Oosterzee to pay him a visit at his summer residence in Holland, but I submitted to him the preface and the proof-sheets of the first three chapters, which met his cordial approval. Dr. Lange wrote to me since, that my visit to Germany had inspired him and his associates with fresh courage and zeal in the vigorous prosecution of the *Commentary*, and that most of the Old Testament books are now distributed among sound and able divines, although it is impossible to say when the whole will be completed. As for the American edition I can only say that nearly all the parts published in German are already taken in hand, and several of them are approaching completion. The Acts of the Apostles, the Catholic Epistles, and the Book of Genesis will probably be published before the close of this year.

P. S.

NEW YORK, *February* 17, 1866.]

AT the request of my honored friend, Dr. SCHAFF, I consented to continue the *Commentary on Luke*, which is now happily brought to a close. I did this with reluctance, being sensible to what disadvantage the bulk of the translation, with its comparative meagreness of illustrative addition, would appear by the side of the first three chapters, enriched as these are with the affluence of annotation which the studies of many years have enabled the Editor to add. I have been fortunate, however, in being admitted, through the great kindness of the officers of the American Bible Union, to the free use of their admirable library, of which I have availed myself especially in the Notes on the Text, as the comparative fulness of these will show. These have also been compared with the Codex Sinaiticus throughout, which had not been published when the original appeared.

The notes on the other parts of the work, though reasonably numerous, will usually be found brief, as, from the prevailing soundness and judiciousness of Dr. VAN OOSTERZEE'S own discussions, I found but little occasion for enlarging. In those which have been added, the names of BLEEK, MEYER, and ALFORD appear most frequently, the two former because of their high eminence in Biblical science, the latter because of his special relation to the Anglo-Saxon student of the gospels.

A great many modifications of the Common Version have been made, but solely with a view to critical exactness, and, therefore, with no particular regard to diction. No archaisms or points of style have been touched which were not supposed to obscure the sense.

The Revised Version of the American Bible Union in its final form was not published till the *Commentary* was about half printed. Several corrections have been adopted from it, and a good many are common to both works, being such as are naturally suggested by an effort to gain critical clearness.

Nothing whatever has been retrenched from the original except some mere references to German writers of little note, whose works it may fairly be presumed that those who read only English will never see. But every thought, it has been my aim to retain.

The translation of my portion is an entirely new one. There is, indeed, an Edinburgh translation, but I have not even seen it, and have not, at first or second hand, made any use whatever of it. The great simplicity and peculiar agreeableness of Dr. VAN OOSTERZEE'S style has rendered the work of translation a comparatively easy and exceedingly pleasant one. The remarks of Dr. SCHAFF, made above, as to the character of the Dutch mind, as mediating between the German and the Anglo-Saxon mind, will be found, I think, fully borne out by the character of this *Commentary*. While thoroughly familiar both with the results and with the processes of German criticism, the author judges them all with that sober simplicity which we are disposed to claim as a main characteristic of our own race. The work, however, shows abundantly that sobriety and simplicity do not necessarily mean dryness, for it is pervaded by a genial glow, rising not unfrequently into a rich eloquence, worthy of the first living preacher of Holland. It has been a progress of no common pleasure and spiritual profit, guided by him, to accompany the GODMAN through all the stages of His wondrous life, as laid out before us in the less methodical, but free and rich delineation of St. Luke, from the Baptism to the day when, having passed through the grave and gate of death to His joyful resurrection, He crowns His patient training of the disciples whom He had chosen by His last great charge, and is then taken up to sit at the right hand of God, leaving them full of joyful adoration, and ready for the coming of the Paraclete. Seeing that in our day the affections of believers, and the defence of the faith are both gathering more closely around the person of our Lord, those render the most eminent service who enable us most clearly to behold His image in the fulness of His theanthropic love and majesty. To this clearer vision of our Redeemer, we are persuaded that the present *Commentary* will contribute in no mean measure, and with a living force derived from the author's experiences as a Christian preacher, whose work is so much more nearly like that of our Lord than the work of the merely critical scholar.

In conclusion, it gives me pleasure to acknowledge the assistance of my friend, the Rev. JAMES B. HAMMOND, who acted as my amanuensis, and whose intellectual sympathy with the work rendered his services of a much more than merely mechanical value.

CHARLES C. STARBUCK.

NEW YORK, *February* 19, 1866.

THE AUTHOR'S PREFACE TO THE FIRST EDITION.

It was at the commencement of last year that my esteemed friend Dr. J. P. LANGE communicated to me the plan of his Theological and Homiletical Commentary, and, at the same time, expressed the wish, which surprised as much as it honored me, that I should take part with him in this work, by furnishing a Commentary on one of the Gospels. It will not seem surprising that I did not give my consent to this proposal till after much delay. When I considered, on the one hand, my numerous professional engagements and other occupations; on the other, the measure of my ability; I felt that I would rather see so important a work in other hands. When I remembered that I had been hitherto accustomed to learn from so many excellent German theologians, I could not quickly familiarize myself with the idea of becoming their fellow-laborer, and in this work even one of their leaders. And, finally, when I surveyed the peculiar difficulties under which every author must labor, in appearing before a public for the most part unknown to him, I felt, notwithstanding the favorable reception which some of my translated writings have met with abroad, almost constrained to return a negative answer. On the other hand, however, there was something very attractive to me in the plan of this Commentary. The thought of being associated in a work with a theologian whom I so highly esteem as Dr. LANGE, and with others of a kindred spirit, and of thus discharging a portion of the debt of gratitude for the rich instruction I had derived from their writings, possessed unusual interest. The opportunity offered me of being useful in another and more extensive manner than I could hope for in my immediate neighborhood, seemed to me an evident indication from the Lord of the church, which I felt I must by no means leave unheeded. The difficulty concerning the language was soon removed with the help of friends who are thoroughly masters of the German, so that I need not fear the application of the old adage to my work: *His ergo barbarus sum, quia non intelligor olli.* Besides, as I wrote here for foreign divines and ministers, I was at liberty to make such selections from my Dutch writings as seemed to me useful and necessary for the purpose. I therefore took courage to put my hand to the plough, without further hesitation; and have now the pleasure of presenting to the friends of Dr. LANGE's *Bibelwerk* the fruit of the comparatively few, and frequently interrupted, leisure hours which my professional occupations allowed me.

I may be permitted to take this opportunity of saying a few words on the manner in which I have performed my share of this great and noble undertaking. It is obvious that, for the sake of maintaining the uniformity which was on all accounts desirable, the plan and arrangement of my work should be strictly prescribed to me, both by the prospectus which first appeared, and by the subsequently published Commentary on Matthew. Even if it had been my opinion that a different arrangement of the material was preferable, it was my duty to remember that I was not called upon to execute a building of my own, but only to furnish a stone towards the completion of an edifice already planned and partly reared by others. It need scarcely be mentioned, also, that in writing on Luke's Gospel, I was obliged continually to have regard to what had already been said in the Commentaries on Matthew and Mark. It was desirable to avoid repetitions as much as possible, especially with respect to exegetical and archæological matters; while, on the other hand, I wished to make my work on Luke something more than a mere appendix to those on Matthew and Mark. It will then be believed, without further explanations, that it was by no means an easy task to avoid both Scylla and Charybdis; and that a glance at the copiousness of the ideas developed in the treatment of the parallel passages in the two first Evangelists, could not fail to convince me that the commentator on the third would have a difficult position to occupy. The attempt, however, had to be made, to say again that which should be, in the main points, the same in a different manner; and I shall rejoice if competent judges can testify, that a comparison of my work on Luke with Dr. LANGE's on *Matthew* and *Mark* presented them with neither a mere echo nor a jarring discord.

In the translation of the text, I adhered generally to Luther's version except where accuracy and clearness justified an alteration. This modesty, with regard to the master-work of the hero of the Reformation, may be expected from a foreigner who feels no calling to produce a radical reform in this department. As regards the *varietas lectionum*, I have only noticed those readings which have a bearing on the translation and exposition. The character of the exegesis has been accommodated to its homiletical purpose. It would not, perhaps, have been difficult to produce a more extensive apparatus of theological learning; but, mindful of the task imposed upon me, of writing chiefly for practical theologians and clergymen, I thought I should best satisfy this condition by giving a more historical and psychological, than a philological, character to my exposition, and by caring more about clear explanations of things, than extensive explanations of words. Among ancient expositors, I have chiefly consulted CALVIN and BENGEL; among moderns, DE WETTE, STIER, and MEYER; and even where I have felt obliged to differ from them, I have found no difficulty in recognizing the service done to the exposition of the Gospel by these celebrated men. In the division entitled "*Leading Doctrinal and Ethical Thoughts,*" I have endeavored to penetrate somewhat more deeply into the nature of events than was possible in the "*Exegetical and Critical Notes;*" and, here and there where it seemed necessary, to bring forth the apologetic element which, in a work like the present, intended for so many different hands, ought never to be wholly wanting. In this part, and also in the "*Homiletical Hints,*" I have had respect not only to the rich stores of German literature, but also, occasionally, to the productions of other countries, and especially to the theologians and preachers of my own, and the creations of sacred art.

If aught useful or profitable should be found in this division of the *Bibelwerk*, part at least of the thanks is due to the revered Editor, who not only encouraged me to venture upon this work, but, with true liberality, neither wished nor required me to withdraw or to modify my views of certain passages, where they did not coincide with his own. This state of affairs is indeed attended with this inconvenience, that I am entirely responsible for my own work, with all its faults and defects. . . . I could say much, on the great distance—greater perhaps on this occasion than ever—which I find between my performance and my own ideal. But it is needless to increase this sufficiently lengthy book by a long preface. The work must speak for itself; and if I have anywhere contributed merely combustible material to the great temple, I could not myself wish that it should stand the fire.

The views concerning the person of our Lord, and the divine authority of the written Word, on which this Commentary on Luke is based, and which I hope are brought forward with mildness and dignity, will perhaps find more echo in the German than in the Dutch Church and theology. But what does it matter to their defenders, whether the majority or the minority of the moment be on their side, so long as they are conscious of serving the cause of truth, and of always finding a response in many hearts and consciences? May this be at least the case in the circle for which this work is more immediately intended: the Author would then, perhaps, feel encouraged, in accordance with the wish of the Editor, to undertake another portion of this Commentary; the success of which will be best promoted by the concurrence of a select number of like-minded fellow-laborers. Be this as it may, however, he does not regret the many precious hours devoted to this difficult, but very attractive task. Spiritual intercourse with the Gospel of perfect humanity has a peculiar worth in days when, on the one hand, so many look upon humanity and Christianity as in irreconcilable opposition, while others again believe that if humanity is to attain its highest perfection, Christianity must be shorn of its special characteristics, and Christ of His superhuman dignity. May this work, then, be the means of bringing many to a higher appreciation and more profitable distribution of the treasures hidden in the third Gospel; and may the κρίσις of Him of whom Luke testified, be a κρίσις ζωῆς καὶ δόξης for my work.

J. J. VAN OOSTERZEE.

ROTTERDAM, *November*, 1858.

FROM THE PREFACE TO THE SECOND EDITION.

WHEN, a few months ago, I was informed by the esteemed publisher of the *Bibelwerk* that a new edition of my *Luke* was called for, I felt equally surprised and rejoiced. As a stranger in the ecclesiastical and theological world of Germany, I could hardly expect to be so favorably received and even admitted to the rights of citizenship. I embrace this opportunity to return my hearty thanks for the many kind and cheering words expressed to me from near and far, both privately, and by older and younger brethren in the ministry, and in public notices. I feel especially indebted to an unknown reviewer in the monthly journal: *The News of the Churches, and Journal of Missions*, for March, 1860, for the manner and spirit in which he directed the attention of England and Scotland to this book. I would have been still more gratified, if the criticism had been as thorough and searching as it was encouraging. I regret to say that the author of the notice in RUDELBACH and GUERICKE's *Zeitschrift für Lutherische Theologie* for 1860, p. 499 sqq., raises a number of objections without having more than superficially glanced at the work; at least, he charges me with views directly opposed to those which I have expressly stated in more than one place, and he even doubts my full faith in the true Divinity of the Saviour, simply because I call the Gospel of Luke, the Gospel of the purest humanity! . . .

The time since the appearance of the first edition was too short to allow of a thorough reconstruction of the work, especially since I was occupied at the same time with the preparation of a commentary on the *Pastoral Epistles*, and on *Philemon* for the *Bibelwerk*. I confined myself to improvements in style and expression; I added what was neglected, and removed defects which, in my own opinion, as well as in the opinion of others, clung to the first edition. The careful reader will find on many pages the traces of a zealously improving hand, and the word "*revised*," on the title-page, is by no means merely an *ornamentum tituli*. For whatever defects still remain, I ask anew the indulgence of the reader, and commend my *Luke*, in his further journeys, humbly to the blessing of Him who guides and directs with His wisdom, not only the events of our life, but also our writings.

J. J. VAN OOSTERZEE.

ROTTERDAM, *February*, 1861.

III.

THE GOSPEL ACCORDING TO LUKE;

OR,

THE GOSPEL OF UNIVERSAL HUMANITY.

(*SYMBOLIZED BY THE IMAGE OF MAN.*)

[THE COLLECT: Almighty God, who calledst Luke the physician, whose praise is in the gospel, to be an Evangelist and physician of the soul: may it please Thee, that, by the wholesome medicines of the doctrine, delivered by him, all the diseases of our souls may be healed; through the merits of Thy Son Jesus Christ our Lord. Amen.—From FORD'S *Commentary on the Gospel of St. Luke.*—P. S.]

INTRODUCTION.

§ 1. LUKE THE EVANGELIST.

CONCERNING the person and history of the third Evangelist we know little that is perfectly certain. From the Epistles of Paul we learn that he held a conspicuous rank among the friends and fellow-laborers of the great Apostle of the Gentiles (Philemon 24; 2 Tim. iv. 11). He is expressly distinguished (Col. iv. 14) from the brethren who were of the circumcision (vers. 10, 11), and was therefore a Christian of Gentile extraction; having, probably, been first a proselyte to the Jewish religion,* and afterward a convert to the faith of Christ. According to Eusebius [*H. E.* iii. 4] and Jerome he was born at Antioch in Syria; † this tradition rests on no evidence, but is preferable, on account of its antiquity, to all other conjectures concerning his origin. Perhaps it was there that he became acquainted with Paul, and associated himself with that Apostle; at least it is not proved that the view of Eusebius arose simply from an erroneous inference from Acts xiii. 1. ‡ His Greek education and learning are apparent from the philological excellence of his writings. According to Col. iv. 14, his original avocation

---

* [The author must mean a *half*-proselyte, or proselyte of the *gate*, who embraced only the moral law and the Messianic hopes of Judaism, as distinct from the *full* proselytes, or proselytes of *righteousness*, who conformed to the ceremonial law also, and were generally more bigoted than native Jews. Some regard Luke as a Hellenist or a Greek Jew (as distinct from the Hebrews proper), and thus account for his pure Greek style and liberal views. But the comparison of Col. iv. 14 with ver. 11 favors the conclusion that he was uncircumcised, since Paul does not mention him among his companions ἐκ περιτομῆς. Dr. Lange, in his *Life of Jesus* (i. p. 252, German ed.), ingeniously supposes, though without proof, that Luke was one of the Greeks who visited the Saviour shortly before the crucifixion, John xii. 20, and one of the two disciples of Emmaus, Luke xxiv. 13.—P. S.]

† [Jerome, in his short but interesting sketch of Luke, in his *Liber de viris illustribus*, cap. vii.: *Lucas medicus Antiochensis, ut ejus scripta indicant, Græci sermonis non ignarus fuit, sectator apostoli Pauli, et omnis peregrinationis ejus comes*, etc.—P. S.]

‡ [By confounding Luke with Λεύκιος ὁ Κυρηναῖος, Lucius of Cyrene. The name *Lucas* may be a contraction of *Lucanus*, or even *Lucilius*, but not of *Lucius*.—P. S.]

was that of a physician.* It has been often supposed, but cannot be proven, that he was one of the seventy disciples, and one of the two travellers to Emmaus, whose history he has so touchingly narrated. It is at Troas that we first find him in company with St. Paul (Acts xvi. 10). He accompanied him thence to Philippi, where he seems to have remained during the second sojourn of the Apostle at Corinth. He afterward again travelled with Paul to Jerusalem (xx. 5, 6), where he would certainly meet with James and the elders of the Church (xxi. 18), and not lose the opportunity of personal intercourse with the first witnesses of the life and resurrection of Christ. And since, according to Acts xxiv. 23, free access was allowed to his friends during Paul's two years' imprisonment in Cæsarea, it is probable that Luke remained near him during this interval. He afterward accompanied the Apostle to Rome (Acts xxvii. and xxviii.), undergoing the perils of his shipwreck, and, according to 2 Tim. iv. 11, sharing his imprisonment, a few months before his martyrdom, when most of his friends had forsaken him. He has been supposed, and not without reason, to have been the brother "whose praise was in the gospel throughout all the churches," and of whom it is said (2 Cor. viii. 18), that he was sent to Corinth with Titus, to make the collection there for the poor saints at Jerusalem. At all events, he was, during Paul's life, not only his fellow-traveller, but also his fellow-laborer; and there is no doubt that he would continue, after the death of the great Apostle, to be both zealous and active in the cause of the kingdom of God.

He is said by Epiphanius to have preached mainly in Gaul; and by Nicephorus, to have suffered martyrdom in Greece, where, after having been condemned by the unbelievers without even the form of a trial, he was, for want of a cross, nailed to the nearest olive-tree, in the eightieth or eighty-fourth year of his age. His body is said to have been removed, together with the remains of Andrew, from Achaia to Constantinople, and to have been there deposited in the Church of the Holy Apostles, by the Emperor Constantine, or his son Constantius.† All these accounts, however, are as little deserving of belief as the very recent tradition, that he was a painter, and painted the portraits of our Lord, the Virgin, and the principal Apostles. This tradition, however, is a fact in a higher sense; for are not the writings of Luke truly pictures, full of high and holy art, delighting us by their interesting groups and animated portraits of the best and purest of men?

The Catholic Church dedicates the 18th of October to the memory of Luke, assuming, on insufficient ground, that this was the day of his death. The Evangelical Church is willing to leave untouched the curtain which conceals the cradle and grave of Luke, in order to contemplate, with more undivided attention, the precious legacy of his writings, the earliest and most important of which we are now about to consider.

[LITERATURE.—On the person, history, and writings of Luke comp. HIERONYMUS: *De viris illustribus*, cap. vii. (tom. ii. pp. 826 and 827 in *Vallarsi's* edition of Jerome's works); WINER: *Bibl. Realwörterbuch*, art. *Lukas* (vol. ii. pp. 34, 35); GÜDER: art. *Lukas* in Herzog's *Real-Encyklopædie* (vol. viii. p. 544 ff.); WM. SMITH's *Dictionary of the Bible*, art. *Luke* (vol. ii. p. 150 ff.); and the relevant sections in the Critical Introductions to the N. T. and the Commentaries on Luke.—P. S.]

§ 2. THE GOSPEL ACCORDING TO LUKE.

On turning from the reading of the Gospels of Matthew and Mark to that of Luke, we are conscious of receiving a very peculiar impression. It is the same Gospel, but announced in a manner quite different from that of the two first synoptical Gospels. Luke gives much more than Matthew and Mark: witness his account of events preceding our Lord's birth in chs. i.

---

* [Jerome (*Epist. ad Paulinum*) says of Luke: *Fuit medicus, et pariter omnia verba illius animæ larguentis sunt medicinæ.* Allusion is made also to his medical profession in the ancient lines:
    Lucas, Evangelii et medicinæ munera pandens,
     Artibus hinc, illinc religione, valet:
    Utilis ille labor, per quem vivere tot agri;
     Utilior, per quem tot didicere mori!—P. S.]

† [So says Jerome, *Lib. de viris illustribus*, cap. vii. at the close: *Sepultus est Constantinopoli, ad quam urbem vicesimo Constantii anno, ossa ejus cum reliquiis Andreæ apostoli translata sunt.*—P. S.]

§ 2. THE GOSPEL ACCORDING TO LUKE.

and ii., the parables in chs. xv. and xvi., and many other *singularia Lucæ;* and even where his facts coincide with those of the other narratives, he relates them in a manner of his own. He is far more careful than Matthew to preserve the strict order of events (καθεξῆς), and to comply with the requirements of a history, properly so called. His important preface (i. 1–4), which is written in pure Greek, implies previous diligent investigation of the various sources open to him. He tells us that many had already attempted (ἐπεχείρησαν)—for so we understand his account—a written history of the occurrences of the life of Jesus. They had endeavored to take for their guidance, the real instructions of the first witnesses for Jesus, the Apostles, from whom Luke distinguishes both himself and them. It seems very improbable that Luke is here alluding to the Gospels of Matthew and Mark.* He seems rather to have in view certain literary efforts of Christian antiquity, of which some might be better than others; but among which not one was, in his opinion, quite satisfactory. He, at least, considers them inadequate for the "*certainty*" (ἀσφάλεια) of the faith of Theophilus; and having weighed and examined the various documents to which he had access, he felt himself powerfully impelled to undertake such a work also, and, as far as in him lay, to improve upon the accounts of his predecessors.

The third Gospel bears the plainest traces of the individuality of its composer, as far as we know him from the few hints of the Acts, and of the Epistles of Paul. As Luke was a Christian of the Gentiles, his work bears a decidedly universal character [*i. e.*, he represents Christianity as the religion for the whole race, and for all societies, classes, and conditions of men]. It is he who traces the genealogy of our Lord, not to Abraham only, as Matthew, but to Adam, and cares less to represent the Messiah of God in His relation to Israel than in His relation to all mankind. Is he represented to us as a scientifically educated man, living in the polished city of Antioch, which Cicero commends† as a seat of science and learning? The style as well as the contents of his writings plainly show that *he* was not brought up at the receipt of custom, or beside the nets of the fisherman. Again, we recognize the physician (Col. iv. 14) by the minute accuracy with which he describes certain diseases, and find, from other remarks, that the physician was at the same time an excellent psychologist.‡ Ch. iv. 38; xxii. 43, 44, and 51, may be cited as proofs of the former; while in ch. ix. 54–61; xviii. 34; xxiii. 12, and xxiv. 41, we find significant hints of his insight into the mysteries of human nature. And, lastly, does it appear from the Epistles of Paul that Luke was his friend and fellow-traveller? No other Gospel bears such visible traces of the genuine Pauline spirit. It is not indeed probable, that when Paul speaks of *his* Gospel (Rom. ii. 16; 2 Tim. ii. 8), he is alluding to the written narrative of Luke; yet both coincide, in a remarkable manner, in their descriptions of the institution of the Lord's Supper (Luke xxii. 19, 20; comp. 1 Cor. xi. 23–29), in their mention of the appearance of Christ to Peter (comp. Luke xxiv. 34 and 1 Cor. xv. 5), and in other special circumstances. In the form, too, of his expressions, as well as in the choice of his incidents, we recognize in Luke a genuine follower of Paul. Consider, in this view, his narrative of the preaching of Jesus at Nazareth, and the mention of divine favors bestowed upon Gentiles under the Old dispensation (ch. iv. 16–30); the anointing of the Lord by the repentant sinner in Simon's house, and the pardon vouchsafed to her faith (ch. vii. 36–50); the parable of the Pharisee and publican, who went down to his house *justified* (δεδικαιωμένος, ch. xviii. 14); the history of Zacchæus (ch. xix. 1-10), of the penitent thief on the cross (ch. xxiii. 39–43), and other incidents which might be mentioned. As Paul led the people of the Lord out of the bondage of the law into the enjoyment of gospel liberty, so did Luke raise sacred history from the standpoint of the Israelitish *nationality,* to the higher and holier ground of universal *humanity.*

---

* [The word "*many*" must at all events imply more than two, and applies to imperfect accounts which are to be superseded in whole or in part by the more full and exhaustive narrative of Luke. Alford (*Prolegomena* to vol. i. of his *Commentary,* p. 50) gives it as his opinion that Luke never saw the Gospels of Matthew and Mark, else "he would most certainly have availed himself of those parts of their narratives, which are now not contained in his own."—P. S.]

† In Verrem. ch. 2.

‡ Proofs of the scientific acquirements of the physicians of those times, and of Luke in particular, are abundantly furnished by Tholuck in his *Glaubwürdigkeit der evangelischen Geschichte,* p. 160 ff.

And hence it is no difficult task to characterize in a few words the distinctive peculiarities of the third Gospel. Matthew presents Christ to us as the Messiah of Israel; Mark announces the Gospel of the Son of God; while Luke depicts the Son of man, appearing indeed in Israel, but for the benefit of the whole race of man.* Most justly, therefore, may the figure of a *man* be appropriated to him from among the symbols by which the ancient Church designated the four Evangelists. He does not, indeed, soar to such heights as the Eagle (John), but chooses our earth as his sphere of action, and shows us the incarnate Son of God, "in all things made like unto His brethren," sin only excepted. And as the Epistle to the Hebrews teaches us to contemplate the humanity of the Son of God as gradually developing, and attaining the highest degree of perfection (Heb. ii. 10; v. 9; xii. 2), so also does the Gospel we are now considering. The two former Gospels show us *who* Jesus *was:* this informs us *how* He *became* what He was; pointing out to us *successively* the καρπὸς τῆς κοιλίας (ch. i. 42), the βρέφος (ch. ii. 16), the παιδίον (ch. ii. 27), the παῖς (ch. ii. 40), the ἀνήρ (ch. iii. 22). No other Gospel is of so strongly antidocetic a character; it is a continuous commentary on those suggestive words of the Apostle, "God sending His Son in the *likeness* (ἐν ὁμοιώματι) of sinful flesh" (Rom. viii. 3). In studying it, we are more attracted by the loveliness than even by the dignity of the Lord; and the Holy One, born of Mary, appears before our eyes as the *fairest* of the children of men (Ps. xlv. 2). Does it not even seem as if Luke had felt the necessity of transferring to his Master the very calling to which his own life had been hitherto devoted, while depicting to us, far oftener than the other Evangelists, the great Ἰατρός, the Physician who came, not only to "*minister*" (Matt. xx. 28), but "*who went about doing good*" (Acts x. 38), who felt compassion for all diseases both of mind and body, and whose power was present to heal? (Luke v. 17). Even in recording such words and deeds of our Lord as are also noticed by his two predecessors, Luke generally adds some important hints, which give greater prominence to the genuine *humanity* of His *person*, and the *healing nature* of His *redeeming work*. All, for instance, narrate the temptation in the wilderness, but Luke alone adds that "the devil departed from Him *for a season*." All describe His agony in Gethsemane, but Luke alone has preserved the touching account of His *bloody sweat*, and of the *angel* who *strengthened* Him. All speak of the repentance of Peter, but Luke alone of that *look* of the Lord which accompanied the crowing of the cock. And this genuine human greatness of the Redeemer, appears the more striking in this Gospel, from its continuous contrast with the poverty of His outward condition, and the opposition of His enemies. The angels and shepherds at the nativity; Simeon and Anna at the presentation of the child in the temple; Simon and the "woman who was a sinner;" the tears of Jesus over Jerusalem, and the hosannas of the multitude; the silent seriousness of the sufferer, and the noisy jesting of Herod and his men of war; His prayer on the cross for His enemies, and the apathy and hatred of the crowd:—what striking contrasts, depicted by Luke alone, and greatly enhancing the beauty of his Gospel! Not only remarkable copiousness, but surprising variety, characterize this history, and render it, both from its contents and style, of the first importance toward a right acquaintance with the life and character of the Lord Jesus Christ. It is the crown of the synoptic Gospels, as the symbol of man (Luke) rises above that of the bullock (Matthew) and the lion (Mark).

§ 3. AUTHENTICITY AND COMPOSITION OF THE GOSPEL ACCORDING TO LUKE.

After what has been said, the *genuineness* of the third Gospel can scarcely be doubted. We have found it bearing, throughout, that peculiar stamp which would characterize the spirit of the friend and fellow-traveller of Paul. But there is also no lack of external evidence. The most ancient is that offered by Luke himself, in the beginning of the Acts, where he plainly declares that both books were the composition of the same person. The supposition that the

---

* It is, of course, understood by all reflecting readers that such remarks concerning the peculiarities of the Evangelists are meant not in an *absolute*, but in a *relative* sense only. We speak not of *exclusive* advantages of the Evangelists, but only of the prevailing standpoint from which a *parte potiori* each represents the inexhaustible wealth of the life of the God-Man.

§ 3. AUTHENTICITY AND COMPOSITION OF THE GOSPEL.

companion of Paul (Acts xvi. 10; xx. 5) was another than Luke, either Timothy (Mayerhof) or Silas (Hennell and others), already rank among the antiquarian curiosities of historical criticism. It will be shown hereafter, how certain it is that the book called the Acts of the Apostles, is the production of Luke;* but the same evidence proves also the authenticity of his Gospel.

Further external testimony is abundantly furnished by Irenæus, Origen, and Tertullian, while Eusebius also, without any hesitation, places this Gospel in the rank of the ὁμολογούμενα. For details, see the various Introductions, especially also Kirchhofer's *Quellensammlung*, or Collection of the Sources for the History of the New Testament Canon (Zurich, 1844).

It might seem surprising that Papias, who speaks so decidedly of the two former Gospels, should have left no notice of the third; but, on the other hand, we may be certain, that if a spurious Gospel had, in his days, been in circulation under the name of Luke, so conscientious a man would hardly have failed to warn his readers against it. Besides, the preface of Luke seems to have been present to his mind, if he did not exactly follow it in writing the commencement of his now unfortunately lost συγγράμματα (Eusebius *H. E.* iii. 39). *See* Credner's *Introduction to the N. T.* vol. i. p. 202. If the ingenious conjecture of Lange (*Leben Jesu*, i. p. 252), that Luke was one of those Greeks who came to Jesus shortly before His death (John xii. 20), and indeed the same whom Papias calls Aristion (*lucere* = ἀριστεύειν), could be substantiated, this silence would be sufficiently explained. But be this as it may, it is abundantly compensated by the involuntary but powerful testimony of the well-known Marcion, in the second century. It is certain that this Gnostic was well acquainted with this Gospel, which he has both used and mutilated, incorporating much of it in his own, to support his heretical opinions, and thus proving that it existed, not only in his days, but in those of his teacher Cerdo (Tertullian, *de præscript. hæret.* cap. 51).

Certain critics of our days have represented the so-called Gospel of Marcion (chiefly known to us through the writings of Epiphanius and Tertullian), not as a corruption of the original, but as one of the sources whence the present (ungenuine) Gospel of Luke is derived. Dr. A. Ritschl especially, in his *Das Evangelium Marcions und das kanonische Evangelium des Lukas* (Tübingen, 1846), has zealously defended the hypothesis, "that the Gospel of Marcion is not a mutilation of the third Gospel, but the basis of it;" but he himself afterward abandoned this view.† Schwegler (*Nachapost. Zeitalter*, i. pp. 260–284), Baur (*Kritische Untersuchungen über die kanonischen Evangelien*, p. 397), and Zeller (*Theol. Jahrbücher*, ii. 1843, pp. 50-90) have sought to explain the Gospel of Luke as being written with a distinct party-purpose, in the sense of the Tübingen school; namely, either for the purpose of reconciling the Petrine and Pauline parties, or of giving a certain triumph to the Pauline tendency. ‡ Such criticism, which sees in the most evident traces of mature Christian individuality only the fruit of cool calculation, and the craftiness of party spirit, is morally condemned, even before it is scientifically refuted. Such criticism killed and buried the hypotheses of its immediate predecessors, Strauss, and Bruno Bauer, but the feet of them that shall carry it out dead are already at the door (Acts v. 9); and, meanwhile, we may rest contented with the refutation of the monstrous hypothesis, concerning the inverted Marcion, furnished by Hahn, Olshausen, and de Wette.

---

* Comp. Lechler on *Acts*, p. ii. (in Lange's *Commentary*).

† [In an article on the subject in the Tübingen *Theol. Jahrbücher* for 1851.—P. S.]

‡ [I add a judicious remark of the archbishop of York, Dr. WILLIAM THOMSON, in his article on the Gospel of Luke, in SMITH's *Dictionary of the Bible*, vol. ii. p. 155: "The passages which are supposed to bear out this '*Pauline* tendency,' are brought together by Hilgenfeld with great care (*Evangelien*, p. 220); but Reuss (of Strassburg, a liberal critic) has shown, by passages from St. Matthew which have the same tendency against the Jews, how brittle such an argument is, and has left no room for doubt that the two Evangelists wrote facts and not theories, and dealt with those facts with pure historical candor (Reuss: *Histoire de la Théologie*, vol. ii. l. vi. ch. vi.). Writing to a Gentile convert, St. Luke has adapted the form of his narrative to their needs; *but not a trace of a subjective bias, not a vestige of a personal motive, has been suffered to sully the inspired page*. Had the influence of Paul been the exclusive or principal source of this Gospel, we should have found in it more resemblance to the Epistle to the Ephesians, which contains (so to speak) the Gospel of St. Paul."—P. S.]

Compare also the learned *Dissertatio de Marcione, Lucani Evangelii adulteratore*, of Dr. Harting, Traj. ad Rhenum, 1849.*

The *aim* of Luke in writing his Gospel is sufficiently clear from his preface. Concerning Theophilus, *see* the remarks on ch. i. 1–4. His chief source of information was undoubtedly oral tradition. This had, however, been already, in various instances, reduced to writing. We will not venture to assert (with Dr. Baur) that he also knew and used the Gospel of Matthew; at least this is by no means "a long-established result of critical research." But according to the testimony of Irenæus (*Adversus hæres*. iii. 1, 14), of Origen (in Eusebius' *H. E.* vi. 25), and of Tertullian (*Adv. Marc*. iv. 2), the Apostle Paul exercised a direct influence in the composition of this Gospel. The different accounts of the Fathers of the ancient Church may be so harmonized, that Paul was not only the enlightener (*illuminator*) of Luke during the progress of his work, but that, when completed, it received his approbation. It is true, indeed, that our Evangelist does not name Paul as an authority, but this was unnecessary to accredit his narrative to Theophilus; and its early and undisputed reception as canonical, proves that the primitive Church soon recognized in this Gospel the marks of a genuine apostolicity. Indeed, it was never discredited, except by the Cerinthians and Ebionites.

As to the *time* of composition, Luke, as well as Matthew and Mark, seems to have written his Gospel before the destruction of Jerusalem. The abrupt conclusion of the Acts (ch. xxviii. 30, 31) leaves us to suppose that Paul was still alive when this second record was completed. Nor is it by any means proved, by ch. xxi. 24, that this Gospel was not written till after the year 70. If we had here only a *vaticinium post eventum*, the Evangelist would undoubtedly have made a far more precise distinction between the destruction of Jerusalem and the second coming of our Lord.

The *place* where this Gospel was composed can only be conjectured. Alexandria, Bœotia, Achaia, Cæsarea, Asia Minor, and Rome, have all been mentioned, with more or less reason. Perhaps the latter seems the least arbitrary supposition; but the whole question is one of minor importance, the saying of Paul holding good in this instance: ὁ λόγος τοῦ Θεοῦ οὐ δέδεται (2 Tim. ii. 9).

[According to Irenæus (*Adv. hær*. iii. 1) Luke wrote after the death of Peter and Paul, *i. e.*, after 64. But it seems to me intrinsically very probable (with Thiersch) that the Gospel of Luke was written at Cæsarea in Palestine during Paul's imprisonment there, A. D. 58–60; while his Acts were composed at Rome before the close of the first imprisonment of Paul, between 61–63; for his martyrdom would hardly have been ignored in Acts xxviii. 31, if it had occurred before. Alford (in *Prolegomena* to his Commentary on the Gospels, p. 46, 4th ed.) places the composition of the third Gospel even earlier, before A. D. 58, consequently before the traditional date of the Gospel of Matthew. But according to the almost unanimous testimony of the early Church, Matthew's Gospel was written first. Jerome, in his biographical sketch of Luke, *De viris illustr*. cap. vii., mentions that some understand Paul to refer to the written Gospel of Luke *quotiescunque in epistolis suis Paulus dicit* JUXTA EVANGELIUM MEUM. But this is no doubt the gospel which Paul preached himself (comp. Gal. i. 8, 9); and as to the passage 2 Cor. viii. 18 which Jerome quotes, it is not certain that Luke is intended, and in any case, ἐν τῷ εὐαγγελίῳ refers not to a written Gospel, but to the affairs of the preached gospel and its spread among the Gentiles. On the other hand, de Wette, Reuss, Bleek, Meyer, and others, place the composition too late, viz., soon after the year 70, on the false assumption that Luke, xxi. 24 f., already presupposes the destruction of Jerusalem. *See* Com. *in loco*.—P. S.]

The *integrity* of this Gospel is beyond all doubt. The objections formerly made to the first two chapters are not more weighty than those made, on doctrinal grounds, to Matt. i. and ii.

---

* [Comp. also Bishop THIRLWALL's *Introduction* to Schleiermacher on *Luke*, and especially VOLCKMAR, *Das Evangelium Marcions*, Leipzig, 1852, who, though some of his views are untenable, has conclusively proved that our Gospel of Luke is older than the mutilation of Marcion. The original always precedes the caricature; truth is older than heresy.—P. S.]

§ 4. THEOLOGICAL AND HOMILETIC COMMENTARIES. 7

With respect, finally, to its *dignitas canonica et auctoritas divina*, the third Gospel is certainly not the work of one of the first Apostles; but who can prove that the promises of our Lord, John xiv.–xvi., concerning the Paraclete, were limited to the Twelve; and may we not rather apply to the calling of Luke to be an Evangelist, the apostolic word: ἑκάστῳ δὲ δίδοται ἡ φανέρωσις τοῦ Πνεύματος πρὸς τὸ συμφέρον (1 Cor. xii. 7)?

§ 4. THEOLOGICAL AND HOMILETIC COMMENTARIES ON THE GOSPEL ACCORDING TO LUKE.

The great value of the third Gospel easily explains the large number of investigations and comments. We confine ourselves to such works as are specially devoted to Luke, and omit the general commentaries and works on the Bible, which include Luke among the rest.

Above many others we mention J. Piscator: *Analysis logica Evangelii secundum Lucam*, Siegen, 1596; Morus: *Prælect. in Lucæ Evang., ed. Donat.*, Lips. 1795; F. Schleiermacher: *Ueber die Schriften des Lukas, ein kritischer Versuch*, Berlin, 1817 [transl. into English by Bishop Thirlwall]; H. Planck: *Observationes quædam de Lucæ Evangelii analysi critica a Schleiermachero proposita*, Göttingen, 1819; K. W. Stein: *Commentar zu dem Evang. des Lukas*, Halle, 1830; F. A. Bornemann: *Scholia in Lucam ad supplendos reliquorum interpretum commentarios*, Lips. 1830; Lisko: *Die Parabeln, und Wunder Jesu*, 1836 and 1841; Lange: The Exposition of the Gospel of Luke in his *Leben Jesu*, 3d Part, 3d Division; R. Stier: *Die Reden Jesu nach Marcus und Lukas*, Barmen, 1844 [the same in English: *The Words of the Lord Jesus*, transl. by Rev. Wm. B. Pope, vols. iii. and iv. of the new Philad. ed.—P. S.]; J. ab Utrecht Dresselhuis: *Over het Evangelie van Lucas* (a crowned prize-essay of the Society of Haag *pro vindicanda religione Christiana*), 1839; J. da Costa: *Beschouwing v. het Ev. v. Lucas*, Amsterdam, 1850; Dr. H. E. Vinke: *Het Ev. v. Lucas met opheld. en toepass. aanmerkingen*, Utrecht, 1852; W. F. Besser: *Das Evangelium Lucæ in Bibelstunden für die Gemeinde ausgelegt*, 3d ed., Halle, 1854 [homiletical and practical]; Heubner: *Praktische Erklärung des Neuen Testaments*, 2d vol. containing the Gospel of Luke, Potsdam, 1856.

Among older commentaries the work of the Dutch divine Segaar: *Observationes philol. et theolog. in Evang. Lucæ capita priora*, Ultraject., 1766, should not be forgotten. Special treatises on single chapters and verses will be noticed at their proper places.

[The *English* and *American* commentaries on the Gospel of Luke are chiefly those contained in the general commentaries (either of the whole Bible or of the N. T., or at least of the Gospels) of Hammond, Whitby, Burkitt, Matthew Henry, John Gill, Adam Clarke, Scott, Doddridge, Bloomfield, Webster and Wilkinson, Alford, Wordsworth, Barnes, Owen, Crosby, Jacobus (and, in course of preparation, Nast, and Whedon). In addition to these we mention James Ford: *The Gospel of S. Luke illustrated* (*chiefly in the doctrinal and moral sense*) *from ancient and modern authors*, Lond. 1851 (684 pages); (N. N. Whiting:) *The Gospel according to Luke, translated from the Greek, on the basis of the Common Version, with (philological) Notes*. New York: Am. Bible Union, 1860.—Of the *Fathers* we have Homilies and imperfect Commentaries on Luke by Origen, Eusebius, Cyril of Alexandria (the last two first published by Cardinal Angelo Mai, in *Patrum Nova Bibliotheca ex Vat. Codd.* Rom. 1844, vols. ii. and iv.), Ambrose (tom. i. col. 1261–1544, in the Bened. ed. of Ambr. Opera, Par. 1686), and others. Jerome wrote a brief Commentary on all the Gospels (as also on the Epistles and the Apocalypse, and the greater part of the Old Testament); but his Commentary on Luke is rather superficial. See the Vallarsi edition of Jerome's works, tom. x. pp. 772–828. Of Chrysostom we have a series of Homilies on Matthew and John (in tom. vii. and viii. of Montfaucon's ed. of Chrys.), but none on Mark and Luke. The *Patristic* interpretations, including extracts from certain Homilies of Augustine, Gregory, Bede, etc., are conveniently (though not completely) brought together for the English reader in the Oxford translation of Thomas Aquinas' *Catena Patrum*, vol. iii. Part i. Oxford, 1843.—P. S.]

§ 5. FUNDAMENTAL IDEA AND ORGANIC ARRANGEMENT OR DIVISION OF THE GOSPEL ACCORDING TO LUKE.

"The second man is the Lord from heaven" (1 Cor. xv. 47). These words of Paul might well be chosen as the inscription of the most Pauline of all the Gospels. On the one hand, we are taught to see in Christ the Lord from heaven, whose miraculous conception in the womb of a virgin, and visible ascension after the accomplished victory, are far more minutely and precisely related by Luke than by any of his fellow-witnesses. On the other hand, he represents Him to us as the second, the perfect, the ideal man, in whom the saying, "*Homo sum, nil humani a me alienum puto,*" becomes a sacred reality. And beyond any of his fellow-laborers, does he portray the genuine human purity and beauty, the human love and pity, and the human dignity and glory, of our Lord; while he bears no less emphatic testimony to his Divinity. From ch. i. 4, 5; iii. 1, 2; ix. 28, and other passages, we learn that Luke aims more fully than Matthew or Mark at chronological order in the arrangement of events. The higher unity of the different parts is found in the central idea: Jesus Christ, *the Son of Man.*

Part First.

The Miraculous Birth and Normal Development of the Son of Man. (Ch. i. and ii.)

1st Section.—EVENTS PRECEDING THE BIRTH OF CHRIST (ch. i. 5–80).
    A. Annunciation of the birth of His forerunner (vers. 5–25).
    B. Annunciation of the birth of the Messiah (vers. 26–38).
    C. Hymns of praise, with which the expectation of the Messiah's birth and the actual birth of the Baptist are greeted (vers. 39–80).

2d Section.—THE HISTORY OF THE NATIVITY (ch. ii. 1–20).
    A. The highest gift of Heaven (ch. ii. 1–7).
    B. The first Gospel upon earth (vers. 8–12).
    C. Heaven and earth united in celebrating the Nativity (vers. 13–20).

3d Section.—THE HISTORY OF THE DEVELOPMENT OF THE SON OF MAN (ch. ii. 21–52).
    A. The eighth day; or, submission to the law (ver. 21).
    B. The fortieth day; or, the redemption from the service of the temple (vers. 22–40).
    C. The twelfth year; or, the growth in wisdom and favor (vers. 41–52).

Part Second.

The Beneficent Activity and Holy Pilgrimage of the Son of Man. (Ch. iii. 1–xix. 27.)

1st Section.—TESTIMONY BORNE TO MESSIAH* (ch. iii. and iv. 1–13).
    A. By the preaching and baptism of John (vers. 1–22).
    B. By the genealogy (vers. 23–38).
    C. In the wilderness (ch. iv. 1–13).

2d Section.—THE JOURNEYINGS OF JESUS (ch. iv. 14 to ix. 50).
    A. Nazareth (ch. iv. 16–30). The first rejection of the holy Son of Man by the sinful children of men.
    B. Capernaum (ch. iv. 31–vii. 50). The Prophet mighty in deed and word before God and all the people.

---

* [The German titles for the three sections are shorter than the translation: *Die Beglaubigung; die Wanderschaft; der Todesweg.*—P. S.]

§ 5. FUNDAMENTAL IDEA AND ORGANIC ARRANGEMENT. 9

    a. The first settlement, the first miracles, the first choice of Apostles at Capernaum (ch. iv. 31–v. 11).
    b. The first departure from Capernaum to journey in its neighborhood. The Son of Man the Physician of the sick, the Friend of the publicans, the Lord of the Sabbath, the Lawgiver of the kingdom of God (ch. v. 12–vi. 49).
    c. The first return to Capernaum; the first fruits of the believing Gentiles (ch. vii. 1–10).
    d. A second departure from Capernaum. The Son of Man manifested as a compassionate High-Priest at the gate of Nain, and at the table of Simon; and also as the holy Messiah, to the scandal of John, of the people, and of the Pharisees (vers. 11–50).
  C. Galilee and its neighborhood, including Capernaum (ch. viii. 1–ix. 50).
    a. The first Christian sisterhood (ch. viii. 1–3).
    b. The parables of the kingdom of God (vers. 4–21).
    c. The King of this kingdom, also the Lord of creation, of the world of spirits, and of death (vers. 22–56).
    d. The Son of Man proclaimed by the twelve Apostles, feared by Herod, honored by the multitude whom He had fed (ch. ix. 1–17).
    e. The glory of the Son of Man acknowledged on earth, and accredited by Heaven. The scenes on the summit and at the foot of Mount Tabor (vers. 18–50).

3d Section.—THE WAY OF DEATH (ch. ix. 51–xix. 27).
  A. The divine harmony exhibited in the Son of Man, and the four temperaments of the children of men (ch. ix. 51–62).
  B. The seventy disciples (ch. x. 1–24).
  C. Lessons of love, faith, and prayer (ch. x. 25–xi. 13).
  D. The Son of Man dealing with sanctimonious enemies and weak friends (ch. xi. 14–xii. 59).
  E. The Son of Man dealing with the sin of some and the misery of others (ch. xiii. 1–17).
  F. The nature of the kingdom of God; the way to the kingdom of God; the struggle for the kingdom of God (vers. 18–35).
  G. The Son of Man eating and drinking (ch. xiv. 1–24).
  H. The Son of Man opening His mouth in parables (ch. xiv. 25–xvii. 10).
  I. Journey in the borders of Samaria and Galilee, with the remarkable events occurring there (ch. xvii. 11–xviii. 14).
  K. Toward Jericho, in Jericho, from Jericho toward Jerusalem (ch. xviii. 15–xix. 27).

Part Third.

The last Conflict, and highest Glory of the Son of Man. (Ch. xix. 28–xxiv. 53.)

1st Section.—THE LAST CONFLICT (ch. xix. 28–xxiii. 56).
  A. The preparation for the conflict (ch. xix. 28–xxii. 38).
    a. The entrance into Jerusalem (ch. xix. 28–44).
    b. Disputes with His adversaries (ch. xx).
    c. Revelations and parting communications to His friends (ch. xxi–xxii. 36).
  B. The increase of the conflict (ch. xxii. 39–xxiii. 43).
    a. Gethsemane (ch. xxii. 39–53).
    b. Caiaphas (vers. 54–71).
    c. Pilate and Herod (ch. xxiii. 1–25).
    d. Golgotha (vers. 26–43).
  C. The end of the conflict (ch. xxiii. 44–56).
    a. The rest of death (vers. 44–46).

  b. The mourning of nature and humanity (vers. 47–49).
  c. The Sabbath of the grave (vers. 50–56).

2d Section.—THE COMPLETE TRIUMPH (ch. xxiv. 1–48).
 A. Over the power of death and of sin (vers. 1–10,).
 B. Over the doubts of unbelief (vers. 11–45).
 C. Over the opposition of Israel, and of the Gentile world (foretold), (vers. 46–48).

3d Section.—THE DAZZLING CROWN (ch. xxiv. 49–53).
 A. The promise of the Prophet (ver. 49).
 B. The blessing of the Priest (ver. 50).
 C. The glory of the King (vers. 51–53).

THE
GOSPEL ACCORDING TO LUKE.

THE HISTORIOGRAPHICAL PREFACE.

CHAPTER I. 1-4.

1 FORASMUCH[1] as many have taken in hand[2] to set forth in order [to draw up] a declaration [narration][3] of those things which are most surely believed [concerning the things
2 fulfilled][4] among us, Even[5] as they [those] delivered them [handed them down, παρέδωσαν] unto us, which [who] from the beginning were eye-witnesses [οἱ ἀπ' ἀρχῆς
3 αὐτόπται], and ministers of the word; It seemed good to me also, having had perfect understanding of all things from the very first [having accurately traced down all things from the first, παρηκολουθηκότι ἄνωθεν πᾶσιν ἀκριβῶς],[6] to write unto thee in order,[7] most
4 excellent [most noble, κράτιστε][8] Theophilus, That thou mightest know [know accurately, ἐπιγνῷς] the certainty of those things [words, or doctrines, λόγων][9] wherein thou hast been instructed [catechized].[10]

[1 Vs. 1.—*Forasmuch*, antique but not antiquated form for *inasmuch*, *in consideration of*, *since*, well corresponds to ἐπειδήπερ (only here in the N. T.), which is more full-sounding and grave than ἐπειδή, like *quoniam quidem* and the German *sintemal* in Luther's and de Wette's versions, which van Oosterzee exchanged for *nachdem*.

[2] Vs. 1.—Or *undertaken*, *attempted*, ἐπεχείρησαν, which, not of itself (Origen, Ambrose, Theophylact), but in connection with ver. 3 (Meyer), implies the insufficiency of the older διηγήσεις.

[3] Vs. 1.—Ἀνατάξασθαι διήγησιν, *to draw up*, *to arrange*, *to compose a narration* (Rheims Version, Alford), or *narrative*, *history* (Genevan B.). The improper version: *declaration*, is from Cranmer's Bible.

[4] Vs. 1.—Διήγησιν περὶ τῶν πεπληροφορημένων ἐν ἡμῖν πραγμάτων. Dr. van Oosterzee (following de Wette, in the third ed. of his *Commentary on Luke*): *eine Erzählung von den unter uns (Christen) vollständig gewordenen Geschichten;* Vulgate: *quæ in nobis completa sunt;* Meyer: *welche vollendet sind unter uns*. So also Luther, Hammond, Bretschneider, Ebrard, etc. But the Peschito, Theophylact, Beza, Grotius, Kuinoel, Olshausen, Ewald, Alford explain with all the older English Versions, except those of Wiclif and Rheims: *quæ satis atque abunde nobis probata sunt, quæ sunt compertissima, certainly,* or *fully believed*, or *certified*. The verb πληροφορέω means: (1) *to bring out fully, to complete, to fulfil* (like πληρόω, which is the word used in this sense very often in the N. T.); (2) in the passive: *to be fully assured* or *persuaded:* so Rom. iv. 21; xiv. 5 (comp. also the noun πληροφορία, *full assurance;* Col. ii. 2; 1 Thess. i. 5; Heb. vi. 11; x. 22). But in this second sense the verb is used of *persons* only, and not of *things*, πράγματα, as would be the case here according to the Authorized E. V. It is improper to speak of *things* fully persuaded. Another objection to the Authorized Version is, that the full assurance, or πληροφορία, of the gospel history could not be taken for granted at the outset, but was to be effected in the mind of Theophilus by the narrative of Luke, comp. ver. 4. Meyer brings the expression into pragmatic connection with the following ἀπ' ἀρχῆς, ver. 2. The accomplished facts of the gospel history are regarded as standing in close contact with the events of the apostolic age, so that they were completed among those who, like Luke and Timothy, were no more immediate witnesses to the life of Christ.

[5] Vs. 2.—*Even*, which dates from Tyndale, is not required by the Greek καθώς, and is omitted by Wiclif, the Rheims Version, and the N. T. of the Am. B. U.

[6] Vs. 3.—Παρακολουθεῖν, *to follow up, to trace down* (by research), and so *to know fully*, is used in precisely the same sense by Demosthenes, *Pro corona*, p. 285: παρηκολουθηκότα τοῖς πράγμασιν ἐξ ἀρχῆς, κ.τ.λ. Comp. Alford *in loc.*, Tyndale, and Cranmer: *as I had searched out diligently all things from the beginning;* Genevan B.: *learned perfectly all things from the beginning.* I prefer to retain *from the first* (or *from the very first* in the C. V.), ἄνωθεν, to distinguish it from ἀπ' ἀρχῆς, ver. 2. See EXEGETICAL and CRITICAL NOTES.

[7] Vs. 3.—Or *consecutively*, καθεξῆς. Genevan B.: *from point to point*.

[8] Vs. 3.—Κράτιστος is here and often an official title, like our *honorable*. Hence *honorable*, or *most noble* (Genevan B.), is preferable to *excellent*, which is apt to be applied to moral character. The E. V. renders the word twice *most excellent*, here and Acts xxiii. 6, and twice *most noble*, Acts xxiv. 3; xxvi. 25.

[9] Vs. 4.—Van Oosterzee, Luther, de Wette, Meyer, etc., render λόγοι here *doctrines;* the Latin Vulgate, Wiclif, Rheims Version, van Ess: *words;* Beza, Kuinoel, and all the older Protestant English versions: *res, things:* Alford: *histories, accounts.* The living words and doctrines of Christ are meant, which rest upon the great facts of the gospel history and derive from them their ἀσφάλεια. For Christianity is not simply a system of doctrines, but first of all a system of divine human facts of salvation, God manifest in the flesh, living, dying, rising, and ever living for us.

[10] Vs. 4.—Lit.: *catechized, catechetically taught*, κατηχήθης. The specific word should have been retained here and elsewhere instead of the more indefinite *instruct* or *teach.* Catechizing is a primitive and most important institution of the Church, and a preparatory school for full membership. Archbishop Usher says: "The neglect of catechizing is the frustrating of the whole work of the ministry."—P. S.]

EXEGETICAL AND CRITICAL.

Vs. 1. **Have taken in hand.**—The expression is happily chosen, to enhance the importance and difficulty of the work, which many (πολλοί) had undertaken. It seems almost adventurous, in Luke's eyes, to take up the pen for such a composition. Yet does he by no means intend to commence his work by blaming his predecessors, but rather, by the word κἀμοί, **to me also** (ver. 3), he places himself in their ranks. It is nevertheless obvious, that if he had considered their labors perfectly satisfactory, he would not have felt impelled to attempt his present composition. With reason, therefore, does Origen write (see Hieronymus, *Homilia I. in Lucam*): "*Hoc quod ait:* 'CONATI SUNT,' *latentem habet accusationem eorum, qui absque gratia Spiritus sancti ad scribenda Evangelia prosilierunt. Matthaus quippe et Marcus et Johannes et Lucas non sunt* CONATI *scribere, sed* SCRIPSERUNT."
Many.—It is perfectly arbitrary to refer this to the apocryphal Gospels, which were the product of later times. Luke had in view rather the very earliest literary attempts, made by persons more or less authorized, at the commencement of the apostolic age; and it may be reasonably concluded from this preface, that, during the composition of his Gospel, he had before him many written documents and records (διηγήσεις), which, when they seemed worthy of acceptation, he incorporated in its pages. *The relative coincidence between this and the two former Gospels is certainly most simply accounted for, by supposing them to have been freely drawn from common sources.* The very comparison of this literary preface (ch. i. 1–4), written in pure Greek, with the immediately succeeding history of events before Christ's birth (ch. i. 5–80), abounding in Hebraisms, would lead to the supposition, that the latter was derived from some more ancient record. Concluding expressions, which seem originally to have stood at the end of shorter narratives, are also found in various places; *e. g.*, ch. i. 80; ii. 20, 52; iv. 13, etc. It was Schleiermacher who first directed attention to these facts; but he pushed his conclusion from them too far, when he considered Luke as almost exclusively a compiler and arranger, and allowed too little for the influence of his individuality in the selection and treatment of his materials.

Vs. 2. **As they delivered them to us.**—This delivering (παράδοσις) is here certainly the oral tradition, which formed the basis of the *written* Gospels, and contained the matter of the ἀνάταξις, which had already been attempted, with various degrees of success. It began with the baptism of John, and the public ministry of Jesus (Acts i. 21 and John xv. 27), and did not originally include the narratives either of His birth or childhood; though Matthew and Luke could have found no difficulty in obtaining accounts of these from authentic sources. The eye-witnesses and ministers here mentioned, are the same persons, viz., the original Apostles; and **the word** here spoken of is by no means the personal *Logos*—for no interpreter can be justified in thus confusing the respective senses in which Luke and John employ the same term—but the word of the Gospel, delivered by them to Luke and his fellow-laborers.

Vs. 3. **It seemed good to me also.**—The addition of some old translators, *mihi et Spiritui sancto*, the product of a theory of mechanical inspiration, is not needed, to make us conscious that we have, in the Gospel of Luke, a striking revelation of the true Spirit of Christ.
Having accurately traced down all things from the very first.—This **very first** (ἄνωθεν) reaches farther back, as may be seen by the first two chapters, than the **from the beginning** (ἀπ' ἀρχῆς) of ver. 2. Paul uses the same word in Acts xxvi. 5 to designate the beginning of his life among the Jews, before his conversion. Luke, who, according to Acts xxi. 17, saw James at Jerusalem, might have become acquainted, through him, with Mary or the so-called brothers of the Lord, and have learned much from them. The conjecture of a Dutch divine (Dresselhuis), that Luke, in writing the history of the Nativity, made use of an original written narrative, by James the brother of our Lord, which was afterward lost, and replaced by the apocryphal Gospel of James (Protevangelium Jacobi), deserves mention.
Most noble (or honorable) Theophilus.—For the various conjectures that have been made concerning the pedigree, dwelling-place, and rank of this Christian, *see* Winer, *art. Theophilus*. We feel most inclined to favor the supposition which fixes his residence in Italy, and perhaps in Rome. For why is Luke so increasingly precise (Acts xxvii. and xxviii.) in topographical hints, as his narrative is hastening to its close, unless this locality were better known to his friend and first reader, than any other? From Acts xxiii. 8, we may conclude that Theophilus was not of Jewish extraction. Whether he had already made a profession of Christianity, in which he had at first been instructed, must remain uncertain. Κράτιστος was probably a civil official title.

In order.—It does not appear from the word itself, whether by καθεξῆς is to be understood the order of time, or of things. It may denote both; *see* Acts iii. 24, and xi. 4. Since, however, the καθεξῆς γράφειν is spoken of as a result of the ἄνωθεν παρακολουθεῖν, and Luke often shows that he is aiming at chronological exactness, we are inclined to prefer the former meaning. This does not, however, necessarily imply that he always had this exactness equally in view, nor that he was always equally successful in attaining it.

Vs. 4. **Wherein thou hast been catechized.**—One of the earliest historical traces of ancient Christian catechizing, of which, according to verses 1 and 2, the history of our Lord formed the basis. Thereon, however, were built specific Christian λόγοι, whose doctrinal θεμέλιον, or foundation, is pointed out, Heb. vi. 1, 2. These λόγοι could not remain unshaken, unless the most important facts of the gospel history were distinctly understood, and their truth recognized as beyond all doubt. The various, and, perhaps, often contradictory, accounts of these facts, which came to the ears of Theophilus, furnished Luke with a motive for strict historical research, that his friend might know the ἀσφάλεια of the Christian ἀλήθεια.

[This historiographic preface, vers. 1–4, is a model of brevity, simplicity, and modesty, as well as of purity and dignity of style. ALFORD remarks: "The peculiar style of this preface—which is purer Greek than the contents of the Gospel, and also more labored and formal—may be accounted for, partly because it is the composition of the Evangelist himself, and not translated from the Hebrew sources like the rest, and partly because prefaces, especially when also dedicatory, are usually in a rounded and artificial style." The difference of the periodic Greek style of the preface and the simple Hebraizing language of the following narrative is very striking, and shows the conscientious use of the Hebrew traditions or writings on the history of the infancy. Yet these sources were not slavishly translated, but fully appropriated by Luke and interwoven with the peculiarities of his own style which are found even in the first two chapters. Comp. CREDNER: *Einleitung*, i. p. 132 ff.; WILKE: *Rhetorik*, p. 451; EWALD: *Bibl. Jahrbücher*, ii. p. 183; MEYER *in loc.*, and Doctrinal Note 5 below.—P. S.]

DOCTRINAL AND ETHICAL.

1. We see that, even in the first decades of the apostolic age, many felt themselves authorized, or rather compelled, to take up the pen, to instruct their contemporaries and successors with respect to the things that had happened concerning Jesus of Nazareth; and this in an age and country in which the modern passion for writing was entirely unknown. How can this enthusiasm be accounted for, unless the history of the crucified Jesus were the most remarkable and most glorious of all histories? It is perfectly inexplicable how Christ could have set so many tongues, hearts, and pens in motion, if He had not been something more than the modern criticism of a Strauss, or of the Tübingen school, [or Renan] would make Him. Comp. Acts iv. 20; 2 Cor. iv. 13.

2. Even during the lifetime of the Apostles, the need of an accurate, well-arranged life of Jesus, which should be the work of some competent and duly authorized agent, was felt. And if oral tradition was thus early in danger of becoming corrupted (comp. John xxi. 22, 23), how little certainty concerning the Christian revelation should we now possess without the written testimony! Oral tradition is undoubtedly more ancient than the written gospel; nor was the Church exclusively founded upon the latter. But who could instruct us with any certainty, with respect to the contents of the apostolic παράδοσις, without access to the γραφή? Luke, indeed, wrote his Gospel only for Theophilus and his immediate circle; but the question is not concerning the intentions of Luke, but concerning the design of his glorified Lord, under whose special guidance this Gospel was at first composed, and has since been preserved, for the edification of all succeeding ages.

3. Luke speaks of his study of the human sources of information; he says nothing of his divine inspiration. Are we then to conclude that he was unconscious of the latter, or that it was rendered superfluous by the former? By no means; but rather, in this case, the maxim: *subordinata non pugnant* holds good. The Holy Spirit, through whose operation he first became a believer in Christ, and afterward a fellow-laborer with Paul, did surely not forsake him, but descended upon him in far more abundant measure, when he took up the pen to bear testimony for his Lord in this more permanent form for all ages to come. Paul has not said in vain: "God is not the author of confusion, but of order;" and the possession of supernatural power, by no means supersedes the use of natural assistance.*

4. The grand distinction between Christianity and all systems of philosophy, and all other religions, so called, consists in this, that it is not a mere system of notions, but a series of facts. Its first promulgators could all adopt, as their own, the words of John: "That which we have *seen* and *heard* declare we unto you" (1 John i. 1–3). It is this that makes it *everlasting;* for deeds once done can never be altered: it is this that makes it *universal;* for duly accredited facts fall within the reach of those also who could not follow a chain of abstract reasoning: it is this that makes it so *mighty;* for simple facts are stronger than the most elaborate arguments. That a thorough investigation of these facts is a duty, may be taught us by Luke; but their reality being once ascertained, it results, from his words to Theophilus, that the ἀσφάλεια of the faith can no longer be called in question. Would that they who, in reading the Gospel narratives, have continually in their mouths the words, myth, tradition, legend, might enter into the spirit of Luke's prologue, and, after due research, might feel and experience that here, if anywhere, they are treading on the firm ground of the most unquestionable reality!

[5. Luke is the only one of the Synoptists who begins his Gospel with a Preface. His preface is historico-critical, while the Introduction of John is historico-doctrinal. The prominent points in this short *Preface* are: (1) It cautions us against erroneous or defective statements of facts; (2) it directs us to the apostles as eye-witnesses of the life of Christ; (3) it proves the faithfulness of the Evangelist in tracing the facts to the primitive source; (4) it brings out the *human* side in the origin of the sacred writings; showing that the Evangelists were not passive instruments, but free, conscious, intelligent, and co-operative agents of the Holy Spirit in producing these books; (5) it teaches that "faith cometh by hearing," and that the gospel was first taught by catechetical instruction or oral tradition, but then written down by reliable witnesses for all ages to come. This written gospel is essentially the same with the preached gospel of Christ and the Apostles, and together with the Epistles is to us the only pure and infallible source of primitive Christianity.—P. S.]

[6. AMBROSE: *Scriptum est Evangelium ad Theophilum, hoc est, ad eum quem Deus diligit. Si Deum diligis, ad te scriptum est.* If you are a lover of God, a Theophilus, it is written to thee. JAMES FORD: The name *Theophilus* imports the temper of mind which God will bless in the Scripture student; "charity edifieth" (1 Cor. viii. 1); and who are the *most excellent* of the earth, but they whose minds are most imbued with this divine love, with this knowledge of the Lord?—P. S.]

HOMILETICAL AND PRACTICAL.

Luke a physician, like the few; Theophilus a patient, like the many.—Historical belief in the divine truth of Christianity: 1. Its necessity; 2. its certainty; 3. its insufficiency, when unaccompanied by

---

* ["Nature and the supernatural together constitute the one system of God." This sentence, which Dr. HORACE BUSHNELL has chosen as the title of his book on *Nature and the Supernatural*, may be applied also to the doctrine of inspiration. The Bible is the result of divine inspiration and of human labor, and is *theanthropic*, like the person of Christ. See the Preface to the Am. ed. of Lange, vol. i. p. v. MATTHEW HENRY remarks on Luke's Preface: "It is certain that Luke was moved by the Holy Ghost not only *to* the writing, but *in* the writing of it (his Gospel); but in both he was moved as a *reasonable creature*, and not as a mere machine."—P. S.]

a living faith.—Luke: 1. The predecessor of believing searchers; 2. the condemner of unbelieving searchers of Scripture.—The history of the Son of Man, the beginning and foundation of a new world of literature.—The highest aim which a Christian author can propose to himself: to correct what is faulty, to strengthen what is weak, to arrange what is confused.—The spoken word, the first testimony and announcement of the truths of salvation, and the foundation of all future testimony to the Lord and His kingdom.—Assured faith indispensably necessary to those who would bring others to the knowledge of faith.—Assured faith the aim of Christian instruction.—From faith to knowledge, from knowledge to still firmer faith.*—Civil dignities and honors not destroyed, but ennobled, by citizenship in the kingdom of God.—Luke a pattern of profitable trading with intellectual gifts and power in the Christian cause.—The criticism of faith, and the faith of criticism.—"Not for that we have dominion over your faith, but are helpers of your joy" (2 Cor. i. 24).

STARKE:—In a good cause, imitation is a good work.—Nothing should be undertaken inconsiderately, especially in important matters (Prov. xix. 2).—Full assurance and conviction are necessary for writing or speaking with comfort.—The fear of God makes men truly great and excellent.

HEUBNER:—The providence of God in raising up sincere, earnest, and credible men, for the task of writing the history of Jesus Christ.—The end of Christian authors should be the promotion of Christianity. The real value of an author proportionate to his attainment of this end.

* [The author has in mind, no doubt, the famous maxim of Augustine, Anselm, and Schleiermacher: *Fides praecedit intellectum, faith precedes knowledge*, and supplies it by the equally correct principle, that *true Christian knowledge confirms and increases faith*. There is a reciprocal friendly relation between πίστις and γνῶσις. Anselm recognized the latter truth also. For while he said, on the one hand: *Neque enim quaero intelligere ut credam, sed credo ut intelligam*, he laid down the principle, on the other hand: *Negligentiae mihi videtur si quae credimus, non studemus intelligere.* Such study, far from leading away from faith, confirms and strengthens it.—P. S.]

PART FIRST.

The Miraculous Birth and Normal Development of the Son of Man.

FIRST SECTION.

EVENTS PREPARATORY TO THE BIRTH OF CHRIST.

CHAPTER I. 5–80.

A. *Annunciation of the Birth of His Forerunner.* CH. I. 5–25.

5 There was, in the days of Herod, the king of Judea, a certain priest named Zacharias,¹ of the course of Abia: and his wife *was* [he had a wife]² of the daughters of
6 Aaron, and her name *was* Elisabeth. And they were both righteous before God, walk-
7 ing in all the commandments and ordinances of the Lord blameless. And they had no child, because that Elisabeth was barren; and they both were *now* well stricken [far advanced] in years.
8 And it came to pass, that, while he executed the priest's office [ἐν τῷ ἱερατεύειν] be-
9 fore God in the order of his course, According to the custom of the priest's office [of the priesthood, τῆς ἱερατείας],³ his lot was to burn incense when he went into the temple
10 of the Lord. And the whole multitude of the people were praying without at the time
11 [the hour, τῇ ὥρᾳ] of incense. And there appeared unto him an angel of the Lord
12 standing on the right side of the altar of incense. And when Zacharias saw *him*, he
13 was troubled, and fear fell upon him. But the angel said unto him, Fear not, Zacharias: for thy prayer is heard; and thy wife Elisabeth shall bear thee a son, and thou
14 shalt call his name John. And thou shalt have joy and gladness; and many shall re-
15 joice at his birth. For he shall be great in the sight of the Lord, and shall drink neither wine nor strong drink; and he shall be filled with the Holy Ghost, even from his

CHAP. I. 5–25.   15

16 mother's womb. And many of the children of Israel shall he turn to the Lord their
17 God. And he shall go before Him in the spirit and power of Elias [Elijah], to turn the hearts of the fathers to the children, and the disobedient to the wisdom of the just; to make ready a people prepared for the Lord.
18 ·And Zacharias said unto the angel, Whereby shall I know this? for I am an old
19 man, and my wife well stricken [far advanced] in years. And the angel answering, said unto him, I am Gabriel, that stand in the presence of God; and am sent to speak
20 unto thee, and to show [bring] thee these glad tidings. And, behold, thou shalt be dumb, and not able to speak, until the day that these things shall be performed, because thou believest not [didst not believe, οὐκ ἐπίστευσας] my words, which shall be fulfilled in their season.
21 And the people waited [were waiting, ἦν ὁ λαὸς προσδοκῶν] for Zacharias, and mar-
22 velled [wondered, ἐθαύμαζον] that he tarried so long in the temple. And when he came out, he could not speak unto them: and they perceived that he had seen a vision
23 in the temple; for he beckoned unto them, and remained speechless. And it came to pass, that, as soon as the days of his ministration were accomplished [completed], he departed to his own house.
24 And after those days his wife Elisabeth conceived, and hid herself five months, say-
25 ing, Thus hath the Lord dealt with me in the days wherein He looked on *me*, to take away my reproach among men.

(¹ Vs. 5.—As a question of principle, I would advocate a uniform spelling of Scripture names, conforming Hebrew names as much as possible to the Hebrew, and Greek names to the Greek original. This would require an alteration of *Zacharias* into *Zachariah, Abia* into *Abijah, Elias* into *Elijah, Jeremy* into *Jeremiah*, etc. But as *Zacharias* occurs so often in this chapter, I left it undisturbed. Comp. my *Critical Note* to *Commentary on Matthew*, i. 10, vol. i. p. 48.
² Vs. 5.—The E. V. follows the *textus rec.* and Cod. A.: ἡ γυνὴ αὐτοῦ (*uxor illius*). But the best uncial MSS. (Sinait., B., C.*, D., L., X.), and the modern critical editions of Lachmann, Tischendorf, Alford, and Tregelles, read γυνὴ (without the article) αὐτῷ, *uxor illi, he had a wife;* and so also van Oosterzee in his German Version: *er hatte ein Weib*. The received text is a correction for perspicuity sake. The other differences of reading in this section are still less insignificant and not worth mentioning in this *Commentary*, as they are also passed by in the original. *See* the Critical Apparatus in Tischendorf's Greek Testament, editio septima of 1859, and Tregelles' Greek Testament, Part ii., containing Luke and John.
³ Vs. 9.—Van Oosterzee likewise observes the (unessential) distinction between ἱερατεύειν, ver. 8, and ἱερατεία, ver. 9, and renders (with Luther) the first *Priesteramt*, the second *Priesterthum*. The Latin Vulgate, however, has in both cases *sacerdotium*, and de Wette *Priesteramt*. The E. V. renders ἱερατεία, which occurs twice in the Greek Testament, the *priest's office*, Luke i. 9, and the *office of the priesthood*, Heb. vii. 5, and ἱεράτευμα, *priesthood*, 1 Pet. ii. 5, 9.— P. S.)

EXEGETICAL AND CRITICAL.

Vs. 5. **In the days of Herod.**—*See* remarks on Matt. ii. 1.
A certain priest.—Zachariah has been supposed, on insufficient grounds, to have been the high-priest. It is worthy of remark, how the meaning of both the names (Zachariah, *i. e., the Lord remembers;* and Elisabeth, *i. e., God's oath*) was explained and fulfilled by what happened to those who bore them.
Of the course (class) of Abijah.—The descendants of Eleazar and Ithamar, the sons of Aaron, were exclusively called to the service of the sanctuary, and divided into four and twenty classes or orders (1 Chron. xxiv.), each of which ministered in the temple during a week. The descendants of Eleazar, the elder son, formed sixteen of these classes or courses; those of Ithamar, the younger, only eight, —that of Abijah being (1 Chron. xxiv. 10) the eighth. From the days of Solomon, these four and twenty courses relieved each other weekly in the temple-service; it is, therefore, not to be wondered at, that attempts have frequently been made to ascertain the exact time of the year at which the Lord was born, by means of the chronological date of the week of the course of Abijah. The result of these researches, made chiefly by Scaliger, Solomon van Til, and Bengel, is communicated and criticised by Wieseler (*Chronologische Synopse*, pp. 140–145). It is, however, self-evident, that all such calculations must be uncertain and rash, until it can first be proved that the pregnancy of Elisabeth commenced *immediately* on the return of Zachariah, and that the several courses continued, each *suo loco et tempore*, to perform their services in unintermitted succession.

Vs. 6. **Righteous before God.**—A declaration not only of their truly Israelitish and theocratic character, but also that they were persons to whom the divine approval pronounced upon Noah, Gen. vii. 1, might rightly be applied, and who knew, from their own experience, the "blessedness" of which David sung in Ps. xxxii. When the promise made to Abraham is on the point of fulfilment, we suddenly find that the true Abrahamic character (Gen. xv. 6; xvii. 1), however rare, has by no means utterly disappeared in Israel.

Vs. 9. **According to the custom of the priesthood.**—In the service of the sanctuary, nothing was left to accident, or to human arrangement. The *lot* determined who was to perform each separate portion of the sacred service, and, especially, who was each morning and evening to burn incense before the Lord. This office was considered exceedingly important and honorable. According to Josephus (*Antiq. Jud.* xiii. 10), a heavenly vision was also vouchsafed to John Hyrcanus during its performance. It seems impossible, however, to determine whether the vision of Zachariah took place at the time of the morning or evening offering.

Vs. 10. **Were praying.**—The pious were accustomed to unite in the outer court (ἔξω) in silent supplication, while the priest in the sanctuary offered the incense, which was ever regarded as the symbol of acceptable prayer. Comp. Ps. cxli. 2; Rev. v. 8; viii. 3, 4.

Vs. 11. **There appeared unto him.**—It may be taken for granted, that the quiet and solitary sojourn of Zachariah in the Holy Place had both quickened and elevated his susceptibility for beholding the angelic appearance; yet the narrative certainly bears no traces of any ecstatic state, properly so called. Indeed, the fact which he must have told himself, that he saw the angel, "standing at the *right* side of the altar of incense" (which he may have considered a good omen), vouches for his clearness of perception, and sobriety of mind.

Vs. 13. **Thy prayer is heard.**—It is generally thought, that the secret prayer of Zachariah for a son, known to God, and long uttered in vain, is here intended. But would the aged Zachariah have limited himself to this request? Did no higher aspiration, than a merely personal one, arise from the heart of a priest in the Holy Place? Must not Zachariah have been among the προσδεχόμενοι λύτρωσιν ἐν Ἱερουσαλήμ, spoken of ch. ii. 38? And is it not therefore probable, that the chief matter of his prayer might be expressed by the words of the Psalmist (Ps. xiv. 7): "Oh that the salvation of Israel were come out of Sion?" For all these reasons, we conclude, with Meyer, that the prayer of the priest had special reference to the coming of Messiah. A twofold answer to this prayer is promised: first, that Messiah shall indeed appear in his days; and secondly, that he shall himself be the father of the forerunner, who was to prepare His way (Mal. iv.)—an honor he could not have ventured to anticipate. Zachariah sought first the kingdom of God and His righteousness, and all other things—earthly joy of a father, etc.—are added to him (Matt. vi. 33).

John.—Hebr.: *Jochanan* (*i. e.*, *God is gracious;* equivalent to the German *Gotthold*). According to an old Greek glossary: Ἰωάννης, ἐν ᾧ ἐστιν ἡ χάρις. The name of the forerunner, as well as that of Jesus (Matt. i. 21), was prescribed before his birth. Was this distinction vouchsafed also to the mother of our Lord, whose name has since been so idolized?

Vs. 15. **He shall be great in the sight of the Lord.**—Truly great, then; for just what a man is in God's eyes, that is he indeed, neither more nor less. A silent hint also, that no earthly greatness is to be expected; for "that which is highly esteemed before men is an abomination in the sight of the Lord."

He shall drink neither wine nor strong drink.—Plainly referring to the condition of the Nazarites, for the origin and laws concerning whom, *see* Num. vi. Acts xxi. 24 shows that such vows were not unusual in Israel in New Testament times. This appointment places the forerunner, in this respect also, on a level with Samson and Samuel, who, as well as himself, were born to their parents contrary to all natural hopes and expectations.

From his mother's womb—*i. e.*, not merely *inde a puero*, according to Kuinoel's lax interpretation, but before he shall have seen the light of life (comp. ver. 41), from his earliest origin.

Vs. 17. **In the spirit and power of Elijah.**—An evident reference to the last of the prophets, Mal. iii. 1; iv. 5, 6, whose words are thus endorsed by the angel. The expression, "*the Lord their God*," ver. 16, alludes not exclusively to the Messiah, but to the Jehovah of Israel, of whom it is said, that He Himself should appear in glory when the divinely commissioned Messiah should come into the world. The true subjects of Messiah are also the "*people prepared for the Lord*," the God of Israel.

To turn the hearts of the fathers to the children.—The feeling of the paternal relationship had grown cold in many hearts, in the midst of the moral corruption of Israel: when the forerunner lifts up his voice, the ties of family affection shall be strengthened. Others interpret this, to restore to the children the devout disposition of their fathers.

Vs. 18. **For I am an old man.**—According to the law of Moses the Levites were not permitted to serve beyond their fiftieth year, Num. iv. 3; viii. 24. But this law did not apply to the priests, and Zachariah was probably much older than fifty. His objection seems, in itself, as natural as that of Mary, ver. 34; but the Lord, who sees the heart, knows how to distinguish between the objections of unbelief, and the natural questionings of innocence.

Vs. 19. **I am Gabriel.**—An answer full of dignity, and at the same time perfectly intelligible to a priest well instructed in the Holy Scriptures, who would recognize, by this name, the heavenly messenger, revealed to Daniel (viii. 16; ix. 21) as one admitted to very intimate relations with the Godhead. The belief in different classes of angels, though a development of later days, was the fruit of direct revelation. They who look on the Book of Daniel as the invention of a later age, cannot credit his angelology; and the angelic world, which was opened to Zachariah and to Mary, is closed to them, as a punishment of their unbelief.

Vs. 20. **Thou shalt be dumb, and not able to speak.**—This is no mere repetition, but the first member of the sentence is the consequence of the second. The notion, that a natural dumbness, arising from an apoplectic stroke, is here meant, is one of those curiosities of Rationalism, which have only an antiquarian interest.

Vs. 21. **And the people were waiting for Zachariah.**—According to many interpreters, they were waiting to receive the blessing. It does not, however, appear that this was always the office of the priest who offered incense. It seems more probable, that, not being accustomed to find the priest remain longer in the sanctuary than was strictly necessary, some might have feared, when Zachariah had been some time expected in vain, that some misfortune, or sign of the divine displeasure, had befallen him.

Vs. 22. **They perceived that he had seen a vision.**—Dumbness having fallen upon him in the temple, it was a natural supposition, that this might be the result of an angelic appearance. Zachariah makes signs that the supposition is correct. Interpreters have given due prominence to the symbolic signification of this moment in the sacred history. Bengel says: "*Zacharias, mutus, excludebatur tantisper ab actionibus sacerdotalibus. Præludium legis ceremonialis finiendæ, Christo veniente.*"—Chemnitz: "When the voice of the preacher (Isa. xl.) is announced, the priesthood of the Old Testament becomes silent. The Levitical blessing is silenced, when the Seed comes, in whom 'all the families of the earth are blessed.'"

Vs. 24. **And she hid herself five months.**—Neither, as it seems to us, from shame on account of her advanced age, nor to secure rest, nor from unbelief, nor for the sake of observing an ascetic retirement, and then suddenly making her situation known; but to leave to God, through whose extraordinary intervention she found herself in this condition, the care of making it manifest, and of taking away her reproach among men (comp. ver. 25). There is a remarkable coincidence in the frame of mind of Elisabeth and Mary, under similar circumstances. Elisabeth was συγγενής to Mary, not merely κατὰ σάρκα, but also κατὰ πνεῦμα.

DOCTRINAL AND ETHICAL.

1. "*Introite, et hic Dii sunt*," seems to resound in the ear of the believer, as Luke leads him into the sanctuary of the gospel history. We are indebted to the fact, that he begins his previous narrative at an earlier period than Matthew, for the advantage of recognizing fresh proofs of the "manifold wisdom of God," in the course of events which preceded the birth of the Lord. The new revelation of salvation begins in the days of Herod, when sin and misery had reached their climax, and when the yearning for Messiah's appearance was more intensely felt than ever. The temple, so often the scene of the manifestation of the glory of the Lord, becomes again the centre, whence the first rays of light secretly break through the darkness. Every circumstance, preceding the birth of John, testifies to a special providence of God. He is born of pious parents, and of priestly blood, that the genuine theocratic spirit may be awakened and produced in the forerunner of the Lord. He is trained for his high destination, not in corrupt Jerusalem, but in the retirement of a remote city of the priests (ver. 39). It is not revealed to all, that the voice of "him that crieth" shall soon resound over hill and valley. The first witness to this is only the pious old man, who greets the prophet as his child. An angel assures Zachariah of the distinction conferred upon him. What human tongue could have foretold it to him; or how could he have ventured to hearken to the voice of his own heart, without direct revelation? The angel appears to him in the retirement of the sanctuary, while he is employed in the faithful discharge of his priestly office, and standing on the *right* side of the altar, he intimates that the days are past in which the appearance of beings from another world betokened death and destruction to mankind. To enhance his enjoyment of it, the blessing is announced as an answer to prayer; and the very name given to the child, speaks to him of the graciousness of his God. As a son begotten in old age, John ranks with Isaac; as granted to the barren in answer to prayer, with Samson and Samuel. His office and mission are stated in words which must have recalled to Zachariah the prophecy of Malachi; while the description of his habits, as those of a Nazarite, and of his character, as in the spirit of Elijah, must have pointed out to his father a life of sorrow and strife. And when the astonished priest desires a sign, his want of faith is visited with a proof of the severity, but at the same time of the goodness, of God. As faith is to be the chief condition of the new covenant, it was needful that the first manifestation of unbelief should be emphatically punished; but the wound inflicted becomes a healing medicine for the soul. Zachariah is constrained to much silent reflection, and, according to the counsel of God, the secret is still kept for a time. The sight of the priest struck dumb, awakens among the people an expectation of some great and heavenly event; and soon will "the things" done in the priest's house be "noised abroad throughout all the hill-country of Judæa" (ver. 65).

2. So many traces of divine wisdom are apparent in the narrative, that scepticism itself has no exceptions to make, but to its miraculous character. In this case the appearance of an angel is especially offensive to the tastes and notions of modern criticism. This being the first account of the kind, which we meet with in Luke's Gospel, we may be allowed the following remarks. The existence of a higher world of spirits, can as little be proved, as denied, by any *a priori* reasoning; experience and history can alone decide the point. Now it is certain, on purely historical and critical grounds, that angels have been both soon and heard by well-known and credible individuals; and if this be so, a higher world of spirits must exist. It has, indeed, been said (by Schleiermacher), that belief in the existence of angels has no necessary basis and support in the religious self-consciousness (or subjective experience) of the believer;[*] but the question here is merely concerning the historical truth of biblical angelology, and not concerning the subjective experience it produces. Angels are not merely "transient emanations and effulgences of the divine essence" (Olshausen); but personal, conscious, holy beings, related, like men, to the Father of spirits. God, being the supreme and absolute Spirit, is able to employ such λειτουργικὰ πνεύματα in His service; and man, having received a spiritual element from God, cannot lack the ability of perceiving, with an enlightened eye, the appearance of beings so nearly related to himself. It is not when the bodily eye has been directed to the material world, but when a higher and more spiritual organ has been developed, and the ear opened to the voice of God, in the hours of prayer and solitude, that angelic appearances have been perceived. This power of perception, produced by God Himself, must be distinguished from the trance or vision, properly so called, wherein angels have sometimes, but by no means always, been perceived. Comp. Acts x. 10; 2 Cor. xii. 1 ff. The angelic apparitions were by no means the fruit of an overstrained imagination, but objective revelations of God, by means of personal spirits; yet only capable of being received under certain subjective conditions. With respect to the angel who appeared to Zachariah, if unbelief, on hearing his name, should cavil, and doubt whether such definite names are borne in heaven, this conclusion cannot be escaped under the pretext, that Gabriel (*the hero of God*) is no *nomen proprium*, but merely an *appellativum*; and we have only to answer, *neganti incumbit probatio*.

3. There is a remarkable *coincidence* between Zachariah and *Abraham* on the one side, and *Elisabeth* and *Sarah* on the other; not only in the fact of their unfruitfulness during so many years, but also in the frame of mind in which they at length received the glad tidings. But in these parallel histories, it is, in the Old Testament, the man who is strong, the woman weak, in faith (Gen. xviii. 12); while here, on the contrary, it is the man whose faith falters. Even in the very first chapter of Luke, woman, who had so long been thrown into obscurity in the shadow of man, begins, in the persons of Mary and Elisabeth, to take her place in the foreground, by the heroism of a living faith; as if to show that she is no longer the slave of man, but a fellow-heir

---

[*] [It should not be inferred from the text that Schleiermacher denied the existence of angels altogether. He only denied the existence of Satan and the evil angels.—P. S.]

with him of the grace of life (1 Pet. iii. 7). It is, however, quite in keeping with divine wisdom that in this case unbelief in view of the rising sun of the gospel salvation is much more severely punished than under the old dispensation. The clearer the light, the more intolerable the shade in the eyes of God. On the psychological ground of the doubt of Zachariah, compare the fine remarks of Dr. LANGE, *Leben Jesu*, ii. 1, p. 65 (German ed.).

4. It is a striking proof of the divine wisdom, that John is announced as the second *Elijah*. This name gives the earliest indication of his mission, as reformer, in an extremely corrupt nation; of his struggle, in resisting single-handed the false gods of his age, as Elijah did Ahab and Jezebel; of his fate, in being first persecuted and rejected, but afterward honored. The likeness of John the Baptist to Elijah, strikes us not only in his outward appearance, his clothing, and way of living, but in his spirit and character, as a preacher of repentance. The difference between them—consisting chiefly in the fact, that the second Elijah performed no miracles—is explained by the peculiarity of his relation to the Messiah. If the latter were to appear as a prophet mighty in word and deed, His forerunner could do no miracles, without dividing the attention, and provoking a comparison, which must have been to the prejudice of one or the other. He who would cavil because the head of the greatest of the Old Testament prophets is encircled by no halo of miracles, will find his answer, John x. 41.

5. On the formerly often-questioned *genuineness* of the two first chapters of Luke, comp. CREDNER, "*Einleitung in das N. T.*," p. 131; on the whole of Luke's narrative of events preceding the birth of Christ, J. P. LANGE, "*On the Historical Character of the Canonical Gospels, especially on the History of the Childhood of Jesus*," Duisburg, 1836; and (though with critical discrimination) "*Die Jugendgeschichte des Herrn*," by Dr. E. J. GELPKE, Born, Chur (Coire), and Leipzig, 1842.

HOMILETICAL AND PRACTICAL.

The announcement of the birth of John the Baptist, appointed by divine wisdom, received in human weakness, confirmed by striking signs, crowned with surprising results.—God's way in the sanctuary: 1. *The dark* sanctuary, or dwelling-place of the Infinite; 2. *the divine*, where His glory is manifested.—The answer to the prayer of Zachariah was: 1. Earnestly desired, 2. long delayed, 3. promised in a surprising manner, 4. incredulously waited for, and 5. gloriously vouchsafed.—The happiness of pious couples, even when the blessing of children is denied.—The high value of tried fear of God in the eyes of the Lord.—The life of faith a continual priesthood.—A lonely old age cheered up and made serene by the light of the Lord.—God's revelation hidden from the eye of the world.—The holy angels present, even now, in the Lord's house.—The fear with which the revelation of great joy fills the heart of a sinner.—John a gift of God.—The birth of John still a matter of rejoicing to many.—John, the second Elijah: their similarity and dissimilarity.—John, great in the sight of the Lord: his superiority to all the Old Testament prophets, his inferiority to our Lord.—The gift of abstinence even under the new covenant.—No meetness for the kingdom of heaven, without sincere repentance.—The desire to see signs and wonders: 1. Easily explicable; 2. very reprehensible; 3. entirely superfluous, where a greater sign has already been vouchsafed.—The angel who stands in the presence of God: his mysterious name, exalted work, and hidden origin.—Zachariah dumb, yet preaching to believers and unbelievers.—The announcement of the birth of John the Baptist, a proof of the truth of the prophetic word (Isa. xlv. 15): 1. God, a God that hideth Himself; 2. the God of Israel; 3. the Saviour. —Elisabeth, a type of the faith which receives God's blessing, enjoys God's peace, and waits God's time. —When the reproach of his people is taken away, the Lord has been looking down on them favorably. —The Lord's second coming is, like His first, openly announced, incredulously doubted, patiently expected.—The Lord will give more to His people than He withholds from them.—Does Zachariah tremble at the sight of an angel? Where will the ungodly and the sinner appear, when the Lord cometh with ten thousand of His saints?—The punishment of unbelief is in the end a blessing.—The less, the preparation for the greater.—Who hath despised the day of small things? Zech. iv. 10.—"Children are an heritage of the Lord, and the fruit of the womb is His reward."—Gabriel standing in the presence of God in heaven, and John great in the sight of the Lord on earth.—The interest of the angels in the coming of God's kingdom on earth.—Even in times of the greatest corruption, there are still houses which are temples of God.—"The vision is yet for an appointed time; but at the end it shall speak, and not lie: though it tarry, wait for it; because it will surely come, it will not tarry." Hab. ii. 3.

STARKE:—In prayer, we should remember the presence of angels.—Even one of the holiest of men cannot stand before an angel.—Even the true servants of God are not without infirmities.—Nothing is great, but what is great before God.—God is able to do exceeding abundantly above all that we ask or think, Eph. iii. 20.—The more intimate the communion of a Christian with his God, the more certain his chastisement when he offends Him.—He who sins with his mouth, is punished in his mouth.—God has an eye upon His people, though no one else should see them.—There are times when the children of God bear reproach; there are also times when God takes away their reproach before men: in both His grace is shown.

CHAP. I. 26-38.   19

B. *Annunciation of the Birth of the Messiah.* Ch. I. 26-38.

(The Gospel for the day of the Annunciation of Mary.)

26 And in the sixth month[1] the angel Gabriel was sent from God unto a city of Gali-
27 lee, named Nazareth, To a virgin espoused [betrothed] to a man, whose name was
28 Joseph, of the house of David; and the virgin's name *was* Mary. And the angel [he][2]
    came in unto [to] her, and said, Hail, *thou that art* highly favoured [thou highly favour-
29 ed! κεχαριτωμένη],[3] the Lord *is* [be] with thee: blessed *art* thou among women.[4] And
    when she saw *him*,[5] she was troubled at his [the] saying, and cast in her mind what
30 manner of salutation this should [might] be. And the angel said unto her, Fear not,
31 Mary: for thou hast found favour with God. And, behold, thou shalt conceive in thy
32 womb, and bring forth a son, and shalt call His name JESUS. He shall be great, and
    shall be called the Son of the Highest: and the Lord God shall give unto Him the
33 throne of His father David: And He shall reign over the house of Jacob for ever; and
    of His kingdom there shall be no end.
34 Then said Mary unto the angel, How shall this be, seeing I know not a man?
35 And the angel answered and said unto her, The Holy Ghost shall come upon thee, and
    the power of the Highest shall overshadow thee; therefore also that holy thing, which
36 shall be born of thee,[6] shall be called the Son of God. And, behold, thy cousin
    Elisabeth, she hath also conceived a son in her old age: and this is the sixth month
37 with her, who was [is] called barren. For with God nothing shall be impossible.
38 And Mary said, Behold the handmaid of the Lord; be it unto me according to thy
    word. And the angel departed from her.

[1 Vs. 26.—"In the sixth month," *i. e.*, of the pregnancy of Elisabeth.
2 Vs. 28.—The ὁ ἄγγελος of the *text. rec.*, though sustained by Codd. A., C., D., and the Latin Vulgate (*angelus*), is omitted by the Vatican and other uncial Codd. and thrown out by Tischendorf and Alford, but retained by Lachmann, and Tregelles who includes it in brackets. The Sinaitic MS. comes to its aid, and reads: πρὸς αὐτὴν ὁ ἄγγελος εἶπεν (the *text. rec.* places ἄγγελος *before* αὐτήν, so also Lachmann and Tregelles). It is easier to account for its insertion than for its omission.
3 Vs. 28.—*Highly favored, Begnadigte* (Luther less literally: *Holdselige*), is the proper translation of the passive participle κεχαριτωμένη, and not *full of grace, gratia plena, gnadenvolle*, as the Latin Vulgate and the Romish versions render it in the service of Mariolatry. Alford: "Though χαριτόω is not found in classical writers, the analogy of all verbs in -όω must rule it to mean, the passing of the action implied in the radical substantive (χάρις) on the object of the verb—the *conferring of grace or favor upon.*" The word occurs besides here once in the N. T., viz., Eph. i. 6: τῆς χάριτος αὐτοῦ, ἐν ᾗ ἐχαρίτωσεν ἡμᾶς ἐν τῷ ἠγαπημένῳ, which the Vulgate renders: "in qua gratificavit nos," etc., the E. V.: "wherein he hath made us accepted," lit.: *has graced* us.
4 Vs. 28.—The words of the *text. rec.*, εὐλογημένη σὺ ἐν γυναιξίν, *blessed* thou among women, are generally regarded as a later insertion from ver. 42, and thrown out of the text by the recent critical editors. Tregelles retains the words, but in brackets. Cod. Sinait. likewise omits them. The original reading of the angelic salutation then is simply: "*Hail, highly favoured one, the Lord* [be] *with you!*" The reading here in connection with the proper translation of κεχαριτωμένη has some bearing upon the question of the worship of Mary.
5 Vs. 29.—The word ἰδοῦσα, *when she saw him*, for which the Vulgate reads *cum audisset*, is wanting in Codd. Sin., Vatican., and other ancient authorities, and thrown out of the text by Griesbach, Tischendorf, Alford, and Tregelles, while Lachmann retains it. The correct reading is: ἡ δὲ ἐπὶ τῷ λόγῳ διεταράχθη, *and she was troubled at the saying.* Meyer, and after him Alford, suppose that the original mistake was, passing from ΔΕ to ΔΙΕταράχθη (hence Cod. D. reads only the verb, simplex), which gave rise to the glosses, transpositions, and reinsertions of ἐπὶ τῷ λόγῳ.
6 Vs. 35.—Or: *The Holy One that is born*, τὸ γεννώμενον ἅγιον; Vulgate: *quod nascetur* (other Latin authorities: *nascitur*) *sanctum*. The particularizing addition, ἐκ σοῦ, *ex te, of thee*, of the received text, is without sufficient authority and thrown out or put in brackets by the critical editors.—P. S.]

EXEGETICAL AND CRITICAL.

Vs. 26. **Nazareth.**—See remarks on Matt. ii. 23.

Vs. 27. **To a virgin.**—Joseph is the most prominent person in Matthew's narrative of events preceding the birth of Christ, Mary in Luke's; an indication that in all probability she was, whether mediately or immediately, the source whence he derived the account of these facts. (Comp. Acts xxi. 17.)

Of the house of David.—These words, relating solely to Joseph, show that he was also of the blood-royal. That they by no means deny the descent of Mary from David, will appear hereafter.

Vs. 28. **And [the angel] came in unto her.** —Here is no mere apparition of an angel in a dream, as to Joseph; but a visit in open day, although, of

course, in a quiet hour of retirement, as more befitting and satisfactory under the circumstances.—The words, *the angel*, although wanting in the best manuscripts, is intended. The substitution of any human being is inadmissible.

Highly favored.—It is apparent from ver. 30 that this is not spoken of the external beauty of Mary, but of the favor or grace she had found in God's sight. The same epithet is bestowed upon all believers, Eph. i. 6, orig.

[The greeting of the angel in ver. 28 is called the *Angelic Salutation* or *Ave Maria*, and forms the first part of the famous Roman Catholic prayer to the Virgin Mary:

"*Hail, Mary, full of grace, the Lord is with thee.*"

The second part of this prayer is taken from the address of Elisabeth to Mary, ver. 42:

"*Blessed art thou among women, and blessed is the fruit of thy womb, Jesus.*"

To this was added, in the beginning of the sixteenth century (1508), a third part, which contains the objectionable invocation of the Virgin:

"*Holy Mary, Mother of God, pray for us sinners, now and at the hour of our death. Amen.*"

The concluding words, however, *nunc et in hora mortis*, are a still later addition of the Franciscans. Even the first two parts of the *Ave Maria* were not used as a *standing form of prayer* before the thirteenth century.—P. S.]

Vs. 29. **She cast in her mind.**—A proof of her serenity and presence of mind at a critical hour. How different were Zachariah, and many before him!

Vs. 32. **Shall be called;**—*i. e.*, not only shall *be*, but shall one day be publicly *recognized* as what He really is.

The Son of the Highest.—This name seems here used by the angel, not in a metaphysical, but a theocratic sense. It points to the anointed King, so long foretold by the prophets, and to whom the words, 2 Sam. vii. 14; Ps. ii. 7; lxxxix. 28, so fully applied. Very deserving our consideration is the following observation of O. von Gerlach: "It is worthy of remark, that the proper divinity of her son was not definitely revealed to Mary: otherwise, neither she nor Joseph could have been in a position to bring up the child; for the submission, which was a necessary condition of His humanity, would have been submission only in appearance. But this promise, while it by no means abolished the parental relationship, would yet direct the reverential attention of the parents toward the child. From the very beginning of our Lord's incarnation, we see that the knowledge of His divinity was not to be communicated in an external and awe-inspiring manner, but to be gradually manifested by His humanity and His work of redemption."—For Mary, who was so intimately acquainted with the Old Testament, this prophecy would contain the essence of the most remarkable Messianic promises: 2 Sam. vii.; Isa. ix.; Micah v., etc.

Vs. 33. **Over the house of Jacob.**—The announcement of His universal spiritual reign would have been, at this time, even more incomprehensible to Mary. It lies hidden, however, in the promise: "*Of His kingdom there shall be no end.*" We must not regard these words of the angel as an accommodation merely to the exclusively Jewish expectations then prevailing, concerning the kingdom of Messiah. Salvation is really of the Jews, and will one day return to Israel.

Vs. 34. **How shall this be?** etc.—A natural objection, and a question as much allowed by the angel, as that of Zachariah (ver. 18) was arbitrary and blamable. Comp. Num. xxxi. 17; Judg. xi. 39; Matt. i. 18.

Vs. 35. **The Holy Ghost—the power of the Highest.**—The parallel between these two expressions, exacts that the one should be interpreted by the other; and their *mutual* light teaches, that the Holy Spirit has verily a life-producing power, but by no means, that He is *only* power, without personality.

Shall come upon thee—shall overshadow thee.—Again two phrases reflecting light upon each other. Both point to the supernatural operation of the Holy Spirit, in bringing to pass that which ordinarily occurs only through conjugal intercourse. The word ἐπισκιάσει can no more be understood to denote a special divine protection (Kuinoel), than a cohabitation (Paulus, the rationalist).

Therefore also.—His miraculous birth is here spoken of as the natural, but by no means the only reason, why He, who had no human father, should receive the name of the Son of God.

Vs. 36. **Thy cousin**, or: **kinswoman** (ἡ συγγενής σου).—It does not quite appear what was the relationship between Mary and Elisabeth, the daughter of Aaron (ver. 5). This relationship, however, whatever it might be, proves nothing against Mary's descent from David, as different tribes might be united by marriage. (Num. xxxvi. 6 offers no difficulty, as it relates only to heiresses, whose family was in danger of becoming extinct.) There is, therefore, no reason to conclude that Mary, by reason of her relationship to Elisabeth, was of the tribe of Levi (as in the *Testam. XII Patriarcharum*, p. 542, and Schleiermacher's *Lukas*, p. 26).

Vs. 37. **With God nothing shall be impossible.**—*Nothing*, *i. e.*, no word (ῥῆμα) of promise. A powerful support for Mary's faith, who might infer from the *mirabile* the possibility of the *miraculum*. It is at the same time the last, and indeed the only sufficient, answer to the horror of the miraculous, which characterizes modern criticism.

Vs. 38. **Be it unto me.**—Not only the utterance of obedient submission, but also of patient, longing expectation. The heart of Mary is now filled with the Holy Spirit, who can also prepare her body to be the temple of the God-Man.

DOCTRINAL AND ETHICAL.

1. Concerning the person of Mary, her youth, and legends of her after history, *see* Winer *in voce* "Mary." The beauty of her character, as "the handmaid of the Lord," and the chosen instrument of the Holy Spirit, strikes us at the first glimpse at her. (A. H. Niemeyer gives a short but beautiful description of her, in his *Characteristik der Bibel*, i. pp. 40–42.)

2. Two views, which have obtained in the Christian world, concerning the person and character of Mary, are condemned by these early pages of Luke's Gospel. The first is that of the Roman and Greek Church, which transforms the handmaid of the Lord into the queen of heaven; the mother of Jesus into the mother of God; the redeemed sinner into the mediatrix and intercessor. The other is that of *Rationalismus vulgaris*, which deprives the humble bride of the carpenter of the chastity and purity which were her richest dowry, and necessarily rejects the miracle of the supernatural birth; there being no reason for concluding that Jesus was the son of Joseph. The first idea was chiefly supported by the apocryphal Gospels, which surrounded the head of her, upon whom the light of the divine favor had indeed richly fallen, by a halo of celestial glory. Its result was an almost heathen apotheosis of the virgin-mother, producing all the follies of an unlimited Mariolatry. The second notion was first conceived in the brain of the heathen Celsus, who derides the mother of Jesus, as the victim of seduction; while the Jewish version of this fable names one Panthera or Pandira as her seducer. To the shame of Christendom, we have seen this blasphemy revived, in va-

rious forms, in the eighteenth and nineteenth centuries (Bahrdt, and, in some degree, Paulus and others). Its own intrinsic beauty, truth, and sublimity commend the Gospel narrative, in opposition to both these products of a diseased imagination.

3. With respect to the descent of Mary from David, it is undeniable that the words, ἐξ οἴκου Δαβίδ, Luke i. 27, refer exclusively to Joseph; yet they by no means assert, that our Lord did not descend from David on His *mother's* side. We shall soon see that Luke iii. presents us with the genealogy of Mary, as Matt. i. does with that of Joseph. The angel, too, who announces to her that she shall conceive a son, through the power of the Holy Spirit, could not possibly have added: "*The Lord God shall give unto Him the throne of His father David,*" had not Mary herself been a daughter of David. Her song of praise, also, clearly shows what expectations she cherished for the house of David, and can only be fully understood, *psychologically,* when it is regarded as uttered by the daughter of a royal house, who, though that house was then in the depths of degradation, was yet looking forward to the elevation of the rightful dynasty, and the abasement of the foreign tyrant who then usurped the throne. The *Magnificat* (as Mary's Psalm is called) is as unambiguous a proof of Mary's royal descent as the genealogy, ch. iii.

4. The miraculous conception of our Lord, by the power of the Holy Spirit, is related by Luke, as a fact which cannot be doubted, and leaves no room for the hypothesis that we have here a myth or legend. It has often been said, but never proved, that the Jews of those days were expecting that Messiah would be born of a virgin, in some miraculous manner; but even then, it would not follow that the narrative was composed merely in obedience to the dictates of such an expectation. The analogy of certain heathen theogonies may perhaps prove the *possibility* of inventing such a narrative, in a polytheistic or pantheistic sense; but its *reality*, in a Christian and theistic sense, can by no means be thus accounted for. A comparison with the accounts in certain apocryphal Gospels on this point speaks more for, than against, the historical fidelity of Luke. Our Lord Himself, indeed, so far as we know, never spoke of this miracle; but His silence may be satisfactorily accounted for. His mother's honor, the nature of the circumstance, the enmity of the Jews, all forbade Him to bring to light a mystery, for the truth of which He had only His own or Mary's word to offer. Nor need it astonish us, that His contemporaries speak of Him as the son of Joseph (John i. 45); nor that Mary, speaking of her husband to Jesus, then twelve years of age, should say, "Thy father" (Luke ii. 48); nor, least of all, that His brothers should not believe in Him (John vii. 5); for, from all in the domestic circle, except Mary and Joseph, the affair was concealed with profound secrecy. We have already seen that Matthew also speaks of a miraculous birth; while Mark passes over in silence the history of Christ previous to His entry upon His public ministry, although he presents the person of our Lord in so divine a light, as naturally to lead to the supposition of His heavenly origin. John is also silent on the subject, though, in his description of the children of God, as born οὐκ ἐξ αἱμάτων, οὐδὲ ἐκ θελήματος σαρκὸς, οὐδὲ ἐκ θελήματος ἀνδρός, immediately before the words, ὁ λόγος σὰρξ ἐγένετο, there seems contained a latent reminiscence of what he must have undoubtedly heard from Mary during his long and intimate intercourse with her. For if he says, that "that which is born of the flesh is flesh," and that the λόγος ὃς ἦν ἐν ἀρχῇ πρὸς τὸν Θεόν, became *flesh,* we must, according to this Evangelist also, believe that this took place in some other way than through the θέλημα σαρκός. Nevertheless, though the conception by the power of the Holy Spirit may be deduced from his doctrine concerning the Logos, he certainly does not expressly declare it. Paul also contents himself with the general statement, that the Lord was *born of a woman,* and of the *seed of David* (Rom. i. 4; Gal. iv. 4); and it seems clear that this miracle, though an indispensable element of gospel history, did not originally belong to the apostolic κήρυγμα, which, according to Acts i. 21, began with the baptism of John.

5. This does not, however, interfere with the fact, that the miraculous conception stands on a firm historical foundation, and is of great dogmatic importance. For the first assertion, they who deny it, *a priori,* as absolutely impossible, deserve no other answer than: πλανᾶσθε μὴ εἰδότες τὰς γραφὰς μηδὲ τὴν δύναμιν τοῦ Θεοῦ [Matt. xxii. 29]. Yet, far rather than say, with a modern theologian (Karl Hase), that "birth of a virgin cannot be proved to be impossible," would we comfort ourselves with the words of the angel [to Mary, Luke i. 37]: ὅτι οὐκ ἀδυνατήσει παρὰ τοῦ Θεοῦ πᾶν ῥῆμα. The laws of nature are not chains, wherewith the Supreme Lawgiver has bound Himself; but cords, which He holds in His own hand, and which He can lengthen or shorten as His good pleasure and wisdom dictate. And surely, in the present case, an end worthy of divine interference justified the deviation. When the Eternal Word was, in "the fulness of the time," to take upon Him the form of a servant, the new member could only be introduced into the human series in an extraordinary manner. He, who was in the beginning with God, and who came of His own will to sojourn in this our world, could hardly enter it as one of ourselves would. He, who was the light and life of men, must surely see the light of day, not by carnal procreation, but by an immediate exercise of omnipotent power. Besides, how could He be free from every taint of original sin, and redeem us from the power of sin, if He had been born by the fleshly intercourse of sinful parents? The strong and healthy graft which was to bring new life into the diseased stock, must not originate from this stock, but be grafted into it from without. To deduce hence the need also of an *immaculata conceptio,* in the case of Mary, would be to lose sight of the fact, that we do not lay the chief stress upon the article "*natus e virgine M.*," but upon the preceding "*conceptus e Sp. S.*" From the moment of our Lord's conception, the Holy Spirit certainly continued to influence and penetrate the mind and spirit of Mary, to suppress the power of sin, and to make her body His consecrated temple. If it be said (by Schleiermacher) that Christian consciousness is perfectly satisfied by accepting the fact, that God removed from the normal development of the Son of Man all the pernicious influences and consequences attending an ordinary human birth, the question here is not, What can the Christian consciousness of an individual bear? but, What saith the Scripture? We believe, on the authority of Luke, who took all pains and had the best means of reliable information (comp. i. 1–4), that the power of the Holy Spirit overshadowed Mary in a mysterious manner. The moment of conception is simply hinted at by the

words, "*Behold the handmaid of the Lord,*" and seems to coincide with the departure of the angel.* Moreover, the true humanity of the Son of Man is by no means abolished, but rather explained by this miracle; for was Adam no real man, because he also, in a physical view, was a υἱὸς Θεοῦ? In short, the miraculous conception is a σκάνδαλον to those alone who will see in our Lord nothing more than His pure humanity, and who put the sinlessness of the perfect man Christ Jesus in the place of the real incarnation of God in Him. To us, who believe in the latter, His miraculous conception is the natural consequence of His superhuman dignity, the basis of His normal development, and a symbol of the ἄνωθεν γεννηθῆναι, which must take place in every member of the kingdom of God. Compare J. J. VAN OOSTERZEE: *Disputatio Theologica de Jesu e virgine Maria nato.* Traj. ad Rh. 1840.

6. The conception of the Son of God, by the Holy Spirit, is the beginning of the intimate union between the λόγος ἔνσαρκος and the πνεῦμα οὐκ ἐκ μέτρου, John iii. 34. Thirty years later, the Spirit descended upon Him in a bodily shape; and after He was glorified, He sent the Spirit upon all that believed on Him. The same Spirit who formed the *body* of Christ, forms also the *corpus Christi mysticum,* the Church.

HOMILETICAL AND PRACTICAL.

The calm, unostentatious entrance of the Divine into the world of man.—God hath chosen the weak things of the world to confound the things which are mighty.—The true veneration of Mary: 1. Exhibited; 2. justified; 3. carried out.—The present worship of Mary [in the Roman and Greek Churches] judged before the tribunal of Gabriel: 1. Mary is called by him, *highly favored;* by her worshippers, the *dispenser of favors;* 2. by him, blessed *among* women; by them, raised *above* women; 3. by him, the *handmaid* of the Lord, a sinful daughter of Adam; by them, the *Queen* of angels [and saints]; 4. in his eyes, a sinful daughter of Adam [nowhere exempt in the Bible from the general depravity of Adam's posterity]; now [according to the papal dogma proclaimed in 1854], conceived without sin (*immaculate concepta*).—Mary a type of faith; in her just astonishment, natural fear, gentle boldness, quiet reflection, and unlimited obedience.—The blessed among women: 1. Poor, yet rich; 2. "troubled," yet meditative; 3. proud as a virgin, yet obedient as a wife; 4. first doubtful, then believing.—The angelic appearances to Zachariah and Mary compared.—Jesus a gracious gift: 1. To Mary; 2. to Israel; 3. to the world.—The greatness of Jesus, and the greatness of John, compared (vers. 15 and 32): 1. Jesus greater than John in Himself; 2. a greater gift of God; 3. therefore worthy of our greater appreciation.—The throne of David: 1. Raised up after deep abasement; 2. raised up amongst Israel; 3. raised up amongst us; 4. raised up to fall no more.—The question: "How shall this be?" may be asked: 1. In a sense

lawful for man, and reverential toward God; or 2. in a sense unlawful for man, and dishonoring God.—The operation of the Holy Spirit in creation (Gen. i. 2), and in redemption or the new creation (Luke i. 35), compared: 1. In both, a long and silent preparation; 2. in both, a life-giving and fructifying operation; 3. in both, a new world created.—The support which those, who are "highly favored," find from contemplating others also highly favored: This support perfectly lawful, often indispensable, always limited, and the highest, and often the only, support of faith, in a power to which nothing is impossible. —With God nothing shall be impossible, an answer by which: 1. Unbelief is put to shame; 2. weak faith strengthened; 3. and faith excited to thankful adoration and unlimited obedience.—Behold the handmaid of the Lord! 1. Her hidden conflict; 2. her complete victory; 3. her full reward; 4. her happy peace.—The messenger of Heaven and the child of earth united, to perform the counsel and good pleasure of God.—The greatest miracle in the world's history, encompassed with the thickest veil of obscurity.

STARKE:—God knows where to find His children, however hidden they may be (2 Tim. ii. 19).—God is wont to bestow His favors in times of quiet and retirement, Isa. xxx. 50.—All believers are the "blessed" of the Lord (Eph. i. 3).—The holier, the humbler.—The "troubles" of holy minds always end in comfort.—The members of Christ's kingdom have in Him an everlasting King, an everlasting support, and an everlasting joy.—Let even thy nearest and dearest forsake thee, so thou make sure the Lord Jesus be with thee, and abide in thee.

HEUBNER:—Mary and Eve: their similarity and dissimilarity, their relation to the human race.—Mary the happiest, but also the most sorely tried, of women.—Christians born of the house of Jacob, according to the Spirit.—Humility the best frame of mind for the reception of grace.—Our birth is also a work of God.—The miraculous birth of Jesus, a glorification of the whole human race.

WALLIN:—The angel's salutation of Mary may be applied to Christians in all the holy seasons of life: baptism, confirmation, the time of chastening, the day of death.

FR. ARNDT:—How does the time of regeneration begin in the world, and in the heart? By an announcement of the grace of God, which is: 1. Heard in humility; 2. received with patience and entire self-resignation.

VAN OOSTERZEE [in sermons previously published]:—Mary the handmaid of the Lord. This saying the inscription of the history of Mary, as maid, wife, and widow.—Her character presents a rare combination of: 1. Genuine humility, with joyful faith; 2. of quiet resignation, with active zeal; 3. of faithful love, with unwavering heroism.—That the Word was made flesh, is: 1. An undoubted fact; this proved by: (*a*) the life, (*b*) the words, (*c*) the works of the Lord; 2. an unfathomable miracle; (*a*) the unprecedented, (*b*) the intimate, (*c*) the voluntary, nature of the union of the Divine Word with flesh; 3. an ever-memorable benefit; for this incarnation is: (*a*) the glory, (*b*) the light, (*c*) the life of mankind. To conclude, the questions: Do you believe in the fact? adore the miracle? highly esteem the benefit?

---

* [Older divines generally date the supernatural conception from the words of the angel, ver. 35, which were the medium of the mysterious operation of the Holy Spirit.—P. S.]

C. *Hymns of Praise, with which the expectation of the Messiah's Birth, and the actual Birth of the Baptist, were greeted.* CH. I. 39–80.

(Vers. 57–80, the Lesson for the day of John the Baptist, 24th of June.—Vers. 67–79, the Gospel for the first day of Advent in the Grand-Duchy of Hesse and elsewhere.)

39 And Mary arose in those days, and went into the hill-country with haste, into a
40 city of Juda; And entered into the house of Zacharias, and saluted Elisabeth.
41 And it came to pass, that, when[1] Elisabeth heard the salutation of Mary, the babe
42 leaped in her womb; and Elisabeth was filled with the Holy Ghost [Spirit]: And she spake out with a loud voice, and said, Blessed *art* thou among women, and blessed *is*
43 the fruit of thy womb. And whence *is* this to me,[2] that the mother of my Lord should
44 come to me? For, lo [behold], as soon as the voice of thy salutation sounded in mine
45 ears, the babe leaped in my womb for joy.[3] And blessed is she that believed: for [believed that][4] there shall be a performance [fulfilment, τελείωσις] of those things which were told her from the Lord.

46 And Mary said,
My soul doth magnify the Lord,
47 And my spirit hath rejoiced in God my Saviour. [,]
48 For [In that] He hath regarded the low estate of His handmaiden; [handmaid.][5] for [For], behold, from henceforth all generations shall call me blessed.
49 For He that is mighty hath done to me great things; and holy is His name. [,]
50 And His mercy is on them that fear Him from generation to generation.[6]
51 He hath showed [wrought] strength with His arm:
He hath scattered the proud in the imagination of their hearts.
52 He hath put down the mighty from *their* seats [princes from thrones],
and exalted [raised up] them of low degree.
53 He hath filled the hungry with good things;
and the rich He hath sent empty away.
54 He hath holpen [helped] His servant Israel [Is., His servant],
in remembrance of *His* mercy; [,]
55 As He spake to our fathers, [(As He spake to our fathers)][7]
to Abraham, and his seed for ever [to A. and his seed, for ever].[8]

56 And Mary abode with her about three months, and returned to her own house.
57 Now Elisabeth's full time came that she should be delivered; and she brought forth
58 a son. And her neighbours and her cousins [kindred, συγγενεῖς] heard how the Lord had showed great mercy upon [toward] her; and they rejoiced with her.
59 And it came to pass, that on the eighth day they came to circumcise the child; and
60 they called him Zacharias, after the name of his father. And his mother answered and
61 said, Not *so;* but he shall be called John. And they said unto her, There is none of
62 thy kindred that is called by this name. And they made signs to his father, how he
63 would have him called. And he asked for a writing-table [tablet, πινακίδιον], and
64 wrote, saying, His name is John. And they marvelled all [they all wondered]. And his mouth was opened immediately, and his tongue *loosed*, and he spake, and praised
65 [blessing, εὐλογῶν] God. And fear came on all that dwelt round about them: and all
66 these sayings were noised abroad throughout all the hill-country of Judea. And all they that heard *them* laid *them* up in their hearts, saying, What manner of child shall this be! [What then will this child be?][9] And [For][10] the hand of the Lord was with him.

67 And his father Zacharias was filled with the Holy Ghost, and prophesied, saying,
68 Blessed be the Lord [, the, ὁ] God of Israel;[11] [,]
for [that] He hath visited and redeemed His people,
69 And hath raised up an [a] horn of salvation for us in the house of His servant David [of David, His servant, Δαβὶδ τοῦ παιδὸς αὐτοῦ];

70 As He spake by the mouth of His holy prophets, which have been since the world began [of His holy prophets of old];[12]
71 That we should be saved [salvation, σωτηρίαν][13] from our enemies, and from the hand of all that hate us;
72 To perform the mercy *promised* [to show mercy, ποιῆσαι ἔλεος] to our fathers, and to remember His holy covenant,
73 The oath which He sware to our father Abraham [to Abraham, our father],
74 That He would grant [to grant] unto us, that we, being delivered out of the hand of our enemies, might serve Him without fear,
75 In holiness and righteousness before Him, all the days of our life [all our days].[14]
76 And [also] thou,[15] [O] child, shalt be called the Prophet of the Highest: for thou shalt go before the face of the Lord to prepare His ways;
77 To give knowledge of salvation unto His people, by [in, ἐν] the remission of their sins,[16]
78 Through the tender mercy [mercies, διὰ σπλάγχνα ἐλέους] of our God; whereby the day-spring from on high hath visited us,
79 To give light to them that sit in darkness and in the shadow of death, to guide our feet into the way of peace.

80 And the child grew, and waxed [became] strong in spirit, and was in the deserts till the day of his showing [manifestation, ἀναδείξεως] unto Israel.

---

[1] Vs. 41.—Better: *And it came to pass, as Elisabeth . . . that the babe . . .* So the Revised N. T. of the Am. B. U. The best authorities place ἡ Ἐλισ. after τῆς Μαρ., while the Elzevir text reads: ἡ Ἐλ. τὸν ἀσπασμὸν τῆς Μαρ. (an intentional transposition).

[2] Vs. 43.—This is the shortest rendering of πόθεν μοι τοῦτο, so. γέγονεν, and preferable to what would be otherwise more in keeping with the modern *usus loquendi*: *How hath this happened to me.* Comp. the Vulgate: *Unde hoc mihi;* Luther and van Oosterzee: *Woher (kommt) mir das.*

[3] Vs. 41.—An immaterial difference in the order of words in the Greek text. Griesbach, Scholz, Tischendorf read: τὸ βρέφος ἐν ἀγαλλιάσει, for the *text. rec.*: ἐν ἀγ. τὸ βρ. The latter is supported by B., C., D., F., L., and Cod. Sin., and should be retained with Lachmann, Alford, and Meyer.

[4] Vs. 45.—There is a difference of opinion as to the meaning of ὅτι. Van Oosterzee agrees with Luther, the old Latin and the English Versions, and translates: *denn.* See his Exegetical Note. But Grotius, Bengel, de Wette, Ewald, Meyer, etc., render it *that*, making it depend upon πιστεύσασα, as in Acts xxvii. 25: πιστεύων γὰρ τῷ θεῷ ὅτι οὕτως ἔσται. I prefer the latter, because the supernatural conception foretold by the angel, vers. 31 and 35, had then already taken place.

[5] Vs. 48.—Ἐπὶ τὴν ταπείνωσιν τῆς δούλης αὐτοῦ, the lowliness, humility, humble condition of his handmaid. Ταπείνωσις refers not to the humility of mind, but the humility of station or external condition. Luther and van Oosterzee: *Niedrigkeit.*

[6] Vs. 50.—Better with the Latin Vulgate, Luther, van Oosterzee, the Revised N. T. of the Am. B. U., etc.: *His mercy is from generation to generation, to them that fear Him,* τὸ ἔλεος αὐτοῦ εἰς γενεὰς γενεῶν (or with the older MSS.: εἰς γενεὰς καὶ γενεάς, or with Cod. Sin.: εἰς γενεὰν καὶ γενεάν, which corresponds literally to the Hebrew לְדֹר וָדֹר, and is preferable to the other readings) τοῖς φοβουμένοις αὐτόν. The C. V. favors the connection of *from generation to generation* with φοβουμένοις instead of ἔλεος.

[7] Vs. 55.—The clause: *As He spake to our Fathers*, should be inclosed in parenthesis, and the punctuation changed thus: *In remembrance of His mercy (as He spake to our fathers) to Abraham*, etc. For μνησθῆναι ἐλέους and τῷ Ἀβραάμ belong together; while the E. V. connects *to Abraham* with *spake*, which is inadmissible in the Greek (ἐλάλησεν πρὸς τοὺς πατέρας ἡμῶν, not τοῖς); comp. Ps. xcviii. 3 and Micah vii. 20, to which our passage alludes. In any case the words *for ever* must be connected, not with *spake*, nor with *seed*, but with *in remembrance of his mercy*, and should therefore be separated from *seed* by a comma.

[8] Vs. 55.—The Codd. are divided between εἰς τὸν αἰῶνα and ἕως αἰῶνος. Lachmann, Tischendorf, Meyer, and Tregelles adopt the former.

[9] Vs. 66.—Τί ἄρα (*quid igitur*) τὸ παιδίον τοῦτο ἔσται; The force of the ratiocinative ἄρα should not be lost; it refers to the peculiar circumstances and auspices of the birth of John; comp. viii. 25; Acts xii. 18, where the ἄρα is likewise overlooked in the E. V.

[10] Vs. 66.—The Sin. and Vatic. MSS. and other ancient authorities read καὶ γάρ, *etenim, denn auch;* while the Elzevir text omits γάρ, which could easily be missed by a transcriber on account of the following χεὶρ. The words: "*For the hand of the Lord was with him,*" are a remark of Luke in justification of the preceding question of astonishment, as if to say: The people had good reason to expect great things from such a child.

[11] Vs. 68.—Εὐλογητὸς Κύριος ὁ Θεὸς τοῦ Ἰσραήλ is the literal version of the Hebrew בָּרוּךְ יְהֹוָה אֱלֹהֵי יִשְׂרָאֵל, Ps. lxxii. 18; cvi. 48 (*see* Septuag.). The sentence: *the God of Israel*, is explanatory and should be separated by a comma, and the article retained (with Norton, Kendrick, Sharpe, Wakefield, Campbell, Whiting, the N. T. of Am. B. U., and the German versions).

[12] Vs. 70.—Διὰ στόματος τῶν ἁγίων (τῶν) ἀπ' αἰῶνος αὐτοῦ προφητῶν. The second τῶν after ἁγίων in the *text. rec.* is omitted in Codd. Sin., B., L., etc., and by Tregelles and Alford, but retained by Lachmann and Tischendorf (ed. septima), and defended by Meyer. Ἀπ' αἰῶνος is not to be understood here in the absolute sense, *ab orbe condito*, as the E. V. implies (also Calov: *imo per os Adami*), but relatively, like the Hebrew מֵעוֹלָם. Comp. ἀπ' αἰῶνος, Gen. vi. 4 (where the E. V. renders: *of old*); Ps. xxv. 6 (likewise: *of old*). Meyer (and Alford) quotes Longin. 34: τοὺς ἀπ' αἰῶνος ῥήτορας. Luther translates the word: *vor Zeiten*; van Oosterzee: *vor Jahrhunderten*; Stier better: *von Alters her*; Ewald: *seiner heiligen uralten Propheten*; Norton: *from the beginning*; Kendrick, Whiting, the N. T. of the Am. B. U.: *of old*.

[13] Vs. 71.—Σωτηρίαν, etc., is anaphora and further explanation of κέρας σωτηρίας, *a horn of salvation*, ver. 69, *i. e., a mighty, strong salvation; horn* being a metaphorical expression with reference, not to the *horns of the altar*, which served as an asylum merely (1 Kings i. 50; ii. 28 ff.), but to horned beasts, which are weak and defenceless without, but strong and formidable with, their horns; comp. the Hebrew קֶרֶן, 1 Sam. ii. 10; Ps. lxxxix. 18, etc.

[14] Vs. 75.—The true reading of the oldest authorities, including Cod. Sin., is: πάσας τὰς ἡμέρας ἡμῶν (without τῆς ζωῆς of the Elzevir text), *all our days.*

¹⁵ Vs. 76.—The oldest reading, confirmed by Cod. Sin., is: καὶ σὺ δέ, instead of καὶ σύ. MEYER: "Kal — δέ ward gewöhnlich von den unfeinen Abschreibern verstümmelt."
¹⁶ Vs. 77.—Van Oosterzee: "Erkenntniss des Heils zu geben [bestehend] in Vergebung ihrer Sünden." Ἐν ἀφέσει ἁμαρτίας belongs not to σωτηρίας alone, but to γνῶσιν σωτηρίας; that they might know that Messianic salvation comes in and through the remission of their sins. ALFORD: "The remission of sin is the first opening for the γνῶσις σωτηρίας: see ch. iii. 7. The proposition ἐν has its literal meaning, 'in.'" There should be no comma after 'people.'—P. S.]

EXEGETICAL AND CRITICAL.

Vs. 39. Into a city of Juda.—It does not seem probable that these enigmatical words denote so much as a city of the tribe of Judah, much less that they point out Jerusalem or Hebron. The supposition, that Ἰούδα has been substituted for Ἰούτα (mentioned Josh. xv. 55), is far more credible; nor is it unlikely that this less strictly correct orthography is derived from Luke himself. Juta is to this day a considerable village, inhabited by Mohammedans. *See* Röhr's *Palestine*, p. 187.

Vss. 39, 40. Mary arose—and entered.—According to Jewish customs, it was improper, or at least unusual, for single or betrothed females to travel alone. Mary, however, may have undertaken this journey with Joseph's consent, and, perhaps, partly in the company of others. Extraordinary circumstances justify extraordinary measures, and Lange correctly remarks: "the obedience of the cross makes truly free."—The supposition, that Joseph had taken his betrothed bride to his home, after a public solemnization of their nuptials, before this journey (Hug, Ebrard), seems improbable; but still more so, that Mary had already apprised him of the fact of the angelic visitation. Her part throughout was to announce nothing, but simply to wait till He, who had destined her to the highest honor ever bestowed, should, in His own good time, also make clear her innocence to the eyes of her husband and the world. By this state of affairs only, can Luke's account be reconciled with Matthew's, who, after the words εὑρέθη ἐν γ. ἔχ., describes the discovery of Mary's state as an unexpected, and hence a disquieting, discovery to Joseph. Mary leaves it simply to God to enlighten Joseph, as He had enlightened her. Nor does she undertake a journey to Elisabeth to consult with her, or to avoid her husband, but to seek that confirmation of her faith pointed out to her by the angel.

Vs. 41. And it came to pass.—The salutation of Mary, the ecstasy of Elisabeth, and the leaping of the babe in her womb, are three circumstances occurring at the same moment. At Mary's arrival, Elisabeth is filled with joy, and her babe moves. Luke mentions the latter circumstance first, as being the most extraordinary, although, in itself, it was rather the consequence than the cause of the emotion felt by Elisabeth at Mary's salutation. The aged woman, filled with the Holy Spirit, recognizes, by the extraordinary movement of the child, the presence of the future mother of her Lord; and thus the yet unborn John already offers involuntary homage to the καρπὸς τῆς κοιλίας of Mary.

Vs. 42. Blessed art thou—and blessed is the fruit, etc.—The first beatitude of the New Testament, and, in a certain sense, the root of all the rest. Elisabeth, while extolling the blessedness of Mary on account of her faith and obedience, was undoubtedly reflecting with compassion on the condition of Zachariah, whose unbelief had been reproved with loss of speech, while the believing Mary was entering her house with joyful salutations.

Vs. 45. For there shall be a fulfilment, etc.—It is grammatically possible, yet not logically necessary, to refer the ὅτι to the *object* of Mary's faith ("which believed *that* there," marg.). The assurance, that verily the things promised should be fulfilled without exception, though not indispensable in Mary's case, must yet have been a confirmation of her faith, which she would most gladly welcome. It is self-evident how much the abruptness of the sentences in which Elisabeth pours out the fulness of her heart, enhances the beauty of this passage. A psalm-like tone, better felt than expressed, seems to resound in her words, forming a prelude to Mary's "*Magnificat*."

[**Vss. 46–55.** The MAGNIFICAT of the Virgin Mary (so called from the old Latin version of Μεγαλύνει, vs. 46: MAGNIFICAT *anima mea Dominum*), and the BENEDICTUS of Zachariah, vss. 68–79 (so called from its beginning: Εὐλογητός, vs. 68, BENEDICTUS *Dominus Deus Israel*), are the Psalms of the New Testament, and worthily introduce the history of Christian hymnology. They prove the harmony of poetry and religion. They are the noblest flowers of Hebrew lyric poetry sending their fragrance to the approaching Messiah. They are full of reminiscences of the Old Testament, entirely Hebrew in tone and language, and can be rendered almost word for word. Thus μεγαλεία corresponds to גְּדֹלוֹת (Ps. lxx. 21; lxxi. 29; cxxvi. 2, 3); ὁ δυνατός to גִּבּוֹר (Ps. xxiv. 8); εἰς γενεὰν καὶ γενεάν (as Cod. Sin. reads) to לְדֹר וָדֹר. It is worth while to read the first two chapters of Luke in the Hebrew translation of the New Testament. These hymns form a part of the regular morning service in the Anglican liturgy, and resound from Sabbath to Sabbath in Christian lands. Dr. BARROW says of the *Magnificat*: "This most excellent hymn is dedicated by a spirit ravished with the most sprightly devotion imaginable; devotion full of ardent love and thankfulness, hearty joy, tempered with submiss reverence." WORDSWORTH: "This speech, full of Hebraisms, has a native air of originality, and connects the eucharistic poetry of the gospel with that of the Hebrew dispensation. . . . Thus the voices of the Law and the Gospel sound in concert with each other; and utter a protest against those who would make the one to jar against the other."—The *Magnificat* is divided into four stanzas, each of which contains three verses, viz.: (1) vss. 46–48 (to αὐτοῦ); (2) vs. 48 (from ἰδοὺ) to vs. 50; (3) vss. 51–53; (4) vss. 54, 55. The *Benedictus* of Zachariah contains five stanzas, each with three verses. So Meyer and Ewald. *See* Ewald's translation in his: *Die drei ersten Evangelien*, pp. 98 and 99, where he divides the *Magnificat* into 12, the *Benedictus* into 15 lines. —P. S.]

Vs. 46. And Mary said.—The angel's visit was vouchsafed to Mary later than to Zachariah, yet her song of thanksgiving is uttered long before his: faith is already singing for joy, while unbelief is compelled to be silent. The *Magnificat* is evidently no carefully composed ode, but the unpremeditated outpouring of deep emotion, the improvisation of a happy faith. It was easy for Mary, a daughter of David's royal race, well acquainted with the lyrics of the Old Testament, favored by God and filled with the Holy Spirit, to become in an instant both poetess and prophetess. The fulfilment of the angel's words with respect to Elisabeth, in which she saw a pledge and token of the full performance of his other promises, and of the realization of her most cherished hopes, seems to have been the immediate cause of this song of praise.

My soul doth magnify the Lord.—Mary's hymn recalls, besides the song of Hannah (1 Sam. ii. 1), several passages in the Psalms, especially in Ps. cxiii. and cxxvi. The beginning plainly refers to Ps. xxxi. 8, according to the Septuagint. The whole may be divided into three or four strophes, forming an animated doxology. The grace of God (vs. 48), His omnipotence (vss. 49-51), His holiness (vss. 49, 51, 54), His justice (vss. 52 and 53), and especially His faithfulness (vss. 54 and 55), are here celebrated. It sounds like an echo, not only of David's and Hannah's, but also of Miriam's and of Deborah's harps; yet independently reproduced in the mind of a woman, who had laid up and kept in her heart what she had read in Holy Scripture.

Vs. 47. **God my Saviour.**—Undoubtedly Mary was looking for civil and political blessings, through the birth of the Messiah; but we overlook the clearness of her views, and the depth of her mind, by thinking that her expectations were only, or chiefly, fixed upon these. The temporal salvation which she expected, was in her eye only the type and symbol of that higher salvation, which she desired above all things.

Vs. 48. **The low estate.**—Not humility, or lowliness of mind, but of condition, *humilis conditio*.

From henceforth.—The first beatitude, uttered by Elisabeth, is a token of an unutterable number, of which one at least is recorded, Luke xi. 27: "*Blessed is the womb that bare Thee, and the paps which Thou hast sucked.*" *

Vs. 49. **And holy is His name.**—No mere apposition to δυνατός (Kuinoel), but a new and independent sentence (comp. 1 Sam. ii. 2).

Vs. 52. **The mighty** (δυνάστας).—Mary would have been no true daughter of David, if she could have spoken these words without primary reference to Herod; but no believing Israelite, if she had thought of Herod alone. The overthrow of all anti-Messianic power seems, in her imagination, to begin with the fall of the Idumean usurper.

Vs. 53. **He hath filled the hungry with good things.**—The supposition, that only the good things of this world are here alluded to (Meyer), is as little to be entertained, as that the satisfying of a spiritual hunger is exclusively intended (de Wette). Such an alternative is certainly unnecessary in the case of Mary, whose earthly hunger and nourishment were both the type and resemblance of a higher need and a higher satisfaction, and who had certainly felt what Goethe afterward sung: "*Alles Vergängliche ist nur ein Gleichniss.*" † At this time, the spiritual craving was most powerfully felt among the outwardly needy. How exclusively materialistic, or how exclusively spiritualistic, would Mary have been, if she could have wholly confined her meaning to either of these ideas!

* [Christ did not rebuke the woman for this exclamation, but foreseeing the future excesses of Mariolatry, He significantly replied, vs. 28: "*Yea rather* (μενοῦνγε is both confirming and correcting = *utique* and *imo vero*), *blessed are they that hear the word of God and keep it*,—P. S.]

† ["Every thing transient is only a parable." From the conclusion of the second part of Goethe's *Faust*.—P. S.]

Vs. 55. **Abraham and his seed.**—A remarkable proof that Mary's expectations concerning the Messiah's appearance were not of a particularistic and exclusive, but of a universal nature. For the seed promised to Abraham was to be a blessing to the whole world.

Vs. 56. **And returned to her own house.**—To keep silence before Joseph, as she had broken silence before Elisabeth. Even the distasteful manner in which what passed between the betrothed pair is embellished in apocryphal literature (*Protevang. Jac.* ch. 11, 12; see THILO's *Codex Apocr. N. T*, p. 215), is better than the opinion that Mary made a sort of *confessio auricularis* to her husband. To suppose it psychologically and morally impossible that Mary kept silence and waited, even after her visit to Elisabeth, betrays a very superficial appreciation of her frame of mind. Hers was no transient kindling of mere enthusiasm, but a constant and steadily burning flame of divine inspiration.

Vs. 59. **To circumcise the child.**—On the origin, intention, and sacredness of circumcision, see de Wette, *Archæologie*, § 150 [also Jahn's *Archæology*, and the Bibl. Cyclopædias of Winer, Kitto, Smith, Herzog, etc., *sub voce*]. According to Gen. xxi. 3, 4, the performance of circumcision, and the bestowing of a name, had been simultaneous from the very origin of the rite. It is remarkable how much the custom of giving the name on the *seventh* or on the *eighth* day after a child's birth has been practised in the East, even where the rite of circumcision has been unknown. According to Ewald, *Israel. Alterthümer*, p. 110, the first of these practices is found to exist among the Khandi in India, and the second among the Negroes; he also connects their use with the ancient sacred division of time into weeks. Among the Greeks and Romans also it was customary to name the child on the day of purification.

Vs. 60. **And his mother answered.**—*Ex revelatione*, according to Theophylact, Euthym. Zigabenus, Bengel, and Meyer. But it is not said here, that she was filled with the Holy Spirit; and it is highly improbable that Zachariah should have kept the matter concealed from her during so many months. Needless multiplication of the miraculous is quite as censurable as arbitrary denial.

Vs. 62. **And they made signs.**—Certainly not because he was also deaf, as Ewald and many ancient writers have supposed; for the very fact that a sign was considered *sufficient* for Zachariah, shows that he had already silently *heard* the friendly contention.

Vs. 63. **A writing-tablet.**—Tertullian well says: "*Zacharias loquitur in stylo, auditur in cera;*" and Bengel: "*Prima hæc scriptura N. T. incipit a gratia.*" [Πινακίδιον was "a tablet smeared with wax, on which they wrote with a style."—P. S.]

Vs. 64. **And his mouth was opened immediately.**—Neither by the force of joyful emotion (Kuinoel), nor by his breaking a voluntary silence (Paulus), but by a miracle, whereby the word of the angel (vs. 20) was fulfilled at exactly the right time. Now that his soul is fully released from the chains of unbelief, his tongue is released from the chains of dumbness. His first use of his recovered faculty is not to utter a complaint, but a doxology: a proof that the cure had taken place in his soul also.

Vs. 65. **And fear came on all.**—Not a remark in anticipation of the history (de Wette), but the first immediate impression produced by what occurred at the birth and naming of the child. The Evangelist does not say that Zachariah uttered his song of praise on this eighth day. In the whole of Luke's previous history, as well as in other parts of Holy Scripture, fear has always been the first effect produced upon man by the consciousness that heavenly beings are entering into nearer and unusual intercourse with him (ch. i. 12, 29; ii. 9). This fear, which now spread only through the hill-country of Judæa, afterward filled the heart of all Jerusalem. It was undoubtedly kept up, as well as the expectation of some greater thing to follow, by the unusual manner in which the child John was brought up.

Vs. 66. **For the hand of the Lord was with him.**—An evident reference to the prophecy of the angel (vs. 15), and a summing up of the whole history of John's childhood. With Lachmann and Tischendorf, we prefer the reading καὶ γὰρ χείρ to καὶ χείρ of the *Recepta*. The question of surprise is thus modified, and the surprise indirectly expressed as constantly increasing.

Vs. 67. **And prophesied.**—This word, both here and in many other places, must not be understood in the sense of *vaticinium edere*, but of uttering inspired words of praise to God. The last prophecy concerning Christ before His birth, by the mouth of Zachariah, has the character, not of an oracle of Delphi, but of a psalm of David. It can scarcely be better described than in the words of Lange, *Leben Jesu*, ii. p. 90: "The song of praise now uttered by Zachariah, had so gradually and completely ripened in his soul, that he could never forget it in future. This song depicts the form and stature of his faith; it is the expression of the gospel, as his heart had received it. It is with a truly priestly intuition that Zachariah sees the reconciliation and transformation of the world in the advent of the Messiah. The coming Christ appears to him the true altar of salvation for His people, who henceforth, delivered from their enemies, shall perform true, real worship, celebrating the service of God in perpetual freedom. It is this that is his heart's delight as a priest. His heart's delight as a father is, that his son John shall be the herald of the Lord, to give the knowledge of His salvation, even to them who sit in darkness and the shadow of death."

Vs. 68. **For He hath visited and redeemed.** —Here, as also in Mary's song, the aorist is most properly used to express the prophetic consciousness, to which the salvation, still partly hidden in the future, appears already present. In the eyes of Zachariah, all the benefits to be bestowed by the Messiah are summed up in the one word λύτρωσις; and this λύτρωσις is the fruit of the gracious look, which God has just cast (ἐπεσκέψατο) upon Israel. Zachariah passes over from speaking of Israel only, in vs. 68, to describe these benefits as bestowed generally (vs. 79) on all those who sit "in darkness and the shadow of death;" a beautiful climax, and worthy of notice.

Vs. 69. **A horn of salvation.**—The well-known Biblical meaning of קֶרֶן (1 Sam. ii. 10; Ps. cxxxii. 17, and elsewhere) must be here understood, and not the horns of helmets, nor the horns of the altar. A strong, powerful defender is pointed out; nor does Zachariah forget that this horn is to spring from David's race, though it is remarkable how much less the Davidic element prevails in his song than in Mary's.

Vs. 70. **As He spake by the mouth of His holy prophets.**—Zachariah is here taking up the golden thread which had dropped from Mary, vs. 55.

Vs. 71. **Salvation** (σωτηρίαν) **from our enemies.**—Undoubtedly the political element was chiefly present to Zachariah. The priest is at the same time the patriot in the best sense of the term, deeply moved by the sight of Roman tyranny. But he chiefly prizes this political liberation as the means to a higher end, the reformation of divine worship: vss. 74 and 75.

Vs. 72. **The mercy promised to our fathers.** —The fulfilment of the promises concerning Messiah, is not only a matter of rejoicing for the present, and a source of hope for the future, but also a healing balm for past sorrows. The fathers had, for generations, wept over the decay of their nation, and were now living with God to look down from heaven upon the fulness of the time. Comp. Luke xx. 37, 38; John viii. 56.

Vs. 74. **That He would grant unto us.**—We are not to understand here the *matter* of the oath, but the *purpose* for which God once swore it, and was now about to fulfil it. For the oath itself, *see* Gen. xxii. 16–18.

Without fear.—Not the fear of God, which is rather the Old Testament token of piety, but the fear of *enemies*, which had often made Israel incapable of serving the Lord with joy. "How many times had the Macedonians, especially Antiochus Epiphanes, and the Romans, hindered the Jews in the exercise of their worship!" (De Wette.)

Vs. 75. **In holiness and righteousness before Him.**—Ὁσιότης and δικαιοσύνη are so far different, that the former refers more to piety considered in itself, the latter to piety with respect to God. [This expression sufficiently proves that the song of Zachariah looks by no means simply to the temporal greatness of the Messianic kingdom, but to the spiritual also.—P. S.]

All the days of our life, or rather **all our days.**—Both the number and weight of critical authorities justify us in expunging the words τῆς ζωῆς from the Greek text. Zachariah, then, is here speaking, not of the lives of individuals, but of the continuous national existence of highly favored Israel. Uninterrupted national prosperity, based upon true religion, is the ideal of his aspirations.

Vs. 76. **And also thou, O child.**—Zachariah, as a prophet of God, now begins to foretell the career of the last and greatest of the prophets. A striking proof of the prevalence of the theocratic over the paternal feeling in his song, is seen in the fact, that the Messiah is always placed in a more prominent position than His forerunner. Zachariah, however, at last, cannot forbear speaking of the latter, and with evident reference to Isa. xl. 3 and Mal. iv. *He is to go before the face of the Lord* (Jehovah), whose glory appears in the advent of the Messiah. The foundation of the salvation which he proclaims is forgiveness, and the *conditio sine qua non* of this forgiveness is the *knowledge of salvation;* comp. Heb. viii. 11, 12.

Vs. 78. **The day-spring from on high.**—An emblematic allusion to Messiah and His salvation, again referring to Mal. iv. 2. There is a remarkable coincidence between the last Messianic prophecy of the Old Testament, and the very last before the incarnation of the Divine Word.

Vs. 79. **Those sitting in darkness and the shadow of death.**—The glance of the prophet here takes a far wider range than Israel. He beholds very many, deprived of the light of truth and life, sitting in darkness and the shadow of death, but sees in spirit the Sun of Righteousness rising upon them all: Isa. ix. 2; lx. 1.

To guide our feet.—The end for which the day-spring should "*give light*," as this again was the end for which it "*visited*" our dark world. The hymn concludes with a boundless prospect into the still partly hidden future.

[ALFORD: "Care must be taken, on the one hand, not to degrade the expression of this song of praise into mere anticipations of temporal prosperity, nor, on the other, to find in it (except in so far as they are involved in the inner and deeper sense of the words, unknown save to the Spirit who prompted them) the minute doctrinal distinctions of the writings of St. Paul. It is the expression of the aspirations and hopes of a pious Jew, waiting for the salvation of the Lord, finding that salvation brought near, and uttering his thankfulness in Old Testament language, with which he was familiar, and at the same time under prophetic influence of the Holy Spirit. That such a song should be *inconsistent* with dogmatic truth, is *impossible*: that it should unfold it minutely, is in the highest degree *improbable*."—AUGUSTINE (*Medit*.): "O blessed hymn of joy and praise! Divinely inspired by the Holy Ghost, and divinely pronounced by the venerable priest, and daily sung in the church of God; Oh, may thy words be often in my mouth, and the sweetness of them always in my heart! The expressions, thou usest, are the comfort of my life; and the subject, thou treatest of, the hope of all the world."—P. S.]

Vs. 80. **And the child grew.**—A summary description of the twofold development of the youthful Nazarite, both in mind and body. Thirty years passed before the "*fear*" which arose at his birth (vs. 65), was replaced by the universal agitation caused by his powerful voice. It is certainly possible, but neither certain nor probable, that during his sojourn "in the wilderness," he came in contact with the Essenes who dwelled in the neighborhood of the Dead Sea (Plinius: *Hist. Nat.* v. 17). [Comp. the similar conclusion on the physical and spiritual development of the child Jesus in ch. ii. 40.—P. S.]

DOCTRINAL AND ETHICAL.

1. The new covenant is greeted, at its first appearance, with hymns of joyful praise. What a contrast to the fear and terror accompanying the introduction of the Old! These songs present a happy interfusion of the letter of the Old, with the spirit of the New Testament. That of Mary is more individual, that of Zachariah more national, in its character. The former is more nearly akin to David's thanksgiving after the promise made to him, 2 Sam. vii. 18; the latter, to his hymn of praise at Solomon's anointing, 1 Kings i. 48. It is worthy of remark, how entirely in the spirit of the Old Testament are the Messianic expectations expressed in both songs, and how pure and free they are from narrow and exclusively Jewish notions.

2. The three songs of Elisabeth, Mary, and Zachariah contain important contributions to the right understanding of their Christology. Each is thoroughly persuaded that the Messiah is to be the head of the prophetic brotherhood, the source of temporal as well as spiritual prosperity to Israel, the highest blessing to the world, the highest gift of grace, the supreme manifestation of the glory of God. We may easily disregard the absence of metaphysical speculations in the compositions of those whose views are so purely theocratic. Their hopes are just as material as might be expected from pious Israelites of their times, but at the same time so indefinite, that they could only belong to the period of the beginning of the sacred narrative. The relative want of *originality* in the song of Mary, which is full of reminiscences, offers a psychological proof of its authenticity. Such songs as these would never have been composed so many years after the appearance of Jesus. Indeed, they may be considered as representative of the state of Messianic expectation just before the "rising of the Sun of Righteousness;" and are, in tone, form, and spirit, much older than the apostolic preaching of Christ's spiritual kingdom. At what other time could such lays have gushed forth, than just at that happy season, when the most exalted poetry became reality, and reality surpassed the ideal of poetry?

3. It is striking, that while it is said of both Elisabeth and Zachariah, before they uttered their songs, that they were filled with the Holy Spirit (vss. 41, 46), the same is not said of Mary. The Spirit seems no longer to have come upon her, after the Old Testament manner, for a few moments, but to have dwelt in and acted upon her in the gospel manner. The royal spirit is more expressed in her song; the priestly character, in that of Zachariah. In his, the Old Testament type, in hers the New, prevails.

4. The enthusiasm of faith attains its highest point just before the time of vision begins (Luke x. 23, 24). It makes the aged Elisabeth young; transforms the youthful bride of the carpenter into the inspired prophetess of her future Son; renders the priest the herald who announces the coming of the forerunner; and even communicates its rapture to the child unborn. The dogmatizer has as little right to build upon this latter circumstance a doctrine of *fides infantium* (as Calovius, a strict Lutheran divine of the seventeenth century, did), and thus make the exception the rule, as the neologian has, to deride a phenomenon of a history, whose religious importance and world-wide influence he is utterly unable to appreciate. Comp. also Aristot. *Hist. Anim.* vii. 3, 4.

5. The song of Zachariah is a proof how much his spiritual life, and his insight into the divine plan of salvation, had increased, during the months of silence which succeeded his reception of the angelic message.

6. Theologians who deny the existence of Messianic prophecies so called—*i. e.*, of special promises given by God Himself, with respect to the coming of Christ—should take a lesson from Mary and Zachariah. In their view, "*God spake by the mouth of His holy prophets;*" spake for centuries past; spake to *Abraham and to his seed*, of the coming Christ; spake so, that all future ages should believe, and expect, that all that was yet unfulfilled, would surely come to pass in due season. We have here a complete outline of Old Testament Christology, to be remembered by the divines and preachers for all time to come.

[7. "*And (John) was in the deserts till the day of his manifestation unto Israel,*" vs. 80. Here we see combined the wisdom of temporary retirement (the truth underlying the monastic system), and the duty of public usefulness in society (which the system of Protestant ethics makes most prominent). The former is a preparation for the latter. "*L's bil-*

det ein Talent sich in der Stille, sich ein Character in dem Strom der Welt" (Goethe). On temporary retirement Bishop HORNE (*On the Life and Death of John the Baptist*) remarks: "He who desires to undertake the office of guiding others in the ways of wisdom and holiness, will best qualify himself for that purpose by first passing some time in a state of sequestration from the world; where anxious cares and delusive pleasures may not break in upon him, to dissipate his attention; where no skeptical nor sectarian spirit may blind his understanding, and nothing may obstruct the illumination from above; where every vicious inclination may be mortified through grace, by a prudent application of the proper means, and every fresh bud of virtue, sheltered from noxious blasts, may be gradually reared up into strength, beauty, and fragrance; where, in a word, *he may grow and wax strong in spirit until the day of his showing unto Israel*. Ex. iii. 1; Ezek. i. 1–3; Dan. ix. 3, 23; Rev. i. 9; Acts vii. 23." On the other hand, MILTON (*Areopagitica*) justly censures the permanent monastic retirement of idleness or selfish piety in these words: "I cannot praise a fugitive and cloistered virtue, unexercised and unbreathed, that never sallies out and sees her adversary, but slinks out of the race, where the immortal garland is to be run for, not without dust and heat. Assuredly, we bring not innocence into the world; we bring impurity much rather: that which purifies us is trial; and trial is by what is contrary."—P. S.]

HOMILETICAL AND PRACTICAL.

The silence of faith and the silence of unbelief contrasted in the cases of Mary and Zachariah.—Meeting of Elisabeth and Mary, emblematic of that of the Old and New Covenant at their respective limits.—Mary's greeting a comfort to Elisabeth in her sorrow, at her husband's loss of speech.—The Holy Spirit in the yet unborn John glorifying the Divine Word, before His birth in the flesh.—The great hymn of praise of the dispensation of grace begun.—Humility perplexed at the ineffable manifestations of grace.—The blessing pronounced: 1. Upon her who first believed; 2. in her, upon all believers of the New Covenant.—Faith leads to sight; sight to increase of faith.—Mary's song of praise: 1. The climax of all the hymns of the Old, 2. the beginning of all the hymns of the New, Covenant.—Deep conviction of the reception of the highest favors combined with personal humility.—The manifestation of righteous retribution combined with unlimited grace.—All the perfections of God glorified in the gift of the Saviour: 1. Grace, 2. power, 3. holiness, 4. mercy, 5. justice, 6. faithfulness.—The new day of salvation, the fruit of ancient promises.—The fruit of faith in Christ's salvation is joy; which is: 1. A thankful joy; 2. an humble joy; 3. a hopeful joy; 4. a God-glorifying joy.—A heart devoted to God, the best psalter.—Mary and Eve: Faith in God's word the source of supreme joy; unbelief of God's word the source of deepest sorrow.—Mary, the Hannah of the New Testament, and, like her, despised, exalted, rejoicing.—The coming of Jesus is: 1. The exaltation of the lowly; 2. the putting down of the mighty; 3. the satisfying of the hungry; 4. the leaving empty of those who regard themselves as spiritually rich.—God's faithfulness and Israel's unfaithfulness.—The mercy of God shown: 1. To Mary; 2. through Mary to Israel; 3. through Israel to the world.

The three months of Mary's sojourn with Elisabeth, an emblem: 1. Of the communion of saints on earth; 2. of the intercourse of the blessed in heaven.—The birth of John, a sign of God's faithfulness and truth.—The silence of Heaven at the birth of John, and the rejoicing of the angels at the birth of Jesus.—The import of bestowing a name: 1. In the case of the forerunner; 2. generally.—Every child a gift of God.—The obedience of faith, in the case of Zachariah: 1. Tried, 2. shown, 3. rewarded.—The Hallelujah of man succeeds the Ephatha of God.—The "report" of God attentively received, at first awakens a just fear, and afterward drives away all fear.—A question and answer at the birth of a child: 1. The natural question, What manner of child shall this be? 2. the satisfactory answer, The hand of the Lord will be with him.

The true father also a priest: the true priest filled with the Holy Spirit; the true fulness of the Holy Spirit manifested in words of praise to God.—Redemption, a visit made by God to His people, by Heaven to earth.—*Novum Testamentum in Vetere latet, Vetus in Novo patet* [St. Augustine].—No national prosperity without the fear of God; no fear of God unaccompanied with beneficial effects upon national prosperity. — Redemption, God remembering His God-forgetting people.—The true service of God is a service *without fear:* 1. Without timid fear of man; 2. without slavish fear of God.—No salvation without forgiveness of sins; no forgiveness of sins without knowledge of the truth; no knowledge of the truth without divine revelation; no divine revelation without divine mercy, grace, and faithfulness.—The rising sun an emblem of Christ: 1. The darkness preceding both; 2. the light spread by both; 3. the warmth given by both; 4. the fruitfulness caused by both; 5. the joy with which both are hailed.—Darkness and the shadow of death: 1. cast down, 2. enlightened, 3. dissipated.—The Prince of Peace, the guide into the way of peace.

The threefold hymns of praise.—Variety and oneness in the minds of those who here glorify the grace of God in Christ.—Mary begins with what is individual, and ascends to what is general; Zachariah begins with what is general, and descends to what is individual; Elisabeth must precede, before Mary can follow.—In the case of Zachariah, the silence of unbelief is exchanged for the song of praise; in that of Mary, the song of praise is exchanged for the silence and expectation of faith.—All three sing on earth the first notes of a song which shall perfectly and eternally resound in heaven, the one song of an innumerable multitude of voices.

The hidden growth of one designed for a great work in the kingdom of God.—Solitude the school of the second Elijah.—The last silence of God, before the first words of the desert preacher.

STARKE:—Christians should not travel from sinful curiosity, but for some good purpose.—The loving salutation of the children of God.—When the heart is full, the mouth overflows.—We may well be filled with grateful astonishment, that the Lord should come unto us in His incarnation, in His Supper, through His word, and through faith.—As we believe, so it happens to us.—Mary says, *My Saviour:* she is then a sinner, needing a Saviour like any other child of Adam.

QUESNEL:—The more God exalts an individual, the more should he humble himself.—LANGII *Op. Bibl.:*—Pride of heart the greatest sin before God.—ZEISIUS:—Christians should give their children names which tend to edification.—BRENTII *Op.*:—God makes the speaker dumb, and the dumb man to speak.—OSIANDER:—Hymns of praise, from sanctified hearts, are the most acceptable sacrifice to God.—Compare Luther's exposition of the *Magnificat*, for Prince John Frederick of Saxony (*Werke*, vii. 1220-1317), wherein he well says: "It is the nature of God to make something out of nothing; therefore, when any one is nothing, God may yet make something of him."

HEUBNER:—The faith of the less (Elisabeth) may strengthen the stronger (Mary).—Mary the happiest of all mothers.—Religion the foundation of true friendship.—Pious mothers a blessing to the whole race of man.—The Spirit must open a man's lips, or he is spiritually dumb.—John a guide into the way of peace, because a guide to Christ.—God carries on His work in secret.—Mature prepara-tion for public work, especially for the work of the preacher.

ARNDT:—Mary's visit to Elisabeth: 1. How it strengthens her faith; 2. how it called forth her praise.

PALMER:—To the art of praising God (Luke i. 46–55) belong: 1. A clear eye to estimate the works of God; 2. a joyful heart to rejoice in them; 3. a loosened tongue to express this joy aright. (The first might also be exemplified in Elisabeth, the second in Mary, the third in Zachariah, and thus the theme and parts be applied to the *whole* pericope, vss. 39–80.)

SCHROTER (in a baptismal sermon on Luke i. 66):—In what sense was this question asked? How ought it to be asked?—F. W. KRUMMACHER:—The dayspring from on high.—The festival at Hebron.—The *Benedictus* of Zachariah. (*Adventsbuch*, Bielefeld, 1847, pp. 140–172.)

SECOND SECTION.

THE HISTORY OF THE NATIVITY.

CHAPTER II. 1–20.

A. *The highest Gift of Heaven.* VERS. 1–7.

(Vers. 1–14, the Gospel for Christmas.)

1   And it came to pass in those days, that there went out a decree [or edict, δόγμα]
    from Cæsar Augustus, that all the [ROMAN] world should be taxed [registered, enrolled].
2   (*And* this taxing [enrolment, ἀπογραφή]^2 was first [the first, πρώτη]^3 made when Cyre-
3   nius [Quirinius]^4 was governor of Syria.) And all went to be taxed [enrolled], every
4   one into [to] his own city. And Joseph also went up from Galilee, out of the city of
    Nazareth, into Judea, unto the city of David, which is called Bethlehem (because he
5   was of the house and lineage [family, πατριᾶς] of David), To be taxed [enrolled] with
6   Mary his espoused [betrothed] wife^5 being great with child. And so it was, that,
7   while they were there, the days were accomplished that she should be delivered. And
    she brought forth her first-born son, and wrapped him in swaddling-clothes [bands],
    and laid him in a manger;^{6} because there was no room for them in the inn.

[^{1} Vs. 1.—*To register* or enrol is the proper term for ἀπογράφεσθαι (lit. *to write off, to copy, to enter in a list;* see the Greek Dictionaries). This may be done with a view to taxation (ἀποτίμησις, census), or for military, or statistical, or ambitious purposes. We know from Tacitus, *Annal.* i. 11, Suetonius, *Aug.* 28, 101, that Augustus drew up with his own hand a *rationarium* or *breviarium totius imperii,* in which "*opes publicæ continebantur; quantum civium sociorumque in armis: quot classes, regna, provinciæ, tributa aut vectigalia et necessitates ac largitiones*" (Tacitus). Tyndale, Coverdale, Cranmer, the Genevan Version, the Bishops,' and King James' have all *taxed*; Rheims Version: *enrolled*; Norton, Sharpe, Campbell, Whiting, the revised N. T. of the Am. B. U.: *registered*; Luther: *schätzen*; Ewald: *aufschreiben*; Meyer, van Oosterzee: *aufzeichnen.*

^{2} Vs. 2.—The usual reading is αὕτη ἡ ἀπογραφὴ πρώτη ἐγένετο. But Lachmann, on the authority mainly of the Vatican MS., omits the article ἡ, and this omission to which Wieseler assents, is now sustained by the Sinait. MS. The article is not necessary where the demonstrative pronoun takes the place of the predicate; comp. Rom. ix. 8: ταῦτα τέκνα τοῦ Θεοῦ sc. ἐστίν; Gal. iii. 7; iv. 24; 1 Thess. iv. 3; Luke i. 36; xxi. 22, and BUTTMANN: *Grammatik des N. T.* 1859, p. 105.—Dr. van Oosterzee translates: *die Aufzeichnung SELBST geschah als erste, the registering* ITSELF *took place as the first,* etc. He reads with Paulus, Ebrard, Lange, Hofmann αὐτή, (*ipsa*) *itself,* instead of αὕτη, *this* (which may be done, since the sacred writers and oldest MSS. used no accents at all), and he bases upon this his solution of the chronological difficulty of the passage. *See* his *Exeg. Notes.* I cannot agree with this solution.

^{3} Vs. 2.—Αὕτη (ἡ) ἀπογραφὴ πρώτη ἐγένετο, κ.τ.λ., *This enrolment was the first made when, i. e., the first that was made or took place,* Quirinius being then governor of Syria. The Vulgate: *Hæc descriptio prima facta est a præside Syriæ Cyrino.* This is, grammatically, the most natural rendering of πρώτη, which probably refers to a *second* census under Quirinius, held about ten years after Christ's birth, and mentioned by Luke in Acts v. 37 (ἐν ταῖς ἡμέραις τῆς ἀπογραφῆς), and by Josephus at the close of the 17th and the beginning of the 18th book of his *Antiquities.* Meyer translates likewise: *Dieser Census geschah als der erste während Quirinius Prœses von Syrien war.* There are, however, other translations of πρώτη, which arise from a desire to remove the famous chronological difficulty involved in this incidental remark of Luke. (1) The authorized E. V., Bishop Middleton, Whiting, and others, take the word adverbially = πρῶτον, πρῶτα, *primum*: "*This enrolment was first made when,*" etc., *i. e., did not take effect until* [text cut off]

CHAP. II. 1–7.

governor of Syria. But this sense would require a very different phrase such as οὐ πρότερον ἐγένετο πρὶν ἤ, or τότε πρῶτον ἐγένετο ὅτε, or ὕστερον δὴ ἐγένετο, κ.τ.λ. (2) Huschke, Tholuck, Wieseler, Ewald, and other eminent scholars solve the chronological difficulty by taking πρώτη in the sense of προτέρα, *prior to*, or *before* Quirinius was governor. Ewald compares the Sanscrit and translates: *Diese Schatzung geschah* VIEL FRÜHER ALS *da Quirinus herrschte* (*Geschichte Christus*, p. 140; but not in his earlier translation of the Synoptical Gospels of 1850 where he translates: *Dieser Census geschah als der erste während Quirinus über Syrien herrschte*). Meyer objects to this interpretation, but both he and Bleek admit that πρῶτός τινος may mean *before some one*. This *usus loquendi* is justified by John i. 5, 30: πρῶτός μου, *prior me;* John xv. 18: πρῶτον ὑμῶν, *priorem vobis;* Jer. xxix. 2: ὕστερον ἐξελθόντος (צֵאת אַחֲרֵי) 'Ιεχονίου τοῦ βασιλέως, *after the departure of Jeconiah the king* (here, however, ἐξελθόντος is gen. abs., and πρώτη does not occur), and by several passages from profane writers (see Huschke, Wieseler, Meyer, and Bleek). But it cannot be denied that this sense of πρώτη is at least very rare, and no clear case can be adduced where it occurs in connection with a *participle;* while, on the other hand, Luke might have expressed this sense much more clearly and naturally in his usual way by πρὸ τοῦ ἡγεμονεύειν (comp. vs. 21 of this chapter; xii. 15; Acts xxiii. 15), or by πρίν or πρὶν ἤ. Hence this translation, though not impossible, philologically, is yet not natural, and should only be adopted when the chronological difficulty can not be solved in a more satisfactory way. *See* the *Exeg. Notes*.

[4] Vs. 2.—Κυρήνιος is the Greek form for the Latin *Quirinius* (not *Quirinus*, although Meyer insists on this form). His full name was PUBLIUS SULPICIUS QUIRINIUS; he was first consul at Rome, then præses of Syria, and died at Rome A. D. 21. *See* Tacitus, *Annal.* iii. 48; Sueton. *Tiber.* 49, and Josephus, *Antiq.* Book xvii. at the close, and Book xviii. at the beginning.

[5] Vs. 5.—The oldest and best authorities, including Cod. Sin., omit γυναικί, which is no doubt a later supplement.

[6] Vs. 7.—The *text. rec.* (and Tischendorf in ed. 7) reads the article, ἐν τῇ φάτνῃ, *in* THE *manger;* but the article is wanting in Codd. Sin., A., B., D., L., etc., and thrown out by Lachmann, Meyer, Alford, so that the Authorized Version is here (accidentally) correct. The article was added here and in vs. 12 by a copyist, in order to designate the *particular*, well known manger of our Saviour. Sharpe, Wakefield, Scarlett, Campbell, and Whiting have prematurely corrected the E. V. and inserted the definite article on the basis of the Elzevir text.—P. S.]

EXEGETICAL AND CRITICAL.

Vs. 1. **In those days.**—Shortly after the date of John's birth. Comp. ch. i. 36.

All the world.—Πᾶσα ἡ οἰκουμένη denotes not merely the country of the Jews, but the whole Roman empire (*orbis terrarum*); and the enrolling (ἀπογράφεσθαι) was undertaken to obtain a registry of the inhabitants of the country, and of their respective possessions, whether for the purpose of levying a *poll-tax*, or of *recruiting the army*.

Vs. 2. **The registering itself took place as the first, when Quirinius was governor of Syria.***—The difficulties found in this remark of Luke, and the various efforts which have been made to solve this chronological enigma, are well known. (*See* among others, WINER, *in voce, Quirinius, Realwörterbuch*, ii. 292 ff.)

[The difficulties are found in the following statements:

1. That the emperor Augustus ordered a general census throughout the empire (vs. 1). But it is certain from heathen authorities that Augustus ordered at least three times, A. U. 726, 746, and 767, a *census populi*, and also that he prepared himself a *breviarium totius imperii*, which was read, after his death, in the Roman senate. Comp. the *Monumentum Ancyranum;* Tacitus, *Annal.* 1, 11; Sueton. *Octav.* 28, 101. The census of 726 and that of 767 can not be meant by Luke; that of 746 *may* be the same, but it seems to have been confined to the *cives Romani*. It is more probable that the census here spoken of was connected with the *breviarium totius imperii*, in which was noted also *quantum sociorum* (including King Herod) *in armis*.

2. That a Roman census was ordered for Judæa at the time of Christ's birth (vs. 3), *i. e.*, during the reign of Herod the Great and before Palestine became a Roman province (A. U. 750). But Herod was a *rex socius*, who had to pay tribute to the Romans; and, then, this census may have been ordered not so much for taxation, as for statistical and military purposes to make out a full estimate of the whole strength of the empire. The same object is

* [We give here, as usual in the *Exegetical* and *Critical Notes*, the author's own version, which reads: *Die Aufzeichnung selbst geschah als erste, da*, etc. He bases upon it his solution of the chronological difficulty, with which I cannot agree. *See* my *Crit. Note* 2, on vs. 2.—P. S.]

contemplated in the decennial census of the United States.

3. That Luke assigns the census here spoken of to the period of the presidency of Quirinus (Cyrenius) over Syria, while, according to Josephus, *Antiq.* xvii. cap. 13, § 5; xviii. 1, 1, this Quirinus became governor of Syria after the deposition of Archelaus and the annexation of Judæa to Syria, A. U. 758 or 760, that is about eight or ten years *after* Christ's birth, which preceded Herod's death in 750 A. U. (According to the isolated, and hence unreliable, statement of Tertullian, *Adv. Marc.* iv. 19, Christ was born when Q. Saturninus was governor of Syria.) I shall give the passage of Josephus in full, that the reader may judge better of the nature of the difficulty and the attempts to solve it.

(*Antiq.* xvii. ch. 13, § 5): "So Archelaus's country was laid to the province of Syria; and *Quirinius*(Cyrenius), *who had been consul was sent by Cæsar to take account of the people's effects in Syria*, and to sell the house of Archelaus. (B. xviii. ch. i. § 1.) Now *Quirinius, a Roman senator, and one who had gone through other magistracies, and had passed through them till he had been consul, and one who, on other accounts, was of great dignity, came at this time into Syria, with a few others, being sent by Cæsar to be a judge of that nation, and to take an account of their substance*. Coponius, also, a man of the equestrian order, was sent together with him, to have the supreme power over the Jews. Moreover, *Quirinius came himself into Judæa, which was now added to the province of Syria, to take an account of their substance*, and to dispose of Archelaus's money. But the Jews, although at the beginning they took the report of a taxation heinously, yet did they leave off any further opposition to it, by the persuasion of Joazer, who was the son of Bœthus, and highpriest; so they being over-persuaded by Joazer's words, gave an account of their estates, without any dispute about it. Yet was there one Judas, a Gaulonite, of a city whose name was Gamala, who taking with him Sadduok, a Pharisee, became zealous to draw them to a revolt, who both said, that this taxation was no better than an introduction to slavery, and exhorted the nation to assert their liberty, as if they could procure them happiness and security for what they possessed, and assured enjoyment of a still greater good, which was that of the honor and glory they would thereby acquire for magnanimity."

The census of Quirinius here described by Josephus, is evidently the same to which Luke alludes in Acts v. 37: "After this man arose Judas the Galilean, in the days of the enrolment (ἐν ταῖς ἡμέραις τῆς ἀπογραφῆς), and drew away much people after him," etc. Josephus calls this rebellious Judas a Gaulonite because he was of Gamala in Lower Gaulanitis; but in *Antiq*. xx. 5, 2 and *De Bello Jud*. ii 8, 1 he calls him likewise a Γαλιλαῖος. In regard to this census, then, the Jewish historian entirely confirms the statement of the sacred historian.

But now the trouble is to find room for another census in Palestine under the superintendence of the same Quirinius and at the time of Christ's birth. This is the real and the only difficulty, and has given rise to various solutions, which are noticed below.

Besides the article of Winer to which Dr. van Oosterzee refers, the following authorities may be consulted on this vexed question: PHILIPP EDUARD HUSCHKE (a learned lawyer of Breslau): *Ueber den zur Zeit Christi gehaltenen Census*, 1840. THOLUCK: *Glaubwürdigkeit der evang. Geschichte.* WIESELER: *Chronologische Synopse*, pp. 73–122. HENRY BROWNE: *Ordo Sæclorum*, Lond. 1844, pp. 40–49. FR. BLEEK: *Synoptische Erklärung der drei ersten Evangelien*, 1862, p. 67 ff. A. W. ZUMPT: *De Syria Romanorum provincia*, &c., 1854 (pp. 88–125). R. BERGMANN: *De inscriptione latina, ad P. Sulpicium Quirinium referenda*, Berol. 1851. H. GERLACH: *Die röm. Statthalter in Syrien u. Judäa von 69 a. C. bis 69 p. C.* Berl. 1865, p. 22. H. LUTTEROTH: *Le recensement de Quirinius en Judée*, Par. 1865.—P. S.]

We reject as inadmissible: 1. The attempt to remove the difficulty in a critical way, whether by rejecting the whole verse as an erroneous gloss (as Venema, Valckenaer, Kuinoel, Olshausen, and others), or by altering the well-supported reading as by the omission of the article (with Lachmann). 2. The conjecture, that Quirinius instituted this census, not as ordinary Proconsul of Syria, but as *extraordinary legatus Cæsaris;* * for, in this case, Luke would certainly have employed another word than ἡγεμονεύειν. 3. The explanation, that this enrolment took place *before* Quirinius was governor of Syria (Tholuck and Wieseler). Luke writes better Greek than to use πρώτη in the sense of προτέρα.† 4. The evasion, that ἀπογραφή means *registration* as well as *taxation* (Ebrard), and that the former took place now, the latter eleven years after under Quirinius. 5. Entirely arbitrary and gratuitous is the supposition of Schleiermacher, that it was merely a *priestly* taxing that took the parents of Jesus to Bethlehem, which Luke incorrectly confounds with the Roman census.

Setting these aside, we believe we may render the passage thus: *the taxing itself was made, for the first time, when Quirinius was governor of Syria.* With Paulus, Lange, and others, we read αὐτή for αὕτη; a reading which no one can deem inadmissible, who considers that Luke himself wrote without accents. We believe that the Evangelist inserts this remark, to distinguish the *decree* for the enrolment, which brought Mary and Joseph to Bethlehem, from the *enrolment itself*, which was not carried into execution till several years later. From the mention of the governor of Syria and Judæa it is evident that vs. 2 speaks of the enrolment in the country of Judæa, while vs. 1 refers to the enrolment of the whole Roman empire. Nothing prevents us from supposing that the ἀπογραφή was really ordered and begun at the birth of Christ, but was interrupted in Judæa for a time by the death of Herod, and the political changes consequent on that event, and subsequently resumed and carried out with greater energy under Cyrenius, so that it might rightly be said to have been *made*, or completed, when he was governor.‡

---

* [Browne, also, in his learned work on Biblical chronology, entitled *Ordo Sæclorum*, p. 40 ff., solves the difficulty by taking ἡγεμών in a wider sense and assuming that Quirinius was at the head of an imperial commission of the census for Syria.—P. S.]

† (Comp., however, πρῶτός μου, John i. 15, 30; xv. 16, and my *Critical Note* 3 above.—P. S.)

‡ [The objection to this solution of the difficulty is, that

The remark of Luke, that this taxing was the *first* that was made in Judæa, is no doubt designed to make prominent the fact that the birth of Jesus occurred just at the time when the deepest humiliation of the Jewish nation by the Romans had begun. Perhaps also in the fact that our Lord should, so soon after His birth, have been enrolled as a Roman subject, he may have discovered a trace of that *universality* which characterizes his Gospel.

Thus viewed, the account of Luke contains nothing that compels us to charge him with a *mistake of memory*, in so public and important a fact. Had he not investigated everything from the beginning (Luke i. 1–3), and does he not show (Acts v. 37) an accurate acquaintance with the taxing which took place eleven [ten] years later, and was the cause of so many disorders? The decree of Augustus was not improbable in itself; and from the account of Tacitus (*Ann.* i. 11) it may be inferred, that it was actually promulgated. For he tells us, that after the death of Augustus, Tiberius caused a statistic account, in the handwriting of Augustus, to be read in the senate, in which, among other particulars, were stated the revenue and expenditure of the nation, and the military force of the citizens and allies. Now, Augustus could not have obtained such information concerning Judæa without an ἀπογραφή, nor is it at all inconceivable, that the territory even of an ally, such as Herod was, should have been subjected to so arbitrary a measure. It appears also from Josephus (*Ant. Jud.* xvi. 4, 1; xvii. 5–8, 11), that Herod was not at all indulged at Rome, but was regarded with a considerable measure of disfavor, and perhaps the enrolment could be affected in a milder manner in the dominions of an ally, than among the inhabitants of a conquered province. The *monumentum Ancyranum* at all events, proves, that in the year 746 A. U. C. an enrolment of Roman citizens took place, and that, therefore, such enrolments were by no means uncommon in the days of Augustus. The notices of this enrolment by Cassiodorus (*Var.* iii. 52) and Suidas (*in voce,* ἀπογραφή) prove less, since both these authors, being Christians, might have drawn their information from Luke. But the silence of Josephus, concerning this whole transaction, may easily be accounted for, especially if we allow that the enrolment was indeed begun under Herod, but not at once completed. Suetonius speaks but very briefly of the whole period; while in Dion Cassius we find no notice at all of the history of the five years preceding the Christian era. They cannot, therefore, be cited as evidence against Luke; and we should certainly be mistaken in supposing, that the complete imperial δόγμα was, in all places, immediately complied with, as if by magic. Should any feel, however, that all these considerations fail to remove the existing difficulties, we can only advise them to assign such *data* to the ὀστρακίνοις σκεύεσι, in which the great treasure of the gospel is deposited.

[There is another and better solution of the chronological difficulty which should be mentioned, viz., the assumption that Quirinius was *twice* governor of Syria, once three years before Christ down to the birth of Christ (A. U. 750–753), and once about 6–11 after the birth of Christ (760). A double legation of Quirinius in Syria has recently been made almost certain by purely antiquarian researches from two independent testimonies, viz.: 1. From a passage in Tacitus, *Annales*, iii. 48, as interpreted by A. W. ZUMPT:

---

vss. 3 ff. relate the enrolment itself, or the *execution* of the imperial *edict*.—P. S.]

De Syria Romanorum provincia ab Cæsare Augusto ad T. Vespasianum (*Comment. Epigraph. ad antiq. Rom. pert.* Berl. 1854, vol. ii. pp. 88–125), and approved by MOMMSEN: *Res gestæ divi Augusti*, pp. 121–124; comp. also ZUMPT's recent article in Ilengstenberg's *Evang. Kirchenzeitung* for Oct. 14, 1865 (against STRAUSS: *Die Halben und die Ganzen*). 2. From an old monumental inscription discovered between the Villa Hadriani and the Via Tiburtina, and first published at Florence, 1765, and more correctly by Th. Mommsen, 1851, which must be referred, not to Saturninus (as is done by Zumpt), but to Quirinius (according to the celebrated antiquarians, Mommsen and Bergmann), and which plainly teaches a second governorship in these words: *Proconsul Asiam provinciam ob[tinuit legatus] Divi Augusti iterum [i. e., again, a second time] Syriam et Ph[œnicem administravit or obtinuit]*. Comp. RICH. BERGMANN: *De inscriptione latina, ad P. Sulpicium Quirinium, Cos. a. 742 U. C., ut videtur, referenda,* Berol. 1851, together with a votum of MOMMSEN, ibid. pp. iv.–vii.; also HERM. GERLACH: *Die römischen Statthalter in Syrien und Judäa von 69 vor Chr. bis 69 nach Chr.* Berl. 1865, p. 22 ff. We hold, then, to a double census under Quirinius: the first (πρώτη) took place during his first Syrian governorship, and probably in connection with a general census of the whole empire (the *breviarium totius imperii*), including the dominion of Herod as a *rex socius*, and this is the one intended by Luke in our passage; while the second took place several years afterwards, during his second governorship, and had reference only to Palestine, with the view to fix its tribute after it had become a direct Roman province (A. U. 759), and this is the census mentioned in Acts v. 37, and Josephus, in *Antiq.* xviii. 1, § 1. It is certain that Augustus held at least three *census populi* of the empire.—P. S.]

Vs. 4. **Joseph also went up.**—The usual expression for going from Galilee to the much more elevated region of Jerusalem. The enrolment would naturally take place in Judæa, in consideration of the claims of nationality. The policy of Rome, as well as the religious scruples of the Jews, demanded it. For this reason, each went to be registered, every one to his ancestral city; though, in other cases, the Romish census might be taken either according to the place of residence or the *forum originis*. **Bethlehem.**—Comp. the remarks of Lange on Matt. ii. 1.

Vs. 5. **With Mary.**—The conjecture that Mary was an heiress (Olshausen and others) who had possessions in Bethlehem, and was obliged to appear there to represent an extinct family, cannot be proved, and is also unnecessary. Undoubtedly, according to the Roman custom, women could be enrolled without their personal appearance; nor did the Jewish practice require their presence. But if no edict obliged Mary to travel to Bethlehem, neither did any forbid her accompanying her husband; and her love for the city of David seems to have overcome all difficulties. Would not a contemplative spirit like hers, perceive that the δόγμα of Cæsar Augustus was but an instrument, in the hand of Providence, to fulfil the prophecy of Micah (ch. v. 1), with respect to the birth-place of Messiah; and now that all was cleared up between her and Joseph, could she have been willing to await the hour of her delivery alone in Galilee, while he was obliged to travel into Judæa?

Vs. 7. **In a manger.**—Probably some cave or grotto used for sheltering cattle, and perhaps belonging to the same shepherds to whom the "glad tidings" were first brought. Justin Martyr, in his *Dial. c. Tryph.*, speaks of a σπηλαίον σύνεγγυς τῆς κώμης. Compare also Origen, *Contra Cels.* 1, 55. At all events, even if this tradition be unfounded, it cannot be proved that it arose from a misunderstanding of Isa. xxxiii. 16. In any case, it deserves more credit than the account in the *Protevangelium* of James, ch. 18, and *Hist. de nativit. Mariæ*, ch. 13, that during her journey the time of Mary's delivery arrived, and that she was obliged to seek refuge in this cave. Luke, on the contrary, gives us reason to conclude that she had arrived at Bethlehem, and sought, though in vain, a shelter in the κατάλυμα. It is not probable that the φάτνη formed part of the caravanserai; nor can we agree with Calvin's view, that descendants of the royal race were designedly harshly and inhospitably treated by Roman officials. It is more likely that Mary and Joseph would not, in their state of poverty, be thought worth the distinction of any special mortification.

DOCTRINAL AND ETHICAL.

1. The days of Herod form the centre of the world's history. Every review of the state of the Jewish and heathen world at the time of Christ's birth, confirms the truth of the remark of St. Paul, ὅτε δὲ ἦλθεν τὸ πλήρωμα τοῦ χρόνου, κ.τ.λ., Gal. iv. 4.

2. As the time of Herod is the turning-point between the old and new dispensations, so is it also the most brilliant period in the revelations of God. God, man, and the God-Man, are never presented to us under a brighter light.

3. *God* manifests all His attributes in sending His Son: His *power*, in making Mary become a mother through the operation of the Holy Ghost; His *wisdom*, in the choice of the time, place, and circumstances; His *faithfulness*, in the fulfilment of the word of prophecy (Micah v. 1); His *holiness*, in hiding the miracle from the eyes of an unbelieving world; and especially His *love* and *grace* (John iii. 16). But, at the same time, we see how different, and how infinitely higher, are His ways and thoughts than ours. His dealings with His chosen ones seem obscure to our finite apprehension, when we see that she who was most blessed of all women, finds less rest than any other. God brings His counsel to pass in silence, without leaving the threads of the web in mortal hands. Apparently, an arbitrary decree decides where Christ is to be born. Still, when carefully viewed, a bright side is not wanting to the picture. God as the Almighty carries out His plan through the free acts of men; and without his knowledge Augustus is an official agent in the kingdom of God.

4. *Man* also manifests himself at the birth of the Lord: his nothingness in the midst of earthly greatness is shown in Cæsar Augustus; his high rank and destiny, in the midst of earthly meanness, in Mary and Joseph.

5. The *God-Man*, who here lies before us as a πρωτότοκος, is at the same time the absolute miracle and the most inestimable benefit. God and man, the old and new covenants, heaven and earth, meet in a poor manger.

"*Den aller Weltkreis nie beschloss
Der liegt hier in Mariens Schooss*," etc.

He who, either secretly or openly, denies this truth, can never understand the significance of the Christmas festival—perhaps never experience the true Christmas joy. The denial of the divinity of Christ by the Rationalist preacher is annually punished at the return of every Christmas celebration.*

6. When we are once convinced *who* it is that came, the manner *in which* He came becomes a manifestation not only of the love of the Father, but also of the grace of the Son. 2 Cor. viii. 9.

The lowly birth of the Saviour of the world coincides exactly with the nature of His kingdom. The origin of this kingdom was not of earth; its fundamental law was to deny self, and for love to serve others; its end, to become great through abasement, and to triumph by conflict: all this is here exhibited before our eyes as *in compendio*.

7. The more our astonishment is excited by the miracle of the incarnation, the more must we be struck by the infinite simplicity—we could almost say barrenness, and chronicle-like style—of St. Luke's account of it. Few internal evidences of authenticity are more convincing than those furnished by a careful comparison of the canonical and apocryphal narratives of the Nativity. The contrast is as indescribable, as between a calm summer night enlightened by tender moonbeams, and a stage-scene of tree and forest lit up with Bengal lights. Such a delineation could only be the work of one resolved to say neither less nor more than the truth.

8. In contemplating what the sacred history says, we must not overlook what it passes over in silence. Of a birth without pain, *salva virginitate, nulla obstetricis ope*, and other similar *commenta*, in which a fancy not always pure has delighted itself, not a jot or tittle is mentioned. How early, however, such play of human wit began and found favor, may be seen, among others, in the example of Ambrosius, who in his treatise *De instit. Virg.*, Opera, tom. ii. p. 257, finds the maternal lap of Mary described in Ezek. xliv. 2, of which he sang:

"*Fit porta Christi pervia,
Referta plena gratia,
Transitque rex et permanet
Clausa, ut fuit per sæcula.*"

9. The designation, "her first-born son," does not necessarily imply that the union of Joseph and Mary was blessed with other children. The first-born might also be the only child.† The question, therefore, whom we are to understand by the ἀδελφοί of Jesus must be decided independently of this expression.

[Comp. on this difficult question my annotation to LANGE's *Matthew*, p. 256 ff.; the commentators on Matt. i. 25; and also BLEEK: *Synoptische Erklärung*, etc., vol. i. p. 76. Bleek remarks, that πρωτότοκος may indeed apply to the only child of a mother, but only at the time of his birth, or at least as long as there is some prospect of other children. The Evangelists, however, looking back to the past history, could not well use this term of Jesus, if they had known that Mary had no other children.—P. S.]

10. The first reception which Jesus met with in this world, is in many respects of a typical character. Comp. John i. 11. Bengel well remarks: "*etiam hodie Christo rarus in diversoriis locus.*"

[11. ST. BERNARD: "Why did our Lord choose a stable? Evidently that He might reprove the glory of the world, and condemn the vanities of this present life. His very infant body has its speech." Dr. PUSEY: "Christ's attendants were the rude cattle, less rude only than we, the ox and the ass, emblems of our untamed rebellious nature, yet owning, more than we, 'their master's crib.' Is. i. 3; Ps. xxxii. 9."—P. S.]

HOMILETICAL AND PRACTICAL.

The decree of the earthly emperor, and the over-ruling arrangement of the heavenly King.—The lowly birth of the Saviour of the world is, 1. *surprising*, when we consider *who* He is that comes; 2. *intelligible*, when we ask *why* He comes; 3. a *cause of joy*, when we see *for whom* He comes.—The King of Israel, a Roman subject.—"The king's heart is in the hand of the Lord; He turneth it whithersoever He will."—The stem of Jesse hewn down, yet shooting anew, Isa. xi. 1.—Bethlehem, the house of bread for the soul, John vi. 33.—The journey of Mary and Joseph to Jerusalem, a type of the believer's pilgrimage: dark at its beginning, difficult in its progress, glorious in its end.—The city of David, the least of all the cities of Judah, and the most remarkable of all cities on earth.—Mary's first-born son, the only-begotten Son of God, and the First-born among many brethren.—Room in the inn for all, except Him.

The manger of Jesus, 1. the scene of God's glory, 2. the sanctuary of Christ's honor, 3. the foundation-stone of a new heaven and a new earth.—The Saviour of the world is (2 Cor. ix. 15), 1. a gift of God, 2. an unspeakable gift, 3. a gift for which we must give Him thanks.—The birth of Jesus, the new birth of the human race: 1. Without it, the new birth of mankind is impossible; 2. with it, the new birth is begun; 3. by it, the new birth is assured.—The Christmas festival the festival of the faithfulness of God.—The coming of the Son of God in the flesh, a manifestation of the infinite wisdom of God: this wisdom evidenced in the time (vers. 1 and 2), the place (vers. 3 and 5), and the mean circumstances (vers. 6 and 7) of His appearing.—The manger, 1. what it conceals, 2. what it reveals.—The whole world summoned to be enrolled as subjects of this King.—"Behold, I make all things new!" 1. A new revelation, 2. a new covenant, 3. a new man, 4. a new world.—Father, Son, and Holy Ghost, equally manifested and glorified in the manger of Bethlehem.—Christmas, the celebration of, 1. the highest honor, and 2. the deepest disgrace, of man.—The manger of the Nativity, a school of, 1. deep humility, 2. steadfast faith, 3. ministering love, and 4. joyful hope.—The coincidences between the birth of Christ in us, and the birth of Christ for us: The birth in us is, 1. carefully prepared for, 2. quietly brought to pass, 3. as much misunderstood by the world, yet, 4. as quickly manifested upon earth, and rejoiced over in heaven, as the birth for us.

STARKE:—The first lesson given us by the new-born Christ is, Obey.—Even before we are born, we are wanderers in the world.—Jesus has consecrated

---

* [The author, in the second edition, has a long note protesting against a superficial and inconsiderate review in Rudelbach and Guericke's *Zeitschrift* for 1860, p. 502, which did him great injustice, and asserting his unqualified belief in the full Divinity of our Saviour for which he has long borne the reproach of Christ in Holland.—P. S.]

† [So Jerome on Matt. i. 25, Theophylact in Luke ii. 7 (πρωτότοκος λέγεται ὁ πρῶτος τεχθείς, κἄν μὴ δεύτερος ἐπετέχθη), and all the Roman Catholic commentators, but evidently under the influence of the dogma of the *perpetual* virginity of Mary which obtained from the fourth century.—P. S.]

all the hard places on which we are obliged to lie in this world.

HEUBNER:—Earthly kingdoms are obliged to serve the heavenly kingdom.—The enrolment of Jesus among the children of men, the salvation of millions. —Our birth on earth, an entrance into a strange country.

F. W. KRUMMACHER:—The threefold birth of the Son of God, 1. begotten of the Father before all worlds, 2. born of flesh in the world, 3. born of the Spirit in us.

C. HARMS:—Christ in us conceived by the operation of the Holy Spirit, born in poverty and weakness, exposed to peril of death soon after birth, remains for years unknown, experiences, on appearing, great opposition, is persecuted and oppressed, but soon rises again, raises itself into heaven, and in His spirit they that cleave to him carry forward and complete His work.

KUCHLER:—It is necessary for a due celebration of Christmas, that we should recognize the Son of God in the new-born child; for, without this recognition, we should lack, 1. the full reason for, and due appreciation of, this celebration; 2. we should observe it without the right spirit; and 3. fail to obtain its true blessing.

FUCHS:—The Son of God born in the little town of Bethlehem, a proof, 1. that the Lord certainly performs what He promises; 2. that with God nothing is impossible; 3. that nothing is too mean or too lowly for God.

FLOREY:—The festival of Christmas, a children's festival: 1. It leads us to a child; 2. it fills the world of children with joy; 3. its due celebration demands a childlike spirit.

AHLFELD:—The birth of the Lord the greatest turning-point of history: 1. The world and the heart before the birth of Christ; 2. the world and the heart after the birth of Christ.

THOLUCK:—The characteristics of Christmas joy; it is a secret, silent, childlike, modest, elevating joy.

JASPIS:—How the celebration of the first Christmas still glorifies itself in the heart of believing Christians.

Dr. THYM:—Christmas joy over the Christmas gift.

[M. HENRY:—Christ was born *in an inn*, to intimate: 1. That He was homeless in this world; 2. that he was a pilgrim on earth, as we ought to be; 3. that He welcomes all comers, and entertains them, but *without money and without price.*—P. S.]

B. *The first Gospel upon Earth.* CH. II. 8–12.

8 And there were in the same country shepherds abiding in the field, [and, καί] keep-
9 ing watch over their flock by night. And, lo, the [an] angel of the Lord came upon them, and the glory of the Lord shone round about them; and they were sore afraid.
10 And the angel said unto them, Fear not: for, behold, I bring you good tidings of great
11 joy, which shall be to all [the] people.[1] For unto [to] you is born this day, in the city
12 of David, a Saviour, which [who] is Christ the Lord. And this *shall be* a sign unto you [and this shall be the sign to you, τοῦτο ὑμῖν τὸ σημεῖον·]; ye shall find the [a] babe wrapped in swaddling-clothes,[2] lying[3] in a[4] manger.

[1 Vs. 10.—Παντὶ τῷ λαῷ. The omission of the article in the Authorized Version unduly generalizes the sense. The people of Israel are here meant, for whom the angelic message was first, though, of course, not exclusively, intended.
2 Vs. 12.—Ἐσπαργανωμένον, swathed, or wrapped up in swaddling clothes or swathing bands. The paraphrastic rendering of the English Version from Tyndale to James was perhaps suggested by that of Erasmus: *fasciis involutum.* See vs. 7.
3 Vs. 12.—The usual reading καί before κείμενον has no sufficient critical authority and was inserted to connect the two participles. Cod. Sinait. omits also κείμενον and reads simply βρέφος ἐσπαργανωμένον ἐν φάτνῃ.
4 Vs. 12.—The definite article τῇ before φάτνῃ in the *text. rec.* is wanting in the best authorities, also in Cod. Sin., and cancelled by the modern critical editors.—P. S.]

EXEGETICAL AND CRITICAL.

Vs. 8. **Keeping watch over their flock by night,** φυλάσσοντες φυλακάς.—The expression seems to indicate, that they were stationed at various posts, and perhaps relieved one another. On the authority of Lightfoot, *ad Luc.* ii. 8, many commentators have remarked, that the Jews were not accustomed to drive their cattle to pasture after the first half of November, and that we have, in this verse, indirect evidence of the worthlessness of the tradition which has assigned the 25th of December as the day of our Lord's birth. It is well known that this date was chosen on account of the contemporary *natalis invicti solis*, without finding any other support in the gospel. On the other hand, however, we might contend that, from Luke ii. 8 alone, it cannot be deemed impossible that the birth of our Lord should have occurred in winter. This winter may have been less severe than usual. Several travellers (*e. g.*, Rauwolf, *Reisen* 1, p. 118) inform us, that in the end of December, after the rainy season, the flowers bloom and the shepherds lead out their flocks again. Besides, these shepherds may have formed an exception to the general rule, whether from poverty, or as being servants. The Lord Himself, in the first night of His life on earth, did not rest on roses. It is also worthy of note, that the ancient Church, to whom the peculiarities of the climate of Palestine were certainly known, was never hindered in its practice of celebrating the Nativity on the 25th of December by the consideration of Luke ii. 8. May not the difficulty, then, be more imaginary than real?

[NOTE ON THE DATE OF THE NATIVITY OF CHRIST.—The fact mentioned by Luke, that the shepherds pastured their flock in the field of Bethlehem, is of itself not inconsistent with the traditional date of our Saviour's birth. Travellers in Palestine differ widely in their meteorological accounts, as the seasons themselves vary in different years. But Barclay, Schwartz and others who give us the result of several years' observations in Jerusalem, agree in the statement that during the rainy season from the end of October to March there generally occurs an interregnum of several weeks' dry weather between the middle of December and the middle of February, and that during the month of December the earth is clothed with rich verdure, and sowing and ploughing goes on at intervals. Schubert says that the period about Christmas is often one of the loveliest periods of the whole year, and Tobler remarks, that the weather about Christmas is favorable to the feeding of flocks, and often most beautiful. The saying of the Talmudists, that the flocks were taken to the fields in March and brought home in November, had reference to the pastures in the wilderness far away from the cities or villages. Comp. on this whole subject S. J. ANDREWS: *The Life of our Lord upon the Earth*, p. 16 ff.

But while the statement of Luke cannot disprove the tradition of the Nativity, it can as little prove it. This tradition is itself of late origin and of no critical value. The celebration of Christmas was not introduced in the church till after the middle of the fourth century. It originated in Rome, and was probably a Christian transformation or regeneration of a series of kindred heathen festivals, the Saturnalia, Sigillaria, Juvenalia, and Brumalia, which were celebrated in the month of December in commemoration of the golden age of universal freedom and equality, and in honor of the unconquered sun, and which were great holidays, especially for slaves and children. (*See my Church History*, N. Y., vol. ii. p. 395 ff.) In the primitive Church there was no agreement as to the time of Christ's birth. In the East the 6th of January was observed as the day of His baptism and birth. In the third century, as Clement of Alexandria relates, some regarded the twentieth of May, others the twentieth of April, as the birth-day of our Saviour. Among modern chronologists and biographers of Jesus there is still greater difference of opinion, and every month, even June and July (when the fields are parched from want of rain), have been named as the time when the great event took place. Lightfoot assigns the Nativity to September, Lardner and Newcome to October, Wieseler to February, Paulus to March, Greswell and Alford to the 5th of April, just after the spring rains, when there is an abundance of pasture, Lichtenstein places it in July or December, Strong in August, Robinson in autumn, Clinton in spring, Andrews between the middle of December, 749, to the middle of January, 750 A. U. On the other hand, Roman Catholic historians and biographers of Jesus, as Sepp, Friedlieb, Bucher, Patritius, also some Protestant writers, defend the popular tradition, or the 25th of December. ❦Wordsworth gives up the problem, and thinks that the Holy Spirit has concealed the knowledge of the year and day of Christ's birth and the duration of His ministry from the wise and prudent to teach them humility.

The precise date of the Nativity can certainly be no matter of vital importance, else it would have been revealed to us. It is enough for us to know that the Saviour was born in *the fulness of time*, just when He was most needed, and when the Jewish and Gentile world was fully prepared for this central fact and turning point in history. For *internal* reasons the 25th of December, when the longest night gives way to the returning sun on his triumphant march, is eminently suited as the birth-day of Him who appeared in the darkest night of sin and error as the true Light of the world. But it may have been instinctively selected for this poetic and symbolical fitness rather than on historic grounds.—P. S.]

Vs. 9. **And, lo, an angel.**—The whole narrative is evidently designed to impress us with the sudden and unexpected manner of the angelic apparition; while, at the same time, it is not denied that the susceptibility of the shepherds for the reception of the heavenly message may have been enhanced by their waiting for the redemption of Israel, their mutual discourse, and their sojourn, in the quiet solemn night, beneath the starry heavens. Meanwhile, the first preacher of the gospel stands suddenly before them.—**The glory of the Lord which shone round them** (δόξα Κυρίου περιέλαμψεν αὐτούς), is the הָבוֹד יְהוָה, already known to them from the Old Testament. And it was the sight of this that filled them with fear.

Vs. 9. **And they were sore afraid or feared greatly** (ἐφοβήθησαν φόβον μέγαν).—The fear which we so often find mentioned in the sacred narrative, when man comes into immediate contact with the supernatural and the holy (comp., *e. g.*, Luke v. 8 and xxiv. 5), is not to be wholly attributed to the fact, that such contact was unexpected, and still less to a conviction of moral impurity before God, only. It seems rather, that the old popular belief, that he who had seen God would die (Judg. xiii. 22), had by no means disappeared even after the Babylonian captivity. This belief might also have been strengthened by traditional remembrance of the cherubim with the flaming sword at the gate of Eden. In any case, this superstitious fear is surely a better ὀσμὴ εὐωδίας before God, than the incredulous scepticism of modern days concerning any angelic visitations.

Vs. 10. **To all the people.**—Namely to Israel, to whom they belonged, as is expressed with the same particularity, Luke i. 33; Matt. i. 21. The announcement of this truth to the shepherds, indirectly intimates, that other pious Israelites were soon to hear from *them* of the birth of their King. In vs. 17 we are told of the first fulfilment of this indirect command.

Vs. 11. **Christ, the Lord.**—Not the Christ of the Lord, as He is called ch. ii. 26, but the Messiah, who equally with the Jehovah of the Old Testament, bears the name Κύριος (com. ch. xxiii. 2, and Acts ii. 36). The intimation that He was born in the city of David would recall Micah v., which, according to Matt. ii. 5, was in those days universally understood to refer to Messiah.

[ALFORD: "This is the only place where these words (Χριστός and Κύριος) come together. In ch. xxiii. 2, we have Χμ. βασιλέα, and in Acts ii. 36, Κύριον καὶ Χρ. And I see no way of understanding this Κύριος, but as corresponding to the Hebrew JEHOVAH." So also WORDSWORTH. This reference is the more probable, since Luke in vs. 9 uses Κύριος twice of Jehovah. The connection of *Christ* with *Lord* occurs also in Col. iii. 24, though in a somewhat different meaning, τῷ Κυρίῳ Χριστῷ δουλεύετε. —P. S.]

Vs. 12. **And this shall be the sign to you.**— It happens here, as in the annunciation of the birth to Mary (ch. i. 36). A sign was vouchsafed, where none was asked,—God seeing that it was indispensably necessary, on account of the extraordinary nature of the circumstance; while Zachariah, who requested a sign, was visited with loss of speech. The sign now granted, is as wonderful as the occurrence just announced, yet one suited to the capacity of the shepherds, and at the same time infallible. The fear, as to whether they may approach the new-born King, and offer Him their homage, is dispelled by the intimation of His lowly condition, while their carnal views of the nature of His kingdom are thereby counteracted. Unless we suppose that the shepherds forthwith made inquiry in all the possible φάτναι of Galilee, whether a child had lately been born therein, we must conclude that their own well-known, and perhaps not far distant φάτνη, was the one pointed out. If they would naturally have hastened thither first, we are not left to suppose, with Olshausen, that they were led by some secret influence upon their minds. Conjectures, which give offence to the sceptical, are best avoided, when not indispensably necessary.

DOCTRINAL AND ETHICAL.

1. This narrative may be called, The history of the first preaching of the gospel upon earth. It became Him, of whom are all things, and by whom are all things, to send such a message by the mouth of an angel. The last preaching of the gospel, the glad tidings of the last day, "Behold, He cometh again," will also be announced with the voice of the archangel, and the trump of God.

2. It will not seem without significance, to any who appreciate the symbolic element of the Scriptures, that the first announcement was made to shepherds. Jehovah had Himself borne the name of the shepherd of Israel, and the Messiah had been announced under this designation by the prophets (Ps. xxiii.; Ezek. xxxiv.). David had pastured his flocks in this very neighborhood; and since the rich and mighty in Jerusalem were looking only for an earthly deliverer, it was undoubtedly among these humble shepherds that the poor in spirit and the mourners would be found, to whom the Lord Himself afterwards addressed His own preaching. There is something indescribably divine and touching in the care of God to satisfy the secret yearnings of individuals, at the same time when He is occupying Himself with the eternal salvation of millions. Man overlooks the masses in the individual, or neglects the individual in the masses; God equally comprehends the interests of both in His arrangements.

3. The glory of the Lord, which shone round the shepherds, consisted not alone in the dazzling brightness of the angel, but was manifested by the fact of his appearing, at such a moment, in such a place, to such men. An angel announces the birth of Jesus; no such announcement distinguishes the birth of John; and thus it is made evident from the very first, how much the King surpasses the forerunner. But for this angelic manifestation, how could the glad tidings have been communicated with infallible certainty, and who could have been more worthy of so august a proclamation than the Word made flesh? Yet the angel appears not in the manger, but visits the shepherds in the silent night-watches, in the open field; a circumstance which powerfully testifies, that the greatness which is to distinguish the Lord's coming is a silent and hidden greatness. He appears to shepherds: God has chosen the mean things of the world to confound the things which are mighty. He speaks too in a manner suited to their comprehension and to their need, and impresses on the first preaching of the gospel that *character indelebilis* of all its after-announcements: "Great joy." Surely we can hardly fail to perceive here also, somewhat of the πολυποίκιλος σοφία τοῦ Θεοῦ, spoken of in Eph. iii. 10.

4. The Redeemer is here called *Saviour*, not Jesus. This name was first to be bestowed upon Him eight days later, in the rite of circumcision.—Born unto *you:* the word must have directed the attention of the shepherds to the fact, that a supply for the felt necessity of each individual soul was now provided. The sign granted to them is so peculiarly an exercise of their faith, that we might almost imagine we heard the new-born Saviour exclaim to those who were the first to come unto Him: "Blessed is he whosoever shall not be offended in Me."

[5. From Dr. RICHARD CLERKE (abridged): God has in every birth His admirable work. But God to be a child, Θεὸς ἐγγάστριος, God in a woman's womb, that is the *miraculum miraculorum*. The great God to be a little babe (μέγας Θεὸς μικρὸν βρέφος, St. Basil); the Ancient of days to become an infant (*coinfantiari*, St. Irenæus); the King of eternity to be two or three months old (βασιλεὺς αἰώνων to be *bimestris, trimestris*), the Almighty Jehovah to be a weak man; God immeasurably great, whom heaven and earth cannot contain, to be a babe a span long; He that rules the stars to suck a woman's nipple (*regens sidera—sugens ubera*, Augustine); the founder of the heavens rocked in a cradle; the swayer of the world swathed in infant bands;—it is ἔργον ἀπιστότατον, a Greek father says, a most incredible thing. The earth wondered, at Christ's Nativity, to see a new star in heaven; but heaven might rather wonder to see a new Sun on earth.—P. S.]

HOMILETICAL AND PRACTICAL.

The "quiet in the land," not forgotten of God.— The glory of the Lord shining in the fields of Bethlehem.—The glory of God,—1. majesty, 2. wisdom, 3. love, 4. holiness,—seen in the angelic appearance at the birth of Jesus.—The angel a model for all preachers, the shepherds a pattern for all hearers, of the Christmas message.—The gospel, though centuries old, an ever new gospel: 1. The hearers, vs. 8; 2. the preachers, vs. 9; 3. the key-note, vs. 10; 4. the principal contents, vs. 11; 5. the sign, vs. 12.—No fear which may not be exchanged for great joy by the glad tidings of a Saviour; but also, no great joy can truly pervade the heart, unless preceded by fear.—The message of Christmas night, a joyful message for the poor in spirit.—The Christmas festival, a festival for the whole world; 1. this it is designed to be; 2. this it can be; 3. this it must be; 4. this it will be.—The child in the manger, 1. the Son of David; 2. the Lord of David; 3. the Lord of David because He was born His Son.—The shepherds of Bethlehem, themselves sheep of the Good Shepherd.

STARKE:—With God is no respect of persons.— MAJUS:—The glory of the Lord, of which the proud see nothing, shines round about the lowly.—The servants and messengers of the Lord must walk in the light.—OSIANDER:—The birth of Christ a remedy against slavish fear.—Divine revelation does not supersede our own diligence, investigation, and research, but extends to them a helping hand.

HEUBNER:—Everything here turns upon, 1. *Who* the new-born child is; 2. *for whom* He is born; 3. and

where.—Christmas joys, a foretaste and pledge of the joys of heaven.
  HARLESS:—In Christ is joy for all the world; viz., 1. the divine message for the lowly; 2. the consolation for the fearful; 3. the satisfying of the individual yearnings; and 4. the appearance of the Salvation of the whole world.
  PALMER:—The three embassies of God: He sends, 1. His Son to redeem us; 2. His angels to announce Him; 3. men to behold Him.
  HOFACKER:—The extensive prospect opened to our faith at Christ's birth: 1. How far backward; 2. how high upward; 3. how far forward, it teaches us to look!—What should a heart filled with the devout spirit of Christmas consider? 1. The excellence of the first Christmas preacher; 2. the humility of the hearers; 3. the importance of the angelic Christmas sermon.
  COUARD:—Unto you is born this day a Saviour: 1. A Saviour is *born*; 2. a *Saviour* is born; 3. a Saviour is born unto *you*; 4. a Saviour is born unto you *to-day*.
  VAN OOSTERZEE:—The light appearing in the night.—The birth of Jesus a light in the darkness, 1. of ignorance; 2. of sin; 3. of affliction; 4. of death.
  THOMASIUS:—The birth of the Lord in its relation to the history of the world: 1. As the end of the old world; 2. as the beginning of the new.
  ARNDT:—The first Christmas sermon. Nothing less is incumbent upon us than, 1. to understand it; 2. to believe it; 3. to obey it.

C. *Heaven and Earth united, in celebrating the Nativity.* CH. II. 13–20.

(Vss. 15–20. The Gospel for the Day after Christmas.)

13 And suddenly there was with the angel a multitude of the heavenly host praising
14 God, and saying, Glory to God in the highest, and on earth peace, good will [εὐδοκία] toward men [peace among men of His good will, *i. e.*, among the elect people of God,
15 εἰρήνη ἐν ἀνθρώποις εὐδοκίας].¹ And it came to pass, as the angels were gone away from them into heaven, [and the men]² the shepherds said one to another, Let us now go even unto Bethlehem, and see this thing which is come to pass, which the Lord
16 hath made known unto us. And they came with haste, and found Mary and Joseph,
17 and the babe lying in a manger. And when they had seen *it*, they made known
18 abroad the saying which was told them concerning this child. And all they that heard
19 *it* wondered at those things which were told them by the shepherds. But Mary kept
20 all these things, and pondered *them* in her heart. And the shepherds returned,³ glorifying and praising God for all the things that they had heard and seen, as it was told unto them.

[¹ Vs. 14.—Here we meet with one of the most important differences of reading which materially affects the sense. Dr. van Oosterzee follows the Received Text and defends it in the *Exegetical Notes*. I shall supply here the necessary critical information. The *text. rec.*, which reads εὐδοκία, and puts a comma after εἰρήνη, is supported by some later uncial MSS., E., G., H., K., L., M., P. (but not by D., as was generally stated before Mai's edition), even by Lachmann, Tischendorf, ed. 7, and Bleek), also by most of the Greek fathers, as Origen (?), Eusebius, Athanasius, Epiphanius, Greg. Naz., Chrysostom, Cyr. Alex., Const. Apost. (the Gloria in excelsis), and most of the interpreters. The Authorized English Version, Luther, and most of the Protestant Versions follow the *text. rec.* On the other hand, εὐδοκίας (the genitive depending on ἀνθρώποις and connected in one sentence with ἐπὶ γῆς εἰρήνη) is the reading of the oldest and weightiest uncial MSS., Cod. Sinait. (as edited by Tischendorf), Cod. Alex. or A., Cod. Vatic. or B. (as edited both by Angelo Mai, who derives εὐδοκίας *a prima manu*, and by Buttmann), Cod. Bezæ or D. (Cod. C. or Ephræmi Syri has a lacuna in ch. ii. 6-41, and can be quoted on neither side), the Itala and Vulgata (*hominibus bonæ voluntatis*, to which Wiclif and all the Roman Catholic Versions conform), Irenæus, the Latin fathers, as Ambrose, Hieronymus, Augustine, and it was approved by Beza, Bengel (though not in his *Gnomon*), Mill, R. Simon, Hammond, and adopted in the text by Lachmann, Tischendorf (ed. 7), Tregelles (Alford is doubtful); among modern commentators by Olshausen, Meyer (who translates: *unter Menschen, welche wohlgefallen*), and Ewald (*unter Menschen von Huld*). The internal evidence also is rather in favor of εὐδοκίας. For it is easier to suppose that a transcriber changed the genitive into the nominative, to make it correspond with δόξα and εἰρήνη, than that he changed the nominative into the unusual phrase ἄνθρωποι εὐδοκίας. Tischendorf says *in loc.* (ed. 7 critica major): "*Incredibile est εὐδοκίας a correctore profectum esse, εὐδοκία vero facile se offerebat. Praeterea lectio a nobis recepta ab ipso sensu imprimis commendatur; aptissime enim hymnus iste duobus membris absolvitur, quorum alterum verbis δόξα usque Θεῷ, alterum verbis καὶ ἐπὶ usque εὐδοκίας continetur.*" But I shall have more to say on the interpretation of the passage in the *Exegetical Notes* below.
² Vs. 15.—The reading καὶ οἱ ἄνθρωποι before οἱ ποιμένες is supported by A., D., E., etc., adopted by Tischendorf, and Alford, also by de Wette, Meyer, and van Oosterzee (who defends it as forming a beautiful antithesis to ἀγγελοι); but it is omitted by Codd. Sin. and Vat., the Latin Vulgate, Eusebius, Augustine, etc., and is included in brackets by Lachmann and Tregelles.
³ Vs. 20.—Ὑπέστρεψαν is the proper reading, sustained by Cod. Sin., etc., and adopted in the modern critical editions against ἐπέστρεψαν of the Elzevir text.—P. S.]

EXEGETICAL AND CRITICAL.

Vs. 13. **A multitude of the heavenly host,** צְבָא הַשָּׁמַיִם.—A usual appellation of the angels, who are represented as the body-guard of the Lord. Comp. 1 Kings xxii. 19; Dan. vii. 10; 2 Chr. xviii. 18; Ps. ciii. 21; Matt. xxvi. 53; Apoc. xix. 14. To include among the multitude spoken of, the spirits of the Old Testament saints, as well as angels, is a conjecture unsupported by the text.

Vs. 14. **Glory to God in the highest.**—The song of the angels may be divided into three parts, the last of which contains the fundamental idea, which evokes the praise of the two preceding strophes. God's good-will toward men: this is the matter, the text, the motive of their song. The reading, ἐν ἀνθρώποις εὐδοκίας, followed by the Vulgate and received by Lachmann, is indeed supported by considerable weight of external testimony, but presents the internal difficulty of introducing a weak repetition in this short doxology: ἐπὶ γῆς and ἐν ἀνθρ. being merely equivalents. This difficulty can only be obviated by understanding εἰρήνη in its literal sense of *peace*, altering the punctuation, and reading as the first member of the sentence, δόξα ἐν ὑψίστοις Θεῷ καὶ ἐπὶ γῆς, and as the second, εἰρήνη ἐν ἀνθρώποις εὐδοκίας. Yet even then, this last expression, in the sense of men who are the objects of the divine good-will, or of those who are themselves men of good-will (*homines bonae voluntatis*), is harsh and unexampled in New Testament phraseology. It is far more suitable to consider the divine εὐδοκία ἐν ἀνθρ., so gloriously manifested in sending His Son, as the theme of the song. It is because of this good-will that he receives δόξα ἐν ὑψίστοις in heaven, Matt. xxi. 9; and ἐπὶ γῆς εἰρήνη, *i. e.*, praise and honor. The parallelism of the members requires this explanation, and a comparison with Luke xix. 38 favors it. The connection of ideas, then, stands thus: the good-will of God towards man is the subject of His glorification, both in heaven and earth. The usual explanation of peace as the cessation of a state of enmity through the birth of Messiah, the Prince of Peace, Isa. ix. 5, must in this case be given up. The εἰρήνη appears in this song, not as a benefit vouchsafed to man, but as an homage offered to God.

Good-will.—The word expresses not only that God shows unmerited favor to men, but that they are also objects of complacency to Him. The same fact is expressed by Christ, Matt. iii. 17; xii. 18; xvii. 5. The solution of the mystery, how a holy God can feel complacency towards sinful man, lies in the fact, that He does not look at him as he is *in himself*, but as he is in Christ, who is the Head of a renewed and glorified humanity.

[I beg leave to differ from the esteemed author in the interpretation of the *Gloria in excelsis*, especially for the reason that εἰρήνη never means *praise* or *honor*, but always *peace*, and is so uniformly translated in the English Version in the 80 or more passages where it occurs in the N. T. (except Acts ix. 31, where it is rendered *rest*, and Acts xxiv. 2, where it is translated *quietness*). See BRUDER's Greek Concordance. If we retain the reading εὐδοκία, I prefer, as coming nearest the interpretation of Dr. v. Oosterzee, that of Bengel: "*Gloria in excelsissimis Deo* (sit), *et in terra pax* (sit)! *cur? quoniam in hominibus beneplacitum* (est)." In other words, God is praised in heaven, and peace is proclaimed on earth, because He has shown His good-will to men by sending the Messiah, who is the Prince of peace (Isa. ix. 5) and has reconciled heaven and earth, God and man. Or, according to the more usual and natural interpretation, the third clause is taken as an amplification simply of the second, forming a Hebrew parallelism. Hence the absence of καί after εἰρήνη. This will undoubtedly remain the meaning of the *Gloria in excelsis* for the common reader of the authorized Protestant Versions of the Bible which read εὐδοκία in the nominative.—But as I have shown above in the *Critical Notes*, the weight of external testimony is strongly in favor of the reading εὐδοκίας, in the genitive, so that the angelic hymn consists of two, not of three, clauses: Δόξα ἐν ὑψίστοις Θεῷ—καὶ ἐπὶ γῆς εἰ ρήνη ἐν ἀνθρώποις εὐδοκίας,—the last three words qualifying and explaining ἐπὶ γῆς. There is a threefold correspondence: (1) between δόξα and εἰρήνη; (2) between ἐν ὑψίστοις or ἐν οὐρανοῖς and ἐπὶ γῆς; and (3) between Θεῷ and ἐν ἀνθρώποις εὐδοκίας. (Cp. Meyer and Bleek.) The sense is: Glory be to God among the angels in heaven for sending the Messiah, —and peace or salvation on earth among men of His good pleasure (*unter Menschen des göttlichen Wohlgefallens*), *i. e.*, among God's chosen people in whom He is well pleased. Εὐδοκία (רָצוֹן) is, in any case, not the good-will of *men* toward God or toward each other (as the Vulgate and the Roman Catholic Versions have it: *hominibus bonae voluntatis*, Rheims Version: *men of good-will*), so as to limit the peace to those men who are disposed to accept the Messiah and to be saved; but it means here (as in all other cases but one) the good-will or the gracious pleasure of *God* toward men, by which He reconciles the world to Himself in Christ (2 Cor. v. 19). Comp. Matt. xi. 26 (οὕτως ἐγένετο εὐδοκία ἔμπροσθέν σου); Luke x. 21; Eph. i. 5 (κατὰ τὴν εὐδοκίαν τοῦ θελήματος αὐτοῦ); Eph. i. 9; Phil. ii. 13 (ὁ Θεὸς . . . ἐνεργῶν . . . ὑπὲρ τῆς εὐδοκίας); 2 Thess. i. 11. In the same sense the *verb* is used Matt. iii. 17: "This is My beloved Son *in whom I am well pleased*, ἐν ᾧ εὐδόκησα); xvii. 5. For the unusual *genitive* we may compare the analogous phrases: σκεῦος ἐκλογῆς, Acts ix. 15, and ὁ υἱὸς τῆς ἀγαπῆς αὐτοῦ, Col. i. 13.

I will only add that this angelic song is the keynote of the famous *Gloria in excelsis*, which was used as a morning hymn in the Greek Church as early as the second or third century, and thence passed into the Latin, Anglican, and other Churches, as a truly catholic, classical, and undying form of devotion, sounding from age to age and generation to generation. Sacred poetry was born with Christianity, and the poetry of the Church is the echo and response to the poetry and music of angels in heaven. But the worship of the Church triumphant in heaven, like this song of the angels, will consist only of praise and thanksgiving, without any petitions and supplications, since all wants will then be supplied and all sin and misery swallowed up in perfect holiness and blessedness. Thus the glorious end of Christian poetry and worship is here anticipated in its beginning and first manifestation.—P. S.]

Vs. 15. Let us now go.—Not the language of doubt, which can scarcely believe, but of obedience desiring to receive, as soon as possible, assurance and strength, in the way of God's appointing.

Vs. 16. And found Mary and Joseph, and the babe.—Here, as usual in the history of the Nativity, the name of Mary comes before that of her husband. Natural as it was that they should not find the child without His parents, yet this meeting was specially adapted to give most light to the shepherds concerning the mysterious occurrence. The Evangelist leaves it to our imagination to conceive the joy with which this sight would fill the hearts of the simple shepherds, and what strength the faith of Mary and Joseph must have drawn from their unexpected and wonderful visit.

Vs. 17. They made known abroad the saying that was told them, διεγνώρισαν.—The διά obliges us to believe that they spoke to others besides Joseph and Mary concerning the appearing of the angels. Probably by daybreak there might have been many persons in the neighborhood of the φάτνῃ. Though the influence of the shepherds was too little for their words to find much echo beyond their immediate circle; yet they were the first evangelists *pro modulo suo* among men.

Vs. 18. **And all that heard it wondered.**—It is a matter of rejoicing, that the good news left no one who heard it entirely unmoved. The contrast, however, between these first hearers (ver. 18) and Mary (ver. 19), forces upon us the conclusion, that their wonder was less deep and less salutary than her silent pondering.

Vs. 19. **But Mary.**—Mary appears here, as well as in ch. i. 29, and ii. 51, richly adorned with that incorruptible ornament which an apostle describes (1 Pet. iii. 4) as the highest adorning of woman. Heart, mind, and memory are here all combined in the service of faith.

Vs. 20. **And the shepherds returned.**—A beautiful example of their pious fidelity in their vocation. Their extraordinary experience does not withdraw them from their daily and ordinary duties, but enables them to perform them with increased gladness of heart. They probably fell asleep, before the beginning of our Lord's public ministry, with the recollection of this night in their hearts, and a frame of mind like that of the aged Simeon. Their names, unknown on earth, are written in heaven, and their experience is the best example of the first beatitude. Matt. v. 3. Undoubtedly, their early and simple testimony to the new-born Saviour was not entirely without fruit; though they might soon have been convinced that such a messsage, brought to them from heaven, was not calculated for the ears of every one, nor intended to be proclaimed upon the house-tops.

DOCTRINAL AND ETHICAL.

1. Granting, as is reasonable to suppose, that the announcement of the first angel produced a heavenly and extraordinary frame of mind in the shepherds, yet the fact of the angels' song loses none of its historic reality from this admission. The first message of salvation made them capable of entering into the rejoicings of the heavenly world on this unparalleled occasion. It is easier to believe that the words κατὰ ῥητόν were imprinted on their memory, than that they could possibly forget them. Happily, however, there is now no need of mentioning or refuting the rationalistic explanations of this occurrence, as they have already died a natural death. The arbitrary assumption, that the history of the song of angels *must* have immediately resounded through the whole land, could alone have emboldened any one to find, with Meyer, "in the subsequently prevailing ignorance and non-recognition of Jesus as the Messiah," a real difficulty against the objective truth of this whole occurrence.

2. Although St. Luke's declaration (ch. i. 3), that he had " perfect understanding of all things from the very first," must be applied to every part of the history of the Nativity; yet the historic credibility of the angels' song is best demonstrated when it is considered in connection with the personal dignity of the Redeemer. A just estimate of the whole is the best preparation for appreciating isolated facts, in the history of our Lord's manifestation in the flesh. The divine *decorum* manifested in the early history will be evident to those only, who honor and understand the great facts of Christ's public life. The supernatural occurrences with which the history opens, can offend those alone who forget the exalted nature of its progress, and the miraculous splendor of its conclusion. (For remarks on the *Gloria in excelsis*, see the *Dissert. theol. de hymno angelico* by Z. B. MUNTENDAM, Amsterdam, 1849.)

3. He who acknowledges in Jesus of Nazareth the Christ, the Lord, the Son of the living God, will find no difficulty in the miracles attending His entrance into the world. Four things are here especially in unison with the rank of the King, and the spiritual nature of His kingdom:—*Angels* celebrate the birth of Jesus; angels celebrate the birth of Jesus *on earth;* angels celebrate the birth of Jesus in the *quiet night;* angels celebrate the birth of Jesus in the presence of *poor shepherds*. The first denotes the exalted dignity of His person; the second, the purpose of His coming (Col. i. 20); the third, the hidden nature of His glory to the eye of sense; the fourth, the subjects to be admitted into His kingdom. There is something so unspeakably great and glorious in this union of earthly obscurity with heavenly splendor, of angels with shepherds, of the form of a servant with the majesty of a king, that the well-known saying, "*ce n' est pas ainsi qu' on invente*," can never be better applied than to the whole narrative.

[Rousseau, in the famous Confession of the Savoyard Vicar in his *Emile*, says against the theory of poetic fiction that the poet (of the gospel history) would be greater than the hero; and Theodore Parker, though himself addicted to this false system, inconsistently, yet truly and forcibly remarks, that "it takes a Jesus to forge a Jesus." This is a strong argument against the mythical hypothesis of Strauss, and the legendary hypothesis of Renan. By denying the miracle of the historical Jesus of the gospel, they leave us the greater miracle of the Jesus of fiction.—P. S.]

4. It will conduce to our due estimation of the work of redemption, to consider the point of view from which the angels contemplate it. These holy spirits, who desire to look into the depths of these mysteries (1 Pet. i. 12), who admire the manifold wisdom of God in His dealings with His church (Eph. iii. 10), and rejoice even over one sinner that repenteth (Luke xv. 10), held but one such festival as that they celebrated in the night of the Nativity. It is no marvel, since by the birth of Jesus sinners are not only reconciled with God and with each other, but things in heaven and on earth are also gathered together in one (Eph. i. 10). To the question, why the Logos should receive fallen *men*, and not fallen *angels*, they know but *one* answer: εὐδοκία!

5. The excellent way in which the wonders of the holy night have been glorified by art, deserves special admiration. We need but call to mind the church hymn of CŒLIUS SEDULIUS (about A. D. 405); *A solis ortus cardine;* the *Quid est quod arctum circulum* of PRUDENTIUS; the *Jesu redemtor omnium* of an unknown author; the *Agnoscet omne seculum* of FORTUNATUS, not to refer to later ones. Among painters, JOHN ANGELICUS DA FIESOLE has admirably represented the Annunciation; CORREGGIO the suggestive image of the night of the Nativity; RAPHAEL the ideal conception of the Madonna with the holy child. In the representation of the entire holy family the Italian school is distinguished above all others. [Roman Catholic art glorifies too much the Madonna in the Divine Child and reflects the doctrinal error of Mariolatry; Protestant art glorifies the Divine Son above His earthly mother and every other creature. The perfection of art will be the perfection of worship, whose only proper object is the triune God.—P. S.]

HOMILETICAL AND PRACTICAL.

The salvation of sinners, the joy of angels.— God's good-will towards men, the matter of His glorification in heaven and earth.—What does the angels' song announce to men? 1. Bethlehem's miracle; 2. Jesus' greatness; 3. the Father's honor; 4. the Christian's calling; 5. heaven's likeness.—The praise of the sons of God in the first hour of creation (Job xxxviii. 7), and in the first hour of redemption.— The hymns of heaven, contrasted with the silence of earth.—The angel, the best instructor in true Christmas rejoicing.—The song of the seraphim of the Old (Isa. vi. 1 ff.), and the song of the angels of the New Covenant.—Every Christmas carol a distant echo of the angels' song.—The song of the angels on earth, and the song of the redeemed in heaven (Rev. v. 9). —Angels came into the fields, but not to the manger.—Angels return to heaven, their Lord remains on earth.—The light which disappeared from the shepherds, contrasted with the light which continued to shine before them.—The journey to the manger: What must be, 1. left behind, 2. taken, and 3. expected on this journey.—The earnest inquiry after the incarnate Redeemer.—Through faith to vision; through vision to higher faith.—The first act of worship before the child in the manger.—The first messengers of the gospel (vs. 17).—The birth of Christ in us: 1. Its commencement, by wondering (vs. 18); 2. its progress, by pondering (vs. 19); 3. its end, thankful glorifying of God (vs. 20).—The testifying faith of the shepherds contrasted with the silent faith of Mary.—The first communion of saints around the manger of the Lord, a communion of faith, of love, and of hope.—Mary's faith tried, strengthened, and crowned on the night of the Nativity.—Contemplative faith at the manger of the Lord.—The first pilgrims to the stable of Bethlehem: 1. Their pilgrim mind; 2. their pilgrim staff; 3. their pilgrim hope; 4. their pilgrim joy; 5. their pilgrim thanksgiving.—The glad tidings of salvation, 1. demand, 2. deserve, and 3. reward, the strictest investigation.—Not one indifferent witness to the new-born Saviour.—The Sabbath hours of the Christian life, a preparation for renewed God-glorifying activity.—To glorify God in our daily work, the best thankoffering for the sight of His grace in Christ.

STARKE:—*Nova Bibl. Tub.*: Jesus honored in heaven, however much He was despised on earth.— MAJUS:—In Christ heaven and earth, God, men and angels, are reconciled.—*Bibl. Wurt.*:—As soon as we hear of Christ, we should run to find him.—We should excite one another to exercises of piety.—We must seek Christ, not according to our own notions, wit, or reason, but according to the word of God.— *Nova Bibl. Tub.*:—They who wonder at the mysteries of God, though they believe not yet, are not far from faith.—Be not a forgetful hearer, but a doer of the word.—LUTHER:—It is praiseworthy to imitate the angelic virtues (vers. 13–20).

ARNDT:—True celebration of Christmas, after the pattern of the shepherds: 1. Their going; 2. their seeing; 3. their spreading abroad the saying; 4. their return to their avocations.

HEUBNER:—A childlike disposition is not disturbed by the meanness of outward appearances.—Ver. 19: St. Luke here gives us a hint of one of his sources of information.—What effects should the announcement of the birth of Jesus produce in us? 1. Desires after Jesus, a longing to know Him by our own experience; 2. zeal in testifying for Jesus, for the encouragement of others;, 3. renewed activity in duty, and constant glorifying of God by a holy walk and conversation.

KITTEN:—The festival of the Nativity, a festival for both heaven and earth: 1. For heaven; for it was, (*a*) prepared in heaven, (*b*) suited for heaven, (*c*) celebrated in heaven. 2. For earth; for it is the festival which commemorates, (*a*) our illumination, (*b*) our elevation to the rank of God's children, (*c*) our transformation into heirs of glory.

FLOREY:—Our heart, the birth place of the Lord: 1. Hidden from the world; 2. favored by the Lord; 3. blessed within.

HERBERGER:—Christmas day, 1. a day of miracle; 2. a day of honor; 3. a day of grace.

HÖFER:—In Christ we receive, 1. the love of heaven; 2. the light of heaven; 3. the peace of heaven.

AHLFELD:—The shepherds as patterns for imitation: 1. They seek the child in the stable and the manger; 2. they spread the gospel message everywhere; 3. they praise God with thankful joy.

HARLESS:—The faith of the shepherds, true faith. 1. Its foundation—(*a*) God's word, (*b*) God's deed; 2. its properties—(*a*) emotion of heart, (*b*) activity of life; 3. its aim—(*a*) the spreading of the kingdom of God upon earth, (*b*) the glory of God.

BRANDT:—Joy in the Saviour is, 1. the greatest, 2. the noblest, 3. the most active joy.

KRAUSHOLD:—A true Christmas blessing consists in our becoming, 1. more desirous of salvation, 2. firmer in faith, 3. more abundant in testimony, 4. more joyful in praise.

FUCHS:—The Christian's celebration of Christmas: 1. His visit to his Saviour (vss. 15, 16); 2. his sojourn with his Saviour (vss. 18, 19); 3. his return from his Saviour (vss. 17, 20).

["With malice toward no one, with charity for all." This truly Christian motto of President Lincoln, in his second inaugural address, spoken in the midst of a fearful civil war, March 4, 1865, is an earthly echo of the Divine εὐδοκία.—P. S.]

THIRD SECTION.

THE HISTORY OF THE GROWTH.

CHAPTER II. 21-52.

———

A. *The Eighth Day; or, Submission to the Law.* Vs. 21.

(The Gospel for New Year's Day.)

21 And when eight days were accomplished for the circumcising of the child [for circumcising Him],[1] his name was called JESUS, which was so named of [by] the angel before he was conceived in the womb.

[1 Vs. 21.—The Received Text reads τὸ παιδίον, *the child*, to mark the chief person; but this word is unnecessary in the connection and not sustained by the best authorities and critical editions which read αὐτόν. So also Cod. Sinait. The second καὶ before ἐκλήθη is simply redundant, and hence properly omitted in the E. V.—P. S.]

EXEGETICAL AND CRITICAL.

Vs. 21. **The circumcising.**—See the *Exegetical Notes* on ch. i. 59.

[ALFORD:—"The Lord was made like unto His brethren (Hebr. ii. 17; iv. 15) in all weakness and bodily infirmity, from which legal uncleannesses arose. The body which He took on Him, though not a body of sin, was mortal, subject to the consequences of sin,—in the likeness of sinful flesh; but incorruptible by the indwelling of the Godhead (1 Pet. iii. 18). In the fulfilment therefore of His great work of redemption He became subject to legal rites and purifications—not that they were absolutely *necessary* for *Him*, but were included in those things which were πρέποντα for Him in His humiliation and 'making perfect'; and in His lifting up of that human nature, *for which* all these things were *absolutely necessary* (Gen. xvii. 14), into the Godhead."—BENGEL remarks ou πρὸ τοῦ, *antequam: "Exquisite hic denotatur beneplacitum Patris in Christo, atque innuitur simul, nunc infantem circumcisione per se non egnisse. Conf. Gal. 1. 15."*—P. S.]

Jesus, Ἰησοῦς.—Hebr. יְהוֹשֻׁעַ, or contracted, יֵשׁוּעַ,—*Jehovah auxilium.* It appears from Col. iv. 11, and Matt. xxvii. 16, 17, where the correct reading is *Jesus Barabbas*, that the name was not an usual one at this time. For mystical derivations of the name *see* Wolf and others.

Which (name) was so named (or: the name given by the angel).—The naming of our Lord was not less an act of faith in obedience to the divine command, than the naming of the Baptist (ch. i. 63). In this instance, the direction was not given to Joseph alone (Matt. i. 21), but also to Mary (Luke i. 31).

DOCTRINAL AND ETHICAL.

1. It is remarkable that Luke relates the circumcision of the Baptist in a far more detailed and circumstantial manner than that of the Messiah. This is surely no proof that the two narratives were derived from entirely different sources (Schleiermacher); while this very brevity and simplicity offer a fresh token of the truth of the history. A mere inventor would never have omitted enhancing the occurrences of the eighth and fortieth days, by appearances of angels. The detailed account of the circumcision of John, contrasted with the brevity with which that of Jesus is narrated, is the more striking, when we consider that the first stands entirely upon Old Testament ground; while the Mosaic law, and the rite of circumcision itself, were about to be done away with by the second (Lange.)

2. In a certain point of view, circumcision had not the same meaning for the child Jesus, as it bore for every other son of Abraham. The spotless purity of His body needed no symbol of the putting off of the sinful Adam; and even without περιτομή, He would doubtless, in the eye of Heaven, have been sanctified and hallowed in a peculiar sense of the word. But the King of the Jews could not, and would not, omit the token that He belonged, according to the flesh, to that elect people; and when the Son of God appeared in the likeness of sinful flesh, He chose also to receive the emblem of purification from sin, that He might be in all things like unto His brethren, sin only excepted. The principle, so prominently laid down by our Lord at His baptism, also applies in this instance, Matt. iii. 15. It shows a deep insight into the nature and reality of His incarnation, that the mother of our Lord never thinks of withdrawing either Him or herself from the duties of the eighth or of the fortieth day.

3. He who was ἐκ γυναικὸς γενόμενος, came also at the appointed time ὑπὸ νόμον by circumcision. His reception of this rite is an incident in the history of the self-humiliation of Him who, being originally in the form (μορφή) of God, took upon Him the form of a servant. By it He became symbolically bound to perform that will of the Father, for whose fulfilment He had come into the world. Olshausen well remarks, that "the harmony of the divine plan of salvation required His submission to even this form of human development, according to which He was received as a member of the theocracy of the Old Testament, by means of the same sacred treatment which brought all His brethren within the bonds of the covenant, in order that He might, after attaining to the perfectly developed consciousness of His higher existence, elevate to the higher degrees of His own life, that community to which He was united by so many various ties."

4. Now that Christ is circumcised, the law is in this respect also both fulfilled and repealed. Baptism takes the place of circumcision (Col. ii. 10-12), as the form of admission into the new covenant; and

Paul rightly opposes the judaizing zeal for the re-introduction of circumcision, as a virtual denial of Christian principle.

5. The most important fact of the eighth day, is, after all, the naming of the Saviour. What name was ever given which promised more, and which less disappointed the expectations excited, than this? Comp. Acts iv. 12.

HOMILETICAL AND PRACTICAL.

Jesus made under the law, that He might redeem us from the law.—Jesus both humbled and exalted, on the eighth day.—The circumcision of the flesh, and the circumcision of the heart, Rom. ii. 28, 29.—Circumcision and baptism.—The first fruits of the blood of Christ, a sacrifice of obedience.—The name Jesus is, 1. a name given by God; 2. a name whereby we must be saved; 3. the only name under heaven given for this purpose.—The solemn manner in which circumcision was instituted (Gen. xvii.), contrasted with the silent and almost imperceptible manner in which it disappeared, Heb. viii. 13.—The harmony between the name and work of Jesus.—The name Jesus: 1. The dignity with which the Lord is invested; 2. the work which He performs; 3. the homage He receives, as bearing this name.—Joseph and Mary, patterns of the unquestioning obedience of faith.—The name of Jesus, and our name.—New Year's day, the Lord's name-day: 1. The knowledge of the name of Jesus, the best New Year's blessing; 2. the faithful confession of this name, the chief New Year's duty.—The New Year considered in the light of the name of Jesus, the name of Jesus in the light of the New Year.—Our earthly destination also, is appointed by God before our birth.

STARKE:—Christ was esteemed unclean, according to the law, that, by His satisfaction, He might take away our uncleanness.

PALMER:—The name of Jesus in the mouth of His believing people who are in the world: 1. All that we believe and confess in the world is summed up in this *one* name; 2. what we do for the world, we do in the name of Jesus; 3. what we shall take out of the world is this name alone; (or, more shortly, the name of Jesus, with respect to the faith, the works, and the hope of the Christian).

RAUTENBERG:—The name of Jesus, our light in the darkness of the New Year's morning: 1. The light of grace for the darkness of our conscience; 2. the light of power for the darkness of our life.—This name on New Year's day, 1. throws the right light on our reminiscences; 2. gives the right weight to our resolutions; 3. and provides the anchor of true confidence for our hopes.

SPITZLER:—We must begin with Jesus Christ, the true "beginning."—Through Him we have, 1. new life; 2. new hopes; 3. new righteousness; 4. new peace.

V. GERLACH:—The New Year, a year of salvation.

STIER:—The right way of beginning the New Year: 1. Not in our own name; 2. not only in the name of God alone, but in the name of the Lord Jesus.

HEUBNER:—The Christian resolution to lead a new life in the New Year: 1. What this resolution requires—circumcision of the heart and fulfilment of duties; 2. what gives it strength—the name of Jesus; 3. what promises its accomplishment—the protection of Providence (vs. 21).

B. *The Fortieth Day; or, the Redemption from the Temple Service.* CH. II. 22–40.

22 And when the days of her [their]¹ purification, according to the law of Moses, were accomplished [completed], they brought Him to Jerusalem, to present *Him* to the Lord;
23 (As it is written in the law of the Lord [Ex. xiii. 2], Every male that openeth the womb
24 shall be called holy to the Lord); And to offer a sacrifice, according to that which is said in the law of the Lord [Lev. xii. 8], A pair of turtle-doves, or two young pigeons.

25 And, behold, there was a man in Jerusalem, whose name *was* Simeon; and the same man *was* just and devout, waiting for the consolation of Israel: and the Holy
26 Ghost was upon him. And it was revealed unto him by the Holy Ghost, that he should not see death, before he had seen the Lord's Christ [the Christ of the Lord].
27 And he came by the Spirit unto the temple: and when the parents brought in the child
28 Jesus, to do for Him after the custom of the law, Then took he [he took] Him up in his arms, and blessed God, and said,

29 Lord, now lettest Thou Thy servant depart in peace, according to Thy word:
30, 31 For mine eyes have seen Thy salvation, Which Thou hast prepared before the face of all people [all the nations, πάντων τῶν λαῶν];
32 A light to lighten [for a revelation to, εἰς ἀποκάλυψιν] the Gentiles, and the glory of Thy people Israel.

33 And Joseph [His father, ὁ πατὴρ αὐτοῦ] and His mother² marvelled at those things
34 which were spoken of Him. And Simeon blessed them, and said unto Mary His mother,

Behold, this *child* [οὗτος] is set [appointed] for the fall and rising again of many in Israel; and for a sign which shall be spoken against;

35 (Yea, [And] a sword shall pierce through thy [thine] own soul also),
That the thoughts of many hearts may be revealed.

36 And there was one Anna, a prophetess, the [a] daughter of Phanuel, of the tribe of Aser [Asher]: she was of a great age [of great age], and had lived with an [a] hus-
37 band seven years from her virginity; And she *was* a widow of about [till]³ fourscore and four years, which [who] departed not from the temple, but served *God* [serving]
38 with fastings and prayers night and day. And she,⁴ coming in that instant [at that very hour, αὐτῇ τῇ ὥρᾳ], gave thanks likewise unto the Lord [God],⁵ and spake of Him to all them that looked for redemption in ⁶ Jerusalem.
39 And when they had performed all things according to the law of the Lord, they returned into Galilee, to their own city Nazareth.
40 And the child grew, and waxed strong⁷ in spirit, [being] filled with wisdom; and the grace of God was upon him.

[¹ Vs. 22.—Αὐτῶν is better authenticated (also by Cod. Sinait.) than αὐτοῦ, and still better than αὐτῆς, and refers to Mary and Joseph (not the child, nor the Jews; comp. the following ἀνήγαγον αὐτόν. In this instance the translators of King James followed the Complutensian reading αὐτῆς, which is almost without authority and a manifest correction from the misapprehension of a transcriber who thought that αὐτοῦ or αὐτῶν would imply the impurity of Christ. Wiclif and the Genevan Bible have *Maries purification*, the Rheims Test. *her purification*, but Tyndale and Cranmer correctly *their* purification.

² Vs. 33.—The original reading, which is sustained by Codd. Sinait., B., D., L., Origen, Vulgate (*pater ejus et mater*), etc., was no doubt: ὁ πατὴρ αὐτοῦ καὶ ἡ μήτηρ (Cod. Sinait. adds a second αὐτοῦ), and is adopted in the text of Tischendorf, Alford, and Tregelles (not of Lachmann). The substitution of Ἰωσήφ for πατὴρ αὐτοῦ is easily explained from prejudice. The word is, of course, not to be taken in the physical, but in the legal and popular sense.

³ Vs. 37.—The usual reading is ὡς, which is very usual in connection with numbers; but Lachmann, Tischendorf, Alford, and Tregelles read ἕως, *till*, according to Codd. Sinait., B., L., Vulgate (*usque ad*), etc.

⁴ Vs. 38.—Αὕτη is wanting in the best authorities and modern critical editions, and could easily be inserted from vs. 37.

⁵ Vs. 38.—Τῷ Θεῷ is the true reading (sustained also by Cod. Sinait.), and now generally adopted instead of the *lect. rec.* τῷ Κυρίῳ.

⁶ Vs. 38.—Ἐν is wanting in Codd. Sinait., Vat., etc., and dropped by Lachmann, Tischendorf, Tregelles. Alford puts it in brackets. In this case Ἱερουσαλήμ must be taken as the genitive; *for the redemption of Israel*. But Meyer defends the ἐν, and explains its omission from vs. 25.

⁷ Vs. 40.—Πνεύματι seems to have been inserted from ch. i. 80, and is excluded from the text by Lachmann, Tischendorf, Alford, Tregelles, on the best ancient authorities. Cod. Sinait. is likewise against it. Dr. van Oosterzee omits it in his German Version.—P. S.]

EXEGETICAL AND CRITICAL.

Vs. 22. **Their** (not her) **purification.**—The law of Moses declared, that the mother was unclean seven days after the birth of a son (fourteen days after the birth of a daughter), and must remain separate for thirty-three days from this period. These forty days are together denoted the days of the καθαρισμός. If several persons are spoken of (αὐτῶν, *their*), we must not refer it to the *Jews* in general, nor to the mother and *the child* (for the Mosaic precept, Lev. xii. 4-6, had regard only to the mother, not the child), but to the mother and *the father*. Joseph was not obliged to be present in the temple, yet he might take part in the solemnity of purification, as it was his part to present the first-born to the Lord. It appears from the reference to Lev. xii. 8, that Mary brought the offering of the poor.

Vs. 24. **In the law of the Lord.**—According to Exod. xiii. 2, all the first-born were dedicated to God. In remembrance of the deliverance from Egypt, when the destroying angel spared the first-born of the Israelites, it was ordered, that the eldest son of every family should be considered as God's special property, and be redeemed from the service of the sanctuary by the payment of five shekels (Num. xviii. 16). The tribe of Levi afterward took the place of the first-born thus dedicated and redeemed. The fact that Mary was unable to bring a lamb and a turtle-dove [Lev. xii. 6], as she would undoubtedly desire to do, is a fresh proof of the truth of the apostolic word, 2 Cor. viii. 9.

Vs. 25. **Simeon.**—The principal traditions concerning this aged saint are to be found in Winer *in voce*.* The very manner in which Luke mentions him, as ἄνθρωπος ἐν Ἱερουσ., while he speaks with so much more of detail concerning Anna, supports the conjecture that, though acknowledged by God, he was not famous among his fellow-men. He may have been, however, one of the leading men of his country, and was probably aged, while he must certainly be numbered among those who waited for the redemption of Israel, vss. 25, 38. A later tradition, describing him as blind, but receiving his sight on the approach of the child Jesus, suitable as its allegorical sense may be, is without historical foundation.

Vs. 26. **Revealed unto him by the Holy Spirit.**—By an inward revelation, which it would be as impossible to describe as presumptuous to doubt. We prefer supposing an infallible consciousness, wrought by God, that his prayer in this respect was certainly heard, to imagining the intervention of some wonderful dream. If the spirit of prophecy had departed from Israel since the time of Malachi, according to the opinion of the Jews, the return of this Spirit might be looked upon as one of the tokens of Messiah's advent.

Vs. 26. **See death.**—Or, as it is elsewhere expressed, *taste death*, Matt. xvi. 28; Heb. ii. 9. It means, not merely falling asleep, but the experience of death as death, with its terrible accompaniments. That he should depart immediately, or soon *after* seeing Christ, was not indeed revealed to him in so many words, but might naturally be expected by

* [According to some, Simeon was the son of the famous Rabbi Hillel, and father of Gamaliel, the teacher of St. Paul (Acts v. 34). The Rabbis say: "The birth of Jesus of Nazareth was in the days of R. Simeon, son of Hillel." But this is, of course, a mere conjecture, without inherent probability.—P. S.]

him. Lange beautifully remarks: "Simeon is in the noblest sense the eternal Jew of the Old Covenant who cannot die before he has seen the promised Messiah. He was permitted to fall asleep in the peace of his Lord before His crucifixion."

Vs. 27. **And he came by the Spirit.**—Perhaps he was accustomed, like Anna, to go daily into the temple; at all events, he now felt an irresistible impulse from God to enter it. It is possible that he might have heard the narration of the shepherds of Bethlehem; but such a supposition is not necessary for the understanding of the gospel account.

Vs. 29. **Now lettest Thou**, etc.—Simeon's song of praise is genuinely Israelitish, not exclusively Jewish. Compared with the hymns of Zachariah and Mary, it is more peculiarly characterized by its psychological truth than even by its æsthetic beauty. The internal variety and harmony of these three compositions is a proof of the credibility of the early chapters of Luke which must not be overlooked. **According to Thy word.**—A retrospect of the previous revelation.

Vs. 30. **Thy salvation.**—His mind fastens on the thing, not the person; and he sees the world's salvation, while beholding the form of a helpless child.

Vs. 31. **Before the face of all nations** (πάντων τῶν λαῶν).—The true union of the particular and universal points of view. Salvation goes out from Israel to all people without distinction, in order to return to Israel again. The Sun of Righteousness makes the same circuit as the natural sun, Eccles. i. 5.

Vs. 32. **A light for a revelation to (to lighten) the Gentiles,** εἰς ἀποκάλυψιν ἐθνῶν.—The κάλυμμα is now taken away from the eyes of all nations, that they may see the Christ, the Light of the world.—**And the glory.**—Not a declaration that glory is the end proposed, but used as apposition to σωτήριον, vs. 30. The highest glory of Israel consists in the salvation of Messiah.

Vs. 33. **And His father and mother marvelled.**—Not because they learned from the song of Simeon anything that they had not heard of before, but they were struck and charmed by the new aspect under which this salvation was presented. Simeon sees fit to moderate their transports, by alluding to the approaching sufferings which must precede the glory. His words, however, contained nothing new or strange. The prophets had already announced, that the Servant of the Lord would undergo sufferings and persecution; and even the apparent poverty of the mother and of the holy child could not but convince the pious man, who well knew the carnal expectations of his fellow-countrymen, that a Messiah born in so lowly a condition could not fail to encounter the opposition of the nation. With regard to the ῥομφαία (vs. 35), it did not pierce Mary's soul for the first time, but only for the last time, and the most deeply, on Golgotha.

His father.—[Our Saviour never speaks of Joseph as His father, see vs. 49; but he was His father in a *legal* sense and in the eyes of the *people*, and, as Alford observes *in loc.*, in the simplicity of a historical narrative we may read ὁ πατὴρ αὐτοῦ and οἱ γονεῖς, without any danger of forgetting the momentous fact of the supernatural conception.—P. S.]

Vs. 34. **Set for** [κεῖται εἰς, **is appointed for**] **the fall.**—Comp. Isa. viii. 14; Rom. ix. 33. This divine setting or appointing is always to be considered as *caused* by their own fault, in those who fall, by wilfully continuing in unbelief and impenitence. Mary had already expressed the same truth, in a more general form, ch. i. 52, 53; while the Lord Himself still further develops it, John ix. 39, 41; Matt. xxi. 44. We have here the first hint, given in New Testament times, of the opposition which the kingdom of Messiah would experience from unbelief. The angels had only announced great joy: it was given to the man of God, who saw heaven opened before his death, to go a step further.

[**And for a sign which shall be spoken against,** σημεῖον ἀντιλεγόμενον, *signum, cui contradicitur*.—BENGEL: "*Insigne oxymoron. Signum alias tollunt contradictionem: hoc erit objectum contradictionis, quanquam per se signum est evidens fidei* (Is. lv. 13, *Sept.*); *nam eo ipso, quia lux est, illustris et insignis est. Magnum erit spectaculum.*" The fulfilment of this prophecy culminated in the crucifixion. —P. S.]

[Vs. 35. **And a sword shall pierce,** etc.—This sentence is coördinate to the preceding one, and hence should not be inclosed in parenthesis, as in the E. V. The grief of Mary corresponds to the rejection and suffering of Christ. The **sword** that shall pierce the ψυχή of Mary, must be referred to her sympathizing motherly anguish at beholding the opposition of the world to her Son, and especially His passion and crucifixion. It is a prophecy of the *mater dolorosa apud crucem lacrymosa*, who represents the church of all ages in the contemplation of the cross.—I cannot agree with Alford, who refers the ῥομφαία to the sharp pangs of sorrow for her *sin* and the struggle of *repentance;* referring to Acts ii. 37. This would require πνεῦμα or καρδίαν rather than ψυχήν, and is hardly consistent with the character of Mary. She was probably one of those rare favorites of Divine grace who never forsake their "first love," who are always progressing in goodness, and from their infancy silently and steadily grow in holiness, without passing through a violent change, or being able to mark the time and place of their conversion. Such were St. John, Zinzendorf, Mary of Bethany and other female saints.—P. S.]

Vs. 35. **That the thoughts of many hearts may be revealed.**—The thoughts of Mary, who now as before (ver. 19) ponders and is silent, and the thoughts of all who, whether for their fall or rising again, should come in contact with her Son. Lasting neutrality with respect to the Lord is impossible; he that is not for Him is against Him; comp. Luke xi. 23. His appearing brings to light the latent good and evil, as the same sun which dissipates the clouds that obscure the sky, also draws up the mists and vapor of earth.

Vs. 36. **A daughter of Phanuel.**—It is remarkable that the name of Anna's father should be mentioned, and not that of her husband. Perhaps he also was known as one who waited for the consolation of Israel. The pious words of Anna, ver. 38, cannot be the only reason of her being called a **prophetess;** such an appellation must have been caused by some earlier and frequent utterances, dictated by the Spirit of prophecy, by reason of which she ranks among the list of holy women who, both in earlier and later times, were chosen instruments of the Holy Ghost. **Eighty-four years** (fourscore and four) is mentioned as the sum of her whole life, not of that portion of it which had elapsed since the death of her husband. It is specially mentioned, to show also that, though she had passed but few years in the married state, she had reached this advanced age as a widow; a fact redounding to her honor in a moral sense, and ranking her among the comparatively small number of "widows indeed," whom St. Paul especially commends, 1 Tim. v. 3, 5. That her piety was of an entirely Old Testament character, gives no support to the opinion of certain Roman Catholic theologians, e. g. SEPP; *Leben Jesu*, ii. p. 54, that Mary was brought up under her guidance in the house of the Lord.

Vs. 38. **Likewise gave thanks,** ἀνθωμολογεῖτο, *vicissim laudabat*, Ps. lxxix. 13.—She took up the theme of praise which had just fallen from the aged Simeon. We believe, with Tischendorf, that the correct reading here is τῷ Θεῷ; but even if we read τῷ Κυρίῳ, with the *Textus Receptus*, we still have to apply it to the Jehovah of Israel. It is no acknowledgment of the new-born Christ, but a doxology to the Father who sent Him, that is here spoken of; while the words immediately following, **and spake of Him,** evidently allude to the child of Mary, whose name needs not to be repeated here, as He plays the chief part in the whole history.

Vs. 38. **That looked for redemption in Jerusalem.**—There were then a certain number of pious persons dwelling in the capital, who lived in and upon the hope of salvation through the Messiah, and among whom the report of His birth was soon spread. Who knows how soon this report might not have spread also throughout the whole country through their means, had not the secret departure of the holy family to Egypt and Nazareth caused every trace of them to disappear from the eyes of this little band at Jerusalem? Perhaps, too, it was chiefly composed of the aged, the poor, and the lowly, whose influence would certainly not be very extensive. The new-born Saviour, now recognized, through the testimony of Simeon and Anna, by the noblest in Israel, was soon to receive the homage of the Gentile world also, through the arrival of the wise men from the east.

Vs. 39. **And when they had performed all things—they returned into Galilee, to their own city Nazareth.**—The question naturally occurs here, whether the visit of the wise men, and the subsequent flight into Egypt, took place before or after the fortieth day. Although the former is by no means impossible (see LANGE, *Leben Jesu* ii., p. 110), we think the latter conjecture preferable. The narrative of Luke (ch. ii. 22-24), at least, gives us the impression, that the presentation in the temple took place at the customary time; and we should therefore find some difficulty in inserting the matter contained in Matt. ii. between the eighth and fortieth days. As long as Mary had not brought her offering of purification, she was obliged to remain at home, as unclean; and if Joseph, on his return from Egypt, as we find from Matt. ii. 22, 23, was obliged to settle at Nazareth, instead of Bethlehem, from fear of Archelaus, it was not likely that he would then have ventured to go to Jerusalem, and even into the temple. We need not necessarily conclude, from Matt. ii. 1, that the event there mentioned took place in the days immediately following the birth of Jesus; nor can Luke ii. 39 be considered a complete account of the whole occurrence. This would have required the return to Bethlehem, and its sad results, to be mentioned before the settlement at Nazareth. The passage is rather a concluding paragraph, wherewith the Evangelist closes his account of the early infancy of our Lord, before passing on to a somewhat later period. Completeness not being his aim in this preliminary history, he has no need to speak of the visit of the Magi, and the flight into Egypt, even if he were as well acquainted with these circumstances as Matthew was; but hastens on to the definitive settlement at Nazareth (ch. i. 26; ii. 4), where Mary and Joseph had previously dwelt; and even of this period he gives only a general account, ver. 40, and a single occurrence, vss. 41-52.*

Vs. 40. **And the child grew,** etc.—Comp. ch. i. 80. The same expressions are made use of concerning John, while somewhat more is added when Jesus is spoken of. There is no need of insisting on the anti-docetic character of the whole narrative.

DOCTRINAL AND ETHICAL.

1. Even the second occurrence in the life of our Lord, His presentation in the temple, is elucidated by a reference to what *is written*. From this time forth, the ἵνα πληρωθῇ ἡ γραφή will continually recur, and the whole life of the God-Man present a realization of the ideal, depicted in the prophetic writings of the Old Testament. The offering of doves, brought by Mary on this occasion, while it shows the poverty of her condition, testifies at the same time to the depths of humiliation to which the Son of God descended. Mary cannot bring a lamb for an offering: she brings something better, even the true Lamb of God, into the temple.

2. In Simeon and Anna we see incarnate types of the expectation of salvation under the Old Testament, as in the child Jesus the salvation itself is manifested. At the extreme limits of life, they stand in striking contrast to the infant Saviour, exemplifying the Old Covenant decaying and waxing old before the New, which is to grow and remain. Old age grows youthful, both in Simeon and Anna, at the sight of the Saviour; while the youthful Mary grows inwardly older and riper, as Simeon lifts up before her eyes the veil hanging upon the future.

3. The coming of Simeon into the temple, "by the Spirit," is entirely according to Old Testament experience. The Spirit does not dwell *in* him, permanently, as his own vital principle, as in the Christian believer; but comes *upon* and *over* him, as a power acting from without. Such exceptional manifestations among the saints in Israel, by no means prejudice the statement of St. John, ch. vii. 39. There is a remarkable coincidence between the expectation of Simeon and that mentioned Isa. xlix. 6. [ALFORD: "Simeon was the subject of an especial indwelling and leading of the Holy Ghost, analogous to that higher form of the spiritual life expressed in the earliest days by *walking with God*, and according to which God's saints have often been directed and informed in an extraordinary manner by His Holy Spirit."—P. S.]

4. A divine propriety, so to speak, seems to require that the new-born Saviour should receive first the homage of the elect of Israel, and afterward that of the representatives of the Gentile world. If so, the visit of the Magi must have been subsequent to the presentation in the temple. Besides, if the gold they offered had come into the hands of Mary and Joseph before this event, would they have brought only the offering of poverty?

---

* [For an examination of the conflicting views of harmonists on the order of these events, the reader is referred to SAM. J. ANDREWS: *The Life of our Lord*, N. Y., 1863, p. 84 ff., who places the visit of the Magi and the flight into Egypt soon *after* the presentation in the temple. This is the view of the majority of modern harmonists; while the old traditional view puts the arrival of the Magi on the sixth day of January, or on the thirteenth day after the birth of our Saviour.—P. S.]

CHAP. II. 22–40. 47

5. The shepherds, Simeon, and Anna agree in this, that they all become, in their respective circles, witnesses to others of the salvation of God. They do not wait, or seek for suitable opportunity, but seize upon the first, as the best. Comp. Ps. xxxvi. 1; Acts iv. 20. When the Saviour is seen by faith, the true spirit of testimony is already aroused.

6. The sacred art has not forgotten to glorify the presentation of Jesus in the temple. Think of the beautiful pictures of JOHN VAN EYK, RUBENS, GUIDO RENI, PAUL VERONESE, RAPHAEL, TITIAN, REMBRANDT, and many others.

7. [AMBROSE, on Luke ii. 22 (Opera, tom. i. p. 1301):—" Christ received a witness at his birth, not only from prophets and shepherds, but also from aged and holy men and women. Every age, and both sexes, and the marvels of events, confirm our faith. A virgin brings forth, the barren becomes a mother, the dumb speaks, Elizabeth prophesies, the wise men adore, the babe leaps in the womb, the widow praises God . . . Simeon prophesied; she who was wedded prophesied; she who was a virgin prophesied; and now a widow prophesies, that all states of life and sexes might be there (*ne qua aut professio deeset aut sexus*."—P. S.]

8. We shall have to speak more particularly, in the next division, of the manner of the genuine human development of Jesus. But the hint here given, is sufficient to direct our attention to its reality. Not only the body, but the soul and spirit of the Lord, grew incessantly and regularly. When He was a child, He spake as a child, before He could, with full consciousness, testify of God as His Father. Undoubtedly the awakening of His divine-human consciousness, His recognition of Himself, formed part of the filling with wisdom. As Sartorius says in his lectures on Christology, "The eye which comprehends heaven and earth within its range of vision, does not, by betaking itself to darkness or closing its lid, deprive itself of its power of sight, but merely resigns its far-reaching activity; so does the Son of God close His all-seeing eye, and betake Himself to human darkness on earth; and then as a child of man open His eye on earth, as the Light of the world, gradually increasing in brilliancy till it shines at the right hand of the Father, in perfect splendor."

HOMILETICAL AND PRACTICAL.

The offering of pious poverty acceptable to God. —The inconsiderable redemption-money paid *for* Christ; the infinite price of redemption paid *by* Christ.—Simeon, a type of an Israelite indeed: 1. Just and devout; 2. waiting for the consolation of Israel; 3. filled with the Holy Ghost.—The Holy Ghost, 1. witnesses of Christ; 2. leads to Christ; 3. and teaches to praise Christ.—The song of Simeon, the last note of the psalmody of the Old Testament. —He who has seen the salvation of Christ can depart in peace.—Christ, according to the prophecy of Simeon, 1. the glory of Israel; 2. the light of the Gentiles; 3. the highest gift of God to both.—The death that glorifies God, has, 1. a song on the lips; 2. Christ in the arms; 3. heaven in view.—Christ set for the fall of some, and the rising of others: 1. It is not otherwise; 2. it cannot be otherwise; 3. it ought not to be otherwise; 4. it will not be otherwise.—The sign that is spoken against, 1. in its continual struggle; 2. in its certain triumph.—Christ,

the touchstone of the heart.—The Saviour came into this world for judgment, John ix. 39.—The sword in Mary's heart: the depth of the wound; the balm for its healing.—Anna the happiest widow of Holy Scripture.—A pious old age, cheered with the light of Christ's salvation.—The first female testimony to Christ, a testimony, 1. excited by longing expectation; 2. based on personal vision; 3. given with full candor; 4. sealed by a holy walk; 5. crowned by a happy old age.—The Annas of the Old and New Testament, 1 Sam. ii.: Both tried, heard, and favored in a peculiar manner.—In Christ there is neither male nor female, old nor young, etc.; but faith which worketh by love.—The significancy of the events of the fortieth day, 1. to Simeon and Anna; 2. to Mary and Joseph; 3. to Israel; 4. to Christendom in after ages.—The holy childhood.— The grace of God on the holy child.—The most beautiful flower on the field of Nazareth.

STARKE:—The duty of all parents to present their children to God.—MAJUS:—Vows and sacrifices must be offered according to the law of God, not according to the notions of men.—The most pious are not always the richest; therefore despise none for their poverty.—God has a people of His own, even in the darkest seasons of the Church, 1 Kings, xix. 18.—QUESNEL:—The elect of God never die, till they have beheld, here on earth, the Christ of God with the eye of faith.—HEDINGER:—The duty of yielding immediately to special impulses toward that which is good.—The death of God's children, a loosening of the bondage of His life of misery.— The prosperity and adversity of the saints, determined beforehand in the counsels of God, even from eternity (vs. 34).—Whatever happens to Christ the Head, happens also to His members (vs. 34).— ZEISIUS:—Mary (vs. 35), a type of the Church, upon whom, as the spiritual mother, all the storms of affliction fall.—God, the God of the widow, Ps. lxviii. 6.—Holy people cannot but speak of holy things: what is the chief subject then of our discourse?—LANGII *Opus Bibl.*:—Children should imitate the mind of Jesus, and grow stronger in what is good.—Jesus remained a child but a short time, and His believing people should not long remain children in faith.

HEUBNER:—Christian dedication of children: 1. Its nature; 2. its blessing.—Simeon's faith, and Simeon's end.—The prelude of the " *Stabat mater* . . . *cujus animam trementem, contristatam et gementem, pertransivit gladius.*"—Anna, the model of the Christian widow, forsaken by the world, and living alone and bereft; but not forsaken of God, and living in the happy future, and in the faith of Christ. —Early announcement of the destination of Jesus: 1. How and why it happened; 2. its truth and confirmation.

RIEGER:—Of the spiritual priesthood of Christians.—J. SAURIN:—Simeon delivered from fear of death by the child Jesus: 1. He cannot desire to see anything greater on earth; 2. he has the sacrifice for sin in his arms; 3. he is assured of eternal life, why then should he desire to remain any longer on earth?—F. W. KRUMMACHER beholds, in the history of Simeon, 1. a divine "Forwards," 2. a happy halt, 3. a safe anchorage, 4. a peaceful farewell, 5. a joyful welcome.—O. VON GERLACH:—Jesus our all, when we, 1. have found in Him rest for our souls; 2. are resolved to fight for Him; and 3. to bear His reproach.—RAUTENBERG:—Simeon's hope: 1. To what it was directed; 2. on what it was founded; 3.

and how it was crowned.—BOBE:—Simeon in the temple: 1. The Holy Spirit his leader; 2. faith his consolation; 3. piety his life; 4. the Saviour his joy; 5. departure for his home his desire.—KRUMMACHER:—Anna a partaker of a threefold redemption: 1. From an oppressive uncertainty; 2. from a heavy yoke; 3. from a heavy care.—FLOREY:—Directions on our pilgrimage for a new year (from vss. 33–40). We must go on our journey, 1. steadfast in the faith (vs. 34); 2. submissive to the divine will (vs. 35); 3. diligent in the temple of God (vs. 34); 4. waiting for the promises of God (vs. 38); 5. faithful in our daily work (vs. 39); and 6. growing in the grace of God (vs. 40).—L. HOFACKER:—Simeon, one of the last believers of the Old Covenant, an encouraging example for the believers of the New.

C. *The Twelfth Year; or, the Growth in Wisdom and Favor.* CH. II. 41–52.

41 Now His parents went to Jerusalem every year at the feast of the passover.
42 And when He was twelve years old, they went up to Jerusalem, after the custom of
43 the feast. And when they had fulfilled the days, as they returned, the child Jesus tarried behind in Jerusalem; and Joseph and His mother [parents, οἱ γονεῖς]¹ knew not
44 of it [knew it not]. But they, supposing Him to have been [that He was] in the company, went a day's journey; and they sought Him among *their* kinsfolk and acquaint-
45 ance. And when they found Him² not, they turned back again [they returned] to Jerusalem, seeking him.
46 And it came to pass, that after three days they found Him in the temple, sitting in the midst of the doctors [teachers], both hearing them, and asking them questions.
47, 48 And all that heard Him were astonished at His understanding and answers. And when they saw Him, they were amazed: and His mother said unto Him, Son, why hast
49 Thou thus dealt with us? behold, Thy father and I have sought Thee sorrowing. And He said unto them, How is it that ye sought me? wist ye not [Did ye not know] that
50 I must be about my Father's business [ἐν τοῖς τοῦ Πατρός μου]?³ And they understood not the saying which He spake unto them.
51 And He went down with them, and came to Nazareth, and was subject unto them:
52 but His mother kept all these sayings in her heart. And Jesus increased in wisdom and stature [age],⁴ and in favour with God and man.

[¹ Vs. 43.—It is more probable that the original reading οἱ γονεῖς αὐτοῦ, *His parents*, which is sustained by Codd. Sinait., Vatic., Vulg. (*parentes ejus*), etc., recommended by Griesbach, and adopted by Lachmann, Tischendorf, Alford, Tregelles (also by van Oosterzee in his Version), was changed for dogmatic reasons into the *text. rec.*: Ἰωσὴφ καὶ ἡ μήτηρ αὐτοῦ, than *vice versa*. Comp. *Crit. Note* 1 on ch. ii. 33. Meyer, however, defends the *lect. rec.*, and regards οἱ γονεῖς αὐτοῦ as an addition from vs. 41.
² Vs. 45.—Αὐτόν, after εὑρόντες, is wanting in the best authorities, and a superfluous insertion *a seriore manu*.
³ Vs. 49.—Literally: *in the things of My Father; in rebus Patris Mei; in dem, was Meines Vaters ist*. Comp. 1 Tim. iv. 15, ἐν τούτοις ἴσθι. So Maldonatus, Wolf, Valckenaer, Rosenmüller, de Wette, Ewald, van Oosterzee, Alford (who, however, strangely translates: *among My Father's matters*), and all the older English Versions. But the fathers and the majority of modern commentators, including Meyer, also the revised N. T. of the Am. B. U., give the phrase a local reference: *in My Father's house, i. e.*, in the temple. This is grammatically equally correct, but it improperly limits and weakens the rich meaning, since Christ could only occasionally be in the temple. The preposition ἐν denotes the life-element in which Christ moved during His whole life, whether in the temple or out of it. *See also the author's Exeg. Note*, p. 49, in which I entirely concur.
⁴ Vs. 52.—The primary meaning of ἡλικία (from ἧλιξ, *of age, in the prime of life*) is *age*, the *flower or prime of life*, *manhood*, and is so correctly understood here by the Vulgate (*aetate*), Erasmus, Luther, Wiclif, Tyndale, Cranmer, the Rheims N. T., Kuinoel, de Wette, Alford, Whiting, van Oosterzee, and many others, comp. John ix. 21, 23; Heb. xi. 11; also Luke xii. 25 and Matt. vi. 27 (*are* Lange's note, vol. i. p. 134). The Genevan and the Authorized E. V., Beza, Grotius, Bengel, Ewald, Meyer, Robinson (Diction.), the revised N. T. of the Am. B. U., etc., translate: *stature, growth*, as in Luke xix. 3 (τῇ ἡλικίᾳ μικρός). But the only reason urged by Meyer against the former version, applies rather to the latter; for *growth* in *age* is more comprehensive than growth in *stature*. The meaning of the passage is that Jesus grew *in wisdom as well as in age*.—P. S.]

EXEGETICAL AND CRITICAL.

Vs. 41. At the feast of the Passover.—See Lange's remarks on the Passover, Matt. xxvi. 2 [vol. i. p. 459]. The celebration lasted seven days, from the 15th of Nisan, and was appointed for all time to come. Every Israelite was bound to be present, except such as were unable to perform the necessary journey, viz., the sick, the aged, and boys under the age of twelve, who, as well as the blind, the deaf, and the lunatic, were permitted to remain at home. At the beginning of the month of Nisan, messengers were despatched to all parts, to remind the people of the approaching festival, that none might have ignorance to plead as an excuse for absence. A detailed description of the rite is not necessary for the elucidation of Luke's narrative; we need only here remark, that every Jewish child of twelve years old was permitted, as "a son of the law," to take part in the celebration of the sacred festival. According to Jewish custom at a later time, a child was, in his fifth year, instructed in the law; in his tenth, in the Mishna; and in his thirteenth, was fully subjected to the obedience of the law. There existed, also, no longer any reason that Jesus should absent Himself from Judea, as Archelaus, whom Joseph had reason to fear, was already banished by Augustus, after a reign of ten years. Women were by no means obliged to go up to the feast (see SCHÖTTGEN, Horæ in Luc. ii. 41); yet the fact of Mary's accompanying her son on the occasion of his first celebration, needs neither defence nor explanation.

Vs. 43. The child Jesus tarried behind in Jerusalem.—Luke neither tells us that Jesus remained behind at Jerusalem intentionally, nor that Joseph and Mary lost sight of Him through want of necessary care. A circumstance must here have been omitted; and we may safely suppose, that Joseph and Mary joined their elder fellow-travellers in the persuasion that Jesus, who knew of the time and place of departure, was among the younger ones. The more Mary was accustomed to trust to His obedience and wisdom, the less necessary would it be always to watch Him. An involuntary mistake, of whatever kind it might be, separated the child from the parents. Perhaps, too, they might have become uneasy on His account earlier in the day; but the multitude of the caravans at a time when, as Josephus tells us, Galilee contained more than four million inhabitants [?]* would render an instantaneous search impracticable; and a day's journey being generally not very long, inquiry was delayed till the end of the day. It must not, besides, be forgotten, that in the East even an ordinary child of twelve would be equal to one of fourteen or fifteen among us; and that they could not, therefore, be extremely uneasy, especially about such a child as He was.—See Tholuck's apologetic treatment of this subject in his *Glaubwürdigkeit der evangelischen Geschichte*, p. 210, etc.

Vs. 46. After three days.—If we understand, with de Wette and others, that these three days were spent in seeking for the child in Jerusalem, it is almost inexplicable that it should only so late have come into their thoughts to go to the temple. It seems more probable that we must allow one day for their departure, vs. 44; one for their return, vs. 45; and the third, vs. 46, for their search; and that they found Him in the sanctuary at the close of the latter. (See Grotius and Paulus *in loc.*)

In the temple.—Probably in one of the porches of the Court of the Women, where the schools of the Rabbis were held, and the law regularly expounded. The *Evang. infant. Arab.* ch. 50–53, gives a lengthy apocryphal account of the conversation of Jesus with the Jewish Rabbis in the temple.

Sitting in the midst of the teachers.—It has been often said, that it was the custom of the times for scholars to receive the instructions of the Rabbis standing, as a mark of reverence. This has been, however, well disproved by Vitringa (*de Synagog. Vet.* i. p. 167). We have to understand it in the same sense as St. Paul speaks of his *sitting* at the feet of Gamaliel (Acts xxii. 3). De Wette insists, notwithstanding, that the child Jesus appears here in a *consensus* of discussing Rabbis, entering into the argument as a member of it would do. Surely he has not sufficiently considered the following words, ἀκούων καὶ ἐπερωτῶν, which plainly show, that the idea of receiving is here made far more prominent than that of communicating. Olshausen far more suitably remarks, that "a lecturing, demonstrating child would have been an anomaly, which the God of order would never have exhibited." The astonishment of His hearers at the intelligence manifested in His answers, need not surprise us, if these answers were even as excellent as that which He gave to Mary's somewhat hasty demand.

Vs. 48. Thy father and I.—Not merely the only possible manner in which Mary could publicly speak to her son of Joseph, but also an indisputable proof of the wisdom with which she brought up the child; a wisdom, which taught her to say nothing yet to Him of the mystery of His birth, and which had faith enough to wait, till His own consciousness should be fully and clearly awakened to the fact of His being the Son of God. The more surprising, therefore, must His answer have seemed to His mother, as containing a hint, intelligible to her alone, that He already knew who His Father was.

Vs. 49. How is it that ye sought Me?—The quiet repose of this answer, contrasted with Mary's natural agitation, produces an impression quite peculiar. He is apparently astonished that He should have been sought, or even thought of, anywhere else, than in the only place which He felt to be properly His home.—Perhaps this was the moment in which His immediate intuition of His destination was aroused. Thus the magnet, if it could speak, would express its astonishment, if it were assigned another than a northward direction, or the sunflower, if it was supposed not to be always turned toward the sun. [ALFORD:—"This is no *reproachful* question. It is asked in all the simplicity and boldness of holy childhood."—P. S.]

About My Father's business.—The rendering of some, "*in My Father's house*," unnecessarily narrows the fulness of the expression. He stays in the temple as such only, inasmuch as it is there that τὰ τοῦ πατρὸς are for the present concentrated, according to His view. Better: *in the things or affairs* of my Father, in that what belongs to His honor and glory. A beautiful exposition of this inexhaustible text may be found in STIER's *Words of the Lord Jesus*, vol. I. [**I must be**, δεῖ.—It signifies a *moral* necessity which is identical with perfect freedom.—P. S.]

Vs. 50. And they understood not the saying.—If Meyer and others are right, in concluding that the meaning of these words was totally incomprehensible to His parents, this inexplicable ignorance might perhaps be adduced, as evidence against the truth of the history of the Nativity and its miracles. We do not, however, see any reason why we should not attribute their astonishment to the fact, that he should, *sponte sua*, so plainly express what He had learned neither from men nor from the doctors. Besides, twelve years of quiet oblivion had elapsed, between His birth and this moment; and even the faith of a Mary would not be always equally clear and strong.

Vs. 51. And was subject unto them.—It seems almost as if Luke were trying to oppose the

---

* [This must be an oversight. The author meant probably *Jerusalem* instead of *Galilee*; for the number of inhabitants of Galilee is not to the point in this connection. And as regards Jerusalem, the number is overstated. The ordinary number of inhabitants of the holy city, according to Hecatæus, was 120,000; and at the time of the passover, the population, according to Josephus, *De bello Jud.* vi. 9, 3, exceeded the number of 2,700,000 male individuals, including, of course, all foreigners from Syria, Egypt, etc.; the number of paschal lambs slaughtered amounting once to 136,500. Counting the women and children it may by a bare possibility have reached four millions. The number of the inhabitants of Galilee at the time of Christ must have been over five millions, if the statement of Josephus be correct, that the smallest of the 401 towns and villages of Galilee numbered over 15,000 inhabitants (*De bello Jud.* iii. 3, 2; *Vit.* 45). But at the time of David the whole population of Palestine furnished 1,300,000 men capable of bearing arms (2 Sam. xxiv. 9), which would give us only a total population of nearly five millions.—P. S.]

4

notion, that the child, whose faculties were developing in so heavenly a manner, had even for an instant spoken in an unchildlike manner to His mother and foster-father. If His heart drew Him to the temple, the voice of duty called Him back to Galilee; and, perfect even in childhood, He yielded implicit obedience to this voice. The blossom of His inner life, which had opened and spread abroad its first fragrance in the temple, was to continue expanding in the obscurity of Nazareth; and Mary was to wait eighteen years, keeping " all these sayings in her heart," before anything else unprecedented should occur.

Vs. 52. **In wisdom and age.**—*Age* (margin) would seem the preferable rendering of ἡλικία, for, though increase in *age* is as inevitable a consequence as increase of *stature*, yet the former expression is important to Luke, who, having spoken of His twelfth year, and being about to mention His thirtieth (ch. iii. 23), characterizes, by this concluding formula, the whole of these eighteen years as a period of development.

DOCTRINAL AND ETHICAL.

1. We may compare the appearance of Jesus on earth to the course of the sun. The first light appeared above the horizon on the night of the Nativity at Bethlehem; when His public ministry began, this light had gained its meridian height; but as the sun's journey from east to south is often performed amidst darkening clouds, so is the history of these thirty years for the most part veiled in obscurity. Only once, in this long morning, is the veil of clouds drawn aside, and we get a glimpse of the increasing glories of this Sun of Righteousness; and this moment of brightness is the epoch of this Passover feast.

2. Perhaps there are few passages in Luke's history of the birth and childhood of Jesus, which bear such incontestable marks of truth and reality as this. A comparison with the apocryphal Gospels is even unnecessary, as the whole narrative breathes throughout a truth and simplicity, with which nothing else can be compared. What writer of a fiction would ever have imagined an occurrence, from which the miraculous is so entirely banished, in which no angel is introduced to assist in the discovery of the lost child, but his parents are represented as finding Him again in an ordinary manner, and one in which even an appearance of disobedience to Mary is cast upon Jesus! To be unable to imagine so precocious a development, is to place the Lord behind many children, of whom remarkable traits of early maturity are related. Nor should we forget here the remark of a Christian apologist, that "in Christianity, and in its sacred records, the motto of cold intellectual culture, '*nil mirari*,' is less applicable than the principle of the most sublime of its predecessors: τὸ θαυμάζειν τῆς φιλοσοφίας ἀρχή." Osiander.

[" Of the boyhood of Jesus, we know only one fact, recorded by Luke; but it is in perfect keeping with the peculiar charm of His childhood, and foreshadows, at the same time, the glory of His public life, as one uninterrupted service of His heavenly Father. When twelve years old, we find Him in the temple, in the midst of the Jewish doctors, not teaching and offending them, as in the apocryphal Gospels, by any immodesty or forwardness, but hearing and asking questions, thus actually learning from them, and yet filling them with astonishment at His understanding and answers. There is nothing premature, forced or unbecoming His age, and yet a degree of wisdom and an intensity of interest in religion, which rises far above a purely human youth. ' He increased,' we are told, ' in wisdom and stature, and in favor with God and man.' He was subject to His parents, and practised all the virtues of an obedient son; and yet He filled them with a sacred awe as they saw Him absorbed in the things of His Father, and heard Him utter words, which they were unable to understand at the time, but which Mary treasured up in her heart as a holy secret, convinced that they must have some deep meaning, answering to the mystery of His supernatural conception and birth. Such an idea of a harmless and faultless heavenly childhood, of a growing, learning, and yet surprisingly wise boyhood, as it meets us in living reality at the portal of the Gospel history, never entered the imagination of a biographer, poet, or philosopher before. On the contrary, as has been justly observed by Dr. H. Bushnell (*on the Character of Jesus*, p. 19), 'in all the higher ranges of character, the excellence portrayed is never the simple unfolding of a harmonious and perfect beauty contained in the germ of childhood, but is a character formed by a process of rectification, in which many follies are mended and distempers removed, in which confidence is checked by defeat, passion moderated by reason, smartness sobered by experience. Commonly a certain pleasure is taken in showing how the many wayward sallies of the boy are, at length, reduced by discipline to the character of wisdom, justice, and public heroism, so much admired. Besides, if any writer, of almost any age, will undertake to describe not merely a spotless, but a superhuman or celestial childhood, not having the reality before him, he must be somewhat more than human himself, if he do not pile together a mass of clumsy exaggerations, and draw and overdraw, till neither heaven nor earth can find any verisimilitude in the picture.'—This unnatural exaggeration, into which the mythical fancy of man, in its endeavor to produce a superhuman childhood and boyhood, will inevitably fall, is strikingly exhibited in the myth of Hercules, who, while yet a suckling in the cradle, squeezed two monster serpents to death with his tender hands, and still more in the accounts of the apocryphal Gospels, on the wonderful performances of the infant Saviour. These apocryphal Gospels are related to the canonical Gospels as the counterfeit to the genuine coin, or as a revolting caricature to the inimitable original; but, by the very contrast, they tend, negatively, to corroborate the truth of the evangelical history. The strange contrast has been frequently urged, especially in the Strauss controversy, and used as an argument against the mythical theory. While the evangelists expressly reserve the performance of miracles to the age of maturity and public life, and observe a significant silence concerning the parents of Jesus, the pseudo-evangelists fill the infancy and early years of the Saviour and His mother with the strangest prodigies, and make the active intercession of Mary very prominent throughout. According to their representation, even dumb idols, irrational beasts, and senseless trees, bow in adoration before the infant Jesus, on his journey to Egypt; and after His return, when yet a boy of five or seven years, He changes balls of clay into flying birds, for the idle amusement of His playmates; strikes terror round about Him, dries up a stream of water by a mere word, transforms His companions into goats, raises the dead to life, and performs all sorts of miraculous cures, through a magical influence which proceeds from the very water in which he was washed, the towels which he used, and the bed on which he slept. Here we have the falsehood and absurdity of *unnatural fiction*, while the New Testament presents to us the truth and beauty of a *supernatural*, yet *most real history*, which shines out only in brighter colors by the contrast of the mythical shadows." (From SCHAFF's *Person of Christ, the Miracle of History.* Boston, 1865, p. 28 ff.)—P. S.]

3. The first words which drop from the lips of the Word made flesh, are especially important in a doctrinal point of view. They are the childlike and naïve expression of direct and infallible self-consciousness, now gradually developing into higher knowledge. This is the moment in which the long-closed and slowly-growing bud first breaks through its outer covering. The child Jesus excites astonishment, but shows none, except at the fact that they knew not where to find Him. But the deep mysteries of His nature are still covered with a garment of the purest innocence. The temple is to Him, in the fullest sense, the dwelling-place of His Father, of whom He will soon declare, that "*God is a Spirit.*" His ear, desirous of instruction, is seeking answers to important and vital questions from those Rabbis, against whose perversions of Scripture He will soon denounce a terrible woe. His foot, which an irresistible yet inexplicable attraction draws toward the temple, soon submissively follows the track which the will of His parents points out. We feel that the *child* Jesus must have acted thus, and could not have acted otherwise.

4. But this passage of Christ's early history is of extreme importance for other reasons. It is important in its influence on *the present*. Hitherto pious Jews and lowly shepherds, waiting for the salvation of Israel, have borne testimony to the infant Messiah: He now bears testimony to Himself; and the whole occurrence, which would surely be impressed on the mind of certain doctors of Jerusalem, was a fresh hint to the whole Jewish nation, to give a becoming reception to Him who would shortly appear among them. It is also important in its relation to *the past*. A seal is now set to the word of the angel, "He shall be called the Son of the Highest" (Luke i. 32). The consciousness of Jesus is aroused to this unique relationship, and a ray now gilds the obscurity of Nazareth, which must recall to Mary's mind the miracles of Bethlehem, and direct her hopes to a future full of blessings. Finally, it is important as a sign of *the future*: if ever the saying of a child was prophetic, it was the saying of Jesus in the temple. It is the programme, the key-note, of the whole future earthly and heavenly life of our Lord. His consciousness of divinity, His obedience, His self-denial, His speech, as never man spake, all are here present *in nuce*, soon to be manifested *in luce.* Luke ii. 49 is the germ of John iv. 34; viii. 29; ix. 4; and even His farewell to life, John xvii. 4, naturally refers to this beginning.

5. The outer life of Jesus, during the next eighteen years, is covered with a veil of obscurity, which not even the writers of the apocryphal Gospels have ventured to lift. His days seem to have been quietly passed in the privacy of the domestic circle. Even Nathanael, who lived at Cana, only three leagues off from Nazareth, John i. 46, 47, had never yet heard anything of the son of Joseph. The death of His foster-father probably happened during this interval. Miracles would have been without purpose in the retirement of home; and John ii. 3 cannot be understood to denote that any had yet been performed by him. Mark vi. 3 (according to the true reading, ὁ τέκτων) shows decidedly that He had worked at His father's trade; a fact supported also by tradition. See JUSTIN'S M., *Dialog. cum Tryph.* ch. 88. Compare the account of a remarkable statement of Julian the Apostate, in Theodoret, *H. E.* iii. 23, and Sozomen, vi. 2. The family of Nazareth seems not to have lived in a state of extreme poverty, but still less in the possession of any temporal superfluity.

6. The increase of Jesus in wisdom during this period was,—(1.) *real.* Jesus had to learn from the words of others what as yet He knew not; and that was entirely unknown to Him as a child, which He had a glimpse of as a boy, conjectured as a youth, and first clearly perceived as a man.—(2.) *Unchecked.* In attributing to the Lord Jesus the relative imperfection of childhood, we must carefully avoid imputing to Him the *failings* of childhood. His life showed no trace of childish faults, to be hereafter conquered. The words of John, Matt. iii. 14, show, on the contrary, what impression was made by His moral purity when thirty years of age; and the voice from heaven, vs. 17, sets the seal of the divine approval on the now completed development of the Son of Man, a seal which the Holy One of Israel would only have affixed to absolute perfection.—(3.) It was *effected by means.* We may exclude from the means whereby this development was effected, (*a*) a learned education by Jewish doctors (John vii. 15); (*b*) an Eastern, Egyptian, Greek, or Alexandrian training, which was formerly thought of; (*c*) an instruction in the principles of the various Jewish sects, viz., the Pharisees, Sadducees, and Essenes. On the other hand, we may ascribe more or less influence to—(*a*) His training by the pious Mary, and the godly Joseph, in the ways of a quiet domestic life; (*b*) to the natural beauties of the neighborhood of Nazareth;* (*c*) to the Scriptures of the Old Testament, which He undoubtedly read, understood, and delighted in, more than any other child; (*d*) to the annual journeys to Jerusalem, which must certainly have opened His eyes to the corruption of His nation and its leaders; and (*e*) above all to prayerful communion with His heavenly Father. But, allowing for all these, we are forced to recur (*f*) to that essential singularity of the personality of the Lord, whereby, with such comparatively weak and disproportioned means, he could become *actu*, what He had been from His birth *potentiâ.* —Lastly, [4] the development of the God-Man was *normal*, inasmuch as it holds up to His people an example of what they must more and more approach unto, in fellowship with Himself, growing by the

---

* [RENAN, in the second chapter of his *Vie de Jésus*, gives, from personal observation, the following graphic description of the beauty of nature around Nazareth: "Nazareth was a little town, situated in a fold of land broadly open at the summit of the group of mountains which closes on the north the plain of Esdralon. The population is now from three to four thousand, and it cannot have varied very much. . . . The environs are charming, and no place in the world was so well adapted to dreams of absolute happiness. Even in our days, Nazareth is a delightful sojourn, the only place perhaps in Palestine where the soul feels a little relieved of the burden which weighs upon it in the midst of this unequalled desolation. The people are friendly and good-natured; the gardens are fresh and green. . . . The beauty of the women who gather there at night, this beauty which was already remarked in the sixth century, and in which was seen the gift of the Virgin Mary (by Antonius Martyr, *Itiner.* § 5), has been surprisingly well preserved. It is the Syrian type in all its languishing grace."—P. S.]

faithful use of every means of grace, from "little children" to "young men," and from "young men" to "fathers" in Christ: 2 Cor. iii. 18; 2 Pet. iii. 18. —On the whole subject of the human development of the Son of Man, compare ATHANASIUS, *Orat. III. contra Arian.* ch. 51 (tom. i., p. 475), and GREGORY NAZIANZEN, *Oratio* 43 *in laud. Basilii*, ch. 38. See also the excellent remarks of ULLMANN, *Sinlessness of Jesus* (p. 104 f. of the 5th German edition), and those of MARTENSEN in his *Dogmatik* ii., p. 315. The latter well observes, that "we see in this narrative, not only that the consciousness of His peculiar relation to His Father is dawning within Him; but that in His sitting in the midst of the teachers of His nation, not merely listening, but astonishing them by His questions and answers, we may also perceive the earliest revelation of His productive relation to those around Him (*discendo docuit*)."

[P. SCHAFF (*The Person of Christ*, etc., 1865, p. 31 ff.): "Jesus grew up among a people seldom and only contemptuously named by the ancient classics, and subjected at the time to the yoke of a foreign oppressor; in a remote and conquered province of the Roman empire; in the darkest district of Palestine; in a little country-town of proverbial insignificance; in poverty and manual labor; in the obscurity of a carpenter's shop; far away from universities, academies, libraries, and literary or polished society; without any help, as far as we know, except the parental care, the daily wonders of nature, the Old Testament Scriptures, the weekly Sabbath services of the synagogue at Nazareth (Luke iv. 16), the annual festivals in the temple of Jerusalem (Luke ii. 42), and the secret intercourse of His soul with God, His heavenly Father. These are, indeed, the great educators of the mind and heart; the book of nature and the book of revelation are filled with richer and more important lessons, than all the works of human art and learning. But they were accessible alike to every Jew, and gave no advantage to Jesus over His humblest neighbor. Hence the question of Nathaniel, "What good can come out of Nazareth?" Hence the natural surprise of the Jews, who knew all His human relations and antecedents. "How knoweth this man letters?" they asked, when they heard Jesus teach, "having never learned?" (John vii. 15.) And on another occasion, when He taught in the synagogue, "Whence has this man this wisdom and these mighty works? Is not this the carpenter's son? is not His mother Mary and His brethren (brothers) James and Joses and Simon and Judas? And His sisters, are they not all with us? Whence, then, hath this man all these things?" These questions are unavoidable and unanswerable, if Christ be regarded as a mere man. For each effect presupposes a corresponding cause. . . Jesus can be ranked neither with the school-trained nor with the self-trained or self-made men, if by the latter we understand, as we must, those who without the regular aid of *living* teachers, yet with the same educational *means*, such as books, the observation of men and things, and the intense application of their mental faculties, attained to vigor of intellect and wealth of scholarship, like Shakspeare, Jacob Boehm, Benjamin Franklin, and others. All the attempts to bring Him into contact with Egyptian wisdom, or the Essenic Theosophy, or other sources of learning, are without a shadow of proof, and explain nothing after all. He never quotes from books except the Old Testament, He never refers to secular history, poetry, rhetoric, mathematics, astronomy, foreign languages, natural sciences, or any of those branches of knowledge which make up human learning and literature. He confined himself strictly to religion. But from that centre He shed light over the whole world of man and nature. In this department, unlike all other great men, even the prophets and the apostles, He was absolutely original and independent. He taught the world as one who had learned nothing from it and was under no obligation to it. He speaks from divine intuition as one who not only *knows* the truth, but who *is* the truth, and with an authority, which commands absolute submission, or provokes rebellion, but can never be passed by with contempt or indifference. His character and life were originated and sustained in spite of circumstances with which no earthly force could have contended, and therefore must have had their real foundation in a force which was preternatural and divine."—P. S.]

7. We may be thankful that St. Luke, compared with the other Evangelists, has communicated to us so much of the early history of our Lord; nor less so, that he has told us so little; as this very reticence furnishes a proof of his *fides historica*, checks vain curiosity, and shows us how infinitely more important for our faith is the history of His ministry, passion, death, and glorification, than that of His youth and childhood.

HOMILETICAL AND PRACTICAL.

The first Passover of Jesus: 1. The history; 2. the significance of this journey for Jesus, for His parents, for Israel, for the world.—The first appearance of the Messiah in the sanctuary.—The glory of the second house greater than that of the first, Hag. ii. 10.—The first Passover of Jesus: 1. Visited with desire; 2. celebrated worthily; 3. left obediently.—The parents and the child united before the Lord.—The Son of Man once a lost son.—Seeking for Jesus: 1. The anxiety of deprivation; 2. the joy of finding. —The interchange of joy and sorrow during our earthly pilgrimage.—Jesus lost in the hurry and hustle of the world, but found again in the temple.—Jesus sitting in the midst of the teachers whom He was afterwards to oppose.—The school of Rabbis at Jerusalem, a model for parents and children.—Mary's astonishment excited by Jesus, comp. vss. 18 and 33. —The over-hasty zeal of Mary, and the heavenly tranquillity of Jesus.—God, the Father of the Lord Jesus Christ, in a sense applicable to Him alone.—The Son of Man aroused to the consciousness of His being the God-Man.—To be about His Father's business, the vocation, 1. of Christ; 2. of the Christian. —Even the first recorded saying of the Lord too deep to be entirely understood, the explanation of all His deeds, and the key to His whole life.—Christ's first Passover journey: 1. A glimpse into the history of His youth; 2. a turning-point in the history of His development; 3. a turning-point in the history of salvation.—The return from Jerusalem to Nazareth, a specimen of the voluntary self-denial and obedience of Christ.—Jesus, even at Nazareth, about His Father's business.—The contemplative faith of Mary, 1. in its secret conflict, 2. in its final triumph. —The growth in secret, both in wisdom and stature, from the imperfect child to the perfect man, of Him who was the Most High and Most Glorious.—The increase in grace.—He who finds favor with God, finds favor also with man.—The season of waiting.—Faithfulness in little things.—The fifth commandment not destroyed but fulfilled by Jesus.—The fear of the Lord the beginning of wisdom.—Increase in wisdom and age, the work of grace; favor, the crown put upon wisdom and age.—That which is most precious, though ripening in the world, 1. was then, 2. is now, 3. will be ever, hidden from the eye of the world.

STARKE:—The care parents should have for their children.—To public worship must be added domestic worship.—QUESNEL:—Jesus is more often lost in time of prosperity than in times of misfortune and persecution.—HEDINGER:—We often, from erroneous judgment, seek Christ among our kinsfolk and acquaintance, where He is not to be found.—We often have to seek long for Jesus; and this is our best employment, even if we have to spend more than one spiritual day's journey upon it.—Sorrow for the loss of Jesus, a reasonable sorrow.—He who would be a teacher of others, must first be a learner.—CRAMER:—Christ has hallowed instruction by question and answer.—The more spiritual gifts any one has received, the more careful will he be to avoid boasting. —*Nova Bibl. Tub.*:—Jesus more learned than His teachers (Isa. l. 4): let us hear Him.—Parents transgress when they reprove and punish their children unseasonably or unreasonably, Prov. xx. 1–6; xxii. 6.—MAJUS:—Children may instruct their parents, if they do it respectfully and modestly, 1 Sam. xix. 4.— We must not despise what we do not understand.— OSIANDER:—Christ has, by His obedience, made satisfaction for the disobedience of children; while, by His example, He teaches children to obey their parents.—Faith keeps in her heart even what she does not understand.—There is little hope of children who increase in age and stature only, and decrease in wisdom and favor.

HEUBNER:—The care of man is not sufficient for children, if God does not add to it the care of His angels.—Even good children may innocently cause grief.—As Jesus grew and ripened in retirement, so the ministers of the gospel often have long to wait before God calls them into full work.—Jesus commanding respect even as a boy.—The family of Jesus a model for Christian families.—The charms of the history of Jesus for the young.

STIER:—The holy child Jesus and our children (a continuous contrast).—ARNDT:—1. The tokens; 2. the excitements; 3. the fruits of early piety, visible in the holy child Jesus.—The early history of Jesus: 1. Jesus *in* Nazareth; 2. Jesus *of* Nazareth.—A DES AMORIE V. D. HOEVEN (preacher in Utrecht, died 1849): 1. Behold the child Jesus! 2. Behold in the child the man Jesus! 3. Become children in Christ, that you may become men!—GERDESSEN:— The appearance of Christ in the sanctuary: Ought He not to be, 1. about His Father's business; 2. in the midst of the teachers; 3. according to the usage of the feast; 4. sought for sorrowing; and 5. manifesting a childlike disposition?—M. G. ALBRECHT (died 1835): The child Jesus is often lost in our days, after a spiritual manner.—GAUPP:—The Mediator between God and man discernible in Jesus, even in His twelfth year: 1. In the holy privacy of His life in God; 2. in the consciousness of His relation to the Father; 3. in the unintermitted occupation of His spirit with the work which the Father had given Him to do.—RAUTENBERG:—Our children our judges: 1. What this means; 2. how this happens; 3. to what this leads.—Finally, an excellent sermon by ADOLPHE MONOD (died 1856): *Jésus enfant, modèle des enfants*. Paris, 1857.

PART SECOND.

The Beneficent Activity and Holy Behavior of the Son of Man.

FIRST SECTION.

TESTIMONY BORNE TO MESSIAH.

CHAPTER III.

A. *By the Preaching and Baptism of John.* CH. III. 1–22.

1 Now, in the fifteenth year of the reign of Tiberius Cæsar, Pontius Pilate being governor [procurator] of Judea, and Herod being tetrarch of Galilee, and his brother Philip tetrarch of Iturea and of the region of Trachonitis, and Lysanias the[1] tetrarch
2 of Abilene, Annas and Caiaphas being the high priests,[2] the word of God came unto
3 John, the son of Zacharias [Zachariah], in the wilderness. And he came into all the country about [the] Jordan, preaching the baptism of repentance for the remission of
4 sins; As it is written in the book of the words of Esaias [Isaiah] the prophet, saying,[3] The voice of one crying in the wilderness, Prepare ye the way of the Lord, make His
5 paths straight. Every valley shall be filled, and every mountain and hill shall be

brought low; and the crooked shall be made straight, and the rough ways *shall be*
6 *made smooth*; And all flesh shall see the salvation of God.
7   Then said he to the multitude [multitudes, ὄχλοις] that came forth to be baptized of
[by] him, O generation [Brood] of vipers, who hath warned you to flee from the wrath
8 to come? Bring forth therefore fruits worthy of [meet for] repentance; and begin
not to say within yourselves, We have Abraham to [for] *our* father: for I say unto
9 you, That God is able of these stones to raise up children unto Abraham. And now
also the axe is laid unto the root of the trees: every tree therefore which bringeth not
forth good fruit is hewn down, and cast into the fire.
10, 11 And the people asked him, saying, What [then] shall we do then? He answereth
and saith unto them, He that hath two coats, let him impart to him that hath none;
and he that hath meat [food], let him do likewise.
12   Then came also publicans to be baptized, and said unto him, Master, what shall we
13 do? And he said unto them, Exact no more than that which is appointed you.
14 And the[4] soldiers likewise demanded of him [asked'him], saying, And what shall we
do? And he said unto them, Do violence to no man [one], neither accuse *any* falsely;
and be content with your wages.
15   And as the people were in expectation, and all men mused [all were reasoning,
διαλογιζομένων πάντων] in their hearts of [concerning] John, whether he were the Christ,
16 or not; John answered, saying unto *them* all [answered them all, saying, ἀπεκρίνατο ὁ
'Ι. ἅπασιν λέγων], I indeed baptize you with water [ὕδατι]; but one mightier than I
cometh, the latchet of whose shoes I am not worthy to unloose: He shall baptize you
17 with [in, ἐν] the Holy Ghost, and with fire: Whose fan *is* in His hand, and He will
thoroughly purge His [threshing-] floor, and will gather the wheat into His garner;
18 but the chaff He will burn with fire unquenchable. And many other things, in his
exhortation [And with many other exhortations he], preached he unto the people.
19   But Herod the tetrarch, being reproved by him for Herodias his brother Philip's
20 [brother's][5] wife, and for all the evils which Herod had done [did, ἐποίησε], Added yet
this above all, that he shut up John in prison.
21   Now, when all the people were baptized, it came to pass, that Jesus also being bap-
22 tized, and praying, the heaven was opened, And the Holy Ghost descended in a bodily
shape, like a dove, upon Him; and a voice came from heaven, which said,[6] Thou art
My beloved Son; in Thee I am well pleased.

[[1] Vs. 1.—The article *the* should be omitted as in *governor* and the preceding *tetrarch*.
[2] Vs. 2.—Or more correctly, according to the oldest readings: *Annasbeing high-priest and Caiaphas*, ἐπὶ ἀρχιερέως
'Ἄννα καὶ Κ., for which the *text. rec.* reads ἐπ' ἀρχιερέων—a manifest correction on account of the two names. On
Annas or Ananus, and Joseph or Caiaphas, his son-in-law and successor in the office of high-priest, see Matt. xxvi. 3;
John xviii. 13; Joseph. *Antiq*. xviii. 2, 2; and *Exeg. Notes*.
[3] Vs. 4.—The word *saying*, λέγοντος, is unnecessary and should be omitted on the authority of Codd. Sin., B., D.,
L., etc., and the modern critical editions. It was inserted from Matt. iii. 3.
[4] Vs. 14.—The article should be omitted as in the Greek.
[5] Vs. 19.—The *text. rec.* inserts from Mark vi. 17, Φιλίππου after γυναικός, against the best ancient authorities, including Cod. Sin. The modern critical editions omit it.
[6] Vs. 22.—The words *which said*, λέγουσαν, should be thrown out of the text, according to Codd. Sin., B., D., L.,
Vulg., etc. Insertion from Matt. iii. 17.—P. S.]

EXEGETICAL AND CRITICAL.

Vs. 1. **In the fifteenth year,** etc.—With this chronological notice, Luke points out, as his predecessors had omitted doing, the exact position which the sacred narrative occupies on the wide platform of universal history. We will endeavor to point out, as briefly as possible, what may be deduced from his indication concerning the precise period of the public appearing of John and of Jesus.—(*a*) **The fifteenth year of the reign of Tiberius Cæsar** is easily ascertained. Augustus died A.U.C. 767, which, taking this event as the *terminus a quo*, gives the year 782. It seems, however, probable, that our computation must be made from the time when Tiberius was associated with Augustus in the government of the Empire, two years earlier, which would give us the year 780. The reigning years of a Roman emperor were, indeed, commonly dated from the time when he governed alone; but as Luke is here speaking of ἡγεμονία, and not of μοναρχία or βασιλεία, he seems to include the two preceding years, in which Tiberius, indeed, possessed a power no way inferior to that of Augustus.—(*b*) **Pontius Pilate,** the successor of Valerius Gratus, and sixth **governor** (*procurator*) **of Judea,** possessed this dignity for ten years under the above-named Emperor, viz., from 779–789 A.U.C., until he was deprived of his office in consequence of the accusations of the Jews.—(*c*) **Herod** (Antipas) became **tetrarch of Galilee** after the death of his father, Herod the Great, 750, and continued in his government till his deposition in 792.—(*d*) **His brother Philip** received, contemporaneously with himself, the tetrarchy **of Iturea** and **Trachonitis,** and remained in this post till his death in 794. According to Josephus (*Ant. Jud.* xvii. 8, 1), his jurisdiction extended also over Batanæa and Auranitis, while his brother also governed Peræa.—(*e*) **Lysanias, tetrarch of Abi-**

lene, was not the ruler from Chalcis, between Lebanon and Anti-Lebanon, who was put to death, four and twenty years before Christ, by Antony, at the instigation of Cleopatra,* but may have been a second Lysanias, whom Josephus passes over in silence, as less celebrated than the former. It will not seem improbable to any, that two princes of the same name should have ruled over the same district, during the course of so many years.—And lastly, (*f*) with regard to **the high-priests, Annas and Caiaphas.** For remarks concerning the latter, see LANGE on *Matt.* xxvi. 3 [vol. i. p. 460]; the former had been made high-priest by Cyrenius, but deposed seven years after by Vitellius. He was succeeded by three others, and lastly by Caiaphas. That he should have continued, after his deposition, to bear the name of high-priest in the sacred history, seems owing to the influence he still possessed,—an influence originating in his own character, strengthened by his relationship to Caiaphas, and always employed in opposition to Christianity. He is even always mentioned first, either on account of his age, or because he first bore the office of high-priest, or perhaps because he exercised the office alternately with Caiaphas.† See, with respect to this latter supposition, Huc, *Einl. in's N. T.* ii. p. 218, and FRIEDLIEB, *Archäologie der Leidensgeschichte.* We shall not be mistaken if, using this notice of Luke as a foundation, we reckon the date of John's ministry to have been the year 780, and that of our Lord's birth, thirty years earlier, viz., 750, or about four years before the usual Christian era.—Compare the exact, and, in our estimation, not yet superseded, calculations of WIESELER, in his *Chronological Synopsis.*‡

Vs. 2. **The word of God came.**—We can see no reason for supposing (with Wieseler) that this refers, not to the first preaching, but to some later appearance, of the Baptist, which was the immediate cause of his imprisonment. The solemnity of this introduction leads us rather to conclude, that the Evangelist intends to point out the time when John began to exchange his solitary life in the wilderness for one of public activity. And this circumstantial chronology is the more suitable, since the eras of John and of Jesus are inseparable; the baptism of the King of the heavenly kingdom following the public appearing of the forerunner, and taking place in the same year.

Unto John, the son of Zachariah.—See Luke i. 5, etc.—**In the wilderness.**—The locality is thus indefinitely mentioned by Luke, while the sphere of his activity is only generally stated as extending εἰς πᾶταν τὴν περίχωρον τοῦ 'Ιορδ. For Theophilus, who lived so far from the scene of the sacred history, a more exact indication was unnecessary. Compare, however, John i. 28; iii. 23, and the remarks on Matt. iii. 1 [vol. i. p. 68].

Vs. 4. **The voice of one crying in the wilderness,** etc.—There is no reason for so closely uniting

* [Joseph. *Antiq.* xv. 4, 1; xix. 5, 1; xx. 7, 1; *De bello Jud.* i. 13, 1; ii. 11, 5; Cass. Dio, 49, 32. Meyer concludes against Strauss that the statement of Luke is confirmed rather than refuted by Josephus.—P. S.]

† [WORDSWORTH *in loc.*: "St. Luke, in a spirit of reverence for the sacred office—instituted by God Himself—of the High-Priesthood, which was hereditary and *for life,* does not acknowledge that the High-Priest could be *lawfully* made and unmade by the civil power. He still calls Annas the *High-Priest,* and yet, since Caiaphas was *de facto* High-Priest, and was commonly reputed so to be, he adds his name in the second place to that of Annas."—P. S.]

‡ [Comp. also the careful essay of ANDREWS on the date of Christ's birth, in his *Life of our Lord,* pp. 1–22.—P. S.]

these words, as to make them designate the voice of John, as a *vox clamantis in deserto.* The word בַּמִּדְבָּר (Isa. xl. 3) does not belong to the preceding קוֹל קוֹרֵא, but to the immediately following, *præparate viam Domini.* The parallelism exacts that we should translate, Prepare ye *in the wilderness* the way of the Lord, make straight *in the desert* a highway for our God, Isa. xl. 3. The voice of the caller is the same mentioned in ver. 8. Luke gives this prophetic passage more correctly, and more closely follows the Septuagint, than the other Synoptists, especially in the closing phrase, ὄψεται πᾶσα σάρξ, κ.τ.λ.

Vs. 5. **Every valley,** etc.—That the whole of this passage, from Isaiah, is figurative language, derived from the march of a monarch, preceded by his herald, scarcely needs mentioning. The particular, however, which must not be overlooked is, that the prophecy of Isaiah xl. (Luke knows nothing yet of a *second* Isaiah), though it has a *real,* has no *direct* or *exclusive* reference to John the Baptist. A manifestation of the glory of God is announced, which, beginning with the return from Babylon, is beheld in incomparable splendor at the coming of Christ, and since goes on in growing fulfilment, but is not completed till the last day. Every prophet of the Old Testament going before the face of Jehovah, was a type of John the Baptist, who was to announce the advent of the God-Man; and John again was the type of every apostle, preacher, or missionary, who causes "the voice of one crying" to be heard, before the King Himself can appear. This voice began to sound when Isaiah first perceived and interpreted it; it was heard with unusual power through John's instrumentality; it will not be silent till the last trumpet shall be heard.

Vs. 7. **To the multitudes—Brood of Vipers!** —This mode of address might seem strange to us, without the more detailed account of St. Matthew, who informs us (ch. iii. 7), that the people, addressed in this discouraging manner, were by no means anxious inquirers after salvation, but rather Pharisees and Sadducees, or at least such as were infected by their pernicious leaven. Among this multitude must then be reckoned the crowds attracted to the banks of the Jordan by idle curiosity, if by no worse motive, whom the penetrating glance of John appreciates at their proper value. John, on the banks of the Jordan, appears, as Jesus did afterward, with the fan in his hand; and before we accuse him of harshness, we should do well to remember, first, that love itself can be severe, and that the meek Saviour Himself was inexorably so, toward hypocrites; and secondly, that the judgment here announced was not inevitable, but only impending over obstinate impenitence, while John earnestly desires that they may yet escape it, and points out the way of safety. By the terms, "serpents," "brood of vipers," the diabolical nature of hypocrisy is pointed out. Comp. 2 Cor. xi. 14; Rev. xx.—**Who hath warned you?**—in other words, who hath taught you, and how came you to think that, while you remain as you are, and without an inward change of mind, you can escape the wrath to come, by compliance with an outward sign alone? The last of the Old Testament prophets had also spoken of the judgment to be executed by the Messiah (Mal. iv. 5, 6); but the Jews pacified themselves with the idea, that this threat applied to the Gentiles, and not to themselves.

Vs. 8. **Bring forth therefore fruits worthy**

of repentance.—These are the ἔργα mentioned Acts xxvi. 20, and detailed in the same connection, ver. 11. John requires these, because without them they could not possibly escape the wrath to come (οὖν).

And begin not, etc.—Descent from Abraham, the national boast of the Jews, had now a higher importance in their eyes, because they believed that this, though standing *alone*, would give them a right to share in the blessings of the Messiah. This idea was, as it were, the shield under which they sought to shelter themselves from the sharp arrows of the preaching of repentance, and which John thus snatches from them.—Of these stones.—He points to the stones of the wilderness, with reference too, perhaps, to the creation, when God made man of the dust of the earth. The notion, that the call of the heathen was now present to the mind of the Baptist, is at least unimproved; nor is there in his preaching any reference to this event.

Vs. 9. The Axe is laid.—There is, in these words, a passing on from the notion of the possibility, to that of the certainty, of the wrath to come. The axe laid, not near to the unfruitful branches, but to the very roots, points to the judgment of extermination about to break forth on the impenitent.—Every tree, etc.—A fruitless fig-tree was afterward made, by our Lord, the representative of the whole Jewish *nation* (Luke xiii. 6); but here each tree, about to be hewn down, denotes an impenitent *individual*, receiving his sentence. John at least does not teach an ἀποκατάστασις πάντων.

Vs. 10. And the people asked him.—The question of perplexed penitents; not unlike that put to Peter, at the feast of Pentecost, Acts ii. 37. The answer is given entirely in the Old Testament fashion, and from a legal point of view, without any mention of the higher requisites of faith and love; and is remarkable, as showing how thoroughly practical, temperate, and even comparatively rigorous, was the morality of the preacher of repentance. A man who made the duties of mercy and justice, of brotherly love and fidelity in daily intercourse, so prominent, could scarcely be an enthusiast. Luke is the only Evangelist who has communicated, from some unknown source, these special features of the Baptist's teaching. His whole answer shows with what penetration he had, even in his secluded life, observed the chief defects of each different class. He who would influence men, must not live so severed from them, that he ceases to know and understand them.

Vs. 11. He that hath two coats, etc.—They are not required to leave their several callings, but to sacrifice their selfishness while remaining in them. Comp. Isa. lviii. 3–6; Dan. iv. 24.

Vs. 13. Exact no more, etc.—The covetousness and selfishness of the publicans, the "*immodestia publicanorum*," had become proverbial; John pronounces an irrevocable veto against their exactions.

Vs. 14. Soldiers.—It is uncertain whether these soldiers were used for purposes of police (Ewald), or whether they belonged to some foreign legion employed by Herod in his wars (Michaelis). At all events, they were men actually employed in military service, and were perhaps, by their question, kindred spirits to the pious centurion Cornelius (Acts x.)—Διασείειν, to extort by fear, to lay under contribution. Συκοφαντεῖν, to play the spy, thence to slander, to do injustice (to cheat). How much opportunity the military service afforded for such practices, and how much the hardships of the times were thereby enhanced to many, needs no explanation.

[John did not say to the soldiers: Throw away your arms and desert your colors; but: Do not abuse your power. His exhortation plainly implies the lawfulness of the military profession, and consequently the right of war under certain circumstances. Aggressive wars, it is true, are always wrong, but defensive wars against foreign invasion and domestic rebellion are justifiable. War is always a dread calamity, but in the *present* state of society, it is often an unavoidable necessity, and the only means of defending the rights, the honor, and the very existence of a nation, and may thus prevent still greater evil. It is a destroyer and barbarizer, but in the overruling providence of God it may become a civilizer and even a Christianizer.—P. S.]

Vs. 15. Whether he were the Christ.—A surprising proof of the deep impression made, by the moral strictness of the Baptist, upon the susceptible mind of the multitude. There was *some* foundation of truth in this delusion, since, by means of John, Christ Himself, though invisibly, was standing at the door and knocking. The moral greatness of John is shown in the fact, that he made no use of this delusion of the people, but hastened to withdraw within those limits which they would almost have compelled him to pass. Similar conduct was shown by Paul and Barnabas, Acts xiv. 15.

Vs. 16. John answered them all, saying.—And if we also read that, on an entirely distinct occasion, he gave the same answer to a small section of the Sanhedrin (John i. 25), we are by no means forced to the conclusion, that one Evangelist contradicts the other, but rather that John repeated this saying at different times; a saying whose purport was so important, and whose form was figurative language so entirely in the spirit and after the heart of the Baptist, that, having once uttered it, he could not have expressed himself more powerfully and naturally with respect to this vital question.

Vs. 16. One mightier than I.—A general expression for what he elsewhere declares in a more definite manner, *e. g.*, John i. 30. The greater might of the Messiah is here made, by the context, to consist especially in the fact, that His baptism can effect what John's baptism is powerless to produce. Consequently, He more deserves the reverence and attention of the people, while His forerunner deems himself unworthy to perform the most menial office for Him.

He shall baptize you with [better in] the Holy Ghost, and with fire.—He will, so to speak, wholly immerse you in the Holy Ghost, and in the fire.* The baptism of the Spirit, which produces re-

---

* [The difference between βαπτίζειν ὕδατι without ἐν, and βαπτίζειν ἐν πνεύματι ἁγίῳ καὶ πυρί, should be noticed in the translation by *with* in the former and *in* in the latter case; the instrumental dative signifies the element *by which*, the preposition *ἐν* the locality or element *in which* the baptism is performed. Matthew, however, in the parallel passage, iii. 11, 12, uses *ἐν* in both cases, while in Mark i. 8 there is a difference of reading; some authorities have *ἐν* before ὕδατι and πνεύματι, others omit it before both, still others (as Cod. Sin.) read ὕδατι and ἐν πνεύματι. I prefer the latter as being more consistent with Scripture usage, comp. Luke iii. 16; John i. 33; Acts i. 5; xi. 16, as well as with the nature of the case. Water may be regarded both as the element *in which*, and as the element *by which* baptism is performed, and hence may or may not be connected with *ἐν*; but the Holy Spirit could not properly be conceived as the mere instrument of an act, and hence should in every case be construed with the local preposition *ἐν*.—As regards the bearing of the phrase *to baptize in the Holy Ghost*, on the

newal, is contrasted with the baptism of water, which can only represent it. The baptism of fire is appointed for the unconverted, as that of the Holy Spirit for believers.* As Simeon had announced that Christ was set for the fall of some and rising of others, so does John here describe Him as coming with a twofold baptism. Some are renovated by His baptism, others buried in the fiery baptism of final judgment.

Vs. 17. **Whose fan**, etc.—*See* Matt. iii. 12 [vol. i. p. 72.] The same figure occurs also Jer. xv. 7, and Luke xxii. 31; while the internal connection between the κήρυγμα of John and that of Malachi iv. 1 is self-evident.

Vs. 18. **He preached the Gospel unto the people.**—The announcement of the most fearful judgments belongs, then, no less than that of an abundant baptism of the Spirit, to that work of evangelization which the Baptist had commenced. A significant hint to those who consider a representation of the judgments of the Lord fundamentally incompatible with the full and free preaching of the Gospel.

Vs. 19. **But Herod.**—The first appearance upon the scene, of the tetrarch, who is hereafter to play so terrible a part in the Baptist's history. He was the son of Herod the Great, and of Malthace, a Samaritan. He married first the daughter of King Aretas, but afterwards entered into an adulterous connection with his brother Philip's wife. The account here given by Luke should be specially compared with that of Mark (ch. vi. 17–20). Mark tells us that this punishment did not hinder Herod from esteeming John in a certain sense; Luke, that he had not brought it upon himself by reproving this crime alone, but also **all the evils that Herod did.** There can be no ground for doubting (with Meyer) the historical character of a narrative so psychologically probable. He who is in any measure acquainted with the character of the tetrarch, will not doubt that a preacher of repentance would find material enough for reproving him concerning πονηρά. That these reached their climax in the imprisonment and execution of John, was a conviction which Luke undoubtedly shared with all Christian antiquity, and which needs no justification.

Vs. 20. **That he shut up John in prison.**—It is not impossible that he allowed him less and less liberty in the prison to which he had been condemned, and at length cut off all access to him. The whole of Luke's account of John is summary, and written without regard to chronology: he here collects all that he has to say concerning the forerunner, that he may confine himself for the future to the history of Jesus alone; the narrative of the baptism forming the point of transition.

Vs. 21. **It came to pass,** etc.—The necessity of comparing together the accounts of the different Evangelists, in order to obtain an exact description of the chief events of the Gospel history, is here very apparent. Not one Evangelist communicates a complete account of what happened at our Lord's baptism; and it is only by collating their several contributions, that we obtain a complete view of the occurrence. Matthew gives us the most copious account, and also the dialogue which took place between the Baptist and the Saviour; Mark, according to his usual custom, narrates very concisely, but with the addition of some fresh and graphic incident,—here the opening of the heavens (σχιζομένους τοὺς οὑρ.): John depicts the subjective side of this event, in its high significance to our Lord's forerunner; Luke presupposes an acquaintance with the occurrence, through the apostolic κήρυγμα, and touches upon it for the sake of completeness, and especially to render conspicuous the testimony borne by the Father to the Son on this occasion. In this condition of things, it is unfairness itself to understand our Evangelist's expressions, which certainly were never penned with diplomatic exactness, so *ad literam* as to cause an irreconcilable discrepancy between himself and his fellow-witnesses. Plainly, the words, that Jesus was baptized **when all the people were baptized,** do not necessarily imply, that both the baptism of the Lord and the opening of the heavens happened in the *presence* of a numerous multitude,—such a publicity would have been a violation of both human and divine *decorum,*—but only, that, at the period when the greatest number of baptisms was taking place, the baptism of Jesus of Nazareth took place (and naturally in private) among others. The object of Luke is, not to narrate the baptism for its own sake, but for the sake of the heavenly authentication which the Lord then received.

Vs. 21. **Jesus also being baptized, and praying.**—It is one of the *singularia Lucae,* that he often mentions that Jesus prayed, even when the other Evangelists make no mention of the circumstance; as, for example, on the night preceding the choosing of His Apostles (Luke vi. 12.) By uniting the accounts of all the Evangelists, with reference to our Lord's practice of private prayer, we find that He, who always lived in uninterrupted communion with the Father, specially and emphatically hallowed every turning-point of his earthly career—His baptism, choice of Apostles, renunciation of a throne (John vi. 15), transfiguration, and his journey towards his last sufferings—by solitary prayer. Those who accept the view that the Evangelist describes a public baptism, must surely have lost sight of his account of this act of prayer. Or did He then so pray *publice,* that the heavens were opened, a sort of show-prayer in fact? As well might we infer from Luke's words, literally interpreted, the incongruity, that He was baptized with all the people, *in massa,* and at the same time.

Vs. 21. **The heaven was opened.**—The objective character of the narrative is remarkable. According to Matthew and Mark, it is Jesus who sees heaven opened, and for whose sake this occurrence takes place. John expressly states, that the ray fell upon the mind of the Baptist; while Luke relates the event as though uncaused by the subjectivity of any, and in this respect satisfies the higher requirements of historic narrative.

---

immersion controversy, it is hardly fair to press it one way or the other, since in this case the term is evidently used figuratively, though, of course, with reference to the sacred rite. It means to be overwhelmed or richly furnished with the Holy Spirit. Dr. van Oosterzee, like Dr. Lange and most of the German commentators, adheres to the original and prevailing usage of βαπτίζω; but they do not intend to deny the wider Hellenistic use of the term, much less to convey the idea that immersion is the *only* proper mode of baptism, the effect and validity of which does not depend either on the quantity or quality of water, or the mode of its application, but upon the power of the Holy Spirit accompanying the water and the administration of the rite in the name of the Holy Trinity and with the intention to baptize. Comp. on this controversy the lengthy remarks in my *History of the Apostolic Church,* § 112, p. — (of the English edition).—P. S.]

* [So also Dr. Lange. Comp. my annotation on Matt. iii. 11, vol. i. p. 72. In *dissent* from this reference of the baptism of *fire* to the final judgment.—P. S.]

Vs. 22. **In a bodily shape, like a dove.**—The mention of the *dove* by all the four Evangelists, plainly shows, that the descent of the Spirit was usually compared, by the Baptist who saw it, and afterwards by those who related it, to the descent of a dove. It is, however, by no means necessary to infer, from the σωματικὸν εἶδος of Luke, the *actual* form of a dove. Luke does not say, σωματικῷ εἴδει περιστερᾶς, but ὡς περιστεράν. By supposing a ray of light to have descended from the opened heaven, gently, swiftly, and evenly, like the downward flight of a dove, and to have shone around the head of the praying Saviour for some space of time, we escape many difficulties, and obtain a representation beautiful in itself, and becoming the divine majesty. It is by no means proved, that the dove was, in the days of Jesus, regarded by the Jews as an emblem of the Holy Spirit. The very shy nature of the dove renders it difficult to conceive its descending from heaven, and *abiding* on a newly baptized person, even in a vision. And if ancient Christian art, exchanging the figure for the fact, constantly introduced a visible dove into every representation of the baptism, it is only probable that this unæsthetic treatment was the result of an exegetical error. Our view also will satisfactorily explain why Justin Martyr (*Dial. cum Tryph.* c. 88), as well as the Gospel of the Hebrews (Epiphanius, *Hæres.* xxx. 13), mentions a vivid ray of light as suddenly surrounding the banks of Jordan. By a very natural symbolism, light was regarded by the Jews as an emblem of the Divinity; and we can see no reason why the descent of a ray of light should not also have been compared to the descent of a dove.

[I beg leave to differ from the esteemed author in his ingenious attempt to get rid of the dove. The Holy Spirit did not use, indeed, a *real, living* dove as His organ (as Satan used a serpent in the history of temptation), else the Evangelists would not connect ὡς or ὡσεί with περιστερά, but He assumed, in His form of manifestation to the inward vision of John (comp. the parallel passage of John i. 32, *I* (John) saw, and Matt. iii. 16, "*he* saw"), an organized bodily shape, σωματικὸν εἶδος (Luke), and this was, according to the unanimous testimony of all the Evangelists, the shape of a *dove*, or looked like a dove, ὡς περιστερά, which is the natural symbol of purity and gentleness. The comparison is between the *Spirit* and the dove, and not (as Bleek and others assume) simply between the *descent* of the Spirit and the flight of a dove, for this would leave the σωματικὸν εἶδος of Luke unexplained. The whole phenomenon was, of course, not material, but supernatural (a πνευματικὴ θεωρία), yet none the less objective and real.* Why should the creative Spirit, who in the beginning was brooding (*like a dove*, as the *Talmud* has it) over the face of the waters (Gen. i. 2), brought cosmos out of chaos, not be able to create an organized shape of deep symbolical significance? A dove is decidedly a more appropriate and expressive medium of His manifestation than the form of "a ray of light from heaven." There is no good reason, therefore, to deviate here from the old interpretation, which is adopted also by de Wette, Meyer, and Alford, as the plain and natural meaning of Luke.—P. S.]

Vs. 22. **A voice from heaven.**—There is no reason for understanding this, either of a so-called

---

* [Comp. Jerome in *loc.*: "*Aperiuntur autem cœli non reseratione elementorum sed spiritualibus oculis, quibus et Ezechiel in principio voluminis sui apertos eos esse commemorat.*"—P. S.]

בַּת קוֹל, a pure invention of the later Rabbis, or of thunder, which, indeed, is often called the voice of the Lord in the poetical, but never in the historical, books of the Old Testament. Everything compels us to accept this as an actual, extraordinary, and plainly audible voice from heaven; yet such a one as would be understood and interpreted only in a peculiar state of mind and spirit, such as that in which Jesus and John then were. Any interpretation which impugns either the reality or the agency of the voices from heaven, heard during the life of Jesus, is objectionable. Certainly Jesus understood, still better than John, the full force and meaning of the Father's voice. For the servant it was the decisive intimation, "This same is He;" for the Son, the definite declaration, "**Thou art My beloved Son.**" The reference to Ps. ii. 7,.Isa. xlii. 1, is evident; but the opinion, that Jesus is here called *the Son, in whom the Father is well pleased*, only because he is the Messiah of Israel, the theocratic King, is derived from the exegetic *commentum*, that, in New Testament diction, Χριστός and ὁ υἱὸς Θεοῦ are only two terms to denote the same idea. (On the whole narrative, compare the *Disputatio theol. inaug. de locis evang. in quibus Jesum baptismi ritum subiisse traditur*, by Dr. J. J. Prins, L. B., 1838; and on John the Baptist, a monograph by G. E. W. DE WYS, Schoonhoven, 1852.)

DOCTRINAL AND ETHICAL.

1. In the beginning of the third chapter of Luke, compared with the close of the second, we feel how remarkable is the transition from quiet seclusion to unbounded publicity, in the incidents recorded. On the preaching and ministry of John, see the remarks on Matt. iii. [vol. 1. p. 67 ff.]

2. In the choice of the time at which the voice of the Baptist, and so shortly after that of the Lord, should begin to be heard, we see another manifest proof of the wisdom of God. What civil, political, and moral misery is associated with the names which Luke here (vs. 1 and 2) mentions! All Israel had, indeed, become a barren wilderness, when "the voice of one crying" was loudly and unexpectedly heard.

3. The preaching of John, as Luke communicates it, is, even in its form, of a prophetic, Old Testament character. The Lord comes in the wind, in the earthquake, and in the fire, but not yet in the still small voice. It is easy to remark the difference between the voice of the law, which resounds here, and that of the gospel, which was afterward heard; but not less necessary, perhaps, to observe their still more striking agreement. Even in the severest tones of the preacher of repentance the evangelical element may be recognized, while we meet with expressions in the discourses of Jesus quite as strong as any which we hear from the lips of John (*e. g.,* Matt. xi. 20-24; xxiii. 13 f.). If we shrink from the notion, that the Lord Himself, on such occasions, was standing on lower ground, Old Testament ground, from which He afterward rose to greater heights, we shall be obliged to conclude, that the New Testament also recognizes a revelation of wrath not less terrible than was threatened under the Old. Matt. xix. 6 may aptly be cited in this case.

4. The morality preached by John differs from that of the Lord, inasmuch as the former lays more stress upon the regulation of the external conduct, while Jesus lays more upon that of the inner life.

It is, however, self-evident, that all which John requires from the people, the publicans, and the soldiers, is only valuable in his eye so far as it is the fruit and proof of an inward change of mind. John could not be contented with fruits externally united to a dead tree, but must recognize the truth of Matt. vii. 18. But the more he knew himself to be unable to communicate the new life, the more strenuously would he insist on such conduct as would give unambiguous proof of an inward desire of salvation; and the more emphasis he laid upon the inflexible demands of the law, the more intense must be the desires awakened in the hearts of many.

5. The character of John, as exhibited by his lowly testimony to himself, contrasted with the lofty expectations of the people, is one of the most exalted which the history of the kingdom of God can show. To have been able to enlist thousands on his side by a single word, and not to utter that word, but to direct the attention of these thousands to another, whom they had not yet seen, and as soon as He appears, humbly to retire to the background, yea, even to rejoice in his own abasement, if only this other be exalted (John iii. 29, 30),—when has a more elevated character been seen, and how can such moral greatness be explained, unless the words of Luke i. 15, 80 were the expression of unmixed truth?

6. The inquiry concerning the aim and purpose of John's baptism, is quite independent of that concerning the antiquity and meaning of the baptism of proselytes. He who submitted to it, confessed himself, by this very act, to be impure, and worthy of punishment; acknowledged his obligation, as one called into the kingdom of the Messiah, to lead a holy life; and received the assurance that God would forgive his sins. Even here, then, forgiveness was not to be earned by the sinner's own previous amendment; but with the announcement of the kingdom of God was revealed the preventing grace of the Father, which promised forgiveness of sins; and only faith in this grace could afford strength for moral improvement, which could alone enable him who was the subject of it fully to taste the joy of pardon. This baptism differed from all former Old Testament washings, by its special reference to the now nearly approaching kingdom of Messiah; while the distinction between the baptism of John and the subsequent Christian baptism was, that the former prepared and separated for the kingdom of God, and the latter admitted within it. On this account, baptism by the disciples of Jesus, and even by the Lord Himself, at the commencement of His public ministry (John iii. 22; iv. 2), can be regarded as only a continuation of this preparatory baptism of John. Christian baptism, the baptism of consecration, could not be instituted till the New Covenant had been instituted in Christ's blood, the throne of the kingdom of heaven ascended, and the promise of the Holy Spirit fulfilled.

7. Not only did John and Christ stand in external connection with each other, but they are inseparably united. As John preceded Christ, so must the preacher of repentance still cause his voice to be heard in the heart, before Christ can live in us. Through anxiety to peace, through repentance to grace, was not only the way into the kingdom of the Lord for the Jews in those days, but also for Christians in those. Holy strictness is still the true initiation into the exalted joy of the Christian life. He who remains the disciple of John without coming to Christ, endures hunger without obtaining food; he who will go to Christ without having been spiritually a learner in the school of John, finds food, without having any appetite for it.

8. Every answer to the inquiry, why Jesus suffered Himself to be baptized, may be considered unsatisfactory, which either regards baptism as necessary for the Lord, in the same sense as it was for the sinful Israelites, or, on the other hand, sees in this fact only a compliance with an existing usage of no special importance to Himself. John immediately perceived that baptism, as an acknowledgment of guilt and impurity, was unnecessary for Jesus (Matt. iii. 14.) Nor do we read that any requirement of μετάνοια was made. Perhaps we may even regard the mention, by Matthew, that "when He was baptized, He went up straightway (εὐθύς) out of the water," as a hint at the difference between *His* baptism and that of the other Jews, who probably remained some time under the water. If we inquire into the Lord's own *view* of the *necessity* of baptism in His own case, He calls it a fulfilling of all righteousness. He considers it as fitting that He should now submit to this rite, as, thirty years before, it was considered fitting that He should be circumcised and presented in the temple. He was hereby brought into personal relation with that kingdom of God, the future subjects of which were to be set apart in like manner, and entered into communication with an impure world whose sins He was to bear. And, though no acknowledgment of obligation was necessary in His case, yet a holy and solemn consecration to His high vocation was by no means superfluous. Needing no purification for Himself, He yet receives it, as head of His body the Church, for all His members; and thus proves that He will be in all things like unto His brethren, sin only excepted. Besides, it is seen by the incidents which accompanied and followed it, what it was the will of the Father that this baptism should be to Him, even the heavenly consecration of the Son to the work which the Father had given Him. He consecrates Himself, and at the same time the Father consecrates him, to the kingdom of God.

9. It is apparent, from Isa. xi. 2, that the anointing with the Holy Spirit was among the characteristics of the Messiah. The peculiarity, however, is, that while He *came* momentarily upon the elect of the Old Testament, He *remained upon Jesus*. The same thought is paraphrastically expressed in the old *Evangelium Nazaræorum*, where the Holy Spirit is introduced at the baptism of the Lord as saying: " My Son, I was waiting in all the prophets till Thou shouldest come, that I might rest upon Thee. Thou art My resting-place (*tu enim es requies mea*), My only-begotten Son, who rulest forever."

10. The revelation at the Jordan was neither new nor unnecessary to the God-Man. Undoubtedly the consciousness of the Lord, with respect to His work and person, had been continually increasing in strength, clearness, and depth, since the occurrence recorded of His twelfth year. His very first word to John shows how He places Himself upon a level with the greatest of the prophets; and He who will fulfil all righteousness must well know who He is, and wherefore He is come. But now the revelation from above impresses its unerring seal upon the perfect revelation within, and Luke represents this sealing (John vi. 27, ἐσφράγισεν) as a definite answer to prayer. As the voice from Heaven (John xii.) consecrated Him the atoning High Priest, and that upon Tabor declared Him the greatest of the prophets, who was to be heard before Moses and Elias, so was His

formal appointment as King of the heavenly kingdom bestowed upon Him in the presence of the Baptist.

11. The descent of the Holy Spirit at the baptism, and the miraculous birth of our Lord by the power of the Holy Spirit, are by no means inconsistent facts. Undoubtedly, the Son of Man had not lived thirty years upon earth without the Holy Spirit: and it is an arbitrary assumption to suppose that miraculous power was specially bestowed upon Him at this instant. Our Lord, however, had hitherto possessed the gifts of the Holy Spirit only by means of his continual communion with the Father, and of the Father's unceasing communications to Him. There is nothing unfounded in the opinion, that the Father communicated still more to Him, who already possessed so much, and that the indwelling element of His life was developed, in all its fulness, by a new and mighty afflation from above. We should not be able to determine with certainty *what* He now received, unless we could compare His inner life before and after His baptism; but for this we are not furnished with sufficient data. It is enough for us to know that the Holy Spirit, who had been for thirty years the bond of communion between the Father and His incarnate Son, now, at the beginning of His public ministry, entered into new relations with Him. He anointed Him as King of the kingdom of heaven, and at the same time as a Prophet, mighty in deed and word before God and the people.

12. The whole history of the baptism of Jesus is highly and abidingly valuable in a doctrinal point of view. It is a pledge to us that our Lord voluntarily undertook His work upon earth, began and ended it with full consciousness, and was furnished with all the gifts and powers which it required. It gives to our faith in the Son of God the objective foundation of divine testimony, which can neither be denied nor recalled. And it presents us with so striking a revelation of the fulness of the divine nature, when the Father gives testimony to the Son, and the Holy Spirit descends in a visible form, that we can scarcely read it without recalling the words of one of the Fathers: *I ad Jordanem et videbis Trinitatem.*"

HOMILETICAL AND PRACTICAL.

John and Jesus in their mutual relation.—The history of the kingdom of God, in its connection with the history of the world.—Tiberius and Herod in princely robes; Annas and Caiaphas in priestly garments; John in the rough clothing of a preacher of repentance.—The forerunner: 1. His severity toward the unholy multitude; 2. his humility toward the holy Christ.—Preparing the way of the Lord, is, 1. a difficult work; 2. an indispensable necessity; 3. a blessed employment.—The voice of the caller; 1. How much it requires; 2. how gravely it threatens; 3. how gently it comforts and promises.—John must still precede Jesus.—The abasement of all that is high, and the elevation of all that is low, in the heart whereinto Christ enters.—Fruitless efforts to escape the wrath to come.—The fruits of conversion: 1. No true religion without conversion; 2. No true conversion without godliness.—Descent from Abraham gives no precedence in the kingdom of God.—What the power of God can make out of stones: 1. Of stones of the desert, children of Abraham; 2. of stony hearts, hearts of flesh.—The axe laid to the root of the trees: what justice has laid it to the *root;* what mercy leaves it *still lying* at the root!—The judgment on unfruitful trees is, 1. surely to be expected; 2. perfectly to be justified; 3. still to be avoided.—The great inquiry, What shall we do? 1. A question becoming all; 2. a question answered to all.—The answer to the great inquiry of life, 1. from the stand-point of the law (Luke iii. 10-14); 2. from the stand-point of grace (Acts ii. 38.)—No true peace, without a vigorous struggle against besetting sins.—The fundamental law of the kingdom of God, in its application to daily life.—No condition too lowly, or too unfavorable, to allow a man to prove himself a subject of the kingdom of God. The beneficial influence of conversion upon the military profession.—How would it have been, if John had been the Christ?—Baptism with water and the Spirit: 1. The distinction; 2. the connection between them.—Deep humility, the greatness of John the Baptist.—The exalted nature of Jesus, freely owned by John, a confession, 1. honorable to John; 2. due to Christ; 3. important to the world, to Israel, to us.—Jesus the true Baptist.—Baptism with the Holy Spirit: with the Spirit, 1. of truth, to enlighten us; 2. of power, to renew us; 3. of grace, to comfort us; 4. of love, to unite us to each other, to Christ, to God.—Baptism with fire considered, 1. on its terrible; 2. on its inevitable; 3. on its beneficial side.—The preaching of the gospel by John is especially the preaching of repentance: 1. As such, it was prophesied of; 2. as such, it was carried on; 3. as such, it worked; 4. as such, it is still needed. The thresher and the fan, the wheat and the barn, the chaff and the unquenchable fire.—John before Herod: 1. The strict preacher of repentance; 2. the innocent victim; 3. the avenging accuser.—John, a faithful court-preacher.—John and our Lord on the banks of the Jordan.—The most exalted solemnity during the Baptist's life.—The voice from heaven at the Jordan, a revelation for John, for Jesus, for us.—The time of baptism, a time of prayer.—The voice of the Father, the Amen to the prayer of the Son.—Jesus baptized with the Holy Spirit.—The anointing of Christ, the anointing of the Christian.—The first voice from heaven to the Lord's honor, the key-note of the subsequent voices from heaven.—The heavenly authentication after thirty years of solitary separation.

STARKE:—Everything happens at the right time.—The light arises in darkness, when it looks most gloomy.—The chief work of the preacher must ever be to prepare the way to the Lord Jesus.—Repentance no easy matter: it costs time and labor to level mountains.—The Church of God is not confined to any special people.—God seeks fruit; is not contented with mere leaves; and, however high a tree thou mayest be, is no respecter of persons.—The work of God, for the most part, begins with people of low condition.—A preacher must inculcate not merely general, but special duties, according to the condition of his hearers. The multitude generally knows no medium, but would either raise a man to heaven, or plunge him into hell.—Christ can, and will, in His own good time, purify His Church; a comfort for those who mourn over its present corruption.—The Church is not without chaff; heart-Christians and lip-Christians are always mingled.—Christ receives baptism in the same manner as sinful men; what humility!—The mystery of the Trinity is here plainly enough depicted: away with the vain babbling of Jews and Socinians.

HEUBNER:—The faithful preaching of repentance,

an act of heroism.—The solemn voice of truth does not repel, but attracts. The mere preaching of the law cannot lead to salvation; the preaching of the gospel can alone do this.—Christ knows the genuine and the spurious among His followers; what teacher is like Him? Jesus received a heavenly consecration to His calling: we too may enter upon our calling, if we have the inward consciousness that God has chosen us for our work, and the inward witness that we are the children of God.

ARNDT:—How does the light arise upon mankind, and upon individual men? The appearance of John may teach us. Day dawns quietly yet powerfully; gravely yet full of promise.—The baptism of Jesus in the Jordan considered, 1. as strange in the sight of man; 2. as pleasing in the sight of God. SCHLEIERMACHER:—What must precede the Lord's entrance into human hearts.—HARLESS (in a sermon on Luke iii. 15-17): On the question, what kind of prophets do we require? Such as (a) think humbly of themselves; (b) know how to reprove the folly of the multitude; and (c) direct attention from themselves to Him who came with the baptism of the Holy Spirit, and will come with the fiery baptism of judgment. STRAUSS:—[Late court-preacher and professor at Berlin.]—The greatest man and Christ: 1. What is the greatest of men compared with Christ? 2. What is Christ compared with the greatest of men? PALMER:—Testimony for Christ must always be, 1. a voluntary; 2. a just; 3. a constant testimony. F. W. KRUMMACHER:—The kingdom of Christ, according to the preaching of John, is, 1. a kingdom not of this world, though a world-wide kingdom; 2. a kingdom not of outward show, but a kingdom of truth; 3. a kingdom not of false peace, but of substantial help; 4. not a kingdom of the law, but of salvation; 5. not a kingdom of demands, but a kingdom of grace.

B. *Testimony of the Genealogy.* CH. III. 23-38.

23 And Jesus Himself began to be about thirty years of age [Jesus Himself was about thirty years of age when He began (His ministry)];[1] being (as was supposed) the son
24 of Joseph, which [who] was[2] *the son*[3] of Heli,[4] Which was *the son* of Matthat, which was *the son* of Levi, which was *the son* of Melchi, which was *the son* of Janna, which
25 was *the son* of Joseph, Which was *the son* of Mattathias, which was *the son* of Amos, which was *the son* of Naum, which was *the son* of Esli, which was *the son* of Nagge,
26 Which was *the son* of Maath, which was *the son* of Mattathias, which was *the son* of
27 Semei, which was *the son* of Joseph, which was *the son* of Juda, Which was *the son* of Joanna, which was *the son* of Rhesa, which was *the son* of Zorobabel, which was *the son*
28 of Salathiel, which was *the son* of Neri, Which was *the son* of Melchi, which was *the son* of Addi, which was *the son* of Cosam, which was *the son* of Elmodam, which was *the son*
29 of Er, Which was *the son* of Jose, which was *the son* of Eliezer, which was *the son* of
30 Jorim, which was *the son* of Matthat, which was *the son* of Levi, Which was *the son* of Simeon, which was *the son* of Juda, which was *the son* of Joseph, which was *the son* of
31 Jonan, which was *the son* of Eliakim, Which was *the son* of Melea, which was *the son* of Menan, which was *the son* of Mattatha, which was *the son* of Nathan, which was *the*
32 *son* of David, Which was *the son* of Jesse, which was *the son* of Obed, which was *the*
33 *son* of Booz, which was *the son* of Salmon, which was *the son* of Naasson, Which was *the son* of Aminadab, which was *the son* of Aram, which was *the son* of Esrom, which
34 was *the son* of Phares, which was *the son* of Juda, Which was *the son* of Jacob, which was *the son* of Isaac, which was *the son* of Abraham, which was *the son* of Thara, which
35 was *the son* of Nachor, Which was *the son* of Saruch, which was *the son* of Ragau, which was *the son* of Phalec, which was *the son* of Heber, which was *the son* of Sala,
36 Which was *the son* of Cainan, which was *the son* of Arphaxad, which was *the son* of
37 Sem, which was *the son* of Noe, which was *the son* of Lamech, Which was *the son* of Mathusala, which was *the son* of Enoch, which was *the son* of Jared, which was *the son*
38 of Maleleel, which was *the son* of Cainan, Which was *the son* of Enos, which was *the son* of Seth, which was *the son* of Adam, which was *the son* of God.

[¹ Vs. 23.—Καὶ αὐτὸς ἦν Ἰησοῦς ὡσεὶ ἐτῶν τριάκοντα ἀρχόμενος, *And Jesus Himself was about thirty years old* (or *of age*) *when He began* (His ministry). So Tyndale, Wesley, Norton, Whiting, de Wette, Meyer, Alford, etc. The rendering of Cranmer, the Genevan and the Authorized Versions is ungrammatical and makes ὡσεὶ unmeaning. We may say ἄρχεσθαι εἶναι ἐτῶν τριάκοντα, or ἔτους τριακοστοῦ, *to enter into the thirtieth year*, but not ἄρχ. ἐτῶν τριάκοντα. Ἀρχόμενος adds an explanation, and hence is put last. We must supply *to preach*, or *to teach*, or *His ministry*, comp. Acts i. 1, 22. So Euthymius: ἀρχ. τῆς εἰς τὸν λαὸν ἀναδείξεως αὐτοῦ, ἤτοι τῆς διδασκαλίας.

² Vs. 23 ff.—The insertion *which* (who) *was* of the E. V., in this verse and throughout this section, is heavy and unnecessary, and hence properly omitted in the translations of Wesley, Campbell, Sharpe, Kendrick, Whiting, the Revised N. T. of the Am. B. U., etc. If it be retained, it should be italicized rather than *the son*.

³ Vs. 23 ff.—*The son.* This is implied in the Greek construction τοῦ Ἡλί, etc., and need not be italicized.

⁴ Vs. 23 ff.—In the spelling of these proper names there is considerable variation in the MSS. and ancient transl., but not of sufficient account to justify a deviation from the Received Text. In a popular revision of the English Version, the

spelling of Hebrew names here, as in the genealogy of Matthew, should be conformed to the Hebrew spelling, as in the E. V. of the O. T. Hence *Eli* for Heli, *Naggai* for Nagge, *Shimei* for Semei, *Judah* for Juda, *Johanah* for Joanna, *Zerubbabel* for Zorobabel, etc. *See* the *Crit. Note* on Matt. i. vol. i. p. 48.—P. S.]

EXEGETICAL AND CRITICAL.

Vs. 23. **When He began,** ἀρχόμενος (His ministry).—The rendering, *And Jesus was, when He began (i. e.,* to preach), *about thirty years of age,* is not free from difficulties, but is recommended by its connection with the context. For, in the preceding verses, the Evangelist has been describing the dedication of the Lord to His work as Messiah; and what more natural than that he should now speak of His entrance thereupon? Besides, it is entirely according to his custom to specify dates: he has already mentioned that of the ministry of John, and those of the birth, circumcision, presentation in the temple, and first Passover of Jesus; and he now indicates to his readers the date of the things ἃ ἤρξατο Ἰησοῦς ποιεῖν τε καὶ διδάσκειν, Acts i. 1. In any case this construction is preferable to the exposition: "*incipiebat antem Jesus annorum esse fere triginta,*" *Jesus began to be about thirty years of age.** If Luke had meant to say this, he would certainly have expressed himself very obscurely.

About thirty years of age.—All attempts at fixing an exact chronology of our Lord's life, from this indication of Luke, have split upon this word "about" (ὡσεί).† We are only informed by it, that when Jesus began His public ministry, He was not much under, or much above, thirty years of age. This was, according to Num. iv. 3, 47, the age at which the Levitical services were entered upon, though undoubtedly there was no need of applying such a law to the Lord's entrance upon His work as Messiah. On the other hand, however, it was at the age of thirty that the Jewish scribes were accustomed to enter upon their office as teachers; and John the Baptist also commenced his ministry at this age. Perhaps the contemporaries of Jesus might not have been disposed to recognize the authority of a teacher who had not attained the age appointed to the Levites.

Vss. 23-38. **Being (as was supposed the son of Joseph) the son of Eli, etc.**—We prefer including υἱὸς Ἰωσήφ also in the parenthesis. The passage then stands, ὢν . . . τοῦ Ἠλί, being the son of Eli, *i. e.,* though supposed to be the son of Joseph. This manner of introducing the parenthesis will show at once that we agree with those who consider that, while Matthew gives the genealogy of Joseph, Luke gives that of Mary. Compare the important remarks of Lange on Matt. i. [vol. i. p. 48 ff.]. The difficulties of this view are not unappreciated by us, but still greater difficulties attend every other hypothesis; whether that of the Levirate marriage, or that of the total irreconcilability of the two genealogies. Considered in itself, it was far more likely that Luke would give the genealogy of Mary than that of her husband. She is the principal figure throughout his early chapters; while Joseph occupies a far more subordinate position than in Matthew. He is very explicit in narrating that Mary became the mother of the Holy Child, through the miraculous operation of the Holy Spirit; why then should he, who was not writing for Jews, give the descent of His foster-father, when he is intent upon asserting that the Lord was not related to Joseph according to the flesh? He is expressly contrasting His true descent from Eli, the father of Mary, with His supposed descent from Joseph; and Mary is simply passed over, because it was not customary among the Jews to insert the names of females in their genealogies. We find it then here stated, that Jesus was the descendant of Eli, viz., through Mary, his daughter. It is true that the word τοῦ is used throughout to denote the relation of father and son, not of grandson and grandfather; but Luke was obliged, this once, to use this word in another sense, *since through the miraculous birth, which he had himself described, one member in this line of male ancestors was missing*. The Ἀδὰμ τοῦ Θεοῦ, too, at the end, shows that τοῦ need not, in this passage, be invariably supposed to apply to physical descent. If Mary became the mother of our Lord through the power of the Holy Spirit, He could have no male ancestors but hers, and the name of Eli, His grandfather, must stand immediately before that of Jesus, in His genealogy, since the introduction of the mother's name was not customary, and that of the father impossible in this instance.

The difficulties raised against this view are easily met. Is it urged, 1. that the Jews did not keep genealogies of women?—the answer is, that this is the genealogy of Eli, the father of Mary, and grandfather of Jesus. 2. That Mary, being a cousin of Elisabeth, must have been a daughter of Aaron, and not of the tribe of Judah? But her mother might have been of the house of Aaron, and related to Elisabeth, while her father was descended from the royal line. 3. That, according to an ancient Jewish tradition, one Joachim was the father of Mary? But this tradition is quite unworthy of belief, and is also contradicted by another, which asserts that Mary, the daughter of Eli, suffered martyrdom in Gehenna (see Lightfoot *ad Luc.* iii. 23). 4. That while the genealogies of Luke and Matthew have nothing else in common, they both contain the names of Salathiel and Zerubbabel? We answer, that both Mary and Joseph seem to have descended from Zerubbabel, the son of Salathiel. The fact, that this latter is called by Luke the son of Neri, and by Matthew the son of Jeconiah, may be explained by supposing a Levirate marriage, the name of the natural father being given by Luke, and that of the father according to the law, by Matthew. Besides, why might not both lines meet at least once, during a period of so many centuries? Jeconiah was carried captive to Babylon at the age of eighteen, and remained there a prisoner thirty-seven years; Neri, his brother (Matt. i. 11), would then, in his place, "raise up seed unto his brother," and become the natural father of Salathiel, whose son Zerubbabel had several children, from one of whom (Abiud) descended Joseph, and from another (Rhesa), Eli, the father of Mary. (For the defence of this hypothesis, compare also the treatise of WIESELER, in the *Theol. Studien und Kritiken,* ii. 1845, and the article, *Genealogy of Jesus,* in the Bibl. Dictionaries.)

On comparing the genealogies in Matthew and Luke, we are immediately struck with the differences between them. The former is written in the descending, the latter in the ascending line: the former ex-

---

* [So Erasmus, Luther, Bez<small>a</small>, and the authorized Engl. Version. Comp. my *Critical Note* 1 on vs. 23; also Meyer *in loc.*—P. S.]

† [For a full discussion of the date of Christ's baptism, the reader is referred to A<small>NDREWS</small>: *The Life of our Lord,* etc., pp. 22-35.—P. S.]

tends to Abraham, the common ancestor of the Jewish nation; the latter to Adam, the common parent of mankind: the former is divided into three parts, each of fourteen generations, and thus exhibits a more artificial arrangement, while it wants the completeness which we discover in the latter. Both tables give fourteen names from Abraham to David; while from David to the Babylonian captivity, Matthew gives fourteen, and Luke twenty-one names. Symmetrical arrangement causes Matthew to omit certain names; while a desire for historical completeness is more strongly manifested in Luke, who, during his stay with Paul at Jerusalem (Acts xxi. 17), might easily have found opportunities of obtaining important particulars concerning Mary and her genealogy. The universal character of his genealogy is explained by the fact, that his Gospel was not written, as that of Matthew, for the Christians of Palestine. It presents no other difficulties, except the mention that Zerubbabel was the son of Rhesa, while 1 Chron. iii. 19–21 gives very different names. It has been, however, supposed, that the last-named statement is less accurate, and that the original text has been corrupted in this place.

The historical authority of this genealogy has been vainly contested, on the ground of a statement of Eusebius (*H. E.* i. 7), that the genealogies of the distinguished Jews were burnt in the time of Herod. This statement bears on its very surface marks of internal improbability; while the authority of J. Africanus, which is cited in its support, is highly problematical. Josephus, too, says nothing of this measure, and publishes his own genealogy, as it existed in the public registries. Besides, in this case, the "taxing" (Luke ii. 2) would have been impracticable; while the same informant (J. Africanus) states, that some few, among whom he expressly mentions the family of our Lord, prepared genealogical tables from copies, or from memory. The apocryphal Gospel of James also speaks of the existence of the genealogies, as a thing publicly known. See THILO, *Cod. Apocryph. N. T.* 1, p. 166.

DOCTRINAL AND ETHICAL.

1. The often contested descent of Mary from David is raised above all possibility of refutation by the genealogy of Luke. The Lord Jesus was therefore naturally, as well as legally, descended from David; and this descent is with perfect justice made prominent by both Peter and Paul (Acts ii. 30; xiii. 23; Rom. i. 3; 2 Tim. ii. 8); while Jesus designates Himself the Son of David, Mark xii. 35–37. This descent from David was important to the Jews of those days, as one of the legitimate proofs of His Messiahship, and is still of the highest significance. It is a fresh proof of the faithfulness of Him who performed the promises which He had sworn to David and His seed, and a specimen of His divine arrangement, which may well fill us with adoring admiration. As the Christ could only be born in Israel, the nation which alone worshipped the true God, so was it also necessary that He, in whom the ideal of the old theocracy was to be realized, should be a descendant of the man after God's own heart, under whose sceptre the theocratic nation had reached the climax of its prosperity. This royal origin of our Lord is the key to the psychological explanation of the royal and exalted character, continually impressed upon His words, deeds, and silence. It makes us understand also, with what perfect right He could, even in His glorified state, declare that He was not only the bright and morning star, but also the root and offspring of David. (Rev. xxii. 16; comp. ch. v. 5.)

2. The genealogy of Jesus stands here immediately after His baptism. As soon as Luke has related how He was acknowledged by His heavenly Father as His Son, he proceeds to narrate who He really was related to, according to the flesh.—Starke.

3. The genealogy of Luke offers complete proof that the Lord was "very man," the promised seed of David; and also, by human descent, the Son of God, as the first Adam is therein said to have been.

4. The second Adam, like the first, sprang immediately from a creative act of Omnipotence. The Messiah belongs not to Israel alone, but to the whole world of sinners. The prophetic word (Micah v. 2), that His "goings forth have been from of old, from everlasting," applies, in a certain sense, even to His human origin.

HOMILETICAL AND PRACTICAL.

The genealogical tree of Christ: 1. The root; 2. the branch; 3. the crown; 4. the fruit of His race. —The genealogy in connection with the work of redemption: It presents us: 1. with the image of humanity, which needs redemption; 2. with the greatness of Christ, who undertakes redemption; 3. with the glory of God, who ordains redemption.—The first and the second Adam: 1. Their natural relationship; 2. the infinite difference in their relations, (*a*) to God, (*b*) to man, (*c*) to each other.—The wonderful difference between the apparent and the actual in the person of the Redeemer. Luke gives us a glimpse of it in His descent; but it strikes us also when we consider the lowly outward appearance and exalted dignity: (*a*) Of His person; (*b*) of His work; (*c*) of His kingdom; (*d*) of His future.—The great importance of the Bible genealogies.—Christ the aim and end of the Bible genealogies.—God's faithfulness in the performance of His ancient promises.—Jesus, the son of Adam: 1. The Son of God became a son of Adam; 2. the Son of Adam truly the Son of God, the promised Redeemer.—Concealment of the true descent of Jesus, even at the beginning of His public ministry.—The miraculously begotten Son of Mary suffers Himself to be supposed to be the son of Joseph.—For further ideas, *see* LANGE on Matt. i. 17 [vol. i. pp. 50, 51]. Consult also KÖPPEN: *Die Bibel, ein Werk göttlicher Weisheit,* i. 26–40; ii. 199, etc., on the value of these, and the other genealogies.

ARNDT:—The significance of the genealogy of Jesus: 1. For His person; 2. for His work. "This remarkable genealogical tree stands forth, a unique memorial of the faith and expectation of the Old Testament saints. To our imaginations, its boughs and branches had been vocal for centuries with the words: 'Oh that Thou wouldest rend the heavens,' etc., while tears of thankfulness and ecstasy water its root, and these names, which brighten, like stars of heaven, the history of Israel, seem moistened with the dew-drops of joy and ardent desire. Oh, not one single word of Holy Scripture was written in vain!" etc.

C. *In the Wilderness.* Ch. IV. 1–13.

1 And Jesus being full of the Holy Ghost returned from [the] Jordan, and was led
2 by [in] the Spirit into the wilderness, Being forty days tempted of [by] the devil.
And in those days he did eat nothing: and when they were ended, he afterward[1] hun-
3 gered. And the devil said unto him, If thou be the Son of God, command this stone
4 that it be made bread. And Jesus answered him, saying, It is written, That man shall
5 not live by bread alone, but by every word of God[2] [Deut. viii. 3]. And the devil,
taking him up into a high mountain,[3] shewed unto him all the kingdoms of the world in
6 a moment [instant] of time. And the devil said unto him, All this power will I give
thee, and the glory of them [*i. e.*, of the kingdoms]: for that [it] is delivered unto me
[has been committed or entrusted to me *by God*]; and to whomsoever I will, I give it.
7 If thou therefore wilt worship [fall down before] me, all shall [it shall all] be thine.
8 And Jesus answered and said unto him, Get thee behind me, Satan:[4] for it is written,
9 Thou shalt worship the Lord thy God, and him only shalt thou serve. And he brought
him to [into] Jerusalem, and set him on a [the] pinnacle of the temple, and said unto
10 him, If thou be the Son of God, cast thyself down from hence: For it is written, He
11 shall give his angels charge over [concerning] thee, to keep thee [safe]: And in *their*
hands they shall bear thee up, lest at any time thou dash thy foot against a stone [Ps.
12 xci. 12]. And Jesus answering said unto him, It is said, Thou shalt not tempt the
13 Lord thy God. And when the devil had ended all the temptation, he departed from
him for a [until a *convenient*] season.

[1] Vs. 2.—The adverb is wanting in Codd. B., D., L., [Cod. Sin.], etc., and probably is to be expunged as by Lachmann, Tischendorf and Meyer, because apparently inserted from the parallel passage, Matt. iv. 2.
[2] Vs. 4.—Van Oosterzee omits the clause, ἀλλ' ἐπὶ παντὶ ῥήματι Θεοῦ, supported by Tischendorf, but against Lachmann and Meyer. Meyer remarks that "it is supported by almost all the old versions and fathers, and that, if it had been inserted from Matt. iv. 4, would as a *vox solennis* have doubtless been more precisely like that passage." Alford omits it, Tregelles brackets it. Cod. B. and Cod. Sin. both omit it.—C. C. S.]
[3] Vs. 5.—*Text. rec.*: εἰς ὄρος ὑψηλόν. The genuineness of this reading is at least doubtful [omitted by Codd. B., L., Cod. Sin.], and to be regarded as a paraphrastic emendation from Matt. iv. 8, and is therefore omitted by Tischendorf, [Tregelles], Alford, and defended by Meyer, with reason, as absolutely necessary in the text.—C. C. S.]
[4] Vs. 8.—*Text. rec.*: Ὕπαγε ὀπίσω μου, σατανᾶ. Apparently an interpolation from Matt. iv. 10. At least it is wanting in Codd. B., D., L., [Cod. Sin.], most versions, and in fathers of authority, and is moreover a serious (and, at the same time, critically suspicious) obstacle to the harmony of the evangelical narratives.

EXEGETICAL AND CRITICAL.

The narrative of the temptation has in Luke a peculiar character. While Mark contents himself with relating the event in a brief mention (ch. i. 12–13), Luke is almost as detailed as Matthew, but deviates in his order of arranging the different temptations from this his predecessor in narration. The third temptation, with Matthew, is with Luke the second, and the reverse. We give the preference to the arrangement of the first Evangelist. Matthew keeps the order of time more in mind (vss. 1, 5, 8) than Luke, who speaks quite indefinitely (vss. 1, 2). In the arrangement of the former, moreover, there is a more natural climax, and it is in itself improbable that the Lord, after He had repulsed the demand of the tempter that He should worship him, would have tolerated still a third attempt from this side or would have entered into any intercourse with him. On this account, Ambrosius and also other fathers of the church, even in commenting upon the narrative of Luke, have preferred the arrangement of Matthew. In another respect, also, the praise of greater exactness belongs to the first of the Evangelists. Matthew makes the temptation proper only begin after the fortieth day; Luke represents this whole space of time as a period of inward temptations, nevertheless it is evident that at least the temptation to turn stones into bread, represented as the first of all, could only begin at the end of the period of time, after long fasting. Perhaps the two narratives may be, without violence, reconciled in this way; that the forty days, also, were, in a more general sense, a time of inward temptations (Mark and Luke), while immediately thereafter (Matthew) the more concrete cases of temptation which are adduced in the first and third Gospels, present themselves.

Vs. 1. **In the Spirit**, ἐν τῷ πνεύμ.; in Matthew, ὑπὸ τοῦ πνεύμ.—There appears to be no doubt that this signifies the Holy Spirit, which had just been poured out in all its fulness upon the baptized Jesus. Full of the Holy Spirit, that now more than ever penetrated and inspired Him, He was driven with irresistible might not only toward (εἰς) the wilderness, but into (ἐν) the wilderness, where He abides awhile, not only with the unexpected *consequence*, but with the definite purpose (πειρασθῆναι, Matthew), that He there, according to God's supreme providence and under His especial permission, should be tempted of the devil.

Vs. 2. **Forty days tempted by the devil**.—If we read with Lachmann, ἐν τῇ ἐρήμῳ, which appears to deserve the preference, we may perhaps refer the designation of time, viz., forty days, to the immediately preceding words, ἤγετο εἰς τὴν ἔρημον, and translate: "He was led in the Spirit into the wilderness forty days, and tempted by the devil." In this way even the appearance of a discrepancy between Matthew and Luke, in regard to the actual point when the temptation began, is avoided.

Into the wilderness.—We are to understand the word "wilderness" not with some of the older expositors in a figurative, but in a literal, sense, and probably (agreeably to tradition) to refer it to the wilderness of Quarantania, between Jericho and Jerusalem. As to the locality, *see* the Gospel of Matthew by Lange, p. 81. There is still shown the mountain upon which the tempter is said to have taken the Lord, lying over against Abarim, from whose summit Moses overlooked the promised land. Trustworthy travellers relate, that in the neighborhood of this mountain there are found many stones whose form and whose color even agrees with that of bread, so that they could easily deceive the hasty observer. *See* Sepp, *Leben Jesu*, ii. p. 92.

By the devil.—We come here to the natural question, what we are to think as to the agent of the temptation and the manner in which the tempter approached the Lord. As to the former, the views may properly be divided into two classes. Some will acknowledge here no working of the devil whatever, and understand it either of one or of several human tempters, or, of tempting thoughts and conceptions, which are supposed to have arisen in the mind of Jesus Himself in view of His Messianic work. Others assume an actual temptation of the devil, whether in visible form as the Gospels relate, or through the working of the invisible evil spirit upon the pure ψυχή of the Lord, capable as it nevertheless was of temptation. The different advocates of these explanations may be found named in Hase, Meyer, and De Wette. It cannot be difficult for us to make a choice among these different explanations. That the narrative can scarcely be understood literally appears hardly to need an intimation. A corporal appearance of the devil, a temporary ἐνσάρκωσις of the evil principle, is without any analogy in the Holy Scriptures. How should the devil have had power over the body of the Lord to carry Him through air and clouds whither he would? If the Lord did not know him, what should we have to think of His all-surpassing knowledge? And if He did know him, how could He consent to hold discourse with such a tempter? Where lies the mountain from which all the kingdoms of the earth can be viewed with a glance, and how could the Lord during the forty days in which He abides in the silent wilderness all at once stand upon the pinnacle of the temple? But this impossibility of understanding the narrative κατὰ ῥητόν does not for all this give us a right to find here an historical or philosophical myth. If even the previous history exhibits a purely historical character, still less do we move in a nebulous, mythical sphere at the beginning of the public life of Jesus. Analogies which are presented with the history of the temptations of Job, David, and others, would at most only prove the possibility, but by no means the probability or certainty of the invention of a narrative of a temptation of the Messiah. We see plainly that the Evangelists are persuaded that they are relating an historical fact, and we have no right, upon philosophical grounds, to bring in doubt the possibility of the chief fact here related.— Quite as unsatisfactory is the interpretation of it as a dream, vision, or parable. If the Lord had wished to teach His apostles in a similitude from what fundamental principles He started in His Messianic activity, and to what temptations they also were exposed, He would certainly have availed Himself of another form of instruction. Moreover, it is hard to see how such a parable could with any ground have been understood as history. The difficulty does not lessen but increases, if we assume that the parable in this form does not come from Jesus Himself, but from one of His disciples, who invented it in order to warn the first believers against sensuous Messianic expectations; and if we understand it as a dream or a vision, the narrative then really loses all significance. What value has a conflict that has arisen from self-deceit, and does he deserve the name of a victor who strives against spectres of the night? If this vision was effected by the devil in the soul of Jesus (Olshausen), we do not then comprehend what significance is to be attributed to a temptation that was not combated with rational self-consciousness. Or if this dream was a product of the fantasy of Jesus Himself (Paulus), we could then no longer ascribe any perfect sinlessness to Him whose imagination could, *sponte sua*, defile itself with such odious conceptions.

As respects the opinion that we have here to understand a *human* tempter, this, in its older form, has been already too often combated for us to lose now even a word in disputing it. The only form in which it deserves consideration is that in which Lange (*Leben Jesu*, p. 218) brings it up. He is far from denying the diabolical ground of the temptation, but maintains that the medium of it was a visit of the Sanhedrim, who, after John—subsequently to their interview with him—had referred them (John i. 19-28) to Jesus, had, in Lange's view, approached Him with the full pomp and impetuousness of their Messianic expectations, and laid before Him a plan of Messianic activity wholly different from that which had originally come to maturity in His own mind. We cannot possibly read the brilliant exposition of this view in its details without recognizing the author's gift of intuition and combination. If we saw ourselves necessitated to look for historical foundation of this kind for our present narrative, we should undoubtedly seek in vain to project a better. But, on the other hand, it must not be overlooked that the Evangelists themselves do not make the least mention of so early a meeting of the Lord with the Sanhedrim; that there is as little proof of John's having designated the Messiah to the Sanhedrim as there is probability of any such interview with the yet unknown Nazarene; that, finally, the offence speedily taken by the Sanhedrim against the Lord after His public appearance admits of a sufficient explanation even without assuming so secret a back-ground. All these reasons now give weight to the question whether we should not do better (Ullmann) to understand here tempting thoughts, which had come up in the soul of the Lord from the worldly form of the Messianic expectations among the Jews, which, however, He at once, through the might of His holy will, repelled from Him, and which, when He afterward communicated these inner experiences of His to His disciples, He ascribed, in oriental style, to the devil, the prince of this world. However, on considering the matter more closely, this interpretation also offers difficulties, so that Strauss for once did not say untruly that the Lord in this case would have communicated to His disciples "a confused mixture of truth and fiction." Why He should have related to His friends this history of His inward conflict in such a form, can scarcely be understood. As to the first and second temptations at least, we do not see how they could proceed from the worldly-minded expectation of the contemporaries of the Lord. This, at all events, would have sprung more from the consciousness of His own miraculous power and the certainty of the protection of God than from the corrupt notions of the spirit of the times. "If Jesus had

had even in the most fleeting manner such thoughts, He would not have been Christ, and this explanation appears to me as the most wretched neoteric outrage that has been committed against His person" (Schleiermacher). If these tempting thoughts were purely theoretical and objective, occasioned by conceptions having nothing attractive for the Lord, where is the temptation? and if these evil thoughts proceeded actually from the heart of the Son of Man (Matt. xv. 19), where is His sinlessness? We, for our part, believe that we can only explain the origin of the temptation by assuming the *direct operation of the (invisible) evil spirit upon the mind and the sensibility of the Redeemer*. In this case, 1. the credibility of the narrative is recognized, and we are as little necessitated to understand the devil at the beginning as the angels at the end of the narrative, in a merely figurative sense; 2. the sinlessness of the Lord is preserved: the tempting thoughts originate not from within, but are brought upon Him from without; 3. and, finally, the abandonment of a spiritless literal interpretation is vindicated. But if the Evil One worked directly, although invisibly, upon the God-man, the temptation must have taken place ἐν πνεύματι, alone, and we are justified in representing to ourselves the Lord upon the pinnacle of the temple without His having left the wilderness. There is no other conception which, like this, holds fast to what is essential in the purely historical interpretation without falling into the absurdities that necessarily spring from the assumption of a bodily appearance of the devil.

We feel conscious that this opinion can find no favor in the eyes of those who despise the doctrine of a personality of the Evil One as a superstition of the middle ages. But we cannot join with them, since we are thoroughly persuaded that very many scruples against the biblical demonology proceed from exaggeration or misunderstanding. That Jesus and the apostles did speak of a personal evil spirit and of his operations, is subject to no doubt, and that in this they accommodated themselves to a superstitious popular fancy, is wholly without proof. If any one, philosophically reasoning, persists in seeing in their expressions only the personification of an abstract idea, let him look to it how he can answer for it; but let him not at all events impose this conception on Jesus and the apostles. *Never is Rationalism weaker than when it seeks to vindicate itself exegetically.* That the old demonology did not receive its fuller development among the Jews until after the Babylonian captivity, we must no doubt concede; but so far is it from being of Chaldean and Persian origin, that, on the other hand, it distinguishes itself in essence and character from this and every dualistic theory, intended to explain the riddle of sin. That even in higher regions of the spiritual world freedom has been misused to sin, is as far from being unreasonable as is the conception that the fallen angels unite with a high degree of intellectual development a deep moral degeneracy. Both facts are daily to be seen among men, and whoever is willing to believe in personal good angels, but not in a personal Satan, is thoroughly inconsistent. The possibility of a direct working of the Evil One upon the spirit of the Lord, admits of being opposed neither with psychological nor with scriptural arguments. Its intention could be no other than to bring Him to a fall, and thus to frustrate the work of Redemption, and its permission by the Father can seem strange to no one who understands what this means: "Though He were a Son, yet learned He obedience by the things which He suffered!"

And He did eat nothing in those days.—A comparison with Matt. xi. 18 shows, that it is not indispensably necessary to understand such an expression of an entire abstinence from all food. "He might have been able, as well as John, to partake of locusts and wild honey without essentially annulling the fast." (Lange.) On the other hand, however, nothing hinders us from understanding this fasting of the Lord in its strictest sense. If there are examples of an uncommonly long fasting, even in men whose physical and psychical development has been disturbed by sin, how much more conceivable is it with Him whose bodily organism had been weakened by no sin, whose soul, more than that of any one, could control the flesh and constrain it to obedience. Immediately after such a fast, hunger must necessarily have made itself felt with unexampled power; and undoubtedly by the abstinence from bodily nourishment, the susceptibility of the soul to the influence of the Prince of Darkness, and the combat with him, was not a little heightened. According to Matthew and Luke, the hunger makes itself felt not in the course of the forty days, but only at the end of them.

Vs. 3. **If Thou be the Son of God command.**—The voice of the evil spirit evidently links itself with the remembrances of the heavenly voice at the Jordan. Here also, is the devil a *Simia Dei*, since he permits an echo of the word of truth to be heard. —**This stone**, τῷ λίθῳ τούτῳ, more δεικτικῶς, than in Matthew, who retains his ordinary plural, οἱ λίθοι οὗτοι, in an *oratio indirecta*. The point of attachment for the temptation is partly the exalted self-consciousness, partly the painful necessity of the Lord; the purpose of the temptation, to have Him use His miraculous power for the satisfaction of His own necessity.

Vs. 4. **That man shall not live by bread alone.**—In Matthew the citation, Deut. viii. 3, is quoted more fully, and moreover from the LXX. We need not deny that the Lord uses the declaration in a somewhat different sense from that in which Moses means it; nor is there any reason for referring the appellation "Man" exclusively or principally to the Messiah. In a divinely free manner He uses the word of Scripture to indicate that man, even without the use of bread, may behold his life lengthened and sustained by any means whatever of which God may avail Himself to strengthen his bodily energies. In other words: God does not need His miraculous power in order to allay painful hunger. For that He possesses innumerable means, and the Son will await the way which the Father may please to use.

Vs. 5. **Taking Him up into a high mountain.** —As already remarked, Luke assigns to the third and severest temptation the middle place. "*Matthæus eo temporis ordine describit assultus, quo facti sunt, Lucas gradationem observat in locis, et describit desertum, montem, templum. Quæ ordinis non modo innoxia sed etiam salubris varietas, argumento est, non alterum Evangelistam ab altero scripsisse.*" (Bengel). The difficulty, however, which the narrative of Luke v. 8 offers, according to the *Recepta*, namely, that the Lord, after He had recognized and unmasked the Evil One, can yet admit for the third time discourse with him; this difficulty vanishes if we assume, with Tischendorf and others, that the words, "Get thee behind me, Satan," are here spurious, and have been transferred from the parallel passage in Matthew.

Showed unto Him.—Of course, ἐν πνεύματι, not one after the other, but all together, ἐν ῥιπῇ ὀφθαλμοῦ, 1 Cor. xv. 52.

All the kingdoms of the world.—Not the Jewish land, but the heathen world surrounding it and extending beyond the sight, which is several times spoken of in the New Testament as subject to the prince of this world, while Jehovah is the head of the theocratic state. Besides this, it deserves consideration that the address of Satan to the Lord on this occasion is communicated by Luke somewhat more at length than by Matthew.

For it has been committed to me, etc.—A paraphrase of the preceding words for the benefit and edification of Theophilus and other readers, who were unacquainted or little acquainted with the demonology of the Jews.

Vs. 7. **If Thou, therefore, wilt fall down before me.**—We need not here understand an actually idolatrous adoration. It is sufficient if we understand it of an Oriental homage which is often rendered to mighty monarchs, Matt. ii. 2. As the first temptation is addressed to sensual *appetite*, this is addressed to the craving for the possession of kingly dignity, upon which the Messiah is conscious of being assuredly able to reckon. The temptation lies in the alternative; dominion without conflict on the one hand, bloody strife on the other, against the might of darkness, if its alluring voice should be repelled. The lie which is at the bottom of the arrogant promise of the tempter ("to me is it committed," etc.), is truly Satanic; but it is this very arrogance of demand which enables the Lord (Matt.) to know with whom He is striving in this moment, and He has at once the "ὕπαγε ὀπίσω μου" ready against Satan, in that He yet again hurls upon him a decisive word of the Scripture.

Vs. 8. **Thou shalt worship the Lord thy God,** Deut. vi. 13.—According to the LXX., with a variation of προσκυνήσεις instead of φοβηθήσῃ, on account of the preceding words of Satan. The Lord does not only publicly express the monotheistic principle, but shows at the same time that He will rather dispense with all the kingdoms of the world, however by right they belong to Him, than obtain them in an unlawful way. His answer is a declaration of war; His rejection of the homage He paid for with His life; and so repulsed, Satan could not return the third time. Before it came to this pass, however, that he retreated, still another temptation took place previously; according to Matthew's accurate account, the second, which, however, Luke relates as the third.

Vs. 9. **And he brought Him to Jerusalem.**—Although in itself it is very probable that the Lord, during this period, spent a single day, κατὰ σάρκα, at Jerusalem (Lange), it nevertheless appears more probable to us that He did not in body leave the wilderness at all before the combat was quite ended. Before the inner consciousness of the Lord, *it was*, without doubt, *as if* He stood upon the πτερύγιον, and as respects the ability of the Evil One to transport Him in spirit to a place so entirely different, we may well call to mind the expression of Gregory: "*Nil mirum est, si Christus a Diabolo se permisit circumduci, qui a membris illius se permisit crucifigi.*"

On the pinnacle of the temple, not ναοῦ, but ἱεροῦ.—The access to the κορυφή was apparently permitted to no one but the priests and Levites alone, but nothing hinders us from understanding one of the accessory buildings, whose pinnacle constituted a sort of cornice (ἀκρωτήριον), and of which Josephus also relates that from it one could throw a look that made him dizzy, into an incalculable depth (*Ant. Jud.* xv. 15, 11). It is true, if any one cast himself down there he would not descend before the eyes of the citizens of the city, but in the obscure vale of Kedron. But the promise, moreover, is precisely this, that in falling He should not reach the bottom, but in His fall should be held up by the angels, and doubtless be brought into the midst of the astonished inhabitants of the city and frequenters of the temple, who a moment before had seen him, with shuddering terror, upon the eminence.

Vs. 10. **For it is written, He shall give.**—"The devil can quote Scripture for his purpose." And this time he combats the Lord with His own weapons. The passage, Ps. xci. 11, 12, is not Messianic (Usteri), but speaks of the saints in general, and the devil leaves the Lord to draw a conclusion *a minori ad majus* from the safety of the saints to that of the Messiah, the chief favorite of God. By a literal interpretation of the figurative utterance he tempts the Lord to work a *miracle of display*, not upon the heart and conscience but upon the imagination of the people, and thus in a few moments to bring about an extraordinary success. This time he works not upon the desire of enjoyment or possession, but of honor and elevation. Now it will undoubtedly have to be shown, whether the Lord really believes the word of the Scripture with which He has already repeatedly defended Himself. He is tempted on the side of that same believing confidence which has just held Him back from turning stones into bread, and the greatness of His triumph consists in this, that He at once discovers the just limit that separates confidence and presumption.

Vs. 12. **And Jesus answering.**—The Lord answers a third time with a word of Scripture, out of Deut. (vi. 16), still more striking in Matt., πάλιν γέγραπται, ruxus. The word of the law which He mentions contains no contradiction of the devil's quotation from the Psalm, but a rectification of the misuse which the Evil One had made of it. Apart from the special signification of the utterance for the Israelitish people (on occasion of the strife at Marah, Ex. xvii. 2) the Lord gives him to feel that whoever throws himself uncalled into danger in the hope that God will deliver him, displays no heroic courage of faith, but commits an act of presumptuous folly.

Vs. 13. **And when the devil had ended all the temptation.**—The coming and ministration of the angels is to be supplied from Matthew and Mark. See, as to this, LANGE, *Matthew*, p. 86. Without doubt, it is in the spirit of the narration if we conceive to ourselves these as invisible witnesses of the combat and triumph of Jesus. (Comp. 1 Cor. iv. 9.) While they, soon after the departing of Satan from Him, serve Him whether spiritually or bodily. (Comp. 1 Kings xix. 5.)

Until a season.—It is a very significant intimation for the apprehension of the whole history of the temptation which Luke gives us in these concluding words. Unwittingly he gives us occasion in these forty days to see not only the beginning but also the type of the different temptations which were perpetually returning for the God-man. Without doubt he has regard, moreover, particularly to the time when Satan entered into Judas (Luke xxii. 3) and the whole power of darkness rose against the Suffering One. Yet he may also have thought on the activity of the Evil One in opposing the Lord previously to this. Comp. ch. x. 18; xiii. 16; xxii. 31.

DOCTRINAL AND ETHICAL.

1. The history of the temptation in the wilderness constitutes partly the end of the history of the hidden, partly the beginning of the history of the public life of Jesus. The silence of John respecting this event, proves nothing against the truth of the narrative of the Synoptics. Had none of those uttered a word of a *tentatio a Diabolo*, the believer himself, who sees in Christ the God-man, and assumes the reality of a kingdom of darkness over against the kingdom of Heaven, would of himself have come to the supposition that a life and working such as that of the Lord could not possibly have begun without such a preceding inward conflict. Of what kind this conflict was is now communicated to us by his witnesses in a way which leaves us no other choice, than here either to understand it as one of the σεσοφισμένοι μῦθοι, whose origin, on historical Christian ground, an apostle of the Lord denies (2 Pet. i. 16), or to believe that Jesus Himself instructed His disciples in reference to this remarkable event of His inner life. For us the latter admits of no controversy, and thus is the inquiry as to the source of the historical narrative answered in a satisfactory manner. But at the same time it is self-evident that the Lord could not communicate to His friends in reference to what took place in the wilderness more than they were in a condition to bear. John xvi. 12. Without doubt, therefore, He clothed His narrative in a form which was calculated for their receptivity and their necessity, and there remains to us the privilege of distinguishing carefully between the fact itself and the peculiar way in which it was represented by Him and has been described by them. Here, also, does the utterance, John vi. 63, hold good.

2. The fact now, which can be derived with sufficient certainty from the different narrations, is apparently this: 1. At the beginning of His course, the Saviour was exposed to temptations to act in direct opposition to the high principles to which He showed Himself faithful through life. 2. These temptations were directly occasioned by the Prince of this world, who wished to bring the second Adam, like the first, to apostasy, in order thus to destroy the work of redemption. 3. The Lord, with clear consciousness and steadfastness, combatted these temptations with the sword of the Spirit (Eph. vi. 17), and left the field of conflict without a single wound. 4. The Victor, as a sign of the Father's approbation, was served by the angels of heaven and received their homage. —Every explanation of the history of the temptation which acknowledges what is essential in these great elements of it, deserves from the Christian point of view to be admitted and weighed. In respect to the external side of the fact (the condition of the Lord, the manner of the temptation, the locality, etc.), it will, perhaps, never be possible to find an explanation which satisfactorily resolves all difficulties. Yet this is of less consequence if only the inner significance of the above named facts remains acknowledged, and these, themselves, are not assailed.

3. The history of the temptation throws the brightest light upon the person of the Lord. On the one hand, we learn to know Him here from His own word (vs. 4) as a man like His brethren in all things (Heb. ii. 17); on the other hand, Satan himself proclaims Him as God's Son (vs. 3), and this time, at least, has the father of lies become a witness of the truth. The true humanity of the Lord reveals itself not less in the hunger which He feels than in His capacity of being tempted. His divine majesty shows itself in the manner in which He combats, in the victory which He achieves, in the crown which He wins.

4. Dogmatics has in the treatment of the history of the temptation, the difficult problem, on the one hand, to regard the Lord as truly tempted, so that the temptations do not glide from Him as something merely external, as water from a rock, without making any impression upon His sensibility; on the other hand, to vindicate the word of the apostolic writer, χωρὶς ἁμαρτίας (Heb. iv. 15). That both the one and the other, are impossible, if an absolute *non potuit peccare* is asserted of the Lord, is self-evident. The ἀναμαρτησία of the Lord by no means excluded the possibility of sinning; but on the other hand consisted in this, that He, filled with boundless abhorrence of sin, combatted and overcame it under whatever form it might show itself. Only the Father is ἀπείραστος κακῶν (James i. 13), but the Logos, once entered within the bounds of finite humanity, comes through his ὁμοίωμα σαρκὸς ἁμαρτίας (Rom. viii. 13) into personal contact with sin. Like every true man, the Lord had a sensuous perception of the pleasant and the unpleasant. For this feeling natural enjoyment must have been preferable to want, honor to shame, riches to poverty, life to death. Upon this feeling the might of temptation works, and whoever in this of itself could already find something sinful, would have to prefer an accusation against God, who originally so constituted our human nature. He would, moreover, be obliged to consider the first man as a sinner born, for in the very commandment of probation and in the added threatening (Gen. ii. 16, 17) the existence of this feeling is presupposed. Every representation by which there is ascribed to the Lord even a *minimum* of the *peccatum originale* (Irving) is condemned by the Christian consciousness in the most decided manner.

5. On the other hand, the *potuit non peccare*, can and must, be vindicated here as vigorously as the *realiter non peccavit*. He did not awaken the conception of what was evil, of Himself within Himself, but it came from without to Him through the operation of another spirit upon His own. This would have amounted to an inward sin only in the case that the Lord's will had inclined a moment to practise that which He had learned to know as morally evil. That the three thoughts: to work a miracle for Himself; to work upon the people through outward display; and to attain earthly dominion—considered altogether for itself and as yet without reference to God's will—had something attractive for His delicate and pure moral sense, is so little to be denied that the opposite, in a true man, would scarcely be conceivable. It lay in the very nature of the case that such conceptions at this moment must produce upon the spirit and sensibility of the Lord a double impression. Why should He otherwise have at once reached out for a weapon with which to combat the enemy? But here we could speak of sin, only in case that the desire for evil had really been awakened, that the wish to be able to give an ear to the Evil One had come up in His sensibility. But of this we

perceive no trace. The temptation comes before His eyes in its most alluring colors; He has a living sense of all that it possesses which is attractive; He reflects that He might be able to succumb, yet instantaneously He repels it from Him as something foreign and unhallowed. It places itself before His imagination, but finds no point of attachment in His will; it works upon the ψυχή, yet before this can be stained the tempter is already conquered through the πνεῦμα.

Two examples for a more particular elucidation. There was as yet no sin when Eve saw that the forbidden tree had its attraction, nor yet when the permission to eat of this tree appeared to her desirable, so long, that is, as she was considering this act without any relation to the prohibition that had been received; only when in unconscious and conscious conflict with the commandment the actual desire rose in her mind, and she was filled with dissatisfaction at the commandment, did sin then creep into her heart, even before she had stretched out her hand after the apple.—It was as yet no sin that the Lord in Gethsemane exhibited a natural dread of death, a natural longing for life; no sin as yet that He in the immediate presence of death, and in the consciousness of being able to escape it, had a double sense of the worth of life, nor was it even as yet any sin that He prayed and wished that the cup might pass from Him: only if He had allowed this wish to prevail contrary to the will of God, after He had clearly perceived this will; if the resolution to submit Himself to God's recognized will had been preceded by reluctance and conflict; if, in a word, not His deed but His will even had then moved in another direction from God's will, then would the Man of Sorrows have been also a child of sin.

6. The temptations here vanquished perpetually returned in the public life of the Lord. The first, e. g., Matt. xxvii. 40; the second, John vii. 3, 4; the third, John vi. 14. It cannot surprise us that the Lord, therefore, saw in the entreaty of Peter, Matt. xvi. 22, a Satanic back-ground. To whichever of these temptations He had given a hearing, still either His perfect obedience or His perfect love of man would have been stained, and herewith His perfect capability of being a Redeemer of sinners would have been annihilated.

7. The history of the temptation throws light upon the work of the Lord. We learn here to recognize this as a work that was given Him by the Father Himself to do, which He entered upon with clear self-consciousness, which was preceded by severe conflict, and which was directed entirely to destroying the works of the devil. 1 John iii. 9. In His perfect obedience, the second Adam, He here stands over against the first as the Restorer of the Paradise which Adam lost by his sin. "Adam fell in Paradise and made it a wilderness; Christ conquered in a wilderness and made it a paradise, where the beasts lost their savageness and the angels abode." (Olshausen.)

8. The threefold temptation of Jesus is the symbol and type of the temptations against which every Christian has to strive. 1 John ii. 16. First temptation = the lust of the flesh; the second = the lust of the eye; the third = pride, of which John says: "It is not of the Father, but of the world."

9. The temptation of Jesus as it repeats itself, as well in His own life as in the lives of His people, was, on the other hand, in a certain sense adumbrated in the temptations and trials of the most eminent men of God under the ancient covenant. (Joseph, Job, David, and others.) It lies in the nature of the case, from that in proportion as one is placed on a higher eminence in the kingdom of God, he is also exposed to severer temptations. It is remarkable that almost at the same time with this temptation of the Lord a similar temptation encountered His Forerunner. See LANGE, Leben Jesu, p. 451 ff.

10. The origin of all these temptations, and very especially of the temptation of Jesus, was the working of the devil. The history of His temptation may be called a striking revelation of the existence, the might, the laws, and the working of the kingdom of darkness. The existence of this kingdom of the personal Evil One, is not revealed by the Holy God. It reveals itself in facts like these. It is here shown that there is an Evil Spirit, an enemy of God, and of His kingdom. He knows Christ and hates Him. He uses the Scripture and perverts it; to lead astray is his joy, and lying is his power; God's word the only weapon that vanquishes him. It is noticeable how the most exalted moments of development for the kingdom of God have been at all times accompanied by an intenser reaction of the kingdom of darkness. Where the history of mankind begins, there the father of lies shows himself. When Israel is about to become a theocratic people, he imitates the miracles of Moses through the Egyptian sorcerers; when the Son of God appears in the flesh, He increases the number of the δαιμονιζόμενοι, and seeks to bring Him Himself to apostasy; and when the last development of the kingdom of God approaches, there does he rage most vehemently because his time is short. Rev. xx. 7.

11. With the best right, at all times, has the Saviour's "It is written" been considered as one of the strongest proofs for the divine authority of the Holy Scripture. The Christian who regards the whole Bible with the eye with which the Lord viewed the Old Testament, cannot possibly restrict the rule which He gave on another occasion, ὅτι οὐ δύναται λυθῆναι ἡ γραφή. John x. 35. It is remarkable, moreover, of what high importance even *those* parts of Scripture can be, which to us, superficially considered, appear less important for Christian life and faith. All three citations of the Lord are taken from one book (Deuteronomy), and yet the word of God, out of this one book, is for Him enough to put the Devil and his power to flight. 1 Cor. xii. 22, 23, holds good, also, of the organic whole of the Scripture.

12. In the inquiry respecting the historical reality of the angelophanies in the life of the Lord, we must above all not overlook their infrequency, which affords the strongest argument against an invention. From the settlement of the child in Nazareth we have met no angels on His way, and after this appearance we shall not see them in visible form again before the night of Gethsemane falls. Would a writer of myths have been able to content himself with so little? But if now, after the decisive ὕπαγε ὀπίσω μου had been addressed to Satan, no angels had appeared, we should almost have had occasion to doubt the reality of their existence. Comp. LANGE, *Gospel of Matthew*, p. 86: *Jésus tenté au désert, trois méditations par Ad. Monod*, Paris, 1854.

13. An eminent work of art, setting forth the history of the temptation in a genuine Protestant spirit, has proceeded from Ary Scheffer.

HOMILETICAL AND PRACTICAL.

The history of the temptation offers for homiletical treatment peculiar difficulties, which are easier to feel than to avoid. It is certainly easier to point out how it must not, than how it must be, handled suitably for the edification of the church. On the whole, a sharp separation of the exegetico-critical and the practico-ascetical element is to be commended, and the counsel of the apostle, 2 Tim. ii. 23, must not be lost out of mind. Superficial criticism of opposing opinions is in the pulpit as superfluous as an extended defence of personal views. Where there is strife the Devil comes into the midst of the children of God. Job i. 6. It will be best to leave the disputable points in a sacred obscurity and to keep to that which is clear and evident. To those who, in reference to the New Testament demonology, stand on a sceptical or negative position, the treatment of this material is least of all to be commended. They have, if they cannot withhold themselves from it, at least to take heed that they advance no principles by which the expression of the Christian self-consciousness in reference to the absolute sinlessness and purity of the Lord shall be in the least wounded. On the whole, if one is disposed to treat the entire narrative altogether, it will perhaps be best to consider it either as an image of the conflict which the Lord had to sustain His life long, or as a type of the spiritual conflict to which every believer in His name is called. That, nevertheless, both in the whole narrative, as well as in its particular parts, there lies a rich treasure of thoughts homiletically serviceable, may be seen from the following hints.

From the Jordan of glorification to the wilderness of temptation. This is the way of God; as with Christ, so with the Christian; and, moreover: 1. An old, and yet an ever new; 2. a hard, and yet a good; 3. a dark, and yet a light; 4. a lonesome, and yet a blessed way.—The temptations which follow a Christian, even into solitude.—Christian fasting in its opposition: 1. To Judaizing fasting, which sees in abstinence from food something in itself meritorious; 2. to heathenish wantonness, which says: "Let us eat and drink, for," etc.; again, 3. to the ultramontane: "Touch not, taste not, handle not;" 4. to the ultra-Protestant: πάντα ἔξεστιν, but without the limiting οὐ πάντα συμφέρει.—Doubt of the truth of God's word the first way to sin; so, 1. In Paradise, Gen. iii. 2; so here, vs. 3; 3. so always.—The temptation to misuse, ever united with the possession of peculiar power.—The unpermitted ways of providing one's bread.—"It is written" (γέγραπται), the sword of the Spirit: 1. How beautifully it glitters; 2. how deeply it wounds; 3. how decisively it triumphs.—Man lives not by bread alone; he cannot, he may not, he need not.—God can in all manner of ways remove the need of His own.—The dangerous mountain heights in the spiritual life.—The Evil One, the prince of this world: 1. Extent; 2. limits of his might.—Never does Satan lie more outrageously than when he promises.—The worship of the Devil in its more refined forms: 1. How old it is; 2. how richly it appears to reward; 3. how miserably it ends.—To worship the Lord and serve Him alone: 1. A difficult; 2. a holy; 3. a blessed requirement.—Even the sanctuary is no asylum against severe and renewed temptation.—The Lord of the temple upon the pinnacle of the temple and—upon the brink of the abyss.—The highest standpoints border on the deepest abysses.—The Devil also a Doctor of Divinity.—The misuse of Holy Scripture: 1. In many ways the letter used as a weapon to combat the spirit; a poetical word as a weapon to contest the requirement of the law; an Old Testament declaration as a weapon to combat a declaration of the New Testament; 2. dangerous, because the word of Scripture, in and of itself, is holy, finds an echo in the spirit, and is used with so much craft; to be vanquished only by a right, that is, an intelligent, persevering searching of the Scriptures, prompted by the longing for salvation.—No angels' help to be expected for him that would tempt God.—The ministration of angels to the saints: 1. How far to be expected; 2. how far not.—What is it to tempt God? Why is this sin so great? How is this sin best avoided?—When the Scripture is used believingly, wisely, and perseveringly, there must the Devil at last give way.—When the Devil gives way, it is still always "for a season;" every time he comes back in order: 1. To mislead; but also, 2. to be combatted; and, 3. to be conquered anew.—The angels come to serve Him who has refused their help when it would tempt God.—The noblest triumphs over the kingdom of darkness are celebrated in secret.—Heaven is a sympathizing witness of the conflict carried on on earth.—God permits no one to be tempted above his power of resistance, but gives with the temptation the way of escape. 1 Cor. x. 13.

STARKE:—Whoever gives himself to be guided by God's spirit, like Christ, comes, it is true, into temptation; but yet he also comes out again.—Satan seeks in particular to make God's children doubtful of their being his children.—The weapons of Christ and His Christians are not carnal, but yet mighty before God.—The glory and joy of the world is brief and momentary.—When the Devil is not ashamed to lie to Christ's face, of what, then, is he to be ashamed?—OSIANDER:—Whoever, to obtain honor and happiness, professes a strange religion, worships the Devil.—*Nova Bibl. Wirt.*:—The Devil is a lofty-seeming spirit; let us, in the might of God, destroy all high things, and in the low valleys of humility be quiet and still.—The Devil can, it is true, strongly draw saints toward sin, but not constrain them by force; *persuadere potest, precipitare non potest.*—JEROME:—The Scripture is the only rule and standard of our faith and life; to that let us cleave. Ps. cxix. 105.—As Satan continually comes back, so does God come ever back to help us.

STIER:—How the threefold tempter of the wilderness repeats himself with added strength in the passion.—RAUTENBERG:—Christ is tempted even as we, yet without sin. This word is: 1. A light for our blindness; 2. a spur for our slackness; 3. a staff for our weakness.—BACHMANN:—The temptation of Jesus was a temptation: 1. To doubt of God; 2. to presuming upon God; 3. to apostasy from God's word.—OETTINGER:—In the kingdom of God there is: 1. No spiritual consecration without spiritual trials; 2. no spiritual trials without spiritual weapons; 3. no spiritual weapons without spiritual victory.—ARNDT:—The temptation of the Lord: 1. Its character; 2. its importance so far as it is set forth, (*a*) representatively, (*b*) figuratively, for us.—FUCHS:—The means to a victory over the temptations of the Devil: 1. Watch continually, in every place; 2. watch and pray evermore; 3. use diligently God's word.—VAN OOSTERZEE:—The temptation in the wilderness the image of the conflict of the Christian life: 1. The temptation; 2. the enemy; 3. the attack; 4. the weapon; 5. the victory; 6. the crown. Finally, the question: If you fight against Christ, how can you still have courage, if you fight under Christ, how can you still be anxious?—The three temptations of the Lord: that in the morning, the noon, the evening of life. Sensuality especially the sin of the youth, ambition especially that of the man, avarice especially that of the old man. Whoever has overcome the first of these three temptations must count upon the second, whoever sees the second behind him will soon be covertly approached by the third. But in these all, we are more than conquerors through Him that loved us. Over against forty days' temptation in the first stand the forty days' peace and joy in the second life of the Lord.

SECOND SECTION.

THE JOURNEYINGS (Chap. IV. 14—IX. 50).

A. *Nazareth.*—*The First Rejection of the Holy Son of Man by the Sinful Children of Men.* Ch. IV. 14–30.

14 And Jesus returned in the power of the Spirit into Galilee: and there went out a
15 fame of him through all the region round about. And he taught in their synagogues,
16 being glorified [receiving honor] of all. And he came to Nazareth, where he had been brought up: and, as his custom was,[1] he went into the synagogue on the Sab-
17 bath day and stood up for to read [stood up to read]. And there was delivered unto him the book of the prophet Esaias. And when he had opened [unrolled] the book,
18 he found the place where it was written, The Spirit of the Lord *is* upon me, because he hath anointed me to preach the gospel [or to bring good tidings] to the poor; he hath sent me to heal the broken-hearted,[2] to preach deliverance to the captives, and
19 recovering of sight to the blind, to set at liberty them that are bruised, To preach the
20 acceptable year of the Lord. And he closed the book, and he gave it again to the minister [attendant] and sat down. And the eyes of all them that were in the syna-
21 gogue were fastened upon him. And he began to say unto them, This day is this
22 Scripture fulfilled in your ears. And all bare him [honorable] witness, and wondered at the gracious words [words of grace[3]] which proceeded out of his mouth. And they
23 said, Is not this Joseph's son? And he said unto them, Ye will surely say unto me this proverb, Physician, heal thyself: whatsoever we have heard done in Capernaum,
24 do also here in thy country [native place]. And he said, Verily I say unto you, No
25 prophet is accepted in his own country. But I tell you of a truth, many widows were [there were many widows] in Israel in the days of Elias [Elijah], when the heaven was shut up three years and six months, when [a] great famine was throughout [came
26 upon] all the land; But unto none [no one] of them was Elias [Elijah] sent, save unto
27 Sarepta [Zarephath], *a city* of Sidon, unto a woman *that was* a widow. And many lepers were [there were many lepers] in Israel in the time of Eliseus [Elisha] the prophet; and none [no one] of them was cleansed, saving [save] Naaman the Syrian.
28 And all they in the synagogue, when they heard these things, were filled with wrath,
29 And rose up, and thrust him out of the city, and led him unto the brow [or, a cliff]
30 of the hill whereon their city was built, that they might cast him down headlong. But he, passing through the midst of them, went his way.

[1 Vs. 16.—From the position of this clause it might appear as if His custom had been not only to visit the synagogue on the Sabbath, but also to read in the public service, but the position of κατὰ τὸ εἰωθὸς in the Greek, makes it best to confine the reference to His habitual attendance in the synagogue.—C. C. S.]

[2 Vs. 18.—The *Rec.* inserts ἰάσασθαι τοὺς συντετριμμένους τὴν καρδίαν, which, however, appears to be an interpolation from the LXX., Is. lxi. 1, rightly put in brackets by Lachmann, and rejected by De Wette and Meyer. [Wanting in B., D., L., and Sin.—C. C. S.]

[3 Vs. 22.—Χάριτος does not refer to the ethical character of His words, but to their persuasive beauty. *Anmuth*, not *Gnade*.—C. C. S.]

EXEGETICAL AND CRITICAL.

Vs. 14. **And Jesus returned in the power of the Spirit into Galilee.**—With these words Luke begins to portray the public activity of the Lord in Galilee. Respecting this activity in general, *see* LANGE's *Matthew*, p. 91. That Luke speaks of a return of the Lord to Galilee, while Mark only speaks in general of a *coming* (i. 14), is easily explicable from the fact that he had already spoken of a longer abode of Jesus in Galilee (chap. ii. 39–52). And in saying that this took place in *the power of the Spirit*, he indicates not obscurely that the Spirit which was poured out at His baptism upon the Saviour, far from being suppressed or departing from Him in consequence of the temptation in the wilderness, on the other hand, exhibited itself for the first time in full power in Him after the triumph there achieved. As Bengel also has it: *Post victoriam corroboratus*.

A fame.—Not a "fame of the return of the man that had been so marked out at His baptism and then hidden more than forty days" (Meyer); for it is quite as destitute of proof that the testimony given to the Lord at His baptism took place *coram populo congregato* as that John should have spoken of the miracle at the baptism to any one. Vs. 14 plainly anticipates vs. 15, in which latter the actual cause of this fame is first stated. The doctrine which He preaches draws astonished attention, and finds at the beginning acceptance. This account of Luke deserves attention the more, from the fact that hitherto he has mentioned no miracles as the cause of the φήμη. The word of the Saviour in and of itself, independently even of the way in which He afterwards confirmed it, appears at once to have come home to many.

Vs. 15. **And He taught.**—Luke in this expression gives only a general account of the earliest activity of the Lord in Galilee, and moreover passes over all that preceded His appearance in Nazareth (vs. 16 *seq.*) in silence. It is not here the place to adventure ourselves in the labyrinth of the New Testament harmony and chronology. If any one, however, wishes to know how we believe that after the forty days' temptation the different events are to be arranged, they appear to us to have followed one another in the following order:

1. The first friends (John i. 35–52);
2. The first miracle (John ii. 1–12);
3. The first passover (John ii. 13–22);
4. Jesus and Nicodemus (John ii. 23–iii. 21);
5. The Messiah in Samaria (John iv. 1 *seq.*);
6. The second miracle in Cana (John iv. 43 *seq.*);
7. The first sermon in Nazareth (Luke iv. 16–30).

Luke iv. 14, therefore, according to our opinion, proceeds parallel with John iv. 43. The first sermon at Nazareth was immediately preceded by the second miracle of Cana, John iv. 43 *seq.*, and was followed immediately by the removal to Capernaum, Matt. iv. 13.

Vs. 16. **And He came to Nazareth.**—The question is, whether this visit to Nazareth was the same as that related in Matt. xiii. 55–58, and if this is the case, which of the Synoptics has communicated this circumstance in its most exact historic connection. The first question we believe, with others and with Lange (*Matthew*, p. 255), that we must answer affirmatively; and in respect to the second inquiry, that we must give the preference to Luke. The opinion that the Lord preached twice in this way at Nazareth encounters, according to our view, insurmountable difficulties. That Jesus, after such treatment as is related by Luke, vs. 30, should have returned yet again; that He should have preached there again, should again have heard the same reproach, should again have given the same answer, is a supposition that perhaps no one would have defended had not his harmony been guided by doctrinal considerations and interests. Luke, it is true, does not speak of the miracles which are reported Matt. xiii. 58. But nothing hinders us from assuming that He had already performed these before the sermon in the synagogue, since (vss. 27–29) immediately after that the attack upon His life followed, although Matthew and Mark end their account respecting Nazareth with the mention of these miracles. It appears that the Lord even before the sermon communicated by Luke had thought in this way to dispose their hearts in His favor,—and let it not be said that this is an artificial interpretation (Stier). Is it not improbable that the Lord should only have remained one day at Nazareth and should only have come into the town on the same Sabbath on which He entered the synagogue? Even the Jewish Sabbath laws, which restricted travelling on this day, forbade this, and, on the supposition that the Lord had already wrought some miracles at Nazareth, His severe discourse acquires double force, and the comparison with the miracles of Elijah and Elisha, moreover, is fully in place. We do not admit the objection that then the words which the Lord puts in their mouths, vs. 23, would no longer be applicable. On the contrary, they were not content with the miracles wrought among themselves, but, on the other hand, desired miracles like those at Capernaum (John iv. 45), miracles such as awaken astonishment at a distance. Why should not the report of that which had been done for the βασιλικός at Capernaum have made its way to Nazareth? and is there indeed anything that is harder to appease than the craving for marvels? If any one, however, believes that all the difficulties are not in this way, either, removed out of the way, he will yet have to acknowledge that the difficulties which spring from the repetition of all these events are at any rate somewhat more numerous.

Where He had been brought up.—Evidently this account points back to the history of His childhood. A holy moment in the life of the Lord, when He for the first time should teach in the synagogue of the town in which He has spent so many years in silence. Respecting Nazareth, *see* LANGE on Matt. ii. 23.

As His custom was.— *Videmus, quid egerit adolescens Jesus Nazarethæ, ante baptismum*. Bengel. Apparently (*see* above) this Sabbath was the first after His return to Nazareth, where the Lord, before this public appearance, had already wrought some miracles in a smaller circle, and appears to have remarked the first traces of unbelief (Matt. xiii. 58; Mark vi. 5), the rebuke of which, in His first discourse, would otherwise not have been immediately necessary.

And stood up to read.—Hitherto He had always been accustomed to sit among the hearers. The public reading in the synagogue consisted of a portion of the Law, which, in regular order, was followed by a section of the Prophets. Besides this, opportunity was sometimes given to respectable strangers to give a free word of exhortation or consolation (Acts xiii. 15), and the Saviour's rising served as a token that He also wished to make use of this liberty. The public reading of the Law had already taken place, and that of the Prophets was about to begin. He, therefore, receives from the hand of the attendant the roll, out of which on that day, according to the customary sequence, the lesson was to be read. It was that of Isaiah, and after He had unrolled this holy book, He finds, certainly without seeking, yet not without special higher guidance, the prophetic passage referred to.

Vs. 17. **The place where it was written.**—Strictly speaking, this passage (Isaiah lxi. 1) was the *haphthara* appointed for the morning of the great Day of Atonement (the 10th Tishri), and on this account Bengel, in his *Ordo Temporum*, p. 220, believed himself to have here come upon an infallible chronological datum; yet, even if it were assumed that this division of the lessons was already in use in the Saviour's time, it would then be surprising that Luke has not said a word here of His seeking an appointed prophecy: exactly the opposite.

Vs. 18. **The Spirit of the Lord is upon me.** —Isaiah lxi., freely quoted after the Septuagint. Jesus probably read the passage aloud in Hebrew, but Luke appears to communicate it from memory according to the Alexandrian version. From this arises the difference between the original text and the citation, which is more particularly stated by De Wette (*ad locum*). He has even taken the words: ἀποστεῖλαι τεθραυσμέν. ἐν ἀφ. from Isaiah lviii. 6, so that accordingly he gives not so much the letter as the main thought of the text of this sermon. This text appears, however, to have been designedly ended at the words: *The acceptable year of the Lord* (that is, the definite time in which the Lord is gracious), although commonly not less than 21 verses were read from the Prophets. The freedom was used, according to later authors also, of often deviating from this usage, and then 3, 5, or 7 verses were sometimes read aloud. *See* Sepp, *Leben Jesu*, ii. p. 123. As respects the passage in itself, the prophet undoubtedly speaks primarily of his own vocation and dignity, but as the servant of Jehovah he was in his work and destiny the type and image of the Messiah, the perfect servant of the Father. What at the time of Isaiah was only relatively true for himself, could hold good in its full significance only of the Messiah, who had brought in an eternal redemption. Therefore Jesus can with the fullest right begin: ὅτι σήμερον, κ.τ.λ. Comp. Hoffmann, Weissag., and Erf. ii. p. 96.

Vs. 20. **And when He had rolled up the book.**—It is, of course, to be understood that the words: "To-day is this Scripture fulfilled," &c., constituted not properly the contents but the beginning of this discourse. The text chosen gives the Lord occasion to set forth the work to be accomplished by Him on its most amiable side; no wonder, therefore, that the eyes of all are directed upon Him. With this one picturesque stroke, Luke (Pictor) gives to his narrative the greatest distinctness, and places us, as it were, in the midst of the citizens of Nazareth. What here took place he probably learned from Mary, or one of the ἀδελφοί, who were certainly present at this first discourse of Jesus of Nazareth, and therefore, he is able to go more into detail than Matthew and Mark, and even to communicate the prophetic text. Respecting the fulfilment of a prophecy, comp., moreover, the remark in O. von Gerlach, *N. T.* on Matt. ii. 16.

Vs. 22. **And all bare Him witness.**—To the gracious words of the Saviour is this testimony given, and from this it becomes very soon evident that it does not respect the *contents* but the *form* of the discourse of the Lord. They admired not *what* but the way *in which* the Saviour spoke, especially when they remembered His humble origin, which would have given occasion to no such expectation; for it is, of course, certain that the inhabitants of Nazareth could not have known of the mystery of His conception by the Holy Ghost. This passage, as well as John vii. 46, is noteworthy, since it gives an unimpeachable evidence of the irresistible impression which the graciousness of the manner of Jesus in His discourse and preaching, produced even in the case of imperfectly developed or hostilely disposed persons.

Vs. 23. **Surely,** πάντως.—The Lord has the certain expectation of that which they will allege against Him, since He sees the captiousness of prejudice arising already in their hearts, and He makes use of the proverbial expression: "Physician, heal thyself," not only in order to express His meaning more plainly, but also to give them an intimation in respect to the blessed purpose of His appearance as Israel's physician. From comparison of Matt. xiii. 57 and Mark vi. 4 with Luke iv. 24 it appears that the Synoptics deviate in some measure from each other in the report of the words in which the Lord expressed the idea that a prophet usually has nowhere less authority than in his own country. It is very possible that He used this apophthegm often, and that with slight variations; the most original and simple form of the proverb, however, we believe that we find in this passage of Luke. As to the causes why the prophet in his own immediate circle receives less honor than elsewhere, Neander deserves to be compared in his *Leben Jesu*, at this passage.— **Heal thyself,** not: "Undertake the remedy of thine own poverty before the world," or, "Take better care than hitherto of thy prophetic dignity;" but: "Help thine own countrymen, who are naturally the nearest to thee." The figurative words are sufficiently explained by the literal words immediately following them: "What we have *heard*," &c. To the craving for the marvellous, which of itself, indeed, knows no bounds, there is added now, moreover, the reckoning how great a fame their despised village would attain if He should make it the centre of a brilliant miraculous activity. On this account they indirectly reproach Him with having already bestowed an honor on Capernaum, to which they properly had the nearest claim. Of the many miracles which the Lord had already at an earlier point of time performed in Jerusalem (John ii. 23), they appear as yet to have learned nothing.

Vs. 25. **Many widows were in Israel.**—With the greatest humility He, who was so much more than a prophet, places Himself so far on an equality with the prophets in the Old Testament as this, that He together with them must be content to suffer an unbelieving rejection, which, it is true, is most severely requited by God. This we see from two examples taken from the life of Elijah and Elisha, which are doubly noteworthy for this reason, that here at the beginning of the public life of Jesus in somewhat covert wise the same thing is announced which the Saviour at the end with explicit words threatens the Jews with, as punishment for their unbelief. *See* Matt. xxi. 43.

As respects now the first of these examples, comp. 1 Kings xvii. 18. There has some difficulty arisen, from the fact that the duration of the drought here (as well as in James v. 17) is stated as three years and six months, while from 1 Kings xviii. it appears to result that Elijah in the 3d year returned to Ahab, and very soon after his return the rain commenced. We cannot agree with De Wette, who here, by comparison with Dan. xii. 7, maintains that he has deduced the fact, that it was a Jewish custom to give to a period of calamity the average duration of three and a half years, and as little can we assume with others (*e. g.*, GEBSER, *Commentary on James*), that in the New Testament another reckoning of time has been followed from that in the Old. We prefer supposing, with Olshausen, that the third year, 1 Kings xviii. 1, must be reckoned from the arrival of Elijah at Sarepta, 1 Kings xvii. 9, which, however, had been already preceded by a year of drought, during which the prophet had abode at the brook Cherith, vs. 7.—That Elijah was actually sent only to this one and to no one of the many widows in Israel besides, we should not be absolutely obliged to conclude from the Old Testament, but we assume it upon the infallible word of the Saviour. [As our Lord here evidently proceeds upon the common ground of the history, which both parties were alike acquainted with, this last remark appears superfluous.—C. C. S.]

Vs. 27. **Many lepers.**—Comp. 2 Kings vii. 3.—In the time of Elijah, ἐπί. Comp. chap. iii. 2; Mark ii. 26; Acts xi. 28.—**Naaman.** *See* 2 Kings vi. 1-19. "Then might," the Lord means to say, "the Jews also have been able to say to Elijah and Elisha: Do the same also here in your country." But it was not possible, because the Jews did not seek the help which they had at the door, and closed their hearts against the Lord. "Theophilus, doubtless, when he read this, rejoiced in the God who is truly also 'the God of the Gentiles.'" Besser. The mention of the history of Naaman was the more humiliating since he had first been unbelieving, but afterwards, on the representations of his simple-minded servants, had become believing.

It would be most unjust to accuse this turn, which the Saviour gave His discourse, of excessive harshness (Hase, De Wette), since we must not forget what an unloving judgment (vss. 22, 23), respecting His person and His work had preceded it, and how here everything depends on the tone and the voice of the speaker. Moreover, since Luke communicates to us only the main substance of the whole address, we must be very careful of rendering here a precipitate judgment; we have rather here to admire the wise Physician who does not shrink from heroic methods in order to attack the very heart of the chief moral disease of His contemporaries, namely, sensuousness and earthly-minded expectations, and who will rather set at stake His own safety than spare their perverseness. And ought not He who had spent so many years of retirement at Nazareth, and had carefully observed the moral condition of its inhabitants, to have been better able to judge how sternly and severely He was obliged to rebuke, than modern criticism, which here also is very far from being without pre-suppositions?

Vs. 28. **And all they in the synagogue . . . were filled with wrath.**—The *veritas odium parit* never belied itself less than in respect to the Saviour, in whom the ἀλήθεια itself was personally manifested upon earth. How little do the embittered hearers apprehend that precisely by this they give the proof of the justice of the rebuke which they had heard! The reception which Jesus here found, agrees remarkably with that which afterwards Stephen found (Acts vii. 51). And if this rise of bitterness is compared with the earlier enthusiasm, vs. 22, it shows in a striking manner the inconstancy of human honor as well as the untrustworthiness of human passions. Not at Rome alone did the Capitoline border hard on the Tarpeian rock.

Vs. 29. **A cliff of the hill.**—Nazareth still lies at the present day on a mountain precipice of from 400 to 500 ft. high, which lifts itself above a valley of about a half a league in circumference; *see* RÖHR, *Palestine*, pp. 126-129, and the other eminent narratives of travel. Near the Maronite church they still show the rocky wall on the west side of the town, from 40 to 50 ft. high, where the event of the text is said to have happened, and from which He could easily escape them through the narrow and crowded streets of the town (Robinson, p. 423). That the monks show at a distance of two English miles from Nazareth another Mount of Precipitation, where there are yet two stones against which (they say) the Lord leaned in defending Himself, and which yet show traces of His hands and feet, is doubtless one of the grossest errors which tradition has committed in the sphere of the Saviour's life.

Vs. 30. **But He.**—It will hardly be necessary to vindicate the historic reality of this fact against critics who are throughout disposed to place the Jews somewhat higher, and the Lord, indeed, somewhat lower than the Gospel does. Proofs of the turbulence, the cruelty, and the revengefulness of the Galileans can be found in abundance in Josephus, even in the history of his own life. As respects the escape of the Lord, we can here no more assume, with Olshausen, De Wette, and Strauss, something mysterious, than we can subscribe to the prosaic explanation: That He owed His deliverance only to the courage and the resoluteness with which He warded them off from Him (!!) and voluntarily expelled Himself from the synagogue, John xvi. 2 (Von Ammon). With Hase, Stier, and Lange, we ascribe Jesus' escape to the composure with which He made a way for Himself, strong in the consciousness that His hour was not yet come. He goes thus, not in order to escape His Passion, but in order actively to await the agony of His Passion appointed for Him hereafter. Examples of the daunting influence which composure and self-control have often exercised on raging crowds are too numerous to be all mentioned here. Let the reader only call to mind the effect of the crushing word: "Slave, wilt thou slay Marius?" and better than this, John xviii. 6. It is, then, unnecessary also to understand here a particular protection of God (in the sense of a miracle, Meyer), but it is better to bring all *mirabilia* of the kind, in the wider sense of the word, into connection with the elevated and wholly unique personality of the Lord—the absolute *miraculum*—to which, in a certain sense, it was innate to make such an impression on the rude rabble surrounding Him. "Not in any such sense as that they were struck with blindness does He go forth, invisible and with an outward miracle, for this is precisely what the Evangelist by διελθὼν διὰ μέσου means to deny; but He only beholds them with a look of His hitherto restrained majesty, reserved for this last need, and they, receiving yet another sign of His spiritual might as a parting token, are bound and incapable of touching Him. Nay, they are compelled on the right and left to make place reverently for His going forth. They stood, stumbled, sought, grew ashamed, fled, and went apart, as Pfenninger with striking pencil paints the close of the scene." R. Stier.

DOCTRINAL AND ETHICAL.

1. The Saviour comes forward in the might of the same Spirit with which He was baptized and with which He overcame Satan. The account of His preaching at Nazareth is especially noteworthy, because it shows how His personality and His word, even without doing miracles, made an irresistible impression so long as the sensibility was not closed up through hostility and prejudice. We remark the same in Samaria, John iv. 41, 42. The history of the Saviour's first preaching in the town of His bringing up, may also serve as a proof how fully applicable to Him is the word of the Psalm, Ps. xlv. 3.

2. Jesus' discourse at Nazareth may be named at the same time an opening sermon of His whole activity in Galilee. Impossible, indeed, would it be to find a more admirable text than the Saviour found in turning over the prophetic roll; it is a gospel in brief, the best description of the *Christus Consolator.* The poor, the prisoners, the blind are indeed the best representatives of the whole mass of suffering mankind. Their names present before our eyes misery and sin in their whole compass. Freedom, light, healing—what noble images of the salvation given in Christ! "Christ finds all those to whom He comes blind, without knowledge of God, bound of Satan, and kept prisoners under death, sin, and the law. For out of the Gospel there is nothing but utter darkness and captivity, so that even if we have some little knowledge, yet can we not follow the same, because we are bound." Luther.

3. This sermon is of moment, because from it it appears in what relation Christ as Prophet placed Himself to the Old Testament. He grounds His proclamation of the Gospel upon the Scripture, cleaves not merely to its letter, but presses through to its spirit and proclaims Himself as the end of the Law and the Prophets. The Prophetic Scripture is the mirror in which He beholds His own image and shows it to His contemporaries. The genuine evangelical spirit comes to manifestation in an Old Testament form. Even the *parallelismus membrorum,* to be observed in the diction of the Old Testament, is not wanting in the way in which He opposes the widows in Israel in the days of Elijah, to the lepers in those of Elisha, and repeatedly declares: "To none of them," &c. After such remarks the inquiry may well be called superfluous whether the Saviour, in the place where He was brought up, received into His soul the inmost spirit of the Scriptures of the Old Testament.

4. The Saviour at Nazareth reveals at once His double character as Physician and Prophet; as physician, who is treated with scorn when he wishes to prepare help for others and at once is bidden to heal himself; as prophet, who deserves the highest honor and does not receive the least. Upon the miracles wrought by the Lord in Nazareth, *see* LANGE, *Matthew,* p. 255.

5. The first discourse of the Saviour at Nazareth bears so far as this a typico-symbolic character, that, on the one hand, it serves as a prototype of every true preaching of the gospel as to substance, ground, and tenor, and, on the other hand, as in a mirror brings to sight the cliffs on which the effects of a discourse commonly suffer shipwreck—earthly-mindedness, prejudice, pride. Of the four classes of persons who are designated in the parable of the Sower, we find here particularly the second and the third.

6. The manner in which the Saviour begins His sermon at Nazareth deserves, in form as well as matter, to be called a model for every true preacher of the gospel. Comp. the chapter: "Jésus Christ, modèle du prédicateur," in the admirable tractate of Nap. Roussel, *Comment il ne faut pas prêcher,* Paris and London, 1857.

7. Nazareth's synagogue is an image of unbelieving Israel, Nazareth's rock an image of the unshakable composure and inward tranquillity of Jesus.

HOMILETICAL AND PRACTICAL.

The triumphal return from the wilderness of temptation.—Whither Jesus comes, the fame of Him always precedes Him.—The beginning of His pilgrimage takes place under the most favoring presages.—Jesus returns to Nazareth, the place of His bringing up, as a prophet mighty in word and deed. —The heart-winning art of Jesus.—The visit to the synagogue on the Sabbath a settled custom of the Lord.—The public reading of the word of God an important part of the joint worship of God.—The high value of the prophetical word: 1. Before, 2. during, 3. after the time of the Saviour.—All mourners are comforted when Christ appears.—The true preacher of the gospel one anointed with the Holy Spirit.—The time of the New Covenant an acceptable year of the Lord; as such, the day of salvation is: 1. Announced, 2. manifested, 3. confirmed in the case of all believers.—The gracious year of the Lord precedes the day of vengeance of our God, yet the latter follows immediately.—Christ: 1. The consolation of the poor, 2. the freedom of the prisoners, 3. the light of the blind.—How admiration for the preacher may be united with the rejection of the preaching.—The might of prejudice against the truth.—The unbelief of earlier and later days at all times self-consistent: 1. Manifested, 2. punished, in the same way.—God's greatest exhibitions of grace are lost on those who give ear only to the voice of flesh and blood.—The history of the Old Testament a *testis temporum, lux veritatis, magistra vitæ.*—A believing Gentile more acceptable to God than an unbelieving Jew.—No respect of persons with God.— Craving for miracles easily excited, never contented, severely rebuked.—"Unless ye see signs and wonders, ye will not believe."—The poor of this world hath God chosen, &c., 1 Cor. i. 26 *seq.*—The inconstancy of human laudations and emotions, vss. 22–28; comp. Acts xiv. 18, 19.—Jesus rejected in Nazareth an argument for the truth of the declaration John i. 11. It is striking that unbelieving rejection of the Saviour: 1. Still shows the same character, 2. still betrays the same origin, 3. still deserves the same judgment as the behavior of the inhabitants of Nazareth.—Christ the Vanquisher of His enemies even when He appears to give way to them.—The immovable composure of the Lord over against the blind rage of His enemies.—The servant of the Lord inviolable so long as his hour is not yet come.— What a distinction between the mountain in the wilderness where the Lord surveys the kingdoms of the earth, and the rock at Nazareth where He beholds His own life threatened! And yet upon both is He victorious, and even the Mount of Precipitation is a step to His enthronement and dominion over all.

STARKE:—True preachers have to go through good and evil report, 2 Cor. vi. 8.—New preachers of the gospel are wont to be praised, but not long, for the people get tired and their ears itch again for new doctrines, 2 Tim. iv. 3.—To visit the public assembly on the Sabbath is all Christians' duty, Heb. x. 25.—HEDINGER:—The ground of all divine truth and its means of proof must be Scripture.—When men first begin with despising the person of a teacher, they are wont also commonly to despise his words and office.—ZEISIUS:—So long as the gospel is preached with sweet words, the godless also put up with it, but so soon as the application is made, the best appearing are often ready to burst with anger.—OSIANDER:—It is a folly of men to esteem highly what is strange, but to account as nothing what has come up among themselves.—QUESNEL:—Truth embitters those whom it does not enlighten and convert (the gospel a cause of tumult, Luther).—Men are often worse than the devil, who did not do what the Jews wanted to do, vs. 29.—CANSTEIN:—There is no might nor counsel against the Lord.—It is often prudence and magnanimity to give way to inflamed dispositions.

HEUBNER on vss. 18 and 19:—The order of salvation is given in these verses as in 1 Cor. i. 30: 1. Wisdom = to preach the gospel to the poor; 2. righteousness = to heal the broken hearts (these words are, however, spurious. *See* above); 3. sanctification = to proclaim deliverance to the captive, &c.; 4. redemption = preaching the acceptable year of the Lord; in other words: 1. The prophetical, 2. the high-priestly, 3. and 4. the kingly office of the Lord. (*Ingeniose magis quam vere!* Van Oosterzee.)—ARNDT:—The first sermon of Jesus at Nazareth: 1. How rich in matter it must have been; 2. what an impression must have been made!—PALMER:—How the people are astonished at the speech of the Lord! [*Vere sed insipidissime.*—C. C. S.]—DRÆSEKE:—The acceptable year of the Lord.—VAN OOSTERZEE (inaugural discourse in his native town Rotterdam upon Luke iv. 16–22):—The first sermon of Jesus at Nazareth a standard for the minister of the gospel at the beginning of his work. The narrative imparts to the minister of the gospel pregnant suggestions: 1. In reference to the *point of view* from which he is to consider his work: *a.* origin, *b.* matter, *c.* object, of preaching (vss. 18, 19). 2. In relation to the *manner* in which he must perform his work: as here the preaching must be: *a.* Grounded on Scripture, *b.* accommodated to the necessity of the hearers, *c.* presented in an attractive manner. 3. In relation to the *fruit* upon which he can reckon in this labor. Nazareth shows us: *a.* That blossoms are as yet no certain sign of fruit; *b.* that this fruit may be blasted by the most unhappy causes; *c.* that the harvest may turn out yet better than at the beginning it appears (there in the synagogue were Mary, and also the ἀδελφοί, who afterwards believed, and if the Saviour did not work many miracles at Nazareth, He yet wrought some, Matt. xiii. 58). 4. In relation to the *temper* in which he is to begin a new work: *a.* With thankful recollections of the past (vs. 16); *b.* with holy spiritual might for the present (vs. 18); *c.* with joyful hope for the future (vs. 21). Happy the teacher who is permitted to begin his preaching under more favorable presages than Jesus began His in the city where He was brought up.

B. *Capernaum.—The Prophet mighty in Works and Words before God and all the People.* CHS. IV. 31–VII. 50.

1. The first Settlement, the first miraculous Acts, the first Choice of Apostles at Capernaum.

a. ARRIVAL AND ACTIVITY AT CAPERNAUM, AND EXCURSION FROM THENCE INTO THE REGION ROUND ABOUT (Vss. 31–44).

31 And [he] came down to Capernaum, a city of Galilee, and taught[1] them on the
32 sabbath days. And they were astonished at his doctrine: for his word was with
33 power. And in the synagogue there was a man, which had a spirit of an unclean devil,
34 and cried out with a loud voice, Saying,[2] Let *us* alone [or, Ha!]; what have we to do
   with thee, *thou* Jesus of Nazareth? art thou come to destroy us? I know thee who
35 thou art; the Holy One of God. And Jesus rebuked him, saying, Hold thy peace,
   and come out of him. And when the devil had thrown him in the midst, he came out
36 of him, and hurt him not. And they were all amazed [there came an awe upon all],
   and [they] spake among themselves, saying, What a word *is* this! for with authority
37 and power he commandeth the unclean spirits, and they come out. And the fame [a
   rumor or report, ἦχος] of him went out into every place of the country round about.
38 And he arose out of the synagogue, and entered into Simon's house. And Simon's
   wife's mother was taken with [suffering under] a great [severe] fever; and they be-
39 sought him for her. And he stood over her, and rebuked the fever; and it left her;
40 and immediately she arose and ministered unto them. Now when the sun was setting,
   all they that had any [*friends*] sick with divers [various] diseases brought them unto
41 him; and he laid his hands on every one of them, and healed them. And devils
   also came out of many, crying out, and saying, Thou art Christ[3] the Son of God. And

he rebuking *them* suffered them not to speak: for⁴ they knew that he was Christ. 42 And when it was day, he departed and went into a desert place: and the people sought him, and came unto him, and stayed him, that he should not depart from 43 them. And [But] he said unto them, I must preach the kingdom of God to [the] 44 other cities also: for therefore [thereto] am I sent. And he preached in the synagogues of Galilee.

[¹ Vs. 31.—'Ην διδάσκων, expressing His doing it habitually.—C. C. S.]
² Vs. 34.—*Rec.:* λέγων before 'Εα. Critically dubious. See Lachmann, *ad loc.* [Om. inter al. B., L., Sin.—C. C. S.]
³ Vs. 41.—*Rec.:* 'Ο Χριστὸς ὁ υἱὸς, κ.τ.λ.; a somewhat superfluous paraphrase, which is omitted by B., C., [Sin.], D., L., F., X., Vulgata, Origenes, Griesbach, De Wette, Meyer, &c.
[⁴ Vs. 41.—Not: "to say that they knew," &c., λαλεῖν is never *to say*, but *to speak*, *to discourse.* Alford.—C. C. S.]

EXEGETICAL AND CRITICAL.

Vs. 31. **And He came down to Capernaum.**—Comp. the remarks on Matt. iv. 13. Plainly enough Luke brings the removal of the Saviour to Capernaum into connection with the unfavorable reception which He finds at Nazareth. Herein he is indirectly supported by Matthew (ch. iv. 13), while Mark (ch. i. 21) does not contradict it. John, it is true, gives no account of this settlement of Jesus at Capernaum, but it is known how incomplete his Galilean reports are. That he also knows of an abode of the Saviour at Capernaum, appears from ch. ii. 12; vi. 59. The suitableness of this dwelling-place for Jesus, nevertheless, strikes the eye at once: He finds Himself here in the centre of a very active traffic, between Tyre, Sidon, Arabia, and Damascus, upon the great road to the Mediterranean, where continually great throngs were streaming together. From here He could easily travel to Judæa, Ituræa, and Upper Galilee, in order to preach the gospel. Here the influence of the sacerdotal party was not so strong as in Jerusalem; here He found, moreover, the dwelling of Simon Peter, a friend's house, whose hospitable rooms He was doubtless glad to use as His shelter during His sojourn there, even if He did not exactly live in this house, especially as His brothers at Nazareth did not yet believe on Him. If He wished for rest He could find this nowhere better than on the shore of the lake, of whose exquisite environs Rabbinical scholars write: "Seven seas have I created in the Holy Land of Canaan, saith the Lord, but only one of all these have I chosen, namely the Sea of Gennesareth," and if danger threatened Him, He could at once betake Himself to the opposite jurisdiction of the tetrarch Philip. That the moral wretchedness of the town above many others, might recommend it only the more to the great Physician of sinners, is easily intelligible.

And taught them.—What He preached there is given in Mark i. 15. Particularly in the beginning of His public life does He attach Himself to John the Baptist, yet He distinguishes Himself at once from Him in this, that with the requirement of μετάνοια He connects that of faith on the gospel, and explicitly declares, that the time is not only come near, but is fulfilled.

Vs. 32. **And they were astonished.**—The preaching of the Saviour produces, therefore, at Capernaum at once a much deeper impression than at Nazareth (vs. 22). A similar explanation to that here, in relation to the might of the word of Jesus in opposition to that of the spiritually dead doctrine of the scribes and Pharisees, is also given by Matthew, ch. vii. 28, 29.

Vs. 33. **Which had a spirit of an unclean devil.**—According to Mark i. 21, compared with vss. 16–20, this healing took place not before but after the calling of the first four apostles, which Luke does not mention until ch. v. 1–11. Matthew passes over this miracle entirely in silence. As respects the possessed, of whom we here meet one, it will hardly be necessary here again to refute the rationalistic assertion, that the Saviour and His Evangelists, when they speak of demoniacal infirmities, accommodated themselves only to a superstitious popular conception. With everything figurative which they contain, yet expressions such as Luke xi. 24–27; Matt. xvii. 21, and other passages, appear to lead to the presupposition that these unhappy ones were actually tormented by demoniacal influence. Modern science has as yet by no means proved that an actual possession, even nowadays, is unheard of and impossible. How much less is it inconceivable in the fulness of time, when the kingdom of darkness concentrated its full power against the kingdom of light!

Here indeed the ontological objection has been brought forward that there are no demons, and that, if there were, the possession of men by them would be utterly impossible. But a modest science would indeed have to take the word "impossible" not quite so quickly upon its lips, and not in its self-conceit to decide in a sphere of which, outside of historic revelation, it knows nothing. The whole connection of our bodily and spiritual nature, as well as the operation of spirit upon spirit, remains for us still, in part, a *terra incognita*. This we know, however: the soul operates through the nervous system upon the body and receives by the medium of these nerves its impressions from the outer world. Not less certain is it, that the natural connection between the nervous life and consciousness may be relaxed for a shorter or longer time; the magnetic sleep and insanity are witnesses for this. If, therefore, as the Lord Himself declares, demons exist, why should they not be able so to work on the nervous system that the soul subjected to this strange influence is fettered and rendered inactive? Why should we not be able to experience the operation of the world of spirits upon us most strongly just at the time when the regular operation of the world of sense upon us is restrained? Undoubtedly, if we understand such an *indwelling* of the demons that by it two or three subjects are united in one material organism, we fall into psychological monstrosities. But if we assume a personal operation of evil spirits upon their victims which takes place in a psychical way and does not expel the human spirit but suppresses it, there are then no insurmountable difficulties remaining, even if the demoniacally infirm are not precisely to be called greater sinners than others. Yet there may have been in their own physical or psychical condition a peculiarly great receptivity for the operation of the demons. The accounts which we have of these infirm in the Synoptics give us warrant for such a conception. But as respects the silence of John upon this, we can by no means infer too much from the argument *e silentio*. Perhaps the Saviour healed fewer possessed in Judæa than in Galilee. Perhaps John considered it unnecessary to amplify the few miracles related by him with reports of this particular character. Perhaps, also, he was disposed to consider the combat between darkness and light more on its ethical than on its metaphysical side. In brief, there is just as little reason for the assumption that he himself was unbelieving in the matter of demonology, as for the assumption that he preferred to pass this Jewish superstition over in silence before his readers in Asia Minor. In order to maintain this assumption, we should be obliged to overlook entirely such passages as 1 John iii. 8; John xiii. 27; x. 20. In the last named passage the word καὶ μαίνεται is by no means synonymous with the preceding δαιμόνιον ἔχει, but this latter is in the opinion of the Jews the ground of the former. In a similar way they connect, John viii. 48, the charge that Jesus was possessed, with the injurious epithet *Samaritan*. Comp., moreover, respecting the demoniacs, LANGE, *Matthew*, p. 96; IDELER, *Geschichte des religiösen Wahnsinns*, I., and the weighty article of Ebrard in HERZOG's *Real Encyklopädie*, iii. pp. 240–255.

Vs. 34. **What have we.**—The demoniac, therefore, knows Jesus in His high dignity, although He had just appeared publicly for the first time in Capernaum. If we have once recognized the possession, there is nothing in this extraordinary. Analogies in abundance are presented by natural presentiments, the gift of second sight, &c. The mystery concealed from the human world of the origin of Jesus and the purpose of His incarnation, is already known to the world of spirits, which almost instinctively is compelled to tremble when it recognizes its future conqueror. Noticeable is the plural in which the demon makes itself heard, although Luke has spoken in the singular of a πνεῦμα δαιμ. ἀκαθ. It is possible that he speaks, as it were, in the name of the whole demon-world, which he feels threatened in himself, or also that he makes himself heard in the name of the whole throng assembled in the synagogue, in the definite purpose of arousing a bitterness against Jesus and bringing His life into danger. Certainly this would have been a worthy attempt for the vassal of the Prince of Hell, since the latter had been so brilliantly beaten back in the wilderness, and was now bent upon vengeance and new assaults. Comp. the Satanology of Boss in RUDELB. and GURIKE's *Zeitschrift*, 1851, iv., and the prælection of Sartorius upon the Doctrine of Satan in HENGSTENBERG's *Evang. Kirchenzeitung*, 1858, i.

Vs. 35. **And Jesus rebuked him.**—Here also we see at once that in the therapeutics of the heavenly Physician threatening takes a far more important place than sympathizing lamentation. He passes over for a moment the sufferer Himself in order to direct at once His word of might against the evil spirit controlling him. The word of might with which He commands the demon has a noticeable agreement with that with which He afterwards bridles the seas and the winds.

And when the devil had thrown him.—Here also, as often, the most violent paroxysm precedes the healing of the sufferer. To undertake fully to explain such phenomena in sickness is perhaps as foolish as to call them wholly inconceivable. Whoever has understanding will call no philosophical presuppositions to his help in order to judge *a priori* of facts, but will rather observe facts, in order upon them to build his theories, and, moreover, especially in cases like the present, will be mindful of the word of the English poet-king: "There are more things in heaven and earth, Horatio, than are dreamt of in your philosophy."—**Threw him,** ῥίψαν; somewhat stronger Mark: σπαράξαν, *quum discerpsisset cum.* "*Meliore verbo usus est Lucas, in sensu tamen optime conveniunt, quia uterque docere voluit, violentum fuisse Dæmonis exitum. Sic ergo miserum hominem prostravit, quasi discerpere vellet: irritum tamen fuisse conatum dicit Lucas, non quod impetus ille prorsus absque læsione fuerit, vel saltem obsque ullo doloris sensu, sed quia integer postea fuit homo a diabolo liberatus.*" Calvin.—As to the rest, the ground on which the Saviour imposed silence on the demon strikes us at once. He would not have His Messianic dignity prematurely declared before the ears of all, and repulsed every homage which was offered Him from impure lips or in an equivocal intent. In this last respect, we see Paul following the footsteps of His great Master, Acts xvi. 18. Here also the declaration, Psalm l. 16, holds good.

Vs. 36. **What a word is this!**—Mark: What sort of *new* doctrine, καινὴ διδαχή. The newness in this case is found not so much in the matter as in the effect of the words of Jesus.—**With authority and power.** Authority which endures no contradiction, power which endures no resistance.

Vs. 38. **And He arose.**—Comp. Mark i. 29–31. The position of the miracle wrought upon Peter's mother-in-law in Mark and Luke, immediately after the first casting out of a devil in the synagogue at Capernaum, appears to deserve the preference to that in Matthew (ch. viii. 14–17), who mentions this event after the Sermon on the Mount. According to Mark, Andrew also dwelt in this house, who, however, does not, like Simon, appear to have been married. That the sickness of the πενθερά was of a serious nature appears not only from the technical expression used by the physician Luke πυρετῷ μεγάλῳ (*see* Galen, *De diff. febr.*, 1., cited by Wetstein), but also especially from the fact that it hindered her even from entertaining, in a manner somewhat befitting Him, the so greatly desired guest. The εὐθέως of Mark, in his mentioning their prayer for help to the Saviour, belongs again to the pictorial peculiarities of this evangelist.

Vs. 39. **Rebuked the fever.**—As just before the demon. According to Matthew and Mark, who omit this circumstance, He lays hold of her hand in order to lift her up. That the one does not exclude the other is easily understood; apparently the Saviour considered this contact as necessary in order to awaken the faith of the sick woman, who was too severely attacked by the fever herself to entreat His help. That she is able at once to rise, bears witness to the completeness of her recovery; that she at once girds herself for serving, shows that the bodily benefit was also sanctified to her heart. As to the rest, this miracle is related by all the Synoptics, not so much because it was remarkable above others, but especially because it belongs to the first period of the Saviour's activity in Capernaum, and increased enthusiasm to ecstasy. At the same time, also, because it was followed by a series of other miracles in the town and region round about, concerning which there is not more particular mention. Especially was it important as a proof of the particular care which the Saviour devoted to the fashioning and training of Peter for an apostle. Among the twelve there was none whose house, person, boat, in short, whose whole circle of life was so made the theatre of remarkable miracles as that of Peter, who on this day also was bound with new bonds to the Master.

Vs. 40. **Now when the sun was setting.**—According to Matthew and Mark: when it had already become late. It is almost as if the Synoptics, even by the choice of their words, wished to put their readers in the position to follow almost step by step the Saviour on the first day of His unwearied and blessed activity at Capernaum. While the sun is going down, the report of two astonishing miracles has caused the light of a new hope for the sick in the town and its vicinity to rise. Among the various infirm of whom Luke gives account, Matthew and Mark mention also many possessed. The former He appears to have healed especially by laying on of hands, the other through His words (Matthew). The graphic trait which Mark adds to this whole representation, vs. 33, namely, that the whole city assembled before the door, betrays evidently the influence of Peter, the eye-witness.

Vs. 42. **And when it was day.**—According to Mark i. 35, so early that it might well have been called still night. From his account it also appears that the Saviour withdraws Himself into solitude in order in prayer to seek rest for some few moments of the night. Here also, as elsewhere (Matt. xiv. 23), is there the same alternation of prayer and labor in the life of the Saviour, such as in truth might be called a praying without ceasing. This short repose, however, is disturbed by the disciples following Him even here (κατεδίωξαν, Mark), with Peter at their head (Mark i. 36), who do not rest until they have found Him, in order to make known to Him the entreaty of the inhabitants who were waiting for His return.

Vs. 43. **I must preach ... to the other cities also.**—Δεῖ, of course, not in the sense of an absolute necessity, but of a Divine decorum, of a moral obligation which springs from His very relation as the Messiah of Israel, and not of Capernaum alone. Elsewhere also must He preach the gospel: upon this, not upon doing miracles, does the Saviour here lay the greatest emphasis—**For thereto am I sent.** That is: "Thereto have I publicly come forward, have been manifested as Divine teacher among My contemporaries," equivalent to the expression in Mark: "For that have I come out," ἐξελήλυθα. Here we have no more to understand a proceeding forth from the Father, as in John xvi. 28 (Euthymius, Stier), than a mere going forth from Capernaum. The latter gives an insipid sense—the former, the apostles would now perhaps have understood least of all. The Saviour speaks simply of the purpose for which He now appeared publicly as a teacher.

Vs. 44. **And He preached.**—According to Mark i. 39, He at the same time casts out devils and traverses all Galilee. This journey appears to have been very extended and to have wound up with the ἑορτὴ τῶν Ἰουδαίων (John v. 1).

DOCTRINAL AND ETHICAL.

1. Like the wilderness of Quarantania, so does also the synagogue at Capernaum show the combat of the Lord against the might of hell. Now, when the prince of this world had been repulsed, his satellites assay the assault. At both points Christ triumphs through the might of His word, and the demons' cries of terror are so many voices to His honor as well as the acclamations of praise of the enthusiastic people. In a striking manner does this narrative already confirm what James (ch. ii. 19) says of the faith of devils; but at the same time also by the side of their power, their powerlessness here becomes manifest. Where the demon cannot drive back the Lord, he still seeks to do mischief to the poor man, but he succeeds as little in one as in the other.

2. Word and deed are here, as everywhere, united in Christ. With justice, therefore, says Augustine, *Tract.* 24 *in Joh.:* "*Interrogamus ipsa miracula, quid nobis loquantur de Christo; habent enim, si intelligamus, linguam suam. Nam quia ipse Christus Verbum est, etiam factum Verbi verbum nobis est.*"

3. For the first time in the Gospel of Luke we meet in this passage with a report of miracles. Of course, we cannot here go into any particular investigation respecting these works of the Lord and His apostles, which, indeed, is much the less necessary after the fruitful hints of Lange. Only in general we must recollect in respect to these and all subsequent accounts of miracles: 1. That the impossibility of miracles admits of no proof whatever, either from the empirical, or from the logical, or from the metaphysical side. 2. That the conception: "laws of nature," which are presumed to be infringed by miracles, is in the nature of the case elastic, so that Goethe is right when he says (*Zur Farbenlehre*): " As on one side experience is limitless, because ever new and yet newer things can be discovered, so are maxims also, which, if they are not to grow petrified, must not lose the capability of extending themselves and of receiving what is greater, nay, of consuming and losing themselves in a higher view." 3. That the distinction between *miracula* and *mirabilia* will become clearly evident only if we consider the fact not in and of itself, but connected with the moral character of the wonder-worker and of the purpose of his activity. 4. That the miracles of the Saviour are worthily esteemed only as they are in a certain sense regarded as the natural revelations of His divinely human personality, which itself might be called the greatest, the absolute, nay, if one will, the sole miracle. 5. That miracles were in no sense given in order to constrain to faith, but rather in order to take away from unbelief every excuse, John xv. 24. The direct intention of miracles was to serve as a proof of the Divine mission of the Saviour, John v. 36, and so far also to awaken confidence towards His person and His words. That the miracle in and of itself, without any reference to the personality of the doer, is no decisive proof of the inner truth of his preaching, is something which modern Apologetics may frankly concede without losing anything. She may the rather agree with the beautiful expression of Jean Paul: "Miracles on earth are nature in heaven."

4. The miracle in his dwelling is of special moment for the history of Peter's apostolic development. Through the first word of the Saviour (John i. 43), he becomes His friend; through the miracle of the draught of fishes (Luke v. 1–11), he becomes His apostle; finally, by the miracle wrought on his mother-in-law, the apostle is bound to the Master in thankful affection. That, moreover, the apostle was married, and is not required wholly to break this bond, is evident also from 1 Cor. ix. 5. As to the manner in which the Romish Church seeks to wrest the argument against the celibacy of the clergy de-

duced from these passages, the reader can find much that is interesting in SEPP, *Leben Jesu*, ii. p. 154. This question itself, however, must not detain us here.

5. Even though Peter had carried away no other remembrances from the life of the Lord than those of this first sojourn at Capernaum and the first visit in the region round about, he would already have had a right to introduce his first preaching to the Gentiles with a ὃς διῆλθεν εὐεργετῶν. The door of his dwelling, besieged by all manner of sick, who offered the Lord not even an hour of praying night-rest, is the worthy theatre of the *Christus Consolator*, and the citation of Isaiah liii. 4 in Matthew is in this connection one of the most felicitous of the whole sacred history. Comp. LANGE on Matt. viii. 16, 17.

6. From the comparison with Matt. iv. 23-25 it appears how great the impression was which the Saviour already made at His public appearance in Galilee and the region round about. It is so much the more remarkable that He makes no use for Himself of this enthusiasm, and does not so much foster as avoid it, and so soon leaves Capernaum, where yet so many hearts beat for Him. This also is a proof of the truth of John ii. 23-25, and at the same time a proof of the wisdom of the Saviour in the fashioning of His first disciples. He wishes to call them to self-denial, to accustom them to a life of journeying, and to bridle awakening earthly expectations.

HOMILETICAL AND PRACTICAL.

Jesus' arrival at Capernaum the fulfilment of the prophetic word, comp. Matt. iv. 15.—The King of God's kingdom a preacher of the gospel.—The deep impression of the word of the Lord: 1. Astonishing, 2. explicable, 3. important; *a*. for faith (apologetically), *b*. for life (practically).—The One anointed with the Holy Spirit and the one plagued by the evil spirit in the same synagogue together.—The synagogue at Capernaum glorified by the visit of the Lord of the temple.—Capernaum by the coming of the Lord raised even to heaven.—The people that sat in darkness have seen a great light.—The early enthusiasm for the Saviour at Capernaum compared with the subsequent lukewarmness.—Where Jesus comes, the devil cannot possibly abide.—The Son of God appeared that He might destroy the works of the devil.—The power and powerlessness of the kingdom of darkness: 1. Its power: *a*. to have dominion over men, *b*. to cast scorn on the Son of Man; 2. its powerlessness: *a*. to withstand the Lord's word of command, *b*. mortally to wound His redeemed; 3. the last revelations of the power of the Evil One precede the exhibitions of his powerlessness.—How the Evil One stands over against Christ and Christ over against the Evil One: 1. The Evil One stands over against Christ with hypocritical homage, irreconcilable hate, and anxious fear; 2. Christ stands over against the Evil One with immovable peace, compassionate love, and triumphant might.—Heaven, hell, and earth meet one another on the same place.—The Stronger who disarms the strong.—The demons wish to have nothing to do with Jesus, but Jesus has all the more, therefore, to do with the demons.—The Saviour's word of might: 1. Unique in majesty; 2. unique in power.—Before the Lord goes anywhere, the report

of Him goes already before Him.—The house of Simon: 1. Chosen by the Messiah, 2. visited by sickness, 3. made glad by Omnipotence, 4. changed by thankfulness into a house of the Lord.—The dwelling of Peter the theatre of great unhappiness, great redemption, great thankfulness.—Grace and gratitude: 1. In order to be able to serve the Lord, we must first have been healed by Him; 2. in order to manifest genuine thanks for His healing love, we must serve Him. No service without a foregoing healing, no healing without subsequent service.—The busy Sabbath rest of the Saviour.—The bright evening after a beautiful day of His life.—Sick ones of many kinds, only one Physician; healings of many kinds, only one miraculous might; voices of many kinds, only one key-note: He has done all things well.—The demons knew Christ even before men knew Him, but what good does this knowing do them?—The solitary prayer of the Saviour: 1. His refreshment after labor, 2. His balsam amid pains, 3. His shield in temptations, 4. His staff for the further journey of life.—Seeking Jesus: 1. In order to find, 2. without finding, 3. till found.—Obedience the key-note of the Saviour's free manifestations of love.—John remains long in one place, Jesus must go forth as widely as possible in order to preach the gospel.—The first journey of the Lord a triumphal journey.

STARKE:—Whoever has a soul possessed by uncleanness, is much more wretched than he whose body is possessed of the devil.—*Bibl. Wirt.*:—The devils themselves shame the unbelief of men, vs. 34. —The heaviest temptations are sometimes the last ragings of Satan.—CRAMER:—The works of Christ are meant to create in us wonder; wonder, inquiry; inquiry, a good report; the report, the knowledge of Christ; the knowledge of Christ, eternal life, John xvii. 3.—Christ does not draw back from going to the sick and visiting them for our reminder and imitation, Matt. xxv. 43.—QUESNEL:—A single individual that stands well with God may bring a blessing upon his whole family.—HEDINGER:—For health recovered, the best thanks are: with new obedience to serve God.—OSIANDER:—We should not be angry if now and then some desire our help at inconvenient time, but ascribe it to necessity, or excuse their simplicity.—BRENTIUS:—Christ brings with His word for towns and villages no harm, but pure grace and blessing.—QUESNEL:—It is praiseworthy for preachers of the gospel often to betake themselves to solitude (comp. the beautiful meditation of VINET: *La solitude recommandée au pasteur*).—MAJUS:—Jesus, when He hides Himself and appears to be lost, must with all diligence be sought.—Christ is to be preached as well in the schools as in churches, yet when will Christendom be with earnestness intent thereon?

LISCO on vss. 31-36:—The might of the Saviour: 1. It is acknowledged even by the kingdom of darkness; 2. it manifests itself in gracious redemption; 3. it reveals to us the Divine origin and the Divine power of His doctrine.—On vss. 38 and 39:—Jesus truly our Saviour: 1. He heals of all manner of sickness, 2. He bestows new powers for activity.—VAN OOSTERZEE:—Christ, the Divine physician of souls, how He ever yet: 1. Discovers the same wretchedness, 2. feels the same compassion, 3. desires the same temper of heart, 4. follows the same method of healing, 5. excites the same opposition, 6. deserves the same homage as here at the healing of bodily ills.

b. THE MIRACULOUS DRAUGHT OF FISHES (CH. V. 1-11).

1 And it came to pass, that, as the people pressed upon him to [1] hear the word of
2 God, he stood by the lake of Gennesaret, And saw two [little] ships [2] standing by [*the
shore of*] the lake: but the fishermen were gone out of them, and were washing *their*
3 nets. And he entered into one of the ships, which was Simon's, and prayed him that
he would thrust out a little from the land. And he sat down, and taught the people
4 out of the ship. Now when he had left speaking, he said unto Simon, Launch out
5 into the deep [*water*], and let down your nets for a draught. And Simon answering
said unto him, Master, we have toiled all the night, and have taken nothing: never-
6 theless at Thy word I will let down the net. And when they had this done, they
7 inclosed a great multitude of fishes: and their net brake [*began to break*]. And they
beckoned unto *their* partners, which were in the other ship, that they should come and
8 help them. And they came, and filled both the ships, so that they began to sink. When
Simon Peter saw *it*, he fell down at Jesus' knees, saying, Depart from me [Go out
9 from me, *i. e.*, from my ship]; for I am a sinful man, O Lord. For he was astonished
[astonishment seized him], and all that were with him, at the draught of the fishes
10 which they had taken: And so *was* also [and so also did it seize] James, and John, the
sons of Zebedee, which were partners with Simon. And Jesus said unto Simon, Fear
11 not; from henceforth thou shalt catch men.[3] And when they had brought their ships
to land, they forsook all, and followed him.

[1] Vs. 1.—*Rec.*: τοῦ ἀκούειν, instead of which we read with Tischendorf καὶ ἀκούειν. Not the purpose, but the circumstance is expressed. [Inter al. c. A., B., Sin.—C. C. S.]
[2] Vs. 2.—*Rec.*: πλοῖα. With A., C.*, L., &c., it appears that we must read πλοιάρια for πλοῖα. [Sin. has πλοῖα, but omits the preceding δύο.—C. S.]
[3] Vs. 10.—'Εσῃ ζωγρῶν. The resolved form expressing that it should be his calling.—C. C. S.]

EXEGETICAL AND CRITICAL.

General Remarks.—In the narrative of the miraculous draught of fishes, the main question is whether this occurrence is identical with the calling of four disciples, which is related by Matthew (ch. iv. 18-22) and Mark (ch. i. 16-20), or whether it is actually distinct from this and did not occur till later. The distinction between the narrative of Luke and that of the other Synoptics is so great that many have maintained the latter opinion (Krabbe, Sepp, Hug). Yet in the nature of the case it is less probable that a calling crowned with such a conclusion should have been repeated twice in so short a time, and it can be shown that the narratives admit without great trouble of being brought into agreement. As respects the distinction in the notation of time, Matthew tells us only that the calling of the four took place while Jesus was walking on the shore; Mark, that the Lord after this calling returned into the city, and healed the demoniac in the synagogue, while Luke, on the other hand, has placed this last miracle before the miraculous draught of fishes. We believe that the arrangement of the events which Mark under Peter's guidance maintains, deserves the preference, and that therefore Luke (ch. iv. 31-44) already relates by anticipation what did not take place till after the miraculous draught. Perhaps he has let the events in the synagogue at Capernaum follow immediately after the portrayal of the occurrences in the synagogue at Nazareth, that faith and unbelief in the two places might be the more strongly contrasted. Vs. 31 he only speaks in general of one of the Sabbaths which Jesus spent at Capernaum. The distinction in locality is removed when we observe that here also the one in no wise denies what the two others say. We do not read in Matthew and Mark any such thing as that our Lord standing on the shore *from there* called the four, but only that He was walking on the strand. Nothing hinders us from subjoining, what Luke alone relates, that thither also the people followed Him, and He, in order to preach, ascended a ship. If Luke also had failed to make us acquainted with this, we should have had to conclude, even from Matthew and Mark, that our Lord went *into* the ship. If Peter was mending nets, is it probable that Jesus would have called out to them from the shore: Leave all and follow me? A third difficulty, that Luke does not mention Andrew at all, is solved by the consideration that Peter in his narrative is so entirely the main person that even the sons of Zebedee are thereby thrown more or less into the shade. Besides he speaks also of other persons who were present in Peter's ship (vss. 2, 5, 9), and taken with amazement at the astonishing miracle, and (ch. vi. 14) enumerates Andrew among the twelve. The question left by him unanswered as to how the latter came to the Lord, is answered by Matthew and Mark, and if there still appears to be a difficulty in the fact that Luke alone relates the miracle and Matthew and Mark only the word of the Saviour, we know no better answer than this: "Undoubtedly to him who stands in Strauss' point of view every single miracle would of necessity occasion afresh so much astonishment and headache that he would not be able to pass over *one;* but it being presupposed, on the other hand, that Jesus really wrought miracles and, moreover, many miracles, we cannot see why every evangelist was obliged to relate every miracle" (Ebrard). Perhaps Mark has omitted this circumstance of so much moment to Peter, even as he does not relate the walking of the apostle upon the water, because the humble apostle, under whose influence he wrote, wished rather to see it passed over. With Luke this reason did not weigh, and he freely communicates what redounds to the honor of the Lord as well as of the disciple. In brief, if only we make no unreasonable demands, we account it possible and easy to unite the three Synoptic accounts into a whole without needing to do violence to any one of them.

As respects John, he does not communicate this miracle, but has, on the other hand, related a similar calling of five disciples, among whom are three of these here named (ch. i. 35–52), and the question spontaneously presses itself on us how the one can be brought into agreement with the other. We believe that there is not here the least reason for speaking of a contradiction between the evangelists (Strauss, Weisse, B. Baur, Fritzsche, De Wette, Theile, Von Ammon). John describes the first becoming acquainted on the occasion of an unexpected meeting; the Synoptics relate the nearer connection between the Saviour and the disciples. After the first stay of Andrew, John, and Peter with Jesus (John i.), they had gone away as His friends and had accompanied Him upon His Galilean journey, so that they, even at the beginning, as His disciples baptized (John iv. 2). But still it was as yet a free, not a binding, intercourse, in which they were at liberty from time to time to return to the fish-net. Therefore we have, for instance, in the synagogue at Nazareth (ch. iv. 16–30) not met them in the Saviour's company. But in what way now this preliminary connection passes over into an abiding relation and in what way the apostles were called and set apart to the apostolic function, this is related to us in reference to these four in the narrative of the miraculous draught of fishes.

Vs. 1. **The lake of Gennesaret.**—See Lange on Matt. iv. 18.

Vs. 2. **And were washing their nets;** *ut per acto opere*, Bengel, comp. vs. 5. That these fishers here appear almost as strangers cannot surprise us, since Luke has as yet not made mention of these friends of the Saviour with even a word.

Vs. 3. **Which was Simon's.**—It appears that Simon had not left the ship. That the Saviour ascended *this* ship, not that of the sons of Zebedee, has probably its ground only in the fact that the latter at that moment chanced to be ashore, not on board their vessel. If Simon was older than Andrew, it becomes so much the plainer why he as owner of the ship is first named.

Vs. 4. **Launch out into the deep water.**—As the first command had put the obedience of Peter to a slight test, so here his faith is exercised by an apparently arbitrary demand of the Saviour. To him as steersman the command is addressed in the singular; the plural χαλάσατε, κ.τ.λ., has its force with reference to the rest of the crew of the boat, who must have been active therein. That Peter considers this latter command also as addressed to himself personally appears from the answer, vs. 5. Without doubt, after a night of unsuccessful toil this injunction to take up his work again in full day must have appeared singular to him, but he already knows enough of the Lord to bring his fisherman's theory as a sacrifice to his faith at Jesus' word alone.—**Master.** Not the common διδάσκαλε, but ἐπιστάτα; about the same as the Hebrew רַבִּי, a title which was given even to such teachers as any one entertained respect for, without as yet standing in a personal relation to them, comp. Luke xvii. 13.

Vs. 6. **Their net began to break.**—If there was here an actual rent, it was, of course, only a beginning of tearing, since otherwise the whole draught might have been immediately lost again. So in like manner the allusion to the sinking of the vessels must be understood *cum grano salis*, without, however, our being actually obliged with De Wette to see here an exaggeration.

Vs. 7. **And they beckoned.**—According to Matthew's and Mark's account, also, the two ships lay close enough together to be able with a slight signal to join each other, the more easily as the crew of the second ship had doubtless observed the uncommon occurrence on the first with intense curiosity. That they for astonishment and fear were incapable of speaking, and, therefore, had to limit themselves to beckoning like Zacharias (ch. i.), is not said by Luke, but only by Euthym. Zigab. and Theophylact.

Vs. 8. **Go out from me.**—The cause of this crushing impression of wonder upon Peter is easy to explain. His words by no means entitle us to compare him to a credulous fool who trembles when he unexpectedly espies an arch-magician near him (Von Ammon, *Leben Jesu*, ii. p. 378). It appears to us, on the other hand, that the sequel must not be overlooked. Peter had as yet been able to judge no other miracle which he had seen, so well as this. It belonged to his *calling*, it took place on *his* vessel, with *his* fish-net, after *his* own fruitless endeavors, in *his* immediate presence. In the case of earlier works of the Saviour, his understanding had indeed doubtless given silent acquiescence, but here both understanding and heart were constrained to bow themselves before a present majesty. Thankfulness and surprise, after so long disappointment, unite themselves with a deep consciousness of his unworthiness, so that he is no longer able to abide in the presence of the Holy One. Had his conscience, perhaps, something to reproach him with that he after a voluntary association of a month with Jesus had again returned to his calling? Had the words: "We have toiled the whole night and have taken nothing," been expressed in a tone of displeasure and doubt? Or did there perchance in this place concur an instinctive dread of danger when he felt the sinking of the ship, and did he entreat for preservation? In such a disposition as that of Peter, various causes may work together so as to call forth such a cry of distress. That he did not confess any particular offence, but his general sinfulness in the presence of the Holy One, hardly needs, we presume, any proof. The entreaty: "Depart from me," the Lord heard in spirit, while He dealt exactly against its letter and turned in to be with the man who with trembling hand waved Him from himself.

Vs. 10. **And so also did it seize James and John.**—See on Matt. x. 2–4. In respect to their relationship to the Saviour, we must refer the reader to the dissertation of Wieseler in the *Studien und Kritiken*, 1840, p. 648 ff., who has convincingly demonstrated that Salome, the wife of Zebedee, was an own sister of Mary, the mother of the Lord, so that her children were own cousins of Jesus. In John xix. 25 there are not three, but four women named, and Mary, the wife of Cleopas, must be carefully distinguished from His mother's sister Salome, the wife of Zebedee. [It will be noticed that among the women mentioned as being present at the crucifixion, Matt. xxvii. 56, three are named as conspicuous: Mary Magdalen, Mary the mother of James and Joses, and the mother of Zebedee's children. Mark xv. 40 the same three are mentioned, only that Zebedee's wife is mentioned by the name of Salome. We have, however, no reason to doubt that Salome and Zebedee's wife are one and the same. In John xix. 25, besides the mother of Jesus, whose presence is not mentioned by the other two evangelists, we find mentioned Mary Magdalen and Mary, the wife of Cleopas, whose identity with Mary, the mother of James and Joses, we have no reason to call in question. But where is Salome? The whole passage reads thus: "Now there stood by the cross of Jesus His mother and His mother's sister, Mary, *the wife* of Cleopas, and Mary Magdalene." The question here is: Besides the mother of our Lord, are there two women mentioned here, or three? Is Mary, the wife of Cleopas, to be taken as identical with His mother's sister, or as different? If the former, Salome is not to be found, and John has omitted bearing witness to this fidelity of his own mother. If the latter, Salome is identical with our Lord's mother's sister, and the three whom the first two Synoptics mention, are also mentioned here.—C. C. S.]

Vs. 11. **They forsook all.**—Not only the ship, but the rich haul. Zebedee soon returned without his sons to Bethsaida (Mark i. 20), while they proceed with the Lord through Capernaum's gate, where He immediately after (*see* above), in the synagogue and in the house of Peter, works the miracles already related by Luke in anticipation (ch. iv. 31–42), to enter with Him afterwards upon the journey through Galilee, which had been already, ch. iv. 43, 44, mentioned with a word, to be afterwards, ch. v. 12 f., described more in detail.

DOCTRINAL AND ETHICAL.

1. We have here in Luke the first account of an anticipatory choice of apostles, which is the less to be passed over unnoticed since the Saviour evidently lays so much weight upon it. Our attention is from the beginning drawn to it by the fact that the Saviour seeks the disciples and does not wait until they approach Him of their own impulse, but takes the first step towards them, so that He can afterwards say to them: Ye have not chosen Me, but I have chosen you. In this act the word, vs. 10, which the Saviour spoke on this occasion, bears the stamp of the deepest wisdom. It is a word of might, precisely fitted to come home to a heart like that of Peter; a brief word, but which, therefore, could the less be obliterated from the memory; a figurative word, borrowed from Simon's own calling, which could the less be unintelligible to him as it was at the same time in congruity with the Old Testament manner of speech (Jer. xvi. 16; Is. xlii. 10). It is, finally, a word full of promise, which, it is true, commanded that which was hardest, but promised also that which is highest and was immediately ratified by a sign.

2. It has been asked whether Peter's draught of fishes was a miracle of omniscience or omnipotence. In other words, whether the Saviour, because of His higher knowledge, because He wished to see, saw at this moment, at a certain part of the sea, the largest number of fishes which were together, or whether He, through the mighty operation of His will, drove the finny tribes together to one point. It is not to be denied that the former admits of being received into the realm of our conceptions more easily than the latter. On the other hand, we are not to overlook the truth that according to the nature of things and the poetic declaration of the Psalm (Ps. viii. 8), the dominion over all that passeth through the paths of the seas belongs to the ideal of the perfect Son of Man.

3. The miracle here accomplished deserves to be called a striking revelation of the majesty of the Saviour. It took place within a sphere which these four disciples could judge better than any one else, and only after faith had been required of Peter and this faith had been found approved. It stands forth at the same time as a symbol of their whole subsequent apostolical activity: abundant draught of fishes at the simple word of the Lord, after a night also of fruitless wearying toil, without, however, losing the draught. It is noticeable that here there is mention of the tearing of the nets; but afterwards, in the case of a similar miracle, it is no longer mentioned, John xxi. 11. [Trench, not inaptly, regards the former miracle as symbolical of the gathering of men into the outward kingdom of God on earth, from which they may be lost; the latter one, as symbolizing the gathering of the elect souls into the kingdom of glory, none of whom will be lost.—C. C. S.]

4. In this whole work of wonders, Christ reveals Himself as the Fisher of men. It is known how dear this symbol was to the early Christians; this is testified by their monuments, rings, cups, &c., and by the characteristic word ἰχθύς itself, in which they recognized the initials of Jesus Christ, God's Son, Saviour; but especially by the beautiful words from the hymn of Clemens Alexandrinus:

ἁλιεῦ μερόπων
τῶν σωζομένων,
πελάγους κακίας
ἰχθῦς ἁγνούς
κύματος ἐχθροῦ
γλυκερῇ ζωῇ δελεάζων, κ.τ.λ.

[Fisher of mortals
The saved
From the sea of wickedness
Pure fish
From the hostile wave
For sweet life enticing.]

5. "Where the blessing of God operates aright, there does it operate as coals upon the head, and brings to the knowledge of sin and of grace. To be caught by the Lord, is on earth the greatest blessedness; after this there is no greater than to be able to catch men for the Lord." Lühe.

HOMILETICAL AND PRACTICAL.

Jesus in the midst of a throng longing for salvation.—The Fisher of men on the shore of the most remarkable sea.—All that on earth we name our own must be ready for the service of the Lord.—The Lord's ways: 1. Other, 2. higher than man's ways.—Even the Lord's disciples know dark nights.—After a dark night a bright morning.—The faith of Peter: 1. Tried, 2. enduring, 3. changed into sight.—The obedience of faith: 1. Its ground, 2. its nature, 3. its blessing.—All is yours, if ye are Christ's.—The remarkable transitions in the life of faith: 1. From disappointment to surprise, 2. from want to plenty, 3. from joy to terror, 4. from fear to hope.—The humility of Peter, vs. 8, compared with that of Paul, 1 Tim. i. 15.—Where a contrite heart exclaims: "Depart from me, O Lord," there does He certainly turn in.—The beholding of the great deeds of the Saviour must lead us to holy wondering.—Whoever has once rightly feared need never fear again.—The preacher of the gospel a fisher of men.

—Only he who leaves all can gain all.—The wonderful draught of fishes an image of the preaching of the gospel: 1. The wide-reaching command (vs. 4), 2. the hard labor (vs. 5 *a.*), 3. the sole might (vs. 5 *b.*), 4. the rich fruit (vss. 6, 7), 5. the right temper (vs. 8), 6. the highest requirement of the evangelical function (vss. 10, 11).—Whoever is himself caught of Jesus, must again catch others. —How admirably does Jesus understand the art of winning hearts for Himself!—CANSTEIN:—To the Christian all places are hallowed for the transaction of divine things, whether for himself or for others.— J. HALL:—Labor in our calling, however simply it may be done, makes us fitted for the blessing of God (Ps. cxxvii. 1, 2).—MAJUS:—The Lord brings His own wonderfully into the deep and into the height. —*Nov. Bibl. Tub.*:—Whoever receives Jesus to himself, such a one does He reward with abundance, not only of spiritual but of temporal blessing.— Abundance makes not less care and trouble than lack.—Before we let the blessing of God perish, we should beckon to others and have them enjoy it with us.—HEDINGER:—Spiritual poverty is the nearest way to the greatest riches in God.—BRENTIUS:— Whoever is faithful in that which is least, to him is more committed.—HERDER:—"Launch out into the deep" is God's word of command to every one in his vocation, and let: "Lord, at Thy word," be the answer of every one in order to draw God's blessing with his net.—HEUBNER:—The miraculous draught of fishes a prophetic type of Acts ii. 41.—The humility of the Christian in good fortune, first makes the blessing truly a blessing.—The blessed fishermen: 1. Blest by Jesus' gracious presence, 2. by the rich gift, 3. by the gracious call of Jesus.—The just means of gaining temporal blessing: 1. God's word, 2. labor, 3. trust in God, 4. acknowledgment of personal unworthiness, 5. right use of the blessing.—RIEGER:— How nothing humbles man so much as grace.—FUCHS: —Peter an example for us: 1. Hear when the Lord speaks; 2. labor when the Lord commands; 3. believe what the Lord promises; 4. follow whither the Lord calls.—BACHMANN:—Concerning a blessing in our vocation: 1. We should desire it according to this order; *a.* hear willingly and diligently God's word, *b.* go faithfully on in thy toil, *c.* trust the Lord thy Helper. 2. We should rightly apply it after this rule; *a.* recognize in receiving it thy unworthiness, *b.* prove therewith thy thankfulness, *c.* follow after Jesus with joyfulness.—THOMASIUS:—Man as he is: 1. *Before* the Lord comes to him, 2. *when* the Lord comes to him, 3. *after* the Lord comes to him. —FR. ARNDT:—The Christian a fisher of men.— LISCO:—Blessing in our temporal calling: 1. On what it depends; 2. of what nature it is; 3. for what it inspirits us.

---

2. The first Excursion from Capernaum to the surrounding Districts. The Son of Man the Physician of the Sick, the Friend of Publicans, the Lord of the Sabbath, the Lawgiver in the Kingdom of God.

CHS. V. 12—VI. 49.

a. THE SON OF MAN, THE PHYSICIAN OF THE SICK (CH. V. 12-26).
(Parallels: Matt. viii. 1-4; Mark i. 40-45.—Paralytic: Matt. ix. 1-8; Mark ii. 1-12.)

12 And it came to pass, when he was in a certain city, behold a man full of leprosy;
13 who seeing Jesus fell on *his* face, and besought him, saying, Lord, if thou wilt, thou canst make me clean. And he put forth *his* hand, and touched him, saying, I will: be
14 thou clean. And immediately the leprosy departed from him. And he charged him to tell no man: but go, [*said he,*] and shew thyself to the priest, and offer for thy
15 cleansing, according as Moses commanded, for a testimony unto them. But so much the more went there a fame abroad of him [did the report concerning him go abroad]: and great multitudes came together to hear, and to be healed by him¹ of their infirmi-
16 ties. And [But] he withdrew himself into the wilderness, and prayed [kept himself
17 secluded in the solitary places, and gave himself to prayer]. And it came to pass on a certain day [on one of the days], as he was teaching, that there were Pharisees and doctors [teachers] of the law sitting by, which were come out of every town [village] of Galilee, and Judea, and Jerusalem: and the power of the Lord [*God of Israel*] was pres-
18 ent [*in Jesus*] to heal them. And, behold, men brought in a bed a man which was taken with a palsy [who was paralyzed]: and they sought *means* to bring him in, and to lay
19 *him* before him. And when they could not find by what *way* they might bring him in because of the multitude, they went upon the housetop, and let him down through the
20 tiling with *his* couch [pallet] into the midst before Jesus. And when he saw their
21 faith, he said unto him,² Man, thy sins are forgiven thee.³ And the scribes and the Pharisees began to reason, saying, Who is this which speaketh blasphemies? Who
22 can forgive sins, but God alone? But when Jesus perceived their thoughts, he answer-
23 ing said unto them, What reason ye in your hearts? Whether [Which] is easier, to
24 say, Thy sins are forgiven thee; or to say, Rise up and walk? But that ye may know

that the Son of man hath power upon earth to forgive sins, (he said unto the sick of the palsy,) I say unto thee, Arise, and take up thy couch, and go into thine house. And immediately he rose up before them, and took up that whereon he lay [had been lying], and departed to his own house, glorifying God. And they were all amazed [utter astonishment seized all], and they glorified God, and were filled with fear, saying, We have seen strange [unheard of] things to-day.

¹ Vs. 15.—*Rec.:* ὑπ' αὐτοῦ. To be omitted, as by Griesbach, Lachmann, Tischendorf, Meyer, [Alford,] &c., not only on account of authorities of weight, but also of its uncertain position [om. B., Sin.].
² Vs. 20.—*Rec.:* αὐτῷ, apparently only a gloss [om. B., Sin.].
[³ Ἀφέωνται. The old grammarians are not at one as to the explanation of this form. . . . The correctest view explains it as perf. pass. of the Doric form, related to the perf. act. ἀφέωκα. Winer.]

EXEGETICAL AND CRITICAL.

General Remarks.—Mark and Luke relate the healing of the leper immediately after the Saviour's leaving Capernaum; Matthew, on the other hand, puts it after the Sermon on the Mount. To us the former order appears to be the most exact. A glance at Matt. viii. and ix., compared with Mark and Luke, gives clear indication that in this chapter of the first Gospel many miracles are chrestomathically connected without respect to an exact chronology. As Luke relates (ch. v. 12) that this miracle took place when Jesus was in one of their towns, and Mark (ch. i. 43) that the Saviour drove from Him (ἐξέβαλεν) him whom He had healed (apparently from a house in which the leper had stopped), this of itself proves that this miracle could not have taken place as Matthew appears to indicate to us (ch. viii. 7; comp. vs. 5), on the way between the Mount of Beatitudes and Capernaum, but after His entrance into an unnamed town. From Mark i. 45 it appears, moreover, that Jesus cannot have returned immediately after the healing of the leper to Capernaum, which we should otherwise conclude from Matt. viii. 1–13. From all these grounds we adhere to the order of Mark and Luke. Another view will be found represented by LANGE, *Matthew*, p. 150. *Audiatur et altera pars.*

Vs. 12. **In a certain city.**—The name is not given, but from the connection it appears that it was a town in Galilee which the Lord visited on this journey, undertaken (*see* above) in order to visit Jerusalem at the Feast of Purim, and ending there, and which, therefore, probably lay in the direction of Judæa.

Full of leprosy.—*See* LANGE, *Matthew*, p. 150, and the there cited authors.

Lord, if Thou wilt.—It may be assumed that the faith of the leper had been aroused and strengthened by the report that had gone out concerning Jesus (*see* ch. iv. 37), and which may have extended even to his neighborhood.

Vs. 13. **And He.**—Mark alone adds: σπλαγχνισθείς. The stretching out of the hand, a token of miraculous power, was at the same time a revelation of condescending love, since He by touching a leper might have been accounted Levitically unclean.

Be thou clean.—"Such an imperative as the tongue of man had hitherto never uttered. Thus has hitherto no prophet healed. Thus speaks only He in the might of God who speaks and it is done." (Stier.) That here it is no declaring a leper clean by already discovering the beginning of recovery (VON AMMON, *Leben Jesu*, p. 113), but a miraculous cleansing of a sick man whom the physician Luke designates by πλήρης λέπρας, is self-evident. Why else should silence be imposed upon the man, and to what serves the εὐθέως of Mark?

Vs. 14. **And He charged Him.**—According to Mark even in a sharp vehement tone, ἐμβριμησάμενος, from which, however, it by no means follows that the Saviour displayed any resentment against him whom He had delivered, as Von Ammon will have it.—**To tell no man.**—For the different explanations of this command by earlier and later expositors, *see* LANGE, *Matthew*, p. 151.—In order to judge rightly here we must take special note of the place where, the time when, and the person on whom, the miracle was done. The Saviour finds Himself now in the heart of Galilee, in the land of longing after freedom, of enthusiasm, of insurrection. The fame of His miracles at Capernaum had undoubtedly intensified expectation in a high degree. The one healed was a man who by his coming and crying to Jesus had already shown great courage and strength of faith, who now was bound to his deliverer by bonds of most intimate gratitude, and who doubtless was thereby lacking in the necessary considerateness needful to apprehend when he should speak of Him or be silent. Here, therefore, a sharp reminder was just in place, and we do not, therefore, at all need to assume that the Saviour gave it from fear of being Himself accounted Levitically unclean, on account of His contact with the leper.

But go . . . and offer.—A transition from the *oratio indirecta* to the *directa* not strange in the *usus loquendi* of the New Testament. *See* WINER, § 63, 2. The here-mentioned sacrifice we find prescribed, Leviticus xiv. 10, 21. The Saviour stoops so low as to permit His miracle to be judged by the priest as to its genuineness and completeness.

Εἰς μαρτύριον αὐτοῖς. For the priests themselves, and of what else than of Jesus' Messianic dignity and redeeming power?

Vs. 15. **But so much the more went there a fame abroad of Him.**—The cause Mark gives (ch. i. 45); the delivered one forgets the injunction, 1 Sam. x. 22. Thankful joy makes silence impossible for him. We will not censure his behavior too severely, for it must have come hard to him not to venture to utter the name of his deliverer. It is noticeable also, that in the Gospels we never find the behavior of those who transgress such a command very severely censured. Yet, certainly he did the cause of Christ no service, since, indeed, on every hand the enthusiasm of the people soon reaches such a height that the Saviour holds it advisable to abide in a desert region, where He devotes Himself to solitary prayer. This latter, moreover, is emphasized with peculiar force by Luke, agreeably to his custom.

Vs. 17. **And it came to pass.**—In view of the slender thread by which this narrative is connected with the foregoing one, nothing constrains us to suppose that this miracle took place precisely on this journey and very soon after the former one. The variance mentioned here as existing between the Saviour and the Pharisees, testifies to a later period. (See LANGE, *Matthew*, p. 166.)

Καὶ δύναμις κυρίου.—Not to be understood of the Lord Jesus, who, in Luke, is commonly called ὁ κύριος ("the healing power dwelling in Him revealed itself," Olshausen), but of the Father who operated through the Son. Here also the Divine energy does not manifest itself before faith has shown itself. But while in the foregoing miracle the faith of the sick man himself appears in the foreground, here the sufferer is passive, and is, not only in a bodily but also in a spiritual respect, borne by the faith of those who at any cost will bring him before the feet of the Lord. There is nevertheless no ground for the supposition that he himself did not share in this faith. Would he have been brought wholly against his will in so extraordinary a way to the Saviour? On the contrary, we may name him "infirm in limb but fresh in heart, a chief warrior of faith on the litter." LANGE, *Leben Jesu*, ii. p. 665.

Vs. 18. Παραλελυμένος. The cessation of nervous activity is a disease that is found everywhere in various forms. Sometimes it attacks the whole body, sometimes only parts of it. The old authors named the former ἀποπληξία, the latter παράλυσις; but now I see that they call both παράλυσις. Commonly those who are attacked in all their members by severe nervous debility, are quickly taken away; if not, they live, it is true, but seldom recover their health, and for the most part drag on a miserable life, losing, moreover, their memory. The sickness of those who are partially affected, is, it is true, never severe, but often long and almost incurable." From the physician CONN. CELSUS, *L. iii. Medicinæ*, ch. 27, cited by Heo, "Criticism upon the Life of Jesus by Strauss," ii. p. 20.

Vs. 19. **They went upon the housetop.**—Heo, *l. c.* p. 22, shows that such a thing could be done without any danger. Comp. the valuable statements of WINER, i. p. 283. Even if in this dwelling there was no stair-case outside, a way could have been made over the roof of another to gain access to the place where Jesus was stopping. A breaking up of the roof right over the place where Jesus was, is the less inconceivable, inasmuch as corpses were often in this way removed from the house of death. See SEPP, ii. p. 160.

Vs. 20. **Man, thy sins are forgiven thee.**—Only the most superficial unbelief can from this word, spoken for an entirely definite case, draw the conclusion that the Saviour at all times regarded special suffering as punishment for special sins. Here, however, trouble of conscience appears actually to stand in the way of restoration of the body, and the Saviour, who with unerring glance looks through the outward and inward condition of the sick man, begins in this way to heal his soul.

Vs. 21. **Who is this.**—This very wondering of the Pharisees shows plainly that here not only was forgiveness promised but also bestowed, which was exclusively a Divine work.—**Who can forgive sins, but.**—And, therefore, whoever forgives sins must be infinitely more than man. So think they, much more justly than many later scribes.

Vs. 23. **Which is easier.**—Which was easier could be well made out without trouble. Miracles had other prophets also performed, but really to bestow forgiveness, that belonged to the Searcher of hearts alone, or His highest representative on earth. They think, however, that to *say* that sin is forgiven, is undoubtedly the easiest, particularly so long as inquiry is not made respecting the credentials of the speaker's authority; that they may not, however, doubt longer of these latter, the Saviour accomplishes the miracle of healing, whereby the blessing of the forgiveness of sins is at once manifested and sealed.

Vs. 25. **Took up that whereon he had been lying.**—*Suavis locutio, lectulus hominem tulerat, nunc homo lectulum ferebat.* Bengel.

Vs. 26. **They glorified God.**—An admirable antithesis, the enthusiasm of the people over against the murmuring of the scribes. The dissonances dissolve themselves in harmony, the shadows in light and life.

DOCTRINAL AND ETHICAL.

1. Were we disposed with a certain school of criticism to make a distinction between more difficult and more easy miracles, the healing of the leper, undoubtedly, would belong to the category of the first. To make, by the utterance of a word, a man full of leprosy so clean that he can freely show himself to the most searching eye, is a deed which deserves a place not only in the sphere of the *mirabilia*, but also in that of the *miracula* in the strictest sense of the word. Comp. 2 Kings v. 7. It is no wonder that the Saviour mentions this kind of miracle also with special emphasis to the disciples of John the Baptist as proofs of His Divine mission, Luke vii. 22. Moreover, like all miracles, this kind of healing especially has a symbolical character. As even in the Old Testament leprosy was an image of sin, see Ps. li. 9; Is. i. 6, and elsewhere, so was purification from leprosy a type of the forgiveness of sins. This and the following miracle give us to behold the Saviour as the living image of Him who once said to Israel: I am Jehovah, thy physician, Exodus xv. 26.

2. As the miracle itself is a symbol of the highest blessing of the New Covenant, the confirmation of the miracle takes place altogether in an Old Testament manner. The Saviour is not come to destroy the law and the prophets, but to fulfil them, Matt. v. 17. Moreover, the priests must by the testimony here required of them be hindered from denying afterwards that the man had actually been leprous.

3. The forgiveness of sins bestowed by the Saviour on the paralytic is an unequivocal proof of His celestial dignity. With entire justice, therefore, does Bengel say: *cælestem ortum hic sermo sapit.* But it may justly be called incomprehensible that sometimes men have imagined themselves to have found in the bestowal of this benefit of the Saviour before His death an argument against the indispensable necessity and power of His atoning death. Was not then, considered from the Divine point of view, the sacrifice of perfect obedience, an *eternal* deed? And could He who was to bring it, not bestow the highest gift of grace on a sinner even before this deed was as yet in the fulness of time perfected?

4. The connection between natural and moral evil is undoubtedly placed by the Lord here, but by no means everywhere in a similar manner, in the foreground. Before the assertion was ventured that Jesus was in this respect as much in error as the Jews with their limited notions, it would have been better first to take more account of declarations such as Luke xiii. 5; John ix. 3. Is the Saviour to be regarded as standing below the author of the book of Job, or below Moses, who undoubtedly represents

misfortunes of the people as punishments of the people (Deuteronomy xxviii.), but by no means concludes from personal misfortune as to personal transgression? We must rather assume *here* an especially immediate connection existing between sin and sickness, which, it is true, was not known to the superficial view of the beholder, but doubtless well known to the Searcher of hearts. [The disease was certainly one which is one of the most frequent consequences of sinful profligacy.—C. C. S.] Besides, it might yet be a question, which stood the lower, the Jews who considered misfortune and punishment ordinarily as synonymous words, or so many nominal Christians who will never behold in their own fate a direct retribution of sinful action.

HOMILETICAL AND PRACTICAL.

The cleansing of the leper, the image of the redemption of the sinner.—How the sinner stands with respect to the Lord and the Lord with respect to the sinner: 1. *a.* With an incurable malady, *b.* with awakened faith, *c.* with eager entreaty; 2. *a.* with a mighty arm, *b.* with a compassionate heart, *c.* with an earnest injunction.—Whither Jesus comes there He finds wretchedness; where Jesus finds wretchedness He is ready for healing.—Deep misery, great grace, imperfect thankfulness.—The prayer of faith; how sweetly it sounds; how much it desires; how richly it rewards.—The healing of the leper a revelation of the compassionate love, of the boundless might, of the adorable wisdom of the Saviour.—The redeemed of the Lord called: 1. To show himself, 2. to offer sacrifice, 3. to be silent when the Lord will not have him speak.—The injunction of silence which the Saviour here and elsewhere imposes on the healed: 1. Seemingly strange, 2. fully explicable, 3. most momentous: *a.* for our knowledge, *b.* for our faith, *c.* for our following the Lord.—Offer unto God thanksgiving and pay thy vows unto the Most High, Ps. l. 14.—Obedience is better than sacrifice, 1 Sam. xv. 22.—Unenjoined testifying of Christ: 1. Whence it comes, 2. whither it leads.—Solitary prayer the best refreshment, consolation, strengthening, as for the Saviour so also for all His people.—The healing of the paralytic a proof of the truth of Simeon's prophecy, Luke ii. 34: Christ to the one a Rock of hope, to the other a Stone of stumbling.—The great impulse to hear the word of God why: 1. Then often so great, 2. now often so slight?—The Saviour's miraculous cures the revelation of a heavenly might.—No better service of friendship than to bring the sick to Christ.—Access to Jesus never barred.—Jesus the Searcher of hearts: 1. Over against praying faith, 2. over against murmuring unbelief.—The greatest message of joy for the sinner.—The connection between sin and sickness.—The first accusation of blasphemy in the public life of the Saviour: 1. Its occasion, 2. its injustice, 3. its result.—Two things, both alike impossible with man, both alike easy for the Son of Man. —The authority of the Son of Man upon earth: 1. An extended, 2. a beneficent, 3. a vehemently disputed, 4. a triumphantly vindicated authority.—The mournful coming to Jesus, the believing waiting on Jesus, the God-glorifying return from Jesus.—The result of this miracle, a confirmation of the old word of the sacred poet, Ps. ii. 11, 12: 1. Serve the Lord with fear, 2. rejoice with trembling, 3. kiss the Son —blessed are all they that trust in Him!—The benefit of the forgiveness of sins: 1. Missed with pain, 2. sought with earnest desire, 3. graciously bestowed, 4. unbelievingly denied, 5. convincingly scaled, 6. thankfully enjoyed.—Jesus: 1. The Searcher of hearts, 2. the Physician of the sick, 3. the Bestower of eternal life.

STARKE (on the first miracle):—Temporal things we pray for with conditions, but spiritual things, for the most part, wholly without conditions.—Thus does it often fare with us that we doubt not, to be sure, of the might of God, but do doubt somewhat of His will, 2 Chron. xx. 6, 12.—It is to the almighty Saviour easy to help by a word.—MAJUS:—A faithful servant of Christ must seek neither honor or renown with his works.—QUESNEL:—Sometimes, after Jesus' example, we must prefer to the exercise of Christian love, solitude and prayer.—(On the second) QUESNEL:—The faith, the prayer, and the love of pious people often help towards the conversion of the sinner.—It must needs come inwardly and outwardly to a thorough breaking through all hinderances to Jesus.—MAJUS:—The faith of another may well in some respects be serviceable to one, but to the forgiveness of sins he can give no help at all.—BRENTIUS:—God gives us the most useful and best things always first.—A healthy soul in a healthy body a great benefit.—HEDINGER:—Respecting Divine things and works partisan reason judges as the blind of color.—People of over-brisk wit must be met in love, and with speeches spiced with salt, Col. iv. 6.— CANSTEIN:—The enemies of Christ must often against their purpose further the honor of Christ.

HEUBNER:—Jesus, the Pure, is infected by no impurity.—What would avail us an impotent even though benevolent Saviour?—The healing of the paralytic: 1. Christ begins it in the soul, 2. vindicates it against suspicious thoughts, 3. accomplishes it victoriously and gloriously on the body of the man. —Christ's power to forgive sins: 1. The nature of this power (vs. 20), 2. its certainty (vss. 22–24), 3. its importance (vs. 26).—RIEGER:—Jesus, a Saviour after the heart of the men who have begun to be heartily disposed towards God.—STEINHOFER:— Three states of the soul in reference to the forgiveness of sins: 1. When one seeks it, 2. when one believes it, 3. when one has it.—RANKE:—Happy he who seeks his help with Christ, for: 1. For His love there is no man too mean, 2. for His power there is no misery too great, 3. the condition of His help is for no one too hard.—RAUTENBERG:—Pray for one another: 1. How this is done, 2. what fruit this brings forth.—OTTO:—The leper: 1. The sufferer's lamentation; he entreats: *a.* believingly, *b.* patiently. 2. The Physician's gracious promise; He utters: *a.* words of comfort and promise, *b.* words of might and command.—FUCHS:—The paralytic; theme: the blessing of sickness: it leads: 1. To knowledge of ourselves, 2. to the Physician of our souls, 3. to the exercise of Christian virtues, 4. to the praise of the Lord.—BRASTBERGER:—Forgiveness of sins, the source of all comfort.—AHLFELD:—1. The sick man, 2. his friends, 3. the Physician.—BACHMANN:— Christ's power to forgive sins: 1. A most comforting, 2. a variously misapprehended, 3. an irresistibly attested, 4. a much to be glorified power.—STIER:—Concerning the comfort of the forgiveness of sins: 1. How much we all need it, 2. how Christ has it ready for us all, 3. how each one may receive for himself this comfort.—J. P. HASEBROEK:—We have seen strange things to-day. A glance: 1. At the subject, 2. the means, 3. the fruit of true spiritual recovery, of which this miracle is a type.

b. THE SON OF MAN, THE FRIEND OF PUBLICANS (Ch. V. 27-39).
(Parallels: Matt. ix. 9-17; Mark ii. 13-22.)

27 And after these things he went forth, and saw [noticed, ἐθεάσατο] a publican [tax-gatherer] named Levi, sitting at the receipt of custom: and he said unto him, Follow
28, 29 me. And he left all, rose up, and followed him. And Levi made him a great feast in his own house: and there was a great company of publicans [tax-gatherers] and of
30 others that sat down [were reclining at table] with them. But their[1] scribes and Pharisees murmured against his disciples, saying, Why do ye eat and drink with publicans
31 and sinners?[2] And Jesus answering said unto them, They that are whole need not a
32 [the] physician; but they that are sick. I came not to call the righteous, but sinners
33 to repentance. And they said unto him, Why do [om., Why do[3]] the disciples of John fast often, and make prayers, and likewise *the disciples* of the Pharisees; but thine
34 eat and drink? And he said unto them, Can ye make the children of the bridechamber
35 fast, while the bridegroom is with them? But the [om., the] days will come, when[4] the bridegroom shall be taken away from them, and then shall they fast in those days.
36 And he spake also a parable unto them; No man putteth a piece of a new garment upon an old; if otherwise, then both the new maketh a rent,[5] and the piece that was
37 *taken* out of the new agreeth not with the old. And no man putteth new wine into old bottles [skins]; else the new wine will burst the bottles, and be spilled, and the
38 bottles [skins] shall [will] perish. But new wine must be put into new bottles [skins];
39 and both are preserved.[6] No man also having drunk old *wine* straightway[7] desireth new; for he saith, The old is better [good[8]].

[1] Vs. 30.—*Rec.* om. αὐτῶν.
[2] Vs. 30.—The last words, καὶ ἁμαρτωλῶν, are omitted by Tischendorf on the authority of D., but, as it still appears to us, without preponderating reasons.
[3] Vs. 33.—The interrogative form of the *Rec.*: Διατί, κ.τ.λ., seems borrowed from the parallel passage in Mark. According to the most correct reading in Luke we have not a direct question, but an affirmative objection [Cod. Sin. inserts Διατί.—C. C. S.].
[4] Vs. 35.—*Rec.*: καὶ ὅταν ἀπαρθῇ. The καὶ is found in A., B., D., R., omitted by C., F., L., M., Sin. Retained by Tischendorf, Meyer, Alford, and Tregelles. Put in brackets by Lachmann. The difficulty of giving an exact sense to it, favors its originality. Meyer says: "It *might* be taken as explicative. But it is more congruous with the sorrowful tone of the discourse to take ἐλεύσονται, &c., by itself as an interrupted thought, and καὶ as *and: But there will come* (not be always absent) . . . (namely, when that will be found, which you now miss), *and when the bridegroom shall be taken away*, &c."—C. C. S.]
[5] Vs. 36.—"The latter part of this verse is peculiar, and is to be thus understood: '*if he does, he will both rend the new garment*' (by taking out of the ἐπίβλημα), '*and the piece from the new garment will not agree with the old.*' The common interpretation (which makes τὸ καινόν the nom. to σχίζει, and understands τὸ παλαιόν as its accus.) is inconsistent with the construction, in which τὸ καινόν is to be coupled with ἱμάτιον, not with ἐπίβλημα. In Matthew and Mark the mischief done is differently expressed. Our text is very significant, and represents to us the spoiling of both systems by an attempt to engraft the new upon the old; *the new* loses its completeness, the *old*, its consistency." Alford.—C. C. S.]
[6] Vs. 38.—The clause in the *Rec.*, καὶ ἀμφότεροι συντηροῦνται, is omitted by Tischendorf, principally on the authority of D., L.; apparently these words are borrowed from Matt. ix. 17, and, therefore, justly declared by Griesbach to be at least doubtful. [Omitted by Sin., which, however, differs from D. in having βάλλουσιν instead of βλητέον.—C. C. S.]
[7] Vs. 39.—Whether the word εὐθέως actually stood in the original Greek text may well be doubted, but even regarded as *interpretamentum*, it is certainly entirely in the spirit of the Saviour's words.
[8] Vs. 39.—*Rec.*: χρηστότερος with A., C., R., χρηστός, B., L., Sin. "The sentence seems to have been tampered with by some who wished to make it more obvious, and to bring out the comparison more strongly: εὐθέως being inserted, better to correspond with the fact, and the matter in question, and the comparative substituted for the positive; but the sentence loses much of its point and vigor by the change: the old wine is not *better than the new* (which has *not been tasted*), but merely 'GOOD,' *i. e., good enough,* therefore no new is desired." Alford.—C. C. S.]

EXEGETICAL AND CRITICAL.

Vs. 27. **Named Levi.**—It is superfluous to give here a detailed proof of the identity of Levi and Matthew. Comp. LANGE, *Introduction to Matthew*, § 2, and HERZOG's *Real-Encykl. in voce*. We also assume that our first Evangelist was originally called Levi, but that later, as Simon was named by the Lord, Peter, received from Him the new name of Matthew. If now this was sufficiently known by tradition to the Christians among whom the second and third Gospels first came in use, there was then no longer need that Mark and Luke should instruct them particularly any further in respect to the identity of the person distinguished by the two names. The new name *God's gift*, is certainly doubly fitting in the mouth of the Lord, who in all of His disciples recognized those given by His heavenly Father and now remarked with joy Matthew's willingness to follow Him.

Follow Me.—Nothing hinders us from believing that Matthew had already belonged, for a shorter or longer time, to the most attentive hearers of the Saviour. But now he is called to accompany Him continually as an apostle, and to leave all for His sake; comp. ch. v. 11. The feast which, however, he yet prepares before going, assumes thereby the character of a farewell meal, but serves also at the same time as a testimony of the prompt and thankful temper with which the former publican entered upon his new vocation. Vs. 29. **A great feast in his own house.**—Matthew says in general, ἀνακειμένου αὐτοῦ ἐν τῇ οἰκίᾳ, without speaking expressly of the size of the company or of the honor bestowed on his dwelling. Even in that which he passes over, there reveals itself the humility of the newly-called apostle.

Vs. 30. **Their scribes and Pharisees.**—Luke does not by any means say that these men were among the company at table, for they would then undoubtedly, according to their own opinion, have defiled themselves. We must, on the other hand, conceive the matter thus: that, where Jesus abode, access was forbidden to no one, and that this feast so far bore in some measure a public character. The desire of His enemies to observe the Saviour was doubtless stronger than their disinclination to enter the house of a publican, with whom, moreover, in daily life, they necessarily came from time to time in contact. Matthew, on the other hand, was so little disposed to forbid them that, on the contrary, he now with so much the greater joy admitted those as witnesses of the honor unexpectedly fallen to his lot, who once so deeply despised his station.
Murmured against His disciples.—It is noticeable that they had not ventured to address their fault-finding directly to the Saviour Himself. The defeat suffered by them shortly before at the healing of the paralytic had probably deterred them from coming too frequently in contact with Himself. Perhaps also they addressed the disciples in order to frighten back others from attaching themselves, like Matthew, to such a Lord, who makes no scruple of bringing them into such bad company.
Why do ye eat and drink?—According to Matthew and Mark, the question is asked more with their eye upon the Master, with whom the disciples meanwhile were also eating and drinking. See BENGEL: *ἐσθίετε, plurale, sed Jesum præcipue petebant*, vs. 31. The Saviour answers not merely to shame them and to maintain His own cause, but also especially in order to come to the help of His perplexed disciples, who are not yet in a condition suitably to defend themselves and Him.

Vs. 31. **They that are whole.**—The sententious form of this utterance might half incline us to suppose that we have here before us a proverb from daily life. Certainly it afterwards became such. The sentence has an entirely ironical character, and the here designated "whole" are no others than the ninety-nine righteous who need no conversion, ch. xv. 7.—There is also a holy mockery. See Proverbs i. 26; Ps. ii. 4.—It is noticeable how the Saviour here speaks not only of a Physician, but of *the* Physician, and, therefore, very emphatically, though indirectly, proclaims Himself the Physician of souls. According to Matt. ix. 13, He on this occasion cites also the prophetical proverb, Hosea vi. 6.

Vs. 32. **To call ... to repentance.**—The words εἰς μετάνοιαν are, according to the best reading, only found in Luke. The absolute καλέσαι in Matthew and Mark has, however, no other sense. Repentance is for the just-named sick, the restoration of the health of the soul.

Vs. 33. **And they said unto Him, The disciples of John.**—According to the more exact account of Matthew and Mark, the disciples of John themselves come, in union with the Pharisees, to the Saviour with this objection. Perhaps the Pharisees had incited the disciples of John in this matter to make common cause with them. The antithesis: Jesus at the Feast and John in Prison could not fail yet more to put them out of humor. They avow their surprise without reserve, and the answer received by them perchance embittered them not a little, and may very well have contributed to their giving their master a report through which his singular question and message to the Messiah was hastened, Luke vii.

19. If we find them here united with the Pharisees, we must not forget that these latter on this occasion had not yet appeared as blood-thirsty enemies of the Saviour, but only as crafty liers in wait, perhaps under the guise of interest in the cause of the Saviour. In ascetic rigorism they had with the disciples of John several points of contact. Moreover, momentary coming together is not of itself any actual league of two hostile powers, as we see with the Pharisees and Sadducees towards the end of the public life of Jesus. The Pharisees must have been the more eager to join with the disciples of John, as it must have filled them with great joy if they could bring into public discussion a difference of principles between Jesus and the John who was so highly honored among the people, and, therefore, indirectly oppose the Saviour. Who knows whether this very feast in Levi's house may not have taken place on one of their weekly fast-days? Luke xviii. 12.

Καὶ δεήσεις ποιοῦνται.—Luke alone mentions this element of their question, which circumstance, however, does not warrant us to count it unhistorical. (De Wette.) Fasting and praying are often united as signs of a strict religious life. See Matt. xvii. 21. John had instructed his disciples in the latter also, Luke xi. 1. The fact that Jesus in His answer does not return to this point, may have occasioned Matthew and Mark to pass it over in silence.

Vs. 34. **Can ye make?**—An evident allusion to the last testimony of John the Baptist (John iii. 29), given with a look at his murmuring disciples. He is the Bridegroom, the chief person of the Messianic feast; the time of His walk upon earth is, so long as it endures, a festival for His faithful disciples; yet this time hastens soon to an end.

Vs. 35. **But days will come.**—The Lord intimates a time as coming in which a much greater sorrow impends over His disciples than even that which had now smitten the sorrowing disciples of John. He was not only to be separated from them in body, not only to go away, but to be taken away. Not ἀπελθῇ, said He, but ἀπαρθῇ, from ἀπαιρεσθαι, a word which, in the New Testament, is found only here, and is not unfittingly rendered by "*tear away*." The Saviour certainly would not have used it, had He foreseen nothing but a peaceful dying. Moreover, that He as yet speaks only figuratively and cursorily of His approaching decease, ought not to occasion us surprise, John xvi. 12.

Vs. 36. **No man putteth.**—The special fitness of a parable taken from wine and clothing just here, while He sat at the feast, strikes the eye of itself. Comp., as to the sense, LANGE, *Matthew*, p. 171. Both express the incompatibility of a life in the spirit of the Old and of the New Testament at once. The interpretation, however (Neander), that the Saviour here would teach the great truth that the old sinful nature cannot by outward service of God be really amended, but only through the new birth, is, indeed, very pregnant, but is in conflict with the connection and purpose of this discourse, especially, moreover, in conflict with the words with which the Saviour, according to Luke, concludes His address. No, both parables illustrate the incompatibility of the Old and the New, of the life under the law and that under grace, with the distinction, however, that in the former the new (the cloth) is represented as something added with the intent of mending the old; while, on the other hand, in the second the new (the wine) is more the principal thing, and comes into prominence in its peculiar force and working.

Vs. 39. No man also having drunk old wine—This last sentence belongs to the communications peculiar to Luke, and there is, therefore, no ground for the assumption that the Saviour uttered it on an entirely different occasion (Kuinoel). It is evidently the intention of the Lord to intimate here that the scandal taken by the Pharisees and the disciples of John is intelligible, nay, that in a certain sense it may even be excusable. Accustomed to their old ideas, as to old wine, they can feel as little at home in His principles as any one, who has drunk his old wine with appetite, can at once long for the new. Was it a wonder that they judged so awry concerning His disciples? At the same time there is implied an indirect justification of the Baptist in this respect, that the latter had not dissuaded his disciples from strictness in fasting and praying. If he had done this, standing as he did in other things entirely upon the legal footing, he would only have set a piece of new cloth upon an old garment. He had done (the Saviour intimates) quite as well in leaving everything on the old footing as Jesus would have done ill if He had restrained the free spirit of His teaching and of His disciples within the narrow forms of Judaism.

The old is good.—So does it read literally: χρηστός, while a few Codd. (B., L.) have the comparative, χρηστότερος. It is, of course, understood that in the reading accepted by us also, it cannot be used absolutely, but of a relative and subjective goodness of the old wine as respects the taste of the drinker. The old remains good only so long as one is not accustomed to the new, which in and of itself is better.

DOCTRINAL AND ETHICAL.

1. The calling of Matthew does not only enlarge the circle of disciples with a new apostle, but permits us also to contemplate the image of the Divine Son of Man in a light in which Luke has not hitherto placed Him before our eyes, as the Friend of publicans and sinners. Such a point of view is wholly in the spirit of the third Gospel, which promulgates to us the Pauline doctrine of justification by free grace in the Saviour's own words and deeds. But at the same time this whole narrative is a gospel in miniature; and exhibiting Jesus, as it does, sitting at table in the midst of publicans and sinners, it offers one of the most beautiful symbols of the whole purpose of His coming.

2. Scarcely does the gospel of grace begin to come in its most lovely form into manifestation, when the scandal taken by those who remain standing in a legal position comes also to view in its full strength. The kingdom of God no sooner comes to the spiritually poor, than the rich, who are left empty, are inflamed with intense anger. The Saviour suffers this displeasure to manifest itself, since the revelation of it prepares the surest way for its annihilation.

3. He who exhibits Himself here as the Physician of the sick, makes Himself known also as the heavenly Bridegroom. Here, too, is a point in which the Christology of the fourth Gospel concurs with that of the Synoptics. Comp. John iii. 29 with Matt. ix. 15; xxii. 2. Through this figurative speech beams a cheerfulness with which the deep melancholy of the words immediately following contrasts the more strikingly. The thought of death accompanies the Saviour even to the social meal; and in the as yet weak manifestations of the hatred of His enemies, He sees a presage of all that is afterwards to come to pass. The mysterious intimations of the fourth Gospel (John ii. 19; iv. 37, 38) being excepted, we find here the first, as yet covert intimations of the bloody death which is, before they expect, to sever Him from His disciples. It is noticeable how even in this prophecy of His death a regular climax from a less to a more definite, from a figurative to a literal, statement takes place. Yet we shall soon find occasion to come back more particularly to this.

4. The Saviour gives here an important instruction in reference to fasting. When the Romish Church derives from it the doctrine that He ordained fasts as an abiding usage after His death, this comes from the fact that she overlooks the full force of the promise, Matt. xxviii. 20; for is not the Bridegroom taken away in body simply for this purpose, that He may come again in the spirit and remain forever? Without doubt, there is also a Christian fasting (Acts xiii. 2; 1 Cor. vii. 5), and the Protestant polemics against Rome, which almost represent the matter as if the Saviour had forbidden fasting and as if this abstinence was in no case to be commended, are not free from gross one-sidedness. There is a liberty *for* fasting as well as a liberty *from* fasting, and here also, the apostolic rule, Rom. xiv. 5, holds good. On the other hand, however, we do not venture from the Lord's words to conclude definitely that the Christian, in days of spiritual darkness and spiritual conflict, when he feels the presence of the Saviour little or not at all (Olshausen, Neander), is called to fast. Jesus does not say that in the days when *they* are not with the *bridegroom* they are to fast, but "in the days when the *bridegroom is not with them*." Those days, however, since His glorification, have never returned. How literally, moreover, this prophecy was fulfilled with the first disciples of the Saviour, appears in John xvi. 20.

5. The whole parable of the wine and the bottles throws a clear light upon the distinction between the Old and the New Covenant. It shows how clearly the Saviour was conscious of infusing into mankind a wholly new life, with which the old forms of worship of God were not capable of being lastingly united. So powerful was the new spirit, that it must needs destroy and remove entirely the obsolete form; so peculiar, that every mixture with heterogeneous elements could only injure at once the new and the old. Therefore He could with such assurance commit to time that concerning which He knew that it would certainly come to pass. He could composedly leave those who with good intentions held fast to the old to entertain awhile the opinion that their wine was better than any other. Afterwards they would of themselves come to juster views.

6. The concluding words of the parable in Luke are at the same time the expression of one of the ground-thoughts which the Saviour in the training of His first disciples kept continually in view. He did not take from them the old wine at once, before they were in a condition to relish the new. He began with giving milk, and not at once the strong meat, comp. 1 Cor. iii. 2. Thus does He stand before us, on the one hand, as infinitely more than Moses and ready to break the yoke of the law, on the other hand, as meeker than Moses and concerned not to quench the smoking wick. A wholesome doctrine does this whole passage contain, on the one hand, for those who would weaken the quickening power of the gospel by the imposition of legal fetters, and, on the other hand, for those who wish to lead the

weak brother at once to the highest position of faith and freedom, without allowing the leaven time for gradual development. On the whole, we may perhaps say that Rom. xiv. contains the best practical commentary on this word of the Lord. Never were the *suaviter in modo* and the *fortiter in re* more harmoniously united than here. Comp. the development of this doctrine in LANGE's *Leben Jesu*, p. 679.

HOMILETICAL AND PRACTICAL.

The calling of Matthew the striking image of the vocation to a Christian life: 1. The grace glorified in Matthew, 2. the career appointed for Matthew, 3. the sacrifices required of Matthew, 4. the compensation provided for Matthew, 5. the blessing arising from Matthew, 6. the throne of honor ascended by Matthew (Matt. xix. 28).—The distinction between Levi and Matthew the image of the distinction between the old and the new man. The old man in servitude, the new free, &c.—Follow me! 1. A command of resurrection for the spiritually dead; 2. a word of life for the newly awakened.—Only he who leaves all is on the way to win the highest.—The feast of farewell to the world the feast of communion with the Lord.—Whoever will follow Jesus must not do it sighingly.—Jesus sitting in the midst of publicans: 1. There is His place, 2. there shines His glory, 3. there resounds His voice of peace.—The Wherefore of the natural man in opposition to the words and deeds of the Lord: 1. Its partial right, 2. its actual wrong.—The distinction in principle between the ascetic disciple of John and the free disciple of Christ.—So many who are called Christ's disciples and yet essentially are still nothing but John's disciples.—Whoever becomes only a disciple of John, without passing over into the school of Christ, ends with subjection under the Pharisaical spirit.—Jesus the vindicator of His disciples who are wrongly attacked for His own sake.—The well need not a physician, but the sick: 1. A perpetual rule: a. the well are nothing for the physician, b. the physician cannot be anything for the well; 2. a powerfully arousing voice: a. to the well, that they may become sick in their own eyes, b. to the sick that they may become well.—For whom Christ: a. is not, for whom He b. is certainly come.—The distinction between fasting and prayer on the legal and on the evangelical position.—The fast which God chooses, Is. lviii.—The alternation of the time of mourning and the time of feasting in the life of the disciples of the Lord. 1. Even the time of feasting is followed by the time of mourning; 2. the time of mourning is something transient; 3. the time of rejoicing is abiding.—The conflict between the old and the new in the spiritual sphere: 1. The ground, 2. the requirements, 3. the end of the conflict.—The kingdom of God like to a new strongly-working wine.—The endeavor in the spiritual sphere to unite the incompatible: 1. Often made, 2. never successful, 3. in the end ruinous.—The new spirit aroused by Christ is: 1. Mighty enough to break to pieces all old forms, and also 2. actually destined thereto.—The demeanor of the disciple of Christ towards the old and the new: 1. No mechanical adherence to the old, 2. no premature urging of the new, but 3. a gradual transition, by which the friend of the old is made receptive for the new.—The spirit of the Saviour equally far removed from absolute conservatism and from radical liberalism.—New wine must go into new bottles: 1. So was it in the time of the Saviour, 2. so was it again at the time of the Reformation, 3. so does it remain forever.

STARKE:—God has in the calling of men His own time and way.—*Nova Bibl. Tub.*:—The order of conversion: 1. Jesus beholds the sinner in grace, 2. He calls him by His word, 3. faith follows without delay, 4. and love shows itself active and busy.—The church of God here on earth is a lazaretto and hospital.—*Bibl. Wirt.*:—The old bottles and rags of papistical ordinances fit themselves in no way to the doctrine of the Holy Gospel, therefore no Christian's heart should cleave to the same.—QUESNEL:—We must not teach the souls of the unconverted everything good that we know, but feed them with the truth according as their necessities and the capacity of their spiritual appetite demands.—In religion also, every age needs its own food, 1 John ii. 13, 14.

LUTHER to Staupitz (on vss. 34, 35):—"I let it content me, that I find in my Lord Jesus Christ a sweet Redeemer and a faithful High-priest; Him will I extol and praise so long as I live. But if any one will not sing to Him and thank Him with me, what matters that to me? If it likes him, let him howl by himself alone."

HEUBNER:—Matthew won is himself in turn to win others. So should we!—Syncretism (as they were of old wont to call the mixture of entirely heterogeneous doctrines and institutes distinct in their spirit, after the law which existed in Crete of forgetting all domestic strife when war broke out) endures not long.—LISCO:—The foolishness of making half-work with Christianity.—ZIMMERMANN:—How with the Christian the old must be wholly overcome by the new: 1. The old unbelief and error by the new faith; 2. the old death by the new life; 3. the old habit by the new hunger and thirst.—ARNDT:—All that is old must become new, and then all that is within must be expressed without.—How Jesus out of a publican makes an apostle: 1. The history (vs. 27), 2. the justification of this calling (vss. 28-32).—The Saviour's instructions concerning fasting.—F. W. KRUMMACHER:—Wherefore came Christ?

HAMANN:—Christianity does not aim at patching up all our understanding, will, and all our other powers and necessities even to the potsherds of our treasure, and the main matter does not rest upon any religious theories and hypotheses, else the promise to make all new (2 Cor. v. 17; Rev. xxi. 5), were not then a baptism of Spirit and fire with new tongues.

c. THE SON OF MAN, THE LORD OF THE SABBATH (CH. VI. 1-11).

(Parallels: Matt. xii. 1-14; Mark ii. 23—iii. 6.)

1 And it came to pass on the second sabbath after the first,[1] that he went through the corn fields; and his disciples plucked the ears of corn, and did eat, rubbing *them* in *their*
2 hands. And certain of the Pharisees said unto them,[2] Why do ye that which is not
3 lawful to do [om., to do[3]] on the sabbath days? And Jesus answering them said, Have ye not read so much as this [lit.: Not even this have ye read?], what David did, when himself was a hungered [he himself hungered], and they which were with
4 him; How[4] he went into the house of God, and did take and eat the shewbread, and gave also to them that were with him; which it is not lawful to eat but for the priests
5 alone? And he said unto them, That the Son of man is [a, V. O.] Lord also of the sab-
6 bath. And it came to pass also on another sabbath, that he entered into the synagogue and taught: and there was a man [there, ἦν ἐκεῖ ἄνθρωπος] whose [lit.: and his] right
7 hand was withered. And the scribes and Pharisees watched him, [to see] whether he would heal[5] on the sabbath day; that they might find an accusation [or, whereof to
8 accuse him[6]] against him. But he knew their thoughts, and said to the man[7] which had the withered hand, Rise up, and stand forth in the midst. And he arose and
9 stood forth.[8] Then said Jesus unto them, I will ask [I ask[9]] you one thing; Is it lawful on the sabbath days to do good, or to do evil? to save [a] life, or to destroy *it?*
10 And looking round about upon them all, he said unto the man, Stretch forth thy
11 hand. And he did so: and his hand was restored whole[10] as the other. And they were filled with madness[11]; and communed [or, consulted] one with another what they might do to Jesus.

[1] Vs. 1.—If our critical conscience allowed us to expunge entirely the puzzling δευτεροπρώτῳ from the text, we should certainly have disburdened ourselves in the most convenient way of one of the most desperate *cruces interpretum*. However, although a not inconsiderable number of testimonies is for the omission, and, therefore, the possibility that we have here before us only an old marginal gloss, must be conceded, yet we cannot avoid supposing that this ἅπαξ λεγόμενον has been expunged by some only out of exegetical perplexity, *ignoratione rei*, as Bengel expresses himself. Respecting the presumable sense, see *Exegetical and Critical* remarks. [Ins., A., C., D., R.; om., B., L. Cod. Sin. has ἐν ἑτέρῳ σαββάτῳ. Meyer regards it as spurious. Tischendorf inserts it; Lachmann and Alford put it in brackets; Tregelles omits it.—C. C. S.]

[2] Vs. 2.—*Rec.:* αὐτοῖς. Critically too weakly supported. [Om., Sin.]

[3] Vs. 2.—*Rec.:* ποιεῖν, as *interpretamentum* correct, but as reading suspicious. [Supported, however, by Sin.—C. C. S.]

[4] Vs. 4.—*Rec.:* πῶς εἰσῆλθεν. Πῶς rightly, as it appears, omitted by Tischendorf, according to B., D., Cantabrig., and some cursives. It is more intelligible how πῶς should have been interpolated from Matthew, than why it should have been omitted, if it had actually stood here originally.

[5] Vs. 7.—With Lachmann and Tischendorf we give the preference to θεραπεύει over θεραπεύσει. The latter appears borrowed from Mark iii. 2. [Cod. Sin. has θεραπεύει.—C. C. S.]

[6] Vs. 7.—*Rec.:* κατηγορίαν αὐτοῦ with A., R., D. has κατηγορῆσαι. B., S., R., Cod. Sin.: κατηγορεῖν.—C. C. S.]

[7] Vs. 8.—'Ἀνδρί. *Rec.:* ἀνθρώπῳ. Meyer's remarks *ad loc.* are entirely correct. "Τῷ ἀνδρί was omitted in consequence of the following τῷ (as in D., Cant.), and then the hiatus supplied by τῷ ἀνθρώπῳ according to vs. 6 and Mark iii. 3."

[8] Vs. 8.—Entirely without reason are the last words: ὁ δὲ ἀναστὰς ἔστη, omitted in De Wette's translation of this passage.

[9] Vs. 9.—*Rec.:* ἐπερωτήσω. With Tischendorf, [Alford, Tregelles,] we prefer the present ἐπερωτῶ, which is supported by B., L., [Sin.,] 157, and five ancient versions, and heightens the vividness of the whole scene. By the same authorities, [including Sin.,] the reading εἰ, instead of τί, is strongly supported.

[10] Vs. 10.—The ὑγιής which the *Rec.* subjoins to ἡ χείρ αὐτοῦ, is doubtless only an interpolation from the similar passage in Mark. [But Tischendorf and Lachmann, and Alford, following them, omit the whole clause, ὑγιής ὡς ἡ ἄλλη, in Mark iii. 5, supported by A., B., C., D., [Sin.,] and 3 other uncials. It seems more likely to have been introduced from Matthew, where its genuineness is undoubted. In Luke it is omitted by A., D., D., Sin., and 6 other uncials.—C. C. S.]

[11] Vs. 11.—"It does not appear that this word can ever mean, as in the former editions, 'madness,' rage of a senseless kind. . . . The proper meaning, 'senselessness,' 'wicked folly,' must be kept to. *See* Ellicott's note on 2 Tim. iii. 9." Alford. I give this note, although I am not persuaded that the not difficult transition from "utter senselessness" to "madness" has not been made in this passage. It is hard to see how they could have been "filled" with "senselessness," "unwisdom," as Wiclif has it, otherwise than through rage.—C. C. S.]

EXEGETICAL AND CRITICAL.

Δευτεροπρώτῳ.—Without here entering into a statement or *crit*[*ique*?] of all the different explanations of this designation, we will here only briefly justify the view taken by ourselves. So much appears at once, that this Sabbath was no ordinary but an extraordinary one, and that it must have fallen in the month Nisan, since it was not till this month that the barley was ripe. In the second half of this month fell the passover. But if the miracle of the loaves and fishes took place before the second passover in the public life of the Saviour, John vi. 4; and if the plucking of the ears, according to all the Synoptics, preceded the miracle, the second-first sabbath must have fallen between the feast of Purim, John v. 1, and the passover, ch. vi. 4. Since now the word δευτεροπρώτῳ of itself points us to a *terminus a quo*, it appears that the question what terminus is here meant cannot be answered more naturally than by WIESELER, *Chron. Syn.* pp. 226–234, that it was the first sabbath after the beginning of the second year in a cycle of seven years. We understand it, therefore, of the first sabbath in Nisan, with which the Jewish church-year began, and believe that in relation to that of the former year, which was the first in the week of years, it is named the second. That such a division of years was known among the Jews is sufficiently plain from Dan. ix. 24, only it cannot be absolutely demonstrated that they were accustomed also to number the years according to their place in the cycle, and the first sabbath in each year according to the cyclical yearly number. This, however, is so simple and natural that little can be objected against it. But that here, according to the view of Scaliger, which is followed by Kuinoel and De Wette, the first sabbath after the second passover is meant, can only be assumed if with them the feast of the Jews, John v. 1, is regarded as a passover. Bengel's view, that here the sabbath before the new moon in Nisan, 14 days before the passover, is meant, is indeed apparently supported by his reckoning, that on this day 1 Sam. xx. 18–42 had been read, and that, therefore, the Saviour's answer, when He appealed to 1 Sam. xxi. 6, stood in connection with the pericope just heard. But Wieseler justly remarks that the present division of the Parashas and Haphtharas is of later origin. Other views are presented in De Wette and Meyer. For the history of the exegesis, comp. WOLF, *in curis;* WINER, art. *Sabbath,* &c. Upon the grammatical signification of the word δευτεροπρώτῳ, see HITZIG, *Ostern und Pfingsten,* p. 19.

Vs. 1. He went through the cornfields.— Comp. LANGE, *Matthew,* p. 217. Apparently the Lord had found the morning's spiritual nourishment in the word of the Scripture in the synagogue, but of earthly bread His disciples have as yet enjoyed nothing, or, at least, so little that they feel the need of instantly allaying their hunger. A striking proof of the πτωχεύειν of the Saviour, 2 Cor. viii, 9. They make use of the right which the law, Deuteronomy xxiii. 25, gave to the needy. On the position of a pure Mosaism there was certainly no breach of the sabbath, since certainly their act could not be called a daily *labor;* they followed rather the precept of the later Rabbins, not to fast on the sabbath, but by enjoyment of food and drink to strengthen themselves. See MAIMONIDES, *Schabb.,* ch. 30. But the Pharisees who followed the Saviour, perhaps for the purpose of spying out whether He would go any further than the usual sabbath-day's journey, saw here, according to their bigoted views, work, and so a criminal breach of the sabbath.

Vs. 2. Τινὲς δὲ τῶν φαρ.—According to the first two Gospels they address themselves to the Lord, according to Luke more directly to the disciples; they may have done both. It is entirely agreeable to the spirit of the Pharisees to make Jesus Himself answerable for the conduct of His disciples; on the other hand, if there were several present, some may have turned directly to the guilty ones. At all events, the Saviour takes up the cause of His own, and the way in which He does it, at the same time gives us to recognize the holy sabbath-rest of His soul.

Vs. 3. What David did, 1 Sam. xxi. 6.—If we read, Mark ii. 26, that this took place at the time of Abiathar the high-priest, this appears to be a lapse of the pen for Abimelech. The example was in the highest degree fitted to show how necessity knows no law, and the more strikingly as the Rabbins themselves said: "In the sanctuary there is no sabbath, the slaughtering expels the sabbath." See Lightfoot on the passage.

Vs. 5. The Son of Man.—As the sabbath must give way before the temple-service, so must sabbath and temple-service both give way before something greater (μείζων in Matthew), namely, the Son of Man. If the day of rest and glorifying God must yield even to the rational inhabitant of earth, how much more might the Son of Man, the Redeemer and the Ideal of mankind, have dominion over the sabbath-service! The true sabbath-breakers were those who would sacrifice man to save the sabbath. As to the rest, vs. 5 appears in Luke very abrupt (De Wette), but this does not warrant us with Cod. D. to place this declaration of the Saviour after vs. 10, and still less on this testimony alone to receive the addition: "τῇ αὐτῇ ἡμέρᾳ θεασάμενός τινα ἐργαζόμενον τῷ σαββάτῳ εἶπεν αὐτῷ· ἄνθρωπε, εἰ μὲν οἶδας τί ποιεῖς, μακάριος εἶ· εἰ δὲ μὴ οἶδας, ἐπικατάρατος καὶ παραβάτης εἶ τοῦ νόμου." In and of itself this utterance is by no means unworthy of the Lord, but it is not probable that at this time any one in the Jewish land would have labored unpunished, and, moreover, with a good conscience [on the sabbath], and quite as little that the Saviour, by such a declaration, exposed to various abuse, would have needlessly angered His enemies. If we do not choose to assume that the narration was invented *a Marcionita quodam* (Grotius), or that it was suggested by the words of Paul, Rom. xiv. 22, 23 (Neander), yet at least it may be supposed that it was inserted by some one who fully agreed with the view commended by the apostle in the above passage.

Vs. 6. On another sabbath.—In all probability on the one immediately following. Luke, to be sure, does not expressly say this, but all the Synoptics connect this miracle immediately with the foregoing, which could the more easily happen if we assume with Wieseler, p. 237, that the day after the δευτεροπρώτῳ was again a sabbath, and that, therefore, not seven but only one day intervened between the two sabbaths. Then it is also intelligible how Mark and Matthew do not even definitely distinguish the days, and how the Pharisees so shortly after their discomfiture come to renew their attack.

A man.—According to Jerome on Matt. xii. 10, who takes his account from the Hebrew Gospel of Matthew, *quod a plerisque vocatur Matthaei authenticum,* it was a mason, who entreated to be healed that he might not have to beg. The allegorical manner in which this father sets forth this person as a type of Judaism, which in the days of Jesus had become quite incapable of building the spiritual temple of God in Israel, does not of itself justify us in doubting the truth of this account, which may actually proceed from a pure tradition.

Vs. 7. Παρετηροῦντο.—The snare was not laid without cunning. The healing of a sick man by any one who was accustomed to render help to sufferers, might with better title call forth the charge of breaking the sabbath than plucking ears during a walk, as this was at all events no actual work. There even existed a controversy between the schools of Hillel and Shammai, whether even the comforting of the sick on the sabbath was to be regarded as allowed. See SCHÖTTGEN, *Horæ Hebr.* 4, p. 123.

Vs. 9. I ask you.—One must enter fully into the spirit of the embittered enemies in order to feel the crushing force of the question. It contains a searching antithesis (intelligible, however, to them alone) between the beneficent plan of the Saviour and the murderous intent of the assailants. He says in other words: "Which really breaks the sabbath, I, who am preparing myself for a work of beneficent healing, or you, who in secret cherish a purpose of murder against Me, the innocent one?" He will thus not only impress upon them that not to do good is of itself to do evil, but at the same time show that they cannot conceal themselves before Him. This whole address of the Saviour, moreover, united with His searching look (Mark iii. 5) is a practical commentary on Paul's word (Eph. iv. 26). The word which Matthew (vs. 14) alone has in addition, appears by Luke to be more correctly used on another occasion. See ch. xiii. 10; xiv. 5.

Vs. 11. 'Ανοίας.—Rage made them mad; comp. 2 Tim. iii. 9 and the passage in proof from the classic literature in Meyer.—The Æolic optative form expresses in a striking way the uncertainty and wavering of their deliberations. See WINER, N. T. Gram. 6th ed. p. 275 : "What they might perchance do with Jesus," quid forte faciendum videretur (balancing the different possibilities in a wavering frame of mind).

DOCTRINAL AND ETHICAL.

1. The first sabbath miracles which we here see the Lord perform, spontaneously suggest the question in what relation He placed Himself to the Law and the Old Covenant. On one hand it must be acknowledged that He actually held Himself bound to the law of Moses, and from His first visit to the temple even to His last passover, showed that in this respect also He wished to fulfil all righteousness. The words of the Sermon on the Mount, Matt. v. 17, remained His principle of life, so that He could composedly leave it to time for the new spirit awakened by Himself to destroy also the old form. But as little as He freed Himself or His own from obedience to the commandments of God, just as little could He endure to have this weakened by human ordinances. And this was actually done when the Pharisees and others explained and enjoined the commandment of the sabbath in such a way, that it must often appear as if man had been made for the sabbath. The thirty-nine different activities which they regarded as forbidden on the sabbath, were an invention of trivial narrowness, not commanded by the letter of the law, and in manifold ways at variance with its spirit. The Saviour maintains the spirit of the law precisely when He incurs in their eyes the guilt of a formal breach of the sabbath.

2. As the Lord of the sabbath He shows, on the one hand, the obligation, and, on the other hand, the freedom, of His disciples in reference to the sacred day of rest. The Lord, in visibly distinguishing the sabbath from other days, and on this day visiting the synagogue, gives us plainly to see that His disciple is also enduringly under obligation to hallow to God a weekly day of rest. But, on the other hand, He also passes through the corn, performs labors of love, and powerfully vindicates the maxim : " Necessity knows no law." A mechanical Judaistical celebration of Sunday is, therefore, by His example as little favored as a reckless contempt of Sunday. The Christian also, the one anointed by the Holy Spirit, is a lord of the sabbath, and where the spirit of the Lord is there is liberty, but also order, obedience, glory given to God, and fear of offending a weak brother.

3. When the Lord, appealing to Scripture, asks: "Have ye never read?" this is not only an accommodation to the prejudices of the Jews, but also an expression of His principle to remain in all things faithful to the standard here established. David's son mirrors Himself in the history of His illustrious ancestor. While He with compassionate care vindicates the interests of His own, He shows here at the same time the most exalted self consciousness. He feels that in Him yet more than in the temple the Father's glory dwells. And if He does not at once give it to be understood that He will make use of this His exalted dignity and abrogate the law of the sabbath and the temple-service, He actually did at least here what He says in the fourth Gospel, John v. 17 : " My Father worketh hitherto, and I work."

4. In the Saviour's sabbath miracles also His exalted character reveals itself. When once a prophet was despised by Jeroboam, the hand of the presumptuous king was dried up (1 Kings xiii. 4). Jesus heals a withered hand, and is far from punishing the hands recklessly lifting themselves against Him. His miracles are no punishments but benefits, and even though the enemies of God's kingdom think to destroy life, the King's delight is to preserve it.

HOMILETICAL AND PRACTICAL.

General point of view for both narratives: the Son of Man, the Lord of the sabbath, who as such 1. rules in unrestricted might, 2. serves in love.

SPECIAL :—Vs. 1. The celebration of the sabbath in the bosom of nature.—Enjoyment of nature on the sabbath: 1. Tasted, 2. embittered, 3. vindicated. —The Divine harmony of the sabbath disturbed by the discord of sin.—The hostile looks which beset even the most innocent movements of the disciples of the Lord.—The Scripture, authority in every point of religious controversy.—David, a prophetic type of evangelical freedom, in the midst of legal servitude.—The Scripture, no shew-bread in the sanctuary, for the priests alone.—Our Lord, His position towards a twofold view of the sabbath, that of freedom and that of servitude.—The dry morsel, with quietness, is better than, &c. (Prov. xvii. 1.)—The Son of Man, the true Son of David, the true Lord of David.—How the sabbath may be disturbed even without working. —Vs. 6 seq. No corruption in the Israelitish worship keeps Jesus back from visiting the synagogue. —The hostility of the Pharisees augmented by every discomfiture.—The afflicted one in the house of the Lord : 1. What he seeks, 2. how much more he finds. —Healing of the sick man, furthered : 1. By the malice of enemies, 2. by the compassion of the Lord, 3. by his own faith.—Evil thoughts in the house of the Lord : 1. Entertained, 2. penetrated, 3. frustrated.— Jesus overcoming His enemies by 1. the questioning of righteousness, 2. the powerful word of love.—It is permitted to do good on the sabbath.—Holy anger and compassionate love united in one look of the Lord.—The greater Jesus' love the deeper the hate of His enemies.—The madness of enmity : 1. It thinks that it can destroy Jesus ; 2. it does not once see how deeply it condemns itself.—No faith is demanded that is not also crowned.—The synagogue the theatre of the glory of our Lord: 1. His impartial judgment, 2. His heavenly knowledge of hearts, 3. His compassionate sympathy, 4. His delivering might, 5. His forbearing long-suffering.

BOTH TOGETHER :—Two sabbath-works in the life of the Lord ; difference and agreement between these two: 1. Difference of acts but oneness of end ; 2. difference of enjoyment but oneness of consecration ; 3. difference of strife but oneness of triumph.—The Christian sabbath celebration: a. Negatively: 1. no absolute equalizing of all days, 2. no slothful inactivity; *b.* positively: 1. glorifying of God in the house of prayer and in the temple of Creation, 2. labor of love for others.—The sabbath-rest of the Saviour like that of the Father: *a.* An active, *b.* a holy, *c.* a blessed sabbath-rest.—The Lord of the sabbath and the slaves of the law.—The sabbath a day on which the Saviour: 1. Refreshes His friends, 2. vanquishes His foes, 3. helps His afflicted ones, and by all this 4. advances the coming of the kingdom of God.

STARKE:—Love and need know no law.—MAJUS: —It is a shame to those who will be masters of the Scripture when they do not know what is written in the law.—QUESNEL:—The use of holy things, when it takes place through love, can never desecrate them, because God's love sanctifies all things.—*Nova Bibl. Tub.*:—Those must be of evil disposition to whom even benefits can be an occasion of persecution, and even good an inducement to evil.—CANSTEIN:—The solicitousness of Christ's enemies to hinder His kingdom shames the sluggishness of the children of God.—OSIANDER:—The papistical corner-miracles (Winkel-wunder) are mere cheatery; Jesus did His miracles publicly before the world.—We are not to mind the blasphemy of the godless when we do what our vocation brings with it.—When the truth shines brightest hardened ones nevertheless are thereby not amended, but only made worse and more venomous, 2 Tim. iii. 13.—With despisers of the truth, even miracles will accomplish nothing.

HEUBNER:—The excessively anxious care of the Jews in the old temple for the sabbath is a reproof to Christians.—Zeal for religion without love is an abomination.—ARNDT:—Jesus the Friend of the church, since He 1. uses the means of the church, 2. furthers the ends of the church.

CALVIN:—"*Monemur etiam, cavendum esse, ne cærimoniis tribuendo plus quam par est, quæ longe pluris sunt coram Deo, et quæ præcipua legis Christus alibi vocat* (Matt. xxiii. 23), *effluere sinamus.*"

---

d. THE SON OF MAN, THE LAWGIVER IN THE KINGDOM OF GOD.
CHAPTER VI. 12-49.

a. THE CHOICE OF APOSTLES (Vs. 12-16).
(Parallels: Matt. x. 2-4; Mark iii. 13-19.)

12 And it came to pass in those days, that he went out into a [the] mountain to pray,
13 and continued all night in prayer to God. And when it was day, he called *unto him* his disciples: and of them he chose twelve, whom also he named apostles [that is, mis-
14 sionaries]; Simon, (whom he also named Peter,) and Andrew his brother, James and
15 John, [and¹] Philip and Bartholomew, [and, V. O.] Matthew and Thomas, James the
16 *son* of Alpheus, and Simon called Zelotes [*i. e.,* the zealot], And Judas *the brother* [the son, V. O.²] of James, and Judas Iscariot, which also³ was the traitor [became traitor].

¹ Vs. 14.—For the insertion of καί—καί before the names James and Philip also, among others, we have B., D., L., [Sin.]. In the same way it appears that this particle must be read before all the following names, vss. 15, 16. Luke, therefore, does not give the names of the apostles in pairs, but *singulatim*. [Before Ἰακ., vs. 15, om. καί A., B., D.², 11 other uncials, itm. καί D.¹, Sin., L. Considering that καί is so strongly supported before all the other names, it is evident that if it is to be omitted here, it is a mere taking of breath on the part of the evangelist, and does not introduce a pair.—C. C. S.]

[² Vs. 16.—"Usually, and I believe rightly, rendered Jude *the brother* of James, see Jude, vs. 1, and note." Alford. Winer supports the same opinion as Alford, Meyer the same as Van Oosterzee. It appears to me that the former is preferable.—C. C. S.]

³ Vs. 16.—Καί here has not sufficient manuscript testimony (*see* Tischendorf). At least it gives room for the conjecture that it is taken from the parallels in Matthew and Mark. [Om. B., L., Sin.—C. C. S.]

EXEGETICAL AND CRITICAL.

Vs. 12. **In those days.**—From the comparison with Matthew and Mark it appears that the choice of apostles took place at a time in which the fame of the Saviour had mightily increased in Galilee. The healing of the man with the withered hand was followed by a number of miracles (Matt. xii. 15-21; Mark iii. 17 *seq.*). Even from Tyre and Sidon do the throngs stream together. The voice of the supplicating sick unites itself with the cry of the demons. With difficulty does He escape the throng, withdraws Himself to the solitary mountain, and finds in communion with the Father the rest which earth gives Him not.

In prayer to God.—It is of the greatest moment that the choice of the apostles is preceded by a night of prayer, and that it may thus be denominated the fruit of the most immediate communion of the Son with the Father. An echo of this prayer we hear in the heartfelt supplication of the Lord for all those given Him by the Father. (John xvii. 6-9.)

Vs. 13. **His disciples.**—According to the definite account of Luke, we are to conceive the matter thus, that the Saviour caused a great number of the disciples to come to Him, and now out of this number called the twelve apostles. We have, therefore, to distinguish clearly this choice of apostles, on the one hand, from the later mission of the apostles indicated by Matt. x. in giving their names (vss. 1, 5), on the other hand, from the earlier relation in which at least some of these men had already stood to Jesus. First had they become friends, then disciples of the Lord in a wider sense, afterwards are they called as apostles to leave all (Luke v. 10, 11, 27, 28), but now united in a distinctly formed circle of apostles. And even within this there are still grades in respect of their intimate communion with Christ. Even as apostles He calls them at first servants (Matt. x. 24), afterwards friends and children (John xiii. 33; xv. 15), finally even brethren (John xx. 17).

Whom also He named apostles.—The complete college of the twelve did not, therefore, first arise after Jesus' ascension by gradual selection from a wider circle of His adherents (Schleiermacher, Weisse), but it was founded by Jesus Himself. Only on this supposition do we understand the character of the Sermon on the Mount as a dedicatory discourse, as well as the connection between this act of the Saviour and the previous solitary prayer. Although John does not mention the formal choice of apostles, yet it appears from John vi. 70; xv. 16, that he by no means contradicts it. It is true that the name apostle in other places in the New Testament is not exclusively given to the twelve (*see* Gal. i. 19; Acts xiv. 14; Hebr. iii. 1). But the Saviour Himself never, so far as we know, used this name otherwise than as the designation of the twelve to whom He entrusted the apostolic function.

The apostolic catalogue of Luke agrees almost entirely with that of Matthew; *see* LANGE *ad loc.*, who also communicates particularly what is most worth knowing respecting the names of each one. We wish chiefly to suggest the heavenly wisdom of the Saviour in the manner in which they have been paired. Although Luke does not give the names in pairs but individually (*see* vs. 14), yet from the comparison with other specifications of the names it is easy to see how the pairs must have been arranged.

a. **Peter and Andrew.** In all catalogues of the apostles Peter stands at the head. The man full of fire and energy, the son of Jonah (a dove), who is to become a rock of the doves, the mouth of the apostolic circle, as John constitutes its heart; of fiery spirit, as the latter of deep sensibility; ever ready for combat, as the latter is patient in enduring—and by his side Andrew, his brother, whose personality is less prominent, but who brought his brother to Jesus (John i. 42), and afterwards appears a single time as the fourth intimate companion of the Saviour along with the three specially chosen ones, Mark xiii. 3.

b. **John and James,** his brother, sons of Zebedee and own cousins of the Lord, the first prophet and the first martyr among the twelve. The question why they received the name Boanerges appears to have been best answered by Theophylact, who says this name designated them, ὡς μεγαλοκήρυκας καὶ θεολογικωτάτους. Against the view that this name was meant to be a censure of their fiery zeal (Luke ix. 51 *seq.*), maintained by Gurlitt, *see* LANGE in the *Studien und Kritiken*, 1839, i. Comp. *Leben Jesu,* ii. p. 696.

c. **Philip and Nathanael,** the son of Tholmai (Bartholomæus), two friends (John i. 45 *seq.*), the one of Bethsaida, the other of Cana in Galilee. Nathanael is known for his uprightness (John i. 47), Philip for his frankness, through which he ventured to open every difficulty to the Lord (John vi. 7; xii. 22; xiv. 9). Two men involved in similar prejudices, but also animated by like love to the truth, belonged in the apostolic circle together.

d. **Matthew and Thomas.** In this fourth pair the name Matthew in Luke and Mark stands first, but he himself gives himself a second place, perhaps in the same feeling of humility in which he has added to his name the phrase ὁ τελώνης. Both are apparently of Galilee. If Thomas was of a heavy, melancholy temper, on the other hand Matthew, as we know from the narrative of his calling (Luke v. 27, 28), was distinguished by the capability of easily surmounting great difficulties; and while the one, moreover, was disposed to solitary thought, the other appears from his former calling to have gained a certain facility in intercourse with men. Thus does one supplement the other.

e. **James,** the son of Alphæus or Cleophas, and **Lebbæus,** surnamed Thaddæus. The former certainly is not one and the same with James, the brother of the Lord (John vii. 5). The other, agreeably to his two names, לֵב, *cor*, חַם, *mamma*, a courageous, spirited man. It is unnecessary to understand here two different persons, and far less can we believe (Von Ammon) that some apostles, because they did not come up to the Saviour's expectations, were even in His life replaced by others. No, Lebbæus and Thaddæus-are one person; however, the question remains: what was the proper name of the man who possessed this double surname? Here Luke (vs. 16) shows us the way with his : καὶ Ἰούδαν Ἰακώβου, only we must not understand by this the brother but the *son* * of an otherwise unknown James. From John xiv. 22 we know that besides Judas Iscariot there was yet another Judas among the twelve. This similarity of name may have been the cause why he was not commonly called Judas, but by one of his surnames, as indeed Jerome with reason called him the Three-named.

f. **Judas Iscariot and Simon Zelotes,** or Canaanites. These two names, the one Greek and the other Hebrew, signify "The Zealot." The germ of zealotism, which first developed itself in the last Jewish war, already existed in the days of the Saviour; perhaps Simon had already appealed to the law of the Zealots and belonged to the followers of Judas Gaulonites, before he became an apostle. Apparently the Lord placed the high-spirited, vigorous man beside the dark form of Judas Iscariot, on account of the moral preponderance which Simon might exercise upon his character, but also because Judas could most easily unite himself with a brother who had already previously striven for a political and outwardly theocratical end. It is noticeable, moreover, that Judas Iscariot, in Luke, is not coupled with Simon Zelotes, but with Judas, the son of James. We need not, however, conclude from this alone that tradition, in respect to the pairing of the apostles, had already become uncertain. We incline the rather to suppose that the Saviour, who quite early penetrated the character of Judas, did not always associate the same companion with him. By change, the danger of being infected by Judas was averted, and from different sides an influence was exerted for the ennobling of his character. The vigorous, hearty Lebbæus might for his part have been as well fitted for that as the courageous zealot.

As to the choice of the apostles in general, comp. an admirable dissertation by LANGE in his miscellaneous writings, part iv. p. 158, and the authors cited by HASE, *Life of Jesus.* Some names of apostles which are mentioned in the Gemara, namely, Nazar, Nabi, Bohi, are of later and fabulous origin, and can, therefore, by no means be turned as weapons against the evangelical tradition. Respecting the conjectural fate and deeds of these twelve, which were very early embellished by tradition, *see* WINER *in voce.*

DOCTRINAL AND ETHICAL.

1. The calling and training of His apostles was one of the most momentous parts of the work which the Father had committed to the Son. With a little

* [*See* Notes on the text.—C. C. S.]

reflection, we can by no means be surprised that the Saviour (John xvii. 4–6) defines the declaration: τὸ ἔργον ἐτελείωσα, κ.τ.λ., more precisely by adding almost immediately afterwards: ἐφανέρωσά σου τὸ ὄνομα τοῖς ἀνθρώποις, οὓς δέδωκάς μοι, κ.τ.λ. The ἔργον of His public life was, as it were, concentrated in the training and guidance of His elect witnesses. He Himself could indeed only lay the first foundations of the extended temple of God, and therefore He was obliged to look around for skilful workmen who should carry the temple up. Therefore, even during His life, He gathered a little company whose spiritual head He was, first visibly, afterwards invisibly. Therefore does He begin immediately after His baptism, to prepare for the vocation of the twelve. To their training the greatest part of His time and energies is devoted, and even when He acts upon the people, He has regard at the same time to their peculiar needs. His death even has to contribute to their education, since by it their earthly expectations are at the same time slain; and even after His resurrection He continues for yet forty days to labor personally in their training, until finally they are fully capable and prepared to receive the promised Holy Spirit. We have accordingly here approached the proper centre of His public life.

2. The choice of apostles is one of the most brilliant proofs of the adorable wisdom of the Saviour. 1. He chooses *simple-minded*, yet already measurably *prepared*, men. To some has the Baptist's instruction, to others the toilsome fisherman-life, or the active publican's office, been a more suitable school of preparation than a scientific preparation by Hillel or Shammai. 2. *Few*, yet very *diverse*, men. He works intensively before He begins to labor extensively on the kingdom of God that is to be founded. He will rather perfect some than only partially train many. Accordingly He trains them with and also by means of one another, and shows how fully His gospel accommodates itself to every point of human development, and how it is perfectly calculated for every one's individual necessities. 3. Some *prominent* to go with several less noticeable men whom He gathers together into a little company. So far as we can see, the beautiful figurative language used in 1 Cor. xii. 14–27 is also completely applicable to the organism of the apostolic circle. Had all been as distinguished as a Peter, a John, and as afterwards a Paul, the unity would have suffered by the diversity, and the one light would have been broken into altogether too many colors.

3. With this wisdom the preëminence which He gives to three of His apostles above the others is not in conflict. Unquestionably the preëminence is undeniable (Mark v. 37; ix. 2; Matt. xxvi. 37), but it was at the same time relative, natural, beneficent. *Relative*, for it by no means excluded sharp rebuke of personal failings and close observation of the necessities of each single one (Matt. xvi. 23; Luke ix. 54, 55). Not Peter and the sons of Zebedee, but Andrew and Philip, make the Lord acquainted with the request of the Greeks (John xii. 22). The former we find sitting with the three on the Mount of Olives (Mark xiii. 3), with the latter the Lord counsels as to how He shall feed the people (John vi. 5), *Natural*, on account of their individuality and the need of the Son of Man for personal intimacy. A Christ who, among twelve intimate associates, had not one bosom-friend, we should scarcely understand or be able to love. *Beneficent*, for the training as well of the elect three for their special work as of the other nine, who must thus have learned to see that as well the Saviour's vocation as the preëminence accorded by Him was only free grace.

4. Quite as little difficulty does the primacy of Peter offer, which we, understanding it in a sound sense, do not need to deny. Only one-sided ultra-Protestantism can assert that the Lord did not concede to Peter the slightest preëminence. Certainly it is not accidental that his name in all the apostolic catalogues is the first; and that the word of the Saviour (Matt. xvi. 18) refers not alone to the confession but also to the person of Peter, is scarcely to be denied. Yet over against this, observe: 1. That the Lord also most sharply rebukes or humbles the highplaced apostle; 2. that his prerogatives are communicated to all the apostles, see Matt. xviii. 18; John xx. 22; 3. that the other apostles and first churches conceded to him no primacy in the Roman Catholic sense (Acts xi. 12; ch. xv.; Gal. ii. 11); 4. that he did not claim it for himself (1 Peter v. 1–4); 5. that even the most ancient church fathers do not acknowledge it in respect to him. See J. ELLENDORF, *The Primacy of the Roman Popes*.

5. As respects, finally, the choice of Judas, we are to avoid, on the one hand, the Docetic conception that Christ had at His very first meeting with him seen through the future traitor, and chosen him entirely *ad hoc;* on the other hand, the Ebionitic one, that He erred like a common man, and found a devil where He had expected an angel. According to the first, we must pity Judas as the victim of an unavoidable destiny, while the other view presents not indeed the love, yet so much the more the wisdom, of the Saviour in an unfavorable light. The only correct view is this, to see in the choice of Judas, the highest stake of adventurous love, which finds in him the germ for much that is excellent, and does all that is possible to win him wholly, but soon discovers that the evil is much stronger than the good, John vi. 69, and now expressly warns him, Matt. vi. 19–21; Mark vii. 21–23; Luke xii. 16–20; repeatedly leaves him free to go, John vi. 67; xiii. 27; with long suffering endures him, John xiii. 11; finally, with majesty removes him, but now henceforth can look back even upon the son of perdition with tranquillity, because He has not on his account the least thing with which to reproach Himself, John xvii. 12. Living and dying, therefore, even Judas preserves the rank of a witness of the Lord, so that the scoff of unbelief upon this point, from Celsus on (see *Origen Contr. Celsum*, ii. p. 11) even to Strauss and later than he, rebounds on the head of its own authors. Comp. the weighty judgment of Lavater on Judas, communicated by NIEMEYER, *Charakteristik der Bibel*, i. pp. 83, 86.

6. The result has justified the wisdom of the Saviour in the choice of apostles most admirably. The kingdom of heaven founded by so frail and weak instruments on earth, stands as a work of God in the strictest sense of the word before us. When we compare what the twelve originally were with what they afterwards became, we obtain the convincing proof of the power of the grace of the Lord, but see at the same time how the Holy Spirit works not for the destruction but for the purifying and ennobling of each particular individuality.

7. "First they become disciples, then apostles; not at once are they sent out to preach, and not at once into all the world. Christ was no enthusiast, to have called His apostles without instruction, and as it were with unwashed hands to the ministry. Dur-

ing a long time did He instruct them with great diligence, and carefully train them up for their future vocation, and yet upon the apostles a special miracle of the Holy Spirit was to be shown forth! How much more does it become us to insist that the servants of the Lord shall right earnestly study with persevering diligence and holy eagerness to learn in order to become fit to teach." Chemnitz.

HOMILETICAL AND PRACTICAL.

The Lord will have witnesses of His manifestation; He chooses them, He trains them.—The choice of apostles an image of the choice of grace.—The choice of apostles prepared for with care, brought into effect with wisdom, and by the result most admirably vindicated.—Important steps must be prepared for in prayer.—Difference and unity among the first witnesses of the Lord.—The grace of the Lord: 1. How low down it seeks its elect; 2. how high it lifts its elect.—" Diversities of gifts, but the same Spirit," 1 Cor. xii. 4-6.—" Ye have not chosen Me, but I have chosen you," John xv. 16.—One must already be a disciple in order to be able to testify as an apostle.—The apostolate and the later ministry: 1. Precedence, 2. equality.—The preacher of the gospel not less called than the apostles to be His witness.—The word of the Saviour, "Ye also shall bear witness" (John xv. 27), addressed to every preacher of the gospel. Thereby: 1. The extent of his office is defined ; 2. the nobility of his office is confirmed ; 3. the conflict of his office is declared ; 4. the power of his office is assured ; 5. the blessing of his office is prophesied ; 6. the requirement of his office is renewed.

STARKE:—The affairs of the kingdom of God we should prefer to all convenience and earthly repose.

CRAMER:—Teachers and preachers must not crowd themselves into their office, but wait till they are sent by Christ, the Lord of the harvest.—*Bibl. Wirt.:* —We should not form such an idea to ourselves of the church of Christ on earth, as if it could be without hypocrites and ungodly.—ARNDT:—The names of the twelve apostles: 1. Their choice ; 2. their importance. We may: *a.* not overvalue, *b.* but quite as little fail to recognize their incomparable preëminence. " Their preëminence in the church has been, moreover, through all centuries in such wise recognized, that never has an important teacher of it, never has a martyr or a reformer, ventured to attribute to himself the appellation of an apostle, as little as any one since then has again borne the name of Jesus. Only high-minded fanatics have now and then chosen twelve apostles and two and seventy disciples from their adherents, but all these sects have long since fallen under the judgment of history (and the Irvingites ?)."

BURGER:—The apostolic catalogue. I. Historically. 1. What was the work of the apostles? 2. What were the men whom the Lord chose to this work ? 3. Why did He choose just such men ? II. Apologetically. 1. These apostles the best witnesses of the Lord ; 2. proofs for the divinity of the gospel ; 3. even the traitor witness of the truth.— VAN OOSTERZEE:—The catalogue of the apostles: I. *A source of knowledge.* This catalogue fills 1. a brilliant chapter in the history of mankind, 2. a sublime chapter in the history of Jesus, 3. a noteworthy chapter in the history of the Divine government. II. *A support of faith.* It witnesses of 1. the truth, 2. the sublimity, 3. the divinity, 4. the imperishableness, of the gospel. III. *A school of life.* It displays the image 1. of the condition, 2. of the intended work, 3. of the prerogatives, of the Christian church even in our days.

β. THE SERMON ON THE MOUNT (VSS. 17-49).

17 And he came down with them, and stood in the plain [having come down with them], he stood upon a level place, ἐπὶ τόπου πεδινοῦ], and the [a] company of his disciples, and a great multitude of people out of all Judea and Jerusalem, and from the seacoast of Tyre and Sidon, which came to hear him, and to be healed of their diseases ;
18 And they that were vexed [harassed] with unclean spirits : and they[1] were healed.
19 And the whole multitude sought to touch him : for there went virtue out of him, and
20 [he, V. O.²] healed *them* all. And he lifted up his eyes on his disciples, and said, Bless-
21 ed be [*are*] ye poor; for yours is the kingdom of God. Blessed *are ye* that hunger now :
22 for ye shall be filled. Blessed *are ye* that weep now : for ye shall laugh. Blessed *are ye,* when men shall hate you, and when they shall separate you *from their company,* and shall reproach *you,* and cast out your name as evil, for the Son of man's
23 sake. Rejoice ye in that day, and leap for joy : for, behold, your reward *is* great in
24 heaven : for in the like manner did their fathers unto the prophets. But woe unto you
25 that are rich ! for ye have received your consolation. Woe unto you that are full ! for
26 ye shall hunger. Woe unto you that laugh now ! for ye shall mourn and weep. Woe unto you [om., unto you³], when all men shall speak well of you ! for so did their
27 fathers to the false prophets. But I say unto you which hear, Love your enemies, do
28 good to them which hate you, Bless them that curse you, and[4] pray for them which de-
29 spitefully use you. And [om., And] unto him that smiteth thee on the *one* cheek offer also the other; and him that taketh away thy cloak forbid not *to take thy* coat also.
30 Give to every man that asketh of thee; and of him that taketh away thy goods ask

31 *them* not again. And as ye would that men should do to you, do ye also to them like-
32 wise. For if ye love them which love you, what thank have ye? for sinners also love
33 those that love them. And if ye do good to them which do good to you, what thank
34 have ye? for sinners also do even the same. And if ye lend *to them* of whom ye hope
   to receive,[5] what thank have ye? for [6] sinners also lend to sinners, to receive as much
35 again. But love ye your enemies, and do good, and lend, hoping for nothing again;
   and your reward shall be great, and ye shall be the children [lit.: sons] of the Highest:
36 for he is kind unto the unthankful and *to* the[7] evil. Be ye therefore[8] merciful [or,
37 compassionate], as your Father also is merciful. [9] Judge not, and ye shall not be
   judged: condemn not, and ye shall not be condemned: forgive, and ye shall be for-
38 given: Give, and it shall be given unto you; good measure, pressed down, and shaken
   together, and running over [or, heaped up],[10] shall men [they] give into your bosom.
   For with the same measure that ye mete withal [measure with] it shall be measured to
39 you again. And he spake a parable unto them; Can the blind lead the blind [a blind
40 man lead a blind man]? shall [will] they not both fall into the ditch? The disciple is
   not above his [the, V. O.[11]] master: but every one that is perfect shall be as his mas-
41 ter [when completely trained, every one will be like his master]. And why beholdest
   thou the mote that is in thy brother's eye, but perceivest not the beam that is in thine
42 own eye [but the beam in thine own eye dost not perceive]? Either [12] how canst thou
   say to thy brother, Brother, let me pull out the mote that is in thine eye, when thou
   thyself beholdest not the beam that is in thine own eye? Thou hypocrite, cast out first
   the beam out of thine own eye, and then shalt thou see clearly to pull out the mote
43 that is in thy brother's eye. For a good tree bringeth not forth corrupt fruit; neither
44 [yet again [13]] doth a corrupt tree bring forth good fruit. For every tree is known by
   his own fruit. For of thorns men do not gather figs, nor of a bramble bush gather they
45 grapes. A good man out of the good treasure of his heart bringeth forth that which
   is good; and an evil man out of the evil treasure of his heart [om., treasure of his heart,
   V. O.[14]] bringeth forth that which is evil: for of the abundance of the [his] heart his
46 mouth speaketh. And why call ye me, Lord, Lord, and do not the things which I
47 say? Whosoever cometh to me, and heareth my sayings, and doeth them, I will shew
48 you to whom he is like: He is like a man which built a house, and digged deep [build-
   ing a house, who dug deep], and laid the foundation on a [the] rock: and when the
   [a] flood arose, the stream beat vehemently upon that house, and could not shake it;
49 for it was founded upon a rock [because that it was well built [15]]. But he that heareth,
   and doeth not, is like a man that without a foundation built a house upon the earth;
   against which the stream did beat vehemently, and immediately it fell [in a heap, συνέ-
   πεσεν]; and the ruin of that house was great.

---

[1] Vs. 18.—The *Rec.*: καί before ἐθεραπεύοντο has A., B., [Sin.,] D., L., Q., and 33 other Codd. against it. The independent sense which this omission gives to vs. 18 directs the attention still more definitely to these possessed, as a special class of sick. [This omission of καί is accepted by Lachmann, Meyer, Tregelles, and Alford, but disapproved by Tischendorf.—C. C. S.]

[2 Vs. 19.—This insertion of "He" before healed, appears unnatural, and seems to proceed from an unnecessary anxiety to emphasize the voluntariness of the Saviour's healings.—C. C. S.]

[3] Vs. 26.—Ὑμῖν is here, as before γελῶντες, vs. 25, spurious. [Om., ὑμῖν, vs. 25, B., Sin., K., L., S.; ins., A., D., E., 10 other uncials. Om., ὑμῖν, vs. 26, A., B., Sin., E., 15 other uncials; ins., C., D., Δ.—C. C. S.]

[4] Vs. 28.—The [E. V.] has "*and* pray, &c.:" the καί is critically untenable.

[5] Vs. 34.—The reading of Tischendorf, λαβεῖν, appears preferable to that of Lachmann, ἀπολαβεῖν. [Sin. has λαβεῖν.—C. C. S.]

[6] Vs. 34.—The *Rec.*: καὶ γὰρ οἱ ἁμ., κ.τ.λ., appears to be taken from the preceding verse. [Cod. Sin. omits γάρ.—C. C. S.]

[7 Vs. 35.—'Επὶ τοὺς ἀχαρίστους καὶ πονηρούς, "the unthankful and evil." One class designated by two qualities; not "the unthankful and the evil," two classes.—C. C. S.]

[8] Vs. 36.—*Rec.*: γίνεσθε οὖν οἰκτίρμονες. Οὖν appears to have crept in quite early on account of its connecting the sentences more exactly. [Lachmann, Tregelles, and Alford omit the οὖν, supported by B., D., L., Ξ., [Sin.]; Tischendorf and Meyer retain it, supported by A., R., X. Meyer remarks: "How easy to overlook it before the syllable ΟΙ! An internal ground of omission, considering the congruousness of οὖν to the sentence, is hardly to be assumed."—C. C. S.]

[9] Vs. 37.—At the beginning of vs. 37 καί is to be retained, in the second clause, on the contrary, to be expunged (against *Rec.*). [All the critics agree in retaining the first καί, opposed only by D. But Tischendorf and Alford retain the second καί also, supported by B., L., S., X., Sin.—C. C. S.]

[10] Vs. 38.—The repeated καί—καί before the last two adjectives, can without danger to the purity of the text very well be dispensed with. [Om., Sin.]

[11] Vs. 40.—*Rec.*: διδάσκαλον αὐτοῦ. [Αὐτοῦ approved by Tischendorf, om. by Lachmann, Tregelles, Alford, Cod. Sin.—C. C. S.]

[12 Vs. 42.—Ἢ πῶς, κ.τ.λ. *Rec.* approved by Lachmann, bracketed by Tregelles. Cod. Sin. gives πῶς δὲ δύν., κ.τ.λ.—C. C. S.]

[13] Vs. 43.—Tischendorf has rightly received into the Greek text the word πάλιν, which was bracketed by Lachmann. Weighty authorities support it, and many appear to have omitted it only because it is not also found in the similar passage, Matt. vii. 18. [Ins., Cod. Sin.]

[14] Vs. 45—We read with Tischendorf: ὁ πονηρὸς ἐκ τοῦ πονηροῦ προφέρει τὸ πονηρόν. What more the *Rec.* has are pleonastic supplements, whose genuineness is doubtful. [Tischendorf's reading is confirmed by Cod. Sin.—C. C. S.]

¹⁸ Vs. 48.—*Rec.*: τεθεμελίωτο γὰρ ἐπὶ τὴν πέτραν. Comp. Matt. vii. 25. One cannot help supposing that the reading defended by Tischendorf: διὰ τὸ καλῶς οἰκοδομεῖσθαι αὐτήν, although only supported by a few manuscripts (D., L., and cursives), was the original one, which, however, quite early was supplanted by the *Rec.*, from a harmonistic striving. [Tischendorf's reading is not supported by D., but by B., L., Ξ., and Cod. Sin., the latter, however, having οἰκοδομῆσθαι. —C. C. S.]

GENERAL SURVEY.

1. As to the question whether the Sermon on the Mount was twice delivered by the Lord, or whether we meet in Matthew, chapters v.–vii.; Luke vi. 20 –49, with the same discourse, the views have always been different. We feel obliged to concur with the interpreters who maintain the identity of the discourse. Its commencement, contents, course of thought, and conclusion, certainly agree remarkably, in Matthew and Luke. Each is followed immediately by the healing of the centurion at Capernaum, and although the one mentions a mountain and the other a τόπος πεδινός, yet even this discrepancy can be reconciled. [Robinson and Stanley both describe the Tell Hattûn, which the Latin, though not the Greek tradition, connects with the delivery of the Sermon on the Mount, as consisting of a ridge, from which rise two horns or peaks, known as the Horns of Hattûn. If the tradition is correct, as Stanley is disposed to regard it (and even Robinson finds nothing contradictory to it in the situation of the hill), our Lord ascending the ridge into one of the peaks, would have gone up "into the mountain," and coming down afterwards, for greater convenience, upon the ridge, would have been upon a τόπος πεδινός, without having left the mountain.—C. C. S.] If Jesus appears, according to Matthew (ch. v. 1) to have sat, according to Luke (ch. vi. 17), to have stood, yet this latter may be regarded as having been the case, some moments before the beginning of the discourse, while as yet the sick were coming to Him, and the people were sitting down to hear. The Jewish teachers were certainly accustomed to impart their instruction sitting, and even if Matthew's report were unknown to us we should have to supplement that of Luke in this way: that Jesus, first standing, soon sat down. In this way the two accounts can be brought into unison. Many single proverbial expressions of this discourse the Saviour may often without doubt have repeated, but that He, at different periods in His life, should have made use of the same commencement and the same conclusion of His discourse we consider as on internal grounds improbable. It would only be conceivable if we assume with Lange that the Sermon on the Mount, as given in Luke, immediately followed that of Matthew, and that the former was an esoteric one, delivered on the summit of the mountain before the disciples—the second an exoteric one, delivered on the same day on a less elevated part of the mountain. See the more detailed developments of this view in his *Leben Jesu*, ii. pp. 568–570. Nevertheless even in this view it is conceded that "the two discourses in their fundamental ideas and essential substance are one discourse and two different redactions."

2. As to the questions, when, where, before whom, and for what purpose, this discourse was held, we believe that we find the most exact account in Luke (*contra* Meyer). Altogether unfounded is the assumption that it was uttered even before the calling of Matthew; on the contrary, it was, as far as we know, the first extended discourse which Matthew, after his own calling and after the setting apart of all twelve apostles, heard. From this very fact it is explicable that he assigns it a place so early in his gospel, although it at once strikes the eye that Matthew here binds himself to no strict chronological sequence; as indeed even his statement, ch. iv. 23–25, refers not obscurely to a point of time not in the beginning, but about in the middle of the public life of our Lord. Even the open opposition to Phariseeism and the not obscure declaration of the Saviour's Messianic dignity in this discourse appear to intimate a later point of time. As to the place, *see* LANGE, *Matthew*, p. 100. Comp. JOSEPHUS, *De Bell. Jud.* iii. 108. Among the hearers we have to distinguish the nearer circle of his μαθηταί, including the just-called apostles and the wider circle of the people, who also listened to it, and left the Mount in holy rapture. Matt. vii. 28; Luke vii. 1. From the substance of every utterance in it, it is perfectly easy to conclude to which part of this numerous audience it was especially directed, and as respects the purpose of the whole discourse: "Jesus must undoubtedly, after He had gradually gained so great a following and attracted so much attention, and after He had by parables intensely excited the expectation of His hearers, have certainly at last been obliged for once frankly to declare what He meant. All His working hitherto took the form of menus,— the end had not yet been manifested. The sick He had healed, the dead He had raised, of a βασιλεία τοῦ Θεοῦ, which He had come to found, He had spoken in enigmatical images. The people had opened their ears; all, more clearly or more obscurely, more purely or more impurely, had surrendered themselves to the hope that Jesus was the promised Messiah. They followed after Him; they were willing to take part in His kingdom: should He therefore now any longer keep silence? must He not give to this wavering, perplexed mass definite form: Such and such is the nature of my kingdom; this is its form, this the true disposition for it; these are my requirements?" (Ebrard.)

3. The praise of the greatest originality and exactness in the report of the Sermon on the Mount we do not give to Luke (Schneckenburger, Olshausen, B. Bauer, and others), but to Matthew. We believe that the more systematic arrangement of the thoughts in Matthew does not proceed from him, but from the Saviour Himself. The view of Sepp (II. p. 261), that Matthew as well as Luke does not properly communicate anything here but "the complex whole and sententious summary of all the didactic deliverances, as it were the themes of the sermons which our Lord, during His whole Messianic activity, delivered," is too arbitrary to receive any particular critical notice. He has no other ground than "the explications which the godly Catharine Emerich von Dülmen gave" in her visions, an authority which the Protestant can hardly acknowledge.

4. The question why Luke communicates the Sermon on the Mount in a much less regular and perfect manner than Matthew, may be differently answered. It may be that Luke only found this short extract in his written authorities (Ebrard), or that oral tradition preserved this instruction of the Saviour in more than one form (Meyer a. o.) In no case must we overlook the fact that Luke has indeed proposed as his end exactness in his accounts, but not complete-

ness, and might pass over much, e. g., of the controversy against Phariseeism, Matt. v. 20–48, which for his friend Theophilus was unnecessary and perhaps not even intelligible. Other portions of the Sermon on the Mount he communicates in another connection, and it is therefore very possible that the Saviour delivered them more than once. On the other hand, he has even in his shorter redaction some additional sayings of the Saviour, which perhaps Matthew communicates in a more correct connection. (Accordingly Stier himself, in reference to Luke vi. 45 compared with Matthew xiii. 52, is obliged to acknowledge "that Luke has made a mistake." *Reden Jesu,* i. p. 302.) By no means is the opinion well grounded (Bauer, Schwegler) that the redaction of the Sermon on the Mount in Luke bears a thoroughly Ebionitic character. *See* below in the exegetical remarks.

5. The peculiar character of the Sermon on the Mount comes in Luke also into sufficiently clear relief. Even 1. considered in and of itself, the substance as well as the form is incomparably beautiful. It is perhaps possible, in respect to some particular sayings which are here found, to adduce parallels from Rabbinical, nay, from heathen authors, but the whole is inimitable, and the spirit which streams through all its parts and joins them all together is completely unattainable. 2. In its historic connection, without being an actual consecratory or inaugural discourse of the Twelve, it is nevertheless in the highest degree adapted for the frame of mind and need of the moment. It was intended, more than had hitherto been the case, to draw the attention of a numerous throng to His person and His work, and by the very reason of its great difference from the mode of teaching of the Pharisees and Scribes, it called forth of itself an impression all the deeper. If we consider it 3. finally as well in relation to the Old Testament as to the chief substance of the Gospel in its strict sense, it soon becomes clear to us that the requirements here uttered are at the same time the expression of the eternal spirit of the Mosaic law, from which even the Saviour could not absolve. And lastly, if we give ear to the Beatitudes, the distinction in principle between Law and Gospel comes at once unmistakably to light. The doctrine of faith and grace is here, it is true, not announced in many words, and so far there is truth in the pregnant expression of Hase: "The Sermon on the Mount is not the completion but the one side of Christianity." On the other side, it must however be remarked, that silence as to that which the people from their position could not yet bear, is by no means a contradiction of it; that the doctrine of sin and its wretchedness is here manifestly presupposed; that even in Luke there is no want of intimation as to the Saviour's person (vss. 22, 40–46), and that therefore R. Stier is not without reason in saying (*Reden Jesu,* i. p. 312) : " Oh, ye rationalists, who are so willing to hear the ethics of the Sermon on the Mount, hear, hear, I pray you, also its dogmatics!" —The Sermon on the Mount is the Magna Charta of the kingdom of God, and at the same time places before the eyes of all the disciples of the Lord the unchangeable principles by which the new life of faith must be guided. It is a practical commentary on the word of the Baptist, Matt. iii. 8. Whoever finds difficulty in the ethical requirements of the Sermon on the Mount has an unhealthy, and whoever will hear of no truth of salvation which is not contained in the words of the Sermon on the Mount has a superficial, a one-sided Christianity.

6. Since the Sermon on the Mount in Luke is, in respect to form, inferior to that of Matthew, it is not possible to give so organic a disposition of its contents as was the case in the notes on Matthew; but if any one is disposed, in order to make the general survey, at least to attempt a division, we may distinguish

I. The Salutation of Love (vss. 17–26).
II. The Requirement of Love (vss. 27–38).
III. The Importunity of Love (vss. 39–49).

FIRST SECTION : *Salutation of Love.*

(VSS. 17–26.)

EXEGETICAL AND CRITICAL.

Vs. 17. **And He came down with them.**—We have therefore to conceive the Saviour as surrounded by a threefold circle of hearers ; the first indicated by μετ' αὐτῶν (the recently chosen Twelve), the second described as an ὄχλος μαθητῶν, and this latter again closed around by πλῆθος πολὺ τοῦ λαοῦ, who come partly even from beyond the boundaries. Comp. Matt. iv. 23–25.

Vs. 19. **For there went virtue out of Him.**—Comp. Luke v. 17 ; viii. 46. As therefore the choice of apostles is preceded by silence and prayer, so is the Sermon on the Mount immediately preceded by miraculous works. Here in fullest significance is the sublimest symbolism of the kingdom of heaven whose fundamental laws He will forthwith reveal to the world. The might of deed must support the might of the word. So is the faith of the just-chosen ones strengthened and the people prepared for hearing.

Vs. 20. **And He lifted up His eyes.**—It belongs to the peculiarities of Luke that he in some passages gives us to feel the eloquence of the look of Jesus even when this is not indicated by others. See here and in ch. xxii. 61.

Blessed are ye poor.—"This is indeed an admirably sweet friendly beginning of His doctrine and preaching. For He does not proceed like Moses or a law-teacher with command, threatening, and terrifying, but in the friendliest possible way, with pure, enticing, alluring, and amiable promises" (Luther). The question whether the most original and exact form of the Beatitudes is to be found in Matthew or Luke appears to us to admit an answer in favor of the former. This gives us the right even at this point to call to our help as a legitimate *subsidium interpretationis,* the τῷ πνεύματι of Matthew. That the Saviour means no other than the spiritually poor is quite as plain as that those at this day were commonly found among the poor in worldly respects; comp. James ii. 5. Luke is here as far as in chs. xii. or xvi. from the thought of conceding to external poverty, considered in and of itself, even the least advantage. With the confessedly universal and Pauline character of his Gospel such an Ebionitic tendency is incompatible. Comp. moreover LANGE on the passage, and upon the inner connection of the different Macarisms, KIENLEN in the *Studien und Kritiken*, ii., 1848.

Vs. 21. **Ye that hunger now—ye that weep now.**—According to what is said above, only spiritual hunger and trouble for sin and the suffering arising from the same can be understood. As only such come with eager longing to the kingdom of God, so could God's kingdom and truth only come to these. In answering the question how satisfaction and comfort should fall to their lot, we have not only to bear in mind the word of the kingdom of heaven, which was perfectly to satisfy their spiritual necessities, but especially also the new spiritual life, which was to be bestowed upon them in communion with the King Himself.

Vs. 22. **Blessed . . . when men shall hate you.**—Comp. Matt. v. 11, 12. A noticeable climax is found in the description of this hatred in Luke, *first*, as the foundation of all that follows, ὅταν μισήσωσιν, then the severing of the thus hated from general and special intercourse (ὅταν ἀφωρίσωσιν), and moreover, alongside of this negative persecution, also the more positive and more malicious (καὶ ὀνειδίσωσιν), finally, the formal excommunication from the synagogue (καὶ ἐκβάλωσιν); comp. John ix. 34; xvi. 2.—And all this is not purely personal injuriousness, but is an opposition in principle against the principle of faith represented by them: "*and cast out your name as evil;*" to be understood of the name which they bore as Jesus' disciples. What, however, alone can make such a suffering the ground of a beatitude is the adjoined: "*for the Son of Man's sake.*" Not every ignominy, only the ignominy of Christ gives the ground for joy and renown. Comp. Acts v. 41; Heb. xi. 26.

Vs. 23. **Rejoice ye.**—Comp. Acts xvi. 25; Romans v. 3; viii. 35-39. "Great is your reward in heaven. *Deus est debitor noster, non ex congruo, sed ex promisso.*" (Augustine.) At the same time an indirect intimation that they for their approved faithfulness must not expect too great a reward on earth. It is especially noticeable how the Saviour at once places His scarcely-called apostles in one rank with the prophets of the Old Testament, and in the demand that they should be ready for His name's sake to suffer shame, shows the sublimest self-consciousness. Such intimations must also, above all, not be overlooked by those who are paying attention to the Christology of the Synoptical gospels. As to the rest, it scarcely needs pointing out how completely the idea that they were to suffer in such society, surrounded by such a νέφος μαρτύρων, was adapted to strengthen the courage and the spiritual might of the witnesses of the Lord.

Vs. 24. **But woe unto you.**—The force and application of these four οὐαί, which are only found in Luke, is, after what has been said, self-evident. Had the Saviour been able to find among the rich also the spiritually poor, He would not the less have pronounced them blessed. The rich Chuza with his wife (ch. viii. 2, 3), or the family of Bethany (ch. x. 38-42), had surely never for an instant drawn this οὐαί upon themselves. But if even a Nicodemus ventured only in the night to come to Jesus, if the rich young man went away sad, and if there were innumerable proofs of the truth of the declaration Matt. xix. 23, 24, no wonder that here there proceeded forth a terrific Woe over the rich, who for the greater part were self-satisfied and proud characters; sumptuous livers who suffered a pious Lazarus to pine away at their gate, unrighteous ones who stinted the wages of the poor (Luke xvi. 20; James v. 4). These threatenings also are, therefore, directed against a moral degeneracy, which however at that time was a chief sin of the rich and powerful. A poor man who merely on account of his neediness should have made claim to the kingdom of heaven, must have been pride itself, have been no truly hungry soul, but one spiritually full, who should be left empty. Comp. Luke i. 53; Rev. iii. 17, and from the Old Testament, Is. lxv. 13, 14; Hosea ii. 9. — **Ye have received your consolation.** — "As something perishable" (De Wette); comp. Matt. vi. 2; Luke xvi. 25.—The retribution which here is first described only as a coming short of the expected consolation is in the two following threatenings, πεινάσετε, πενθήσετε καὶ κλαύσετε, represented as a direct feeling of hunger, pain, and sadness.

Vs. 26. **Woe, when all men shall speak well of you.**—Is this Woe like the first three addressed to unbelievers (Meyer), or to the disciples, in opposition to the Beatitudes of vss. 22, 23? (De Wette, Kuinoel, and most.) Without doubt the former is demanded by symmetry. Those who accept the praise of the hostile world are compared by the Saviour with the ψευδοπροφῆται; but disciples who could so far forget themselves as to take any special pains to secure the praise of *all* men, would be properly no longer disciples. The Saviour first begins again in vs. 27 to address Himself directly to the circle most nearly surrounding Him. It is, however, of course, self-evident that the rule here expressed by the Lord can be easily applied to His first disciples and to all further witnesses of His name.

As to the rest, there is not the slightest ground respecting the four Woes in Luke "to assign them to the later formation of the later tradition" (Meyer), in other words, to deny that the Saviour Himself uttered this fourfold judgment. If one is not disposed to assume that He delivered it immediately after the seven Beatitudes of Matthew, there is yet nothing against the supposition that the Saviour first uttered this Woe on another occasion, and that Luke has (very fittingly) taken it up into his abridged redaction. Respecting all the Beatitudes, comp. the admirable homily of HERDER in his complete works.

DOCTRINAL AND ETHICAL.

1. There are moments in the public life of the Lord in which, if possible, even more than at others, He does everything to prepare the coming and founding of His kingdom in Israel. To such culminating points of the light of His glory belongs also that to which we have now drawn near. The calling of the twelve apostles is in the fullest sense of the word a decisive step towards His goal. A rich fulness of miracles shown forth urges at the same time the enthusiasm every moment higher. An incomparable sermon exalts and intensifies this impression. Even before the beginning of the Sermon on the Mount it is already shown into how wide a circle the report of His words and deeds had gone out, and certainly this circle now enlarges itself to a yet more significant extent. Within a few hours there is concentrated thus a work of love which at another time might have been divided through several days. It is the hour of the preparation for a great decision. That Israel did not know and use such a καιρὸν τῆς ἐπισκοπῆς increases its shame and guilt.

2. There exists an inward connection between the choice of apostles and the Sermon on the Mount. Now when the heralds of the King are appointed, the Magna Charta of the kingdom of heaven is proclaimed. All which the recently called hear is, on the one hand, adapted to inflame the holy fire on their altar, on the other hand, fitted to extinguish the fire that is fed by the stubble of earthly expectations.

3. The Beatitudes present to us, even in the imperfect form given in Luke, a clear mirror of the kingdom of heaven. The first and the last of the Beatitudes preserved in the evangelical history (Luke i. 45; John xx. 29) agree in this, that they promise salvation to those who believe even without seeing. Between these two Beatitudes stand those of the Sermon on the Mount in the midst. They reveal to us the glory of the King of the kingdom of heaven as the *Christus Consolator* of suffering and sorrowing mankind (an admirable work of art representing this by Ary Scheffer); comp. ch. iv. 18, 19. They give us to see the final purpose of the kingdom of God as in the highest degree adapted to satisfy the deepest spiritual interests of man. They present before us the image of the citizen of heaven, as well as the character that is peculiar to him, and the destiny that stands before him. The highest blessings of the kingdom of heaven, perfect satisfaction, joy, and consolation, do they make known to all that desire salvation; yea even into the future of this kingdom of God there is granted us here as in a prophetic sketch a glance. Thus does already the beginning of the Sermon on the Mount deserve to be called a short summary of the whole preaching of the gospel, as indeed the words in Nazareth's synagogue, Luke iv. 18, 19, already were.

4. The four "Woes," which in Luke follow the Macarisms, are as little unworthy of the Saviour as the fact that in the Old Covenant over against mount Gerizim there stood mount Ebal, and that in the Gospel of Matthew (ch. xxiii.) the eight "woes" uttered by the Saviour stand over against the eight Beatitudes of the Sermon on the Mount. He might have reiterated here what Moses at the end of his last address testified, Deut. xxx. 18, 19. In this respect there exists a noticeable agreement between the beginning and the conclusion of the Sermon on the Mount, which in Luke also ends with a proclamation of a blessing and a curse in a parabolic form. This blessing and this woe might even be named a typical symbol of that which in sublimest wise shall hereafter repeat itself; comp. Matt. xxv. 34-40. It is the audible resonance of the אָרוּר and of the בָּרוּךְ of the prophets (comp. Jer. xvii. 5-8), with the distinction that here in true evangelical wise the μακάριος precedes the οὐαί.

HOMILETICAL AND PRACTICAL.

The King of the kingdom of heaven for the first time in the circle of His future ambassadors.—Christ the Physician of body and soul.—The might of deed and word.—The Saviour's gracious look upon weak yet sincere disciples.—The Beatitudes of the New Testament: 1. In their sweetness, 2. in their holy earnestness.—Blessing and cursing, life and death.—The common character of the Macarisms as: 1. Enigmatical utterances, 2. utterances of truth, 3. utterances of comfort and life.—The Mount of Beatitudes and the Mount of the Law-giving: 1. How they stand over against one another; 2. how they condition one another.—The first beatitude on earth, the last in heaven, Rev. xxii. 14.—What is foolish before the world that hath God chosen, 1 Cor. i. 26-31.—The beatitude and description: 1. Of the character; 2. of the salvation of the heavenly citizen: 1. *a.* poor, *b.* hungry, *c.* weeping, *d.* hated by men; 2. *a.* riches, *b.* full contentment, *c.* joy, *d.* reward of a prophet.—The identity in the reception of the prophets of the Old and the apostles of the New Covenant in the unbelieving world: 1. The exactness, 2. the ground, 3. the significance of this identity for all succeeding centuries.—The King of the kingdom of heaven: 1. The Friend of the poor, 2. the Bread of the hungry, 3. the Joy of the sorrowing, 4. the Judge of the oppressed. —Even under the day of grace a Woe.—Self-righteousness and unrighteousness the two hindrances to entering into the kingdom of heaven.—The distinction between reality and semblance among those called to the kingdom of heaven: 1. The unfortunate not seldom least to be commiserated, 2. those worthy of envy not seldom furthest removed from the salvation of the Lord.—The kingdom of heaven: 1. The riches of the poor, 2. of all poor, 3. of the poor alone.—It is blessed, 1. To need consolation, 2. to receive consolation, 3. to enjoy consolation.—The alternation of joy and pain in the life of the disciple of the Lord: 1. Joy of the world must become sorrow for sin, 2. sorrow for sin must become joy in Christ—1. No disciple of Christ without hatred of the world; 2. no hatred of the world without rich compensation; 3. no compensation without steadfast faithfulness.—The great reward in heaven: 1. To whom it was once given and why; for whom it is even now prepared and how.—How the self-righteous man stands in respect to Christ and how Christ stands in respect to the self-righteous.—The hungering of the already satisfied; 1. a painful, 2. a self-caused, 3. an unending hungering.—Universal praise of the world a stigma for the Saviour's disciples, since it brings them into the suspicion, 1. of unfaithfulness, 2. of characterlessness, 3. of the lust of pleasing. —False prophets can ever reckon upon loud applause.

STARKE:—Jesus has an entirely different office from Moses.—Love of riches and love of God can never agree together in one heart.—Rich enough, whoever has the kingdom of God.—QUESNEL:—Tears belong to time, but true joy to eternity.—Whoever finds it irksome to bear the cross of Christ understands not its worth.—OSIANDER: Godless rich men have their heaven on earth, and after this life hell is made ready for them.—For a good Christian name we must certainly strive, but not against our consciences speak to please every one. Galatians i. 10.—Many a one might come to repentance if flattery did not, so to speak, bar the door against conversion. Jeremiah xxiii. 15-22.

ST. MARTIN (*l'homme de désir*, 1790):—*Voulez-vous que votre esprit soit dans la joye? faites que votre âme soit dans la tristesse.* [Would you have your spirit joyful? Contrive that your soul may be in heaviness.]—KERN:—Heaviness and highness, sadness and gladness of true Christians.

Entirely original treatment of the Sermon on the Mount (according to Matthew) by Dr. C. Harms, in twenty-one sermons, Kiel, 1841. Examples: The first Beatitude: 1. It opens the door of the kingdom of heaven that we may look in, 2. bids us stand still to inquire: Are we therein? 3. It is the call at the door of the kingdom of heaven to enter in, and 4. a word of encouragement to those entered in, that they may also remain therein.—The second: 1. the

Who, 2. the When, and 3. the How.—The third: We discourse 1. of righteousness, 2. of the longing after it, and 3. of the promise which is given to this longing.

SECOND SECTION: *The Requirement of Love.*
(Vss. 27–38.)

EXEGETICAL AND CRITICAL.

Vs. 27. **But I say unto you which hear.**—Antithesis to the foregoing, vs. 26. Meyer very happily: "Yet although I utter against *those* these Woes, yet I enjoin on you not hatred but love towards your enemies. It is therefore no accidental antithesis" (Köstlin). As the Saviour in vs. 26 had shown what treatment Christians have to *expect* of their enemies, He unfolds, vss. 27–38, what *return* they must give to this treatment. Comp. Matt. v. 38–48; vii. 12. Here is connected in *thetic* form what was given by Matthew *antithetically*, over against the ἐρρέθη τοῖς ἀρχαίοις.

Ἀγαπᾶτε, κ.τ.λ.—The doctrine of love to enemies is here communicated in the most complete the fourfold form, while in Matt. v. 44 the second and the third member appear to be spurious. (*See* Tischendorf.)—Respecting the subject itself comp. LANGE, *Matthew*, p. 117. Although it cannot be denied that love to enemies is in a certain sense required even by Jewish and heathen moralists, it must yet be remembered that the thought of requiring acts of enmity with devout intercession could only arise in the heart of Him who has Himself prayed for the evil doers. Such sayings of the Saviour, particularly, may well have elicited from even a godly man, on reading the Sermon on the Mount, the exclamation: "Either this is not true, or we are no Christians."

Vs. 29. **And unto him that smiteth thee on the one cheek.**—The sense and application of this and similar precepts will occasion no difficulties, if we only bear in mind the simple rule: "The ethical commandments of Christ, or His explanations of the Old Testament, must themselves in turn be explained in the spirit of Christ." (THOLUCK, *Bergpredigt*, p. 163.) Let us in this matter consider well, *first*, that in proportion as civil life is more and more guided and sanctified by the spirit of Christ, it must continually be and become less and less possible that any one should unrighteously smite us, or take away our mantle, or force us to accompany him a mile. *Secondly*, that the Saviour did not here intend to project a definite rule of behavior, but to inculcate certain essential principles, as Augustine very justly remarks on the passage: "*Ista praecepta magis ad praeparationem cordis, quae intus est, pertinere, quam ad opus, quod in aperto fit, ut teneatur in secreto animi patientia et benevolentia, in manifesto autem id fiat, quod iis videtur prodesse, quibus bene velle debemus.*" Respecting the views of the ancient Christians as to the allowableness or inadmissibleness of military service, we find important statements in NEANDER's *Denkwürdigkeiten*. If we remember, finally, the time of closely impending persecutions in which this precept was given, and the conflict in which a *literal* following of vss. 29, 30, would bring us with the unchangeable and chief principle of vs. 31, the way is then as it were of itself prepared for a right explanation of this precept. We do not even need to form the supposition that "the sentence: 'From him that taketh thy goods ask them not again,' is hardly original with Luke, since it unnecessarily exaggerates the endurance" (Ewald), for it requires nothing more than what had immediately preceded. Better is Bengel's remark: "*Nimis hic cumulatae sunt ingenii humani exceptiones.*"

Vs. 31. **And as ye would.**—Here connected still more closely with the duty of love to enemies, in Matt. vii. 12 more generally stated. Justly Theophylact: νόμον ἔμφυτον ἐν ταῖς καρδίαις ἡμῶν γεγραμμένον. The Saviour gives a touch-stone into the hands of His disciples, by which they might prove themselves as to whether their demeanor towards neighbors and enemies was in agreement with their duties. His utterance contains no principle, but a touch-stone of morality, since it only refers to an outer form of action. Neither is it new (comp. Jesus Sirach xxx. 15, and the passages cited by Tholuck, p. 488 seq.), and might even be misused by egoism and perversely interpreted by scoffers, except as it is understood and applied with the whole spirit of Christianity. Where it is so used we shall discover in it a plain, simple, universally applicable precept of the practical wisdom of life, fully fitted for the purpose for which the Saviour has given it. Only let a special emphasis be laid upon the καθώς. Very happily Lange: "Not what people desire of us, but *according to* all that we desire of them, agreeably to that should we do to them." We subjoin that here the standard is not intrusted to the hands of every natural man, but to those of the disciples of Christ.

Vs. 32. **What thanks.**—"*Qualis vobis gratia, ut qui uberius quidam, mercede dignum, praestiteris.*" Bengel. It is, of course, to be understood that we are not here to think of human, but of Divine recompense. Comp. Matt. v. 46, 47.

For sinners also.—Here and vss. 33, 34, each time ἁμαρτωλοί, in Matthew τελῶναι καὶ ἐθνικοί (see TISCHENDORF on Matthew v. 47). In Luke, from his position of liberality towards the Gentiles, it is not the *ethnic* but the *ethic* antithesis which comes most into prominence; but the meaning remains the same. The Saviour will raise His disciples above the position of the ordinary morality of the natural man. Comp. the beautiful essay of A. VINET in his *Nouveaux discours sur quelques sujets religieux*, entitled, *L'extraordinaire*, pp. 146–184.

Vs. 34. **And if ye lend.**—Lending in the hope of receiving again is human; but without this hope it becomes Christian. And yet, how many found their right to the Christian's name almost on nothing else than on services of love so carefully measured and egoistic that every heathen or Jew equals them therein, perhaps even excels them.

Vs. 35. **Hoping for nothing again.**—It is plain that the Saviour here only forbids the expectation of *human* recompense, inasmuch as He has already confirmed the hope of heavenly reward, vs. 23, and immediately animates this again with the words: **And your reward shall be great.** The different explanation of Meyer: "*nihil desperantes*," is, without doubt, philologically admissible; yet it appears to us to be less favored by the connection.

Ye shall be the children of the Highest.—We find no reason to restrict the enjoyment of this dignity (with Meyer) to the future life. The Pauline doctrine of the υἱοθεσία even in the earthly life of believers, appears to us, on the other hand, to have its ground in such sayings of Jesus. If the ethical relationship with God manifests itself even here, why should its reward be incapable of being enjoyed until the next life?

Vs. 36. **Be ye therefore merciful.**—In Matthew, τέλειοι, here, οἰκτίρμονες; explicative: (for only in His moral attributes can God be an ideal to be imitated, and of this His love is the centre). Even without the spurious οὖν the nexus idearum is of itself evident.

Vs. 37. **And judge not.**—Comp. Matt. vii. 1. Κρίνειν is not the same as κατακρίνειν (Olshausen), or here there would be a tautology with the immediate sequel: μὴ καταδικάζετε, κ.τ.λ.; but what is here understood by *judging*, is the considering of the faults of our neighbor with a look only sharpened by mistrust, and not tempered by love and self-knowledge. It is the not "judging of a righteous judgment," John vii. 24. Undoubtedly, to the spiritual man, who judges all things (ἀνακρίνει, 1 Cor. ii. 15), the right to judge, in and of itself, cannot be forbidden; yet it is only granted by the Lord when one has previously cast a look of searching examination upon himself. "Luke conceives as a consequence what Matthew designates as that to be avoided." (De Wette.) **Forgive, &c.**—A practical commentary on this saying *see* in Matt. xviii. 23-35.

Vs. 38. **Good measure, pressed down and shaken together, and heaped up.**—The distinction of Bengel: *in aribus, mollibus, liquidis*, appears to be more ingenious than true. At least it cannot be denied that all the epithets here used can be used of a measure for *dry* substances. The climax brings into relief in a vivid manner the riches of the Divine retribution. Since now the Saviour does not at all say *whom* He uses for the impartation of such a recompense to His disciples, it is not at all necessary to restrict the matter exclusively to the future life, and to understand it of the angels (Meyer). Even in this life His disciples might at least now and then expect a superabundant recompense of their labor of love.—**With the same measure.**—Very well Theophylact: τῷ αὐτῷ, οὐ μὲν τοσούτῳ.

DOCTRINAL AND ETHICAL.

1. The high value of the ethical precepts here given will not become fully evident unless we consider how the Saviour Himself fulfilled them His life long in the most perfect manner; so that they contain not only the expression of His will, but also the living image of His own heart and life. By the comparison with the Saviour's own conduct, moreover, will the arbitrary application of the rules here given be best avoided. Comp. for instance John xviii. 21, 22.

2. In the fulfilling, moreover, of the precepts here given, vss. 29, 30, the main requirement of the gospel, love to God before all, and to our neighbor as ourselves, still remains at once principle and corrective. It is self-evident that an unthinking obedience to the letter would often bring with it dishonor to God, and would strengthen our neighbor in his injustice. Or should we have to give a supplicant everything, for instance even a dagger or poison to the madman who incessantly begs for them? Just as well might then the old Carpocratians derive from this passage the doctrine that a woman is obliged to follow the voice of temptation to forbidden lusts! But then the Saviour himself sinned against His own precept, when He permitted the Canaanitish woman first to entreat fruitlessly for help, and forbade one healed by Him to accompany Him, although entreated by him to permit it. The understanding, enlightened by the spirit of Christ, and the moral sense, guided by a tender conscience, must and can, in particular cases, decide whether love itself does not command to act directly contrary to the letter of the precept, in order to act agreeably to its spirit.

3. The peculiar Christian command of love to enemies must, on the one hand, not be exaggerated, nor, on the other hand, thrown aside. The former is done when the fact is overlooked that even heathen philosophers have given the most striking hints in this respect; *see* Tholuck on the passage. The other takes place when it is forgotten that the ground, impulse, form, measure, and ideal of this love, in the Christian sphere, are something entirely different from what they are in the extra-Christian sphere.

4. This whole pericope of the Sermon on the Mount is important for the answer of the question, how far the Saviour required an entirely *pure* love (*Amour pur* in the sense of Fénelon), or whether He has encouraged a respect to the reward promised to obedience. That He would never command a desire of reward, as the *essential principle*, hardly needs to be suggested; and quite as little, that genuine Christian effort does not seek its reward without, but within, itself. On the other hand, however, we see that He adds the incitement of the love of reward as a counterpoise to so many things that might be able to depress zeal and obedience. The question, Matt. xix. 27, although placed upon a legal position, is not of itself anti-Christian.

5. The exalted excellence of the Christian ethics comes convincingly into view when we compare its highest requirement, Likeness to God in love, with what heathen philosophers have given as the highest precept.

HOMILETICAL AND PRACTICAL.

Love to enemies: 1. A human virtue, 2. a Christian virtue, 3. a Divine virtue.—Love to enemies: 1. A severe conflict, 2. its noble trial, 3. its glorious crown.—The vengeance of love: 1. Its fervor, 2. its loveliness.—The invincible might of voluntary defencelessness.—Better suffer wrong than do wrong.—The relation of Christian love of our neighbor to befitting self-love.—The ordinary in the life of man, the extraordinary in the life of a Christian.—Whoever, in a Christian sphere, only does what is common, has no extraordinary reward to expect.—The love of sinners to each other, and of nominal Christians, compared with one another: 1. Often the former is even greater; 2. often both are like; 3. the latter must always rise above the former.—The Christian a follower of God as a dear child, Ephes. v. 1.—What God *is*, Christ's disciples must *become*.—Regard to reward in the Christian sphere: 1. How far is it permitted, 2. how far not permitted.—Compared with the goodness of God, all are unthankful and evil.—Compassion that which is divinest in God and in man.—The judicial function, as exercised by pride and by love.—Even the righteous receive reward here below.—The disciple of the Saviour before a threefold judgment, before that: 1. Of his conscience, 2. of his neighbor, 3. of the Lord. Comp. 1 Cor. iv. 4.—God's righteousness keeps measure, but God's love is immeasurably rich. "It gives for a penny more than ten thousand pounds, for a peck more than a hundred thousand bushels, for a little drop of comfort to my neighbor whole streams of refreshments; for a little tear, shed from love to Jesus, a whole sea of blessedness; for brief temporal suffering an everlasting and far more exceeding weight of glory." Brastberger.

STARKE:—Be ashamed, ye scoffers, that pretend that the gospel teaches nothing concerning friendship: He who commands to love our enemies, presupposes that true friends are much more to be loved.—HEDINGER:—In all wrong suffered we must leave room for the wrath of God, Rom. xii. 19.—A Christian heart is easily entreated, and willingly assumes the necessities of the saints.— NOVA BIBL. TUB.:—Better is it to lose land and goods, and to let all go, than to suffer harm to the soul. Matt. xvi. 26.—To love enemies and do them good, is the Christian's art and test.—OSIANDER:—An honest man seeks his own, but a Christian Jesus Christ's.—A bought or bartered love is no love of God that has reward.—CRAMER:— Children of God have their Father's temper, and do not let themselves be rebuffed by the unthankfulness of man from doing them good.—*Nulla re sic colitur Deus, ut misericordia*, Gregor. Nazianz.—MAJUS:—It is a desperate blindness, rather to rush upon Divine vengeance, than to show kindness and meekness towards our own brother.—HEDINGER:—Be not angry if thou gettest back again just the coin which thou hast given out.—Why do others trouble thee? Look to thyself! Gal. vi. 1.—It ought not to go hard with love to give that which Divine truth promises to give back. Prov. xix. 17.—The Christian loses by liberality nothing, but gains very much. 2 Cor. viii. 10; Acts xx. 35.—To be parsimonious and niggardly is not the right way to become rich, but to be beneficent and free-handed is the way.—The *jus talionis* is with the righteousness of God fully in accord, and never fails. Therefore be warned, whosoever thou art. Judg. i. 7; 1 Kings xxi. 19–24. Comp. 1 Kings xxii. 38, 39.

UDDER:—The Christian eye for human faults: 1. Strict against itself, 2. gentle towards its neighbor.— AHLFELD on vs. 36:—1. The source from which compassion springs; 2. the fields on which it brings forth its fruit; 3. the hindrances with which it wrestles.— UHLE:—How we are wont to demean ourselves: 1. Towards our neighbor's faults; 2. in the case of suffering wrong from him; 3. in the case of his necessity being made known to us.—RAUTENBERG:—The Divine compassion: 1. The type, 2. the ground, 3. the reward of our compassion.—BURKE:—The love of compassion: 1. Who gives it? 2. How is it exercised? 3. Who rewards it?—SCHMALTZ:—Without self-conquest no true love.—ALT:—Who can constrain his enemies to esteem?—STIER:—Concerning the evil habit of judging others.—VAN OOSTERZEE:— *What do ye more than others?* The Christian called to distinguish himself. This a requirement: 1. Whose scope is extensive; 2. the urging of which is legitimate: 3. the remembering is needful. On 1. The Saviour demands that His disciples should be more *upright*, more *disinterested*, more *steadfast* in good than others. On 2. The Christian *must* distinguish himself above others; he *can* do it, and, as history shows, he does it in *fact*. On 3. By this remembrance, Humility, Faith, Heavenly longing, is awakened.

THIRD SECTION: *The Importunity of Love.*

(Vss. 39–49.)

EXEGETICAL AND CRITICAL.

Vs. 39. **And He spake.**—From transitions of this sort we see how loose the thread is which connects the different elements of the Sermon on the Mount in Luke. Respecting the understanding of the παραβολή, see Lange, on Matthew 13, and below on ch. viii. The here cited parabolic saying appears according to the more exact report of Matthew, ch. x. 24; xv. 14, to have been spoken on another occasion, and not to belong to the original Sermon on the Mount, although in and of itself it is quite possible that the Saviour frequently used such gnome-like *dicta.*

Can the blind.—If one is inclined to insist upon some connection between the four parables here following and what precedes, it would be best to settle it as follows: "The disciples might, after these words of the Lord, think in their hearts: It is not easy to be a Christian! They were called to show to the world by their preaching and by their walk the way which the Lord showed them: therefore this above all was needful, that they themselves should allow the light to penetrate themselves, and should establish themselves upon the right and only ground. To this now does the Lord admonish them." (Besser.)

Τυφλός.—Whoever himself is blind for the light of truth cannot possibly serve another as leader, but draws him with him into destruction which reaches its fearful culmination in Gehenna. This was plainly manifest by the example of the *Pharisees*, comp. Matthew xv. 14, from which the disciples could see what leaders they should not be. Although all men by nature are spiritually blind, the judgment here pronounced is perfectly righteous, since the blindness of the leaders of the blind to the light of the Lord is a self-caused one.

Vs. 40. Οὐκ ἔστιν μαθητής.—If the Sermon on the Mount in Luke consists in part of a collection of different sayings of the Saviour apart from their original historical connection, it is then indeed superfluous to inquire after the connection of the preceding saying with this. Yet vs. 40 may serve to illustrate the naturalness and justness of the judgment pronounced in vs. 39. In this way, namely: only if a disciple surpassed his master could he hope to be preserved from the ditch into which he sees his blind leader fall. Since, however, the disciple does not commonly surpass the master, he has also the same danger to fear. As a rule every one is constituted like his master.—We must not overlook the fact that here at the same time an indirect intimation is given to the Twelve to fashion themselves in all things after the character of their new Master.

Vs. 41. **And why beholdest thou.**—Comp. Matt. vii. 3. Not merely "a climax upon the preceding" (Gerlach), but a pointing out of the way to be kept from the character and fate of the blind leader of the blind. Self-knowledge and amendment is required of the disciples of the Lord before they judge the failings of others and offer themselves to them as leaders.

Κάρφος.—"That He may warn us the more diligently He finds a palpable comparison and paints it before our eyes,—gives such a sentence as this, that every one who judges his neighbor has a great beam in his eye, while he who is judged has only a little splinter, so that he is ten times more worthy of judgment and condemnation even in this, that he condemns others." (Luther.) As to the rest, moral defects, as well as those of knowledge, appear to be spoken of here, such as the Saviour relatively likens to a little splinter. The δοκός can then be nothing else than just that foolish imagination of a greater excellence compared with our faulty brother: therefore the man with the δοκός is immediately called ὑποκριτά because he demeans himself as if free of faults.

Διαβλέψεις.—The composite, perhaps chosen ("*intenta acie spectabis.*" Meyer) in order to place in a strong light the difficulty and delicacy of the work, in which the greatest carefulness is necessary. How surely every one has first to look to himself appears particularly from the following parable.

Vs. 43. Οὐ γάρ.—First of all this parabolic saying is connected with what immediately precedes, "If thou dost not see the beam in thine own eye thou wouldst be like the corrupt tree, which cannot possibly bring forth good fruit." So Bengel: *qui sua trabe laborans alienam festucam petit est similis arbori mala bonum fructum affectanti.* Yet, since the Sermon on the Mount is hastening to its end, we may at the same time refer this word back to all the preceding requirements, the fulfilment of which is specially dependent on the condition of the heart.

A good tree.—Comp. Matt. vii. 15–20, and Lange on the passage. The fruits can here be nothing else than *works*. That the Saviour is here particularly thinking of misleading spirits in the Christian Church we do not believe, although we willingly concede that His saying may also be applied to these: as the sign of such it is not the walk, but the doctrine, that is given. In a striking way did the misleaders of the people who shortly after His appearance stirred up the unhappy Jews show the truth of this His utterance. They knew how with brilliant promises to allure great throngs to their side, but their behavior was so entirely in conflict with the essential principles of religion and of the state, that by this alone they could not but forfeit all confidence. The credulous multitude who gave credence to their words learned too late what evil fruits these trees of abundant promise brought forth.

Vs. 45. The good man.—Comp. Matt. xii. 35. Probably no part of the original Sermon on the Mount, but communicated out of its historical connection by Luke. The Saviour regards no man as naturally good in the Pelagian sense of the word, but speaks of the sinner who has become good through grace. Both the good and the evil man He sets forth as they commonly reveal themselves outwardly, without however denying his weak side even the good has his weak and the evil man his better side. The heart of the one and of the other is the magazine (θησαυρός), out of which perpetually proceeds what therein was in no small measure hidden.—For out of the abundance, comp. Ps. xxxvi. 2.

Vs. 46. And why call ye Me.—This same dictum is communicated in a complete form, Matt. vii. 21, with reference to the Pharisaic pretended holiness. Yet it is also applicable to the disciples of the Lord so far as in their disposition remnants of the old leaven are still found. It is only possible for the greatest misunderstanding, the most perverted apprehension of the οὐ πᾶς ὁ λέγ. in Matthew to find here a ground for declaring the external confession of the Saviour to be wholly indifferent. (Kant.) Comp. Matt. x. 32, 33. In the connection in which Luke reports this saying of the Saviour, it constitutes of itself the transition to the concluding parable, which he has in common with Matthew. Before any one comprehends the requirements of the ποιεῖν in an anti-evangelical sense, let him consider what the Saviour himself demands as the essence of the ἔργον τοῦ Θεοῦ, John vi. 29.

Vs. 47. Πᾶς ὁ ἐρχόμενος, κ.τ.λ.—A commencement of the concluding parable peculiar to Luke, in a more lively form than in Matthew. The whole conclusion of the Sermon on the Mount shows sharply, from word to word, a striking climax. Very vivid is the representation of the man who not only begins to build but also incessantly digs deeper (ἐβάθυνε), and does not rest before he reaches the firm rock (ἐπὶ τὴν πέτραν). That this is done in Palestine even now by solid builders is stated by Robinson, *Biblical Researches*, vol. iii. The rock can here hardly be primarily the person of Christ, as in 1 Cor. x. 4, but is primarily the word, wherein however He Himself is. Who builds thereupon the house of his hope builds secure; whoever out of Him seeks firmness and security proceeds towards certain destruction. The work of both builders becomes plain by the test. Comp. 1 Cor. iii. 11–15.

Vs. 48. A flood.—De Wette: "an inundation." Comp. Job xl. 23, LXX.—Symbol of all possible tests which the edifice of faith and hope can have to undergo in hours of doubt, of temptation, and of danger of death. Then is true for the disciple of the Lord the word—Proverbs xii. 7. The antithesis is so much the more striking as He does not here oppose the morally good to the morally bad, but simply the careful to the heedless.

For it was well built.—"For it was founded upon a rock."—The steadfastness of the building does not lie in *what* is built, but in the foundation on *which* it is built.—Comp. Ezekiel xiii. 11.

Vs. 49. Without a foundation.—ἐπὶ τὴν ἄμμον, Matthew. All that is not πέτρα remains ἄμμος, even if it were outwardly like a rock.—The breach, in Matthew the fall, the one is consequence of the other. In both redactions the Sermon on the Mount ends as it were in a storm of wind, earthquake, and fire, 1 Kings xix. 11, 12. The supposition that a rising tempest or rain hastened the end of the discourse and placed on the lips of the Saviour this last word is *ingeniose magis quam vere.* Now and then without doubt the Saviour has found occasion from the nature surrounding Him to the choice of His figurative language, *e. g.*, John iii. 8; xv. i. But did He also in Matt. xv. 14, or in John xvi. 21? —*Credat Judæus Apella.*

DOCTRINAL AND ETHICAL.

1. The four parables with which the Sermon on the Mount in Luke concludes contain the most admirable proofs of the Saviour's wisdom as a Teacher. They were all taken from daily life, and also from histori-

cally given circumstances. One had not far to go to seek blind leaders of the blind, or to see beautifully appearing trees with evil fruit. So far as such manifestations continually repeat themselves in the church of the Lord, an eternal significance may be ascribed to them. The example of the Saviour moreover shows plainly how far those are from the ideal of Christian eloquence who condemn a great richness of noble imagery. Here there is no abstract development of ideas, but all alike pictorial and intuitive. The presentation of the subjects becomes plain in that these are made visible in persons acting very variously. Alternately we hear the voice of the deepest love, and that of the earnestness which menaces with judgment. The discourse unfolds itself regularly; is as rich in surprises as in gradual climax, and ends with an utterance which must leave the deepest impression in the conscience. "*Non opus est, omnes homilias desinere in usum paracleticum,*" remarks Bengel, with great truth, on Matt. vii. 29. After the reading of the Sermon on the Mount we repeat the declaration, John vii. 46.

2. Without the word μετάνοια being mentioned, the last part of the Sermon on the Mount also contains a most obvious intimation of the indispensable necessity of the new birth. The blind who leads the blind into destruction; the hypocrite who overlooks his own faults compared with those of his brother; the corrupt tree which in its present condition cannot possibly bring forth good fruit; the fool who builds his house upon the sand—all give us to recognize in various forms the image of the natural man in his delusion and pride, in his ruinous fall and destruction. In vain is it to will to do good so long as one has not become good, and good can no one have himself without Christ. Comp. Jeremiah xiii. 23. Thus does the Lord repeat here in a practical popular form essentially the same thoughts which He in John iii. has expressed before Nicodemus. On the other hand He states the one infallible sign of the genuineness of the great change which takes place in the heart of His true disciples: the joyful doing of His will.

3. When we observe how the Saviour in this part of the Sermon on the Mount also insists especially upon an active Christianity, it is almost incomprehensible how, in the course of the centuries, and even to-day, so much Antinomism could show itself in the Church. For, according to His intimations also, His disciple can and will be blessed alone ἐν τῇ ποιήσει αὐτοῦ. Comp. James i. 25. Never can the vindicator of a lax and shallow morality appeal to His words so long as He has not rent the Sermon on the Mount out of the Gospel. Yet, alas, to many an antinomistic theory is the profound saying of Gregory of Nazianzen applicable: πρᾶξις ἐπίβασις θεωρίας.

4. If we apply the saying: "Out of the abundance of the heart the mouth speaketh," to the Saviour Himself, how deep a look do we then obtain through the clear current of His preaching on the Mount into the golden recesses of His Divinely human heart! The less He says unequivocally in the Sermon on the Mount, who He is, the more clearly does it show itself.

5. Not unjustly has the conclusion been drawn from this part of the Sermon on the Mount, how much easier it is to take note of others than of ourselves; how much more convenient to show a brother the way than to walk therein ourselves; how great the danger of ourselves being found reprobates while we work for the salvation of others. Comp. 1 Cor. ix. 27. Perhaps it was similar considerations which in the end of the last century gave occasion to the singular question, "Whether it is a miracle when a *clergyman* is saved?" (Bretschneider, † 1792.)

6. The concluding parable of the Sermon on the Mount unites in itself allegory and prophecy in the most beautiful manner. In three verses there is here compressed the primeval, and yet ever fresh, history of all that which has been built, is building, and until the end of all days shall be built; on the one hand without, on the other hand in and upon, the word and the Spirit of the Lord. The μεγάλη πτῶσις of the house built upon the sand, was, among other instances, heard at the fall of unbelieving Judaism, as well as at that of all unbelieving philosophical systems which have overlived themselves, and at that of every state, of every church which is not built upon the only true foundation; and all this will repeat itself in continually greater measure, the nearer the last crisis of the future approaches, until the word is wholly fulfilled: 1 John ii. 17.

HOMILETICAL AND PRACTICAL.

He who allures to love, threatens also with the terrors of judgment.—The blind and his leader: 1. The way of both; 2. the fate of both, *a.* mournful, *b.* inevitable.—The disciple must be as his master, 1 John ii. 6.—Whoever will be to others not a mischief, but a blessing, must begin to know himself aright.—Unloving judgment a fruit of blindness in the judge.—Humility before God leads to love towards man.—A serviceable hand not seldom coupled with a loveless heart.—A brother's name and a brother's service without true brother's love, an abomination before God.—Only the absolutely Holy One is able and entitled to judge completely.—A hypocritical judge of his brother a corrupt tree in the garden of God.—The connection between tree and fruit: 1. In the realm of nature; 2. in the realm of grace.—Christian diagnosis.—What is to be expected of men whose hearts are like thorns and brambles.—The heart a treasure-chamber for very different treasures.—A full heart and a closed mouth agree ill together.—The Christian cannot be silent concerning Jesus. Acts iv. 20.—First to become, than to be, last to do.—The spiritual vintage: 1. Here on earth; 2. in the future. —A fourfold relation to the Lord; there are men who 1. Neither say Lord! Lord! nor do His will; 2. say, indeed, Lord! Lord! but without doing His will; 3. do His will, indeed, but without saying Lord! Lord! (upright but anxious souls); 4. as well do His will, as also say Lord! Lord! The last, the concurrence of deed with word, is in every respect the best.—Nominal Christianity: 1. In its guise of great promise: 2. in its wretched reality.—The different builders: 1. One plan of building, but two manner of foundations; 2. one crucial test, but two manner of results. —How the genuineness of faith is tested: 1. In the tempest of doubt; 2. in the tempest of affliction; 3. in the tempest of death.—The magnificent Plan; the swelling Flood; the deep Fall; the heavy Ruin.

STARKE:—In the choice of a leader, whether temporal or spiritual, all foresight and prudence is to be used; the danger is great, the mischief often irreparable, of hasty choice.—From the ignorance of pastors rises adulteration of the true service of God, superstitious sermons, abuses, and numerous disorders. 2 Tim. iii. 13.—The least splinter can destroy the whole eye; slight seeming sins also are ruinous and damnable. Canticles ii. 15; 2 Sam. vi. 6, 7.— QUESNEL:—Whoever diligently proves himself, will not easily chastise others. Sir. xxiii. 2.—True self-knowledge the beginning of our own amendment, and the way to edify our neighbor.—The wisdom from above makes humble and compassionate, but earthly wisdom presumptuous and unmerciful men.—Self-complacence corrupts all good.—OSIANDER:—He is no pious man, out of whose mouth poisonous calumnies are heard. Ps. xv. 2, 3.—QUESNEL:—The fruits of a carnal or of a spiritual heart are the works of the flesh or of the Spirit. Gal. v. 16 *seq.*—*Bibl. Wirt.:* —The evil heart of man becomes then good when Christ the fruitful olive tree is, by faith, planted in the same. Acts xv. 9.—He is only a mocker that calls God his Lord, yet obeys not His commandments. Malachi i. 6.—To know and do the Lord's will, manifests a faithful servant. Luke xii. 47, 48.— OSIANDER:—Believers are in all storms of temptation preserved to eternal life. Isaiah xxxii. 2; xxxiii. 16.— Ye teachers, ye hearers, ye parents, ye children, think on a right laying of foundations in religion, that in the hour of temptation and distress ye may not find yourselves deceived.

HEUBNER:—The disposition to give a verdict against others, the fruit of a false eagerness to quiet one's self.—The Christian must be severe against himself, mild-judging towards others.—The culture of grace first fashions a man into something noble.— The inward disposition in man, what the sap is in a tree.—What a destruction shall come upon apostate teachers!—COUARD (on vs. 46):—The confessing of Jesus Christ in Christendom. It comes to pass that 1. With many the confessing of Christ is wholly want-

ing (they deny the Lord); 2. with many this confession is the thoughtless language of custom (they are Christian in name); 3. with some only an assumed pretence of godliness (hypocrites); 4. with others a matter of the heart and expression of living faith (true Christians).—JASPIS:—Hypocrisy in religion: 1. How easily it creeps over us; 2. how quickly it grows; 3. how slowly it cures; 4. how deep it casts us down.—HOFFNER:—Four things of principal concern in Christianity: 1. Faith *makes* the Christian; 2. the life *shows* the Christian; 3. suffering *proves* the Christian; 4. dying *crowns* the Christian.—KRUMMACHER:—Who shall enter into the kingdom of heaven? (on vs. 46. Comp. Matt. vii. 21–23.) From this saying appears the threefold necessity: 1. Of saying "Lord! Lord!" 2. of the new birth through the Holy Spirit; 3. of incorporation into the despised *ecclesiola in ecclesia.*—CLAUS HARMS (on the Pericope Matt. vii. 15–22):— Deeper Christian truths in the text read. They respect: 1. The teachers, especially the false; 2. the conditions of our salvation, the rule and the exception; 3. the future decision, when and by whom, and according to what it is made.

"Let not him who is established and built upon the rock, imagine that he can now be no more overtaken by all manner of affliction or danger. Rather is he like a house that is situated on the shore of the sea, upon which the waves beat heavier than is known to houses inland. This house must be the target and mark of all the beating storms of the world. But because it is founded on the rock, it may indeed be shaken to the centre, and its rafters creak, yet fall shall it never, for its foundation stands fast and unmovable." CHEMNITZ.

---

3. The First Return to Capernaum. The First-fruits of the Believing Gentiles (CH. VII. 1–10).

(Parallel: Matt. viii. 5–13.)

1 Now when he had ended all his sayings in the audience of the people, he entered
2 into Capernaum. And a certain centurion's servant, who was dear unto him, was sick,
3 and ready to die. And when he heard of Jesus, he sent unto him the [om., the] elders
4 of the Jews, beseeching him that he would come and heal his servant. And when they came to Jesus, they besought him instantly [urgently], saying, That he was worthy for
5 whom he should do this [to have this done for him]: For [*said they*] he loveth our
6 nation, and he hath built us a synagogue [and our synagogue he himself built]. Then Jesus went with them. And when he was now not far from the house, the centurion sent friends to him, saying unto him, Lord, trouble not thyself; for I am not worthy
7 that thou shouldest enter under my roof: Wherefore neither thought I myself worthy to come unto thee: but say in a word, and my servant shall be healed [let my servant
8 be healed, V. O.¹]. For I also am a man set under authority, having under me soldiers, and I say unto one, Go, and he goeth; and to another, Come, and he cometh; and to
9 my servant, Do this, and he doeth *it*. When Jesus heard these things, he marvelled at him, and turned him about, and said unto the people that followed him, I say unto you, I have not found so great faith, no, not in Israel [not even in Israel have I found so
10 great a faith]. And they that were sent, returning to the house, found the servant whole [well] that had been sick.

¹ Vs. 7.—Tischendorf, after B., L., καὶ ἰαθήτω, instead of the *Rec.* καὶ ἰαθήσεται. The former appears more agreeable to the humble tone of the suppliant. [And the latter more expressive of his strong faith. This is supported by the other MSS. and by Cod. Sin.—C. C. S.]

EXEGETICAL AND CRITICAL.

Vs. 1. **He entered into Capernaum.**—Comp. Matt. viii. 1-13, and LANGE on the passage. The healing of the Leper, which Matthew places immediately before the recovery of the sick servant, had, according to the more exact account (Luke v. 12-16), preceded the Sermon on the Mount.

Vs. 2. **Servant.**—That we are here not to understand the son, but the servant (παῖς here = δοῦλος, עֶבֶד, Acts iii. 26), appears not only from the statement of Luke, that this sick person was very dear to the centurion, which in the other case would have been superfluous, but also from that of Matthew that he was sick in the house of the centurion, which certainly would have needed no mention if it had been his son. The cause why he so highly valued particularly this servant, apparently his only one, see vs. 8 b.—[To refer the centurion's concern to the mere fear of losing a valuable servant, appears an exceedingly frigid interpretation of the phrase "was dear unto him."—C. C. S.]

Vs. 3. Πρεσβυτέρους.—Not necessarily ἀρχισυνάγωγοι (Acts xiii. 15), but *elders of the people* in the ordinary sense of the word. It need not surprise us to see such πρεσβύτεροι τοῦ λαοῦ come to the Saviour with an entreaty for help; for why should *all* adherents of the sacerdotal party at that period have been alike hostile to the Saviour? Even if they did not themselves share his expectation and his faith, yet they must have been afraid of turning their friend and protector, by the refusal of his request, into an enemy, since he, moreover,—as Jewish selfishness would easily calculate—if his servant should recover, would not feel himself indebted alone to Jesus, but also under personal obligation to them. They, therefore, bring his request to Jesus, adding commendation and urgent entreaty thereto, assuring Him: "He is worthy that thou shouldest do this for him." And the Saviour, who had refused the weakly believing βασιλικός at Capernaum (John iv. 46-54) to make him a visit, refuses this not to the afflicted centurion, and counts him worthy of this honor, not because he had built the synagogue, but because he had shown the heroic courage of faith.

Vs. 5. **And our synagogue he himself built.**—There are several examples on record of individuals who had founded Jewish synagogues, *see* Lightfoot *ad loc.* Even the founding of one by a heathen suggests no difficulty, since the sanctity of the place did not depend upon the founder, but on the religious consecration. So did Herod also renew the temple. Moreover this centurion was, in all probability, a proselyte of the gate, like Cornelius (Acts x.) and so many others besides.

Vs. 6. **Sent friends.**—This second sending is related by Luke alone, whose account supplements that of Matthew, without being in conflict with it. Now, when once the centurion believes that Jesus is on his way to his dwelling, he holds himself bound not only to await the Lord, but also to go to meet Him (πρός σε ἐλθεῖν, vs. 7), and it is just this that makes him diffident. Yet now he sends in his place —a very delicate and thoroughly natural touch—no intercessors, for these he needed no longer, but intimate friends of his family, who can in some measure take his place in greeting the highly honored Guest. It is much more probable that the Saviour addressed to the friends of the centurion the praise bestowed upon his great faith, which Matthew and Luke give account of, than that He should have uttered it to his face. Even though he did address himself by others to Jesus, Matthew could very well declare of the centurion, that he came to Jesus and entreated Him, according to the well-known rule: *Quod quis per alium facit, ipse fecisse putatur*, in the same manner in which it is said of Noah and of Solomon: "He built the Ark, or the Temple."

Vs. 7. **Say in a word.**—Even his affliction about his sick servant redounds to the honor of the heathen centurion, since commonly slaves were hardly treated by the Romans as persons, but rather as things. Still more to his honor is his humility, and most of all his vigorous faith, even though this was not free from heathen superstition. Without doubt he has already heard about Jesus, and represented the matter thus to himself, that the good Genii of health appeared, the evil fled before Jesus like troops at the will of the general. How mighty to him must the help of such a ruler of spirits have appeared! He asks nothing more than the word of command, before which the paralysis shall give way. From the power of his own words he concludes as to the might of the words of Jesus. As to the rest, that this centurion was no other than Chuza, Herod's steward (Luke viii. 3), is a supposition (Sepp) that is entirely without proof.

Vs. 10. **The servant well that had been sick.**—There is just as little reason (Lachm., Tischend.) to expunge the phrase τὸν ἀσθενοῦντα, as (Paulus, a. o.) to understand ὑγιαίνοντα only in the sense of *recovering*. Much better Bengel: "*Non modo sanum, sed sanitate utentem.*"—According to Matthew as well as Luke, therefore, the healing took place at a distance, as in John iv. 46-54. This is, however, no good reason for considering these two accounts as different relations of the same miracle. "The distinct character of the Synoptical narrative, the humble power of faith of the stranger in Israel and its deep impression upon Christ, this anti-Judaistic feature, pregnant of the future, if it was once extant in the tradition of the church, could not possibly have been so obliterated by the fourth Evangelist, considering his own character, and have been perverted almost into the opposite" (Hase).—How much attraction, moreover, this miracle must have had for Luke, not only as *physician*, but also as *Paulinist*, needs no suggestion. The prophetic declaration of the bringing in of the Gentiles, which the Saviour, according to Matt. viii. 11, 12, uttered on this occasion, Luke gives in another connection, ch. xiii. 28, 29.

DOCTRINAL AND ETHICAL.

1. For the first time we find here in the Gospel of Luke witnesses of a miracle *at a distance*. An example of something of the kind we find in the life of Elisha (2 Kings v.), without, however, discovering a warrant in this agreement for finding here a mythical or legendary narrative in the gospels (Strauss), or for supposing the basis of both narratives to be a parable (Weisse). The point of attachment for the miraculous activity of the Saviour was undoubtedly given in the faith of the centurion and in the sympathy of his friends: "An invisible highway, we may say, for the victorious and saving eagles of the great Imperator." LANGE, *Life of Christ*, ii. p. 648. But the last ground of all must, however, be sought in the entirely unique personality of the Saviour. If

He was really the one whom He affirmed Himself to be, distance in space could not then hinder His holy will, united with that of the Father, from working where He held it needful. What was possible to the prophet with the heathen Naaman certainly could not be impossible to the *Son* with the heathen centurion. By this very fact He exhibits to us the image of the working of the Father (John v. 17; xiv. 9), which is impeded as little by time as by space. At the same time, we behold here as in a mirror, how He in heaven, exalted above all limits of the material world, can work directly even to the extreme limits of the earth. Much that is beautiful and striking respecting this and other miracles of the Saviour is found in the Notes on the Miracles of our Lord, by Archbishop Trench.

2. Only twice do we read in the Gospel that the Saviour marvelled; He who at other times exercised the *nil mirari* in Divine perfection; once at the unbelief of His fellow citizens at Nazareth (Mark vi. 6), once at the faith of this heathen. And at this *His* wondering, we need *not* wonder; it is a proof the more for His true humanity. The whole history of the world may be called a continuous history of faith and unbelief, and by these two is the infallible judgment of the Lord respecting men and sinners determined. The praise which He bestows on this heathen is the more remarkable, because it evidently shows that the Saviour can praise and crown a great faith even where it is yet mingled with erroneous conceptions of the understanding.

3. A strong *apologetical* value lies in the impression which the report of the miraculous power of the Saviour had made upon a heathen, and in the expectation that a word at a distance would be sufficient to fulfil his wish. Respecting the Christ of the negative criticism, we understand just as little how He could give occasion to such a report as how He could excite so bold a hope in the heart of a heathen.

4. This whole history is a striking proof of the indispensable necessity of faith as a *conditio sine qua non*, as well of desiring anything of the Lord as also of receiving much from Him. At the same time the character of true humility, in opposition to the counterfeit, is here made evident. False humility suffers itself to be kept back from coming to Jesus by the sense of personal unworthiness; true humility confesses: "I count myself not worthy," but—comes. Very beautifully Augustine says: "*Dicendo se indignum præstitit dignum, non in cujus parietes, sed in cujus cor Christus intraret.*"

5. While the Saviour concedes to the heathen centurion such a benefit, He is not unfaithful to His own principle. (Matt. xv. 24.) More than by his building of the synagogue and the intercession of the elders for him was this centurion by his faith received into the Israel according to the Spirit, and made partaker of the περιτομὴ τῆς καρδίας (Romans ii. 29), which is the real requirement in the kingdom of God.

6. The manifestation of faith in a heathen in contrast with the unbelief of the Jews has a strong symbolic side; comp. Matt. viii. 11, 12; John i. 11–13.—For a doctrine of prayer also the intercession of the elders and friends has a great significance, as a striking argument for the necessity and blessing of this service of love. Comp. James v. 16. "These elders, although they were not without faith, had nevertheless less faith than he who sent them (vs. 9). Yet do they entreat not in vain for him. Thus can often less favored ones profit others that are farther advanced more than they do themselves. Even so also the friends" (vs. 6). (Gerlach.)

HOMILETICAL AND PRACTICAL.

The first heathen who experiences the miraculous power of the Saviour.—Great faith: 1. Courageous in entreaty; 2. humble in approach; 3. joyful in receiving the benefit of the Lord.—The entreaty of the Jews for a heathen considered from its singular, touching, and successful side.—No greater love for Israel than the care for its highest interests.—Jesus ready to go wherever need and faith call Him. Urgent intercession the best service of friendship.—Prayer and faith most intimately connected together: 1. How true humility leads to faith; 2. how true faith never forgets humility.—Christ the true Ruler over sin and sickness.—Heathen precede the Jews into the kingdom of heaven.—There is more faith on earth than we know of.—Great faith, by Jesus 1. Remarked; 2. praised; 3. crowned; 4. held up for imitation.—The centurion of Capernaum before a threefold forum: 1. The judgment of man, vs. 4 (*a*): "He is worthy," &c.; 2. the judgment of conscience, vs. 6: "I am not worthy," &c.; 3. the judgment of the Saviour, vs. 9: "Such faith," &c.—The great faith of the master of the house a blessing for all his household.—How distress drives to Jesus and how Jesus comes to the distressed.—Great faith a singularity: 1. This is not otherwise, 2. this cannot be otherwise, 3. this will not be otherwise.—The good which we remark in others, we ought to praise with cordiality.—Time and space no barriers to the helpful love of the Lord.—In order to be highly praised by the Lord, one must be humbled most deeply before Him.—A School of Love: 1. Of a heathen towards Jews; 2. of Jews towards a heathen; 3. of the Saviour towards both together; *a*, in the deed, *b*, in the word of His love.

STARKE:—God is no respecter of persons. Acts x. 34, 35.—*Nova Bibl. Tub.*:—Christian governors ought duly to acknowledge the faithfulness and obedience of their subjects, take their necessities upon them, not leave them in their spiritual and bodily distress.—For their benefits men willingly entreat God and men.—Outward works are by men, on account of their own profit, most praised, but Jesus looks at the heart, and praises faith.—HEDINGER:—Become nothing, that thou mayst be something in Christ, 1 Corinthians xv. 9, 10; 1 Peter v. 5—"Who has, to him shall be given, that he may have abundance." The true grace of God is ever in growth and increase.—To the hero in war a heroic faith is well beseeming.—God has, even in the military profession, without doubt, His own.—Our best way to become worthy of the grace of Christ, is to count ourselves unworthy of it.—MAJUS:—The better a man knows God and himself, the humbler will he be.—CANSTEIN:—Weak faith God does not despise, but a stronger faith nevertheless is more acceptable to Him.

LISCO:—Strong faith, 1. As to its nature; 2. as to its reward.—Coming to Jesus: 1. From what it springs: *a*. from believing confidence, *b*. from love to the brethren; 2. how manifested: *a*. with hearty humility, *b*. with unreserved confidence; 3. how rich in blessings it is: *a*. it procures us the applause of Jesus, *b*. it is salutary for others.—PALMER:—What is the faith which is well pleasing to the Lord, but which He does not find in Israel? 1. It is faith which springs from humility; 2. which is joined with love; 3. which aims after what is highest, and strives to appropriate it.—An entirely original application of vs. 8 in *Cassianus Collat.* vii. 5: One must even so bring his thoughts under military command, summon the good, to the evil at once give their discharge.—FUCUS:—Concerning Christian faith: 1. Its source; 2. its expression; 3. its blessing.—RANKE:—Blessed he who seeks help of Christ, 1. For His love there is no man too mean; 2. for His power there is no wretchedness too great; 3. the condition of His help is for no one too hard.—THYM: —The sick servant at Capernaum: 1. The lord of the servant, 2. the sick man, 3. the Physician.—BENGEL: —Faith: 1. Kind and test; 2. profit and praise.

---

4. A second Excursion from Capernaum. The Son of Man manifested as Compassionate High-Priest at Nain's Gate and Simon's Table; but at the same time as the Holy Messiah as opposed to the Offence taken by John, the People, and the Pharisees.

CH. VII. 11–50.

a. THE YOUNG MAN AT NAIN (Vss. 11-17).
(Gospel on the 16th Sunday after Trinity.)

11 And it came to pass the day after, that he went into a city called Nain; and many
12 [a good many] of his disciples went with him, and much people. Now when he came nigh to the gate of the city, behold, there was a dead man carried out, the only son of
13 his mother, and she was a widow: and much people of the city was with her. And
14 when the Lord saw her, he had compassion on her, and said unto her, Weep not. And he came and touched the bier [the coffin]: and they that bare *him* stood still. And he
15 said, Young man, I say unto thee, Arise. And he that was dead [the dead man] sat up,
16 and began to speak. And he delivered him to his mother. And there came a fear [an astonishment] on all: and they glorified God, saying, That a great prophet is risen up
17 among us; and, That God hath visited his people. And this rumour of him went forth throughout all Judea, and throughout all the region round about.

EXEGETICAL AND CRITICAL.

Vs. 11. **The day after.**—By this noting of the time, Luke gives us full liberty to make the raising of the young man at Nain to follow immediately after the healing of the servant of the centurion at Capernaum. It took place τῇ ἑξῆς sc. ἡμέρᾳ. If with some we were obliged to read τῷ, then surely καθεξῆς (χρόνῳ) would have followed. *See* DE WETTE *ad loc.*

Nain.—Ναΐν, perhaps נָעִים, now only a little hamlet, NEIN, only inhabited by a few families, then a small town in the tribe of Issachar, hard by the source of the brook Kishon, not far from Endor, two and a half leagues from Nazareth. The name signifies "The lovely," perhaps on account of the pleasant situation in the plain of Esdraelon. Except in this passage it does not occur in the sacred history. The fathers Eusebius and Jerome knew it as a village two Roman miles southward from Tabor. *See* WINER *in voce.*

Of His disciples.—We may understand here μαθηταί in a more extended sense of the word, without thereby excluding the twelve apostles, who had been the day before called and consecrated, and to whose further training and strengthening in faith such a miracle as that now to be accomplished at the very beginning of their apostolic life was as desirable as beneficent. The multitude doubtless consisted partly at least of hearers of the Sermon on the Mount, who now were to see anew how the Saviour fulfilled His own precept, "Be merciful as your Father is merciful."

Vs. 12. **Carried out.**—Comp. Acts v. 6. Graves were commonly outside the towns. Τεθνηκώς was apparently omitted by A. 54. because it was of course understood, for which reason there is no ground to put it in brackets, (Lachmann.) Respecting the variations of the reading αὕτη χήρα (sc. ἦν), which moreover only slightly change the sense, *see* MEYER *ad loc.*

Vs. 13. **The Lord.**—An appellation peculiarly frequent in Luke; comp. ch. x. 1; xi. 39; xii. 42; xiii. 15; xxii. 61, especially adapted to indicate the majesty revealing itself in His discourse and action. Bengel has a fine remark: "*Sublimis hæc appellatio jam Lucæ et Johanne scribente usitatior et notior erat, quam Matthæo scribente. Marcus medium tenet. Initio doceri et confirmari debuit hoc fidei caput, deinde præsupponi potuit.*"

Weep not.—As with Jairus, his fear, so with this widow her grief is first allayed, before the Lord displayed His miraculous might, ἐσπλαγχνίσθη. Comp. Matt. ix. 36. It is the manifestation of the compassionate High-priest, which is so conspicuously dwelt on by the writer of the epistle to the Hebrews also, kindred as he is in spirit with Paul and Luke (Heb. ii. 16, 18; iv. 14).

Vs. 14. **The coffin** (σορός). It was open above. Since the bearers and the funeral train had of themselves stopped at the approach and the address of Jesus, who certainly was not wholly unknown to them, it is not necessary with Meyer to remark in their instantly standing still a trace of the extraordinary. "*Miracula præter necessitatem non sunt multiplicanda.*" If the bearers also felt compassion for the mother, it is more probable that they themselves expected help.

Young man.—The mighty word of the Prince of Life; comp. Luke viii. 56; John xi. 44. The instant rising and speaking of the dead, shows that not only life but also strength and health have returned, and the Lord, by giving him back to his mother, completes the miracle of His power by the highest act of His love. It is remarkable how the Saviour immediately after their restoration, manifests a visible care as to the dead raised by Him. To the daughter of Jairus He causes food at once to be given; Lazarus He causes to be relieved of his grave-clothes.

Vs. 16. **An astonishment.**—Not with all, it is true, equally deep, and perhaps not wholly free from superstition, but yet so far of genuine stamp as it led to a thankful glorifying of God and the Lord Jesus. That they extol Him as a prophet will not surprise us if we consider that the prophets not only foretold future things, but also performed miracles, and among them the raising of the dead.

Hath visited.—Comp. Luke i. 68. In respect to the æsthetical explanation of the miracle, there is a beautiful homily of Herder's, which deserves to be compared.

DOCTRINAL AND ETHICAL.

1. The raising of the dead belongs in the fullest sense of the word to that class of σημεῖα, which serve as symbols of the life-giving activity of our Lord, John xi. 25, 26. They do not become fully conceivable unless we hold fast to the union of the Divine and human in the person of Jesus, and to the certainty of His own resurrection. To consider the three dead persons whose resurrection is related to us as only apparently dead, is rationalistic caprice. But even though we acknowledge on good grounds the reality of their physical dying, it is by no means implied in this, that all receptivity for the influence of the miraculous word of the Saviour had departed from them. From the very fact that they heard this miraculous voice (allowing their raising to be once established by a purely historical criticism) we may, it seems to us, infer the opposite. For this voice makes its way, not to the body, but to the spirit, of the departed. And who now will decide when the separation of the spirit from the body is irrevocable, and their re-union utterly impossible? This only takes place when the bodily organism is wholly destroyed or rendered uninhabitable, and this is in these instances by no means the case. It is not mutilated, wholly decayed bodies which the Lord revives, but bodies that have just died, whose corporeal organism needs not to be re-created and restored, but only to be reanimated. "There was still a thoroughly trodden way between the corpse and the spirit which had left it, and so much is clear, that the corpse of the departed in its earliest stage is very different from a mummy or from a corrupt mass." (Lange.) This remark is perhaps of no interest for those who conceive the connection between soul and body as external, such as there is between bird and cage; but the more deeply modern science considers, along with the undeniable distinction, the intimate connection also of spirit and matter, the less venturous appears the conjecture that the spirit immediately after death stands as yet in a closer connection with its scarcely-abandoned dwelling-place than many are disposed to believe. This appears especially to have been the case with the dead persons whom Jesus raised. Departed in a time in which life and immortality had not yet been brought to light, they could at most surrender themselves to death with composure, without longing after death; they were moreover still bound to the earth by holy bonds of blood or sympathy. If ever tears, prayers, and entreaties might still fetter a spirit to the earth or call forth a longing after life, it was here the case, and scarcely do they hear the voice of Omnipotence when they can and will obey.

2. If, therefore, the possibility of the raising of the dead, as related in the Gospel, cannot be denied *per se*, its reality is sufficiently established. The Saviour Himself enumerates νεκροὶ ἐγείρονται (vii. 22) among the signs of His redeeming activity, and what had already been performed by the prophets, beseemed Him, the highest Ambassador of the Father, yet more. Of the witnesses of these facts there were many, and those not exposed to suspicion, and even in a later period, testimonies as to this point are not wanting. *See* particularly the fragment of Quadratus, an Evangelist of the apostolic age, in Eusebius (*H. E.* iii. 3), who moreover declares that this apostolical writer was yet extant in his time, and was known to him as well as to the most of his brethren. Jerome also (*Catal. Script.* ch. 19) gives an account of it. When this account was written the youthful persons raised by the Saviour might have been still living.—The strongest proof of their truth lies however in the internal character of these narratives of miracles. Whoever, with freedom from prejudice, reads the account of the raising at Nain or at Bethany will always repeat the exclamation: *ce n'est pas ainsi qu'on invente*. As respects the silence of Matthew and Mark with reference to this miracle, it is difficult to give any other answer than conjecture. Perhaps it arises from the fact that the name of the youth or his mother was not more particularly known. The silence of Matthew could also be explained if we were at liberty to assume that in this expedition from Capernaum he had perhaps remained behind a single day in order to finish the settlement of his affairs. That of Mark is sufficiently explained by the fact, that his Gospel is laid out on a much more limited scale. In view of the great abundance of matter, moreover, no one of the narrators undertook to be complete, and the distinction into more ordinary and more difficult miracles, which latter especially they were not to pass over if these should not be controverted, was to them in their simplicity apparently wholly unknown.

3. In comparing the raisings of the dead on the part of the Saviour with those of the prophets on the one hand and those of the apostles on the other, there comes into view as well a remarkable distinction as a beautiful agreement. The Saviour's raisings of the dead are attended with an exalted composure and majesty and acting from His own completeness of might, before which that tension and strain of all the powers of the soul which we more or less observe in the prophets and apostles, wholly vanishes. What to us appears supernatural, for Him appears the highest nature.

4. The event at the gate of Nain might be called one of the most striking proofs of the consoling doctrine of a *providentia specialissima*. The time of

the death and the burial of the young man—the road taken by the funeral train—the meeting with the Lord directly at the decisive moment—nothing of all this is casual here. Time, place, and circumstances, all are ordered to reach a glorious goal; comfort to the afflicted; glory for the Lord; revelation of the quickening power of God.

5. The Saviour's raising the dead was on the one hand a symbol of the life which He causes to arise in the spiritually dead world through His word and His spirit; on the other hand, a prophecy of that which in the ἐσχάτη ἡμέρα shall take place in far greater measure. Both points of view He Himself conjoins in the strictest manner. John v. 24–29.

HOMILETICAL AND PRACTICAL.

Nain's gate, the sanctuary of the glory of God. We see, here has He revealed His glory as: 1. The great Prophet who confirms His preaching with the most astonishing signs; 2. the compassionate High-Priest who dries the tears of the sorrowing; 3. the Prince of life who snatches from the grave its booty.—The journey of the Saviour in the midst of His disciples a perpetual confirmation of His promise, John i. 51.—The personal meeting together of the Prince of Life with the spoil of Death.—How Death strives with Life and Life with Death: 1. Death: a. strikes down the most vigorous age; b. rends the holiest bonds; c. occasions the bitterest tears; 2. Life is here: a. revealed; b. restored; c. dedicated to the glory of God.—The meeting of the Saviour with the funeral train a proof of the most special Providence of God.—Nain's gate, a school for Christian suffering and consolation.—"Weep not:" 1. How easy to use this word; 2. how difficult to obey the injunction; 3. how blessed to dry the tears.—Christ the Life of man: 1. In the creation; 2. in the renovation; 3. in the resurrection.—The resurrection's word of might: 1. The exalted tone; 2. the mighty working; 3. the God-glorifying echo of this word.—How the Lord: 1. Comforts the sorrowing; 2. awakens the dead; 3. unites the severed.—The dawn of eternity breaking over the gate of Nain.—Glory rendered to God, the best fruit of the miracles of Jesus.—How the word of the Saviour's might transforms everything: 1. A funeral train into an array of witnesses of His miracles; 2. a bier of the dead into a field of resurrection; 3. a mourning widow into a thankful mother; 4. a public road into a sanctuary of the glory of God.—He who marvels at great faith has also compassion on the deepest misery.—The love of the Lord: 1. A prevenient; 2. a comforting; 3. an all-accomplishing love.—Ephesians iii. 2–6.—The youth raised from the coffin; Jairus' daughter from the death-bed; Lazarus from the grave.—The journeyings of Christ a gracious visitation of God to His people.—Nain, in a few moments changed from a vale of misery into a vale of beauty (Nain the lovely).—The work of the Lord: 1. On the soul of the mother; 2. on the body of the son.—Spiritually awakened children a gift of the Lord to parents.—Fear and joy here most intimately united.—The renown of the Saviour at this period of history of His life as yet continually on the increase.

STARKE:—Genuine Christians follow Christ whether the way goes towards Cana or towards Nain—towards Tabor or towards Golgotha.—BRENTIUS:—The Lord passes over no city with His grace. The dayspring from on high visits even the meanest villages and hamlets at the right time; oh, excellent consolation!—CRAMER:—The world is a lovely Nain, but death destroys all pleasure therein.—Weep with them that weep, rejoice with them that rejoice.—*Bibl. Wirt.*:—Young people should not put the thoughts of death so far from them, but pray with Moses, Ps. xc. 12.—*Nova Bibl. Tub.*:—How often does the Lord call to one spiritually dead, "Arise"; and he nevertheless continues to lie there.—MAJUS:—Those who are awakened to spiritual life speak with new tongues and walk in a new life.—OSIANDER:—Upon noble deeds follows a good report, a renowned name.

LISCO:—Christ the Vanquisher of Death: 1. In His gracious affection for man; 2. in His divine might and majesty.—The funeral.—HEUBNER:—Life presses in; death flies; admirable change: life is victorious over death.—Jesus' look is even yet directed upon the suffering ones in His church.—"Whoever is afraid of death is afraid of the Lord Jesus." Scriver.—The joy of reunion.—ARNDT:—This history a mirror of sorrow and consolation: 1. A mirror of sorrow: a. Vanity of the world; b. return to the dust; c. the uncertain goal and hour; d. the vanishing of worldly comfort; e. the funeral train, the way of all flesh, *processus mortis.* 2. A mirror of consolation: a. Christ's countenance, the friendly countenance of God; b. the compassionate heart of Jesus; c. His gracious voice: "Weep not;" d. His stretching forth the hand; e. His vivifying word.—Focus:—The preaching of the young man at Nain to the Christians of our time: 1. Who lives shall die; 2. who dies inherits life.—A glance upon: 1. The dead young man; 2. the weeping widow; 3. the almighty Lord; 4. the astonished people.—RIEGER:—Two mighty dominions: 1. A dreary one of death; 2. a joyful one of life.—PETRI:—The wholesome knowledge: 1. Of our true need; 2. of the Almighty help of the Lord.—WESTERMEIER:—The funeral train in the gates of Nain: 1. The dead man who is carried out; 2. the mourners who follow after; 3. the Comforter who suddenly appears.

N. B. We may remark that the homiletical treatment of this narrative should be guarded against a too sentimental representation of the death of the young man, the sorrow of the widow, the joy of reunion, and the like. Nothing is easier than in this way to elicit from the hearers a stream of tears, but the sublime simplicity of Luke remains in this also an unsurpassed model, and the development of the specifically Christian element in this Pericope promises more fruit than the fanciful treatment of its merely human or dramatic elements.

CHAP. VII. 18-35.   115

b. THE EMBASSY OF THE BAPTIST (Vss. 18-35).
(Comp. Matt. xi. 2-19 in part, Gospel for the 3d Sunday in Advent.)

18, 19 And the disciples of John showed him of all these things. And John calling *unto him* two of his disciples sent *them* to Jesus [the Lord, V. O.¹], saying, Art thou he that should come? or look we for another [are we to look, προςδοκῶμεν, prob. subj.]?
20 When the men were come unto him, they said, John [the] Baptist hath sent us
21 unto thee, saying, Art thou he that should come? or look we for another? And in that same hour [or, In that hour²] he cured many of *their* infirmities and plagues, and
22 of evil spirits; and unto many *that were* blind he gave sight. Then Jesus [And He, V. O.³] answering said unto them, Go your way, and tell John what things ye have seen and heard; how that the blind see, the lame walk, the lepers are cleansed, the
23 deaf hear, the dead are raised, to the poor the gospel is preached. And blessed is *he,*
24 whosoever shall not be offended in me [or, take offence at me]. And when the messengers of John were departed, he began to speak unto the people concerning John, What went ye out into the wilderness for to see? A reed shaken with the wind?
25 But what went ye out for to see? A man clothed in soft raiment? Behold, they which are gorgeously apparelled, and live delicately [sumptuously], are in kings' courts.
26 But what went ye out for to see? A prophet? Yea, I say unto you, and much more
27 than a prophet. This is *he,* of whom it is written, Behold, I send my messenger [angel,
28 V. O.] before thy face, which shall prepare thy way before thee [Malachi iii. 1]. For [om., For, V. O.⁴] I say unto you, Among those that are born of women there is not a greater prophet than John the Baptist: but he that is least in the kingdom of God is
29 greater than he. And all the people that heard *him,* and the publicans, justified God,
30 being baptized [or, having been baptized] with the baptism of John. But the Pharisees and [the] lawyers rejected [set at nought] the counsel of God against themselves,
31 being not baptized of [by] him. And the Lord said [om., And the Lord said, V. O.⁵], Whereunto then shall I liken the men of this generation? and to what [whom] are
32 they like? They are like unto children sitting in the marketplace, and calling one to another, and saying, We have piped unto you, and ye have not danced; we have
33 mourned to you, and ye have not wept. For John the Baptist came neither eating
34 bread nor drinking wine; and ye say, He hath a devil. The Son of man is come eating and drinking; and ye say, Behold a gluttonous man, and a winebibber, a friend of pub-
35 licans and sinners! But wisdom is justified of [by] all her children.

¹ Vs. 19.—*Rec.:* πρὸς τὸν Ἰησοῦν. [With A., Sin., 13 other uncials; π. τ. κύριον, with B., L., R., Ξ.—C. C. S.]
[² Vs. 21.—For *Rec.: ἐν αὐτῇ δὲ τῇ ὥρᾳ,* Tischendorf, Tregelles, and Alford read: *ἐν ἐκείνῃ τῇ ὥρᾳ,* as Meyer says, "on insufficient authority and insufficient internal evidence." They are supported by B., L. Cod. Sin. has *ἐν ἐκείνῃ τῇ ἡμέρᾳ.*—C. C. S.]
³ Vs. 22.—*Rec.:* ὁ Ἰησοῦς. [Om., ὁ Ἰησοῦς, Tischendorf, Tregelles, Alford; in Lachmann, bracketed; om., B., D., Ξ., Cod. Sin.—C. C. S.]
⁴ Vs. 28.—*Rec.:* Λέγω γὰρ ὑμῖν. [Om. γαρ, D. Cod. Sin., L., X., Ξ. read αμην λεγω. Tischendorf reads γάρ, and remarks: "*nisi conjunctio adscripta fuisset, vix tam varie legeretur.*"—C. C. S.]
⁶ Vs. 31.—The words at the beginning of the 31st verse: Εἶπε δὲ ὁ κύριος, are in all probability spurious, and have been introduced from some evangelistarium, which might the more easily make a new address begin here, as vss. 29, 30 did not appear to contain a saying of the Lord Himself, but an interposed observation of the evangelist, which, however, is not to be assumed. See below. [Om., Cod. Sin.]

EXEGETICAL AND CRITICAL.

Vs. 18. **Of all these things.**—The miracles which the Saviour had performed of late, especially moreover the raising of the young man at Nain, the report of which, vs. 17, had resounded so far. Respecting the place in which John lay in prison, *see* LANGE on Matt. xi. 2. Matthew brings this embassy into another historical connection, but to us it appears that the order of the occurrences in Luke deserves the preference. From both accounts, however, it appears that although the Baptist was deprived of his freedom, yet the intercourse between him and his disciples still continued in some measure.

Vs. 19. **Art Thou.**—We also cannot possibly assume that John doubted respecting the person of the Lord. With reason has the interpretation as well of the ancient Christian Church as of the reformers, controverted this view as untenable.—But as little conceivable is it that he asked this question for the sake of his disciples alone, or that he would in this way even from his prison offer yet a last public homage to the Lord. (Osiander.) It is rather a question not of secret unbelief, but of increasing impatience. Not the Saviour's person but His mode of action is to John a riddle. Matters move too slowly for him, especially as he himself is now condemned to involuntary inactivity. In vain does he wait for a speedy and public declaration of the Lord in respect to His Messianic dignity. It annoys him that the Saviour speaks more by deeds than by words, since these deeds, moreover, are not miracles of punishment, like those of the old prophets, but benefits, which perhaps did not so well correspond with the expectation which he had formed to himself of the

Lord of the threshing-floor with His fan in His hands (Matt. iii. 11, 12). Perhaps, moreover (Ebrard), it was not pleasing to him that the Saviour hitherto had as yet made no sharply-marked separation among the people, as he himself had begun to do, but let this building fall, while, working formlessly, He journeyed here and there. We do not need, therefore, to assume "that it had become doubtful to him, how the revelation of God, made to himself, was to be understood." (Hofman.) But certainly it must, from his point of view, have surprised him, that the Saviour as yet appeared more in a prophetical than in a properly kingly character. So far, but only so far, can we speak of a doubt, a temptation of the faith of the imprisoned Baptist, which will surprise us the less if we consider how completely as yet he stood within the limits of the Old Covenant, whose heroes distinguished themselves more in conflict than in endurance, and whose great reformer, Elijah the Tishbite, whose image he bore, had also known hours of abandonment and anguish of soul in his own experience. (1 Kings xix. 2–4.) Why should a soul like that of the Baptist have only had its Tabor heights, and not also its Gethsemane depths? And this all becomes the plainer, if we consider that John perhaps in spirit foresaw his end, and, therefore, must have desired the more intensely to see yet before his death the revelation of the kingdom of God, to which his whole life had been devoted. Whoever condemns him, has certainly become acquainted with a life of faith more by description than from personal experience. At the same time he is no less an example worthy of our imitation, that he does not turn himself with his difficulty away from the Lord, but directly to the only one who can solve the riddle for him. As respects the objection, moreover, that he could not in his imprisonment have heard such remarkable reports, comp. WINER on the article *Gefängniss*, and Acts xxiv. 23.

Vs. 21. **In that hour.**—The disciples of John, according to this, find the Saviour in the midst of His miraculous activity; and this account of Luke, which is far from being "a merely explicative addition from his own hand" (Ewald), on the contrary explains to us why the Saviour gives to them just this answer taken from His employment at the time. In the account of the sick here healed, it must not be overlooked that Luke also, the physician, distinguishes the demoniacs from naturally sick persons (Meyer), and with peculiar emphasis designates the recovery of the blind as a gracious gift of the Lord (ἐχαρίσατο).

Blind.—While the Lord points to these tokens of His Messianic dignity (comp. Isa. xxxv. 5, 6; lxi. 1), He shows, on the one hand, that the greater publicity wished for by John was already sufficiently attained; on the other, that He was not yet minded to speak otherwise than through these. The Baptist's question itself was, moreover, affirmatively answered, for he received in this form the assurance: Jesus is truly the CHRIST. And so far as he himself, in a spiritual sense, had become poor, the gospel was also announced to him. The question whether here by the πτωχοί is to be understood outwardly or spiritually poor, is to be answered thus, that, as a rule, the latter were mostly to be found among the former, and that, therefore, both meanings are to be here united.

Vs. 23. **And blessed is he.**—An intimation which was by no means superfluous, either for John, or still less for his disciples, and least of all for later times.—**Whosoever shall not be offended in Me:**—"*rara felicitas*," Bengel, comp. 1 Peter ii. 8.

Vs. 24. **And when—were departed.**—In Matthew, τούτων δὲ πορευομένων ἤρξατο. It is as if the Saviour could scarcely wait for the departure of the messengers to remove immediately the unfavorable impression which the question of the Baptist had, perhaps, made upon the people. Not alone to vindicate the honor of John, but also to anticipate further difficulties conceived as to His person and His work, does He direct an explicit address to the people, in which He extols the character of John, but rebukes the wavering disposition of the people. If any one, perchance, thought that John had not remained consistent with himself, the Saviour lets this reproach so far as this fall upon the nation itself, that neither John, nor Himself, had as yet been able to please them. He makes no scruple of recalling to their memory the image of the Baptist in his most brilliant period.

A reed shaken with the wind?—The Saviour begins with intimating what John had not been; no reed, no weakling, and the like. The assurance that John had not been by nature a wavering and inconstant man, was at the same time a sure implication that the Baptist, therefore, did not doubt respecting the person of the Saviour, as Chrysostom has already justly remarked in his thirty-seventh homily. This first question is followed by no answer, since each one could give this for himself. Observe further the fine climax in the arrangement of the interrogations, κάλαμον, ἄνθρωπον, προφήτην.

Vs. 25. **A man.**—The question is intended to contradict the conjecture, that John had sent to Christ because his imprisonment was burdensome, and he hoped to be free therefrom. An antithesis between his camel's-hair garment in the wilderness on the one hand, and the sumptuous clothing of his enemies at the court on the other. In order to seek a weakling, one had to go not to the prison, but to the palace.

Vs. 26. **A prophet?**—Instead of allowing that John had in any respect lost his claim to this name, the Saviour shows how far he was even exalted above ordinary prophets. He is something greater (Neuter) than all his predecessors, since he could claim to be the herald of the Messiah.

Vs. 27. **This is he.**—Comp. Malachi iii. 1. "He is, if ye will hear, Elijah who is to come, as Malachi prophesied; and before whom is Elijah to go to prepare the way? Malachi says: 'Before God the Lord Himself.' What does Jesus, therefore, testify of Himself, when He says, John has gone as Elijah before Him? Who hath ears to hear, let him hear!" J. Riggenbach.

Vs. 28. **Among those that are born of women.**—Comp. Matt. xi. 11. Luke has correctly adjoined the word προφήτης, which was already presupposed in the ἐγήγερται of Matthew. Among all the prophets John deserves to be called the greatest, because he was the messenger of whom Malachi has spoken. Respecting the ethical worth of his character, the Saviour does not here speak directly, but yet He would not have bestowed this praise upon His Forerunner, if the latter had only possessed prophetical dignity without high excellence of character. The second part of the declaration is by no means to be explained as a testimony of our Lord in reference to Himself (Fritzsche, a. o.). How can the King of the kingdom of heaven place Himself on an equality with those who are in His kingdom? No, He speaks of the least of His disciples, and this not only so far as they appear as apostles or evangelists, but without any distinction. He thinks of their preëminence above the most distinguished men of the Old Covenant, the array of whom closed with John. They had, through the light of the experience of His redeeming power, deeper insight into the nature, the course of development, and the blessings of the kingdom of heaven, than had been the portion of John. If this was true even of those who then believed in Jesus, how much more of us to whom, by the history of the centuries, His greatness has been so much more gloriously revealed.

Vs. 29. **And all the people.**—It is a question, whether we have here a remark of Luke, meant to give, vss. 29, 30, his hearers who dwelt out of Palestine a more particular account of the various reception which the baptism of John had found (Bengel, Paulus, Lachmann, Bornemann, Stier), or whether it constitutes a continuation of the discourse of the Saviour. The latter appears to deserve the preference, as the words εἶπε δὲ ὁ κύρ., vs. 31, are on internal and external grounds suspicious, while, moreover, vss. 29, 30 contain nothing additional which the Saviour Himself might not have said; and besides, there is no second example of so extended an interpolation of Luke without any indication of it. It is a statement of how differently the preaching and baptism of John had been judged, by which, therefore, the reproach, vss. 31, 34, is prepared.—[" Vs. 29 f. does not contain an intervening comment of Luke, which is opposed by his usage elsewhere, and is disproved by the spuriousness of εἶπε δὲ ὁ κύριος, vs. 31 (b. Elz.), but is *the language of Jesus*, who states the *different results* which the appearance of this greatest prophet had had with the people and with the hierarchs. It must, however, be admitted that the words, in comparison with the force, freshness, and oratorical liveliness of the preceding, bear a more *historical* stamp, and therefore may with reason be regarded as a later intercalation of tradition." MEYER.—C. C. S.]

Ἐδικαίωσαν τὸν Θεόν, *i. e.*, not only: "They declared in act that His will, that they should receive the baptism of John, was right" (Meyer): but they approved the judgment of God, which called them sinners, that needed such a baptism unto repentance.

Vs. 30. Ἠθέτησαν. It was God's counsel (βουλή) that the Jews through the baptism of John should be prepared for the Salvation of the Messianic age. Since now the Pharisees and Scribes held themselves back from this baptism, they frustrated this counsel in relation to themselves (εἰς ἑαυτούς), and exhibited themselves, indeed, the bitterest enemies of themselves, as has been in all times the case with the rejectors of the Gospel. The Saviour in this whole remark, just as in John v. 33–35, looks back upon the period of John's activity as one already concluded, and since He is conscious that the opposition against Him, at bottom, springs from no other source than that against John the Baptist, he finds the way prepared of itself for the following parable.

Vs. 31. **Whereunto then shall I.**—Here the inquiry of perplexity, as in Mark iv. 30 that of intimacy with His disciples. The answer is an irrefragable proof with how attentive and tranquil a look He observed daily life even in the plays of the childish world. In children He sees miniature men, in men grown-up children.

Vs. 32. **Like unto children.**—We must declare against the common explanation, as if the children (the Jews) had so played and spoken *among one another*, for who should then have been the ones who would not dance when others played, nor weep when others lamented? Yet as little do we believe with Fritzsche, that Jesus and John are here reckoned *in with* their contemporaries, that the former were to be the speakers, and the latter the addressed. We reverse it rather, and consider Jesus and John indicated (according to Matthew) as ἑταῖροι, over against whom the people are introduced speaking, and complaining that these friends had always wanted something different from what themselves wanted and did. They had demanded of John cheerfulness, and he had come μήτε ἐσθίων μήτε πίνων; from Jesus they had expected strictness and sadness, and He manifested a mild and joyous spirit. In this view no feature of the comparison is lost, and yet the application is not forced or stiff. Comp. LANGE, *Life of Christ*, ii. p. 761, with whose objections against the explanation of R. Stier we fully agree.

Vs. 33. **Neither eating bread, nor drinking wine.**—Comp. Luke i. 15. John's austere mode of life was wholly agreeable to the spirit of his teaching, but displeasing not only to the small court-party, but to all who, pervaded by the leaven of the Sadducees, held unrighteousness dear. They accused him not only of lunacy, but also of actual possession (the Scripture distinguishes the two, John x. 20). No wonder, for he would not dance when they piped before him.

Vs. 34. **The Son of Man.**—Here is this appellation very especially fitting, as it comes at the beginning of a declaration which refers us to the Lord's ideal Humanity. He was come eating and drinking, in no way despising the comforts of social life, but temperately enjoying them, even in company with publicans and sinners. But herein had legal self-righteousness found a heavy stone of stumbling. What they had not been able to endure in John, they appeared now to demand in Christ: austere, unbending sternness. And when He did not give ear to this demand, they had ready at once the names of glutton and wine-bibber, friend of publicans and sinners, in which, however, they did not consider that these latter words indicated His highest titles of honor (comp. Luke xv. 2). Not only had the disciples of John taken offence at Him (comp. ch. v. 33), but also the Pharisees and all that were accustomed to see through their eyes. The greater part did not receive Him because He had not chosen to weep when they began a gloomy lay of mourning. It would have been a hopeless attempt to labor at the conversion of such a nation, if no exceptions to this sad rule had been found. To these the Saviour refers in the following words. [Notwithstanding that the author's application of the similitude of the complaining children to the Jews is supported by the names of Bleek, De Wette, and Meyer, I cannot see sufficient reason for abandoning the usual interpretation, which reverses the application. It is confessedly the *unreasonableness* of the Jews in being satisfied neither with John's mode of life, nor with our Lord's, which is the point of comparison. Exactly parallel to this is the unreasonableness charged by the children in the parable upon their fellows. To say that the complaining children were the unreasonable ones, in expecting their fellows to accommodate themselves to every whim of theirs, appears rather an afterthought, than one suggested naturally by the parable. It is true, the words are, "This generation is like unto children," &c.; but, as Bleek admits, passages like Matt. xiii. 24 show that these words do not necessarily mean that the generation itself is like the complainers, but that the *relation* between this generation and our Lord and John, was like that set forth in the parable. There is certainly weight in Bleek's objection, that this indefiniteness can hardly go so far as to liken the generation addressed to one class of the children, when it was meant to be represented as like the exactly opposite class. But this, it appears to me, does not turn the scale against the evident correspondence between the generation complained of by Christ and the children complained of in the parable.—C. C. S.]

Vs. 35. **But wisdom.**—*See* different views in LANGE *ad loc.* Perhaps we meet here with a proverb not unknown to the contemporaries of our Lord; at least this declaration has a gnome-like character. Wisdom can here be no other than the Divine Wisdom which had been revealed by John and Jesus, and in Jesus was personally manifested: her children are those who are not only born of her, but also related to her, in that they possess a wise heart; and the justification of wisdom takes place where she is acquitted of accusations of this kind, and acknowledged in her true character. Such a justification was to be expected from her children alone, but also from *all* her children. We are not to understand this saying as a complaint, but as an antithesis of the preceding; an encouragement at the same time for the disciples of Jesus, when they should afterwards experience something similar to that which He and John had experienced.

DOCTRINAL AND ETHICAL.

1. It is a striking argument for the great difference between the Old and the New Testament, that even the greatest of the prophets can, at the beginning, accommodate himself only with difficulty to the Saviour's way of working. Among all those lofty and brilliant expectations which had been excited by the prophetic word, the meek, still spirit of the Gospel could only gradually break a way for itself. John must continually take secret offence against Jesus, before he had become in spirit a disciple of the best Master. Thus this whole history is a continuous proof of the truth of the saying, Matt. xviii. 7: "It must needs be that offences come," and as here, the σκάνδαλα have served the purpose of hastening the revelation of the glory of the Lord, and the coming of His kingdom.

2. Here also, as in John v. 36, the Saviour adduces His ἔργα as arguments for the certainty of His heavenly mission,—a new proof of the agreement between the Synoptical and the Johannean Christ, but at the same time also a troublesome sign for every one who still with the apostles of unbelief demands: "*dites-moi ces miracles de votre Évangile.*" The Saviour did not perform the miracles that they might become stones of stumbling; on the other hand, they are intended to be means of advancement on the way of faith, and now as ever His answer to every one who secretly takes offence, but turns himself with his doubts to Him that they may be solved, and has remained receptive for rational persuasion, is: "The blind see," &c. But whoever cannot, by the spiritual workings of Christianity in man and in mankind, be convinced of the fact that something superhuman is working concealed therein, for such an one all abstract grounds of proof are fruitless. From this follows, moreover, that only those who in person belong to the τυφλοῖς and κωφοῖς spiritually healed by Jesus, will possess a persuasion of faith which can be shaken by nothing subsequent. This is the true demonstration of the Spirit and of power, which constitutes the crown of all Apologetics. But precisely because the Saviour knows this, and foresees how much it costs flesh and blood to remove out of the way all offences taken at Him and His work, He pronounces all blessed who raise themselves to such a height. Another Macarism faith may perhaps subjoin: "Blessed he who, when he might take offence, turns himself to Jesus for healing!"

3. In an exalted tone and, moreover, with perfect justice, does the Saviour praise His imprisoned Forerunner. The whole life of John is a continuous commentary on that which is here said in a few words; and it impresses, therefore, its seal on the correctness of this description of his character. Not less, moreover, does a praise bestowed on such an occasion redound to the honor of the Saviour Himself. In the first place, we admire here His deep wisdom, which takes pains to obliterate in the best manner a perverted impression; and then quite as much the holy severity with which He, without respect of persons, censures the faults of His contemporaries. While the Saviour avoids making a direct declaration of His Messianic dignity, He places it indirectly in a clear light, inasmuch as He points as well to His distinction from, as also to His exaltation above, the position and spirit of the Baptist. And as the people, after what had just taken place, were, perhaps, already disposed to look down upon the prophet of the wilderness with contempt, He constrains them rather to throw a searching and shaming look into their own hearts.

4. "The least in the kingdom of heaven is greater." One of the most admirable testimonies respecting the inestimable preëminence of the sincere disciples of the Saviour; but at the same time also a witness of Christ to Himself that may not be slightly esteemed. What a consciousness must He bear within Him who exalts His least disciple above the greatest of the prophets, and yet can declare: "I am meek and lowly of heart" (Matt. xi. 29).

5. The diverse behavior of the publicans and Pharisees, in relation to the baptism of John, gives a convincing proof that self-righteousness sets a far greater obstacle to the coming of the kingdom of God in the heart, than the unrighteousness of the most deeply-sunken sinners. Comp. Matt. xxi. 31, 32.

6. The reception on the part of their changeable contemporaries which fell to the lot of John and Jesus, recurs in all manner of forms as well in the history of the Theocracy under Israel, as in that of the Christian Church. This manifestation repeats itself continually where men judge after the flesh, where men judge the truth according to a previously settled system, instead of unconditionally subjecting themselves with their system to the wisdom of God; where, in a word, the natural man bears dominion. Only of the spiritual man does the apostle's word hold good, 1 Cor. ii. 15. Each time the man wills otherwise than God, or he wills that willed by God at another time, in another way, and in another measure. The only infallible touch-stone, therefore, as to whether we already belong to the τέκνα τῆς σοφίας or not, lies simply in the relation in which we stand to God's word and testimony. The truth of God is recognized with such assurance by the children of wisdom, because, even when it is in conflict with their natural feelings, it finds the deepest echo in the sanctuary

of the heart and conscience. The children of wisdom are essentially identical with the νήπιοι (Luke x. 21), to whom the things of God have been revealed.

7. The crown of all the σημεῖα of the Lord, and at the same time the means whereby these are continually propagated in the spiritual sphere, is the preaching of the Gospel to the poor, which is, moreover, the highest signature for the divinity of the Gospel. Comp. 1 Cor. i. 26, 31.

HOMILETICAL AND PRACTICAL.

The fame of the Saviour finds its way to a solitary prison: 1. How John stands here with reference to Jesus: *a.* with a secret displeasure, *b.* with a question implying desire; 2. Jesus with reference to John: *a.* with a satisfying answer, *b.* an earnest warning, *c.* an emphatic commendation.—Doubts must bring us the quicker to Christ.—Doubt dies only in the immediate neighborhood of Him through whom it was raised.— "Art thou He that should come?" This question is answered, *a.* with the "No" of unbelief, *b.* the "Yea" of faith, *c.* the Hallelujah of thankfulness.—The great Advent question: *a.* its high significance, *b.* its satisfactory answer.—The miracles of the Saviour in the natural and moral world, His best credentials.—Christ yet continues to perform what He did in this hour.—Christ's healings of the blind.—Christ's raisings of the dead.—The preaching of the Gospel to the poor: 1. A clear credential for the Saviour, 2. an inestimable benefit for the world, 3. an infinitely exalted, yet holy commission for the Christian.—How poverty is related to Christ, and Christ to poverty.—The blessedness of those who are not offended in Christ: 1. An unusual, 2. a rich, 3. an obtainable blessedness.—The holy love and the holy earnestness of the Saviour over against honest doubters.—The flexible reed and the inflexible character of John.—One needs not go to the shore of Jordan to see shaken reeds.—The prophets in camel's hair, the courtiers in sumptuous clothing.—The morally free man in bonds, and the slave of the world in freedom.—John *a.* equal to, *b.* exalted above, the prophets of the Old Testament.—The herald's function of John the Baptist: 1. In its origin, 2. its significance, 3. its abiding value.—The greatness and the littleness of John the Baptist: 1. His higher position above other prophets. No prophet was *a.* enlightened with clearer light, *b.* privileged with a more excellent commission, *c.* crowned with a higher honor, *d.* adorned with a purer virtue than John; 2. his littleness, as compared with the genuine disciple of the Saviour. The true Christian is, on his part, *a.* enlightened with clearer light, *b.* privileged with a more exalted commission, *c.* crowned with a higher honor (John xv. 15), *d.* called to purer virtue than John.—The word of the Saviour concerning the greatness or littleness of John the Baptist: *a.* humbling for those that stand below him, *b.* encouraging for those that stand beside him, *c.* cheering for those who really stand above him.—The reception of the Baptist with Pharisees and publicans: 1. Very diverse, 2. fully explicable, 3. now as then of important consequences.—John and Jesus found and find the same friends and the same foes.—Knowledge that God is in the right is the beginning of conversion.—Enmity against the truth is at the same time enmity against one's own soul.—The world of children the image of the world of men.—The alternation of frolicsome joy and complaints is after the manner of children,

great and small.— The servant of the Truth never called to dispose himself according to the changing humors of his contemporaries.—How far is it permitted, or not permitted, the preacher of the Word to take account of the demands which others make of him?—Now, as ever, strict seriousness is condemned by the world as lunacy.—The Son of Man is come eating and drinking.—The temperate enjoyment of life approved and consecrated by the word and the Spirit of the Lord.—Christ the Friend of publicans and sinners: 1. A vile calumny, 2. a holy truth, 3. an exalted eulogy, 4. a joyful message, 5. an example worthy of imitation.—The Lord Himself a proof of the truth of His word, Luke vi. 26.—The justification of Wisdom by her children: 1. Necessary, 2. certain, 3. satisfactory.—As long as there are children of Wisdom, that which is foolish has nothing to fear before God, 1 Cor. i. 25.

STARKE:—It is something beautiful and pleasant when teachers and hearers stand in good accord, and diligently edify one another.— QUESNEL:—A Christian can draw profit even from novel tidings, if he applies them to his own edification and that of others. —MAJUS:—Learn to answer rightly the most weighty inquiry of all, who the true Saviour of the world is, and thou shalt be well enlightened.—According to Christ's example we should rather prove with deeds that we are Christians, than with words.—CANSTEIN: —It is something great when one can fearlessly appeal to truth and deed. 2 Cor. i. 12.—MAJUS:—Those that walk after Christ find many hindrances and offences in their way, but these must be taken out of the way and overcome, Isa. lvii. 14.— OSIANDER:—Steadfastness in all good is the most excellent ornament of a servant and child of God.—BRENTIUS:—Careless and rough people are oftentimes easier to be persuaded by the word of truth, than presumptuous hypocrites and reputed wise men.—Whoever despises the counsel of God which is meant for his soul's health, will experience God's counsel against him with harm and pain.—HEDINGER:—God can manage it so as to please no one: to say nothing then of a frail man with censorious fault-finders.—God's former servants have been ever calumniated, how then should His present ones fare better?—The world cleaves to its wonted way, and calls evil good and good evil (Isa. v. 20); wonder not thereat.— OSIANDER:—The teacher is not to be born that can please all men.— MAJUS:—Independent wisdom calls all fools to herself, and will make all wise, but few hear her and follow her.—HEUBNER:—Whoever does not find in Christ his salvation may wait therefor in vain.—Only one coming will overpass all our expectations, the coming of Christ.—Christianity is founded upon history, upon facts.—Christianity a religion of the poor.— GUYON (on vs. 28):—John is the type of the condition of penitence. Whoever has truly pressed into the sanctuary, into the kingdom of grace, whoever has arrived at the full enjoyment of grace, is greater, more blessed than he that remains still in penitence. —LUTHER (vss. 32-34):— "If one preaches the Gospel, it amounts to nothing; if he preaches the Law, it amounts to nothing again: he can neither make the people really joyous, nor really sorry."

The PERICOPE (vss. 18-27, comp. Matt. xi. 2-10). The double testimony which Jesus renders before the people: 1. The testimony concerning Himself, vss. 18-23; 2. respecting John the Baptist, vss. 24-27.— COUARD:—John, 1. As to his faith; 2. as to his walk; 3. as to his works.—PH. D. BURK:—When Jesus will hold up before a soul its wretchedness out of Him,

He tells it of the blessedness of those that abide in Him. *Contraria contrariis curantur.*—THYM:—The question of the Baptist. We take: 1. The question for testing: *a.* from whom it proceeds, *b.* how it arose, *c.* what it aims at. 2. The answer from experience: *a.* who gives it, *b.* to what it refers, *c.* what prize it proposes to us. 3. The testimony in truth: *a.* by whom it is given, *b.* what it sets forth, *c.* what aim it has.—HÖPFNER:—The glory of Jesus who came into the world in a servant's form.—FLOREY: — What the Saviour requires of those who will prepare His way in the hearts of men.

---

c. THE DINNER IN THE HOUSE OF SIMON THE PHARISEE (Vss. 36-50).

(Gospel on St. Mary Magdalene's Day.)

36 And one of the Pharisees desired him that he would eat with him. And he went
37 into the Pharisee's house, and sat down to meat [reclined at table]. And, behold, a woman in the city, which was a sinner[1] [or, a woman who in the city was a sinner], when she knew that Jesus sat at meat [was reclining at table] in the Pharisee's house,
38 brought an alabaster box [or, flask] of ointment, And stood at his feet behind him weeping, and began to wash [moisten] his feet with tears, and did wipe them with the
39 hairs of her head, and kissed his feet, and anointed *them* with the ointment. Now when the Pharisee which had bidden [invited] him saw *it*, he spake within himself, saying, This man, if he were a prophet, would have known who and what manner of woman
40 *this is* that toucheth him; for [that] she is a sinner. And Jesus answering said unto
41 him, Simon, I have somewhat to say unto thee. And he saith, Master [Teacher], say on. There was a certain creditor which had two debtors: the one owed five hundred
42 pence [denarii], and the other fifty. And [om., And, V. O.[2]] when they had nothing to pay, he frankly forgave them [remitted it to] both. Tell me therefore, which of
43 them will love him most? Simon answered and said, I suppose that *he*, to whom he
44 forgave [remitted] most. And he said unto him, Thou hast rightly judged. And he turned to the woman, and said unto Simon, Seest thou this woman? I entered into thine house, thou gavest me no water for my feet: but she hath washed [moistened]
45 my feet with tears, and wiped *them* with the hairs of her head [om., of her head, V. O.[3]]. Thou gavest me no kiss: but this woman, since the time I came in, hath not
46 ceased to kiss my feet. My head with oil thou didst not anoint: but this woman hath
47 anointed my feet with ointment. Wherefore I say unto thee, Her sins, which are many, are forgiven; for [because, V. O.] she loved much: but to whom little is for-
48, 49 given, *the same* loveth little. And he said unto her, Thy sins are forgiven. And they that sat at meat [reclined at table] with him began to say within themselves,
50 Who is this that forgiveth sins also? And [But] he said to the woman, Thy faith hath saved thee; go in peace.

[1] Vs. 37.—Agreeably to the most probable arrangement: ἥτις ἦν immediately after γυνή. [Cod. Sin. places the words so.—C. C. S.]
[2] Vs. 42.—*Rec.*: Μὴ ἐχόντων δὲ. Δέ is to be omitted. [Ins., Cod. Sin. and 15 other uncials; om., B., D., L., P.—C. C. S.]
[3] Vs. 44.—*Rec.*: ταῖς θριξὶ τῆς κεφαλῆς αὐτῆς. [Om., τῆς κεφ., A., B., D., Cod. Sin. al.—C. C. S.]

EXEGETICAL AND CRITICAL.

General Remarks.—1. CHRONOLOGY. Although Luke makes the narrative of the feast in Simon's house follow immediately on the embassy of the disciples of John, yet it by no means results from this, that the one took place immediately after the other. It is not improbable that, among others, the discourses of the Saviour given in Matthew, ch. xi. 20-30, preceded it. But at all events both occurrences belong to the history of the public life of the Saviour in Galilee shortly before the second passover (John vi. 4).

2. HARMONY. It is a question whether this anointing is the same which the three other Evangelists mention at the beginning of the history of the Passion. Although distinguished men have given an affirmative answer to this question (Schleiermacher, Strauss, De Wette, Ewald), we have no scruple, nevertheless, to attach ourselves to those who declare for the original diversity of the two narratives. For both accounts agree only in this, that in the two cases the host is named "Simon," and that the woman who anoints the Saviour dries His feet with the hair of her head. But on what grounds it is impossible that two Simons may have lived, of whom one was a disciple in Galilee, who treated Jesus with distrust, and the other a recovered leper in Judea, who clave to Jesus with faithful affection, we comprehend as little as why those whose doubts arise from the agreement of the two names, leave us yet two Judases, two Simons, and two Jameses in the circle of the apostles. And as respects the other circumstances, it scarcely needs suggestion that two affectionate and thankful women, quite independently of

each other, might have the thought occur to them of bringing the Saviour an homage of such a kind. Besides these, all the features of the case are different: In this, the host is an enemy, there a friend, of the Saviour; here it was an anointing from thankful love, there, at the same time, an anointing for death; here Jesus is censured by a Pharisee, there the woman by a disciple; here it is haughtiness, there it is selfishness, which is the source of this hostility; here the sinner is pronounced blessed, there the female disciple is honored with the highest distinction. "A criticism which in these representations can see images with no solidity, dissolving into one another, because in them accidentally there are two hosts of the name of Simon, or some other similarities, would more easily become skilled in assigning titles and uniforms, than in distinguishing the highest delineations of character and exhibitions of peculiar dispositions in the higher region of the primitive Christian history or the Christian spiritual life." LANGE, *Leben Jesu.* Even the conjecture (Neander) that the name *Simon* has through an incorrect tradition been transferred from the second host to the first, we consider as arbitrary as unnecessary. With greater justice it might perhaps be assumed that Mary of Bethany had knowledge of the act of the Galilean woman, and had therefore the earlier come to the thought of showing her love and her thankfulness to the Saviour in a similar manner. The endeavor to identify the two accounts with one another presupposes a view of the incorrectness of the evangelical tradition, to which we are in principle opposed.

Vs. 36. **And one of the Pharisees desired Him.**—Time and place are not particularly indicated. There is as little reason for ascribing the very invitation of the Pharisee to hostile intentions as for believing that it sprung from the good ground of esteem and affection. Perhaps pride itself impelled him to receive a Rabbi at his table, whose name was already upon so many tongues, and in respect to whom one did not know how high he might yet rise. And the Son of Man, who was come "eating and drinking," yielded willingly to his invitation, although we may well suppose He was not unaware (John ii. 25) that it had sprung from an impure intent.

And reclined at table.—It appears from the sequel, without having His feet washed or being anointed. "Jesus lay supported on His left arm with His head turned towards the table, upon a pillow, and His feet were turned outward to where the attendants stood; moreover they were naked, as He had laid off His sandals." De Wette.

Vs. 37. **A woman who in the city was a sinner.**—The name of the town is not given. The conjecture that it was Jerusalem (Paulus) is quite as unfounded as many others. In any case, we are to seek the theatre of the event in Galilee. "Sinner" appears here to intimate especially an unchaste life, by which she stood in evil repute among her fellow townsmen. (*See* vs. 39.) Respecting the different ways in which a woman among the Jews might procure to herself the name ἁμαρτωλός, comp. Lightfoot, *ad loc.*

Very early has this sinner been regarded as one and the same with Mary Magdalene, on which account the church has appointed this gospel for her memorial. *See* WINER, *in voce*, and SEPP, *Leben Jesu*, p. 281–292, who has also collected the most noticeable legends in regard to her person. Undoubtedly the identity of the persons is not mathematically demonstrable, but much less can we designate the difficulties which have been raised against it as entirely unremovable, and we doubt whether the Catholic church in this point deserves the opposition which, as a rule, falls to her share from the most of modern expositors. Tradition, which was acquainted with the second anointing by Mary, the sister of Lazarus, would not also, without some special occasion, have given the name Mary to the woman first anointing. That Mary Magdalene is first mentioned, ch. viii. 2, certainly does not prove that she could not before this have anointed the Saviour in Simon's house. Perhaps she had belonged to the unhappy ones, out of whom Jesus, only a short time before, about the time of the visit of John's disciples (ch. vii. 21), had expelled unclean spirits. A sinner like Magdalene had certainly not been received in the ordinary way into the most intimate circle of friends, and assuredly one can scarcely imagine a more beautiful occasion for it than the act here recorded in Simon's house. We may add that precisely such a behavior as that recorded of the woman in Simon's house agrees entirely with what is known to us respecting the loving Magdalene (John xx. 11–18), especially if she had only lately been healed of her terrible plague. But enough concerning a conjecture, which certainly cannot be fully proved, but which still less deserves to be rejected without further inquiry. Comp. LANGE, *Life of Christ*, *ad loc.* [I do not see what occasion the author has to regard Mary Magdalene as an extraordinary sinner. As Trench has well observed in his work on Miracles, demoniac possession appears to have implied a peculiar deficiency of the energy of personal will in the afflicted, whether natural or induced by weakening disease, but by no means to have implied of course any peculiar criminality. Undoubtedly sin, and especially sins of voluptuousness, tend very greatly to weaken the moral and voluntary energies. But there are so many other causes that may effect the same result, that to bring such an imputation against Mary Magdalene on no other ground, appears to me, I confess, little better than a posthumous slander. Then the mention of Mary Magdalene immediately afterwards, viii. 2, in a manner that does not betray the faintest consciousness of her having been mentioned before, is certainly very little agreeable to this identification. Our Saviour, moreover, although He came to seek and to save the lost, and although to His inward view one saved sinner was even as another, appears in the choice of His intimate companions to have maintained a Divine decorum, such as breathes through all His words and acts, and which may not without reason have been supposed to be operative in this case.—C. C. S.]

Vs. 37. **When she knew.**—The meals at which Jesus took part appear to have had a somewhat public character. The entrance stood open to all, not because they were invited with Him, but because the concourse could not be hindered.

An alabaster flask, ἀλάβαστρον μύρου.—A very fine, mostly white species of gypsum, but not so hard as marble, and therefore not so serviceable for finely polished furniture. "*Unguenta optime servantur in alabastris*," writes Pliny, xiii. 3, and to this notion apparently it is to be ascribed that they were accustomed to transport unguents and perfumes in alabaster flasks, which were sealed at the tops, and opened by breaking the long neck. Perhaps we are here to understand alabaster from Damascus and Syria, which was distinguished especially by its clearness, while the best Nard ointment was prepared at Tarsus in Cilicia. Comp. FRIEDLIEB, *Die Archæol. der Leidensgeschichte*, on Matt. xxvi. 6 *seq.* —Moreover, among the ancients there prevailed elsewhere also the custom of kissing the feet of those to whom it was intended to display a very especial reverence, especially of the Rabbis (Wetstein), and the noting of the moment when the whole transaction began (ἤρξατο), contributes not a little to heighten the vividness of the whole narrative.

Vs. 38. **And began to moisten His feet with tears, and did wipe them with the hairs of her head.**—The question spontaneously presents itself to us, what may have given occasion to all this burst of feeling in the homage rendered by the woman. Without doubt she had previously seen and heard the Lord, and, in whatever way it may have come to pass, had already received a great benefit from Jesus. We are most disposed to understand this as a bodily healing and benefit, certainly not worth less than the debt of five hundred denarii. For this mercy she will manifest to the Lord her thankful love. Perhaps He had, in order to put her to the proof, delivered her indeed from the malady which was the consequence of her sinful life, but as yet withheld the word of pardon and grace, of which she stood in most need. So there burns along with the flame of gratitude the secret longing after a higher, a spiritual salvation in her heart. The impure wishes to be declared pure, the fallen to be raised up, the sorrowing to be comforted, the thankful for recovery to be blest with yet greater fulness of grace. For a shorter or longer time she has already been looking for an opportunity to draw near to the Saviour without being thrust back by an incompassionate hand, and now when she hears He is a guest in Simon's house, she is withheld as little by false shame as by fear of man from following the drawing of her heart.

Vs. 39. **Now when the Pharisee . . . saw.**—Without doubt the first feeling of the Pharisee was that of displeasure that such a woman had ventured to pollute his pure threshold. But with that is next joined dissatisfaction and doubt in reference to his guest, who, as he sees, is well content to be touched by such hands. Without any organ by which he is able to place himself in the woman's condition or to estimate the beauty of her action, he judges according to the logic of the natural man and of the Jew imprisoned in prejudices. The major term of the syllogism which, in secret, he forms to himself, is double. A prophet would, in the first place, know what is hidden, and know accordingly the history of this ἁμαρτωλός, and, secondly, shudder at the contact of that which is unholy. That the former may be true of Jesus and the latter not, does not even enter his mind. The minor and the conclusion from his point of view need no statement. Among the Jews the idea commonly prevailed that a prophet must know everything secret, and that in particular the Messiah must be at a loss for an answer to no question; therefore the ensnaring questions which even to the end of His life they continued to propose to Him; therefore also the inference of the disciples (John xvi. 29, 30).—As respects our Simon, moreover, it is scarcely to be doubted that he, how much soever he may have been λέγων ἐν ἑαυτῷ, yet also gave vent to his displeasure by looks, gestures, and light murmurs. The Saviour, however, has no need of that to hear him, He already reads in Simon's thoughts. He vindicates the honor of the woman and His own in a noble parable, which He presents in so striking, so powerful a manner that we scarcely know which we should most admire: the skill with which He causes the accuser to appear as witness against himself, or the moderation with which He still spares His host, inasmuch as He forbears any severer censure; whether the holy irony with which He explains Simon's deficiency in love, or the lofty seriousness with which He gives him to feel that his sin is yet unforgiven.

Vs. 41. **A certain creditor.**—Under the image of the creditor the Lord depicts Himself, while, in the debtor that owed the more and the one that owed the less, we behold respectively the portrait of the sinner and of Simon. It results, therefore, from this, that the Saviour declares the action of the sinner to be a work of thankful love in consequence of a benefit received. It does not however necessarily follow from this that Simon also had been restored by a miracle from a sickness (Paulus, Kuinoel); the benefit bestowed on him (=50 denarii) was the honor of a visit from the Lord, the value of which, however, must have been exceedingly small in his eyes.

Δηνάρια, a Roman silver coin, =1 drachma = 16 asses [about 7¼*d.* sterling, or 15 cents; 50 denarii = $7.50; 500 D. = $75.00: both sums worth then many times their present value.—C. C. S.].

Vs. 43. **I suppose.**—The gravity of the Pharisee, before whom a problem is laid for solution, does not belie itself. With greater modesty than that with which he had just murmured in secret does he give his opinion, and is rewarded by the Saviour with an ὀρθῶς of holy irony, an ὀρθῶς which is about to turn itself immediately as a weapon against him.

Vs. 44. **Seest thou this woman?**—Apparently Simon had as much as possible avoided looking at her. At least he must, after the parable he had heard, have regarded her with quite different eyes, and have seen in a great sinner a great lover, and so far a great saint, if he compared her with himself, the proud egoist. But now the word of rebuke breaks as a flood over him. The great distinction which the Lord had rendered to Simon by His coming He brings at once, with the noblest sense of dignity, into view.—**I entered into thine house.**—The σοῦ at the beginning of the address gives emphasis to the tone of reproach, of which Simon is made conscious in a threefold comparison of his behavior with that of the sinning woman. No washing of the feet, no kiss of welcome, no anointing has he, at the entrance of his Guest into his dwelling, had ready for Him. What Meyer, *ad loc.*, in reference to the first adduces as an excuse, namely, that the washing of His feet had not been absolutely necessary, since the Saviour had not come directly from His journey, is to our apprehension not satisfactory; for if this neglect had been entirely unimportant or accidental, the Saviour would certainly not have brought it up to him. As opposed to his lovelessness and his avarice, the benevolence and bounteousness in the sinning woman's exhibition of love strikes the eye so much the more. Simon gives no water—she her tears, *aquarum preciosissimas* (Bengel), and instead of a linen cloth, the thousand hairs of her head. Simon gives no kiss upon the mouth, she kisses much more humbly the feet, of the Lord; Simon gives no ἔλαιον, but she something much more precious, μύρον. And this proof of her homage she presented to the Lord from the very time of his entrance, ἀφ' ἧς εἰσῆλθον. (See the textual notes on vs. 45.) The reading εἰσῆλθεν, has perhaps arisen from the fact that the woman was supposed to have entered after Jesus, so that she could not well have manifested her love to Him from His very entrance. This difficulty, however, vanishes if we consider that the woman, seeking for an opportunity for her work of love, would probably have entered very soon after the Saviour; and thus at the same time the antithesis is most distinctly preserved between that which the two, Simon and the woman, had done at His entrance into the house.

Vs. 47. **Wherefore I say unto thee.**—We consider it forced and unnatural to regard λέγω σοι as standing in a parenthesis (De Wette), and separated in some measure from οὗ χάριν. Better Meyer: "On this account I say to thee; for the sake of these her exhibitions of love, I declare to thee: Forgiven are her sins," &c.

Ἀφέωνται—ὅτι ἠγάπησε πολύ.—According to the Roman Catholic exegetes, with whom, among others, De Wette also agrees, the words: **Because she loved much**, must indicate the proper cause, the *antecedens* of the forgiveness of the debt. The Romish church has here found a support for the doctrine of the meritoriousness of good works, and the Protestant polemics have undertaken to confute it by often in some measure doing violence to the text. To the unsuccessful attempts to escape from this difficulty must apparently be added the following: "Her sins are forgiven her (this she knows, and) therefore has she exhibited much love;" or this: "Her sins are forgiven her, that she might love much," or " that the Pharisee, from her thankfulness, might be well able to conclude that already much must have been forgiven her," &c. All these interpretations suffer shipwreck on the simple signification of the words, especially of ὅτι, and the parable also, vss. 41, 42, shows evidently that the Saviour received her work as a token of thankful love. Had the woman really already received entire assurance of forgiveness, and her rich love now been the proof of it, as it is asserted, then the assurance, vs. 48, would have been, at least in a good measure, superfluous. No, the progress of the case is this: The woman held herself, by a former benefit (bodily healing perhaps, but not as yet any full assurance of forgiveness), quite as much favored by Jesus as if a debt of five hundred denarii had been remitted to her. Out of thankfulness for this benefit she had come believingly to Jesus (vs. 50), and had shown to Him in her love the strength of her thankful faith, and now she receives, in such a temper of mind, not out of merit, but out of grace, the assurance of the forgiveness of sins. Simon, on the other hand, considers himself as little favored by the visit of Jesus as by the remission of a debt of fifty denarii; therefore also he has shown the Lord little love.—"But to whom little is forgiven the same loveth little,"—and because he had so little faith and love he could moreover have little (or no) part in the forgiveness which he did not even earnestly desire.—However, the holiness of works seeks in vain a support in these words, for Jesus Himself says (vs. 50): "Thy faith hath saved thee," and by this of itself makes known that her love had flowed from the fountain of faith. Because she believes and has manifested this her faith by love, therefore does forgiveness fall to her lot.—We can hardly see that now any other difficulty remains to be removed, since at all events we read elsewhere also that love covers even the multitude of sins, and that mercy rejoiceth against judgment, 1 Peter iv. 8; James ii. 13; Matt. xxv. 31—

40. That she has deserved forgiveness by her love, the Saviour is as far from saying as that she has deserved it through faith; but only through the faith which works by love (Galatians v. 6), was she receptive for the benefit of forgiveness, which He immediately bestowed upon her purely out of grace. [Meyer's explanation appears to me better: "This ὅτι ἠγάπησε πολύ does not contain the *cause* and therefore not the *antecedent* of the forgiveness. So Catholics interpret it, proving therewith their doctrine of the meritoriousness of works, and of late also De Wette, apprehending love to Christ as one with faith in Him; Olshausen, seeking to surmount the difficulty of the thought in his way, and interpreting love as *receptive* activity; Paulus, B. Crusius. The contrary is established, not by dogmatics (see the admirable remarks of MELANCHTHON, in the *Apol.* iii. 31 *seq.*, p. 87 *seq.*, ed. Rech.), but, as appears by the context, because this interpretation is entirely inconsistent with the παραβολή lying at the basis, vss. 41, 42, as well as with the immediately following ᾧ δὲ ὀλίγον ἀφίεται, &c., if love does not appear as the *consequence* of forgiveness; the *antecedent*, that is, the subjective cause of forgiveness, is not Love, but Faith, as appears from vs. 50. According to the context, therefore, it is correct to interpret ὅτι . . . of the *ground of knowledge;* Forgiven are, &c., *which is certain, since she has exhibited love in a high degree.* . . . Calov. *Probabat Christus a posteriori.*"—C. C. S.]

Vs. 48. **Thy sins are forgiven.**—With celestial love the Lord ascends a yet more and more exalted climax in His language. First has He shown that He receives the homage of the sinful woman without any scruple; then has He said to a third person what a privilege is meditated for her, one much more excellent than she had hitherto enjoyed, namely, the full certainty of the forgiveness of sins; finally this assurance is personally addressed to herself, and sealed in her heart through the peace of God that passeth all understanding. The word αἱ πολλαί was uttered, it is true, in her presence, yet not to herself; the Lord, before this company, will not humble her more deeply, but on the contrary kindly raises her.

Vs. 49. **Began to say.**—Just as in ch. v. 21. It would appear almost inconceivable that the same censure should have been already repeated, if we forgot that a Pharisaic heart at all times remains the same; besides, these guests need not of course have been acquainted with that which had already taken place at the healing of the paralytic.

Vs. 50. **And He said.**—Not spoken at precisely the very instant when these thoughts were rising (Meyer), but probably because the Saviour heard the approach of the storm which would rise against the woman if she did not immediately withdraw herself. He gives her an intimation to leave the house before the peace which He had given her could be assailed or disturbed by any one.—Faith helped the woman, inasmuch as it brought her soul into the disposition in which she could entreat and receive the most ardently desired of all benefits from the Lord. A similar word of comfort was received by another woman, Mark v. 34. Comp. also the words of Eli to Hannah, 1 Samuel i. 17.

DOCTRINAL AND ETHICAL.

1. The readiness with which the Saviour could accept an invitation so grudgingly given as that

of this Simon, belongs undoubtedly to the self-denial of His ministering love. He wished especially not to repel the Pharisees any more than was absolutely necessary, and knew moreover that many an ear that elsewhere would be closed to formal preaching might perhaps catch up the word of life when He clothed it as table-talk in the forms of daily life. Here also He may have had a special reference to the training of His apostles, who, brought up in a simpler condition, had hitherto observed the dark side of Pharisaism more from a distance. Finally, He could, by His personal presence, best put to shame the calumnious reports which, without doubt, were spread abroad in His absence in reference to Him and His disciples. Worthy of notice, moreover, is it that when He trod this threshold a sinning woman also sees the door open to her, for whom, according to Pharisaic severity, the entrance would assuredly have been forbidden. Καὶ ἰδού. Where Christ appears the law loses its power, and grace bears the sceptre.

2. The whole narrative of the penitent sinner is a gospel within the gospel, as well in relation to the inward temper which the Lord demands of repentant sinners as also in respect to the salvation which His grace affords them. In this sense the whole narrative, which redounds to the honor of Luke's delicate taste, as physician and artist, deserves to be named an eternal history, and so far it is indifferent whether the chief character be Mary Magdalene or another. The chief matter is still her voice and her experience, which may be the share of every one among us. With justice did Gregory the Great write concerning this Pericope: "As oft as I think upon this event, I am more disposed to weep over it than to preach upon it." It fits perfectly into the Pauline Gospel of Luke, which proclaims to us the justification of the humble sinner out of free grace.

3. The parable which the Lord presents to Simon for consideration is for this reason above all so remarkable, that on the one side it sets forth as well the self-righteous Simons as the unrighteous ἁμαρτωλοί as debtors, and on the other hand strongly emphasizes the great benefit of the New Covenant, the blessing of the forgiveness of sins.

4. Whoever so understands the word of the Lord, vs. 47, as that the love of the woman was the meritorious cause of her pardon, such an one reverses the sense and the meaning of the parable, as if it taught that the two debtors had begun to love their creditor in an unequal measure, and that the creditor in consequence of this had remitted to them the debts of unequal amount, which then we should have to call: wishing to reap the fruit before the tree has been planted. For a debtor who is not in condition to pay will not love his creditor, but flee from him, and love awakes in his heart only when he, on good grounds, can believe that the debt at one stroke is remitted to him. So judges Luther also when he writes: "The Papists bring up this declaration against our doctrine of faith, and say that forgiveness of sins is attained through love and not through faith; but that such is not the meaning is proved by the parable, which clearly shows that love follows from faith. 'To whom much is forgiven,' says the Lord, 'the same loveth much;' therefore if a man has forgiveness of sins, and believes it, there follows love; where one has it not, there is no love."

5. "And He said to her, Thy sins are forgiven thee." If we will not assume that the sinner here received nothing more than she already possessed, we are then certainly necessitated to suppose that the certain assurance of the forgiveness of sins had not been bestowed upon her before this meeting with the Lord. The benefit for which she comes to testify her thankfulness to Him cannot therefore possibly have been this assurance.

6. Simon and the sinner, with respect to the Lord, are two admirable types of the Roman Catholic and of the Evangelical church. The former is as little as Simon free from the leaven of self-righteousness, and takes secret or open offence at every revelation, at every confession, of the free grace of the Saviour. Like the proud Pharisee, she makes void the commandment of God for the sake of her own notions, and is not perfect in love for the very reason that she does not regard love as a consequence but as a condition of the forgiveness of sins. Here holds good the declaration of John, 1 John iv. 17, 18. The other, on the contrary, feels herself in many respects as polluted as the sinning woman at the table, but as one entirely unworthy she lies at the feet of the Lord, and does Him homage, not in order thereby to merit anything, but out of pure thankfulness that He has merited and earned all for her. So long as she has not yet entirely unlearned the significance of the word δωρεάν (Romans iii. 24), the saying holds good for her: Thy faith hath saved thee; and she may go in peace. And this very faith will make her so much the richer in love and thankfulness, since she deeply feels that to her not fifty but five hundred denarii have been remitted out of grace. Thus does the gospel cherish and tend the fruit of obedience, which the law can indeed demand, yet cannot bring forth.

7. In order to understand the true relation between forgiveness and love, the parable Matt. xviii. 23–35, deserves especially to be compared.

HOMILETICAL AND PRACTICAL.

The dinner in Simon's house a proof of the truth of the word of the Lord, Luke v. 31, 32.—Jesus ever ready to come wherever the sinner invites Him.—Great sin, great repentance; great faith, great love.—True and pretended honor shown to the Lord in one and the same dwelling.—The poverty of an unloving, the riches of a loving, heart.—No sinning woman too bad to come to Jesus.—Love and honor united in her homage.—The steps upon which the Lord leads the sinner out of the depth upon the height: 1. He suffers her to approach Him; 2. He accepts her homage; 3. He assures her of the forgiveness of sins; 4. He causes her to go in peace.—The steps upon which the Lord leads the Pharisee from the height into the depth: 1. He seats Himself at his table; 2. He casts a look into his heart; 3. He makes his lovelessness manifest; 4. He puts him to shame before the sinner, and places him far below her.—Thankful love, how it is: 1. Richly attested, 2. unjustly censured, 3. powerfully vindicated, 4. blest a thousandfold.—The inventiveness of love.—The costliest thing not too costly for the Lord.—Frugality ill applied where love is to be shown to the Highest.—The blessed feeling of a heart that finally has pressed through to Jesus' feet.—Here at Jesus' feet, yonder on Jesus' heart.—To every Simon has the Lord even yet something special to say.—The table-talk of the Saviour tested according to the apostolic rule, Colossians iv.

6.—Christ beholds all other men stand in relation to Himself as debtors.—Every one receives forgiveness for as many or as few sins as he himself feels and repents of.—Thankful love cannot possibly precede the highest revelation of grace, but must necessarily follow it.—The self-righteous one his own judge. —One can judge rightly and yet condemn himself.— Seest thou this woman? 1. A sinner, and yet a sanctified person; 2. a mourner, and yet one blessed; 3. one condemned, and yet one crowned for eternal life.—The picture of the sinning woman in accord with the apostle's confession respecting himself, 2 Cor. vi. 9, 10.—God forgives in order that we may hold Him dear.—The penuriousness of disdain towards the Lord.—What disdain neglects, penitence supplies.—In Christ Jesus neither circumcision availeth anything nor uncircumcision, but faith which worketh by love, Galatians v. 6.—Set for the fall of one, for the rising of another.—The deepest ground of want of love towards Christ and the natural spring of love to Him.—Faith in the forgiveness of sins no dead letter, but an active principle of life. —The assured certainty of the forgiveness of sins, 1. An indispensable, 2. an invaluable, 3. an attainable benefit.—Who is this that forgiveth sins also? —Even the secret thoughts of the heart known to the Saviour.—Faith the only but also the certain way to deliver us.—No going in peace without faith; no faith without going in peace.

STARKE:—J. HALL:—He is a wise teacher who accommodates himself to be all things to all men that he may gain all, 1 Cor. ix. 22.—The Christian, even a preacher, may indeed go to the festive meal, yet must he have regard of place, time, and occasion, to accomplish some good even there.—The female sex has also a part in the kingdom of God, 1 Peter iii. 7.—The soul which truly feels its sins counts nothing too good and too dear for Christ.—Shamefacedness is both a sign and an effect of grace.— MAJUS:—Those converted to God give their members, which they have aforetime consecrated to sin, as instruments of righteousness, Romans vi. 19.— Who hath not himself repented knows not the heart of penitent sinners.—QUESNEL:—Sweet mildness of Jesus: happy he that also deals thus when he will amend his neighbor.—To convince and instruct one by questions is the best mode of teaching.—BRENTIUS:—Sin a great and heavy debt, which we in and of ourselves cannot discharge.—Nova Bibl. Tub.: —When the veil of our prejudices is removed, our own heart condemns us.—The penitent kisses continually the feet of the Lord Jesus.—Even in the holiest place one has often evil thoughts.—To forgive sins is God's work alone, and therefore Jesus has by this also demonstrated His Godhead.—Whom God and his conscience absolve from sin, he has no cause to be troubled at the blind judgment of the world.

HEUBNER:—Tears of repentant sinners are precious to God.—Pride has no sense of the love which God bestows on repentant sinners.—God knows, like a careful creditor, just how much every one owes Him.—What love to Jesus is, and how it arises.— Jesus teaches us here how we should deal with fallen ones.—Great sinners, great saints.—PALMER:—How love to Christ arises in a heart. It arises: 1. From the hope of attaining through Him forgiveness of sins; 2. from the certainty of having obtained forgiveness.—SCHLEIERMACHER:—Respecting the connection of forgiveness of sins with love, *Pred.* i. p. 522.

Admirable work of art representing the Magdalene [or rather, this woman.—C. C. S.], by Correggio, Battoni, and many others.

C. *Galilee and the Surrounding Regions, without excluding Capernaum.* CHS. VIII. 1—IX. 50.

1. The First Christian Family Circle. CH. VIII. 1-3.

1 And it came to pass afterward, that he went throughout every city and village preaching and shewing the glad tidings of the kingdom of God: and the twelve *were*
2 with him, And certain women, which had been healed of evil spirits and infirmities,
3 Mary called Magdalene, out of whom went seven devils, And Joanna the wife of Chuza Herod's steward, and Susanna, and many others, which ministered unto him [them, V. O.¹] of their substance.

¹ Vs. 3.—*Rec.*: αὐτῷ. Αὐτοῖς has preponderating authority, see TISCHENDORF *ad loc.* "The singular appeared more obvious to the copyists, partly because ἦσαν τεθεραπ. preceded, partly through reminiscence of Matt. xxvii. 55; Mark xv. 41." Meyer. [Αὐτῷ, A., L., M., X., Cod. Sin.; αὐτοῖς, B., D., E.², 10 other uncials.—C. C. S.]

EXEGETICAL AND CRITICAL.

Vs. 1. **Afterward,** ἐν τῷ καθ. sc. χρόνῳ.—Luke is here not concerned to arrange the different events in a strict chronological succession, but only in general to call attention to the fact that the activity of the Saviour, in His journeys through Galilee, was continued uninterruptedly, while he now adjoins a mention of the services rendered by women in this period, of which none of the other Evangelists make mention. Occasion to do this he more than probably found in the immediately preceding narrative. Κατὰ πόλιν καὶ κώμην. From town to town, and from village to village; comp. Acts xv. 21. The unweariedness of the Saviour's activity comes here with especial clearness into view.

Vs. 2. **And certain women.**—In the earlier period the disciples still wondered when they saw their Master in conversation with a woman, John iv. 27. Now there has already been formed a circle of female disciples, who were joined to the Master by thankful love.—**Mary of Magdala.** *See* above. Respecting Magdala, see LANGE, on *Matthew* xv. 39.

Vs. 3. **Joanna** is only here and in ch. xxiv. 10 referred to by name, as the consort, perhaps the widow, of Chuza, steward of Herod. If we assume with some that Chuza was the βασιλικός (John iv. 46–54), we might suppose that grateful love for the deliverer of her son had brought the mother to Jesus.—**Susanna,** that is, Lily, שׁוֹשַׁנָּה, is not further known.—**And many others.**—Comp. Matt. xxvii. 55.

Which ministered unto them.—The female friends of our Lord appear for the most part to have belonged to the well-circumstanced higher class, since the here-mentioned ministration doubtless consisted principally in support rendered to earthly necessities from their property. This ministration was rendered to the whole travelling company. The reading αὐτῷ is perhaps in some manuscripts a correction, which visibly arose from the effort to represent the service of these women as an act of Divine service, which was exclusively limited to the Master.

DOCTRINAL AND ETHICAL.

1. The brief account which Luke gives us respecting these women is peculiarly adapted to awaken a vivid conception of the journeyings of the Saviour through Galilee. We see Him proceeding from one town to another, wearing as clothing the simple yet becoming tunic, which was not sewed but woven from above throughout, perhaps the gift of love; the sandals bound crosswise over His uncovered feet; the disciples near by without money in their girdles, without shoes, staff, or wallet; perhaps a little flask with oil, after the Oriental usage, hanging over their shoulders, for the refreshment of their wearied limbs (Mark vi. 13; Luke x. 34; Genesis xxviii. 18); and at a becoming distance the women covered with their veils, who were concerned with tender affection for the wants of the company, now and then preparing for their beloved Master a refreshing surprise, and now holding discourse with one another, now with Him. The view of such a circle of brethren and sisters, whose centre the Lord is, makes an impression that elevates the heart.

2. The unhesitating way in which the Saviour admitted and accepted the loving services of these women is a striking proof not only of His condescending love, which endures services rendered to Him, although He did not come to be ministered unto (Matt. xx. 28), but at the same time of His firm confidence in the purity and faithfulness of these Galilean friends, which indeed did remain, even beyond His death, unchangeably the same.

3. We see here an emancipation of woman in the noblest sense of the word, and the beginning of the service of women in the church of Christ (Wichern), and at the same time also a decided triumph of the evangelical spirit over the limitation of the Jewish Rabbinism, and the prophecy of the new world of love called into being through Christ.

HOMILETICAL AND PRACTICAL.

In Christ Jesus there is neither Jew nor Greek, man nor woman, but a new creature.—Thankful ministration of love well pleasing to the Lord.—Diversity and agreement among the first female friends of Jesus.—What the Saviour is for woman, and what woman must be for the Saviour.—Woman in Christ no longer slave of the man, but a fellow-heir of the grace of life, 1 Peter iii. 7.—Women of high condition also cannot possibly dispense with the Saviour.—The Head of the church served *by* and *in* His members.—The destination of earthly good also to the advancement of the kingdom of God.—The first Christian circle of sisters united for a work of love, 1. Whose origin is pure, 2. whose character is that of power, 3. whose fruit is abundant, 4. whose duration is perennial.—The service of the poor, Divine service (Angelus Merula).—Among the women of the evangelical history not one enemy of the Lord.

STARKE:—Whoever hath tasted that the Lord is gracious, such an one cannot abandon Him.—If Christ was not ashamed of the ministrations of others, why should we be ashamed when we find ourselves in like circumstances?—QUESNEL:—Godly women have at all times helped to build up the kingdom of God by the exercise of love towards Christ's servants and His poor members, Romans xvi. 1, 2, 6.—MAJUS:—For spiritual benefits to render something temporal is becoming, and yet a poor payment.—For His poor children God knows well how to provide.

---

2. The Parables concerning the Kingdom of God. VSS. 4–21.

(Parallels: Matt. xiii. 1–23; xii. 46–50; Mark iii. 31—iv. 23.—Vss. 4–15, Gospel for Sexagesima Sunday.)

4 And when much people were gathered together, and were come [when they were
5 coming] to him out of every city, he spake by a parable: A sower went out to sow his seed: and as he sowed, some fell by the way side; and it was trodden down, and the
6 fowls of the air devoured it. And some fell upon a rock [the rock]; and as soon as it
7 was sprung up, it withered away, because it lacked moisture. And some fell among [the] thorns; and the thorns sprang up with it, and [having sprung; om., and] choked
8 it. And other fell on [the] good ground, and sprang up, and bare fruit a hundredfold. And when he had said these things, he cried, He that hath ears to hear, let him hear.
9 And his disciples asked him, saying [om., saying, V. O.¹], What might this parable
10 be [*i. e.*, mean]? And he said, Unto you it is given to know the mysteries of the kingdom of God: but to others [the rest *only*] in parables; that seeing they might not
11 see, and hearing they might not understand. Now the parable is this: The seed is the
12 word of God. Those by the way side are they that hear; then cometh the devil, and

taketh away the word out of their hearts, lest they should [that they may not, ἵνα μὴ]
13 believe and be saved. They on the rock *are they*, which, when they hear, receive the word with joy; and these have no root, which for a while believe, and in time of temp-
14 tation fall away. And that which fell among thorns are they, which, when they have heard, go forth, and are choked with cares and riches and pleasures of *this* life, and
15 bring no fruit to perfection. But that on the good ground are they, which in an honest and good heart, having heard the word, keep *it*, and bring forth fruit with patience [or,
16 persevere in bringing forth fruit]. [But] No man, when he hath lighted a candle, covereth it with a vessel, or putteth *it* under a bed; but setteth *it* on a candlestick, that
17 they which enter in may see the light. For nothing is secret, that shall not be made
18 manifest; neither *any thing* hid, that shall not be known and come abroad. Take heed therefore how ye hear: for whosoever hath, to him shall be given; and whosoever
19 hath not, from him shall be taken even that which he seemeth to have. Then came to
20 him *his* mother and his brethren, and could not come at him for the press. And it was told him *by certain* which said, Thy mother and thy brethren stand without, desiring
21 to see thee. And he answered and said unto them, My mother and my brethren are these which hear the word of God, and do it.

[1] Vs. 9.—*Rec.:* λέγοντες. At least doubtful. [Om., Cod. Sin.]

EXEGETICAL AND CRITICAL.

General Remarks. — CHRONOLOGY: Luke correctly places the preaching of the kingdom of God on the part of the Saviour in this period of His Galilean activity. The comparison with Matthew and Mark teaches us, however, that he passes over several important particulars. Without here entering upon a criticism of the different earlier and later arrangements of the evangelical narrations, we simply state what order appears to us most worthy of credit: 1. The meal in Simon's house (Luke vii. 36–50). 2. Beginning of a new journey through Galilee (Luke viii. 1–3). 3. Return εἰς οἶκον (Mark iii. 20). 4. Blasphemy respecting a covenant with Beelzebub (Mark iii. 20–30. Comp. Matt. xii. 22–37). 5. His mother and His brethren (Mark iii. 31–35. Comp. Luke viii. 19–21; Matt. xii. 46–50). 6. The parables (Matt. xiii.; Mark iv.; Luke viii.),—that of the Sower first, according to all the Synoptics.

Vs. 4. **Much people.**—Here, too, the Evangelists are not at variance, but complement one another. According to Luke the cities of all Galilee furnished their contingent to swell the company of hearers of the Lord—"*ex quavis urbe erat cohors aliqua*," (*Bengel.*) According to Matthew and Mark this concourse is so great that the Saviour has to ascend a ship on the shore in order there to be heard better. Of the different parables which, according to Mark and Luke, were delivered at the same time on this occasion, Luke communicates only the first, together with its interpretation.

Vs. 5. **By the wayside.**—"*Eo, ubi ager et via inter se attingunt.*" Here the first portion of the seed is threatened by a double danger—the feet of travellers and the birds of heaven. Notice how much the vividness of the parable is heightened by this last feature.

Vs. 6. **Upon the rock.**—To be understood of a rocky soil covered with a thin layer of earth, so that the seed is repelled as soon as it attempts to shoot out roots. It grows comparatively high (ἐξανέτειλε, Matthew and Mark), but can only unfold itself above and not below.

Vs. 7. **Among the thorns.**—Not an overgrown thistle-field, but a place in the arable ground where formerly thorns have grown up, which now come (from the roots) into development together with the seed, and finally entirely suffocate this, since they grow much more quickly, and, and first repressing the slow growing of the seed, soon make it entirely impossible.

Vs. 8. **On the good ground.**—Which, through the care of the husbandman in preparation, has *become* good. Luke only mentions summarily the hundredfold increase, while Matthew and Mark speak of the thirty and sixtyfold.

When He had said these things.—Just so Matthew and Mark. According to the latter an ἀκούετε had also preceded. This whole parable is intended to constitute not only one out of many, but as the first in a closely connected series to form as it were His inaugural discourse as a teacher of parables. Comp. Mark iv. 13.

Vs. 9. **Asked Him.**—Here also the brief report of Luke must be filled up from the more detailed one of Matthew and Mark. It then appears that they asked not only for the interpretation of this parable, but in general concerning the cause why He speaks to the people in parables. The answer which Luke gives, vs. 10, is the answer to the question, which he himself does not state.

Vs. 10. **Unto you it is given.**—According to all three Evangelists the kingdom of God is agreeably to this word of the Saviour: 1. A μυστήριον, which, however, 2. His disciples know, but, 3. only after it is *given* to them through the preparing grace of God, δέδοται γνῶναι. The true reconciliation between the Supernaturalism and Rationalism of the more ancient and the more modern form will have to proceed from this, that justice is done at once to each of these three thoughts.

But to the others only in parables.—We are not to supply: *With the rest speak I in parables*, but: to the rest it is *given* to understand the mysteries of the kingdom of God only when they are laid open to them in parabolic form.

That seeing they might not see.—Comp. Is. vi. 9, 10, where, however, we are never to lose from view, that: "The effect of hardening through prophecy is an eliciting, and so revealing, of the hardening which already exists and which through their fault reveals itself in reference to the word." *Stier.* Comp. LANGE on *Matthew* xi. 12.

Vs. 11. **The seed.**—In the explanation it is,

according to Luke, the Seed, according to Mark, the Sower, that stands in the foreground.

Vs. 12. **They that hear.**—That is, who *merely* hear, without the word of preaching being mixed with faith. It is to be noticed that the Saviour only ascribes the miscarriage of the first, and not of the second and third portion of the seed to direct diabolical influence. The evil one is as quickly at hand (εὐθέως, εἶτα) as the birds by the just-sown seed.

The distinction between the second and third kind appears especially to lie in this, that those sown upon the rock are the superficially touched, who are soon offended by persecution; those sown among the thorns, the half-hearted, who are soon seduced by temptation. " *Hic ordo,*" says Calvin very correctly of the former, "*a superiore differt, quia temporalis fides, quasi seminis conceptio, fructum aliquem promittit, sed non ita bene et penitus subacta sunt corda, ut ad continuum alimentum eorum mollities sufficiat. Et sane, ut aestu solis probatur terrae sterilitas, ita persecutio et crux eorum vanitatem detegit, qui leviter tincti, nescio quo desiderio, non probe serio pietatis affectu imbuti sunt. Sciendum est, non vere esse incorruptibili semine regenitos, quod nunquam marcescit, quemadmodum Petrus docet.*"

Vs. 14. **Cares and riches and pleasures.**—Here, as in Mark iv. 19, a threefold cause for the miscarriage of the third class, earthly *care, possession,* and *enjoyment.* Luke very beautifully describes these hearers as going away among the one and the other (πορευόμενοι), after they had listened for a while. "A picturesque addition" (De Wette).

And are choked.—*See* Meyer *ad loc.*

Vs. 15. **In an honest and good heart.**—Not in an absolutely ethical sense (Meyer), for purity of heart cannot precede faith, but must follow it. Yet honest and good to receive seed and to bear fruit. An intimation of the right disposition for hearing, which itself in turn is a fruit of the *gratia praeveniens.* Comp. Acts x. 35.

Vs. 16. **But no man.**—The same saying appears again, ch. xi. 33. Nothing stands in the way of our supposing that the Saviour repeated words of this kind on fitting occasions. In Mark also, vss. 21, 22, it appears immediately after the parable of the Sower, and the connection of thought is not very difficult to give. The Saviour does not mean to say that as He had sufficiently illustrated to them the preceding parable, so they also should now on their part spread this abroad among others (Meyer, De Wette), but He utters it to be applied to what He had said in relation to the different reception of the word of God among men: namely, that the fruit of preaching would one day be known, and that it is therefore of the greatest importance actually to keep the word in a good and pure heart in order that in time to come it may become evident that it has brought forth fruit an hundredfold.

Vs. 18. **Take heed therefore.**—In Luke the πῶς, in Matthew the τί, is brought more into prominence, while that which in Matt. xiii. 12, appears in another connection, Luke here very fittingly adjoins. By this connection the significance of the—in all appearance—proverbial way of speaking is in a peculiar manner more precisely defined.—**For whosoever hath,** namely, of fruits of the word which he obtained by the fact that he heard in the right way. The productiveness is conditioned by the receptivity. Whoever first bears in himself a germ of the higher life, such a one will in the use of the pre-

pared means continually receive more of spiritual blessing. Whoever neglects that which is deposited by God within him loses what he never rightly possessed. *Ὁ δοκεῖ ἔχειν ἀρθήσεται,* an exact *interpretamentum* of the original form in Mark, ὃ ἔχει. The so-called possession had been the fruit of a mere imagination.

Vs. 19. **Then came to Him.**—Originally this occurrence belongs before the parable (*see* above), but apparently Luke communicates it here because it might serve very well to commend the right hearing, inasmuch as it indicates the high rank which the doers of the word (James i. 25), according to the Saviour's judgment, enjoy.

And could not come at Him.—We gain a clear conception of the fact only by comparing Mark iii. 21–30. The simplest understanding of Mark iii. 20, 21, is however apparently this, that no one else than the relatives of the Lord on this occasion had been afraid that He was beside Himself; in respect to His brothers, who, according to John vii. 5, even later did not yet believe on Him, we can at least not call this inconceivable. Intentional malice existed here as little as Acts xxvi. 24. If we remark, however, that mother and brothers wait very quietly until He has finished speaking, and that the latter publicly requested Him to come unto them, we can just as well conceive that they lay hold of the calumny set afoot by the Pharisees: ὅτι Βεελζεβοὺλ ἔχει, as a means of withdrawing Jesus, out of well-meaning yet misguided affection, from this stormy sea. In no case does the account say that Mary uttered or believed these words of blasphemy. She stands here more in the midst than at the head of His relatives, and not possibly could she name the holy thing that was born of her, lunatic. Yet of one error she makes herself, together with her family, guilty. She wishes to withdraw the Saviour (perhaps out of provident care that He might take food, Mark iii. 20), from the work which He regards as His food. This Jesus refuses with holy sternness, yet at the same time with tender forbearance. Of the self-denial which He demands in respect to earthly kindred, Matt x. 37, He Himself gives a brilliant example. What is said of Levi, Deut. xxxiii. 9, is true now in a higher measure of Him.

Vs. 20. **And it was told Him.**—Perhaps by one who would have been glad to see the immediately preceding discourse of rebuke, Mark iii. 23 *seq.*, continue no longer, and therefore with some eagerness makes use of this welcome interruption in order to direct the Saviour's attention to something else.

Thy mother and thy brethren.—The difficult question, whom we have actually to understand by the ἀδελφοῖς of the Lord, has been even to the latest times answered in different ways. The view of those who here understand natural brothers of the Lord, children of Joseph and Mary, born after Jesus, has, according to the opinion we have hitherto held, at least the fewest difficulties. This view is powerfully vindicated by Dr. A. H. Blom, in his *Disput. Theol. Inaug. de Christi ἀδελφοῖς καὶ ἀδελφαῖς,* L. B. 1839. On the other side those who are among the later scruples of Lange and others, who here understand cousins of the Lord, may not be condemned. The question appears yet to demand a continued investigation in order finally to come to full decision. Comp. meanwhile the valuable essay of Wieseler, Stud. und Krit. 1842, i., but particularly also the appendix to the 9th prælection on the Life of Jesus, by C. J. Riggenbach, Basel, 1858, where the grounds for and against each principal view have been very judiciously set forth. S. 286–304.

Vs. 21. **And He answered.**—Comp. LANGE on *Matt.* xii. 50. According to the picturesque trait in Mark, vs. 34, He in saying this looks with a benevolent glance over those immediately surrounding Him. With full consciousness He sacrifices, if it must be so, earthly relationships to higher ones. Thus does He assure His disciples of the higher rank which they enjoy in His eyes, while they are forgotten by the world. His mother and brothers, on the other hand, when they have come near enough, hear the only condition upon which He in truth can call them His own: namely, if they honor the will of the Father, who has assigned Him another circle than their limited dwelling. Doubtless at this word a voice in Mary's heart testified that she belonged in a yet higher sense than κατὰ σάρκα to the kindred of Christ. From the fact that the Saviour speaks alone of mother, brother, and sister, but not of His father, as indeed the latter nowhere appears in the history of His public life, it may with great probability be concluded that Joseph was now already dead. [The fact that Joseph nowhere appears in the course of our Lord's ministry, renders it sufficiently probable that he was dead. But the fact that our Lord, among the possible relations which human beings can sustain to Him, does not include that of Father, may well be explained from His unwillingness to attribute to any human being that relation which God alone sustained to Him.—C. C. S.] His disciples He calls brethren, comp. Heb. ii. 11; but from this it by no means follows that His disciples themselves had the right to give to Him in too familiar a manner the name Brother.

DOCTRINAL AND ETHICAL.

1. For the first time in the Gospel of Luke we here meet with the Lord teaching the people in parables, which of itself certainly could not have been strange to His hearers. The fiery orientals, whose fancy is so rich, whose thoughts are so accustomed to poetical vesture, early availed themselves of a form of teaching which could at once excite to reflection and satisfy the taste. Prophets like Nathan, sages like Solomon, poets like Isaiah, had veiled their oracles in the guise of the parable (2 Sam. xii. 1–7; Eccl. ix. 14–16; Isaiah v. 1; xxviii. 23–29); and in the days of our Lord also the Jewish Rabbis availed themselves of this inviting mode of representation. One of the Rabbis, in particular, afterwards distinguished himself in this, namely, R. Nahorai, who lived a century after Christ, shortly before Bar-Cochba, and whose parables remind us in many respects of those of the Saviour. It would be indeed well worth the trouble to institute a distinct investigation upon the point how much the moral portion of the Talmud is indebted in this respect to the gospel. Comp. SEPP, *L. J.* ii. p. 243. And if we ask what, why, and how the Saviour taught in parables, we find new occasion to repeat the declaration, John vii. 46.

2. By a *parable* we understand an invented narrative taken from nature or daily life, wherein weighty duties, truth, or promises, are set forth in a pictorial manner. While the philosophical *myth* must bring an abstract *idea* within the sphere of our conception; under the garb of the parable, on the other hand, a present or impending *fact* is placed before the eyes. While the *simile* gives only a simple agreement between two different things, it lacks the dramatic development and the striking issue which we meet with in a completed parable. Even from the *fable* is it distinguished, inasmuch as it moves within the bounds of possibility, and not only, like the fable, presents moral teaching, but also religious truth. The chief thought around which all the parables of the Saviour more or less directly revolve is the hidden character of the kingdom of God. It has therefore been attempted in many ways to arrange the different parables of our Lord into a complete whole, in which the doctrine of the kingdom of Heaven in all its parts is contained (Neander, Lisco, Lange, Schweitzer, &c.). Nothing is easier than to derive a Theology, Anthropology, Soteriology, and Eschatology of Jesus from His parables, in which, however, it must be borne in mind that not every delicate feature of the representation can be used as a stone for a dogmatic edifice, but that only the *tertium comparationis*, the leading idea, is to be made prominent according to the particular design.

3. The purpose of the parable is twofold, comp. Matt. xiii. 13, and LANGE *ad loc.* Justly, therefore, has Lord Bacon already said: "*Parabola est usus ambigui, facit enim ad involucrum, facit etiam ad illustrationem, in hoc docendi, in illo occultandi artificium quaeri videtur.*" Comp. John ix. 39. However, we must not overlook the fact that the veiling of the truth in parables was only relative and temporary. They were not like the bushel under which the light was hid, but more like the veil of mist which indeed obscures the brilliancy of the sun, yet also more often allows it to stream through. The explanation which the Saviour gives of some parables in particular He would undoubtedly have given of all, had He been inquired of with the desire of salvation.

4. In respect to the parables also the Gospel of Luke shows an indisputable wealth. It is true we miss here individual parables which are found in Matt. xiii., Mark iv., and elsewhere, but on the other hand several of the most exquisite parables have been preserved to us by Luke alone. Without speaking now of many gnome-like sayings which he communicates as parables, *e. g.* ch. xiv. 7, let us consider particularly the rich treasure of parables which he has preserved in the narrative of the Saviour's last journey to Jerusalem, ch. ix. 51 *seq.* To these belong: 1. The Good Samaritan, ch. x. 30–37; 2. The Importunate Friend, ch. xi. 5–8; 3. The Rich Fool, ch. xii. 16–21; 4. The Unfruitful Fig-tree, ch. xiii. 6–9; 5. The Great Supper, ch. xiv. 6–24; 6. The Tower and The War, ch. xiv. 28–32; 7. The Lost Sheep, Coin, and The Prodigal Son, ch. xv. (of which, however, the first two appear with another design in Matt. xviii. 12, 13); 8. The Unjust Steward, ch. xvi. 1–9; 9. Lazarus and Dives, ch. xvi. 19–31; 10. The Servant Ploughing, ch. xvii. 7–10; 11. The Unjust Judge and the Widow, ch. xviii. 1–8; 12. The Pharisee and the Publican, ch. xviii. 9–14; 13. The Parable of the Pounds (to be distinguished from that of the Talents, Matt. xxv. 14–30), ch. xix. 12–27. Even when Luke narrates parables given in the other Evangelists, he is not wanting in new peculiar features of them. Comp. for instance ch. xii. 35–48, with Matt. xxiv. 42–51. Especially does he communicate the parables which are in agreement with the broad Pauline position of his Gospel, while we scarcely fear a contradiction when

we maintain that it is among the parables preserved by him that the most exquisite in detail appear. Who would give up the dogs in the parable of Lazarus and the rich man? Who the trait of the haughty Pharisee standing by himself, σταθεὶς πρὸς ἑαυτόν, or of the eldest of the two sons who does not come out of the house, but directly from the field where he has served his father by his labor? How much would the parable of the Good Samaritan have lost in beauty if over against this friend of man, not a priest and Levite, but a simple citizen of Jerusalem, had been placed! Even if some of the parables in Luke contain particular *cruces interpretum*, yet the labor of investigation is richly compensated, as in reference also to all the parables related by him, the fine expression is applicable: "The miracles of Jesus are manifestly great individual parables of His general activity,—parables in act. His parables, on the other hand, unfold themselves as miracles of His word. The miracle is a fact which comes from the word and is converted into the word. The parable is a word which comes out of a fact and stamps itself in the fact. The common birthplace of these ideal twin forms is therefore the world-creating and world-transfiguring Word." Lange.

5. Although in judging of the prophetic character of the parable, men have not always been temperate enough, and have certainly gone too far in finding in many the indication of individual periods in the development of Christianity beyond the general intimation of earlier or later times, it is nevertheless entirely beyond doubt that precisely like many prophecies, so do also many parables realize themselves continuously in ever-augmenting measure in the history of the kingdom of God [or, as Bacon says: "have a springing and germinant fulfilment in every age."—C. C. S.]. This is true of the very first parable, the Sower. Considered in the most general way, it contains truth in reference to God's word in the world as to *when, how, and where*, it has been sown at all times. But very especially is it applicable to the activity of the Great Sower in the kingdom of God, Christ; and certainly it is of moment how He here Himself communicates in parabolic form the result of His experience up to that time among His mainly unbelieving contemporaries. But continually does the fulfilment of the parabolic sketch repeat itself in the preaching of the gospel by apostles, martyrs, reformers, nay, and that of the most obscure country pastor. And so long as the world remains *the world* it will not cease to be true that a good part, nay the greatest part, of the seed is continually lost through the fault of men.

6. That the Saviour, not in the parable, but in the explanation of the parable to His disciples, speaks so unequivocally of the Evil One, is a convincing proof that the New Testament Satanology is to be regarded as something entirely different from a pædagogic accommodation to a superstitious popular fancy.

7. The cause why the seed with some bears no fruit and with some bears fruit more richly than with others, is not to be found in the fact that the heart of the one is by nature so much better than that of the other. Whoever would bring up Luke viii. 15 as a proof against the doctrine of general depravity would do well first to read over once more Mark vii. 21-23. The καλὸν καὶ ἀγαθόν is in the spirit of the Saviour's teaching the fruit of the *gratia praeveniens*, from which the man has not withdrawn himself since God Himself has wrought in him the will, Philippians ii. 13. It belongs to the work of the modern believing Dogmatics to develop the doctrine of prevenient grace in its deep religious and Christian ground more than has hitherto been done.

8. It is to be understood that among those of whom the Lord says that they fall away in time of temptation, there are no genuine believers. He Himself has declared that they believe πρὸς καιρόν, and the distinction between *fides temporalis* and *salvifica*, even on the ground of this expression, has a deep significance. Everywhere where the seed is lost there is lacking that ὑπομονή to which Luke viii. 15 makes so emphatic allusion. Much may go on in a heart without its becoming in truth a partaker of the new life. Every conversion which has effect only in the sphere of the intellect, the feeling, the imagination, or the course of action itself, without having penetrated into the innermost sanctuary of the will, may be a blossom that endures long, but yet finally falls off without bearing fruit.

9. By the different measure of fruitfulness in good are indicated the different degrees of faith, love, sanctification, hope, &c., which have been attained in consequence of hearing. Therefore also the different measures of talents, gifts, and capacity to carry on the sowing for the kingdom of God through the ages (Lange). The cause of the great distinction is as little to be sought exclusively on the side of man as on the side of God. Here also both factors work together, and it must be well considered on the one hand that not every place of the field is ploughed and harrowed equally long; on the other hand, that not every spiritual gift bestowed is used with equal care. Here also the rule holds good that grace works ever mystically, yet never magically, and again: "Whoever will keep firm hold of the Lord's gifts must use them in diligent labor for increase; for that are they in their nature given; keeping and gaining increase therewith are one. Works are faith's nourishment, the diligence of faithful use is the oil for the burning lamp; to do nothing in the might of grace and to reap no fruit from its sowing is enough to bring with it the judgment which takes again what one appeared to have, and thought he had, but which was already no longer a true having." Stier.

10. What the Saviour here says very definitely of the fruit of the word may be also asserted in a wider sense of all mysteries of the kingdom of heaven. Publicity before the judgment and in God's hour is here emphatically the watchword.

11. What Paul declares of himself, 2 Cor. v. 16, is to be seen in a yet higher sense in the Son of Man. The saying respecting His mother and His brothers is essentially only the repetition of the same principle which the boy of twelve years, Luke ii. 49, had already uttered as His own. That Mary, even after the instruction received, John ii. 4, could yet again have a thought of interfering to some extent actively in the plan of His labors is a new proof how far the Mary of the Gospels is still below the *Immaculate Concepta* of Rome. If Mary became great in the kingdom of God, this is not because she was after the flesh the mother of the Lord, but because she on her part fulfilled the will of His Father. [On the other hand, doubtless, for the mother of the Lord not to have been a believer would have been something too monstrous for Divine grace and providence to have for a moment permitted.—C. C. S.] Here also, as ever, the natural relation of the Saviour,

compared with the spiritual, recedes far into the background.

HOMILETICAL AND PRACTICAL.

Where Jesus preaches there is never lack of hearers.—The shore of the sea of Gennesaret a sowing field.—The word of God a seed: 1. Of heavenly origin; 2. of inestimable worth.—Let three quarters of the seed be lost, if only the last quarter prospers.—The feelingless heart is like a hard-trodden path.—The Evil One under the guise of innocent birds.—Inward hardening not seldom coupled with superficial feeling.—A lively impression of the word seldom also a deep one.—Prosperous growth must go on at once upward and downward.— Thorns grow up quicker than wheat-stalks.—Apostasy in the time of persecution: 1. A speedy; 2. an intelligible; 3. a miserable apostasy.—Faith for a time and faith for eternity.—Earthly care, earthly possession, earthly enjoyment in its relation to the word of preaching.—One can promise fruit without actually bringing it forth.—The effect of the word conditioned by the state of the heart.—Perseverance in good a token of genuine renewal; comp. Matt. xxiv. 13.—The different measure of fruitfulness and good, or what it has: 1. Remarkable; 2. humble; 3. encouraging.—The disciple desiring to learn must go with his questions, not from, but to, Jesus.—The kingdom of God: 1. A secret; 2. which, however, is intended to be understood; 3. the right understanding of which is granted, but; 4. only to the disciple of Christ. —The hiding of the truth in the parable for the not yet receptive mind, a manifestation of the Divine: 1. Holiness; 2. wisdom; 3. grace.—The disciple of the Lord not the light—but yet the candlestick.—Publicity the watchword of the kingdom of God; here all things; 1. Can; 2. must; 3. shall, at some time, come perfectly to light.—The perverse and the right way to hear the word.—Take heed how ye hear! 1. To the hearing itself you are obliged; 2. but one can hear in very different ways; 3. it is by no means indifferent in what way we hear; 4. therefore take heed.—Who hath, to him shall be given, &c.: 1. A marvellous saying; 2. a saying of truth; 3. a saying of wisdom.—The kindred of the Lord after the flesh and His kindred after the Spirit.—The pure and impure desire of seeing Christ.—A wish that appears laudable is not always really devout.—The high value which the Lord attaches to the hearing and fulfilling of the word.—His saying concerning His mother and brethren, the application of the fourth part of the parable of the Sower.—The spiritual family of the Saviour: 1. The wide-spread family likeness; 2. the firm family bonds; 3. the rich family blessing.

Starke:—Cramer:—Many hearers, few devout ones.—*Nova Bibl. Tub.*:—Formerly the people hasted from the cities to Christ, now, when one has not so far to go, they hasten from Him.—Christian teachers in their many unfruitful labors must possess their souls in patience and not hastily give up all for lost, Isaiah xlix. 4.—If grace does not moisten our heart and make it full of sap, the seed of the Divine word therein must dry up, for our heart is a rock.—Majus:—Take good note of the hindrances to thy conversion, and remove what stands in the way.—*Auris condita est ad audiendum quæ conditor loquitur*, Gordius Martyr.—Quesnel:—The understanding of the Holy Scripture and its mysteries is not given to all; one must humbly seek it from the fountain of wisdom.—Satan also knows that God's word is the blessed means of conversion and salvation.— Canstein:—God gives no one the light of His knowledge for his own use merely, but also for the common benefit, 1 Cor. xii. 7.—Often for the punishment of unbelief even in this life all is taken away and the light turned into darkness, Matt. xxv. 28.—Quesnel:—Whoever fervently loves Christ cannot long do without Him.—The Virgin Mary has no better right to Christ than other people, Luke xi. 27, 28.—A Christian in what concerns the service of God must forget even his parents, Matt. xix. 29.—Believers are spiritually related to Christ, and as dear to Him as children never are to their parents, Hebr. ii. 11; Is. xlix. 15.

Luther (XII. 23, 24):—"This is it that has the most fearful sound, that such pious hearts as have a good root, are full of holy intention, of fixed purpose and fervent effort, yea to whom not even perseverance itself is lacking, have nevertheless been robbed of fruit. These are therefore those who will serve two Lords, please both God and the world together, and who do many and great things for God's sake, and even that becomes a snare to them, because they take pleasure in that they become aware that they are filled with gifts and make profit. Such also are those who serve God most devoutly, but they do it for the sake of enjoyment and honor, or at least for the sake of religious benefit, either in this life or that to come."

Heubner:—Similarity of the preaching of the Divine word and of sowing.—Two main classes of human character: 1. Evil: *a*. hardened, *b*. frivolous, *c*. impure, earthly minded (all human characters may be thrown into these classes, as indeed Kant has done it according to this very parable, *Religion Innerhalb*, &c., § xxii. pp. 21, 22); 2. Hearts full of longing after salvation, &c.—The main part in preaching belongs to the hearer.—The preaching of the gospel never wholly fruitless; a ground of comfort, especially for young ministers.—Ahlfeld:—The husbandry of our Lord Jesus Christ: 1. The husbandman; 2. the field.—Stier:—1. The word of God is a seed; 2. even this seed's thriving depends on the field; 3. what now is the good ground or heart for God's word?—From whence comes such good ground?—G. Schweder:—The hearts of believers also are like to the various ground.—Baumeister: —The seeming Christian and the true Christian.—There are, namely: 1. Christians with a merely outward religion; 2. Christians with a shallow religion; 3. Christians with a half religion; 4. Christians with a true religion.—Thym:—Whose fault is it if few hearers of the word are saved? 1. Is it God's who causes the word to be proclaimed?—2. Is it the fault of the word which is proclaimed to men?—3. Or is it that of the man to whom the word is proclaimed?— Berk:—The might of the word of God: 1. Through how manifold hindrances it breaks away; 2. what a rich and mighty fruit it brings forth.—Ritter:—As the man so his religion.—Florey:—What is required if God's word is to bring forth fruit in us?—Rautenberg:—The complaint that God's word brings forth so little fruit: 1. What ground for it; 2. what comfort against it; 3. what duty concerning it we have.— Harless:—The word of the kingdom an open secret.

3. **The King of the Kingdom of God at the same time the Lord of Creation, of the World of Spirits, of Death. Vss. 22–56.**

a. THE STILLING OF THE STORM IN THE LAKE. Vss. 22–25.

(Parallels: Matt. viii. 23–27; Mark iv. 35–41. Gospel for the 4th Sunday after Epiphany.)

22 Now it came to pass on a certain day [one of the days], that he went into a ship with his disciples: and he said unto them, Let us go over unto the other side of the
23 lake. And they launched forth. But as they sailed, he fell asleep: and there came down a storm [gust] of wind on the lake; and they were filled [were filling] *with water*,
24 and were in jeopardy. And they came to him, and awoke him, saying, Master, Master, we perish. Then he arose, and rebuked the wind and the raging of the water: and
25 they ceased, and there was a calm. And he said unto them, Where is your faith? And they being afraid wondered, saying one to another, What manner of man is[1] this! for he commandeth even the winds and [the] water, and they obey him.

---

[1] Vs. 25.—'Ἐστιν is according to Tischendorf and Lachmann (A., B., L., X., cursives) an addition whose genuineness is doubtful. [Tischendorf in his 7th ed. has it with Cod. Sin. and 13 other uncials; om., A., C., L., X.—C. C. S.]

EXEGETICAL AND CRITICAL.

HARMONY.—Without doubt the stilling of the tempest took place on the same evening on which the Saviour had delivered the parable of the Sower and some others. The parable of the Mustard Seed, and of the Leaven (Matt. xiii.), Luke gives in another connection (ch. xiii. 18–21); that of the Tares, of the Treasure in the Field, of the Pearl, of the Fishing-net, and of the Slow Growing of the Seed (Mark iv. 26–29) he passes over. The question, whether it is in and of itself probable that the Saviour delivered all these parables almost *uno tenore* on one and the same day on which so much had already taken place (Mark iii. 20–35), may here remain provisionally undecided. Enough that the stilling of the tempest, which, according to Luke, took place on one of the days (vs. 22), took place, according to Mark (vs. 35), on the same day at evening. According to Matthew, who is as far from contradicting as from confirming these chronological statements, the Saviour wished at the same time to withdraw Himself in this way from the people, ch. xviii. If it should appear that he transposes the miracle into an earlier period of the life of the Lord than it occurred, we are not to forget that Matt. viii., ix. is a collection of different miracles of the Saviour without the apostle's having observed any very strict chronological arrangement. On internal grounds, however, we consider it probable that the offer of the two men who wished to follow Jesus (Matt. viii. 19–22) immediately preceded the tempestuous voyage. Luke communicates this particular in the account of another voyage, narrating those two, moreover, with a third similar case, ch. ix. 57–62. Taking it all together now, it no longer is difficult to represent distinctly to ourselves the whole course of events. The long day—one of the few in the public life of the Lord where we find ourselves in a condition to follow Him almost from step to step—was visibly hurrying towards evening, but still Jesus beholds around Him numerous throngs desiring instruction and help. If, therefore, He is to enjoy the rest which at last has become absolutely necessary, He must withdraw Himself from the throng and give the multitude opportunity to reflect upon the parables they have heard. Accordingly He gives immediate command to His disciples as to the departure, after He had previously left behind on the shore the scribe who had desired to follow Him, and another whom He called in vain. His disciples took Him with them in their vessel, according to the graphic expression of Mark: ὡς ἦν, that is, without any further preparation for the journey. As to the rest, the Synoptics give essentially the same account. If Mark communicates particulars which confirm the surmise that the personal remembrances of Peter have not been without some influence upon the form of his account, he nevertheless agrees perfectly with Luke. From the two, Matthew deviates in this twofold respect; namely, that he, in the first place, has given the address of the Saviour to His disciples as if preceding His word of might to the tempest; and secondly, that he has put the exclamation of astonishment at the very end, not exclusively in the disciples' mouths, but in those of the men (ἄνθρωποι) who were in the ship. But as respects the last, we do not see what improbability there is in the view, that besides the Twelve some other persons also, attendants and the like, may have been present in the ship, and may have joined with the disciples in the tone of wonder to which the disciples (Mark and Luke) undoubtedly give louder and stronger expression than all the rest. With regard to the first mentioned point, the representation of Matthew, it appears, has the most probability in its favor, for we know that the Saviour was wont first to awaken faith, before He performed a miracle; and on a later occasion also the wind did not sink until He had asked the sinking Peter: "Oh, thou of little faith, wherefore dost thou doubt?" The address to the disciples and the mighty word of deliverance followed one another so quickly, that Mark and Luke might easily reverse the order without making themselves guilty of a censurable inaccuracy.

Vs. 22. **That He went into a ship.**—According to Mark iv. 36, there were other vessels also accompanying the Saviour near by, which is least of all to be wondered at, at the end of such a day. If one is not disposed, therefore, to seek the ἄνθρωποι of Matthew (vs. 27) upon the vessel of the apostles, the conjecture then that the companions of the voyage on the ἄλλοις πλοιαρίοις had been, at some distance, witnesses of the miracle, and, therefore, made manifest their astonishment without reserve,—such a conjecture certainly will not be too hazardous.

Unto the other side.—The eastern shore is here meant. According to Mark, the Saviour seats Himself in the πρύμνα, hinder part of the ship, comp. Acts xxvii. 29, 41, and falls fast asleep upon a προσκεφαλαίῳ. Now awakes the storm,—according to Matthew and Mark, a σεισμός (by which also an earthquake is signified, Matt. xxviii. 2); according to Luke, more precisely, a λαῖλαψ ἀνέμου, which precipitates itself from above upon the sea.

Vs. 24. **Master, Master.**—If we assume that Luke has most accurately communicated the words of the troubled disciples, we should then notice in the expression itself the trace of the anxious fear that was in them. They call the Lord, we may note, with a double ἐπιστάτα to help, while Mark puts in their mouths a διδάσκαλε, and Matthew even a κύριε. But more than the expression, the exclamation itself bears witness of utter faintness of heart. So ὀλιγόπιστοι (Matthew) are they, that really it may be said of them, they have *no* faith (Mark and Luke), yet now as ever their faith manifests itself in this, that in their distress they flee to none but Jesus. Without doubt the storm must have been very unexpected and violent, for experienced sailors like these to be attacked by so violent a terror. But the malady of unbelief also has an epidemic character, and undoubtedly the unwonted view of the sleeping Saviour did not a little augment their distress.

Vs. 24. **A calm,** γαλήνη = דְּמָמָה, Psalm cvii. 29 in Symmachus.—An additional sign of a miracle, since otherwise, even when the storm has subsided, a disturbed movement of the air and the water always continues for a time. According to Mark, the Saviour gives His rebuke with the words: "σιώπα, desiste a sonitu, and πεφίμωσο, obmutesce, desiste impetu." Bengel. First of all the Lord rebukes the storm in the heart, afterwards the storm in nature.

Vs. 25. **What manner of man is this?**—No question, we may believe, of doubt, but of the deepest astonishment, which is heightened by the unexpectedness and unexampled character of the miracle. Here also, as in Luke v. 8, the astonishment is so great because the miracle is wrought in a sphere familiar to them. It is as if they had never yet conceded to the greatness of the miraculous worker its full rights. It is true, they knew Him previously, and yet their feeling is like that of the Baptist when he exclaimed: "I knew Him not," John i. 31.

DOCTRINAL AND ETHICAL.

1. A miracle such as this we have not yet met with in the Gospel of Luke. We have, in miracles of nature like this, as well as at Cana and elsewhere, to meet the objection that wholly inanimate nature appears to offer no point of attachment whatever to the mighty will of the miracle-worker; but that this difficulty gives us no warrant whatever for the fallacies of the naturalistic interpretation, needs hardly be mentioned. The vindicators of this show that they have as little knowledge of nature, as true knowledge of the human heart. As little can we accede to the view of those (Neander) who, by sharply distinguishing the objective and the subjective side of the account, suppose that the Saviour actually only quieted His disciples; so that now before the eyes of their enlightened faith the raging of nature displayed itself in another form, and their ear, as it were, no longer heard the raging of the storm, while later, when the storm had actually subsided, that was ascribed to the working of Jesus upon *nature,* which was only the consequence of His influence upon their *mind.*—[This of Neander may fairly be called as flat and vapid a rationalizing away of a simple narrative as Paulus himself was ever guilty of.—C. C. S.] This error, moreover, could hardly remain concealed from the Saviour, and at least could have exercised no influence on the less susceptible shipmen, who did not belong to the Apostolic circle, and least of all could it have been favored by the Saviour Himself. Whoever leaves it undecided (Hase) whether the Saviour professed or wrought the miracle, contradicts in fact the sacred record. No, that they here mean to relate a miracle is plain to the eye, and the question can only be simply this: did it take place or did it not take place? Have we here history or myth?

2. The mythical explanation stumbles not only against these general obstacles, but has here, moreover, the particular difficulty to solve that not a single Old Testament narrative has so much agreement with the Evangelical as to allow of the assumption that the latter arose from the former. It is undoubtedly not hard with lofty air to explain this whole miracle as "an anecdote of the kind that have been related of every century and of the miracle-workers of all times, and whose origin may be explained in a thousand ways" (Weisse). Such arbitrariness, however, condemns itself, so long as the genuineness of one of the Synoptical gospels is still admitted. Nothing else, accordingly, is left but to acknowledge the reality of the miracle, and if one wishes to seek a medium of it, to say with Lange: "The Saviour rebukes the storm in the inner world of His disciples, in order to find a medium of rebuking the storm in nature. He removes the sin of the microcosm, in order to remove the evils of the macrocosm." We have here the concurrence of the will of the Father with that of the Son, which belongs to the deepest mysteries of His Theanthropic being. In His whole fulness Christ stands here before us as an image of Him who "sitteth upon the waters and drinketh up the sea by His rebuke." Pss. xxix., xciii. What Moses performed in the might of Jehovah when he opened with his staff the way through the waters for himself, that the Son of the Father does through the efficacy of His will alone. Here also we meet with that union of the Divine and human nature and operation which we so often discover in the Gospel. He who wearied with His day's work lays Himself a while to sleep, because He needs bodily rest, and remains quiet in the most threatening danger, rises at once in Divine fulness of might and commands the tempestuous wind and bridles the sea. As sinful man can work mechanically upon the creation, so does the God-Man work dynamically, and thus does this whole activity become a prophecy of the future in which the spirit of redeemed mankind will govern matter, and the hope of Paul, Rom. viii. 19-23, will be fully realized.

3. The purpose of this miracle soon strikes the eye. It was to make the companions of the apostles in the voyage for the first time or renewedly attentive to the Lord; it was to exercise and strengthen the disciples in faith, but above all it was to hold up before them a sensible image of that which afterwards, when they were entered upon the apostolical career, would befall them. As their little ship was now thrown around, so should also the young church, at whose head they stood, appear often given over to the might of the waves and billows. But then also they should become aware at the right time of the Lord, who would arouse Himself to change the darkness

into light. This is the deep sense of the symbolical explanation of the miracle, which deserves censure only when it is put in opposition to the purely historical, instead of being grounded upon it. No wonder if many have essayed it, if not always so beautifully as, for example, Erasmus, when he writes, *Præfat. in Evang. Matth. in fine:* "*hinc nimirum illa periculosa tempestas, quia Christus dormit in nobis.—Diffisi præsidiis nostris, inclamemus Jesum, pulsemus aures illius, vellicemus, donec expergiscatur. Dicamus illi flebili voce: Domine, tua non refert, si pereamus? Ille, ut est exorabilis, audiet suos, suoque spiritu repente sedabit tempestatem mundano spiritu agitatam. Dicet vento: quiesce,*" &c. Comp. the Hymn of Fabricius: "*Hilf, lieber Gott, was Schmach und Spott,*" &c., and the spiritual interpretation of this narrative in LUTHER's *Kirchen-Postille, ad loc.* The homage which was offered to Christ after He had performed the miracle, is an echo of the Old Testament Choral: Ps. cvii. 23–30.

HOMILETICAL AND PRACTICAL.

Wherever Jesus goes, thither must His disciples accompany Him.—The duty of the disciples of the Lord: 1. To follow Him upon every way; 2. to call on Him in every distress; 3. to glorify Him after every deliverance.—The calm is followed by a tempest, the tempest by greater calm.— Jesus sleeping in the storm; by this one feature of the narrative, 1. The greatness of the Lord is manifested; 2. the perplexity of the disciples explained; 3. the rest of the Christian prophesied.—The distress of the disciples of Jesus: 1. Its causes; 2. its culmination; 3. its limits.—Whoever, even in distress, can call on Jesus, has no destruction to fear.—No storm so vehement but the Lord can still it: 1. In the world; 2. in the Church; 3. in the house; 4. in the heart.— The question, "Where is your faith?" now as of old: 1. A question for the life; 2. a question for the conscience; 3. a question for the times.—What manner of man is this that he commandeth even the wind and the water?—Jesus' greatness revealed in the obscure night of tempest. On the little ship He exhibits Himself as: 1. The true and holy Man; 2. the wise and gracious Master; 3. the almighty and adorable Son of God.—The storm on the sea an image of the Christian life: 1. The threatening danger; 2. the growing anxiety; 3. the delivering might; 4. the rising thanks.—If the storms within us are still, those without us then also subside.—Trial and deliverance work together: 1. To reveal the Lord; 2. to train His people; 3. to advance the coming of His kingdom.

STARKE:—QUESNEL:—The present life is, so to speak, only a passage from one side to the other, and finally from time into eternity.—CANSTEIN:—Sleeping and rest has even in the ministry its season. Enough that the Keeper of Israel neither slumbers nor sleeps. Ps. cxxi. 4.—Where Christ is there is danger, and sometimes even greater than where He is not; yet not for destruction, but for trial.—MAJUS:—Danger at sea is a mighty arouser to prayer.—OSIANDER:—Christ is the Lord of the sea and of the winds, and to Him, even after His human nature, all things are subject. Ps. viii. 2 *seq.*—So oft as we receive a benefit from the dear God, our faith should become stronger.

HEUBNER:—*Nil desperandum, Christo duce.*—Christian fearlessness in danger: 1. Its necessity, 2. its nature, 3. the means of attaining it.—Dr. J. J. DOEDES, Prof. in Utrecht, a homily:—1. The commencement of the voyage; 2. the raging of the tempest; 3. the fear of the disciples; 4. the rest of the Lord; 5. the rebuke of the weak in faith; 6. the power of the word of might.—RAUTENBERG:—The heavier the cross, the more earnest the prayers. —GERDESSEN:—The appearance of Christ in earthly tumult: 1. He lets it rage, *a.* as if without measure, *b.* without concern, *c.* without remedy; 2. He stills it, *a.* the stormy world, *b.* the stormy life, *c.* the stormy heart.— LISCO:—Concerning trust in the Lord: 1. Wherein it reveals itself; 2. what its nature is; 3. how it is rewarded.—FLOREY:—The words in the ship at the storming of the sea: 1. The word of terror; 2. the word of censure; 3. the word of might; 4. the word of astonishment.—HÖPFNER: —The disciples of Christ according to this Gospel: 1. Willingly following, 2. anxious, 3. praying, 4. ashamed disciples.— DENNINGER:— The wondrous ways of the Lord: Wonderfully does He bring His own: 1. Down into the deep, 2. up out of the deep. —FUCHS:— Why sleeps the Lord so often in the tempests of this life? He will lead us: 1. To the knowledge of our powerlessness; 2. to faith in His almightiness; 3. to prayer for His help; 4. to praise of His name.

---

b. THE DEMONIAC AT GADARA (Vss. 26–39).

(Parallels: Matt. viii. 28–34; Mark v. 1–20.)

26 And they arrived at the country of the Gadarenes,[1] which is over against Galilee.
27 And when he went forth [had gone out] to land, there met him out of the city a certain man [a certain man of the city met him], which had devils [was possessed by demons] long time, and ware [wore] no clothes, neither abode in *any* house, but in the tombs.
28 When he saw Jesus, he cried out, and fell down before him, and with a loud voice said, What have I to do with thee, Jesus, *thou* Son of God most high? I beseech thee,
29 torment me not. (For he had [om., had] commanded the unclean spirit to come out of the man. For oftentimes [for a long time] it had caught [seized upon] him: and he was kept bound with chains and in fetters; and he brake the bands, and was driven of
30 [by] the devil [demon] into the wilderness [desert places].) And Jesus asked him, saying, What is thy name? And he said, Legion: because [for] many devils [demons]

31 were entered into him. And they [or, he²] besought him that he would not command
32 them to go out into the deep [abyss]. And there was there a herd of many swine
feeding on the mountain: and they besought him that he would suffer them to enter into
33 them. And he suffered them. Then went the devils [demons] out of the man, and
entered into the swine: and the herd ran violently down a steep place [the cliff] into
34 the lake, and were choked [drowned]. When they that fed *them* [the keepers] saw
35 what was done [had happened], they fled, and went and told *it* in the city and in the
country. Then they went out to see what was done [had happened]; and came to
Jesus, and found the man, out of whom the devils [demons] were departed, sitting at
36 the feet of Jesus, clothed, and in his right mind: and they were afraid. They also
which saw *it* told them by what means he that was possessed of the devils [by the
37 demons] was healed. Then the whole multitude of the country of the Gadarenes round
about besought him to depart from them; for they were taken with great fear: and
38 he went up [om., up] into the ship, and returned back again. Now the man, out of
whom the devils [demons] were departed, besought him that he might be with him:
39 but Jesus [he, V. O.³] sent him away, saying, Return to thine own house, and shew
how great things God hath done unto thee. And he went his way, and published
throughout the whole city how great things Jesus had done unto him.

¹ Vs. 26.—Respecting the different readings: Gadarenes, Gergesenes, Gerasenes, &c., *see* below in *Critical* and *Exegetical* remarks.
[² Vs. 31.—Van Oosterzee has "*he* besought him," &c. Παρεκάλει might have as its subject either ἀνήρ or the neuter δαιμόνια. The fact that παρεκάλεσαν in the next verse is used, where δαιμόνια is the subject, may incline us to prefer the singular subject here.—C. C. S.]
³ Vs. 38.—*Rec.*: ὁ Ἰησοῦς. [Om., B., D., L., Cod. Sin.—C. C. S.]

EXEGETICAL AND CRITICAL.

Vs. 26. **The Gadarenes.**—That in Matt. viii. 28, the reading Γαδαρηνῶν deserves the preference appears hardly to admit of a doubt. *See* Lange *ad loc.* But in Luke also we find no sufficient ground to read with Lachmann and Tischendorf, on the authority particularly of B., D., Γερασηνῶν, and still less again to read with L., Δ. [*Cod. Sin.*] and a few others, Γεργεσηνῶν. The very distinction between these two latter readings shows how much hesitation there has been, and how soon the old and true reading Γαδαρηνῶν was supplanted. We cannot possibly understand Gerasa, one of the ten cities of the Decapolis, the present Djerasch, since it lay more than ten [German, fifty English] miles distant from the sea, and as respects Gergesa, we find, it is true, mention made of Gergesites, Deut. vii. 1; Josh. xxiv. 11 [E. V., Girgashites]; but I do not from that alone venture to affirm the existence of a city of this name at the time of Jesus. The authority of Origen is not a sufficient support for the reading Γεργεσηνῶν, since he chose this only on geographical and not on critical grounds, and besides, he assures us that even at his time, in some manuscripts, the reading Γαδαρηνῶν was found, which he only rejects because this city was too far distant from the shore. In respect to this last objection, there is nothing in the way of the conjecture that Jesus had proceeded a certain distance inland when He saw the demoniac, and that, according to the very accurate calculation of Ebrard, *ad loc.* S. 381, the city was at least a league distant from the sea. We for our part are of the opinion that the region of the shore of the sea is likely in the mouth of the people to have still retained the name of "the land of the Gergesenes" after the Gergesites of Joshua's day, and that a copyist, for more exact definition of the original expression, "land of the Gadarenes," first wrote on the margin the words, "of the Gergesenes," which afterwards in many manuscripts supplanted the original reading. In this way the comparatively wide diffusion of the incorrect reading is perhaps best explained.

Vs. 27. **A certain man of the city.**—So also Mark. According to Matt. there were two. This plural in Matt. which several times recurs when the other Synoptics have a singular, belongs to the peculiarities of his gospel, for whose explanation a general law must be sought for. There is no want of conjecture in favor of there having been two (Strauss, De Wette, Lange), and it is no doubt possible that Luke and Mark mention only one, namely, the most malignant; but on the other hand we cannot regard it as probable that the original two should thus have been reduced to a unity, and we find moreover in the whole account no one proof that the Saviour here had really two demoniacs to deal with. Nor may we forget that the whole account of Mark and Luke as to this event is much more precise and complete than that of Matthew. We therefore give to them, here also, the preference, and have only to inquire now, from whence the second demoniac has come into the narrative of Matthew. The conjecture (Ebrard, Olshausen) that he joins in mind the demoniac in the synagogue at Capernaum with this one (Mark i. 23) is wholly without proof. More happy appears to us the opinion (Da Costa) that the raging demoniac precisely at the moment when the Lord arrived was involved in strife with one of the passers by (Comp. Matt. viii. 28 *b*), so that Matt. relates κατ' ὄψιν, without diplomatic exactness. Or should we assume (Neander, Hase, De Wette) that the plurality of the here-mentioned demons led to the inexact mention of a plurality of demoniacs? Perhaps if we assume that Matthew originally wrote in Hebrew, this difference might possibly be laid to the account of the Greek translator. But if none of these conjectures is acceptable there is nothing left then but to acknowledge here one of the minute differences, for whose explanation we are wanting in the requisite data, and which can give offence only from the point of view of a one-sided and mechanical theory of inspiration. More ancient attempts at explanation, *see* in Kuinoel *ad loc.* In no case is it admissible with Von Ammon to explain the variation in this subordinate point by assuming that none of the apostles were personally present, inasmuch as they, when the Saviour disembarked, probably remained on the ship in order to fish ; and at the same time also, not improbably to sell some fish in Gadara while the Master preached or performed miracles !!

Vs. 27. **In the tombs.**—There are still found in the neighborhood of the ancient Gadara (the present Omkeis) many caves and chalk ranges which served as places of burial, and from other accounts also we know that the inhabitants carried on an active traffic in cattle and especially in swine. No wonder, for they consisted of a mixture of Jews, Greeks, and Syrians, of whom the former stood in very low esteem with their countrymen in Judea and Galilee, because they had assimilated themselves more than the latter to other nations. Only seldom did the Saviour visit these regions, in which He found but few lost sheep of the house of Israel. The first time that we meet Him here, He performed a miracle which more perhaps than any other has been to many expositors a λίθος προσκόμματος. What the ass of Balaam is in the Old Testament that are the swine of Gadara in the New Testament, foolishness and a stumbling-block to the wisdom of this world.

Possessed by demons.—*See* remarks on ch. iv. 33.

Vs. 28. **Jesus, Thou Son of God.**—Perhaps the demoniac was a Jew not wholly unacquainted with the Messianic hope; but certainly it is in the spirit of the Evangelists if we believe that the knowledge of the Lord which the demons usually exhibited had been attained in a supernatural way.

Vs. 29. **For He commanded,** παρήγγειλεν.—" Not in the sense of the pluperfect, but like ἔλεγεν, Mark v. 8." Meyer. According to Luke the Saviour had therefore commanded the spirit to come out before the latter had begged for forbearance, but we do not therefore need to assume that He had uttered this command to the unfortunate man from some distance, even before the latter had come to Him. Perhaps the words of the demoniac in the extreme tension of his mental condition had only been ejaculated interruptedly. First the question: "What have I to do with thee Jesus thou Son of God?" Afterwards the answer of the Saviour, who never accepted public acknowledgment from demoniacs, ἔξελθε, κ.τ.λ. Mark v. 8. Afterwards the abrupt entreaty : " I beseech thee torment me not," and then the inquiry after the name.

For for a long time.—A more particular explanation of Luke, which throws into more relief on the one hand the misery of his condition, on the other the miraculousness of the deliverance; comp. Mark v. 2–4.—**Seized upon.**—So that he hurried him along unresistingly with himself.—**He was kept bound with chains and fetters.**—Whenever his relatives or keepers had succeeded in bringing him back home for a while, out of the wilderness.

Vs. 30. **What is thy name?**—The answer to the question whether the Saviour here speaks to the demoniac himself, or to the demon tormenting him, depends entirely on the conception which we form of such unfortunates. In the first case it is an attempt to bring the demoniac in a psychological way to reflection and to help him to distinguish his own conceptions from those of the unclean spirit. In the other case it is an inquiry of the King of the personal world of spirits, which He addresses to the author of so much misery, and we must say with Stier:

" We interpreters will here modestly remain without when the Son of God speaks with one from hell, only with the just conviction that the two have well understood one another."—**Legion.**—The demoniac is in feeling entirely identified with the evil powers that control and torment him. Respecting the name " Legio," *see* LANGE on Matt. xxvi. 53.

For many demons.—Less accurately this reason stated for the name given, is in Mark put in the mouth of the demons themselves.

Vs. 31. **And he besought Him.**—The demon, that is; who in this instance was still working with unlimited power upon the unhappy man, and at the same time uttered himself in the name of the whole Legion. Why the demons desire to go into the swine is a question which we, so far as we are concerned, can answer only with a confession of the entire incompetence of our intelligence on this mysterious ground. Only one folly would be yet greater than that of a presumptuous decision: the folly, namely, of those who are as little acquainted with the nature of demons as of swine, and yet at once utter, *ex cathedra*, the word "absurd; impossible." Much better: " *Potestas Christi etiam super animalia, dæmones, abyssum porrigitur. Idque agnovere dæmones.*" Bengel.

Into the abyss.—That is, into hell; comp. Rev. ix. 11; xx. 3. " The evil spirits also have their wishes and understand their interest as well as man. As they therefore in this ever-intensifying conflict between themselves and the Messiah, become aware that they must in some way yield before Him, they entreat at least to be handled in the mildest way and to be permitted to go into a tolerably near herd of swine (and only too fully does their man concur in this wish, because otherwise he fears that he must die): against this wish Christ has nothing to object. But so powerful is yet, from fear before the Messiah (?), the momentum of the evil spirits in going out, that they enter into a corresponding number of swine and drive these again into wild flight ; nay more, precipitate them down the cliff into the water, and so against their will must, nevertheless, go out of the dying man (rather the sick man) into hell, while the man, liberated from them, comes to his long sighed-for repose." Von Ewald. The terror and the precipitation of the herd into the sea, we should, however, rather explain, with Lange and many others, as resulting from the last terrible paroxysm which, as usual, preceded the healing. The number of the swine (Mark v. 13) may moreover be stated in a round number, either according to the reckoning of the spectators or according to the statement of the embittered possessors.

Vs. 33. **And entered into the swine.**—It is of course understood that we here have not to understand individual *indwelling*, but dynamic *influence*, of the demoniacal powers upon the defenceless herd. But if philosophy declares that such an influence is entirely impossible, we demand the proof for the right of deciding in so lofty a tone upon a matter which lies entirely outside of the limits of experience, and are, therefore, on the contrary, fully in our right when we, after the credibility of Luke is once established, conclude *ab esse ad posse*. If the psychologist accounts it impossible that irrational beings should experience the influence of spiritual forces, we will wait till he gives us a little more assurance with regard to the souls of beasts than we have hitherto possessed. And if the critic wishes to know for what end the demoniacal power caused the swine to rush so quickly into the lake, we will acknowledge our ignorance, but simply desire that one should not declare incomprehensible and ridiculous to be synonymous. It is indeed possible that the swine were precipitated against the will of the demons into the lake, because the organism of these animals proved too weak to resist their overmastering influence. In this case it plainly appears from the result that the entreaty had been an unintelligent one; but then, does not mental confusion belong to the nature of evil? Enough; one thing stands fast, that it was by no means wholly unexpected or against the intention of Jesus that the swine were controlled by demoniacal influence (against Paulus, Hase, Von Ammon). The Saviour must have known what He conceded with the word of might ὑπάγετε; moreover He afterwards does not excuse Himself for an instant to the owners of the herd by saying that He had not been able to foresee their loss. He simply goes His way and listens to the entreaty of the demons, unconcerned whether the herd shall be able to endure this terror or not. With His special concurrence does it take place, that the possession of the rational man passes over upon the irrational herd. We believe, if we may compare the supernatural with a mysterious natural fact, that here something similar took place to what even now often takes place by magnetic forces, when some bodily evil is transferred from one object to another, even from man to animals. Undoubtedly Jesus found such a miraculous diversion of the malady necessary for the restoration of the sick man, and the possibility that demoniacal conditions may pass over upon others, even upon beasts, appears not to admit of denial. Comp. Kiesen, *System des Tellurismus*, ii. p. 72.

Finally, as respects the question how far a permission of the Saviour is to be justified which occasioned so considerable a loss, *see* Lange on Matt. viii. 31. Some answers to this question have certainly turned out rather unlucky, *e. g.*, that of Hug, that the flesh might have been still fished up and salted and used. Without entirely excluding the thought that here there is a just retribution for the defilement of the Jewish population (Olshausen), the answer suffices us that Jesus' word: "not come to destroy, but to save," applies indeed to men, but not to beasts. At any price He will pluck this soul from the powers of darkness. He exerts His miraculous might, not with the immediate *purpose* of destroying the herd; but if the loss of these is the inevitable consequence of His beneficent activity, this loss can be made good, while the opportunity to save this man is not likely ever to return. He who afterwards gave Himself up for a pure sacrifice does not here account the life of unclean beasts at a higher rate than it deserves. The imputation that He in this way infringed upon the property-rights of strangers, made by Woolston and others, was not once brought forward by the Gadarenes themselves, and the attempt to vindicate their rights more strongly than they themselves in this case thought necessary, may be dismissed with a *ne quid nimis*. Finally it must not be overlooked that the healing was a benefit not only for the demoniac, but also for the whole region. Comp. Matt. viii. 28 *b.*

Vs. 35. **Clothed.**—The Evangelist says not from whence or by whom. Perhaps we may here understand the intervention of the Saviour's disciples, who here also accompanied Him. The healed one moreover now sits παρὰ τοὺς πόδας τοῦ Ἰησοῦ, as a disciple at the feet of his Master.

Vs. 36. **They also which saw it.**—Matthew also speaks, v. 33, of keepers, who had been witnesses of the miracle.

Vs. 37. **To depart from them.**—A longer stay of the Saviour could have had little attraction for men who, above all, calculated the material loss, and were seized with superstitious and half heathen fear. The abode of the dangerous demoniac in the midst of them is less burdensome to them than the longer sojourn of such a worker of miracles. A sad contrast to the entreaty of the Samaritans, John iv. 40. But the Saviour here and there alike yields to the desire expressed.

Vs. 38. **Now the man.**—Comp. Mark v. 18-20. The prayer with which the recovered demoniac follows the departing Saviour may serve as an unequivocal proof of the completeness of his healing, as well as of the warmth of his thankfulness. The Saviour does not grant the request, partly perhaps for the reason that for the perfectness and duration of his recovery somewhat more of rest was required. But that He here encourages the one whom He had delivered to a proclamation of the benefit bestowed upon him, while on those who were healed elsewhere silence is imposed, is a proof the more that He had not the intention to return into the land of the Gadarenes; there must, therefore, at least one living and speaking memorial of His miraculous power abide there. Moreover, in Peræa the diffusion of such accounts was less critical than in Galilee, which was so inclined to insurrection. In the directing of the man back to his home, it is at the same time implied that the Saviour remembers his perhaps distressed or anxious relatives, for whom now his untroubled domestic life is to be the theatre of his gratitude and obedience. Yet not only to his own friends, but throughout the whole of Decapolis, does the man proclaim what had been done, so that the astonishment which he at all events awakens, without doubt became a beneficent preparation for the later preaching of the gospel in these dark regions.

Vs. 39. **How great things.** Ὅσα.—In a remarkable manner are the great works of God and Jesus at the conclusion of the narrative co-ordinated. Without doubt it is the intention of the Evangelist here to indicate that it was God Himself who in and through the miraculous power of the Messiah displayed in extraordinary wise His workings.

DOCTRINAL AND ETHICAL.

1. There is no revelation of Christ as the King of the world of spirits which contains so much that is obscure as that which took place at Gadara. In relation to such miracles also does the Saviour's own word hold good, ch. vii. 23, and this Macarism can only be fulfilled in him who with Paul continues mindful of the φρονεῖν εἰς τὸ σωφρονεῖν.

2. The miracle here narrated conflicts in no way with the well-known summing up of the biography of the Saviour, διῆλθεν εὐεργετῶν, Acts x. 38. It is no miracle of punishment, any more than the drying up of the fig-tree was one, and that for the reason that swine and fig-tree are irrational creatures, to which therefore as a class the conception of punishment is only very loosely applicable. Moreover, the Saviour acts here as representative of the Father on earth, who daily destroys the lesser that the higher may be nourished and preserved, and has never yet forbidden

His lightnings to purify the atmosphere for fear they might perchance strike the trunks of some trees. Had the herd of swine been driven by a tempest into the sea, who would accuse God of the wickedness of having infringed upon the property-rights of legal possessors? How many a murrain has taken off far more than 2,000 victims!

3. "That the diseased life of the soul falls into the duality of a so-to-speak subjective and an objective, of a dominant and a suppressed, Ego, can be a matter of surprise only to him who does not know or does not clearly keep in mind that the Ego even in itself and in a healthy condition is this duplicity of a subject-object." Strauss, in a review of Justin Kerner's Essay on Demoniacs of Modern Times.

4. The healing of the demoniac of Gadara is a striking symbol on the one hand of the conflict which the kingdom of God continually carries on against the realm of darkness; on the other hand of the triumph which it finally, although after heavy sacrifices, attains; at the same time a proof how much in earnest the Saviour was in His own declaration, Matt. xvi. 26.

5. In the command with which the Saviour parts from the recovered man, there lies an honor put upon devout domestic life, which is the less to be overlooked, inasmuch as it is a striking revelation of Christianity as the principle of the purest Humanity.

6. Peter, too, had once begged that the Lord would depart from Him, Luke v. 8, and yet the Lord had turned into his house more than ever before; but the prayer of the Gadarenes He accepts in fearful earnestness, because He penetrates their unbelief, their sin. This mournful result of the miracle at Gadara, moreover, is a striking proof how even the most astounding miracles cannot constrain to faith when the requisite disposition of heart and conscience is lacking.

HOMILETICAL AND PRACTICAL.

To the storm on the sea succeeds the contest with the world of spirits.—When Israel amalgamates with the heathen, the demons find a roomy dwelling prepared for themselves.—The deep wretchedness of the man who is ruled by demoniacal powers.—Domestic life most direfully desolated by the might of darkness.—The Lord of Heaven known to the dwellers of hell.—The Evil One feels that his Vanquisher draws nigh.—Evil also is fruitful and multiplies.—Even where the Lord leaves the night of darkness free, its own destruction is the wretched end of this freedom.—Beasts, men, and demons alike subject to the Son of Man.—The worth of the soul: 1. No harm so great as when harm occurs to the soul; 2. no price too dear, if only the soul is redeemed; 3. no thankfulness so heartfelt as when the soul feels itself delivered.—The miracle at Gadara a revelation of the glory of the Saviour: 1. As the Son of the living God; 2. as the King of the world of spirits; 3. as the Deliverer of the wretched; 4. as the Holy One, who does not suffer Himself to be entreated in vain to depart.—Whoever is saved by the Lord must, as a disciple, sit at His feet.—The great things which Jesus did by this miracle: 1. In the world; 2. in the house; 3. in the land of the Gadarenes.—The enmity of the flesh is to be changed by no benefit, however great it be.—The redeemed of the Lord wishes nothing more ardently than to abide with Him.—Domestic life the worthy theatre of active gratitude.—Through the redeemed of Christ must the Father be glorified.—Even when Jesus departs He leaves yet witnesses of His grace behind.—The might of darkness runs ever into its own destruction.—Presumptuous transgression of the law is ever sooner or later visited.

STARKE:—Christ neglects no land in the world with His grace.—The angels rejoice over a sinner's conversion, but the devil is sorely disgusted when a soul is freed from his tyranny.—J. HALL:—Those are no true Christians who deny the Godhead of Christ, since the devil nevertheless acknowledges it, 1 John iv. 15.—God sets the devil also his bounds and says finally: "It is enough," Job xxxviii. 11.—OSIANDER: —There must an astonishing number of the angels have fallen away from God.—Satan has not even power over irrational creatures except as it is permitted him of God.—BRENTIUS:—God often lets outward possessions escape from us that we may receive spiritual good.—*Nova Bibl. Tub.*:—That is the way of the godless world; they love swine more than Christ.—BRENTIUS:—Christendom is full of Gergesenes.—QUESNEL:—It is a fearful judgment of God upon sinners when He hears their prayer to their hurt, as He does the demons' prayer.—Teachers and preachers must at their expulsion be resigned and content.—New converts are wont to fall into all manner of self-devised ways, therefore they need faithful admonition and direction.—Obedience is better than sacrifice.—CANSTEIN:—To glorify the grace of conversion helps much to the edifying of our neighbor.

On the whole, the treatment of this narrative offers to the preacher peculiar difficulties not less great than that of the Temptation in the Wilderness. It is therefore, unless one is obliged to it by ecclesiastical ordinances, not to be commended to any one at least, who in reference to the Biblical demonology occupies a sceptical or negative position. But even if one in this respect takes the Lord at His word, we have here especially to take heed of being wiser than the Scripture and, in an ill-applied apologetical zeal, of vindicating the conduct of the Saviour in such a way as involuntarily to remind those who think differently of the maxim, "*Qui excusat, accusat.*" Perhaps it is best to leave the metaphysical question wholly or mainly untouched, and to give especial prominence to the practical side of the deliverance of the soul from the powers of darkness, as to its greatness, its worth, and the like. As an example of an admirable sermon upon this δυσνόητον we may adduce *les Démoniaques*, in the sermons par *Adolph Monod*, 2 Recueil, *Montauban, Paris*, 1857. So also, Fr. Arndt, who in his Sermons upon the Life of Jesus, iii. p. 39–52, found in this narrative occasion to preach with wholly practical aim respecting: 1. The character; 2. the causes; 3. the healing of the malady of the demoniac.

c. THE RAISING OF JAIRUS' DAUGHTER (Vss. 40-56).

(Parallels: Matt. ix. 18-26; Mark v. 21-43. Gospel for the 24th Sunday after Trinity.)

40 And it came to pass, that, when Jesus was returned, the people *gladly* received
41 him: for they were all waiting for him. And, behold, there came a man named Jairus, and he was a ruler [the president] of the synagogue; and he fell down at Jesus'
42 feet, and besought him that he would come into his house: For he had one only daughter, about twelve years of age, and she lay a dying. But [And it came to pass,
43 V. O.¹] as he went the people thronged him. And a woman having [who had had] an issue of blood twelve years, which had spent all her living upon [for] physicians,
44 neither could be healed of [by] any, Came [Approached] behind *him*, and touched the border [fringe, Num. xv. 38] of his garment: and immediately her issue of blood
45 stanched. And Jesus said, Who touched me? When all denied, Peter and they that were with him said, Master, the multitude throng thee and press *thee*, and sayest thou,
46 Who touched me? And Jesus said, Somebody hath touched me: for I perceive that
47 virtue is gone out [perceived virtue to have gone out] of me. And when the woman saw that she was not hid, she came trembling, and falling down before him, she declared unto him² before all the people for what cause she had touched him, and how
48 she was healed immediately. And he said unto her, Daughter, be of good comfort [om., be of good comfort, V. O.³]: thy faith hath made thee whole; go in peace.
49 While he yet spake [is yet speaking], there cometh one from the ruler of the syna-
50 gogue's *house*, saying to him,⁴ Thy daughter is dead; trouble not the Master. But when Jesus heard *it*, he answered him, saying, Fear not: believe only, and she shall
51 be made whole [lit., saved]. And when he came into the house, he suffered no man to go in [with him⁵], save Peter, and James, and John [John and James, V. O.⁶], and
52 the father and the mother of the maiden. And all wept, and bewailed her: but he
53 said, Weep not; [for, V. O.⁷] she is not dead, but sleepeth. And they laughed him to
54 scorn, knowing that she was dead. And he put them all out [omit this clause, V. O.⁸],
55 and took her by the hand, and called, saying, Maid, arise. And her spirit came again, and she arose straightway: and he commanded to give her meat [something to eat].
56 And her parents were astonished: but he charged them that they should tell no man what was done.

¹ Vs. 42.—Καὶ ἐγένετο ἐν τῷ πορεύεσθαι αὐτόν. *Rec.*: Ἐν δὲ τῷ ὑπάγειν αὐτόν. [Former reading accepted by Tischendorf, Alford, Meyer, Lachmann with C.¹, D., P. Cod. Sin. agrees with *Recepta*.—C. C. S.]
² Vs. 47.—*Rec.*: αὐτῷ, which, however, is to be expunged. [Om., Cod. Sin.]
³ Vs. 48.—*Rec.*: θάρσει, which the Saviour undoubtedly said according to Matt. ix. 22, and perhaps also according to Mark v. 34, but certainly not according to the original text of Luke. *See* MEYER and TISCHENDORF *ad loc.* [Om., Tischendorf, Lachmann, Meyer, Tregelles, Alford with B., D., L., Ξ., Cod. Sin.—C. C. S.]
⁴ Vs. 49.—*Rec.*: λέγων αὐτῷ. Not sufficiently attested. [Tischendorf, Alford, Lachmann retain αὐτῷ with A., C., D., E., 11 other uncials; om., B., Cod. Sin., X., Ξ.—C. C. S.]
⁵ Vs. 51.—The words σὺν αὐτῷ have sufficient authority for themselves, to be received with a good conscience into the text, although they are wanting in the *Recepta*. [The Cod. Sin. agrees substantially with this, but has συνεισελθεῖν αὐτῷ instead of εἰσελθεῖν σὺν αὐτῷ.—C. C. S.]
⁶ Vs. 51.—*Rec.*: *James and John*. From Mark v. 37. [*Recepta* supported by Cod. Sin., A., I., S., X., A.—C. C. S.]
⁷ Vs. 52.—*Rec.* omits γάρ. The number of witnesses for γάρ in Luke is too great to allow us to regard it as merely a copulative borrowed from Matt. ix. 24. [Lachmann, Tregelles, Alford insert γάρ with Cod. Sin., B., C., D., L., X., A. Meyer and Tischendorf omit it with A., E., and 9 other uncials.—C. C. S.]
⁸ Vs. 54.—*Rec.*: Αὐτὸς δὲ ἐκβαλὼν ἔξω πάντας. These words appear to have been with good reason expunged by Lachmann and Tischendorf, as Griesbach had already suspected them. B., D., [Cod. Sin.,] L., X., and other MSS. have them not, and it is much easier to explain how they have been interpolated from Matthew and Mark, than why they should have been omitted, if they had really stood in the original text of Luke. The variation in the arrangement of the words also (C.¹ does not read ἔξω, and several MSS. and versions place it after πάντας) appears to strengthen the probability of interpolation.

. EXEGETICAL AND CRITICAL.

HARMONY.—According to Mark and Luke, the raising of Jairus' daughter follows immediately after the return of Jesus from the land of the Gadarenes. According to Matthew, on the other hand, this raising immediately preceded the healing of the paralytic and the calling of Matthew to the apostleship. It appears to us that the former arrangement deserves the preference (similarly Wieseler, a. o.). The words of Matthew, vs. 18, ταῦτα αὐτοῦ λαλοῦντος αὐτοῖς, seem occasionally to be rather a standing formula to adapt one narrative to another, than a diplomatically exact indication of the actual state of the case. Matt. viii. 9 and ix. bear rather a chrestomathic than a strictly chronological character, while the arrangement in Mark and Luke is much more natural and simple. The opposite view is represented by Olshausen, Lange, Stier. We believe that one must lose himself in a sea of insurmountable difficulties, if he makes Matt. ix. 18-26 follow immediately upon vss. 1-17.

Vs. 40. **The people gladly received Him.**—According to the concurrent accounts of Mark and Luke, the people wait upon the shore for the Saviour while He was returning from the land of the Gadarenes. It appears as if the throngs that had streamed together, also interested themselves for the fate of Jairus. Respecting his office as president of the synagogue, see LANGE on Matt. ix. 18.

Vs. 41. **And he fell down at Jesus' feet.**—A revelation of the life of faith in the president of a synagogue certainly not too friendly to Jesus, of no mean significance. By distress he also was impelled to Jesus, although it could not previously be observed that the healing in the synagogue at Capernaum (ch. iv. 31–44), the miracle upon the paralytic (ch. v. 12–26), or that on the servant of the centurion at Capernaum (ch. vii. 1–10) had made upon this ruler a decisive impression. But now when he is himself in need he without doubt calls to mind all this, and derives therefrom boldness to come with his own sorrow to Jesus.

Vs. 42. **One only daughter, about twelve years of age.**—The statement of the age Luke alone has; it interested him doubtless as physician also. That the woman with an issue of blood had also been ailing twelve years is a coincidence such as real life affords thousands of. An inventor would without doubt have taken care that these two numbers should *not* have agreed with one another.

She lay a dying.—'Ἀπέθνησκεν, imperfect, not "*obierat, absente mortuamque ignorante patre*" (Fritzsche). According to Matt. ἄρτι ἐτελεύτησεν. From vs. 49 it appears, however, that Jairus at this moment did not yet regard her as dead. The different accounts admit of easy combination, if we only consider the excited state of the speaker, who certainly did not weigh his words in a gold-balance. "He left her as one who was dying, and might therefore express himself waveringly." Lange. As to the rest, the prayer of Jairus shows a singular mixture of faith and weakness of faith; he stands below the heathen centurion and almost on a level with the βασιλικός, John iv. 46–54. He desires not only healing, but stipulates moreover expressly that the Saviour must, above all, Himself come and lay His hands on his little daughter. He conceives the miracle only under one, and that the most ordinary, form, instead of entreating, "Speak in a word." But just this brings him also into perplexity, since the Saviour allows Himself to be detained on the way.

As He went.—The Saviour therefore does not allow Himself to be kept back by the exceedingly imperfect form of Jairus' faith, since He is persuaded of its sincerity. Comp. Matt. xii. 20.

'Ἰατροῖς, "for physicians." With his psychological tact Luke brings into relief how much the wearisome suffering of this woman had been aggravated by the fact that with all her suffering she had in addition made so many fruitless essays to be relieved (προσαναλώσασα). Mark expresses himself less favorably for the faculty: "πολλὰ παθοῦσα ὑπὸ πολλῶν ἰατρῶν καὶ μηδὲν ὠφεληθεῖσα, ἀλλὰ μᾶλλον εἰς τὸ χεῖρον ἐλθοῦσα."

Vs. 44. **The fringe of His garment.**—The κράσπεδον, צִיצִת, comp. Numb. xv. 38, and WINER, *Realwörterbuch*, Art. *Saum*.

Vs. 45. **Peter and they that were with him.**—Peculiar to Luke, since Mark only speaks of the disciples in general. Entirely in agreement with the precipitate character of Peter, who thinks merely of an accidental, and not in the least of a believing, touch.

Vs. 46. **Somebody hath touched Me.**—"*Hoc absurdum videtur, quod gratiam suam effuderit Christus nesciens, cui benefaceret. Certe minime dubium est, quin sciens ac volens mulierem sanaverit, sed eam requirit, ut sponte in medium prodeat. Si testis miraculi sui fuisset Christus, forte non fuisset ejus verbis creditum, nunc vero, quum mulier, metu perculsa, quod sibi accidit, narrat, plus ponderis habet ejus confessio.*" Calvin.

I perceived virtue to have gone out of Me.—It is and remains a difficult question how we are to conceive this going forth of virtue. Certainly not in any such way as if His healing power resembled an electric battery, which was obliged to discharge itself involuntarily at the least touch. There proceeds nothing from Him unless He *will*, but He has ever the will to help when and so soon as He only meets with believing confidence. It is therefore not unconsciously, but with full consciousness, that He permits healing power to stream forth when the hand of faith lays hold upon Him. The people press Him on all sides, but experience nothing of the ever-ready healing power, even though one or another might have had a concealed disease, simply because this confidence is lacking in them. And that this virtue proceeds from the Lord need occasion as little perplexity as that the Holy Spirit proceeds from the Father, John xv. 26. Of this going forth of His miraculous power now, the Saviour has no sensuous feeling, but an intellectual knowledge; He knows it within Himself (ἔγνων). Into what definite individual the virtue had passed the Saviour did not know directly. The miraculous knowledge of the Godman was no magical clairvoyance, and His question, "Who is the one (Masc. ὁ, not ἡ) who has touched me?" was by no means a mere feigning. He looks around that the concealed believer might come forward, for this He knows, that without faith the beneficent power would in no case have been elicited from Him. In the spirit He has already heard the cry of distress of a suffering and trusting soul. That His garment was the cause of the healing, the mechanical conductor of the healing power, of this the Evangelist says nothing; but by the touch of His garment faith might be as well tested as by the grasping of His mighty hand. Designedly, therefore, does He cause the woman to come forward from obscurity to the full light, that she may be brought back from the fancy of a magical, to the apprehension of a freely intended working of the Saviour. Not Jesus' garment, but her own faith, has saved her, even though this faith in the beginning was by no means wholly free from superstition.

Vs. 47. **And how she was healed immediately.**—According to tradition, Eusebius, *H. E.* vii. 18; Sozomenus v. 21, the woman erected at Paneas, her birthplace, a memorial of this benefit, which the Emperor Julian is said afterwards to have removed and to have erected his own statue in the place of it. Elsewhere, as in the Gospel of Nicodemus, ch. vii., and in Thilo i. 561, this woman appears under the name of Veronica, who, in the presence of Pilate, proclaimed Jesus' innocence in loud voice, and on the way to Golgotha wiped His face with the handkerchief that is still preserved. Without being obliged to criticise the genuineness and value of these accounts, they may, however, serve as proofs how, even in Christian antiquity, the faith and the hope of this sufferer were esteemed. Compare, moreover, the similar miracles Matt. xiv. 36; Acts v. 15; xix. 11. In SEPP, *Leben Jesu*, II. § 399, we find important particulars in reference to the manner of healing the ῥύσις αἵματος by Jewish physicians. The completeness of the miraculous healing is admirably expressed by Luke the physician in the παραχρῆμα ἔστη ἡ ῥύσις τ. αἵμ.

Vs. 49. **While He is yet speaking.**—By the use of the present in the narrative the vividness and dramatic power of Luke's representation is not a little heightened. It appears, moreover, from this message, that Jairus had come forth with the knowledge and approbation of his family to call the Master. Perhaps, however, this resolution had produced a reaction with some; at least these messengers, probably sent by the distressed mother to the sorrowing father, show now plainly enough that they expect no further benefit from the Teacher.

Vs. 50. **Fear not.**—The whole delay with the woman had been for Jairus a trial of fire. His just awakened faith had been most intensely shaken; but now, when about to succumb, he is strengthened by the Saviour.—Καὶ σωθήσεται. Still more accurately, as it appears, this word is omitted by Mark, although, of course, the event showed that this indirect promise had been comprehended in the "*Only believe*." In that the Saviour at such an instant forbids all fear and demands only faith, He causes Jairus already to expect something great, but does not as yet tell him definitely *what*.

Vs. 51. **He suffered no man to go in.**—As the Saviour did not bring with Him all His disciples, it appears to have been His intention to keep the miracle as much as possible concealed. That He causes Himself to be accompanied by the three disciples, who also upon Tabor, and in Gethsemane, entered into the innermost sanctuary, is a proof of the high significance which He Himself attributes to this raising of the dead.

Vs. 52. **And all wept and bewailed her.**—Comp. Matt. ix. 23 and DE WETTE, *Archæology*, § 263, who makes mention of this expression, among others, from the Talmud: "*Etiam pauperrimus inter Israelitas, uxore mortua, præbebit ei non minus quam duas tibias et unam lamentatricem.*" We can easily imagine how great a din, in the house of an Israelite of distinction, after the loss of his only daughter, there must have been.

She is not dead.—Against the explanation of it as a swoon, Lange justly declares: Matt. *ad loc.* It is true, Von Ammon concludes, from the small number of witnesses that Jesus takes with Him, that the awakening maiden above all things had need of rest and quiet, and therefore was not really dead; but just as well might he, from the command given to the bearers at Nain to stand still, have been able to conclude that the motion of the bier might have been injurious to the only seemingly dead man. The explanation of Olshausen and others is in conflict with the ethical character of the Lord, who was never wont to surround His deeds with an illusory glitter, with the consciousness of the parents and family, vs. 53, and with the express account of Luke: "her spirit returned," vs. 55, comp. 1 Kings xvii. 22. It is not to be doubted, moreover, that the figurative speech taken from sleep serves still more to veil the miracle. A vaunter would have said of one apparently dead: "She sleeps not, but she is dead." The Prince of life says of one dead, "She is not dead, but sleepeth." In the eyes of the Saviour she was at this moment already living, although she as yet lay there fettered corporeally by the power of death.

Vs. 55. **To give her something to eat.**—

Here also there appears in the miracle of the Saviour a trait of benevolence and provident care which forgets nothing, for which nothing is too trivial. Thus does He elsewhere take care that the crumbs should be gathered; that Lazarus should be freed from the grave-clothes,—at once a proof of the truth of the account, and of the completeness of the miracle.

Vs. 56. **That they should tell no man.**—The opinion that the command to keep silence is here interpolated in the wrong place, and was given, not at this miracle, but at a former one (Hase), is destitute of all proof. The command, on the other hand, is occasioned by the intense expectation of the people at the time, who might easily have given themselves up to insurrectionary commotions. Besides, it was a training school for Jairus and his family, who, after they had now beheld the miraculous power of the Saviour, had to be guided to further faith and obedience. And as respects the little daughter, awakened by Jesus to new life, who does not feel how injuriously the continual questions and expressions of astonishment and curiosity would have worked upon the higher and inward life in her case.

DOCTRINAL AND ETHICAL.

1. It is important to note the different forms in which faith reveals itself in Jairus and in the woman with the issue of blood. The former comes courageously forward, but is secretly anxious, and appears stronger than he really is. The other approaches timorously, but is secretly strong in faith, and is really far more than she appeared. Both types have in the Christian world many spiritually related to them.

2. This double narrative of miracle bears in almost every trait the stamp of truth, simplicity, and quiet sublimity. This anxiety of the father and this timidity of the woman; this restlessness of the people and this composure of the Saviour; this surprise of the disciples and His own decisively repeated "Some one hath touched me!" this laugh of unbelief over against the outbreak of sorrow; this majesty in revealing, and this care in concealing, His miraculous power; all this forms a so inimitable whole that one may grasp the truth almost with his hands. Matthew, according to his custom, relates concisely and objectively; with Mark the influence of the eye-witness Peter is unmistakable; the particulars of Luke reveal the physician, and his statement of the age of the child is in some measure supported by Mark, inasmuch as the latter says that she *walked*. All the accounts admit of combination in a most unforced manner, and if any one could take them merely for artfully interwoven threads of a pious invention, we should with reason have to doubt not only his religious sense, but also his natural sense of beauty and truth.

3. A striking similarity appears between the raising of Jairus' daughter and that of Lazarus. Both times does the Lord delay before He brings the help, and permits the sick one to whom He is called, to die. Both times He gives a mysterious promise of deliverance. Both times finally does He declare the death a sleep. Here also the Synoptic agrees with the Johannean Christ. [It may be questioned whether in either case the death had not occurred when the message of entreaty reached Him. It seems, at least, hard to believe that the Saviour would have

permitted any mortal to pass through the agonies of death, merely for the purpose of displaying His miraculous power more fully. On either interpretation, however, the similarity between the present miracle and the raising of Lazarus remains.—C. C. S.]

4. "The journey to this miracle is a remarkable type of many an inward leading. When Jesus has already arrived with the man almost at the goal of his conversion and perfection, just then comes often the hardest shock; by which even what of faith has been gained, appears to fall again completely in ruins. Yet it is only meant to serve for the complete overcoming of all misgiving in the man, for the perfecting of faith and for the glory of the divine Benefactor." Von Gerlach. Comp. moreover the remarks on the raising of the young man of Nain, ch. vii. 11–17.

HOMILETICAL AND PRACTICAL.

When Jesus has been missed for a time, He is received with the greater joy.—How life's distress drives to Jesus.—Jesus the best refuge for the troubled parent's heart.—No youth or strength secures from death.—Jesus looks not mainly at the completeness, but at the sincerity of the faith that calls upon Him.—Jesus the Physician of our hidden infirmities.—The hopeless essays to heal one's self.—The world a physician under whom the sick man grows continually worse and worse.—The bold grasp of faith: 1. What it ventures; 2. what it wins.—How many surround Jesus outwardly, but how few touch Him believingly!—Hidden faith must finally come to light: 1. For the glory of the Lord; 2. for its own attestation; 3. for the encouragement and for the comfort of others.—The tranquillity of the Saviour in opposition: 1. To the thronging of the people; 2. to the contradiction of the disciples; 3. to the perplexity of the woman; 4. to the anxiety of Jairus.—The faith of the woman with the issue of blood: 1. Secretly nourished; 2. courageously shown; 3. immediately discovered; 4. humbly acknowledged; 5. nobly crowned.—Even the hidden benefits of the Lord come at their time to light.—"Fear not, only believe!" 1. An astounding, 2. a legitimate, 3. a possible, 4. a most salutary requirement.—Jesus the best guide on the way of faith. (Jairus.) We see, 1. Supplicating faith heard by Jesus; 2. eager faith tried by Jesus; 3. sinking faith strengthened by Jesus; 4. steadfast faith crowned by Jesus; 5. thankful faith perfected by Jesus.—The way of the Saviour between mourners on the one hand, and laughers on the other.—A hopeless sadness, once for all, proscribed by Jesus when He called death a sleep.—Sleep the image of death; both are, 1. Preceded by weariness; 2. accompanied by a rest; 3. followed by a wakening.—The raising of the spiritually dead also is performed by the Saviour for the most part in holy stillness.—Unbelief which will be wiser than Jesus, is ever put to shame.—The spiritually awakened also need, and at once, nourishment.—Self-denial the best proof of the gratitude of faith.—Even in reference to the Saviour's deeds, there is time for silence as well as for speech.

STARKE:—If Jesus with His Gospel is repulsed in one place, He is bidden welcome in another.—God often permits men to wait a while before He comes, that they may be the more eager and the more fitted to receive Him.—BRENTIUS:—Great the man, great the cross.—In coming to the help of sufferers, there should not be long delay.—The miracles that in our day are said to be wrought by touching the bones of saints, are mere cheatery.—God heals also our secret infirmities, of which we are ashamed.—CRAMER:—Christ is a Searcher of hearts, and one can undertake nothing so secret that He does not see it.—OSIANDER:—God lets His children sometimes be put to shame, that He may afterwards honor them the more.—The Saviour knows how to speak a word in season to the weary.—Christ Lord of both dead and living.—Romans xiv. 9.—Learn thou to accommodate thyself to the *horas* and *moras* of our God.—J. HALL:—It is better to go to the house of mourning than to the house of feasting.—Christ and His own are by the unbelieving world continually laughed to scorn.—The scoffing of the world must not keep the Christian back from good works.

HEUBNER:—When a spiritual father calls on Jesus for a soul entrusted to Him, he may hope of Jesus not to entreat in vain.—The folly of men appeared of old also as now, partly even in excessive funeral pomp.—The trust which Jesus knew how to inspire in Himself.—LISCO:—How faith is assaulted and strengthened.—The mighty help of the Lord Jesus.—PALMER (The Pericope):—As there, the Saviour's eye sees ever in secret; as there, the Saviour's hand helps ever in secret.—The Lord's dealings with a believer here amid the tumult of the world, yonder in the eternal Sabbath-stillness.—FUCHS:—The example of the two sufferers in the Gospel teaches us, what Paul says, Rom. v. 3: 1. Tribulation worketh patience; 2. patience worketh experience; 3. experience worketh hope; 4. hope maketh not ashamed.—SOUCHON:—The Lord's leadings for our salvation.—COUARD:—We have a God that helps, a Lord God that delivers from death.

---

4. The Son of Man proclaimed by the Twelve, feared by Herod, honored by the Company which He had fed.

CHAPTER IX. 1–17.

(Parallels: Matt. x. 5–15; xiv. 1; xiv. 13–21; Mark vi. 7–16; vi. 31–46; John vi. 1–14.)

a. THE SENDING FORTH OF THE TWELVE APOSTLES (Vss. 1–6).

1 Then he called his twelve disciples [the twelve; om., *disciples*] together, and gave
2 them power and authority over all devils [the demons], and to cure diseases. And he
3 sent them to preach [proclaim] the kingdom of God, and to heal the sick.[1] And he

said unto them, Take nothing for *your* journey, neither staves, nor scrip [wallet], neither
4 bread, neither money; neither have two coats [tunics] apiece. And whatsoever house
5 ye enter into, there abide, and thence depart. And whosoever will not receive you,
when ye go out of that city, shake off the very dust from your feet for a testimony
6 against them. And they departed, and went through the towns, preaching the gospel,
and healing every where.

[¹ Vs. 2.—Tischendorf, supported by Meyer, has simply ἰᾶσθαι, without a following accusative. The variations: τοὺς ἀσθενοῦντας, τοὺς ἀσθενεῖς, τοὺς νοσοῦντας, πάντας τοὺς ἀσθενοῦντας, and *omnes infirmitates* (Brix.), are so numerous, that it is almost certain that they were introduced by different transcribers as natural complements of ἰᾶσθαι. Tregelles brackets the accusative. B. is the only uncial, however, which omits it.—C. C. S.]

EXEGETICAL AND CRITICAL.

HARMONY.—The raising of Jairus' daughter is immediately followed by two other miracles, which Matthew alone relates, ch. ix. 27–34. Hereupon the Saviour appears to have undertaken a new journey through Galilee, and to have convinced Himself repeatedly of the exceeding spiritual necessity of the people. (*Ibid.* vss. 35, 36.) He therefore exhorts His disciples to entreat the Lord of the harvest for laborers (vss. 37, 38), and gives them finally opportunity with this praying to unite working, and themselves to lay their hand to the plough.

In the narrative of the sending out of the twelve apostles, also, the briefer account of Luke must be complemented by that of Matthew and Mark. It then appears that the Saviour sent them out two and two, and in their instructions, according to the statement of all the Synoptics, adduces the expulsion of the demons as a special and main part of their activity, clearly distinguished from the healing of ordinary illnesses. The discourse given on this occasion is communicated by Matthew far more in detail and more precisely than by the two others. Luke merely, vss. 3–6, communicates somewhat of the first part of it (Matt. x. 5–15), while we find again some elements of the continuation in the tenth and twelfth chapters.

Vs. 1. **The Twelve.**—Although weighty testimonies declare for the reading τοὺς δώδεκα μαθητὰς αὐτοῦ, it must not be overlooked that Luke usually uses οἱ δώδεκα as a standing formula, and that other manuscripts use the word ἀποστόλους, which appears to be an interpolation by a later hand, as well as the former, which is borrowed from a parallel passage in Matt. x. 1. At the same time, Matthew here gives the names of the twelve apostles, which Luke had earlier communicated in another connection (ch. vi. 12–16). Luke, on the other hand, is more particular in stating the substance of their instruction, and mentions also the κηρ. τὴν βασ. τοῦ θ., while the two others speak only of miraculous acts. As to the manner in which the δύναμις καὶ ἐξουσία may have been imparted to them, comp. LANGE on *Matthew*, x. 1.

Vs. 3. **Take nothing.**—There is some difference among the Synoptics in reference to the instruction given to the Twelve as to their preparations for the journey. According to all three, they were to take no money in their purses, no change of coats, and no provision of food. According to Mark and Luke, the taking of bread with them is also not permitted, as to which Matthew is silent. But while according to Matthew and Mark, vs. 8, they might take a staff *alone*, we find according to Matthew and Mark, this also forbidden them (for the reading ῥάβδους is apparently not genuine). We believe that Mark, who here alone gives the narration in an *oratio obliqua*, expresses himself more freely than the two others. The spirit of the command is, however, according to all, the same. The Saviour speaks of that which they must procure for the journey. If they already had a staff they were permitted to take it with them (Mark), but if they possessed none, they were not to buy one (Matthew and Luke). Nothing were they to take with them, nothing were they to take to them in requital of their benefits. Their history instructs us how the apostles understood these commands; the last literally, as the curse of Peter upon Simon Magus shows, Acts viii. 20, the former in the spirit of wisdom, *e. g.* 2 Corinthians xi. 12; 2 Timothy iv. 13.

Vs. 4. **There abide.**—Comp. ch. x. 7. Wander not from house to house.—**Thence depart.**—From thence continue your journey without having capriciously chosen another abode.

Vs. 5. **And whosoever will not receive you.**—Comp. Matt. x. 14. With Lachmann and Tischendorf, it seems that we must unquestionably read δέξωνται, since δέχωνται is borrowed from parallel passages. The shaking off of the dust, a symbolical action, as a testimony against them, as Theophylact says: εἰς ἔλεγχον αὐτῶν καὶ κατάκρισιν. From Acts xiii. 51, we see how the apostles *eius quo* followed this command of the Saviour literally.

DOCTRINAL AND ETHICAL.

1. In investigating the purpose of this missionary journey of the Twelve, too little notice perhaps has been taken of the word of the Saviour, Matt. ix. 38. With no warrant whatever has this journey been often considered as a kind of *practising* for the future work of the Twelve. The Saviour at least gives not a single hint that He will have it so understood. Nor was the practice of having probationary sermons by destined preachers of the gospel at His time as yet in use. As little did this mission serve to prepare for the personal arrival of Jesus in some towns and villages of Galilee. It is at least not to be proved that the apostles came into towns where He was wholly unknown; moreover, it would have little accorded with His wisdom to have let the gospel even during His life to be brought into places, and that by inexperienced men, where as yet they did not know Himself. No. The Twelve were not to go before, but here and there to return upon His track; not in order to sow but in order first to reap, does He bid them to go forth: not to begin what He will continue, but rather to continue what He Himself has already begun. Thus does all become clear. Thus does it appear why they had at each time to inquire who was worthy to receive them; in other words, who was favorably disposed in reference to the Saviour and the cause of His kingdom. Thus does their right to shake off the dust become

manifest, which for the rejection of a first preaching was almost too stern, but for the spurning of a renewed essay, was fully justified. Thus first do we get a true light as to the prohibition of extensive preparations for journeying. For they were not going as strangers among enemies, but as friends unto a region where the Saviour Himself had already prepared a way for them. And thus does it at the same time become plain why He let them just now undertake this journey. Already had He denounced against the impenitent cities of Galilee the judgment threatened them, Matt. xi. 20–24, but now He will through His apostles make a last attempt to win the apostates to Himself. The more He beholds in the spirit the unfolding of the great drama of His life, the more does He proceed with the thundering tread of decision. Ever more threateningly do the parties begin to stand over against one another; in order that now the thoughts of hearts may become more manifest does He now send forth His apostles. They are to water the seed already sown by Him for the kingdom of heaven: to tend with care what promises fruit: and what shows itself as tares to make known to Him as such: in a word, to be workers for the harvest.

2. As respects the duration of this journey, it can be as little determined as the names of the towns and villages visited. But surely it endured longer than a day (against Wieseler, *l. c.* p. 291), as certainly some time is always required to go from town to town, to seek out the worthy, and abide there, &c. But if we consider that they, divided into six pairs, traversed only one part of Galilee, and were as yet in no way adapted to get on independently, it is not then probable that the Saviour was many days or weeks separated from the Twelve. Apparently He waited for them meanwhile at Capernaum, and when, after their return, the miracle of the Loaves took place, the second passover was no longer far distant, John vi. 4. As we hold the view that the sermon at Nazareth only took place once, and that at the time indicated by Luke, ch. iv. 16–30, it is therefore not necessary for us to intercalate immediately after this mission of the Twelve the narrative Matt. xiii. 54–58; Mark vi. 1–6.

3. Although the exercising of the apostles was not here the main matter, yet even on our view there is displayed in this mission, in a lovely light, as well the wisdom of the Saviour in the training of His witnesses, as also His love to the lost sheep of the house of Israel. The healing activity for which power is bestowed upon them, is at the same time a striking symbol of that which evangelization and missionary labor must even now everywhere accomplish wherever it directs its steps. And the spirit which the Saviour, even according to the brief redaction of Luke, has here commended to His witnesses, unconcern about earthly matters, freedom from pretension, but also holy zeal where their word is obstinately disdained, must even now not be missing in any one who will bear His name with honor among baptized or unbaptized heathen.

4. "Love to a convenient life is a great hinderance to the work of God in an evangelist, for it is with the poor who cannot afford it him that he has most to do, ch. vii. 22, and the rich are far more apt to draw him into such a life than he to draw them from it. The world must know that one does not seek it for its goods, and that he has no communion with it but for its salvation. If it will not hear of that, then we must go forth from it." O. Von Gerlach.

HOMILETICAL AND PRACTICAL.

The apostolic authority: 1. Its extent, 2. Its grounds, 3. its purpose, 4. its limits.—The missionary of the gospel at the same time the physician of souls.—The evangelizing journey of the witnesses of the Lord, their equipment, aim, fruit.—Who first seeks the kingdom of God and its righteousness may trust that all other things shall be added to him.—Freely ye have received, freely give.—The testimony for the believing and against the unbelieving world.—How the faithful servant cares for the honor of the Lord, the Lord for the necessity of His faithful servant.—The gospel of the kingdom must everywhere be preached.—The preaching of the gospel an act of the obedience of faith.—The spirit of domestic missions.

STARKE:—CRAMER:—The sacred ministry still delivers man from the power of Satan.—To the ministry pertains a regular call, both internal and external.—HEDINGER:—Whoever serves the gospel is to live therefrom, 1 Corinthians ix. 14.—CANSTEIN:—If the disciples of Christ, for the sake of convenience, were not to go from one house to another, much less should preachers, for greater accommodation, seek after better parishes.—The ministry not an *otium*, but a *gravissimum negotium*.

---

b. THE ALARM OF HEROD (VSS. 7–9).

7 Now Herod the tetrarch, heard of all that was done by him [om., by him, V. O.[1]]: and he was perplexed, because that it was said of [by] some, that John was risen from
8 the dead; And of [by] some, that Elias [Elijah] had appeared; and of [by] others,
9 that one of the old prophets was risen again. And Herod said, John have I beheaded; but who is this, of whom I hear such things? And he desired to see him.

[1] Vs. 1.—*Rec.*: ὑπ' αὐτοῦ. Om. B., C.[1], D., L., [Cod. Sin.].

EXEGETICAL AND CRITICAL.

Vs. 7. **Now Herod the tetrarch.**—Comp. Matt. xiv. 1–12; Mark vi. 16–29. Matthew and Mark have united the account of Herod's trouble of conscience with that of the beheading of John. Luke, who had already, ch. iii. 19, 20, related the imprisonment of the Baptist, intimates here, with only a word, its end; on the other hand, his Gospel is, in its turn, particularly rich in traits of importance for the psychology of Herod, which at the same time depict to us the ever-deepening degeneracy of the tyrant in a moral respect. Comp. ch. xiii. 31–33; xxiii. 6–12.

All that was done.—As well by the Lord Himself as by His messengers, who in these very days were in His name casting out devils. The terror of Herod becomes more comprehensible if we consider that the beheading of the Baptist had taken place in the same period, and that therefore his conscience had had as yet no time to go to sleep. Although John, during his life, did no miracles, John x. 41, yet it might be very easily imagined that he, if after his death he had once again returned to life, was equipped with miraculous powers. Elijah might be thought of, as he had not died; one of the old prophets finally, since the return of some of them in the days of the Messiah was expected.

Vs. 9. **John have I beheaded.**—Not so much the language of a terrified conscience (Meyer) as rather a painful uncertainty. Scarcely has he known how to relieve himself of John, than he already hears of another, to whom they now again ascribe in addition a so astonishing and miraculous energy. What must he now think of this one, or fear from him? Just because he does not know, he desires to see Him himself, as also afterwards to kill Him, ch. xiii. 31. In Luke it is the expression of uneasy uncertainty, in Matthew and Mark the fixed idea of an awakened conscience, that comes especially into view. One moment the one, another the other, feeling might be the predominant one.

DOCTRINAL AND ETHICAL.

1. The terror of Herod at the report of Jesus is an indirect argument for the reality and multiplicity of His miracles, and has so far an apologetical worth. A Herod is not a man to allow himself so quickly to be perplexed by an insignificant or ungrounded rumor.

2. In the person and activity of the Saviour there is this peculiarity, that those with whom the moral and religious perceptions are wholly blunted and choked, do not know what to make of Him. They are terrified by the very sound of His footsteps, but they themselves scarcely know why.

3. Conceptions whose reality the understanding cannot earnestly believe may yet be terrifying to the conscience. Herod undoubtedly scoffs at the Pharisees' ideas of immortality, and yet he trembles at spectres.

HOMILETICAL AND PRACTICAL.

The fame of the Saviour makes its way everywhere.—The gospel a savor of death unto death. —The might and the impotency of the conscience. The might: 1. It faithfully reminds of the evil committed, 2. judges it righteously, 3. chastises it rigorously. Its impotency; it is not in condition: 1. To undo the past, 2. to make the present endurable, 3. to make the future hopeful.—The influence of the awakened conscience on the conceptions of the understanding.—The unworthy desire to see Jesus. (For the opposite, see John xii. 20–22.)

STARKE:—Truth makes its way more easily to ordinary hearers than to great lords.—There have been many mistaken opinions concerning Christ spread abroad, but faithful teachers must be skilled to refute the same.—The evil conscience is fearful, and takes fright at a shaken leaf, Job xv. 20.—Comp. two admirable sermons of A. MONOD, upon the beheading of John the Baptist, in the second collection of his *Sermons.*

---

c. THE MIRACLE OF THE LOAVES (Vss. 10–17).

10 And the apostles, when they were returned, told him all that they had done. And
11 he took them, and went aside privately into a desert place belonging to the city called Bethsaida.[1] And the people, when they knew it, followed him: and he received them,
12 and spake unto them of the kingdom of God, and healed them that had need of healing. And when the day began to wear away, then came the twelve, and said unto him,[2] Send the multitude away, that they may go into the towns [villages] and country
13 round about, and lodge, and get victuals: for we are here in a desert place. But he said unto them, Give ye them to eat. And they said, We have no more but [than]
14 five loaves and two fishes; except we [*ourselves,* ἡμεῖς expressed] should go and buy meat [food] for all this people. For they were about five thousand men. And he
15 said to his disciples, Make them sit down by fifties in a company. And they did so,
16 and made them all sit down. Then he took the five loaves and the two fishes, and looking up to heaven, he blessed them, and brake, and gave to the disciples to set before
17 the multitude. And they did eat, and were all filled [satisfied] : and there was [were] taken up of fragments that remained to them twelve baskets.

[1] Vs. 10.—In view of the great diversity of readings in this passage, it seems to us that the reading of Tischendorf, which Meyer also has adopted, εἰς πόλιν καλουμένην Βηθσαϊδά, has, especially on internal grounds, the greatest probability in its favor. *Lectio difficilior præferenda.* "Εἰς πόλιν must have occasioned difficulty, since what follows took place not in a city, but in a wilderness (comp. vs. 12, and also Mark vi. 31)." [Tischendorf, supported by B., L., X., Ξ., Cod. Sin., has simply τοπον ερημον. Alford says: "the text not appearing to meet the requirements of the narrative following, was amended from the parallels in Matthew and Mark."—C. C. S.]

[² Vs. 12.—More exactly: "And the day began to wear away, and the twelve coming said to him," &c.—C. C. S.]

EXEGETICAL AND CRITICAL.

Vs. 10. **And the Apostles, when they were returned.**—In order to get a right conception of the whole connection of the occurrences, we must especially compare Mark vi. 30, 31. The Saviour receives almost simultaneously the account of the return of the Twelve and of the death of the Baptist. To this is added the rumor that Herod desires to see Him, which occasions Him to pass over from the province of Antipas to that of Philip. He will afford His disciples and Himself a quiet hour, which, however, becomes impossible on account of the thronging of the people. We may here make the general remark, that, above all, a comparison of the different accounts is requisite in order to come to a correct understanding of the miracle of the Loaves. We shall then find confirmed the remark of LIC. S. RAU, in an admirable essay upon John vi. found in the *Deutsche Zeitschrift für christliche Wissenschaft und christliches Leben*, 1850, p. 263: "That as well by the point of time which the representations of the Synoptics and of John assign to this history, as by the significance which they ascribe to it, they equally place this miraculous act of the Saviour in the clearest light, and, as it were, upon that highest summit of the life of Christ up to which the fateful way to the sacrificial death leads to higher and higher self-unfolding, in order from now on to lead on to the fate necessarily following this self-unfolding, and lurking in the depth." Especially for the examination of the Tübingen views respecting the Gospel of John, does the whole essay deserve to be compared.

Βηθσαϊδά.—Not the western (Winer, De Wette), but another town of this name on the northeastern shore of the lake, belonging to the province of Philip, who had given it the name Julias, and had considerably embellished it. Built near the shore at the place where the Jordan pours itself into the lake of Tiberias, it was surrounded by a desolate region which now, however, in the spring, was covered with a carpet of grass, large enough to receive a numerous throng. Thither does the Saviour proceed with the disciples, according to Matthew and Mark, in a ship, while Luke does not say that He goes *by land* (Meyer), but leaves the mode of the journey entirely undetermined. Apparently Capernaum was the place where the Saviour and the Twelve had, after the return of the latter, met one another again.

Vs. 11. **Followed Him.**—As appears from Matthew and Mark, on foot by the land-way after they had seen Him depart, taking also sick persons with them, who were healed by Jesus. Von Ammon draws from the statement that these sick people also had come on foot, the conclusion that they could not, after all, have been so very sick; as though blind or deaf people, who could travel very well, might not have been among them; and as though the others who were not capable of walking, might not have been carried.

Vs. 12. **And when the day.**—Here we must insert especially from Mark and John the preceding circumstances and deliberations which Luke, in his more summary account, passes over for the sake of brevity.

That they may go.—This demand of the disciples to send the multitude away, does not speak favorably for the view that the people had brought a tolerably large provision of their own with them, to the common distribution of which they were about to be prompted.

Vs. 13. **Give ye.**—"With emphasis, for previously they had counselled to let the people get food for themselves." Meyer.

Should go and buy.—It is self-evident that this whole language of the disciples is only the expression of the most pitiable perplexity, which had no other means at command. Whoever can assert in earnest that the disciples now actually did buy food with two hundred denarii, and then distributed it (Von Ammon), appears to expect that men are going to believe his rationalistic tidings at his word, without demanding any further proofs therefor.

Vs. 14. **By fifties.**—We find no sufficient reason to insert ὡσεί (Lachmann). "*Numerus commodus propter quinarium panum.*" Bengel.

Vs. 16. **Blessed,** εὐλόγησεν.—According to Jewish usage before the beginning of a meal. Here it becomes in the fullest sense of the word a miraculous blessing, whereby the deed of Almighty love is brought to pass. Between Matthew and Mark there exists no actual difference. It is noticeable that all four Evangelists take note of the act of prayer.

THE MIRACLE ITSELF.—The miracle of the Loaves is certainly one of those whose possibility is quite as hard to bring within the sphere of our comprehension as its form within the sphere of our conception. See statement and criticism of the different views in LANGE on Matt. xiv. 20. So much the less can we overlook the fact that the external proofs of the reality of the miracle are so unanimous and decisive that concerning them scarcely a doubt is possible. It cannot be denied that the relative diversities of the individual accounts are less essential (Strauss). In the main points all the Evangelists give the same account, and the difficulties of the mythical explanation are here in fact insuperable. Or is perchance the whole historical narration to be taken as a mere symbol of the evangelical idea that Christ is the bread of eternal life? (Von Baur). As if this idea could not have been expressed and stated as well in a fact! How, then, would the enthusiasm of the people be explicable, and the mutual discourse, John vi., which is connected with this miracle, and, moreover, the great schism which in consequence of it took place among the μαθηταί, John vi.? No, this very point is the great proof for the reality of the miracle, that it is indispensably necessary in order satisfactorily to explain the decrease then beginning in the following of Jesus. So far something had here taken place similar to that at the Lord's resurrection; and this, at least, becomes immediately obvious, that here something must have taken place by which the great revolution in so many minds is sufficiently explained. Up to this day we see the following of Jesus increasing: He stands before us, as it were, on the steps of the throne, John vi. 15; a few hours later, the enthusiasm has cooled and the throng of His followers noticeably diminished. Only a miracle like this could have roused so intense an expectation, and, when this expectation on the following day was not fulfilled, so great a bitterness as we have account of, especially in the fourth Gospel.

With this, however, we do not mean that we are blind to the difficulties which offer themselves here, even from a believing point of view. We can as little represent to ourselves that the fragments of bread had multiplied themselves in the hands of the people as in those of the disciples; and even if we make the miracle to have taken place immediately by the Sariour's own hands, we can as little conceive continually growing loaves as continually reappearing fish; and although one should speak of a quickened process of nature (Olshausen; a representation, moreover, of which there is found an indication even in Luther), yet there is little gained by this, since, indeed, it appears no process of nature, but a process of art, to multiply in a miraculous way baked bread and cooked fish. Here one feels, more than ever, how difficult it is to enter in any way into transaction with the inconceivable, since, after all, everything finally depends upon our conception of God, upon our Christology, and upon the credibility of the evangelical history. Yet, on the other hand, we must not pass over the fact that the Saviour here by no means makes something out of nothing, but out of that already existing makes something more, and does not, therefore, pass the limits which the Incarnate Word has fixed for Himself, and that it could not be for Him too miraculous to raise Himself, if need were, over the artificial processes of preparing bread and fish for human use. We may call to mind, at the same time, that the ethical receptivity for this miracle must have existed in the people in consequence of all which they had this day already seen and heard of the Lord, and by which their faith had been first awakened, or their already awakened faith had been strengthened. And inasmuch as we now believe ourselves obliged to follow the example of the Evangelists, who do not more particularly describe the form of the miracle, we at the same time rejoice that the sublimity and the purpose of this sign are beyond all doubt. But if Christian science believes itself obliged to go a step further, and to venture an attempt to seek a modal, or perhaps a mystic, medium of bringing into effect what here took place, then certainly the profoundly-conceived attempt of LANGE, *L. J.* ii., S. 309, deserves a careful examination. Comp. his remarks upon it in the Gospel of John.

DOCTRINAL AND ETHICAL.

1. The deep impression which the death of the Baptist produces upon the Saviour, is a striking proof, on the one hand, of His genuine human nature and feeling; on the other hand, of His clear insight into the connection of the martyr-death of the Baptist with His own approaching Passion. He shows at the same time His tender care for the training of His disciples, when He, after some days of unusual exercise of body and soul, considers some hours of rest and solitude as absolutely necessary. Comp. the beautiful essay by A. VINET: *La solitude recommandée au pasteur.*

2. The miracle of the Loaves is one of the most striking proofs of the truth of the word of the Lord to Philip, John xiv. 9. We admire here in the Saviour a veritably Divine *might* which speaks and it is done; in virtue of which He, in higher measure and from His own fulness of might, can repeat what in the Old Testament had already, in smaller measure, been brought to pass by prophets and at Divine command. (Comp. the manna-rain of Moses, and the multiplication of food by Elijah and Elisha.) Besides deep *wisdom*, which helps at the right time and by the simplest means, we see here, at the same time, in Jesus, the image of the God of *peace* (1 Cor. xiv. 33), inasmuch as He takes care for the orderly division of the multitude and for the preservation of the fragments remaining. More than all, however, does His *compassion* attract us, which has at heart the fate of the unfortunate, which, with tenderest attention, chooses even the softest place for couch and table, and with ungrudging wealth bestows not only what is absolutely necessary, but also more than what is necessary. This whole miracle must serve as proof how He, like the Father, can out of little make much, and bless what is of little account. Above all, however, it is an image of the great truth which He the following day so powerfully develops (John vi.), that He is the bread of eternal life.

3. The miracle of the Loaves is the faithful miracle of the way in which the Saviour satisfies the spiritual necessities of His own; but at the same time with all that is extraordinary, the concurrence of this miracle with the continuous care of Providence for the bodily support of its human children, is unmistakable. The whole narrative of the miracle is a practical commentary on the declaration, Psalm cxlv. 15, 16.

HOMILETICAL AND PRACTICAL.

The first report in the Gospel of labor accomplished.—Mournful accounts shake as little as joyful ones the holy rest of the Lord.—The Lord grants His faithful laborers rest.—Even unto our places of rest not seldom does earth's disquiet follow us.—The unwearied Saviour never indisposed to beneficence.—Jesus the Physician of body and soul.—Human-perplexity over against Divine knowledge; human sympathy over against Divine compassion; human counsel over against Divine action; human poverty over against Divine wealth.—Jesus refers the hungry multitude to His apostles.—Let all things be done with order.—Daily bread hallowed by thanksgiving and prayer.—"That nothing be lost:" a fundamental law in the kingdom of God in the use of all that which the Lord has bestowed.—The miracle of the Loaves a proof of the truth of Matt. vi. 33.—The Saviour keeps in the wilderness a feast with the poor, while He is awaited with longing at the court of Herod.—The Lord makes of little much. —The Lord never gives only so much that there is nothing left over.—They that seek the Lord shall not want any good thing.—The satisfying of earthly, the type of the satisfying of heavenly, necessities.— The conditions under which the Christian even now may expect the satisfying of his earthly necessities: 1. Believing trust; 2. befitting activity; 3. well-regulated order; 4. wise frugality, joined with, 5. thanksgiving and prayer.—"Open thy mouth wide, that I may fill it." Psalm lxxxi. 10 b.—The Lord permits us to suffer hunger only, in His own time, the more richly to relieve it.—He hath filled the hungry with good things.—The miracle of the Loaves a revelation of the glory of the Son of God and the Son of Man.—He dismisses no one empty but him who came full.

STARKE:—*Nova Bibl. Tub.*:—Who loves Jesus follows Him even through rough ways.—QUESNEL: —God lets us first recognize our human impotence before He displays His omnipotence.—Spiritual shepherds should feed their sheep.—By gold one can obtain all perishable goods, but the rich God can throw to us all that we need, even when we have little or no money.—It is to the Almighty Saviour all one to help by little or by much. Upon that, faith can venture all. 1 Samuel xiv. 6.—*Nova Bibl. Tub.*: —No one should imagine himself too good or too high to serve the needy.—BRENTIUS:—In distress of hunger, the best refuge is to Christ.— God's blessing one must not lavish away at once, but lay up for future need. Proverbs xi. 27.— HEUBNER:—To be agents in the distribution of Divine gifts, like the disciples here, is a high honor and grace.—The requirement of that which man ought to do, according to God's will, appears often very surprising, surpassing all capacity, for God has beforehand already taken care for all, and Himself concurs. His is properly the main act.—The feeling of compassion in Christ much mightier than the need of rest.—VAN OOSTERZEE :—Jesus the bread of life. Intimation how He even now: 1. Meets with the same necessity; 2. exhibits the same majesty; 3. prepares the same refreshment; 4. deserves the same homage; 5. provokes the same schism as at the miracle of the Loaves.

---

5. The Glory of the Son of Man confessed on Earth and ratified from Heaven. The Scene on the Summit and at the Foot of Tabor.

CHAPTER IX. 18–50.

a. THE JOURNEY TO THE TRANSFIGURATION (Vss. 18–27).

(Vss. 18–21, parallel to Gospel for Sts. Peter and Paul's Day; Matt. xvi. 13–20.)

18 And it came to pass, as he was alone praying, his disciples were with him; and he
19 asked them, saying, Whom [Who] say the people that I am? They answering said, John the Baptist; but some *say*, Elias [Elijah]; and others *say*, that one of the old pro-
20 phets is risen again. He said unto them, But whom [who] say ye that I am? Peter
21 answering said, The Christ of God. And he straitly [strictly] charged them, and com-
22 manded *them* to tell no man that thing [this]; Saying, The Son of man must suffer many things, and be rejected of the elders and chief priests and scribes, and be slain, and
23 be raised [rise again, V. O.¹] the third day. And he said to *them* all, If any *man* will
24 come after me, let him deny himself, and take up his cross daily, and follow me. For whosoever will save his life shall lose it: but whosoever will lose his life for my sake,
25 the same shall save it. For what is a man advantaged, if he gain the whole world,
26 and lose himself, or be cast away? For whosoever shall be [have been] ashamed of me and of my words, of him shall the Son of man be ashamed, when he shall come in
27 his own glory, and *in his* Father's, and [that] of the holy angels. But I tell you of a truth, there be some standing here, which shall not taste of death, till they see [have seen] the kingdom of God.

¹ Vs. 22.—According to the reading of Lachmann and Tischendorf ἀναστῆναι instead of ἐγερθῆναι. ('Ἀναστ., A., C., D., 2 other uncials; ἐγερθ., Cod. Sin., B., R., Σ., al. longe. pl. 'Ἀναστ. approved by Tischendorf, Lachmann, Meyer, Alford.—C. C. S.]

EXEGETICAL AND CRITICAL.

Vs. 18. **And it came to pass.**—By comparison with Matthew and Mark, it appears at once that Luke, after the mention of the miracle of the Loaves, passes over all the words and deeds of the Lord which are related Matt. xiv. 22; xvi. 12; Mark vi. 45; viii. 26. Harmonistics must take note of this, and Isagogics give the grounds of this. The best explanation is given perhaps by the conjecture that the written sources (*Diëgesen*) of which Luke made use were in relation to this period of the public life of the Saviour less complete, less rich in comparison with what follows. At least no cause can be discovered for an intentional omission.

As He was alone praying.—According to Matthew and Mark the Saviour was now in the region of Cæsarea Philippi. (*See*, respecting this place, LANGE on *Matthew* xvi. 13.) Here also, as we have several times remarked, Luke brings into view the praying of the Saviour. Justly does Bengel say: "*Jesus Patrem rogarat, ut discipulis se revelaret.* *Nam argumentum precum Jesu colligi potest ex sermonibus actionibusque insecutis.*" Comp. vi. 12, 13. Apparently we must understand the matter thus— that the disciples had found the Saviour praying in solitude, as in ch. xi. 1, while from vs. 23 it appears to be the case that besides the Twelve, other listeners had soon approached, so that He, in a few moments, found a wider circle gathered around Him to which He could address His words.

And He asked them.—From the preceding prayer we must conclude that the Saviour Himself considered the conversation now following as in the highest degree momentous, and this will not surprise us if we only transport ourselves into His circumstances during this period of time. The more unequivocally He had lately experienced the irreconcilable enmity of His adversaries, the more clearly did the end of His course, now drawing nearer, rise before His soul. The time had now come when He must speak more openly than hitherto to His disciples of His approaching suffering and death. The prayer which the Saviour offered afterwards for Simon, ch. xxii. 32, can hardly have been excluded here. But before He now grants to the Twelve a deeper view into the nature of His *work*, He will convince Himself of their manner of thought respecting His *Person* and His character.

Who say the people that I am?—He wishes to know for what the [common] people, this interpreter of public opinion, took Him, Him who commonly designated Himself by the somewhat mysterious name of the Son of Man. Other views see in LANGE, *ad loc.* The inquiry after the views of men, in which one only heard the voice of flesh and blood, might justly surprise us if we forgot that it only constituted the transition to a far more momentous one.

Vs. 19. **John the Baptist.**—The opinions are different, yet fully explicable. That John the Baptist had risen, was perhaps an echo of that which was talked of at Herod's court, perhaps also an inference drawn by high esteem, to which it appeared impossible that such a man of God should have been actually and forever taken away from the world.—**Elijah.**—Comp. Malachi iv. 5.—**One of the old prophets.**—Men believed, from Micah v. 5 and other passages, that they were warranted to conclude that at the time of the Messiah different prophets would again appear. (*See* LIGHTFOOT on *John* i. 21.) In brief, for something ordinary and insignificant no one took the Nazarene: a messenger of God they could not fail to recognize in Him; perhaps He was the Forerunner. For the Messiah public opinion did *not* now take Him to be. It was divided, and moreover had not in the main become more favorable to the Saviour. If there had formerly existed among the people a disposition to believe in His Messianic dignity, now there is no more talk of this. After the great schism, John vi. 66 *seq.*, the sum of popular favor is set. Carefully considered, therefore, the popular voice is now no longer a homage, but only a denying of the Lord.

Vs. 20. **But who say ye that I am?**—Plainly the emphasis falls upon ὑμεῖς, in opposition to the ὄχλοι. First the Lord will hear the echo of the people's views; He will hear now His powerful witnesses' own voice, the expression of their living, personal, and independent faith. It appears how highly the Lord esteemed the confession of faith of His disciples, and how He is the farthest possible from reckoning their Christology among the Adiaphora.

The Christ of God.—The complete form of the answer, *see* Matt. xvi. 16. It is wholly impossible to prove that it was only the theocratical and not the supernatural dignity of the Saviour which here hovered before the mind of Peter. If before this even rough shipmen had recognized something superhuman in Jesus, Matt. xiv. 33, the Saviour would certainly not have pronounced His disciple blessed for his confession, had this side of His being yet remained wholly hidden to him, although, of course, it is evident that this faith of the heart in Peter had not for that as yet become in his mind a fully rounded dogma. As to the rest, we must very decidedly declare ourselves against the view that takes this confession of Peter for the same which is related John vi. 69 (Wieseler, Ran). This last is much less decided and powerful, at least according to the true reading in Tischendorf. Besides, the two are in their historical connection heaven-wide apart, and the two confessions cannot be identified without most arbitrarily accusing John of inaccuracy.

Vs. 21. **To tell no man.**—The more detailed answer of the Saviour, and His praise bestowed upon Peter, *see* Matt. xvi. 17-19. Comp. LANGE, *ad loc.* That the Saviour was almost, as it were, "terrified" at the confession of Peter (Fritzsche, Schneckenburger, Strauss), is as little implied in the letter as in the spirit of the narrative. As to the ground on which especially He commanded silence, this is at once evident. For the first time it has now become manifest that His self-consciousness agrees in substance with the confession of faith of the Twelve. He Himself has impressed upon the language of faith the seal of His attestation, and therefore, in fact, from this moment there already existed a little congregation in which the faith on Jesus as the Christ was the centre of union. If this community, with its manner of thinking, manifested itself externally, it would here have found premature adherents, and there have roused renewed opposition. Therefore the Saviour will have them keep silence respecting His person so long as His highpriestly work was not yet accomplished, but at the same time now declares His apostles capable of receiving more particular instructions respecting the nature of this work.

Vs. 22. **The Son of Man must suffer many things.**—In antithesis to the figurative and covert allusions to His approaching death, which they had already heard, comp. Matt. ix. 15; John ii. 19; iv. 37, 38, the Saviour now begins to speak in a literal manner. He makes known, 1. who the accomplishers of this suffering shall be, 2. in what form it is to be prepared for Him, 3. the necessity of this suffering, 4. the issue of this suffering, namely, His resurrection. The view (De Wette, a. o.) that the last is here added only *ex eventu*, is with right denied and refuted by LANGE, *Gospel of Matthew*, p. 302. The offence taken by Peter at this word and the rebuke suffered by him are related only by Matthew and Mark.

Vs. 23. **If any man will come after Me.**—Here, as in John vi. 67, the Lord gives His apostles the choice whether they will follow Him even now, when the way goes for a time into the depth. If they do it, they shall know beforehand what it will cost them. Whoever follows Him, **let him take up his cross daily,** a symbol of self-denial which the Saviour would certainly not have adopted by preference if He had not Himself, even already in the distance, beheld this instrument of His own pain and ignominy. There exists no ground for declaring the remarkable καθ' ἡμέραν, which Luke alone has, an interpolation *a seriore manu*. From Jesus Himself does it proceed, and places the extent and the difficulty of this requirement of self-denial in the clearest light. Worthy of notice is it that it is no other than Peter who afterwards so deeply apprehended and so powerfully reëchoed this requirement. (*See* 1 Peter iv. 1-3; and comp. Rom. vi.; Col. iii. 1-4, &c.)

Vs. 24. **Whosoever will save his life.**—In order to make evident the indispensable necessity of self-denial, the Saviour uses a double motive. The first is taken from the present, vss. 24-26, the other from the future, vs. 27. Only by self-denial, He says, can a man become partaker even here of the higher life of the Spirit, so that he has therefore the choice between temporary gain and eternal loss. Here also is a proof of the higher unity between the Synoptical and the Johannean Christ. Comp. John xii. 25. The *life*, which the man will commonly preserve at any price, is the natural, selfish life, whose centre is the ψυχή, considered out of its relation to the πνεῦμα. Whoever will preserve this life, and therefore walk in accordance with his natural inclinations, may reckon upon it that he loses his true, his proper life: but those who, for the sake of Christ and His cause, set at stake the possession of life and the enjoyment of life in the common sense of the word, will through this very temporary perishing become partakers in perpetually richer measure of the true and higher life of the Spirit. A word of infinitely deep significance for the first apostles of the Lord, who for His sake left all, yet not less significant for the history of the development of the Christian life of each one. (*See* the profound remarks of LANGE, *Leben Jesu*, ii. p. 899.) In the most striking manner has Luke, vs. 25, expressed the antithesis, the gaining of the whole world, and the ἀπολέσας δὲ ἑαυτόν, the loss of the personality, to whose preservation the man had brought such sacrifices. "As if thou in a general conflagration hadst saved and preserved around thee thy great and full palace, but hadst thyself to be consumed, what wouldst thou then have gained in comparison with him who out of the conflagration of his goods had rescued his life? Therefore, also, on the contrary: what does it harm a man to set at stake the whole world, which after all shall one day pass away, and burn up, if only the soul is delivered? A human soul's true, everlasting salvation is more worth than the whole world. Thus must one reckon gain and loss over against one another, and whoever has not so reckoned will at the end experience, to his everlasting loss, how enormously he misreckons! Then will the bankrupt break out with his τί δώσει ἄνθρωπος, whereto the Psalm has already answered: It ceaseth forever!" Stier.

Vs. 26. **Whosoever shall have been ashamed.**—A word of the Lord which reminds us of the sublimest declarations of the fourth Gospel. The Ἰουδαῖοι there appearing (ch. xii. 42, 43), show us by their example what it is to be ashamed of the Saviour, as Paul, Romans i. 16, is an example of the opposite. It is noticeable that the Saviour does not say: Whoever has been ashamed of the *Son of Man*, but: Whoever has been ashamed of *Me* and of *My* words—a manifest proof that here the discourse is of a being ashamed which is possible even with outward intellectual knowledge of Him and of His Messianic dignity.—**Of him shall also the Son of Man be ashamed.**—A milder form of the threatening, Matt. vii. 21 ; xxv. 41, and therefore so much the more impressive, since the Saviour here represents Himself as surrounded with a threefold glory: 1. His own, 2. the Father's, 3. that of the holy angels, who now become witnesses of the well-deserved shame that is prepared for the unfaithful disciple. It is scarcely to be doubted that the Saviour directs His eye towards His last παρουσία, at the συντέλεια τοῦ αἰῶνος. But before the thought of its possibly great distance could weaken the impression of the warning, He concludes with a nearer revelation of His kingly glory.

Vs. 27. **But I tell you of a truth.**—Even this solemn exordium, which the parallel passages in Matthew and Mark also give, causes us to expect that it will appear that the Lord Himself attributes especial importance to the assurance which He is now about to give. More plainly can He hardly intimate that His disciples shall outlive Him, that His cause shall triumph over all hostility, and that He, by the name of the Son of Man, means to designate Himself as the Messiah, for He speaks now of a kingdom in which the Son of Man gives law. Nay, scarcely can we avoid the belief that this very saying, which the first three Evangelists have with so great unanimity preserved in the same connection, was one of the strongest supports for the hope of the apostolic age, that there would be a speedy and visible return of Christ. The longing for its fulfilment contributed also to preserve the letter of the promises, and the love of the heart sharpened understanding and memory. However, it cannot be difficult to decide which coming of the Saviour He wished to be immediately understood by this saying. He has here in mind, as in Matt. xxvi. 64, the revelation of His Messianic dignity at the desolation of the Jewish state, which should take place within a human generation. (For a statement and criticism of other views, *see* LANGE, on *Matthew*, xvi. 28.) Thus, also, the beginning of this whole conversation is beautifully congruous with the end. For as the Saviour in the beginning had alluded to the humiliation which was about to be prepared for Him by the Jewish magnates, vs. 22, He now ends, vs. 27, by making mention of the triumph which He should win over the Jewish magnates, when the ruins of the city and of the temple should proclaim His exaltation. This His coming in His kingdom, which at least John (ch. xxi. 22) beheld, and apparently also others of his fellow-disciples, is at the same time a type and symbol of His last παρουσία, that mentioned vs. 26. The shorter form in Luke: ἰδεῖν τὴν βασ. τ. θεοῦ must be more particularly explained from the fuller one in Matthew and Mark, in the parallel passages. Comp. moreover Matt. x. 23, as a proof how not alone the Johannean but also the Synoptical Christ speaks of a continuous coming of the Messiah in different phases. In view of the intimate connection which, according to the Synoptics, exists between this saying of the Lord and the Transfiguration which is soon after related, it may be justly supposed that the disciples, even in this event, beheld the actual, even though only preliminary, fulfilment of this prophecy of the Lord.

DOCTRINAL AND ETHICAL.

1. Although the discourse here given opens no new period in the life of our Saviour, it may yet be said that in the region of Cæsarea Philippi, there began a new period of the intercourse of our Lord with the Twelve. After He had persuaded Himself of their independent and living faith, He now opens to them the sanctuary of His Passion, in order to guard them against apostasy when hereafter the critical period should dawn. Comp. John xiii. 19. With deep wisdom He nevertheless connects the first unequivocal declaration of His Passion with the setting forth of His future Glory, into which He was to enter in this very way. Comp. Luke xxiv. 26.

2. Mark indicates very happily the distinction between the Saviour's earlier and present intimations of His sufferings by the word παρρησία, viii. 32. Instead of covert there come now express, instead of general more particular, intimations. Without doubt this higher truth was closely connected with the development of Jesus' own consciousness in reference to His approaching fate, which consciousness became continually clearer the longer He looked upon the prophetic image of the Messiah and observed the course of circumstances. But quite as certain is it that there is no ground to deny the possibility of such a foreknowledge *a priori*

(De Wette, Von Ammon, Strauss,) and that the criticism which will explain such prophecies merely *ex eventu* is no way purely historical, but is an entirely arbitrary dogmatism. Further on we hear from Jesus Himself, Luke xxiv. 44–46, from the angels, *ibid.* (vss. 7, 8), nay, even from His foes, Matt. xxvii. 62, 63, that He prophesied not only His dying, but also His resurrection. As respects the stiff-necked doubting and afterwards the unbelieving sadness of His disciples, which there has often been a disposition to use against the genuineness of the prophecy of the Resurrection, this was certainly not the first and only time that the Saviour was better understood by crafty enemies than by friends full of prejudice. Very often the disciples took a figurative expression as literal (*e. g.* Matt. xvi. 11, 12); why can they not, on the other hand, have viewed a literal expression as figurative? From their point of view they could not possibly conceive that the Messiah should die, and could not therefore accommodate themselves to the prophecy of the Resurrection, and still less could they imprint it deeply in their souls. And when our Lord, according to Matthew and Mark, said that He would return definitely τῇ τρίτῃ ἡμέρᾳ into life, this is only the repetition of that which He had earlier intimated in another form, Matt. xii. 40; John ii. 19. Comp. HASERT, *Ueber die Vorhersagungen Jesu von seinem Tode und von seiner Auferstehung.* Berlin, 1839.

3. As to the question by what means the Saviour, in the way of His theanthropic development, came to the clear insight of the certainty and necessity of His death, we are warranted by His own declaration to give the answer that He viewed the image of His Passion in the mirror of the prophetic Scriptures. Assertions that He would then have understood the Old Testament incorrectly, as this, rightly explained, says nothing whatever of a suffering or dying Messiah (De Wette, Strauss), make only then some show when one places the hermeneutics of modern science higher than those of the Lord Jesus and of His apostles enlightened by the Holy Spirit. Comp. STEUDEL, *Theol. des A. B.* p. 402, and HOFFMANN, *l. c.* ii. p. 121. Drawn from these sources, the foresight of the Saviour was much less the fruit of a grammatical exegesis of particular *Vaticinia* than of a typico-symbolic apprehension of the whole Ancient Covenant. In the fate of the Servant of the Lord in Isaiah, He saw His own, and in all which former men of God had experienced and suffered, He beheld the image of His own future [or as some one has excellently said, He looked into the Old Testament and found it full of Himself.—C. C. S.]. Comp. Mark ix. 13; Luke xiii. 33. Once familiarized with thoughts of death, the Saviour could, even by looking at the political condition of His people, come in a simple and natural way to the conception that heathens, and those heathens Romans, would be the accomplishers of the sentence of death, executioners, therefore, by whom the punishment of the cross had been introduced among conquered nations. And who would consider it as impossible that the God-man should come in still other ways than those of natural reflection to such a thought? In the most intimate communion with the Father, the Father's will had without doubt become so clear to Him that He could with full certainty speak of a Divine δεῖ.

4. The first prediction of His Passion is of so high an importance because it gives us to view this Passion not only from the human but especially from the Divine side. In that which shall come upon Him the Saviour recognizes not only the abuse of the freedom of men, but also the fulfilment of the eternal counsel of God, who not only foresaw and permitted, but expressly willed that Christ should suffer all this. Through the voluntary obedience with which the Son submits Himself to the plainly recognized counsels of the Father, He, at the same time, converts the fate awaiting Him into the highest *deed* of His love.

5. The necessity of the way of suffering in order to arrive at glory is so great that this way has been ordained not only for the Master, but also for all His disciples without distinction. Here also does the word of J. Arnd hold true: "Christ has many servants, but few followers." Only he will gradually attain to bear καθ' ἡμέραν what the Lord had to take upon Himself, who can as thoroughly deny and abjure the old man in himself as Peter once denied the Lord.

HOMILETICAL AND PRACTICAL.

No specially important turning-point of life but must be hallowed with solitary prayer.—To the Saviour it is not indifferent what men say of Him. Neither can it be indifferent to His disciples.—Public opinion we must be as far from slavishly following as from haughtily despising.—The affinities and the difference between the Saviour on the one hand, John, Elijah, and the prophets on the other hand.—The spirit of the faithful prophets reappearing in Jesus far more gloriously.—The disciple of the Saviour called, 1. To hear the *vox populi* respecting Him, but, 2. to raise himself above it.—But who say ye that I am? 1. A question of conscience; 2. a question of controversy; 3. a question of life; 4. a question of the times.—Jesus will have His disciples, 1. Independently recognize Him as the Christ; 2. voluntarily confess Him as the Christ.—No sincere faith without confession, no genuine confession without faith.—The confession of Peter the first of the million voices of the Christian confession.—What then had to be kept silent is now loudly proclaimed.—Silence and speech have each their time.—The first prediction of the Passion: 1. Its remarkable contents; 2. its high significance.—Expectation of suffering and expectation of glory in the consciousness of our Lord most intimately joined together.—The way of suffering: 1. How far it must be trodden by Him alone; 2. how far it must be trodden by all His disciples after Him.—The disciple of the Saviour a cross-bearer day by day, willingly coming after Christ.—The Christian calculation of profit and loss.—To win the highest the highest must be staked.—The all-surpassing worth of a soul.—The spiritual bankruptcy of him that gains the whole world but loses himself.—Even the gain of the whole world is only vain show and harm so long as a man has not won Christ.—The Saviour's saying concerning the gain and loss of life compared with Paul's experience, Philipp. iii. 6–9.—How a confessor of the Gospel may even to-day be ashamed of the Master: 1. In his heart; 2. in his words; 3. in his deeds.—The Christian, 1. Needs not to be ashamed of his Lord; 2. may not, and, 3; will not, if he is a Christian in truth.—The seeking of honor with men, the way to shame before God.—He who willingly humbled Himself, shall come again in glory.—No disciple of the Lord shall die till he has in greater or less measure seen the coming of the kingdom of God.—The coming of the Lord, 1. A bodily, afterwards, 2. a spiritual, and finally, 3. a spiritual and bodily (*geist-leibliches*) coming.—The history of the world, the judgment of the world, but not the final judgment.—The way of suffering, 1. Clearly foreseen by Jesus; 2. plainly pointed out to His disciples to be walked in; 3. for Him and His disciples issuing in glory.—The requirement of self-denial for Jesus' sake: 1. A difficult, 2. a necessary, 3. a wholesome, 4. a reasonable requirement.—The Saviour in relation to His faithful disciples: 1. How much He requires; 2. how infinitely more He promises.

STARKE:—CANSTEIN:—The truth is only one, but errors and lies are many.—BRENTIUS:—That Christ's kingdom is a kingdom of the cross must not be concealed, that no one may take offence thereat.—True self-denial distinguishes the genuine Christian from every one else.—It requires much to become a Christian, still more to remain one.—So blind is our fleshly heart that it seeks life in that which brings it death.—In religion nothing comes according to our plans, but all according to God's.—The *jus talionis* holds good with Christ in both directions.—*Nova Bibl. Tub.*:—It is an unhappy dying when one tastes death before he has seen the kingdom of God.—Salvation is certainly very often nearer to us than we think. Romans xiii. 11.

HEUBNER:—The Christian's independence of popular opinions.—GERLACH:—The bearing of the Cross is not something that is reserved for certain extraordinary occasions; whoever feels his own and the world's sin deeply, bears it daily.—J. SAURIN:—Discourse on the soul, drawn, 1. From the excellence of its nature; 2. from the infiniteness of its duration; 3. from the price of its redemption.—DIETRICH:—Sermon on the day of St. Peter and St. Paul upon the partially parallel Gospel, Matt. xvi. 13–20.—THOLUCK:—The daily crossbearing of the Christian: 1. In what it consists; 2. why to the very end of life it should be a daily one.

---

b. THE TRANSFIGURATION (Vss. 28–36).

28   And it came to pass about an eight days after these sayings, he took Peter and John and James [James and John, V. O.¹], and went up into a [the] mountain to pray.
29   And as he prayed, the fashion of his countenance was altered, and his raiment *was*
30   white *and* glistering [ἐξαστράπτων, lit., flashing forth light]. And, behold, there talked
31   with him two men, which were Moses and Elias [Elijah]: Who appeared in glory, and spake of his decease [or, departure] which he should [was about to] accomplish at
32   Jerusalem. But Peter and they that were with him were heavy [weighed down] with sleep: and when they were awake,² they saw his glory, and the two men that stood
33   with him. And it came to pass, as they departed from him, Peter said unto Jesus, Master, it is good for us to be here: and let us make three tabernacles; one for thee,
34   and one for Moses, and one for Elias [Elijah]: not knowing what he said. While he thus spake, there came a cloud, and overshadowed them: and they feared as they
35   [*i. e.*, Jesus, Moses, and Elijah] entered into the cloud. And there came a voice out of the
36   cloud, saying, This is my beloved [elect, V. O.³] Son: hear him. And when the voice was past, Jesus was found alone. And they kept *it* close, and told no man in those days any of those things which they had seen.

[¹ Vs. 28.—The *Rec.* is approved by Tischendorf, Lachmann, Tregelles, Alford, with Cod. Sin., A., B., C.¹, 12 other uncials. Van Oosterzee's order only by C.³, D., 2 other uncials.—C. C. S.]

[² Vs. 32.—"Some difficulty is here occasioned by διαγρηγορήσαντες. The verb διαγρηγορεῖν signifies elsewhere: *to watch through*; so Herodian, III. iv. 8: πάσης . . . τῆς νυκτὸς διαγρηγορήσαντες. Accordingly Meyer wishes it to be so taken here: *Since they, however, remained awake, did not actually fall asleep*. But according to the connection with the preceding it is altogether improbable that such is the meaning: 'since they, notwithstanding their disposition to sleep, yet remained awake,' but rather that Luke meant this word, in any case an unusual one, in the sense: After they as it were had passed through their slumber to awaking again, had again waked; as the Vulgate had already rendered it by *evigilantes* (Luther: *da sie aber aufwachten*)." Bleek. Van Oosterzee takes Meyer's interpretation against the preferable one, as it seems to me, of Bleek.—C. C. S.]

³ Vs. 35.—According to the reading of B., L., [Cod. Sin.,] ἐκλελεγμένος, approved by Grieshach, Schulz, Tischendorf, and Meyer. The *Recepta* ἀγαπητός, although strongly attested, appears to be taken from the parallels in Matthew and Mark.

EXEGETICAL AND CRITICAL.

Vs. 28. **Eight days.**—According to Matthew and Mark, *six* days after the just-mentioned conversation. If we assume that Luke has reckoned in the day of the discourse and a second day for the Transfiguration, which had perhaps already taken place in the morning, the difference is then almost reconciled, and it does not even need the assumption of some, that the Saviour spent one or two whole days on the mountain, the Transfiguration taking place after their expiration.

Into the mountain, τὸ ὄρος.—More definite than Matthew and Mark, who only mention an ὄρος ὑψηλόν. The tradition which has pointed to Tabor has been often contradicted, yet the objections raised against this are, according to our opinion, not well tenable. That this tradition existed even in the time of Jerome, and that the empress Helena for this reason erected a church on Tabor, proves of itself not much, it is true. Yet it may still be called remarkable, that tradition designates a place so far distant from Cæsarea Philippi, where our Saviour had just before been found (Matt. xvi. 13). Without sufficient ground in the apostolic tradition, it appears probable that they would not have assumed the theatre of the one event to be so far removed from

CHAP. IX. 28–36.

that of the other. For the other mountains which have been thought of instead of Tabor, namely, Hermon or Paneas, there is almost less yet to be said. Yet it must not be forgotten that about a week intervened between the Transfiguration and the first prediction of the Passion, in which time the Saviour may very well have traversed the distance from Cæsarea to Tabor, which, it is true, is somewhat considerable. Comp. Matt. xvii. 22. If the Saviour, moreover, shortly after He left the mountain, returned to Capernaum, Matt. xvii. 24–27, this town was scarcely a day's journey distant from Tabor. The single important difficulty is that raised by De Wette, following Robinson, that at this time there was a fortification on the summit of Tabor. But although Antiochus the Great fortified the mountain 219 B.C., it is not by any means proved that in the time of Jesus this fortification was yet standing, and though, according to Josephus, this mountain, in the Jewish war, was fortified against the Romans, this, at all events, took place forty years later. Traces of these fortifications are found apparently in the ruins which have since been discovered especially on the south-western declivity; but in no case is it proved that the whole mountain was built over at the time of Jesus. Moreover, it must not be overlooked how exceedingly well adapted the far-famed beauty of this place was for its becoming a theatre of the earthly glorification of the Lord.—According to a Dutch theologian (Meyboom), we are to understand the southern summit of the Anti-Lebanon, a snowy peak, which now bears the name Dschebel Escheik.

Peter, James and John.—Already previously witnesses of the raising of Jairus' daughter, and later than this of the agony in Gethsemane, the most intimate of His friends, those who were initiated into the most mysterious and sublime scenes. The influence of the autopsy of Peter is, in Mark ix. 3, 6, 8, 10, unmistakable.

Vs. 29. **The fashion of His countenance was altered.**—We have here the first feature in the narrative which requires special attention; the alteration of the outward appearance of the Saviour. We cannot possibly assume (Olshausen) that the body of the Saviour, even during His earthly life, underwent a gradual process of glorification, which here entered into a new stadium. This view leads us to a Docetic conception, and moreover explains, it is true, the shining of His countenance, but not the gleaming of His garments, on which account even Olshausen sees himself necessitated to conceive the Saviour not only as glittering, but also as shined upon. Justly does Lange call attention to the fulness of the Spirit which, from within, overstreamed His whole being. Even with this, however, the brilliancy of His garments is not yet sufficiently explained, so that there is occasion to connect with the inward outstreaming of glory an external illumination. But why might not this latter have arisen from the brilliancy with which undoubtedly we must conceive the appearance of the two heavenly messengers as attended? For we nowhere read that the Saviour shone so miraculously before they had appeared to Him. Even in the case of Moses, Ex. xxxiv. 29, the brilliancy of his countenance is occasioned by an external heavenly light. [With all deference to the author, this anxious analysis of the Transfiguration appears to us artificial and puerile.—C. C. S.]

Vs. 30. **Two men.**—How the apostles learned that it was Moses and Elijah no one of the narrators tells us. They may have become aware of it either by intuition, or by some outward token have understood it from the nature of the discourse, or have heard it afterwards from Jesus. In no case does the uncertainty as to the manner how they learned it give us authority for the assertion that they could not have known it at all, and still less for the rationalizing conjecture that it was two human strangers, secret disciples, confederates with Jesus, and the like.

Which were Moses and Elijah.—That these words were meant to be only the subjective judgment of the relator, but in no way the objective expression of the fact, has, it is true, been often said, but never yet been proved.

Vs. 31. **Spake of His decease.**—Luke alone has this intimation as to the subject and the purpose of the interview, by which the true light is first thrown upon this whole manifestation. That Luke's account has arisen "from the later tradition, which very naturally came to this reflexion," we cannot possibly believe with Meyer *ad loc.* The witnesses who saw the rest may also have heard this and remembered it afterwards.—It is noticeable that Peter, 2 Peter i. 15, calls his own death also, to which he is looking forward, an ἔξοδος.—**When they were awake,** διαγρηγορήσαντες.— Lange: "Sleeplessly watching." De Wette: "When they had waked up."—At all events it is an antithesis to the preceding ὕπνῳ βεβαρημένοι, by which we are forbidden to draw from this last expression the inference that they had been hindered by sleep from being competent witnesses. However drunken with sleep they may have been, they had not, however, at all gone to sleep, but remained so far awake that they could become aware of all that here took place with the bodily eye and with the ecstatic sense of the inward man alike. Even had we no other proof, yet this very feature in the narrative would show us that we have here before us no dream of the three sleeping disciples, or phantasm of their own heated imagination. That Luke, more than the other two Synoptics, would warrant us to assume something here merely subjective (Neander), is at least wholly unproved.

Vs. 33. **And it came to pass.**—The first feeling which animated the disciples in the view of the heavenly spectacle was naturally fear, Mark ix. 6. But scarcely have they recovered from that when an indescribable feeling of felicity fills them, to which Peter, almost with child-like transport, lends words. The heavenly temper of the spiritual world communicates itself to the dwellers of earth, and as it were with their hands will they hold fast to the heavenly presence before it vanishes from their eyes.—**Three tabernacles.**—From the fact that Peter does not propose to build six, but three booths, it may be assuredly concluded that by ἡμᾶς he means only himself and his fellow-disciples,—not all who were there present (De Wette). SEPP, ii. p. 408, takes the liberty of finding in the tabernacles a symbol "of the threefold ministry in the Church."

Not knowing what he said.—Not because he was yet entirely overcome with sleep, but because he was wholly taken captive by the extraordinariness of the whole scene. Else he would not have expressed himself with so little suitableness, a subjective reflection which manifestly proceeds from Peter himself.

Vs. 34. **A cloud.**—The Shekinah, the symbol of the glory of God. "*Hæc, ut ex sequentibus patet, ad ima se demisit.*" Bengel. The cloud of light which formerly filled the sanctuary of the Lord now receives the three as into a tabernacle of glory, and ravishes the end of the manifestation from the eyes of the disciples, as its beginning also had remained hidden from them.

Vs. 35. **A voice.**—The same which was heard before on the Jordan and afterwards in the Temple. As the Saviour, by the Divine voice on the Jordan, had already been consecrated as the King of the kingdom of heaven, and afterwards, John xii. 28, as the High-priest of the New Testament; so here, on the part of the Father, His Prophetic dignity is in its elevation above that of the two greatest messengers of the Lord in the Old Testament proclaimed to His disciples.—**Hear Him.**—At the same time an echo of an utterance of Moses, Deut. xviii. 15. Comp. Ps. ii. 7; Isaiah xlii. 1.

Vs. 36. **And they kept it close.**—According to Matt. xvii. 9, at the express command of our Lord. The whole conversation respecting Elijah, which Matthew and Mark now give, Luke passes over, perhaps because he considered it for his Gentile Christian readers partly as little intelligible and partly as less important.

DOCTRINAL AND ETHICAL.

1. For the statement and criticism of the different interpretations, *see* LANGE on Matt. xvii. 1.

2. As well those who interpret the Transfiguration on the mountain as a purely objective manifestation from the spiritual world without any subjective mediation, as also those who derive all from the quickened receptivity of the disciples, supported by some outward circumstances, such as the morning light, the gleaming of snow, and the like, misapprehend both the letter and the spirit of the narrative. The point of view from which what here took place must be considered, is presented to us by the Saviour Himself when He speaks of a ὅραμα, a word which in the New Testament is often used of an objectively real phenomenon (Acts vii. 31; xii. 9). It is, as Lange very justly names it, "a manifestation of spirits in the midst of the present state." But he who ascribes the whole miracle to the subjectivity of the apostles will scarcely be able to explain how the so simple, and as yet so earthly-minded, disciples, should all at once have been transported out of themselves into such an ecstasy that they could believe that they saw heaven opened above the very head of the Messiah. No, the language of the three Synoptics warrants decidedly the opinion that the disciples, fully awake, perceived with their eye and ear an objective appearance. For even if Peter did not know what he said, he yet knew very well what he saw; but had they been misled by their heated imagination, and had he or his companions afterwards shown it, the Saviour would certainly not have neglected to instruct them more perfectly thereupon. But on the other hand, this also must be maintained with as much decision—that they by that which they outwardly saw were transported into the condition of an exalted [intensified, *potenzirten*] life of the soul, and thereby became receptive for the hearing of the heavenly voice. Whoever, like Peter, finds in dwelling together with citizens of the spiritual world nothing terrifying, but on the contrary, wishes that this might endure as long as possible, shows by that very fact that he is completely exalted above himself. Here, apparently, there took place a similar union of sensuous and spiritual intuition, of a miraculous fact with an exalted inward life, to that which we can also perceive in the miracle at the Baptism.

3. When philosophy, *a priori*, doubts the possibility of such a revelation of the spiritual world perceivable by mortals, we shall simply answer her that she is incompetent from her own resources to decide anything in reference to an order of things which is known to us as little by conclusions of reason as by intuition. If, however, historical criticism inquires whether there is sufficient ground to assure to the narrative of the Transfiguration its place in the series of the facts in the public life of our Lord, we would recall that the grounds which elsewhere speak for the credibleness of the Synoptics whenever they relate the most astonishing miracles, hold good here also in undiminished force. Some have, it is true, asserted that such enigmatical and isolated events did not belong to the original apostolic Kerygma; but this is mere rationalistic caprice. The command of the Lord to keep silence *until* His resurrection, implied not only the permission, but in a certain measure the command, to speak of what took place here *after* His resurrection; and it would have been psychologically inconceivable if His disciples had neglected to do so. It is sufficiently evident how high a place this narrative occupies in the Synoptics; higher even than the miracle at the Baptism. The difference of the several accounts in respect of some points is in fact insignificant. It is true John says not a word of what here took place: his silence, however, cannot by any means throw any reasonable suspicion on the testimony of his predecessors in narration. On the other hand it is entirely in the spirit of his Gospel, that he gives us to see the glory of the Only-begotten Son of the Father less in such single details than in the grand unity of His manifestation. Only a simple spiritualism, which, moreover, forgets that the fourth Gospel also speaks of voices from heaven, John xii. 28, can from this silence deduce anything against the objectivity of the history of the miracle. And, what above all may not be overlooked, the testimony of the Synoptics is in a striking manner supported by the second epistle of Peter, ch. i. 16–18, whose spuriousness, it is true, has often been asserted, but, in our eyes at least, has been as yet by no means proved. Comp. DIETLEIN, *Der 2te Brief Petri*, p. 1–71; GUERICKE, *Neutestamentl. Isagogik*, p. 472; STIER, *Brief Judä*, p. 11; THIERSCH, *Apost. Zeitalter*, p. 209; *et al. plur.*

4. The inquiry as to the purpose of the heavenly manifestation is not difficult to answer. The representatives of the Ancient Covenant come in order to consecrate the Messiah for death. The Lord must have longed to speak of that which now lay so deeply at His heart, and yet could find no one on earth who could fully comprehend Him, to whom He could with confidence have unbosomed Himself. His subsequent agony in Gethsemane would certainly have been still more overpowering and deep had the hour of Tabor not preceded. If we read elsewhere that even the angels desire to look into the work of redemption (1 Peter i. 12), we here become aware how it awakens not less the inmost interest of the blessed departed. For our Lord, this manifestation and interview was a new proof that His plan of suffering was in truth comprehended in the counsel of the Father, and to the disciples the remembrance of this night might afterwards become a counterpoise against the scandal and the shame of the cross. Finally, as respects the heavenly voice, the exaltation of Jesus even over the greatest men of God in the Ancient Covenant was

thereby established, the testimony at the Jordan was repeated, and therefore a new proof of His sinlessness and of His being well pleasing to God was given, whereby the scoffings which He should afterwards hear were more than lavishly even beforehand compensated to Him. As respects the further purpose of the manifestation in its whole, and in its different parts, see LANGE ad loc.

5. The Christological importance of this whole event for all following centuries is self-evident. A new light from heaven rises upon Jesus' *Person*. On the one hand it rises upon His true Humanity, which needed the communication and strength from above. On the other hand, His Divine dignity, as well in relation to the Father, as also in comparison with the prophets, is here made known to earth and heaven. Considered from a typico-symbolic point of view, it is significant that the appearance of the prophets is represented as a vanishing one, Jesus, on the other hand, as alone remaining with His disciples. Their light goes down, His sun shines continuously.

6. Not less light here falls upon the *Work* of the Saviour. The inner unity of the Old and the New Covenant becomes by this manifestation evident, and it is shown that in Christ the highest expectations of the law and the prophets are fulfilled. His death, far from being accidental or insignificant, appears here as the carrying out of the eternal counsel of God, and is of so high significance that messengers of heaven come to speak concerning it on earth. The severity of the sacrifice to be brought by Him is manifest from the very fact that He is in an altogether extraordinary manner equipped for this conflict. And the great purpose of His suffering, union of heaven and earth, Coloss. i. 20, how vividly is it here presented before our souls when we on Tabor, although only for a few moments, see heaven descending upon earth, and dwellers of the dust taken up into the communion of the heavenly ones.

7. The manifestation on Tabor deserves, moreover, to be called a striking revelation of the future state in this. We see here: the spirits of just men made perfect live unto God, even though centuries have already flown over their dust. In a glorified body they are active for the concerns of the kingdom of God, in which they take the holiest interest. Although separated by wide distances of time and space beneath, Moses and Elijah have met and recognized one another in higher regions. The centre of their fellowship is the suffering and glorified Jesus, and so blessed is their state, that even their transient appearance causes the light of the most glorious joy to beam into the heart of the child of earth. Earthly sorrow is compensated and forgotten; the Canaan which Moses might not tread in his life, he sees unclosed to him centuries after his death. Thus do they appear before us as types of that which the pious departed are even now, in their condition of separation from the body, and as prophets of that which the redeemed of the Lord shall be in yet higher measure at His coming.

8. The inseparable connection of suffering and glory, as well for the Lord as for His disciples, is here in the most striking manner placed before our eyes. Tabor is the consecration for Calvary, but at the same time gives us a foretaste of the Mount of Olives. At the same time the carnal longing for the joy of Ascension without the smart of Good Friday, is here for all time condemned. The hours of Tabor in the Christian life are still as ever like those of Peter and his companions. "Even with the purest feeling of the joy of faith there mingles here on earth much that is sensual and self-seeking; such exaltations of the spirit wrought by God Himself, are not bestowed on us in order for us to revel here in the intoxication of unspeakable emotions; there follows upon them the cloud, which withdraws from us all sensible sweetness of the enjoyment given us, and in our poverty and sinfulness causes us to feel the terrors of God, that we may ever learn to serve Him the more in the Spirit." Von Gerlach.

9. There are admirable paintings of the Transfiguration, especially by Raphael. See STAUDENMAYER, *Der Geist des Christenthums, dargestellt in den heiligen Zeiten, Handlungen und Kunst*, ii. p. 430-437, and the chief histories of art. Comp. the Essay on the History of the Transfiguration by Dr. C. B. MOLL in PIPER's *Evang. Kalender*, 1859, p. 60 seq.

HOMILETICAL AND PRACTICAL.

The mountain-heights in the life of the Saviour.—Prayer the night-rest of Jesus.—The inward glory of the nature of our Lord revealed without.—The eye of the fathers of the Ancient Covenant directed full of interest upon the Mediator of the New.—The conflict which is carried on on Earth, is known to the dwellers of Heaven.—Jesus consecrated to His suffering and dying by a visit from the dwellers of heaven. This consecration was: 1. Necessary, on account of the true Humanity of the Saviour; 2. fitting, on account of the high momentousness of the event; 3. of great value for the disciples, as well then as afterwards; 4. continually important for the Christian world of following centuries.—Servants of God on earth separated from one another, in heaven united with one another. — The high importance which heaven ascribes to the work of redemption on earth.—The gleaming heaven in contrast with the sleeping earth.—The blessed view of the unveiled world of spirits.—" Master, it is good for us to be here." 1. That *we are* here; 2. that we are *here*; 3. that we are here *with Thee and heaven.*—Tabor delights endure only for instants.—Even in communion with the dwellers of heaven, Peter cannot deny his individuality.—When I was a child, I spake as a child.—Alternation of rapture and fear in the consecrated hour of the Christian life.—The voice of God from the cloud contains even yet important significance: 1. For the Saviour, 2. for the disciples, 3. for the world.—God wills that all men should hear the Son of His love. 1. This the Father requires; 2. this the Son deserves; 3. this the Holy Spirit teaches us.— The prophets vanish, Jesus remains alone.—Jesus alone: 1. So appears He even now to His own in the holiest hours of life; 2. so will it also be hereafter. Even heaven vanishes to the eye which may behold the Lord of heaven face to face.—Christian silence.—Even to his fellow-disciples the disciple of the Saviour cannot relate all which the Saviour has often let him taste.—[How some Christian people are perpetually tormented with a notion that they must testify to whatever manifestation of God is granted to themselves, at the risk of bringing shallowness and weakness upon their own experience!—C. C. S.]—How well it is with the friend of the Saviour on Tabor: 1. How well it was there for His first disciples; they saw there a manifestation: *a.* most sublime in itself, *b.* most momentous for the Master, c. most pregnant of instruction for themselves. 2. How well it is continually with the Christian there; he finds, a. support for his faith, b. a school of instruction for his life, c. a living image of his highest hope.—The light which Tabor throws: 1. Upon the majesty of the person of Jesus; 2. upon the fitness of His suffering; 3. upon the sublimity of His kingdom.—Hear ye Him: 1. With deep homage; 2. with unconditional obedience; 3. with joyful trust.—The near connection of Old and New Covenant.—Tabor the boundary: 1, Between the letter and the Spirit; 2. between the ministration of condemnation, and the ministration of righteousness; 3. between that which vanishes away, and that which abides. 2 Cor. iii. 6–11.—Jesus' Transfiguration, considered in connection with His Passion: On Tabor, 1. The prediction of His Passion is repeated; 2. the necessity of His Passion is confirmed; 3. the conflict of His Passion is softened; 4. the fruit of His Passion is prophesied.—The ascent [*Aufgang*] to Tabor, and the decease [*Ausgang*] at Jerusalem. We receive here light upon: 1. The exalted character of the Person who accomplishes this decease; 2. the worth of the work which is accomplished in this decease; 3. the glory of heaven which through this decease is disclosed.—Jesus the centre of union of the Church militant and the Church triumphant.—From the depth into the height, from the height again towards the depth.

STARKE:—The prayer of believing souls brings a foretaste of eternal life with it.—Oh, Saviour, if Thou wert so glorious on the Mount, what must Thou now be in heaven!—Christ, Moses, and all the prophets speak with one voice concerning our redemption. Be not then unbelieving, but believing.—*Nova Bibl. Tub.*:—When Jesus shall waken us to His glory, we shall be as those that dream.—QUESNEL:—Whoever will enjoy rest and glory before labor and suffering, has never yet become acquainted with true religion.—The saying, "It is good to be here," may be spared till we are in heaven.— *Nova Bibl. Tub.:*— Our future blessedness is yet encompassed with a cloud; "It doth not yet appear what we shall be." 1 John iii. 2.—My Redeemer, it is nothing to me who abandons me, if only Thou remain. Ps. lxxiii. 25.

WALLIN:— Desire no heaven upon earth.— ARNDT:—Jesus' Transfiguration the opening scene of His passion. 1. The connection in which it stands with the Passion; 2. the significance which it has especially for the Passion.— FUCHS:—The Transfiguration of Christ: 1. Where did it happen? 2. how did it happen? 3. whereto did it happen?—COUARD:—The importance of this narrative: 1. For our faith, 2. for our life, 3. for our hope.—In KRUMMACHER'S Elijah the Tishbite, the concluding discourse upon: Jesus Alone.— SCHLEIERMACHER:— 4th vol. of sermons, p. 338.—PALMER:—"Lord, it is good to be here." An admirable text for occasional sermons, remarks at communions, weddings, at the grave, &c., useful also at dedications.

c. THE RETURN (Vss. 37–50).

(Parallels: Matt. xvii. 14–23; Mark ix. 14–21; Matt. xviii. 1–5.)

37 And it came to pass, that on the next day, when they were come down from the
38 hill [mountain], much people met him. And, behold, a man of the company cried out, saying, Master [Teacher], I beseech thee, look upon my son; for he is mine only child.
39 And, lo, a spirit taketh him, and he suddenly crieth out; and it teareth him that he
40 foameth again, and bruising him, hardly departeth from him. And I besought thy
41 disciples to cast him out; and they could not. And Jesus answering said, O faithless [unbelieving] and perverse generation, how long shall I be with you, and suffer you?
42 Bring thy son hither. And as he was yet a coming, the devil [demon] threw him down, and tare [convulsed] *him*. And [But] Jesus rebuked the unclean spirit, and
43 healed the child, and delivered him again to his father. And they were all amazed
44 at the mighty power [μεγαλειότητι, majesty'] of God. But while they wondered every one at all things which Jesus [om., Jesus, V. O.[1]] did, he said unto his disciples, Let these sayings sink down into your ears: for the Son of man shall be [or, is about to
45 be] delivered into the hands of men. But they understood not this saying, and it was hid from them, that they perceived [comprehended] it not: and they feared to ask
46 him of that [concerning this] saying. Then there arose [There arose also] a reasoning among them, [as to] which of them should be greatest [was the greatest; lit., greater].
47 And Jesus, perceiving the thought [reasoning, διαλογισμόν, as in vs. 46] of their heart,
48 took a child, and set him by him, And said unto them, Whosoever shall receive this child in my name receiveth me; and whosoever shall receive me, receiveth him that sent me: for he that is least [lit., less] among you all, the same shall be [is, V. O.[2]]
49 great. And John answered and said, Master, we saw one casting out devils [demons]
50 in thy name; and we forbade him, because he followeth not with us. And Jesus said unto him, Forbid *him* not: for he that is not against us is for us.

[1] Vs. 43.—Van Oosterzee's omission of ὁ Ἰησοῦς is according to Tischendorf, Tregelles, Alford with Cod. Sin., B., D., L., X., Ξ.—C. C. S.]
[2] Vs. 48.—*Rec.*: ἔσται. For ἐστι we have the authority of B., C., L., X., Cursives, [Vulgate, Origen, Cyprian, &c., and the probability that ἔσται is a correction according to Matt. xviii. 4. [This reference to Matt. xviii. 4 is unintelligible, since the undisputed text there is ἐστιν.—C. C. S.]

EXEGETICAL AND CRITICAL.

HARMONY.—Luke continues his narrative with an account of that which took place on the morning after the Transfiguration of the Saviour, and by this moreover gives a proof that we must regard this last event as having taken place in the night (otherwise LICHTENSTEIN, *L. J.*, see p. 309). The conversation in descending from the mountain he passes over, not from an anti-Judaistic tendency (Baur), but as indifferent for Theophilus. With Matthew and Mark he relates the healing of the demoniac lad, and the prediction of the Passion following thereupon. After this the account of the return to Capernaum and of the stater in the fish's mouth must be inserted, which we find only in Matt. xvii. 24–27. The disputation of the disciples as to their rank, communicated by Luke (vs. 46-48), proceeds parallel with Matt. xviii. 1–5, and what he adds in relation to John and the exorcist, vss. 49, 50 (comp. Mark ix. 38–41), appears actually to stand in the correct historical connection, and must immediately follow Matt. xviii. 5.

Vs. 37. **Much people met Him.**—Somewhat more in detail and with more vividness does Mark portray this meeting (ix. 14, 15), in whose whole account the influence of the autopsy of Peter cannot be mistaken. But we find in comparing the accounts of the three Evangelists no artificial climax therein, arising from a certain desire of glorifying the Saviour (Strauss). In a very unforced manner, on the other hand, they may be united by supposing that a part of the throng had hurried to the Saviour, while another part waited for Him. Besides, the ἐξεθαμβήθησαν of Mark affords an unequivocal proof of the deep impression which His sudden appearance made. If we, however, consider that the people, as it appears, had not expected Him, and in their conscience were convinced of an unrighteous temper towards Him and His disciples at this instant, then His unexpected appearance must have caused them a so much stronger shock of surprise the more His composure and majesty in the descent from the mountain contrasted with the restless tumult of the people.

Vs. 38. **Look upon my son**, ἐπιβλέψαι.—Not Imp. 1st Aor. Mid., but Inf. Act. depending on δέομαι. It is therefore not necessary with Lachmann to give the preference to the reading ἐπίβλεψον. The prayer that the Saviour would regard and help the unhappy demoniac is made more urgent by the mention that he is the only child, a trait which Luke alone preserves, but which is not therefore the less historical.

Vs. 39. **And, lo, a spirit.**—According to Matthew the sick child was at the same time a lunatic. The epileptic attacks, interrupted only by short intervals, by which the youthful sufferer was tortured, were aggravated periodically, as it appears, with the waxing of the moon. That lunacy and demoniacal suffering do not at all exclude one another, has been with the best right remarked by LANGE *ad loc.*—**He crieth out.**—Not the boy (Meyer, De Wette) but the spirit, which so soon as he has possessed himself of the boy, suddenly (ἐξαίφνης), by working upon the bodily organs of the possessed, causes the most hideous tones to be heard, and inflicts upon him moreover the further mischief described in the sequel of the verse. There is nothing which intimates or requires a sudden change of subjects.

Thy disciples.—Doubtless the unhappy father had come with the purpose that Jesus should help him, and found himself not a little disappointed when he learned that the Saviour with His three intimate disciples was absent. But when he was told that the demons had often been subjected to the disciples also (Matt. x. 8), he had appealed to them for compassion, and apparently expected that they should be able at least to do that which, as was said, the disciples of the Pharisees accomplished (Matt. xii. 27). The sight of the fearful condition of the boy had, however, filled them with mistrust as to their own powers; perhaps they had also become lately weary in fasting and prayer (Matt. xvii. 4); at all events the attempt had failed, the evil spirit had not yielded at their word, and the consequence of this had been shame before the suppliant, displeasure with themselves, and shame before the Master. Mistrust had been sown, discord awakened, perhaps already scoffing speeches thrown out; it was high time that the Saviour should intervene when it appeared in so striking a manner that His disciples even yet were very little suited to work independently even for so short a time.

Vs. 41. **O unbelieving and perverse generation.**—To whom the Saviour so speaks Matthew and Mark do not tell us, and the true reading, αὐτοῖς, in Mark, admits of many conjectures. *See* the principal views stated in LANGE on Matt. xvii. 17. That we have here by no means to exclude the apostles appears even from Matt. xvii. 20, and if we in some measure place ourselves in the frame of mind in which to-day the Saviour found Himself, and think once again on the great contrast which, for His feeling, existed between the scene on the summit and that at the foot of the mountain, we then understand how He could in this moment name all that surrounded Him, although in different measure, a γενεὰ ἄπιστος: a single word, which, however, betrays a world of melancholy. All the conflict, the self-denial, the tension of His powers which it cost His love to tarry continuously in an environment which in everything was the opposite of His inner life and effort, resounds overwhelmingly therein. How much harder this strife had become to Him, after that which He had just heard, seen, and enjoyed in the same night, we only venture in silence to conjecture. But we ask boldly whether this lamentation also may not be considered as a psychological proof of the fact that the Transfiguration on the mount was really an objective fact.

Bring thy son hither.—As to the more particular circumstances, the graphic account of Mark is especially worthy of comparison with this. The command is intended to contribute towards awakening the believing expectation of the father and making him thus receptive for the hearing of his prayer. Just at the approach to the Saviour the last paroxysm supervenes in all its might. "*Quod atrocius solito in hominem sævit diabolus, ubi ad Christum adducitur, mirum non est, quum quo proprior affulget Christi gratia et efficacius agit, eo impotentius furit Satan.*" Calvin.

Vs. 43. **At the majesty.**—Here also, as often in Luke, the glory redounding to God by the healing is the crown of the Saviour's miracle. Comp. ch. v. 26; vii. 16.

Vs. 44. **Let these sayings sink down into your ears.**—We see that the Saviour is to be misled by no false appearances; on the other hand, He will draw His disciples' attention to the close connection between the "Hosannas!" and the "Crucify Him! Crucify Him!" They are to give heed to those words, that is, to those eulogies of the people. "In your ears," *primus gradus capiendi.* Bengel.— **For the Son of Man,** γάρ, not in the sense of "namely," as if the words referred to were those that now followed, but as Meyer takes it: "The disciples are to bear in memory these admiring speeches on account of the contrast in which His own fate would now soon appear with the same. They are, therefore, to build no hopes upon them, but only to recognize in them the *mobile vulgus.*"

Vs. 45. **But they understood not.**—A description of the ignorance and uncertainty of the disciples, which gives us to recognize in Luke the admirable psychologist. The word of the Saviour is not understood by the disciples: this chief fact stands at the beginning. The ground of it: ἦν παρακεκαλ.: there lies a κάλυμμα upon the eye of their spirit, in consequence of which they cannot comprehend the meaning of the Lord, and because this *perceptio* is lacking, neither can there be any *cognitio.* The only one who could have cleared up the obscurity for them would have been the Master Himself, but Him they do not venture to interrogate personally, and remain therefore in the dark. The natural consequence of these obscure anticipations, which do not come to clearness in their minds, can only be sadness, which Matthew (xvii. 23) gives as their prevailing mood after the prediction of the Passion has been renewed.

Vs. 46. **A reasoning . . . which of them was the greatest.**—That just in this period of time such a strife could arise, shows most plainly how little the Saviour's repeated prediction of His suffering had yet taken root in the mind of His disciples. In their thoughts they had already distributed Crowns, while the Master had the Cross in His eye. Occasion for such a strife they had been able to find a sufficiency of in the days last preceding, even if the germ of rivalry had not been already existent in their hearts. The declaration to Simon that he should be the rock of the church ; the singling out of the three intimate disciples in the night of the Transfiguration, in whose demeanor it was easy to see that they had something great to keep silence concerning ; the miraculous payment which the Saviour had but just before discharged for Himself and Simon (Matt. xvii. 24–27); finally, the awakened enthusiasm of the people subsequently to the healing of the lunatic boy, all these might easily coöperate to quicken their rivalry and earthly-mindedness. According to Luke the Saviour saw the thoughts of their hearts. According to the more exact and vivid account of Mark (ix. 33, 34), He Himself first asks after the cause of their dispute, which they scarcely venture to name to Him.

Vs. 47. **Took a child.**—Just as in the Gospel of John (ch. xiii. 1–11), so does the Saviour in the Synoptics also give force to His instruction by a symbolic act. The tradition of the Greek church that the here-mentioned child was no other than the afterwards so renowned Ignatius (Christophoros ; see Euseb., *H. E.* iii. 30.; *Niceph.* ii. 3) rests probably on his own anticipation in his *Epist. ad Smyrn.* ch. iii. : ἐγὼ γὰρ καὶ μετὰ τὴν ἀνάστασιν ἐν σαρκὶ αὐτὸν οἶδα. Even assuming that the Epistle is genuine and that οἶδα is to be understood of a meeting in the body, yet that which this father here states of the time after Jesus' resurrection does not of itself give any ground for the assumption that he had even earlier come into personal intercourse with the Saviour.

Vs. 48. **Whosoever shall receive this child.** —No reminiscence from Matt. x. 40, the reception of which in this passage takes from the Saviour's whole discourse in Luke all continuity (De Wette), but one of the utterances which the Saviour might fittingly repeat more than once. By the fact that Jesus shows how high He places the child, He commends to them the childlike mind ; and in what this consists, appears from Matt. xviii. 4. The point of comparison therefore is formed, not by the receptivity, the striving after perfection, the absence of pretension in the child (De Wette), but most decidedly by its humility, which was so entirely lacking in them. By this humility, the child's understanding was yet free from vain imagination, the child's heart from rivalry, the child's will from stubbornness. That the Saviour, however, does not by this teach any perfect moral purity of children, or deny their share of the general corruption brought by sin, is very justly remarked by Olshausen, *ad loc.*

In My name, ἐπὶ τῷ ὀνόματί μου, that is, because he confesses My name. It is here self-evident that the expression : "Whosoever receives one such child, receives Me," is applicable not to the child in itself, but to the child as a type of childlike minds. Such an one is not only the true subject, but even the legitimate representative of the humble Christ, even as He is the image of the Father, who is greatest when He humbles Himself the lowest. Erasmus : *Quisquis igitur demiserit semet ipsum, hic est ille maximus in regno coelorum.* Subjective lowliness is here designated as the way to objective greatness.

Vs. 49. **And John answered and said.**— Comp. Mark ix. 38–40. It gives us a favorable view of the spirit and temper of the apostolical circle in this moment, that the word of the Lord commending humility, instead of wounding their self-love, awakens their conscience. John at least calls to mind a previous case, in which he feels that he dealt against the principle here uttered by the Lord, inasmuch as he had not received one of the little ones who had confessed His name. Although he already conjectures that the Master cannot approve of this behavior, he modestly discloses it to Him.

We saw one.—Even as in Acts xix. 13, here also had the name "Jesus" served as a weapon in the hand of one of the exorcists. An admirable proof of the authority which even a stranger attributed to the name of the Saviour. The man had actually more than once succeeded in its use, but the disciples out of ill-concealed rivalry and ambition had forbidden it him, inasmuch as the command : "Cast out devils," had been by the Master exclusively given to them. Perhaps this prohibition had been given to the exorcist only lately, when the nine disciples had failed in the healing of the lunatic boy, and were therefore still less able to bear that another should succeed in this respect better than they. Undoubtedly the Saviour would have reprehended this arbitrary conduct of His disciples more sharply if they had not thus voluntarily and humbly acknowledged to Him their perverse behavior.

Vs. 50. **He that is not against us.**—It is not to be denied that many manuscripts here read ὑμῶν for ἡμῶν, see LACHMANN, *ad loc.* According to Stier this passage belongs to those where the correction of the Lutheran translation appears urgently important ; since the "*us*" here in the mouth of the Saviour destroys almost the whole sense of this language. Olshausen, De Wette, and others also read ὑμῶν. Two reasons however exist, which move us to give the preference to the *Recepta.* In the first place, the reading ἡμῶν is the most difficult, and it is easier

CHAP. IX. 37–50.

to explain how ἡμῶν could be changed into ὑμῶν, than the reverse. Besides, the preceding γάρ appears to favor the common reading, since they had just been speaking of casting out devils in the name of the Saviour. But, however this may be, the difference of the sense, even with the reading changed, is far less than, superficially considered, it might appear; for, even if the Lord said, "He that is not against *you* is," etc., yet He still means the cause of the disciples only so far as this might be at the same time called His own cause, and therefore indirectly He includes Himself also. The fuller form of the answer is found in Mark; *see* the remarks there. Suffice it, the Saviour considers the doing of miracles in His name as an unconscious homage to His person; this homage as a proof of well-wishing, and this well-wishing as a pledge that He, in the first instance at least (ταχύ), had no assault to fear on this side, as, for example, the charge of a covenant with Beelzebub. It appears here, at the same time, how painfully this blasphemy, to which He had lately been exposed, affected Him.

DOCTRINAL AND ETHICAL.

1. The going down from the mount of Transfiguration, where He had been consecrated for His Passion, may, in the wider sense of the word, be called for the Saviour already a treading of the way of the Passion. The might of hell grins with hidden rage upon the future Conqueror of the realm of darkness, over whom heaven had just unclosed. The bitterness of the Pharisees had during this absence not diminished but increased, and the discomfiture which His disciples suffered is only the presage of greater ignominy which awaits them when the hour of darkness shall have come in with power. In the midst of all discords of sin and unbelief which become loud at the foot of the mountain, the word of the Saviour is so much the more affecting: "How long," etc. It is the expression of homesickness, and of the sorrow with which the Son longs after His Father's house, which, on the summit of the mountain, had disclosed itself to His view. Comp. Luke xii. 50. How many secret complaints to the Father does this one utterance of audible complaint presuppose.

2. The childlike mind which the Saviour demands from His disciples is so far from standing in contrast with the doctrine of a general corruption through sin, that on the other hand there is required for the attaining of this mind an entire transformation of the inner man. In truth, Matt. xviii. 3 says nothing else than John iii. 3. And here also the agreement of the Synoptical with the Johannean Christ comes strikingly into view.

3. The answer of the Saviour to John in reply to his inquiry respecting the exorcist, is an admirable proof of the holy mildness of our Lord. It breathes a similar spirit to the expression of Moses, respecting the prophesying of Eldad and Medad, Num. xi. 26–29, and that of Paul respecting those who preach Christ through envy and strife, Philipp. i. 18, and gives at the same time a standard, according to which in every case the philanthropic and Christian activity even of those must be judged respecting whose personal life of faith we may be uncertain. It is true the Saviour had declared, in the Sermon on the Mount, that it is possible to cast out devils in His name and yet be damned (Matt. vii. 22, 23), but even if this should hereafter come to light on that day before His judgment-seat, still it was something which His disciples could not as yet decide. They were continually to hope the best, and the more so as he who with hostile intentions, and without any faith at heart should attempt exorcism in His name would certainly not succeed in it. The favorable result of such an endeavor was a proof that, for the moment, they had to do with no enemy of the cause of the Saviour. The rule given here by Jesus is not in the least in conflict with His saying given Matt. xii. 30. The rule: "He that is not for Me is against Me," is applicable in judging of our *own* temper; the other: "He that is not against Me," etc., must guide us in our judgment respecting *others*. The first saying gives us to understand that entire neutrality in the Saviour's cause is impossible, the other warns us against bigoted exclusiveness. Read the two admirable discourses of A. VINET upon these two apparently contradictory sayings under the title: *La tolérance et l'intolérance de l'Évangile*, found in his *Discours sur quelques sujets relig.*, p. 268–314, and the essay of ULLMANN in the *Deutschen Zeitschrift*, by H. F. A. SCHNEIDER, 1851, p. 21 seq.

HOMILETICAL AND PRACTICAL.

The passage from the summit to the foot of the mountain.—In order to be glorified with Christ, we must first suffer with Him.—Jesus the best refuge for the suffering parental heart.—The best disciples cannot replace the Master Himself.—Conflict without triumph against the kingdom of darkness, 1. Possible; 2. explicable; 3. ruinous.—The name of the Saviour blasphemed on account of His people's weakness of faith.—Every failure of the disciple of the Lord is the Master's shame.—The happiness of childhood and youth destroyed by the might of the devil.—The strife between faith and unbelief in the suffering father's heart, comp. Mark ix. 24. 1. Jesus knows; 2. relieves; 3. ends this strife.—Over against the Saviour, the whole world stands as a perverse and unbelieving generation.—"Bring thy son hither," the best counsel to suffering parents.—A last, vehement conflict often immediately precedes triumph.—Jesus the Conqueror of the might of hell.—The glory rendered to the Father the best thanks for the Son.—No outward praise can deceive the ear of the Saviour.—When the world testifies honor, the Christian has, above all, to consider how quickly its opinion changes.—Misunderstanding of the plainest words of the Saviour: 1. How it reveals itself; 2. from what it arises; 3. whereby it is best avoided.—The dispute as to rank among the disciples of the Saviour: 1. An old; 2. a dangerous; 3. a curable evil.—Without genuine childlikeness, no citizenship in the kingdom of God. 1. In what this childlikeness consists: in humility, by which *a.* the child's understanding is yet free from vain imagination; *b.* the child's heart is yet free from ignoble jealousy; *c.* the child's will is yet free from inflexible stubbornness; *d.* the child's life is yet free from the dominion of unrighteousness. 2. Why one, without this disposition, can be no genuine disciple of the Saviour. Without this disposition, it is impossible, *a.* to recognize the King of the kingdom of God; *b.* to fulfil the fundamental law of the kingdom of God; *c.* to enjoy the blessedness of the kingdom of God.—The world makes its servants great, the Saviour makes His disciples little.—The high value which the Saviour ascribes to the receiving of one of His own.—Tolerance and intolerance in the true disciple of the Saviour.—Narrow-minded exclusiveness, 1. Not strange even in distinguished disciples; 2. in direct conflict with the word and the example of the Master.—The allies whom the cause of the Saviour finds even outside of His immediate circle of disciples.—Christian labor on independent account: 1. How often even now it is met with; 2. how it is to be rightly judged. —How the church, collectively, may rightly judge the free activity of Christian individuals.

STARKE:—*Langii Op.*:—Oh, how many parents experience the extremest grief of heart on account of their children; but how few there appear to be of them, who permit themselves thereby to be drawn unto Christ.—BRENTIUS:—The devil is a fierce enemy of man, if he gets any leave of God.—CRAMER: —Christ is far mightier than all the saints; therefore in distress flee not to these, but to Christ Himself.—When man's help disappears, God's help appears. — BRENTIUS :— The wise and long-suffering Saviour knows still how to bring in again and to make good that which His servants have neglected and delayed; O excellent consolation!—Christ and Belial agree not together, 2 Cor. vi. 15.—OSIANDER:— When it is well with us, let us think that it might also be ill with us, that we fall not into carnal security.— HEDINGER:—The flesh does not like to hear of suffering, and will not understand it.—If there is even yet so much ignorance in spiritual matters in the regenerate, how must it be with the unregenerate?—Jesus is thinking of suffering, the disciples of worldly dignity; how wide apart is the mind of the Lord Jesus and of man!—*Nova Bibl. Tub.*:—How needful to watch over one's heart, since, even in enlightened souls, such haughty thoughts arise.'—In children there is often more good to be found than any look for in them.—True humility of heart an infallible sign of grace.—QUESNEL:—God is in Christ, and Christ in His members.—True elevation is in humility.—HEDINGER:—Let Christ only be preached in any way, Phil. i. 18.—Blind zeal for religion is the greatest error in religion, Rom. x. 2.—True love approves the good, let it be done where and by whom it will, 1 Thess. v. 21.—CRAMER:—When servants and children of God agree in the main matter, it is no harm though they be somewhat different in words or ceremonies.

LISCO:—Defective faith.—The might of sin over man: 1. How it reveals itself; 2. how it is overcome by Jesus.—HEUBNER:—John (vs. 49), an example of well-meant but unwise zeal and sectarianism. —The spirit of Christ is not bound.—There is a displeasure at good when found in others, to which even the good are tempted.—The boundary between true liberality and indifference.—PALMER:—1. What do our children bring us? 2. What have we prepared for them?—MAREZOLL:—The noble simplicity of the Lord: 1. Where and how it displays itself; 2. what profit it brings.—BECK:—Zeal for the honor of the Saviour may be, 1. Well-meant, and yet, 2. un-Christian.—ARNDT:— The true dignity of the Christian.

THIRD SECTION.

THE JOURNEY TOWARDS DEATH.

CHAPS. IX. 51—XIX. 27.

A. *The Divine Harmony in the Son of Man and the Four Temperaments of the Children of Men.*
CH. IX. 51–62.

(Parallel to Vss. 57-60. Matt. viii. 19-22.)

51 And it came to pass, when the time was come [when the days were fulfilling] that
52 he should be received up, he steadfastly set his face to go to Jerusalem, And sent messengers before his face: and they went, and entered into a village of the Samaritans,
53 to make ready for him. And they did not receive him, because his face was as though
54 he would go to Jerusalem. And [But] when his disciples James and John saw *this*, they said, Lord, wilt thou that we command fire to come down from heaven, and con-
55 sume them, even as Elias [Elijah] did? But he turned, and rebuked them, and said, Ye know not what manner of spirit ye are of [Know ye not of what spirit ye are chil-
56 *dren*? V. O.¹]. For the Son of man is not come to destroy men's lives, but to save
57 *them* [om. this sentence]. And they went to another village. And it came to pass, that, as they went in the way, a certain *man* said unto him, Lord, I will follow thee
58 whithersoever thou goest. And Jesus said unto him, [The] Foxes have holes, and [the] birds of the air *have* nests [habitations, κατασκηνώσεις]; but the Son of man hath not
59 where to lay *his* head. And he said unto another, Follow me. But he said, Lord,
60 suffer me first to go and bury my father. Jesus said unto him, Let the dead bury their
61 dead: but go thou and preach the kingdom of God. And another also said, Lord, I will follow thee; but let me first go bid them farewell, which are at home at my house.

62 And Jesus said unto him [om., unto him, V. O.²], No man, having put his hand to the plough, and looking back, is fit for the kingdom of God.

[¹ Vs. 55.—Tischendorf omits all between ἐπετίμησεν αὐτοῖς and καὶ ἐπορ. according to A., B., C., Ξ., Cod. Sin. As to this, Alford says, "It is hardly conceivable that the shorter text, as edited by Tischendorf, should have been the original, and all the rest insertion." "The words have such a weight of authority against them, that they would be worthy of rejection, if it were explicable how they came into the text. How easily, on the other hand, out of regard to Elijah, could an *intentional* omission take place! Moreover, the brief, simple, and pregnant word of rebuke is so unlike a copyist's interpolation, and as worthy of Jesus Himself, as it is, on the other hand, hard to conceive that Luke, on an occasion so unique, limited himself to the bare ἐπετίμησεν αὐτοῖς." Meyer. "It is in itself something very improbable, that the original narrative should have been expressed with such boldness as according to this text: 'He turned and rebuked them,' without the communication of the Redeemer's own expressions, and, on the other hand, it is not less improbable, that if the text had originally read barely [as proposed], it should have been already in the ancient church supplemented as it now appears in the Received Text. For it is already so found in the Vulgate, four manuscripts of the Itala, and in most of the other ancient versions, as well as in Marcion, Clemens Alexandrinus, Cyprian, Augustine, Ambrosius, and others. The early omission of the words was perhaps originally occasioned by an accidental error in copying, the eye of the copyist being misled from καὶ εἶπεν to καὶ ἐπορ., as Meyer supposes, and then this shorter text being retained in the church from dogmatical considerations also, namely, because the words of Christ were used by Marcion, who already read them, as we see from Tertull. adv. Marc. iv. 23, and other anti-Jewish Gnostics, to justify their rejection of the Old Testament and the Jewish economy." Bleek. The spuriousness of the words: "For the Son of Man is not come," &c., is not much contested. It appears to be "the interpolation of a sentence customary" with our Lord, from Matt. xviii. 11, or Luke xix. 10.—C. C. S.]

[² Vs. 62.—Om., πρὸς αὐτόν. The variations show this to be an interpolated supplement to the verb: some insert it before, some after ὁ Ἰησ., some giving αὐτῷ. Alford. Cod. Sin. has it.—C. C. S.]

EXEGETICAL AND CRITICAL.

CHRONOLOGICAL.—We believe that the here-mentioned journey must be coördinated with John vii. 1 (Friedlieb, Krafft, Hug, Lücke, Wieseler, a. o.). The grammatical expression of Luke ix. 51 admits of this, and the remark, John vii. 10, that the Saviour went up secretly, agrees admirably with Luke's account that He travelled through Samaria. The arrangement of the events in Stier, who places John vii. 1 immediately after Matt. xvi. 12, and makes the Saviour remain three whole months at Jerusalem, appears to us supported by no sufficient reasons, and to offer internal difficulties. We consider it, on the other hand, entirely probable that the Saviour, between the feast of Tabernacles, John vii., and the feast of the Dedication, John x., spent yet some time in Galilee.

Vs. 51. **When the days were fulfilling that He should be received up.**—With these words Luke begins a new particular narrative of travel, and for Harmonistics the question is naturally of great importance what we are to understand by the expression ἡμ. τῆς ἀναλ. We should be relieved of great difficulties if we found ourselves allowed to understand by it the coming to an end of the days in which the Saviour found a favorable reception in Galilee (Wieseler, Lange), but even if the grammatical possibility of this interpretation was sufficiently proved, yet the whole way of conceiving the first period of the public life of the Saviour, as a time of favorable reception in contrast with the conflict afterwards arising, appears to be hardly in the spirit of Luke. The translation of συμπληροῦσθαι in the sense of: "To come to an end," is at least not favored by Acts ii. 1, and moreover the whole Pauline usage of our Evangelist is decidedly in favor of interpreting the ἀνάληψις in the ecclesiastical sense of *Assumtio*. Comp. Acts i. 2; xi. 22; 1 Tim. iii. 16. We believe, therefore, that this is here indicated as the final term of the earthly manifestation of the Saviour, to which even His death was only a natural transition. But we are not obliged, therefore, as yet to assume that here the journey to the last Passover is meant; on the other hand, the opposite seems to be deducible from xiii. 22; xvii. 11. Quite as little can we assume that here two journeys to feasts have been confounded (Schleiermacher), and least of all that it is not even an account of any particular journey which begins here

(Ritzschl). It appears, on the other hand, that here one of the last journeys is designated which the Saviour, on the approach of the end of His life, had entered upon with His view directed to His exaltation, and at the same time that in this whole narrative of journeying, ch. ix. 51 to ch. xviii. 14, different details do not appear in their strict historical sequence. This was fully permitted to the Evangelist, since on his pragmatical position the whole public life of the Lord might properly be called a journey to death, as Bengel strikingly explains it: "*Instabat adhuc passio, crux, mors, sepulcrum, sed per hæc omnia ad metam prospexit Jesus, cujus sensum imitatur stilus Evangelistæ.*" Moreover, it clearly appears that this whole account of this journey in Luke is drawn from one or several distinct written sources (διηγήσεις); yet respecting their nature and origin it is impossible to determine anything certain, and for the credibility of this part also we must be contented with the declaration which Luke has made respecting his whole Gospel in the introduction, ch. i. 1–4.

He steadfastly set His face, ἐστήριξε τὸ πρόσωπον.—We cannot agree with the opinion (Von Baur) that nothing is here meant to be intimated than that Jesus, in all of the journeys which He was now making, never lost the final goal out of His mind, but made them with the continual, unshaken consciousness that they, wherever they led, were properly a πορεύεσθαι εἰς Ἱερουσ. True, there lies in the word ἐστήριξε the conception of a steadfast, undaunted beholding of the final goal of the journey, but that nevertheless an immediate commencement and continuance of the journey itself was connected therewith is sufficiently apparent from vs. 53–56.

Vs. 53. **And they did not receive Him.**—It is true that the caravans for Jerusalem often journeyed this way (see JOSEPHUS, *Ant. Jud.* xx. 6. 1; and LIGHTFOOT, on John iv. 4), but for all that, hospitality might very well have been refused to a company travelling separately, and, above all, to the Saviour; if the report of the increasing hatred against Him had already made its way even to Samaria, and obtained there some influence. [The fact that the company were Jews is quite sufficient to account for the refusal, without the wholly superfluous and ungrounded supposition that they were influenced by any condition of parties among the Jews. If Jewish hatred against the Saviour had had any influence among the Samaritans, it would have been in His favor.—C. C. S.] Respecting the hatred between

Samaritans and Jews, comp. LANGE, on the *Gospel of John*.

Vs. 54. **James and John.**—There is just as little ground for assuming (Euth. Zigab.) as for denying (Meyer) that the sons of Zebedee themselves were the messengers. The exasperation that filled them is as easily comprehensible as the entreaty for vengeance which they uttered. 1. They had seen the Lord upon Tabor, where Moses and Elijah did Him homage; shortly after, a conversation of high moment had directed their attention to Elijah and his relation to the kingdom of God. Is it a wonder that an image from the history of this prophet came up before their souls, and a spark of his fiery zeal set their hearts into a flaming glow? Comp. 2 Kings xix. 12. That the name Boanerges was given them for a humiliating reminder of what here took place, is, as already remarked, without any ground.

As Elijah did, ὡς καὶ 'Η. ἐποίησεν.—Upon the authority of B., L., and some cursives and variations, these words have been often suspected (Mill, Griesbach), and finally omitted by Tischendorf. We believe, however, that their early omission must be explained on the ground that "in the answer of Jesus an indirect censure of this example was discovered" (De Wette). On the other hand, it is probable that the words proceeded from the disciples themselves, since such an apparently unreasonable inquiry could be best justified by an express appeal to the man who had also performed such a miracle of punishment.

Vs. 55. **Know ye not of what Spirit ye are?** —The Saviour does not disapprove this Elijah-like zeal unconditionally. He knows that this, on the plane of the old Theocracy, was not seldom necessary; but this does He seriously censure: that His disciples so entirely overlooked the distinction between the Old and the New Testament, that they, in the service of the mildest Master, still continued to believe that they could act as was permitted the stern reformer of Israel on his rigoristic position. They ought far rather to have considered that they, in His society, had, from the very beginning, become partakers of another Spirit, which knew no pleasure in vengeance. Not only of this does the Master powerfully admonish them, that they should be the bearers of this Spirit, but also that they in His society were already the dwelling-places of this Spirit. We find no ground for removing these words as spurious from the text, notwithstanding that they had been quite early suspected and expunged by many. (*See* TISCHENDORF, *ad loc.*) Their rejection, however, is sufficiently explained by the fact that they seemed to contain an indirect censure of Elijah's way of dealing, and therefore gave offence to the copyists, although from a mistaken understanding of them. Perhaps it was feared also that by retaining these words the ancient Christian zeal in the persecution of heretics would be seen to be condemned, and they were therefore discreetly left out. In both cases the omission is at least fully intelligible, but not in what way they had come into the other manuscripts if the Saviour had not uttered them. And would Luke have written only ἐπετίμησεν αὐτοῖς without adding anything more; precisely as he had previously, vs. 42, said in reference to an evil spirit? On the contrary, as respects the last words in the *Recepta:* "The Son of Man is not come," &c., the number as well as the weight of the authorities for their spuriousness is in our eyes decisive. They are in all probability, as a fitting conclusion of an ecclesiastical lesson, transferred either from Matt. xviii. 18, or Luke xix. 10. The grounds, at least, on which, for example, STIER, iii. p. 95, will still vindicate them, appear to us rather subjective and unsatisfactory.

Vs. 57. **And it came to pass.**—The correct historical sequence of this occurrence appears to have been observed by Matthew, ch. viii. 19, 20. The second may have taken place almost contemporaneously with it, the third probably on another occasion; but it is related by Luke here, on account of the similarity of the case, in one connection with the others. Our Evangelist apparently gives them at the beginning of this last narrative of travel, for the reason that they have all relation to *one* most momentous subject, the following of the Saviour in the way of self-denial, of toil, and of conflict.

A certain man.—According to Matthew, a scribe. If we proceed upon the presupposition that the Evangelist, in the case of very special callings of disciples, had in mind only the calling of apostles, and that therefore the here-mentioned person must necessarily have been one of the Twelve, the conjecture of Lange is then in the highest degree happy, that we here in the two following accounts have the history of the calling of Judas Iscariot, Thomas, and Matthew. On the other hand, we do not know whether the first was a scribe: we believe, moreover, that we must assume, on chronological grounds, that the calling of Matthew had already taken place. The first of these three men is moreover not called by Jesus, but, unrequested, offers himself to Him as companion of His journey. He utters the language of excited enthusiasm, follows the impression of the moment, and is the type of a sanguine nature.

Vs. 58. **The foxes.**—The answer of the Saviour does not of itself entitle us to accuse the scribe who offers himself as a disciple, of an interested end; but it only presupposes that his resolution had been taken too hastily to be well matured and well considered. The Saviour therefore desires that he should first consider how little rest and comfort he had to expect in this journey. He Himself had less than even the wildest beasts possess, and can therefore call His followers also only to daily self-denial. The Saviour here does not primarily refer to the humbleness and poverty of His life, but to His restless and wandering life, although the first of these thoughts need not be wholly excluded. Does, perchance, the presentiment also express itself in these words that even dying He should lay His head to rest in a place which was not even His own property? At all events, we have to admire the deep wisdom of the Saviour in this, that on this occasion He calls himself the Son of Man, as if He would intimate that He who requires so much self-denial, also fully deserves it. As far as we from other passages are acquainted with even the better-minded scribes, we shall be very well able to assume that this one, at such a word, went from thence with a disturbed mind. The interpretation, moreover, that the Saviour with this pregnant answer only meant to say, "But I know not as yet for the coming night where I shall sleep" (Herder), or, that "The Divine Spirit which restlessly worked in Him, suffered itself to be hemmed in under no roof, within no four walls" (Weisse), belongs fitly in a collection of exegetical curiosities. The view of Schleiermacher, that the scribe wished to follow the Saviour to Jerusalem on whichever of the many roads to Jerusalem He might travel, we cannot approve, since it rests upon an improbability, in presupposing that not Matthew but Luke has given this occurrence in the right historical connection. To better purpose may we, in order to understand this man's meaning, compare the language which Ittai used towards David, 2 Sam. xv. 21.

Vs. 59. **And He said unto another, Follow Me.**—According to Matthew's intimation also: πρῶτον, Jesus first called this man to follow Him, and encouraged him, therefore, while He rather deterred the former. The melancholy temperament is treated by the Lord very differently from the sanguine. According to Matthew, he is one of the μαθηταί, belonging to the wider circle which is alluded to also in John vi. 66. If the scribe was too inconsiderate, this man is too melancholy, and even in the most immediate neighborhood of the Prince of life, he sees himself pursued by gloomy images of death. The Lord knows that this man must choose at once or without doubt he will never choose, and deals with him, therefore, with all the strictness, but at the same time with all the wisdom, of love.

First to go and bury my father.—The sense is not that the father was already old, and that he wished to wait for his death (so, among others, HASE, Leben Jesu, second edition), for then he would have demanded an indefinite, perhaps a long postponement, and would have deserved a sharper answer. No, without doubt his father had died, and he had perhaps only quite lately received the intelligence of his death. It is not, however, probable that he would have mingled among the people and approached the Saviour, immediately from the house of death, after he had become Levitically unclean. He wishes, on the other hand, to go to his dead father, and cherishes the hope that the Saviour, for his sake, will postpone His departure or else permit him to follow afterwards.

Vs. 60. **Let the dead.**—*See* LANGE, *ad loc.*, in Matthew. With a man of such a character the Saviour considers it absolutely necessary to insist on the exact fulfilment of the high principle, that for His sake, one must unconditionally leave all. If even the Nazarites were not permitted to defile themselves by touching the mortal remains of their kindred (Num. vi. 6, 7), without this prohibition having been viewed as too strict, the Saviour also does not require too much when He here demanded the leaving of the dead father; the more so since He made good a thousandfold that which was given up for His sake, by the joyful calling to preach the Gospel of the kingdom of God. Duty to a handful of dust must now give way before duty towards mankind. It is of course understood, that the Saviour here by the first mentioned νεκροί means the spiritually dead, and it at once appears how much, by the double sense in which the word νεκροί is here used, the expression gains in beauty and power. Here also, in the use of language by the Synoptic and the Johannean Christ, there is discernible an admirable agreement. Comp. John v. 24, 25.

Vs. 61. **Lord, I will follow Thee.**—Luke does not state definitely whether the initiative proceeded from the Saviour or the disciple. It may be that Jesus had first called him, yet it is also possible that he here offers himself. This history has a remarkable concurrence with the prophetical calling of Elisha, 1 Kings xix. 19, 21, and the form of the Saviour's answer also appears borrowed from what took place with Elisha, who was called when ploughing. Here the Saviour insisted upon undivided devotion, as He in the first case insisted upon ripe consideration, in the second upon courageous decision. The inquirer is either not to follow, or to follow wholly and perfectly.

Vs. 62. **No man.**—Before all things the Saviour will give the man to feel that in the kingdom of God a severe labor must be accomplished,—a labor which will be doubly severe and certainly unfruitful, if the whole man does not take part in it. He portrays to us from life the plougher whose hand is on the plough, whose eye is turned back, and whose work must thereby become toilsome, ill regulated and insignificant. [The light, easily overturned plough of the East lends force to the image.—C. C. S.] What should He have to do with such laborers in His kingdom? To be compared with this, although not to be identified with it, is the example of Lot's wife, Luke xvii. 32, and the apostolic saying, 2 Peter ii. 22.

Remarks on the whole Section.—It has often been remarked that Luke, without observing a strict chronological sequence, brings together here four different characters: vss. 51–56 the Choleric, vss. 57, 58 the Sanguine, vss. 59, 60 the Melancholic, vss. 61, 62 the Phlegmatic. Without precisely asserting that the Evangelist had the definite purpose to portray the Saviour's manner of dealing with men of the most different temperaments, we yet cannot deny that he is much more concerned for the union of similar facts than for strict chronological arrangement. It is not probable that in the last period of the public life of the Saviour, when enmity against Him had already so considerably increased, a scribe would have followed Him even then; on the contrary, it is much more credible that this, as Matthew relates, took place at an earlier period of time. That this last case occurred twice (Stier), appears to us on internal grounds hardly admissible.

DOCTRINAL AND ETHICAL.

1. It has more than once been inquired what temperament is to be ascribed to the Son of Man, and the decision has been made in favor of some one of the four, *e. g.* the choleric (Winkler). But the comparison of our Saviour's temper of soul and manner of dealing with that of the four different men coming here into view, gives us plainly to perceive that every strongly pronounced temperament necessarily represents something one-sided, while it is precisely in the perfect harmony of His predispositions, powers, and movements of soul, that the characteristics of the entirely unique personality of Jesus must be sought.

2. The insult which the Saviour received from the Samaritans must have been the greater, the more widely the fame of His Messianic dignity had penetrated even among them. To a Messiah who was going up to Jerusalem instead of restoring the temple-service on Gerizim, they could not possibly extend hospitality. But at the same time, this hatred is also a striking symbol of the reception which is now as ever prepared for the Christian in the midst of an unbelieving world, as soon as this becomes aware, or conjectures, that his countenance also is directed towards the heavenly Jerusalem.

3. The heavenly mildness of the Saviour over against religious hatred on the one hand and the desire of vengeance on the other, only becomes rightly apparent, if we not only compare Him with Elijah, but

above all consider who He was, and what reception He was entitled to demand. His vengeance on Samaria for the refusal of recognition here, we read in Acts viii. 14–17.

4. It is quite as incorrect to overlook the special necessity of the requirements, vss. 60–62, for those times, as to suppose that they were exclusively suitable for those times. On the contrary, there is here expressed in a peculiar form the high principle which binds all His disciples immutably, without respect to time or place, and with which we have already become acquainted, ch. ix. 23–25.

5. The very strictness of the requirements which the Saviour imposes on His followers, is an incontrovertible proof of the exalted self-consciousness which He continually bore within Himself. Who has ever demanded more, but who also has promised more and rendered a greater reward than He? And in that which He here demands of others, He Himself has gone before in accomplishing the will of His Father at every time without rebuke.

HOMILETICAL AND PRACTICAL.

Vss. 51–56. The steady step with which the Saviour goes towards His Passion and His Glory.—The distinction between this village of the Samaritans and Sychar, John iv. 40.—The power of deep-rooted religious hatred.—The strife between exaggerated religiosity and genuine humanity.—The hatred in Samaria the presage of the conflict in Jerusalem.—The fiery zeal of the sons of Zebedee: 1. Flaming out, 2. rebuked, 3. purified.—The Saviour over against: 1. Bigoted enemies, 2. unintelligent friends.—Jesus the meek Servant of the Father.—True and false religious zeal. Comp. Romans x. 2.—Religious hatred, false zeal, and meekness.—The distinction between the spirit of the Old and that of the New Covenant.

Vss. 57–62. The following of Jesus; a threefold precept: 1. No very hasty step; the Master requires earnest consideration; 2. no melancholy resolution; the Master requires a courageous walk; 3. no unresolved wavering; the Master requires entire devotion.—Well-meaning but ill-considered steps, Jesus dissuades from.—The restless life of the Lord.—Whoever will follow the Son of Man, must count on self-denial.—What is heaviest, must weigh heaviest.—The dead father and the living Gospel.—To the spiritually dead commit the care of the lifeless dust.—Forgetting what is behind, reaching on to what is before.—The love of the Saviour in an apparently arbitrary refusal.—The undecided man between the Saviour and them of his house.—The useless plougher on the field of the kingdom of God: 1. His type; 2. his work; 3. his sentence.—Three stones of stumbling on the way of following Jesus: 1. Overhastiness, 2. heavyheartedness, 3. indecision.

The whole Section. The Divine harmony in the Son of Man, and the different temperaments of the children of men.— The wisdom of the Saviour in converse with and in guiding men of the most different kinds.—How: 1. Different temperaments are related to the Saviour; 2. how the Saviour is related to different temperaments.—Severity and love, holiness and grace, in the Son of Man united in noblest wise.—Comp. especially the admirable sermons of Fr. Arndt on Luke ix. 52–62.

STARKE:—The consideration of death must not depress us, since we know that we are travelling towards the heavenly Jerusalem.—J. HALL:—Oh, deep humiliation, that He whose is the heaven and all the habitations therein, entreats for a lodging, and does not even find it.—QUESNEL:—When one has once begun in good earnest the journey to heaven, he has little credit thereafter in the world.—Not to be hospitable, especially towards those who follow Christ, is unrighteous. Hebr. xiii. 2.—ZEISIUS:—How thirsty for vengeance after all is flesh and blood!—Against sin we must be zealous, but not against the persons of the sinners.—Although one may indeed follow the saints, yet herein considerateness is to be used.—CANSTEIN:—To the church of Christ there has no might and power for the destruction of men been given.—*Nova Bibl. Tub.*:—Whoever with Christ seeks only easy days, let him stay away from Him.—BRENTIUS: —A Divine call must be accepted without conferring with flesh and blood, let it cost what it may. Gal. i. 16.—Parents one must honor, but for the sake of the kingdom of heaven let them also go. Matt. xix. 29.—The ministry demands the whole man.—ZEISIUS:—It is easy and hard to be a Christian.

HEUBNER:—How many profitless and superfluous drones there are in the ministry. Such workers are corpses that will all yet be buried.—Jesus commonly comes even to us not unannounced.—AUGUSTINE:—*Opus est mitescere pietate.*—PALMER:—Earthly desire, earthly love, earthly sorrow—these are the three powers that scare men away from Christ.—BECK (on vss. 51–56):—Know ye not what Spirit ye are children of? 1. What Spirit we *are* children of; 2. what Spirit we *ought to be* children of.—GEROK:—The four temperaments under training of Jesus Christ, the Searcher of hearts.—SCHAUFLER (on vss. 61, 62):—Anything but a conditional following of Jesus!

B. *The Seventy Disciples.* CH. X. 1–24.

(Partial parallel to Matt. xi. 20–30.)

1 After these things the Lord appointed other seventy [seventy others[1]] also, and
2 sent them two and two before his face into every city and place, whither he himself would [was about to] come. Therefore said he [And said, V. O.[2]] unto them, The harvest truly *is* great, but the labourers *are* few: pray ye therefore the Lord of the
3 harvest, that he would send forth labourers into his harvest. Go your ways: behold,
4 I send you forth as lambs among wolves. Carry neither purse, nor scrip [wallet], nor
5 shoes; and salute no man by the way. And into whatsoever house ye enter, first say,

CHAP. X. 1-24.

6 Peace *be* to this house. And if the [a] son of peace be there, your peace shall rest
7 upon it: if not, it shall turn [return] to you again. And in the same house remain, eating and drinking such things as they give: for the labourer is worthy of his hire.
8 Go not from house to house. And into whatsoever city ye enter, and they receive
9 you, eat such things as are set before you: And heal the sick that are therein, and say
10 unto them, The kingdom of God is come nigh unto you. But into whatsoever city ye enter, and they receive you not, go your ways out into the streets of the same, and say,
11 Even the very dust of your city, which cleaveth [from your city, transferred from last clause] on us [to us upon our feet²], we do wipe off against you: notwithstanding, be ye sure of this, that the kingdom of God is come nigh unto you [om., unto you, V. O.⁴].
12 But [om., But, V. O.⁵] I say unto you, that it shall be more tolerable in that day for
13 Sodom, than for that city. Woe unto thee, Chorazin! woe unto thee, Bethsaida! for if the mighty works [αἱ δυνάμεις, *Kräfte*, V. O.] had been done in Tyre and Sidon, which have been done in you, they had [would have] a great while ago repented,
14 sitting in sackcloth and ashes. But it shall be more tolerable for Tyre and Sidon at
15 the judgment, than for you. And thou, Capernaum, which art [who hast been ⁶] exalt-
16 ed to heaven, shalt be thrust down to hell. He that heareth you heareth me; and he that despiseth you despiseth me; and he that despiseth me despiseth [despiseth—in all
17 four places—ἀθετῶν, lit., sets at nought] him that sent me. And the seventy returned again with joy, saying, Lord, even the devils [demons] are subject [subjected] unto us
18 through [lit., in] thy name. And he said unto them, I beheld⁷ Satan as lightning fall
19 [fallen, πεσόντα] from heaven. Behold, I give [I have given, δέδωκα⁸] unto you power [ἐξουσίαν] to tread on serpents and scorpions, and over all the power [δύναμιν] of the
20 enemy; and nothing shall by any means hurt you. Notwithstanding, in this rejoice not, that the spirits are subject [subjected] unto you; but rather [om., rather⁹] rejoice,
21 because your names are written in heaven [the heavens]. In that hour Jesus rejoiced in spirit, and said, I thank thee, O Father, Lord of heaven and earth, that thou hast hid these things from the wise and prudent, and hast revealed them unto babes: even so,
22 Father; for so it seemed good in thy sight. [And turning himself to his disciples, he said, V. O.¹⁰] All things are delivered to me of [by] my Father: and no man [one] knoweth who the Son is, but the Father; and who the Father is, but the Son, and he
23 to whom the Son will reveal *him*. And he turned him unto *his* disciples, and said [turning himself . . ., he said] privately, Blessed *are* the eyes which see the things that ye
24 see: For I tell you, that many prophets and kings have desired to see those things which ye see, and have not seen *them;* and to hear those things which ye hear, and have not heard *them*.

¹ Vs. 1.—The δύο added here and in vs. 17, which the Vulgate has received and Lachmann bracketed, is too slenderly attested to be received into the text, and is, therefore, correctly rejected by most critics. [Om., Cod. Sin., A., C., L., Z.—C. C. S.]
² Vs. 2.—According to the better reading δέ instead of οὖν. See TISCHENDORF *ad locum*. [Tischendorf, Lachmann, Tregelles read δέ, Alford οὖν, regarding δέ as substituted, because the more common copulative. For οὖν are A., E., 11 other uncials; Cod. Sin., B., C., D., L. have δέ.—C. C. S.]
³ Vs. 11.—With Griesbach and Tischendorf we believe that we may receive the words εἰς τοὺς πόδας ἡμῶν without scruple into the text. They have been omitted from many manuscripts only because they appeared to be superfluous [ins. A., B., C., D., R., Z., Cod. Sin.—C. C. S.]
⁴ Vs. 11.—The reading of the *Recepta* ἐφ' ὑμᾶς is only a repetition from vs. 9, by which the force of the word of leave-taking, which is here put into the mouth of the Seventy, is without reason weakened. [Om., ἐφ' ὑμᾶς, B., D., L., Cod. Sin.—C. C. S.]
[⁵ Vs. 12.—Cod. Sin. retains δέ with D., M., V.—C. C. S.]
⁶ Vs. 15.—The reading of Tischendorf: μὴ ἕως τοῦ οὐρανοῦ ὑψωθήσῃ, finds, it is true, in B., D., L., [Cod. Sin., Z.,] and in the Ethiopic and Coptic versions, and in the Itala, important support, and, superficially considered, it may appear as if the pathos of the address is heightened by the interrogative form. On the other hand, however, such a reflection appears less congruous, indeed has even more or less a sarcastic and ironical character, which accords as little with the solemnity of the occasion as with the frame of mind of the Saviour. [As Bleek and Meyer remark, this reading, so weakening to the sense and real solemnity of the denunciation, has arisen from an inadvertent doubling of the last letter of καφαρναουμ, thus changing the following η into μη, and involving afterwards the necessity of changing ὑψωθεῖσα into ὑψωθήσῃ to make sense. This change was supported by the fact that the original reading in the parallel passage, Matt. xi. 24, was probably η . . . ὑψωθῆς, which passage both acted upon this and was acted upon by it.—C. C. S.]
[⁷ Vs. 18.—Ἐθεώρουν. Imp., *I* [already] beheld [when you went forth]. Meyer.]
⁸ Vs. 19.—Δέδωκα is the reading approved by the author, following Tischendorf, and agreeing with Meyer and Alford. I see that Cod. Sin. also gives the Perfect.—C. C. S.]
⁹ Vs. 20.—The word μᾶλλον, which Elzevir here receives into the text in addition to the other adversatives (with S., X.], and which from his Greek text has passed over into several translations, is critically worthless and logically a hindrance, since it weakens the force of the exquisite antithesis.
¹⁰ Vs. 22.—'There is no ground whatever for omitting this beginning of vs. 22, as has been done, *inter al.*, by Luther and also by Griesbach. The words have but few authorities against them (D., L., cursives, versions), and appear to have been neglected on account of the similar commencement of vs. 23. That, however, they have not been transferred from this latter verse, appears from the fact that here κατ' ἰδίαν is wanting. [The uncials omitting the words are, however, more numerous and weighty than he states, being in addition to D. and L., M., Z., and especially the two important Codd., Cod. Sin. and, according to Alford and Tischendorf, B., although the latter hesitates, as in Woide's and Mai's editions; at least, they are omitted.—C. C. S.]

EXEGETICAL AND CRITICAL.

General Remarks.—From different quarters the credibility of the account of Luke respecting the Seventy has been disputed (Strauss, De Wette, Theile, Weisse, Von Ammon, Baur, Köstlin, Schwegler, a. o.). Inner improbability appeared to cast doubt on this account, while the silence of the other Synoptics was also suspicious. Commonly, however, the attacks have been directed against a manner of viewing the fact, which is demanded neither by the letter nor the spirit of the evangelical narrative. The Seventy, namely, have been too much regarded as a fixed number, as a continually active circle of the Saviour's servants *besides* the Twelve, and *exclusive* of them, and were supposed to have preached the kingdom of God afterwards also. In this case, it certainly would have been extremely surprising that there is no other trace to be found of this circle of disciples, nay, that even Eusebius was no longer able (*H. E.* i. 12) to give the catalogue of the names of these disciples. But on attentive consideration it soon appears that the Seventy received no other commission than at this particular time to prepare for the coming of the Saviour in some towns and villages, and that they, after the accomplishment of their charge, were absorbed in the wider circle of His followers. Thus are they a remarkable luminary in the public life of the Saviour, whose brilliancy, however, endured only a brief time, and Luke therefore cannot be justly charged with having here, for the first time, not " precisely investigated " everything. That Jesus, besides the Twelve, had yet a wider circle of disciples, appears also from John vi. 66 ; Acts i. 15–26 ; 1 Cor. xv. 6. But if we had here to understand an intentional invention, then, without doubt, many more particulars respecting the great deeds of these men would have appeared both here and in the Acts. The number Seventy also occasions not the least actual difficulty. Perhaps it is an indefinite round number (comp. Matt. xviii. 22), or the Saviour may have had His reasons for sending out neither more nor less than thirty-five pairs of such ambassadors in different directions. But even if we assume that we have here a symbolical number before us, which referred to the elders of Israel (Exodus xxiv. 9), or to the members of the Sanhedrim with the exclusion of their president, or finally to the seventy heathen nations, according to the ancient Israelitish reckoning, the symbolism is not, therefore, by any means unhistoric (Schwegler). The number of the apostles also was a symbolical one, and if we assume that this number Seventy is to indicate the universal direction of the gospel, it then becomes doubly intelligible that Luke, the Paulinist, brings forward this circumstance so distinctly. Matthew and Mark might the more readily pass over these, as they had already communicated more in detail the discourse of the Saviour in the sending out of the Twelve, which in many points coincided with this one.

Vs. 1. **Seventy others.**—If this circle existed only a few days or weeks, it is the less surprising that it soon became uncertain who had belonged to it. Fancy had then free play, and very soon men used this company as a charitable foundation in order to provide for men who did not belong to the Twelve, but who were of some account [in the church], such as Mark, Luke, Matthias. (Strauss). A peculiar list of candidates is found in SEPP, iii. 26, who here, at the same time, finds prefigured the number of the cardinals of the papal see.

And sent them.—The chief purpose of this sending was not to fashion and train these messengers for a later independent activity (Hase, and after him Krabbe, who appeals, *N. B.*, for proof of it to vs. 20), but it was a new attempt, in order to influence to, decision at least a part of the people, and by word and deed to prepare the coming of the kingdom of God in the midst of them. " This whole journey of Jesus was intended, before the departure of the Lord from His previous theatre of activity, to present to the people the last decision, to be everywhere the Messianic entrance, which, in connection with the final entry into Jerusalem, was to culminate in the latter." Meyer.

* **Into every city and place whither He Himself was about to come.**—According to LANGE, *Leben Jesu*, ii. p. 1057, we are to understand exclusively towns in Samaria, and to consider this whole mission as a noble vengeance for His rejection, Luke ix. 51–56. It is, however, a question whether the Saviour really had the intention of visiting so many as thirty-five towns and villages of the Samaritans. If we keep in mind the direction of His own journey, we should undoubtedly rather have to assume that the Seventy preceded Him to Judæa. In this whole investigation, however, we must not overlook the fact that it is as yet very much in question whether Luke communicates this whole sending forth of the Seventy in its exact historical connection. The expression μετὰ ταῦτα, vs. 1, is at least very indefinite, and since he in vs. 17 relates also the return of these messengers immediately after their departure, it brings us almost to the conjecture that he here as frequently follows rather the order of subject than that of time. If we are obliged to assume that our Saviour afterwards actually visited all the places whither these messengers had gone before Him, this probably would have happened shortly after the feast of Tabernacles, John vii. But in no case are we obliged to conceive the matter as VON AMMON, *ad loc.*, does, who, from very peculiar sources, seems to know that the Saviour on this journey sent forth a great number of His disciples, and selected them to give special probationary instructions in the nearest synagogues !! Better Riggenbach : " The seventy disciples are to be regarded as a net of love which the Lord threw out in Israel."

Vs. 2. **And said.**—As the Seventy are distinct from the Twelve, so is the instruction which is communicated to both distinct. The difference between the two inauguration addresses is great enough to refute the conjecture that transferences and transpositions of single expressions have taken place from one discourse into the other. It is noticeable how these admonitions of the Saviour to the Seventy agree with the precepts which He, according to Luke, ch. ix. 1–6, gave to the Twelve in sending them forth. If the Evangelist is not to be charged with very great inconsistency, we shall be forced to assume that the words of Jesus on the second occasion were at least partially the same. But the distinction comes much more strongly into view in comparing this with Matt. x. The gift bestowed on the Twelve of working miracles is far more extended than that which is here bestowed in vs. 9 on the Seventy. Of the persecutions which He foretells the Twelve, and of the extraordinary help of the Holy Spirit which He promises them, Matt. x. 17–24, and of which there was to be further speech only after the day of Pentecost, the

Seventy in entering upon their only momentary and soon accomplished work, have communicated to them not a word. The earlier command not to go into a town of the Samaritans is this time omitted, as the journey perhaps went through a part of Samaria. On the other hand, the remarkable injunction given to the Seventy alone, to salute no man on the way, appears doubly congruous, as the Saviour sees His public life hurrying to an end. Such differences are as far from being unimportant as accidental, but have sprung rather from the different nature of the persons and facts. The Twelve had to return upon the traces of Jesus, in order to gather in the harvest of that which He had sown. The Seventy must go before His face, in order to prepare a way for Him.
The harvest truly is great.—According to Matt. ix. 37, 38, the Saviour uttered this word before the sending of the Twelve, and it is very possible that He now repeated it. But if we assume that it was only spoken once, then undoubtedly its position in Matthew is the most exact.
Vs. 3. **As Lambs.**—According to Matthew x. 16, the Twelve are sent out ὡς πρόβατα. It is undoubtedly possible that this distinction is to be explained merely from a different form of the tradition (Meyer); on the other hand, however, it is quite as conceivable that the Saviour, for this case, intentionally modified the figurative language. But if He did, it was certainly not to attribute to the Seventy a lower place than to the Twelve (Euth. and Zigab.), but "in order this time to lay emphasis on simplicity together with defencelessness (Matthew has 'doves')." Stier.
Vs. 4. **Salute no man.**—It is well known that salutations in the Orient were much more essential than with us, and that, e. g., inferiors remained standing until their superiors had passed by. Comp. 2 Kings iv. 29. Respecting the different formulas of salutation among the Jews, see LIGHTFOOT, ad loc.
Vs. 5. **And into whatsoever house.**—The preliminary investigation enjoined in Matthew, ch. x. 11, is here omitted. From everything it appears that the Saviour's affairs demanded haste. His whole instruction may be comprehended in the saying, John xiii. 27b.
Vs. 6. **A son of peace.**—Not pace dignus (Bengel), but one for whom peace is prepared, because the needful receptivity for the word of peace is found in his heart. Upon this one is the salutation of peace to rest, for peace shall fill his heart, Phil. iv. 7. In the opposite case it was only an empty sound in his ear, and returned without delay to him from whom it had proceeded.
Vs. 7. **And in the same house.**—In the one, that is, where they are received by children of peace. They must thus avoid even the appearance of seeking from the inhabitants theirs instead of them, and are not permitted, therefore, even in a meagre entertainment to find any cause of speedy departure. Comp. Matt. x. 11; Luke ix. 4.
Vs. 9. **Heal the sick.**—The brevity of this commission in comparison with the detailed instruction to the Twelve (Matt. x. 8) is not to be overlooked. It is remarkable, however, that the Seventy, on their return, speak of no other healing of the sick than the casting out of the demons. The connection of healing and preaching here gives the former a symbolical character.
Vs. 11. **Even the very dust.**—See the remarks on ch. ix. 5, and LANGE on Matthew x. 14. What there was not yet enjoined on the Twelve is here pre-

scribed to the Seventy: to follow even this last act of displeasure with the repetition of the word of love, that the kingdom of God was come near. But now no longer: "To you" (spurious), but quite generally. "It is and remains true that it is come near, even though you contemn it."
Vs. 12. **I say unto you that it shall be more tolerable in that day for Sodom.**—According to the common conception, the judgment of retribution has already smitten Sodom and Gomorrah. According to the steady teaching of the New Testament, on the other hand, this judgment, terrific though it was, is only a forecaste of that which is to be expected at the end of days. Comp., for instance, Jude vs. 7. The terrible judgment, moreover, with which the Lord here threatens those who reject His servants, is an unequivocal proof of the high rank which He ascribes to them, compared with the most eminent men of God, and indirectly, at the same time, a striking revelation of His own entirely unique self-consciousness.
Vs. 13. **Woe unto thee, Chorazin!**—Comp. Matt. xi. 20-24. Here again it is as before; whoever assumes that the Saviour uttered this Woe only once, will, at the same time, have to concede that it is communicated by Matthew in the most natural connection. Luke then introduces this saying on this occasion apparently because he had just given the exclamation over Sodom, and also communicates it with less fulness and particularity. On the other hand, no one can dispute our right to assume here too that the judgment of these Galilean towns lay so heavily on the heart of Jesus that He more than once uttered forth the exclamation of woe (Meyer). Something subjectivistic in remarks of this kind is indeed hardly to be wholly avoided. Respecting the locality of the here-mentioned places, see LANGE on Matthew, xi. 20-24. It is noticeable, and at the same time wise, that the Saviour, among the towns whose judgment He denounces, does not speak expressly of Nazareth. This might have had the appearance of a personal revenge.
They would have . . . repented.—"These words are remarkable inasmuch as the Saviour, even as respects the past, speaks of nothing as absolutely necessary. He here plainly recognizes the freedom of self-determination and possibility of the contrary event." Olshausen.—Undoubtedly, there must have been so many miracles performed as well at Chorazin as at Bethsaida, that this judgment was fully deserved. And yet the Evangelists relate nothing whatever of them. A proof certainly that they have been rather frugal than lavish in the writing of their accounts of miracles. Comp. John xxi. 24, 25.
Vs. 16. **He that heareth you.**—As the Seventy, although they were not invested with the apostolic office, nevertheless saw themselves called for a time to an apostolic activity so weighty, we cannot be surprised that the Saviour gives also to them an assurance similar to that with which He had formerly sent forth the Twelve, Matt. x. 40.
Vs. 17. **Returned again with joy.**—Although it is of course evident that the return of the different messengers could not have taken place at the same time, Luke, however, so represents the matter as if they had simultaneously rendered account to the Lord of the result of their journey, and had received His approbation and indeed His eulogy. Not a solitary trace of the permanent gain which they brought to the kingdom of God has been preserved to us;

yet a single hint is given of the momentary impression which they elicited.—" **Even the demons.**"—To their eye every other fruit of their labors recedes before this recollection. If we consider that a command to cast out demons had not been expressly given them, and that this attempt a little before had failed even when made by nine apostles, ch. ix. 37 seq., we can still better understand this joy of the Seventy, and must at the same time entertain the most favorable ideas of their courage and of their strength of faith. Their righteous joy is in the answer of the Saviour confirmed, augmented, and sanctified.

Vs. 18. **I beheld Satan.**—That in this figurative speech the whole fall of the kingdom of darkness in and with its personal head is portrayed, can as little be contested as that here it is a beholding with the eye of the spirit that is spoken of. The answer to the question, when or how long previously the Saviour had seen this spectacle, is determined entirely by the connection of the discourse. If this saying stood entirely alone there would not be the least difficulty in understanding an earlier period in the public life of our Lord (Lange), or even in going back before His Incarnation (Hofman). In a very sound sense of the word we may call the whole inner life of Jesus a continuous spiritual beholding of the discomfiture of the kingdom of darkness; one which is to be restricted to no particular time. But when the Saviour utters this word in answer to the Seventy, He can scarcely mean to say anything else to them than that they have by no means deceived themselves, since He, accompanying them in spirit, had seen the sudden downfall of Satan, whose servants the demons were. It is not an isolated vision which is here spoken of, but a spiritual intuition of the God-man, before whom even the secrets of the world of spirits are discovered and lie open.

Vs. 19. **I have given unto you power.**—Thus does the Saviour, by a new assurance, augment the joy which He had just confirmed. Δέδωκα, according to the corrected reading of Tischendorf. The Preterite is not merely a reminiscence of the previously given plenitude of power, but also a confirmation and renewal of the same.—" **To tread on serpents and scorpions.**"—Undoubtedly here also similar miracles are indicated to those related in Mark xvi. 17, 18; Acts xxviii. 5; Ps. xci. 13, yet only so far as they were revelations of the higher spiritual ability which Christ had bestowed upon them. Not only to shake off poisonous serpents and adders, which, comparable to intertwining lightning-streams, are types of the fallen Evil One, but to cast down all might in the spiritual world which exalted itself in hatred against Christ—this was their holy function. Through the Spirit of truth they had to make subject to themselves the spirits of lies; but in this noble task there lurks also a dark danger. The Lord knows how the nets of temptation are first stretched for the favored among His own, and therefore does He sanctify their righteous and augmented joy by a word of most earnest warning.

Vs. 20. **Notwithstanding, in this rejoice not . . . are written in heaven.**—The word μᾶλλον appears here added to the text only to bring more clearly into view that the Saviour disapproves their joy at the subjection of the spirits not unconditionally, but only relatively. This, however, even without such an addition, is sufficiently obvious from the whole spirit and connection of this admonition. The Saviour wishes them not to rejoice too much over anything which they may accomplish for the kingdom of God. For this joy might easily and unconsciously be joined with self-seeking and pride, and besides, would not always dwell in their hearts, and might perhaps be followed by conflict and disappointment; and it must moreover at last lead them to keep their eye directed more without than within and above. Besides, what any one does is a very deceiving standard for the judgment of his inner worth. One may cast out devils and yet himself be still a child of darkness (Matt. vii. 22); therefore our Lord gives to their joy a better direction. Even the greatest talents and gifts cannot be compared with the prerogative of him who obtains in heaven a place of honor.—" **That your names.**"—The Seventy knew undoubtedly, as we also do, the beautiful figure of the Old Testament which depicts to us the Eternal One with a book before His face, wherein He notes down the names and deeds of His faithful servants. Exodus xxxii. 32, 33; Malachi iii. 16. Comp. Rev. iii. 5. Our Lord now rejoices them with the transporting assurance that their names also shone there, and directs their attention in this way to the truth that their own deliverance from the power of the devil ought to dispose them far more to thankful joy than their most glorious triumph over his disarmed servants. This prerogative should remain to them even though Satan should again exalt himself, even though their name should not be renowned upon earth, even though it should be there forgotten. "*Contrarium de prævaricatoribus, in terra scribentur*, Jer. xvii. 13." Bengel. Comp. also Psalm lxix. 28; Phil. iv. 3.

Vs. 21. **In that hour.**—Comp. Matt. xi. 25, 26. That the here-following words of the Saviour are given by Matthew in a far more significant connection is admirably proved by Lange, *ad loc.* That, however, Luke states correctly the definite occasion on which the Saviour gave utterance to this God-glorifying declaration, appears not only from the ἐν αὐτῇ τῇ ὥρᾳ, but also from the whole connection, unless one should also wish to reckon this saying among the *bis repetita*, which undoubtedly has its difficulties if too often resorted to.

Jesus rejoiced.—If from the preceding words, vs. 20, it might appear as though the Saviour did not wholly share the transport of His disciples, and regarded the joy which they reaped in their work with less satisfaction than they themselves, we see here the contrary, and by the one word ἠγαλλιάσατο, Luke offers to our heart and our imagination the most delightful conception: the hour of joy in the life of Jesus.

That Thou hast hid.—That by the wise and prudent here only fancied wise men, and by the νήπιοι not ignorant persons in themselves, but simply childlike souls, are understood, is evident. It is also evident that as well in the time of the Saviour as in the following ages, it has been commonly rejected by the former and received by the latter. But what are we to understand by this, that *God* has hidden these things from the wise and prudent? To say that God has permitted it, but in no wise ordained it, is a confession that testifies of perplexity; was it then only permission that God revealed it to the simple? To maintain that God has arbitrarily so ordained it, would sound like a blasphemy of God; can God Himself blind me, and at the same time make my blindness the ground of my condemnation? Without doubt we have here to understand a direct, yet at the same time a holy, wise, and loving disposition of things by the Father, one which is thoroughly grounded in the nature of things. To the haughty man it is morally impossible to bow before Christ, and the connection between his inner corruption and his great destitution is effected by God Himself. God has connected the participation in His kingdom with a condition which lay within the reach even of the most simple: namely, lowliness and humility of heart; wise and prudent men wantonly made themselves unreceptive of this blessing, and became in consequence of this obnoxious to this judgment, that God hid these things from them. And if our Lord gives thanks therefor, it is not for this hiding in and of itself, however deserved it may be, but for this, that even if these things were hidden to the wise, they at least did not remain concealed for all. An example of similar construction we find, among others, Rom. vi. 17. This Divine ordinance, by which so many stood outside of His kingdom, was at the same time the source of manifold conflict in His life, and yet the Saviour is not only perfectly at one with the will of the Father, but rejoices thereat, and declares: ναί, ὁ πατήρ, κ.τ.λ.—In the idea of a εὐδοκία of course everything arbitrary must be avoided, which really indeed appears also from what follows, ἔμπροσθέν σου. The counsel of the Father may be sovereign, but never tyrannical.

Vs. 22. **All things are delivered to Me by My Father.**—Again, one of those passages where the Christology of the Synoptics and that of John surprisingly concur. Comp. John xvii. 2. By the limitation of the πάντα to the *teaching* of Jesus, Grotius has prepared the way for the rationalistic interpretation of this saying, an interpretation which may be named arbitrariness and superficialness itself. It appears, moreover, that the most original form of this saying is found in Matt. ch. xi. 27. Comp. LANGE *ad loc.* and that the form in Luke: οὐδεὶς γινώσκει, τίς ἐστιν ὁ υἱός must be considered as an (undoubtedly correct) *interpretamentum*. The peculiar phenomenon that this saying of the Lord is, in the writings of Justin Martyr, even three times, as also in the Clementines, and in Marcion and Tertullian, read in exactly the reverse order: "No one knows the Father but the Son," is sufficiently explained by that with which IRENÆUS, *adv. Hær.* iv. 14, prefaces the mention of this deviation: "*Hi autem, qui peritiores Apostolis esse volunt, sic scribunt,*" &c. *See* OLSHAUSEN, "*Genuineness of the Four Gospels,*" p. 205.—"**No one knoweth.**"—The Saviour declares therefore that a man can be guided only by the knowledge of the Son to that of the Father, but also conversely that a man can be guided only by the Father to the knowledge of the Son. And that the complete form of the expression would also require the addition, "No one knoweth the Son but the Father and he to whom the Father will reveal Him," appears evident from vs. 21*b*, and from Matt. xvi. 17. Respecting the conception of Revelation here presented, Dr. VON BELL, *Diss. Theol. de vocibus φανεροῦν et ἀποκαλύπτειν,* L. B. 1849, p. 51, deserves to be compared. Of the Seventy and of all who had believed through their word, it could without doubt be said that the Father had revealed Himself through the Son in their souls. This whole expression of the most exalted self-consciousness might at the same time serve to counteract the scandal which one or another might take at the rejection of the Gospel by the wise and prudent.

[The exact correspondence, in substance, spirit, and form, of this passage, Luke x. 21, 22, and the parallel passage, Matt. xi. 25-27, with the Gospel of John, has always attracted attention. Yet its isolated character in the two Synoptical Gospels is equally apparent. It is not in the least discordant with their contents, and in Luke especially is seen to be in thorough harmony with the context. Nevertheless, it is in an essentially different vein from the general tone of our Lord's discourses as given by the Synoptics. Yet that our Lord only once in His public life broke forth into a distinct declaration of His inner relation to the Father, to which, nevertheless, in the Synoptics, He so frequently alludes, is hard to believe. This passage lies embedded in the Synoptical discourses as a vein of rich ore, which by a sudden "fault" breaks off, showing us that a continuous mass of it exists somewhere, and at the same time that it is at a considerable remove from this isolated fragment. This original matrix we find in the Gospel of John.—C. C. S.]

Vs. 23. **Unto His disciples . . . privately.**—Already here and there one (*see* vs. 25) presses more closely to the circle of the Seventy who gather around Jesus and receive His exalted eulogy. The Saviour unites the highest wisdom with the holiest transport of soul, and therefore addresses the words now following to them apart. In Matt. xiii. 16, 17 also this saying is found: yet surely it appears on *this* occasion doubly congruous. Whether the Saviour originally named *kings* or *righteous men* along with the *prophets*, is on internal grounds exceedingly difficult, and on external grounds not at all, to be determined.

Vs. 24. **Many prophets and kings.**—One of the sublimest utterances of our Lord which appear in the Synoptical Gospels. He proclaims Himself as Him in whom alone not only the expectation of the earlier time is fulfilled, but in whom also the Ornament and Crown of mankind has appeared. The image of a David and Hezekiah, of an Isaiah and Micah, rises clearly before His soul, and their inner life stands before His spirit as a life of expectation, as whose centre and fulfilment He recognized Himself. Over against all these He looks upon the scanty circle of His disciples, who are infinitely higher privileged, and as if He feared even the appearance of self-exaltation when He testifies of Himself, He says unto them in the ear what soon is to be proclaimed upon the housetops: "More than Solomon, more than Jonah is here." At the same time this felicitation for the Seventy is an indirect admonition not only to look with continual faith upon Him, but also moreover to listen to Him with all the devotion of which kings and prophets would certainly have counted Him worthy. Doubly fitting is this intimation, since the messengers now recoiled again into the circle of His ordinary hearers, and the placing of such a saying at the conclusion of the interview with the Seventy appears therefore on internal grounds exact.

DOCTRINAL AND ETHICAL.

1. *See Exegetical* and *Critical* remarks.
2. The sending forth of the Seventy is a new revelation of the glory of the King of the kingdom of Heaven. It is a repetition of that which had already begun in smaller measure in the journeyings of the Twelve through Galilean towns and villages; an evangelization in a field that is yet strange or hostile, a Home Mission upon a continually enlarging scale. Here also do the messengers of Christ go two and two, as it were

in remembrance of the word of the Preacher, Eccl. iv. 9, 10. According to the Lord's own word, vs. 18, their journey at the same time bears the character of a vigorous assault upon the powers of darkness; there is something moreover indescribably naïve and touching in the manner in which they reveal their joy over the success of their momentous undertaking. But especially is this new preaching a powerful voice of awakening for the lost sheep of the house of Israel to come to the Good Shepherd, and the Woe over towns in which such works were done was certainly doubly deserved.

3. The image of the genuine minister of the Gospel is, in the address of the Saviour to the Seventy, placed vividly before our eyes. The substance of His preaching is a message of peace, comp. Isa. lii. 7, which finds echo in the heart of the son of peace, and in his heart alone. The demeanor which becomes him is meekness, contentment, self-denial, on the one hand—see as an example of the manner in which the precepts here given were applied by Paul, 1 Cor. ix. 5; 2 Cor. x. 16; Rom. xv. 20—on the other hand a demeanor of dignity when despised and opposed. The authority which is bestowed upon him is, since he stands in the service of the truth, in a certain sense like that of the apostles, nay, like that of the Lord Himself, notwithstanding all other differences in office and sphere of activity. And his honor, which is continually unacknowledged by the world, will be brilliantly established by Him that hath sent him, when once the judgment upon the rejecter of the Gospel shall be revealed.

4. The enduring might which the Saviour has bestowed on His witnesses in the spiritual sphere is at the same time an indirect argument against the correctness of the limited view of those who would restrict the gift of miracles almost exclusively to the circle and the age of the Apostles; instead of believingly receiving the Saviour's word, John xiv. 12. Comp. the weighty dissertation of Tholuck upon the miracles of the Catholic Church, in the first part of his miscellaneous writings.

5. In the well-known letter of Publius Lentulus to the Roman Senate, which is alleged to contain a description of the person of the Saviour, there is contained among other things the testimony: *qui nunquam visus est ridere, flere autem sæpius.* To this rigoristic and ascetic view, what Luke here relates of the Saviour's joy of soul is strikingly opposed. Here at least His countenance is refulgent with inmost joy, His head He raises triumphantly towards Heaven, and from His whole being shines forth a glow of blessedness. The sublimity of this joy we feel the more, when we compare with it that of the Seventy. They rejoice in the great things, He in the good brought to pass; they have their joy directed to the outer, Jesus His to the moral world; they rejoice alone in the present, Jesus also in the past and the future; they are disposed to self-praise, Jesus to thankful adoration. Only once besides do we hear Him with such complete publicity glorify the name of the Father. It is just before the raising of Lazarus (John xi. 42), both times, therefore, when spiritually dead awake to higher life. The subject and the character of His joy is, therefore, a proof of the saying, John xiv. 9.

6. The utterance, "No one knows the Son save the Father," is one of the most convincing testimonies for the true Godhead of Christ. One who was only a created spirit or an immaculate man could not possibly without blasphemy against God testify this of Himself. If only the Father knows perfectly who the Son is, we must then give up all hope of searching out, on this side of the grave, so much of this depth that the object of faith shall have become *wholly* the object of the Christian Gnosis. Touching the Almighty, we cannot find Him out, Job xxxvii. 23. On the other hand, we must be careful to make a distinction between *cognitio vera et adæquata*, and doubt only of the latter and not of the former. It is therefore as over-precipitate as superficial when this saying of the Saviour has not seldom been used as a catchword in order to repress as impossible or unprofitable a more than superficial investigation of the person and work of the Saviour. The saying, "No one knows the Son but the Father," can at most be a result but never a hindrance of a renewed Christological investigation, and least of all a cloak for indifferentism or ignorantism. The remark of Otto Von Gerlach on Matt. xi. 27 is well worthy of being compared here.

7. The Gospel stands not below but above the understanding of the wise and prudent in their own eyes. One misuses the word of the Lord concerning babes and the simple if he reads therein an authorization of stupidity and narrowness, and a sentence of condemnation against science and a true Christian depth of apprehension. True wisdom, however, can only be that which is joined with child-like simplicity, and as true knowledge leads to faith, so can faith alone bring us to true science. It is, however, no shame but an honor to the Gospel that it can be nothing for those who will not learn but judge, will not humble themselves but bear rule, comp. 1 Cor. i. and ii.

8. "Rejoice that your names are written in heaven," a *dictum probans* for the doctrine of the Evangelical Church that a believer even in this life may be assured of his eternal salvation. When Möhler [the eminent Roman Catholic Symbolist] asserts that he "in the neighborhood of a man who without any restriction declared himself sure of his salvation should be in a high degree uneasy," nay, "that he could not repel the thought that there was something diabolical beneath this," he thereby affords us a deep glance into the comfortlessness of a heart which seeks the ultimate ground of its hope in self-righteousness [as many Protestants do, who agree with the Roman Catholic church in making their own assurance of salvation depend upon their attainments in holiness, instead of resting in simple faith in the consciousness that they have committed themselves to Christ.—C. C. S.]. but he shows at the same time that he has not comprehended the word of the Lord to the Seventy in its whole depth. It is well known that this, "Rejoice that your names are written in heaven," was the worthy answer of the dying Haller to the friends who congratulated him on the honor of a visit in his last hours from the Emperor Joseph II.

HOMILETICAL AND PRACTICAL.

The Saviour's work of love an unwearied and continual work of love.—The preaching of the word of the kingdom of Heaven must be continued in ever-increasing measure.—Even yet the Lord often sends forth His servants two and two.—Value and difficulty of collegial relations among the ministers of the Gospel.—The husbandry of God: 1. Great is the harvest; 2. few are the laborers; 3. God alone can restore the just relation between harvest and laborers.—God the Lord of the harvest, who 1. Determines the time of the harvest; 2. appoints the laborers for the harvest; 3. guards the success of the harvest; 4. deserves the thank-offering of the harvest.—Prayer to the Lord of the harvest: 1. Its contents; 2. its ground; 3. its blessing.—The vocation of the messengers of the Gospel on its bright and dark side; 1. Christ Himself sends them out, but, 2. as lambs in the midst of wolves.—The Christian freedom from care of those who serve the kingdom of Heaven.—The preaching of the Gospel at the same time a salutation of peace and a declaration of war.—Only the son of peace can receive and appropriate the salutation of peace. —The coming of the Gospel into the circle of domestic life.—"We seek not yours but you."—The fundamental features of a future Halieutics and Poimenics [or, in other words, of a theory of the two branches of the minister's work, the conversion of men as a fisher of souls, and the training of converts as a shepherd of souls.—C. C. S.] comprised in the instructions given to the Seventy.—The laborer is worthy of his hire: 1. However imperfect he be he certainly deserves it; 2. however late it may come he always receives it.—'Ιατρὸς γὰρ ἀνὴρ πολλῶν ἀντάξιος ἄλλων.—Even the severest utterance of the rejected witnesses of Christ may never bear the character of a personal vengeance.—Holy wrath and inexhaustible love united in the ambassadors of Christ. —The greater the privileges the greater the responsibility.—The wrath of the Lamb, Rev. vi. 16.— What the desolated cities of antiquity testify to unbelieving posterity.—A future judgment awaits even sinners already condemned.—Capernaum the image of unbelieving Christendom: 1. The darkness resting upon Capernaum; 2. the light rising upon Capernaum; 3. the enmity reigning in Capernaum; 4. the judgment passed upon Capernaum.—The Saviour regards the cause of His ambassadors as His own.— Whoever rejects the Gospel rejects not man but God. —Whoever as the servant of Christ seeks not his own honor, him, sooner or later, shall his Master bring to honor.

Whoever has gone forth into the service of the Lord owes Him first of all an account thereof.—Before the name of Jesus all the powers of darkness must bow. Satan's fall: 1. Perceived by Jesus; 2. effected by Jesus; 3. celebrated by Jesus.—The falling of Satan and the falling of lightning: 1. The height of both; 2. the quickness of both; 3. the depth of both.—The greatest triumphs over the might of darkness are known to the King alone, not to the servants. —Jesus, treading on serpents, gives the same power also to His church, Rom. xvi. 20.—Naught can harm him who harms not himself.—Dominion over the world of spirits, however desirable it may be, is yet not the deepest ground for the joy of the disciples of Jesus.—The highest eulogy: "Your names are written in Heaven:" 1. How it is to be understood; 2. how desirable it is; 3. how alone it is to be obtained,— The certainty of salvation: 1. Its only ground; 2. its all-surpassing worth.—Can even a name written in the book of life be blotted out of it again? Rev. iii. 5.

"In the same hour Jesus rejoiced in spirit:" 1. An example of the joy which the Lord sometimes experiences upon earth; 2. an image of the joy which He now experiences in Heaven; 3. a presage of the blessedness which He shall hereafter taste when the kingdom of God shall be fully perfected.—The joy of the Saviour and the joy of His people.—How true Christian joy elevates itself to praise and thanks.—The sovereignty of the Father of light: 1. The Father in Heaven at the same time Lord of Heaven and earth; 2. the Lord of Heaven and earth at the same time a heavenly Father.—The kingdom of God, now as ever, hidden from the wise and prudent, and revealed unto babes: 1. This *is* not different, *a*. in the days of the Saviour, *b*. in later ages, *c*. in our time; 2. this *cannot* be different, *a*. objective cause in the nature of the Gospel, *b*. subjective in the human heart, *c*. supernatural in the counsel of God; 3. this *may not* be different, for even in this way, *a*. the divinity of the Gospel is confirmed, *b*. the requirements of the Gospel are satisfied, *c*. the trial of the Gospel is assured.—God's good pleasure in concealing and revealing the truth of salvation: 1. An uncensurable, 2. an inalterable, 3. an adorable good pleasure.—Even though it appear enigmatical, yet must faith approve the good pleasure of the Father.—It is possible to be wise and prudent and at the same time to be a child and simple, 1 Cor. xiv. 2.—Not the developed understanding but the soul longing for salvation is the first point of attachment for the things of the kingdom of God.—The power bestowed on the Lord Christ by the Father: 1. An unlimited; 2. a legitimate; 3. a beneficent; 4. an ever-enduring power.—The whole unique relation between the Son and the Father: 1. How far it is the object of our faith; 2. how far it can be the object of our knowledge.—How: 1. The Son reveals to us the Father, but also, 2. the Father reveals to us the Son.—The relation between the Father and the Son: 1. The highest mystery; 2. a revealed mystery; 3. even after the revelation yet continually a partially concealed mystery.—The blessed lot of the sincere disciples of the Lord.—In Christ: 1. The highest expectation of antiquity fulfilled; 2. the highest ideal of mankind realized; 3. the highest revelation of the Godhead bestowed.—No prophet or king of the Ancient Covenant so blessed as the heir of the new.—In order to see that which is highest on earth, there is no need to be prophet or king, but only a disciple of Jesus.

STARKE:—HEDINGER:—For faithful teachers God must be entreated.—Faithful laborers in church and school grow not of themselves, nor are they taken from the trees; God gives and sends them.—Those who are sent of God must possess the qualities of sheep and lambs, 1 Tim. iii. 3.—OSIANDER:—Preachers should be content with little, and remain mindful of this, that the kingdom of God is not meat and drink, Rom. xiv. 17.—When the common usages of the country have nothing sinful in them, they are undoubtedly by all means to be observed.—*Nova Bibl. Tub.*:—Happy are they who are sons of peace, on whom rests the peace of the children of God, Gal. vi. 16.—Woe to the houses where the blessing brought turns back again.—"If we have sown spiritual things for you, is it a great matter if we shall reap your carnal things?" 1 Cor. ix. 11.—CRAMER:—In hell there will doubtless be grades of damnation, Luke xii. 47, 48.—QUESNEL:—This is a holy abyss of the judgment of God, that the Gospel is preached even to those who reject it, and that it has not been preached for those who would have repented, Rom. xi. 33.—*Nova Bibl. Tub.*:—By repentance one can avert from himself temporal and eternal destruction, 1 Kings xxi. 29; Jer. xxvi. 3; Jon. iii. 10.—The condition of very great exaltation is dangerous, for it is exposed to very heavy falls, Obadiah iv.—BRENTIUS:—Joy from divine blessings bestowed must keep within bounds, and lead to the watchword, Psalm cxv. 1.*—MAJUS:—The holy ministry has the destruction of the kingdom of Satan as its design.—CANSTEIN:—That God's children often rejoice more over lesser than greater heavenly benefits is a sign of their imperfection.—HEDINGER:—Not gifts but faith saves.—In the kingdom of God one has not only occasion to weep, but also heartily to rejoice over the goodness of God and the marvellous things which He does for the children of men.—OSIANDER:—Not all the wise are rejected, and not all the simple enlightened; they who lay off their wisdom and go to Christ to school shall be instructed unto the kingdom of Heaven.—CANSTEIN:—The natural knowledge of God is not enough to salvation, else had we needed no special revelation.—ZEISIUS:—Oh, what an admirable preëminence of the New Testament above the Old, but also much heavier condemnation of unthankful Christians than of the Jews, Heb. ii. 2.—BRENTIUS:—The fathers of the Old Testament were saved as much by the cross of Jesus Christ as we, only that for us the light shines clearer than for them, Acts xv. 11.

HEUBNER:—With Christ man can do more than he believes; our faintheartedness is often put to shame. How many simple missionaries accomplish by faith what the profoundest theologians without faith would not lay hand to.—Christ plainly took the kingdom of evil spirits for something real.—If we are purely bound to Christ no enemy is dangerous to us.—How different worldly and heavenly praise.—BENGEL:—How can one know whether his name is written in the book of Life? With this point one must not

[* The German here has *lösung*, which appears to be a misprint for "*losung*."—C. C. S.]

make the beginning of the salutary doctrine, which first brings forward repentance and faith, but make a conclusion thereunto, as the epistle of Paul to the Romans in particular exhibits. Only look to it that thou ever hold faithful to the name of the Lord Jesus Christ, for the rest let Him take care. If thy name appears with renown in human registers, that helps thee nothing, but hurts thee rather.—SCHLEIERMACHER:—Rejoice not over what you accomplish (Sermon 3, page 24), for the reason : 1. That it cannot be the standard of our own value ; 2. that it conflicts with love to judge any one according to this; 3. that we cannot always hold fast this joy.

VON GERLACH:—There comes the hour of fulfilment of all longings and hopes, as it has come for the world in Jesus Christ. What the prophets had portrayed in individual, ever-clearer traits of His image in their prophecies, this appeared in Him Himself in full glory. Thus could no prophet have conceived Him, and still less have portrayed Him. Although there is no doctrine of the New Testament, of which the beginnings were not already to be found in the Old, although everything concerning Christ has been said, scattered here and there ; yet who, before His appearance, could have had even a presentiment of this union of the highest, holiest, Divine majesty and the deepest lowliness of humility, of the most powerful might and the fiercest zeal with the stillest meekness and patience. Of the inestimable privileges of the true Christian, the word of Saint Bernard holds good:

Quocumque loco fuero,
Jesum meum desidero,
Quam lætus, quum invenero!
Quam felix, quum tenuero!

C. *A School of Love, of Faith, and of Prayer.* CH. X. 25—XI. 13.

1. The Good Samaritan (CH. X. 25-37).

(Vss. 23-27, Gospel for the 13th Sunday after Trinity.)

25 And, behold, a certain lawyer stood up, and tempted him [putting him to the
26 proof], saying, Master [Teacher], what shall I do to inherit eternal life? He said unto
27 him, What is written in the law? how readest thou? And he answering said, Thou shalt love the Lord thy God with all thy heart, and with all thy soul, and with all thy strength, and with all thy mind; and thy neighbour as thyself [Deut. vi. 5; Lev. xix.
28 18]. And he said unto him, Thou hast answered right: this do, and thou shalt live.
29 But he, willing to justify himself, said unto Jesus, And who is my neighbour?
30 And Jesus answering said, A certain *man* went down from Jerusalem to Jericho, and fell among thieves [robbers], which stripped him of his raiment, and wounded *him*, and
31 departed, leaving *him* half dead. And by chance there came down a certain priest that
32 way; and when he saw him, he passed by on the other side. And likewise a Levite [also], when he was at [having come to] the place, came and looked *on him*, and [and
33 seeing him] passed by on the other side. But a certain Samaritan, as he journeyed,
34 came where he was; and when he saw him, he had compassion *on him*, And went to *him*, and bound up his wounds, pouring in [on] oil and wine, and set him on his own
35 beast, and brought him to an inn, and took care of him. And on the morrow when he departed,[1] he took out two pence [denarii], and gave *them* to the host, and said unto him, Take care of him: and whatsoever thou spendest more, [I] when I come again,
36 I [om., I] will repay thee. Which now of these three, thinkest thou, was neighbour
37 unto him that fell among the thieves [robbers]? And he said, He that shewed mercy

CHAP. X. 25–37.   173

[τὸ ἔλεος, the merciful act] on him. Then [And²] said Jesus unto him, Go, and do thou likewise.

¹ Vs. 35.—'Εξελθών (vox molestissima, Schultz). It is possible that it was omitted on account of the following ἐκβαλών (Meyer), but more probable that it is an explicative addition, since the mention of the αὔριον would of itself direct attention to the continuance of the journey. [Om. B., D., L., Sin.; Tischendorf, Meyer, Alford retain it.—C. C. S.)
² Vs. 37.—Rec.: εἶπεν οὖν. The reasons for δέ preponderate.

EXEGETICAL AND CRITICAL.

Vs. 25. **A certain lawyer.**—According to Strauss we have here only a different tradition of the occurrence which is related by Matthew, xxii. 37–40, and Mark, xii. 28–34. But whoever compares the two accounts attentively will probably come with us to the conclusion, that Luke relates something entirely different. Although almost superfluous, compare moreover LANGE, *Leben Jesu*, ii. p. 1242.

Putting Him to the proof.—It is as if Luke would by the very commencement: καὶ ἰδού, draw our attention to the contrast between the joyful emotions of the circle of friends which had but just heard from Jesus' mouth words of approbation and joy, and the cold stranger who bestirs himself to prepare for the Master new snares. It is a νομικός, who is perhaps distinguished from the Pharisees in this (comp. Luke xi. 44, 45), that he, more than these, holds to the letter of the law of Moses; but in no case a Sadducee, or a Herodian, since his highest striving appears directed towards eternal life. He appears as an ἐκπειράζων, and as this word is always used in an unfavorable sense, we are at least to assume that he wished to find out whether the Saviour also would teach anything which was in conflict with the law of Moses. His question springs therefore from a very different source from that of the rich young man, Matt. xix. 16, and without doubt he expects a very different answer from this one, which, on the position of the law, was the only possible one. He is first put to shame by the very fact that the Saviour gives him to hear nothing strange, but simply that which was perfectly familiar.

Vs. 27. **Thou shalt love.**—It speaks perhaps favorably for this νομικός that he does not name one or several special precepts, but immediately brings forward the spirit and main substance of the law, which the Saviour, in a case not wholly dissimilar, was obliged first to remind the inquirer of, Matt. xxii. 38, 39. So much the sadder was it here that with so clear a knowledge of the law, there was joined an utter lack of self-knowledge.

Vs. 29. **Willing to justify himself.**—Perhaps the scribe took the reply, "this do," as an indirect reproach that he, to his own amazement, had not yet done it, and now apparently his conscience begins to speak. But he will justify himself, inasmuch as he intimates that he, in this respect at least, had already fulfilled the requirement of the law, unless it were that Jesus perhaps by the words "thy neighbor" might have some different meaning from himself. But better still, we are perhaps to conceive the matter thus: if the answer was so simple as it appeared to be from the words of our Saviour, there might undoubtedly be need of an excuse that he had approached Jesus with so trifling a question. He wishes, therefore, by this more particular statement to give the Saviour to feel that precisely this is the great question, namely, whom he is to regard as his neighbor and whom not; and as to this, our Lord now, in the immediately following parable, gives him a definite exposition.

Vs. 30. **From Jerusalem to Jericho.**—According to Lange, the journeying of the Saviour in Samaria, and the sending of the Seventy into the towns and villages of the Samaritans, had possibly offended this scribe, and our Lord, by the delineation here following, wishes indirectly to shame this narrow-heartedness. It may also be conjectured that our Lord on His own journey through Samaria towards Jerusalem was at this very moment on the way between Jericho and the capital, and had therefore chosen the scene of the parable precisely *in loco*. If we now add to this that the village, vs. 38, was Bethany, whither He must come before He entered the city, we then obtain at least some conception of the course of this journey of our Saviour.

And fell among robbers.—The wilderness between Jericho and Jerusalem was known as insecure. See JOSEPHUS, *De Bello Judaico*, iv. 8, 3, and HIERONYMUS, *ad Jerem.* iii. 2. Wholly encircled by robbers (περιέπεσεν), he addresses himself fruitlessly to defence, and remains lying wounded on the road, while they, with his garments and the remaining booty, take themselves off. Already half dead, he must infallibly expire if help does not with all speed appear for him.

Vs. 31. **By chance.**—"*Multæ occasiones bonæ latent sub iis, quæ fortuita videntur. Scriptura nil describit temere, ut fortuitum; hoc loco opponitur necessitudini.*" Bengel.—**A priest—a Levite.**—It is well known that at Jericho many priests had their abode, who, when their turn came, discharged the service of the sanctuary at Jerusalem. Commonly they appear to have chosen the longer but safer road by Bethlehem, so that it was an exception when they travelled through the wilderness. It here brings into so much the more striking light their want of feeling, that the two do not pass on without first having come nearer and, more or less exactly, taken note of the state of the case. This inspection, however, merely persuades them of the greatness of the danger that awaits them also if they delay even for an instant, and therefore they make haste to quit the way of blood as quickly as possible. Neither the voice of humanity, nor that of nationality, nor that of religion, speaks so loudly to their heart as the desire of self-preservation.

Vs. 33. **A certain Samaritan, as he journeyed.**—From the very choice of this example, it is evident that the injured man was certainly no heathen (Olshausen), but a Jew, in whom, however, his benefactor views, before all, an unhappy *man*.—**Oil and wine.**—Customary remedies, see Isa. i. 6 and WETSTEIN, *ad loc.*—**He had compassion on him.**—"*Animi motus sincerus præcedit, quem sequuntur facta, animo congruentia.*" Grotius. Mark the beautiful climax. First the compassionate heart, then the helping hand, next the ready foot, finally the true-hearted charge.

Vs. 35. **He took out two denarii.**—'Ἐκβαλών, "graphic: out of a girdle," Meyer. He leaves the unhappy man in rest, but takes care also that no difficulty shall arise to him after his departure on the score of payment. From his promise to make good what may be lacking on his return, we may perhaps draw the inference that the ὁδεύων expresses not only the *conditio*, but also the *habitus*, of the Samaritan.

Vs. 37. **The merciful act**, τὸ ἔλεος.—The definite species of compassion, that is, which was described in the parable. It has been often remarked that the scribe by this circumlocutory answer wished to avoid mentioning the name of Samaritan. *See,* *e. g.,* BENGEL, *ad loc.* So has Luther also written in his *Kirchenpostille, ad loc.*: "Will not name the Samaritan by name, the haughty hypocrite."

DOCTRINAL AND ETHICAL.

1. By the question, "How readest thou?" the Saviour ascribes to the law absolute authority in the answer of the question proposed by the scribe. Here also the same principle as in John x. 34–36, and elsewhere. ¡ After such declarations from the Saviour, the answer to the inquiry hardly continues difficult, what authority must be ascribed to the Scripture in the decision of the highest question of life for mankind.

2. The answer given by the scribe stood, at least as far as concerns Deut. vi. 5, upon the broad phylactery which was worn by the Jews, and so far it may be said that this τοῦτο ποίει is to be taken as having been uttered by Jesus δεικτικῶς. As to the rest, it need not surprise us that the Saviour here gives another answer than, *e. g.,* John vi. 29. From the point of view of the scribe, the requirement of faith, if made to him would have been unintelligible. It is moreover literally true, that if any one indeed so fulfilled the law that his act in God's eyes really bore the stamp of perfection, he would certainly enter into life. It is only if the scribe had answered that it was impossible to him to fulfil the law as God requires on account of his sin and weakness; it is only then that he would have been receptive of further instruction. The Saviour places first precisely the duty required by the law, in its full emphasis, in order to bring him to a knowledge of himself, and to give him a clear insight into his own imperfection in contrast with the supreme ideal. This conversation is, therefore, a striking proof of the deep didactic wisdom of the Saviour.

3. The parable of the Good Samaritan is certainly one of the most beautiful, considered from an æsthetic point of view. The antithesis of the Samaritan on the one hand, of the Jew, the priest, and the Levite on the other; the extended description of his work of love in its full and entire compass; the perfect completion of the picture by the trait at the end,—all this contributes to exalt the graphic vigor of the portraiture. No wonder that this parable has become one of the most popular, and that it has been seriously inquired whether here also an occurrence from actual life may not have been related, of which the Saviour in some way or other had obtained knowledge. This view, however (Grotius a. o.), natural as it is, appears nevertheless hardly admissible, for the reason that the Saviour was not wont to bring up without necessity, and in their absence, the *chronique scandaleuse* of the priests and Levites.

4. The purpose of the parable would be understood amiss, if we thought it was intended to serve directly to commend the duty of love to enemies. The Saviour does not once say that the object of the love here exhibited was a Jew, but only that it was a man, and will give the inquirer to feel that the word "neighbor" must be applied in a far wider sense than only that of Friend, Companion, or Countryman. It is the more beautiful that the Saviour makes no other than a Samaritan the type of the genuine love of man, if we consider that it was very shortly before that He had experienced the intolerance of the Samaritans in its full strength. Ch. ix. 51, 56.

5. Here, however, there is a special distinction to be made between Christian love of the *brethren*, which is commended in John xiii. 34, and the general love of our *neighbor*, which is commended in this passage. The first has for its object the fellow-believer, the love of Christ for its standard, and faith on Him as its condition. The second embraces all men, loves them as one's self, and is grounded in the natural relation in which all the sons and daughters of Adam stand to each other as members of one great family here on earth. It is not uncommon that those in the right way, zealous for that which is specifically Christian, give themselves less concern regarding this general human duty. It is, therefore, well worth the trouble to consider somewhat more particularly the portrait here drawn by the Lord. We see then at the same time, also, why this parable is found in the Pauline and broadly human Gospel of Luke.

6. The *element* of the general love of man is that most pure feeling which does not ask, "Who is my neighbor?" but in every man beholds a brother, and in the unhappy man first of all (ἐσπλαγχνίσθη). Its *extent*, therefore, is entirely unlimited; it does not ask whether it has to do with a Jew, Samaritan, or heathen, but only whether it has to do with a man, as such. Its *tokens* reveal themselves in unrestricted helpfulness (oil and wine), self-denial (giving up of his own beast), heartiness (the commendation to the host), and continuance (afterwards as well as now he will pay all). And its *reward* is, besides the approving voice of conscience and the involuntary praise even of those far differently minded, above all, the testimony of the Lord, who sets such a deed of love before others as their example. A whole chapter of Christian ethics is, therefore, here written down in a few words.

[GR. There is one thing to be taken note of in connection with the parable of the Good Samaritan, which we are apt to neglect, and thereby to lose much of its force. We are so much accustomed to look upon the Good Samaritan as a model of excellence, as to forget that he was a heretic, not in the Jewish notion merely, but in reality; and that our Lord, in His conversation with the Samaritan woman, John iv. 22, distinctly and severely condemns his heresy. This parable, therefore, teaches us not only that true love to man knows no distinction of nationality or creed, but that this genuine philanthropy may be exhibited by one involved in grave speculative errors, and neglected by those whose speculative belief is sound. We have here Heterodoxy with Humanity, and Orthodoxy without Humanity. Our Lord has shown elsewhere, abundantly, that He has no thought of conniving at Heterodoxy, or of disparaging Orthodoxy. Only, He teaches that Humanity is better than Orthodoxy, if only one may be had, and that Inhumanity is worse than Heterodoxy, if one must be endured.—C. C. S.]

7. If we inquire who has perfectly set forth the character of the Good Samaritan, and perfectly accomplished his work, then we know of only one—our Lord. So far we may say that He has depicted the

portrait of perfect philanthropy with traits from His own immediate self-consciousness.

8. What has been hitherto said, already prepares the way for an answer to the question, how far the Christian homilete is at liberty to view in the Samaritan the image of the Saviour. As is well known, this was done very early by many of the ancient fathers, and by Luther and Melanchthon, and among the moderns by Stier and others [Alford]. This has been, on the one hand, powerfully defended, and it has been asserted that if we stop at the common conception, "it is hard to find a Christian theme" in this whole Pericope (Cl. Harms). On the other side, it has been wholly condemned as pious fantasy, and certainly not with injustice, if we remember how every particular of the parable has been expounded even to trifling, so that, for instance, Jerusalem must denote Paradise,—Jericho, the world,—the lodging, the Church,—the two denarii, the two sacraments. This can only be reconciled when one knows how to make a distinction between historical *exposition* and practical *application* of the instruction here given. From the position of the former it is entirely inadmissible to say that the Saviour had here the intention to designate Himself as the Redeemer of man from sin and misery. No, the purpose is no other than to portray actual love of man in the sphere of actual life; this must, therefore, be and remain the chief point. But if now it is asked, in conclusion, in whom the ideal of the highest love of man is perfectly realized, then it is almost impossible to overlook here the image of the Saviour, and to pass over in silence what He, the Heavenly Samaritan, has, become for Humanity sick unto death, already given up by priest and Levite, &c. For the love of Christ is not only the type, but is also no less the most powerful impulse to such an active love of our neighbor as is here required. A distinguished example of the treatment of this parable, in which the ethical and the Christological element alike receive full consideration, has been given by A. Vinet in the dissertation: *Le Samaritain*, in his *Nouveaux discours sur quelques sujets religieux*. Thus does this parable become in a certain sense the sublimest allegory of Sin on the one hand, and Grace on the other. Comp. THOLUCK, *Die wahre Weihe des Zweiflers*, p. 63, and LISCO, *ad loc.*, p. 239. It is, however, self-evident, that we are not therefore permitted to build on individual details a doubtful dogmatic view (*c. g.*, Semipelagianism on the expression that the man lay *half* dead on the way), and that in a tropical use of it the great central thought must be adhered to, without pressing the particulars overstrongly. A certain spiritual tact will here show the way better than could be done by definite rules, and this of itself already introduces the

HOMILETICAL AND PRACTICAL.

The way to life the highest question of life.—Jesus the best guide on the way to eternal life.—A just question proposed from a perverted motive.—Necessary and unnecessary questions in the sphere of religion and of life.—The highest questions of life satisfactorily resolved in God's word.—Not "What thinkest thou?" but "How readest thou?"—To the Law and to the Testimony, Isa. viii. 20.—The requirement of love to God: 1. The extent, 2. the justice, 3. the reward of this requirement.—Whoever actually fulfilled God's commandment, would actually also live. —Hopeless efforts to justify one's self against the Lord.—The question: "Who is my neighbor?" 1. Its high moment; 2. its only answer; 3. its manifold application.—A man plunged by men into wretchedness.—Stand we not every hour in jeopardy? 1 Cor. xv. 30.—The value of apparently fortuitous occurrences. —A priest without love.—The might of selfishness: it is stronger than the voice *a.* of humanity, *b.* of patriotism, *c.* of religion.—Faithful Samaritan service. —There is more evil, but also more good than we know.—The attentive look, the compassionate heart, the helpful hand, the willing foot, the open purse.— Service of love: 1. Willingly begun, 2. unweariedly continued, 3. never completed.—The debt of love, Rom. xiii. 8: 1. A measureless debt, 2. an undeniable debt, 3. a blessed debt.—True love gives not only its own, but itself wholly.—Love not in word, neither in tongue, but in deed and in truth, 1 John iii. 18.— True love of our neighbor: 1. Its motive; 2. its character: open-handedness, self-denial, heartiness, steadfastness; 3. its reward.—The Good Samaritan service of the disciples of the Saviour.—The Good Samaritan the image of the Saviour.—How He, the Saviour of sinners, still, 1. Lights upon the same misery; 2. expresses the same compassion; 3. prepares the same redemption; 4. demands the same temper of mind as is set forth in this parable.—Who, then, is our neighbor?—Not knowing, but doing, the first requirement of the Lord.—As this scribe, so are, sooner or later, all put to shame who will take Jesus in their snares.

STARKE:—As the question, so the answer.—CRAMER:—The law aims high and demands the whole heart, &c.—QUESNEL:—Piety consists not in having, but in doing.—*Nova Bibl. Tub.*:—Oh! the shameful priests, who pass by the poor.—Ecclesiastics that have not the Spirit, are bare, fruitless trees, Judges ix. 14.—True love takes on itself with much danger the necessity of the saints.—Compassion has so bright a brilliancy that it shines even in the eyes of enemies.—MAJUS:—No one must be ashamed to follow even simple and mean people in good.—LISCO: —Christian love of our neighbor should be: 1. Universal; 2. self-sacrificing.—The active compassion of the citizens of the kingdom: 1. Its sphere of activity; 2. its nature; 3. its portion.—HEUBNER:—Man does not lack so much the knowledge of his duty as the will for it.—How little is close contact with, and administration of, that which is holy often wont to sanctify the heart. How deep has the priesthood often sunk!—How often have the followers of the true religion been excelled by professors of false religions! —Love seeks, where its means are not sufficient, to win others also to its ends.

On the Pericope:— HEUBNER:—How Jesus demands true love of man: 1. By His example; 2. by the most perfect doctrine.—The peculiarity of Christian love of our neighbor: 1. Sources, 2. manifestations.—The double eye of the Christian: 1. The eye of faith, vss. 23, 24; 2. the eye of love, vss. 25-35. The Christian is not to be one-eyed.—Love, the true proof of faith.—PALMER:—How love again makes good what sin has ruined.—FRCHS:—Who is counted blessed by the Lord, is truly blessed.—SCHULTZ:— How we in this world can become partakers of eternal life: 1. If we see that which Christ has revealed, vss. 23, 21; 2. if we so love as Christ requires, vss. 25-35; 3. if we so work as Christ has enjoined, vss. 36, 37.—Happy he, 1. Who is a Samaritan; 2. happy he who finds one!—VON HARLESS:—Good Samaritan love: 1. Whom it profits; 2. how it manifests itself; 3. whence it comes.— FLOREY :—The glory of true love: 1. It inquires not, vss. 25, 29; 2. it hesitates not, vs. 33; 3. it is not afraid; 4. it tarries not, vs. 34; 5. it willingly sacrifices, and leaves nothing unfinished, vs. 35.— F. ARNDT :—Active, helpful love. —BURK :—How we without the Lord Jesus nowhere, but with Him everywhere, may see our way. The Pericope is admirably adapted for missionary sermons also.

---

2. Mary and Martha (Vss. 38–42).

38 Now it came to pass, as they went [were journeying], that he entered into a certain
39 village: and a certain woman named Martha received him into her house. And she
40 had a sister called Mary, which also sat at Jesus' feet, and heard his word. But Martha was cumbered about much serving, and came to him, and said, Lord, dost thou not care
41 that my sister hath left me to serve alone? bid her therefore that she help me. And [But] Jesus [the Lord¹] answered and said unto her, Martha, Martha, thou art careful and
42 troubled [or, anxious and perplexed] about many things: But one thing is needful;² and Mary hath chosen that good part, which shall not be taken away from her.

¹ Vs. 41.—The reading ὁ κύριος has not only the authority of B., L., [Cod. Sin.,] in its favor, but also the connection, and the *usus loquendi* of Luke in many other passages. [*Rec.* supported by Lachmann, Tregelles, Alford. The other by Tischendorf.—C. C. S.]
² Vs. 42.—"The reading ολίγων δὲ ἐστιν χρεία ἢ ἑνός (B., C.¹, L., 1, 33, Copt., Æth., some fathers, [Cod. Sin.,] has arisen out of understanding the answer as referring to a dish" [!!!].

EXEGETICAL AND CRITICAL.

Vs. 38. **Now it came to pass.**—In view of the indefiniteness of this beginning, there is as little reason for the assertion that this event took place immediately after the discourse with the scribe as for assuming that it did not take place for some time after. Here also it appears plainly enough that Luke does not arrange the event with a strict chronology.

Into a certain village.—If we assume that all related by Luke from chap. ix. 51 to xix. 27, occurred during one and that the last journey to Jerusalem, then unquestionably there is room for doubt whether the here-named κώμη is Bethany, and we must rather suppose (Meyer) that Luke speaks here of one of the villages of Galilee. But we know not what should hinder us from distributing the historical matter of this narrative of travel between two or three journeys to feasts, so that the present one should be about to end very soon with the feast of Tabernacles, which was near at hand, John vii. And if this is so, we can then very well imagine that the Saviour had now behind Him the boundary between Samaria and Judæa, and had tarried yet a day at Bethany before He went up ὡς ἐν κρυπτῷ to the feast, John vii. 10. So taken, therefore, Luke transports us on to the same ground which we, guided by John in his 11th chapter, afterwards tread, and it at once appears that the brief portraiture of character in the text is an indirect, psychological, but powerful argument for the truth of the Johannean representation. This proof is by no means weakened by the fact that Luke makes no mention whatever of Lazarus (Strauss), for having in view only the difference between the two sisters, he had not the least occasion to speak of the brother also. It still remains remarkable that Luke describes the character of Martha and Mary wholly in the same manner as John; nor is it at all proved that Lazarus inhabited the same house with his sisters. As to the locality of Bethany itself, comp. WINER *in voce*.

Into her house.—The care of the entertainment appears to have been assumed by Martha, perhaps the elder of the two sisters, while it is wholly unproved that she was a widow (Grotius), and had been formerly married to Simon the leper (Paulus). That Jesus now appeared for the first time in this family, and that therefore the lovely beginning of the friendship of the Saviour with this domestic circle is portrayed, Luke does not tell us. So active a hostess, so deeply interested a friend, as Martha, would certainly have received Him as joyfully, even if His arrival had no longer had the surprise of novelty. In hearty and affectionate zeal, the best that the house can afford is brought forth in order right worthily to receive the beloved Guest. Martha knows not how to make her entertainment choice enough; she lacks hands for it; she wants to give the meal a thoroughly festal air. Is it a wonder that she took offence at Mary's inactivity?

Vs. 39. **Mary ... at Jesus' feet.**—There is not yet a reference to reclining at table (Paulus and Von Ammon), for the meal is not yet prepared, but a sitting like that of the disciples at the feet of the Master, as Paul afterwards—[Was it not at this very time?—C. C. S.]—sat at the feet of Gamaliel. In John xi. 20 also, Mary is represented as seated, in contrast with the unquiet, busy Martha.

Vs. 40. **Lord, dost Thou not care.**—What is censurable in Martha's behavior consists especially in this, that she, in a difference with her sister, seeks to win the Saviour as her confederate.—**Hath left me to serve alone,** κατέλιπεν.—Perhaps Mary had at the beginning, before the Saviour's arrival, also assisted in the domestic labors, but soon afterwards had seen that she could now use the precious time more profitably, and therefore left her sister. Martha demands that the Saviour shall send Mary back again to her post, which she has left too early, since she can no longer be spared there.

Vs. 41. **Martha, Martha.**—"Jesus' reply is not to be taken in the earnest tone of preaching, but in the half jest [a hardly appropriate term.—C. C. S.] of friendly humanity." The double utterance of the name, as also afterwards, "Simon, Simon," "Saul, Saul," is, however, meant to express the quiet dissatisfaction of the Saviour, not so much with the act as rather with the disposition and temper of Martha.—**About many things.**—It is not at all necessary to insert here any word having reference to food or to the meal.

Vs. 42. **But one thing is needful,** ἑνὸς δέ ἐστι χρεία.—The explanations of this expression would have been far less divergent if the distinct inquiry had been proposed: Needful—for what? The answer can, according to the connection, only be this: "To receive the Lord aright;" for this was after all the main thing in Martha's feelings, and even Mary also, little occupied as she appeared, must have been anything but indifferent. But for that, said the Saviour, "Not much," but "one thing is needful."—All explanations must be rejected which by the ἑνὸς will have us understand only one dish, or anything else than that which the Saviour Himself, a moment afterwards, names the good part, κατ' ἐξοχήν. The ἕν is plainly = ἡ ἀγαθὴ μερίς. And what, according to that, is the one thing that is needful in order rightly to receive the Saviour? The disposition which Mary was manifesting at this moment, the sitting at the feet of Jesus, the receptivity for hearing and laying up the words of eternal life. Where Jesus comes, He comes to give, and where, therefore, there is a receptivity of faith for the spiritual good which He bestows, there is He at the same time received according to His own will, in the best manner. The Saviour does not say that Martha was wholly lacking in this disposition; she also was a disciple and friend; but He gives her to feel that she might incur the danger, amid all the bustle and tumult of life, of losing this temper of mind. In contrast with this stands the prerogative of Mary, whose part shall not be taken away from her. Her sister is not to call it in question, and if she remains of the same mind as now, her good part will also remain for her an imperishable one. "By ἥτις, which does not = ἥ, what follows is marked as belonging to the essence of the ἀγαθὴ μερίς, *quippe quæ.*" Meyer.

One must certainly view this narrative with very singular eyes, if he is disposed, with SCHWEGLER, *Nachapost Zeitalter,* ii. p. 52, to remark here an emphasized contrast between the Jewish and the Pauline Christianity, which are here, according to him, both presented, and of which, according to this, the latter was praised by Jesus. If the little narrative had been invented with such an intention, then without doubt the censure which Martha has to hear, would have turned out much stronger. For such an arbitrary fancy, we can merely give our opponent a "Duly received." Tholuck.

DOCTRINAL AND ETHICAL.

1. It is a view as incorrect as superficial to wish to regard Martha as the type of an earthly-minded woman, and Mary as the type of a heavenly-minded disciple of the Saviour. It is, therefore, also amiss to understand by that one thing which is needful, the care for eternal things in an entirely general sense, as if this was to be found in Mary alone, and was wholly neglected by Martha. Both—this must always be first held fast—are friends and disciples of Christ, whose heartfelt pleasure it is to serve Him according to their best ability, only that in relation to the manner how this must be done, each has her own idea. Martha is of the opinion that the Saviour would be best served by a carefully prepared entertainment; Mary, longing for salvation, hears the words of His mouth. With Martha the pleasure of giving Him much is preëminent; Mary feels the necessity of receiving much. With Martha, productivity, with Mary, receptivity, stands in the foreground. Martha is the Peter, Mary the John, among the female disciples of Christ. Both have, therefore, their peculiar calling and special Charisma. In Martha, the fact is not in itself censured that she will approve her love by a carefully prepared entertainment, if she only take care that the higher things also do not take harm by this. What is amiss in her consists rather in this, that she demands that Mary shall become like her, instead of recognizing that her sister in a certain relation is right, nay more, is in the enjoyment of a still higher privilege; for with all her attachment to the Saviour, Martha yet lacks that composed calmness of soul which can alone make her receptive for intimate and abiding communion with Jesus, which hitherto had only become Mary's inestimable portion.

2. Martha is not the type of earthly-minded friends of the world, but the type of numerous Christians, who work restlessly for the cause of the Saviour and their own salvation, but forget the personal possession and enjoyment of Christ for and in themselves. Mary stands before us, on the other hand, as a lovely symbol of those blessed ones who have found rest with Him, and therein possess as well the ground of the highest blessedness, as also the activity most pleasing to Him. The heart of the former is often as a sea which the storms have too greatly agitated for it to be able clearly to reflect the image of the Sun, while with the second the light of heaven shines upon a still, clear, watery mirror. Here also does Tersteegen's word hold good: "Thou must not bind thyself so much to form and manner. One is not continually seeking God. One must forsooth also find Him. Whoever is not in the search, he runs and works much; who hath found Him, enjoys and works quietly." [*Du musst dich nicht so sehr an Form und Weisen binden. Man suchet Gott nicht stets, man muss ihn ja auch finden. Wer noch im Suchen ist, der läuft und wirket viel. Wer ihn gefunden hat, geniesst und wirket still.*] The first character predominates in the Roman Catholic, the other in the Evangelical Church. In its degeneracy, the Martha character becomes proud work-holiness, the Mary nature, on the other hand, slothful quietism. But if they are sanctified by faith both have their right; although without doubt the latter stands higher, yet both have in the kingdom of God their value, and may develop themselves independently beside each other, without any necessity that the one individuality should be suppressed or absorbed by the other. The more intimately the zealous Martha's hand is united with the composed, quiet Mary's heart, so much the nearer does one come to the ideal of a harmonious Christian life.

3. Mary also would have something one-sided, if she regarded every work of Martha without restriction as below her dignity. The two sides of character represented by the two, activity and passivity, direction towards the external and towards the internal, the practical and the more contemplative temper, spontaneity and receptivity, love and faith, unwearied activity and unmovable rest, we find them in the

most perfect manner united in the perfect Son of Man, the God-man.

HOMILETICAL AND PRACTICAL.

Jesus the best friend of the family: 1. He heightens its joy; 2. He softens its sorrow; 3. He sanctifies the duty of the calling; 4. He strengthens its union; 5. He conducts towards the most exalted destiny in the domestic life of His people.—The right receiving of the Saviour.—The true service of the Lord consists in this, that we allow ourselves to be served by Him. —Mary and Martha, two grand forms of the Christian life, in their different relation to Him.—Great difference of character often with unity of principle and endeavor.—*Non multa sed multum.*—Much is not enough, but enough is much.—How sad it is when Christians reciprocally accuse each other instead of being helpers of their mutual joy.—How the Saviour, 1. Compassionately hears; 2. seriously answers the complaints of His people; 3. makes them serviceable for their own amendment.—One thing is needful: 1. In order rightly to employ the time of life; 2. in order rightly to enjoy the joy of life; 3. in order rightly to endure the burdens of life; 4. in order rightly to await the end of life.—The good part: 1. Which cannot, 2. may not, 3. will not be taken away.—Jesus the defender of His misunderstood friends.

STARKE:—J. HALL:—The female sex also does Christ esteem, and He will gladly enter into the house of their heart if they will only receive Him.—

Blessed is the family when all with one accord are knit together in entertaining the Lord Christ.— Christians must be hospitable, Heb. xiii. 2.—MAJUS: —A soul eager to learn the heavenly truth must have rest from earthly business and be humble, especially if it will learn.—LANGII *Op.:*—If our mode of life brings much distraction with it, we have the more cause often to collect ourselves therefrom, in order to enter into a *Sabbatismum sacrum,* into secret converse with God.

HEUBNER:—Two different kinds of love towards Jesus, a more natural and a more holy one.—The preëminence of the *vita contemplativa* above the *activa.*—How many learned, subtle theologians are like Martha—take care and trouble for the merest trifles, while the substance escapes their attention.— DRÆSEKE: a Sermon, 1824. Jesus and the Sisters of Bethany (one-sided apology for Martha).—THEREMIN: —The brother and sisters whom Jesus loved.— SCHMIDT:—One thing is needful: 1. What the many things are, about which man strives in vain; 2. what the one thing is which is needful, and how with this one thing all things fall to our lot.—J. MULLER:—The true relation to our earthly occupations of the care for celestial things.—ARNDT: —Jesus the family friend without compare, because He, 1. feels Himself happy in this domestic circle; 2. makes it happy.—GEROK:—The good part which our Evangelical Church has chosen.—Comp. also the beautiful hymn *Eins ist Noth, ach Herr dies eine,* and the Essay of F. W. Krummacher upon Mary and Martha, in PIPER's *Evang. Kalender,* 1851, p. 74 *seq.*

---

3. Lord, Teach us to Pray (CH. XI. 1–13).
(In part parallel to Matt. vi. 9-13; vii. 7-11.)

1 And it came to pass, that, as he was praying in a certain place, when he ceased, one of his disciples said unto him, Lord, teach us to pray, as John also taught his dis-
2 ciples. And he said unto them, When ye pray, say, Our [om., Our¹] Father which art in heaven [om., which art in heaven], Hallowed be thy name. Thy kingdom come.
3 Thy will be done, as in heaven, so in earth [omit this sentence²]. Give us day by day
4 our daily bread. And forgive us our sins; for we [ourselves, αὐτοί] also forgive every one that is indebted to us. And lead us not into temptation; but deliver us from evil
5 [omit this clause³].—And he said unto them, Which of you shall have a friend, and
6 shall go unto him at midnight, and say unto him, Friend, lend me three loaves; For a friend of mine in his journey [from a journey, transf. after is come] is come to me, and
7 I have nothing to set before him? And he from within shall answer and say, Trouble me not: the door is now shut, and my children are with me in bed; I cannot rise and
8 give thee.⁴ I say unto you, Though he will not rise and give him, because he is his friend, yet because of his importunity [lit., shamelessness, ἀναίδειαν] he will rise and
9 give him as many [*loaves*] as he needeth. And I say unto you, Ask, and it shall be
10 given you; seek, and ye shall find; knock, and it shall be opened unto you. For every one that asketh receiveth; and he that seeketh findeth; and to him that knock-
11 eth it shall be opened. If a son shall ask bread of any of you that is a father, will he
12 give him a stone? or if *he ask* a fish, will he for a fish give him a serpent? Or if he
13 shall ask an egg, will he offer him a scorpion? If ye then, being evil, know how to give good gifts unto your children; how much more shall *your* heavenly Father give ⁵ the Holy Spirit to them that ask him?

¹ Vs. 2.—*Rec.:* Πάτερ ἡμῶν ὁ ἐν τοῖς οὐρανοῖς. [Ἡμῶν ὁ ἐν τοῖς οὐρανοῖς omitted by Tischendorf, Meyer, Bleek, Tregelles, Alford, as formerly by Mill, Bengel, Wetstein, &c.; supported by B., Cod. Sin. (and L. after ἡμῶν), several cursives, the Vulgate, some MSS. of the Itala, and Origen once.—C. C. S.]

CHAP. XI. 1-13.

[² Vs. 2.—The same critics approve this omission, supported by B., L. (Cod. Sin. inserts the sentence), 2 cursives, all the manuscripts of Luke compared by Origen, the Vulgate, the Armenian version, the Corbeian Itala, and Tertullian, Jerome, and Augustine. Lachmann, who otherwise has the Received Text, brackets the words ὡς ἐν οὐρανῷ καὶ ἐπὶ γῆς.—C. C. S.]

³ Vs. 4.—*Rec.:* ἀλλὰ ῥῦσαι ἡμᾶς ἀπὸ τοῦ πονηροῦ. All three additions are, as it appears, taken from the perfect redaction of the Lord's Prayer in Matthew, while there are no arguments of sufficient weight to establish their genuineness in Luke. Respecting the state of the question, see TISCHENDORF *ad locum.* (The same critics support this omission who approve the two former ones. It has also the authority of B., L., 10 cursives, Vulgate, Coptic, and Armenian versions, Tertullian or Marcion, Jerome, Augustine. It is easy to see how, if these clauses were originally wanting in Luke, they might have been supplied afterwards from Matthew, to reduce to uniformity the two forms of the Lord's Prayer, but if they had been original with Luke, no motive could be assigned for their omission. According to the overwhelming weight of critical opinion, therefore, the Lord's Prayer, as given in Luke, should read thus: *Father, Hallowed be Thy name: Thy kingdom come: Give us day by day our daily bread: And forgive us our sins, for we also forgive every one that is indebted to us: And lead us not into temptation.*—C. C. S.]

[⁴ Vs. 7.—Van Oosterzee renders this verse as a question: "*Would he then?*" &c., in which, however, he is not supported by critical authority. The sentence, as Meyer remarks, begins as if to end thus: *Would he not be answered: Trouble me not?* &c. Nevertheless, *I say*, &c., but the length of the intervening sentence interrupts the construction.—C. C. S.]

[⁵ Vs. 13.—Ὁ Πατὴρ ὁ ἐξ οὐρανοῦ δώσει. The language of this passage is very closely moulded on that of Matthew, and, as Bleek remarks, ὁ ἐξ οὐρανοῦ δώσει is to be regarded as a contraction of ὁ ἐν οὐρανῷ δώσει ἐξ οὐρανοῦ.—C. C. S.]

EXEGETICAL AND CRITICAL.

Vs. 1. **In a certain place.**—The place is not more particularly designated by Luke, but if we may allow play to conjecture, the school of prayer was opened in the neighborhood of the same place in which the school of faith had lately been opened, namely, Bethany; for Luke attaches this account immediately to the domestic scene in the house of Mary and Martha, and since from other passages it is known that the Saviour was especially accustomed to pray on the summits of mountains, we are almost spontaneously brought to think here of the Mount of Olives, the subsequent theatre of His conflict and of His coronation (comp. ch. xxi. 37). That the historical trait, Luke xi. 1, has been invented by the Evangelists merely in order to find a suitable occasion for the communication of the Lord's Prayer (Strauss), is an unsupported conjecture. Do we not know from other passages that our Saviour was often accustomed to seclude Himself for solitary prayer, that John had actually taught his disciples to pray (Luke v. 33), and that some of these disciples had passed over to Jesus, and might yet very well remember this fact?

Vs. 2. **Father.**—First of all the question is whether the Saviour gave the precept of the most perfect prayer twice or only once. From internal grounds, the latter appears to us more probable, and we therefore believe that not Matthew but Luke has communicated the same in its original historical connection. If the Saviour had already communicated the Lord's Prayer in the Sermon on the Mount to His auditors as a model of prayer, He would then have hardly omitted, at the question, "Teach us to pray," to have referred them to His former instruction. At the same time it appears to us less congruous that the Saviour should for the first time have uttered this precept as a portion of a longer discourse before thousands of hearers; far more probable is it that it was first imparted to a smaller circle of disciples on a different occasion, and from this centre was more generally diffused. The view (Stier, Tholuck) that what was uttered in the Sermon on the Mount was not till afterwards given as a fixed precept, is a way of relieving the difficulty that testifies of perplexity. The words in Matthew, οὕτως οὖν προσεύχ. ὑμεῖς, certainly do not properly convey any other sense than the commencement here in Luke, ὅταν προσεύχ. λέγετε, κ.τ.λ. Matthew does not give the Lord's Prayer in the Sermon on the Mount because it was there for the first time uttered, but because the preceding instruction of our Lord respecting prayer in secret offered him a fitting occasion for it.

Thy name . . . Thy kingdom.—See LANGE on Matt. vi. 9.

Vs. 3. **Our daily bread.**—Ἐπιούσιος is that which we need for our οὐσία, our existence, and therefore not *daily* bread, for this is already implied in the σήμερον of Matthew, as also in the καθ' ἡμέραν of Luke; and tautologies in such a prayer ought certainly not to be presupposed; but it signifies, sufficient bread for the sustenance of our life, *panis sufficiens.* The most one-sided spiritualism alone can take offence that here at least one prayer ascends for temporal necessities. Jesus designed His precept not for angels but for men, and were the view of Stier and others true, that here we are to understand spiritual bread *also*, it might then be doubted whether in this case a limiting σήμερον would stand with it. The Jews, at least, had scarcely heard of heavenly bread when they immediately pray: "Lord, evermore give us this bread," John vi. 34.—The precept, Matt. vi. 34, is alone applicable to temporal but not to eternal affairs, and this whole petition contains, even when it is exclusively used of earthly necessities, a striking reminder of the saying, Matt. vi. 33. Other views see given in LANGE, *ad loc.*

The words which according to Gregory of Nyssa (vs. 2) must have been read instead of the ἐλθέτω ἡ βασ. σου, namely, ἐκθέτω τὸ ἅγιον πνεῦμά σου ἐφ' ἡμᾶς καὶ καθαρισάτω ἡμᾶς, appear to be nothing more than an old gloss arising from vs. 13. The external authority of this reading is at least too insignificant to allow it to be regarded with Volkman, Hilgenfeld, Zeller, as the original.

Vs. 4. **For we ourselves also forgive.**—In Matthew ὡς. By no means is the willingness of the supplicant a ground upon which God can bestow on him forgiveness, but rather a subjective condition without which he has no boldness to entreat the forgiveness of his own sins. Comp. 1 John iv. 18, 19.

Lead us not into temptation.—As the prayer for daily bread raises us above care for *to-day*, and the prayer for *the forgiveness of sins* is meant to quiet us concerning the past, so is the prayer against temptation a weapon for the uncertain *future.* The sense of the difficult expression can only be determined *ex opposito* in Matthew: ἀλλὰ ῥῦσαι, κ.τ.λ. We pray, therefore, that God would not lead us into *such* temptation as would certainly occasion us to fall under the might of evil, as it is that from which we wish to be redeemed. God leads us into such temptation when He gives us over to the evil desires of our heart. (See *e. g.* 2 Samuel xxiv. 1.) "The temptation is here the more critical probation occasioned by the previously-named guilt, and the 'Lead us not into it' the consequence of the 'Forgive us.'

Let us not experience the consequences of our guilt in intenser probationary trials." Lange.

As respects, moreover, this precept in general, nothing hinders us from complementing the imperfect account of Luke from that of Matthew; and if we do this we obtain six—or according to the more apparently correct enumeration, seven—petitions, in which all is expressed which the disciple of the Saviour has to pray for, as well for the glory of God as also for the advancement of his own temporal and spiritual well-being. "All the tones of the human breast which go from earth to heaven sound here in their key-notes." Stier. Although it cannot be that the Saviour meant to establish here a formula that was to be repeated every time *ad literam*, He however answers here the question of His disciples, vs. 1, in so far as He plainly shows them *what* and *how* they must pray. With the exception of one petition—the fifth—the Lord's Prayer expresses all that the Saviour in the days of His flesh could beg from the Father, and also all which according to His will His own should entreat for themselves in His name. As respects, 1. the contents of the prayer, He teaches them *a.* to pray as well for temporal as also for spiritual necessities, but, *b.* still more for spiritual than for temporal: one petition is only for daily bread; five, on the other hand, are devoted to higher concerns; *c.* that the glorifying of the name of God must stand yet more in the foreground than the fulfilment of our necessities: we first hear a threefold *Thy* before we hear a threefold *us*. And as respects 2. our frame of mind in this prayer, the Saviour here teaches us to pray, *a.* in deep reverence, *b.* in child-like confidence, *c.* in a spirit of love for others.

As respects the value of this precept, the singular fancy of Herder in his explications of the New Testament, that the *Pater Noster* could be derived from an oriental source, from the *Zend Avesta*, has been weighed by later science and found wanting, and even so does the assurance of Wetstein: "*tota hæc oratio ex formulis Hebraicis concinnata est*," at all events affirm too much. For the fourth and fifth petitions there are no parallels whatever extant; for the third and sixth only imperfect ones. For the first two there are the most, yet by no means literal ones; and here also, with reference to the Saviour, we are not to overlook the truth: "Even when the popular culture offered Him what was noble and true, it worked ever only as a stimulus for His own inner development, and even that which He has received He reproduces renovated from His creative power of life." Olshausen. In no case can this partial agreement with others take from this model anything of its high worth. Not so much in particular expressions, as rather in the tenor and spirit, in the arrangement and climax of the whole, lies its peculiar worth, and those who can assert of the *Pater Noster* that it is only a joining together of Rabbinic expressions, might assure us with the same right that from a suitable number of single arms, legs, and members, one could compose an animated human body. We honor much more the wisdom of the Saviour in this, that He would teach His disciples no chords which would have been entirely strange to their unpractised lips, and in vain do we seek here for the traces of a limited Judaistic spirit. So brief is it, that it does not even weary the simplest spirit, and yet so perfect that nothing is therein wholly forgotten: so simple in words that even a child comprehends it, and yet so rich in matter that the principal truths and promises and duties are here presupposed,

confirmed, or impressed, and that Tertullian with right named it a *breviarium totius evangelii*. How often soever it may have been misused, especially where it has been turned into a spiritless formula of prayer, while men have forgotten that it only expresses the lofty fundamental ideas which must prevail in the exercise of prayer, it remains yet continually a goldmine for Christian faith, a standard for Christian prayer, a prop for Christian hope. Respecting the history and use of this prayer, comp. Tholuck, *Bergpredigt*. Respecting its value, Stier, *Reden Jesu*, vol. i. pp. 194-224; Lange, *L. J.* ii. pp. 609-618, Lange on *Matthew, ad loc.*

Vs. 5. **Which of you.**—A parabolic representation which is only found in Luke, and is attached so loosely to the preceding instruction, that possibly the Master delivered it at another time, and it is given here only on account of the connection of thought. The purpose is, as also in the parable of the Unrighteous Judge (ch. xviii. 1-8), to encourage to perseverance in prayer. The example is taken entirely from daily life, and shows anew with what sharp penetration our Lord observed the common occurrences and experiences of the same.—**Three loaves.**—"*Unum pro hospite, unum pro me, unum supernumerarium, honoris causa. Mire popularis h. l. est sermo.*" Bengel. It is striking how much more friendly the request is than the first answer, which does not begin with φίλε, and very plainly betrays ill-humor.

Vs. 8. **Because of his importunity,** ἀναίδεια here in direct reference to prayer as unweariedness, perseverance in its highest energy. God wishes a faith which is not ashamed of endurance, and which therewith entertains the highest expectations.

Vs. 9. **Ask, and it shall be given you.**—A definite assurance of a special hearing of prayer, from which it results that prayer has not only a *subjective* influence for our tranquillizing, our comfort, etc., but also an *objective*, procuring us from God what He without the prayer would certainly not have bestowed upon us. Here also, as so often throughout the Old Testament, we have a God who permits Himself to be entreated, and in the conflict with praying faith to be voluntarily overcome. "The inexorableness of a stone and the exorableness of a free being are things which can be proved or refuted by experience alone, which can make an end of all philosophical contradiction even in spite of or rather for the bettering of our Sophia, yet certainly always to the contentment of our Philosophia." Pfenninger. Respecting the climax in this saying of our Saviour, see Lange on the parallel passage.

Vs. 10. **For every one that asketh.**—As the Saviour has just urged perseverance in prayer, He now speaks of the certainty of being heard, and gives His disciples to understand that prayer is in no case in vain, and that an uttered wish is surely fulfilled, that is, if it belongs to those *good gifts* which are now represented under the image of bread, fish, and egg. But if any one should in his foolishness beg a scorpion or a snake, the father would be no father if he could fulfil such a wish.

Vs. 12. **Or if he shall ask an egg.**—This third example is found only in Luke, the two others also in Matthew, ch. vii. 9, 10. From that which the *friend* will do, the discourse of the Saviour rises even to that which one could expect of a *father;* from that which an imperfect earthly father does, even to that which the perfect Father in heaven bestows.

Vs. 13. **If ye then, being evil.**—Not a comparison of the morally corrupt man with God (Meyer), but rather a contrast. How should it be possible that a holy God should not do that which even sinful man does!

The Holy Spirit — ἀγαθά in Matthew. A remarkable *interpretamentum*, which teaches us with the best right to consider the Holy Spirit as the essence of all good gifts which the Father in Heaven can bestow on His praying child. Ὁ ἐξ οὐρανοῦ δώσει, abbreviated form for ὁ πατὴρ ἐν οὐρανῷ δώσει ἐξ οὐρανοῦ.

DOCTRINAL AND ETHICAL.

1. When we meet the Saviour in this period of His life praying in a solitary place, we behold at the same time in what a holy frame of soul He has traversed the last steps on the way to the Feast of Tabernacles, the theatre of His thickening conflict. Before His praying eye, the earth with its wickedness has for a short time sunk away. Heaven listens to His words, the disciples hold their peace while they regard Him at a reverent distance. What is more natural than that the view of their praying Master should awaken the desire of the disciples also to pray, and that they go to Him with this wish, who was as much more than John as the Son stands above the servant?

2. The instruction as to prayer which the Saviour gives on this occasion, answers all main questions which are to be solved with reference to secret converse with God. As to the question *what* and *how* we have to pray, the Lord's Prayer gives a satisfactory answer. As to the not less natural question, as to the *ground* on which we can expect to be heard, the Saviour restricts Himself to an appeal to the parental feeling of even sinful men. In reality, the difficult question as to the possibility and conceivableness of special hearing of prayer is best decided before this forum. With a fatalistic and strictly deterministic conception of God, the hearing of prayer becomes an impossibility, and nothing more than merely the psychological effect of prayer conceivable. But whoever believes in a living, freely-working God, who projects and executes His counsel not without but with reference to the praying man, will cleave fast to prayer, even if, in relation to the connection of the prayer with the receiving, questions were to be asked which He could not fully answer.

3. The Lord's Prayer is a short compendium of the principal truths of the Christian faith, of the highest demands of the Christian life. Theology finds here the idea of a personal, living, freely-working God, distinct from the creature and yet standing to the same in direct relation (Immanence). For Anthropology we gain here the conception of man as a dependent, sinful, easily misleadable being; of sin as being debt towards God; of the destiny of man, that it consists in this, to be united in a Kingdom of God. Pneumatology may appeal for a doctrine of angels as well as of the personal evil spirit to the Lord's Prayer; and the highest benefits which Soteriology gives us to hope for, Forgiveness and Sanctification, they stand here by right in the foreground. That the special Christological element is not here so sharply emphasized as might be expected, must be conceded; but, on the other hand, it is self-evident that this prayer is intended exclusively for disciples of the Saviour, who know that it is through the Son that they go to the Father, and can expect to be heard only when they thus pray in His name, John xvi. 24. The chief requirements of the Christian life, as well in and of itself as in relation to the Father, and even to the brethren on earth, can with equal ease be derived from this model.

4. The perseverance in prayer which the Saviour commands on this occasion must be well distinguished from the praying without ceasing of which Paul speaks, 1 Thess. v. 17. The latter is a continual prayerfulness and living of the soul in connection with God, even when it has nothing definite to entreat. The former, on the other hand, is persevering prayer for something which one does not immediately receive, but as to which, nevertheless, we may expect that God will give it to us in His own time and way, Luke xviii. 1–8.

5. Although the Saviour in the well-known saying, *Ye who are evil*, opposes His hearers not to Himself but to the pure and holy Father, it is, however, none the less true that He here, inasmuch as He speaks of ὑμεῖς, not of ἡμεῖς πονηροί, renders an indirect but unequivocal testimony to His own ἀναμαρτησία. No teacher would, excluding himself, be able to speak of his hearers as evil, without bringing on himself the appearance of presumption, unless he were himself without sin.

6. Inasmuch as the Saviour at the end of this instruction comprehends all which God gives to prayer in the single πνεῦμα ἅγιον, He gives us at the same time to know to what prayers we may expect *unconditional*, to what, on the other hand, only *conditional*, answers. Prayer for spiritual gifts is always heard; the desire after special temporal blessings only when one has really prayed for bread, not for stone, a fish, or a snake. [The author has here omitted to mention, what without doubt he would readily admit, that a *selfish* prayer for particular spiritual gifts is no more secure of being heard than a selfish prayer for temporal gifts. By spiritual gifts he here means, probably, those graces which serve for the more perfectly doing God's will, and which are desired for that end. The prayer for such, of course, cannot remain unheard.—C. C. S.]

7. "Where a Christian is, there is really the Holy Spirit, who does nothing there than continually pray; for although He does not continually move the mouth or make words, yet the heart goes and beats, even as the pulses of the veins and the heart in the body, without cessation or ceasing; so that one can find no Christian without prayer, as little as a living man without the pulse, which stands never still, but stirs and beats ever on, although the man sleeps or does other things, so that he does not become aware of it." Luther.

HOMILETICAL AND PRACTICAL.

The solitary prayer of the Saviour, "Lord, teach us to pray:" 1. The disciple of the Saviour must *pray*; 2. must *learn* to pray; 3. must learn to pray of *Jesus*; 4. must *go* to Jesus with the entreaty, "Lord, teach us to pray."—How the Saviour teaches His disciples to pray: 1. By His word; 2. by His example; 3. by His Spirit; 4. by His ways and dealings with them.—The wish to learn to pray most pleasing to the Lord. It is: 1. The joyful token of life; 2. a means to farther development of life.—God, our Father who is in heaven: 1. *Father*; 2.

heavenly Father; 3. *our* heavenly Father. These three words a doctrine for faith, love, and hope.—Hallowed be Thy name: 1. The first prayer; 2. the dearest prayer; 3. the last prayer of the disciple of the Saviour. It is yet continued in heaven and even when the kingdom is already come, sin forgiven, &c.—Thy kingdom come: 1. *Whither?* into heart, house, church, world; 2. *why?* then only is the Father's name glorified, the purpose of the Son attained, the fellowship of the Spirit complete; 3. *how are we to pray for this?* With thankfulness, with zeal, with steadfast hope.—Give us to-day our daily bread. Every word a doctrine: 1. *Give,* the doctrine of dependence; 2. *bread,* the doctrine of contentment; 3. *our bread,* the doctrine of industriousness; 4. *to-day,* the doctrine of freedom from care; 5. *daily* bread, *panis sufficiens,* the doctrine of trust; 6. give it to *us,* the doctrine of love.—The noticeable relation in which this part of the Lord's Prayer stands to the great whole: 1. The Saviour teaches us, it is true, to pray also for daily bread, but, 2. over against one prayer for earthly things stand six for heavenly, Matt. vi. 33; 3. this one prayer is preceded by three for the glory of God, and, 4. is followed immediately by three others which respect something infinitely higher than its own object. All is most pregnant with instruction and significance.—Forgive us our debts: 1. Even the disciple of the Saviour sins continually; 2. these sins also are debts before God; 3. for these debts also is daily forgiveness ready; 4. this forgiveness becomes our portion only when we for our part are disposed to forgiveness towards others.—For also we forgive: 1. No ground of our hope; 2. no means of compelling an answer to prayer; 3. no intimation of the measure according to which we expect forgiveness, but a sign: 1. Of humility, which is conscious of its own debt; 2. of love, to which the "Forgive *us*" is more than an idle sound; 3. of uprightness before God, which cannot possibly have a controversy with our brother, since the Father has remitted so infinitely more, Matt. xviii. 23–35.—Lead us not into temptation: 1. Thy way is often so dark; 2. the temptation is so great; 3. our heart is so weak; 4. the consequences of an eternally repeated fall are so lamentable.—The Lord's Prayer: 1. A prayer for the closet; 2. a prayer for the church.—The circle of the Saviour's disciples an association of prayer.—Prayer the pulse-beat of the Christian life.—The Heavenly Father bestows more upon prayer than does the best friend here on earth.—The importunity of faith: 1. How hard it is; 2. how richly it rewards.—True perseverance in prayer.—The certainty of the hearing of prayer: 1. Its limits: the prayer must be befitting, the prayer must be believing, the will must be united with God's will; 2. its grounds: God's attributes, God's promises, God's deeds manifest from history and experience.—The question, *Is* there an actual hearing of prayer? answered successively with: 1. The No of doubt; 2. the Yea of faith; 3. the Hallelujah of thankfulness.—How often we in our shortsightedness beg stones instead of bread, snakes instead of fishes and the like.—The "I say to you" of the Saviour maintains its prerogative against all rebuffs and doubts of the darkened understanding.—The commendation of prayer for the Holy Spirit: 1. The Holy Spirit the Christian's first necessity; 2. the Holy Spirit the Father's holy gift; 3. the Holy Spirit in the heart the fruit of believing prayer.

STARKE:—Teaching in the ministry has its time, but praying also. One coal kindles the other.—BRENTIUS: To pray a believing *Pater Noster* is a weighty and grave matter; there is a child-like spirit required thereto, Rom. viii. 16.—*Nova Bibl. Tub.:*—God is much kinder towards His friends than men towards theirs.—If God instantaneously heard our sighing, it would be a harm to us, for faith, love, and hope would have no room for exercise.—OSIANDER:—If God holds still at thy prayer, continue thou on valiantly, vigorously, and joyfully: He will indeed soon answer: Thy faith hath saved thee.—CANSTEIN:—Parents are under obligation to provide for their children in bodily respects also, and to give them, according to ability, what they need.

To the Sermons on the Lord's Prayer mentioned by LANGE on *Matthew*, p. 130, add: 1. Claus Harms' eleven Sermons, Kiel, 1838; John Zimmerman and others, Tholuck, four Sermons in the second volume of his Sermons.—THE SAME:—How one in such times as the present should use the Lord's Prayer, in his Sermons for the Times, 1848.—2. On the Parable, LISCO:—Concerning the persevering entreaty of oppressed citizens of the kingdom: 1. Ground; 2. occasion; 3. power of the same.—The Christian boldness in prayer.—ARNDT:—Of the converse of the Christian with his God: 1. That we should pray; 2. what we have to entreat; 3. how our prayer must be fashioned.—The Lord's Prayer the model prayer of all Christians.—W. HOFACKER:—Concerning prayer as the inner pulse of the spiritual life.

D. *The Son of Man in His relation to hypocritical Enemies and Friends weak in Faith.*

CHAPTERS XI. 14—XII. 59.

1. The Kingdom of Satan and the Kingdom of Christ (CH. XI. 14–28).

(Parallel to Matt. xii. 22-30; 43-45; Mark iii. 22-30.)

14 And he was casting out a devil [demon], and it was dumb. And it came to pass, when the devil [demon] was gone out, the dumb spake; and the people wondered.
15 But some of them said, He casteth out devils [the demons] through Beelzebub the
16 chief of the devils [demons]. And others, tempting *him*, sought of him a sign from
17 heaven. But he, knowing their thoughts, said unto them, Every kingdom divided against itself is brought to desolation; and a house *divided* against a house falleth [and

CHAP. XI. 14–28.

18 house is precipitated against house[1]]. If Satan also be divided against himself, how shall his kingdom stand? because [for] ye say that I cast out devils [the demons]
19 through Beelzebub. And if I by Beelzebub cast out devils [the demons], by whom do
20 your sons cast *them* out? therefore shall they be your judges. But if I with the finger of God cast out devils [the demons], no doubt the kingdom of God is come upon [unto]
21 you. When a [the] strong man [one] armed keepeth his palace, his goods are in
22 peace: But when a stronger than he shall come upon him, and overcome him, he taketh from him all his armour wherein he trusted, and divideth [distributeth] his spoils.
23 He that is not with me is against me; and he that gathereth not with me scattereth.
24 When the unclean spirit is gone out of a [the] man, he walketh through dry places, seeking rest; and finding none, he saith, I will return unto my house whence I came
25, 26 out. And when he cometh, he findeth *it* swept and garnished. Then goeth he, and taketh *to him* seven other spirits more wicked than himself; and they enter in, and dwell there: and the last *state* of that man is [becomes] worse than the first.
27 And it came to pass, as he spake these things, a certain woman of the company [multitude] lifted up her voice, and said unto him, Blessed *is* the womb that bare thee,
28 and the paps which thou hast sucked. But he said, Yea, rather, blessed *are* they that hear the word of God, and keep it.

[1 Vs. 17.—Οἶκος ἐπὶ οἶκον πίπτει. This appears to be a continuation of the figure. When a kingdom comes to ruin everything in it shares that ruin, and house is dashed against house. Οἶκος ἐπὶ οἶκον may, indeed, be taken as a pregnant expression for οἶκος ὢν ἐπὶ οἶκον. But, as Bleek remarks, in this case, instead of ἐπὶ οἶκον we should at least expect ἐφ' ἑαυτόν. It is better, therefore, with the Vulgate and various distinguished critics, to take it as a variation of the idea in Matthew and Mark, rather than as an exact equivalent of it.—C. C. S.]

EXEGETICAL AND CRITICAL.

Vs. 14. **And He was casting out.**—This miracle is not to be paralleled with Matt. ix. 32–34 (Neander, Tischendorf), but with Matt. xii. 22 *seq.* The demon here driven out was, according to the more precise account of Matthew, also blind. As to the rest, we must carefully distinguish this sufferer from the ordinary infirm man who suffers under organic defects of sight and hearing. He is by no means called demoniac because he was blind and deaf, but he was blind and deaf because he was in a high degree demoniac. "He was dumb through psychical influence. Undoubtedly this manifested itself as a kind of insanity, only this insanity is not to be considered as merely one of imagination, but as the consequence of the real work of hostile potencies. Its overcoming through the light and might of the Redeemer restores again the normal psychical and physical relation, in the sufferer." Olshausen.

And the people wondered.—According to the parallel passage in Matthew, they are even on the point of publicly proclaiming Jesus as the Messiah. It is this very culmination of enthusiasm which awakened the strongest reaction of the Pharisees, who now declare our Lord not the Elect of God, but the instrument of Satan. "*Ubi ad extremum cœcitatis venit impietas, nullum est tam manifestum Dei opus, quod non pervertat.*" Calvin.

Vs. 15. **Through Beelzebub or Beelzebul.**—The name Beelzebub signifies properly: Fly-god, 2 Kings i. 2, 3, 16; Beelzebul signifies: god of dung. See LIGHTFOOT, *ad loc.* That by this name another spirit is signified than the one that in other places is called Satan, or the head of the fallen angels, is without proof. Except in the gospels, Beelzebul appears nowhere as a name of the devil. As to the rest, not Beelzebub but Beelzebul appears to be the more correct reading.

Vs. 17. **And house is precipitated against house.**—Graphic representation of the desolation of a city divided within itself, in which the one falling house necessarily draws down the other with it in its fatal fall. It is quite as arbitrary to take οἶκος here in the sense of *family* (Bornemann) as to understand here merely a falling of the separated house ἐφ' ἑαυτόν (Paulus, Quesnel, De Wette).

Vs. 18. **If Satan also.**—The Saviour places Himself entirely on the position of His opponents. If He actually cast out the demons through their Chief, then it would follow that Satan was now busy in destroying his own work. Every kingdom, every town, every family stands in itself a complete whole; so soon as it breaks this unity, it breaks up with its own hand the foundation of its independent existence. So was also the kingdom of darkness a whole, which had risen against the kingdom of truth and of light. Satan could not, therefore, possibly drive out evil spirits without doing injury to his own realm. Perhaps the Pharisees might here have made the objection that Satan, for the accomplishment of a *higher* purpose, might admit a *lesser* hurt, and might drive out one of his satellites in like manner as Caiaphas (John xi. 50) wished to have one man die that the whole people might perish not. As they, however, in this passage, betray no acquaintance with these higher tactics of the kingdom of darkness, it was not necessary for our Lord to remove this objection or anticipate it. Respecting this whole polemics against the blasphemy of the Pharisees, comp. NEANDER, *ad loc.*

Vs. 19. **By whom do your sons cast them out?**—To the *argumentum ex absurdo*, the Saviour adds here an argument *e concessis*. By the sons of the Pharisees we have doubtless to understand none other than their spiritual sons, their disciples, the exorcists. Comp. Acts xix. 13. From the lack of adequate information respecting these, it is difficult to form a perfectly correct judgment respecting the driving out of devils by the disciples of the Pharisees. Without doubt charlatanism was connected therewith, and many a healing would be found to be only temporary and apparent, although they must, nevertheless, more than once have succeeded, by adjuration in the name of the Lord, in expelling a condition of possession that would not yield to other means. See the very remarkable passages of

Irenæus and Tertullian, which GROTIUS, *ad loc.*, cites. And why might not individual better-minded Pharisees accomplish such an act in faith and the Spirit of God, and see their weak endeavors crowned with heavenly blessing?

Vs. 20. **By the finger of God.**—According to Matthew, ἐν πνεύμ. Θεοῦ, comp. Exodus viii. 19.

Vs. 21. **When the strong one.**—Our Lord now passes over to a third counter-argument—this time of an entirely empirical nature. He first gives us to see in what light He views the prince of this world, whom the Pharisees had here so unbeseemingly mentioned, and the opposing of whom they regarded as a comparatively unimportant matter. He was a strong man who, well accoutred, relied upon his equipment and his secure rocky castle. Whoever can fall upon, bind, and despoil such an one, must not stand below but above him, and be stronger than he. How could the victor stand in a covenant of peace and friendship with the vanquished, and how would it be possible to overmaster the Strong One, except only ἐν δακτύλῳ Θεοῦ? Comp. Isaiah xlix. 24, 25. With right Bengel: "*Gloriosior victoria Christi, postquam vicit Satanam tot sæculis grassatum et confisum.*" If any one thinks that he is obliged to explain all the particular features of the figurative language, he can, with Stier, by the house of the strong man = Satan, understand the world; by σκεύη understand men, whom he uses as his instruments, after he has previously robbed them themselves, and in the preceding blind man see a concealed allusion to the death of Christ, and His descent into hell. But it is more natural to have regard here simply to the *tertium comparationis*, and to stop with the chief thought: Only the stronger can overcome the strong.

Vs. 23. **He that is not with Me.**—Respecting the connection of this saying with an apparently opposite declaration, *see* before on Luke ix. 50. The discourse advances regularly: after the triple refutation of the blasphemers, follows now a word of warning. It is this time addressed especially to such as on the one hand seized with astonishment at the miracle, on the other hand struck by the blasphemous allegation of the Pharisees, did not know what they should think of Jesus, and were secretly inclined, at least for the moment, to remain neutral in respect to the two parties. These He gives to understand that in the case of so intense a conflict of principles such a neutrality was impossible, and at bottom was no better than open enmity. It was not sufficient that they did not join in with the blasphemy of the Pharisees; they must decidedly take a stand. The so-called *juste milieu* between friendship and enmity could not possibly be longer maintained; indifference would of itself be injury. But how much more worthy still of punishment were those who openly opposed themselves to Him! For them is meant the saying that now follows.

Vs. 24. **When the unclean spirit.**—Luke gives this parabolic discourse before, Matthew, on the contrary, after the discourse of Jesus concerning the sign of the prophet Jonas. Comp. Matt. xii. 43–45. Apparently this latter arrangement is to be taken as the original. Luke moreover again places what is similar together, and gives this declaration as early as this because it belongs to the sphere of demonology, with which the preceding accusation and vindication also stood in relation, and perhaps for this cause also omits the words with which, according to Matthew, vs. 45, the Saviour concluded the whole address: "Even so shall it be also unto this wicked generation." The sense and the intention of the imagery here is, moreover, in and of itself not hard to understand. Not He was possessed or in covenant with Beelzebub, as His enemies blasphemously alleged, but Israel itself, which stood under the influence of its blind leaders, was now the possessed party. A demon had been driven out after the Babylonian captivity, the demon of idolatry; but that the unhappy nation was now in so much better case, was by no means true; as a sevenfold worse scourge had blasting Pharisaism taken the place of the first demon. No wonder! his former house he, the demon, finds empty, σχολάζοντα (Matthew). Forsaken indeed by him, it is yet by no means inhabited by a better,—by the Holy Spirit. He finds therefore abundant room for return; finds the house as if in festal adornment already prepared for him, as it were demoniacally tricked out by the ruling spirit of lies. He now takes seven other spirits with him worse than he, that is, in not a moral respect, for the Scripture does not teach us to know any degrees of demoniacal wickedness, but worse, inasmuch as they can accomplish yet more than he. With these he takes possession of his former dwelling-place, so that the temporary redemption of the poor possessed is followed by a sevenfold greater misery. "*Reperit domum vacantem: eos procul dubio designat Christus, qui vacui Dei spiritu ad recipiendum diabolum parati sunt, nam fideles, in quibus solide habitat Spiritus Dei, undique muniti sunt, ne qua rima Satanæ pateat.*" Calvin.

How shaming this representation was for the Pharisees, strikes the eye quite as quickly as in what a striking manner it was fulfilled, in the continually deeper fall of this whole generation. At the same time, however, it must not be overlooked that this whole instruction contained a weighty intimation for the man who had just been healed by the Saviour (vs. 14). It was to remind him of this truth, that it did not suffice for this instant to be redeemed from the evil spirit, if his heart was not at once united in sincerity with Jesus, and if he did not by that alone remain in security against renewed demoniacal influence; nay, for the whole multitude the portraiture of a man was instructive, who, after he had been, in the first instance, purified from sin, gives himself again into its service, and now sinks deeper than ever before. Nor does it indeed admit of any doubt that this word found an echo in the consciences of many. A trace we find in the enthusiasm which it awakened, according to Luke's account alone, in one of the female hearers.

Vs. 27. **A certain woman of the multitude.**—That it was a mother (according to tradition, Marcella, a maid-servant of Martha) appears from the nature of her felicitation. Her enthusiasm is by no means incomprehensible after such a severe discourse (Strauss), for without doubt she admired more the *how* than the *what* of the words of the Saviour. "The whole anecdote betrays a fresh and living remembrance, which appears to have inserted it on the very spot where it occurred." Schleiermacher. The unnamed woman listened to the words as only a mother can listen who, perhaps herself childless, or it may be unhappy in her children, in silence envies Mary. Her words form a striking contrast with those which the Saviour Himself, on the way to the cross, utters over the daughters of Jerusalem, Luke xxiii. 28, 29. He does not gainsay her utterance, but He rectifies it (μενοῦνγε, immo vero, as in Rom.

ix. 20; x. 18). "Very true, blessed," &c. An intimation for the woman not to let herself be borne along too much by transient impressions, but rather to hear still farther; an eulogy of Mary, whom He already perhaps discovered among the throng (comp. Luke ii. 19-51); a transition to further instruction of the people, which however was now interrupted by the intelligence that His mother and His brethren were calling Him. Comp. Matt. xii. 45, 46; Luke viii. 19-21. "It may not be impossible that even during Jesus' discourse in vindication of Himself, the rumor of the arrival of His relatives had made its way, and had given this woman occasion for the exclamation which she made, but it is more probable that Jesus addressed two separate answers, one to the woman, the other to those who gave Him notice of the arrival of His mother, because Luke distinguishes altogether too definitely the two utterances from each other for us to suppose them to have been one. Therefore, we shall be able to conclude that the actual information of His mother's arrival did not itself reach Jesus until after this exclamation of the woman, and that it then gave Him occasion to that saying respecting His disciples." Lichtenstein.

DOCTRINAL AND ETHICAL.

1. Not unjustly has there often been found in this whole discourse of our Lord one of the strongest proofs of the objective truth of the New Testament Satanology. How much of its force does the whole argument of this discourse lose if we should assume that our Lord here accommodated Himself to a popular belief, above which He Himself was infinitely elevated! If it is not true that He cast out actual demons and that by the Spirit of God, then the conclusion derived from it that the kingdom of God therefore had come to them, is in this passage an assertion without proof. That the Saviour, in the form of His representation, attaches Himself to the prevailing ideas, especially in vss. 25, 26, must be conceded; but He would never have permitted Himself such an accommodation had He not, in the substance of these conceptions, recognized the elements of higher truth. There exists a remarkable contrast between His portrayal of the strong man who keeps his palace and can only be overcome by a stronger one, and the slight importance which many rationalistic theologians attribute to the *locus de Diabolo*.

2. The energetic manner in which the Saviour on this occasion insists upon a decided position, for or against Him, proves sufficiently how intensely the opposition of parties had then increased; but at the same time this declaration gives indirectly a powerful testimony to the entirely unique value of His person and His work, towards which it is impossible permanently to maintain a strict neutrality, and which lay claim to so undivided an interest, that indifference is itself a kind of covert enmity.

3. The parable of an evil spirit who returns with seven others, was strikingly fulfilled, first upon the Jewish people, not only in the days of our Lord, but also in the apostolic age. The first impression which was made upon some, after the death of the Saviour, passes away again, and shortly before the destruction of Jerusalem, it may be especially said that the nation was possessed not only by seven, but by seventy times seven devils. Moreover, this phenomenon recurs perpetually in the Christian church, when, after a time of commencing growth, a period of mournful retrogression, and when, after short awakening, a time of spiritual stiffening into dead forms, begins. So was it when, after the Reformation, the letter-worship of ecclesiastical orthodoxy established itself; so does it now perhaps threaten to be in some regions after that religious awakening of the first half of this century has cooled off; and, finally, there is here portrayed the image of every one who has made the first step on the way to conversion, but afterwards has fallen from this height into the most unhappy depth (2 Tim. iv. 10; Heb. vi. 4-6; 2 Peter ii. 20-22). How far this remains possible even after genuine conversion, is a question which cannot here be answered. In no case can one, in the dwelling out of which only one demon had been driven, and which is only empty, swept, and garnished, recognize the image of one *truly* regenerate.

4. The woman that lifts up her voice to bless Jesus, is the prototype of all those who have honored the mother of the Saviour more than they have her Son, and have incurred the guilt of *Mariolatry*. If the Saviour does not favor this honoring of His mother, even here, where it moves within modest bounds, what judgment will He then pass upon the new dogma of *Pio Nono*, upon which an entirely new Mariology is built?

HOMILETICAL AND PRACTICAL.

The threefold temper towards the miracle-working Saviour: 1. Enthusiasm and its right; 2. hatred and its blindness; 3. neutrality and its impossibility. —The Son of God was manifested that He might destroy the works of the devil, 1 John iii. 8.—He hath done all things well: the dumb speaking, Mark vii. 37.—No sign great enough to overcome the repugnance of unbelief.—The might of Satan a fearful, well-ordered, but yet vincible might.—The enemies of the Lord condemned, 1. By their conscience; 2. by those holding their own views; 3. by the Saviour. —Satan's defeat a sign that the kingdom of God has come near.—The strife of the Strong with the Stronger: 1. The Strong One, *a.* his palace, *b.* his booty, *c.* his false rest; 2. The Stronger, *a.* His courageous assault, *b.* His complete triumph, *c.* His brilliant crown.—Neutrality in the Christian sphere no virtue, but a chimera.—The Saviour would rather have to do with open foes than with half-friends.—Whoever begins to stand apparently neutral towards truth becomes, for the most part, at last an opposer of the same.—The dangerousness of half-conversion. —Not easily does the Evil One give up his rights over the heart which he has for a while had dominion over.—The Spirit of Evil finds nowhere abiding rest.—What matters it that one is in a measure free from the Evil Spirit, if he is not filled with the Holy Spirit?—The wretched reëntrance upon the hardly forsaken way of sin: 1. Undoubtedly possible, 2. in the last degree ruinous.—Hypocrisy the worst kind of possession.—All the seven deadly sins come up at once in the heart that is sold under sin.—" It had been better for them not to have known the way of righteousness," &c., 2 Peter ii. 22.—The female mind more receptive than many a masculine one of the greatness of the Saviour.—The first Mary-worship.—The woman that blesses Jesus' mother the type of superficial religious feeling: 1. Nature of this feeling, *a.* it is easily aroused, *b.* promptly revealed, *c.* soon evaporated; 2. value of the same, *a.* the Saviour does not disapprove it wholly, *b.* still less does He approve it unconditionally, *c.* He will have it pass over to something better—the hearing and keeping of His word.—Blessed are they that hear the word of God and keep it. Their blessedness has, 1. A higher character; 2. a firmer ground; 3. a longer duration than any other.

STARKE:—HEDINGER:—The mockers blaspheme God's work; they that are better doubt.—BRENTIUS:—It is the way of perverse people to count devils' works for God's works, and God's works for devils' works.—Christ is also Judge of the word and the thoughts. Comp. *Ps.* cxxxix. 1, 2.—It is undoubtedly permitted to defend ourselves against all those who blaspheme our function, which we discharge to God's honor.—Here on earth even children are often the judges of their parents, 1 Sam. xix. 5. —Nothing but the finger of God—no human power—is capable of driving Satan out of the heart.—Christ and Belial agree not together.—QUESNEL:—The converted sinner is a Judge which the devil has lost, but of which he knows all the weak quarters and entrances, and where he often even yet has secret confederates. [*Diabolonians in Mansoul.*]—With children of Satan it fares as with their wicked father, Isaiah lvii. 20, 21.—All presumptuous sins are garnishings of the heart for the habitation of many devils.—ZEISIUS:—Spiritual relationship with Christ is more excellent than all natural connection of blood.—BRENTIUS:—True Christianity consists not in word but in deed and in truth, 1 Cor. iv. 20.

STARKE:—One must be free if he will make others free.—Moral relapses risk the soul's salvation. —MASSILLON:—*Sur l'inconstance dans les voies du salut, sermon sur Luc.* xi. 26, *pour le troisième dimanche de la carême.*—MARHEINEKE:—How ingenious the human heart is when the question is of closing itself against the impressions of manifest truth! —ULBER:—The many enemies of Jesus, who yet is all men's Friend.—FUCHS:—Enmity against Christ: 1. It testifies of unthankfulness; 2. betrays folly; 3. prepares wretchedness.—AHLFELD:—How standest thou with reference to Christ? 1. Art thou His enemy? 2. Art thou indifferent? 3. Makest thou half work? 4. Believest thou on Him?—PALMER:— The kingdom of the world and the kingdom of Christ: 1. Nature; 2. relation of these two kingdoms.—VON GERLACH:—How Christ overcomes the kingdom of the devil, 1. Without us; 2. in us.—RAUTENBERG:—The reproach of Christ our honor. A reproach: 1. For us; 2. from us; 3. upon us.— WANKEL:—The fearful power of the Evil One: 1. Fearful by its unnoticed commencement; 2. rapid progress; 3. wretched issue.—ALT:—"Who is not with Me," &c.: 1. Who does not believe with Me, he speaks against Me; 2. who does not walk with Me, he strives against Me; 3. who does not work with Me, he labors against Me; 4. who does not combat and sacrifice with Me, he betrays Me.

2. A Sign for the Eye and an Eye for the Sign (Vss. 29–36).

(Comp. Matt. xii. 38–42; vi. 22, 23.)

29 And when the people were gathered [gathering] thick together, he began to say, This [generation[1]] is an evil generation: they seek [it seeks] a sign; and there shall no sign be given it, but the sign of Jonas [Jonah] the prophet [om., the prophet[2]].
30 For as Jonas [Jonah] was [became] a sign unto the Ninevites, so shall also the Son of
31 man be to this generation. The queen of the south shall rise up in the judgment with the men of this generation, and condemn them: for she came from the utmost parts of the earth to hear the wisdom of Solomon; and, behold, a greater [πλεῖον, neuter; lit., some-
32 thing more] than Solomon *is* here. The men of Nineveh shall rise up in the judgment with this generation, and shall condemn it: for they repented at the preaching of Jonas
33 [Jonah]; and, behold, a greater than Jonas [πλεῖον 'Ιωνᾶ] *is* here. [And] No man, when he hath lighted a candle, putteth *it* in a secret place, neither under a [the] bushel,
34 but on a [the] candlestick, that they which come in may see the light. The light of the body is the [thine[3]] eye: therefore when thine eye is single [sound], thy whole body also is full of light; but when *thine eye* is evil [diseased], thy body also *is* full of
35 darkness. Take heed therefore, that the light which is in thee be not darkness.
36 If thy whole body therefore *be* full of light, having no part dark, the whole shall be full of light, as when the bright shining of a [the] candle [with its brilliancy, τῇ ἀστραπῇ; om., the bright-shining] doth give thee light.

[1] Vs. 29.—According to the reading approved by Tischendorf on preponderating grounds: ἡ γενεὰ αὕτη γενεὰ πονηρά ἐστιν. [Supported also by Cod. Sin.]
[2] Vs. 29.—*Rec.*: τοῦ προφήτου, taken from the parallel passage in Matthew. [Omitted also by Cod. Sin.]
[3] Vs. 31.—*Rec.*: ὁ ὀφθαλμός—Matt. vi. 22—σου is, however, decidedly supported and already approved by Griesbach. [Supported also by Cod. Sin.]

EXEGETICAL AND CRITICAL.

Vs. 29. **He began to say.**—The occasion for this discourse of rebuke on the part of the Saviour Luke has already, vs. 16, communicated at the same time with the judgment of the Pharisees. Matthew keeps the two elements, ch. xii. 24 and 38, more exactly apart, arranging them chronologically. According to his account it is principally Pharisees and Scribes who desire to see the sign from heaven, in whom, however, the Saviour, with the most perfect right, views the legitimate representatives of the whole evil and adulterous generation of His contemporaries. According to Luke they are indeed ἄλλοι than those who had before spoken, yet by no means animated with a better spirit. They will tempt Jesus (πειράζοντες) in that they laid for Him a snare, indirectly support their humiliated and castigated friends, and desire something of Him which He could not refuse them without exciting much remark. If we are not disposed by the sign from heaven to understand an actual revelation of the Shekinah, they have at all events some kind of cosmic phenomenon in mind, either an eclipse of the sun or moon, or a meteor, or something of the sort, which, however, must be so far different from the other miracles of our Lord as this, that it was to be performed, not on men who surrounded Him, but on objects which were apparently elevated above Him, and was therefore to strike the eye so much the more strongly. Perhaps they find occasion for this inquiry in the definite assurance of the Saviour that He cast out demons ἐν δακτύλῳ Θεοῦ, at which they in a hypocritical tone declared themselves ready to acknowledge Him as soon as He should have given them an incontestable proof of His heavenly mission. It is in this case much easier to understand that the Saviour, agreeably to His principle, performed no sign before them, since He found in them not the slightest receptivity for the moral impression of His miracles : comp. Matt. xiii. 58.

There shall no sign be given it.—This whole answer of the Saviour breathes, besides righteous displeasure, a heavenly composure and wisdom : for it gave all to whom the truth was dear, plainly to understand that His refusal to give a sign was perfectly just, and besides that only conditional, and finally, that it was only temporary.

The sign of Jonah.—The briefer expression of Luke must be explained by the more developed statement of the language of our Lord in Matt. ch. xii. 40, of whose genuineness and exactness there is no occasion whatever to doubt. "The reference of the sign of Jonah merely to the preaching and manifestation of the Saviour in Paulus, Schleiermacher, Neander, a. o., needs no refutation." Lange. Had the Saviour wished to refer to that alone, He would then have had to express Himself more exactly, and to say: As Jonas was a sign to the Ninevites, so is also the Son of man for this generation. The ἔσται itself points to the future. As Jonah from the belly of the fish had come forth, to appear to the Ninevites, so should the risen Jesus be for His contemporaries a sign, but not from heaven; from the depth of the earth shall this sign be given, but yet it should serve for their condemnation. The parallel consists in this, that Jonah goes down into the fish's belly, and after three days' abode therein, comes again out of the same, while Christ descends into the heart of the earth, Sheol (Meyer), and also after the same time again gloriously appears. And if we must also, according to Jonah ii., conceive the prophet as living in the belly of the fish, this takes nothing from the general correctness of the comparison. As respects, however, the difficulty as to the designation of time, a νυχθήμερον does not need always to endure just twenty-four full hours. See 1 Sam. xxx. 12, 13, and in the Talmud Hieros. it is expressly stated: "Day and night make together a period (עונה), and the part of such an one is as the whole." Comp. STIER, R. J. II., p. 53.

Vs. 31. **The Queen of the South.**—Comp. LANGE on *Matt.* xii. 42. Less precisely has Luke placed the comparison with Solomon before that with Jonah and the Ninevites, because then the beautiful climax of the discourse is lost. The Queen of Sheba had given yet greater proofs of faith and exhibited yet more interest than the Ninevites, who believed on the word spoken in their immediate vicinity; for out of distant lands had she come to hear the wisdom of Solomon, while the Jews contemned what they could find in their immediate neighborhood, and yet there was more here than Solomon !

More than Solomon.—In order to feel the power of this comparison, in which the wisdom of Solomon is to be kept carefully in mind as the *tertium comparationis*, we must not only realize to ourselves what is written in the Old Testament regarding Solomon, but also especially what tradition had added to this, in reference to his magic words, his ring, his knowledge of the secrets of the spiritual world, &c., in consequence of which Solomon stood in almost unearthly glory before the eyes of the contemporaries of Jesus. [The simple reference to the scriptural account of Solomon appears quite sufficient, without supposing our Saviour to have taken any account of the superstitious fables respecting Him. —C. C. S.]

Vs. 32. **The men of Nineveh.**—It cannot be stated with certainty whether Jonah made to the Ninevites any intimation of the miracle that had happened to him or not. But even supposing he did not, the contrast is then so much the stronger. The Ninevites believed Jonah upon his word, without knowing anything of the miracle. The Jews, on the other hand, had not only heard the preaching of Jesus, but also afterwards an account of His resurrection, and yet they believed not. In no case, therefore, is the judgment here uttered by Jesus too hard.

Vs. 33. **And no man.**—Course of thought : I am more than Jonah (vs. 32); but in order to know this one does not (as you do) put the light under a bushel. Unquestionably Jesus, according to Luke, appears to wish to denounce the insincerity of His adversaries (De Wette). Comp. Matt. v. 15 ; Luke viii. 16.—εἰς κρυπτήν, that is, in a vault, a cellar, the familiar *crypta* of ancient buildings and churches. *See* MEYER, *ad loc.*

Vs. 34. **When thine eye is sound.**—Comp. Matt. vi. 22, 23. If the light is to be permitted to shine brightly before the eyes of others upon the candlestick, then it is above all things necessary to preserve to one's self the light of his own power of perception undarkened and bright. Respecting the inner eye, *see* LANGE on the parallel passage in *Matthew.* There appears to be indicated by this an immediate original consciousness of God, to which also Paul, Acts xvii. 27, alludes. It appears, therefore, that according to the doctrine of the Saviour, the organ exists even in fallen man by which revealed truth can be viewed, and it may be said that here, as also in Matt. xiii. 12, the general law is stated according to which an increase of the inner light and of the spiritual life takes place in man. If we assume that Luke communicates this saying of the Saviour in its exact historical connection, then especially must we not leave out of view that Jesus here speaks of the people (vs. 29), but not exclusively of His disciples, so that by the eye and the light of which here He speaks, we must understand, not anything specifically Christian, but something generically human.

Vs. 35. **Take heed, therefore.**—Only in Luke does the admonition appear in this definite form. The same thought is uttered in the τὸ σκότος πόσον in Matthew. The Saviour fears that the here-indicated darkening is already found in part in His hearers, and warns them therefore to look to it that it do not become a total darkening.

Vs. 36. **If thy whole body therefore.**—This saying also only Luke has preserved. The appearance of a weak tautology, of which expositors complain, is best avoided if in the *protasis* we let the emphasis fall upon ὅλον, in the *apodosis* upon φωτεινόν, ὡς ὅταν, κ.τ.λ. The sense is then this: Only when thy body is wholly illumined, without having even an obscure corner left therein, will it become so bright and clear as if the full brilliancy of a bright lamp illumined thee; in other words, then wilt be placed in a normal condition of light.

DOCTRINAL AND ETHICAL.

1. It is from a Christologico-psychological point of view noticeable how it is the repelling of the charge of diabolical agency, which disposes and occasions the Lord to give forth one of the most elevated expressions of His self-consciousness, in that He places Himself far above Jonah and Solomon. As this comparison gives proof of His true humanity, it at the same time places the superhuman in His activity in the brightest light.

2. The sign of the prophet Jonah is essentially the great sign which the Saviour, even in the beginning of His ministry, had intimated to the hostile Ἰουδαίοις, John ii. 19–21. Thus, therefore, does the Saviour in Jerusalem and Galilee, over against similar opposers, and now, after the lapse of a year, remain fully consistent with Himself.

3. The craving for wonders is a diseased condition of soul, which can never be satisfied, and which, therefore, is combated by the Saviour with all His might. Comp. John iv. 48. And so much the stronger opposition did He present to this temptation since it was in its deepest ground a Satanic one, and really a repetition of the request that He should perform a miracle of display. Comp. Luke iv. 9, 10. The Saviour could so much the less satisfy the demand of His contemporaries, as these were wholly wanting in the holy sense of light [*Lichtsinn*] which had animated the Ninevites in reference to Jonah and the Queen of the South in reference to Solomon.

4. It is manifestly here expressed that the truth revealed to man in the Gospel stands, not as something entirely foreign, over against and outside of him, but as related to the inmost constitution and the highest receptivity of his nature, as the eye and the light are, as it were, made for one another. Here holds good the beautiful expression of Goethe: *Wär' nicht das Auge sonnenhaft, wie könnten wir das Licht erblicken*, &c. [Were not the eye akin to the sun, how could we behold the light?] And the Christian hymn, *Heil'ge Einfalt, Gnadenwunder*. [Holy simplicity, miracle of grace.]

5. "So can and should the receptivity of light in the spiritual sense (reason, feeling, and conscience) be cherished and kindled to the light of life and of the body. The essence of the care of the same is the simplicity, that is, the completeness, concentration, and consistency of the inner life. For this light-sense the word of God now necessarily becomes the inner light of life, which gradually drives out even from the corporal and sensual sphere of life all elements of obscuration, all fragments of the old night, till the whole being of the man, even his exterior, is not only illumined, but also diffuses light, a clear, beautiful, and consecrated beam of God." Lange.

[" *And in clear dream and solemn vision*
Tell her of things that no gross ear may hear,
Till oft converse with Heavenly habitant
Begins to cast a beam on th' outward shape,
The unpolluted temple of the mind,
And turns it by degrees to the soul's essence,
Till all be made immortal." Comus.]

HOMILETICAL AND PRACTICAL.

Outward hearing of the word joined with inward enmity and perverted designs.—The unappeasable greediness for ever greater and greater wonders.—The request for a sign from Heaven an indirect proof of the reality of the other signs on earth.—The resurrection of the Lord the highest sign of His Messianic dignity.—Jonah and the Son of man: 1. What advantage the former appears to have over the latter; 2. wherein both stand on a level; 3. wherein the latter infinitely excels the former.—More than Solomon is here. We consider in reference to this saying: 1. How strange it sounds; 2. how true it is; 3. of what moment it continues to be.—The wisdom of the Saviour and the wisdom of Solomon: the first had: 1. A higher originality (John vi. 46); 2. a wider extent (John vi. 68); 3. a more salutary purpose (Matt. v. 48) than the latter.—The different grades of the damnableness of sin: 1. Penitent heathen rise up against unbelieving Jews; 2. Jews longing for salvation against hypocritical nominal Christians.—The greater the privilege the heavier the responsibility.—The brightest light is lost when it is either: 1. Set under a bushel, or 2. viewed with diseased eyes.—As the light for the eye and the eye for the light, so are Christ and man made for one another.—The hopeless condition of the man in whom the inner light is wholly darkened; it is darkness: 1. In him; 2. around him; 3. above him.—The single eye and the illumined body, the diseased eye and the darkened body.—What must there be in man if he will rightly understand and esteem revealed truth? Comp. John vii. 17.—Between truth and man there exists the same inner relation as between the light and the eye.

STARKE:—BRENTIUS:—In the work of salvation God does nothing new for any man: the matter proceeds in the way once shown in the Holy Scriptures.—CRAMER:—The Old and the New Testament explain one another clearly.—HEDINGER:—Terrible is it that the poor yet right-minded heathen, the blind people who yet have striven after virtue, shall herein condemn many Christians.—The doctrine of the last judgment is a fundamental article of the Christian religion, and must therefore be often urged with great earnestness.—*Bibl. Wirt*.:—Christian preachers should be in an exceptional manner a light in the Lord.—Man needs that his soul should be filled with the divine light if he will do the works of light.—Enter diligently into thine heart and be for its enlightenment and amendment unweariedly concerned. Ps. cxxxix. 23, 24. The condition of a man before,

CHAP. XI. 37-54.   189

in, and after, conversion may be well compared with the night, with the break of day, and with day itself.

HEUBNER:—Christ must have accounted the history of Jonah a true history, for, a. He would not have compared Himself with a fabulous hero; b. nor could the Ninevites, if their repentance after Jonah's preaching is a mere fable, judge the Jews of that time.—Every converted man is for the unconverted that know him a judging, condemning example.— How often do people run and study for the sake of earthly wisdom, while Christ's wisdom, so near at hand, is despised; men have a disgust at it, and deify the wisdom of the dust.

---

3. Two Manner of Enemies (Vss. 37-54).

37 And as he spake, a certain Pharisee besought him to dine [breakfast, ἀριστήσῃ]
38 with him: and he went in, and sat down to meat [reclined]. And when the Pharisee
39 saw it, he marvelled that he had not first washed before dinner. And the Lord said
40 unto him, Now do ye Pharisees make clean the outside of the cup and the platter; but
    your inward part is full of ravening [rapacity] and wickedness. Ye fools, did not he,
41 that made that which is without, make that which is within also? But rather [om.,
    rather] give alms of such things as ye have [the contents, τὰ ἐνόντα]; and, behold, all
42 things are clean unto you. But woe unto you, Pharisees! for ye tithe mint and rue
    and all manner of herbs, and pass over judgment and the love of God: these ought ye
43 to have done, and not to leave the other undone. Woe unto you, Pharisees! for ye
44 love the uppermost seats in the synagogues, and[1] greetings in the markets. Woe unto
    you, scribes and Pharisees, hypocrites [om., scribes and Pharisees, hypocrites! V. O.[2]]!
    for ye are as graves which appear not, and the men that walk over [men in walking
45 over] them are not aware of them. Then answered one of the lawyers [or, men learned
    in the law], and said unto him, Master [Teacher], thus saying thou reproachest [art
46 reviling] us also. And he said, Woe unto you also, ye lawyers! for ye lade men
    with burdens grievous to be borne, and ye yourselves touch not the burdens with one
47 of your fingers. Woe unto you! for ye build the sepulchres of the prophets, and your
48 fathers killed them. Truly [So then] ye bear witness that ye allow [are witnesses and
    consent to] the deeds of your fathers: for they indeed killed them, and [but] ye build[3]
49 their sepulchres. Therefore also said the wisdom of God, I will send them prophets
50 and apostles, and some of them they shall slay and persecute: That the blood of all the
    prophets, which was shed from the foundation of the world, may be required of this gen-
51 eration; From the blood of Abel unto the blood of Zacharias, which perished between
    the altar and the temple [lit., the house]: verily [yea] I say unto you, It shall be re-
52 quired of this generation. Woe unto you, lawyers! for ye have taken away the key
    of knowledge: ye entered not in yourselves, and them that were entering in ye hinder-
53 ed. And as he said these things unto them [And when he had gone out from thence[4]],
    the scribes and the Pharisees began to urge him vehemently [to be intensely embittered
54 against him], and to provoke him to speak of many [various, πλειόνων] things: Laying
    wait for him, and seeking [om., and seeking[5]] to catch something out of his mouth,
    that they might accuse him.

[1 Vs. 43.—Τοὺς ἀσπασμούς. Those to which they were accustomed, from the reverence of the people.—C. C. S.]
[2 Vs. 44.—The Rec. has here γραμματεῖς καὶ Φαρισαῖοι, ὑποκριταί; in all probability taken from the similar passage in Matthew. [Om., Tischendorf, Tregelles, Meyer, Bleek, Alford with B., C., L., Cod. Sin.—C. C. S.]
[3 Vs. 48.—The following words of the Rec.: αὐτῶν τὰ μνημεῖα, are wanting in B., D., L., [Cod. Sin.,] Copt., Cantabrig., and other authorities, and are therefore bracketed by Lachmann, and rejected by Griesbach, Tischendorf, [Meyer, Tregelles, Alford. But Bleek vindicates their genuineness and necessity.—C. C. S.] It is supposed with reason that they contain an interpolated supplement, as οἰκοδομεῖτε can stand very well alone.
[4 Vs. 53.—The reading κἀκεῖθεν ἐξελθόντος αὐτοῦ, approved by Tischendorf, [Meyer, Tregelles,] on the authority of B., C., L., [Cod. Sin.,] has internal probability. The Recepta varies, and it is much easier to assume that this complot took place after the Saviour's departure than in His presence.
[5 Vs. 54.—The additional words of the Recepta, ζητοῦντες ἵνα κατηγορήσωσιν αὐτοῦ, are in all probability spurious. See MEYER, ad locum. [The text, as Van Oosterzee accepts it, is Tischendorf's. Supported by B., L., Cod. Sin.—C. C. S.]

EXEGETICAL AND CRITICAL.

Vs. 37. Ἐν δὲ τῷ λαλ.—That the Pharisee's invitation came to Jesus while He was uttering what immediately precedes, Luke does not tell us, but only that it was given while the Saviour was engaged in speaking. It is therefore not impossible that this event belongs to a later period of the Saviour's sojourn and activity in Galilee, when the hostility against Him had risen to a still higher pitch. On the other hand, the invitation of the Pharisee just at the moment becomes doubly intelligible if we compare Mark iii. 20. Perhaps this breakfast was offered the Saviour by a Pharisee dwelling in the neighborhood, who might fear that Jesus through the press of the people could not reach the dwelling of his host.

Breakfast, ἀριστήσῃ.—We are here not to understand the chief meal, but a lighter *prandium*, which was taken earlier and required less time. That the disposition of the entertainer towards the Saviour was not on that account by any means a friendly one, sufficiently appears from the connection.

Vs. 38.—**Had not first washed.**—Respecting the washings and purifications of the Pharisees before a meal, *see* the detailed statements of LIGHTFOOT on Matthew xv. 2; SEPP, *L. J.* ii. p. 343.—We have no ground for supposing that the Saviour did not commonly wash Himself before a meal. Now, perhaps, He omitted it because He had just accepted the invitation, or because He was wearied by the day's work which He had hitherto accomplished.

Vs. 39. **And the Lord said unto Him.**—Against the charge that the Saviour in the herefollowing conversation at table in some measure lost out of mind the requirement of courtesy towards His host, we have simply to bring to mind that "such a divine rudeness is everywhere in place" (Ebrard). If we consider that the host by his surprise had at the very beginning violated the duty of hospitality and benevolence; that they had scarcely even sat down when this injurious remark was made to the Saviour; that the Saviour had respect not merely to the matter but especially to the principle and the intention of the charge, we cannot then be in the least surprised that He emphatically vindicates Himself, and combats the hypocrisy of those who had censured Him. Every-day decorum gives place here to an infinitely higher duty. We must, however, doubtless assume that the Pharisee had expressed his astonishment in some way or other, since the Saviour would otherwise have taken a different occasion for uttering such a *Philippic*.

Now do ye Pharisees.—It is known how remarkable an agreement there is between this rebuke of the Saviour's and that which Matthew, ch. xxiii., has given much more in detail. The question which of the two Evangelists has communicated this rebuke in the most exact connection has been alternately answered in favor of Matthew and Luke. *See, e.g.* the view in Meyer on Matt. xxiii. 1. It is, however, to be remarked, 1, that the first reproach which, according to Luke, the Saviour addresses to the Pharisees, vss. 39, 40, bears internal traces of having been uttered at a meal, and that also the coming forward of the scribe, vss. 45, 46, by which a new rebuke is called forth, has internal probability. On the ground of this it appears not to admit of doubt that the Saviour really directed against a Pharisee in Galilee, on occasion of a breakfast, several similar rebukes to those which we find in Matthew, ch. xxiii., directed in yet greater number against the scribes and Pharisees at Jerusalem. 2. On the other side, however, the denunciatory discourse in Matthew affords so many proofs of an internal connection and a living totality, that the originality and exactness of its redaction cannot possibly be denied. It is, 3, undoubtedly possible that the Saviour, as occasion offered, repeated several rebukes against the Pharisees in Galilee and those of like mind in Judæa, but less probable that a whole series of rebukes, with citation of the same passage of Scripture and the same denunciation at the end, was twice delivered. It is more simple, therefore, 4, to assume that Luke is indeed

right in representing the Saviour during a meal as uttering a discourse of rebuke against the Pharisees and scribes, but that in this he has taken the liberty of inserting at the same time *per anticipationem* several similar expressions, which, as appears from Matthew, the Saviour actually uttered only in the last days of His life, which Luke, however, on account of their similar character, communicates here, while in consequence of this he does not recur to the last denunciatory discourse. As to the whole matter, the opinion that "the Evangelists have taken up elements of earlier discourses of Jesus in later ones and the reverse" (Lange) can only be rejected in principle by those whose harmonistics are controlled by a somewhat mechanical theory of inspiration.

Νῦν, κ.τ.λ.—Not an antithesis merely of ΝΟΝ in opposition to an understood πάλαι (Meyer); for we have not a single proof that the Saviour considers the former generation of Pharisees as better than the present, but rather in the sense of *eo jam perventum est*, which, perhaps, in view of the character of holy irony borne by the whole discourse, is best translated by "full well," equivalent to "this is the way, they are on the right way to," &c.

Vs. 39. **But your inward part.**—Not a contraction for "the inside of your cup," to which Matt. xxiii. 25 appears to point, but the interior of the persons in contrast with the exterior of the cup. In Matthew the opposition between outer and inner side of the enjoyment of life appears more prominent. In the form given by Luke the outwardly purified cup is opposed to the inwardly corrupted heart of the drinker.

Vs. 40. **Ye fools.**—Since God has created the inside as well as the outside, one as much as the other must be held holy; and it is not only evil but foolish to wish to separate, even in thought—to say nothing of act—that which in the nature of things is absolutely inseparable.

Vs. 41. **But rather give alms.**—It appears to us entirely against the spirit and intent of this discourse of the Lord, to wish to find here an actual precept how alone they could bring about genuine purity. In this case certainly there would have had to follow in the future as the motive πάντα καθαρὰ ὑμῖν ἔσεται; and what now stands: καὶ, ἰδ. ὑμ. ἐστιν appears to be meant to indicate to us how soon anything in their eyes was purified,—so soon, that is, as only they had lavished τὰ ἐνόντα for an ostentatious almsgiving. The Saviour said *date* not *datis*, since they already actually did it, but He will urge them in the Imperative only to continue this. We thus come spontaneously to the ironical interpretation (Erasmus, Kuinoel, a. o.) in this way: "What more would be yet necessary than to designate, set apart, the contents for alms; for thereby the whole inward impurity has at once disappeared." That there is also a holy irony appears from Proverbs i. 26, and elsewhere. All attempts to find here a definite moral commandment which is meant in earnest, appear to us forced in the extreme, nor may we forget that the Saviour ends with: πάντα καθαρὰ ὑμῖν ἐστιν, that is, *e vestro (perverso) judicio*. Had He here wished to speak of actual objective purity, this addition would have been entirely superfluous. [This is a very doubtful interpretation. There seems no sufficient reason for doubting that our Lord means to commend practical benevolence as better than any scrupulosity about ceremonial purity. "Instead of any excessive anxiety," He says, "about having the outside of your vessels duly purified, it would be better to give their contents to the poor. Such a spirit of beneficence will render any merely ceremonial defects of small account."—C. C. S.]

Vs. 42. **Ye tithe.**—Moses had aforetime required that they should bring the tenth of all their possessions, as an offering to the sanctuary. Numbers xviii. 21 ; Deut. xiv. 23. The perverseness of the Pharisees consisted in this, that they applied the command to the most insignificant trifles, e. g. mint and rue, and on the other hand neglected inviolable requirements of the Divine law. They forgot judgment respecting themselves first of all, in the sense, that is, in which the Saviour had required it, John vii. 24 ; and at the same time the love of God, considered as the *genitive of object*, and according to Matthew, moreover, faithfulness, τὴν πίστιν (vs. 23). Thus did they violate the noblest duties towards God, their neighbor, and themselves.

These ought ye to have done.—It is an admirable proof of the heavenly composure and impartiality of our Lord, that instead of abrogating the fulfilment of the minor duties, or declaring it unimportant, He on the other hand permits and commands it, but then also insists with the best right that the higher duties should at least be fulfilled not less conscientiously than the rest. Comp. Matt. xxiii. 23.

Vs. 43. **The uppermost seats ... greetings.** —Comp. Matt. xxiii. 6, 7, and *see* LANGE, *ad loc.*

Vs. 44. **Graves which appear not.**—In a somewhat different form the same rebuke is expressed in Matt. xxiii. 27. There the Saviour condemns especially the ornamenting and decking out of a thing that was inwardly abominable ; here the consequence of it is brought forward : the whitewashed grave as such is scarcely to be recognized any longer, and one can therefore go over it without knowing it ; so may one come in contact with the Pharisees, without at once receiving an impression of their inward moral corruption. [I should here suppose that in the two passages two different classes of graves are referred to. Here the humbler grave of the common people, which in time might sink into the earth and be walked over without notice, thereby defiling the passers-by ; and in the passage in Matthew, on the other hand, the more pompous sepulchres of the rich, whose magnificent decorations were so poorly in agreement with the corruption which they concealed within. The application of the two images is not essentially different. —C. C. S.].

Vs. 45. **One of the lawyers.**—There is no ground for thinking that this νομικός belonged himself to the sect of the Sadducees (Paulus). On the other hand, it seems that we must assume that the learned caste of the νομικοί maintained a somewhat aristocratic position with reference to the great mass of the Pharisees, and that this man wished to remind our Lord : "If thou speakest thus, thou wilt not only raise against thee the *plebs*, but also the men of science ; not only, so to speak, the *laici*, but also the *clerici*." He wishes to conjure down the tempest of denunciation, and to overawe the Saviour ; with what poor success will immediately appear.

Vs. 46. **Woe unto you also, ye lawyers.**— Comp. Matt. xxiii. 4. "*Gradus: digito uno attingere, digitis tangere, digito movere, manu tollere, humero imponere. Hoc cogebant populum, illud ipsi refugiebant.*" Bengel.

Vs. 47. **Ye build the sepulchres.**—Comp. Matthew xxiii. 29–31.—Not the building of the sepulchres in and of itself, but the connection which they thereby proved themselves to have with the prophet-murdering race of old, is condemned by our Lord. Fathers and children together did only one work,—the former killed the messengers of God, the latter buried them ; the former incurred, the latter perpetuated, the damnable guilt of blood ; and while they apparently honored the prophets, they had towards God, who had sent them, the same enmity at heart as the murderers of the prophets. For other views, *see* LANGE, *ad loc.*

Vs. 48. **But ye build.**—It is of course understood that it is still the graves of the prophets which are meant. If they had been of a better sort than their fathers, they would have erected no monuments of a damnable deed, which ought rather to be buried in the dust of oblivion. Now, however, when they spoke with so much ado of their fathers, they with their μνημεῖα apparently honored the prophets, but in effect their murderers, and—themselves.

Vs. 49. **Therefore also said the wisdom of God.**—"Therefore, that is, because you have part of the guilt and are ripe for the punishment of your fathers ; the wisdom of God has also said," &c. The Lord appears hereby to mean that through Him the wisdom of God speaks personally to the children of men. The view that the Saviour here cites an ancient declaration of God, lost to us (Paulus, Von Hengel), is inadmissible, as "contrary to the analogy of all other citations of Jesus, as well as to the evangelical tradition itself, which attributed these words, with Matt. xxiii. 34, to Jesus." Meyer. Perhaps we have here to understand a former declaration of the Saviour Himself, and to compare Matt. xi. 19. As the Son of the Father, who spoke what He had formerly seen and heard with the Father, the Saviour could with the best right name Himself ἡ σοφία τοῦ Θεοῦ, and perhaps it is the recollection of similar declarations which has given John occasion to designate Him decidedly as the λόγος τοῦ Θεοῦ. That here only a ὕστερον πρότερον of form occurs (Neander, Twesten, Meyer), has no proof. It was certainly not unworthy of the Saviour to cite His own formerly-uttered word as that of the Incarnate Wisdom of God, and if He did this we cannot then assume that He understood by the prophets and apostles any one else than those of the New Covenant now soon to appear in His place, and by whose rejection the measure of wickedness should be fulfilled, and the murder of the prophets reach its culmination. The colors in which here the fate of His witnesses is depicted are probably all taken from their subsequent life. Even crucifixion is in Matthew not mentioned without ground, if the familiar tradition contains truth that Peter suffered the martyr's death in this form, not, it is true, at the hands of the Jews, but yet after he had been condemned by the Jews and delivered to the heathen world. Persecute, ἐκδιώξ, so that it was no longer granted to them to remain quiet in the land. Comp., *e. g.*, Acts xiii. 50.

Vs. 50. **The blood of all the prophets.**—*See* LANGE on the parallel in Matthew. The view of Hug, Sepp, and others, that the Saviour here predicted the murder of Zacharias, the son of Baruch, shortly before the destruction of the temple (comp. JOSEPHUS, *De Bell. Jud.* iv. 5, 4,) belongs already to the history of exegesis. We too cannot see anything else in it than that the Saviour has in mind 2 Chron. xxiv. 21, and in this way brings together the murder of the prophets from the first to the last book of the Old Testament canon. He mentions therefore the ancient, as yet unatoned-for blood-guiltiness, which soon, augmented by new, will reach its fearful culmination. As respects finally the well-known difficulty that Zacharias was not the son of Barachias, but of Jehoiada, we prefer on the whole the view (Ebrard, pp. 5, 6,) that Zacharias according to the Old Testament also was a grandson of Jehoiada, and that the Saviour here correctly states Barachias, who is not mentioned in the Old Testament, as his father. Respecting this whole passage the Essay of Müller deserves to be compared, *Stud. u. Krit.*, 1841, 3.

Vs. 51. **Yea, I say unto you.**—It belongs to the fearful earnestness of the Divine retributive righteousness, that when a generation concurs in heart with the wickedness of an earlier generation, it receives, in the final retribution of the accumulated guilt, as well the punishment for its own, as also for the former sins which it had inwardly made its own.

Vs. 52. **Woe unto you, lawyers!**—Comp. Matthew xxiii. 14. Here is said definitely to the νομικοί what had there been said to the scribes and Pharisees in general. The position of this saying in Luke, after the fearful denunciation of the previous verse, breaks more or less the climax of the discourse, and may perhaps with other things serve as a proof that he on this occasion has inserted single sayings which were actually not uttered till afterwards. By the key of knowledge we can, as to the rest, understand nothing else than the way of the knowledge of Divine truth which had been revealed and manifested in Christ. By their hierarchical influence upon the people they barred them from access thereto, and by their disposition towards the Saviour, they closed the access to it against themselves.

Vs. 53. **And when He had gone out from thence.**—*See* the note on the text. It may be plainly noticed that either anger or conscience made immediate answer impossible to the host and the scribes. In silence therefore did they permit the Saviour to depart from the *prandium*, but remained together in order to consult what attempts were now further to be made. They soon seek Him again, in order to interrogate Him about all manner of things (ἀποστοματίζειν), apparently trifling sophistical questions which Luke does not even account worthy the honor of mention. In case of necessity they are even ready to suffer even new castigations, by the answer which the Saviour certainly is not to be supposed to have forborne giving them, if only they could at last succeed in drawing something from Him which should in some way give them the right of denouncing Him either before the secular or before the spiritual authorities.

DOCTRINAL AND ETHICAL.

1. The holy anger of the Saviour at the breakfast of the Pharisee (Mark iii. 5, comp. Ephesians iv. 26), far from being below His dignity, or standing at all in conflict with His character, is on the other hand a striking revelation of His heavenly greatness. It is well known that He towards all that had deeply fallen was affectionate and forbearing, and only towards hypocrites was inexorably severe. The cause of this lies in His character as King of truth, with which no sin stands in so direct opposition as hypocrisy, because it vaunts itself of the guise of a virtue, of the essence of which it is entirely destitute. [So far have we, in our mawkish theories of universal goodnature, sunk below the understanding of this divine severity of our Lord against unworthy teachers of religion, that I have actually seen the declaration attributed to a leading religious journal, that "no man who respects religion will speak ill of a clergyman." Such an impudent identifying of religion with its teachers is hardly credible. How does it consist with the tremendous rebukes of our passage, directed against clergymen?—C. C. S.]

2. Phariseeism, far from being a merely accidental form of the Judaism of that time, is on the other hand the natural revelation of the sinful condition of the heart when men will not give up the hope of becoming righteous before God by their virtue and merits. They are proud of that which they imagine themselves to possess, and continually inclined to assume the guise of that which they well know they do not possess. The enmity of the flesh towards the immutable declarations and contents of the law (Romans viii. 7), they seek to conceal behind respect for outward forms, and in each case they make a compromise with themselves, in order to conceal the transgression of the great commandment by exact fulfilment of the less. But this whole web of self-deceit is penetrated by the sun-like glance of the King of truth, and whoever, like the scribe, vs. 45, takes part with the cause of unrighteousness, receives his righteous proportion of the sharp chastisement.

3. When the Saviour combats the temptations of the Pharisaical hierarchy, it is by no means His intention entirely to forbid all distinctions of offices of honor in His kingdom. The same one who wills not that one of His people should be called *Rabbi*, has placed some as apostles, &c. Ephesians iv. 11. But this He censures, that the office is desired for the title's sake, instead of the title for the office's sake; that men take honor one of another instead of seeking the honor which is of God alone, John v. 44. How sadly is the Catholic Church, following the Pharisees, gone astray both as to the letter and the spirit of this word of the Lord!

4. Men judge the heart according to the deed; the Saviour judges the deed according to the heart. Therefore He adduces the building of the sepulchres of the prophets, that in and of itself might be permitted and laudable, as a new ground of accusation, inasmuch as He discovers the same temper of mind in the buriers of the dead, as had once dwelt in the murderers. What they undertake against earlier and later messengers of God, is to Him so far from being surprising and unexpected that He, as the personal Wisdom of God, has already seen it beforehand and predicted it, and yet He has not permitted Himself to be held back by this mournful prospect an instant from His uninterrupted labor of love.

5. That the judgment of the Lord, severe as it was, was not at all too hard, appears at once from this fact alone, that the Pharisees have not the most distant thought of humbling themselves under the rod of this word, but only forge new attacks, and therefore fall out of one sin into another and yet worse sin.

6. There is one wisdom which shuts up the kingdom of God from one's self and others, and another which shows and helps to find the entrance. The former is revealed in the Pharisees and scribes, the latter in the Saviour. The appellation σοφία τοῦ Θεοῦ is one of those points of contact which occur in so manifold ways between the Synoptical and the Johannean Christology. Comp. also Proverbs viii. 23. An Ebionitic or Socinianistic Christ could not possibly have spoken in such a way.

7. Inasmuch as the Saviour takes the two exam-

ples of unrighteously-shed blood from the first and last book of the Old Testament canon, He gives testimony for the Scriptures of the Old Testament as being a whole.

HOMILETICAL AND PRACTICAL.

The Saviour's pleasure at table embittered by the malice of man. Prov. xvii. 1. The free Humanity of the Saviour in contrast with the restrictions of a dry Legalism.—The severity of love.—Outward purifying without inward purity.—The mournful opposition between seeming and being, in the religious sphere: 1. The seeming an anxious copy of the being; 2. the being, the mournful contrast of the seeming.—The compromise between conscientiousness and the lust of sin.—Beneficence not seldom a cloak for the exercise of gross sins.—Faithfulness in much and little. There are men who are, 1. Neither the one nor the other; 2. who are conscientious in little and not in much; 3. conscientious in much and on the contrary neglectful in little; 4. who unite both qualities.—The Saviour Himself a noble type of faithfulness as well in the highest as in the lowest duty in His calling.—The striving after vain honor a genuinely Pharisaic vice.—How little do men often conjecture how it is with our hearts!—The principle of solidarity.—Whoever perpetuates the mention of damnable deeds which might better fall into forgetfulness, renders thereby a testimony against himself.— No rejection of the word of God which had not been already predicted.—The blood-stream in Israel's history, the length, the breadth, the depth, the height. —The wisdom of God over against the folly of man. Vs. 49. Comp. vs. 40.—The blood-guiltiness of Israel: 1. An ancient guilt; 2. an accumulated guilt; 3. a righteously visited guilt.—This whole discourse a proof of the truth of the prophetical word: The Lord is patient, yet of great might, Nahum i. 3.—Hostility against the truth even where it is clearly recognized.—*Veritas odium parit*, Acts ix. 5b.

STARKE:—OSIANDER:—It is not a sin to eat and converse with people of another religion, if only we do nothing that is contrary to our profession.—MAJUS: —We should give offence to no one, but if he will without it take offence, he does it on his own responsibility.—Often do men make side-work the main work and the reverse.—*Bibl. Wirt.*:—To please men, one must not conceal the truth, but, when time and place require, confess it, without regard to private gain or loss.—QUESNEL:—Sometimes to address the sinner severely is very necessary in order that he be roused and brought to the knowledge of sin.—BRENTIUS:—Without faith it is impossible to please God, let one give as many alms as he will.—Hypocrisy and avarice, where they coexist, are almost incurable.— Everything in its due order and measure.—QUESNEL: To be first or chief is not pride, but to strive after it is a sign of haughtiness.—The discovery of hypocrisy a hard work.—CANSTEIN:—The evil conscience accuses itself when sin and vices are only rebuked in general terms.—It is the greatest hypocrisy to wish to honor departed teachers with monuments, but persecute living ones, Acts vii. 52.—ANTON:—Evangelical preachers are appointed for this that they suffer tribulation—why do we wonder at that?—The Lord regards and inquires after His servants' blood, Ps. ix. 12.—CANSTEIN:—From one sin into another, from hypocrisy to murder of prophets.—HEDINGER: —It is one thing to think we understand the Scriptures, another thing to be certain of it.—Though children of the world are otherwise at variance, yet they join together when Christ's truth is to be opposed.—The longer, the worse, they mislead and are misled. Isaiah xxvi. 10.

HEUBNER:—If there is a heavenly nobility, this has another character than the earthly.—How dangerous the position of the teacher of religion is!— The easy conscience is none.—The human heart may be a temple and a grave, the best and the worst may conceal itself therein.—There is for every man a measure of sin, he cannot stand half-way, comp. Rev. xxii. 11.—There is a degree of corruption when man cannot escape destruction, but we can never determine that in the concrete.—RIEGER:—A sermon upon the imputation of others' sins in his *Herzens-Postille*, p. 91. Comp. PLUTARCHUS, *De sera numinis vindicta*, ed. Reichii, viii. p. 213-217.—SAURIN:— *Les grands et les petits devoirs dans la Religion, Sermon sur Math.* xxiii. 23 (parallel to Luke xi. 42), tom. x.—A Sermon by ARNDT upon Jesus' denunciation of woe in the temple, Matt. xxiii., in his sermons on the *Life of Jesus*, iv., deserves also to be compared here.

---

4. For what the Disciple of the Saviour has, and for what he has not, to take care (CH. XII. 1-34).

1 In the mean time, when there were gathered together an innumerable multitude [lit., the myriads] of people, insomuch that they trode one upon another, he began to say unto his disciples first of all, Beware ye of the leaven of the Pharisees, which is
2 hypocrisy. For [But¹] there is nothing covered, that shall not be revealed; neither hid,
3 that shall not be known. Therefore, whatsoever ye have spoken in darkness shall be heard in the light; and that which ye have spoken in the ear in closets shall be pro-
4 claimed upon the house-tops. And I say unto you my friends, Be not afraid of them
5 that kill the body, and after that have no more that they can do. But I will forewarn you whom ye shall fear: Fear him, which after he hath killed hath power to cast into
6 hell; yea, I say unto you, Fear him [this one, τοῦτον]. Are not five sparrows sold for
7 two farthings, and not one of them is forgotten before God? But even the very hairs of your head are all numbered. Fear not therefore: ye are of more value than many
8 sparrows. Also I say unto you, Whosoever shall confess me [have confessed] before

9 men, him shall the Son of man also confess before the angels of God: But he that de-
10 nieth [hath denied] me before men shall be denied before the angels of God. And
   whosoever shall speak a word against the Son of man, it shall be forgiven him: but
   unto him that blasphemeth [hath blasphemed] against the Holy Ghost it shall not be
11 forgiven. And when they bring you unto [before] the synagogues, and *unto* [*before*]
   magistrates, and powers, take ye no thought how or what thing ye shall answer [in your
12 defence], or what ye shall say:² For the Holy Ghost shall teach you in the same hour
   what ye ought to say.
13   And one of the company said unto him, Master [Teacher], speak to my brother,
14 that he divide the inheritance with me. And he said unto him, Man, who made [ap-
15 pointed] me a judge or a divider over you? And he said unto them, Take heed, and
   beware of [all³] covetousness: for a man's life consisteth not in the abundance of the
16 things which he possesseth. And he spake a parable unto them, saying, The ground
17 [estate; lit., place, χώρα] of a certain rich man [had] brought forth plentifully: And
   he thought within himself, saying, What shall I do, because I have no room where to
18 bestow [deposit] my fruits [or, crops]? And he said, This will I do: I will pull down
19 my barns, and build greater; and there will I bestow all my fruits and my goods. And
   I will say to my soul, Soul, thou hast much goods laid up for many years; take thine
20 ease, eat, drink, *and* be merry. But God said unto him, *Thou* fool, this night thy soul
   shall be required [lit., they require] of thee: then whose shall those things be, which
21 thou hast provided? So *is* he that layeth up treasure for himself, and is not rich
   toward God.
22   And he said unto his disciples, Therefore I say unto you, Take no thought [Be not
   anxious] for your [the⁴] life, what ye shall eat; neither for the body, what ye shall put
23 on. The life is more than meat [food], and the body *is more* than raiment [apparel].
24 Consider the ravens: for they neither sow nor reap; which neither have storehouse
   nor barn; and God feedeth them: how much more are ye better than the fowls
25 [birds]? And which of you with taking thought can add to his stature [length of life,
26 ἡλικίαν] one cubit?⁵ If ye then be not able to do [even] that thing which is least,
27 why take ye thought [are ye anxious] for the rest? Consider the lilies how they
   grow: they toil not, they spin not [how they neither toil nor spin, V. O.⁶]; and yet I
28 say unto you, that Solomon in all his glory was not arrayed like one of these. If then
   God so clothe the grass, which is to-day in the field,⁷ and to-morrow is cast into the
29 oven; how much more *will he clothe* you, O ye of little faith? And seek not ye what
30 ye shall eat, or [and⁸] what ye shall drink, neither be ye of doubtful mind.⁹ For all
31 these things do the nations of the world seek after: and [or, but] your Father knoweth
   that ye have need of these things. But rather seek ye the kingdom of God [seek ye
32 his kingdom¹⁰]; and all [om., all] these things shall be added unto you. Fear not,
33 little flock; for it is your Father's good pleasure to give you the kingdom. Sell that
   ye have, and give alms; provide yourselves bags [purses] which wax not old, a treasure in the heavens that faileth not, where no thief approacheth, neither moth corrupteth
34 [destroyeth]. For where your treasure is, there will your heart be also.

[¹ Vs. 2.—Γάρ rests only on the authority of D. Cod. Sin. omits even δέ.—C. C. S.]
² Vs. 11.—We find no sufficient grounds for the opinion that the words ἢ τί εἴπητε are taken from the parallel passage
in Matthew.
[³ Vs. 15.—The insertion of πάσης instead of τῆς is supported by convincing agreement of critics and manuscripts, including A., B., D., and Cod. Sin.—C. C. S.]
[⁴ Vs. 22.—The decided weight of authority (including A., B., D., Cod. Sin.) is for the omission of ὑμῶν.—C. C. S.]
⁵ Vs. 25.—The words μεριμνῶν and πῆχυν ἕνα are not sufficiently well attested critically, to avoid the supposition that
they are borrowed from Matthew. [Μεριμνῶν is read by Lachmann, Meyer, Tregelles with A., B., Cod. Sin., with 17 other
uncials, and πῆχυν by Tischendorf also, with all the manuscripts. Van Oosterzee must have meant to say that ἕνα was
weakly supported, as it is omitted by B., D., Cod. Sin.—C. C. S.]
⁶ Vs. 27.—Rec.: πῶς αὐξάνει· οὐ κοπιᾷ οὐδὲ νήθει. D., on the other hand, as also Versions and Clem.: πῶς οὔτε
νήθει οὔτε ὑφαίνει. So Tischendorf. [Also Meyer, Alford.] Although the reading has no preponderance of external
authorities, it is nevertheless internally more probable, as the *Recepta*, on the other hand, is taken from the parallel passage in Matthew.
[⁷ Vs. 28.—Lit.: *If God so clothe in the field the grass which is to-day, and to-morrow,* &c. Εἰ δὲ ἐν ἀγρῷ τὸν χόρτον
ὄντα σήμερον, κ.τ.λ. B., L., Sin. The field is represented as the theatre of God's activity.—C. C. S.]
[⁸ Vs. 29.—Καί, B., L., Cod. Sin., 2 other uncials.—C. C. S.]
⁹ Vs. 29.—Van Oosterzee translates this: *Erhebt* [*verfliegt*] *euch nicht in euren Wünschen.* "Be not too high-raised
in your expectations." Vulgate: *Nolite in sublime tolli.* This meaning is defended by De Wette and Meyer, agrees with
the more usual meaning of μετεωρίζεσθαι, but, as Bleek remarks, and Alford also, is much less congruous with the context
than the signification: *"to fluctuate in doubt,"* which is also an undisputed sense of the word.—C. C. S.]
¹⁰ Vs. 31.—Αὐτοῦ has the authority of B., D., [Cod. Sin.,] Copt., Sahid., Æth., and others, for itself, while, on the
other hand, the *Recepta*, τοῦ Θεοῦ, has against it the suspicion of being transferred from Matt. vi. 33, as also, probably, the
superfluous πάντα after ταῦτα.

GENERAL REMARKS.

1. Although there is no lack of able attempts so to unite the different elements of discourse in Luke xii. that therein a logical connection shall become possible (Olshausen, Stier, Lange, a. o.), yet in our eyes the view is more probable that this whole chapter exhibits a chrestomathic character; in other words, that Luke here places together different admonitions and warnings of the Saviour which actually, according to the other Evangelists, were at least in part delivered on very different occasions. Without doubt the Saviour in this period of His life delivered a detailed discourse before the ears of a numerous multitude, in which He expressly warned against the Pharisaical leaven, vs. 1. Yet even vss. 3–9 remind us, as respects contents and course of thought, too strongly of Matt. x. 26–33 for us to be able to find here anything else than a modified redaction of the sayings given by Matthew in the right place. Vs. 10 stands here much less congruously than Matt. xii. 31, 32. The promise, vss. 11, 12, appears also in Luke, ch. xxi. 14, 15, while we have met with it in a very fitting connection in Matt. x. 19, 20. If we, therefore, will not assume that the Saviour uttered it three times, we shall be obliged to suppose that it does not stand here, ch. xii. 11, 12, in its right place. We come thus almost to the view of De Wette, in reference to the words of Jesus contained in this chapter, when he, with it is true not wholly fitting expression, declares: "mostly compiled, only vss. 13–21 peculiar." The parable of the Rich Fool belongs exclusively to Luke, and since he does not give an intimation that it was originally delivered in another historical connection, we are at full liberty to connect it with this course of thought. In reference to vss. 22–24, on the other hand, we cannot regard it as very probable that the Saviour should have twice adduced the very same example from the realm of nature, in warning His disciples against unprofitable care (comp. Matt. vi. 22–34), while besides this it appears that the thoughts in Matthew are rendered much more naturally and correctly than in Luke. Much more simple is the view that of such words of the Saviour more than one redaction has been preserved by the Evangelists, who certainly in the statement and transcription of His utterances were no more destitute of the guidance of the Holy Spirit than in the delineation of His deeds and destiny. Vs. 32 again is to be found only in Luke, as well as also—to speak here of the contents of the second half of this chapter—vss. 35–38; 47, 48, in this form is only communicated by him. Vss. 39–46 have again so manifest a coincidence with Matt. xxiv. 42–51 that in all probability it belongs originally to the last eschatological discourse of the Saviour. To a similar result do we come if we compare Luke xii. 49–53 with Matt. x. 34–36 (comp. ch. xx., xxii.), vss. 54–56 with Matt. xvi. 2, 3, and vss. 58, 59 with Matt. v. 25, 26. It is certainly conceivable that the Saviour uttered all this twice or oftener before different hearers, and not impossible, *if* one places this hypothesis in the foreground, to *find* then the leading thread also which more or less closely joins together all these heterogeneous elements of discourse: but is it not much more simple to assume that the same saying of the Lord has been given by each of the different Evangelists under higher guidance in his own way, in which case it must be left to a discerning criticism in particular cases to investigate which form is most original? In each particular case so to decide the matter that not the least uncertainty shall remain, will perhaps, and probably, always remain impossible. In the lack of trustworthy historical data, subjective opinion always has more or less play, and dogmatics exercises even unconsciously its influence upon harmonistics. Commonly, however, at least as respects this our chief point, a consideration free of prejudice will lead to the conclusion that the most of the here-cited sayings are given by Matthew in a connection which has the greater probability for itself. This, however, does not hinder us from acknowledging that the way in which they are communicated and arranged by Luke, gives us sometimes a deeper view into the unspeakable riches of the words of the Eternal Word. Therefore, without every time inquiring as to the connection in which they have been preserved elsewhere, we take them up simply as Luke communicates them to us.

2. As respects now vss. 1–34 in particular, we will, in order to be able better to survey the rich matter contained in this portion of the discourse, divide it into three parts. In the first, vss. 1–12, the tone of warning predominates; in the second, vss. 13–21, we perceive a tone of instruction, while in the third, vss. 22–34, a tone of encouragement and comfort becomes evident.

a. WARNING AGAINST THE TEMPER OF THE PHARISEES, AND COMMENDATION OF THE OPPOSITE CHARACTER (Vss. 1–12).

EXEGETICAL AND CRITICAL.

Vs. 1. **In the mean time,** ἐν οἷς.—Manifestly we have so to conceive the matter that while the Pharisees were occupying themselves with ensnaring questions and plotting, the throng around the Saviour was increasing with every moment. There is no actual ground to consider even the mention of the myriads as hyperbolical (Meyer), although undoubtedly it was still further from being a strictly arithmetical computation. Comp. Matt. iv. 23-25; Mark iii. 20; iv. 1. We have here manifestly arrived at a point of the history in which the extremes of love and hatred towards the Saviour extensively and intensively have reached the highest pitch.

First of all.—Thus does the Saviour begin to speak to His disciples, and exhibits hereby His forbearance and self-control, in that He at this moment, when the Pharisees are inflamed with blind rage against Him, does not turn Himself directly to the masses with His warning. Πρῶτον not to be joined with τοῖς μαθητ. (Luther, Bengel, Knapp, a. o.), which would be partly obscure, partly purposeless, partly also without example; but with προσέχετε = Luke ix. 61. After that which had just taken place, the Saviour has no warning so much at heart as just this.

Of the leaven.—Comp. Matt. xvi. 6. As appears from the conversation after the second miracle of the Loaves, the Saviour designated by the leaven of the Pharisees their doctrine, and this not in general, for then it would have contained also pure Mosaic elements, but so far as it had been disfigured by the spirit of their sect. It is thus probable, even *a priori*, that He, inasmuch as He was at a former time zealous against this ζύμη, now also has this doctrine in mind. On this ground we must fully subscribe to the penetrating remark of Meyer: "Here also it is not hypocrisy that is meant (as commonly explained), because otherwise afterward ἡ ὑπόκρισις (with an article) would have to stand, but the pernicious doctrines and ordinances of the Pharisees upon which Jesus but just before had been debating at table. Of this He says: 'Their *essence* is hypocrisy,' which gives an element of the warning with the ground on which it rests."

Vs. 2. **There is nothing covered.**—Comp. Matt. x. 26. As hypocrisy in itself is not permitted, vs. 1, so is it besides fruitless, since the truth sooner or later comes to light.—Concealed—hidden (with entire generality of meaning), both from God and man. Nothing,—Good as well as Evil; that which is greatest as well as that which is least.

Vs. 3. **Therefore, whatsoever ye have spoken in darkness.**—A singular statement, if we bring it exclusively into connection with the apostolic κήρυγμα, for we read indeed of the Saviour that He preached to His disciples in the ear (Matt. x. 27), but their preaching was from the beginning destined to the greatest publicity. Therefore the opinions (De Wette: "an incongruous expression." Bengel: *cum timore aliquo*. Meyer: "All that ye—on account of persecutions—shall have taught in secret, will—at the victory of My cause—be proclaimed with the greatest publicity."). This whole antithesis of persecution and victory is, however, plainly gratuitous. But why, moreover, is it necessary to understand here so decidedly the *apostolic κήρυγμα*? It is much more simple if we understand in general all which, whether by the apostles or by the people, vs. 1, has been spoken in secret and is hereafter to be brought to the light. Vs. 2, it is said of *everything* hidden that it shall come to the light; vs. 3, more definitely of the hidden *words* of each one. By this reminder hypocrisy is opposed in its deepest grounds, and even before the apostles could come into the temptation of concealing truth from the fear of man, it is indicated to them in vss. 4, 5, whom they must not fear, and whom they must beyond question fear.

Vs. 4. **Be not afraid.**—Comp. Matt. x. 28. We have here the question, who is meant by the name: τὸν—ἐξουσίαν ἔχοντα ἐμβαλεῖν εἰς τὴν γέενναν, God or Satan? The majority of commentators have, in agreement with the exegetical tradition, decided in favor of the former view; some voices have been raised for the latter (Olshausen, Stier, Lange, *L. J. ad loc.*, Besser, Arndt, Riechel, Van Oosterzee, *ad loc.*). After the retractation of Lange, also, on Matthew *ad loc.*, we cannot but assume that the truth is on the side of the minority. Grounds: 1. Fear can only be here interpreted in one sense, in that of *being afraid of*, being on one's guard; for this certainly the word denotes in the first part of the admonition, and he whom man has to fear, δὲ μᾶλλον, cannot be the Supreme Love, but must necessarily be Satan. It is true, there is a distinction in the construction. We have first: μὴ φοβηθῆτε ἀπὸ τῶν, κ.τ.λ., then: φοβήθητε δὲ τὸν ἔχοντα, κ.τ.λ. Bengel already remarked: *Plus est, timeo illum, quam timeo ab illo.* But the Saviour uses in the connection of the parallel passage, Matt. x. 26, φοβήθητε with the accusative also in the sense of *being afraid*, and the δὲ μᾶλλον (in Matthew) plainly intimates that here an increase of fear (of being afraid) unto yet much greater fear takes place; that the Saviour, therefore, does not give His disciples the admonition in order, instead of the first named feeling, to awaken another within them, but on the other hand to cherish *the same* fear in yet much higher degree.

2. Besides, Satan is the proper soul-murderer, even as men are murderers of the body: but of God it is never said that He destroys the soul. To the objection that the devil nowhere appears in Scripture as the one who damns to hell (Olshausen), we must answer that he appears here not as judge, but as executor of the retributive judgment of God, under His special permission. [Where in the New Testament is the mediæval notion of the devil as God's bailiff, or executioner, countenanced?—C. C. S.] The body he kills through men who are his instruments, John viii. 40, 41; the soul he destroys through the deadly destruction of sin. From among the many foes who could do them great harm, the Saviour brings one forward who was capable of inflicting the greatest of all upon them, and whom they accordingly must fear much more. Therefore He adds, according to Luke, with visible intensity: "Yea, I say unto you, fear him." "Whoever can think of the Heavenly Father, we understand not how his ear can hear." Stier.

3. Least of all does such a designation of the Father belong to a discourse in which the Saviour speaks to His friends, for their encouragement, of a special Providence, which has numbered even the hairs of their head. On all these grounds we here understand "the fearful unnamed and yet well-known One, whose kingdom is hell, who here already beguiles the soul and there forever tortures body and soul." Besser. [Hell is described as the place of Satan's punishment; where is it described as the place of his dominion?—C. C. S.] The Saviour wishes to fill His disciples with holy fear: "That the evil enemy may not beyond deliverance devour their soul to destruction." Lange, *Bibl. Gedichte.* Or, if any one, perchance, finds a difficulty in this that He addresses such a warning to His disciples, then may we remark with Chrysostom: τί γεέννης χαλεπώτερον; ἀλλ' οὐδὲν τοῦ ταύτης χρησιμώτερον φόβου. Ὁ γὰρ τῆς γεέννης φόβος τὸν τῆς βασιλείας ἡμῖν κομίζει στέφανον. Ἔνθα φόβος ἐστίν, οὐκ ἔστι φθόνος·

ἔνθα φόβος ἐστί, χρημάτων ἔρως οὐκ ἐνόχλει· ἔνθα φόβος ἐστίν, ἔσβεσται θυμός, ἐπιθυμία κατέσταλται πονηρά, ἅπαν ἀλόγιστον ἐξώρισται πάθος. Homil. VI. ad popul. Antioch., tom. vi., p. 560. Yet enough already to justify our doubt that here the friends of Jesus are required to fear God, who in the immediately following verse is, on the other hand, represented as the object of their child-like trust, *Ab utraque parte saltem disputari potest.*

[The following remarks on the parallel passage in Matthew appear to me to present in a clear light the inadmissibleness of the author's interpretation. —C. C. S.

"Stier designates it as 'the only passage of Scripture whose words may equally apply to God and the enemy of souls.' He himself is strongly in favor of the *latter* interpretation, and defends it at much length; but I am quite unable to assent to his opinion. It seems to me at variance with the connection of the discourse, and with the universal tone of Scripture regarding Satan. If such a phrase as φοβεῖσθαι τὸν διάβολον could be instanced as — φυλάξασθαι τὸν δ., or if it could be shown that anywhere power is attributed to Satan analogous to that indicated by ὁ δυνάμενος κ. ψ. κ. σ. ἀπολέσαι ἐν γ., I should then be open to the doubt whether he might not here be intended; but seeing that φοβεῖσθαι ἀπό, indicating terror, is changed into φοβεῖσθαι, so usually followed by τὸν θεόν in a higher and holier sense (there is no such contrast in vs. 26, and therefore that verse cannot be cited as ruling the meaning of this), and that GOD ALONE is throughout the Scripture *the Almighty dispenser of life and death, both temporal and eternal*, seeing also that Satan is ever represented as the *condemned* of God, not ὁ δυν. ἀπολέσαι, I must hold by the general interpretation, and believe that, both here and in Luke xii. 3-7, our Heavenly Father is intended as the right object of our fear. As to this being inconsistent with the character in which He is brought before us in the next verse, the very change of construction in φοβεῖσθαι would lead the mind on out of the terror before spoken of, into that better kind of fear always indicated by that expression when applied to God, and so prepare the way for the next verse. Besides, this sense is excellently in keeping with vs. 29 in another way. . . The parallel passage, James iv. 12, even in the absence of other considerations, would be decisive. Full as his epistle is of our Lord's words from this Gospel, it is hardly to be doubted that in εἷς ἐστιν ὁ νομοθέτης ὁ δυνάμενος σῶσαι καὶ ἀπολέσαι, he has this very verse before him. This Stier endeavors to escape by saying that ἀπολέσαι, barely, as the opposite to σῶσαι, is far from being — ψυχὴν ἀπολέσαι in a context like this. But as connected with νομοθέτης, what meaning can ἀπολέσαι bear except that of *eternal destruction?*"—Alford.]

Vs. 6. **Five sparrows.**—A beautiful version of the same saying, Matt. x. 29. So insignificant is the worth of sparrows in daily life, that whoever buys them for twopence gets one into the bargain, and yet what is regarded among men as almost worthless is with God in heaven not forgotten. To the disciples it is left to calculate how far they excel such sparrows in value.

Vs. 8. **Also I say unto you.**—The repetition several times of this announcement is also to the attentive hearer a proof that here different sayings of the Saviour, originally belonging in an entirely different connection, are chrestomathically put together. With this also the anxious inquiry after the connection between this and the immediately preceding admonition falls away. Respecting the matter itself, the courageous confession of Christ, *see* the remark on Matt. x. 32, and on Luke ix. 26. Here it is especially the reward of a confession *coram angelis ;* in the parallel passage in Matthew, on the other hand, that of a confession *coram Patre.*

Vs. 10. **But unto him that hath blasphemed against the Holy Ghost.**—Respecting the sin against the Holy Spirit, comp. LANGE on Matt. xii. 31, 32, and the authors there stated. As entirely inadequate we may consider the view that this sin is nothing else than "the ascribing those miracles to the power of the devil which Christ wrought by the power of the Holy Spirit." Wesley. It must be placed entirely in one line with the sin which cannot be forgiven, and of which the Scriptures speak also in other places, Heb. x. 26 ; 1 John v. 16. Only then, however, can we speak of the sin against the Holy Spirit where a high measure of religious enlightenment and development exists; and in opposition to the not knowing of that which one does, Luke xxiii. 34, we have here to understand fully conscious and stubborn hatred against God and that which is Divine as it exists in its highest development. The highest grace alone makes the deepest apostasy possible, and only he who has reached an important height can plunge into such a depth. Before his conversion Paul blasphemed the Son of Man and it was forgiven him; had he kicked against the pricks, suppressed with all his might the impression received, then would he have committed the sin which cannot be forgiven. Of Judas we might perhaps say that he committed this sin, and refer to the judgment which, Matt. xxvi. 24, is uttered concerning him.—As respects the punishment for this sin, we have to bear in mind the word of Augustine (*De Civit. Dei.* xxi. 24): "*neque enim de quibusdam veraciter diceretur, quod eis non remittetur, neque in hoc sæculo, neque in futuro, nisi essent, quibus, etsi non in isto, tamen remittatur in futuro.*" A brief but good description of the nature of this sin is given by STIER, ii. p. 44. Respecting the distinction between the Reformed and Lutheran expositors, of whom the former believe that no regenerate person, the latter that such alone, can fall into this sin, we cannot here speak. The grounds for the opinion of the latter are found in Stier and Olshausen; those of the opposite views in J. MULLER, *Christ. Lehre von der Sünde*, ii. p. 566.

Vs. 11. **Before the synagogues.**—One may not unjustly doubt whether the former warning against the sin against the Holy Spirit was wholly congruous for the faithful, devoted disciples of the Saviour; this promise, on the other hand, is very definitely given with reference to their future calling as preachers of the Gospel. The accumulation of expressions is especially adapted to indicate to them that they would be cited not only before Jewish but also before heathen tribunals, and the here-given promise of the Holy Spirit is of such a kind that it promises to them a direct immediate help from above for all cases in which they could need it. Although, however, this help is here limited to that which they should say in their defence, it is understood without doubt that this defence of the apostles was at the same time a testimony, κήρυγμα, in the most exalted sense of the word, and that the assistance already promised them for the lesser should be far less still withheld for the higher. The Book of Acts is an uninterrupted and continuous exposition of the significance and force of this saying. Comp. especially the apologetic discourses of Peter and Paul. Therefore, with right, Bengel: "*aut quid dicatis etiam præter apologiæ necessitatem.*"

DOCTRINAL AND ETHICAL.

1. It is by no means accidental that in one of the discourses of the Lord the warning against the ζύμη τῶν φαρισαίων, ἥτις ἐστὶν ὑπόκρισις stands in the foreground. Hypocrisy is only one of the many sins which He rebukes and opposes in those called to His kingdom; but it is the sin which exceeds all others in meanness, and is in the most irreconcilable conflict with the fundamental law of the kingdom of truth. In the Christian sphere also the Old Testament declaration holds good, Deut. xviii. 13; Psalm li. 10.

2. It is well known how high a rank the mysteries occupy in the heathen religions of antiquity. Those initiated into them believed themselves to have attained a higher degree of piety; from the familiar they mounted up into the region of the unfamiliar, which no uninitiated foot ever dared tread, no indiscreet tongue betray. But in the Christian sphere precisely the opposite is the case. Here the κεκαλυμμένον is not the higher but the lower degree, and not into the chambers but upon the housetops are His followers directed; a proof at the same time of the fact that the restoration of the heathen mysteries in the bosom of the Catholic Church is in principle against the original spirit of Christianity, and that secret orders, that do not venture to come to the light with that which they actually profess or do, have to fear His veto who demanded publicity in the noblest sense of the word, and whose cause more than any other is worthy to face the brightest light.

3. There are words of the Saviour which are best understood and estimated when they are read in the light of a clear starry heaven. To this belongs also the saying of the sparrows and the hairs of the head. "When I consider Thy heavens the work of Thy fingers, the moon and stars which Thou hast ordained; what is man that Thou art mindful of him, and the son of man that Thou hast numbered the hairs of his head?" In order, however, rightly to estimate the whole comfort of this doctrine of a *providentia specialissima*, we must never forget that the Saviour here speaks to His friends, who precisely as such were the objects of the special providence of God.

4. The immortality of the soul in the philosophical sense of the word is as far from being expressly taught and proved by the Saviour as the being and the unity of God; ordinarily He presupposes what indeed cannot be doubted. Not the purely negative conception of immortality, but the positive conception of resurrection and eternal life, stands in the Scriptures of the New Covenant in the foreground. But for this reason we may the less fail to notice that He at least once has in so many words declared that the soul, which is definitely distinguished from the body, *can* in no case be destroyed. The New Testament Demonology also receives by this saying an important degree of light, and the admonition which He gives to His disciples, that they should be perpetually on their guard against Satan's craft and might, they in their turn hold up before their fellow-believers, Ephes. vi. 10; 1 Peter v. 8; James iv. 7, *et alibi*.

5. The sin against the Holy Spirit may in no wise (as *e. g.* Colani does) be made equivalent to the sin against one's own conscience. Conscience speaks even in the breast of the rudest heathen; against the Holy Spirit, however, no one can sin who does not already possess more than usual knowledge and experience of the power of Christian truth.

6. Not unjustly is the Saviour's promise of the assistance of the Holy Spirit regarded as one of the strongest grounds of the high authority in which the word and writings of the apostles stand. Especially according to the parallel in Matt. x. 19, 20, is that which this Spirit speaks in them definitely distinguished from the utterances of their own individual consciousness. The manner of the Spirit's working may be incomprehensible; but so much we see at once, that we have here to understand an entirely extraordinary immediate influence; for it was to be given them ἐν αὐτῇ τῇ ὥρᾳ. The promise of this assistance extended as well to the substance as to the form of their language (πῶς ἢ τί), and this help was to support them so mightily (comp. Luke xxi. 14, 15) that it would be morally impossible for their enemies to persevere in offering them resistance. At the same time this help is promised them for everything which they had to say, not alone respecting their own persons, but also concerning the cause of their Lord. Their writings also, in which this apology of their faith is stated according to the varying necessities of the time, are entirely the faithful expression of that which the Spirit gave them in such moments to ponder, to speak, to write; and this whole promise, communicated by all the Synoptics, is only the brief summary of all that which the Saviour in His parting discourse in John has brought into view in greater detail in reference to the Paraclete.

HOMILETICAL AND PRACTICAL.

The opposition in principle between Pharisaism and Christianity.—How the hypocrite stands related to the Saviour and the Saviour to the hypocrite.—Mysteries whose distinction it is to remain concealed to eternity, the kingdom of heaven does not contain.—Secret speaking and acting must be an exception; sincerity and publicity must be the rule with the disciples of the Saviour.—No fear before many enemies, but only before an adversary fearful beyond measure.—The might of Satan: 1. Its extent; 2. its ground; 3. its limits.—Watchfulness against the enemy of souls united with child-like confidence in the Father of spirits.—The rule of God in little things.—The arithmetic of the Saviour's disciple.—The least is great, the greatest is little before God.—The life of the Christian is invaluable.—The comfort which a look at sparrows and at the hair of the head can give to the disciple of Christ. How much higher do we stand as: 1. Rational beings; 2. as immortal beings; 3. as purchased by the blood of the Son of God; 4. as called to likeness with God. Therefore is it impossible that He who numbers the sparrows should forget the man, the Christian.—The holy function of the Christian to confess his Lord. This function has: 1. A broad extent; 2. unquestionable right; 3. incomparable importance.—According to that which we are here before the Lord can we already judge what hereafter to expect from Him.—How far does even the disciple of the Saviour still need a warning like the Pharisees (Matt. xii. 31, 32) against the sin against the Holy Spirit?—The sin which cannot be forgiven: 1. There is only one sin which absolutely cannot be forgiven; 2. it is now as ever possible to commit this sin; 3. the judgment upon it is perfectly righteous; 4. the mention of it is now as ever fitting: *a.* in order to give a salutary disquiet to individuals; *b.* in order to give a settled composure to troubled souls.—The Holy Spirit the best apologist of the threatened cause of the Saviour: 1. How far this promise regards exclusively the apostles and has been fulfilled in them; 2. how far it holds good of all believers and may be used also for their advantage.

STARKE:—Who does not teach aright, he also lives not aright; and who does not live aright, he also does not teach aright.—QUESNEL:—The saints avoid not the light, and do nothing of which they must be ashamed before God's judgment.—HEDINGER:—God's proclamation of grace is no secret of alchemy, but every one is to know and understand it.—The marvellous simplicity which is found in the Gospel, Psalm xix. 9.—BRENTIUS:—If servants and children of God have much of the suffering of Christ, they are also richly comforted through Christ.—The soul has its own individual existence; therefore it may fare well or ill with it when it is separated from the body.—*Nova Bibl. Tub.*:—It is impossible that God should leave those that trust in Him.—Everything, even the least of things, that happens to man is God's ruling.—It is not enough to believe with the heart on Jesus, but we must also resolutely and joyfully confess Him with the mouth before the world. —There is a sin greater than others, and also worthy of heavier punishment.—MAJUS:—Every Christian must be ready to give account of his hope, 1 Peter iii. 15.—The great ones of the earth have been from the beginning for the most part great enemies to Christ and His Gospel.—The inner ministry of the Holy Ghost is very closely connected with the outer, and must not remain separated from it, 1 Tim. vi. 3-5.

PALMER (on the parallel, Matt. x. 26-33):—The Lord's might and men's impotency: 1. His work He accomplishes, and man cannot hinder it; 2. His faithful ones He protects, and man cannot hinder it; 3. the unfaithful He overthrows, and man cannot hinder it.—VAN OOSTERZEE:—The government of God takes note of trifles. This is truth: 1. Too sure for doubt; 2. too glorious to be slighted; 3. too instructive to be forgotten.—BECK:—Whence comes true courage?

b. THE PARABLE OF THE RICH FOOL (VSS. 13-21).

EXEGETICAL AND CRITICAL.

Vs. 14. **And He said.**—Entirely without reason has the historicalness of the occasion for this parable of the Rich Fool been brought in doubt by De Wette; to us, on the other hand, this trait appears to be probable, and to have been taken from life. But certainly the speaker here appearing is no familiar friend of Jesus (Kuinoel), but a stranger, who perhaps among the myriads, vs. 1, had heard the Saviour for the first time, and while He was speaking of heavenly things had been brooding over earthly. Struck by the might of the personality of the Nazarene, he had considered within himself whether His influence might not perhaps best bring to a happy conclusion the existing family strife. At the same time, this instance shows in a peculiar manner how parties were continually defining themselves more and more sharply for and against the Saviour, inasmuch as in the very place where they had embittered even His meal (ch. xi. 37), there is given Him a special proof, undoubtedly of strong cleaving to earthly things, but quite as much of personal confidence. From the warning against avarice which the Saviour, vs. 15, subjoins, we have not necessarily to draw the conclusion that the petitioner had in mind a thing in and of itself unrighteous.

Man.—The answer exhibits no personal displeasure of the Saviour against the bearer of the unseemly request, but only shows that the Saviour was by no means minded to enter upon a sphere which could not possibly be His own. His answer involuntarily reminds us of the language which once an Egyptian uttered to Moses, Exodus ii. 14.

Vs. 15. **Take heed and beware of covetousness.**—Not only of covetousness which has just before appeared in the definite form of cleaving to a disputed inheritance, but of all exaggerated love of earthly possession. If the petitioner (vs. 13) still remained in the circle of the hearers, the Saviour here renders him a better service than if He had made him rich; He will heal him of his chief malady. To this end serves the parable of the Rich Fool, which Luke alone has preserved, and of which it is not unjustly affirmed, "It is scarcely to be called a parable, so distinctly does it of itself and without any diversion of thought set forth the relation to God" (Riggenbach).

For a man's life ... which he possesseth.— A difficult sentence, in which however the reading of Tischendorf, αὐτῷ, appears to deserve the preference above that of Lachmann, αὐτοῦ. The best construction, on the whole, appears to be this: "ὅτι ἡ ζωὴ αὐτῷ οὐκ ἐστίν τινι ἐν τῷ περισσεύειν (infinitive for the substantive) ἐκ τῶν ὑπαρχόντων αὐτοῦ.—Ζωή is not here to be taken in the sense of the happiness of life but—ψυχή, as Schott paraphrases: "*siquidem quando quis bonis abundat, tamen vita ejus a bonis minime pendet.*" Not from the possession of many goods, but from the will of God, who lengthens or shortens the thread of life, does it depend whether one remains long and quietly here in life or not. One may be preserved in life without possessing goods, and also remain in the possession of goods and unexpectedly lose life. That riches in and of themselves do not give happiness is undoubtedly true, yet not the chief thought of this parable.

Vs. 17. **The estate of a certain rich man.**— Probably a quite considerable space of ground, not χωρίον, but χώρα. Not without intention does the Saviour choose as His example a man who gathers his riches in a customary, legitimate, apparently innocent way. "*Modus hic ditescendi innocentissimus et tamen periculosus.*" Bengel. The first thing which is lacking to this fortunate rich man is complete contentment.

What shall I do?—With discontent is joined anxiety and perplexity, since he does not know how he shall manage with his treasures. A similar perplexity to that which is related, Mark xvi. 3, in which, however, God does not come into the midst and give help. That his increased prosperity offers him opportunity to do something for his poor brethren, does not even come into his mind; selfishness strikes the key-note, even in the four times recurring μου: τοὺς καρποὺς μου, κ.τ.λ.

Vs. 18. **I will pull down my barns.**—By

a forcible tearing down, therefore, he believes he shall open the way to his happiness. The ἀποθῆκαι were for the most part subterraneous dry vaults. It is possible that the Rich Fool is thinking of enlarging them, but also that he is of a mind to build up greater ἀποθῆκαι from the foundation. Here also there is not the least mention of the poor, but, on the other hand, an emphatic exaltation of his γεννήματα as his highest earthly ἀγαθά.

Vs. 19. **Soul.**—To the continuing discontent and rising care of the rich man is added now the self-deceit of the falsest hope. Unconsciously he confesses that he has hitherto not yet found the long sighed-for rest, but expects it, and that for a long time, when the intended work shall have been entirely completed. Very finely, Meyer: "to my *soul*, not exactly *mihi*, but to my soul, the seat of the sensibilities, here of the desire of enjoyment." Not only idleness, no, revelling, is the ideal that this fool mirrors to himself. The reference to the passage, Sirach xi. 17–19, is in this whole representation almost impossible to mistake.

Vs. 20. **Thou fool.**—The searching contrast between the soliloquy of the fool and the judgment of God, belongs to the greatest beauties of the parable. This beauty, however, is lost if we think here merely of a *decretum Dei* (Kuinoel) instead of the invisible King of Heaven appearing in speech and action, and suddenly causing him to feel that not even so many hours are allotted him as he had been dreaming of years—ἀπαιτοῦσιν. Who now is to fulfil this sentence? God Himself (Meyer); the death-angels to whom I have committed the power (Von Gerlach); robbers and murderers (Bornemann, Paulus)? The latter is perhaps the most agreeable to the concrete character of the parable; neither is there any ground whatever for understanding the verb impersonally. If we understand burglars demanding his life of him, the requirement has then double emphasis. There is thereby the image of terror held up before the rich man, to him especially in the highest degree frightful; and the question immediately following thereon, "Whose shall those things be which thou hast provided?" acquires still higher significance if we assume that the murderers, unknown to him and already approaching, shall be at the same time the robbers of his goods. Nor does vs. 21 offer any difficulty to this explanation if we only keep the *tertium comparationis* in mind.

Vs. 21. **So is he that.**—He dreams as illusively as this fool, in order sooner or later to awake in a similarly terrible manner. Θησαυρίζων ἑαυτῷ, *in suum commodum*, so that in his enjoyment consists the chief end which he in the augmentation of his treasures has in mind. To this restless and fruitless θησαυρίζειν is opposed the still and abiding πλουτεῖν εἰς Θεόν which is directed towards God and Divine things, and in another passage is called "laying up treasures in heaven," Matt. vi. 20.

DOCTRINAL AND ETHICAL.

1. That the Saviour does not meditate even an instant the composing of the controversy respecting the inheritance in any way whatever, is worthy of note. Had such a strife arisen among His own, He would then without doubt have composed it, so that undoubtedly the later precept of His apostle (1 Cor. vi. 1–6) was entirely in the spirit of the Master. But here, where it concerned a matter entirely foreign, standing in no relation to the kingdom of God, His answer could only be one of refusal, and accordingly He decidedly repels the temptation to enter upon a sphere which lay so far from that which the Father had appointed Him. Although he had appeared as Israel's King, He mingles as little with the controversies of the Jews as with the political affairs of the Romans, but on the other hand remains faithful to His subsequently uttered principle (John xviii. 36). And as He gives in this relation also an example to all His disciples, who are to be no ἀλλοτριοεπίσκοποι (1 Peter iv. 15), so is His conduct also of importance for the regulation of the principle of the relation of the Church to the State. Not without reason, at least, has the Augsburg Confession, in its 28th article, adduced this declaration of the Saviour (vs. 14) as a proof that the two jurisdictions, the spiritual and the secular, should not be confounded with one another.

2. Not as a judge concerning inheritances, but as a Redeemer from sins, and from avarice among them, not less than from hypocrisy, will the Saviour exhibit Himself on this occasion. Such a consideration is wholly in the spirit of the third, the Pauline Gospel (comp. 1 Tim. vi. 6–10), and deserves the more to be laid to heart, inasmuch as avarice is not seldom especially the sin of the saints, who have already died to the lusts of the flesh, and are made free from the natural pride of the heart. As to the rest, the parable of the Rich Fool is also full of allusions to Old Testament utterances. *See*, *e. g.*, Job xxii. 25; Ps. xxxix. 7; xlix. 12 *seq.*; Jer. xvii. 11; Ps. lxxii. 10, 11.

3. If we consider that the parable of the Rich Fool was uttered in the presence of the disciples of Jesus, and also, therefore, of Judas, we find new occasion to admire the Saviour's wisdom in teaching which so indirectly but powerfully attacks the darling sin of the future traitor.

HOMILETICAL AND PRACTICAL.

Even under the preaching of Jesus there are unreceptive and inattentive listeners.—Care for the earthly inheritance instead of the longing for the heavenly.—The Saviour will not work with force, but renewingly and regeneratingly upon earthly relations. —Avarice the root of all evil.—Let every one abide in that whereunto he is called.—How poor a rich man and how rich a poor man may be.—If riches fall to any one, let him not set his heart thereon.—Even earthly blessing may become a snare.—Cares of earthly riches opposed to the holy unanxiousness of the children of God.—The rich man's self-enjoyment of life in its full beggarliness.—Augmenting disquiet with augmenting wealth.—Delusive hope of rest in later years.—God's thoughts other than the thoughts of men.—The unlooked-for death of the child of the world.—The mournful fate of the man who gathers treasures to himself and is not rich toward God: 1. Painful discontent; 2. increasing anxiety; 3. delusive hope; 4. irreparable loss.—Riches in God: 1. The only true; 2. the inalienable; 3. the universally accessible riches.

For homiletical treatment, either the 15th verse or the 21st verse offers the point of departure. For a harvest-sermon also this parable is especially adapted.

STARKE:—QUESNEL:—The goods of this world give often occasion for discord, disquiet, and offence. —CANSTEIN:—It is not great wealth that preserves the temporal life of man, but God's power and blessing.—God's blessing reaches even over the fields of the ungodly, Matt. v. 45.—They who receive the richest blessing are wont often to forget their benefactor.—*Nova Bibl. Tub.*:—Earthly souls have ever earthly thoughts and purposes.—MAJUS:—Epicurean men soon have their everlasting reward.—The Lord knoweth the thoughts of men that they are vain.—*Bibl. Wirt.*:—The avaricious are unhappy in this world and that to come.—MAJUS:—Whoever is rich in God, like Abraham, David, and Solomon, whom earthly riches hurt not, he uses them according to the Lord's will. [Grave exception may be taken to the last-named of these three examples.—C. C. S.]

HEUBNER:—Even the strictest bands of consanguinity do not protect selfish hearts against discord.—How great is the self-love of the vain-minded?—Cleaving to earthly good a folly.—The poor Rich Fool comes before God's judgment with a lost name, with a lost soul, with a lost world, with a lost heaven (Rieger).—The true wealth of man.—Comp. two homilies of Basil, Opp. ii. p. 43, Edit. Garner.—ARNDT:—Fleshly security: 1. Its form; 2. God's judgment upon it.—LISCO:—Concerning the misleading of many citizens of the kingdom by earthly wealth.—Avarice considered as the destroyer of all the harvest-blessing.—KRUMMACHER:—How faith keeps harvest-home and how unbelief. The two classes of men diverge essentially: 1. In their view of the Divine blessing received; 2. in the use that they make of the same; 3. in the relation of dependence in which they place themselves to the blessing.—GEROK:—The rich man—a poor man; see how one can miscalculate.—COCARD:—What is requisite if our earthly care is not to be a sinful one.—KLIEFOTH:—What shall we take with us through the gates of the grave?

c. THE FREEDOM FROM ANXIETY OF THE DISCIPLES OF THE SAVIOUR (Vss. 22-34).

EXEGETICAL AND CRITICAL.

Vs. 22. **Therefore I say unto you.**—If we presuppose that this admonition to tranquil freedom from care was delivered on the same occasion (*see* however above, and comp. Matt. vi. 22-34), then it is not difficult to give the connection of this part of the Saviour's discourse with the former one. The source of the avarice which He has just been combating is nothing else than the excessive anxiety and fear that we might in some way suffer lack, and this fear certainly becomes no one less than the disciple of the Saviour. Earthly care now is directed first of all to nourishment and clothing. Both forms the Saviour opposes, inasmuch as He points those that are anxious to what they see in the realm of nature, but above all to the truth that He who has already given the higher, will certainly not let them lack the lesser.

Vs. 23. **The life is more than food.**—" You turn it exactly round; food is meant to serve life, but life forsooth serves food; clothes are to serve the body, but the body forsooth must serve the clothing, and so blind is the world that it sees not this." Luther. If God bestows the higher, He by that very fact already gives a pledge that He will not withhold the lesser. Rom. viii. 32.

Vs. 24. **Consider the ravens.**—Ps. cxlvii. 9. Perhaps also an indirect reminiscence of the miraculous history of Elijah, 1 Kings xvii. 6. By κατανοήσατε there is more meant than a superficial view, rather an observing and studying, of the ravens. Matthew, using more general terms, has only πετεινά. Perhaps at this particular moment birds or lilies had in His immediate vicinity drawn the attention of the Saviour to this, and given Him occasion to this figurative mode of speech.

Vs. 25. **To his length of life.**—*See* LANGE on *Matthew*, vi. 27.

Vs. 27. **Consider the lilies.**—The plural designates the κρίνα not necessarily as a mass but also as individuals.—Πῶς οὔτε νήθει, κ.τ.λ., an indirect question, whose more complete form is found in Matthew. *See* the notes on the text.

In all his glory.—When he showed himself in his full royal magnificence. *See* 2 Chron. ix. 15.

Vs. 29. **Neither be ye of doubtful mind,** or, do not exalt yourselves, μὴ μετεωρίζεσθε.—The usage of this word is familiar, which echoes also in our "Meteor." *See* the rich collection of examples in KUINOEL, *ad loc.* Μετεωρίζεσθαι can signify nothing else than: To lift one's self so far on high that one shines like an aerial phenomenon, but must also share the fate of so many wandering lights. Comp. the familiar: "*Tolluntur in altum, ut lapsu graviore ruant.*" Especially does the high flight of fancy appear here to be meant, when one creates imagined necessities for himself, and for this reason is doubly ill-content with reality, and for this very reason allows himself so much the more to be seduced into unbelieving anxiety. The more modest the wishes, the more easily is the heart contented.

Vs. 31. **Seek ye His kingdom.**—There is no sufficient ground for transferring hither from Matt. vi. 33, the adverb πρῶτον. According to Luke it is the Saviour's will that we should seek *absolutely* after God's kingdom; in which case the precept is only apparently different from that given in Matt. vi. 33. The πρῶτον ζητεῖτε which is there enjoined is also a seeking that excludes every further anxiety. In the sense in which they are to seek the kingdom of God, the Saviour's disciples have nothing more to strive after. *See* LANGE on the passage in *Matthew*.

Vs. 32. **Fear not, little flock.**—In the first place, here, without doubt, allusion is made to the fear combated in the foregoing verses, but then also further, fear which might hinder them in the seeking of the kingdom of God. This seeking should in no case be fruitless: for it was the Father's good pleasure to give them what they desired above everything.

Little flock.—Perhaps the intentional contrast of the little circle of disciples with the myriads of the people, vs. 1. At the same time a word of the Good Shepherd. Comp. Matt. xxvi, 31; John x. 11.—

Your Father's good pleasure.—Eph. i. 4-6. Not only a *divinum arbitrium, cui stat pro ratione voluntas,* but also a *beneplacitum amoris divini.*

Vs. 33. **Sell that ye have.**—A strengthening of the admonition which in Matt. vi. 19-21 appears in another form. Undoubtedly this precept may be applied in a very sound sense as addressed to *every* Christian: comp. Matt. xix. 21. Here, however, it is a definite command to the apostles, who, in order to live entirely for the kingdom of God, were to be fettered by no earthly care.

And give alms.—This commandment also must,

like several precepts of the Sermon on the Mount, not be interpreted κατὰ ῥητόν, but in the spirit of wisdom, which is quite as far from egoistic limitations as from communistic extravagances. In caring in this way for others they would make to themselves (ἑαυτοῖς) **purses that wax not old.** To take with them this kind of βαλάντια was not forbidden, as it was to take the other sort, Luke xxii. 35; and in these purses they laid up for themselves a **treasure that faileth not.** This treasure in heaven, of which the Synoptics speak, is already laid up in this life, as also ζωὴ αἰώνιος, according to John, begins even before death. Even because the treasure in heaven is of spiritual origin, of heavenly kind, it is also of absolutely imperishable duration.

Vs. 34. **For where your treasure is.**—A word of the deepest knowledge of men, and capable of the most manifold explication. The human heart little by little appropriates to itself the style and nature of the treasure to which its whole thought is directed. Whoever constitutes his god of gold, his heart becomes as cold and hard as metal; whoever takes flesh for his arm or makes it his idol, becomes more and more sensual, and takes on the properties of that which he loves above everything; but whoever has invisible treasures keeps spontaneously eye and heart directed upon the invisible world, and whoever has no higher good than God, accords to Him in his love also the first place. This is the key to the unspeakably rich patristic word: "*Domine, quia nos fecisti ad te, cor nostrum inquietum in nobis, donec requiescat in te.*"

DOCTRINAL AND ETHICAL.

1. See *Exegetical* and *Critical.*
2. In order to feel the high value of this instruction of the Saviour, we have only to place ourselves in the condition of the apostles, who for His sake left all. Not only were the Eleven by the force of this beyond doubt often preserved from discouragement and anxiety, but also in the soul of a Paul, who did not as yet sit here at the feet of the Saviour, echoes the tone of this encouraging word, which he without doubt afterwards heard. *See* Phil. iv. 6, 7, and comp. 1 Peter v. 7.
3. The holy freedom from care which the Saviour here commends to His disciples has nothing in common with the light-minded carelessness of those who do not think of the morrow; for there is also Christian care, which impels to prayer and also at the same time to labor. Only that anxiety does the Saviour censure which acts as if all in the last resort was dependent on this care alone, instead of thinking on the admirable rule: "*Mit Sorgen und mit Grämen, Lasst Gott sich gar nichts nehmen, es will erbeten sein.*" [Anxiety procures nothing from God, but only prayer]. Very justly does Luther distinguish: "The care that comes from love is bidden, but that which is separate from faith is forbidden."
4. This part also of the Saviour's discourse affords the complete proof how He, the Friend of man, was at the same time the friend of glorious nature. Ravens and lilies does He make for His disciples preachers of the most consolatory truth. But if we will feel the whole power and beauty of this imagery, we must regard Him who used it with the eye of a John, and recognize in Him the Eternal Word without which nothing was made that is made—that has created also the ravens and lilies of the field. The symbols of the fatherly care of God to which He points are not only His own discovery, but what is more, are also His own creation.

5. The encouraging word to the little flock contains the rich germs of the Evangelical and especially of the Pauline doctrine of Predestination. At the same time we obtain here an important intimation in reference to the point of view from which this doctrine must, according to the will of the Saviour, be considered and represented, namely, as a consolation to troubled believers and not as an occasion of idle questions. The comfort here given remains moreover the same, although the number of the disciples of Christ has enlarged itself to many millions. Still, as ever, contrasted with the majority of the unbelieving world, this number is a very small one, and of the friends of the Saviour it may still as ever be said, "Behold I send you as sheep in the midst of wolves" (Matt. x. 16). But these little and defenceless ones have for themselves so much the surer ground of reckoning on the defence and help of the Heavenly Father.

HOMILETICAL AND PRACTICAL.

How far the disciple of the Saviour has to care for his temporal support and how far not.—The distinction between the care of the blind heathen, the God-fearing Israelite, and the believing Christian.—The preaching of the ravens and lilies.—Excessive anxiety for earthly things is: 1. In part needless; 2. in part fruitless; 3. in part injurious to higher interests.—If thou wilt be raised above the care for the lesser good that is yet wanting to thee, look upon the higher that has already been bestowed upon thee.—The impotency of all our caring to alter anything against the will of God in our outward fate. —God clothes; 1. Solomon with glory; 2. the lilies far more gloriously than Solomon; 3. the believer far more richly than Solomon and the lilies together. —Seek not for high things, but condescend to the humble, Romans xii. 16.—"In quietness and confidence shall be your strength," Isaiah xxx. 15.—Your Father knows that ye have need of all these things. 1. There is One who knows what we need; 2. this One is our Father; 3. to this Father Jesus leads us.— Fear not, little flock, a word of comfort: 1. For the circle of apostles over against the unbelieving world; 2. for the evangelical church in the midst of her numerous enemies; 3. for every believing *ecclesiola* over against a degenerate hierarchical church.— Those that buy, that they be as though they possessed not, 1 Cor. vii. 29–31.—Christian communism in opposition to its caricature in our century.—The art of so giving that we become not poorer but richer.—The security of the treasure that is laid up in heaven.—Where the treasure there the heart, either, 1. On earth, or 2. in heaven.

STARKE:—Between anxious care and over-negligence Christians must keep the middle path.—ARNDT: —Let us by all means study diligently the book of nature together with the Holy Scripture.—QUESNEL: —The experience of our impotency even in lesser matters should serve to this, that we surrender ourselves wholly to God in the weightier.—CANSTEIN: —Beautiful attire and boastful glory of other things are wholly vain and come not once near the beauty of a field-flower.—Christ forbids not the labor of the body, but the disquiet and mistrustfulness of the soul.—Children of princes and kings need not to

torment themselves with anxious care, and Christians even much less.—CANSTEIN:—As God means to give us Heaven, why plague we ourselves then anxiously on account of sustenance on earth?—True believers have been at all times few compared with the great mass of the ungodly, Psalm xii. 1.
CRAMER:—To do good to the poor is every Christian's duty, Isaiah lviii. 7.—Whoever will be benevolent, let it be from his own means, not from other people's.—*Nova Bibl. Tub.*:—No funds are better and more safely invested than alms.—Examine thyself, O Soul, where is thy treasure and thy heart?
HEUBNER:—The right precedence among cares,—The miserable folly of earthly cares.—The chief care of the Christian.—Care not how long, but *how* thou livest.—COUARD:—Concerning earthly care, how it, 1. Is unworthy of us; 2. most dangerous; 3. beyond measure foolish; 4. utterly profitless.—WESTERMEYER:—The care forbidden by God: 1. How far forbidden; 2. why.—CLAUS HARMS:—A Harvestsermon in the *Sommerpostille*, 6th ed. p. 349.

---

5. **The Vigilance and the Conflict of the Genuine Disciple of the Lord (Vss. 35–59).**

(Parallel to Matt. xxiv. 43–51.)

a. Vss. 35–48.

35, 36 Let your loins be girded about, and *your* lights burning; And ye yourselves like unto men that wait for their lord, when he will return from the wedding; that, when 37 he cometh and knocketh, they may open unto him immediately. Blessed *are* those servants, whom the lord when he cometh shall find watching: verily I say unto you, that he shall gird himself, and make them to sit down to meat [recline at table], and 38 will come forth [approach] and serve them [wait on them]. And if he shall come in the second watch, or come in the third watch, and find *them* so, blessed are those ser-
39 vants [they¹]. And this know, that if the goodman [master] of the house had known what hour the thief would come, he would have watched, and not have suffered his
40 house to be broken through. Be ye therefore ready also: for the Son of man cometh
41 at an hour when ye think not. Then Peter said unto him,² Lord, speakest thou this
42 parable unto [for] us, or even to [also for] all? And the Lord said, Who then is that faithful and³ wise steward, whom *his* lord shall make ruler over his household [body of servants, θεραπείας], to give *them* their portion of meat [allowance of food] in due sea-
43 son? Blessed *is* that servant, whom his lord when he cometh shall find so doing.
44 Of a truth I say unto you, that he will make him ruler over all that he hath [he will
45 set him over all his possessions]. But and [om., and] if that servant say in his heart, My lord delayeth his coming; and shall begin to beat the menservants and maidens,
46 and to eat and drink, and to be drunken; The lord of that servant will come in a day when he looketh not for *him*, and at an hour when he is not aware, and will cut him in
47 sunder, and will appoint him his portion with the unbelievers⁴ [the unfaithful]. And that servant, which knew his lord's will, and prepared not *himself*, neither did according
48 to his will, shall be beaten with many *stripes*. But he that knew not, and did commit things worthy of stripes, shall be beaten with few *stripes*. For [And] unto whomsoever much is given, of him shall be much required; and to whom men [they] have committed much, of him they will ask the more.

¹ Vs. 38.—Since the words οἱ δοῦλοι are wanting in B., D., [Cod. Sin.,] L., Cant. Corb., and others, it is easy to suppose that they have been inserted here from vs. 37. We have therefore omitted them, with Tischendorf and Lachmann. [Meyer, Alford. Cod. Sin. omits ἐκείνοι also.—C. C. S.]
² Vs. 41.—Perhaps an interpolation, perhaps also genuine, but omitted by B., D., [ins., Cod. Sin.,] L., [R.,] X., as it might appear superfluous.
³ Vs. 42.—Καί before φρόνιμος is of later origin.
[⁴ Vs. 46.—Διχοτομήσει, which has literally the signification given it in our text, is regarded by most critics as used here in a tropical sense, equivalent to "*he shall cruelly scourge him.*" Van Oosterzee takes it so. But the assuming of this meaning is supported by no examples, and is merely inferred from the supposition that the servant is represented as alive after the punishment, in καὶ τὸ μέρος, κ.τ.λ. But this, as Meyer remarks, is simply epexegetical of the preceding, indicating what the punishment is meant to express.—C. C. S.]

EXEGETICAL AND CRITICAL.

Vs. 35. **Let your loins be girt about.**—Very fittingly does the admonition to watchfulness join in with the admonition given in the previous verses to confidence and freedom from care. It is true they could be free from anxiety as to whether it was the Father's good pleasure to give them His kingdom (vs. 32), but they could only inherit if they expected, watching and working, the coming of the Lord. It is true that the now-following admonition alludes to the parable of the Ten Virgins (De Wette), but it contains, nevertheless, a number of peculiar traits, which cause the method, as well as the blessing, of Christian watchfulness, to appear in an entirely new light. As well the form as the substance of the now-following parable in Luke is far more complete than the manner in which Matthew, ch. xxiv. 42-51, has rendered it.

Your lights burning.—Two qualities of the servant who is to receive his returning Lord in fitting wise. The long garments of the Orientals had to be girt up if they were not to hinder them in walking and waiting. See WETSTEIN, *ad loc.* Comp. 1 Pet. i. 13, perhaps a reminiscence of this saying. Even so must the light be kindled when the Lord was about to return in the middle of the night. By the first image it is the activity, by the second the watchfulness, of the faithful servant which is especially indicated.

Vs. 36. **When He shall return from the wedding.**—A trait of the parable somewhat deviating from the common form of the conception, according to which the heavenly γάμοι begin only after the Parusia of the Son of Man. See, *e. g.*, Matt. xxv. 1-13. Here the Messiah is represented as He, surrounded of course by guests and friends, celebrates His wedding in heaven, and now, after the whole banquet is ended, returns to His dwelling, and crowns His faithful servants with honor and joy. That these after His return continue to celebrate the wedding with Him, is here not said. It is now, perhaps, considered as ended. (Otherwise Bengel, Stier.) The servants, however, who have faithfully awaited their Lord when celebrating the wedding, are now refreshed by Him with another feast, prepared in their honor, at which He appears, not as Bridegroom, but as servant. It is, of course, understood that it would be exceedingly forced to press dogmatically every trait of the parabolical representation, and that we must only have respect to the *tertium comparationis*.

Open immediately.—Because they have nothing to hide, and have not fallen asleep. "*Vult suos esse expeditos.*" Bengel.

Vs. 37. **Blessed are those servants.**—By different images the blessedness of the faithful is now portrayed. First stage: The Lord will cause the momentary separation, which had hitherto been between them, to close, and will kindly approach nearer (παρελθών). Second stage: He girds His garment on, in order now, on His side also, to serve *them*. How literally the Saviour has fulfilled this feature of His picture appears from John xiii. 4. Third stage: He causes them to take their place at table, and sets before them His most exquisite viands. It is needless here to understand the viands which had been brought from the wedding-feast, or had been sent to His dwelling. (Kuinoel.) To this is added again, as a fourth feature, vs. 44, that the servants, to whom hitherto only a part of the estate had been committed, are now entrusted with the administration of all the possessions of their Lord. It is, however, not necessary to have in mind the Saturnalia of the Romans (Grotius), among whom it is well known that good and bad servants alike were served by their masters. We might rather call to mind the usage of the ancient Hebrews, of giving their servants a share in sacred feasts (Deut. xii. 18; xvi. 11).

Vs. 38. **In the second watch . . . in the third watch.**—The Romans divided the night into four night-watches, *dici inclinatio, gallicinium, canticinium, diluculum,* a division which the Jews had accepted from them. See particulars among others in FRIEDLIEB, *Archäologie der Leidensgeschichte,* on Luke xxii.

60-62. The opinion is entirely without ground (Lisco, Olshausen), that the Saviour here followed another division into only three night-watches. He says nothing of the fourth, simply for the reason that the disciples, from that, should note that His return was, by no means, to be expected as late as possible, even as He does not name the first; because it would weaken the whole representation of the watchful servants. The Parusia does not come so quickly as impatience, nor yet so late as carelessness supposes, but in the very middle of the night, when the temptation to fall asleep is greatest, and therefore must be most vigorously combated. It may even tarry longer than the servants thought; but, grant that it should take place not till the third, or should come even in the second, watch of the night, whoever perseveres faithfully at his post shall in no wise lose his reward.

Vs. 39. **If the master of the house.**—A modification of the figurative language, in which those who had hitherto been represented as servants, now, during the presupposed absence of their Lord, are compared with the master of the house, who has to take care that his goods be not stolen.

The thief.—Not the ἄρχων τοῦ κόσμου (Olshausen) but the Son of Man, vs. 40, who will come quite as unexpectedly to His disciples. It is noticeable how this comparison of the Parusia with the coming of the thief has passed over, in all manner of forms, into the apostolic writings, and is afterwards heard from the mouth of the glorified Saviour. 1 Thess. v. 2, 6-8; 2 Pet. iii. 10; Rev. iii. 3; xvi. 15. Of course the similitude of the thief is taken entirely from the point of view of those who are sunken in earthly enjoyment and inactive rest, and to whom therefore the Parusia of the Son of Man is no joyful but a terrible event.

Vs. 40. **Be ye therefore ready also.**—*See* LANGE on Matt. xxiv. 43, 44.

Vs. 41. **Then Peter.**—The doubt as to the originality of this question is without any ground. And just as little can it be regarded as an interpolation of Luke (against De Wette). It is, on the contrary, precisely accordant with the character of the apostle, and it is, from a psychological point of view, worthy of remark that this question is proposed by that very apostle who afterwards, Matt. xxvi. 41, most of all needed the admonition, and in so sad a manner forgot it. In view of the well-known earthly-mindedness of the disciples, it is much to be feared that this question was elicited even more by the first than the second part of the parable; by the holding up of the reward even more than by the exhortation to watchfulness, and that Peter wishes to know whether this high distinction (vs. 37) was only intended for him and his fellow-disciples, or also, besides these (ἢ καί), for others.

Vs. 42. **And the Lord said.**—The Saviour is as far from affirming that the parable respects all (Friedlieb), as that it has a special reference to the apostles (Ewald); but He continues in a general sense His figurative discourse, and that in such a way, that Peter, by some reflection, can give himself the answer. This answer amounts to this, that according as a more extended circle of operation is entrusted to a servant of the Lord, his obligation to watchfulness increases, and if he forgets his vocation, he has so much the sharper chastisement to fear. An exceedingly weighty teaching for all the apostles, but, most, for the very Peter who had elicited it. Comp. Matt. xvi. 18.

Who then is that faithful and wise stew-

1 Cor. iv. 2, was a mid-
and the slave, and, as
seph with Potiphar, was
a whole domestic estab-
ost. sense of the word a
herefore, faithfulness in
As the οἰκονόμοι to the
also the apostles stand
vers, and be called to
reward of faithfulness
le of operation received

rvant, ἐκεῖνος. With
alludes very definitely
d. He represents him
wo great sins, to hard-
ers, to slothfulness and
If. Still more strikingly
in Matthew, vs. 49, by
drunken. Precisely this
e of the unfaithful οἰκο-
faithful but defenceless
from them that which is
and, peoples the dwell-
stration with a vile rab-
dissoluteness. While
the unfaithful apostle,
, at the same time, com-
e of the shepherds in
ad of the sheep, feed
ry of the church shows
y ones.

mselves know to hold
o least have learned
art belongs.
they? they are fed:
and flashy songs
of wretched straw.
I are not fed,
rank wind they draw,
ion spread.

MILTON, *Lycidas*.]

le spirit of this whole
s of Peter. *See*, *e. g.*,

ἐν.—For different views
n *Matt.* xxiv. 50. Un-
e said for the view that
word in a milder sense,
literally: "He will split
other hand, it must not
this punishment of the
pointed with the hypo-
sequently as yet living.
and in Matt. xxiv. 51 ;
; 1 Chron. xiv. 10, 11.
nore fittingly chosen if
nt is threatened against
o be faithful but after-
nfaithful, and therefore
n heart. *Qui cor Di-
ngel.
According to Matthew,
he thought comes espe-
he Lord will judge His
lition in which He finds
nifested faithfulness can
ls, in view of the delay
negligence and unfaith-
e find the same thought

Vs. 47. **That servant.**—The Saviour justified the judgment just passed against the possible suspicion of too great severity, by placing a general principle in the foreground, namely, that the more light there beams upon us the greater will be the punishableness of sin, and precisely in the difference of punishment is the impartiality and righteousness of the judge made known. All evil servants are punished, even those of whom it may be said in a certain sense that they have not known the will of their Lord, since in no case is the ignorance absolute, and entirely without their own fault. Some knowledge, how imperfect soever it might be, could be presupposed in them all, because on men there is bestowed not only the light of a special revelation, but also the light of conscience. Comp. the words of Calvin: *Tenendum memoria est, qui regendæ Ecclesiæ præfecti sunt, eos non ignorantia peccare, sed perverse et impie fraudare Dominum suum. Hinc tamen generalis doctrina colligi debet, frustra ad ignorantiæ patrocinium confugere homines, ut se a reatu liberent.*—Comp. James iv. 17.
—**Many stripes.**—Although the fixed number of stripes, according to the Mosaic jurisprudence, amounted to forty, Deut. xxv. 2, 3, it is of course understood that such determining of the number in this case would be in conflict with the spirit of the parable. But the same principle which is expressed, Deut. xxv. 2, namely, that a righteous relation must exist between the greatness of the offence and the punishment, is also emphasized here by the Saviour.

Vs. 48. **To whom much is given.**—In temporal things as well as also in spiritual. The greatest prerogatives bring also the greatest responsibility with them. Ἐδόθη πολύ, not to be restricted precisely to the *magna et accurata religionis scientia*, but in general to be understood of the commission which is given to the high-placed οἰκονόμος, and so far also of the confidence reposed in him.—Πολὺ ζητηθήσεται, in official activity (Meyer), of which strict account shall be required. Although παρέθεντο and αἰτήσουσιν are expressed impersonally, it is nevertheless in this connection scarcely possible to exclude the thought of the Lord of the servant, who has bestowed confidence on him, and will immediately judge his work.
—**The more,** περισσότερον.—According to Meyer: "More than was deposited with him, he is therewith to win a surplus." But where, in the foregoing parable, is the thought expressed that the faithful servant is to get interest with the property of his Lord? The connection appears in this passage much more to favor the interpretation of: *plus quam ab aliis*, which can appear weak and without meaning only in case it is forgotten that this whole expression bears a proverbial character; the parallelism moreover of the two sentences on this interpretation is better preserved.

DOCTRINAL AND ETHICAL.

1. It must not surprise us that the Saviour represents His disciples so decidedly from the point of view of dependent servants, for only in the latter period of His intercourse with them does He address them as Friends and Children, and the high honor which He here promises the faithful servant shows plainly how high a rank His servants possessed in His eyes, and what love He had for His disciples. With the exception of perhaps the promise, Rev. iii. 21, we know no utterance of the Saviour which holds up before the life of the faithful so rich and ravishing a reward as this, vs. 37.

2. It is manifest that the parable of the Faithful and Unfaithful οἰκονόμος is for no one of so high importance as for the preachers of the gospel, who, because they stand upon a higher position than others, are also exposed to greater dangers. After such declarations of the Saviour we comprehend the better the holy fear of the apostle, 1 Cor. ix. 27*b*.

3. We weaken the force of the parable if by the Unfaithful Servant we understand any particular person (Vitringa, *e. g.*, understood the Pope). In the form of a concrete personality, on the other hand, there is a type delineated which is easily found again in all ecclesiastical despots and hierarchs, and verily not at Rome alone. In order to make manifest the inward unfaithfulness of all those who outwardly range themselves among His servants, and perhaps began with a guise of faithfulness and obedience, the Saviour needs to do nothing more than to make some delay. Then the old Adam, who for a while was covered and bedecked, comes spontaneously into manifestation again, and that not seldom in the most hideous forms. Even after the Middle Ages, boundless haughtiness and arrogance towards "the people that know not the law," have often gone hand in hand with equal wantonness and sensuality. But the Saviour treasures up in His memory as much what is committed by an unholy clericalism in His name as what is practised by the spirit of anti-christianity against His defenceless servants.

4. The whole delineation of the terrific punishment just prepared for the unfaithful servant bears the character of the *justitia retributiva*. Those who believe that from the evangelical position one cannot properly speak of any punishment in the juridical sense, but only affectionate chastisements for the moral amendment of the misled, can hardly measure aright the fearful earnestness of declarations such as those of vss. 45–48. It is noteworthy also that the Saviour makes indeed a distinction in the grades, but not in the duration, of the decisive retribution of the future. That those also are threatened with this retributive judgment to whom the Lord's will is less known than to others, admits of entire justification. For if even the heathen, according to Rom. ii. 15, have an ἔργον τοῦ νόμου γραπτὸν ἐν ταῖς καρδίαις αὐτῶν, so that they are not to be excused, how much less can the servant of Christ reckon upon entire exemption from punishment if he in some particular case did not know the will of the Lord.

HOMILETICAL AND PRACTICAL.

The life of the disciples of the Saviour must be a life of watchfulness.—The nature of Christian watchfulness : 1. Alertness, 2. activity, 3. circumspection. —The motive of Christian watchfulness: 1. Certainty, 2. suddenness, 3. decisiveness of the coming of the Lord.—What does the Lord demand of His faithful servants? 1. An eye that is open for His light, 2. a hand that carries on His work, 3. a foot that is every instant ready to go to meet Him and to open to Him. —What does the Lord promise to His faithful servants? 1. Honorable distinction, 2. perfect contentment, 3. beseeming elevation.—The connection between this representation and Luke xvii. 7–10.—Not on the long duration, but on the faithfulness of their working, depends the gracious reward of the servants of the kingdom of God.—According to the state in which the Lord finds us will He judge us.—The thief in the night: 1. How unexpectedly he comes, 2. how carefully his coming must be awaited.—Increasing negligence a sign that the coming of the Son of Man is no longer distant, but near by, even at the door.— The minister of the gospel an οἰκονόμος. By this image there is expressed : 1. His high rank, 2. his holy vocation, 3. his heavy responsibility : "Moreover it is required in stewards that a man be found faithful," 1 Cor. iv. 2.—The οἰκονόμος in the kingdom of God no ruler over the men-servants and maidens, but just as little their slave.—Great temptation to negligence is connected with the tarrying of the coming of the Lord.—Injustice towards the least of His people which is committed by one of His messengers, is to the King of the kingdom of God utterly intolerable. —Excessive severity towards others and excessive laxness towards one's self are not seldom united in hirelings without the shepherd's heart.—The *Jus Talionis* in the theocratic sphere.—Different grades : 1. Of the pardonableness, 2. of the retribution of sin.—Even ignorance in relation to the will of the Lord may be a self-caused ignorance.—For the unfaithful οἰκονόμος it would be better on that day to have been the least of the servants.—He that is privileged above others may only rejoice with trembling, comp. Heb. ii. 3.—The higher one stands the deeper can he fall.

STARKE :—When God knocks we are at once to open to Him the door of our hearts and receive Him as willingly as joyfully, Revelation iii. 20.—BRENTIUS : —Masters must requite their servants' love and faithfulness with love and faithfulness.—To be always found in the doing of good works is the best preparation for eternity, Rom. xiv. 8.—With a blessed death the blessedness of believers begins, Rev. xiv. 13.—MAJUS :—There is an instant on which eternity hangs ; in an instant all may be squandered and lost ; therefore must we ever watch.—All should watch, especially ministers, whose business it is to quicken others to watchfulness.—CRAMER :—A true steward of God must be at once faithful and prudent.—It is the business of all the family to direct themselves according to the beck and will of such stewards.—The unthankful world esteems in general the faithfulness and the diligence of the stewards of God not sufficiently, but God will reward such the more richly.—QUESNEL :—Two vices are common among ungodly preachers: to rule over their hearers with violence, and to live in idleness and voluptuousness.—HEDINGER :—Unfaithfulness smites its own Lord.—CRAMER :—When the people are the securest their destruction is the nearest.—Terrible sins are followed by terrible punishments.—Knowing and doing must never be separated in true religion.— *Nov. Bibl. Tub.* :—Let no one count him happy who has many gifts and acts not accordingly.—God's grace and righteousness detract not from each other, but each establishes His holiness.

LISCO :—The different servants.—Of the readiness of the true citizens of the kingdom for the coming of Christ: 1. Watchfulness, 2. faithfulness.—ARNDT : —Watchfulness in its true character: 1. Its inner essence, 2. its blessed consequences, 3. its indispensable universality.—The glory of the devout and the ignominy of the unfaithful servant.

HEUBNER :—God's judgment takes account of all that can lessen or augment guilt.—All is given by God on credit ; we are only stewards.—KRUMMACHER : —The watching servant in our time, a missionary sermon. (*Sabbath-Glocke*, v. p. 17 *seq.*)—SOUCHON : —Folly in the care for our eternal salvation : 1. Wherein this folly consists ; 2. what can move us to remove from us and to keep far from us this folly.— KLIEFOTH :—The coming of the Lord.—GEROK :—The | excellent day's work of the laborer of God.—THOMA- SIUS :—Readiness for the day of the Lord.

b. Vss. 49–59.

49 I am come to send fire on the earth; and what will I, if it be already kindled [how
50 much do I wish that it were already kindled!¹]? But I have a baptism to be baptized
51 with; and how am I straitened² till it be accomplished! Suppose ye that I am come
52 to give peace on earth? I tell you, Nay; but rather [only] division: For from
    henceforth there shall be five in one house divided, three against two, and two against
53 three. [They shall be divided, father against son³] The father shall be divided against
    the son, and the [om., the] son against the [om., the] father; the [om., the] mother
    against the [om., the] daughter, and the [om., the] daughter against the mother;
    the [om., the] mother-in-law against her daughter-in-law, and the [om., the] daughter-
54 in law against her mother-in-law. And he said also to the people, When ye see a
    [the⁴] cloud rise out of the west, straightway ye say, There cometh a shower; and so
55 it is. And when ye see the south wind blow [blowing], ye say, There will be heat;
56 and it cometh to pass. Ye hypocrites, ye can discern the face of the sky and of the
57 earth; but how is it that ye do not discern this time? Yea, and why even of your-
58 selves judge ye not what is right? When [For as] thou goest [proceedest] with thine
    adversary to the magistrate, *as thou art* in the way, give diligence that thou mayest be
    delivered from him; lest he hale [drag] thee to the judge, and the judge deliver thee
59 to the officer, and the officer cast thee into prison. I tell thee, thou shalt not depart
    thence, till thou hast paid the very last [even the last] mite [λεπτόν].

[¹ Vs. 49.—Τί θέλω εἰ ἤδη ἀνήφθη; Van Oosterzee takes it thus: *What do I wish?* *Would that it were already kin- dled!* This gives essentially the same sense as the rendering proposed above, but, as Bleek and Meyer remark, it is a less natural turn of expression. The use of εἰ for ὅτι, when the object of the wish is less confidently expected, or known not to exist, is sufficiently well established. I will cite one example, adduced by Meyer from Sirach xxiii. 14: θελήσεις εἰ μὴ ἐγεννήθης.—C. C. S.]
[² Vs. 50.—Norton translates this: "What a weight is on me till it be accomplished!"; which, though paraphrastic, appears to express the sense very exactly.—C. C. S.]
³ Vs. 53.—According to the most probable reading, that of Lachmann and Tischendorf, διαμερισθήσονται, with B., D., [Cod. Sin.,] T., U., cursives, Schid., Vulgate, Copt., Itala, and several fathers. The singular of the *Recepta* was sponta- neously suggested by the immediately following substantives. Symmetry, however, requires the verb. [In allusion to Tischendorf's and Lachmann's joining διαμερισθήσονται with the previous clause.—C. C. S.]
[⁴ Vs. 54.—That is, the usual cloud brought by the prevailing west or northwest wind.—C. C. S.] The original τήν appears to have been inadvertently omitted in A., B., [Cod. Sin.,] L., X., Δ., and cursives, on account of the preceding ἰδητε. (Meyer.)

EXEGETICAL AND CRITICAL.

Vs. 49. **I am come.**—To the question in what connection this part of the Saviour's discourse stands with what immediately precedes, the *neutiquam co- hærent* (Kuinoel) is certainly, it seems to me, the sim- plest possible answer. At least the method in which Olshausen and others give the connection of the ideas, is in our eyes excessively forced. But if we insist on having some connection, then the view of Meyer, "that the greatness of the responsibility, vs. 48, as well as the whole momentousness of the pre- viously demanded faithfulness, is still more strength- ened by the difficulty of the state of things, vs. 49, and so is meant to be made the more palpable to the disciples," is perhaps the most simple.

Vs. 49. **Send fire on the earth.**—The question is, what fire the Saviour here means. The answer that we have here to understand a fire of controversy, appears indeed to be the most admissible, but has, however, this difficulty, that then vs. 51 is really only a weak repetition of that which has been already said in vs. 49. If πῦρ is entirely the same with μάχαιρα, Matt. x. 34, and διαμερισμός, vs. 51, it can- not then be well conceived that the Saviour could have unconditionally wished the kindling of such a fire. On the other hand, there is not the least rea- son for here, with many of the fathers and some modern expositors, immediately understanding the fire of the Holy Spirit, for which βαλεῖν would cer- tainly have been no very fitting expression. It is best, without doubt, to proceed from the general sig- nification of the metaphorical expression, and to un- derstand the extraordinary movement of mind which Christ should bring to pass when His Gospel should everywhere be proclaimed, comp. Luke xxiv. 32. As fire has on the one hand a warming and purifying, but on the other a dissolving and destroying, force, not otherwise is it with the manifestation of Christ, of which the Gospel bears testimony. It is, how- ever, by no means to be denied that the Saviour has in mind the latter rather than the former side of the fact. It does not, however, come into the fullest prominence until vs. 51. Division had already been effected by the Saviour's advent, but the fire was not to blaze up in its full power until after His death and His exaltation.

Καὶ τί θέλω εἰ ἤδη ἀνήφθη; The general inter- pretation (Kuinoel, Bretschneider, De Wette, who appeal to Matt. vii. 14): "How much I could wish that it were already kindled," has the signification of εἰ against it. Better Schleiermacher: "And what more do I wish if it is even already kindled?" But it will best agree with the character of the discourse if we with Grotius and Meyer translate: "And what will I? Would that it were already kindled!" This wish, however, the Saviour does not cherish only because between now and the kindling of this fire lay His near and bitter Passion in the midst, which must first be endured (Meyer), but rather because, besides the harmful and ruinous, the salutary force of the fire also stands before His view, and because He knows that only through these flames can all impurity be purged away from the earth.

Vs. 50. **A baptism to be baptized with.**—Over against the heavenly fire which He sends, stands the earthly water of the suffering which previously to that must roll entirely over Him.—**To be baptized.**—An image of the depth and intensity of this suffering, like a baptism performed by immersion. Comp. Matt. xx. 22; John i. 33.—**How am I straitened,** πῶς συνέχομαι.—As far from being only a pressure of longing and desire (Euth. Zigab., De Wette) as from meaning merely, "oppressed by anxiety and fear" (Meyer and others); on the other hand the one must be joined with the other. Without doubt there is here a συνοχὴ καρδίας, not less than John xii. 27; 2 Cor. ii. 4, and whoever in this human reluctance of the Lord against His suffering finds any cause of offence, places himself in a Docetic position. But in the heart of the holy Son of Man such a shrinking back from suffering, and the wish that it might already have been overcome, could not arise without His feeling at the same time the pressure of a love which must be baptized with this baptism, only because it itself has willed it. A similar union of anxiety and longing we see in the woman, John xvi. 21, who when her hour comes is seized with fear and anguish, and yet in the midst of this fear feels love and inward longing soon to press her child to her heart.

Vs. 51. **Suppose ye.**—Comp. Matt. x. 34–36. It was only perplexity on the part of some expositors when they believed that here the language respecting the consequence of the Saviour's manifestation was used exclusively ἐκβατικῶς, not τελικῶς. On the other hand, we may say that the Saviour here speaks not of the highest and ultimate, but yet of a very essential purpose of His manifestation on earth, which, however, was in its turn to be a means for the attainment of a higher end, of a peace, namely, which could be attained through this strife alone. The division which the Saviour brought on earth was and is so general, that He in a certain sense could say of Himself that He establishes nothing less than (ἀλλ' ἤ) discord. This phenomenon is so far from being surprising and fortuitous, that, on the contrary, it has been foreseen and will be met, not as something good and desirable in itself, but as the only way in which He could erect His kingdom of peace here below upon an immovable foundation. An analogous representation, see Luke ii. 34; John ix. 39. Even because Christ is the Sun of Righteousness, it cannot but be that torches of strife and funeral pyres should be kindled by its fiery glow. When the Holy One of God comes into personal contact with an unholy world, a shock and strife is inevitable, and that not only against Him personally, but also among men themselves, inasmuch as these begin to distinguish themselves into adversaries and subjects of His kingdom.

Vs. 52. **Five in one house.**—Here also is the mention of the uneven number five peculiar to Luke, as in the statement of the number of sparrows, vs. 6. When three stand against two and two against three, it is so much the more difficult to bring them together again. The holiest bonds are torn asunder, and as well in the male as also in the female sex does our Lord count friends and enemies, who on account of Him oppose one another. "*Non additur gener, nam hic aliam constituit familiam.*" Bengel. For the whole representation, compare the prophetical utterance, Micah vii. 6. Only when the Saviour appears as the Prince of Peace can the disharmony between the three on the one hand and the two on the other hand be lastingly over.

Vs. 54. **And He said also to the people.**—Luke justly remarks that here the address of the Saviour to the disciples breaks off. What now follows is more adapted to the mixed throng of His listeners, among whom there were found also enemies and those of Pharisaical views. According to Matt. xvi. 1 *seq.*, the Saviour directed the next following censure very particularly against the Pharisees and Sadducees; the expressions, however, in the two Evangelists are more or less different. If we are disposed to demonstrate the connection with the previous section, we may find it in this, that the Saviour now proceeds to the statement of the source from which so much discord and misunderstanding flow as He had just described; namely, the failure to recognize the signs of the times, which unequivocally enough pointed to the Messianic kingdom.

A cloud.—The cloud which rose out of the west, on the side of the sea, was regarded as the sign of approaching rain, *see* 1 Kings xviii. 44, while the south wind was considered as a sign of heat to be expected, Job xxxvii. 17. The here-mentioned καύσων is undoubtedly that glowing heat which was produced in Palestine by the south wind. In the LXX = קָדִים. In most mournful contrast with the sound intelligence of these weather-prophets, which in daily life at once decides (εὐθέως), and whose prophecies also commonly are fulfilled, stands the general blindness in reference to that which was infinitely more momentous and quite as easy to discover.

Vs. 56. **Ye hypocrites.**—We cannot mistake the fact that here towards the end, the discourse again visibly inclines towards its point of departure. Very fittingly could the Saviour address the people in a mass thus, if we consider how deeply the leaven of the Pharisees had already penetrated into their minds. Since they were capable of distinguishing the face of the sky as well as that of the earth (John iv. 35), it could only be from a lack of good-will that they left wholly unnoticed the rain and the vital warmth which in these days had been imparted, in the kingdom of God. What lies nearest to the heart of man his understanding judges best; but since the advent of a spiritual kingdom of God was to them essentially indifferent, they do not account it even worth the trouble of giving heed to these signs in the moral world, which so convincingly afforded proof that the fulness of the time had arrived. The Saviour, on the other hand, will have His contemporaries become meteorologists in the spiritual sphere, and therefore He afterwards also rebukes them that they did not know the time of their visitation, Luke xix. 44.

Vs. 57. **Of your own selves,** ἀφ' ἑαυτῶν, Luke xxi. 30. There was lacking to them, as appears from what precedes, the gift necessary for clearly distinguishing in the spiritual sphere what was right (κρίνειν, *secernere*). When they discerned the face of the sky and the earth (vs. 56), they did this indeed ἀφ' ἑαυτῶν, independently, without any necessity that it should first have been told them by another. So did it beseem them in other relations also to apply the standard of a natural science of truth and duty, without always first awaiting the inspiration of their spiritual guides.—Vss. 58, 59 the Saviour makes a special case in which they could apply such a κρίσις ἀφ' ἑαυτῶν, while He leaves it to their own understanding and conscience themselves to make a profitable application of the here-given rules to much higher and weightier concerns.

Vs. 58. **For as.**—Γάρ here introduces the statement of the special case, by the delineation of which the Saviour more particularly explains His meaning. Comp. Matt. v. 25, 26. He presupposes that they are with their adversary (ἀντίδικος) on the way to their legitimate ruler (ἄρχων), as appears from vs. 59, because a controversy had arisen about an unpaid debt; and if they now should persevere even to the end in the way of litigation, the consequences were very easy to be foreseen. The adversary with whom one cannot reconcile himself drags (κατασύρῃ) the debtor before the righteous judge (κριτής), and he, after he has ascertained the claim of debt to be well established, delivers the accused to the bailiff, who throws him into prison (πράκτωρ, *exactor*, *executor*, a legally appointed functionary of the Roman tribunals, whom Matthew has designated only in general as ὑπηρέτης). And there must one remain, until even the very last and least portion of the debt in its last item is paid. Matthew mentions τὸν ἔσχατον κοδράντην, Luke still more strongly τὸν ἔσχ. λεπτόν. The last farthing equals half a quadrant.—How much mischief, therefore, does one prevent, and how fully he acts in his own interest, when he comes to terms with such an ἀντίδικος, enters into a satisfactory compromise before the last decisive step is taken! Δὸς ἐργασίαν, a Latinism, perhaps as a Roman formula of law sufficiently familiar to Theophilus.

The Saviour, therefore, here urges His hearers in their own interest to placableness, and will have them by such a conduct show that they are in a condition ἀφ' ἑαυτῶν to κρίνειν τὸ δίκαιον. Considered by itself alone the admonition has, therefore, the same intention as in the parallel passage in Matthew, only with the distinction that with Luke the juridical form of the process is brought out somewhat more in detail. If one inquires now in what connection this exhortation, vss. 57–59, stands with the previous verses, vss. 54–56, we acknowledge that we have not found in one of the interpreters an answer perfectly satisfactory to us. The thread connecting the different parts of Luke xii. becomes looser in proportion as the chapter hastens towards its end. In general, we may say that the Saviour here urges His hearers no longer to allow themselves to be so much led in their judgment by others as they had hitherto done, in consequence of which they also did not recognize the signs of the times, vss. 54–56, but to see more with their own eyes. This His meaning He elucidates by an example, vss. 58–59; but neither in the letter nor the spirit of His words is a single proof contained that this example must be interpreted as a parable, and that He wishes thereby to admonish them to repent betimes, "because the Messianic decision is so near, that they may not be exposed to the judgment of Gehenna." (Meyer.) It is wholly arbitrary to see in the ἀντίδικος an allusion to the devil (Euth. Zigab.), to the poor (Michaelis), God (Meyer), or even to the law (Olshausen), and in the φυλακή to see a representation of Gehenna. Nothing but the craving to find in vss. 57–59 a congruous conclusion to a well-connected discourse has here put the expositors on a false track. The Saviour, however, presents not a single proof for the opinion that He here is urging them on allegorically to repentance, and according to the representation of Matt. v. 25, this saying has an entirely different sense. It is, without doubt, better, in case of necessity, to give up making out the connection which undoubtedly exists (Kuinoel, De Wette), which we, moreover, have by no means done, than to find under the simple sense of the words a deeper significance which no one amongst the first hearers, without a more particular intimation of the Saviour, could have found therein.

DOCTRINAL AND ETHICAL.

1. As the Saviour has first admonished His disciples to watchfulness and faithfulness, the remaining part of His discourse, so far in particular as it is addressed to the Apostles, has such a direction as to prepare them for many kinds of strife and troubles, and to take away the scandal which they might otherwise have found when His cause, instead of overcoming, should be suppressed and opposed. The cause of this strife lay at least in part in the unreceptiveness and earthly-mindedness of the people, who neglected to give heed to the signs of the times, and, like blind men, slavishly followed their spiritual guides, instead of seeing with their own eyes.

2. In this whole utterance of our Lord, as far as it stands in direct relation to His own personality and kingdom, we see a striking revelation on the one hand of His truly human, on the other hand His truly Divine, nature. With a genuinely human feeling He shrinks back from His suffering and longs for the beginning of the conflict. But with Divine knowledge He calculates at the same time the consequences of the combat, and utters forth the indispensable necessity of His baptism of suffering, if the fire were really to be kindled upon earth.

3. Already more than once have we heard the Saviour speak with heavy-heartedness and deep feeling of His approaching Passion, but here is the first revelation of this genuinely human reluctance to enter upon the approaching conflict, which afterwards returns in heightened measure, John xii. 27; Matt. xxvi. 38. This inner sorrow and pressure of love also constitutes a part of His hidden history of suffering.

4. It is one of the strongest arguments for the entirely unique significance of the personal manifestation of our Lord, that He calls forth such a discord in the sphere of humanity. The strongest sympathy or antipathy does He arouse, but in no case apathy. So much strife and blood the Gospel could never have caused, had not men been deeply persuaded on both sides that here there was to do with the Highest and Holiest.

5. The recognition of the signs of the times is one of the most sacred obligations which our Saviour imposes on all those who wish to be capable of passing an independent judgment on the concerns of His kingdom. However, the blindness of His contemporaries still shows itself continually under all manner of forms. Men who in the sphere of the natural life display a singular measure of sound

understanding, are, and that in large numbers, dulness and unreceptiveness itself, when it comes to the distinguishing of light and darkness, truth and illusion, from one another in the spiritual sphere. A sad proof of the power which the corruption of the sinful heart exercises upon the darkened understanding. See Rom. i. 18; Ephes. iv. 18.

HOMILETICAL AND PRACTICAL.

The fire which Christ kindles on earth: 1. A fire which warms what is cold; 2. purifies what is impure; 3. consumes what is evil.—Suffering, a baptism.—For the Christian a threefold baptism necessary: 1. The water-baptism of sprinkling; 2. the spiritual baptism of renewal; 3. the fire-baptism of trial.—The intensity of anguish and love with which the Saviour foresees His approaching Passion.—The discord which Christ has brought upon earth: 1. A surprising phenomenon, if we look, *a.* at the King, Ps. lxxii., *b.* at the fundamental law of the kingdom of God, John xiii. 35; 2. an explicable phenomenon if we direct our eye, *a.* to the severity of the Gospel, *b.* to the sinfulness of the human heart; 3. a momentous phenomenon, *a.* this strife is a proof of the high significance, *b.* and means for the establishment, the purification, and the victory of Christianity.—The proclamation of the conflict excited by His appearance a proof: 1. Of the infallible omniscience; 2. of the holy earnestness; 3. of the infinite love of our Lord.—Of all false peace the King of the kingdom of truth makes an end.—The fire kindled in the old earth no curse but a blessing.—Even our nearest earthly kindred we must, in case of need, deny for Christ's sake.—The spiritual world also, like the kingdom of nature, has its signs.—The noticing of the signs of the times a duty: 1. Commended by heavenly wisdom; 2. forgotten by sinful blindness.—The Saviour will have one judge independently what is true and good.—How our own interest urges us to the duty of placableness.—There comes a time in which the law is left to run its course, and every hope of grace is cut off.

STARKE:—CANSTEIN:—When the Gospel is preached in right earnest, it is as if a conflagration breaks out, which every one runs to quench, and thereby is faith proved.—QUESNEL:—Jesus had ever His suffering before His eyes; His love to the cross shames the effeminacy and delicacy of Christians, who are so unwilling to suffer.—Three against two; so was it in Abraham's house: Abraham, Sarah, and Isaac against Hagar and Ishmael.—There is hardly a house in which the evil are not mingled with the good and the good with the evil.—BRENTIUS:—Between the kingdom of Christ and of Satan no peace exists, not even in eternity; let no one, therefore, give himself any fruitless trouble to bring it about.—*Bibl. Wirt.*:—Man, discern the time of grace, which to discern is indeed not difficult.—The proving of spiritual things is a duty even of the simple.—CRAMER:—It is better to compose matters of controversy by friendly dealing and brotherly reconciliation, than by the sharp law and sentence of the judge, 1 Cor. vi. 7.—In hell there is no payment possible, therefore the plague of the same will have no end.

HEUBNER:—If all reforming and heating of people's heads is wrong and illegal, then Christianity would be the most illegal of anything; but everything depends upon whether the revolutionizing and incendiarism comes from selfishness or from God.—Even he who is already resolved to duty feels, nevertheless, shrinking of heart till the conflict is fought out.—When tempests approach thee, strengthen thyself in Jesus.—What is great and noble requires severe conflict.—The false judging of Jesus is our own fault.—EHRENBERG:—Fire as the power: 1. Of separating; 2. of consuming; 3. of warming.—THOLUCK:—" Of what fire does Christ speak here? Is it that which has just now been kindled in the Evangelical Church?" With reference to the separation of the Lutheran from the United Church (in the second volume of his Sermons, p. 412 *seq.*).—SCHENKEL:—The controversy which Christ has brought upon earth, how we have: 1. To wish for it; 2. to fear it; 3. to endure it.—T. MÜLLER:—The destroying might of Christianity: 1. In the outer; 2. in the inner, world.

E. *The Son of Man in relation to the Sin of One and the Misery of Another.* CH. XIII. 1-17.

1 There were present at that season some that told him of the Galileans, whose blood
2 Pilate had mingled with their sacrifices. And Jesus [he] answering said unto them, Suppose ye that these Galileans were sinners above all the Galileans, because they
3 [have] suffered such things? I tell you, Nay: but, except ye repent, ye shall all like-
4 wise perish. Or those eighteen, upon whom the tower in Siloam fell, and slew them,
5 think ye that they were sinners above all men that dwelt in Jerusalem? I tell you, Nay: but, except ye repent, ye shall likewise perish.
6 He spake also this parable; A certain *man* had a fig tree planted in his vineyard;
7 and he came and sought fruit thereon, and found none. Then said he unto the dresser of his vineyard, Behold, these three years I come seeking fruit on this fig tree, and find
8 none: cut it down; why cumbereth it the ground [makes the ground useless]? And he answering said unto him, Lord, let it alone this year also, till I shall dig about it,
9 and dung *it*: And if it bear fruit, *well*: and if not, *then* after that thou shalt cut it
10, 11 down. And he was teaching in one of the synagogues on the sabbath. And, behold, there was[1] a woman which had a spirit of infirmity eighteen years, and was
12 bowed together, and could in no wise lift up *herself*. And when Jesus saw her, he

called *her to him*, and said unto her, Woman, thou art loosed from thine infirmity.
13 And he laid *his* hands on her: and immediately she was made straight, and glorified
14 God. And the ruler of the synagogue answered with indignation, because that Jesus had healed on the sabbath day, and said unto the people, There are six days in which men ought to work: in them therefore come and be healed, and not on the sabbath
15 day. The Lord then answered him, and said, *Thou* hypocrite [Ye hypocrites[2]], doth not each one of you on the sabbath loose his ox or *his* ass from the stall, and lead *him*
16 away to watering? And ought not this woman, being a daughter of Abraham, whom Satan hath bound, lo, these eighteen years, be loosed from this bond on the sabbath
17 day? And when he had said [while he said] these things, all his adversaries were ashamed: and all the people rejoiced for all the glorious things that were done by him.

[1] Vs. 11.—Ἦν, a usual interpolation, by whose omission with B., [Cod. Sin.,] L., X., Lachmann, Tischendorf, [Meyer, Tregelles,] and others, the liveliness of the narrative is heightened.
[2] Vs. 15.—The plural, ὑποκριταί, has externally and internally preponderating authority. The singular of the *Recepta* has only arisen from the fact that the copyist had the preceding αὐτῷ in his eye. But the Saviour addresses Himself, in the person of the ruler of the synagogue, to the whole genus of hypocrites represented by him. [Ὑποκριταί is supported by A., B., Cod. Sin., 13 other uncials, against 3.—C. C. S.]

EXEGETICAL AND CRITICAL.

Vs. 1. At that season.—According to Luke this intelligence comes to the Saviour while He is in Galilee, where he had just (ch. xi., xii.) repelled the imputations of His enemies, and warned the people against the leaven of the Pharisees. Probably we are to conceive the matter thus, that among the listeners to His last discourse there were some who had just received the mournful tidings in respect to the Galileans, and now hastened to communicate them to the Saviour, in order to hear His judgment upon the matter. In all probability the cruel deed had been perpetrated very shortly before, and had excited general exasperation.

Of the Galileans.—Many things here concurred to heighten the hideousness of this deed. Pilate, Procurator of Judæa, had, contrary to law, attacked subjects of Herod. Pilate, the heathen, had not even held sacred holy things, but had perpetrated a massacre in the temple. It is as if the exasperation at this act yet echoed in Luke in the very form of the expression,—**Whose blood Pilate had mingled.**—A tragically graphic delineation, which justifies the conjecture that these unfortunate ones had been wholly on a sudden fallen upon and slain by the Roman soldiers. What the provocation to this deed was cannot be stated with certainty, nor is there any ground to understand here (Euthym. Zigab., Theophil., Grotius, a. o.) particularly followers of Judas Gaulonites. But it is certain that the Galileans at that time were exceedingly inclined to popular commotions (JOSEPHUS, *Ant. Jud.* 17, 9, 3); that even at the feast in Jerusalem tumult not unfrequently arose; and that Pilate was not the man to desist, from regard to the sanctity of a locality, from executing a punishment recognized as necessary. If we call to mind the atrocities which the Romans, particularly afterwards, committed against the Jews, the murder of these Galileans will then appear to us only as a single drop in an unfathomable sea; and we must not be surprised if we find this deed, although it was generally known in the days of Jesus (τῶν Γαλιλ.), only noted down by Luke. An indirect argument for its credibility we find in the enmity subsequently alluded to between Pilate and Herod, chap. xxiii. 12, which perhaps originated from this illegal act. It is, however, not apparent that this intelligence was communicated to the Saviour in any particularly hostile intent, and as Luke moreover gives no intimation in reference to the time when or the feast at which this massacre was committed by Pilate, he takes from us all possibility of drawing any chronological deduction whatever from this isolated historical datum.

Vs. 2. Suppose ye.—In all probability those who brought this intelligence to our Lord were involved in the common error that so sudden a death in the midst of so sacred an employment must without doubt be regarded as a special proof of the terrible wrath of God upon those so slain. Were they perchance thinking of that which the Saviour had just said, ch. xii. 47, 48, upon exact correspondence in the future of retribution with sin, and did they wish over against this to draw His attention to the connection between sin and punishment even in this life? The Saviour at least considers it necessary to contradict the erroneous fancy that these Galileans were in any way stamped as greater sinners than all others by the judgment which had befallen them (ἐγένοντο declarative). He by no means denies the intimate connection between natural and moral evil, but He disputes the infallible certainty of the assumption that every individual visitation is a retribution for individual transgressions, and does not concede to those who are witnesses of a judgment the right, from the calamity which strikes some before others, to permit themselves a conclusion as to their moral reprobacy. But we abuse the declaration of the Saviour if we understand it in such a sense as that these Galileans did not deserve at all to be called ἁμαρτωλοί, but rather martyrs.

Vs. 3. I tell you, Nay.—"*Dominus hoc profert ex thesauris sapientiæ divinæ.*" Bengel.—Our Lord knows and sets Himself against the perverseness of so many who, when they hear of public calamities, are much more inclined to direct their look without than within. In opposition to this He gives the earnest intimation that the fate of individuals ought to be the mirror for all.—**Unless ye repent.**—This declaration is the more apposite if we assume that the momentous intelligence had been brought to the Saviour with the intent to awaken in Him thereby the apprehension that a similar fate might also perchance threaten Him and His followers. No! not He, He declares: they themselves had an approaching Divine judgment to fear. Before Jesus' eyes all Galilee stood forth to view as already ripe to future judgment, and in order to show that Judæa was in no respect securer, He subjoins the reminiscence, vss. 4, 5, of a similar casualty.

Likewise perish.—The reading ὡσαύτως (Tischendorf) appears to deserve the preference above the weaker ὁμοίως (Lachmann). The Saviour does not mean to say that they shall perish in a similar, but that they shall perish in the same manner, namely, through the cruelty of the Romans, who were destined to avenge the evil deed of rejecting the Messiah. What streams of blood were afterwards shed in the same temple, and how many at the same time were buried under the rubbish and the ruins of the city and of the temple!

Vs. 4. **Those eighteen.**—Again the Lord alludes to a similar event, which was yet fresh in every one's memory. From a cause to us unknown, one of the towers standing not far from the brook Siloam had fallen in, and had buried eighteen corpses in its ruins. That it was a tower of the city-wall (Meyer) is not proved.—Here also was the rule and application the same as in the foregoing example, only that to the Saviour now not only the fate of impenitent individuals, but at the same time that of the whole Jewish state, stands before His soul; in spirit He sees much more than a single tower, He sees City and Temple fallen. The question possibly arising, to what circumstances so many who yet were quite as great sinners as those eighteen owed hitherto their preservation from such a lot, the Saviour now answers with the parable of the Unfruitful Fig-tree.

Siloam, comp. John ix. 7, in all probability the same piece of water which in Nehemiah iii. 15 appears under the name Shelah [Siloa in E. V.], a pool in the neighborhood of the fountain-gate, outside of Jerusalem, in the valley of Kedron, which perhaps David or one of his successors had dug (comp. Isaiah viii. 6), and in whose vicinity there was also a village or place of like name. Apparently it received this name (the Sent), because the water with which this pool was supplied was conducted artificially through the rocks. Although Josephus often speaks of Siloah, the archæologists are nevertheless still as ever more or less at variance about the locality in which this pool must be actually sought. The principal views can be seen stated in WINER, *ad loc.*, and as to the question whether Siloah and Gihon must be identified with one another, comp. HAMELSVELD, *Bibl. Geog.* ii. p. 187. As to the rest, nothing more in detail is known about the πύργος ἐν τῷ Σιλ. The view of Stier, however, that the eighteen unfortunate men were prisoners who were confined in the tower, in whose case therefore it might so much the more easily appear as if a Divine judgment had overtaken them, is quite as much without proof as the opinion of Sepp that they were laborers, among whom also was the mason whom, according to the statement of Jerome, our Lord had formerly healed. *See* above on Luke vi. 6.

Vs. 6. **A fig-tree . . . in his vineyard.**—Although the mention of a fig-tree in a vineyard sounds somewhat singular, it is yet by no means incongruous or in conflict with Deut. xxii. 9, which undoubtedly speaks of seed but not of trees. If we assume the fig-tree as the symbol of Israel (Hosea ix. 10; Matt. xxi. 19), the vineyard could then only designate the whole world, in which these people had been planted as an entirely peculiar phenomenon. "*Ficus arbor, cui per se nil loci est in vinea. Liberrime Israelem sumsit Deus.*" Bengel.

Vs. 7. **Then said he.**—If God is the Lord of the vineyard, the gardener can only be Christ. This view deserves at least the preference above the somewhat arbitrary assumption of Stier that by the vineyard the rulers and leaders of Israel collectively are understood, as in Matt. xxi. 33. It is by no means proved that the expression: "Behold I come," vs. 7, applies to Christ alone. The Father Himself is here represented as the comer, because He, since the day of the New Covenant had dawned, might with the fullest right expect peculiar fruits from the fig-tree of Israel. It is undoubtedly certain that everything that is said of the fig-tree is still applicable to each particular individual, and that every one entrusted with the care of souls may recognize his type in the gardener; but quite as manifest is it also, according to the connection of vss. 1-5, that the Saviour here before all has the Jewish state in mind, and that the indirect setting forth of His own person as a gardener agrees perfectly with the care which He had so long expended on this fig-tree, as well as with His character as the Intercessor who prays for the guilty.

These three years I come.—The three years indicated not the previous duration of the ministry of Jesus among Israel (Bengel), and as little the whole ante-christian period (Grotius), and least of all the τρεῖς πολιτείας of the judges, the kings, and the high-priests (Euthym. Zigab.); but denote in general a definite brief time, which here is limited to this particular number three, because the tree when planted brought forth as a rule its fruits within three years. But if one insists on having a definite time for God's work of grace on Israel, we may reckon the time from the public appearance of John the Baptist—a half year before the entrance of Jesus on His office—up to the present moment, which altogether does not make up much less than three years. To this labor of grace, however, Israel had hitherto in no way given answering results. Not only did the fig-tree bear no fruit, but it also withdrew from other trees, by shade, absorption, &c., the warmth and the sap which they might have received if this had not stood in the way (καταργεῖ, see MEYER, *ad loc.*).

Vs. 8. **This year also.**—A sufficient but brief time is still given to the fig-tree to bring forth better fruits.—**Dig about it and dung it.**—Intimation of the condition and augmented labor of grace with which the Saviour in the last weeks and days of His life required the growing hatred of His enemies. To intercession He now joins strenuous activity, and only if this also is in vain will He forbear to make intercession for the unfruitful fig-tree. Yet He does not say that He Himself will hew it down, but only He no longer holds back the Lord of the vineyard, and entreats no longer for something that remains incorrigible. He yet counts it as possible that in the fourth year fruits may become apparent which the three first years had not brought, but He also assumes it as certain that in the opposite case the fig-tree must be removed out of the vineyard.

Vs. 10. **And He was teaching.**—The narrative of the healing of the infirm woman is peculiar to Luke. The time when this miracle took place is not more particularly stated; but the shamelessness with which the Archisynagogus expresses his displeasure against Jesus, allows the conjecture that we have to assign to this event a place in the last period of the public life of our Lord. The reception of the narrative into this connection may at the same time serve as a proof how the Saviour, according to His own declaration, even amid increasing opposition, yet continued to dig about and to dung the unfruitful fig-tree. As to the rest, this Sabbath-miracle has much agreement with others already related, and apparently it is to be attributed to this circumstance also that Matthew and Mark pass it over in silence. Against the credibility of the fact this silence proves nothing, except with those who deny the possibility or profitableness of miracles of this sort *a priori*.

Πνεῦμα ἀσθενείας.—We may plainly recognize that Luke here understands a species of possession; she was plagued by a πνεῦμα, which caused an ἀσθένεια. Her nervous energies were so weakened that she could not raise herself up. "*Ex nervorum contractione incurvum erat corpus.*" Calvin. With the words: "Woman, thou art loosed from thine infirmity," the Saviour calls her unexpectedly to Himself, and therefore works psychically upon her, in order to make her receptive for the benefit which He is about to bestow upon her physically. Finally He lays His hands upon her, and now too the ordinary result does not fail to follow.

Vs. 14. **The ruler of the synagogue.**—In this man anger at the supposed Sabbath desecration is visibly in conflict with a kind of fear which the miracle just performed has aroused in him. What he does not venture to say to the Saviour Himself he says to the people, with so loud a voice that the Saviour also should hear it. But that the miracle can make no other impression whatever upon him, is a strong testimony against him. However, it appears also from vs. 17, that besides him there were yet other ἀντικείμενοι present in the synagogue, which at the same time is an internal proof of the correctness of the reading ὑποκριταί, vs. 15.

Vs. 15. **The Lord,** *cum emphasi*.—The Son of Man makes Himself now heard as Lord of the Sabbath, and that in figurative language similar to that which He had already more than once used in a case of this kind. Take note however of the distinction between the *argumentum ad hominem* which is made use of here, and that which is made use of ch. xiv. 5 (comp. Matt. xii. 11, 12). That it was really permitted on the Sabbath to take out one's beast to drink, is proved by LIGHTFOOT and WETSTEIN, *ad loc.* How was it possible that that which for a beast was regarded as a desirable benefit, should be condemned as a misdeed, so soon as it was performed on a human being?

Vs. 16. **Being a daughter of Abraham.**—Not merely a general antithesis between man and beast, and far less a conception of the human personality deserving of sympathy, restricted according to Jewish popular notions (De Wette), but an emphatic designation of the spiritual relation which existed between father Abraham and this his daughter, comp. xix. 9. That we are entitled to regard this woman as a daughter of Abraham in the spiritual sense, appears even from this, that the Saviour does not once ask as to her faith, doubtless because He had already read this in her heart, while besides, her glorifying of God immediately after the miracle, vs. 13, testifies in her devout disposition of soul; nor is the declaration: "Thy sins are forgiven thee," here made. Where now such a daughter of Abraham was bound by Satan, the Saviour could not forbear to snatch from him this booty.

Whom Satan hath bound.—More plainly than by this otherwise superfluous expression the Saviour could not give it to be understood that He regarded the demoniacal condition of this sufferer as the effect of a direct Satanical influence. Since possession can never be merely corporeal, it may be assumed that along with the spirit of discouragement and privation of power, the spark of faith had maintained or developed itself in the woman.

Vs. 17. **And all the people rejoiced,** comp. ch. v. 26; ix. 43.—The Saviour's words roused the conscience, as His deed roused the sensibility. The view of this miracle renews again the recollection of the former ones, and the continuity (γινομένοις) of this beneficent activity disposes heart and mouth to the glorifying of God. This accord of praise to the honor of the Father was to the Son a proof that He this time also had not tarried in Galilee in vain, and accompanied Him as it were on His way, now when He, as it appears, is leaving this land, in order to repair to the feast of the Dedication, John x.

DOCTRINAL AND ETHICAL.

1. Vss. 1–9, we see the Saviour over against human sin; vss. 10–17, over against human misery: both times in the full glory of His love and holiness. This for justification of the inscription chosen for this division.

2. The Saviour declares Himself on the one hand against the light-mindedness of those who entirely deny the intimate connection between natural and moral evil; on the other hand against the narrowness of those who consider individual misfortune and individual punishment as words of one and the same signification. The true point of view from which national calamities are to be regarded as voices calling to a general conversion, is here brought forward.

3. This parable of the Unfruitful Fig-tree contains not only the brief summary of the history of Israel, but also of the gracious dealing of God with every sinner. For all who live under the light of the Gospel there comes earlier or later a καιρὸς τῆς ἐπισκοπῆς, Luke xix. 4, which when it has passed by unused, makes them ripe for the righteous judgment of God. But the Mediator of the New Covenant is at the same time their Intercessor, as long as deliverance is yet possible. So far then from the long-suffering of God affording any ground for the expectation of a final escape from punishment, it is, on the other hand, a pledge that the contemning of it is finally requited in the most terrific manner. Thus do we find here also the representation of a final judgment followed by no subsequent recovery whatever.

4. As this parable brings before our mind the image of the people of Israel, it permits us at the same time to cast a glance into the holy soul of the Mediator, for to His intercession was it owing that the Jewish state yet stood. The lengthening out of the time of grace for this Unfruitful Fig-tree had also been the object of His still nightly prayers. Undoubtedly if in the words: "How it down," the words and spirit of the Baptist reëcho (Matt. iii. 10), there is heard in these words: "Lord, let it alone this year also," the compassionateness of the Son of Man, who was not come to destroy men's souls, but to save them.

5. Parallels to the parable of the Unfruitful Fig-tree: Isaiah v. 1–7; Hosea ix. 10; Jeremiah xxiv. 3; Psalm lxxx. 9–11; Mark xi. 12–14. Respecting the Sabbath miracles of our Lord, *see* on Luke vi. 1–11.

6. The suffering of the woman in the synagogue is the faithful image of the misery into which Satan plunges man as to his soul; her healing is the image

of redemption. The reality of this miracle is indirectly testified even by the president of the synagogue, who is indeed mean enough indirectly to censure the woman because she has allowed herself to be healed, but does not yet possess shamelessness enough to deny that here a sudden healing took place.

HOMILETICAL AND PRACTICAL.

Jesus, 1. Over against the sin of mankind, vss. 1–9: *a.* with inexorable severity does He rebuke sin, vss. 1–5; *b.* with inexhaustible patience does He wish to preserve the sinner, vss. 6–9; 2. over against the wretchedness of mankind, vss. 9–17: *a.* where Jesus comes He finds wretchedness; *b.* where Jesus finds wretchedness He brings healing.

Many men find satisfaction in being the first bringers of evil tidings.—The Lord often answers us very differently from what we could wish and expect. —Unexpected death.—All who are overtaken by heavy and deserved calamities are sinners, but not for that greater sinners than others.—What befalls others should serve us as a warning, 1 Cor. x. 11. —The riches of the patience and long-suffering of God, Rom. ii. 4.—The parable of the Unfruitful Fig-tree the image of the dealing of God with the sinner: 1. The careful labor, 2. the righteous investigation, 3. the unhappy result, 4. the righteous judgment, 5. the entreating Intercessor, 6. the last delay.—The goodness and severity of God, Rom. xi. 22.—In the heavenly counsel of grace there are days which may outweigh whole years, and years which may outweigh whole centuries.—The acceptable year of the Lord, Isaiah lxi. 2.—All gracious leadings of God have the one purpose that we may really bring forth fruit.—Whoever brings forth no fruit is at the same time injurious to others.—The Lord is patient, but of great power, Nah. i. 3.—The true Sabbath-keeping fixed by the example of the Saviour, vss. 10–17, 1. Indicated, 2. justified.—The house of the Lord the best refuge for sufferers.—No suffering so tedious that the Saviour cannot yet give deliverance.—The Lord understands even unuttered sighs.—The terrible might of Satan over body and soul.—Whom the Son hath made free, he should praise the Father.—Even the most glorious revelations of love are lost for him who has a mind at enmity with God.—Hypocrisy and cowardice not seldom intimately connected. —Even where the Saviour is only indirectly blamed He does not permit it to pass without an answer.— Hypocrisy condemned before the tribunal of the Luman, 1. Understanding, 2. sensibility, 3. conscience.—Ashamed must all be who rise up against Jesus.—How the Saviour vanquishes His enemies: 1. By the deed, 2. by the word of His love.—Jesus breaks asunder the bonds of Satan.—The shaming power of truth.—Glorifying of God the fruit of the work of redemption.

STARKE:—Ever something new, and seldom anything good.—God's open enemies must often be the instruments of His judgment on those who were wont to be called His people.—CANSTEIN:—Men are in no place and in no employment sure that this or that calamity may not befall them.—CRAMER:—Faithful preachers should direct all that they bear to the end of edifying and improving the church.—BRENTICS:—The judgments of God are incomprehensible; it befits us thereat to lay our hands on our mouths and to admire them in holy humility.—QUESNEL:— We ought ourselves to seek the fruit in our lives before God comes to seek it.—Public and private intercessions avail much with God when they are fervent.—When the time of grace is passed Christ intercedes no longer.—The sinner is hewn down when God gives him over to the judgment of reprobacy.—CRAMER:—Examples of tedious sicknesses are necessary, and wholesome for us to know, Rom. v. 3–5.—Jesus looks upon the bowed down, the lowly, and the meek, that He may lift them up and elevate them.—Public assemblies have a promise of blessing; let no one forsake them.—In churches and schools there have undoubtedly been many blind zealots that have more hurt than profited the kingdom of God.—QUESNEL:—Religion must often serve as a pretext to avarice and envy; be watchful against this.—Necessity and love know no law. —CANSTEIN:—Nothing suits better with the day of the Lord than the work of the Lord and the destruction of the works of Satan.—The high value of the souls redeemed through Christ can never be urged and impressed enough.—Although faithful shepherds and teachers must everywhere here go through the valley of misery, yet they obtain one victory after another.

HEUBNER:—Purpose of God in special judgments of calamity.—God sends harbingers before heavy tempests.—The false comfort which men draw from others' calamities.—To perish in the ruin of a city is a small matter compared with the misery of finding one's destruction in the future ruin of the world.—God also counts the years.—The sinner everywhere derogates from the good of earth.— Envy against God even takes on the guise of piety. —Without Christ the spirit is bowed down and not capable of praise.

The Parable.—ARNDT:—The greatness and the duration of the Divine forbearance.—ZIMMERMANN: —How the Divine long-suffering leads the sinner to amendment.—LISCO:—The righteousness of God as it has been made manifest in Christ.—The whole parable admits also of an admirable application for a sermon on New Year's morning.

The Miracle.—PICHLER:—The Lord Jesus such a Saviour as we need: 1. For deliverance out of so manifold need, 2. for the revelation of our inmost heart, 3. for advancement in the life of faith and humility.—PALMER:—Wherever the Saviour comes there does He meet wretchedness and sin.—SCHMIDT: —Opposition to the Saviour, *a.* how it arises, *b.* how it is dissolved (through truth and grace).—LISCO:— The true Sabbath-keeping.

F. *The Nature, the Entrance, the Conflict of the Kingdom of God.* Ch. XIII. 18–35.

1. Parables (Vss. 18–21).

18 Then said he, Unto what is the kingdom of God like? and whereunto shall I re-
19 semble [compare] it? It is like a grain of mustard seed, which a man took, and cast
    into his garden; and it grew, and waxed [became] a great tree; and the fowls [birds]
20 of the air lodged in the branches of it. And[1] again he said, Whereunto shall I liken
21 the kingdom of God? It is like leaven, which a woman took and hid in three measures
    of meal [flour], till the whole was leavened.

[1] Vs. 20.—The καί of the *Recepta*, expunged by Scholz and Tischendorf, but defended again by Meyer, appears to us very suspicious.

EXEGETICAL AND CRITICAL.

General Remarks.—Comp. the remarks on the parallel passage in Matthew and Mark. The manner in which Luke connects these two parables with the preceding (ἔλεγεν οὖν) is so loose that nothing constrains us to assume that the Saviour delivered them immediately after the previously mentioned miracle. The true historical connection in which they originally belong is found exclusively in Matthew and Mark; and on what ground Luke communicates them precisely here, is hard to determine otherwise than conjecturally. According to Meyer, Jesus, after the conclusion of the previous scene, vs. 17, sees Himself warranted in entertaining the most glorious hopes for the Messianic kingdom, which He then expresses in these parables. According to Lange, both parables in the sense of the Evangelist serve to explain the last narrative of healing, each one a particular side of it. According to Schleiermacher, these parables contain a reference to that which the Saviour had just been teaching in the synagogue. It is, however, hard to deny that vs. 17 makes the impression of a formula of conclusion (Strauss), and that with vs. 18 a new Pericope in Luke's account of the journey begins.

Vs. 18. **Unto what is the kingdom of God like?**—According to Mark iv. 30 also, the parable of the Mustard-Seed begins with such a subjective and familiar exclamation; more objective is the representation in Matthew. That, moreover, the question of the Saviour does not give witness to actual uncertainty and perplexity, but rather belongs to the familiar and dramatic form of His address, is, of course, understood.

Vs. 19. **A grain of mustard seed.**—*See* Matt. xiii. 32. The scientific objection that the mustard-seed is by no means the smallest of all the species of seeds on earth, is doubtless most simply refuted by the observation that here it is by no means littleness in and of itself, but littleness in relation to the great plant which came forth from this seed, and which, especially in Palestine, reached often a considerable height. At the time of Jesus, also, the mustard-seed was sometimes used by the scribes as an image to indicate the extreme of littleness. So, for example, was the earth in comparison with the universe compared with a mustard-seed, and this was named "*hardly a seed.*" *See* LIGHTFOOT, *ad loc.*

Into his garden.—In Matthew only "his field," in Mark "the earth," is mentioned. Moreover, the mustard-seed in Luke simply becomes εἰς δένδρον μέγα, while the comparison with other plants mentioned in Mark and Luke is here omitted. Variations of this kind, however, do not entitle us to assume that the Saviour uttered this parable twice. We find, at least here in Luke, rather an express reference back to what has been previously uttered than, so soon again, a repetition of it. In Mark the beautiful conclusion of the parable is elaborated in a most graphic manner.

Vs. 20. Παλίν, **Again.**—Now follows the parable of the Leaven, which Mark has passed over, and which only Matthew in addition, chap. xiii. 33, communicates, with whose account that of Luke agrees *ad literam. See* LANGE, *ad loc.* The view of Stier, who here by the three measures of meal understands, with other things, the three sons of Noah, whose posterity must be thoroughly leavened with Christianity, and afterwards the three parts of the world according to ancient geography (so that Columbus, in 1492, would, in this respect, have destroyed the correctness of this parable), shows, perhaps, much genius, but yet is also tolerably arbitrary. Quite as groundless and untenable is it to find here an allusion to the trichotomy of man, as of a microcosm according to body, soul, and spirit. How much more simple, on the other hand, is Bengel's remark as to this number three, "*quantum uno tempore ab homine portari, vel ad pinsendum sumi soleret.*" Comp. Genesis xviii. 6.

DOCTRINAL AND ETHICAL.

1. Both parables, that of the Mustard-Seed and that of the Leaven, refer to the same fundamental thought, to the blessed spreading abroad of the kingdom of God, first in the extensive, afterwards, also, in the intensive, sense. They belong very especially to those parables of the Saviour which bear the prophetic character, and in every century of Christianity find in greater or less degree their fulfilment. With the first parable this was especially the case in the time of Constantine the Great; with the second, in the middle ages, on the diffusion of Christianity in different European states through the influence of the Catholic Church. Every interpretation, however, which assumes that these parables have been realized not only *a parte potiori*, but exclusively, in a single period of the Christian Church, is to be unconditionally rejected.

2. The intention with which the Saviour refers by a double image to the blessed extension of His kingdom could be no other than this, to take away scandal at the poor, weak, first beginnings of the same, and to encourage His disciples, when they should afterwards have to begin their work with a scarcely perceptible commencement.

3. The here-expressed principle: *maximum e minimo*, is unquestionably the fundamental idea of the kingdom of God, and presents a specific distinction between this and the kingdoms of the world, in whose history commonly the reverse, *minimum e maximo*, is contained.

4. It is from a Christological point of view remarkable how the Saviour here not only expresses an obscure expectation of a quiet faith, but the utmost possible certainty of the triumph of His kingdom, notwithstanding the most manifold opposition. Before the eye of His spirit the Future has become To-day, and the history of the development of many centuries is concentrated into a moment of time. If He now begins to inquire with what He shall best compare this kingdom, we cannot suppress the inquiry, with what shall we compare the King Himself? Compare Isaiah xl. 25.

HOMILETICAL AND PRACTICAL.

The history of the development of the kingdom of God: 1. From small beginnings; 2. with visible blessing; 3. to an astounding greatness.—The parable of the Mustard-Seed the image of the history: 1. Of the Founder of the kingdom of God; 2. of the Church generally; 3. of every Christian life in particular.—The Leaven: 1. Leaven leavens *only* meal (inward affinity of the Gospel to the heart); 2. the *whole* meal (harmonious development of *all* the powers of man and of mankind through Christianity); but, 3. only *gradually*, comp. 2 Cor. iii. 18, and 1 John ii. 12–14; 4. in secret (1 Peter iii. 4), yet so, 5. that it does not rest so long as yet a part of the mass of meal has not been leavened.—Does the parable of the Leaven give a good ground for the doctrine of an ἀποκατάστασις πάντων?—The distinction between the working of the leaven in the mere mass of meal, and of the working of the Spirit of God in the heart; the sphere of physical necessity and of moral freedom to be carefully held separate.—The kneading woman the image of the restless activity which is required in the kingdom of God, and for the same.—Labor for the kingdom of God: 1. Apparently insignificant; 2. continually unwearying; 3. and finally, blessed labor.—If the meal has once been worked through, we must then leave the leaven time and quiet for its effect.—Resemblance of the Gospel and the leaven.—The leaven a minute, powerful, wholesome, penetrating substance.—The Word of God must be carefully mingled with *everything* human: "*nil humani a se alienum putat.*"—The kingdom of God follows, in the whole of mankind, no other course of development than in every individual.—The past, the present, and the future, considered in the light of these two parables.—The development of the kingdom of God from small beginnings a revelation of the glory of God. Even *by this* the kingdom of God stands above us: 1. As a creation of God's own omnipotence; 2. an instructive theatre of the wisdom of God; 3. an inestimable benefit of the love of God.—The development of the kingdom of God from small beginnings an awakening voice: 1. To thankful faith; 2. to spiritual growth; 3. to enduring zeal.—These parables the image of Israel, the glory of Christendom, the hope of the heathen world.—The distinction between human philanthropy and the delivering love of the Lord. The first turns itself as much as possible to the collective mass, and seeks in this way to work upon the individual; the second turns to the single individual, in order to press through to the collective mass.

STARKE:—HEDINGER:—Christianity infects by word, example, and conversation. Happy he who stands in the fellowship of the saints in light.—BRENTIUS:—There are neither words nor similitudes enough to depict the beauty of the kingdom of God.—*Bibl. Wirt.*:—The Gospel changes and renews the man the more, the longer it works upon him.—We must guard well against this, that we be not like such a leavened dough which quickly rises and quickly falls again, and so our conversion and godliness be more a puffing-up than of a firm, abiding character.

EYLERT:—The course of the development of the Divine kingdom on earth: 1. Little is the beginning; 2. gradual the progress; 3. great and glorious the issue.—ARNDT:—The inward activity of the kingdom of heaven: 1. Where; 2. how; 3. what it works.—A. SCHWEIZER:—From the least there comes the greatest.—The penetrating nature of the kingdom of God: 1. Because its aim is to lay hold of everything human; 2. because its power as Divine is victorious; 3. because the whole heart of its ministers is engaged for it (a sermon upon the kingdom of God, Zurich, 1851).—For other ideas see on the parallels in Matthew and Mark.

---

2. A Serious Answer to an Idle Question (Vss. 22–30).

22 And he went through the cities and villages, teaching, and journeying toward Jeru-
23 salem. Then said one unto him, Lord, are there few that be saved? And [But] he
24 said unto them, Strive ['Ἀγωνίζεσθε] to enter in at the strait gate [through the narrow
25 door']: for many, I say unto you, will seek to enter in, and shall not be able. When once the master of the house is risen up, and hath shut to the door, and ye begin to stand without, and to knock at the door, saying, Lord, Lord, open unto us; and he
26 shall answer and say unto you, I know you not whence ye are: Then shall ye begin to say, We have eaten and drunk in thy presence, and thou hast taught in our streets.
27 But [And] he shall say, I tell you, I know you not whence ye are; depart from me,
28 all *ye* workers of iniquity. There shall be weeping and gnashing of teeth, when ye shall see Abraham, and Isaac, and Jacob, and all the prophets, in the kingdom of God,
29 and you *yourselves* thrust out. And they shall come from the east, and *from* the west,

and from the north, and *from* the south, and shall sit down [recline at table, ἀνακλιθή-
30 σονται] in the kingdom of God. And, behold, there are last which shall be first; and there are first which shall be last.

¹ Vs. 24.—Θύρας, according to B., D., L., [Cod. Sin., T.] The *Rec.* πύλης is taken from Matt. vii. 13.

EXEGETICAL AND CRITICAL.

Vs. 22. **And He went.**—According to our view the historical matter which Luke gives in ch. xiii. 22–xvii. 10, should follow immediately after the Saviour's presence at the feast of the Purification of the Temple, John x. 22–39. From Jerusalem the Saviour repaired to the land beyond Jordan, and the region "where John at first baptized," vs. 40. There He remained until the account of the sickness of Lazarus called Him to Bethany, John xi. 6. About this time, therefore, there took place the journey from Perea to Judæa, which lasted about three days, and nothing hinders us in Luke's narrative of travel, vs. 22 *seq.*, from understanding particularly this journey. *See* WIESELER, *l. c.*, p. 322. With ch. 17, then, the account of the Saviour's last journey to the feast of Purification properly first begins. That we are at liberty to understand the words εἰς 'Ιερουσαλ., ch. xiii. 22, quite as well of the direction as of the purpose of the journey, it hardly be disputed; but that it here *must* be taken in the former signification, results from the comparison with John ii. 54. Jesus' answer also to the Pharisees, which He, according to ch. xiii. 31, gave them on the very day of the departure, agrees in respect to the chronological *datum* contained therein in a remarkable manner with John xi. 6; and even the conjecture of the above-named chronologist appears to us by no means without reason, that the name Lazarus in the parable, ch. xvi. 19–31, was also chosen by the Saviour intentionally, in the thought of His just-deceased friend.

Vs. 23. **Then said one.**—Time and place are not particularly stated. Even the matter of the question would not give us any right to pass a less favorable judgment upon the inquirer, if the Saviour's answer did not of itself induce the conjecture that the man hitherto had not been rightly in earnest to procure his own salvation. In any case he was only an external follower of Jesus, vs. 24, who did not suppose that there could be any ground for him to be seriously concerned about the deliverance of his own soul. Apparently the question had been elicited by what he had, either himself or from others, come to know of the lofty strictness of the requirements of Jesus, to which, however, only few gave ear.

Are there few that are saved?—Respecting the peculiar significance of εἰ in such questions *see* MEYER, *ad loc.* " *Dubitanter interrogat, ita ut interrogatio videatur directa esse.*" Saved by reception into the Messianic kingdom under the conditions fixed therefor.

Vs. 24. **Strive,** ἀγωνίζεσθε, " *Certate.*"—From the way in which the Saviour answers, it sufficiently appears how He judges the question and the questioner. It appears from this that the man had not asked this question from inward interest, nor even from compassion upon so many who might perhaps be lost, and least of all out of concern for the salvation of his own soul. It had rather been a question from pure curiosity, which was joined with frivolity and pride. Without giving a distinct decision, the Saviour brings the question immedi- ately from the sphere of abstract theory to that of pure Praxis, and does not even address His words to the questioner alone, with whom He does not further converse, but to all who were to-day listening to Him. That, however, the Saviour's instruction contains an answer—it is true indirect, but yet satisfactory and powerful—to the question addressed Him, strikes us at once on comparing the two, and we cannot, therefore, find any ground for the conjecture that such questions are only employed by Luke, as well here as in ch. xii. 41, as elsewhere, in order to continue the discourse (De Wette). On the other hand, precisely such traits appear to us to bear the stamp of life and movement, freshness and simplicity. We may with safety assume that the questioner was more or less surprised at the small number of the followers of Jesus, but quite as certainly did he hold himself assured, above many, of the inheritance of eternal life, according to the popular faith of the Jews: " *Omni Israelitæ erit portio in mundo futuro.*" *See* LIGHTFOOT, *ad loc.*

The narrow door.—Comp. LANGE on *Matt.* vii. 13. We can find nothing improbable in supposing that the Saviour used so simple and speaking an image in His public instructions more than once, and the less as it is here brought up in a peculiar way.

Many shall seek.—We have doubtless here to understand such a seeking as does not yet deserve the name ἀγωνίζεσθαι,—a seeking, therefore, without true earnestness, and without the firm purpose to obtain entrance at any price. Even when one knows more than a superficial longing to be saved, he often seeks its satisfaction in his own way, and therefore misses the true goal. It is worthy of notice that those who are here represented as ζητήσοντες desire it is true the entrance, but not definitely διὰ τῆς στενῆς θύρας. One may do much for his own salvation, and without success, if he omits the one thing that is needful.

Shall not be able.—Understand principally the moral impossibility of entering into God's kingdom in another way than that of the narrow gate (=μετάνοια). When this shall come to light the Saviour shows, vss. 25–27.

Vs. 25. **When** (namely).—The vss. 25–27 contain two examples of fruitless and vain seeking to enter. First, *they knock*, and call, but too late; then, vs. 27, they appeal, but without reason, to their acquaintance with the master of the house. The similitude is not borrowed from a wedding to which single guests come too late (Matt. xxv. 10–12), but from a family whose head has waited as long as possible for a return of the members of the family wandering about outside; who now, when the time of waiting has expired, inexorably refuses to admit them. Observe the striking climax: first, standing some time without, then knocking, then calling, finally reminding of former acquaintance, but all in vain.

I know ye not whence ye are.—With these words the Lord in the most decided way denies that they, let them be otherwise what they would, are members of *His* family. This declaration is immediately after repeated, yet with still greater emphasis, which sufficiently shows that the judgment is inexorable, and that a stern ἀπόστητε follows it. "How can He call them workers of iniquity if He is so wholly ignorant of them? For this very reason: because they outwardly stood so very near to Him, and have become inwardly so very strange to Him; have become, in the figurative sense, barbarians, whose origin is so wholly from a remote distance, so deeply back in the darkness, that the Lord of worlds, so to say, cannot know their descent: and because they, by the fact that they have for the Saviour of the world so darkened their being, betray that they must have come by great evil deeds to this terrible self-marring." Lange.

Vs. 26. **We have eaten and drunk.**—See on Matt. vii. 22. Here we are especially to emphasize the fact that it is an eating and drinking before the Lord (ἐνώπιον) that is spoken of, without inward communion with Him; while what follows, "in our streets," is meant to signify that He had previously, at all events, known them well, and that it was almost impossible that they should now be so entirely strange to Him. The attempt to bring the apparently so forgetful master of the house in this way to recollection is taken from the very life. The reminder of His teaching and preaching on the streets indicates at the same time that it is no one else that is here spoken of than the very Christ who appeared in the flesh.

Vs. 28. **There shall be.**—In a certain sense a third ἔξεσθε, and that the most terrible of all. The expelled are now represented as those who find themselves in the midst of night (hell), but at this remove are yet witnesses of the joy which awaits the members of the family. As participants of this joy the patriarchs and prophets of the Old Testament come here into the foreground, the spiritual ancestors of the same children who now, through their own fault, have become so wretched. The Marcionitic reading, πάντας τοὺς δικαίους, designedly withdraws from the representation this Israelitish element which the connection necessarily requires, and is, therefore, on this internal ground to be rejected (against Volkmar).

Vs. 29. **And they shall come.**—See on Matt. viii. 11, 12.—It is worthy of note that here the mention of the πολλοί is omitted, which we find in the parallel passage. For the Saviour would, by the repetition of this word, even here, have given a decided answer to the question (vs. 23), which, however, was not in His intention, and was in conflict with His wisdom in teaching. Yet, from the image of a company at table, we may perhaps infer that we are not to understand *individuals only*. As respects, moreover, the significance of the judgment here passed by the Saviour, we must undoubtedly concede that by it, according to the connection, not eternal damnation, but the temporal exclusion of the Jews from the blessings of the Messianic kingdom is meant (Stier), while on the other hand nothing hinders us either from referring the here-applied Biblical method of speech in its whole force to the eternal fate of those who persevere in unbelief and impenitence even to the end.

Vs. 30. **There are last.**—"Respecting the originality of these gnomes, uttered in various places and in different connections, we cannot in any one passage decide." Meyer. The sense is, however, in the different passages, different. Matt. xix. 30 the πρῶτοι are it is true ἔσχατοι, but not for that entirely excluded from the kingdom of God; here they decidedly are. There it is only a putting back, here it is an entire rejection, that takes place. There the Saviour had in mind servants craving reward, here unbelieving rejecters of Himself. Besides, He here speaks (without article) in a wholly general manner of *some* πρῶτοι and of *some* ἔσχατοι, and thereby leads the questioner (vs. 22) back into his own heart, that he may maturely weigh on which side he stands.

What impression this whole instruction of the Saviour made upon this unnamed man the Scripture does not mention. Apparently it was too superficial to enable him to fathom in its whole fulness the deep sense of the word—the decided announcement of the rejection of Israel. It, however, remains remarkable, and also serves as a proof that these chapters in Luke have reference to the last period in the public life of our Lord, that it is precisely here and in the three parables of the following chapter, that this thought of the calling of the Last before the unthankful First, comes so strongly into the foreground. It is shown in this that the fruitless labor of Jesus on the house of Israel is now soon to come to an end.

DOCTRINAL AND ETHICAL.

1. This whole discourse affords a weighty contribution to the right estimation of the kingdom of God. On the one hand this appears before us as something in the highest degree desirable. He who enters therein is blessed (vs. 23); he finds himself in the most desirable company of the blessed (vss. 28, 29), and has received a place among the first (vs. 30); but on the other hand it is impossible to inherit this kingdom without personal conflict, and although not a few sit there at table (vs. 29), yet many seek access in vain (vs. 24). Without doubt the Saviour has here in the mention of these fruitless seekers, not only the unrighteous, but also the self-righteous in mind. Accordingly, the here proposed question is not hard to answer. The entrance to the kingdom of God is not so difficult as many have believed, for the narrow door stands open to all; but this entrance, again, is not so easy as many imagine, for only with hard conflict does one enter therein, and many seek it in vain.

2. As upon the nature of this kingdom, so is there here thrown upon the character of its King a bright light. On the one hand we are seized with a sense of His holy severity; on the other, of His love stooping to the dust. But above all we admire His incomparable wisdom in teaching, by which He knows how to bring back the questioner from the unfruitful domain of speculation to that of Praxis. In this view the Saviour is a never-equalled example, especially for spiritual converse with such members of the Church as direct their eye rather to the dark than to the bright side of the Gospel; who subtilize upon the βάθη τοῦ Θεοῦ; who would rather dispute about predestination than listen to the personal requirements of faith and conversion; in a word, who continually are beginning, where on the other hand they ought to stand-still and conclude. Comp. Deut. xxix. 29. Unnecessary questions the Gospel answers only to a certain degree; but to the one thing that is needful the answer is to be read, Acts xvi. 30, 31.

3. Here also, as in vss. 34, 35, the Saviour gives for the failure of so many to be saved, an ethical, no metaphysical ground. He considers the matter

entirely from the anthropological side. Very especially is this method a fitting and profitable one for popular instruction.

4. What the Saviour here says in relation to the rejection of Israel must be complemented from that which His apostle teaches respecting this (Rom. xi. 25, 26); the gifts and calling of God are without repentance. What, however, gives to this instruction the highest significance for all following times and races, is the earnest declaration that no outer participation in the blessings of the Messianic kingdom can give claim to future blessedness, unless one has really taken in earnest the requirement of μετάνοια.

5. The inexorable sternness with which the householder, even after the repeated calling and begging, unconditionally refuses entrance, contrasts remarkably with the great laxity with which many preachers and theologians continually bring forward the ἀποκατάστασις πάντων as an infallible expectation. Without the solemn conception of an "everlastingly too late," the preaching of the Gospel is robbed of its most salutary salt.

6. Even if we do not venture with Bengel to maintain that in the order of the four regions of Heaven (East, West, North, South), the course of the history of missions, which began in the Orient, and now stand in the South, is given, yet unquestionably the here-uttered principle: "There are last," &c., has its great significance, even for Christian mission labor. Many nations that might be called first, compared with other participants of the faith, and heirs of the kingdom, have retrograded, because they have become sluggish and cold. Others, who were originally poor, unknown, and in the background, come forward in the ranks of Christian nations with honor. And what is here said of first and last has found its literal fulfilment in Israel and the heathen world. Christian Europe may well pray that this may not become true in respect of itself, and that the rain of the Spirit which bedews America and the remote heathen lands, may not continue withheld from its own soil.

HOMILETICAL AND PRACTICAL.

The question: What shall I do to be saved? the most urgent question of life.—The question whether few are saved, may be put from different motives: 1. From idle curiosity; 2. from concealed concern; 3. from secret pride; 4. from true love of man.—Salvation no matter of abstract speculation, but of persevering personal conflict.—Strive to enter in: 1. A weighty requirement; 2. a just requirement; 3. a beneficent requirement; 4. a practicable requirement.—Many seek to enter in but are not able: 1. When they will enter in through another door than the narrow one; 2. when they will enter in through the narrow door indeed, but only if they have made it somewhat wider; 3. when they will enter in through the narrow door indeed, but without leaving behind what cannot be taken along.—Salvation as far from being easy as from being impossible.—The solemn significance of the "everlastingly too late." First are able, but will not; afterwards will, but are not able.—The narrow door: 1. Sought too slothfully; 2. found too late.—The door is closed: 1. When? 2. for whom? 3. for how long?—We must be born of God, or else the Lord Himself does not know whence we are.—No excuses will help when the day of grace has gone by.—Knocking at the door of grace helps on this side, but not on the other side, of the grave.—The increased anger of the Jews when they saw that others were called to the participation of the salvation by themselves refused, revealed itself even in their bitterness towards the first believing Gentiles. Acts xv. 45, 46.—The fathers called out of pure grace, the children thrust out by their own fault.—The kingdom of God is like to a feast: 1. The entertainment; 2. the entertainer; 3. the guests; 4. the spectators.—A too-late repentance is in vain. Many first shall be last; many last shall be first. 1. The truth of this saying: a. in the days of the Saviour, b. in the Christian world of all following days, c. in the sphere of missions; 2. Causes of this phenomenon: a. pride and slothfulness of many first, b. the earnestness and eagerness for salvation of many last, c. the holy love of God which regards all according to their works; 3. Value of this observation: it preaches a. to the last courage, b. to the first humility, c. to both faith on the Lord, who will be the centre of union between first and last.—"This saying should terrify the greatest saints." Luther.

Starke:—It is indeed of moment to know the character of those who are saved, but not the number of the saved.—Canstein:—Men have indeed the desire for future blessedness, but it is the smallest number who value it so highly that for it they are willing to give up the present and visible.—Quesnel:—God has His hours, which man must not let slip by in vain.—Zeisius:—Late repentance seldom true repentance.—Osiander:—Hypocrites are before God, with all their outward holiness, but workers of iniquity.—Brentius:—Who here in the kingdom of grace will not be a citizen, and member of God's family, cannot be such in the kingdom of glory; one has relation to the other.—They who are farthest from the kingdom of God often receive it most eagerly.—Lord, everlasting thanks to Thee that Thou hast also called the heathen!—Canstein:—God has at all times the Church on earth; He is not bound to any nation.—Boast not of thy prerogatives above others; it may before evening turn out otherwise than it was at early morning.—Heubner:—There was here a question of curiosity. Many such there are; so was also the question concerning the salvation of the heathen, and concerning evil angels, among theologians, often more a curious one than otherwise.—The idle expectations of those who imagine themselves to have a right to salvation.—Not rank or nation, or the like, makes worthy of salvation, but doing according to Jesus' will.

3. The Menace of Herod. The Woe uttered over Jerusalem (Vss. 31–35).

(Vss. 34 and 35 parallel to Matt. xxiii. 37–39.)

31 The same day[1] there came certain of the Pharisees, saying unto him, Get thee out,
32 and depart hence; for Herod will [means to, θέλει] kill thee. And he said unto them,
Go ye, and tell that fox, Behold, I cast out devils [demons], and I do cures to-day and
to-morrow, and the third *day* I shall be perfected [or, I shall end *my work here*].
33 Nevertheless I must walk to-day, and to-morrow, and the *day* following: for it cannot
34 be that a prophet perish out of Jerusalem. O Jerusalem, Jerusalem, which killest the
prophets, and stonest them that are sent unto thee; how often would I have gathered
thy children together, as a hen *doth gather* her brood under *her* wings, and ye would
35 not! Behold, your house is left unto you desolate:[2] and verily I say unto you, Ye
shall not see me, until *the time* come when ye shall say, Blessed *is* he that cometh in
the name of the Lord.

[1] Vs. 31.—After the *Rec.* ἡμέρᾳ, which appears to deserve the preference over the reading ὥρᾳ, accepted by Scholz and Griesbach. [Tischendorf, Cod. Sin.)
[2] Vs. 35.—Ἔρημος is omitted by a preponderating number of authorities, and is probably borrowed from Matt. xxiii. 38.

EXEGETICAL AND CRITICAL.

Vs. 31. **The same day.**—This whole narrative is peculiar to Luke, but bears an internal character of probability and consistency, and constitutes unquestionably an essential link in the series of his accounts respecting Herod, with reference to his relation to John and Jesus. Remember that not only Galilee, but also Peræa and the boundary district in which Jesus now was (vs. 22), belonged to the jurisdiction of Herod. If the Saviour, according to ix. 51, was not *in that* province, this is a proof that here another journey than the just-named district is designated (against De Wette).

Get thee out.—The question arises, whether these Pharisees actually spoke in the name of Herod, or whether they only made use of that name in order to expel the Saviour, by the scattering abroad of a false report. The latter view (Olshausen, Stier, Ebrard) appears at first sight not improbable, since such a piece of craft agrees very well with their character, as this is manifested everywhere, and it could hardly be assumed that Herod, who already previously and afterwards again (ch. ix. 9 ; xxiii. 8) manifested so much curiosity in relation to Jesus, should this time have sent such a message to Him. And yet this difficulty, if it is closely considered, is not much more than a mere appearance. Self-contradiction belongs to the character of those whose conscience is ill at ease, and it is therefore psychologically very easily conceivable that Herod, sometimes filled with desire and sometimes with fear, wished at the one time to remove our Lord from him, and at another time to attract Him to him. So had he also trembled before the shade of John the Baptist, although he did not in his heart believe in immortality or eternal life; and so might he just as well sometimes wish the Nazarene at his court, sometimes, again, beyond the boundaries of his province. But that he desired the latter just now, had its ground perhaps in the whisperings of the Pharisees and Sadducees, as well as in anger at the fact that the company of Jesus' followers extended even to families of the court-party, ch. viii. 3. And as now wickedness is most disposed to creep in crooked ways, and is ever of cowardly nature, it is quite agreeable to his disposition that he should use the Pharisees, who in turns flattered and feared him, as messengers to the Nazarene, against whom he did not venture to fight with open visor. These were underhandedly to threaten Him with possible dangers; perhaps, he may have thought, He will then voluntarily withdraw.—On this interpretation the answer of the Saviour is justified, and we do not see ourselves necessitated to discover by a forced interpretation in the ἀλώπηξ the Pharisees themselves, and in this image the fact that the Saviour saw through the craft and the lie. On all these grounds, we believe that the message really proceeded from Herod, and that the answer was directed to this Tetrarch.

Vs. 32. **Tell that fox.**—Intimating craft and slyness. Proofs of this significance (proofs superfluous, as the matter is self-evident), are found in Wetstein, a. o. Against the objection, that such an answer to Herod on the part of Jesus would have been hardly seemly, it must be remarked, that antiquity, in this respect, was not so excessively courtly as modern times; that the man who wasted the vineyard of the Lord (Canticles ii. 15), fully deserved this name, and that surely no one in this respect deserved less to be spared than this tyrant, who had shortly before stained his hands with a prophet's blood. Moreover, the Saviour has here yet more the man than the prince in mind (Lange), and the fear of drawing upon Himself the displeasure of such a man, did not in the least measure arise in Him, as appears from the message which He immediately adds. There is not therefore any need of assuming that this whole message of the Pharisees was only the consequence of an uncertain report, or of a cabal which these had formed with the courtiers of Herod (Riggenbach). In this very thing Herod already showed himself worthy of the name of "Fox," that he availed himself for once of such go-betweens, who at all events wished the removal of the Lord as ardently as he.

Behold I cast out demons.—Intentionally the Saviour speaks not of His words but of His miraculous deeds; because these had most strongly excited the uneasiness of Herod (chap. ix. 9). We have already seen before, that To-Day, To-Morrow, and the Third Day, are no proverbial intimation of a brief but ascertained period of time, but are the exact statement of the time which the Saviour needed for travel from Peræa to Bethany, in the immediate neighborhood of Jerusalem.—Τελειοῦμαι, Present Middle, not in the sense of "I die," which is in conflict as well with the connection as with the *usus loquendi;* but in the sense of "I accomplish." Not My work in general, but this part of My work, the casting out of demons, &c. Not an instant earlier will He leave the domain of the Tetrarch, than the mission to be accomplished by Him is discharged. Herod might therefore have spared himself the trouble of such an embassy. "This is one of the deepest words in the mouth of Jesus, which opens a view into the innermost essence of His history." Baumgarten.

Vs. 33. **Nevertheless I must.**—"No obscure and apparently inaccurately reported utterance" (De Wette), but a very intelligible intimation that He has nothing to fear from Herod, as long as His day of life endures, and that He united the fullest repose in the present with the clearest consciousness of His impending departure. Very well does Meyer give the *nexus* of the thoughts : "Nevertheless (although I do not allow Myself to be disturbed in that three days' activity by your devices), yet the necessity lies before Me that I to-day, to-morrow, and the next day, should follow your πορεύου ἐντεῦθεν, since it is not admissible that a prophet perish out of Jerusalem."—That definite time therefore He still continues to work in Galilee, but at the same time, while He so works, proceeds towards Judæa; not because Herod chases Him away, but because He must follow a higher decree, since it would conflict with all rule that a prophet should be slain out of the capital, which, so to express it, possessed in this respect a sad monopoly. It appears at once that the three days in vs. 33 can denote no other space of time than in vs. 32.

It cannot be.—Holy irony united with deep melancholy. On the third day will the Saviour be at Jerusalem, which is destined afterwards to become the theatre of His bloody death. The view of Sepp (*l. c.* ii. p. 424), that the three days here were meant to be a symbolical intimation of the three years of the public life of the Lord, is arbitrariness itself, and in direct conflict with the connection. The common objection against this saying of the Saviour, that all the prophets nevertheless were not killed at Jerusalem,—among others John was not,—is best refuted by the remark that the latter had not fallen as a victim of the unbelief of the Jews, and that the Saviour here does not mean to give statistics, but a general rule. Besides this, it is less the local situation that is here in view, than the symbolical significance of Jerusalem as the capital of the Theocratic State. Every murder of a prophet committed by the Jews, proceeded mediately or immediately from the elders of the people, who had there their seat; as for example, the horrors of the reign of terror at the end of the last century, in the south of France, proceeded from Paris as the centre. As to the rest, the Pharisees themselves might now judge how insignificant in the eyes of the Lord, after such a δεῖ ordered by a higher hand, a casual and passing threat like that of Herod must be.

Vs. 34. **O Jerusalem, Jerusalem.**—Comp. xxiii. 37–39, LANGE, *ad loc.* If we will not assume that this expression also was used twice by the Saviour (Stier), we have then to choose between its arrangement in Luke or in Matthew. The former is assumed by Olshausen, the other by De Wette, Ebrard, Lange, Meyer, and many others. The lamentation over Jerusalem is unquestionably much more plainly explicable at the end of the public life of Jesus, at His last leaving of the temple, than here, when He was yet far from Jerusalem. This lamentation appears to have been taken up by Luke in this place, only on account of its logical connection with vs. 32, and so far not incongruously.

Vs. 35. **Blessed is He that cometh.**—The view (Wieseler, Paulus) that the Saviour here means the customary Easter greeting of the inhabitants of the city to the arriving pilgrims, and therefore, in other words, means to give notice that He would not be seen before this feast any more in the capital, appears to us unnaturalness itself, and to be only grounded on harmonistic predilections. Why should the Saviour have expressed Himself so indirectly, if He th reby would state nothing else than the term of His impending arrival in the capital ? The true explication see in Lange, on the parallel passage.

DOCTRINAL AND ETHICAL.

1. Already here, as also farther on in the history of the Passion, we see that secular and spiritual might conspire against the Saviour. In a certain measure, the fulfilment of the prophetic word, Psalm ii., Herod appears here allied with the Pharisees, as afterwards (chap. xxiii. 12) with Pilate, both times in opposition to Jesus.

2. In a striking manner, over against the craft and cowardice of the tyrant, does the undisturbed clearness of vision and the steady courage of the Son of man come into view; to this moment also in His history is the declaration John xi. 9, applicable. Over against the fox, the Saviour appears in lamb-like patience, but also in lion-like courage.

3. These words of the Saviour belong to the prophecies of His suffering and dying, in the wider sense of the word. They show that He is plainly conscious to what an end His earthly course will come, where this end awaits Him, and by whom it was to be prepared for Him. Such a departure out of Herod's province is certainly to be regarded as a victory. No one takes His life from Him; He alone has power to lay it down (John x. 18).

4. The heart-thrilling lamentation of the Saviour over Jerusalem, affords a powerful testimony against the fatalistic view, as if Jerusalem must have fallen at all events and absolutely. Either the tears of our Lord over His land and people are an illusive semblance, or we must on the strength of such expressions assume not only an abstract, but a very essential possibility that the chosen people, if it really had known the time of its visitation, would yet have been spared and preserved. "The might of the Almighty appears as powerlessness before the stiffneckedness of the creature, and has only tears to overcome it with. Whose heart will venture to answer here with a system of the head: Thy willing and drawing was now no truly earnest one, Thy lamentation was only a scoffing and sport, for Thy irresistible grace was not present to give them the will ?" Stier.

5. Now as ever is the threat fulfilled upon Israel: "Ye shall no longer see Me." Their senses are blinded, and the veil of the Talmud, which hangs over their eyes, is twice as heavy as the veil of Moses. But the last promise also: "until the time come," &c., points to a happier future, which, *e. g.* Zechariah xii., Rom. xi., and in other places of the Scripture, is yet more precisely designated.

HOMILETICAL AND PRACTICAL.

Jesus over against false friends and irreconcilable enemies.—The dangerous counsel which seeming friendship gives to leave the appointed post.—What the one Herod had begun, the other after thirty years continues. Now that the Saviour will not let Himself be lured to the court of the Tetrarch, He is expelled from His jurisdiction.—How restlessly and yet how restfully does the Saviour strive towards the goal set before Him.—The Fox over against the Hen, Matt. xxiii. 37.—The Christian also is in a certain sense inviolable, so long as he is necessary upon the earth.—The triumphant return from Galilee.—The mournful prerogative of Jerusalem.—Jesus over against Herod. There stand over against one another: 1. Steady courage and wretched cowardice; 2. heavenly simplicity and creeping craft; 3. unshaken fixedness and anxious indecision; 4. certain expectation of departure and powerless threats.—Oh, Jerusalem, Jerusalem!—How Jerusalem stands related to the Lord and the Lord to Jerusalem.—The rejection of Christ the culminating point of the wickedness of Jerusalem.—Whoever will not seek refuge under the wings of the Hen, falls as a booty into the talons of the Eagle.—House left desolate.—Night and morning in Israel's state.—The arousing voice of the Saviour to Jerusalem is addressed to every sinner: 1. The loving care which waits for Jerusalem; 2. the iniquity which reigns in Jerusalem; 3. the compassion which laments for Jerusalem; 4. the retribution which comes upon Jerusalem; 5. the gleam of light which breaks through for Jerusalem.

STARKE:—ZEISIUS:—Satan's way in his children is to draw the saints from good partly through craft, partly through terror, but a Christian must take no account of this.—OSIANDER:—When therefore counsels are brought before us, we should measure them according to the word and our own vocation. If they are contrary thereto, despise them.—The business of true teachers requires that they should call things by their names : who shall take offence with them for that ?—God's work can no man, how mighty soever he be, hinder or set back.—In great cities great sins are committed.—Shame on thee, thou enemy, who often dost not venture to call by name thy real or supposed injurer, while Jesus did it !—ZEISIUS :—Not the loving God, but men's own wickedness, has the fault of their temporal and eternal destruction.—OSIANDER :—The persecution of the Gospel is the principal one of the causes why cities, lands, &c., are laid desolate.—QUESNEL :—What a fearful wilderness is in the heart when God departs from it; what a darkness when the eternal light no longer shines therein !—*Bibl. Wirt.* :—The greater the grace God shows to a people, the greater punishment follows if this grace is unthankfully repelled.

NITZSCH :—*Pred.* v. p. 95 : Christ at Jerusalem : —1. Calling love and obstinate repugnance ; 2. deadly hatred and self-sacrificing faithfulness.— THOLUCK :—*Pred.* i. p. 173 :—So many of them as are lost, are lost not through God, but through their own will (O Jerusalem, Jerusalem !) :—1. What appears opposed to this declaration ; 2. what confirms it ; 3. to what it summons us.

G. *The Son of Man Eating and Drinking.* CH. XIV. 1–24.

1. The Healing of the Dropsical Man and the Beginning of the Discourses at Table (Vss. 1–14).

(Vss. 1–11, Gospel for the 6th Sunday after Trinity.)

1 And it came to pass, as he went into the house of one of the chief Pharisees to eat
2 bread on the sabbath day, that they watched [were watching] him. And, behold,
3 there was a certain man before him which had the dropsy. And Jesus answering spake unto the lawyers and Pharisees, saying, Is it lawful to heal on the sabbath day
4 [or not[1]] ? And they held their peace. And he took *him*, and healed him, and let
5 him go; And answered them, saying,[2] Which of you shall have an ass[3] or an ox fallen
6 into a pit, and will not straightway pull him out on the sabbath day ? And they could
7 not answer him[4] again to these things. And he put forth a parable to those which were bidden [invited], when he marked how they chose out the chief rooms [places];
8 saying unto them, When thou art bidden [invited] of [by] any *man* to a wedding, sit not down in the highest room [place] ; lest a more honourable man than thou be bidden
9 of [invited by] him ; And he that bade [invited] thee and him come and say to thee, Give this man place ; and thou begin with shame to take the lowest room [place].
10 But when thou art bidden [invited], go and sit down in the lowest room [place] ; that when he that bade [invited] thee cometh, he may say unto thee, Friend, go up higher : then shalt thou have worship [honour] in the presence of them that sit at meat [at
11 table] with thee. For whosoever exalteth himself shall be abased ; and he that hum-
12 bleth himself shall be exalted. Then said he also to him that bade him, When thou makest a dinner or a supper, call not thy friends, nor thy brethren, neither thy kinsmen, nor *thy* rich neighbours ; lest they also bid [invite] thee again, and a recompense be
13 made thee. But when thou makest a feast, call the poor, the maimed, the lame, the

14 blind: And thou shalt be blessed; for they cannot [have not wherewith to] recompense thee: for thou shalt be recompensed at the resurrection of the just.

[1] Vs. 3.—According to the reading θεραπεῦσαι ἢ οὔ, accepted by Tischendorf on considerations not without weight, and in some measure already supported by Lachmann. The *Rec.* is taken from Matt. xii. 10.
[2] Vs. 5.—The fuller reading, ἀποκριθ. πρὸς αὐτ. εἶπεν, is critically suspicious. *See* Lachmann and Meyer. [D. omits, Cod. Sin. inserts.]
[3] Vs. 5.—The widely-diffused reading υἱός appears to us, often as it has been vindicated, on internal grounds to be rejected. *See below in the Exegetical and Critical remarks.* [Υἱός supported by A., B., 10 other uncials; ὄνος by Cod. Sin., 3 other uncials. Υἱός accepted by Lachmann, Tischendorf, Meyer, Bleek, Alford, Tregelles. It appears to me that to read it climactically "his son, or even his ox," is the only way in which this reading becomes tolerable, notwithstanding its weight of external authority.—C. C. S.]
[4] Vs. 6.—The αὐτῷ of the *Recepta* is untenable.

EXEGETICAL AND CRITICAL.

Vs. 1. And it came to pass.—The narrative of the healing of the dropsical man, peculiar to Luke, belongs without doubt to the journey communicated ch. xiii. 22, and the here-mentioned meal therefore took place apparently on one of the there-mentioned three days. As in the answer of the Saviour to the Pharisees (ch. xiii. 31-33) a kind of melancholy joy appears, which can be better felt than described, so was it undoubtedly the same frame of mind which impelled Him even in this critical period of His life to accept a dangerous expression of honor, and sit down at the table of a Pharisee.

One of the chief Pharisees.—According to Grotius and Kuinoel, it was a Sanhedrist belonging to the Pharisees, and according to De Wette a president of the synagogue, one of the heads of the Pharisees. They, however, had as a sect no chiefs in the common sense of the word, and we shall hardly be able to understand anything else here than a Pharisee who, by his rank, learning, or influence, had obtained a moral predominance over those of his sect, like Nicodemus, Gamaliel, Hillel, Shammai, or others.

To eat bread.—The Jews were accustomed on their Sabbath days to make visits and give entertainments, Nehemiah viii. 10. It, however, could be done the more easily, without actual desecration of the Sabbath, as they did not need to make a fire for cooking their food, as they had already prepared this the day before; so that the members of their family had to perform no special work on the Sabbath, Exodus xxxv. 3. We are not here to understand, however, a public banquet (Paulus). Our Lord was, on the other hand, as had several times already been the case, invited in with the family, vs. 12. It belongs to the peculiarities of Luke, that he loves to represent to us the Saviour as sitting at a social table, where He most beautifully reveals His pure humanity. This time He glorifies the meal through table-talk which, more than that of any other, was "seasoned with salt," Col. iv. 6, and, according to the exceedingly vivid and internally credible account of Luke, was addressed first to the guests (vss. 7-10), then to the host (vss. 11-14), finally, on occasion being given (vs. 15), to both (vss. 16-24). A Sabbath miracle takes place immediately previously.

Vs. 2. Which had the dropsy.—The commencement καὶ ἰδού evidently emphasizes the unexpectedness of the appearance of the man, who had by no means been invited as a guest, since Jesus, after his healing, sends him away. Since now in this place we read nothing of a great throng of the people, such as appears to have been found at other similar meals, in consequence of which this man might have boldly come in, it is highly probable that the Pharisee had placed him there with a malicious intention. This view is not arbitrary (Meyer), for, vs. 1, we read that the Pharisees were watching Jesus, and although vs. 2 does not begin with γάρ, yet it appears plainly enough that here the very crisis is related which gave occasion to such a lying in wait; a case entirely similar to that in Luke vi. 6, 7. Therefore, also, we find the patient just ἔμπροσθεν αὐτ. in a place where he must meet the eye of the Saviour. The same treacherous disposition lay at the bottom of the hospitality of the Pharisees, as previously at the bottom of their friendly warning, ch. xiii. 31. The sick man, however, probably did not know to what end he had been led there, nay, perhaps they had already, by large promises, awakened in him the spark of faith and hope which the Saviour always made the condition of His miraculous power, of which, however, nothing comes to be mentioned, unless it be that before the healing more had taken place between Jesus and the sick man than the narrative informs us. Perhaps they thought, in view of the helpless condition of the dropsical man, that the healing this time would not succeed, and that their craftiness, therefore, would bring the powerlessness of the Saviour to light. And in the worst case, yet even by a *healing* on the *Sabbath*, would they not have again new matter for an accusation? Grounds enough which might occasion them to grant to this unhappy, perhaps also poor, man, for some moments the honor of their presence in the neighborhood of the festive table.

Vs. 3. And Jesus answering.—These words of the Saviour are an answer to this act of His enemies, and to the secret evil thoughts which He had therewith read in their hearts. He will not perform the miracle without first showing them that He sees through their plan. Therefore He begins of His own accord to speak, while the sick man, out of timidity before so distinguished a company, or, perhaps, in the expectation of a friendly word, stands there in silence.

Is it lawful.—In a certain sense we can say that the Saviour shows them His superiority by this, that He lays for them with so categorical a question a snare. For had they answered unconditionally, Yes, they would thereby have sanctioned His miracle; while their answering No, would, in this particular case, have betrayed their own want of love. On this account they held their peace as before, ch. vi. 9. Only after this triumph does the Saviour go on to speak by deeds: He lays hold of the dropsical man with mighty hand (ἐπιλαβόμενος) and lets him go from Him healed. In this, however, it is worthy of note how He still spares the enemies at whose table He sits, inasmuch as He castigates them not in the presence, but only after the departure, of the recovered man.

Vs. 5. Which of you.—Here also, as before, the act is vindicated with a reference to daily life, yet this time again in a peculiar form, with relation to the nature of the miracle. At the healing of the woman whom Satan had bound eighteen years, ch.

xiii. 16, our Saviour speaks of the loosing of the ox and ass. Here, where a dropsical man has been made sound, He speaks of a well in which the cattle ran the danger of drowning (a minor proof, we may cursorily remark, for the accuracy of the Evangelist in the communication of the sayings of the Saviour). In general, the Sabbath miracles of our Lord, even with inevitable coincidences, present so many fine shades of difference, that the opinion (Strauss) as if all were only mythical variations upon the same monotonous theme, is, by a more exact comparison of them, best shown to be a lie.

An ass or an ox.—The reading υἱός has, it is true, a great number of external testimonies for it (*see* the enumeration in Lachmann and Tischendorf), and has been acutely defended by Rettig (*Stud. und Krit.*, 1838), but brings a disturbing element into the discussion. There is here, at all events, plainly a conclusion *a minori ad majus*, which by the combination of Son and Ox in great part falls away. The appeal to the paternal sensibility of the Pharisees would here, where it was the healing of a stranger that was in question, have entirely failed of its end. The various reading mentioned appears, on the other hand, to require an explanation in this way, that an ignorant copyist wished to put a still stronger expression into the Saviour's mouth than that which He had, according to the common reading, made use of, but for this very reason weakened involuntarily the force of His argument. That the Saviour wished here to express the ethical principle, that what we do in relation to our own on the Sabbath we are also bound to do for others (Meyer), is certainly possible, but, when compared with similar apological *dicta*, is yet by no means probable. Had the Saviour wished to impress the rule, Matt. vii. 12, in this manner, the mention of the ox, at all events, would have been superfluous. Moreover, the son in the well appears, at all events, in a somewhat singular case. On all these grounds, we do not venture to apply here the elsewhere so trustworthy rule, *lectio difficilior praeferenda*. The various reading πρόβατον (D.) also points already to an uncertainty of the reading, in which case it is, perhaps, safest to keep to the *Recepta*.

Vs. 7. **He put forth a parable to those which were invited.**—The word "parable" is here to be taken in the wider sense, not in that of an invented narrative, but in that of a parabolic address. Against the imputation of the indecorum of this table-talk (Gfrörer, De Wette), see the remark on ch. xi. 37. Meyer, "Here, moreover, the occurrence with the dropsical man had prepared another point of view than that of urbanity;" and if we assume, moreover (Lange), that the two brief parables also, vss. 7-14, bear a symbolic character, by which the relation of the guests to the kingdom of God is intimated, there vanishes the lightest semblance of indecorum. But even apart from this, we are not to forget how much here depended on the tone of the speaker, and we may here well remind the reader of the familiar expression, "*Quod licet Jovi, non licet bovi.*"

When He marked.—The unseemly demeanor of the guests gives of itself the occasion for the first parable. It is hard to suppose that the Saviour here wished to instruct them what demeanor became them in reference to the feast in the kingdom of God, since He does not regard the unbelieving Jews as those who really sit at the head of the festal board, but, on the contrary (vs. 18 *seq.*), as those who have, indeed, been invited thereto, but have not made their appearance. No, as yet the instruction is framed entirely according to the circumstances of the moment: "Go and sit down in the lowest place." We might almost suppose that the Saviour Himself, with His disciples, belonged to those who sat below, and with right, but in vain, waited for a higher place, but would, however, in no way appropriate this to themselves. In this case, the noblest sense of dignity and His highest hope for the future also expressed itself in the utterance: "He that humbleth himself shall be exalted," as, on the other hand, a sharp threatening for the Jews lay in the warning, which He for this particular case utters as a general truth: "He that exalteth himself shall be humbled." That this saying was one of those which the Saviour on different occasions could very fittingly repeat, strikes the eye at once, comp. Matt. xxiii. 12; Luke xviii. 14. As to the rest, the whole picture is taken from life, and shows anew with what observant look the Saviour often noticed the most habitual usages of daily life. The feast which is here spoken of is no common δεῖπνον, but a wedding, in which decorum as to the place is yet more important than on other occasions. Where a strife arises about places, it must naturally not be one of the guests but the impartial host who decides, who has invited the one and the other (σὲ καὶ αὐτόν, *te et illum*, Vulg.). To the one pressing forward with so little modesty he says briefly, "Give this man room;" thus put back, he begins then (ἄρξῃ, the lingering beginning of receding, with a feeling of shame, Meyer) to take not only one of the lower but the lowest place (τὸν ἔσχ. τόπ.). "*Qui semel cedere jubetur, longe removetur.*" Bengel. The humble one, on the other hand, who has gone blithely and joyfully to the feast (πορευθείς), and contents himself there with the lowest place, receives a friendly φίλε, that urges him to come up, if not in every case to the highest seat of all, at least higher, ἀνώτερον, and the honor which is herewith connected even in and of itself gains yet double worth by the fact that it falls to him ἐνώπιον his fellow-guests, comp. Prov. xxv. 6, 7.

Vs. 12. **Then said He also.**—The second parable is not a eulogy on the host because he had invited the Saviour, although He did not belong to the high in rank, and to his friends (Ebrard), but is, on the other hand, a sharp rebuke on account of a fault which is almost always committed in the choice of guests at splendid banquets. It is, of course, apparent that the precept of the Saviour must not be understood absolutely, but *a parte potiori*. The Mosaic law had already allotted to the poor and needy a place at the feast-table, Deut. xiv. 28, 29; xvi. 11; xxvi. 11-13, and the Saviour also wills that one should henceforth show his kindness not exclusively or primarily to those who can most richly requite the same. The thought that the origin of the Christian Agape must be derived from this precept (Van Hengel) is purely arbitrary.

Lest they also invite thee again.—The common understanding with which one gives a feast to a man of consequence, namely, that he shall be invited in turn, the Saviour here represents as something that is far more to be avoided than anxiously to be sought. It is of like character with the ἀπέχειν τὸν μισθόν, Matt. vi. 5. "*Metus, mundo ignotus.*" Bengel. Only where one does something, not out of an everyday craving for advantage, but out of disinterested love, does the Saviour promise the richest reward.

Vs. 14. **At the resurrection of the just.**—

CHAP. XIV. 1-14.   225

The last phrase, τῶν δικαίων, would have been entirely purposeless if the Saviour had here had in mind the general resurrection which He describes, e. g., John v. 28, 29. He distinguishes like Paul (1 Thess. iv. 16; 1 Cor. xv. 23) and John (Rev. xx. 5, 6) between a first and a second resurrection, comp. also Luke xx. 34-36, and impresses thereby on this oft-controverted doctrine the stamp of His unerring αὐτὸς ἔφα. At all events, this word contains a germ which is further developed in the later apostolic writings. Comp. BERTHOLDT, *Christol. Judæorum*, § 38. That which according to Paul and John intervenes between the first and second resurrection, the Saviour here leaves untouched, without, however, in any respect contradicting it. That He does not speak of δικαίων in the Pharisaical, but in the ethical, sense, is, of course, understood. Nor is He here concerned to praise His host, who had invited Him, vs. 1, apparently with a perverse intent, but only to lay down the general principle which in social intercourse may never be lost out of mind, and to allude to the joyful prospect at which every one may rejoice who obediently conforms himself to this precept.

and similar passages. Upon the disinterested temper which is here emphatically commanded, all at last depends in the case of His disciples. As to the rest, even heathen antiquity was not wholly without similar precepts. Call to mind Martial's *poscis munera, Sexte, non amicos*, and especially the remarkable words of Plato in the *Phædrus*, Edit. Bipont. X. 293, a proof the more that in this saying of the Lord a purely human feeling, but not a breach against decorum, expresses itself. To the Saviour alone did it belong to bring the here-commended principle into direct connection with the future and everlasting happiness of His people.

6. What the Saviour here commends to others He has Himself fulfilled in the most illustrious manner. To the feast in the kingdom of God He has principally invited not such as were related to Him after the flesh, and from whom He might hope for recompense again, but the poor, blind, etc., in the spiritual sense of the word. But for that reason, also, He has now joy to the full in the kingdom of the Father, and a name that is above every name.

DOCTRINAL AND ETHICAL.

1. See *Exegetical* and *Critical* remarks, and the remarks on Luke vi. 1-11.

2. Here also the Saviour does not reject the offered feast of the Pharisee, and shows thereby the human kindliness of His character. In the miraculous deed which He performs on the occasion, in the humiliating words which He thereby utters, He reveals His Divine greatness. He shows even in social intercourse a free-spokenness, but at the same time a conscientiousness and dignity, according to which His disciple can direct himself in all cases with safety.

3. The warning of the Saviour against seeking after vain honor may be applied also in a wider sense to the seeking after high places and offices of honor in the kingdom of God, when it offends us to see another before us, in which, however, the high-aiming ones draw upon themselves very many a humiliation. So far this admonition coincides with the general principles stated more in detail, Matt. xxiii. 6-8; John xiii. 1-17, and elsewhere. Comp. 1 Peter v. 5; James iv. 6. Here the Saviour represents self-humiliation as an act of holy prudence. Other motives, however powerful, could in this connection not well be touched upon. But certainly he acts most according to the spirit even of this admonition who names himself, with Paul, the chief of sinners, 1 Tim. i. 15.

4. The eternal rule in God's government according to which the humble is raised and the lofty is humbled, was not unknown even to God-fearing heathen. Comp. the admirable answer of Æsop to the question, What God does? "*elata deprimere, humilia extollere.*" Yet we may affirm with certainty that humility such as the Saviour here and in other places required, remained unknown to the heathen, and must be called a peculiar Christian virtue.

5. Not ungrounded is the complaint (Newton) that the Saviour's precept in respect to those whom one must principally invite to a feast is only all too often forgotten by His disciples. On the other hand, however, it must not be overlooked that admonitions of this kind are not possible to be interpreted κατὰ ῥητόν, but rather like Matt. v. 39-42,

HOMILETICAL AND PRACTICAL.

Even in the thickening conflict of His life, the Saviour is not unreceptive of social enjoyment.—The Sunday meals, Sunday dangers, Sunday duties of the Christian.—Even where we should not expect it, hostile looks are often directed against us.—Human misery in the midst of the house of joy.—The house of mourning and the house of feasting (Eccles. vii. 3) here united under one roof; in both the Lord is perfectly in His place.—Jesus understands even the unuttered sighs.—Where Jesus stretches forth His hand there follows healing.—Humanity even towards beasts is also promoted by the Saviour.—Humanity towards beasts not seldom united with inhumanity towards men. [Eminently exemplified among the Hindoos.—C. C. S.]—Powerless silence over against the great deeds of the Lord: 1. from rancor; 2. from perplexity; 3. from inflexible disdain.—The seeking after vain honor: 1. In daily life; 2. in Christian life. —The shame prepared for unrestrained craving after honor, even on this side of the grave.—"Take the lowest place" (Address at the Communion): 1. Even there dost thou as *guest* most fittingly belong; 2. there does the *Host* love best to see thee; 3. there does the *feast* most refresh thee; 4. there dost thou most quickly attain to the *place of honor*.—"Whosoever exalteth himself," etc.: 1. The result of the world's history; 2. the fundamental law of the kingdom of God; 3. the chosen motto of every Christian. —Selfish profit the ground of most of the exhibitions of love of the natural man.—The giving of feasts is by no means forbidden to Christians, but not every feast is alike good in the eyes of the Lord.—Recompense from man and reward from God go seldom hand in hand.—The blessedness of Him who receives no earthly recompense for his love.—True love does not only help the needy, but it quickens and gladdens him also.—He that giveth to the poor lendeth to the Lord.—The resurrection of the just a time of the noblest recompense.

STARKE:—BRENTIUS:—Although learned malice is the worst of all, yet one has not to be too greatly in fear of it.—CANSTEIN:—People of repute and preachers should consider, wherever they are, that notice is taken of them, 2 Cor. vi. 3.—Our entertain-

15

ments should be only feasts of love, but falsehood is the first dish that is served up.—Although we find ourselves among evil people, yet we shall not lack opportunity to do good. — CRAMER: — Silence is sometimes good, but malicious silence, when one should speak, is sin.—CANSTEIN:—Them that need help we should willingly assist, and not allow ourselves to be begged out and moved with long entreaties, but rather anticipate them out of compassion.—According to circumstances, it is fitting and profitable to give account to people of one's doing.—*Nova Bibl. Tüb.*:—Falsehood is put to shame by sincerity, craftiness by wisdom, malice by the light of truth, and must be dumb.—It is good at a meal, even where a number are present, to hold edifying discourse, 1 Tim. iv. 5.—ZEISIUS:—Among the proud there is ever strife, Prov. xiii. 10.—OSIANDER:—Dear Christian, thou must concern thyself not only for godliness, but also for courteousness and good manners, Phil. iv. 8.—*Nova Bibl. Tüb.*:—In lowliness of mind, let each esteem other better than himself, Phil. ii. 3.—BRENTIUS:—Between seeking power, and accepting beseeming honor in humility, there is a great distinction, which one has occasion to take good note of, 1 Thess. ii. 5, 6.—Biblical hospitality belongs especially to the poor and distressed.—HEDINGER:—Love is not covetous; God's children share as long as they have.—To entertain the poor and needy is the same as to receive Christ, and has the promise of this life and that which is to come, Isaiah lviii. 7.—QUESNEL:—Happy indeed does he esteem himself who in case of need advances something to a royal prince who is expecting the crown; (pious) poor people are nothing but needy princes; the kingdom of heaven is theirs; we without doubt make our fortune if we lend to them in need.

HEUBNER:—The dangers in high society.—Jesus brings the man into his heart; he is himself to feel the right and declare it to himself. — Against its will the evil heart must secretly acknowledge the truth.—The discourse of Christ is earnest, convincing, but never satirical against His enemies.—To save a man from danger of life every one accounts a duty, why then not also to save his soul?—Demeanor of Christians in reference to rank.—The power of dispensing with worldly honor makes worthy of honor.—Examples of exact fulfilment of the precept, vss. 12–14, vol. ii. pp. 108–110.

On the Pericope:—Jesus as Guest in the Pharisee's house.—The dangers of Sunday.—The right employment of Sunday. — LISCO: — Occasion for thought in the history of the miracle; Thou shalt sanctify the solemn day.—ULBER:—The bounds of Christian freedom: 1. In reference to Divine service, vss. 1–6; 2. to intercourse with one's neighbor, vss. 7–11; 3. to temporal recreation, vss. 12–14.—FUCHS:—Divine service on Sunday: 1. The Divine service of the temple; 2. Divine service of the house; 3. Divine service of the heart.—Self-exaltation and self-humiliation: 1. Their nature; 2. their expression; 3. their consequences.—AHLFELD:—How celebrates the living Christian Church her Sunday? 1. She has the Lord in the midst of her; 2. exercises love; 3. is humble before the Lord her God.—WESTERMEYER.—Jesus at the table of a Pharisee; how He reveals Himself: 1. In His great-hearted love; 2. in His unsurpassable wisdom; 3. in His humble seriousness.

---

2. The Parable of the Great Supper (Vss. 15–24).

(Vss. 16–24, Gospel for the 2d Sunday after Trinity.)

15 And when one of them that sat [reclined] at meat [at table] with him heard these things, he said unto him, Blessed *is* he that shall eat bread in the kingdom of God.
16 Then said he unto him, A certain man made a great supper, and bade [invited] many:
17 And sent his servant at supper time to say to them that were bidden [invited], Come;
18 for all things are now ready. And they all with one consent began to make excuse. The first said unto him, I have bought a piece of ground, and I must needs go and see
19 it: I pray thee have me excused. And another said, I have bought five yoke of oxen,
20 and I go to prove them: I pray thee have me excused. And another said, I have
21 married a wife, and therefore I cannot come. So that servant came, and shewed his lord these things. Then the master of the house being angry said to his servant, Go out quickly into the streets and lanes of the city, and bring in hither the poor, and the
22 maimed, and the halt, and the blind. And the servant said, Lord [or, Sir], it is done
23 as thou hast commanded, and yet there is room. And the lord said unto the servant, Go out into the highways and hedges, and compel *them* to come in, that my house may
24 be filled. For I say unto you, That none of those men which were bidden [invited] shall taste of my supper.

EXEGETICAL AND CRITICAL.

Vs. 15. **One of them that reclined at table with Him.**—Since, besides Jesus and His apostles, no poor had been invited, this was without doubt one of the rich friends of the Pharisaic host, whose remark gave the Saviour occasion for delivering the Parable of the Great Supper. "The peculiar exclamation, and the exact connection of the following Parable with it, and with all that precedes, speak for the originality of the whole representation in the most decided manner." (Olshausen.) That the form of the exclamation in and of itself "does not allow an inference of Pharisaical and carnal confidence in reference to future participation in the kingdom of God" (Lange), must unquestionably be conceded. The exclamation is intelligible enough. "Ἄρτον φάγ. is, 2 Sam. ix. 7–10, used of entertaining at a royal table. The various reading ἄριστον for ἄρτον is certainly spurious, see DE WETTE, ad loc., and φάγεται is to be taken as Future. But the question is still difficult respecting the disposition in which, and the purpose for which, this remark was uttered on this occasion. If we had met this man in another circle, and if the Saviour had answered him in another way, we could then suppose that here the holy temper of Jesus had communicated itself to this guest, and, with Bengel, explain, "*Audiens coque tactus.*" But in the way in which the remark appears in *this* connection, the exclamation seems to sound more pious than it really was, and not even to have an equal value with the enthusiasm of the Macarizing woman, Luke xi. 27. We find therein a somewhat unlucky attempt, by an edifying turn, to make an end to a discourse which contained nothing flattering for the host, and might perhaps soon pass over to yet sharper rebuke of the guests. With worldly courteousness he seeks, therefore, to go to the help of the Pharisee who had invited him, and to draw off the threatening storm. The parable, however, shows that the Saviour did not by any means let Himself be brought off His course by an interjectional utterance; since He, in other words, answers him to this effect: "What advantage can it be that thou, with all thy seeming enthusiasm, praisest the happiness of them that sit at table in the kingdom of God, if thou, and those like thee, although you are invited, yet actually refuse to come !"

Vs. 16. **A certain man.**—Upon the distinction in connection of this parable with that of the Royal Wedding, see LANGE on Matt. xxii. 2–14. On the comparison it appears that the latter, which is portrayed in much stronger colors, belongs to a later period of the public life of the Saviour, when the opposition between Him and His enemies had declared itself yet much more strongly.

A great supper.—The occasion for the representation of the kingdom of Heaven under this image, was given the Saviour spontaneously by the remark of His fellow-guest, and by the feast of the Pharisee. In other places also, *e. g.*, Matt. viii. 11, 12, He makes use of the same imagery. Great this δεῖπνον may be named, as well on account of the abundance of the refreshing viands, as on account of its being intended to be celebrated by many. The first invitation here designated was that through the prophets of the Old Testament generally; while by the πολλοί we can understand no others than the Jewish nation in general. Although the Saviour does not expressly add this, yet it results from the nature of the case that we have to understand this first preliminary invitation as unconditionally accepted by those invited.

Vs. 17. **And sent his servant.**—Δοῦλος stands here by no means collectively for all the servants (Heubner), but has reference very definitely to one servant, the *vocator* (Grotius), who, according to Oriental usage, repeats the invitation so soon as the feast is prepared, not in order to inquire again whether the guests will come, but in order to make known to them when they should appear. The hereindicated time coincides with the fulness of time, Gal. iv. 4, while the servant can be no other than the Messiah, the עֶבֶד יְהֹוָה of Isaiah. He makes known to Israel that the blessings of the kingdom of Heaven, from this instant on, are attainable for them, and that in such wise, that they have nothing else to do than to come, to take, and to eat.

Vs. 18. Ἀπὸ μιᾶς, some supply γνώμης, others, ὥρας, φωνῆς, ψυχῆς, αἰτίας. The first, doubtless, deserves the preference, although in any case what is meant is self-evident. The motives which they adduce are indeed different; but in this they all agree, that they take back again the word that they have given.—**Make excuse.**—Beg off, *deprecari.* Those invited acknowledge themselves the necessity of an excuse in some manner plausible, and thereby indirectly establish the fact that they were under obligation to appear.

Bought a piece of ground.—Whoever finds it unreasonable that the yet unviewed field was already bought, need not hesitate to conceive the matter thus : that the purchase was not yet unconditionally concluded, and that at this very moment it depended on the viewing whether he should become definitive possessor of it.—**Must needs.**—In courteous-wise the invited guest will give the servant to understand that to his great sorrow it is entirely impossible for him to do otherwise. He begs that he may be held excused, that is, "That he may stand to him in the relation of a person released from his promise."

Vs. 19. **Five yoke of oxen.**—To this invited guest, as to the first, earthly possession stands in the way of becoming a participant of the saving benefits of the kingdom of Heaven. We regard it as somewhat forced to view in this invited guest the love of dominion as intimated, typified in the swinging of the whip over his team of oxen. No, the first and second are so far in line with one another as this, that with both, earthly *possession*, as with the third sensual *pleasure*, becomes the stone of stumbling. But if there yet exists a distinction between the first and second, it is probably this, that the man with the field is yet seeking to acquire the earthly good, while the man with the oxen is thinking of still increasing that which is already gained. The first is the man of business,* whose only concern is to bring what he has just bought into good order; the other is the independent man, who will see himself hindered by nobody; who says to one, "Go, and he goeth," and to the other, "Come, and he cometh," into whom something of the refractory nature of his oxen has passed over, and who has no mind to be incommoded by anybody. His tone is less urbane than that of the first ; he does not beg permission to go, is not merely minded to do this, but is already at that moment actually going. Πορεύομαι—"I am going *even now.*" So says he, already on the point to start, and has only just time to add : "I beg thee," while he already desires to be with his oxen.

Vs. 20. **I have married a wife.**—The third excuse appears to be the most legitimate, on which account, therefore, it is delivered in the tone of self-confidence which does not even account an excuse as necessary. According to the Mosaic Law, Deut. xxiv. 5, the newly-married man was free for a year from military service, and it therefore appeared that it could not be demanded from this man that he should leave his young wife. If, however, one would

---

* [Dr. Van Oosterzee has added this English phrase to the German original; and as our language affords the best term for this character, it would seem that our race is most exposed to the temptation here described.—C. C. S.]

believe on this ground that his excuse was *valid*, then holds good the cutting remark, than which nothing can be better: "Very often do exegetical pedants weary themselves to make reasonable that which in the Gospels is designated as foolish." (Lange.) At all events the invitation to the feast had been already accepted before the celebration of the marriage, and so the marriage set him free, it is true, from the burden of military service, but not from the enjoyment of social intercourse. In case of need he might have brought his young wife also with him; and if she did not wish this, then here, also, the saying, Matt. x. 37, held good. Very rightly says Stier: "Of hindering by the state of marriage generally (I have married!) there is no mention, but of the first heated wedding delight, as the type of all carnal pleasure." No wonder that the *vocator* accuses to his Lord *this* self-excuser no less than the two others.

Vs. 21. **Into the streets and lanes.**—The second class of the invited must still be sought out *within* the city. From this appears, that we have here to understand Jews, not proselytes from among the heathen (Lisco). The Saviour has the publicans and sinners in His mind, comp. Luke vii. 29; Matt. xxi. 32, the poorest part of the nation, the same whom the Pharisee, vss. 12–14, should have invited to his festal board. From this it becomes at the same time evident that by the *first* invited, vs. 17, who begin to excuse themselves ἀπὸ μιᾶς, not the people of Israel, but the representatives of the Theocracy, the Pharisees and scribes, the Ἰουδαῖοι of John were spoken of, to whom, by Divine order, and of right, the invitation had been officially given, and who for their very office' sake were under obligation to take due notice thereof. From these who were now invited in their place, no excuses, as from the first, were to be feared; the blind had no field to view, the lame could not go along behind his oxen, the maimed had no wife who would have hindered him from coming; only the feeling of poverty could have held them back; but this feeling also vanishes, since they must be in a friendly way *led in* by the servant.

Vs. 22. **Sir, it is done.**—We must agree with Meyer when he draws attention to the fact that the servant had by no means, according to the ordinary explanations, again gone subsequently to the second command, and now had again returned. "No, the servant, rejected by the former invited guests, has, of himself, done what the lord here bids him, so that he can at once reply to this command: '*It is done*,' &c. Strikingly does this also apply to Jesus, who, before His return to the Father, has already fulfilled this counsel of God known to Him." According to this explanation the parable is then also the faithful reflection of the reality, and says in other words the same which ch. vii. 29, 30 expresses. Very delicate is the trait that not the lord the servant, but on the other hand the servant brings the lord to take note of the room yet remaining. So great was the feast that, although many had excused themselves, and not a few had been brought in, there was still abundant room for others. Even so in striking manner a strong impulse of delivering love for the salvation of publicans and sinners is brought to manifestation in the "Go out *quickly*," which ταχέως is omitted with the following command, vs. 23, because the labor of grace among the χωλοί, &c., of Israel was limited to a very brief time; while on the other hand the vocation of the Gentiles was to extend itself over many centuries.

Vs. 23. **Into the highways and hedges.**—Here indeed the longers for salvation and the wretched among the heathen, are indicated; Matt. xxii. 9; Eph. ii. 12. "*Sørpes mendicorum parietes.*" Bengel.

Compel them to come in.—The use is well known which has been made of this expression, to justify the compulsion of heretics. There is scarcely however any need of remark that none other than the moral compulsion of love is justified. So did Jesus also compel His disciples to go into the ship, Matt. xiv. 22; Mark vi. 45, certainly not with physical force; Peter also compelled the Gentiles, Gal. ii. 14, to ἰουδαΐζειν, exclusively by the power of his example. Not the way and method in which Saul was zealous for Judaism, but that in which Paul was zealous for Christianity, must be the type for the servant of God who will accomplish the "*compelle intrare*" in His spirit. The house must be *filled*, with such as are not dragged or carried in, but such as are by the power of love moved voluntarily to enter in.

Vs. 24. **For I say unto you.**—It is a question whether we have here to understand the words of the lord of the servant (Bengel, Grotius, Olshausen, De Wette, Meyer), or whether we have before us the words of the Lord Jesus Himself (Kuinoel, Paulus, Stier, &c.). For the first view this speaks, that Jesus in the parable is not represented as Lord, but as servant, vs. 17, and that the δεῖπνόν μου in His mouth sounds somewhat hard; but in favor of the other there are, the solemn tone of the assurance and the ὑμῖν, since in the parable itself there is not found the slightest intimation of the presence of several servants, to whom this word could be addressed. We, for our part, choose the latter; and, far from regarding the form of the parable as having in the slightest degree lost anything by this transition from the image to that which it denotes, since the parable undoubtedly can without difficulty be regarded as concluded in vs. 23, this change of the speaker is to us a beauty the more. Suddenly, we might almost say involuntarily, the Saviour betrays His design, and expresses without concealment His self-consciousness, as it lay at the bottom of the parable. In view of the calling of the Gentiles, there opens before His spirit the noblest prospect; so much the more painfully, on the other hand, does Israel's reprobacy touch Him, so that He suddenly lets fall the veil which hitherto concealed the truth in the words of the parable. "Unfaithful ones," will He say, "*My* supper it is whereto ye are invited; I, who invited you, was at the same time He in honor of whom it has been given; but ye will through your own folly receive no place thereat!" It is as though the truth had become to the Saviour too mighty for Him to conceal it longer in figurative speech. Thus at the same time is the whole discourse at the table concluded in worthy-wise, with a *self-testimony* of Jesus; and in view of the slight echo which this must have found in a circle like this, it may not surprise us if we meet Him immediately after again on His journey.

DOCTRINAL AND ETHICAL.

1. The comparison of the Kingdom of God with a δεῖπνον is very especially fitted to set forth the peculiar nature of this kingdom, on its most attractive side. It is a kingdom of the most perfect *satisfaction*,

of the most blessed *joy*, of the most noble *society*. So much more unpardonable and senseless, therefore, the behavior of the first invited.

2. In a striking way there is depicted to us, in the image of the householder, the reciprocal relation which exists between the Divine wrath and the Divine love. The freer, more unrestricted and more urgent the invitation was, to so much the more vehement anger is the love from which it sprung moved; but this anger leads again to new and yet more intensified revelation of love, which at any price will see its glorious goal attained. "He has therefore so made provision that He must have people that eat, drink, and are merry, though He should make them out of stones." Luther.

3. The representation of the Saviour as a servant who invites to the feast of the kingdom of Heaven, is at the same time, considered in the light of the Old Testament, one of the most beautiful testimonies of Jesus to Himself, comp. Prov. ix. 1–5; Isaiah lv. 1, 2.

4. The vocation to the Kingdom of God appears here as one meant in earnest; the anger of the householder would otherwise be incomprehensible: as an urgent one; no means must be left untried that the house may be filled: but for that reason, at the same time, as one, the inexcusable rejection of which prepares for the stubborn refusers unutterable misery. It remains a *decretum irrevocabile*, that such shall not taste of the Supper.

5. This parable contains an important instruction for all messengers of the Gospel. They have, with all the urgency of love, to invite, without excluding a single one who does not exclude himself. They have to prepare themselves for manifold opposition; but also in all to direct themselves after the commandment of their Lord. If they are repelled, they can with confidence complain of it to Him, and never are they to give themselves over to the thought that there is for any one no more room; and if they are only conscious that in the urgency of their love they avail themselves of no impure means, they have little occasion to fear going too far in this, comp. Luke xxiv. 29; Acts xvi. 5; 2 Tim. iv. 2.

HOMILETICAL AND PRACTICAL.

To declare blessed and to be blessed are two very different things.—One can scarcely utter a great truth, without himself being of the truth.—Happy is he that eats bread in the Kingdom of God; he finds, 1. Full satisfaction; 2. joy; 3. society.—The great feast in the kingdom of Heaven: 1. Hospitably prepared; 2. urgently offered; 3. unthankfully rejected; 4. now as ever standing open.—Many are called but few are chosen.—The course of the history of the Kingdom of God, 1. Before; 2. during; 3. after, the appearance of Jesus.—Many that are first shall be last, and many that are last shall be first.—The vocation to the Kingdom of Heaven: 1. A comprehensive; 2. an actual; 3. an urgent; 4. a strongly-binding, vocation.—The sweet message of the New Covenant: 1. Already *all things* are prepared; 2. already all things are *prepared;* 3. all things are *now* prepared; 4. already all things are prepared for him that will only *come*.—The art of excusing one's self: 1. An old art, Gen. iii. 7–13; 2. a universal art; 3. a good-for-nothing art.—The excuses: 1. Their outward differences; 2. their inward agreement.—The excuses: 1. Abundant in number; 2. nothing in value; 3. pernicious in results.—The more or less courteous form, in which we withdraw ourselves from the fulfilment of our vocation, changes nothing whatever in the essence of the matter.—"I cannot," an euphemism for, "To tell the truth, I will not."—The anger of love, love in anger, comp. Rev. vi. 16.—Yet there is room! This saying: 1. A judgment upon those who should have come but would not come; 2. an attractive voice for those who indeed long, but do not venture, to come; 3. a rousing voice for the servants never to give up their invitation, but rather to extend it as widely as possible.—Yet there is room: 1. In the visible church; 2. in the invisible fellowship of the saints in the many mansions of the Father, John xiv. 2.—The prerogative of the servant who can ever say: "Lord, it is done as Thou hast commanded."—The vengeance of the householder who sees his first invitation rejected: 1. The guests whom he calls; 2. the entertainment which he offers; 3. the number which he will see brought together.—The mournful consequences of not accepting the joyful message: 1. One robs himself of the most glorious privilege; 2. draws on himself the anger of the Lord; 3. sees others go in his place.—The command of the householder, the ground of all domestic and foreign missions.—Whoever has once stubbornly shut himself out, remains shut out.—*Compelle intrare;* use and abuse of this word, degree and limit of the constraint of love.

STARKE:—HEDINGER:—Wishing and commanding accomplish nothing in religion; doing and fulfilling is the will of God, Matt. vii. 21.—CANSTEIN:—The vocation of God is so general, that as well the reprobate as the elect are included therein.—God's Supper has its fixed hour; at that hour must those invited come.—QUESNEL:—Too much leisure and too much business are both dangerous to the attainment of salvation.—The holy bond of marriage, which should be a help to salvation, is often a hindrance to the same.—Servants of God and Jesus always go on in their office with God for a counsellor.—What is despised, foolish, and vulgar before men, on that God confers the greatest honor.—*Nova Bibl. Tub.:*—From the apostasy of the Jews, life has come to the Gentiles, Rom. xi.—(CANSTEIN:—God will finally in His turn despise those that have despised Him.

HEUBNER:—The immeasurable love of God, and the scornful ingratitude of the world.—The loss of the time of grace brings everlasting loss.—Man has no one to accuse but himself, if he is not saved.—The Divine call to salvation.—The truth: God earnestly wills our salvation.—LISCO:—Love of the world a hindrance to salvation for many that are called to the kingdom of God.—ARNDT:—Earthlymindedness: 1. As to its nature; 2. as to its relation to the kingdom of God; 3. as to its blindness; 4. as to its punishment.—ZIMMERMANN:—Christianity, the religion of the poor, for: 1. It makes the poor rich; 2. the spiritually sick well; 3. the spiritually blind to see.—DRÆSEKE:—Yet there is room. This is a summons, *a*. to the poor that they take comfort; *b*. to the faithful that they gather themselves together; *c*. to the sinners, that they be converted; *d*. to the good, that they distinguish themselves (!!!); *e*. to the despised, that they rise up; *f*. for the late born, that they believe themselves not neglected.—AULFELD:—The Great Supper of the Lord: 1. Wherein it consists; 2. how the Lord invites thereto; 3. the excuses; 4. the bitter fruit of the excuses.—BURK:—The straightforward behavior of a faithful and honest servant of God, who invites to the kingdom of heaven.—FUCHS:—Come, for all things are ready ! 1. The entertainment; 2. the entertainer; 3. the entertained.—PETRI:—What should move us to come when God calls : 1. The greatness of His grace; 2. the earnestness of His invitation.—UHLE:—The cheerful and the stern side of Christianity.—KRUM-MACHER:—Why not to Christ? (*Sabb. Glocke,* V. 2.)

This Pericope is exceedingly well adapted also for preparation for the celebration of the Holy Communion, in particular,—also for ordination and installation sermons of Ministers of the Gospel.—Finally also for missionary occasions.

II. *The Son of Man opening His Mouth in Parables.* CHS. XIV. 25—XVII. 10.

1. The Address to the People (CH. XIV. 25-35).

25 And there went great multitudes with him: and he turned, and said unto them,
26 If any *man* come to me, and hate not his father, and mother, and wife, and children,
27 and brethren, and sisters, yea, and his own life also, he cannot be my disciple. And
28 whosoever doth not bear his cross, and come after me, cannot be my disciple. For which of you, intending to build a tower, sitteth not down first, and counteth the cost,
29 whether he have *sufficient* to finish *it?* Lest haply [perhaps], after he hath laid the
30 foundation, and is not able to finish *it,* all that behold *it* begin to mock him, Saying,
31 This man began to build, and was not able to finish. Or what king, going to make war against [marching to a hostile encounter with] another king, sitteth not down first, and consulteth whether he be able with ten thousand to meet him that cometh against
32 him with twenty thousand? Or else, while the other is yet a great way off, he sendeth
33 an' ambassage, and desireth conditions of peace. So likewise, whosoever he be of you
34 that forsaketh not all that he hath, he cannot be my disciple. Salt [therefore¹] *is* good: but if [even²] the salt have lost his savour [become insipid], wherewith shall it
35 be seasoned? It is neither fit for the land, nor yet for the dunghill; *but* men [they] cast it out. He that hath ears to hear, let him hear.

¹ Vs. 34.—On the authority of B., [Cod. Sin.,] L., X., &c., we receive οὖν, with Tischendorf, [Tregelles (brackets it), Alford,] into the text.
² Vs. 34.—According to the testimony of B., D., [Cod. Sin.,] X., &c., καί must be here inserted, by which the force of the language is not a little heightened. "If even the salt itself becomes insipid, which least of all might be expected to lose its taste," &c. Καί appears to have been omitted here only because it is not found in Matt. v. 13; Mark ix. 50.

EXEGETICAL AND CRITICAL.

Vs. 25. **And there went great multitudes with Him.**—This whole Pericope is also peculiar to Luke, and although expressions like vss. 26, 34, appear elsewhere, yet nothing hinders us from believing that the Saviour repeated, from time to time, pregnant sayings of this kind, not to mention that the form of these varies in different passages. The parables of the Building of the Tower and of the Warring King appear to have been delivered at the same time, and are very well suited for the greater number of those who came after the Lord on this occasion. In order to see the suitableness of this method of teaching, it is above all things necessary that we realize to ourselves the point of time in which we here meet the Saviour. He is about to depart from Galilee, *see* ch. xiii. 32, 33, but at this very time He sees Himself surrounded by a continually increasing multitude. Are they impelled by a presentiment that they shall not see the Master again in this region, or by Messianic chiliastic expectations, or by the desire, over against the augmenting hatred of His enemies, to give to the Saviour an unequivocal proof of continued adherence? However this may be, the Searcher of hearts allows Himself as little as before to be deceived by an illusive semblance. He has compassion on the people, since He knows how hard it will soon become for well-meaning but superficial friendship to manifest to Him steadfast faithfulness. From love, therefore, He is stern enough to portray to them in the darkest colors the conditions of being His disciples, that they may be held back from foolish fancy, and led to self-examination. Earlier requirements which He had addressed exclusively to the Twelve, He now extends in yet severer form to all without distinction. Whoever, after such seemingly terrifying, but, in fact, attractive, words, did not yet recede, but persevered in the resolution to follow Him in this way of decision, he was to the best of Masters doubly, yea tenfold, welcome.

Vs. 26. **If any man come to Me.**—The coming to (πρός) Jesus is not the same as the coming after (ὀπίσω) Him, Matt. xvi. 24. The latter presupposes that one is already His disciple, the other that one desires to become such. At the very first, it speaks for the Saviour's deep knowledge of man, that the people who, in the literal sense of the word, are coming along behind Him, so that He must turn Himself around in order to address them, are treated by Him as people who have as yet by no means made the first decisive step to Him, but, in the most favorable case, are in the way now for the first time to take this step.

And hate not.—Comp. Matt. x. 37. "The nearer He is to His end, the more decided and ideal do His requirements show themselves to the people that are inconstantly and undecidedly accompanying Him." The lax interpretation of μισεῖν = minus amare (Kuinoel, De Wette, and many others), dilutes unnecessarily the powerful sense of this declaration, and finds in Matt. vi. 24 no support; rather must we compare what is written, in Deut. xxxiii. 9, of Levi. Not in and of itself is hatred anything antichristian, but only when it is in conflict with the commandment of supreme love, as the Lord, Matt. xx. 37–40; John xiii. 34, 35, has given it. Even to the God of love hatred is ascribed, Rom. ix. 13; our Lord, who loves what is human in Peter, hates and rebukes what is Satanic in Simon Bar-Jonah, Matt. xvi. 21–23, and we may even assert that he who is not capable of hating has never known love in its full power. This is the deep sense of the famous sentiment of tragedy: *Va, je t'aimais trop, pour ne pas te haïr* [Go, I loved thee too much not to hate thee now]. That the Saviour here means no hatred towards one's nearest relatives in itself, needs no explanation, comp. Ephes. v. 29. He has only that in them in mind which intervenes irreconcilably between the heart and His kingdom, and defines plainly enough His meaning still more specifically by the concluding clause, ἔτι δὲ καὶ τὴν ἑαυτοῦ ψυχήν. All, therefore, which stands in relation with the sphere of the ψυχή, instead of that of the πνεῦμα, must be hated and given up. Leave must be taken thereof when it comes into conscious conflict with the requirements of the kingdom of heaven. Certain as it is that one may hold his kindred dear in Christ, and that faith does not dissolve family ties, but knits them closer, and sanctifies them, it is at the same time indubitable that not only at the time of our Saviour, but even now, circumstances may occur in which the union of the duties of faith and of merely natural love is impossible, in which, on the contrary, a conflict is absolutely inevitable. Comp. Matt. x. 34–36.

Vs. 27. **And whosoever doth not bear his cross.**—See remarks on Luke ix. 23, and the parallel passages in Matthew and Mark. We scarcely need remind the reader that here it is by no means all suffering on earth, but exclusively suffering for Christ's sake, that is spoken of.

Vs. 28. **Intending to build a tower,** πύργον.—We are not so particularly to understand a tower in the strict sense of the word, but rather a lofty palace, a sumptuous building, in short, a material erection which requires a more than ordinary development of resources. Here we have the image of seeking after the kingdom of God and of entrance into its discipleship, to which one cannot come without the most strenuous exertion and the most earnest consideration. In a graphic way the Lord sketches the project of the tower-builder. This one has, namely, in the first place, a great plan, which is steadily present to his mind (θέλων). He considers next, not only slightly, but at the fullest leisure, what is required for the carrying out of this plan (καθίσας ψηφίζει. Bengel. "*Sedens duto sibi spatio ad faciendam summam rerum suarum*"). Thirdly, he does not pass to the carrying out of the plan before he has on the ground of this calculation well persuaded himself that he has really τὰ πρὸς ἀπαρτισμόν, that is, that which is necessary for completing it without and within. Thus does he escape scoffing, which does not befall him if he does not begin at all, but certainly will if he begins without consideration.

Vs. 29. **Lest perhaps.**—As in the following parable it is especially the danger and ruinousness, so in this it is the folly and ridiculousness, of an inconsiderate project which is brought to view. We can scarcely avoid the thought that the recollection of the building of the Babylonian Tower, Gen. xi. 1–9, floated before the Saviour's mind. While the decidedly Christian life constrains the world to involuntary respect, half Christianity provokes it to not unnatural scoffing. Not a little is the force of the representation heightened by this, that the Saviour represents the scoffers themselves as saying δεικτικῶς to one another, οὗτος ὁ ἄνθρωπος, κ.τ.λ. In the third person the mockery is yet more delicate than if it were addressed in the second person, directly to the imprudent tower-builder, comp. Matt. xxvii. 40–42.

Vs. 31. **Or what king.**—Plainly the Saviour is concerned to impress on the hearts of His hearers the same thing again, although the representation this time is a somewhat different one. The words themselves are not hard to understand. Συμβαλεῖν belongs together with εἰς πόλεμον: the numbers ten thousand and twenty thousand are designedly chosen to denote a comparatively important, and yet entirely unequal, military power, and the τὰ πρὸς εἰρήνην = to the previous τὰ εἰς ἀπαρτισμόν, designates, not peace itself, but that which he must entreat from the too powerful enemy, in order to come into the enjoyment of a lasting peace. [It appears to me that the author has not brought out the point of the particular disproportion. Many a battle has been gained by a force only half as large as that of the enemy. Yet, unquestionably, the probabilities are very greatly against this. The numbers, therefore, appear to be chosen to indicate a disproportion so great as to make success improbable, but not so great as to make it impossible.—C. C. S.] As respects the subject itself, we may, perhaps, distinguish thus, that the building of the tower is the image of the internal, the war, that of the external, development of the Christian life. So far, Bengel is right in saying that the first image is taken designedly from a *res privata*, the other from a *res publica*. Entirely arbitrary is it, on the other hand, to see in the ten thousand soldiers an allusion to the Ten Commandments, and yet more forced to see in the king with twenty thousand a designation of God the Lord Himself (Stier, Lisco). How it can be said of God, in this connection, that He marches against any one to battle, while yet the ten thousand of His adversaries are to be the type of spiritual forces bestowed by Himself, we do not comprehend. The symmetry of the discourse requires imperatively that we should coördinate the thoughts; not to follow Jesus inconsiderately, not to begin the building of the tower without reckoning of the cost, and to beg for peace (that is, not to give up, but to postpone the strife). Comp. LANGE, *L. J.* ii. p. 1041.

Vs. 33. **So likewise, whosoever he be.**—According to De Wette, this application is not exact. It is, however, at once obvious that the consideration commanded by the Saviour, vss. 28–31, must necessarily lead to self-renunciation, and that the building of the tower remains unfinished, the strife undecided, precisely when one is disinclined in his heart to such a renunciation. Precisely because self-denial is required is earnest consideration absolutely unavoidable. (See the γάρ, vs. 28.)

Vs. 34. **Salt, therefore, is good.**—"*Nil sale et sole utilius.*" PLIN. *II. Nat.* xxxi. 9. According to the οὖν (see the notes on the text) this sentence does not stand here independently, but is in some measure the application of the previous remarks, comp. Matt. v. 13; Mark ix. 50. "*Adagium hoc sæpiuscule Christus usurpavit, ut et alia ejus sæculi.*" Grotius. The saying would here be hardly congruous (De Wette) only in case it were addressed to the people in just the same sense now as formerly it was to the Apostles. This is, however, by no means necessary to be assumed; nothing hinders us from supposing that the sense of the declaration is modified by a look at the hearers. As the disciples were a purifying salt with reference to the unbelieving world, so was Israel (here represented in the people following) called to be such a salt for the heathen nations. The Saviour, by the pregnant concluding remark, will lead the throng following Him to deeper reflection as to whether, and how far, they have satisfied this high vocation, and show them that they, persevering in unbelieving and unfaithfulness, run the danger of being condemned as saltless salt, of being cast out upon the highways of the heathen world, and trodden down by unclean feet. On this interpretation the figurative mode of speech is applicable even to a mixed throng, and expresses thus the thought which, as is visible from the parable of the Great Supper, nay, from more than one expression in the foregoing chapter, hovered continually, just in these days, before the Saviour's soul—the thought, namely, that Israel, in consequence of rejecting the Messiah, should itself be rejected. Such a warning was, more than any other, worth being crowned with the concluding admonition: "Who hath ears to hear, let him hear." Compare, moreover, the remarks on the parallel passages.

Vs. 35. **Not fit for the land, nor yet for the dunghill.**—By this addition the figurative expression of the salt in this connection acquires peculiar force. It belongs to the nature of salt that it can only be used for the purpose peculiar to it, and is good for nothing else. It is as little used for manure, as it is necessary to sow upon salt, Ps. cvii. 34. The people of God, as well as each individual who fails of his original high destination, has, therefore, become not merely in a manner less usable, but wholly unusable. The end of the whole address, such a reminder must make the hearers sensible that it helps nothing, even if one originally might have had some ground to expect something of them, so far as they did not advance to victory in the strife begun, and to the completion of the tower already commenced. Whoever is like the inconsiderate builder, and resembles the presumptuous warrior, he deserves no better name than "Salt that has lost its savor." Neither directly nor indirectly is he good for anything, who has failed of his high destination.

DOCTRINAL AND ETHICAL.

1. The whole Pericope presents before our eyes the lofty earnestness and the severe requirements of the Christian life. The word here spoken has the purpose of deterring the inconsiderate and leading the light-minded to self-examination. What the Saviour here holds up before His contemporaries, is now, as ever, of high significance for all impelled to come to Him by a superficial feeling. There exists a remarkable coincidence between the instruction here given, and the answer which the Saviour once gave a well-meaning scribe, Matt. viii. 19, 20.

2. As this instruction has high significance for the *beginning*, so has it not less for the *continuance* and *completion*, of the Christian life. How many a one accounts all as accomplished when he finds a beginning of the new life, a pietistic awakening in his heart, and believes that therewith *all* is won. The Saviour gives such to consider that it is of the least possible value if one even comes to Him once, but does not go along steadily behind Him, and that a genuine disciple must be recognized at least by two traits of character: by not beginning before all is maturely weighed, and also, after such a beginning, by not ceasing before all is completely accomplished. Thus is the saying justified: "It is easier to throw away the life, than to live it Christianly." Nitzsch. The beginning signifies nothing unless it leads to the end; a good ending is impossible without careful calculation and continually renewed exertion of all inward powers. Only then is the lofty destination of the Christian life, which is comprised in two words, "Building and Warring," happily attained.

3. The scoffing of the world at so much that calls itself Christian loses much of its surprising character if we consider how much half-Christianity there is, showing itself in all manner of forms, and coming forward with the pretension of being already *complete* Christianity. So long as the City of God shows so many incomplete towers and heaps of ruins, it cannot possibly make upon its enemies the impression of an impregnable fortress. The world is fully justified in laughing aloud or in secret at so many who have indeed a desire to distinguish themselves from it, but show no power to vanquish it.

4. But what if, even after careful calculation of forces, it should appear that one is not in a condition to build a tower, not in a condition to overcome the enemy? To this question the parable gives no answer, and we should certainly completely misunderstand the Saviour, if we from His words should conclude that in *this* case it is better not to think *at all* of building or warring. The tower *must* be built; the strife *must* be striven; the kingdom of heaven *must* at any price and above all be sought. But when the severe requirement of self-denial and of conflict has brought the sinner to the consciousness of his own impotency, then the Gospel composes our distress by assuring us that all which the Lord requires He Himself can give, and that what is impossible with men is now as ever possible with God, John i. 17; Matt. xix. 26. This whole instruction, therefore, is admirably fitted to bring home to us the prayer of the old father: *Da quod jubes, et jube quod vis.*

5. Three times the Saviour warns His followers against the fate of the salt that has lost its savor, as He elsewhere speaks of the vine that is cut down and cast into the fire, John xv. 6. To view such warnings as ideal threatenings, because they do not admit of being reconciled with the ecclesiastical dogma of the *Perseverantia Sanctorum*, is as arbitrary as to emphasize them at the cost of other declarations which appear to intimate exactly the opposite, *e. g.*, John x. 28–30. It is obvious enough that the same subject in the Gospel is sometimes regarded from the theological, sometimes from the anthropological side; but that the warnings of the Saviour are quite as earnestly meant as His promises are true and faithful. It belongs to the hardest, but also to the noblest, problems of believing science, to investigate with continually greater profoundness the connection between freedom and the election of grace; to recognize with continually greater impartiality the connection of the Divine and the human

factor in the work of salvation, and when the solution of every difficulty in this relation presents itself, perhaps, as impossible on this side the grave, to accord equally its due to the *one* truth on *both* sides, and to hope for the full explanation of the problem from the world where our knowledge shall no more be in part, 1 Cor. xiii. 9. In no case can a difference of opinion in respect to this mystery justify a lasting separation of really believing Evangelical Christians.

6. What is true of every individual and of Israel, is still true also of the Church of the New Testament, which is planted in the midst of the unbelieving world, in order as a purifying salt to preserve it from destruction. If it fails of this destination, it is wholly unprofitable, and deserves, therefore, to be rejected: comp. Rev. ii. 5; iii. 3-16. This word of the Saviour gives, therefore, into our hands the key to the answer of the question why so many a candlestick, whose flame burned lower and lower, has been finally taken away from its place. In the denunciation of this judgment, love speaks; in the carrying out of it, the most inexorable severity reveals itself.

HOMILETICAL AND PRACTICAL.

The Saviour is as far from being misled by a great number of followers, as from being discouraged by the decrease of their number, John vi. 67.—The preacher of the Gospel also must propose severer requirements when a varied mixed throng follows him.—["Large demands are often more attractive than large concessions"—a thought worthy of being well considered by the minister.—C. C. S.]—The hatred and the love of the genuine disciple of the Saviour.—Not all who outwardly follow Jesus come in truth to Him; not all who in the beginning come to Him persevere in following Him.—The hard and the easy side of the discipleship of the Saviour.—The disinterestedness of the Saviour over against the brief enthusiasm of the people.—The requirement of self-denying love to Jesus: 1. A seemingly preposterous and yet extremely simple; 2. a seemingly arbitrary and yet perfectly warranted; 3. a seemingly exaggerated and yet absolutely indispensable; 4. a seemingly harmful and yet infinitely blessed; 5. a seemingly superhuman and yet certainly practicable, requirement.—How the Saviour calls His disciples: 1. To earnest consideration before; 2. unconditional surrendery in; 3. to enduring watchfulness after, the resolution to follow Him.—The disciple of the Saviour called to build, and at the same time to war, Neh. iv. 17.—Better never begun than only half-ended.—The discipleship of the Saviour a matter of special and earnest consideration.—We have to see to it: 1. What; 2. how; 3. why, we choose.—The Christian a builder: 1. Plan of building; 2. the cost of building; 3. the completion of building.—The scoffing of the world at half-religion: 1. Its fully warranted jest; 2. its terrible earnestness.—The Christian a valiant warrior: 1. The enemy; 2. the armor; 3. the conflict; 4. the event.—Even Christ left all to be our Saviour.—It is precisely the noblest things that are exposed to the greatest corruption.—The cast-away salt: 1. What it once was; 2. what it now is; 3. what it necessarily becomes.

STARKE:—CANSTEIN:—Christ is not concerned about the great number of hearers, but about the honest heart.—*Nova Bibl. Tub.:*—Self-love is death, and the suicide of the old man is life.—Believing, doing, and suffering, admit of no separation in religion.—BRENTIUS:—God is served with no great Babylonian tower.—Christians must at the commencement of all things ever look at the end.—There is no lack of scoffers at true religion, but let us look to it that we give not cause and occasion for scoffing, comp. 1 Peter iii. 16; Titus ii. 7, 8.—Satan and the world leave here no peace to true Christians.—It is not always true that a Christian must forsake his own for Jesus' sake, but a heart prepared thereto is required of all, Acts xxi. 13.—Whoever in and with Christ finds all, such a one can very easily for Christ's sake lose all.—CANSTEIN:—True Christians are profitable to themselves and the world, in words and works, Col. iv. 6, but hypocritical Christians are the most unprofitable men on earth, like spoiled salt.—BRENTIUS:—That a backsliding or apostasy from Christianity may not be accounted a small thing, for this reason has the Lord Jesus added so strong and powerful an awakening voice: Oh that they were wise.

ZIMMERMANN:—Weighty questions for every one that will enter into the kingdom of God: 1. What shouldst and wilt thou build? 2. against what hast thou to combat? 3. hast thou also means and energies for the carrying through of this strife?—The whole Pericope admirably adapted for a confirmation discourse. In the sphere of missions also advantageous for the answer of the question whether one can continue the building and conflict begun or not. The *pro* and *contra* admit of being weighed successively; the result of the consideration cannot be doubtful, but gives then new excitement to arouse to increased zeal.

---

2. The Lost Sheep and the Lost Piece of Money (CH. XV. 1-10).

(Gospel for the 3d Sunday after Trinity.—In part parallel with Matt. xviii. 12-14.)

1, 2 Then drew near unto him all the publicans and sinners for to hear him. And the Pharisees and scribes murmured, saying, This man receiveth sinners, and eateth with
3, 4 them. And he spake this parable unto them, saying, What man of you, having a hundred sheep, if he lose one of them, doth not leave the ninety and nine in the wilder-
5 ness, and go after that which is lost, until he find it? And when he hath found *it*, he
6 layeth *it* on his shoulders, rejoicing. And when he cometh home, he calleth together *his* friends and neighbours, saying unto them, Rejoice with me; for I have found my
7 sheep which was lost. I say unto you, that likewise joy shall be in heaven over one

sinner that repenteth, more than over ninety and nine just [righteous] persons, which need no [have no need of] repentance.

8 Either [Or] what woman having ten pieces of silver, if she lose one piece, doth not
9 light a candle, and sweep the house, and seek diligently till she find it? And when she hath found it, she calleth her friends and her neighbours [τὰς φίλας καὶ γείτονας, fem.] together, saying, Rejoice with me; for I have found the piece which I had lost.
10 Likewise, I say unto you, there is joy in the presence of the angels of God over one sinner that repenteth.

EXEGETICAL AND CRITICAL

Vs. 1. **All the publicans and sinners.**—Πάντες, not in the sense of *all manner of* (Heubner, a. o.), but a popular way of speaking, with which the collective mass of all the there present publicans and sinners is designated. Comp. ch. iv. 40.—**Drew near unto Him.**—The common explanation: *were wont to draw near unto Him* (De Wette), is grammatically not necessary, and has this disadvantage, that thereby the connection with that which precedes is unnecessarily given up. Better: They were at this moment *occupied* with this matter of coming to Him, and that with the distinct intention of hearing Him. We have therefore to represent to ourselves an audience which, at the time of the Saviour's departure from Galilee, had apparently streamed together in a public place, and the majority of which consisted of publicans and sinners, who, at the moment, had pressed before the Pharisees, and by that fact excited their bitterness.

Vs. 2. **Murmured,** διεγόγγυζον. Διά indicates the murmuring of a number among themselves, which for that reason became also plainly audible to others. The cause of this dissatisfaction is, in general, that the Saviour benevolently receives and accepts men of evil name and repute (ἁμαρτωλούς without article). (Προσδέχεσθαι in the sense of *comiter excipere*. Comp. Rom. xvi. 2; Phil. ii. 29.) This is the general accusation, while the following συνεσθίει αὐτοῖς states a special grievance. He receives not only, but permits Himself also to be received. We need not assume that the Saviour on this very day had taken part in a feast of publicans, as, *e. g.*, Sepp will have it, who, without any ground, *l. c.* ii. 169, asserts that the parables here following were delivered immediately after the calling of Matthew, at the feast given by him on that occasion. The Pharisees are now thinking of what the Saviour was often wont to do, and utter their dissatisfaction with it publicly. By such a course of conduct they believed the Master lowered Himself, inasmuch as He showed to the worst part of the nation an undeserved honor, and at the same time injured the Pharisees, who previously had, indeed, now and then, allowed Him the distinction of being received at their table, but who now would have to be ashamed of such a guest.

Vs. 3. **And He spake this parable.**—When we consider that the chief parable, vss. 11–32, is introduced only by a simple εἶπεν δέ, and that the two examples from daily life, vss. 3–7 and vss. 8–10, bear less than the narrative of the Prodigal Son the character of a thoroughly elaborated *parable*, we are then disposed to assume that vss. 3–10 constitute only the introduction to the actual parable, παραβολή, which is announced in vs. 3, but not begun until vs. 11. On the other hand, however, it is not to be denied that Luke uses the word παραβολή in a wider sense also, and that to designate not only an invented narrative, but also a parabolic expression, or an example from daily life; *see*, *e. g.*, ch. iv. 23; v. 36; vi. 39; xiv. 7–11. It will therefore probably be simplest to assume that the παραβολή announced in vs. 3 is actually uttered, vss. 4–7; that the Saviour immediately after that expresses the same thought, vss. 8–10, in a second παραβολή, and finally, vs. 11, after a brief interval, takes up the word again in order once more to present this cardinal truth in more perfect parabolic form.

Vs. 4. **What man of you.**—From this commencement, as also from vs. 8, it immediately appears that the Saviour appeals to that universal human feeling which impels, as well the man as the woman, to seek what is lost, and to rejoice with others over what is found again. With this He introduces the *first* of the three parables contained in this chapter—that of *the Lost Sheep*. It cannot well be doubted that this triplet belongs together, and that we have, therefore, here no chrestomathic combination of parabolic discourses of the Saviour, but a well-connected didactic deliverance, which has as its purpose to express the same main thought in different ways. As to the question whether the first of the here-given parables and that communicated by Matthew, ch. xviii. 12–14, are one and the same, *see* LANGE, *ad loc.* We do not know what there could be against the opinion that the Saviour may have repeatedly availed Himself of the same image, once for the instruction of His Apostles, another time for the shaming of His enemies. The two parables are different: 1. *In form.* In Matthew the ninety-nine remain on the mountains; in Luke, in the wilderness. Luke xv. 5–7 also is very different from the parallel passage in Matthew, and serves as a proof that Luke communicates the more elaborated and later developed—Matthew, on the other hand, the originally simpler, form of the parable. 2. In *purpose and meaning.* With Luke it is God's infinite love for yet lost sinners; but with Matthew, Christ's labor of grace on wandering believers, that is the main thing. According to the connection then, the purpose of the discourse is a different one in Matthew and Luke. Besides this, the image itself is so natural, so taken from life, that it cannot surprise us to learn that even in later Rabbins an analogon of this parable is found. *See* SEPP, ii. p. 169.

Having a hundred sheep.—Ἑκατόν not only used as a round number, but also to bring into view the comparative smallness of the loss in opposition to what yet remains to Him. In the most striking way the Saviour now portrays the faithful love that seeks the lost, so that even on account of the freshness of the portraiture, this parable belongs, with very good right, in the Gospel of Luke. The Good Shepherd at once leaves the ninety-nine ἐν τῇ ἐρήμῳ, the accustomed pasturing-place of the sheep, and leaves them for the moment with entire unconcern as to the great danger to which he exposes the majority. He goes after the lost one (ἐπί), with a definite intention to fetch it back. Not speedily does he give up his efforts. His love is therefore a persevering and continually renewed effort for the deliverance of the lost one; and when it is finally again within His reach, he does not chase the wearied sheep unmercifully back, nor commit it even to the most trusted of his hirelings, but lays it on his own shoulders (ἑαυτοῦ). He bears it joyfully home, and now calls as well his neighbors as also his more distant friends together. Having heard of his loss, the well-known lost sheep, τὸ ἀπολωλός, they must now also share his joy, which even exceeds his thankfulness for the undisturbed possession of that which is *not* lost.

Vs. 7. **Likewise joy shall be in Heaven.**— Here as yet quite general. Afterwards, vs. 10, with more special mention of the angels. It is noticeable how here the Saviour designates the joy in Heaven as something yet future (ἔσται), while He afterwards, vs. 10, speaks of it as of something already actually beginning (γίνεται). We can scarcely avoid the thought that here the prospect of that joy hovered before His soul which He, the Good Shepherd, was especially to taste when He, after finishing His conflict, should return into the celestial mansion of His Father, and should taste the joy prepared for Him. John xiv. 2; Heb. xii. 2.

More than over ninety and nine.—The question whom we have now to understand by these δίκαιοι, has been at all times differently answered. Luther, Spener, Bengel, interpret it of those already become righteous through faith, since they have already repented, and stand in a state of grace with God, such as Manasseh, a. o.—De Wette: The actually righteous, that is, more righteous than publicans, and the like.—Meyer: δίκαιοι characterized from the legal point of view, not from that of inward ethical character.—Grotius: Only an anthropopathic element of the picture, *quia insperata et prope desperata magis nos afficiunt*. According to our opinion, passages like Matt. ix. 13; Luke xviii. 14, are particularly to be brought into the comparison. If we consider, moreover, that the hearers of the Saviour consisted partially of Pharisees, and in what way these had, a little before, manifested their inward spite (vs. 12), we can then no longer doubt that we have to understand fancied righteous ones of a legal type, who, however, if one applied a higher standard, must appear yet more sinful than others. Comp. Matt. xxi. 31, 32. We know not what should hinder us here also, as often already, to assume a holy irony in the words of the Saviour, nor why He should only in the *third* parable have indirectly attacked the Pharisaical pride of virtue. The comparison of the greater joy over one, with that over the ninety-nine, over whom, strictly speaking, there can be no joy at all, is then to be taken just as the declaration Luke xviii. 14.

Vs. 8. **Either what woman.**—In order to indicate that not the material worth of what is lost, in itself, but the worth which it has in the eyes of the possessor, is the cause of the carefulness of the love which seeks it, the Saviour takes a second example from daily life, but not now from something so valuable as a sheep, but from a δραχμή, in itself rather insignificant. For the woman, however, this loss is of great importance, since her whole treasure consists of ten such drachmae.—Δραχμή, the common Greek coin which, at that time, was in circulation among the Jews also. The Attic drachma was = ¼ stater, [17.6 cents]; the Alexandrian twice as heavy. It appears that we have here to understand the first,

which, not seldom even somewhat lighter, was in circulation at the time of the Saviour. The ten drachmae are then about equal to $1 76.* *See* WINER, *in voce.*

Doth not light a candle.—In the most practical manner the labor of the woman to come again in possession of the lost drachma is now sketched after the life. It is as though one saw the dust of the broom flying around in sweeping, until she succeeds in discovering in a dark corner the lost piece, and immediately picks it up. The coin, which was originally stamped with the image of the Emperor, but had been thrown into the dust and become almost unrecognizable, is the faithful image of the sinner. "*Sum nummus Dei, thesauro aberravi, miserere mei.*" Augustine. As to the rest, the lighting of the lamp, the sweeping, and the seeking, belong, in our eyes, so entirely to the pictorial form of the representation, that it appears to us almost arbitrary to see therein (Stier) the indication of the threefold activity of the preacher, the eldership, and the whole Church for the saving of the lost one. "If we would attribute to every single word a deeper significance than appears, we should not seldom incur the danger of bringing much into the Scripture which is not at all contained in it; for as the artist, for the beautifying of his picture, does much that is not indispensably necessary, so has Christ also spoken many words which stand to the main matter which is to be imaged forth by the figure in only a remote, often, indeed, in no relation at all." Zinmermann.

Vs. 10. **Likewise . . . there is joy**, γίνεται. —Here the Saviour speaks not comparatively, but absolutely; not only in general of joy in Heaven, but ἐνώπιον τῶν ἀγγ. τ. Θ. It is, however, not entirely correct, if this word is used as a direct proof of the opinion that the angels rejoice over the conversion of a sinner, for the Saviour is not speaking directly of the *gaudium angelorum*, but *coram angelis*. As the Shepherd and the Woman rejoiced *before* and *with* their friends, so does God rejoice before the eyes of the angels over the conversion of the sinner; but as the friends and neighbors rejoice with the Woman and the Shepherd, so can we also conceive the angels as taking part in this Divine joy. But if it is *God*, in the whole fulness of His being, who is represented, it is then inadmissible to understand it exclusively, either of the Holy Ghost (Stier, Bengel), or of the Church of the Lord (Luther, Lisco). The *applicability* of the parable to both is willingly acknowledged by us, but that the Saviour's intention was here to refer to the *munus*, either of the *spiritus sancti*, or of the *ecclesiae*, *peccatores quaerentis*, can hardly be proved. Equally rash does it appear when Bengel, in the friends and neighbors of the Shepherd and of the Woman, finds an intimation of the different ranks and classes of the angels, *vel domi, vel foris agentes*.

DOCTRINAL AND ETHICAL.

1. Not without reason does the eye rest with continually new interest on the picture: Jesus among the publicans and sinners. It is the Gospel within the Gospel, like John iii. 16; Romans i. 17, and some other passages. This of itself is remarkable, that the greatest sinners feel themselves drawn, as it were, with a secret attraction to Jesus; what an

---
* [Of course then worth at least ten times its present value.—C. C. S.]

entirely unique impression must His personality have produced upon these troubled and smitten hearts! Thus does He reveal Himself at the same time as the Prince of Peace, of whom Psalm lxxii. 12-14, and so many other passages of the prophetic Scriptures, speak; and what the Pharisees impute to Him as a trespass, becomes for faith an occasion the rather for praise and thanks. The feast which He keeps with publicans is a striking symbol of the feast in the kingdom of God, Luke xiv. 21-23, and at the same time the happy prophecy of the heavenly feast which He will hereafter share with His redeemed in the fulness of bliss.

2. The parable of the Good Shepherd sets forth for us, in a striking manner, the image of the pastoral faithfulness of God's searching for the sinner. Israel had already been compared, even under the Old Testament, to a strayed sheep, Isaiah liii. 6; Ezekiel xxxiv. 5; Psalm cxix. 176, etc., and Jehovah also was, even from ancient time, represented under the amiable figure of a shepherd, Ezekiel xxxiv., and Psalm xxiii.; Isaiah xl. 11; as in Homer also, the best kings are designated as ποιμένες λαῶν. But inasmuch as this pastoral faithfulness of God reveals itself most admirably in the redeeming activity of Christ (comp. John x.), we may at the same time, in the first parable, see an image of the earthly activity and of the heavenly joy of the loving Son of Man. But certainly it is going too far to find even the atoning death of the Saviour (Melanchthon) indicated in the shepherd with his sheep on his shoulder: "*Ovem inventam ponit in humeros suos, i. e., nostrum onus transfert in se ipsum, fit victima pro nobis.*" Such an allusion would then at least have been as yet understood by no one of the hearers of our Lord, and yet they had no farther to look than upon Him in order to convince themselves that the Good Shepherd in the parable was no ideal, but a reality; and surprised we cannot be that even the most ancient Christian art laid hold of this symbol with visible affection. *See* the examples, *e. g.*, in Augusti's *Beiträge zur christlichen Kunstgeschichte und Liturgik*, ii. Even the present moment proved how much the Saviour had at heart the seeking of the lost. "*Ideo Jesus Christus secutus est peccatores usque ad victum quotidianum, usque ad mensam, ubi maxime peccatur.*" Bengel.

3. What the Saviour relates of the Woman and the Shepherd was at the same time an admirable model of pastoral prudence and Halieutics for His first apostles. Only when they should care for the wandering and lost with so much pleasure and love would they be fitted for the work of their calling. That they did not forget the teaching appears, among other things, from the beautiful narrative of the aged John and the young man Theagenes, which Clemens Alexandrinus communicates to us in his *Quis Dives Salvetur*, cap. 42,—the best practical commentary on the parable of the Good Shepherd.

4. These two parables, as in particular the third, that of the Prodigal Son, are a palpable proof of the falsity of a one-sided fatalistic deterministic view of the world, according to which the lost coin and the lost sheep must absolutely be found again, and therefore we can scarcely speak of any trouble in seeking, or of a joy in finding.

5. What the Saviour declares of the joy in heaven over that which is found again on earth, deserves to be named one of the most striking revelations of the mysteries of the life to come. To the Saviour the angel-world is more than a poetic dream —more than an æsthetic form; it is to Him a community of self-conscious, rational, and holy beings. These are acquainted with that which goes on in the moral world on earth; they take lively interest in the saving of the sinner; they rejoice as often as in this respect the work of love succeeds: this joy springs from their knowing how, even through the conversion of one sinner, the honor of God is exalted, the kingdom of Christ is advanced, the blessedness of mankind is increased, the future reunion of heaven and earth is brought nearer. The Saviour in this leaves to our faith the reckoning how high their joy, since the foundation of the kingdom of God on earth must have already risen, and what a height it shall hereafter reach when all converted sinners shall have been fully prepared and sanctified. Comp. Ephes. iii. 10; 1 Peter i. 12; and the whole imagery of the Apocalypse.

6. Were anything more necessary for the removal of any doubt in so glorious a revelation, it would be the remembrance that, according to this parable, the joy over the finding of the lost is, in God and His angels, quite as *natural* as in the Woman and the Shepherd. Even in an extra-ecclesiastical sphere, the striking character of this thought has been already recognized and uttered with emphasis, *e. g.*, by Goethe, when he in the ballad, The God and the Bayadere, says:

"*Es freut sich die Gottheit der reuigen Sünder,
Unsterbliche heben verlorene Kinder
Mit feurigen Armen zum Himmel empor.*"

[The Godhead rejoices over repentant sinners; the immortals raise lost children with fiery arms upward to heaven.]

7. See below on the following parable.

HOMILETICAL AND PRACTICAL.

How much attractiveness Jesus has for publicans and sinners. In Him they see, 1. The highest ideal of mankind realized; 2. the highest revelation of the Godhead manifested.—Jesus, even as Friend of the publicans and sinners, is sent for the fall of some and the rising of others.—The joyful message of salvation proclaimed by the blasphemers of the Saviour. See further the ideas in Luke vii. 34.

The Good Shepherd, the image of the love of God in Christ for sinners: 1. Its unexampled compassion; 2. its persevering patience; 3. its forbearing tenderness; 4. its blessed joy.—"Till he find it," the highest goal of Divine love: 1. How much is requisite before it is reached; 2. how heartfelt its joy when it is reached.—Rejoice with them that do rejoice!—Human feeling the best pledge of the riches of the Divine compassion.—The sinner's salvation, the angels' joy.—The worth of a single soul.—Grounds for the joy of heaven when the lost sheep is found.—The angels rejoice then, 1. For God's sake; 2. for Jesus' sake; 3. for the sinner's sake; 4. for their own sake.—The joy of the angels on its practical side: the Saviour's declaration hereupon contains, 1. A striking revelation of the blessed love in heaven; 2. a powerfully rousing voice to conversion; 3. a strong impulse to the work of seeking love; 4. a ground for quickening the longing of the Christian for the life in heaven.—How much the greatest unrighteousness has, on the platform of the Gospel, the advantage above self-righteousness.—The Lost Coin: 1. What the loss of it has to surprise us; it is lost, *a.* out of a well-guarded treasure, *b.* lost in the house,

c. lost, almost without hope of finding again; 2. What this loss has to quicken us. It impels *a.* to kindle a light, *b.* to sweep, *c.* to seek till it is found.—The Lost Coin the striking image of the sinner: 1. Its original brilliancy; 2. its present deterioration; 3. its worth when it shall hereafter be found again.—The soul of the sinner the object of the greatest sorrow, labor, and joy: 1. No loss so great as when the soul is lost; 2. no trouble too great if only the soul is preserved; but 3. no joy so blessed as when the soul is saved.—The human heart needs the sympathy of others in its own joy.—No sinner so mean but that he may become an object of the joy in heaven.—Jesus' love of sinners: 1. The objects (vs. 1); 2. the adversaries (vs. 2); 3. the ground (vss. 3–9); 4. the preciousness of the same (vss. 7–10).

STARKE:—QUESNEL:—The main thing that we have to do in this life is to draw near to Jesus.—The company of bad people one does well to avoid, yet he must not wholly withdraw himself from them.—Hypocrites are harder to convert than open sinners.—What a blessing it is for an evangelical preacher when even the greatest sinners like to hear him.—OSIANDER: —The world puts the worst interpretation on everything in faithful preachers.—Christ's whole discharge of His office is a good summary of pastoral theology; —let us therein diligently study and imitate it.— BRENTIUS:—Returning sinners are to be received with much love and friendship, and all previous evil of theirs to be thrown into forgetfulness.—Philemon vs. 10; Ezek. xxxiv. 16.—QUESNEL:—The church triumphant and the church militant are one heart and one soul.—*Nova Bibl. Tub.*:—A lost sinner cannot be found again so easily but that there needs a heavy bosom of law and discipline thereto.—*Peccatorum lachrymæ sunt angelorum deliciæ.*

HEUBNER:—The living intercourse of a pastor with his church is more than literary activity, at which the world is agape.—The beginning of conversion is: to hear Christ's word.—The holier thou art, so much the milder art thou too.—Even yet the world delights to mock at the conversion of the sinner.—Everywhere does Jesus show the inconsistent self-contradictions of man in earthly and in spiritual things.—As the shepherd knows his sheep and tells them, so does God His children.—God waits not till the lost one returns of himself, He seeks him.— Never has God shown Himself as love more than when He redeemed man.—"Nothing weighs too heavy for love; he is willing to take all costs who for God's sake loves souls, and knows what Christ has done for them."—QUESNEL:—The business of men in the search of temporal, stands in contrast with their negligence in the search of spiritual, things. —By the amendment of a single sinner others again may be saved.

On *the Pericope:*—HEUBNER:—Christian care for the deliverance of lost souls.—LISCO:—How important to Jesus the saving of every sinner is.—The saving love of the Christian a copy of the pastoral faithfulness of Christ: 1. A copy which is like the model; 2. but which never equals the model.— PALMER:—1. Jesus receives sinners *when* they come to Him; 2. Jesus seeks sinners even *before* they come to Him.—FUCHS:—The different hearts of those who are mentioned in this Gospel: 1. The repentant heart of the sinners; 2. the envious heart of the Pharisees; 3. the loving heart of the Lord.—AHLFELD:—The Son of man comes to seek what is lost: 1. His toil; 2. His success; 3. His joy.—REICHHELM: —Seeking love: 1. Whom it seeks; 2. how; 3. why it seeks.—SOUCHON:—Jesus will make the righteous sinners, the sinners righteous.—VON KAPFF:—The joy over a sinner that repents: 1. The joy of the repentant sinner himself; 2. the joy of the saints; and 3. the joy of God over him.—W. THIESS:—Jesus receives sinners: this word is 1. The one centre of the Bible; 2. the true centre of Christian preaching; 3. the chiefest jewel in life.—RAUTENBERG:—Who is found? 1. Whoever is drawn back from wandering; 2. carried by Christ; 3. and brought into the fellowship of His people.—HÖPFNER:—How great is the compassion of the Lord! 1. He seeks the lost; 2. brings again the straying; 3. binds up the wounded; 4. tends the weak; 5. guards what is strong. (Numbers 3 and 5 are, however, hardly to be deduced from the text.)—BURK:—The blessed experience in spiritual things: 1. I am lost; 2. God seeks me; 3. God has found me.

The whole *Pericope* is, either as a whole or in part, admirably fitted to be the foundation of a communion sermon.

---

3. The Prodigal Son (VSS. 11–32).

11, 12 And he said, A certain man had two sons: And the younger of them said to *his* father, Father, give me the portion of goods that falleth *to me.* And he divided unto
13 them *his* living. And not many days after the younger son gathered all together, and took his journey into a far country, and there wasted his substance with riotous living.
14 And when he had spent all, there arose a mighty famine in that land; and he began to
15 be in want. And he went and joined himself to a citizen of that country; and he sent
16 him into his fields to feed swine. And he would fain have filled his belly with the husks
17 [pods] that the swine did eat: and no man gave unto him [*therefrom*]. And when he came to himself, he said, How many hired servants of my father's have bread enough
18 and to spare, and I perish [am perishing here[1]] with hunger! I will arise and go to my father, and will say unto him, Father, I have sinned against heaven, and before
19 thee, And [for "And" read "I[2]"] am no more worthy to be called thy son: make me
20 as one of thy hired servants. And he arose, and came to his father. But when he was yet a great way off, his father saw him, and had [or, was moved with] compassion,

21 and ran, and fell on his neck, and kissed him. And the son said unto him, Father, I have sinned against heaven, and in thy sight, and am³ no more worthy to be called thy
22 son. But the father said to his servants, Bring forth the best robe [a robe, the best⁴],
23 and put *it* on him; and put a ring on his hand, and shoes on *his* feet: And bring hither
24 the fatted calf, and kill *it;* and let us eat, and be merry: For this my son was dead, and is alive again; he was lost, and is found. And they began to be merry.
25 Now his elder son was in the field: and as he came and drew nigh to the house, he
26 heard music and dancing. And he called one of the servants, and asked what these
27 things meant. And he said unto him, Thy brother is come; and thy father hath killed
28 the fatted calf, because he hath received him safe and sound. And he was angry, and
29 would not go in: therefore [and] came his father out, and entreated him. And he answering said to *his*⁵ father, Lo, these many years do I serve [so many years have I served] thee, neither transgressed I [have I transgressed] at any time thy commandment; and yet thou never gavest me a kid, that I might make merry with my friends:
30 But as soon as this thy son was come, which hath devoured thy living with harlots,
31 thou hast killed for him the fatted calf. And he said unto him, Son, thou art ever
32 with me, and all that I have is thine. It [But it] was meet that we should make merry, and be glad: for this thy brother was dead, and is alive again; and was lost, and is found.

¹ Vs. 17.—With Griesbach, Scholz, and Meyer, [Lachmann, Bleek, Tregelles, Alford, Cod. Sin.,] we believe that we must receive ὧδε into the text, but place it before λιμῷ.
² Vs. 19.—*Rec.: καὶ οὐκέτι εἰμί, κ.τ.λ.*, without sufficient grounds; καί may be omitted, and then the broken character of the soliloquy forms a beauty the more.
³ Vs. 21.—*See* note 2.
⁴ Vs. 22.—Τὴν before στολήν should be expunged, *see* TISCHENDORF; this makes the first mention of στολήν quite indefinite, with τὴν πρώτην afterwards added as apposition; *see* WINER, *Grammatik*, § 204. Although ταχύ (D., ταχέως) has some authorities of weight for it, B., [Cod. Sin.,] L., X., &c., yet it is probable that this word was interpolated later, in order to heighten yet more the force of the father's word. [Lachmann, Meyer, Alford retain ταχύ; Tregelles brackets it. Found in B., D., Cod. Sin., L., X.—C. C. S.]
⁵ Vs. 29.—Αὐτοῦ ought, on the authority of A., B., D., P., and others, to be received in the text, as by Lachmann and Tischendorf, [Meyer, Tregelles, Alford.]

EXEGETICAL AND CRITICAL.

Vs. 11. **A certain man.**—The simple, unpretentious beginning of the most beautiful of all the parables, is even in and of itself a beauty. The man is here the image of God; the Son anthropomorphizes the Father in a very unique manner. The two sons denote not exactly the Jews and the Heathen, (Augustine, Bede, and the Tübingen school), nor yet angels and men (Herberger), but the mass of men, as divided at this moment before the Saviour, into Publicans and Pharisees. Strictly speaking, both the sons here sketched are lost,—the one through the unrighteousness that degrades him, the other through the self-righteousness which blinds him.

Vs. 12. **The younger.**—The most light-minded, and as such the most easily led astray. The goods which come to him only after the death of the father, he wishes to possess already in his father's lifetime, in order to be entirely free and his own master.—Τὸ ἐπιβάλλον μέρος, somewhat singular, but yet a genuinely Greek expression (see Grotius), to indicate what he of right can demand as his property out of his father's possessions.—**And he divided unto them,** αὐτοῖς.—Therefore not only to the younger, but also to the elder, with the distinction however that the younger now received in hand his own portion, while the elder could regard his as his property, although the father yet administered it, and he still remained as the child in his father's house.

Vs. 13. **Gathered together.**—It very soon appears what the youngest one really meant to do. The false craving for freedom, which the father does not suppress by violence, drives him to seek his fortune abroad. All that he has received he gathers together, partly, probably, *in natura* (De Wette), and journeys as far as possible away. The far-distant land, an image of the sinner's deep apostasy from God. The beauty of the parable is heightened still more by this fact, that with forbearing tenderness, the depth of his degradation is not depicted in many strokes, but afterwards, vs. 30, is for the first time learned somewhat more in detail from the mouth of the elder son. His mode of life is plainly enough characterized, as ἀσώτως, a word which is found only here, but which is sufficiently explained by the use of the substantive, Eph. v. 18; Titus i. 6; 1 Peter iv. 4. Then does the inward separation from the father become quite as great as the outward was. " *Qui se a Christo separat, exul est patriæ, civis est mundi.*" Ambrosius.

Vs. 14. **And when ... a mighty famine.**—The natural consequences of such a mode of life are only hastened by the famine that arises (ἰσχυρὰ λιμός, here feminine according to the Doric dialect and the latter usage; Luke iv. 25, it still appears as masculine, and the reading of the *Recepta*, ἰσχυρός, is only an emendation, according to the customary usage). The external want which he now begins to suffer, becomes a transition to the turning-point of his inner life. But he does not yet come to this turning-point without a last desperate endeavor to remedy his own distress from his own means.

Vs. 15. **Joined himself,** ἐκολλήθη, attached himself, as it were, to him by force, that he might assist him in his necessity. He has therefore remained a stranger in the land in which he has consumed all. "*Quem reditus ad frugem manet, is sæpe etiam in medio errore suo quiddam a propriis mundi civibus distinctum retinet.*" Bengel. But the tender mercies of the wicked are cruel. The citizen of the strange land sends him (ἔπεμψεν, change of the subject of discourse) to his fields, (ἀγρούς in the plural), in order there to keep swine, where he should by no means lack the necessary sustenance: perhaps an intentional insult which the rich heathen put upon the suffering, necessitous Jew, but certainly a striking image of the inconceivable wretchedness into which sin drags man down. And yet this very deep leads up to the height, and among the χοίροις it will soon fare better with the unhappy man than with the πόρναις.

Vs. 16. **Have filled his belly.**—An uncomely expression in itself, but entirely agreeable to the uncomeliness of the fact, and so far an additional beauty of the parable. Somewhat of (ἀπό) the swine's fodder is now his highest desire, without however his being able even to obtain a part of that.—**With the pods,** κεράτια, a wild fruit, found in Syria and Egypt, which was used for swine's fodder. Perhaps the sweetish fruit of the *Caratonia siliqua* (Linnæus), which, on account of the great abundance of them, was of the least possible value, and although they tasted sweet were not wholesome. "The hull of the marrowy pod, one foot in length (κεράτια), was thrown to the swine; but the kernel (Gerah, grain) passed for the smallest weight among the Hebrews."—**And no one gave unto him** (therefrom).—"Either because the feeding of the swine was committed to others than him that pastured them, or because he saw the access to the swine-trough closed to him; perhaps because the steward under whom he served was avaricious and malicious." De Wette. At all events, the only thing that could have reconciled him to his degrading employment, the satisfaction of his raging hunger, he saw still withheld from him in this way.

Vs. 17. **And when he came to himself.**—An admirable expression for the inward change in the heart of the man who had been hitherto beside himself, but now awakes from the dream. Εἰς ἑαυτὸν δὲ ἐλθών, Luther: *da schlug er in sich.* The sinner must first return unto himself, if he will be truly converted to God. He first compares his external condition with that of the more highly privileged. The μίσθιοι have bread, and indeed περισσεύουσιν ἄρτων. He, the son of the family, has not even κεράτια. By the μίσθιοι, we have to understand laborers that are engaged from day to day. Among the παῖδες, vs. 26, we have to understand the meanest of the permanent domestic servants, who stand without, without taking part in the feast; among the δοῦλοι, vs. 22, on the other hand, servants of higher rank, overseers of farms, vineyards, and the like, who personally took part in the joy of the feast. It appears therefore, that the Prodigal Son actually envies the good fortune of those who stood on the last step. Now, when the pride of his heart is broken, no false shame holds him longer back from considering his condition in its true light.

Vs. 18. **I will arise.**—Not precisely the *primordia pœnitentiæ* (Bengel), for these are already indicated in the εἰς ἑαυτὸν ἐλθών, but the transition from the inward to the now also outward change. In this especially is shown the sincerity of his repentance, that it is joined with the not yet extinguished trust in the love of his father, that he seeks not a single excuse, and without delay arises to carry out the resolution taken.—**Against heaven and before thee;** ἐνώπιον σοῦ, that is, "in relation to thee." Since however this relation is ordained by heaven (general indication of the dwelling-place of the higher spiritual world), he feels at the same time how this holy, heavenly world is injured by the fact, that he on earth has infringed in such a way upon the inalienable rights of his father. It is over a token of the sincerity of repentance, when one views even the sins committed against others, as transgressions against the Heavenly Father.—**Make me as one.**—He wishes not only *tractari tanquam mercenarius*, but to be accounted on a level with such in every respect; on ὡς an emphasis is to be laid. He wishes that there may be no distinction between him and the least of the day-laborers, and promises thereby that he will diligently serve, and be obedient as a day-laborer. That he however hopes in this way once more to *deserve* the name of a son, he does not say a word of, and it is therefore perhaps much too refined (Stier) to remark in this entreaty a trace of self-righteousness. He wishes simply to be released at any price from his wretched condition, and with deeds to prove the sincerity of his confession of sin.

Vs. 20. **But when . . . his father saw him.**—The father is represented as daily expecting the return of the strayed one, with longing desire; he is moved with compassion for the unfortunate one, at the view of the wretched garment, and the pitiable condition in which he sees him coming at a distance. The kiss which he impresses on his lips, comp. Gen. xxxiii. 4; Matt. xxvi. 48, is the token of the prevenient love which is shown even before the confession of sin, which the father reads in the heart of the returned son, has had time to pass over his lips. The conclusion of the previously meditated address: "Make me," &c., is in fact kept back "by the demeanor of fatherly love; the agitated son cannot bring these words out in view of such paternal love; a psychologically tender and delicate representation." Meyer.

Vs. 22. **But the father.**—Ταχέως may certainly be added in thought, even though it should not be inserted in the text.—*See* notes on the Greek text.—The father assures the son of his forgiveness, not by replying to his address, but by giving in his presence a definite command to the servants standing by. First, there must a garment, and that the best (*see* notes on the text), be brought out; the father cannot look on these hateful beggar's rags. Thus is he again brought into his former position of honor; for the *Tular* was the long and white upper garment of the principal Jews, *see* Mark xii. 38. The seal-ring and the shoes are to show that he was recognized as a free man (slaves went commonly barefoot). The (τό) fatted calf, which stands in the stall already prepared for slaughter, can be destined for no more joyful occasion than this. Without delay must all the members of the family assemble at the feast-table, and it is as if now the inventiveness of love exhausted itself to prove to the returned wanderer how welcome he is to the happy father's heart. The ground for all this is indicated in the assurance: **For this my son,** &c. Death and life is in the usage of the Scripture the designation of sin and conversion, *see* Eph. ii. 1; 1 Tim. v. 6, and other passages. The father means not only that the son has been dead *for him* (Paulus, De Wette), but that he in himself has risen in a moral respect from the condition of death to a new and higher life. What he has been and now is in the view of the father—once lost, now found,—is expressed in the second antithesis. The parallelism of the expression is therefore not to be taken tautologically.

Vs. 24. **And they began to be merry.**—Of course at the feast, although, in itself, εὐφραίνεσθαι is not to be taken in the sense of *epulari* (Kuinoel). The parable has here reached the point which is designated in the first parable in vs. 7, and in the second in vs. 10; for the joy in the father's house corresponds perfectly to that in heaven and before the angels of God. Not impossible is it, however, that it was especially this third intimation of the same chief thought, which awakened a visible displeasure among the Pharisaic hearers, and that the Saviour therefore felt impelled so much the more to set forth yet more in detail, in the person of the second son, an intimation already given, vs. 7, by portraying his unloving selfishness. Here also we owe to human opposition and malice one of the most beautiful pages of the Gospel.

Vs. 25. **His elder son.**—The less the Pharisees could recognize in the description of the younger son their own image, so much the more must their conscience hold up before them a mirror in the image of the eldest son. Even at the very beginning, the vividness and beauty of the representation is heightened by the fact, that the eldest son at the return of the youngest brother is not in the house, but has spent the day in hard, self-chosen, slavish service, and now first returns home at eventime, when the feast was already in progress.—**Music and dancing.**—Without the article. As to the customariness of this at the feasts of the ancients, comp. Matt. xiv. 6. Even this fact, that such a thing had taken place in the dwelling entirely without his knowledge, secretly angers him, and with an astonishment which betrays displeasure, he calls one of the servants to him.

Vs. 27. **Thy brother is come.**—Entirely without reason have some found (*Berl. Bibl.*) in the answer of the servant something secretly malicious. He gives to the returned son, after the example of his master, the rank befitting him; he does not relate in what condition the brother had come home, but only that he had returned in good health.—The slave speaks of ὑγιαίνειν undoubtedly in the physical sense, as the father had before spoken of death and life in the moral sense; and at the same time mentions the fatted calf, which he had perhaps slaughtered with his own hand, and which was for him, as a servant, very likely the chief matter. In so good-natured an answer there lies nothing at all, in and of itself, which could have given the elder brother just ground for bitterness. It is rather the state of the case itself that is sufficient (in his temper of mind) to fill him with anger. This last stroke of the pencil also proves satisfactorily the unreasonableness of the singular interpretation, that by the elder brother we are to understand unfallen angels.

Vs. 28. **His father ... entreated him,** παρεκάλει. Luther: Begged him. Kuinoel: Called him to him. Meyer: Summoned him to come in. Only the last is somewhat too strong, since then the refusal of the son would have been, in contradiction to his own declaration, vs. 29, a direct disobedience. We prefer explaining it in the sense that the father with soft words sought to move him to judge otherwise, and then also to act otherwise, comp. Acts xvi. 39. So much the more strikingly does the not-to-be wearied and long-suffering love of the father, who for his sake even leaves for a moment the feast of joy, contrast with the refractory and selfish disposition of the elder son.

Vs. 29. **These many years.**—He addresses the father, yet the youngest son's tender πάτερ does not pass his lips. On the other hand, he brings up to him his external obedience and service for reward, with as little modesty as possible. Reward for it he has, according to his own opinion, never yet received, and indeed has not yet enjoyed the only true reward in his heart. It is noticeable (*see* the notes on the text) that his highest wish appears to have concentrated itself in a kid, ἐρίφιον, (the he-goat, the image of lewdness) [There is not the slightest reason to suppose that any such reference is implied in ἐρίφιον.—C. C. S.], while he looks down with contempt upon the immoral conduct of his brother. Ὁ υἱός σου οὗτος. He visibly avoids giving him the brother's name, which, however, the father does, vs. 32, but he tears the veil which was spread over his sinful life. For him the paternal love also concentrates itself in **the fatted calf**, that had far higher value than the vainly wished for ἐρίφιον.

Vs. 31. **Son, thou art.**—Although self-righteousness has already condemned itself by its own words, it is now even to redundance rebuked by the mild answer of the father. With an affectionate τέκνον, he seeks once again to bring him to a kinder disposition, and show him that his uninterrupted dwelling with his father and his prospect of the whole paternal inheritance, vs. 12, should have raised him above so unloving a judgment. An entirely different disposition was now the natural one, and required by the course of events. *To make merry and be glad* was what one must now do, instead of bringing bitter imputations. The father does not say definitely that the eldest son also should now do this. The σέ is now omitted; but he speaks in general of the ethical necessity that it now must be just thus, and not otherwise. In no event, therefore, will the feast of joy be for his sake interrupted, but he himself must judge whether he, after the explanation received, will yet longer stand without in displeasure. ¶ The father has the last word, and it is as if the Saviour asked therewith His Pharisaical listeners: Decide yourselves how the parable shall end; will you still refuse to take part in the joy of heaven over the conversion of sinners?¶

In relation to the parable *as a whole*, we must remark, in addition, that it belongs perfectly in the Pauline Gospel of Luke. "The Pauline representation of the incapacity of the νόμος to confer the true δικαιοσύνη, and of the necessity of another way of salvation through the πίστις and χάρις, constitutes the best commentary on these parables." Olshausen. But in a pitiable way has the Paulinistic and liberal character of this teaching of the Saviour been misused by the Tübingen school, to the support of their understanding of original Christianity, and of the peculiarity of the third Gospel. Ritzschl (formerly), Zeller, Schwegler, nor least, Von Baur, have, with different modifications, insisted on finding here a symbolical representation of the distinct relation in which Jews and Gentiles stood to the Messianic kingdom. ¶ The Prodigal Son then represents heathenism in its degeneracy, return, and restoration; the eldest son, on the other hand, represents the proud and hostile disposition of the Jewish Christians against these later-called and highly privileged. "Who does not here see the behavior of the Jewish Christians towards the Gentile Christians and the Pauline Christianity which we know from the Epistle to the Romans?" It is impossible to read this whole construction of the oldest church history without doing justice to the extraordinary talent and the brilliant gift of combination of which it is the undeniable fruit. But even the noblest building must fall in ruin when it lacks the firm foundation. The latter is here the case, and it has, therefore, been justly remarked that Hilgenfeld and others confound the *applicability* of the parable to their darling theme, with its original *occasion* and intention. That a noticeable agreement exists between the Jewish Christians and the eldest son, between the Gentile Christians and the youngest, is plain, and should be willingly conceded; but that the Saviour's design was to direct attention to this is in direct conflict with vss. 1, 2, 7, 10. With the same right we might be able to find the antitype of the two sons, in the Catholic and in the Evangelical Church in their mutual relations. As to the rest, we already find a trace of the Tübingen idea in Vitringa and others.

DOCTRINAL AND ETHICAL.

1. There is no parable of the Saviour whose beauty and high value has been so generally and openly acknowledged as that of the Prodigal Son. Nothing would be easier than to collect a Chrestomathy of enthusiastic eulogies on this parable, even from rationalists and unbelievers. "In the style of Lavater, whoever loves this style might speak long and much; might exclaim and wonder: How simple and how deep, how unforgettably retainable in its words, unfathomable and inexhaustible in its sense; related with what dramatic life, this parable of the Saviour, the crown and pearl of all His parables, is!" Stier. But mindful that the Divine, least of anything, needs our human praise, we will rather direct the eye to that which is here portrayed, and to the somewhat more particular consideration of the great antithesis of Sin and Grace, which appears in this so popular and yet so profound instruction.

2. Sin appears here before us not only in one but in a twofold form, as it develops itself not only in the widely wandering but also in the self-righteous man, who remains outwardly within the limits of obedience required by God. Against every theory which explains sin from the metaphysical imperfection of human nature, or interprets the fall as a kind of moral *progress* (Schiller), this parable utters the sentence of condemnation.

3. The essence of sin presents itself to us in the younger son as Self-seeking. This awakens in him discontent with the good that he enjoys in the house of his father, impels him to seek independent freedom, sensual enjoyment and honor, and makes him a wretched slave of his unfettered passions. From the root of self-seeking grow two different branches, the sins of *sensuality* on the one hand and those of *pride* on the other. The former we see coming to mournful development principally in the younger, the latter in the elder, son. Sensuality degrades man, blinds him and leads him finally to the brink of the abyss, but God is far from abridging the sinner's use of his freedom; He permits him, on the other hand, to walk his own ways, and makes even the bitter fruits of evil serviceable to his healing and recovery. Through false craving for freedom the Prodigal Son falls into unhappy wandering; through wandering into wretched slavery; through slavery into an unspeakable depth of misery.

4. Quite otherwise does moral corruption reveal itself in the elder son. Outwardly he remains in the house of his father and serves him, yet he is guided only by a mechanical obedience, to which the impelling power of love is wanting. He seeks his reward not in his father's recognition, but in the kid for which he longs and for which he vainly hopes. He vaunts in his vain pride of his fancied fulfilment of duty, although to this there was lacking the heart, and with this everything, and betrays his inner character by his anger at the gracious reception of his deeply-fallen brother. He believes himself, in his blindness, never to have transgressed a commandment, and yet forgets precisely that which is weightiest in the law, mercy and love. Neither his father nor his brother does he love, and yet believes that he may demand all for himself. How self-righteousness stands related to God and mankind is here drawn from life. On the other side, the Saviour shows also how God demeans Himself towards such fools and blind. He endures them in His long-suffering; He addresses them kindly; He excludes them not at once from the enjoyment of His fatherly favor, but yet lets them feel that they are on the way to exclude themselves therefrom, and that if they persist in their error, the joy of heaven over the conversion of the lost sinner can, on their account, be by no means disturbed or postponed.

5. The nature of the conversion of which no one repents, is in the image of the younger son sketched for all following ages. Its beginning is to be found where the sinner comes to himself, and becomes acquainted, not only with his deep wretchedness, but, above all, with his inexcusable guilt. The consciousness of guilt is, according to this parable, by no means a subjective illusion of the sinner, but the expression of an everlasting truth of the voice of God which is heard in the conscience, and which the father in no wise contradicts, which he, on the other hand, answers with the overwhelming revelation of his forgiving love. The knowledge of the nature of sin—that it is not a weakness but an infinite debt—brings about an inward sorrow, 2 Cor. vii. 10; this sorrow impels to the confession of sin; this confession is joined with longing after immediate return. It is precisely in this that the nature of true repentance is here revealed; that it joins the deepest humility with not yet extinguished faith in the love of the Father; that the good resolution, how much soever it may cost, is *without delay* put into execution, and that the son will rather, if it is possible, take the last place in the house of his Father than even for a moment longer look around for a better lot outside of the Father's house. With undoubted justice, it is true, the remark could be made that in this parable it is especially "human activity in the work of conversion that is portrayed." (Olshausen.) However, it is also true, on the other side, that "the Divine activity also is not lacking in this parable." Lange.

6. The grace of God for the Prodigal Son comes in this parable in its *compassionate* and *all-restoring* side before our eyes. The father does not this time seek for the lost son as the shepherd had sought for the sheep and the woman for the coin. For neither is it here an irrational being but a rational man, who must be brought *himself* to choose the way of conversion. Mediately the father has labored for his delivery, for while he has permitted him to bear all the consequences of the evil committed, he has, moreover, patiently waited and kept his house and heart open to him. Scarcely does the son take the first step homeward, when the father regards him with compassionate look, goes kindly towards him (prevenient grace), and refuses not, it is true, the confession of sin, but remits to him whatever it has of pain and humiliation. He not only testifies his joy over the

returned wanderer, but he gives it active expression, and not only pardons the wanderer, but restores him again to the full possession and enjoyment of his forfeited filial rights. It is not, however, necessary to see in *every* feature of the parable, on this point, the intimation of a definite saving truth of the Gospel. Whoever (Olshausen) finds signified in the ring the seal of the Holy Spirit; in the sandals, the being shod as in Ephes. vi. 15; in the Talar, the garment of the perfect righteousness of Christ, easily loses out of mind the distinction between parable and allegory—a point of view where nothing could reasonably withhold us from going a step farther, and, with Jerome, Augustine, and Melanchthon, seeing in the fatted calf the image of Christ. For other examples of arbitrary interpretation, *see* Lisco, *ad loc.* Here also we are carefully to distinguish between the practical applicability and the historical intention of the parable.

7. It is well known what consequences have been drawn from the fact that in this parable the Prodigal Son is received by the father without the intervention of any mediator. "All dogmatical imaginations of the supralapsarians and infralapsarians, nay, even of the demanders of bloody satisfaction, who have no sense of the heaven-wide distinction between Divine and human righteousness, vanish like oppressive nightmares before this single parable, in which Jesus reveals the heavenly secret of human redemption, not according to a mystical or criminal theory of punishment, but anthropologically, psychologically, and theologically to every pure eye that looks into the law of perfect liberty." Von Ammon, *L. J.,* iii. p. 50. But, with the same right, one from this parable might have been able to deduce a proof against the biblical Satanology, since, forsooth, the young man is allured and misled by sin alone; or against the doctrine of sanctification, since the parable adds nothing concerning the new life of the grateful son in his father's house. *Quod nimium, nihil probat.* Silence is not necessarily contradiction, and it is entirely natural that the Saviour, months before His atoning death, before an audience of Pharisees and publicans, should have left this wholly a mystery. It is well known how little He, especially according to the Synoptical Gospels, spoke of the highest goal of His suffering and death even to His familiar disciples; it belonged to the things which He described, John xvi. 12, concerning which the Paraclete should afterwards instruct His church. Whoever uses this parable as a weapon against the Pauline doctrine of atonement, acts as foolishly as he who, pointing to the friendly morning light, would prove thereby the uselessness of the full mid-day sun. The demand that the Saviour must in a single parable have described the whole way of salvation, is excessively arbitrary; nor does the Gospel teach anywhere that the Father had to be, by the death of His Son, first *moved* to be gracious to sinners. "One parable cannot exhaust the whole truth; but in the parable of the Prodigal Son we may say that the Saviour and Mediator is concealed in the kiss which the father gives the son." Riggenbach.

If we now, in conclusion, direct once again our view to this triad of parables, we find a rich variety, and yet an admirable agreement. The first parable depicts to us the sinner in his pitiable folly: the sheep exchanges voluntarily the green meadow for the barren waste. The second portrays to us the sinner in his wretched self-degradation: the coin falls down upon the earth, and lies, although the stamp is not erased, yet buried under the dust, from which it comes, only after much seeking and sweeping, again to the light of day. The third teaches us to know the sinner especially in his unthankfulness: the free love of the father is requited by the Prodigal Son with the squandering of his inheritance;—the sheep in the wilderness, the coin in the dust, the son at the swine-trough, all show us the image of the sinner's deep wretchedness. But since that which is lost is a man only in the third parable, it is implied in the nature of the case that only here can a wandering soul's conversion be placed before us in different gradations and transitions. The Divine love of sinners, on the other hand, is vividly portrayed to us in all three parables, although each time under a somewhat different character. In all it is God, the Father of our Lord Jesus Christ (who, even in the Old Testament, is compared with a Shepherd and a Woman, Ezekiel xxxiv. 28; Ps. xxiii.; Isaiah xl. 11), from whom the revelation of this love proceeds. But the shepherd is yet especially the image of seeking love, the woman that of restlessly laboring and careful love, while in the father this love comes before us as a prevenient, compassionate, and all-restoring love. In the representation of the value of what is lost there is an unmistakable climax: first, one of a hundred, then one of ten, finally one of two: first a beast, then a coin, finally a man. [But the coin, according to the author's own showing, is worth much less than a sheep. In the relative proportion of each to the wealth of the possessor, however, there is undoubtedly a climax.—C. C. S.] Even so there is found a beautiful harmony in the representation of the persons who rejoice with the finder: the neighbors who rejoice with the shepherd, the female friends who rejoice with the woman, the servants of the house who rejoice with the father, are necessary figures of the picture, and all represent the angels who take part in the joy of God in the conversion of even one that is lost. In the first and second parable all that the Divine love adventures and effects in order to find the lost is represented as on its own plane entirely natural. But on the other hand again the benignity, the beneficence, the sublimity of the Divine love to sinners strike the eye most strongly in the third, as it is here a man, whom love can adorn with robe and ring and sandals: features which in the two other parables could find no place. While, finally, coin and sheep are only passive towards the grace that seeks and recovers them, in the image of the Prodigal Son, on the other hand, the spontaneity of the sinner in his return to God comes into the foreground; yet so that it is by no means in a Pelagian sense the fruit of an isolated act of will, but in the sense that this resolution to return is occasioned by the course of circumstances into which he has come entirely against his own will under higher guidance, and in which he feels the bitterness of sin. The conclusion of the third parable not only adds to this a component part of admirable value over and above the first and second, but by it at the same time the whole triad of parables is applied to the shaming and rebuking of the Pharisaical hearers.

HOMILETICAL AND PRACTICAL.

The parable of the Prodigal Son as it represents to us the history: 1. Of each man; 2. of all mankind.—The parable of the two lost sons, or the two main forms of the essence of sin.

The younger son: 1. The descending way of destruction: *a.* pride, *b.* wandering, *c.* servile bondage, *d.* wretchedness. 2. the ascending way of redemption: *a.* humility, *b.* return, *c.* freedom, *d.* life. —The younger son: 1. In his father's house; 2. in a far country; 3. among the swine; 4. on the homeward way; 5. at the feast.—Self-seeking as it reveals itself: 1. In false craving for freedom; 2. in shameless covetousness; 3. in unbounded craving for enjoyment.—The Prodigal Son first inwardly, soon outwardly also, separated from his father.—Selfishness desires only God's gifts, true love God Himself. —The enjoyment of sin is short, remorse for it long. —The associates of sinful joy remain no longer than the soon-squandered goods.—Often external calamities have the work of hastening the revelation of the inward wretchedness of sin.—The child of the house constrained: 1. To attach himself to one of the citizens of the far country; 2. to keep the swine; 3. to crave their fodder; 4. to find that he cannot even get this.—To "come to himself": 1. The end of the old sinful, 2. the beginning of the new penitent, life.—The awakening: 1. Of the conscience; 2. of the understanding; 3. of the sensibility; 4. of the will.—How infinitely better it fares with the meanest day-laborer of the Father than with the sinner at the swine-trough, and even at the riotous banquet.—He "began to be in want," the last word of the wretched history of every sinner. He suffers lack: 1. Of that which he once enjoyed; 2. of that which the world enjoys; 3. of that which the meanest hirelings of his Father enjoy.—The decisive resolve: "I will arise": 1. How much it says; 2. how hard it is to carry out; 3. how richly it rewards.—The consciousness of guilt no fancy, but the expression of a terrible truth; happy he who has learned at the right time to impute to himself his sins as so many debts to God.—Even sin against others is still as ever sin against God.—The confession of sin before God a necessity of the repentant child.—The first step on the way to conversion.—Even when we are yet far from Him the Father sees us.—God's love to sinners: 1. A compassionate; 2. a prevenient; 3. a forgiving; 4. an all-restoring, love.—God Himself longs not less for the wandering sinner than the sinner for Him, and tears down all the walls of division.—Many a humiliation which the sinner deserves, and which the penitent will impose upon himself, is remitted to him by God's love.—The Prodigal Son reinstated: 1. In the former possession; 2. in the old rank; 3. in the lost happiness.—The best in the father's house is for the lost son not too good.—The children of God and members of His family must rejoice with the Father over the return of the sinner.—The service of sin, death; conversion, a birth unto life.—The joy in the Father's house over the returned son is perfect, even though the self-righteous take no part therein.

The elder son: 1. How much better he appears than the younger: *a.* the younger forsook the father, he remains; *b.* the younger squandered the father's goods, he administered and increased them; *c.* the younger sought the company of harlots, he contents himself with his friends even without a kid; *d.* the younger comes even now from the swine, he from the field. 2. How wretchedly lost he is: *a.* he serves the father with a selfish, not with a childlike, mind; *b.* he has enjoyed the father's love, and complains of having received no reward; *c.* he asserts himself never to have transgressed a commandment, and has never yet fulfilled one; *d.* he vaunts himself of his virtue, and in the same moment his transgression has increased. 3. How immeasurably wretched he becomes: he is on the way to lose, *a.* the love of his father; *b.* the heart of his brother, *c.* the joy in the parental dwelling, *d.* nay even the repute of his seeming virtue.—Did he also forsake his father's house, and how have we then to represent to ourselves the end of his history? Michaelis thinks that we might continue the image so: he forsook his father with indignation, went into a strange land, became there much more unhappy, more despised, more vicious than ever his brother had been; he was held as a slave, and finally captured in company with bands of robbers. [If the Saviour meant us to understand all this, we have a right to believe that He would have expressed it. It is quite as fair to suppose that the son might have been brought to a better mind by this tender admonition. But what He leaves ambiguous here, He probably meant to remain uncertain.—C. C. S.]—How the self-righteous man stands related to God, and how God stands related to the self-righteous man.—"My child, what is mine is thine, and what is thine is mine."—There exists a moral necessity of rejoicing over the conversion of the sinner, which the proud Pharisee despises.—Whom, therefore, does the image of the elder son represent, and which is better, to be like him or like the youngest?

STARKE:—Dissimilar brothers.—QUESNEL:—How dangerous when one will live for himself on his own account, to be subject to no one and rule himself.— If the soul has departed from God, it departs more and more from Him.—*Nova Bibl. Tub.*:—Many a young man goes adventurously into strange lands to make his fortune, but let him look well to it that he does not come to harm.—Let one learn to manage frugally; times change; how good is it then to have a penny in need!—Voluptuous swine belong among the swine.—How holy are God's judgments!—Whoever will not be called God's child may become a swine-herd and slave of the world.

HEDINGER:—Distress furthers self-knowledge, misfortune sharpens the wits. Jeremiah ii. 19.—BRENTIUS:—God disciplines through love and sorrow. If love cannot help, distress and all manner of plagues must come.—To true repentance belongs especially a spirit in which there is no falsehood; tempt God not. —A penitent man holds himself unworthy of the grace of the Heavenly Father.—*Bibl. Wirt.*:—The door of grace stands ever open, and God is much more disposed to forgive us our sins than we to pray for grace.—CRAMER:—God's grace is great, but not so great that a sinner can be partaker of the same without repentance.—CANSTEIN:—Joy in the Lord should be common to all true Christians when they hear of true conversions.—Whoever repents becomes living again and dies never, but lives unto eternity. —Anger makes enmity and finally separation.— *Nova Bibl. Tub.*:—Hypocrites are ever imagining that wrong is done them.—To those that are penitent one must not be bringing up their former sins or troubling them anew.—QUESNEL:—Let us have a brother's heart towards our brother, as God has a Father's heart towards His children.

HEUBNER:—The original relation of man to God is that of a son to the father.—God lets men try to live without God, that it may be for them a memorial to eternity.—"*Omnis locus, quem patre incolimus absente, famis, penuriæ et egestatis est.*"—Out of God everything is husks, though it is tendered thee in gold and silver vessels, and even though it were poundcake.—The sinner finds from the world and its lords no compassion.—No repentance is nobler, even though bitterer, than repentance for having contemned love.—The son, from shame and fear, went timidly; the father ran.—The conversion of the sinner a *high* feast of joy.—Pride of virtue is hard towards the fallen.—Even in long service for the kingdom of God there may creep in a lukewarm, reward-craving temper.—God's grace is never exhausted or diminished.

We may compare the explanations and the homiletical expositions of the parable by EWALD, ARNDT, EYLERT, LISCO, as also an excellent Dutch one by M. COHEN STUART, Utrecht, 1859.—MASSILLON, an excellent sermon upon Unchastity in his Lent sermons.—PALMER:—The parable contains, *a*. the history of us all, *b*. an admonition for us all, *c*. a consolation for us all.—The miracle of grace wrought on the sinner.—BECK:—The sinner's way to life.—MAIER:—That light hearts must become heavy, heavy light.—AHLFELD:—The Prodigal Son: Seven Sermons for the season between Easter and Whitsuntide, 1849, Halle, 1850.—HEUBNER:—Three Sermons upon the parable of the Prodigal Son, Halle, 1840.—COUARD:—Sermons.—CARL ZIMMERMANN:—Four Special Sermons.—VAN OOSTERZEE:—(upon the three parables together) The worth of a single soul: 1. The harm that is wrought on a single soul; 2. the compassion that is felt on account of a single soul; 3. the care that is expended on a single soul; 4. the grace that is glorified in one soul; 5. the joy that is experienced on account of one soul.—From this follows: 1. That carelessness of our soul is the most terrible transgression; 2. care for the good of others' souls the highest duty; 3. glorifying of the Shepherd and Bishop of our souls the most fitting thank-offering.—*N. B.* vs. 18 an excellent text preparatory for the communion, or for New Year's Eve.

---

4. The Parable of the Unjust Steward and its Application (CH. XVI. 1–13).

1 And he said also unto his [the[1]] disciples, There was a certain rich man, which had
2 a steward; and the same was accused unto him that he had [of having] wasted his
3 goods. And he called him, and said unto him, How is it that I hear this of thee? give
   an account of thy stewardship; for thou mayest be no longer steward. Then the steward said within himself, What shall I do? for my lord taketh away from me the stew-
4 ardship: I cannot dig; to beg I am ashamed. I am resolved what to do, that, when I
5 am put out of the stewardship, they may receive me into their houses. So he called
   every one of his lord's debtors *unto him*, and said unto the first, How much owest thou
6 unto my lord? And he said, A hundred measures of oil. And he said unto him,
7 Take thy bill, and sit down quickly, and write fifty. Then said he to another, And
   how much owest thou? And he said, A hundred measures of wheat. And[2] he said
8 unto him, Take thy bill, and write fourscore. And the [his[3]] lord commended the unjust steward, because he had done wisely: for the children of this world are in [in ref-
9 erence to, εἰς] their generation wiser than the children of light. And I say unto you,
   Make to yourselves friends of the mammon of unrighteousness; that, when ye fail [it fails, V. O.[4]], they may receive you into [the] everlasting habitations [lit., tabernacles, σκηνάς].
10 He that is faithful in that which is least is faithful also in much: and he that is un-
11 just in the least is unjust also in much. If therefore ye have not been faithful in the
12 unrighteous mammon, who will commit to your trust the true *riches*? And if ye have
    not been faithful in that which is another man's, who shall give you that which is your
13 own? No servant can serve two masters: for either he will hate the one, and love the
    other; or else he will hold to the [om., the] one, and despise the other. Ye cannot serve God and mammon.

[1] Vs. 1.—On the authority of B., D., [Cod. Sin.,] L., αὐτοῦ should be expunged.
[2] Vs. 7.—The καί of the *Recepta* should be omitted, as by Tischendorf.
[[3] Vs. 8.—The article before κύριος having its continually recurring possessive sense.—C. C. S.]
[4] Vs. 9.—*See Exegetical* and *Critical* remarks.

EXEGETICAL AND CRITICAL.

Vs. 1. **And He said also.**—The opinion that the Saviour uttered this parable on another occasion, and not in connection with the three former parables, is without any ground.—On the other hand, the well-known *crux interpretum*, the parable of the Unjust Steward, has the right light thrown upon it only when we assume that it was uttered before the same mixed audience of publicans and Pharisees, for whom also the parables of the Lost Sheep, of the Lost Coin, and of the Prodigal Son, were intended. A tolerably full catalogue of the latest theological literature upon Luke xvi. 1–9, is found in MEYER, *ad loc.*, to which we add the *Interprétation de la parabole de l'économe infidèle*, par M. ENSFELDER, in the *Revue Théol. de Colani*, 1852, iii. and STÖLBE, *Versuch*

CHAP. XVI. 1-13.

einer *Erklärung der Parabel vom ungerechten Haushalter*, Stud. und Krit. 1858, iii., and among the Dutch exegetes, an important dissertation by the late Dr. B. VAN WILLES, 1842.—Here, also, in particular, we prefer to give, instead of a criticism of the various and exceedingly divergent views, a simple statement of our own opinion.

To the disciples.—Not to be understood of the apostolic circle, although this is by no means to be excluded, but of the followers and hearers of the Saviour, in a wider sense of the word. *See* chap. xiv. 26, 27, 33 ; John vi. 66, and other passages, and comp. also Luke xvii. 1 with xvii. 5. We have, therefore, to conceive the Saviour as surrounded by publicans, whom He had just been comforting, and by Pharisees, whom He had just put to shame. The former He wishes to remind of their high duty now, as His disciples, to make good as much as possible the guilt which they had formerly incurred by extortion and dishonesty; the others He wishes to bring back from their love to earthly good, by drawing their attention to the truth that they are only stewards, for whom a day of reckoning will come. Both, therefore, He desires to lead to that prudent foresight, the image of which He depicts in the narrative of the Unjust Steward.

A certain rich man.—Neither the Romans (Schleiermacher), nor the Roman Emperor (Grossmann), and as little the devil (Olshausen), and, on the other hand, not Mammon (Meyer)—the μαμμωνᾶς τῆς ἀδικ. is, on the other hand, equivalent to the ὑπάρχοντα of the rich man, vs. 1—but God, who here is represented as the paramount owner of all which has been given to man only as a fief, and for use. By the οἰκονόμος we have to understand not exclusively the μαθηταί of the Saviour, but every man to whom the paramount owner has entrusted part of His goods.

A steward.—The wealth of the lord in the parable is visible from the circumstance that he needs an οἰκονόμος.—The property which this steward managed consists, however, not in ready money, but in allotments of land, which he has farmed out for such a price as he has thought fit, without every particular in the farm-contracts having been necessarily known to his lord. For we have here to represent to ourselves no modern steward, who every time gives a complete account, and has to decide nothing by his own full powers: on the other hand, it appears that his lord, who bestowed on him his full confidence, had not previously required any reckoning of him at all, until he, persuaded of the man's dishonesty, had resolved to displace him. If the οἰκονόμος was clothed with so extensive powers, it is then also unnecessary to assume that he falsified the farm-contracts; in earlier times it was probably not at all necessary to lay these before the lord of the manor. But how had he squandered the ὑπάρχοντα? He had made the farmers pay more than he had stated and paid in to his lord as the rent: he demanded of them an excessive, and paid to him only the fair amount, so that the difference between what he received and what he rendered constituted a clear gain to himself. He had, however, not enriched himself; for, with his deposition from his post, he sees himself brought at once to the beggar's staff—he had lived sumptuously and wantonly on that which he had from time to time gained in this way, until his lord, we know not how, came on the track of his villainous transactions. His lord now summons him to the rendering of the definite account, to which he, as well known to him, is obliged (τὸν λόγον), and speaks at once of displacement. In the giving of this account, therefore, the papers, the farm-contracts, must for the first time be produced, and the displacement must naturally follow if the comparison of the rent with the sum accounted for reveals the cheat ; it will, on the other hand, not be necessary, if from a thoroughly consistent account it appears that the suspicion conceived has been an ungrounded one. This must be kept distinctly in mind : the displacement is not yet irrevocably uttered, but only threatened ; it does not precede the account, however this may turn out, but will only follow if the steward cannot justify himself. This appears, first, from the nature of the case, since his lord, by such a condemnation, without hearing him, and on a loose report, would have dealt quite as unjustly as the steward, which undoubtedly Jesus did not mean to represent ; and, secondly, from the expression of the steward himself, who sought a secure maintenance only in case (ὅταν) he should lose his post, and who, it is true, foresees a displacement as being as good as certain, but yet ventures one more attempt to smooth over his accounts a little.

Vs. 3. **What shall I do?**—Striking is the monologue in which the Saviour depicts to us the perplexity of the steward, especially striking, if we conceive these words as spoken in broken sentences —"What shall I do? for my lord takes away my stewardship from me:—I cannot dig ; to beg I am ashamed.—Εὕρηκα—I know—I have discovered (ἔγνων) what I will do." And what now does one expect of a man who is proposed for imitation with very particular reference to his prudence ? he will seek a means either, if possible, to avert even yet the dreaded blow and to keep his place, or, in case he should not succeed in this, to provide for himself a comfortable old age.

Vs. 4. **They may receive me into their houses.**—Not precisely into their families (Schultz), but yet οἶκος, regarded as the seat of the family-life into which he, out of thankfulness, hoped to be received. The whole monologue shows us the steward as a man of mature reflection. "For explanation these reflections are not intended, but for portrayal of the crisis."

Vs. 5. **So he called.**—Not (Brauns, a. o.) in the presence, but, of course, in the absence, of his exasperated lord; for the steward must certainly, if he were to give the required account, have time for it, and his lord has, therefore, gone away again. Neither can the speaking ἑαυτῷ, vs. 3, be easily explained otherwise than as taking place in solitude, and the phrase, vs. 5, καθίσας ταχέως γράψον, is plainly the language of a man who wishes to dispose of something quickly before his lord observes it. The opinion also that the steward makes up the fifty measures of oil and the twenty measures of wheat from his own means, is incompatible with his own assertion, vs. 3, that he must beg if he did not find a remedy. If the Saviour had here intended to depict a repentant Zacchæus, who with his dishonestly acquired treasures will even yet do some good (D. Schultz), he would without doubt have put in some way into the steward's mouth an acknowledgment of his guilt.

How much owest thou?—We must conceive the matter thus : that he has all the farmers come at the same time to him, but that he talks with every one of them apart. His dealing with two of them is communicated, as an example, from which one can easily conclude how he dealt with the others also. He does not, as is commonly believed, have the farmers write a new bond with a smaller amount; this would have cost too long a detention, but simply set a smaller number instead of the former, either by the altering of a single letter in the old agreement, which the Hebrew numerals easily admit, or by the mere filling up of a new agreement already prepared. The numbers fifty and eighty, which he causes to be set down instead of the previous hundred, express the just amount which he had already given account of to his lord, and he gains by this alteration the advantage that the leases agree with the sums previously stated to his lord, who had never yet had a sight of the authentic papers. But the farmers, who, as they suppose, had been required to pay an exorbitant sum to the lord, can by this moderating of the price only feel themselves personally obliged to the steward, from whose hands this deduction is made to them, and who has perhaps represented this unexpected favor as a consequence of his intercession and of his influence with the lord of the manor.—**One hundred baths.**—The Hebrew בַּת is equivalent to the old μετρητής, the tenth part of a Homer; therefore for liquids, the same as the Ephah for dry substances.—**A hundred Kor**, the Hebrew כֹּר, according to Josephus, *A. I.* 15. 9, 2 = 10 μέδιμνοι, about = 4⅔ of the Berlin bushel [11½ English bush.]. See WINER, *ad loc.*

Vs. 7. **Write fourscore.**—By the just-mentioned measure the steward has actually done all which in so critical a case could have been expected from a prudent man: for in the first place he makes good his former dishonesty, although only out of selfishness; in the second place, he makes it possible to give a correct account, so far as the leases are laid before the lord and compared with his ledger, and finally, in case the dreaded dismissal follows, nevertheless, he, by his kindness shown to the farmers, purchases for himself a comfortable maintenance for his old age. That he, after he had protected himself in this way, really remained in his office (Baumgarten-Crusius), the Saviour, it is true, does not say, but He is as far from saying also that he was actually removed (common view). This point, on the other hand, remains entirely conjectural, since it does not lie in the purpose of the Saviour to bring the narrative in and of itself to an end, but only to commend a very judicious course of reflection and mode of dealing, in a critical moment, for imitation in a certain respect.

Vs. 8. **And the lord commended the unjust steward.**—It is, of course, understood that this lord was not the Lord Jesus (Erasmus), but the rich lord in the parable, who had soon learned in what way the οἰκονόμος had helped himself out of the trouble. We have here to place ourselves entirely on the stand-point of worldly wisdom, and conceive the matter thus: that his lord does not commend the motive or the act of the steward in itself, but commends the cleverness of his way of dealing, with which he had, while there was yet time, diverted from himself the threatening storm.—**The unjust steward.**—That this designation does not need absolutely to be brought into connection with his last-mentioned conduct, but may be referred as well to his earlier and now abandoned dishonesty, appears from similar usage. Matt. xxvi. 6; comp. Luke vii. 37.

For the children of this world.—There is as little room to doubt that the Saviour designs to have represented the οἰκονόμος as a child of the world, as that He means him for imitation merely and solely in respect of his prudence. The grounds of the here-mentioned phenomenon are plain enough to be seen, "because the means which prudence manages are worldly, and are, therefore, foreign to the aims of the children of light, and because prudence belongs to the understanding and the experience of the world, while the children of light live in the Spirit." De Wette.—Εἰς τὴν γεν. ἑαυτ.—that is, when they come into contact with such as, like themselves, are children of the present world. The children of the world are, therefore, happily designated as γενεά, a family of similar characters. In their *mutual* intercourse these are wont to go to work with as well-considered plans as the Unjust Steward, and in this respect commonly far surpass the children of light when these have intercourse with one another or with others. Children of light the disciples of the Saviour are named, being those that are enlightened with the light of truth, and are accustomed to walk therein. *See* John xii. 35; 1 Thess. v. 5; Eph. v. 8. As to the rest, the expression γενεὰ ἑαυτῶν is not to be referred to bothnamed classes of men (each in its own sphere), but exclusively to the υἱοὶ τοῦ αἰῶνος τούτου, in contrast with whom the Saviour, vs. 9, addresses His disciples.

Vs. 9. **And I say unto you.**—It is well known into what perplexity this precept has brought early and later expositors,—a perplexity which went so far that some have ventured the bold critical conjecture of causing the Saviour, by the insertion of a single little word, οὐ, to say exactly the opposite. What, however, He means by the phrase: **Make to yourselves friends**, is, if we only recollect the conduct of the steward, intelligible enough. The steward had made the farmers subordinated to him, his friends; even so, the Saviour means, should one make those who need help his friends, by bestowing on them benefits with and out of the same money which is so often acquired in an unrighteous manner and applied to shameful purposes. It is entirely arbitrary and against the spirit of the parable to understand here (Ambrosius, Ewald, Meyer) *angels*, who receive the pious man into heaven. The Saviour, on the other hand, represents the matter thus: that those to whom benefits have been shown, precede their benefactors to heaven, welcome them there, and thus exalt their joy. That the form of this promise is borrowed from the expression of the steward, vs. 4, is, of course, obvious. By the **everlasting tabernacles**, we may understand either heaven, or also (Meyer), according to the analogy, 4 Esdras ii. 11, the future Messianic kingdom, in which, however, we meet with the difficulty that then all the φίλοι whom one has gained with the mammon of unrighteousness are represented *eo ipso* as citizens of the Messianic kingdom. [Doubtless our Lord does not mean that any but such friends as do belong to His kingdom are to receive us into the eternal abodes.—C. C. S.] It is safest to understand, in general, a blessed locality where one can abide, in opposition to an earthly locality which one soon leaves.

Of the mammon of unrighteousness, ἐκ τοῦ μαμμ. τῆς ἀδικ.—Ἐκ, the means by which one procures himself friends. Comp. Acts i. 18. The application of the Mammon must have the consequence indicated by Jesus. Respecting the Mammon, *see* LANGE on Matt. vi. 24.—Μαμ. τῆς ἀδικ.—Not because it is commonly acquired in an unlawful manner (Euthym. Zigab.), or because it is itself perishable and delusive (Kuinoel, Wieseler), or because the disciples of the Saviour were in an unrighteous degree very parsimonious therewith (Paulus); but in the same sense in which before an οἶκον. τῆς ἀδικίας, vs. 8, was spoken of. The ἀδικία is the inherent character of the Mammon, which is here represented as a personal being, and called unrighteous because money, as with the Steward, commonly becomes the occasion and the means of an unrighteous course of conduct; "the ethical character of its use is represented as cleaving to itself." Meyer.

When it fails.—Ὅταν ἐκλείπη, so we believe that we must read with Tischendorf, on the authority of Α., Β., Χ. The *Recepta* ἐκλίπητε has probably arisen from the fact that by the mention of the Everlasting Tabernacles it seemed almost a matter of course to take the verb in the plural and to understand it of departure from this earthly place of abode. Therefore, also, the translation: *cum defeceritis*, with the accompanying thought of dying. With the reading defended by us, the sense becomes much simpler, as the Saviour now speaks of the Mammon τῆς ἀδικίας: *cum Mammon defecerit*, when the Mammon is exhausted. So did it fare with the Steward; so might it fare sooner or later with every one who places his confidence in his goods. We have, therefore, not to understand exactly the moment when Mammon leaves us in the lurch in death (Wieseler), but the day when it comes to an end, as with the Steward, vs. 4.

They may receive you, δέξωνται.—Not to be taken impersonally (Starke), or to be referred exclusively to God and Jesus (Schulz, Olshausen), and quite as little (Grotius) to be understood as if the φίλοι *recipientes* were here the means of effecting the reception into the σκηναὶ αἰώνιοι (*efficient, ut recipiamini*), which would necessarily lead either to the doctrine of the meritoriousness of good works or of the intercession of the saints; but it is to be understood of a reception on the part of the friends acquired with our money, as joyful as that upon which the Unjust Steward in the parable had supposed himself entitled to reckon. These friends are conceived as already present in the everlasting σκηναί, and as there coming to meet their benefactors, as it were, at the entrance, with the purpose of admitting them into their future abode (εἰς). Σκηνάς, "*sic appellantur propter securitatem, amœnitatem et contubernii tanquam hospitii communicati commoditatem. Non additur: sua, ut*, vs. 4, *domus suas, quia tabernacula sunt Dei.*" Bengel. Comp. John xiv. 2.

The expressions thus explained must, in conclusion, be briefly vindicated from two perverted interpretations. The first is the Pelagian, as if the Saviour had meant to say that one might by beneficence, from whatever motives, buy himself a place in heaven, and that, therefore, those on whom benefits had been bestowed opened to their benefactors the everlasting tabernacles. For with the unrighteous mammon one may indeed make himself friends, yet these friends only *receive* their benefactors; they can assure them no place in the everlasting abodes, and to give even this reception they have no right in themselves, but only according to God's will, if their benefactors have entered the way of faith and conversion, and this faith has borne fruits of love. [If Christ Himself could give no place of honor in His kingdom, except according to His Father's will, much less may the saints assign any place whatever therein, except as God may will. Nevertheless, the truly beneficent use of wealth is a powerful means of grace, and so of salvation; and this our Saviour doubtless means to teach.—C. C. S.] We find thus no other moral here than Matt. xxv. 34–40. And as respects the other interpretation, the Ebionitic coloring which has been found in this parable, the Tübingen school has, it is true, imagined itself to find in the μαμωνᾶς τῆς ἀδικίας a new proof for its darling theme, that the Gospel of Luke vindicates an Ebionitic contempt of riches and favoring of poverty (*see* SCHWEGLER, *l. c.* ii. p. 59); but it strikes the eye at once that the Saviour so designates not the use and possession of earthly good in itself, as the source of unrighteousness, but only its prevalent misuse. If an Ebionitic spirit had here prevailed, we doubt very much whether Luke would have put in the Saviour's mouth an admonition also to faithful administration of earthly treasures, and the assurance that this stands in connection with the eternal destiny of men. Had the Saviour really thought that earthly good, in and of itself, is something to be reprobated, He would at all events have withheld the admonition, vs. 9. Among the weapons which an impartial criticism has to avail itself of for the controverting of the Ebionitic interpretation of Luke xvi. 19–31, vss. 1–9 certainly do not occupy the least important place.

As respects, moreover, our interpretation of the parable itself, it offers, as we think, undeniable advantages;—it removes many otherwise obvious difficulties. In the first place, it sees in the Steward even greater prudence than those who assume that he sought nothing more than to secure betimes a good support; according to us, his piece hit the mark on two sides. Secondly, on this interpretation, the Saviour's address is far more adapted for the two classes of His hearers; for the publicans now hear the making good of previous dishonesty commended as a work of true wisdom and prudence, while the avaricious Pharisees are shamed by the portraiture of a man who, although in no respect holy, yet stands far above them. In the third place, the objection is thus immediately set aside, which even the emperor Julian and others afterwards have, on the strength of this teaching, brought up against the character of our Lord, as if Christ had, at least to a certain extent, advocated the Jesuitical principle, that the end sanctifies the means. For although it is a thousand times repeated, that it is not the measure taken by the Steward in itself, but only his prudence in laying hold of a measure (in itself evil), which is proposed to the children of light for imitation, yet even in this there will something offensive remain as long as (common view) it is asserted that the Steward made good his former dishonesty by a new trick, and not (as we believe) by the compensation of the damage. How would it then be explicable, that even the Pharisees find in this no occasion for a new imputation? But if we assume, on the other hand, that the Steward out of self-interest abandoned his former crooked ways, we must, it is true, suppose that he acted only as a genuine child of the world (for of self-humiliation or confession of sin we read nothing); but then we can at all events comprehend that not only from his craftiness, but also from his mode of dealing itself, a weighty lesson was to be deduced for the publicans; for in how many respects could the Steward thus serve them as an example, by that which he had done from a purely worldly point of view! Finally, we learn on only this interpretation to understand the full force of the declarations, vss. 10–13.

Vs. 10. **He that is faithful in the least.**—It is as if the Saviour foresaw the objection, that He put too high a value on the faithful application and administration of so worthless and superficial a good as earthly good. To cut off this objection, He adduces a general principle, which He in the following verse immediately applies. It is impossible at the same time to be really faithful in the greater things, and to be unfaithful in the lesser things. For true faithfulness has its ground not in the greatness of the matter in which it is displayed, but in the conscientious feeling of duty of him that exercises it. He therefore that lacks it in the lesser, will not show it even in weightier relations; he to whom it is really a pleasure to be faithful, such an one will account nothing, whether great or small, trifling or unworthy of his attention. Comp. Sirach v. 18. "All faithfulness in great things, without being accompanied with faithfulness in lesser things, is only a semblance; all micrology, which in straining at gnats can swallow camels; such is indeed no true heart-faithfulness. Consequently also the reverse: whoever will abide or become faithful in that which is great, let him be so principally and continually in the little circumstances which continually come up in the details that are everywhere occurrent; here is an indissoluble connection." Stier.

Vs. 11. **If therefore ye.**—What the faithfulness is which the Saviour in the application of the ἄδικος μαμωνᾶς requires (see vs. 9), has appeared from the parable itself. It is exhibited when one, obedient to the precept of our Lord, makes friends with it, who receive us into the everlasting tabernacles. If His disciples were wanting in this faithfulness, if they were, in other words, like the Unjust Steward in his former dishonest course, but not in the prudence with which he, while there was yet time, made good again the evil he had committed, who should entrust to them the higher good, the true good? Τὸ ἀληθινόν is here a general designation of the benefits of the Spirit of truth and light, which in the Messianic kingdom are attainable for every one; benefits whose administration was first of all entrusted to the apostles, but then also to every believer in his sphere. They are called here by antithesis **the true**, because they are not, like the Unrighteous Mammon, untrustworthy and deceitful, but fully deserve the name of genuine and true good, whereby the highest ideal is realized. Comp. John i. 9; Heb. ix. 24.

Vs. 12. **And if ye have not been faithful in that which is another man's.**—A repetition of the same thought, only in another form. The Mammon is here called the ἀλλότριον, since it is not the property of man, who can only be the οἰκονόμος of earthly treasures, but belongs to the paramount owner, who can at any moment demand it back. Money, as such, has then only a relative worth, and the ἀλλότριον is entirely equivalent to the ἐλάχιστον, vs. 11. In opposition to this stand the spiritual benefits which the Saviour, with reference to His disciples, calls τὸ ὑμέτερον, because they, once attained through faith, are destined in time and eternity to constitute their inalienable property. "That which belongs to your true nature, which was your own originally (in the Creator's purpose), and shall in the redemption again become yours." Von Meyer. In this sense, the Mammon can never be called our property, because it with every generation changes owners, and often unexpectedly takes to itself wings.

Vs. 13. **No servant.**—Comp. Matt. vi. 24 and LANGE, ad loc. A proverbial expression like this the Saviour could properly use repeatedly; and here also there is a psychological connection plain between this utterance and what precedes. Whoever was not faithful in the least, and did not apply the ἀλλότριον to the purpose stated in vs. 9, showed thereby that he was yet a wretched slave of Mammon, and by that very fact could not possibly be a servant of God, who will have us use money in His service, and thereby promote our reception into the everlasting tabernacles. It is precisely this *service* of Mammon which stands most in the way of its true *use*, that use which redounds to the glory of God. If perchance one of the Saviour's hearers had inwardly thought that it was, for all this, possible to be in truth His disciple, even though one did not so literally follow His doctrine given in the foregoing parable, He here declares the union of that which is essentially incompatible to be impossible. It is obvious that the faithfulness praised in vss. 10–13, is at once the best manifestation of the prudence to which He, vss. 1–9, has admonished His hearers, and that therefore the whole instruction deserves the name of a well-rounded whole.

DOCTRINAL AND ETHICAL.

1. If the parable of the Unjust Steward, considered entirely by itself, has been a λίθος προσκόμματος for many interpreters, it is rightly considered, taken in its true historical connection, as one of the most striking examples of the elevated didactic wisdom of our Lord. This appears particularly if we consider that this instruction also was given in the presence of Judas, who carried the purse, and for whom in particular the admonition ἐν ἀλλοτρίῳ was of high importance. Indirect, yet intelligible enough, are the threatening and warning which he here hears, that persistence in the way of dishonesty must end with the utter loss of the apostleship, nay of his own soul. At the same time it deserves consideration, how remarkably adapted this whole delineation was for the case of the publicans and sinners, whom the Saviour had by the three previous parables been encouraging, and whom He now by this wished to lead to sanctification. Where He takes them under His protection, He is gentle in His consolations, but where He admonishes them, strict in His requirements. He shows, as it were, to the lost but now recovered sons of the house, how the father, it is true, at their return gives a feast, but how they now also, after having been refreshed and strengthened at the table, must return to an immediate and faithful fulfilment of the obligations imposed upon them. If they formerly had been only hirelings of the Romans, the Saviour will now have them consider themselves as stewards of God, to administer faithfully in their earthly treasure, *His* property. That He places before them an unrighteous steward as a model for imitation, can, after all that we have said, appear a matter of offence only if we, in opposition to the Saviour's intention, press the comparison beyond the *tertium comparationis*. The parable is in this respect entirely equivalent to that of the Importunate Friend, ch. xi. 5, and that of the Unjust Judge, ch. xviii. 1, and this also belongs to the *Singularia Lucæ*, that with Him alone a triad of parables appears, in which the *cum grano salis* more than elsewhere must be kept in mind, if one will not fall into absurdity.

2. The penetrating light which illumines the darkness of the whole parable, is to be found in the remark, vs. 8: "The children of this world," &c. It is visibly the Saviour's intention that His disciples shall learn something of the children of the world, which for the most part is altogether too much lacking to them; and in fact this parable affords rich matter for antitheses which are very shaming for the children of light. The Steward, type of a genuine child of the world, does not for an instant conceal from himself the greatness of the danger threatening him. Without delay he thinks upon means and ways to assure to himself his future lot. The means that appear unsuitable he rejects, in order at once to consider better ones. He is inventive, and knows with great distinctness what he desires, namely, to gain his daily support in an easy and secure way. He does not stop with projects and plans, but all that he has resolved he carries out upon the spot, and chooses, in speaking and dealing, the form which promises the richest fruits for his own advantage. He so disposes himself that he in any case will be protected, whether he remain yet longer steward or not. What a distinction between the sluggishness, irresolution, want of tact, &c., shown by so many better-minded persons, who have infinitely higher interests to lay to heart! However, it scarcely needs an explanation that the Saviour here speaks of children of light, not in the ideal but in the empirical sense, and that the censure herein indirectly expressed, is applicable, as a rule, more to His incipient, than to His established, disciples.

3. It is a striking proof of the practical tendency of the Evangelical morality, that the Saviour has regarded the use and possession of earthly riches as a subject of sufficient weight to be particularly handled by Him in a triad of parables (ch. xii. 15–21; xvi. 1–9; xvi. 19–31), not to reckon in a number of hints upon this, occurring here and there in His discourses. So much immediately appears from the comparison of the different passages: the Saviour does not disapprove the possession of wealth in itself, and is far from the one-sided spiritualism which denies the temporal, as such, almost any worth. But earnestly does He warn, and repeatedly does He draw attention to the truth, how greatly covetousness, no less than ambition and sensuality, renders difficult and hinders entrance into the kingdom of God. He does not repel the rich from Him, any more than He pronounces the poor blessed for the sake of their poverty, but only insists that earthly good, in comparison with something higher and better, should be viewed as the ἐλάχιστον and ἀλλότριον. Compare the beautiful homily of BASIL, contra ditescentes. As to the rest, it is not capable of proof that in the apostolic writings, e. g. 1 Tim. vi., James v., and elsewhere, we find a view of earthly riches different from that in the teachings of the Saviour Himself.

4. The purity of the faithfulness which the Saviour demands of His disciples is not in the least injured by the fact that He points them to the reward which is connected with the exercise of general philanthropy. The gospel is as far from favoring an impure craving for reward, as from the perhaps very philosophical, but certainly very unpsychological, hypothesis, that man must practise virtue purely for virtue's sake. Only as a stimulus, not as a motive of action, does He propose that which love may hope as a gracious recompense in the future life, and thus the prospect which He here opens to the penitent publicans, is essentially no other than that which He, e. g., Matt. x. 41, 42, held up before His faithful apostles. Besides this, there exists also a natural connection between love and blessedness in the future world, which must by no means be overlooked. The thought of the eternal love of heavenly spirits, into whose fellowship we hope to enter, has also more attractions for the loving than for the selfish heart; and whoever really makes himself friends of the Unrighteous Mammon, shows thereby that he finds his highest joy, not in the attainment of selfish purposes, but in the happiness of others. Taking all this together, we should hardly be able to contradict Luther when he says on the following parable: "It is not works that win to us Heaven, but Christ bestows eternal blessedness out of grace, on those who believe and have proved their faith in works of love and right use of earthly good; since now all this is not the case with the rich man, faith was lacking to him, and the whole parable, ch. xvi. 19–31, is therefore directed against unbelief, in order to warn against it by its terrible consequences." Here also the saying of the old father holds good: *Amicæ sunt scripturarum lites*, and the evangelical doctrines of grace and of reward contradict one another in no respect. It was, therefore, a miserable error, when they would in any way draw from this parable the conclusion, that one need only apply property gained in an unrighteous manner to beneficent and pious purposes, in order thereby to see one's guilt removed, and that one, by a pious foundation at the approach of death, could buy his salvation. Upon this error, which crept very early into the Christian Church, there deserves to be compared AUGUST. *Hom.* 113, *Opera* v. pp. 396–398.

5. Upon nothing does the Saviour insist with more right, than unity and harmony in the inner life of His people. True prudence is inconceivable, if genuine faithfulness is lacking, but on the other hand genuine faithfulness is also inconceivable, if inward discord and division yet dwell in the soul. If the will of two masters is hostile to one another, obedience to one must necessarily lead to unfaithfulness towards the other. To Mammon also the admonition of the Apostle is especially applicable, 1 John v. 21. When he who should serve rules, he who should command soon becomes a slave. There is scarcely a sin which so shrewdly and obstinately disputes with God the first place in the heart, as love to temporal good. Comp. the admirable discourse of ADOLPH MONOD, *L'ami de l'argent*, found in the second part of his "Sermons."

6. Whoever has comprehended in its whole depth the requirement of faithfulness in that which is least, which the Saviour places first with so much emphasis, has at the same time comprehended the hard and easy side of the Christian life, the simplicity and the infiniteness of the requirement of Christian perfection. The requirement of faithfulness in that which is least, is essentially no other than the requirement to be perfect with the Lord our God. Deut. xviii. 13; Ps. li. 6.

7. The right use of earthly treasures, as it is here commanded, leads of itself to the Christian communism, whose ideal we see realized most beautifully in the first Christian church, Acts iv. 32; v. 4. The distinction between this free manifestation of benevolence and the communistic fantasies of our century, is as great as that between selfishness and love.

HOMILETICAL AND PRACTICAL.

God, the Paramount Owner even of earthly treasure.—Man is called on earth to be the steward of God. As such he is: 1. Placed in a dependent position; 2. pledged to conscientious faithfulness; 3. to the rendering of a complete account.—" Give account of thy stewardship" (very excellent text for a sermon at the close of the year): 1. Account of the blessings received, children of prosperity! 2. account of the fruit of trial, members of the school of suffering! 3. account of the time measured out to you, sons of mortality! 4. account of the message of salvation received, ye that are shined upon by that light which is most cheering!—Against God's stewards on earth there are severe accusations preferred, and He who hears them all, will examine them all carefully to the very last one.—Life, a time of grace which precedes the day of reckoning: it is, 1. Short; 2. uncertain; 3. decisive.—" What shall I do?" the question: 1. Of painful uncertainty; 2. of well-considered reflection.—He who cannot dig, must not be ashamed to appear as a beggar before God.—" How much owest thou to my lord?" a fitting question also for the minister of the word to address to every member of his congregation individually.—" If the falsifying of human bonds is evil, how much more the presumptuous falsifying of God's written word!"—Not all have an equally great debt to account for to the heavenly Owner.—Prudent people are praised by their like.—Be wise as serpents and harmless as doves.—The phenomenon that the children of the world not seldom excel the children of light in prudence: 1. A continually recurring; 2. a seemingly surprising; 3. a fully explicable; 4. a justly shaming; 5. a powerfully awakening, phenomenon.—What the Christian can learn from the child of the world; compare: 1. The carefulness of the child of the world over against the carelessness of the children of light: "What shall I do?" 2. the clear recognizing of danger by the one, over against the self-deceiving of the others: "My lord taketh away the stewardship from me;" 3. the inventiveness in the choice of remedies with the one over against the spiritual sluggishness of the others; 4. the resoluteness and versatility of the Steward over against the continual loitering and procrastination of so many Christians.—" The children of this world are wiser," &c.: 1. This is so; 2. but it must be made different.— Earthly treasure, well applied, is a means to heighten the joy of heaven.—With gold we can buy no place in heaven, but we may prepare ourselves a good reception in the heaven already open to faith.—Even when earthly treasure fails, the rents of it may be saved.—Faithfulness in that which is great and in that which is small inseparably coupled.—The infinite excellence of heavenly treasure above earthly: 1. The earthly small, the heavenly great; 2. the earthly illusive, the heavenly genuine; 3. the earthly another man's capital, the heavenly an inalienable property of the disciples of the Lord.—Faithfulness in the earthly and zeal for the heavenly calling most intimately united in the Christian.—The indispensable necessity of unity in principle and action.—" How long halt ye between two opinions?" 1 Kings xviii. 21.— The intimate connection of the various requirements of the Lord: 1. No true prudence without faithfulness; 2. no faithfulness without steadfastness in resolve; 3. no steadfastness in resolve without sacrifice; 4. no sacrifice without rich compensation.

STARKE:—QUESNEL:—If we do not apply the gifts of God to His honor, to our neighbor's good, and to our own necessity, this is the same as to destroy and dissipate them.—BRENTIUS:—The heathen held it unjust to condemn any one when his cause was unheard; much less should that be done in Christendom.—J. HALL:—Let no one deal with entrusted goods as his own property.—The great day of reckoning and examination impends over every one, 2 Cor. v. 10.—*Nova Bibl. Tub.*:—Upon unfaithfulness there follows inevitable punishment, deposition, and condemnation.—Laziness and pride are the two evil sources of the so-common craftiness.—One is oft ashamed when he should not be ashamed and on the other hand, he is often not ashamed, when he ought to be ashamed before God.—There is a sad fact even in the Christian world,—the most of worldly people are wise enough to do evil, but how to do good they will not learn.—For ungodly men it is not enough that they sin for themselves, but they draw others also into their sinful net.—What one owes the lord belongs not to the servant.—CANSTEIN:—It would not be easy for one child of the world to ask any evil of another, that the latter would not be ready to do.—One may praise even in a bad man what is good in him.—BRENTIUS:—A broad fertile intelligence is a precious gift of God, and so far laudable.—ZEISIUS:—Be wise to that which is good, and simple concerning evil, Rom. xvi. 19; 1 Cor. xiv. 20.—The children of light have indeed the light in them, but they have also their natural darkness, which makes them slothful.—J. HALL:—Whoever does good soweth to the Spirit, Gal. vi. 8.—CANSTEIN:—Whoever will do good, must do it especially to those who will come into the eternal tabernacles, and are therefore true members of Christ.—Let no one say: I can do with mine what I will, 1 Cor. iv. 7—God all or nothing.

HEUBNER:—The man who does wrong has always his accuser before God.—Without religion, riches are a very ruinous instrument.—Three things make death frightful to the earthly-minded: their evil conscience, the Divine judgment, and the loss of everything earthly.—Earnest consideration always finds a way.—Heavenly blessedness is the true, the eternal property.

The Pericope.—HEUBNER:—The Christian order of salvation: 1. Repentance for our stewardship (vss. 1-3); 2. belief in God's judgment (vss. 3-4); 3. sanctification—holy use of all (vss. 5-9).—The earnest reminders which Christianity gives the rich man.— The threefold prudence: 1. Of the lord of the manor; 2. of the steward; 3. of the Christian.—The obscurities or apparent difficulties in the parable of the Unjust Steward.—LISCO:—Of the prudence of the citizens of the kingdom.—ARNDT:—Wisdom unto the kingdom of God.—ZIMMERMANN:—The children of the world, our teachers in this, that they: 1. Consider the future; 2. use the past; 3. control the present.— The Christian a servant of God, a lord over Mammon. —F. W. KRUMMACHER:—A sermon in the *Sabbath-Glocke*, i. pp. 140-151.—AHLFELD:—1. What in the Unjust Steward have we to shun? 2. what to learn from him?—COUARD:—What belongs to Christian prudence, in the care for our everlasting salvation?— RAUTENBERG:—How do we secure to ourselves a reception into the everlasting tabernacles?—THOLUCK: —What is true of a faithful steward?—WOLF:—The Unjust Steward about to pass the border of his earthly fortune.—Our refuge when we fail.—STEINHOFER:—The connection of prudence and faithfulness in a steward of God; there is a character: 1. Where there is neither prudence nor faithfulness; 2. where there is prudence without faithfulness; 3. where there is faithfulness without prudence; 4. where prudence and faithfulness are united.—BURK:—The great faithfulness of God, even with man's great unfaithfulness. — FLOREY: — The prudence of the steward in the kingdom of God, vs. 8.

5. The Parable of Lazarus and the Rich Man (Vss. 14–31).

14, 15 And the Pharisees also, who were covetous, heard all these things: and they derided [ἐξεμυκτήριζον] him. And he said unto them, Ye are they which justify yourselves before men; but God knoweth your hearts: for that which is highly esteemed 16 [lofty, ὑψηλόν] among men is abomination in the sight of God. The law and the prophets *were* until John: since that time the kingdom of God is preached, and every man 17 presseth[1] into it. And it is easier for heaven and earth to pass [away], than [for] one 18 tittle of the law to fail [fall]. Whosoever putteth away his wife, and marrieth another, committeth adultery: and whosoever [he that[2]] marrieth her that is put away from *her* husband committeth adultery.

19, 20 There was a certain rich man, which was clothed [and he was wont to array himself] in purple and fine linen, and fared sumptuously every day: And there was a cer-21 tain beggar named Lazarus, which[3] was laid at his gate, full of sores, And desiring to be fed with the crumbs which fell from the rich man's table: moreover [nay, even] the 22 dogs came and licked his sores. And it came to pass, that the beggar died, and was carried by the angels into Abraham's bosom: the rich man also died, and was buried 23 [entombed]; And in hell [hades] he lifted up his eyes, being in torments, and seeth 24 Abraham afar off, and Lazarus in his bosom. And he cried and said, Father Abraham, have mercy on me, and send Lazarus, that he may dip the tip of his finger in water, 25 and cool my tongue; for I am tormented in this flame. But Abraham said, Son, remember that thou in thy lifetime receivedst thy good things, and likewise Lazarus evil 26 things: but now he is [here[4]] comforted, and thou art tormented. And beside all this, between us and you there is a great gulf [chasm] fixed: so that they which would pass from hence to you cannot; neither can they pass to us, that *would come* from thence. 27 Then he said, I pray thee therefore, father, that thou wouldest send him to my father's 28 house: For I have five brethren; that he may testify unto them, lest they also come 29 into this place of torment. Abraham saith unto him, They have Moses and the pro-30 phets; let them hear them. And he said, Nay, father Abraham: but if one went 31 [should go] unto them from the dead, they will repent. And he said unto him, If they hear not Moses and the prophets, neither will they be persuaded [or, won over, V. O.], though one rose from the dead.

[1 Vs. 16.—Εἰς αὐτὴν βιάζεται. Van Oosterzee translates this: *that Gewalt dawider*, "uses violence against it." For his vindication of this rendering, see *Exegetical* and *Critical* remarks.—C. C. S.]
[2 Vs. 18.—The second πᾶς of the *Recepta* is merely a mechanical repetition of the first, and therefore properly omitted by Griesbach, Lachmann, Tischendorf, [Meyer, Tregelles.]
[3 Vs. 20.—The words of the *Recepta*, ἦν . . . ὅς, are wanting in B., D., [Cod. Sin.,] L., X., and on this ground were already suspected by Griesbach and Lachmann. With Tischendorf [Tregelles] we believe we should omit them and give the preference to the shorter reading. [Meyer contends for the *Recepta*.—C. C. S.]
[4 Vs. 25.—Ὅδε, which is wanting in the *Recepta*, is supported by a preponderance of external authority. [All the uncials.]

EXEGETICAL AND CRITICAL.

Vs. 14. **Derided Him**, ἐξεμυκτήριζον [lit., turned up the nose at], 2 Sam. xix. 21; Ps. ii. 4. An unequivocal, and at the same time hateful, token of deep contempt, whose cause is easy to give, especially in this case. The rich Pharisees looked down on the poor Nazarene with contempt, as if they would say: "You have spoken very trippingly about the use or misuse of riches, but we have no mind whatever to trouble ourselves about your counsel." The answer of the Saviour, vs. 15, gives us to see how He views this hypocritical pride as the deepest source of this contempt.

Vs. 15. **Ye are they.**—An expression almost like the well-known one of the prophet Nathan, 2 Sam. xii. 7: "Thou art the man!"—**Justify yourselves.**—Comp. Luke xi. 39 *seq.* and ch. xviii. 10, where the image of a Pharisee is delineated who will justify himself even in the eyes of God.—**But God knoweth your hearts.**—Comp. 1 Sam. xvi. 7; Ps. vii. 10.

For what is lofty.—The Saviour, of course, speaks not of that which actually in a moral respect stands high and may stand high, but only that which in men's eyes is prominent above other things, of which is high κατ' ὄψιν.—Βδέλυγμα, in general, a thing which in the eyes of the holy God is abhorrent and damnable; in a special sense, also, impurity, which was often connected with idolatry; therefore τὸ βδέλυγμα τῆς ἐρημώσεως, Matt. xxiv. 15; Mark xiii. 14, and the union of βδέλυγμα and ψεῦδος, Rev. xxi. 27. Here the word is chosen with the more striking force, because the Pharisees considered themselves as very especial favorites of God.

Vs. 16. **The law and the prophets.**—Even from old time the expositors of vss. 16–18 have been divided into two classes. Some give up all connection; so, e. g., De Wette: "Vss. 16–18 stand isolated; every attempt made to demonstrate a connection has been a failure." Among the Dutch theologians, Van Der Palm believed that Luke, before beginning on a new page a new parable, in order to make use of the yet vacant space of his almost fully occupied former leaf, noted down some disconnected sayings of the Lord, without any historical connection. Others, on the other hand, have, with more or less success, sought to state the connection, as well of these sayings with the rebuke in vs. 15, as also with the parable, vss. 19–31. According to Stier, e. g., "All the single sayings fit exactly into most intimate unity." According to Meyer, the actual centre of gravity falls upon vs. 17, while vs. 16 is merely introductory, and vs. 18 is an example which is intended to explain more particularly the previous declaration of the continuing validity of the law. According to LANGE, L. J., iii. p. 464, the Saviour will give the Pharisees to feel that their time is over, and that without their own notice a new period has dawned. The whole exposition of the latter deserves to be compared in its connection. Even the very great diversity of these attempts proves how difficult the question itself is. We, for our part, are acquainted with no statement of the course of thought of these three verses, whose simplicity and naturalness satisfy us in every respect, and we therefore regard it as easier to explain each of these three verses for itself than to state in a satisfactory manner how they are connected with one another, and why the Saviour on this occasion held up precisely these recollections before the avaricious Pharisees.

Were until John.—Not ἦσαν is to be supplied (Ewald, De Wette), but ἐκηρύσσοντο, or something of the kind. In any case, the Saviour will intimate, not that the Old Testament Dispensation was now abrogated (Olshausen), but that the Old Testament up to John constitutes a whole fully complete within itself, which, as the period of preparation, now gives place to the word of fulfilment—the preaching of the kingdom of God.

And every man presseth into it, or, **Every man useth violence against it.**—Comp. Matt. xi. 12, 13. We cannot agree with the common view that here the impulse of enthusiastic interest and the impetuous longing to press into the kingdom of God is indicated. The connection, vss. 14, 15, appears to lead us rather to the thought that it is here a hostile assault that is spoken of, in which the inward malice of the heart reveals itself. In view of the augmenting opposition which the Saviour found in Israel, He could hardly have meant to say that so general an eagerness for entrance into His kingdom existed. But especially does the necessity of an explanation in an unfavorable sense strike the mind when we compare the parallel passage in Matthew in its whole connection. The βιασταί, the powerful of the earth, were in Jesus' days, at all events, not in fact very much devoted to the cause of the kingdom of God, comp. Matt. xi. 16–19; Luke vii. 29, 30, and what ground could the Saviour have had to speak here of an impulse of heart on the part of many, which, at all events, was wanting to the Pharisees? By our explanation, on the other hand, it is, perhaps, possible to show some connection with vs. 14. The Saviour will then say: How hostilely soever ye are disposed towards a kingdom of God, which (vs. 16) was announced by the law and the prophets, yet the law's demands and threatenings hold continually good (vs. 17) in undiminished force (an example, vs. 18), and ye will, therefore, not escape the judgment of the God who knows your hearts, vs. 15. [I cannot accede to the author's view of this passage. In the first place, his arguments drawn from the connection do not appear to have great weight, for the original connection is evidently that given in the parallel passage, Matt. xi. 12. Then his identification of the βιασταί in Matt. xi. 12 with the powerful of the earth, who were opposed to Christ, is quite gratuitous. Persecution against the kingdom of God, to any considerable extent, between the first preaching of John and the period here mentioned, there had not been; while there had been from that period on, a widespread and enthusiastic pressing forward to bear the preaching concerning the kingdom of God, and, on the part of many, a pressing into it. The "every man" of Luke, besides that it is hardly so exact as the terms used by Matthew, need no more be taken with absolute literalness than Paul's mention of the Gospel as being preached "to every creature under heaven." Besides, the whole complexion of both passages shows that, although our Lord, as Alford remarks, here contrasts the actual existence of the kingdom of heaven, as a present and powerful fact, with the bare prophesying of it by John and the prophets, yet He is aware how much that is ill-considered and external there is in this present enthusiasm. Nor do I see any reason why the Presents ἁρπάζουσιν and βιάζεται, in Matthew and Luke, may not have the tentative sense so frequently found in the Present and Imperfect, and be nearly equivalent to "essay to press into it," or "with vehement exertion to appropriate it," with the implication that the future will show how far this eagerness will accomplish its end.—C. C. S.]

Vs. 17. **And it is easier.**—Comp. Matt. v. 18–20, and LANGE, ad loc. The Saviour, it is true, teaches here no external validity of the law; for, according to his own teaching, heaven and earth will one day pass away, Matt. xxiv. 35, but till the dawn of the new economy the moral obligation of the law remains in inviolable force. "In the world of perfection there is no longer need of a law, since every one purposes the right to himself. As, therefore, for God there is no law, so is there also for the perfected world no law. For, like God, so is also this a law unto itself."

Vs. 18. **Whosoever putteth away his wife.**—According to the most, a special example by which the principle expressed in vs. 17 is further established. The singularity of this example misled Olshausen to the curious view that here we have to understand spiritual idolatry of the Pharisees, who honored Mammon more than Jehovah, and has brought Stier to the conjecture that here there is an indirect allusion to the scandal which Herod had given, Mark vi. 18. Possibly it is true, but, in our apprehension at least, not probable. Is it not much simpler to assume that Luke, who nowhere else in his gospel has a place to take in the doctrine of the Saviour respecting the inviolableness of marriage (comp.

Matt. xix. 3–12), here, on the mention of the inviolableness of the law, without observing the original historical connection, adds the statement of a particular from which it may appear how strictly the Saviour regarded its moral precepts? In a more complete form we find this precept respecting marriage and divorce noted down, Matt. v. 31, 32. But if our Lord really uttered this the second time on this occasion, we may then confidently suppose that He paused in His discourse a moment or so before He proceeded to deliver the parable of Lazarus and the Rich Man.

General Remarks on the parable of the Rich Man and Lazarus.—Manifestly this parable was uttered by reason of that which took place vss. 14, 15, with a look at the Pharisees. It stands in this place very congruously, for it has the unmistakable purpose of teaching these people to see of how little value it is to show one's self pious before men when one is reprobate before God; to give them to feel the baseness of an unloving temper, of which they had already made themselves guilty in their judgment of the publicans, ch. xv. 2; but especially to draw their attention to the terrible consequences of the misuse of earthly good, to which their hearts clave so closely. The intention of the parable, therefore, is not to give a special instruction about future retribution—although we thankfully accept the rays of light that fall upon this also, yet it is immediately obvious that the whole parable is veiled in the costume of the Jewish eschatology—but to proclaim the great truth, that if one neglects the application of wealth to beneficent purposes, this becomes the source of eternal calamity. So far, this parable is the obverse of the foregoing, and stands in a natural connection with it. Whoever, like the Steward, makes himself friends of the unrighteous Mammon, is received into the eternal tabernacles; whoever, out of pride and selfishness, does not expend his treasure to this end, is appointed to everlasting torment!

In particular, the first part of the parable, vss. 19–26, has this definite purpose, while vss. 27–31 must be regarded more as an appendix, which in a parabolical form occupies the place of an application of the whole delineation. In this representation, also, some (De Wette, Strauss, the Tübingen school) have been disposed to see a proof that the Saviour found in earthly riches something to be reprobated, and in poverty itself something meritorious, and have appealed for the truth of this to the fact that here there is no more mention of the moral demerit of the rich man than of the piety of the poor man, and that Abraham only refers to the different lot of the two here below (vs. 25), which is now reversed. Yet the onesidedness and superficiality of this inference is obvious of itself. Faults of the rich man in act, definite examples of his want of love, it is true, do not appear in the parable; yet from this very fact appears the beauty of the representation, the deep earnestness of the moral: not the good which the rich man does, but the good which he omits, is sufficient to condemn him before God. Could the Saviour make His teaching, vs. 9, more impressive than by a representation which shows how a man who omitted this, and gave ear not to love but to selfishness, became everlastingly unhappy? In order to be banished into eternal torment, it was not even necessary that one should have maltreated a poor Lazarus upon earth; even those who allowed him to pine helplessly away and left him to the care of the dogs would have to give a heavy reckoning of it! Just such an apparently blameless gormandizer was the one to be held up as a mirror to the Pharisees who appeared pious before men; in the rich man too there was nothing, so the common opinion was, to blame, and yet—he came to the place of torment. Besides, there are not wanting indirect proofs of the moral condemnableness of the rich man; in Gehenna he still desires bodily refreshment; he repeatedly imagines himself capable of directing Lazarus, as if the latter were in his service; nay, in the entreaty that one might go from the dead to his brothers (vs. 30), there is implied the indirect confession that he himself had not been converted. As respects Lazarus now, he is in this delineation not the chief but a subordinate character, who appears more as suffering than as acting. But hardly would the Saviour have represented him as carried by the angels into Abraham's bosom if he could have shown to his ancestor no other letter of recommendation than his former poverty. And have we here liberty so entirely to overlook the high significance which is implied in his humble silence?

It is, finally, entirely unnecessary, with some expositors, to assume that the Saviour here wished to give a true history of a living or deceased man. Even if it is true, according to tradition, that at that time there had been a well-known beggar at Jerusalem who bore the name of Lazarus, yet it is entirely accidental that the poor man in the parable had the same name with him. The conjecture, indeed, is obvious that the Saviour in naming him so was thinking especially of His but just deceased friend at Bethany, whither His own journey was now directed; but this does not admit of proof. But least of all have we here to find allusion to Annas, with his five sons and his son-in-law, Caiaphas, whose Sadducean frivolity the Saviour in such a way is supposed to have held up to view. Such a thing, certainly, was not according to His spirit, and might also have had the appearance of a personal feud. Had this set at that moment risen before the Saviour's mind, He would, perhaps, have chosen other numbers, in order to avoid even the appearance of so unseemly an allusion. But that here something higher than an isolated historical truth, that the highest ideal really lies at the basis of this whole parabolic discourse, we hope we need not now for the first time remind our readers.

Vs. 19. **A certain rich man.**—The omission of the name is no sign of reprobacy (Euthym. Zigab. and others), but a means of generalizing the representation. That the Saviour undertook to draw from life one of Sadducean sentiments is entirely without proof. "*Nullum adest vestigium vel mentio transitus ullius a Pharisæis ad Sadducæos,*" says Bengel with justice; and it can scarcely be doubted that among the Pharisees also there were not a few to whom the description of the rich man's sumptuous manner of life was fully applicable, comp. Ps. lxxiii. 4–9. As entirely without proof is it that our Lord had the history of historical characters of earlier times, Saul, Laban, or others, in mind.—**In purple and fine linen.**—The first the designation of the Syrian upper garments; the other of the Egyptian upper garments. Fine linen, byssus, an Egyptian linen that was sold for twice its weight in gold, mentioned also in Rev. xviii. 12, in association with silk, comp. Pliny, *H.* iv. 19, 1, and many other passages gathered by Wetstein, *ad loc.* That the rich man was accordingly clothed above his position (Starke), we do not for this reason alone need to assume.

But that under the byssus garment no heart full of love and sympathy beat, appears sufficiently from the sequel of the parable.

Vs. 20. **Named Lazarus.**—Perhaps a symbolical name, לֹא עֶזֶר, the Helpless, Forsaken (Olshausen, Baumgarten, Cramer, Lange). According to Lightfoot and Meyer, a contracted name, which denotes *Deus auxilium* (Eleazar, Godhelp). If we assume that the Saviour was in His thoughts with the dying friend at Bethany (*see* above), then the giving of the name is sufficiently explained. In no event is there here (De Wette) a traditional confusion with John xi.

Laid at his gate, ἐβέβλητο.—He had been laid there by others, who either wished to rid themselves of him, or to secure to him what fell from the rich man's table (Stier, Meyer), and he remained lying there helpless, as if for a daily silent reproach to the unloving temper of the rich man.—**Full of sores** (entirely covered therewith, ἡλκωμένος).—**Desiring to be fed.**—Comp. Matt. xv. 27. Whether this wish was fulfilled or not the Saviour does not directly say; yet quite early the gloss crept into the text, καὶ οὐδεὶς ἐδίδου αὐτῷ. See the Vulgate and Luke xv. 16. Critically untenable, yet as an explanation correct, so far as this, that the wish of Lazarus, as a rule, was *not* fulfilled, as appears from what follows.

Vs. 21. **Nay, even the dogs came and licked his sores.**—The enigmatical ἀλλὰ καὶ οἱ κ. appears to be best understood in such a sense that thereby not a *diminution* but an *augmentation* of his misery is stated. That the poor man got no crumbs at all from the rich man's table, the parable, it is true, does not say; how could he indeed have then remained lying at the gate without famishing? But although he now and then got *only* the crumbs and *scarcely* the crumbs, he yet saw even this meagre fare partially disputed him by the dogs. Understand masterless dogs which ran around on the streets of the capital [as everywhere in Western Asia, comp. Ps. lix. 6.—C. C. S.], and allured by so rich a fall of crumbs as that from the table of the rich man, now robbed even the poor beggar of a part of that which perhaps had now and then fallen to his share. [The crumbs are, of course, not the trifling fragments which would fall from one of our tables, but the soft part of the thin cakes of bread in use in the East, which the wealthy, it appears, are sometimes accustomed to wipe their fingers with, and throw it under the table, themselves eating only the crust.—C. C. S.] These wild and unclean brutes, moreover, licked his sores, and thereby increased the pain of the helpless Lazarus. To describe his suffering as mitigated through the compassion of the brutes, would be directly opposite to the intention of our Lord. The antithesis of ἀλλὰ and ἐπιθυμῶν gives us occasion here to suppose a climax in the mournful scene, rather than an anti-climax. Neither is the suffering of the rich man in Sheol mitigated by anything; and even though we assume that it was the Saviour's intention to oppose the compassion of the brutes for the fate of Lazarus to that of the rich man, a sympathy of this kind, if it stopped there, must have heightened his misery the more. Comp. MEYER, *ad loc*. [It is undoubtedly true that the mention of the dogs licking the sores of Lazarus is meant to heighten our conception of his misery. There are two ways now of heightening this: one is to represent the dogs licking his sores as a new infliction, the other is to represent his misery as so

great that the very dogs had pity on him. The latter, which is the common view, appears at once more forcible and more natural, to say nothing of its agreement with the effects of the touch of a dog's tongue, whose grateful smoothness every one is acquainted with. The view of the author, therefore, though supported by Meyer, is justly rejected by Bleek, De Wette, and Alford.—C. C. S.]

Vs. 22. **And it came to pass.**—With this transition the theatre of the history is at once transferred into another world. "*En subita mutatio: qui modo non hominum tantum, sed et canum ludibrium fuerat, repente Angelorum ministerio honoratur.*" Grotius. —**Carried by the angels.**—As, of course, is understood, *as to his soul*. That Lazarus is not buried at all, but carried, soul and body, into Abraham's bosom, where he now lives again and is happy (Meyer), is an explanation incapable of proof. Respecting other Israelites, concerning whom it is said that they have come into Abraham's bosom, no one doubts that nevertheless their bodies, as usual, were committed to the earth. Why then should it have been otherwise with Lazarus? No, his burial was (Euthymius) so mean, that in comparison with that of the rich man it deserves no mention, and the contrast lies rather in the honor that was shown to the two, to the rich man here, to the poor man yonder—to the rich man by pall-bearers, to the poor man by angels—to the rich man as to his body, to the poor man as to his soul.—**Into Abraham's bosom.**—A metaphorical expression of the blessedness which immediately after death was prepared for pious Israelites in common with their blessed ancestor (John viii. 56). In all probability the expression is synonymous with Paradise, Luke xxiii. 43 (Lightfoot). In Sheol, the general appellation for the abode of departed spirits, the Jews, as is known, distinguish, on the one hand, a place of punishment, Gehenna; on the other hand, Paradise, for the pious. We have to understand the rich man as being in the former; Lazarus as being in the other. The two are so near one another that the inhabitants can see each other and hold converse. *See* DE WETTE, *Bibl. Dogm.* §§ 178–182.

Vs. 23. **And in Hades,** ἐν τῷ ᾅδῃ.—General designation of the abode of departed spirits, while from the immediately following ἐν βασάνοις it appears that he found himself in that special place which is named the place of punishment, the γέεννα τ. πυρός. As this was conceived as being in the deepest part of Hades, one would have had to look up (Lange) in order to be able to discover the condition of the blessed. The rich man is now represented as awakening from a condition of momentary unconsciousness to full consciousness, and one of the objects which he first discovers in Abraham's bosom (κόλποις, the customary plural of the Greeks also) is the familiar Lazarus reposing there.

Vs. 24. **Father Abraham.**—He knows Abraham, therefore, and recognizes him as his ancestor; as Abraham also afterwards does not refuse to address him as τέκνον, without, however, this merely outward relationship availing him anything. He desires that Lazarus may be sent to him to cool with a single waterdrop his burning tongue. The gastronome feels himself now so severely punished, precisely in that part of his frame with which he had so long sinned, and desires only a brief refreshment, "perhaps only so slight a one because he had seen the man in the uncleanness of his sores" (Lange). It is noticeable that he still imagines himself able to direct Lazarus, whom he had all his life lightly esteemed. Even so does he afterwards despise Moses also (vs. 30). Only his external condition, what surrounds him, is altered, but not his individuality.

Vs. 25. **Son, remember.**—It looks very much as if, according to Abraham's declaration, Lazarus is only comforted for the reason that he has suffered on earth, and the rich man only tormented for the reason that he on earth had received only good. But in order to be fair, this answer must be complemented with all which the parable gives us on good grounds to conjecture of the moral condition of both, while at the same time the antithesis between τὰ ἀγαθά σου and τὰ κακά without a pronoun, is not to be overlooked. What the rich man had enjoyed was really *his* good, had been in his eyes the highest good; the κακά, on the other hand, which came upon Lazarus, were not actually his, but as providences of God he had borne them with meekness.—**Now he is here comforted.**—The ὧδε received into the text strengthens the local character of the representation, but the νῦν by no means warrants us in assuming that it is not an irrevocable and final term that is spoken of (Stier). One may surely, in a place of torment, still have room for reflections, without, for that, a better future being disclosed along with this possibility. Or was, forsooth, the παράκλησις of Lazarus also merely something provisional?

Vs. 26. **And besides all this.**—Statement of the ground why it is literally impossible to him to fulfil the rich man's wish, even if he desired it. Χάσμα, literally a cleft when "two places are so parted from one another by a torrent or fall of earth, that an unfathomable depth or immeasurable breadth is between," 2 Sam. xviii. 17; Zech. xiv. 4. The here-indicated thought of an irrevocable separation is in itself intelligible enough, but the form in which the Saviour here expresses it is entirely peculiar. The Greeks, it is true, know of a χάσμα in Tartarus; this, however, is not regarded as a space separating two regions; but the Rabbins speak only of a dividing wall between the two parts of Hades, or of an intervening space of an hand-breadth, nay, even only of a hair's breadth. Then also the hope of, perhaps, even yet getting over this χάσμα is very much weakened by the statement of the particular purpose for which this cleft is established, namely, for the very purpose (ὅπως) of rendering the transition from one to the other side impossible. For the explanation of the imagery, compare the well-known passage of VIRGIL, *Æneid*, vi. 126:

"*Facilis descensus Averni,*
Noctes atque dies patet atri janua Ditis:
Sed revocare gradus, superasque evadere ad auras,
Hoc opus, hic labor est."

Vs. 27. **I pray thee, therefore.**—It appears almost as if the unhappy man sought some mitigation of this torment in continuing the conversation, although he could scarcely have hoped for the granting of his petition. For the second time he addresses himself to Abraham, that he may send Lazarus to his brethren. Perhaps he remembers that he by word and example had encouraged them in their sinful life, and feels himself, therefore, the more constrained to adventure an attempt for their delivery.— "Ὅπως διαμαρτύρηται αὐτοῖς, here without definite object (otherwise, Acts xx. 21, and elsewhere). Διαμαρτύρομαι, Wahl; *per deum hominumque fidem testor vel affirmo; de adhortantibus: graviter moneo.* An actual statement that sin is so terribly punished, he does not consider as any longer necessary for his brothers, but so much the more ardently does he long that by irrefragable testimony that may be confirmed to them, which they know indeed, but in their hearts do not believe.

Vs. 29. **They have Moses and the prophets.**—This time the compassionate τέκνον is omitted, and the tone becomes sterner, in order in the last answer of Abraham, vs. 31, to pass over into a distinct and inexorable refusal. Moses and the prophets here appear as the summary of a Divine revelation of all that which was needful for Israel in order to find the way to life. To *hear* these means, of course, not simply to listen to them externally, but designates also at the same time an actual obedience and following of their precepts. That the Hagiographa are included in this mere summary of the Old Testament is, of course, understood.

Vs. 30. **Nay, Father Abraham.**—The unhappy one now pretends to know his brothers better than Abraham himself, but acknowledges at the same time thereby that he had not repented, and therefore his condemnation was a righteous one.

Vs. 31. **If they hear not Moses and the prophets.**—Comp. Isaiah viii. 19; xxxiv. 16; John v. 45. A reference to Elijah's appearance (Baumgarten-Crusius) is by no means contained here. But the resurrection of Jesus, which was announced to the Jews without moving them to faith, may in a certain measure serve as an indirect confirmation of this declaration of our Lord. The enmity against Lazarus also, who had risen from the dead, John xii. 10, although he, it is true, had brought them no positive intelligence from Hades, affords the proof that no extraordinary signs can constrain the impenitent man to faith when he once refuses to give heed to the word of God and His ambassadors extraordinary. As to the rest, this conclusion of the parable must have shamed the Pharisees the more deeply the less it gave them ground to hope that their unappeasable thirst for miracles (John iv. 48) would afterwards find yet more satisfaction. Quite natural, therefore, that they now again give unmistakable signs of how deeply they are offended with the word of the Saviour, which gave Him then occasion for the immediately succeeding warning in reference to σκάνδαλα.

DOCTRINAL AND ETHICAL.

1. The distinction which appears to exist between the Saviour and Paul, when the former brings forward with emphasis the perfect inviolableness and eternal validity of the law, the other proclaims the abrogation of the law through the New Testament, by no means warrants the hypothesis that the Master thought differently, respecting this question of controversy, from His highly enlightened Apostle, and that, therefore, Christianity in Paul took a step beyond Jesus. On the contrary, here also the well-known rule is applicable: "*distingue tempora, et concordabit scriptura.*" The Saviour, who was speaking to His contemporaries in Israel, could not do otherwise than emphasize the relative truth that the law and the prophets remain in force; but Paul, who appeared in the midst of heathenism, must immediately proclaim that the ministry which preaches condemnation, the ministration of the letter, was abrogated. The word of the Saviour aims exclusively at the spirit, the heart, the eternal substance; the

word of the Apostle, on the other hand, at the form, the letter, the external constraining authority of the Old Testament. How far Paul was in principle from Antinomism appears from Rom. iii. 31.

2. "Whosoever putteth away his wife committeth adultery." According to this saying literally interpreted, it certainly appears as if our Lord declared Himself unconditionally against all divorce, and as if the Roman Catholic Church were fully right when she permits at the most a *separatio quoad torum et mensam*, but never *quoad vinculum*. We must, however, complement this declaration of the Saviour from Matt. v. 32; xix. 9, and assume that the transgression by which marriage is dishonored by the one party gives to the other party also liberty—we by no means say *obligation*—to regard it on his or her side also as broken. Whether it is more Christian to make use of this permission or not, this is not to be deduced from the letter of the Saviour's words, although we believe that it is in His spirit if the question is answered negatively. But, certainly, he who in the case stated avails himself of his liberty for a divorce, is not on this account alone to be condemned, and the innocent party, therefore, of two married people separated on this legitimate ground, need not be forbidden to conclude a new connection. The limitation μὴ ἐπὶ πορνείᾳ is therefore here also by no means to be left out of consideration, for in the case of πορνεία an actual divorce has already taken place, so that the legal one is only the normal continuation of it, and the injured spouse in this case does not abandon "his wife," but an adulteress, who has ceased to conduct herself as his wife. In short: "Jesus negatives the question whether the man could arbitrarily divorce the woman, and declares Himself against every one-sided and arbitrary divorce." De Wette.

3. The parable of Lazarus and the Rich Man is the sublimest delineation of this side and of that side of the grave in its astounding antitheses. What is the trilogy of a Dante, in which he sings Hell, Purgatory, and Heaven, compared with the trilogy of this parable, which places with few but speaking strokes the great whole of Earth, Gehenna, and Paradise at once before our eyes? In the vesture of a figurative discourse which is taken from the eschatology of His time, the Saviour gives here the most astonishing disclosures, and lifts the veil which covers the secrets of the future.

4. The antithesis which in the parable takes place between the rich man and the poor man on earth, exhibits to us the picture of the most mournful reality. Comp. Prov. xxii. 2. The Saviour, like Moses, is far from wishing to annihilate the distinction between the rich and the poor as if by a stroke of magic, Deut. xv. 7–11; Mark xiv. 7. He permits the antithesis here on earth to exist, and therein one of the greatest riddles of the righteous administration of Providence. But at the same time He removes the stumbling-block, inasmuch as He depicts to us *this* life not as *the* life, but only as the first half of our being, and inasmuch as He causes the light of eternity to rise over the dark night of this earth.

5. Although it is not the immediate purpose of this parable (*see above*), to give a special instruction about future things, yet many a question about the other world is here answered in a satisfactory manner. So much is shown to us at once: after death the life of the pious continues uninterruptedly, as well as that of the ungodly. Far from teaching a sleep of souls, the Saviour declares on the other hand that consciousness continues beyond the grave. The rich man sees, it is true, his external condition altered, but in his inner man he has remained the same. He knows who and where he is; he recognizes Lazarus; can speak of his father's house, and his five brothers, and their moral condition is to him not unknown. Quite as puffed up as before, he looks down upon Lazarus, and his character yonder, therefore, still shows the same shadows as here. The pain which he suffers consists in a righteous retribution of the evil which he has done here; to Lazarus the crumb was refused, to him a drop is forbidden. [A refinement hardly borne out by the text.—C. C. S.] Traces of true repentance he does not show, but he does of suffering and despair. He calls not on God but on father Abraham, and is not grieved at his sins but only at their consequences. Natural feeling for his brethren makes him tremble at the thought that they also may come to the place of torment, but indirectly he still excuses himself as if he had been in this life not sufficiently warned. No wonder that when such an inward difference exists between him and the blessed, an outward cleft also exists which can no more be filled up than passed over. Although the Saviour here speaks of the condition immediately after death, not of that after the *Parusia*, it appears, however, that according to His conception the sharp separation beyond the grave, between the children of light and those of darkness, becomes in any event a cleft and abyss. As well the doctrine of purgatory, as that of the *Apocatastasis*, is opposed by this parable, and according to the last word of Abraham to the rich man, we can on this side expect nothing more for the unbeliever than an irrevocable silence.

6. The happiness of the life to come consists, according to this parable, in this, that the redeemed of the Lord is comforted (παρακαλεῖται, vs. 25). The soul, freed from the earthly probationary suffering, is carried by angels to a happier place. What the Saviour here teaches of the *ministerium angelorum* is indirectly confirmed by such passages as Luke xv. 10; Hebrews i. 14, a. o. Paradise, which is here spoken of as the destined place of the blessed, must be carefully distinguished from the third heaven, 2 Cor. xii. 4, the dwelling-place of the perfected righteous. The Paradise is, on the other hand, in the intermediate state a place of incipient, although very refreshing, rest, in which the Jews conceived all the saints of the Old Testament as united in joy. By the bosom of Abraham, we are to understand the most swelling part of the garment, which is made by casting it around upon the breast. Here also, as in Matt. viii. 11, 12; Luke xiii. 25–29, and other passages, future blessedness is designated under the image of a feast, where the favorite of the father of the family, in this case Abraham, so lies upon his couch that he can rest upon his bosom. The ideas of refreshment and fellowship are therefore here most intimately united. The poor Lazarus rests in the bosom of the rich Abraham, as if to show that not poverty or riches in itself, but faith and obedience, constitute the ground of their blessedness. This blessedness is experienced in union with others of the same character, as is also true of the state of perdition (comp. the μεταξὺ ἡμῶν καὶ ὑμῶν); but the thought of the fate of the damned does not disturb the rest of the blessed. With full composure Abraham can address the rich man, Lazarus can hear him without rejoicing, but also without giving him hope. How much more sublime is this representation than that in the Koran, *e. g.*, where the

blessed scoff at the damned, and gloat over the contemplation of their torments!

7. In our predilection for the first and chief end of the parable, we must not overlook the dogmatic and Christological importance of its second purpose. It is noticeable how the Saviour here also in unequivocal tone gives testimony for the *sufficientia scripturæ V. T.* A *fortiori* may this testimony be extended also to the Scriptures of the New Testament. United, these means of grace are, for the enlightenment, for the renewal and sanctification, of the sinner, so perfectly adequate, that it is as inconceivable as fruitless to expect even yet more powerful voices of instruction. That, moreover, if the word is to accomplish this purpose, the operation of the Holy Spirit is absolutely necessary, is by no means denied by our Lord. The word is the seed for the new birth, yet sunshine and rain from above must make the seed fruitful upon the field. But there is no operation of the Spirit to be expected where the power of the word is lightly esteemed; the narrative shows sufficiently, that any extraordinary awakening, which any one believes himself able to bring to pass in any other way than that of the living κήρυγμα, is of brief duration and doubtful significance. No sufferer can, therefore, reckon upon being saved by God in extraordinary ways, if he has despised the common way described in God's word; and could even the sign of Jonah be again repeated, it would be in vain for him who despises the preaching of Jonah.

8. In the conclusion of this parable the Saviour utters at the same time a condemnation of all extraordinary attempts which are made in our time also by knocking-spirits, table-tippings, appearances of ghosts, somnambulism, &c., to come upon the trace of the secrets of the future world. Such a superstition is the less to be excused, because it is commonly united with secret unbelief in God's word and testimony. It appears in this, moreover, only too plainly, that even those who fancy themselves in possession of such extraordinary energies and revelations, yet are often not converted, and therefore their obstinacy itself confirms the last word which Abraham has here uttered.

HOMILETICAL AND PRACTICAL.

The truth, recognized by the conscience, opposed by the sinful heart.—The enmity of the Pharisees against the preaching of the law of love.—The Pharisaical temper exists in every natural man; they wish to appear righteous before God.—"God knoweth your hearts;" this truth may be considered: 1. As a certain; 2. as a terrifying; 3. as a comforting, truth.—The heaven-wide distinction between the judgment of God and the judgment of man, 1 Sam. xvi. 7.—The Old Testament period, a period of preparation.—So soon as the kingdom of God is proclaimed with power it is vehemently opposed.—The inviolableness of the law: 1. In what sense? 2. with what right? 3. for what purpose, does the Saviour proclaim the inviolableness of the law?—Married life transfigured by the Spirit of Christ.—Divorce not something relatively good, but a necessary evil.

The rich and the poor meet together; the Lord is the maker of them both.—How poor a rich man, how rich a poor man, may be: 1. In the present; 2. in the future, world.—The rich man, *a*. poor in true joy; *b*. in sympathizing love; *c*. in well-grounded hope; *d*. in eternal happiness.—The poor man, *a*. rich in calamities; *b*. rich in pain; *c*. rich in everlasting consolation.—The comedy and the tragedy of earthly life only a few steps removed from one another.—How the good living of the earth does not soften, but hardens, the heart.—The inexcusableness of an unloving temper exhibited in the person of the rich man: 1. The poor man is alone; 2. hard by the door; 3. well known; 4. daily before his eyes; 5. incapable of labor; 6. modest enough not to complain; 7. content even with crumbs; 8. an object of the attention of the dogs, and yet is he contemned by the rich man.—Death the end of the inequality of life. Comp. Job iii. 17-19.—Death to one the greatest gain, to the other the most terrible loss.—The care of angels for the dying saint, on its undoubtedly certain, on its indescribably consoling, side.—What avails the last honor shown the dying sinner, if it is immediately after death followed by eternal ignominy?—The awakening in the morning of eternity: 1. What there continues of that which we here possess at every awakening: *a*. our consciousness, *b*. our personality, *c*. our memory; 2. what there falls away of that which we here recover at every awakening: *a*. the illusive joy of the sinner, *b*. the perplexing trial of the saint, *c*. the work of the grace of God on both; 3. what there begins of that which we here at every awakening see approaching somewhat nearer: *a*. a surprising meeting again, *b*. a righteous retribution, *c*. an eternal separation.—The mutual beholding of each other by the blessed and the damned.—The carnal relationship with Abraham is in the spiritual world not denied, but it avails nought.—The *Jus talionis* in the future life.—The sorrow of the damned: 1. Over that which they lack; 2. behold; 3. endure; 4. expect.—Woe to the man who knows no higher good than that which he has received in this life!—The great cleft: 1. Its depth; 2. its duration; 3. its two opposing sides.—Not earthly suffering opens the way to heaven, but the manner in which it is borne.—The terrible recollection, in the place of torment, of relatives whom one has left behind on earth.—If natural relationship does not become a spiritual one, it becomes at last only a source of suffering the more.—If sinners really believed how terrible hell is, they would without doubt be converted.—God's word the only and adequate means for the conversion of the sinner. Whoever contemns this means, has no other to expect.—One risen from the dead even would not be able to bring the sinner to true faith.—Whoever expects another means of grace, outside of those ordained by God: 1. Such an one miscalculates fearfully; 2. such an one sins deeply.

STARKE:—QUESNEL:—There comes a time when God, in turn, scoffs at those who have scoffed at His truth.—The avaricious man likes to deck himself with feathers of hypocrisy.—CRAMER:—There are two kinds of pride—spiritual and worldly; neither pleases God, both are an abomination to Him.—BRENTIUS:—The New Testament age requires New Testament people. Heathen sumptuousness of living prophesies for Christendom nothing good.—HEDINGER:—Piety goes often a-begging, but is rich in God.—QUESNEL:—Sickness of body serves often for healing of the soul; happy he whom the Chief Physician counts worthy to be thus cured.—*Nova Bibl. Tub.*:—Shame on you, ye uncompassionate rich! The rational man is shamed by irrational beasts!—Those who become everlastingly glorious, must before have been wretched.—Ah, how is the leaf turned after death !—CANSTEIN :—False trust in the outward fellowship of the covenant with God is found even in the damned.—HEDINGER :—In cruel eternity all grace and comfort has an end. Prov. xi. 7.—The condemned have in their pain longing for mitigation, but obtain it not, and the vain longing will increase their pain.—They who, through a bad example, give others too occasion to sin, will, in hell, on this account, be tormented by their consciences.—MAJUS:—Each one must indeed have concern for the salvation of his friends, but early and betimes. James v. 20.—CANSTEIN :—Evil men will not accommodate themselves to God's dispensation, but despise and censure it, and will, according to their own fancy, manage yet more conveniently for themselves.—HEDINGER:—Out of love to atheists and those who do not like the Scriptures, God will do no miracles.—Ungodly men do not change, and fear not God, even in hell : let no one wonder at this.—*Nova. Bibl. Tub.*:—Faith is content with the word of God, which is full of miracle and proof; but unbelief nothing will suit.—HEUBNER :—God will hereafter destroy all seeming.—The more lofty one's schemes have been, the deeper will he fall.—Riches easily mislead to living well without doing well.—To be voluptuous and without love is quite enough to be damned for.—Of rich men like Dives, there are enough; of poor men like Lazarus, few.—Death for the pious sufferer a wished-for friend, who brings him redemption.—How various is the entering of men into the other world !—Short pleasure followed by eternal torment.—God punishes not with vehement indignation, but with composed righteousness.—Whoever seeks heaven in earthly things will hereafter lose the true heaven.—One need not be poor and full of sores, and yet may be like Lazarus.—Take heed against building the foundation of salvation on natural kindness of heart.—The damned torment one another.—It may be that the dead think oftener of the living than the living of them.—Faith is content with the proofs which God gives, but unbelief has never enough of them.—Man has no right to prescribe to God how He will lead him to salvation.—Here have we also the ground why Christ, after His resurrection, did not appear to the unbelieving.

On the *Pericope*, comp. four sermons of Chrysostom on this section. Ed. MONTFAUCON, tom. i.—The sermon of MASSILLON, *Sur le Mauvais Riche*.—LISCO :—Of the unbelief of false citizens of the kingdom.—How we have to judge the complaint of the inaccessibleness of the Christian means of salvation.—SCHULTZ:—Our soul retains in the future life its consciousness and its memory.—FLOREY :—Four declarations in the New Testament, which this Gospel proclaims and confirms to us: 1. Matt. xix. 23 ; 2. 1 John ii. 17 ; 3. James i. 12 ; 4. 2 Tim. iii. 14, 15.—WOLF :—That death alters the fate of earthlyminded men, but not their temper.—DETTINGEN:—Eternity—how it judges, how it parts, how it brings together.—RULING :—The gulf between the child of the world and the child of God is not filled up by death, but only fixed in reverse order.—FUCHS :—1. The poor Lazarus, *a*. a poor man, but also a rich man, *b*. a sick man, but also a well man, *c*. a sojourner, but also a citizen ; 2. the rich man, *a*. a rich man and yet a poor man, *b*. a well man and yet a sick man, *c*. a citizen and yet a vagrant.—L. A. PETRI :—The worldly man's wretched life and fate: 1. Poor in life ; 2. wretched in death ; 3. lost in eternity.—RAUTENBERG :—Death on two sides : 1. Oh death, how bitter art thou ! 2. oh death, how beneficent art thou !—VON KAPFF :—What Jesus here teaches of the condition of souls after death : 1. Of those that live without God ; 2. of those that live in God.—UHLE :—Some glimpses over the grave out into the still realm of the dead.—COUARD:—Voluptuousness: 1. Its nature; 2. its source ; 3. its consequences.—SAURIN :—The sermon *Sur le suffisance de la Révélation. Serm.*, tom. i. p. 404.

---

6. Parabolic Address to the Disciples concerning Genuine Faith, which overcomes Offences (CH. XVII. 1–10).

1 Then said he unto the [his¹] disciples, It is impossible but that offences will come:
2 but woe *unto him*, through whom they come ! It were better for him that a millstone were hanged about his neck, and he cast into the sea, than that he should offend [or,
3 cause to offend] one of these little ones. Take heed to yourselves : If thy brother tres-
4 pass against thee, rebuke him; and if he repent, forgive him. And if he trespass against thee seven times in a day, and seven times in a day turn again to thee,² saying,
5 I repent ; thou shalt forgive him. And the apostles said unto the Lord, Increase our
6 faith. And the Lord said, If ye had faith as a grain of mustard seed, ye might say unto this sycamine tree, Be thou plucked up by the root, and be thou planted in the sea; and it should obey you.
7 But which of you, having a servant ploughing or feeding cattle, will say unto him by and by [immediately], when he is come from the field, Go and sit down to meat
8 [recline at table] ? And will not rather say unto him, Make ready wherewith I may sup, and gird thyself, and serve me, till I have eaten and drunken; and afterward thou
9 shalt eat and drink ? Doth he thank that [the³] servant because he did the things that
10 were commanded him⁴? I trow not.⁵ So likewise ye, when ye shall have done all those things which are commanded you, say, We are unprofitable servants: we have done that which was our duty to do.

[1] Vs. 1.—Αὐτοῦ has a decided weight of authority. See TISCHENDORF, ad locum.
[2] Vs. 4.—The more this εἰς σέ is required by the connection, the more probable is the conjecture that, strongly as it is attested, it is an interpolation a scriore manu.
[3] Vs. 9.—The ἐκείνῳ of the Recepta is lacking in A., B., D., [Cod. Sin.,] L., X., &c., and appears to be only an explicative addition.
[4] Vs. 9.—Αὐτῷ. The spuriousness of this word is pretty certain [only found in D., X. of the uncials], and is conceded by most of the modern critics.
[5] Vs. 9.—Οὐ δοκῶ. This sentence is not found in B., Cod. Sin., L., X., although it has 11 other uncials for it, with most of the cursives, the Vulgate, most copies of the Itala, both the Syriac versions, &c. Tischendorf retains it, Lachmann brackets it; Tregelles, Alford omit it. Meyer vindicates it, and Bleek is doubtful. Alford meets Meyer's allegation that it might have been inadvertently left out on account of its resemblance to the following οὕτω, by remarking that this is always written οὕτως in the ancient MSS. If we suppose it an interpolation, it must be the marginal ejaculation of some ancient scribe at the hypothetical presentation of so preposterous an inversion of relations. But it appears more natural to take them as our Lord's own words.—C. C. S.]

EXEGETICAL AND CRITICAL.

Vs. 1. **Then said He.**—It remains a difficult question whether we, in Luke xvii. 1-10, meet with a connected discourse of the Saviour or a collection of sayings which are here communicated without historical connection, and are arranged together chrestomathically by a somewhat loose thread. We might be almost tempted to see here not much more than a brief summary of the teachings which the Saviour, according to Matt. xviii. 6 *seq.*, gave more in detail on another occasion. But if we consider that the parable of the Ploughing Servant, vss. 7-10, is entirely peculiar to Luke; that the parabolic expression of the sycamine tree may have been used in a modified form repeatedly used by the Saviour (comp. Matt. xvii. 20; xxi. 21); that moreover the precept, vss. 3, 4, is not exactly equivalent in substance with Matt. xviii. 21, 22, and that the probable temper of the Pharisees after that which they had heard, ch. xv. 1 *seq.*, afforded a natural occasion for the warning against σκάνδαλα, we then see the scruples against the internal unity of ch. xvii. 1-10, vanish more and more. Several attempts to explain the connection of the different parts of the discourse in an internally probable manner are found in STIER, *R. J.* iii. p. 390. Comp. LANGE, *L. J.* iii. p. 466.

Unto His disciples.—Comp. xvi. 1. Doubtless to be distinguished from the ἀπόστολοι, vs. 5, since now it is rather in part publicans only lately converted, ch. xv. 1, who for this reason are named, as being yet weak in faith, μικροί, vs. 2.

Offences.—Perhaps with definite reference to what had just taken place, ch. xvi. 1. Σκάνδαλον, in the sense here meant, is that which the sincere disciple of the Lord with reason stumbles at, because it is dishonorable to the Lord and harmful to the church. The non-occurrence of these scandals is ἀνένδεκτον, disadvantageous or impossible, οὐκ ἐνδέχεται, *non usu venit*, ch. xiii. 33. It is of course understood that the Saviour speaks not of an absolute but of a relative necessity, proceeding from the sinful state of the world. But although the case is now by no means to be altered, yet this lessens not the responsibility of him who induces the coming and increase of the σκάνδαλα.

Vs. 2. **It were better for him.**—The Perfects indicate that the Saviour will describe the condition of a man, around whose neck the millstone has been already hung, and who *has been* already drowned. He finds this fate, terrible as it is, yet still more desirable than if he were yet in life, in order (ἵνα) to give offence.—**A millstone,** λίθ. μυλικός, so must we doubtless read with Lachmann, Tischendorf, a. o., instead of μύλος ὀνικός, which appears to be taken from the *Recepta*, Matt. xviii. 6. The signification of the imagery is in both cases the same, only it must be remarked that here not only a simple drowning, but at the same time a sinking into the deepest abyss of hell, whose image the sea is, is meant. Comp. further LANGE on Matt. xviii. 6.

Vs. 3. **Take heed to yourselves.**—According to the connection, "Take heed especially of the giving scandals, against which such heavy punishments are threatened." Just such scandals they would give, if they were lacking in forgiving love. The Saviour foresees that, notwithstanding His endeavors to speak a word for the publicans, the chasm between these and the proud Pharisees will still continue. Therefore His new disciples must exhibit more than common love, if the friction with the others is not to be renewed every moment, and for this reason He now gives to them also the precept which He, according to Matt. xviii. 21, 22, had previously already given in another form to Peter. If they were of one accord among themselves, and willing to forgive, then it could not be hard for them to take many a stone of stumbling out of the way even of their enemies.

Vs. 3. **If thy brother.**—From the whole connection it appears that the Saviour is not speaking of sins in general, but particularly of such as one brother commits in intercourse with another. For this case He ordains no judicial rebuke, but a milder brotherly admonition (ἐπιτίμησον), a helping him to come right and to amend himself, in all long-suffering of love. Comp. 1 Thess. v. 14. If such correction brings him to humble acknowledgment of fault, forgiveness must not then be withheld, even if the trespass had already been six times repeated. If the Saviour here speaks only of a sevenfold trespass, He means essentially nothing else than when He spoke at another time of seventy times seven, and expresses therefore here also the qualitative infinity of forgiving love, in a symbolical number. But there prevails here greater moderation in the form of His saying, because He will not, by a seemingly overstrained requirement, repel and offend the μικροί, to whom He speaks. It is moreover worth while to compare the precept which He here gives for private intercourse, with that which He ordained for the exercise of discipline in the church, Matt. xviii. 15-18. To the individual brother, there is *not* permitted what at last may be allowed to the church, namely, to put one out as a publican and heathen. The forgiveness must be repeated as often as even the least trace of repentance is shown.

Vs. 5. **And the Apostles.**—No wonder that in hearing such requirements of the Saviour, which really first of all concern themselves, the apostles feel a pressing necessity of inward strengthening, and with shame acknowledge how much they were yet lacking in that higher principle which could alone enable them in the severe conflict with flesh and blood really to gain the victory. As one man they utter the prayer for increase of faith; and it is noticeable how those who at other times could be so wretchedly divided by pride and emulation, now agree in so amiable a manner in this humble supplication, "really the sole example of such common so designated address in the Gospels," Stier. As often, Luke here names Jesus emphatically THE LORD, comp. ch. vii. 31; xxii. 61, *et alic.* in order to bring into view in what light He stood before the eyes of His apostles, when they felt themselves constrained to address themselves to Him with this supplication.

Increase our faith.—Literally, "Add faith to us," πρόσθες ἡμῖν πίστιν. With thankfulness they feel that they are not wholly lacking in faith, but at the same time they humbly consider that the intensive power of their faith is not yet great enough to enable them for such a work as was proposed to them, vss. 3, 4. To understand here especially the faith of miracles (Kuinoel, a. o.), is entirely arbitrary. The Saviour's answer also by no means requires this. It was something higher than external wonders; it was a victory over themselves that had just been spoken of, a triumph of love that could only be the fruit of an augmented faith. Whether they with this prayer desire a direct immediate strengthening of faith, is hard to state, but certain it is that the Saviour grants immediately a direct hearing to their prayer, and strengthens their faith, inasmuch as He gives them to hear first the word of encouragement (vs. 6), then afterwards also a word of humiliation (vss. 7-10).

Vs. 6. **If ye had faith.**—The Saviour does not deny that they had any faith, but only gives them to feel how far they are removed from faith in the highest ideal sense, which alone can make them capable of fulfilling His own so strict requirement. How much faith accomplishes in the spiritual world, He indicates to them by pointing them to what alterations faith, when it is really necessary, brings forth in the natural world.—**To this sycamine tree,** δεικτικῶς. Perhaps a proof that this address was delivered in the open air, while the Saviour was continuing His journey. By a strong personification, the fig-tree is represented as a rational being which is capable of understanding such a command of faith, and obeying it. The συκάμινος, a tree frequently met with in Palestine. Comp. DE WETTE, *Archäol.*, § 83. Perhaps, however, here the συκομορέα, ch. xix. 4, is meant, which, like our oak, has a sturdy trunk and strong branches, deep and powerful roots, so that it is in a certain sense something as great to command such a tree, as to command a mountain: ἐκριζώθητι. Nay, the Saviour here expresses Himself still more strongly than in the parallel passage, Matt. xvii. 20, since the tree is not to sink itself, but actually to plant itself in the sea, where an ordinary tree can neither take root nor grow; and there is therefore a plain intimation, that often that which according to the ordinary laws of nature is entirely impossible, may in a higher order of things, in which faith has the dominion, come immediately to pass. As to the question how far we may expect a literal fulfilment of such promises, without falling into absurdities, Stier deserves to be compared on Matt. xvii. 20.

Vs. 7. **But which of you.**—The old complaint of lack of connection with what precedes (De Wette), is, with an attentive psychological exegesis, sufficiently disposed of. The Saviour could not have known His disciples, if He had not at once considered that even the bare prospect of the accomplishment of so great deeds was capable of making them immediately again selfish and haughty. He therefore, without delay, calls their attention to the truth, that even if faith strengthened them to the highest deeds, they on their part could never talk of a special merit. The parable of the Ploughing Servant, also, may have been occasioned by the view of one laboring at the plough, under the eyes of the Saviour and the Twelve, and the question: **which of you,** is the less incongruous, since at least the sons of Zebedee belonged to a class above the lowest, and might therefore well have δοῦλοι, comp. Mark i. 20.

A servant ploughing or feeding cattle.—Two kinds of work are mentioned, in order definitely to designate the apostolical labor to which they should afterwards be called, and that on its more difficult as well as on its easier side. By the servant, δοῦλος, we are not to understand a μίσθιος, but a serf, who was entirely dependent on His lord, and was most strictly bound to do in blind obedience what was imposed upon him. "*Quid magni facit ad arandum positus, si arat; ad pascendum, si pascit?*" Grotius.

When he is come.—Εὐθέως is not to be connected with ἐρεῖ (De Wette, a. o.), but with παρελθών (Stier, Meyer), as appears evident from the antithesis μετὰ ταῦτα in the following verse. The work must be indefatigably accomplished. Rest follows afterwards, and there is no need of hurrying for that. When the work on the field is accomplished the domestic labor must then be performed, before one can be seated, and the master's meal of course precedes that of the servant. The slave must be content to remain girded till the lord has at his leisure finished eating and drinking.—Περιζωσάμενος, a figurative mode of speech taken from the long garments of the Orientals, which they had to lay aside or gird up, if they wished to journey or to do any work.

Vs. 9. **Doth he thank that servant?**—A question of holy irony, by which the Saviour does not precisely mean to approve the fact, that so many acts of service in daily life are performed without even a word of thanks, but simply reminds of what is continually wont to happen. On the added οὐ δοκῶ, the stamp of originality is in our eyes too strongly impressed for us, with Lachmann and Tischendorf, to doubt its genuineness. For the interpolation there is no reason, but the omission is easy to explain. MEYER, *ad loc.*

Vs. 10. **So likewise ye.**—The Saviour will have His disciples, even after their work is faithfully accomplished, not esteem themselves higher than such servants.—**Which are commanded you.**—As well in the field as in the house. Everything, even the hardest not excepted. They have even in this case, instead of expecting special thanks, to say in deep humility: **we are unprofitable servants,** ἀχρεῖοι, not "poor, insignificant" (Rosenmüller), and as little in the unfavorable sense in which this word is used, Matt. xxv. 30, but simply such as have done nothing more than might be expected from δοῦλοι. If they had accomplished less they would have been even the cause of loss; had they accomplished more than what they were charged with, they would then have been χρεῖοι; but now they could, as ἀχρεῖοι, expect, it is true, the food and drink which was the servant's portion after his day's work was done, but no reward such as was conceded only to an extraordinary service. The Saviour does not demand that His people shall despise and reprobate themselves; He says still less that He Himself is disposed to view them as unprofitable servants; He disputes least of all that a rich reward awaits them, such as He had promised, ch. xii. 31; but here only *every meritum e* *condigno* is denied, and they are expressly reminded that whatever reward they may at any time receive, it is always a reward of grace, which they are in no case to demand. How very especially this instruction was adapted to the case of the Twelve, and how their faith would increase in the measure in which humility grew in their hearts, they have perhaps even at once felt, and certainly afterwards experienced.

DOCTRINAL AND ETHICAL.

1. What the Saviour says about the necessity of σκάνδαλα, shows us what a living consciousness He had of the antithesis which exists between the holy kingdom of God and the sinful world of man. An ordinary moral teacher would have said: "It is not fit that scandals should come;" the King of the kingdom of God on the other hand: "It is not fit that offences should fail to come: even the stone of stumbling will be the means of effecting My exalted aim;" comp. 1 Cor. xi. 19. Yet although He here out of evil causes good to proceed, the moral responsibility of him who occasions the σκάνδαλον remains terribly great, and—is by far too little considered. We must, however, take good heed not to apply arbitrarily to offences *taken*, the Saviour's threatening respecting offences *given*.

2. It is remarkable how, in this didactic discourse of the Saviour, the direction to exercise forgiving love and that to practise unfeigned humility are connected with one another by the prayer for increase of faith. In order to be able to exhibit love, faith must first exist, but in order for us to have faith, humility must first be deeper and more grounded. It appears here, at the same time, how the Saviour strengthens the faith of His people, not in a magical but in an ethical way. He leads them towards the mountain heights of a more developed life of faith, through the obscure depths of self-knowledge. "Out of the narrow place into the broad, out of the depth unto the height."

3. The Saviour's declaration about the transplanting of the sycamine-tree, must not be overlooked when the question, so variously answered, in respect to the possibility of a continuous gift of miracles in the church of the Lord, is discussed. Without any limitation whatever, He connects the gift of miracles with faith, and the assertion that this promise is exclusively applicable to the Twelve and their immediate successors, is purely arbitrary. The hyperbolical form of the imagery does not entitle us to deny the essence of the fact. And if history offers no perfectly attested proofs of the literal fulfilment of the promise, this comes from the fact that the greatest hindrances which faith must overcome, do not commonly show themselves in the physical, but in the ethical, sphere. It is true, so high a development of the force of faith will ever belong to the rarer facts, so long as there is yet so great lack of that humility which the Saviour here so emphatically commends.

4. The saying respecting the unprofitable servant remains a *locus classicus* for the main doctrine of the gospel, and of Protestantism,—the doctrine of the justification of the sinner by grace alone; and it is therefore for this reason fully in its place in the Pauline gospel of Luke. If the existence of a *thesaurus supererogationis* were possible, then the language which the Saviour here will put in His disciples' mouths would only be the expression of a hypocritical humility. We may, on the other hand, evidently see that whoever refuses to call himself, in the here-indicated sense, a δοῦλος ἀχρεῖος, makes Christ Himself a δοῦλος ἀχρεῖος. Comp. Galatians ii. 21. With the assertion (J. MÜLLER, *Chr. Lehre von der Sünde*, i. p. 48) that here at least the possibility of a virtue is presupposed by which one can do more than what is commanded, since otherwise even Christ would have had to bring His holy life under the category of δοῦλος ἀχρεῖος, we cannot agree. For Christ stood to the Father in an entirely different relation from that of servant, with whom He here puts His people on a level. Nor is there a proof for the view that here it is a limited Jewish obedience that is spoken of, which, on an evangelical position, one could raise himself far above. On the other hand it is plainly shown, that he who believes himself to be able to do more than he is under obligation to do, must have very singular notions of the ideal perfection which the law demands. As to the rest, "this commendation of humility contradicts the passage ch. xii. 37 only in appearance, inasmuch as Christ at that time wished to encourage, at this time to humble." De Wette.

5. The parable of the Ploughing Servant is even yet of special significance for the pastoral office. The Saviour here shows plainly that His disciples are to be used for different labors in His service; the one for hard ploughing—the other for quiet pasturing; that they must never be disgusted if their work in a certain sense is never ended; that all which they really need and can justly expect, even for their temporal life, will be provided for them at the suitable time; but that they, even after the most faithful labor, must forever give up the hope of their receiving a recompense as their right, which they have represented to others as a gift of grace. How much fewer would have been the desolations caused by the cancer of the spiritual pride of hierarchs and clergy, if no minister of the church had ever desired or assumed for himself another point of view than that of the Ploughing Servant.

6. This whole instruction of the Saviour is justly used to controvert the doctrine of the holiness of works in the *Ap. Augsb. Conf.* iii: "*Hae verba clare dicunt, quod Deus salvet per misericordiam et propter suam promissionem, non quod debeat propter dignitatem operum nostrorum. Christus damnat fiduciam nostrorum operum, arguit opera nostra, tanquam indigna. Et praeclare hic inquit Ambrosius: agnoscendu est gratia, sed ignoranda natura, promissioni gratiae confidendum est, non naturae nostrae. Servi inutiles significant insufficientes, quia nemo tantum timet, tantum diligit Deum, tantum credit Deo, quantum oportuit. Nemo non videt, fiduciam nostrorum operum improbari.*"

HOMILETICAL AND PRACTICAL.

A religion without scandals is in this sinful world impossible.—The woe uttered upon the man through whom scandals come: 1. Terrible; 2. righteous; 3. salutary.—There is a punishment which is infinitely heavier than harm to body and loss of life.—The high value which the Saviour attributes to the little ones in the kingdom of heaven.—The greatest man who gives scandals, stands below the lowest who suffers them.—The requirement of willingness to forgive our brother, in its length, breadth, depth, and height, Eph.

iii. 18.—Under the Old Covenant, sevenfold vengeance, Gen. iv. 23, 24; under the New Covenant, sevenfold forgiveness.—Rebuke of sin must be united with compassion for the sinner.—No wealth in love without growth of faith.—In the prayer for increase of faith all Christians must join, like the apostles.—How far this prayer is necessary: 1. In particular for the Twelve; 2. how far it remains necessary in general for all believers.—What this prayer, 1. Presupposes: *a.* that one already has faith, *b.* but has yet too little, and *c.* that the Saviour is the only one from whom we can receive more. What this prayer, 2. demands: *a.* more light, *b.* more power, *c.* more fellowship of faith. What the prayer, 3. effects: *a.* the disciple becomes through the hearing of it perfect, *b.* the kingdom of God is advanced, *c.* the Lord is glorified.—Fitting text for a communion sermon: this prayer the best communion prayer, because it was faith which, *a.* before the communion was most lacking to us, *b.* because it at the communion is first demanded, *c.* after the communion may be put to many severe tests.—The all-overcoming power of faith: 1. From what it is visible; 2. why it is not more seen.—A faith like a mustard-seed has power enough to transplant a whole tree.—The relation of labor to recompense in the kingdom of God.—The minister of the kingdom of God like a ploughing servant, one who 1. Is called to various, often wearying labor; 2. can never regard his work as entirely accomplished; 3. in his service receives and enjoys what is needful; 4. but even after the faithfully accomplished task, can never establish any claim to well-deserved reward.—The unprofitable servant very profitable, the most profitable servant unprofitable.—How true recompense for labor in the kingdom of God only begins when one has given up all prospect of reward.—The Saviour esteems His servants more in proportion as they have learned to esteem themselves less.

STARKE:—QUESNEL:—God, with whom all things are possible, could easily prevent all scandals, but He admits them for holy reasons.—*Bibl. Wirt:*— Take care that thou to no one, but especially to young children, give the least scandal.—Love never grows weary in forgiving.—BRENTIUS:—Christians may well be elevated above all prosecutions for trespass, because God the Lord has in such holy wise reserved to Himself all vengeance.—Faith grows not like tares; because it has its root in God, it must also grow through God.—ZEISIUS:—Even weak faith is a Divine power, does miracles, saves, and is not rejected, Mark ix. 24, 25.—Let one examine himself whether he be in the faith, that he may not account his unbelief for a weak faith.—*Nova Bibl. Tub:*— It is not enough for us to begin our spiritual labor and service of God well,—we must also continue it uninterruptedly till the Lord Himself gives us our holiday.—CANSTEIN:—A devoted and faithful servant gives his lord the honor, and concedes to him in all things of good right the preëminence.—First the work, after that the reward. The first we owe, the latter follows from grace.—HEDINGER:—Away spiritual pride; where is perfection? Genuine servants of God never in their own view do enough; they would ever be glad to have done yet something more, so great is their desire to serve God and to win souls.

HEUBNER:—Faith is the power as for all good, so also for invincible placableness.—Prayer the means of strengthening faith, and therefore daily necessary.—It is not the chief concern that faith should be at the very beginning strong, if it is only fresh, sound, impelling.—To uproot even that which is deeply rooted and appears impossible to move, is through faith in Christ possible.—Without labor no repose, without conflict no enjoyment.—He is the worthiest who esteems himself unworthiest.—Faith bids: Ever at rest; love, faith's daughter: Never at rest.—ARNDT:—The utterance of humility in reference to the good that we have done: 1. It confesses that all good which we do is only our duty; 2. that we succeed in it only through God's grace; 3. that it ever remains imperfect.—LISCO:—How necessary for every citizen of the kingdom humility is.

I. *The Journeyings through the Boundaries between Samaria and Galilee, and the noticeable Events during the same.* CHS. XVII. 11—XVIII. 14.

1. The Ten Lepers (CH. XVII. 11-19).

11 And it came to pass, as he went to Jerusalem, that he passed through the midst of
12 Samaria and Galilee. And as he entered into a certain village, there met him ten men
13 that were lepers, which stood afar off: And they lifted up *their* voices [the voice, or, a
14 cry], and said, Jesus, Master, have mercy on us. And when he saw *them*, he said unto them, Go shew yourselves unto the priests. And it came to pass, that, as they went,
15 they were cleansed. And one of them, when he saw that he was healed, turned back,
16 and with a loud voice glorified God, And fell down on *his* face at his feet, giving him
17 thanks: and he was a Samaritan. And Jesus answering said, Were there not ten
18 cleansed? [Have not the ten (οἱ δέκα) been cleansed?] but where *are* the nine? There are not found that returned to give glory to God [Are there none found returning,
19 &c.?], save this stranger [foreigner, ἀλλογενής]. And he said unto him, Arise, go thy way: thy faith hath made thee whole [lit., saved thee].

EXEGETICAL AND CRITICAL.

Vs. 11. And it came to pass.—An exact harmonistics would have, after Luke xvii. 10, to insert the account of the raising of Lazarus, and the deliberation of the hostile Sanhedrim held in consequence of this, John xi. 1–53. After these events the Saviour tarries some time in the small town of Ephraim, till the approaching Passover calls Him again to Jerusalem, John xi. 54, 55. In the beginning of this last journey to the feast follow the occurrences related by Luke, xvii. 11 *seq.* The healing of the ten lepers did not, therefore, take place during an excursion of our Lord from Ephraim (Olshausen, Von Gerlach), but at the very beginning of the journey to the feast, which Luke alone gives an account of. Once more before He takes leave of His public life, the Saviour will in part wander through the regions which had been the theatre of His earlier activity, and so by words and deeds show that He does not avoid His mighty enemies.

Διὰ μέσου.—There is no ground for altering the reading either into μέσον, διὰ μέσον, or ἀνὰ μέσον. See MEYER, *ad loc.* The expression intimates, not that He was travelling through the midst of the two herenamed lands—for in this case not Samaria but Galilee would have to be first named—but that He was travelling in the midst *between* these two lands, so that He kept on the borders without penetrating into the interior of the country, *in confinio*, Bengel. So also LANGE, *L. J.* ii. p. 1065. The opinion that the mention of Samaria took place only in consequence of the appearance of a Samaritan in this narrative, vs. 16 (Strauss), is one of the frivolities of the negative criticism, which contribute not a little to throw suspicion upon its moral character.

Vs. 12. Ten lepers.—Upon the leprosy see on Luke v. 12–16, and LIGHTFOOT on Matt. viii. 2. In 2 Kings vii. 3 we find an example of leprous men, driven by need, having united themselves with one another in a company. As unclean, they were obliged to remain at least 4 ells distant from the untainted. *See* Lev. xiii. 46 ; Num. v. 2. That even to them in their isolation the report of Jesus had made its way, is a striking proof of the greatness of His fame.

Vs. 13. Jesus, Master, ἐπιστάτα, not κύριε.—Although they do not yet know the Saviour's Messianic dignity, yet they account Him a prophet, mighty in deed and word ; their faith is sincere without being perfect, on which account also the Saviour does not repel them. But in order to show to the disciples that He in the manner in which He accomplishes His benefits is bound to no form whatever, as well as at the same time to try the faith of the lepers, He this time effects the cure in an entirely peculiar way. Full of leprosy as they yet are, they must go to the priests, in order to have themselves declared clean by these. In this, it is true, there is implied the indirect promise that they would actually become clean even before they came to their priests, but yet it was no easy requirement that they should, yet unhealed, begin their journey thither. It appears that the Saviour in this way would not only try them, but also avoid any occasion whatever for scandal, and give the representatives of the Theocracy their due honor, comp. Lev. xiii. 2 ; xiv. 2. Probably the Israelitish lepers now go towards the village lying in the vicinity (the whole scene we have to conceive as yet outside of the κώμη), while the Samaritan went probably to his own priests, who, without doubt, observed the same laws of purification. In the midst of their believing journey the healing at once comes to pass.

Vs. 15. Turned back.—Not after he had really been declared clean by the Samaritan priests (Calvin, Luther, Lange); for in this case the Saviour would not have been able to wonder that the nine others had not returned, since these certainly had to make a much longer journey to their priests. No, ἐν τῷ ὑπάγειν all were healed, and all ought to have returned at once, in order to thank their Deliverer. That the nine had allowed themselves to be kept back by the influence of hostilely disposed priests' (*Berl. Bibl.*), is an entirely arbitrary conjecture. Not hours, but only moments had intervened between the command and the healing, between the healing and the thanksgiving. Or are we to suppose our Lord to have tarried inactive a half day at the entrance of the κώμη, in order to see whether one would perchance return ?

A Samaritan.—The other lepers, without doubt, after the priest had declared them clean, returned joyfully to their dwelling; but the Samaritan does not content himself with having received the benefit, he will also praise the Benefactor. His thankfulness is of the right kind, for it displays itself as a glorifying of God, vs. 15, and that is well-pleasing to the Saviour, vs. 18. But the praise of Him who was the first cause of the benefit brings no prejudice to the honor to which the Mediator of this healing may make claim. With loud voice he praises God, and falls down at Jesus' feet, ready, as is of course understood, after that to obey His command, and now to go to the priests.

Vs. 17. Where are the nine ?—In order to understand the full melancholy earnestness of this inquiry, we must consider this event in its historical connection. The Saviour here also is not concerned for honor from man, but He who knows well what is in man knows also that gratitude towards God could not be very heartfelt, where one did not feel himself obliged even to a word of thanks towards his human benefactor. His complaint, in and of itself a just one, if we regard the extraordinariness, the undeservedness, and the magnitude of the benefit bestowed, becomes the more affecting, if we consider the time in which it was uttered. Well acquainted with the plans which had already been forged in Judæa for His destruction, the Saviour yet once again makes this boundary-tract of Galilee the theatre of His saving love, and even at the first miracle on this journey it is manifested how very much the prevailing tone of feeling is now altered. For formerly a miracle performed on one, animated many hundred tongues to His praise ; now, on the other hand, the healing of ten unhappy ones does not even elicit from the majority of the healed, still less from the inhabitants of the village, even a single word of thanks. He has this time rather concealed than made conspicuous the brilliant character of the miracle by its form, but He experiences at the same time how the Doer of the miracles is at once forgotten, and while He on His part, even in this last period, displays His respect for the law and the priesthood, He is rewarded therefor with a mean slight. The observation of this fact goes to the Saviour's heart ; and as He had just shown Himself the compassionate High-priest, He feels Himself now the deeply contemned Messiah. Yet the complaint to which His sadness gives utterance, is at the same time a eulogy for the one thankful one who had appeared before Him, and with the words: "Rise up, go thy way, thy faith hath saved thee;" the benefit is for this one heightened, confirmed, sanctified.

It was perhaps the learning of this distinction between the Samaritan and the Jews, which occasioned Luke, from his broad Pauline point of view, to note down this occurrence, which, we know not from what special reasons, the other Synoptics pass over. Not improbable is the view that he here by a speaking example wished to place in a clear light the unthankfulness of the Jews towards the Saviour, which showed itself throughout His course. Comp. SCHLEIERMACHER, *l. c.* 215. But that Luke does not for all this show any unwarranted, unhistorical preference for the Samaritans (Schwegler, a. o.) appears sufficiently from chap. ix. 53.

DOCTRINAL AND ETHICAL.

1. The essence of faith manifests itself in the ten lepers. Faith recognizes in Jesus the only willing and all-sufficient Helper, and allows itself to be impelled by life's necessity to take refuge in Him. It is observed by the Saviour with pleasure, exercised by trial, and never put to shame, so far as the heart is upright before Him, even when the conceptions of the understanding, respecting the Redeemer, are as yet extremely defective. It is the only way to salvation, not only in a natural, but also in a spiritual, respect, and must, if it is of the right kind, reveal itself in sincere thankfulness towards God and towards the Saviour.

2. No less appears here the nature of true thankfulness. It can only be required and attested when one knows himself to be healed and redeemed by Christ; but then it can and may not possibly fail to appear. Like love, so also is thankfulness towards God most intimately connected with thankfulness towards man, comp. 1 John iv. 20. "*Deo ingratus, non erit hominibus gratus.*" Melanchthon. It reveals itself with irresistible force, as in the case of the Samaritan, who, after he had first with hoarse voice [*i. e.*, husky with leprosy.—C. C. S.] called on the Redeemer, returns again immediately after his healing, in order with loud voice to give God the glory. And as unthankfulness does not only deny the Saviour, but also perturbs Him, so, on the other hand, genuine gratitude is rewarded by augmented gifts of grace, vs. 19, so that the declaration : "He that has, to him shall be given," finds here also its full application.

3. The ingratitude of the nine, in contrast with the one Samaritan, bears so far as this a symbolical character, that it gives an example of the unfavorable reception which the Saviour ever found in Israel, in opposition to the higher esteem which was accorded Him in the heathen world.

4. The love which the Saviour here also, as often, exhibits for the Samaritans, was for the apostles a pædagogic lesson, which, as appeared from the extended commission that was given them, Acts i. 8, was doubly necessary, and afterwards also bore its fruits in the zeal with which they preached the Gospel to Samaria too. Acts viii.

HOMILETICAL AND PRACTICAL.

Augmenting hostility hinders not the Saviour from working so long as it is day.—Leprosy, the image of the defilement and the misery of sin.—How life's necessity brings together and unites men.—Misery's cry of distress : 1. Unanimously raised; 2. graciously answered.—Jesus, a Master who takes compassion on those who call on Him in distress.—Jesus, in the healing of the ten lepers, revealing Himself as the image of the invisible God, comp. Ps. l. 15.—Perplexing requirements and ways of the Lord have no other purpose than to strengthen the yet weak faith.—The Divine institutions of the Old Testament are by the Saviour in the days of His flesh honored and practised.—What is appropriated in faith on Jesus' word is never resultless.—Not always are good and evil found just where we should expect them *a priori.*—The great contrasts which present themselves in the history of the ten lepers: 1. Great misery on the one hand, great grace on the other hand; 2. great unthankfulness from many, thankful recognition from one; 3. Israel blessed with benefits, but rejected by its own fault—the stranger praised and accepted.—Human thankfulness and unthankfulness in relation to the Lord, and the Lord in relation to them.—How true thankfulness towards God reveals itself in the glorifying of Jesus.—The sad inquiry, Where are the nine? 1. What were they once? 2. where are they now? 3. What do they afterwards become?—The thankful stranger a true citizen of the kingdom of God.—He that honors grace received is worthy of greater grace!—What is the faith that has any true saving power? A faith which is: 1. Humble in entreaty; 2. courageous in approaching; 3. joyful in thanksgiving.

STARKE :—*Nova Bibl. Tub. :*—The world is a hospital full of infirm and sick.—J. HALL :—Like and like agree well; pure to pure, impure to impure.—O Jesus, give us grace to seek Thee and strength to wait on Thee.—*Nova Bibl. Tub. :*—From the leprosy of sin there can no one heal us but He that is called Jesus, Matt. i. 21.—Nothing agrees better together than human misery and Christ's compassion.—HEDINGER :—Whoever will spiritually recover, let him show himself to experienced people and Christians.—Christ is indeed a Physician of all men, but He does not heal all in one way.—O man, if God hath graciously heard thy Eleison, forget not then to bring Him thy Hallelujah.—QUESNEL :—With genuine thanksgiving there is true humility.—*Bibl. Wirt. :*—Shameful is unthankfulness towards our neighbor, but much shamefuller towards God and His many benefits.—Learn to suffer and shun ingratitude.—Follow not the multitude; better be with the one than with the nine.—*Nova Bibl. Tub. :* —On humiliation follows exaltation, on repentance departure in peace.—CANSTEIN :—So great and glorious is faith, that that is attributed to it which yet is only God's grace and benefit.

LAVATER :—Even the thanks that are most His due, Christ rewards with new manifestations of grace.—HEUBNER :—The true penitent goes towards Christ indeed, but remains in humility, nevertheless, standing afar off.—The spiritually sick also, when he needs comfort, should show himself to the priest. —The priests cannot make clean but declare clean.—Those of erroneous belief put to shame very often the confessors of the true religion.—The multitude of evil and the rareness of good examples in human society.—Christ now, as then, experiences the unthankfulness of men.—Unthankfulness so frequent a phenomenon because humility is lacking.—He that prays without giving thanks, closes to himself the door of acceptance of his prayer.—On the Pericope.—COUARD:—Our life must be a continued praying and giving thanks: 1. Praying in relation to our necessities; 2. giving thanks in relation to the Divine benefits of grace.—AHLFELD:—Where are the nine?—How is it as to thy thanksgiving prayers towards God?—RAUTENBERG:—The intent of the Divine help: 1. That we may recognize the Divine help; 2. receive it with thanksgiving; 3. through it grow in holiness.—WESTERMEYER:—Comp. P's. l. 15: 1. The commended call; 2. the promised help; 3. the owing thanks.—W. OTTO:—Unthankfulness is the world's reward; this is· 1. An experience gained in the world; 2. an accusation preferred against the world; 3. a shame lying upon the world; 4. a harm arising for the world.—FECUS:—Christ makes us clean: 1. From what? 2. whereby? 3. whereto?—SOUCHON:—Insincere and sincere faith.—STIER:—How the Lord here to our shame complains of the unthankfulness of men.—J. J. MIVILLE:—Compelled piety.

2. Discourses of Jesus concerning the Kingdom of God (Vss. 20–37).

20 And when he was demanded of [inquired of by] the Pharisees, when the kingdom
of God should come, he answered them and said, The kingdom of God cometh not with
21 observation [*i. e.,* so that it can be gazed at]: Neither shall they say, Lo here! or, lo
there! for, behold, the kingdom of God is within you [rather, in the midst of you].
22 And he said unto the disciples, The [om., The] days will come, when ye shall desire
23 to see one of the days of the Son of man, and ye shall not see *it.* And they shall say
24 to you, See here; or,[1] see there: go not after *them*, nor follow *them.* For as the lightning, that lighteneth out of the one *part* under heaven, shineth unto the other *part*
25 under heaven; so shall also[2] the Son of man be in his day. But first must he suffer
26 many things, and be rejected of [by] this generation. And as it was in the days of
27 Noe [Noah], so shall it be also in the days of the Son of man. They did eat, they
drank, they married wives, they were given in marriage, until the day that Noe [Noah]
28 entered into the ark, and the flood came, and destroyed them all. Likewise also as it
was in the days of Lot; they did eat, they drank, they bought, they sold, they planted,
29 they builded; But the same day that Lot went out of Sodom it rained fire and brim-
30 stone from heaven, and destroyed *them* all. Even thus shall it be in the day when the
31 Son of man is revealed. In that day, he which shall be upon the housetop, and his
stuff [goods] in the house, let him not come down to take it away: and he that is in
32, 33 the field, let him likewise not return back. Remember Lot's wife. Whosoever
shall seek to save his life shall lose it; and whosoever shall lose his life shall preserve
34 it. I tell you, in that night there shall be two *men* in one bed; the one shall be taken,
35 and the other shall be left. Two *women* shall be grinding together; the one shall be
36 taken, and the other left. Two *men* shall be in the field; the one shall be taken, and
37 the other left.[3] And they answered and said [say] unto him, Where, Lord? And he
said unto them, Wheresoever [Where] the body *is*, thither will [also[4]] the eagles be
gathered together.

[1] Vs. 23.—*Rec.:* ἰδοὺ ὧδε ἢ ἰδοὺ ἐκεῖ. The ἢ before the second ἰδοὺ, although Lachmann defends it, appears to be borrowed from Matt. xxiv. 23, and is properly rejected by Tischendorf, (Meyer, Tregelles, Alford.]
[2] Vs. 24.—Καί, although dubious, as it is wanting in many manuscripts, is found, however, in B., D., [om., Cod. Sin.,] and has been on this ground, as it appears, properly retained by Tischendorf and at least bracketed by Lachmann. [Tischendorf in his 7th ed. omits it, as do Meyer, Tregelles, Alford.—C. C. S.]
[3] Vs. 36.—In all probability an interpolation from Matt. xxiv. 40, and therefore rejected by almost all later critics, with the exception of Scholz. De Wette hesitates. [Om., A., B., Cod. Sin., 14 other uncials, and much the larger part of the cursives.—C. C. S.]
[4] Vs. 37.—Καί is rightly received by Tischendorf into the text, on the authority of B., [Cod. Sin.,] L., [U., A.]

EXEGETICAL AND CRITICAL.

Vs. 20. **Inquired of by the Pharisees.**—The ground, occasion, and purpose of this inquiry can only be conjecturally determined. To understand it as put by sympathizing inquirers desirous of salvation, is forbidden by the partially rebuking and partially earnestly warning answer of our Lord. Apparently these Pharisees were not unacquainted with the growing hatred of the Jewish magnates against Jesus, and had in secret their sport at the fact that the kingdom of God, of which John and Jesus had already so long testified, still remained invisible, and that our Lord, after long labor in Galilee, had acquired no greater following, as had just before appeared. But as often good comes out of evil, so have we here also to thank a concealed enmity for an instruction of the Saviour which assails an error of His adversaries at its root, and possesses abiding worth for all future ages.

With observation, μετὰ παρατηρήσεως, literally, with or under observation, so that it can be recognized and observed by outward tokens, and that one could exclaim with assurance, **Lo here, lo there!** We are not primarily to understand this of external pomp and brilliancy (μετὰ πολλῆς φαντασίας, Grotius), but in general everything external that can be seen with the eyes and grasped with the hand. By this answer, the Pharisees are at the same time instructed that it is a fruitless trouble to inquire after a definitely fixed point of time, when it shall suddenly come. Of this unnoticed coming of the kingdom of God, the Saviour could not well give any more striking proof than this, that the kingdom of heaven had already in its incipiency appeared among them, without their having even yet in their earthly-mindedness observed it.

Vs. 21. **In the midst of you,** ἐντὸς ὑμῶν.—From the future to which they were looking, the Saviour directs their eyes back upon to-day. Inasmuch as the King of the kingdom of God was already living and working in the midst of them, this kingdom had already come potentially into their nearest neighborhood. The explanation, *in animis vestris* (Chrysostom, Luther, Olshausen, Heubner, Hilgenfeld, and others, and also the deceased Amsterdam Professor A. des Amorie van der Hoeven), is indeed capable of being philologically defended, and finds also some weak analogies in individual Pauline expressions (1 Cor. iv. 20; Rom. xiv. 17; Col. i. 13), but is not favored by the connection. For the translation, "in the midst of you," there are the following grounds: 1. That in this way the antithesis between the external coming and the being already actually present is kept more sharply defined; 2. that the kingdom of God had not been truly set up in the hearts of these Pharisees; 3. that in John i. 26; xii. 35; Luke vii. 16; xi. 20, the same thought which is expressed in our translation is expressed in another way, while, on the other hand, for the apparently profound but really not very intelligible statement, that the kingdom of God is found *in* the man, no other proofs are to be found in our Lord's own words. It would be better, without doubt, to connect with one another the two significations of ἐντός (Stier, Lange), although there is nothing contained in the connection that decidedly requires us to interpret ἐντός otherwise than as the simple antithesis of ἔξω, *intra vos.* Not with entire injustice, apparently, Meyer calls the idea of the kingdom of God as an ethical condition in the soul, modern, not historico-biblical.

Vs. 22. **And He said unto the disciples.**—The Pharisees have been sufficiently disposed of with the above answer, which Luke has alone preserved to us. But the Saviour does not on this occasion give up the subject which they had brought into discussion, but continues, perhaps in their presence, to instruct His disciples still further about the approaching coming of the kingdom of God. In the eschatological discourse, vss. 22–37, which now lies before us, the same phenomenon is repeated which we have already several times met with. Here also Luke communicates sayings which Matthew has presented in an entirely different connection, and again the inquiry cannot be avoided, which of the two has maintained the most exact chronological sequence. If we compare the first and the third Gospels with one another, it appears that Luke xvii. 23, 24, and Matt. xxiv. 23–27; moreover Luke xvii. 26, 27, and Matt. xxiv. 37–39, as well as Luke xvii. 35–37, and Matt. xxiv. 40, 41, coincide almost verbally. Now, it is true the possibility cannot be doubted that our Lord uttered several of these sayings on several occasions, but, on the other hand, it can hardly be denied that many of the words here given by Luke appear in Matthew in a much more happy and natural connection; that it is much more probable that our Saviour, towards the end of His life, spoke to His intimate disciples alone concerning these secrets of the future, and not some weeks before to a circle of hearers so mixed as that in the midst of which Luke here places us; and that finally it is almost inconceivable that the long eschatological discourse, Matt. xxiv., should have consisted in a great measure only of reminiscences of a previous instruction, Luke xvii. From all these grounds we believe that Luke xvii. 22–37 stands in about the same relation to Matt. xxiv. as Luke vi. 17–49 and ch. xii. 22 *seq.*, to Matt. v. 7. In opposition to Schleiermacher and Olshausen, who concede to Luke the preference, we think, with Ebrard, Lange, and others, that we see in the redaction of the third gospel in this place heterogeneous elements, that is, such as, although in themselves undoubtedly genuine, have yet been here inserted only because of the opportunity, and outside of their original historic connection; but we prefer to assume that the Saviour on this occasion did communicate a certain eschatological instruction, without, however, already, as afterwards, speaking of the destruction of Jerusalem, but that individual striking expressions from a later discourse have been by Luke woven proleptically into this one. How much has been transferred from one discourse to the other, it is probable will never admit of any other than an approximate determination.

Days will come.—The psychological connection of this first word to the disciples, and of the last to the Pharisees, strikes the eye at once. Scarcely has the Saviour uttered the assurance that the kingdom of God already exists in the midst of them, when He thinks also of the prerogative of His disciples, who had been already received into the same, but at the same time—and how could it at such a time be otherwise?—on the pain of impending separation. It is as if He feared that His friends, from the assurance that the kingdom of God had already really come, would now also draw the conclusion that the King would forever abide in the midst of them. As He is far from blowing up again even the weakest spark of an earthly hope which He had previously controverted with so much emphasis, He now makes haste to prepare them for grievous times. Under the pressure of manifold tribulations, they were for the moment to wish in vain to see even one of the victorious blessed days of the revelation of the Messiah. The Saviour is thinking of one of those days of happiness such as only the αἰὼν μέλλων could and should bring. He does not mean that they would long for one of the days which they were now experiencing in converse with the yet humiliated Christ, but that they would sigh after the revelation of the Glorified One, who should bring an end to all their wretchedness and satisfaction to their longing. We must not, therefore, explain with Bengel, "*cupiditatem illam postea sedavit Paracletus,*" but rather, "*hanc cupiditatem tantummodo sedare potest Parusia.*" Impelled by this natural but impatient longing, they might easily incur the danger of allowing themselves to be misled by false Messiahs, against which the Saviour warns them in the following verse.

Vs. 23. **Go not after them.**—Comp. Matt. xxiv. 23–27, and LANGE, *ad loc.* It is without ground that Schleiermacher here disputes that we are to understand false Messiahs. Let the reader call to mind also the Goetæ, who shortly before the destruction of the Jewish state led so many thousands by the promise of miracles into the wilderness and into destruction. See JOSEPHUS, *Ant. Jud.* xx. 8, 6. Comp. *De Bell. Jud.* ii. 13, 4; Acts v. 36, 87; xxi. 38, and Homily 76 of Chrysostom.

Vs. 24. **The lightning that lighteneth.**—The *tertium comparationis* between the Parusia and the swiftness of the lightning which shows itself on the dark sky, is not its unexpected appearance, but its indubitable visibleness; even as one, when the lightning flashes from one region of heaven to the other (ἐκ τῆς, sc. χώρας), does not need to inquire *whither* and *where* the flash shows itself. If the day of the Son of Man is once present, this will no more be a matter of doubt than it is a matter of uncertainty whether ἡ ἀστραπὴ ἡ ἀστράπτουσα has darted through the air or not. Ἡμέρα signifies here the παρουσία, which the days designated in vs. 22, ἡμέραι, do not precede, but follow.

Vs. 25. **First ... suffer many things.**—The prediction of suffering and dying which often returns in this last period is here, too, not wanting. " In vs. 25 He gives the great deciding announcement against all false παρατήρησις, that the Messiah *previously*, in a first manifestation, must suffer and be rejected. See on Matt. **xvi.** 21; xvii. 12." Stier. One must, therefore, not by any means, as the Pharisees do, expect the promised Parusia too early, since this must in any case be preceded by a mournful event. Our Lord cannot with sufficient earnestness impress it on the minds of His disciples that His way goes down into the depth, while they are secretly dreaming of high places of honor.

Vs. 26. **In the days of Noah.**—Comp. on Matt. xxiv. 37–39. Although the coming of our Lord will be the perfect redemption of His disciples out of all tribulations (comp. vs. 22), it is here represented especially as a judgment upon the godless and unbelieving world, and this judgment is typified in the fate of the contemporaries of Noah. The Asyndeton between the different verbs heightens the living and graphic force of the portrayal of their careless life in the midst of the most powerful voices of awakening. We may, perhaps, from the fact that the terrible side of the event is made especially conspicuous, while the delivery of Noah is not mentioned, conclude with some probability that the Saviour addressed these words originally to a wider circle than that of His believing disciples.

Vs. 28. **In the days of Lot.**—The second example, which Luke alone relates, is especially remarkable, not only on account of the peculiar coincidence in character between the here-mentioned time and the antediluvian period, but also on account of the striking application which in vs. 32 is made of the history of Lot's wife. Here also there is no other conception of the destruction of Sodom implied than that in Genesis xix. and elsewhere.

Vs. 31. **He which shall be upon the housetop.**—The Saviour gives the counsel to immediate flight, with the abandonment, in case of need, of all that is possessed on earth. It is true, He has not in this connection, as in Matt. xxiv. 17, as yet spoken of the destruction of Jerusalem; but the admonition is in this place not on that account by any means incongruous, as De Wette precipitately asserts. Nor have we, with Meyer, to understand a flight for deliverance to the coming Messiah. This last explanation has visibly arisen from perplexity, and is only seemingly favored by the example of Lot's wife. We may here, in general, understand a city taken by invading enemies, from which it is only possible to save one's life, if he hurries away at the instant, without, at the danger of life, dragging anything with him. The same is the case with him who is fallen upon in the field, which is here conceived quite as generally as the city. The main thought is evidently this: that no temporal possession ought to engage the interest when eternal good must be won at any price. Comp. Matt. xvi. 25. [I do not see how any one can regard vss. 31–37 as anything else than a fragment of our Saviour's subsequent prediction of the destruction of Jerusalem. It fits perfectly into that, while it is impossible to see any immediate applicableness here. It is doubtless inserted here as an element of the eschatological discourse of our Lord, and so far connected with the preceding context.—C. C. S.]

Vs. 32. **Remember Lot's wife.**—It would be inferring too much from this remark of our Lord to wish to conclude from it that He assumes that Lot's wife was, on account of her momentary transgression, given over to endless misery. Much more temperately has Luther judged concerning it: "For her disobedience' sake, Lot's wife must bear a temporal punishment, but her soul is saved. 1 Cor. v. 5." As to the rest, in what her trespass consisted is sufficiently well known from Genesis xix. 26. Through her unlawful looking back, she has become the type of that earthly-mindedness and self-seeking which wishes to preserve the lesser at any cost, and thereby loses the greater. It is worthy of note, that in the book of the Wisdom of Solomon, also, chap. x. 7, the same warning image is held up before us, so that this passage in the Gospel is one of the very few in which we may, perhaps, find an indirect allusion to one of the Apocryphal books. Respecting the exact manner of the death of Lot's wife, and the legend concerning the pillar of salt, see the Commentaries on Genesis xix., especially the remarks of T. W. I. SCHROEDER, *Das erste Buch Mosis ausgelegt*, Berlin, 1844, p. 373.

Vs. 33. **Whosoever shall seek to save his life.**—*See* on chap. ix. 24, and comp. Matt. x. 39; John xii. 25.—Ζωογονήσει, preserve alive, as in Acts vii. 19, namely, in the last decisive moment at the Parusia. The Saviour's discourse here goes yet deeper, inasmuch as He here speaks not merely, as before, vss. 26–30, of the danger which threatens those entirely careless, but also of that which threatens such disciples as, like Lot's wife, had indeed made the first step towards escaping the future destruction, but, alas! afterwards remained standing midway in the way of salvation.

Vs. 34. **I tell you.**—Comp. on Matt. xxiv. 40 *seq.* The Saviour strengthens His admonition still more by allusion to the definitive terrible *division*, which will coincide with the great *decision*. At His coming, that is torn asunder which outwardly, as well as inwardly, appeared to be as closely as possible joined together. Two examples thereof Luke gives, while the third, vs. 36, appears to be transferred from Matt. xxiv. 40. *See* notes on the text. The first is taken from companionship at night; the other from companionship by day. Ταύτῃ τῇ νυκτί is not in the sense of *tempore illo calamitoso* (Grotius, Kuinoel), but is a simple designation of the time which one is wont to spend upon his bed, perhaps with the secondary thought of the uncertainty of the Parusia, which comes as a thief in the night, Matt. xxiv. 41. At the beginning of the second example, vs. 35, we might, on the other hand, supply: ταύτῃ τῇ ἡμέρᾳ. Unexpectedly does the Parusia come; whether by day or by night is all one; dissimilar, only outwardly united things are then forever severed. By the κλίνη μία we have not necessarily to understand conjugal companionship—at all events both pronouns are masculine—but every connection which is intimate enough to entitle to a common bed, as was the case in the following example with the common labor by day. On the other hand, there appear in the other example two women (μία, ἑτέρα), who, according to the Oriental custom, are grinding upon the hand-mill there in use, Exodus xi. 5, and are, therefore, occupied with one and the same appointed work. No matter now whether the Parusia come by day or by night, one of the two is taken away, the other left;—in which, of course, it is understood that our Lord is not thereby giving any fixed rule. Two may be on one bed and both taken; two, on the other hand, may be laboring in one field and both be left; but it may be that even the most intimate companionship will be interrupted by the Parusia. The one is taken, comp. John xii. 26; xiv. 3, the other surrendered, without respect of persons, to the certain catastrophe.

Vs. 36. **Where, Lord?**—Not an expression of terror (*quomodo,* Kuinoel), but a definite inquiry after the *locality* in which all this should take place; even as the Pharisees, vs. 20, had inquired definitely after the *time* of the revelation of the kingdom of God. Although now the Saviour, in this connection, according to Luke, has not been speaking particularly of the destruction of Jerusalem, it seems, however, as if the disciples had a presentiment that the predicted scenes of terror might, perhaps, come to pass even in their neighborhood, in the Holy Land, and wished now that the Saviour would compose their fears about this. He, however, gives them neither an evasive nor an entirely definite answer; but only recites a proverb, respecting which, comp. on Matt. xxiv. 28.—Τὸ σῶμα, in Matt. τὸ πτῶμα, to be understood especially of the animal body, which as soon as it lies lifeless becomes the welcome spoil of birds of prey. If one does not incline to see here any allusion to the Roman eagles which swept down upon the unhappy Jerusalem, as upon their prey, we can then, in general, paraphrase this answer thus (Stier): "Everything in its time and order, according to what belongs to it! Ask not with importunate curiosity after Where, How, or When, but behold: Where the corruption of death is, there must the eagles come! When it has become night, then will the lightning bring an awful light! Only do you take care to be found as the living and as children of the light!" In no case have we occasion, with De Wette, to complain that the enigmatical proverb has, by the redaction of Luke, lost in perspicuity.

DOCTRINAL AND ETHICAL.

1. The answer of our Lord to the question of the Pharisees, when the kingdom of God shall come, is of the utmost moment for controverting all grossly sensuous chiliastic expectations and notions which in the course of the ages have ever and anon come up in the bosom of the Christian church. The longing of the Pharisees to be able to state: *Lo here, lo there,* has remained alive in the hearts of thousands who bear the Saviour's name. It is the natural consequence of earthly-mindedness and pride, which even in the regenerate is indeed kept down, but not yet eradicated. From such eyes the secret power and the spiritual form of the kingdom of God is even to-day hidden. It is easier, moreover, to comprehend in their full force the parable of the Treasure and that of the Pearl, than that of the Mustard-Seed and that of the Leaven. Very often, also, there is found, even in Christians, the craving for heathen display of signs, which at bottom bears witness, not to a strong, but to nothing else than a weak, faith. Over against this coarser or more refined Chiliasm, there stands a more or less one-sided Spiritualism, which, perhaps, has found acceptance in yet more extended circles. Not seldom has the saying, that the kingdom of God comes οὐ μετὰ παρατηρήσεως, been misused and exaggerated, in the sense that this kingdom will never on earth display itself in a glorious form worthy of itself. No; the kingdom of God comes not with observation, but when it has once come, we shall nevertheless be well able to say: Lo here! For here, too, holds good Oetinger's word: "Corporeality is the end of God's ways." Chiliasm, however, for the most part, in view of the body, overlooks the spirit; Spiritualism, in view of the spirit, the body; both forget that man in this sphere also may not arbitrarily sunder what according to God's ordinance is meant to be forever most intimately united. To grossly sensual Chiliasts we are to hold up the utterance: "The kingdom of God is already in the midst of us," while one-sided Spiritualists must be reminded of the Saviour's declaration to His disciples: "For as the lightning, &c.—so shall also the Son of man be in His day." The kingdom of God comes with gentle, scarcely noticeable step, but not to remain invisible.

2. A threefold coming of the kingdom of God is to be distinguished: First, the Saviour appeared in humility, in an humble servant's form; after that He comes in the Spirit invisible, but with heightened power; finally, in majesty and glory in the clouds of heaven. The first phase endured thirty-three years, the second has endured already more than eighteen centuries, and the last makes of the present economy a decisive end. The first period was concluded by the Passion and Death of our Lord; the second will not end without a sorrowful Passion of His dearly-purchased church; the last reveals the perfect glory which shall come in the place of suffering and striving, for the Head as for the members.

3. It is a great error and gives occasion to many misunderstandings, when that which our Lord here says of the kingdom of God is applied without any limitation to the Christian church. So long as the kingdom of God is not fully come, it becomes no one to say decisively and exclusively: "Lo here! or, lo there!" By this, however, it is by no means intended that there are no definite signs by which the true Church of the Saviour can be known as such, and distinguished from false, apostate churches. Word and sacraments remain the tokens of the true outwardly visible Church, to which every believer must attach himself; and therefore the Evangelical Church of our days is to strive not less against a one-sided Clericalism than against a sickly Darbism, which does not allow the church constitution established by the Saviour and His apostles to assert its rights.

4. The Donatistic striving which has revealed itself in the course of the centuries in all manner of forms among believers, is here condemned by our Lord in its inmost essence. Men are bent upon,

making even now an external distinction upon one bed, upon one field, at one mill, between believers and unbelievers; the Saviour, on the other hand, will not have the external union of that which is dissimilar, if it already exists, destroyed by force until He Himself appear with His fan in His hand. Separatism is an anticipation of the great day of decision.

5. There is a heaven-wide distinction between the eschatological expectations which the friends of modern liberalism cherish, and those which are called forth by this teaching of our Lord. It is commonly supposed that in the proportion in which the principles of humanitarianism, culture, free thought, and the like, are more and more widely diffused, the world will become ever increasingly wiser, better, and happier. The Saviour here opens to us a very different view of the times immediately before the end. Of culture and false semblance of external secular enlightenment, there will then undoubtedly be as little lack as in the days of Noah and Lot. But instead now of the great mass becoming continually better and more earnest, we have to expect, on the other hand, according to the Saviour's words, a time of carelessness, hardening, and carnal security, just like that which preceded the destruction of the ancient world and the ruin of Sodom. These are the perilous times in the last days, of which Paul also speaks, 2 Tim. iii. 1; and all which in the Apocalypse is prophesied of the great apostasy of the last period of the world, is only a wider expansion of the theme here given.

6. The Saviour emphatically teaches us how the human race remains at all times ever alike in the midst of continually growing judgments of God. The contemporaries of Noah and of Lot, the Antichrist who shall arise before the last Parusia, are men of one sort. On these grounds the here-mentioned earlier judgments may also be regarded as types and symbols of the yet following ones, and of the last of all. Because in the neighborhood of Noah and of Lot carelessness had reached the highest grade, these generations are especially fitted to be the type of the last generation which shall see the coming of the Lord. No wonder, therefore, that in the epistles of Peter and Jude the history of the flood and of the destruction of Sodom have attributed to them so great a significance and so high a value. See 1 Peter iii. 19–21; 2 Peter ii. 5–9; Jude 7.

7. There exists a sublime parallelism in the way in which the Saviour, vss. 26–29, has described the days of Noah and Lot. This uniformity and this rhythm of the words acquires, however, a higher significance if we find therein an exact expression of the wonderful agreement which exists between men and things in earlier and later times. The careless worldly life reveals itself from century to century, every time in the same stereotyped phases and forms. But just as unexpected as were the flood and fiery rain, will also the last coming of the Lord be—a day which begins like other days, and finds the one on his bed, another in the field, and a third at the mill; but it will not end like other days.

HOMILETICAL AND PRACTICAL.

The permitted and the unpermitted longing after the revelation of the kingdom of God.—Agreement and difference between the inquiry of the Pharisees, Luke xvii. 20, and that of the disciples, Acts i. 6.— The tokens of the coming of the kingdom of God are: 1. Not so palpable; 2. not so dubious; 3. not so restricted, as human short-sightedness imagines: *a*. not with observation; *b*. it is in the midst of you: *c*. and one shall not say it is (exclusively) here or there.—The still and hidden coming of the kingdom of God in hearts and in the world: 1. The Pharisees forget it; 2. it is explicable from the nature of the kingdom of God; 3. it is confirmed by history; 4. it is assured for the future.—The kingdom of God is in the midst of you: 1. What an inestimable matter of thanksgiving; 2. what a heavy accountability.—The kingdom of God in the midst of us avails us not, so long as it is not come into our heart.—The presages of the last coming of the Lord: 1. Painful longing (vs. 22); 2. dangerous misleading (vss. 23–25); 3. growing carelessness (vss. 26–30).—When the Saviour is missed with sorrow and expected with longing desire, He no longer makes long delay.—Even the best disciple of the Saviour is exposed to the danger of being misled by false seeming.—The *vox populi* in the kingdom of God by no means the *vox Dei*.—The lightning flash which illumines the dark heavens, the image of the appearance of the Son of Man, who makes an end of the dark night of the world.—The Divine necessity of the suffering which precedes the glorifying of the Saviour.—The history of the past a prophecy of the yet hidden future.— What is it that has come to pass? Even that that shall come to pass hereafter, Eccles. i. 9.—The days of Noah an image of the days of the Son of Man. In both we see: 1. A decisive judgment pronounced; 2. a long delay occurring; 3. a careless unconcern maintained; 4. a righteous retribution descending; 5. a sure refuge open.—The unaltered character of careless indifference: 1. In the days of Lot; 2. at the destruction of Jerusalem; 3. at the last coming of our Lord.—Careless unconcern in view of threatening judgment: 1. An ancient evil; 2. a dangerous evil; 3. a curable evil.—The day of the Son of Man a day of terror and glory.—The warranted and the deplorable impulse of self-preservation.—Lot's wife a monument of warning for earthly-minded disciples of the Lord; we see her: 1. Graciously spared; 2. at the beginning delivered; 3. presumptuously disobedient; 4. wretchedly perishing.—Whoever will arrive in Zoar must no longer look back towards Sodom.—No earthly gain can make good harm to the soul.—The unexpected separation of that which was externally united, on its: 1. Terrible; 2. beneficent; 3. powerfully awakening and comforting, side.—True fellowship is that which outlives the last day.—The coming of the Lord the end of: 1. Slothful rest; 2. slavish labor; 3. constrained companionship.—Where the carcass is, thither do the eagles gather: a proverb confirmed in the history: 1. Of the heathen; 2. of the Jewish; 3. of the Christian, world.

STARKE: — CANSTEIN: — Whoever conceives Christ's kingdom as fleshly and earthly, will never learn to know it, much less attain thereto.—*Nova Bibl. Tub.*:—Whoever seeks the kingdom of God without himself, loses it within himself.—HEDINGER: —Christ's comfort, presence, and light often hide themselves in temptation.—QUESNEL:—Let us not follow that which men tell us, but that which Jesus Christ first told us in the Scriptures and confirmed by miracles.—What takes place little by little through faith will take place in one instant when Jesus Christ shall show Himself visibly to all men to judge the world. Now is the day of man, then will it be the day of God.—CANSTEIN:—The securer the world, the nearer Jesus Christ with His kingdom, 1 Thess. v. 3.—BRENTIUS:—It is an evil plague that men, when God's judgments break in, become the worse the longer they threaten; this should of right bring us to consideration.—Like sins occasion like punishments, God in His nature unchangeable.— The end of a thing is better than the beginning; yet let us seek to persevere in the way that we have begun even to the end, that we may not tempt God, Rev. iii. 5.—When people are diverse, so is also the end of the world diverse.—When proverbs have a good Biblical sense, and express a matter briefly, we may very profitably and becomingly avail ourselves of them.

HEUBNER:—The fleshly man esteems all according to the outward pomp and glitter.—It is suspicious for a preacher to create a *furore*, which is often only a fire of straw.—The salvation of the church comes not through intervention of the power of the state, but from within.—KNAPP:—Live thyself continually deeper and more intimately into the kingdom of God. —CHR. PALMER:—How differently our Lord answers the question, When does the kingdom of God appear? in the case of different questioners: *a.* to those who as yet knew nothing thereof He says, It is already here; *b.* those who already bear it in their hearts He points to the future, for which they should watch, wait, and hold themselves ready.—Whereby we may try ourselves as to whether our hope in the coming of the kingdom of God is not a delusive one. —NEANDER:—The kingdom of God cometh not with observation.

---

3. The Judge and the Widow (CH. XVIII. 1-8).

1 And he spake a parable unto them *to this end*, that men [they[1]] ought always to
2 pray, and not to faint [become discouraged]; Saying, There was in a [certain] city a
3 [certain] judge, which feared not God, neither regarded man: And there was a widow
4 in that city; and she came unto him, saying, Avenge me of mine adversary. And he would not for a while: but afterward he said within himself, Though I fear not God,
5 nor regard man; Yet because this widow troubleth me, I will avenge her, lest by her
6 continual coming [coming forever, εἰς τέλος] she weary [stun, or, distract] me. And
7 the Lord said, Hear what the unjust judge saith. And shall not God avenge his own
8 elect, which cry day and night unto him, though he bear long with them? I tell you that he will avenge them speedily. Nevertheless, when the Son of man cometh, shall he [indeed, ἄρα] find faith on the earth?

[1] Vs. 1.—Αὐτούς. See LACHMANN and TISCHENDORF, ad locum.

EXEGETICAL AND CRITICAL.

Vs. 1. And He spake.—Although it is possible that between this and the immediately preceding discourse of the Saviour some intervening discourses were delivered (Olshausen, Schleiermacher), yet this hypothesis is not indispensably necessary, as the connection of the parable of the Unjust Judge with the foregoing discourse about the Parusia, strikes the eye at once. The Saviour had already long before announced that heavy times were coming, in which conflicts and oppression would by no means be wanting to His people; what could He now do better than to admonish them to persevering prayer, that, at last, the long-sighed-for ἐκδίκησις, vs. 7, might become their happy lot? The parable, according to this, is principally addressed to His disciples (αὐτούς, comp. ch. xvii. 22), and the **not becoming discouraged** against which a warning is here given with so much earnestness, is not the neglect of the Christian vocation generally, but especially of prayer, as sufficiently appears from the example of the Widow.

Vs. 2. A certain judge.—According to Deut. xvi. 18, Israel must have in all the gates of the city judges, who in cases that occurred had to deliver sentence, and were under obligation to administer justice, without respect of persons. *See* Exodus xxiii. 6-9; Lev. xix. 15. In the days of our Lord, also, such municipal tribunals existed, Matt. v. 21-22; and it is not impossible that the narrative before us was taken from life. The character of the judge here delineated is of such a kind that he allows himself, with perfect recklessness, to be controlled by the most shameless selfishness. Of the two impulses which often restrain men from evil—the fear of God and respect to men—neither one is able to move him to strict righteousness. He is destitute of the character of genuine Old Testament piety, φόβος τ. Θεοῦ, as well as of respect for the judgment of others. Thus does he stand even *below* the ungodly, who, at least, still have the latter, and what is the worst, he is not even ashamed of this his reckless temper in his soliloquizing.

Vs. 3. Avenge me.—The widow desires not only that he will at last make an end of her tedious suit (Schleiermacher), but that he will deliver her forever from the hand of a mighty adversary, who is obstinately persecuting the helpless woman. Although now every soul that finds itself in similar distress may, in a certain sense, be compared to such a woman, yet the connection of the discourse gives us occasion to find here in particular an intimation of the *Church* of the Lord, which before His παρουσία is in apparent defencelessness exposed to the obstinately assailing might of the world and sin, while it a thousand times appears as if she called on God entirely in vain for deliverance and victory.

Vs. 4. A while, ἐπὶ χρόνον, *aliquamdiu*, Erasmus. Indefinite indication of the comparatively long time during which all entreaty might appear in vain.—In the days of the great tribulations, Matt. xxiv. 21, 22. They must be spent in prayer, these days, but reach an end as surely as the widow's time of trial.

CHAP. XVIII. 1-8.   271

The justice which the Unjust Judge executes by constraint, the Righteous One bestows at its due time willingly.

Vs. 5. **Yet because.**—Comp. chap. xi. 8. The judge gives ear to the widow, because her endless complaining becomes unendurable to him. How greatly the beauty of the parable is heightened by the fact that he communicates his resolution in the form of a soliloquy, strikes the eye at once. The tragical fortune of the widow is related in dramatic form.—Εἰς τέλος, not *tandem* but *incessantly*, LXX = לָנֶצַח,—ὑπωπιάζειν, properly to beat one black and blue under the eyes, but then also proverbial for the designation of any possible torment, comp. 1 Cor. ix. 27. According to Meyer, the judge is to be understood as having really become afraid, or at least having scoffingly presented the case to himself that the woman might become desperate, and undertake to make an attack upon him and strike him in the face. Possible, undoubtedly; but surely this was no feature that would have suited well to the image of a defenceless and supplicating widow, since she in this way would have been transformed into a fury. As to the rest, it appears from the whole monologue that it is only selfishness that determines the judge now to yield, as it had before impelled him to unrighteousness. The Vulgate, *Ne sugillet me.* Luther's marginal gloss: "That she may not plague and torture me, as they say of impetuous and wanton people : How much the man plagues me." Well expressed is the proverbial character of the style of speaking in the Dutch translation : *Opdat zy niet kome en my het hoofd breke.* [That she may not come and break my head for me.]

Vs. 6. **Hear what.**—In surprising wise the Saviour holds the man of power to the word which He has Himself put in his mouth. Here, also, rising from the humanly imperfect to the Divinely perfect as before, ch. xi. 5 ; xvi. 8 ; in which, of course, we have to take careful note of the *tertium comparationis.* The force of the antithesis in the question : **and shall not God,** &c., may be better felt than rendered in a paraphrase. As to the rest, here also the Elect are not conceived so much as individuals, but rather as a collective body, although, of course, what is here said is applicable also to every individual in his measure.

Vs. 7. **Though He bear long with them,** καὶ μακροθυμεῖ ἐπ' αὐτοῖς.—In the reading preferred by us it is not necessary to take καί in the sense of καίπερ, *quamvis*, comp. Acts vii. 5 ; Heb. iii. 9, and elsewhere. With μακροθυμεῖ it is not the idea of *forbearance* in general, but *delaying* of help that is to be adhered to, and the second half of the question, vs. 7, is, with Meyer, therefore, to be paraphrased : "and is it His way in reference to them to delay His help ?" It appears from this that the first member of the question requires an affirmative, the second, on the other hand, a negative, answer; and that the here-designated μακροθυμία stands directly in contrast with the ἐκδίκ. ποιεῖν ἐν τάχει which, vs. 8, is promised in the most certain manner. 'Επί designates the ἐκλεκτοί as objects of a delay, in respect to which, according to the Saviour's word, it cannot be thought that it should endure endlessly. He gives here, therefore, not the assurance that God is forbearing towards His own, which here would not be at all in place, nor yet that He for their sake postpones the punishment of His enemies, which is indeed taught in other places, but not here ; but He denies that God can to the last withhold a help which His elect so ardently entreat from Him.

Vs. 8. **I tell you.**—The fixed assurance of the opposite of the negative μακροθ. ἐπ' αὐτοῖς. God is so far from being more inexorable than the Unjust Judge, that, on the contrary, He will hasten, after shorter or longer delay, to assure the victory to the cause of right. The ἐκδίκησις runs here parallel with the Parusia of our Lord, at which His enemies are most deeply humbled. While this παρουσία was in the last chapter represented as the terror of the careless, it is here described as the deliverance of the oppressed, and as the hearing of the prayers which have day and night ascended from the hearts of the elect towards heaven.

Nevertheless, when the Son of Man cometh.—After the Saviour has assured His own that God will in no case leave their complaints unheard, He emphatically proposes to them the question, whether they would indeed exhibit so much patience and perseverance in prayer as the Widow had displayed, and shows thereby that He, at least in relation to some of them, doubts thereof. There is not the least ground to understand here any other than the last coming of the Son of Man, which, it is true, presupposes an uninterrupted, continually ascending climax of revelations of His glory. The Saviour transports Himself in spirit to the time of the συντέλεια τοῦ αἰῶνος, which shall be preceded by the last conflict and the deepest tribulation of His church, and which His disciples on earth are to endure in faith, prayer, patient waiting. Will their faith, even after the long time of trial, be yet great and persevering enough to be able to reckon on such a deliverance as this widow obtained? ⁷Ἄρα contains a certain intimation of doubt, which must stimulate His own so much the more strongly to remain, along with their praying, watchful also.—Τὴν πίστιν designates, not saving faith in general, which recognizes Jesus as the Messiah (Meyer), nor yet the faithfulness of the disciples, which elsewhere, ch. xii. 35-48, is demanded of them (De Wette); but faith in God as a Righteous Judge, which alone enables to so persevering prayer, and which in His disciples is most intimately connected with personal faith on the Saviour, comp. John xiv. 1. Plainly our Lord presupposes that this faith will have to sustain a severe conflict, on account of the delay of the hearing of prayer and the delay of the Parusia. There is, however, no need whatever on this account to assume (De Wette), that the present redaction of this parable belongs to a later period, comp. 2 Peter iii. 3. In other places also it gleams, not obscurely, through the words of the Saviour, that the παρουσία will not come so quickly as some suppose, comp. Matt. xxv. 5, 19.

DOCTRINAL AND ETHICAL.

1. In the doctrine of Christian prayer, the parable of the Unjust Judge, preserved to us by Luke alone, may with right be named a *locus classicus.* In parabolic form the promise is here repeated which in John, ch. xiv.—xvi., is given without a parable. It is, however, to be observed, in addition, that "to pray ever" is not exactly "to pray without ceasing," of which there is mention, 1 Thess. v. 17. By the latter, the uninterrupted living and breathing of the soul in communion with God is designated ; here, on the other hand, the unwearied praying and calling for the same

thing is meant, as to which one has attained the persuasion that it coincides with God's will. Paul speaks of the prevailing frame of mind of the believer; the Saviour, on the other hand, of the conflict of prayer of the distressed and suffering disciple.

2. In a striking way is the relation of the Church militant to the hostile world placed before our eyes in the image of the Widow.—"Here we see the Church, which in her nature and her destiny is the bride of Christ, and waits for His festal appearance, in the form of a widow. Matters have the look as if her betrothed Spouse were dead at a distance. Meanwhile, she lives in a city, where she is continually oppressed by a grievous adversary, the Prince of this world. But since she continually calls on God for help, it may, in a weak hour, appear to her as if He had become the Unjust Judge over her—as if He were dealing entirely without Divine righteousness, and without love to man. But she perseveres in prayer for His redeeming coming. And although this is long delayed, because God has a celestially broad mind and view, and accordingly trains His children for Himself to the great spiritual life of eternity, yet it comes at last with surprising quickness." Lange. Only we must guard ourselves against the inclination to find here a definite period in the history of the church militant, as, for instance, Vitringa does, who interpreted this parable of the relation of the Roman Emperors to the Christian church, through whom the church was first oppressed, but afterwards protected. The image has, in a greater or less measure, found its fulfilment in all ages, and will in particular be realized in the yet impending grievous times of which Paul speaks, 2 Tim. iii. 1, and elsewhere.

3. This parable deserves so well its place in the Pauline Gospel of Luke for the reason also that the disciples of the Saviour are here very especially represented as ἐκλεκτοί. As such they are, entirely without their own merits, the objects of the gracious complacency of God, and may even regard their cause as His. Persevering prayer is at once the sign and the pulse of their spiritual life, and all their prayers meet in the ἔρχου, which the Spirit and the Bride unceasingly repeat, looking towards the heavenly Bridegroom. Rev. xxii. 17.

4. Before one extols excessively the righteousness and the love of the natural man, it is well worth the trouble for once carefully to distinguish how much of it, as with the Unjust Judge, is begotten of necessity and selfishness. This is precisely the character of that external good which man accomplishes outside of union with God; namely, that it is entirely accidental, springs from caprice—not from a fixed principle—and remains a fruit of carnal calculation, but not of spontaneous obedience.

HOMILETICAL AND PRACTICAL.

The coming of the Saviour must not only be awaited with watching, but also with praying.—Christian perseverance in prayer: 1. A holy; 2. a difficult; 3. a blessed duty.—Injustice here below is not seldom practised under the form of law, and by those who should administer justice.—The image of the church militant: 1. The Widow, Isaiah liv. 1, 2; 2. the Adversary, 1 Peter v. 8; 3. the Judge, Ps. xliii. 1.—God, a Husband of widows and a Judge of orphans.—From His elect God cannot possibly withhold what an unjust judge grants a complaining widow.—God delays long, but only to make haste at last.—All the prayers of the church militant converge at last in longing for the coming of the Lord.—The Lord comes: 1. In order to humble His enemies; 2. in order to redeem His friends; 3. in order on both to reveal His glory.—How small comparatively will the number of those be whose faith and prayer endures to the end.—The Son of Man will, at His coming, find not only careless enemies, but also faint-hearted disciples.—The long postponed deliverance comes certainly, and at last often unexpectedly besides.—The persevering prayer of faith: 1. A widely comprehensive duty of faith; 2. an indispensable support of faith, vs. 2; 3. a painful conflict of faith, vs. 4 a.; 4. a triumphant might of faith, vs. 4 b.; 5. a rare fruit of faith, vs. 8.

STARKE: QUESNEL:—Prayer is a property of the poor, and sighing the salvation of the wretched.—CANSTEIN:—Power in the world often misleads men, so that they concern themselves neither about God nor man.—Where there is no fear of God, there is also no true respect nor regard for man.—Rulers should, according to God's commandment, take especial care of widows and orphans, Isaiah i. 17; Jer. vii. 6.—Complaints are torments, even in the most righteous cause.—God brings to pass justice and righteousness when it pleases Him, even through an unrighteous judge.—CANSTEIN:—One can draw profit even from the worst examples.—HEDINGER:—Beware of impatience: God does not what we prescribe to Him, but what He finds good for us, 1 John v. 14.—ZEISIUS:—When often before believers' eyes all appears to be lost, help is often nearest at hand, Ps. xii. 6.—HEUBNER:—The question whether prayer is a duty, is as sensible as that whether it is a duty to breathe.—Continuous prayer to God the best help of widows.—The prayer of the elect must at last be heard, for the redemption of the saints is God's eternal will.—Without faith in God's father's heart, prayer is grimace.—Faith is the main thing on which all depends.—LISCO:—Motives for the citizens of the kingdom to persevering in prayer.—ZIMMERMANN:—Persevere in prayer; to that should impel us: 1. The consciousness of our dependence on God; 2. the greatness of our need; 3. the so oft delaying help; 4. the certainty of a final answer.—GEROK:—The course of Christians through the school of prayer: 1. The need which brings before God's door; 2. the faith that knocks at God's door; 3. the patience that waits before God's door; 4. the experience that goes in at God's door.—F. ARNDT:—Why should we persevere in prayer? 1. Grounds in us; 2. grounds in God.

4. The Pharisee and the Publican (Vss. 9-14).

9, 10, 11 And he spake this parable unto certain [men] which trusted in themselves that they were righteous, and despised others: Two men went up into the temple to pray; the one a Pharisee, and the other a publican [taxgatherer]. The Pharisee stood and prayed thus with himself, God, I thank thee, that I am not as other men [the rest of 12 men] *are*, extortioners, unjust, adulterers, or even as this publican [taxgatherer]. I 13 fast twice in the week, I give tithes of all that I possess [acquire]. And the publican [taxgatherer], standing afar off, would not lift up so much as *his* eyes unto heaven, but 14 smote upon his breast, saying, God be merciful to me a [the] sinner. I tell you, this man went down to his house justified *rather* than the other:[1] for every one that exalteth himself shall be abased; and he that humbleth himself shall be exalted.

[1] Vs. 14.—The reading of Elzevir, ἢ ἐκεῖνος, has here no adequate critical authority. That of Tischendorf, ἢ γὰρ ἐκεῖνος, is strongly supported, but gives a scarcely intelligible sense. That of Lachmann, παρ' ἐκεῖνον, which Grotius already defended, and which is favored by D., [Cod. Sin.,] L., Cursives, deserves on internal grounds the preference, at the same time that it must be supposed that by an ancient and quite generally diffused error in copying (γάρ instead of παρ'), the true reading was very soon lost.

EXEGETICAL AND CRITICAL.

Vs. 9. And He spake this parable.—That the parable of the Pharisee and the Publican was delivered on the same occasion as the previous one (Meyer), we do not believe. In this case we should have to conceive the Pharisees, ch. xvii. 20, as yet present; and, moreover, it can scarcely be assumed that our Lord in their presence would have chosen the Pharisee as the chief personage of His parable. It appears, therefore, that some time afterwards, among the wider circle of the auditors of Jesus, an occasion offered itself for contrasting with one another these portraits of haughtiness and humility. Perhaps Luke gives the parable in this connection because it also stands in relation to prayer, while its conclusion constitutes a very proper transition to the immediately following narrative, vss. 15–17. That it, however, was actually uttered during this period in the public life of Jesus, appears to be deducible from the fact that both men are described to us as going up to the temple in order to pray there, which certainly is doubly congruous when we consider that just during this time many caravans of pilgrims to the feast were travelling up towards the temple, and that Jesus Himself was making His last journey to the feast.

To certain men.—Πρός is here not, as in vs. 1, to be understood of the bare intention of the parable (De Wette, Stier, Arndt), but as a designation of the persons who were addressed. Among whom we have to seek these τινές is not stated particularly, any more than in what way they had made their self-righteous temper manifest. Pharisees proper they certainly were not, but we know how much our Saviour had to warn even His disciples against the Pharisaic leaven, and how self-righteousness was not only the ruling evil of the Jews of His time, but is also even yet the common evil of every natural man. We need not even assume (Stier) that these proud μαθηταί expressed themselves in some such way as this before the previous parable: "Pray? Oh, that we can do already better than others; nor are we lacking in faith," and the like. We may, however, reasonably conceive that the Saviour read this proud imagination in their hearts, or that He had already remarked in actual life a similar contrast to that which He here places before their eyes. As to the rest, Luke describes the disposition which the Saviour here attacks more precisely than the here-named persons.—

In themselves, ἐφ' ἑαυτοῖς, they believed that they had the righteousness required by the law, comp. Phil. iii. 4; 2 Cor. i. 9. Of others they believed exactly the opposite.

Vs. 10. Two men.—Here also two persons are types of two different essential tendencies. Never does our Lord represent any virtue or vice in the abstract, but always in the concrete, as it shows itself in reality. Ἀναβαίνειν, a literally exact expression for the visiting of the more elevated temple-mountain.—**To pray.**—The main element and compendium of the whole public worship of God. Comp. Isaiah lvi. 7.

Vs. 11. Stood.—Σταθείς can either be taken by itself or be connected with the remark following, πρὸς ἑαυτόν in the sense of *stabat seorsim* (Grotius, Paulus). It would then indicate that he chose a position entirely apart, in order not to be Levitically defiled by the too great nearness of men whom he regarded as unclean. It is, however, more simple to connect the words πρὸς ἑαυτ. with the immediately following ταῦτα προσηύχετο (Lisco, Meyer). The expression εἰπεῖν πρὸς ἑαυτ. is usual. *See* ch. xx. 5, 14. Comp. ch. xii. 17; Luke iii. 15; Mark xi. 31; xii. 7, &c. The simple σταθείς already contains a genuinely graphic touch, which vividly brings out the confident feeling of the Pharisee, and especially by the contrast with the μακρόθεν ἑστώς, vs. 13.

Prayed thus with himself.—Yet so loud that others also hear him. His praying is a thanking, his thanking a boasting, not of God but alone of himself. In unbounded presumption he contrasts himself not only with many or with the most, but with the whole body of other men, οἱ λοιποὶ τῶν ἀνθρώπων. "*Duas classes Pharisæus facit, in alteram conjicit totum genus humanum, altera, melior, ipse sibi solus esse videtur.*" Bengel. Yet soon he begins to distinguish the great mass of sinners into particular groups. There are the ἄδικοι in the more restricted sense, the ἅρπαγες, like a Zacchæus, for instance, the μοιχοί, not in the Old Testament scriptural sense, but in the literal sense of the word, and finally the man who stands behind him as the incarnation of all possible moral faults, οὗτος ὁ τελώνης, whom he had probably seen entering also into the temple, but of whom he knows beforehand that his prayer cannot possibly be acceptable to God. Thus does he vaunt his own *person* in order now in one breath to pass over to the heralding of his good *works*.

Vs. 12. I fast twice in the week.—The law

(Lev. xvi. 29–31; Num. xxix. 7) had only prescribed an annual fast-day; but he in addition keeps twice a week a private fast day, according to the custom of that time, Monday and Thursday. Here also, as in Mark xvi. 9, τοῦ σαββ. is the designation of the week, which was concluded with the Sabbath.—**I give tithes of all.**—Therefore much more even than was demanded in the law, according to which only the fruits of the field and of the cattle were tithed (Lev. xxvii. 30; Num. xviii. 21; Deut. xiv. 22). "Ὅσα κτῶμαι, not "what I possess," which would have to be κέκτημαι, but "what I take in," "what comes in to me." He is not speaking of fixed property in itself, but of the natural profits of that for which he has to thank his own insight and keenness, as to which he therefore from his point of view might easily believe that he could properly keep it for himself. Thus do his thanks in a certain manner become an intimation that God really has to thank him for all which he has the goodness to give up of his legitimate property, and as his soliloquy ends with this enumeration, we may conceive the Pharisee as now continuing in silence to please himself with the thought of the great and good things which he has done or is still doing and will do in the future.

Vs. 13. **The tax-gatherer.**—In everything the direct opposite of the proud fool, whose image has inspired almost even more compassion than disgust. The unfeigned humility of the tax-gatherer reveals itself first in the standing-place which he chooses.—**Standing afar off,** μακρόθεν, not in the court of the Gentiles, 1 Kings viii. 41, 42 (Starke), for he is a Jew; not at a distance from the Pharisee (Meyer), for we do not read that he had observed the latter, as on the other hand the latter had noticed him, but far from the sanctuary, which the Pharisee, σταθείς, has without doubt approached as nearly as possible, while on the other hand the publican's courage to do this vanished even as he first ascended towards the temple-mountain. In the second place, his demeanor indicates his humility. It was usually the custom to pray with uplifted hands, 1 Tim. ii. 8, and with look turned towards heaven, Ps. cxxiii. 1, 2; but he is as far from venturing on the one as on the other, comp. Ezra ix. 6, because he in the temple actually thinks of God and His spiritual holiness. Finally, his humility expresses itself in his words, ὁ Θεός, κ.τ.λ. Certainly he is far from comparing himself with the Pharisee or with other men; he sees only himself in the clear mirror of the law, and feels that he has the worst to fear if God will enter with him into judgment. It is possible, undoubtedly (Stier), that we have here to understand an impulse of *first* repentance, if we only, above all, do not forget that the publican's prayer continually repeats itself out of the depth of the continually renewed contrition of the publican's heart. It is right to lay emphasis on the τῷ ἁμαρτωλῷ. He accounts himself a sinner, κατ' ἐξοχήν, as Paul names himself, 1 Tim. i. 15, the chief of sinners, and all for which he prays is comprehended in the single word "Grace." It is entirely unnecessary to press the word ἱλάσκεσθαι in such a way as to see intimated in it the dogmatic conception of atonement. *See* STIER, *ad loc.*

Vs. 14. **I tell you.**—In view of the high importance of the contrast, the Saviour does not once leave His hearers to judge respecting the two suppliants, but Himself passes the irrevocable judgment, in which it is silently presupposed that no suppliant can become participant of a higher prerogative than to go down again from the temple δεδικαιωμένος.

Therefore, in the eyes of our Lord also, δικαίωσις is the summary of all good which the praying sinner can entreat of the holy God. The question only is, Who has good ground to hope for this privilege, he who prays like the Pharisee or he who prays like the publican? The Saviour expresses Himself, as is often the case, more mildly than abstract logical necessity requires. Although He could, considering the case in itself, have well said that the Pharisee did not go down justified at all, He, however, contents Himself with placing the benefit of the publican far above that of the Pharisee. Παρ' ἐκεῖνον, *see* notes on the text; comp. Luke xv. 7; Matt. xxi. 31. The translation of the reading ἢ ἐκεῖνος in the sense of a question, "Or did he perchance, the Pharisee, go home justified?" appears to us even of itself hard, and, besides that, by no means to be recommended by the immediately following ὅτι. It is, however, at all events, arbitrary from the forbearing judgment which here the Saviour passes upon the Pharisee, to draw the conclusion (Stier) that the consciousness of the possession of justification may gradually begin to give way again, if a δεδικαιωμένος begins again secretly to trust in his righteousness.

For every one that exalteth himself.—*See* Luke xiv. 11. The repetition of such a maxim will cause us the less surprise if we consider that it expresses the unalterable fundamental law of the kingdom of heaven, according to which all men are judged, and at the same time gives the deepest ground why the justification of the Pharisee and the rejection of the publican were each entirely impossible.

DOCTRINAL AND ETHICAL.

1. The two parables of the Judge and the Widow, and the Pharisee and the Publican, although they perhaps were not delivered immediately after one another, constitute, however, together a complete whole. Both have reference to prayer, yet so that in the first, believing perseverance before, in the second, humble approach to, the throne of grace, is commended. In order to end like the Widow, one must have begun like the Publican, and in order to act as recklessly of conscience as the Judge, one must have the heart of a Pharisee in his bosom. Comp. ch. xx. 47.

2. The parable of the Pharisee and the Publican shows a remarkable coincidence with that of the Prodigal Son and his brother—the same contrast of unrighteousness and self-righteousness, of humility and pride, in the one as in the other. As there the two sons represent not only the Pharisees and the publicans, but essentially all mankind, so here the two suppliants give us to recognize the fundamental and chief distinction in the relation of man to God. Every natural man is more or less like the Pharisee; whoever learns to know himself as a sinner is, on the other hand, like the Publican. Here, however, it is by no means denied that in the microcosm of a human heart often something of the Pharisee may be found along with the character of the Publican, even though we ourselves do not take note of it. The question, however, remains simply this, Which disposition in our hearts is the ruling one? According to this God will judge us.

3. As in the previous parable the Pauline idea of ἐκλογή, so in this that of δικαίωσις, comes distinctly into the foreground. "*Hic locus perspicue docet, quid proprie sit justificari, nempe stare coram*

Deo, ac si justi essemus ; neque enim publicanus ideo justus dicitur, quod novam qualitatem sibi repente adquisierit, sed quia inducto reatu et abolitis peccatis gratiam adeptus est, unde sequitur, justificationem in peccatorum remissione esse positam." Calvin. It is, however, of course, understood that in this definition the idea of the forgiveness of sins must be interpreted not only negatively, as acquittal from the deserved punishment, but also positively, as reinstatement in the forfeited favor of God, including all the blessed consequences connected therewith.

4. The Epistle to the Romans is the consistent development of the cardinal evangelical idea which is laid down in this parable, and the Reformation is the triumph of the publican's humility over the Pharisaic self-righteousness, which in the Pelagianism of the Roman Catholic Church had acquired the character of a formal system.

5. This parable is important also as a new proof how strongly and continually the Saviour, in all manner of forms, continued that conflict with the Pharisaical principle which He had already begun in the Sermon on the Mount, and which He was about to crown with an eightfold Woe, Matt. xxiii. Pharisaism and Christianity stand not only relatively but diametrically opposed. It is worthy of remark, however, that the Saviour views this instruction as necessary, not only for Pharisees but also for His disciples.

6. The prayer of the Publican is a short compendium of Theology, Hamartology, Soteriology, and a striking proof that true repentance and living faith are absolutely inseparable from one another. In another form we find here the same temper of mind as in the Prodigal Son, ch. xv. 18. It cannot surprise us that this utterance has become for so many a motto in life and death. It was (to pass over other instances) the answer of the famous Hugo Grotius, when he lay dying at Rostock, and an unknown minister of the gospel referred him to this parable: This publican am I !

HOMILETICAL AND PRACTICAL.

The continual danger of the disciples of the Saviour, of being defiled by the Pharisaical leaven.—Pride and contempt of others are commonly most intimately united with one another.—*Duo, cum faciunt idem, non est idem.*—A man sees what is before his eyes, but the Lord looks on the heart, 1 Sam. xvi. 7.—Pride and humility before God: 1. The diversity of their nature, vss. 10–13 ; 2. the diversity of their destinies, vs. 14.—How one may sin even with his humility.—Many a virtue which is great in men's eyes is damnable before God.—The Pharisee and the Publican : 1. The one so gives thanks that he forgets prayer ; the other so prays that he can afterwards give thanks ; 2. the one compares himself with other men ; the other considers himself in the mirror of the law ; 3. the one recounts his virtues ; the other cannot reckon up his sins ; 4. the one keeps with all his virtues his evil conscience at the bottom ; the other receives with all his sins the full assurance of justification.—The fasting which God chooses, and the fasting of the holiness of works.—The Miserere of the soul which precedes the Hallelujah of redemption.—The publican's heart, the publican's prayer, the publican's lot.—One may give the tenth, yea, all his goods, to God, and yet withhold from Him his heart, that is, all.—The publican's prayer: 1. A prayer as comprehensive as rare ; 2. a prayer as fitting as indispensable ; 3. a prayer as rich in sorrow as in blessing.—Happy he whose transgressions are forgiven, &c., Ps. xxxii. 1.—The way of justification under the Old Covenant.—The true penance.—The whole parable admirably adapted to fast-day and communion sermons.

STARKE :—A teacher of the right kind seeks thoroughly to uncover even to the concealed hypocrites among his hearers their evil heart.—QUESNEL :—If wretched men knew themselves aright, they would not thus so easily despise others, Rev. iii. 17.—CRAMER : —The whole world is full of those that pray, and yet not all by far are pleasing to God ; therefore must we not only pray, but see to it how we pray.—When man deals with God, he must never remember what he is before others.—QUESNEL :—Let not one compare himself with infamous evil-doers, but with perfect saints.—A self-elected worship of God, without the foundation of the Holy Scripture, avails nothing, Matt. xv. 9.—OSIANDER :—O man, hast thou sinned ? deny it not, &c. How many have the "God be merciful to me a sinner " in their mouths but not in their hearts !—*Nova Bibl. Tub.* :—Penitent and believing humility brings light and salvation ; humility belongs in heaven, high-mindedness belongs in hell, Isaiah lvii. 15.—*Bibl. Wirt.* :—Man cannot by his own works or piety stand or become righteous before God.

LISCO :—Religiosity and religion in their most striking contrasts. — ARNDT : — How humility expresses itself in reference to the evil we have done : 1. It acknowledges its sin ; 2. and that in all its magnitude ; 3. and as its own guilt; 4. and prays for grace to God.—H. MÜLLER :—*The Graves of the Saints*, Frankfort, 1700 : Whoever will die happy must die as a sinner and yet without sin.—SCHMID :—The gospel way of salvation, how it leads, *a.* down into the depths; *b.* up to the heights.—HEUBNER :—Prayer a touchstone of the heart.—Tremble to have only the guise of virtue and yet to be proud.—A strict, continent way of living is often joined with inflexible selfishness.—Let us prove ourselves as we go from the church home, whether we go as new men or not.—A. MONOD, *Sermons,* 1er *Recueil,* p. 201, *La peccadille d'Adam et les vertus des Pharisiens.*

On the Pericope.—HEUBNER :—False and true devotion : 1. Nature ; 2. appearance.—Justification before God : 1. How it comes not to pass ; 2. how it always comes to pass.—COUARD :—The true churchgoer.—JASPIS :—Your prayers your judges.—ULBER : —The confession of man that he is a sinner : 1. It is hard even for the mouth to utter it ; 2. still harder if it is to come from the heart ; 3. and yet easy if one knows himself aright.—RAUTENBERG :—A look into the heart of the justified sinner.—That we ought to come to God not on the ground of our righteousness, but on the ground of God's compassion.—AHLFELD : —Of grace is man justified before God ; this is : 1. A true saying ; 2. a worthy saying.—STEINMEYER : —As the devotion, so the reward.—POPP :—There is a division and decision.

K. *Towards Jericho, at Jericho, out of Jericho towards Jerusalem.* CHAPS. XVIII. 15—XIX. 27.

1. Jesus and the Children (Ch. XVIII. 15-17).

15 And they brought unto him also infants [their babes, τὰ βρέφη], that he would
16 touch them: but when *his* disciples saw *it*, they rebuked them. But Jesus called
them [*i. e.*, the children, αὐτά] *unto him*, and said, Suffer [the] little children to come
unto me, and forbid them not: for of such is [to such belongs¹] the kingdom of God.
17 Verily I say unto you, Whosoever shall not receive the kingdom of God as a little
child shall in no wise enter therein.

[¹ Vs. 16.—Revised Version of the American Bible Union.—C. C. S.]

EXEGETICAL AND CRITICAL.

Vs. 15. **And they brought.**—From here on the narrative of Luke proceeds parallel with that of Matthew and Mark; he leaves the source from which he had drawn his narratives of journeying, ch. ix. 51–ch. xviii. 4, in order thenceforth to take his material again from the common evangelical tradition. There is, therefore, not the least ground for extending, with Schleiermacher, the special narrative of journeying of which Luke before availed himself, as far as ch. xix. 48. The ground why he precisely at this point coincides again with the other Synoptics, especially with Mark, can hardly be given otherwise than conjecturally. The conversation of our Saviour with the apostles about divorce, Mark x. 2–12; Matt. xix. 1-12, he passes over in silence, perhaps because he has already on another occasion noted down an important utterance on this subject, ch. xvi. 18. Neither does he define particularly the locality in which the Saviour met with the children, while however it is plainly to be seen, from Matt. xix. 1, that we have here to understand it as taking place on our Lord's last journey to Jerusalem, and at His definite departure from Galilee.

Vs. 15. **Their babes,** τὰ βρέφη, little children, therefore sucklings, ch. ii. 16; while Matthew and Mark only speak in general of παιδία. They are in any case children of the Saviour's auditors, who, not content with having received a blessing for themselves, entreat this now for their little ones also. This scene is the more touching, since it was at the same time a scene of farewell, and this act of the parents appears to have had its ground in the obscure presentiment that they should not again see the Saviour in Galilee. The mothers desire that He might leave for these young souls a parting blessing behind. It was, it is true, quite customary in Israel to entreat Rabbins and rulers of synagogues for such a benefit; but that this was desired from Jesus even yet in the last period of His public life, in spite of the continually increasing opposition to Him, is an unequivocal evidence of the deep and favorable impression which His activity had left behind in these regions.

Vs. 16. **Called them.**—Αὐτά, the children themselves. *Comi voce et nutu*, Bengel. The opposition between the friendly countenance of the Master, and the contracted brow of the disciples, is indescribably beautiful. The disciples rebuked the mothers, in the serious belief that it was incongruous to molest the Great Prophet with such trifling affairs, while they now especially desire that He may continue the interesting elucidation respecting marriage and divorce. But scarcely has Jesus learned who it is that wished to approach Him, and who it is that wished to keep these back, than He takes it very ill, and rebukes His disciples therefor; while they had thought that children belonged *less* than any one in His vicinity, He gives them on the contrary to know that He wishes to have, *more* than many others, precisely these around Him. If the Twelve thought that these children must first become like them, in order to attract the interest of the Saviour to them, our Lord, on the other hand, gives them the assurance that they must first become like children, if they would become the participants of His complacent regard.

Vs. 17. **Whosoever shall not receive the kingdom of God as a little child.**—Comp. Matt. xviii. 3, and LANGE, *ad loc.* Mark also speaks, ch. x. 15, of this utterance of the Saviour on this occasion; while Luke, ch. ix. 47, 48, had passed it over, and therefore brings it in afterwards here. With the requirement to receive the kingdom of God as a little child (δέχεσθαι), the Saviour directs attention to the receptivity for the Gospel which is found in the child's disposition. This temper of mind the disciples would soon lose, if they gave ear to the voice of pride and self-seeking, by which they had just before allowed themselves to be influenced to repel these little ones. In this way they might even incur the danger of forfeiting the blessing of the kingdom of heaven, whose subjects they had already begun to be. As to the rest, we are not to overlook the fact that, at least according to Luke, the warning οὐ μὴ εἰσέλθῃ, κ.τ.λ., can be interpreted as addressed to the wider circle of the auditors, parents, &c., who with the disciples at this moment surrounded the Saviour.

DOCTRINAL AND ETHICAL.

1. The desire of the mothers to see their children blessed by Jesus, sprang from a similar feeling of need from which afterwards the baptism of children proceeded. The Saviour, who approved the first-named wish, would, if asked about it, undoubtedly not stand in the way of the latter. [The connection between the two is admirably expressed in the exhortation contained in the office of the Episcopal Church for the Public Baptism of Infants.—C. C. S.]

2. Precisely when Christ appears surrounded by the little ones, and moves in the world of children, is He the image of the invisible God, whose majesty never shines more gloriously than when He condescends to that which is least and last, Ps. cxiii. 5, 6. Such a High-priest we needed, who bears a whole world on His loving heart, and yet also presses children to His heart and blesses them. In the Prosopography of the Redeemer, the trait must not remain

unconsidered, that the only thing of which we read that He took it ill, was precisely this repelling of the children. After all which had just before been uttered about the sins and the wretchedness in wedded life (*see* in Matthew and Mark), this whole scene makes the impression of a friendly sunbeam which breaks through on a thickly-clouded sky.

3. As for the subjects, so also for the King of the kingdom of God, did the way to true greatness lie precisely in this His deep humiliation. He who requires the childlike temper, has shown Himself also the most perfect Son, Heb. v. 8.

4. The becoming like children, and the ἄνωθεν γεννηθῆναι, John iii. 3, are correlative ideas. How completely indispensable the requirement of humility and the childlike temper was, could not appear more evidently than on this occasion. Scarcely do the children retire from the hallowed scene, when a rich young man enters, who, only for the reason that he is lacking in this childlike humility, does not find the entrance to the kingdom of heaven.

5. *See* the parallels in Matthew and Mark, and observe the intimate connection of this occurrence with the immediately preceding parable.

HOMILETICAL AND PRACTICAL.

The blessing of children: 1. Ardently desired; 2. precipitately forbidden; 3. graciously granted; 4. lastingly confirmed.—From that which we desire for our children, is made manifest what we ourselves think of Jesus.—Christ and the world of children.—The misguided zeal of the disciples is not seldom in direct conflict with the intention of the Master.—What found the Saviour in the little children that was much more welcome to Him than the sight of many adults?—How the true childlike temper teaches us, 1. To find; 2. to receive; 3. to esteem aright, the kingdom of heaven.—The disciple of the Lord is called to be in malice a child, but in understanding full grown, 1 Cor. xiv. 20.

STARKE:—The hasty and precipitate character even yet cleaves strongly to beginners in religion.—HEDINGER:—The child's state a blessed state!—Ah, few become like children, therefore we may well suppose more children than grown people enter into the kingdom of heaven.—BRENTIUS:—The children, as it were, constitute the heart and the noblest part of the kingdom of Christ on earth. Who would not count them dear and precious, and gladly be conversant with them? Mark this, ye parents and schoolmasters!—HEUBNER:—Even love can out of love become indignant; but this is no selfish displeasure, but a holy one.—Love of children a trait in the character of every Christianly religious man.—Whomsoever Jesus presses to His heart, such an one will certainly be warmed by love.—ARNDT's sermons upon the life of Jesus. Jesus, the children's Friend without compare. *See* farther on Luke ix. 46–48.

2. Jesus and the Rich Young Man (Vss. 18–30).

(Parallels: Matt. xix. 16–30; Mark x. 17–31.)

18, 19, 20 And a certain ruler asked him, saying, Good Master [Teacher], what shall I do to inherit eternal life? And Jesus said unto him, Why callest thou me good? none *is* good, save one, *that is*, God. Thou knowest the commandments, Do not commit adul-
21, 22 tery, Do not kill, Do not steal, Do not bear false witness, Honour thy father and thy mother. And he said, All these have I kept from my youth up. Now when Jesus heard these things, he said unto him, Yet lackest thou one thing: sell all that thou hast, and distribute unto the poor, and thou shalt have [a] treasure in heaven [the
23, 24 heavens¹]: and come, follow me. And when he heard this, he was [became] very sorrowful: for he was very rich. And when Jesus saw that he was very sorrowful
25 [saw him²]: he said, How hardly shall [do³] they that have riches enter into the king-
26 dom of God! For it is easier for a camel to go through a needle's eye, than for a rich
27 man to enter into the kingdom of God. And they that heard *it* said, Who then can be
28 saved? And he said, The things which are impossible with men are possible with God. Then Peter said, Lo, we have left all [what was ours⁴], and followed thee.
29, 30 And he said unto them, Verily I say unto you, There is no man that hath left house, or parents, or brethren, or wife, or children, for the kingdom of God's sake, Who shall not receive [back] manifold more [many times as much] in this present time, and in the world to come life everlasting.

¹ Vs. 22.—According to B., D., ἐν τοῖς οὐρανοῖς. [Cod. Sin., ἐν οὐρανοῖς.] The singular of the *Recepta* is from Matthew and Mark.
² Vs. 24.—E. V.: "saw that *he was very sorrowful*." [ἰδὼν δὲ αὐτὸν ὁ Ἰ. εἶπεν, according to B., Cod. Sin., L. Accepted by Tischendorf, Tregelles, Alford.—C. C. S.]
³ Vs. 25.—Εἰσπορεύονται (according to B., L. Cod. Sin. has εἰσελεύσονται.—C. C. S.]
⁴ Vs. 28.—Τὰ ἴδια (without πάντα), according to Griesbach, Lachmann, [Tischendorf, Tregelles, Alford,] on the authority of B., L., 157. Πάντα is taken from the parallels.

EXEGETICAL AND CRITICAL.

Vs. 18. **A certain ruler.**—Ἄρχων, more particular specification of the indefinite εἷς in Matthew and Mark; perhaps the president of a neighboring synagogue, who, concealed among the people, had heard the instruction of the Saviour, been present at the blessing of the children, and excited by both to address himself with a weighty question to Jesus. According to no one of the Synoptics does he come πειράζων, like so many before and after him, but on the contrary with a good intention. Noticeable is the comparatively great fulness with which the three Synoptics communicate this occurrence; it has, as is evident, left a deep impression in the circle of the disciples.

Good Teacher.—It is not hard to sketch a somewhat vivid portrait of the youthful speaker. He is as little lacking in emotion and enthusiasm, as in fluency of speech and demonstration of honor before Jesus. He is better than the common depenters on works [*Werkheiligen*, lit., work-saints] of that time, under whose self-righteousness there flowed not seldom a current of hypocrisy, but he stands far below the God-fearing men of the Old Testament, in whose hearts, along with the strictest conscientiousness, there ever remained alive the feeling of the necessity of atonement. What he seeks is not grace but reward;—the eternal life in which he, probably a member of the sect of the Pharisees, believes, he will earn by his own virtue. Yet still an obscure feeling is ever saying to him that the treasure of his good works is not yet great enough; to his righteousness he wishes to add something more, altogether extraordinary, in order then to be able to be sure of the perfect certainty of his salvation. Before the Saviour departs, he wishes for once to hear from Him the answer to this great question of life. Thus does he stand before us as a man full of good intentions, but without deep self-knowledge; who takes pleasure in the law of God, but at the same time also has complacency in himself, whose words not only express his thoughts, but in a certain sense anticipate them; more worthy of love than of envy,—a curious mixture of honesty and of pitiable self-deceit. Not until he is considered from this point of view, is it possible wholly to understand the wisdom and love, with which the Saviour treats him. He is in a certain sense the Nicodemus character of the Synoptics, comp. John iii. 2, although his history, alas, ends less satisfactorily than that of this teacher in Israel.

Vs. 19. **Why callest thou me good?**—Luke simply follows Mark, in giving this answer of our Lord. Respecting the famous various reading in Matt. *ad loc. see* LANGE. We for our part are of the opinion that in Matthew the *Recepta* must be retained, and that the reading of Lachmann and Tischendorf has no higher value than that of an old *interpretamentum*. The grounds for this persuasion do not belong here, but as respects the Marcionitic reading of the second part of the answer in Luke: ὁ γὰρ ἀγαθὸς εἷς ἐστιν, ὁ Θεὸς ὁ πατήρ, it is nothing but a gloss, which does not even bear a strongly Marcionitic character.—As to the rest, we scarcely need to remark that the Saviour by this answer: οὐδεὶς ἀγαθ., κ.τ.λ., is as far from indirectly expressing His own Godhead (the old Dogmatici), as He is from decidedly denying it (the later Rationalists). He contents Himself with declining an epithet which in this mouth would have had no meaning whatever, even as He previously also did not wish from every one to be greeted as the Messiah. Thus does He here give on the one hand an example of modest humility, which contrasts not a little with the self-praise of the young man, and on the other hand He points him, if he will really do what is good, to the highest ideal of perfection.

Vs. 20. **The commandments.**—The Saviour names the commandments of the second table, because when the rich man had once seen his lack of love to his neighbor, the conclusion as to his lack of love to God could not be difficult. According to Mark and Luke, the μὴ μοιχεύσῃς stands first, with internal probability, if we direct our regard to the youth of the questioner. According to the statement of Luke, the Saviour names only five commandments, the μὴ ἀποστερήσῃς of Mark and the ἀγαπ. τὸν πλησ. σου ὡς σεαυτ. of Matthew, being wanting.

Vs. 21. **All these.**—In vain hitherto has the Saviour endeavored to draw the attention of the young man to the contrast between his duty and his own ability. The youth is still so taken up with his own virtue, that he thinks that he is able to point courageously to his whole past life, although at the same time, in the obscure foreboding that he may yet perhaps come short, he adds (Matthew): τί ἔτι ὑστερῶ. The answer of the Saviour does not confirm the truth of his declaration, but only tells him what he, in case it is really so with him, has yet to do.

Vs. 22. **Distribute.**—Διάδος, *see* the notes on the text. By the peculiar form of the injunction, the salutary strictness of the command becomes evident. He must not only sell his treasure, never to see it again;—even that perhaps in an heroic and high-wrought moment might have been possible;—but to distribute the precious wealth with his own hand, piece by piece, among the poor, and thus see the source of his earthly joy, pride, hope, as it were, drop by drop dry up. "*Distribue, ipse id magnam lætitiam afferre solet piis.*" Bengel. Only when he has in this way killed his selfishness even to the root, may he view himself as perfect in love. Then is the Master ready to give him his recompense and highest good, the place of a disciple, His cross, His heavenly treasure.

Vs. 23. **Very sorrowful.**—Περίλυπος: Matthew, λυπούμενος; Mark, στυγνάσας, λυπούμενος. These are all expressions which show that the answer of Jesus produces an intense impression upon the young man. No wonder, it was also very fitting to cure him forever of his foolish self-conceit. Up to this moment, he had thought that the external observance of the manifold commandments might open for him the way to heaven, while he yet had left the *commune vinculum*, the highest principle of all the requirements of God, until now unconsidered. And now it appears that his selfishness is mightier than his seemingly noble love, and that he his life through had already transgressed the first commandment, inasmuch as he offered base worship to Mammon. He becomes aware that to his fabric of virtue even the foundation is yet wanting, and still he had already been hoping to be able to put the capstone on his perfected work. The chasm which lies between knowing and willing, and between willing and doing, becomes to him now plain; he goes away, and it is not impossible that he afterwards returns again; but even though he saw Jesus no more, he has received an instruction which he his whole life long can no more forget. He knows now what is lacking to him, and even though the look of sadness which the Saviour let fall upon the departing one had been a look of irrevocable farewell, yet the lasting loss of this young man would still have been to the rest a gain, on account of the heart-searching instructions and warnings which Jesus connected with this occurrence.

Vs. 24. **How hardly.**—*See* on Matt. xix. 17-29; Mark x. 17-30. That the Saviour here teaches, it is true, a relative but by no means absolute impossibility that the rich man should be saved, shows again how far He, in the gospel of Luke, is removed from all Ebionitic contempt of riches. Only when money has us, instead of our possessing the money, does it close against us the entrance to the kingdom of heaven. Comp. besides the well-known golden tractate of CLEMENS ALEXANDRINUS, *Quis dives salvetur*, also *Pædagogus*, lib. iii. ch. vi. The double form in which Mark (ch. x. 23, 24) communicates the saying of our Lord, is especially adapted to explain more exactly His actual meaning.

Vs. 25. **A camel.**—*See* LANGE on Matt. xix. 24, and LIGHTFOOT, *ad loc.* Beyond doubt there here hovers before the Saviour's soul, in particular, the image of the many rich and mighty in His day, whose earthly temper hindered them from receiving Him, while He in the rich young man saw a type of thousands, to whom the disciples in their Chiliastic dreams had already conceded a place of honor in the kingdom of heaven, but with reference to whom it was soon to appear that they, on account of their love to earthly goods, were not fit for the kingdom of God.

Vs. 26. **Who then can be saved?**—As well this scene with the ruler, as also this earnest utterance of the Saviour, has taught the disciples to cast a deeper look into their own heart. They feel now that not earthly good in itself closes the entrance into the kingdom of heaven, but that it does so only when one hangs his heart upon it, and that one therefore, even without being in possession of riches, may yet be shut out as a rich man. In the living consciousness that even the poorest may have something of this earthly-mindedness which causes the ἄρχων to go sorrowful away, they now all, instead of surprise at others, feel concern about themselves, and venture the great question, which the Saviour answers with His compassionate look and a comforting word. Comp. Job xlii. 2; Jer. xxxii. 17; Zech. viii. 6.

Vs. 18. **Peter said.**—According to all three Evangelists, it is Peter with whom first, in the place of concern, there follows not only recovered composure, but even self-complacency. Very characteristic is it, but at the same time amiable, that he here does not place himself exclusively first, but utters it as the collective consciousness of the apostolic circle, that all more or less had done what had proved too hard for the ἄρχων. The peculiar form of his utterance in Luke, "we have left τὰ ἴδια, that which is ours," brings the greater difficulty of the sacrifice made still more strongly into view. Instead of the fear of not being able to be saved, there now springs up within them the hope of extraordinary reward; and it is entirely unmistakable that in this whole utterance, an egoistic love of reward expresses itself, of which it is even more easily conceivable how it could arise in the heart of Peter, than how it could be approved by Jesus. Before, however, we find difficulty in this latter fact, let us notice first that the assertion of Peter was no idle vaunt, but pure truth;

that the Saviour Himself had just before attached to the renunciation of earthly good the possession of the heavenly treasure, and that with Peter the craving of reward did not exclude love, but was most intimately connected therewith; and secondly, that our Lord not only approves the hope of recompense, inasmuch as He promises to it the richest satisfaction, but also tempers it and sanctifies it, by the immediately following parable, Matt. xxi. 1-16.

Vs. 29. **Verily I say unto you.**—Luke gives the answer of the Saviour less precisely and less in detail than Matthew and Mark, yet with all, the chief thoughts are the same, in which, however, we have to consider that the strictly Israelitish form in which the hope of hundredfold reward is uttered in Matt. ch. xix. 28, is less prominent in the Hellenistic gospel of Luke.

Vs. 30. **Receive back,** ἀπολάβῃ.—*See* notes on the text. A still stronger form than in Matthew, and a fitting expression to intimate that he receives what belongs to him as a reward. Afterwards the Saviour expressed the same thought in another form, Luke xxii. 25-30. The clause: "Many last shall be first," which Matthew and Mark subjoin here, Luke had already given, ch. xiii. 30. As a proverb, its frequent repetition is easily intelligible.

In this time, and in the world to come life everlasting.—This passage is one of those in which the distinction between the common Synoptic and the Johannean signification of the word ζωὴ αἰώνιος appears most strongly marked. Here, also, as, *e. g.*, Matt. xix. 29; xxv. 46, and elsewhere, it is something absolutely of the other world.

DOCTRINAL AND ETHICAL.

1. *See* on the parallel passages in Matthew and Mark.

2. In the Pauline gospel of Luke also, the history of the rich young man occupies a prominent place, inasmuch as this word serves as a palpable proof of the absolute impossibility of being justified by the works of the law. When the Saviour says to a sinner, in view of the requirements of the law: Do this and thou shalt live, this is done for the very purpose of awakening, by the despair of fulfilling such a requirement, the consciousness of deep sinfulness, and the slumbering longing for grace. In this respect also, the history of the rich young man is a rarely equalled type of the pædagogic wisdom of our Lord, and at the same time a key to the Pauline declaration, Rom. vii. 7-24.

3. For the apologetics of the Evangelical history, it is of moment to compare the form in which this occurrence is related in the gospel of the Hebrews. Comp. on this the happy remark of NEANDER, *L. J. ad loc.*, and respecting this whole narrative, the dissertation of K. WIMMER, *Stud. u. Krit.* 1845, i. p. 115.

4. The evangelical idea of the sinlessness of our Lord is in no way endangered by the negative: τί με λέγεις ἀγαθόν. "The declaration is the expression of the same humble subordination to God, penetrated by which Jesus also, although knowing Himself one with the Father, yet designates the Father as the One sending Him, teaching Him, sanctifying Him, glorifying Him,—in one word, as the greater. Ever, indeed, is the Father the original source, as of all being, so of all goodness; the absolutely Good, in His holiness ever the same, while in contrast with Him

even the Son, as Man, is one developing in goodness and holiness, perfecting Himself through prayers, conflicts, sorrows, and suffering, unto Divine glory." Ullmann.

5. The whole history of the rich young man is a powerful testimony to the spirit of the first commandment in the Decalogue. Evidently the Saviour was not concerned with the wealth of the ἄρχων in itself, —for some misfortune or other might then have easily freed him from his possessions; but He wished to detach him from the idol to which his heart was bound. If his idol had been something else, e. g., ambition, the Saviour would not have given him this commandment; he would have fulfilled it without trouble, nay, perhaps would even have boasted of his beneficence; but since his weak side is the love of money, the commandment of self-denial approaches him precisely in this relatively accidental form, that it may become evident to him how only he who can renounce that which is highest, is on the way to gain that which is best. Hard was the requirement, but it was the severity of love.

[After all, our Lord only required of this young man what the apostles, as Peter declares, had already done; and even worldly wisdom does not now venture to dispute that the preëminent honor which they have gained to all ages of the world thereby, has of itself been a hundred times over worth the sacrifice. What emperor in Christendom would dare for a moment to compare his dignity with that of an apostle, or an evangelist, or even the helper of an apostle? And certainly we may believe that the young ruler, who could have made a still greater sacrifice, and whom Jesus, even at His first and only meeting with him, came to regard with so peculiar an affection, was fitted to occupy no mean place in the kingdom of God. So true is it, that even as respects this world, he missed the opportunity of placing himself on such an eminence, as no potentate of his age ever came within sight of.—C. C. S.]

6. The promise of manifold reward for the sacrifice made for the kingdom of heaven, had already been given to the disciples in another form, ch. vi. 23; xii. 35-37. Here, in particular, must be considered how the Saviour, after He had promised them more than the most glowing imagination could expect, makes haste to oppose every narrow self-seeking and false rest in their soul. He takes from them therewith at once the fancy of their being the only ones so highly distinguished. In an entirely general way He promises for all following times to all a hundredfold recompense who should renounce anything for the kingdom of heaven's sake. They should not lack companions of the high fortune which they desired above all things. But that they might not now too early rest upon their laurels, they are on the other hand disquieted by the thought: Those who are now the first, may afterwards very possibly become the last. How thoroughly in earnest, moreover, the Saviour was as to this promise of the hundredfold recompense even in this life, appears from the history of the kingdom of God in all times, comp. e. g., what Paul offered for its sake and afterwards gained. Or consider the French refugees, who for the cause of truth and reformation left their native country, and even yet in their posterity are visibly and wonderfully blest! [What blood more honorable in our country than the blood of the Huguenots?—C. C. S.]

7. The whole instruction of our Lord, as well concerning the dangers of riches as concerning the rich recompense of that which is offered up for Him, acquires an additional and peculiar importance if we consider that this was uttered in the presence of Judas, only a few days before the germinating in him of the dark plan of betrayal.

[8. We must bear in mind that while as yet the might of Christian love had scarcely begun to be felt in the world, riches were to their possessors a temptation to hard-hearted voluptuousness in a degree scarcely possible now. In Christendom, imperfect as it is, even a worldly man, in spite of himself, is forced in some measure to take a Christian view of his wealth. This does not, by any means, remove the danger of riches, but it increases the probability, in each particular case, that those dangers will be surmounted.—C. C. S.]

HOMILETICAL AND PRACTICAL.

Sacrifices for the kingdom of heaven are: 1. Required, vss. 18-22; 2. refused, vss. 23-27; 3. made, vs. 28; 4. rewarded, vss. 29, 30.—The ruler of the synagogue at the feet of Him who is the Lord of the temple.—Jesus, over against the rich young man, truly the Good Master, although He declines this honorable appellation.—The rich young man the type of the man who has much that is needed for his salvation, but not all: 1. His portrait; 2. his fate.—How little even the knowing of the commandments helps us.—The strictness of the Saviour towards the virtuous, His mildness towards the deeply-fallen sinner, and in both cases His heavenly love.—The advantage of an untroubled retrospect upon a well-spent and unspotted youth: 1. A rare; 2. an inestimable; 3. a dangerous, advantage.—One thing thou yet lackest: 1. A kindly intended felicitation, because only *one thing;* 2. an earnest warning, because in the one *all* is lacking to him.—What the rich young man really lacks is love to God above all things.—Whoever will teach others to recognize their own sins against God, does best when he begins with their duties towards their neighbor, 1 John iv. 20.—The treasure in heaven: 1. Its high value; 2. its dear price.—True care for the poor must be a personal one.—The rich young man: 1. Trebly rich, a. in treasures, b. in virtues, c. in self-conceit; 2. trebly poor, a. in self-knowledge, b. in love, c. in heavenly possessions.—The ruinous power of a single darling sin, Eccles. x. 1; Matt. v. 29, 30,—How earthly-mindedness: 1. Contemns the King of the kingdom of God; 2. despises the fundamental law of the kingdom of God; 3. forfeits the blessedness of the kingdom of God.—How the Saviour will cure man of his earthly-mindedness by leading him to the way: 1. Of self-knowledge; 2. of self-denial; 3. of self-surrender to Him.—The love of Christ over against the might of the *ego:* 1. How deep it looks; 2. how much it requires; 3. how richly it rewards.—Why is it harder for the rich than for so many others to enter into the kingdom of heaven?—"How hardly," &c.: 1. A word of terror for the earthly-minded wealthy; 2. a word of comfort for the heavenly-minded poor; 3. a word of thanksgiving for rich and poor who have really overcome the difficulty and have entered into the kingdom of heaven.—The being saved: 1. On its humanly impossible; 2. on its Divinely possible and easy, side.—How far the question, "What shall we have therefore?" from the Christian point of view is permitted or censurable.—The recompense in the kingdom of heaven: 1. Its extent, *a.* in this, *b.* in the future, life; 2. its conditions: one must, *a.* really have left all, and this then, *b.* not out of mercenariness, but out of love.

STARKE:—CANSTEIN:—Our first and chiefest question should be concerning everlasting life.—BRENTIUS:—The law is spiritual, and requires internal and external obedience.—In religion nature and grace must be well distinguished.—Let man be taught to distinguish well the general and the special calling of God.—HEDINGER:—Woe to you, ye rich, Luke vi. 24; 1 Tim. vi. 9; James v. 1.—*Bibl. Wirt:*—Let not thy mouth water too much after worldly goods, because they are more a hindrance than a help to salvation, Prov. xxx. 8.—Rising concern for salvation must be regarded and welcomed as a messenger of grace.—HEDINGER:—All lost, all gained.—BRENTIUS:—The lust of reward here cleaves even, it seems, to the best dispositions.—To the children and servants of God belongs all the good which the kingdom of grace and glory possesses; what would they more? 1 Cor. iii. 21-23.

PALMER:—What lack I yet? 1. What answer our own heart would be glad to give; 2. what the Lord answers thereto.—Of the unhappy contradiction in which so many men are involved with themselves.—W. HOFACKER:—Good labor brings noble recompense.—C. J. NITZSCH:—No one is good saving God alone: 1. In what sense the expression is meant; 2. how in the light of it Jesus Himself appears to us; 3. whether, then, where it holds good, there yet can be any well-grounded confidence in our neighbor.

---

3. Jesus and the Blind Man (Vss. 31-43).

(Parallel to Matt. xx. 17-19, 29-34; Mark x. 32-34, 46-52.)

31 Then [And] he took *unto him* the twelve, and said unto them, Behold, we go up to Jerusalem, and all things that are written by the prophets concerning [lit., for, τῷ υἱῷ,
32 κ.τ.λ.] the Son of man shall be accomplished. For he shall be delivered unto the Gentiles, and shall be mocked, and spitefully entreated [outrageously handled], and spitted
33 on: And they shall scourge *him*, and put him to death; and the third day he shall rise
34 again. And they understood none of these things: and this saying was hid from them, neither knew [comprehended] they the things which were spoken.
35 And it came to pass, that as he was come nigh unto Jericho, a certain blind man
36 sat by the way side begging: And hearing the multitude pass by [a multitude passing
37 by], he asked what it meant. And they told him, that Jesus of Nazareth passeth by.
38, 39 And he cried, saying, Jesus, *thou* Son of David, have mercy on me. And they which went before rebuked him, that he should hold his peace: but he cried so much
40 the more, *Thou* Son of David, have mercy on me. And Jesus stood, and commanded
41 him to be brought unto him: and when he was come near, he asked him, Saying,¹ What wilt thou that I shall do unto thee? And he said, Lord [or, Sir], that I may
42 receive my sight. And Jesus said unto him, Receive thy sight: thy faith hath saved
43 thee [or, caused thy recovery]. And immediately he received his sight, and followed him, glorifying God: and all the people, when they saw *it*, gave praise unto God.

¹ Vs. 41.—Λέγων (Origen: εἰπών) at the beginning of this verse is omitted by Tischendorf, [Meyer, Alford,] according to B., D., [Cod. Sin.,] L., X. It is at least doubtful.

EXEGETICAL AND CRITICAL.

Vs. 31. And He took.—Comp. LANGE on the parallels in Matthew and Mark. The parable of the Laborers in the Vineyard, which in Matt. xx. 1-16 precedes the repeated announcement of the Passion, and the request of the sons of Zebedee which follows it, and which is given by Matthew as well as Mark, Luke passes over. According to the Synoptics, the journey to the Passover is now continued steadily in the direction of Jericho. That, however, the Twelve were not the Saviour's only companions in travel appears from the fact that He calls them to Himself, κατ᾽ ἰδίαν, Matt. xx. 17-19, in order to impart to them a weighty utterance. Perhaps the women, Luke viii. 2, 3, were also with him, and Salome comes forth from their circle with her petition. The visible distinction between the temper of our Lord and that of the disciples is brought into view by Mark in particular, x. 32, with much graphic force. It is as if the feeling of Thomas, which he so strongly uttered, John xi. 16, had now possessed itself of all the disciples. Perhaps Jesus considers just this discouraged state of theirs best fitted for the communication to them for the third time of a prophecy which He had already delivered twice to almost deaf ears. The greater the vividness which had been given by the just-reported conversation to the prospect of hundredfold reward, the more necessary does it appear to our Lord to obviate the earthly-minded expectation with which they follow Him, even on the fatal way; and of set purpose He severs them from the circle of the others, in order, by the very mystery in the manner of His communication, to prepare them the better for the weightiness of its matter.

Τελεσθήσεται, κ.τ.λ.—The reference to the prophetic declarations on this occasion is peculiar to Luke. The Saviour speaks with emphasis of πάντα τὰ γεγρ., comp. ch. xxii. 37. The Messianic prophecies of suffering stand before His eyes as a great whole put in writing τῷ υἱῷ τ. ἀνδρ. for the Son of Man, a *dativus commodi* by which the proper destination of the word of Scripture, that of being realized in Him, is intimated ; an indirect proof that for every detail of the picture of His Passion which is now sketched, vss. 32, 33, there must also be at least an intimation to be found in the prophetic record.

Vs. 32. **Delivered unto the Gentiles.**—Luke in his more summary report passes over the first delivery to the high-priests and scribes, and the condemnation to death by the Sanhedrim. On the other hand he, like Matthew and Mark, mentions the prediction of the mocking, scourging, and maltreatment of our Lord, and has, in common with Mark, the special mention of the spitting on Him. The more than usual agreement of the Synoptics in the communication of these details is a strong proof for the credibility of this prediction, which can be weakened in no manner by any dogmatic doubt (De Wette and others). According to the Synoptics, the Saviour on this occasion speaks of His resurrection on the third day expressly. The gradual climax καί, καί, καί, disappears therefore at once in an overwhelming antithesis.

Vs. 34. **And they understood none of these things,** &c.—"An emphatic diffuseness." Meyer. It is, of course, understood that this ignorance of the apostles was no wanton, but was yet in a certain sense a self-caused, ignorance ; and that it had not reference to the sound of the words, but to the thing itself. Comp. ch. ix. 45. How little, moreover, they understood our Lord, appeared immediately from the petition of the sons of Zebedee. Strikingly does Luke bring into view the totality of the misunderstanding, οὐδὲν συνῆκαν, and its ground, ἦν τὸ ῥῆμα κεκρυμμ., κ.τ.λ., and the natural consequence, οὐκ ἐγίνωσκον. Because their heart stubbornly repels the only intelligible sense of the words, their understanding seeks in vain for a more endurable sense which, perhaps, might be given to these words. *They are spiritually as blind as the Bartimaeus who now comes into view is in body.*

Vs. 35. **As He was come nigh unto Jericho.** —Respecting the locality of the City of Palms, and respecting the difference among the Synoptics in reference to the number of the blind men, and the question whether the miracle took place at the entrance or the leaving of the city, *see* LANGE, *ad loc*. For the various attempts to remove this difficulty, and their advocates, *see* Meyer, De Wette, and others. If one believes that the accounts must *à tout prix* be brought into agreement with one another, then without doubt the conjecture of Lange that the Saviour went in and out at the same gate of the city, and that the miracle falls into two parts, seems to deserve the preference before the view that a second blind man associated himself with Bartimaeus, and, at all events, deserves the preference above the unlucky harmonistic expedient which makes this miracle take place *twice*. We believe, however, that a spiritually free view of the Evangelical reports must frankly allow such little discrepancies, and, no doubt, institute attempts to reconcile them, but by no means force them. Comp. the admirable remark of OLSHAUSEN, *Comm*. i. p. 28, and that of CHRYSOSTOM, *Praef. in Matt.*, in respect to the difference of the Evangelists in minor matters : αὐτὸ μὲν τοῦτο μέγιστον δεῖγμα τῆς ἀληθείας ἐστίν· εἰ γὰρ πάντα συνεφώνησαν μετὰ ἀκριβείας, οὐδεὶς ἂν ἐπίστευσεν τῶν ἐχθρῶν, ὅτι μὴ συνελθόντες ἀπὸ συνθήκης τινὸς ἀνθρωπίνης ἔγραψαν, ἅπερ ἔγραψαν, κ.τ.λ.

[This itself is the greatest evidence of truth, for if all things had accurately agreed, no one of our enemies would have believed that they had not come together by a human agreement and written what they have written, &c.] Taking all together, we account it probable : 1. That here only *one* blind man was healed, and that when Matthew uses the plural, he, as is more his way, is less intent on giving the number than the description of the healed ; and, 2. that the miracle did not take place before (Luke) but after the entrance of Jesus into Jericho (Matthew and Mark). Two narrators, of whom the one is an apostolic eye-witness, stand here over against one another, and it is not probable that the perverse temper of the people, ch. xix. 7, would so soon and publicly have found expression if only a few moments before enthusiasm had been so powerfully awakened by the healing of the blind man, as we read ch. xviii. 43. Far more probable is it that the Saviour performed this miracle on His departure from Jericho, with the design also of leaving behind there an abiding impression. Only on the platform of a mechanical theory of inspiration can offence be taken at this want of diplomatic exactness in the statement of Luke. Whoever, on the other hand, regards his gospel with impartial view, will hardly be able to deny that, especially in the last period of the public life of our Saviour and in the history of the Passion, the exact chronological arrangement of the events is not to be expected, particularly from Luke, and that he in this respect often remains behind Matthew and Mark. The investigation of the cause of this phenomenon does not belong here.

Vs. 37. **That Jesus of Nazareth passeth by.** —The people name our Lord according to the customary style. The blind man, who greets Him as Son of David, however, shows even by this that his faith has reached a higher grade.

Vs. 40. **Commanded him to be brought unto Him.**—Luke relates, it is true, that the Saviour gave this command, but not that the blind man, upon this command being given, was led by others to Him. His account does not, therefore, conflict with that of Mark, who mentions Bartimeus' throwing away his garment and coming to Jesus. Apparently we have to conceive the matter thus : that the blind man left none of the standers-by time to carry out the exact command of our Lord. As little do the accounts of the manner of the healing contradict one another, for the circumstance that Matthew alone mentions that Jesus here also, as often before, touched his eyes, is by Mark as well as by Luke neither directly nor indirectly controverted.

Vs. 41. **What wilt thou.**—"*Interrogat Christus, non tam caeci privatim causa, quam totius populi. Scimus enim, ut mundus Dei beneficia sine sensu devoret, nisi stimulis excitetur. Ergo Christus voce sua turbam adstantem ad observandum miraculum erigit,*" Calvin.

Vs. 43. **All the people.**—This statement of the impression which the miracle produced upon the whole people has been preserved to us by Luke alone. It is as if he would cause us to hear at the gate of Jericho the prelude to the Hosannas which were soon to resound far more mightily at the gates of Jerusalem, comp. ch. xix. 37. That the Saviour Himself no longer desires to check this triumphant praise, appears even from the fact that He no longer imposes on the blind man any silence about what had been done, nor yet requires that he, like the demoniac,

Mark v. 19, shall go home, but willingly allows Bartimæus to swell the enthusiastic throng and go before it. As to the rest, the mention of the doxology, to which the miracles of the Saviour several times give occasion, is peculiar to Luke, comp. ch. v. 26; vii. 16; ix. 43; xiii. 17, and is wholly in the Pauline spirit. Comp. Rom. xi. 33–36.

DOCTRINAL AND ETHICAL.

1. The Saviour's third prediction to His disciples of His Passion is richer in details than the two former ones. We may conclude from this that His own consciousness of His approaching fate gained continually in clearness, and that even the so-called *Contingentia* of the future—*e. g.*, the spitting on Him—stood before His soul already as present. This can the less surprise us if we consider that even these here-mentioned particulars were not foreign to the prophetic image of the Messiah and His Passion, *see, e. g.*, Isaiah l. 6; Ps. xxii. 8. Phenomena of this kind create difficulty for those who know no higher basis for the prophetic viewing of the future than human presentiment alone, and will explain all phenomena in this sphere exclusively from within outward, instead of from above downward. On the other hand, we have simply to remind the reader, "After all human mediation and substratum is provided for, still the proper innermost nature of prophecy remains an every-time-renewed discovery of hidden things through the omniscient Spirit, an anticipating of the future beyond the preformations and germs of the present; in short, a speaking of God, out of which in its turn the prophesying history can alone form and comprehend itself. We have, therefore, no right to forbid every prediction, and although it stands there to explain it away out of principle, merely for the reason that we do not know how to make way for it in our understanding of history, because it appears to stand forth to us as a soothsaying prediction." Stier. If this principle holds good even of predictions of the Old Testament, in how much higher measure must it then hold good of Him who is conscious of Himself being the end of the law and the centre of all prophecy, and whose capacity certainly no one will in any case be able successfully to dispute of knowing all, even to the minute details, which He had to know, in order, as the Founder of the kingdom of God, to accomplish His mission on earth.

2. Attention cannot be too often directed to the closeness with which the Saviour's consciousness of His Passion attaches itself to the prophetical Scripture. He, the Son of the House, sees in the law and the prophets the Magna Charta of the kingdom of God, to which He, not less than its least subject, is bound. As if He had foreseen that hereafter the days would come in which it should be denied, in the name of science, that Israel's prophets have ever decisively pointed to a suffering and dying Messiah, He points us to their testimony as to the clear mirror of His suffering as well as of His glory. For him who will really penetrate deeply into the sanctuary of the history of the Passion, it is of the greatest importance that he do not let the key of the prophetic Scripture be taken from Him. Here also plainly appears the truth of the maxim: *titubante scriptura, simul titubat fides.*

3. In the inquiry, what gave the Saviour courage and energy to go forward with so unterrified a step towards the way of suffering, we undoubtedly must not overlook the truth that He continually beyond His Passion foresaw the Resurrection on the third day. For him who really believes in the Humanity of our Lord, even His lofty courage unto death is a proof that the prediction of the resurrection in the gospel was by no means a bare *vaticinium post eventum*. On the other hand, it is entirely natural that in the degree in which the Passion pressed more vehemently in upon Him, the heart-exalting prospect of the Resurrection was not, it is true, in any wise shaken, but yet temporarily in His consciousness thrown into the background.

4. The incapacity of the disciples to understand our Lord's announcement of His suffering, is a new proof of the truth that in the Christian sphere true spiritual understanding comes to pass through the organ of the heart. If the soul turns itself from a clearly uttered truth, then is also the understanding incapable of recognizing its substance and importance. Here also the well-known saying of Pascal holds good, that one must know human things in order to love them, but, on the other hand, must love Divine things if he would rightly understand them. Comp. the beautiful essay of VINET, *L'Évangile compris par le cœur.*—At the same time, however, this incapacity of the disciples is an unequivocal proof of the indispensable necessity, as well as of the salutary influence, of their enlightenment through the Holy Spirit, in consequence of which they afterwards learned to regard that same Passion as absolutely necessary and worthy of God, which at first was so offensive to them, and for that very reason so incomprehensible.

5. Every healing of the blind related to us in the gospel shows in a striking symbol how the Saviour opens the eye of the soul also for the heavenly light; but in particular may the history of Bartimæus, in its beautiful gradualness of development, be called a type of that spiritual benefit pregnant with instruction. First there makes its way to him merely the report of Jesus, awakening slumbering remembrances, longings, and presagings; then it becomes evident to the people following Jesus that he has a longing for higher benefit than the multitude which only outwardly encircles the Saviour. As commonly, so here also, they do not want the sufferer to enjoy anything from Jesus apart from them, and seek to suppress his tone of lamentation, as a discord in the jubilant acclaim of joy. But this very reaction excites his longing faith to higher courage, and soon the sufferer cannot any longer rest till every hindrance yet separating him from Jesus is overcome; faith triumphs, and the first thing that he now sees is Christ Himself, before whose face he stands, and in whose light he now beholds the whole creation surrounding him as in the glory of the resurrection, "the image of the truth that in spiritual enlightenment Christ is the first, loveliest, and best of everything that one learns to recognize, upon whom, moreover, the simple eye of the spirit with good reason remains through the whole of life directed." In conclusion, the following of Jesus, the preceding others, the united praise of God, the whole order of salvation, as well on the side of God as on that of man, lies here *in nuce* visibly before us, that is, if our eyes are opened.

6. "O, what power has the prayer of believers! There prayed *Joshua*, and the sun in the heaven stood still that he might fully beat down the enemies. Now JESUS, the Sun of Righteousness, which in mid

course was soon to descend, also stood here still." Bogatzky.

7. The last miracle again—the last performed on a man which is made known to us from the public life of our Lord (Matt. xxi. 14 contains only a general notice)—presents before our eyes the high end of His manifestation in a striking manner, comp. Isaiah xxxv. 5; Ps. cxlvi. 8; and the homage which is here brought to Him at Jericho's gate is a prophecy of the universal homage of the redeemed which hereafter shall be brought to Him, especially in His exalted character as the Light of the world.

8. It is an element of the pædagogic wisdom of our Lord, that He, the more His public life hastens to its end, rather seeks than avoids the opportunity to do miracles, and unconditionally accepts the homage of the healed. This also was soon to serve His weakly believing disciples as a counterpoise against the σκάνδαλον crucis.

HOMILETICAL AND PRACTICAL.

Jesus the Light of the world, as well for the spiritually (the Twelve) as for the corporeally blind (Bartimæus): 1. He creates the light for the eye (vss. 31–34); 2. He opens the eye to the light (vss. 35–42).—How the Saviour labors to make His servants friends and intimate companions, John xv. 15. —Jesus contrasted with His disciples: 1. His clear knowledge in contrast with their ignorance; 2. His lofty courage in contrast with their faint-hearted fear; 3. His willing precedence on the way of humiliation in contrast with their constrained following ["He longs to be baptized with blood, He pants to reach the cross." Cowper.].—The Passion of our Lord the fulfilment of a Divine prophecy.—The relation of suffering to glory.—The courage of Christ unto death, and the shrinking from suffering of so many Christians.—Sluggishness of heart the deepest ground of the not understanding so many a word of the Lord.—Jesus and Joshua before the gates of Jericho: 1. What both find; 2. what both bring.— Whoever feels that he is spiritually blind can do nothing better than to beg.—Where the eye of the soul is yet closed, there must the ear of the body become so much more keenly alive to the report which ever flies before our Lord where He comes with His salvation: 1. Into a land; 2. into a home; 3. into a heart.—Happy for him who does not keep from the blind the knowledge that Jesus of Nazareth passeth by.—How differently the Lord appears to diverse eyes: 1. To the superficial multitude He is Jesus of Nazareth; 2. to the eagerly longing Bartimæus He is the Son of David; 3. to the believing disciples He is the Son of the living God.—The Kyrie Eleison of the soul, which precedes its Hosanna. [Κύριε, ἐλέησον μέ —*Miserere mei Domine.* In some of the German litanies, as well as in the Latin mass, this formula of supplication remains in the original Greek, being afterwards interpreted in the Latin or German.— C. C. S.]—On His way to death the Saviour permits Himself to be detained not a moment by the dissuasions of His friends, but gladly by the cry of a blind man's distress.—"What wilt thou that I should do unto thee?" One must earnestly wish to be made whole by Jesus.—What a faith is it, that really heals the spiritually blind?—In order to be able to follow Jesus one must see Him; in order to follow Him aright, one must praise God.—The good example of a sinner healed finds imitation on the part of others.— Blind Bartimæus a guide to a truly Christian celebration of the communion; his history shows us: 1. The right *temper* for the communion, *a.* steady sense of wretchedness, *b.* eager longing for deliverance, *c.* courageous coming to Jesus; 2. the highest *comfort* of the communion, that the Saviour, *a.* knows us, *b.* calls us, *c.* hears us; 3. the *fruit* of the communion most to be desired: *a.* that our eyes may see Him, *b.* our feet follow Him, *c.* our tongues praise Him.

STARKE:—QUESNEL:—We know not, like Jesus Christ, the time of our sacrifice and death, but we know well that we are ever coming nearer to the moment, and we therefore greatly need to think thereon and prepare ourselves therefor, 2 Tim. iv. 6.—Jews and Gentiles have alike shamefully laid hands on Jesus, why then blame we each the other?—*Nova Bibl. Tub.:*—As God dealt with His child Jesus, so does He deal with all believers: suffering must precede, afterwards follows joy.—*Bibl. Wirt.:*—To judge with fleshly thoughts concerning the kingdom of Christ is not well.—*Nova Bibl. Tub.:*—The blind man a poor man.—HEDINGER:—Would God we were blind, then should we see.—The Lord is in time of distress nearer to us than we think.—CANSTEIN:— Is there indeed anything pleasanter for a sinner to hear than when he learns that the Fount of Light, the Chief Physician, Jesus, is coming towards Him ? —Whoever lets Jesus pass by and detains Him not with his prayer is left helpless.—Many times do we experience from those that go before and have a guise of piety, the greatest temptation and the most numerous hindrances in our Christian life.—Faith cannot hold its peace; whoever believes, he speaks.— CANSTEIN:—How often does a God-fearing soul dwell in a wretched body.—God leads one man not like another.—The friendliness of Jesus in converse with all manner of men, especially the poor and needy, calls us to imitation.—OSIANDER:—We will rejoice from our hearts when to our neighbors also salvation is brought from God.—J. MÜLLER:—The history of the blind man at Jericho a mirror of the spiritual recovery of man. [John Newton's "Mercy, O thou Son of David," gives the very soul of this scene.— C. C. S.]—LISCO:—Pray, and it shall be given you.

On the Pericope.—SCHEFFER:—The last journey of the Redeemer to Jerusalem.—F. W. KRUMMACHER: —The stages on the journey to the cross.—FUCHS: —The Saviour on His last sorrowful journey to Jerusalem: 1. Submissive as to His own suffering; 2. compassionate towards the sorrow of others.—ARNDFELD:—The true evangelical fast-keeping: 1. Concerning the fasting mood; 2. concerning the fasting prayers.—COVARD:—How we may celebrate the approaching Passion-week to the blessing of our heart and life.—STIER:—The present blindness of many Christians to the right understanding of the suffering and death of Jesus Christ: 1. How it is with the blindness; 2. whereby it is healed; 3. what we then see and experience.—BRAUNE:—The light that breaks forth from the Passion of Christ. In the Passion of Christ we learn to esteem aright: 1. The sin of the world; 2. the woe of the time.—BURKHARDT:—How it comes that even to well-disposed innocent souls the word of the cross is yet hidden for a while.—The happy blind beggar.—BOMHARDT: —What the passing of Christ to His suffering says to us.—STAUDT:—The prayer, "Jesus, Son of David, have mercy on me": 1. Its necessity; 2. its power;

3. Its nature.—STEINHAUSER:—What is it that we see when through Christ the eyes of our spirit are opened?

VAN OOSTERZEE (from a missionary sermon):—"The sighing creation shows itself to our eyes like Bartimæus at Jericho's gate. Not yet were his eyes unclosed, but already from afar the footsteps of the coming Saviour sound in his ears; already it is told him who approaches; already does he throw the mantle off that hinders him from making haste towards the Deliverer. Yet a little while and he has received his sight and follows the Lord, and heaven and earth sing praises at the sight to God and His Only-begotten."

4. Jesus and Zaccheus (CH. XIX. 1-10).

1, 2 And *Jesus* entered and passed through Jericho. And, behold, *there was* a man named Zaccheus, which was the chief among the publicans [and he was a chief tax-
3 gatherer], and he [this man] was rich. And he sought to see Jesus who he was; and
4 could not for the press, because he was little of stature. And he ran before, and
5 climbed up into a sycamore tree to see him; for he was to pass that way. And when Jesus came to the place, he looked up, and saw him, and said unto him, Zaccheus,
6 make haste, and come down; for to-day I must abide at thy house. And he made
7 haste, and came down, and received him joyfully. And when they saw *it*, they all
8 murmured, saying, That he was gone to be guest with a man that is a sinner. And Zaccheus stood [or, came forward], and said unto the Lord; Behold, Lord, the half of my goods I give to the poor; and if I have taken any thing from any man by false
9 accusation, I restore *him* fourfold. And Jesus said unto him, This day is salvation
10 come to this house, forasmuch as he also is a son of Abraham. For the Son of man is come to seek and to save that which was lost.

EXEGETICAL AND CRITICAL.

Vs. 2. **Zaccheus.**—Hebrew זַּ!, "Pure," Ezra ii. 9; Nehem. vii. 14. This Hebrew name with Greek ending of itself denotes him as a man of Jewish origin; comp. vs. 9. According to the Clementines, he afterwards became a disciple of Peter, and Bishop of Cæsarea. *See Homil.* iii. 63, and *Recogn.* iii. 65. Later Jewish traditions in reference to his descent are found in SEPP, *L. J.* iii. p. 166. He is ἀρχιτελώνης, an administrator of the taxes, to whom the oversight over the common publicans was committed; perhaps plenipotentiary of one of the Roman knights, who often sustained the dignity of Publicani. At Jericho, where in this time a large amount of balsam was produced and exported, the office of tax-gatherer was doubtless an important post. That Zaccheus was rich, appears not only from the place which he had farmed, but also from the liberal way in which he sought to make good previously committed injustice. But that this wealth did not yet satisfy his heart, is made evident by his eager longing after Jesus.

Vs. 3. **He sought to see Jesus.**—Without doubt, the fame of Jesus had come to his ears, but he did not yet know Him by sight. Herod also had displayed the same longing, ch. ix. 7-9; but is there any need of intimating that the curiosity of Zaccheus sprang from a nobler source? In him we are entitled to presuppose a state of mind like that of the Greeks, John xii. 21. After he has heard the wonderful and in part contradictory reports that were in circulation respecting Jesus, an obscure longing for higher treasures has been awakened in his heart, —a longing of which, however, he cannot as yet give any precise account to himself. A very favorable testimony for him is even the fact that he leaves his dwelling, and places himself on the way where the caravan going to the feast must pass by; yet in vain does he strive to discover a spot that will secure him a comfortable standing-place and an unobstructed view; great as is his interest, his stature is proportionably diminutive, so that at last he climbs a tree, on which he finds both rest and an unobstructed view along the road; and he also feels himself now, in the hope of at last obtaining his wish, so happy that he takes no account of the mockeries to which he, the smallest, and yet in a certain sense a great, man, was doubtless exposed in the midst of the jubilant throng, on account of his singular proceeding.

Vs. 4. **A sycamore tree**, συκομορέα.—*See* Lachmann and Tischendorf: the *Ficus Ægyptia* of Pliny. *Arbor moro similis folio, magnitudine, adspectu.* *See* WINER, *in voce.* The fruit is, according to the accounts of travellers, pleasant and sweet-tasting. But here the sycamore bears a fruit of the noblest and rarest kind, which is to ripen for the refreshment of Jesus.

Vs. 5. **Jesus . . . saw him.**—It is not necessary to explain the acquaintance of Jesus with Zaccheus as supernatural (Olshausen); nor have we any more need of taking refuge in the assumption of a relation unknown to us between the two (Meyer), or conjecturing that some one had designedly mentioned him to our Lord (Paulus). The difficulty disappears if we only transfer ourselves fairly to the scene of the event. By the very exceptionalness of his position, Zaccheus strikes the eye of all. His name goes from mouth to mouth. One shows him to another. Here and there dislike manifests itself against the doubtless not universally beloved chief publican, comp. vs. 7, and, therefore, in an entirely natural way the Saviour's look is directed upon Zaccheus. But what is truly Divine consists in this: that our Lord at once fathoms the heart of the man with the same look which once followed Nathanael into solitude, John i. 48, and that He fulfils his longing for a better good in a way which causes Zaccheus to find more than he had at the moment sought. "*Nomine se appellari, Zacchæus non potuit non et admirari et lœtari.*" Bengel.

To-day I must abide at thy house.—Stop a while to rest. Comp. vs. 7, and Matt. x. 11. "Δεῖ is uttered from the consciousness of the Divine disposition of events, vs. 10." Meyer. If this utterance, on the one hand, indicates the haste which well knows that it has no time to lose and will never come again to Jericho, it also beyond doubt expresses, on the other hand, the joy of the Redeemer, who finds the sinner, as the sinner had sought his Redeemer. For the Saviour there exists here an inward necessity to turn in at no other dwelling than that of the publican; His heart commands it, the constraint of compassion tells Him so. "As now in Zacchæus the longing to see Jesus came from the prevenient grace of God, and was the beginning of faith, so was this spark of faith by Christ's address mightily strengthened."

Vs. 7. **When they saw it they all murmured.**—It is, of course, understood that we have not to understand this of the disciples (Calvin), but of the Jews, who had been witnesses of the joy with which Zacchæus received the Lord at the entrance of his dwelling. With greater haste than he had ever used for the taking in of the most considerable gain, Zacchæus has opened his house for the Exalted Traveller, to whom his heart already feels itself drawn. Yet what prepares for him the most delightful surprise is to others a scandal, and soon the smothered murmur of censure gains distinctness: "He is gone to be guest with a man that is a sinner." Παρά must in the construction not be connected with εἰσῆλθεν but with καταλῦσαι, since the latter has no other significance than ξενίζεσθαι. We do not, however, from these words alone need to draw the conclusion that Zacchæus was a sinner above many others—for publican and sinner were, in the mouths of many, words of one and the same meaning—and quite as little that Jesus really spent the whole night in the dwelling of Zacchæus, and did not continue His journey till the following day. Καταλῦσαι, it is true, is commonly taken in this sense, *e. g.*, by Meyer and De Wette, as also by Schleiermacher, *l. c.* p. 174. But the example John i. 39 does not prove this, and our Lord's concluding declaration: "To-day is salvation come to this house," would be deprived of its natural relation to the other: "To-day must I abide at thy house," if both sayings had not been uttered in *one* day. Apparently, therefore, we have to assume that our Lord, who was manifestly hastening to Jerusalem, spent only some hours, the remnant of the day, with Zacchæus, and this of itself was sufficient to make Him with many an object of offence. While every publican, even as such, was odious to the people, who wished to be tributary to Jehovah alone, they had undoubtedly learned of the numerous priests who dwelt at Jericho to look down upon an ἀρχιτελώνης with double contempt. It also bears witness to the unfavorable feeling against our Lord which had so greatly increased in Judæa, that He could scarcely advance a step without drawing on Himself new censure. But if any think that we must assume that the Saviour really spent the night also with Zacchæus, we must at all events conceive that which is related vss. 8, 9, as not taking place on the following morning, but soon after the arrival of our Lord, under the first fresh impression of His personal appearance.

Vs. 8. **And Zaccheus came forward and said.**—Not as though the admonitions of his Guest had now for the first time exercised such an influence upon this publican (Kuinoel), and still less because he was persuaded that no one would be able to charge upon him the least deceit, because he was honesty itself (F. R. SCHNEIDER, *Gesch. J. Chr.* ii. p. 84), but because he in this way wished to give an unequivocal proof of his thankfulness for the undeserved honor that had fallen to his lot. Strikingly does the liberality of the chief publican contrast with the mean-spiritedness of the multitude, vs. 7. And if ever the saying proved true, that it is indeed difficult yet not impossible for a rich man to enter into the kingdom of God, this now came to pass in the words of Zacchæus. He will requite the honor bestowed on his house by some special act; and already does he know his Guest so intimately as this, that he is well persuaded as to what kind of offering will be to Him even far more acceptable than the most splendid feast. Deeply did he feel his accumulated ill-desert over against the immaculately Holy One; but this compassion shown him encouraged him to rise out of the depth into which he had sunk. With entire spontaneousness he begins to speak of the moral obliquity which had earlier misled him, consciously or unconsciously, to defraud any one of anything, and more than the letter of the law makes his duty will he restore. The hypothetical form of his vow, εἴ-τι, is not merely a milder expression of confession (Meyer); it is, on the other hand, entirely natural in the mouth of a man who has so long and so often offended through the common dishonesty of his calling, that he at the moment does not even call to mind when in particular he had gained anything by chicanery. Enough, the restitution which Moses had required only in a special case of theft (Ex. xxii. 1), he will make in the case of everything that he has gained in a dishonest way, and while, according to the later Jewish writers, even he was distinguished as an eminent Israelite, who destined the fifth part of his property to benevolence, Zacchæus gives not less than the half of his goods to the poor. In truth: "*hæc est sapiens illa stultitia, quam de sycomoro, tanquam fructum vitæ, legerat, rapta reddere, propria relinquere, visibilia contemnere.*" Beza. Zacchæus evidently shows that the principle is not strange to him which is expressed in the old maxim: "*Peccatum non remittitur, nisi ablatum restituatur.*" Whether even previously the requirement addressed by John the Baptist to the publicans had come to his ears: "Exact no more than is appointed," we know not; at all events, he had hitherto not acted agreeably to it. But now it is as if not only a new light had risen to his eyes, but also a new life to his heart. The day when Jesus entered his house is the birth-day of his new better man, and while he of his own free choice becomes poorer in earthly goods, his wealth in heavenly treasures augments, so that To-day in his consciousness draws a sharp dividing line between Yesterday and To-morrow. This consciousness he expresses in a surprising manner: the *ingenua confessio* and the *voluntaria restitutio* complement one another admirably.

Vs. 9. **This day is salvation come to this house.**—Our Lord addresses these words directly to Zacchæus (πρός), not merely in relation to him (De Wette, and others); that He does it in the third person arises from the fact, that this declaration is meant to comprise at the same time a vindication of His own coming to this house, and a well-deserved eulogy for Zacchæus himself. He says that salvation has come to the house of the publican, not because that house had received one of His visits, but because its inhabitant really showed himself another man from what he appeared to be in the eyes of the multitude. While they had even just before named him an ἀνὴρ ἁμαρτωλός, the Saviour now names him a υἱὸς Ἀβραάμ, not because he had before been a heathen, but now showed the character of a true Israelite (Maldonatus and others), nor yet merely because he by his conversion had become a true Israelite (ἐστὶ in the sense of ἐγένετο, Kuinoel), but because it was manifest that he, how much soever the people reviled him, yet belonged to the people of God's choice. The unloving censurers had overlooked the fact that he, as a son of Abraham, was nevertheless still related to them according to the flesh; Jesus bestowed upon him the eulogy that he also belonged, according to the Spirit, to the posterity of the friend of God; comp. Luke xiii. 16.

Vs. 10. **For the Son of Man.**—Statement of the ground of the previous declaration. Where a son of Abraham, according to the flesh, is a lost one, just there is My appearance necessary; where a lost one is renewed unto a spiritual son of Abraham, there is the purpose of My appearance attained.— 'HΛϑε signifies not entirely the same as the ἔρχεσϑαι εἰς τὸν κόσμον of John, where the secondary idea of preëxistence is not to be mistaken; absolutely used, it appears to designate the *public* manifestation and coming forth of the Son of Man.—**To seek,** like the Shepherd, ch. xv. 4. Comp. Matt. ix. 13; xviii. 11.—**To save,** not in the sense of to *bless*ed, but in the sense of *to rescue*. The σωτηρία of the New Testament is the preservation of that which would otherwise have become the certain prey of an irrevocable destruction, as Zacchæus would have become if this hour had not dawned for him.— What afterwards became of him we know not. In all probability he remained in his office of tax-gatherer; at least the Saviour, who sees the end of His own career approaching, does not call him away from it, as he formerly called Matthew and others. He knows that such a man will afterwards be an ornament to the calling of the publican, and prove himself continually a son of Abraham. Yet enough, at all events, when Jesus now soon afterwards left Jericho, He knew that in this city at least one house was found in which He had already bestowed that which He, dying, was soon to procure for a whole lost world—σωτηρία!

DOCTRINAL AND ETHICAL.

1. In the days of Joshua there was a terrible curse uttered upon Jericho, Josh. vi. 26, and in the time of Ahab this curse was fulfilled in a not less terrible manner, 1 Kings xvi. 34. With the entry of the Saviour into Jericho there dawns at least for one house in Jericho a day of inestimable blessing, and more yet would have become partakers of this blessing along with Zacchæus, had they only known the time of their visitation.

2. The coming of our Saviour to the City of Palms in the midst of the tumult of an innumerable throng; the silent inquiry of a longing soul after Him, and the sweet answer of prevenient grace; the entrance of Jesus into the favored house with all His peace, and the sacrifice rendered by the thanksgiving of the surprised inhabitant thereof;—all this has a beautiful symbolical sense, which makes this gospel above any other fitted for the dedication of a church, especially when it is brought into connection with the inexhaustibly rich epistle, Rev. xxi. 1–5.

3. "Little soul, thinkest thou then that for thee no tree has grown on which thou mightest climb, that thy eyes might behold Him that bringeth salvation to thy heart?" Gossner.

4. The very great diversity of the ways in which God leads sinners to conversion becomes manifest when we compare the history of Zacchæus with so many others; for instance, with that of the Penitent Thief, of Saul, Cornelius, of the Jailer, &c. The history of this chief of the publicans reminds us of the parable of the Treasure in the Field, and still more of that of the Pearl of Great Price. At the same time the reception which Jesus makes ready for the publican is an admirable commentary on His own word, Rev. iii. 20.

5. The connection of πίστις with μετάνοια is vividly presented in the history of Zacchæus. On the one hand, no receptivity for faith on the Saviour, unless already in his soul an incipient, secret but powerful change had taken place; on the other hand, no true faith that did not of itself lead to a thorough alteration of the life and the method of business. It is foolish to suppose that Zacchæus, by the restoration of extorted gain, could have compensated his guilt before God, but just as little would his repentance have been a sincere one if he had felt no necessity of setting right his trespasses in this way. The consolatory consciousness that the guilt of sin is blotted out cannot possibly refresh us, if it is not at the same time our highest wish to be relieved from the ruinous dominion of the same.

6. The Pauline doctrine of Justification by Faith is by this narrative both explained and confirmed. Zacchæus is the precursor of the many heathens who have not sought for righteousness and yet have obtained righteousness, Rom. ix. 30–33. The Jews, on the other hand, who in their holiness of works murmured against the bestowal of free grace, remained then and remain yet—shut out.

7. In conclusion, the circumstance deserves well to be brought into use in behalf of future Apologetics, that the whole history of Zacchæus bears a character of freshness, truth, and absence of invention, on which every doubt is broken, as even Strauss, L. J. i. p. 613, has conceded. But with this its historical truth is united its ideal and eternal truth, according to which this journey of the Saviour may be called the symbol of His continuous journey through the world's history, in which He now, as ever, reveals Himself to the individual in His saving power, while the greater part, even yet, continually misunderstand Him or mock Him.

HOMILETICAL AND PRACTICAL.

The hour of blessing for the once accursed City of Palms.—Where Jesus passes by He cannot remain hidden.—The rich Zacchæus in all his poverty; the subsequently impoverished Zacchæus in all his wealth. —The longing to see Jesus: 1. How it arises; 2. wherein it reveals itself; 3. in what way it is satisfied. —How the tumult of the world often hinders us still from seeing and hearing our Lord at hand.—In order to see Jesus well, one must climb; in order to receive Him rightly, one must come down.—He hath filled the hungry with good things, but the rich He hath sent empty away.—The courage of the poor sinner. —The looking of Jesus up to Zaccheus no less proof of grace than His looking down towards many others. —Where the concern is to save a sinner, there to the Saviour a stopping on His way to death is no loss of time.—It is not by the beauty of nature, but by a work of grace, that our Lord allows Himself to be detained at Jericho.—" Make haste and come down, for to-day I must abide at thy house," text for a communion address. This assurance: 1. For whom does it hold true? 2. what does it prove? 3. what does it promise? 4. what does it require?—Jesus a Saviour who: 1. Must come into our house; 2. and can come even to-day; 3. and comes for our salvation.—Jesus invites Himself, if one should not venture to invite Him.—The Good Shepherd calls His sheep by name, John x. 3.—Even to-day does the world take offence when the Saviour turns in at the house of the sinner. —Parallel between this event and Luke vii. 36–50. Here also the displeasure of Simon on the one hand, the penitence of the sinning woman on the other hand.—Zaccheus, the longer for salvation, is: 1. Courageously bold; 2. inwardly rejoiced; 3. by many contemned; 4. highly honored.—The little Zaccheus a great hero of faith: 1. How longingly he waits; 2. how frankly he comes; 3. how bountifully he thanks. —The making good of former trespasses: 1. A necessity naturally felt; 2. a sure token; 3. a blessed fruit, of upright faith.—" To-day is salvation come unto this house," a text for baptismal and marriage addresses.—The day of true conversion the most memorable day of life, 2 Cor. v. 17.— Where Jesus gains disciples, there has Abraham also acquired genuine sons.—Jesus is come to seek, etc.: 1. A most humiliating; 2. an indescribably comforting; 3. a powerfully sanctifying, saying.

STARKE:—J. HALL:—From a great sinner there may come a great saint.— OSIANDER:—God has chosen some souls of the rich as well as of the poor to eternal life.—Many a man does something that in his calling appears to him to be unimpeachable, but faith judges very differently; 2 Sam. vi. 16.—Christ willingly directs His eyes upon penitent sinners; Luke xxii. 61.—QUESNEL:—God gives the longing to know Him, and if that is not despised He then gives more. —The Lord Jesus wishes to come spiritually to us; John xiv. 23.—MAJUS:—We may well be conversant with sinners if we only do not mean to practise sin with them.—Compassion towards the poor avails not for salvation, yet must it be practised for those that will be saved; Deut. xxiv. 17.—LANGII Op.:— How many are like Zaccheus in riches and unrighteousness, but how few in true conversion and restitution.—*Nova Bibl. Tub.*:—Happy the house where Jesus becomes a Guest !—With true conversion there come to pass great alterations in houses, cities, and countries.—The farther from the world, the nearer to God.—HEUBNER:—Jesus is accessible to all classes. —Even yet He finds necessity to abide with those that desire Him.—What an honor to entertain Jesus ! —The days of salvation in our life when Jesus comes especially near to us.—Through faith we come into communion with all the saints of the early time.— The visible church leads into the invisible.—Our churches as dwelling-places of Jesus; they are: 1. Reminders of Him, vss. 1–4; 2. sources of His gracious visitation, vss. 5–7; 3. summonses on the part of Jesus to conscientious fulfilment of duty, vs. 8; 4. awakenings to the care of our own and others' souls, vss. 9–10.—PALMER:—The gracious hour of the Lord: 1. How it comes (unexpected, but not unprepared for); 2. what it brings (Christ, and in Him salvation); 3. what traces it leaves behind (a heart disposed to repentance and love).—ARNDT:—Jesus the Friend of man: 1. Towards whom He reveals His love; 2. what moves Him thereto; 3. how He proceeds; 4. what effects he produces; 5. by what means he accomplishes and crowns His work.—J. DIEDRICH:— How men's souls, truly for their salvation, meet with Christ.—W. HOFACKER:—The beautiful process of development which the noble plant of faith, under the influence of Divine grace, passes through: 1. The tender germs; 2. the beautiful flower; 3. the wholesome fruits of the plant.—GEROK:—The concurrence of human will and Divine grace.—KNAPP:—Concerning the ever-abounding blessing of a true personal acquaintance with Christ.—HARLESS:—Jesus receives sinners [*Jesus nimmt die Sünder an*].

---

5. Jesus in relation to the Sanguine Hopes of His Disciples (Vss. 11–27).

11 And as they heard these things, he added and spake a parable, because he was nigh to Jerusalem, and because they thought [or, imagined] that the kingdom of God should
12 [was about] immediately appear [to be manifested immediately]. He said therefore, A certain nobleman [εὐγενής] went into a far country to receive for himself a kingdom,
13 and to return. And he called his ten servants, and delivered them ten pounds, and
14 said unto them, Occupy [Do business *therewith*] till I come.¹ But his citizens [or, those of his city] hated him, and sent a message [embassy] after him, saying, We will not
15 have [we do not wish] this *man* to reign over us. And it came to pass, that when he was returned, having received the kingdom, then he commanded these servants to be called unto him, to whom he had given the money, that he might know how much
16 every man had gained by trading. Then came the first, saying, Lord, thy pound hath
17 gained ten pounds. And he said unto him, Well [Excellent], thou good servant: be-
18 cause thou hast been faithful in a very little, have thou authority over ten cities. And
19 the second came, saying, Lord, thy pound hath gained five pounds. And he said like-
20 wise to him, Be thou also over five cities. And another² came, saying, Lord, behold,

21 *here is* thy pound, which I have kept laid up in a napkin [handkerchief]: For I feared thee, because thou art an austere man: thou takest up that [which] thou layedst not
22 down [didst not deposit], and reapest that [which] thou didst not sow. And [om., And, V. O.[2]] he saith unto him, Out of thine own mouth will I judge thee, *thou* wicked servant. Thou knewest that I was an austere man, taking up that I laid not down
23 [which I did not deposit], and reaping that [which] I did not sow: Wherefore then [And wherefore, καὶ διὰ τί] gavest not thou my money into the bank, that at my com-
24 ing I might have required mine own with usury [collected it with interest]? And he said unto them that stood by, Take from him the pound, and give *it* to him that hath
25, 26 ten pounds. (And they said unto him, Lord, he hath ten pounds.) For [om., For, V. O.[4]] I say unto you, That unto every one which hath shall be given; and from him
27 that hath not, even that [which] he hath shall be taken away from him. But those mine enemies, which would not that I should reign over them, bring hither, and slay *them*[5] before me.

[[1] Vs. 13.—Van Oosterzee translates: "while I am on the journey," on the strength of the reading ἐν ᾧ for ἕως. 'Εν ᾧ is found in A., B., D., Cod. Sin., K., L., R., and is accepted by Griesbach, Lachmann, Tischendorf, Meyer, Tregelles, Alford. Bleek, however, objects to it as not giving a good sense, as ἔρχομαι cannot well have any other meaning than "come" in the connection.—C. C. S.]
[2] Vs. 20.—Ὁ ἕτερος should be read, according to B., D., [Cod. Sin.,] L., [R.,] cursives, Lachmann, Tischendorf, [Tregelles, Alford. Meyer regards the article as a mechanical repetition of those in vss. 16, 18.—C. C. S.]
[3] Vs. 22.—Δέ is not sufficiently attested.
[4] Vs. 26.—The γάρ of the *Recepta* is apparently borrowed from Matt. xxv. 29. [Omitted by Meyer, Alford; bracketed by Lachmann, Tregelles; retained by Tischendorf. Not found in B., Cod. Sin., L. More reason for adding it, than for omitting it if genuine.—C. C. S.]
[5] Vs. 27.—"Them" being in italics in E. V. indicates the absence of the pronoun in the Greek. Tischendorf, Tregelles, and Alford, however, read αὐτοὺς on the authority of B., [Cod. Sin.,] F., L., R.—C. C. S.]

EXEGETICAL AND CRITICAL.

Vs. 11. And as they heard these things.—The instruction communicated by Luke in the next following parable, our Lord may have delivered while yet in the house of Zaccheus, but we doubt whether it was uttered just at the entrance of this dwelling before the ears of the murmuring throng, vs. 7 (Meyer). With better right, perhaps, we might conclude from vs. 28 that the Saviour delivered this parable immediately before His departure from Jericho. But, however this may be, it stands in direct connection with His declaration, vs. 10. It may be that the mention of the Son of Man having come, threw a new spark into the tinder of their earthly expectations, although it is difficult to state more exactly what precise connection there could be between this declaration and the thought that the kingdom of God should become παραχρῆμα manifest. We know, however, how many looks were directed with the liveliest interest upon the approaching Passover, where it appeared that the intense opposition between Jesus and His enemies was about to come to a public decision. Besides this, they were already in the neighborhood of the capital; and might there not there, even by the last word, be kindled anew the expectation of that which had been most longingly desired? In no case do we need to deny that the now-following parable was addressed to the disciples of the Saviour also. From ch. xviii. 34 it appears that they were as yet by no means cured of their earthly Messianic hopes, and here also, as often, there lay a certain truth at the basis of their error. That the kingdom of God should become manifest, ἀναφαίνεσθαι, was in and of itself subject to no doubt, but that it would come into view at this very point, and that in a palpable, sensuous form—in other words, that Christ would be glorified without a previous separation from His own; in that lay the error of which they must be immediately cured, and to controvert it the following parable is designed.

A parable.—That the parable coincides in many respects with that of the Talents (Matt. xxv. 14-30), and yet is in no way identical with that, but is more or less modified in the redaction, Lange has, *Matthew*, p. 441, convincingly demonstrated. So also the assertion is destitute of any ground (Strauss) that this parable has arisen from an only half-successful amalgamation of two others, namely, that of the Talents and that of the Unfaithful Husbandmen. Undoubtedly the representation of a king who, instead of arms, rather entrusts his money to his servants, has at the first look something strange, but if this admits of sufficient explanation from the purpose of the parable, it can by no means prove anything against the originality and exactness of the rendering of Luke. Precisely in this way would our Lord teach His disciples that His true subjects were not, like those of other kingdoms, to strive with arms in their hands, but that they were to carry on business with the entrusted pound, while not till after His return (vs. 27) should they be called to take part in His victory over His irreconcilable foes. In view of the relative coincidence which exists between this parable and that of the Talents in Matthew, the question can hardly be avoided which of them was first delivered, and may consequently be considered as the foundation of the other. Directly in opposition to the common views (Schleiermacher, Neander), we believe that the parable of the Talents must be regarded as a further explanation of the parable before us, not the reverse; in other words, that the first delivered parable (in Luke) is also the simplest; that the one subsequently uttered (in Matthew) bears, on the other hand, a more complicated character. For here the work for all the servants is alike; there there exists a diversity in the number of the talents. Here there is bestowed on the servant only recompense; there with the recompense an extended eulogy. Here it is only an ignominious loss; there also a terrible judgment, which is the punishment of the slothful servant—grounds enough for the opinion that in reality the parable of the Pounds must have preceded that of the Talents. It is true, there are single features in the last-named parable which are less elaborated than in the former: but this phenomenon is sufficiently explained if we only consider that one was, at all events, delivered shortly after the other, and that the parable of the Talents can be only so far called a variation—or, if we will, a short summary of the one before us—as this, that in it the chief thought is modified according to the necessity of the disciples, and set forth yet more clearly. Because the parable, Matt. xxv., was delivered exclusively for the faithful disciples, and not, like this, in the presence also of secret enemies, it was there unnecessary again to depict the fate of the rebellious citizens, without, however, the parable of the Talents having suffered the least loss in completeness by the falling away of this feature; on the other hand, it has even gained in unity thereby. Thus may the two stand very well independently by one another; and, moreover, the parable of the Pounds has this peculiar character, that it sets forth the King of the kingdom of God on the one hand in contrast with His servants, on the other with His enemies. In the prospect of righteous retribution which is prepared for both at His coming, is the inner unity of the representation grounded.

Vs. 12. **A certain nobleman.**—An indirect intimation of the kingly descent and dignity of our Lord; at the same time a prophecy of His going away from the earth, and a comforting representation of His departure to the Father, as of the means ordained for the obtaining of the kingly dignity and glory. Finally, the definite assurance that the interval between the departure and the return of the Lord is only an *interim*.

Vs. 13. **Ten pounds.**—$\Delta\epsilon\kappa a \mu\nu\tilde{a}s$. It is not probable that we have here to understand a Hebrew *mina* of 100 shekels; rather an *Attic mina* of 100 drachmæ =21 thalers (§14),* about one-sixtieth of the talent, Matt. xxv. 15. The distinction is sufficiently explained from the consideration that the lord in the latter parable leaves behind his whole property in the hands of his servants. Here, on the other hand, he only commits to them a slight gift, by which their faithfulness in the least is to be proved, comp. ch. xvi. 10. In comparison with the great reward which is hereafter bestowed above upon the faithful, even five talents are an $\delta\lambda\iota\gamma o\nu$, in comparison with which ten pounds deserved to be called an $\epsilon\lambda\alpha\chi\iota\sigma\tau o\nu$, vs. 17.—$\Pi\rho\alpha\gamma\mu\alpha\tau\epsilon\acute{\upsilon}\epsilon\sigma\theta\alpha\iota$ is used by the Rabbins also in the sense of $\epsilon\rho\gamma\acute{a}\zeta\epsilon\sigma\theta a\iota$, Matt. xxv. 26= *negotiari*. This must they do, not till the King returns, but while he is on the journey. 'Eν $\tilde{\phi}$, *see notes on the text*. General indication of the period of time which remains allotted them for trading. He spends the time in travelling, they the same time in business.

Vs. 14. **Embassy.**—A peculiar designation, taken from the political history of this period, of the stubborn enmity of the Jews (*see* below), especially as this should exhibit itself after our Lord's departure from the earth. The capriciousness of the enmity appears from this, that the ambassadors do not give even a word of reason for their dislike, and the degree in which they despise the king finds expression in the contemptuous $\tau o\tilde{\upsilon}\tau o\nu$. That this essay has no success, since the king nevertheless receives the kingdom, and returns as judge, appears from the sequel of the parable. Before, however, he punishes his enemies, his servants must give account for themselves.

* [Equal, of course, to many times the present value of that sum.—C. C. S.]

Vs. 15. **How much every man,** $\tau\iota s \tau\iota$, contracted form for two different questions. It must be shown what form of business each one had carried on, and with what success. By the pounds we are to understand in general that which the Lord bestows on His servants that they may labor therewith for the kingdom of God and make profit: as well the external possessions as the inward endowment and energy. In deep humility all the servants acknowledge that this gain is not their own, but the lord's, therefore with emphasis, **Thy pound.**

Vs. 16. **Gained ten pounds.**—Here the thought comes into the foreground that faithfulness, even with the smallest $\chi\acute{a}\rho\iota\sigma\mu a$, may become a source of inexhaustible blessing. In Matthew the emphasis is laid more upon the proportionableness of the capital, the profit, and the reward. In this the faithfulness is rewarded simply with a more extended circle of operation (" I will place thee over many things "), and with the enjoyment of the joy of their Lord. Finally, the praise here bestowed on the first servant is withheld from the second, who with the same pound had only gained the half of what the first had gained, in order thereby to intimate that the reward should be different in just that proportion in which the profit of the labor is greater or less. As to the rest, the government over five cities is of itself distinction enough, especially when we consider that the cities lie in the midst of the land of the rebels, that is now become the king's kingdom, and from which the enemies are now soon to be exterminated.

Vs. 20. **In a handkerchief.**—The conduct of the third had been, therefore, in direct conflict with his calling; without personal faithfulness or love he had in secret calculated that if he had gained much, his lord would pluck the fruit thereof; if he, on the other hand, lost, that the responsibility and the damage would be on his side, since he, at all events, would have to give back the amount entrusted. Thus had he given ear to the voice of self-seeking, suffered himself to be strengthened in his natural slothfulness, and instead of laboring in the sweat of his brow for the interest of his lord, he had hidden the entrusted money in the now entirely superfluous handkerchief [Greek, $\epsilon\nu$ $\sigma o\upsilon\delta a\rho\iota\omega$; literally, sweat-cloth]. To excuse his words and his character (Olshausen) appears to us to conflict as well with the letter as with the spirit of the parable. We see evidently that our Saviour will describe the slothful egoist, who allows himself to be held back by carnal considerations from that which in any event would have been his duty, and who believes that he can excuse his mean conduct by the appeal to the austere character of his lord. So much greater, therefore, must his consternation be, when the very ground made the pretext by him for his vindication prepares the way for his condemnation. *See* further on Matt. xxv. 25, 26.

Vs. 22. **Out of thine own mouth will I judge thee.**—" A wonderfully happy argument *ex concessis* " (Lange). Comp. Matt. xii. 37. His own word is retorted upon the slothful one, and thereon a question is grounded, beginning with $\kappa a\iota$ $\delta\iota\grave{a}$ $\tau\iota$, which brings him into contradiction with himself. The lord does not concede to him that he is actually a hard man, but only refutes the shameless one on the position he had most arbitrarily taken. "*Ne dicas, te invenire non potuisse, quibus pecunia esset opus. Argentarii ab omnibus pecuniam sumunt fænore. Sensus est: non est etiam, quod in collocanda* *pecunia periculum obtendas ; mea erat ; ego jam exegissem non tuo, sed meo periculo.*" Grotius.

Vs. 24. **Unto them that stood by.**—Not the other δοῦλοι (Kuinoel), who had already rendered account, but the halberdiers, who surround him when he appears in his majesty, comp. Matt. xxv. 31. The astonishment which these testify (vs. 25 may be put in a parenthesis, Lachmann and Ewald), gives the king occasion now more particularly to give the reason for his severe determination. Without giving heed to the remonstrance, he repeats the great principle, "Unto every one which hath," &c. *See* ch. viii. 18, and the admirable remarks of NEANDER, *L. J., ad loc.* The positive retribution, Matt. xxv. 30, which is threatened against the unprofitable servant is omitted here, probably because the judgment upon the enemies is yet to be declared. Yet by the loss itself decreed against him his unfaithfulness is sufficiently punished; while he that gained the ten pounds has now, besides the gracious recompense, received a happy surprise in addition.

Vs. 27. **But those mine enemies.**—The command is given to the same guards to whom that in vs. 24 was addressed. Contemptuously the enemies are named τούτους (*see* TISCHENDORF, *ad loc.*), as they previously had named their lawful king, τοῦτον.— **Slay them.**—A strong expression of the severity and hopelessness of the Messianic retribution. The sudden breaking off of the parable heightens not a little its beauty.

DOCTRINAL AND ETHICAL.

1. Far more than any other parable of our Lord, the parable of the Ten Pounds is a picture which, as it were, is framed into the political history of that unquiet period. Native princes of minor territories were then sometimes obliged to repair to Rome, in order there to be elevated to their legitimate rank. This had been the case in the Jewish land also with Herod the First, and with Archelaus, and it belongs to the yet too little considered traits of the deep humility of the Son of Man, that He can compare His Ascension, even though only remotely, with the journey of a Herod to Rome ; a μείωσις, and yet, at the same time, an accommodation beyond compare.—But also a second trait of the parable was taken from life, namely, the embassy of the hostile citizens, who sought to work against the dreaded enthronement. We are to understand the fifty Jews, who had followed Archelaus with this very intention, and the eight thousand who afterwards followed these, and earnestly besought Augustus, in the temple of Apollo, that he would free them from the Idumæan prince, and in case of necessity rather even unite them with Syria. In Jericho, where, perhaps not far from the dwelling of Zaccheus, the kingly palace stood which Archelaus had built with princely splendor (*see* JOSEPHUS, *A. J.* xvii. 13, 1), such an allusion was doubly fitting, and at the same time easily intelligible. The bloody vengeance, with the mention of which the parable ends, was in those days often exercised, if at Rome the intrigues of the prince had triumphed over his opponents. It was, moreover, well remembered by the hearers of our Lord how Archelaus, after he had returned as Ethnarch over Judæa and Samaria, had bestowed on his faithful adherents cities for a reward, and had on the other hand, out of vengeance, deprived his enemies of life. (*See A. J.* xiv, 14, 3 ; xv. 6, 7 ; xvii. 9, 3, a. o.) It scarcely needs an intimation how much freshness and life such an historical background imparts to this parabolical instruction, and how spontaneously the question must have arisen : Who is the king—who his servants—who are the enemies that are here spoken of ?

2. The parable of the Ten Pounds was thoroughly fitted to serve as a wholesome antidote against a fourfold error. It might be fancied that the Messianic kingdom would very soon appear; that it would be at once visible on earth; that every one would willingly and with joy submit himself to the same; and finally, that there could be for its subjects no higher calling than that of an inactive enjoyment. In opposition to the first opinion, there is this feature of the parable, that first, the far journey must be made, and therefore ,a comparatively long interval spent before everything could come to the desired issue ; in contrast with the second expectation stands the remark, that not here but elsewhere must the native prince receive the reins of legitimate dominion, before he could vindicate His high rank on His own soil. Over against the third error, our Lord counts it needful to sketch the image of an enmity which would shamelessly, groundlessly, stubbornly, but at the same time also unsuccessfully, lift its head against the King. In opposition to the fourth opinion, He sets forth the image of the calling of the ten servants,—the type of the collective body of all His servants—to the carrying on of business and obtaining of gain. Not as proud warriors, but rather as humble dealers with a very small capital, does He leave them at His going away, and so must all ideal Utopias of their fantasy recede momentarily, at least, before the requirements of the soberest reality.

3. The whole parable is a strong testimony for the elevated self-consciousness of our Lord in reference to His heavenly origin and His high destiny. At the same time it gives a proof of the lofty courage and the still dignity with which He approaches Jerusalem. It is as if once more were heard the roaring of the Lion of the tribe of Judah, before the lamb gives itself to be led to the slaughter. On the one hand the whole Christology of this parable is an echo of many a royal psalm of the Old Testament, especially of Pss. ii. and cx.; on the other hand, we have here the intimation of the more extended eschatological revelations which are afterwards to be given in the Apocalypse.

4. The promise of a future extension and elevation of their activity as the proper reward for the disciples of our Lord, is wholly in the spirit of the Hellenistic Pauline Gospel of Luke, comp. 1 Cor. xiii. 9-12. With this, however, it deserves consideration, that the promise of a personal return of our Lord to earth, vs. 15, comp. Acts iii. 21, is not only made in the Gospel of Matthew, or in the discourses and Epistles of Peter, but also in Luke. Certainly a proof that this doctrine is something more than the mere offspring of a narrow Judaistic theology, and, therefore, at the same time, for all who reject every hope of a personal Parusia as gross Chiliasm, an important intimation that at all events they are not to throw away husk and kernel together.

5. The parable of the Pounds places visibly before our eyes not only the life-calling of the apostles, but also that of all believers. From the fact that here ten servants appear who all receive the same, the diversity recedes before the unity. As bond-servants of their Lord they are called to wait for His return, and that not in inactive rest, but in zealous

activity. They have not to contend with carnal weapons against His enemies, but in the midst of all opposition quietly to proceed with their labor. In the humble position of witnesses to the faith, they must seek with word and deed to spread abroad God's kingdom, and expect their share in the government of the world, not before, but only after, the personal return of the Lord. The success of their endeavors is differently modified according to the diversity of time, talents, and energies; but the reward is suited to the different deserts. In every case it is in proportion to that which was demanded and accomplished. For the ten pounds which the best one gained, he would scarcely have been able to buy a house, and he is placed over ten cities; but never does a reward fall to the portion of the slothful one, who has contented himself merely with this, that he did no positive harm. To gain nothing is the way to lose all, and the injury which one prepares for himself by his own unfaithfulness appears as irrevocable. Certainly here also agrees the word: γίνεσθε δόκιμοι τραπεζίται, which our Lord, according to some, really uttered on this occasion. (According to Dionysius Alexandrinus, Cyril, and others, the admonition, 1 Thess. v. 21, is also to be taken as proceeding from our Lord, and as belonging to the same connection. *See* LARDNER, *Probab.* ii. p. 38.)

6. In the concluding word of the parable there stands before the eyes of our Lord, without doubt, the terrible fate of Jerusalem, which He soon so sadly weeps over, vss. 41, 42. It is the greater for this, that He immediately after these discourses sets forth, in order, for enemies from whom He foresees such hatred, and who are to be condemned to such a punishment, to die the death of a slave.

HOMILETICAL AND PRACTICAL.

Earthly-minded Messianic expectations a weed: 1. Deeply rooted; 2. hard to eradicate; 3. soon shooting up again.—On the point of accomplishing His Priestly offering, our Lord speaks as a Prophet of His future Kingly dignity.—The opinion that the Lord will never come again is, in its kind, not less to be reprobated than the fancy of His apostles that He would never go away.—The parable of the Ten Pounds sketches for us an image: 1. Of the King of the kingdom of God, *a.* His origin, *b.* His destiny, *c.* His departure and return; 2. of His servants, *a.* their calling, *b.* their giving account, *c.* their reward; 3. of His enemies, *a.* their hatred, *b.* their impotency, *c.* their punishment.—The Christian life, that of the merchant: 1. The capital; 2. the income; 3. the profit.—The absolute refusal to acknowledge the kingly authority of our Lord: 1. The height which it reaches; 2. the depth in which it ends.—We must all be manifested; 2 Cor. v. 10.—On what depends the various profit for the kingdom of God, and according to what standard is the diverse recompense calculated?—They who suffer with Christ shall also reign with Him; 2 Tim. ii. 12.—Faithfulness in the least the Saviour esteems not slightly.—The slothful servant condemned from his own words.—If we have presumptuously neglected good, it helps us little if we believe that we have avoided greater evil.—The sins of omission are not less worthy of punishment than the sins of commission; James iv. 17.—The little pound put into a napkin, the greater talent buried in the earth.—Even the angels do not at once comprehend the πολυποίκιλος σοφία in the sentence of the Lord.—No earthly nor heavenly might can alter the judgment once pronounced.—The greater the Lord's forbearance to His enemies has been, so much the more terrible will their judgment be.—The crime of treason is punished under the eyes of the King.—By the extirpation of the enemies of the kingdom of God, the blessedness of the redeemed is perfected.

STARKE:—This parable, as it were the Testament of Christ, in which He shows the nature of His kingdom, &c.—QUESNEL:—Jesus truly of a high descent.—There is no one that has not received from the hand of the Lord gifts wherewith to get usury.—BRENTIUS:—Even the very wisest rulers never satisfy the rabble.—Their humility of heart is the main character of all true servants and children of God.—The growth of grace in us draws the growth of glory after it.—CANSTEIN:—As to worldly business there appertains not only diligence and laboriousness, but also understanding and prudence, so also in spiritual husbandry; Eph. v. 15.—The eternal glory has its fixed degrees.—*Nova Bibl. Tub.:*—Terrible is it that sinners undertake to divert from themselves the guilt of their wickedness, and to push it upon God.—For unreasonable excuses the ungodly are never at a loss.—God is righteous in His judgments; let man only lay his hand upon his mouth.—God will avenge and punish ungodliness not in secret, but before the tribunal of the whole world.—The Almighty God hath committed all judgment to the Son.—Whoever will not let himself be pastured by the lamb, him shall the lion devour.—Up! Christians that die in the Lord—they are setting out towards Jerusalem.

HEUBNER:—Not the abundance and magnitude of what is done, but faithfulness, makes worthy of reward.—Thou needest be no eminent character.—The selfish heart continually hostile to God.—All that originates from God has an inner fructifying power if it is only used aright.—Divine love knows no limits; it gives *ad infinitum.*—LISCO:—The great responsibility of the Christian, which is imposed upon him through the possession of Divine gifts.—The rule according to which the King of the kingdom of heaven will hereafter judge His subjects.—PALMER: —" Him that hath, to him shall be given," &c.; text for communion sermon.—F. W. KRUMMACHER:— " Out of thine own mouth will I judge thee:" the stinging rebuke of apostasy.—BECK:—How we in the light of eternity have to regard this time below.

PART THIRD.

THE Final Conflict and the Culmination of the Glory of the Son of Man.

FIRST SECTION.

THE FINAL CONFLICT.

CHAPTERS XIX. 28—XXIII. 56.

A. *The Entry into Jerusalem, with its attending Circumstances.* CH. XIX. 28–48.

1. The Entry Itself (Vss. 28–40).

(Parallels: Matt. xxi. 1–9; Mark xi. 1–10; John xii. 12–19.)

28 And when he had thus spoken, he went before, ascending up to Jerusalem.
29 And it came to pass, when he was come nigh to Bethphage and Bethany, at the mount
30 called *the mount* of Olives, he sent two of his [the[1]] disciples, Saying, Go ye into the village over against *you*; in the which at your entering ye shall find a colt tied, where-
31 on yet never man sat: loose him, and bring [and loosing him bring[2]] *him hither*. And if any man ask you, Why do ye loose *him?* thus shall ye say unto him, Because the
32 Lord hath need of him. And they that were sent went their way, and found even as
33 he had said unto them. And as they were loosing the colt, the owners thereof said
34 unto them, Why loose ye the colt? And they said, [Because, V. O.[2]] The Lord hath
35 need of him. And they brought him to Jesus: and they cast their [own] garments
36 upon the colt, and they set Jesus thereon. And as he went, they spread their clothes
37 in the way. And when he was come nigh, even now at the descent of the mount of Olives, the whole multitude of the disciples began to rejoice and praise God with a loud
38 voice for all the mighty works that they had seen; Saying, Blessed *be* the King that
39 cometh in the name of the Lord: peace in heaven, and glory in the highest. And some of the Pharisees from among the multitude said unto him, Master [Teacher],
40 rebuke thy disciples. And he answered and said unto them, I tell you that, if these should [shall] hold their peace, the stones would [will] immediately cry out.

[1 Vs. 29.—Αὐτοῦ omitted by Tischendorf, Alford; bracketed by Tregelles with B., Cod. Sin., L.—C. C. S.]
[2 Vs. 30.—According to the reading of B., D., L., which here place a καί before Λύσαντες.]
[3 Vs. 34.—Ὅτι should be read, as by Lachmann and Tischendorf, [Tregelles; omitted by Tischendorf in his 7th ed.] The witnesses for it are too preponderating to allow the supposition, with Meyer [and Alford], that it has crept in from vs. 31. [Ὅτι found in A., B., D., Cod. Sin., K., L., M. Yet the fact of manuscripts fluctuating here, while none omit ὅτι in vs. 31, favors the supposition that it has crept in from there.—C. C. S.]

EXEGETICAL AND CRITICAL.

CHRONOLOGY.—At the entry into the Passion-week, it becomes possible to us to follow our Lord from day to day, and at last almost hour by hour. According to John xii. 1, He came six days before the Passover to Bethany. Since now this began with the 14th Nisan, our Lord must already on the 8th have come into the circle of His friends in Bethany, and therefore on the Friday or Saturday before His death. If we consider, however, that our Lord on His last Sabbath certainly made no extended journey, that we read nothing of any village before or in the neighborhood of Bethany where He could have spent the day of rest, that on the other hand the last-named village appears to have been also the last stopping-place of the journey, it then becomes extremely probable that He entered before the Sabbath, and therefore on Friday, into the village of Lazarus. After the ending of the weekly Divine service, the feast was held at which Mary anointed the Lord, but which Luke passes over in silence. And if now the entry into Jerusalem, John xii. 12, took place on the day after this feast, there is then no ground to transfer this day to any other than Palm-Sunday. The view of those who, on account of some little difference in the four Evangelists, maintain that two entries took place, may well be regarded as already antiquated; *cx abundanti,* comp. VON BAUR, *Kanonische Evang.* p. 196.

Vs. 29. **Bethphage and Bethany.**—The designation of locality does not proceed from the position of the travellers from Jericho, in which case

Bethany must have been named first, since Bethphage was almost a suburb of Jerusalem. But since the two places were so nearly contiguous that they were scarcely distinct, the account of the approach begins here in a popular manner with the more distant locality lying nearest to Jerusalem. In brief, at the moment when the two disciples are despatched, our Lord has Bethany behind Him, Bethphage before Him, and points to the latter when He says δεικτικῶς: **Go ye into the village over against you.**

Two of the disciples.—From the graphic trait of Mark xi. 4, that they find the colt tied "by a door without, in a place where two ways met," we should almost conjecture that his original authority, Peter, was eye-witness, and therefore one of the two. But that John here also, as in the preparation for the Passover, accompanied, is, on account of the tone of his narrative of the entry, less probable. In vividness, at least, his representation is inferior to that of the Synoptics.

Vs. 30. **Whereon yet never man sat.**—"A creatively fresh *new* time, a *new* prince, a *new* beast," Lange. We may compare the new grave in which no one was ever yet laid, ch. xxiii. 53, and, from the Old Testament, the young heifers on which never yet a yoke had come, which upon a new wagon drew the Ark of the Covenant, 1 Sam. vi. 7.

Vs. 31. **And if any one ask you.**—There is nothing in and of itself improbable in supposing that our Lord had friends in Bethphage, and may have made arrangements with them which He did not think necessary to communicate to His disciples. If, however, we consider the mysterious form of the command; if we consider how little it was in the spirit of our Saviour to give to something very ordinary a guise of singularity; if we compare the preparation of the Passover, and if we keep the very unique significance of this entry with its attendant circumstances well in mind,—it is then undoubtedly most natural to see here also a manifestation of that foreknowledge which, so soon as it was necessary, could penetrate even that which lay beyond the sphere of the senses and of common calculation. Without doubt, however, the owners of the beast of carriage belonged to the many concealed friends of our Lord, and He had in spirit foreseen that a command addressed in His name to those men would not be in vain.

Vs. 32. **They that were sent went their way.**—The purpose of this whole command was not so much to come into possession of a beast of carriage, as rather to exercise the disciples in unconditional obedience, even there where something remained inexplicable to them, and at the same time to strengthen them in their faith in the superhuman foreknowledge and the Messianic character of the Lord; for foreknowledge of hidden things belonged undoubtedly to the traits which were especially expected in the perfect Servant of God, comp. John xvi. 30; and with wisdom does the Lord reveal this trait of His Messianic character, in that very hour in which He permits homage to be offered to Him, in His dignity as the Messiah.

Vs. 33. **The owners thereof.**—In Mark: "Certain of them that stood there." What the Saviour foresaw, takes place actually; objections are raised; but at the appointed watchword (ὅτι, the definite answer to the question διὰ τί) every objection is let fall. "*Non poterre, Domino huic obsequentes, frustrari.*" Bengel.

Vs. 35. **Their own garments.**—"Ἑαυτῶν colors this act of honor." Meyer. A similar hearty homage appears in this, that they, according to Luke, set our Lord upon the colt (ἐπεβίβασαν), while the others only speak in general of His sitting thereon (καθίζειν). Besides the disciples, who in this way displayed their reverence for Him, there are, vs. 36, others named who spread out their garments as a carpet before His feet, while, vs. 37, the jubilant exclamations of the multitude, which here is to be carefully distinguished from the disciples, are spoken of.

Vs. 37. **At the descent of the mount of Olives,** πρὸς τῇ καταβάσει τοῦ ὄρους, κ.τ.λ.—According to Luke, who distinguishes the different elements of the act of homage, even somewhat more accurately than Matthew and Mark, the enthusiasm begins there to reach its culmination precisely when the final goal of the peaceful train is in sight. When they have come near to the point of descent of the mount of Olives, to the height from which the whole city spreads itself out like a great panorama before the view of the beholders, the jubilant joy rises higher and higher, while the way begins to descend.

The mighty works.—Matter for praise is least of all lacking; Bartimæus is found in person among the multitude, ch. xix. 43; the view of the capital city awakens again remembrance of similar miracles, and the name Lazarus is upon the lips of all; comp. John xii. 17. The notice of Luke, vs. 37, although he keeps silence otherwise as to the miracle at Bethany, contains however so far an indirect proof of the truth of the narrative, John xi., as this, that it appears from it that our Lord, without doubt, in the time immediately preceding, must have performed some great σημεῖον, which was yet entirely fresh in memory, and raises enthusiasm even to such a height. What particular miracle this however was, we learn only from John.

Vs. 38. **Blessed be the King.**—It is noticeable that the report of the hymn in Luke shows a less specifically Old Testament character than in Matthew and Mark. In this respect the Paulinist does not belie himself. The parallelism requires us to understand εἰρήνη here not in the literal sense of "peace," *pax*, since this reigns in heaven evermore, and is never troubled, never disturbed; but in the signification of *laus* or *gloria*. In heaven, therefore, is given to God the Lord honor, in the highest [regions] glory. See ch. ii. 14.

Vs. 39. **Some of the Pharisees.**—This feature also is peculiar to Luke, and has the highest internal probability. In their eyes our Lord is nothing but a Rabbi in Israel, who is riding on an ass to the city, and who has it at any moment in his power to repress the enthusiasm of the disciples within the bounds of the most unsympathizing composure. ["Their spirit was just that of modern Socinianism: the prophetic expressions used, the lofty epithets applied to Him, who was simply in their view a διδάσκαλος, offended them." Alford.] He himself is more or less responsible for it, if they in their pious zeal go too far, and he will do well to give the fathers of the people no just cause of offence. We recognize here quite the same men who before also had often attempted to make our Lord responsible for that which displeased them in His friends, who, besides, despised the people, that knew not the law. It was permitted to no one to strike a higher key of joy than Pharisaism found consistent with decorum.

Vs. 40. **If these should hold their peace.**—Proverbial expression, to indicate that it is in individual cases harder to impose silence on men, than to cause that which itself is speechless to speak, comp. Hab. ii. 11. A covert intimation of the destruction of Jerusalem, in which the stones of the city and the temple should proclaim the majesty of our Lord. An intimation which is the more striking, if we imagine to ourselves that at this very moment perhaps the echo of the Hosannas was heard against the marble temple, and the acclamations of the people were thus given back from the heights of Zion. "With these words our Lord at the same time expresses a great law of the life of the kingdom of God. When men hold their peace from praising God, and very especially when a dark despotism imposes silence on the better-minded, when the gospel is suppressed, then the stones begin to cry out: they proclaim the judgments of the Lord, whose glory can have no end." Lange.

DOCTRINAL AND ETHICAL.

1. *See* the parallels on Matthew, Mark, and John.
2. In His entry into Jerusalem, the Lord has been sent to some for a fall, and to others for a rising again. At all times this event in His history has called forth scandal and gainsaying. We may remember the unbelieving heathen who at the time of Tertullian (see *Apol. advers. Gentes*, ch. 10) scoffed at the Christians as *asinarii*; the scoffing Jew who asked them: If thy Christ is a God, why has He then ridden upon an unclean beast? (Lipmannus in his now almost forgotten *Nizachon*), and especially the English atheists, the Wolfenbüttel fragmentists, and many younger heroes in the domain of the negative criticism. Here also holds good the saying: Luke vii. 35.
3. The whole entry of our Lord has no lesser purpose than this, to reveal Himself as King in the spiritual kingdom of God. Before His death He will by an unequivocal act proclaim the great truth which He, as the holy secret of His life, had hidden from most of the uninitiated, and only as it were whispered in the ear of receptive individuals. Once in His life He grants to His own publicly to proclaim what lies so deeply at their heart, and He fulfils intentionally a prophecy which at His time was unanimously interpreted of the Messiah. If He has previously considered the declaration of His dignity as dangerous, He now counts silence inconceivable. It is the day on which He who came to His own and His own received Him not, commits Himself to the love of those who so deeply honored Him, and reveals himself to the gaze of those who look with devotion upon Him. This was for His cause, yea, for the whole Israelitish nation, necessary. It was hereafter never possible to say that He had never declared Himself in a wholly unequivocal manner. When Jerusalem afterwards was accused of the murder of the Messiah, it should not be able to say that the Messiah had omitted to give a sign intelligible for all alike. Our Lord will prove that He is more than a prophet mighty in word and deed; that He is King in the full force of the word.
4. But His kingdom is not of *this* world; can He show it more evidently? His attire, the beast He sits on, His train, His whole demeanor proclaims it. No wonder that afterwards Herod no more than Pilate founded on this entry any imputation whatever. The Roman garrison may remain composedly in the tower Antonia, when this peaceful festal throng enters in at the gates of Jerusalem.
5. The deepest significance of this act of our Lord will be understood only when it is brought into direct connection with the history of His Passion. Voluntarily does the Lamb approach His murderers, now that the time of slaughter has arrived. By such a public step He guards on the one hand against an assassination, and on the other hand brings on more rapidly His suffering and dying, for by this very act the hate of His enemies increases; Judas sees himself again deceived, when the Lord suffers even this opportunity of mounting an earthly throne to pass by unused; and while Jesus does nothing more to keep the enthusiasm of the multitude alive by brilliant miracles, the whole enthusiasm of the multitude at the end is nothing more than the last upstreaming brilliancy of an evening sun, before it vanishes beneath the horizon.

6. In connection with the fate of all Israel, this hour may be named the decisive and irrevocable turning-point. Assuredly we may, if we look at the same time at Jesus' words and tears, vss. 41, 42, regard this entry as a carefully prepared last attempt to preserve Israel as a people. Because Jerusalem contents itself to-day with the fleeting Hosannas, it has drawn upon itself the fulfilment of the judgment that its stones hereafter shall yet cry out: for the entry now gave to all opportunity to show their temper without disguise; the people now did not stand under the influence of the priests; no one's tongue was bound to silence by a command; it was the day which decided whether Jerusalem would become the blessed centre of all nations, or the terrible monument of retributive justice. What would have happened if Jerusalem had considered on this day the things which belonged unto her peace,—this is a question not capable of solution, and therefore also an idle one. Suffice it, since they now remained hidden from her eyes, the die was cast, and after the hen had vainly essayed to gather her brood together, the eagles, forty years after, stretch out not in vain their talons upon the carcass.

7. In this way the event itself becomes of moment for all following times. While it prepared the way for Jesus' death and Jerusalem's destruction, it has at the same time prepared the way for the reconciliation of the whole world, and for the bringing in of the Gentiles. At the same time it serves as proof, that although the kingdom of God comes not with observation, yet where it comes it cannot forever remained concealed. What here took place is in no way in conflict with the parables of the Mustard-Seed and of the Leaven. "When the kingdom of God in its mustard-seed and leaven state has in a hidden way worked for a time, the working thereof must make itself known in great results, as facts which press themselves upon the attention of every one, and it is the great historical epochs of the world which are formed therefrom. What gradually goes on must also come to special view in individually great effects. We should misunderstand the force of the Leaven and of the Mustard-Seed, if we suppose that everything must always remain in this hidden gradual development. It would be just such an error as if we should suppose that the great results striking the eye were to be the first. Only in connection with that inner secretly working power, which comes therein to manifestation, can they be rightly understood. The kingdom of God is indeed also the city that lies upon the hill, and the light that must lighten all." NEANDER, *Der glorreiche Einzug Christi in Jerusalem, eine Palmsonntagsbetrachtung.* Berlin, 1848, p. 10.

8. The entry of our Lord into Jerusalem is the fulfilment of the Old Testament prophecy, Zech. ix. 9. On the other hand, the entry itself is in turn the prophecy of His return in glory, when He, surrounded by His many thousands of saints, whose Hosanna has then become a Hallelujah, shall descend from heaven upon earth. 1 Thess. iv. 16; comp. Zech. xiv. 4.

9. There is a striking contrast between the honor and esteem with which the Pharisees and Sanhedrists received an earthly conqueror, Alexander the Great, and the coldness with which they received the King of Peace three centuries after, when He also will make His entry into Jerusalem. Then no expressions of homage appeared to them strong enough; now even the least is too strong. To a contrast not less striking than that is which is to be noticed between the reception of Jesus and that of an earthly king, Erasmus alludes in his *Paraphr. N. T. ad h. l. Opera, Edit. Basil.* vii. p. 186: to the contrast between the entry of the high-priest of the New and of the Old Testament. Externally considered, Erasmus speaks of the high-priest of Israel, but he means thereby without doubt the Pope of Rome, the so-called Vicar of Christ, whose outward pomp stands in such glaring contrast with this humble entry of the Sovereign of the kingdom of God.

10. The stones of the temple of Jerusalem have not been the only ones which in the most literal sense of the word proclaim the glory of God and His Anointed. More and more does the *testimonium lapidum* become for Christian Apologetics of inestimable worth, and the inscription on the Salzburg rock-gate: *te saxa loquuntur*, proves itself true in the historical sphere also before our eyes and ears. Call to mind for instance the latest excavations of Nineveh, Babylon, &c., and compare the interesting writing of OTTO STRAUSS, "*Nineveh, and the Word of God*," Berlin, 1855.

HOMILETICAL AND PRACTICAL.

As often, so also here, when there is anything of moment to be done, there the Lord sends His disciples two and two.—The obedience of faith: 1. Not easy; 2. never put to shame.—Whoever carries out the command of the Lord, must often reckon on opposition.—"The Lord hath need of him," an answer before which all opposition must be dumb.—In the service of the Lord, even the unclean may be purified, the despised invaluable, that which stands idle be used.—Even earthly good must be applied to the service of the Heavenly King.—Even for the friends of the Lord there comes a time for speaking, which terminates the time of silence.—Even an humble yet upright homage is well pleasing to the Saviour.—"Prepare the way of the Lord, make straight in the desert a highway for our God." Isaiah xl. 3; Ps. xxiv. 7, 8; Ps. lxviii. 4.—The wonderful works of our Lord the glory and joy of His disciples.—Joy in Jesus must terminate in glory rendered unto God.—The Hosanna of the people: 1. The echo of the accord of many a psalm in the Old Testament; 2. the beginning of the lay of praise in the New Testament; 3. the prophecy of the perfect festal lay in Heaven.—The enmity of the flesh against the revelation of the life of the Spirit.—The voice of the stones in honor of Christ: 1. How loud it calls; 2. how powerfully it preaches.—The entry into Jerusalem a revelation of the threefold character of our Lord: 1. Of His prophetic dignity; since He *a.* knows hidden things, *b.* accomplishes marvellous things, *c.* foretells future things; 2. of His high-priestly dignity: He is *a.* the immaculate, *b.* the compassionate, *c.* the willing High-priest of the New Covenant; 3. of His kingly dignity: He reveals Himself at this entry *a.* as the promised Messiah, *b.* as the King of the spiritual kingdom, *c.* as the future Vanquisher of the world.—The question: Who is this? answered out of the history of the Entry into Jerusalem, Matt. xxi. 10.—At the entry into Jerusalem there is a threefold example given us: 1. By the people; 2. by the disciples; 3. by our Lord. The first we have to follow to a certain point, the second exactly, the third only from afar.—Our Hosanna and Hallelujah must be: 1. Of higher mood; 2. as freely rendered; 3. less transient than that before the gate of Jerusalem.—At the entry into Jerusalem, no one maintains neutrality towards our Lord; only enthusiasm on the one, and hatred on the other, side.—The vanity of the praise of a world in which the Hosanna and the "Crucify" follow so quickly on one another. Acts xiv. 8-20.—Behold I come to do Thy will, O my God! Ps. xl.

STARKE:—Christ avails Himself of His Divine right as the Lord and Heir of all things, and causes to come to Him what is His own.—BRENTIUS:—The kingdom of Christ brings along with humility the greatest glory with it: Lord, open our eyes; 2 Kings vi. 17.—Jesus has chosen to have nothing His own. —If things often turn out very differently from what men have thought, yet they always come to pass as God has said.—Without great commotion and manifold speeches of men, there is no making progress in the cause of religion.—Servants of Christ in all emergencies appeal to their Lord's command.—The Lord has in all places hidden friends, who reveal themselves at the right time.—Heaven and earth have been again united through Christ.—QUESNEL :—God's praise is to the ears of the world troublesome. —Zealots without understanding must be answered with forbearance and mildness.—Even to lifeless creatures does God give a tongue when it pleases Him.— HEUBNER :—The night of Jesus over human hearts.— Obedience is better than scrupulosity.—The kingdom of the Messiah brings on a spiritual spring.—Lifeless creatures testify against the blindness and unthankfulness of men.

Advent Sermon :—HARLESS :—1. The character of the King; 2. His coming; 3. those to whom He comes; 4. those with whom He abides.—THOLUCK :— The Advent call: Thy King cometh.—W. HOFACKER : —How Jesus, who comes in the flesh, comes yet continually in the Spirit: 1. To whom He comes; 2. with what intent; 3. with what result.—F. ARNDT :—The entry of the King of all kings into the city of all cities: 1. Unimposing to the outward sense; 2. majestic to the eye of faith; 3. intensely desired by help-imploring hearts.—F. W. KRUMMACHER :—*Passions-buch*, p. 49: How this gospel strengthens us in faith: 1. In the Divine Messianic dignity of our Lord; 2. In the blessed coming of His kingdom.— COUARD :—Thy King cometh: 1. He is come; 2. He is ever coming; 3. He will come.—STIER :—1. To whom comes He? 2. how comes He? 3. how shall we receive Him?—How in the life of Jesus continual loftiness and lowliness are found conjoined.— FUCHS :—The Palm-Sunday acclamation, a salutation of the youthful Christian throng on their confirmation day.—NIEMANN :—Blessed be, &c.: 1. How this acclaim then resounded; 2. and should yet resound; 3. shall hereafter resound aloud.—RAUTENBERG :—The diverse reception of our Lord.—KRAUSSOLD :—Behold thy King cometh to thee.—DITTMAR:—The Advent of Jesus, and the necessity of the present time.— THOMASIUS:—The preparation of the church for the coming of our Lord: 1. Purpose; 2. conditions.— HAUSCHILD:—Blessed be He that cometh: 1. To suffer; 2. to rule; 3. to give everlasting salvation.— FLOREY:—What makes the entry of our Lord into Jerusalem so heart-cheering?—BRANDT:—The final entry of Jesus into Jerusalem a blessed spectacle.

---

2. The Manifestation of the Glory of the King in Word and Deed (Vss. 41–48).

41, 42 And when he was come near, he beheld the city, and wept over it, Saying, If thou [also] hadst known, even¹ thou [om., even thou], at least in this thy day, the things
43 *which belong* unto thy peace! but now they are hid from thine eyes. For the [om., the] days shall come upon thee, that thine enemies shall cast a trench [embankment] about
44 thee, and compass thee round and keep thee in on every side, And shall lay thee even with the ground, and thy children within thee; and they shall not leave in thee one
45 stone upon another; because thou knewest not the time of thy visitation. And he went into the temple, and began to cast out them that sold [the sellers] therein, and them
46 that bought [omit these 5 words²]; Saying unto them, It is written, [And³] My house is [shall be] the [a] house of prayer (Is. lvi. 7); but ye have made it a den of thieves
47 [robbers]. And he taught [was teaching] daily in the temple. But the chief priests
48 and the scribes and [also⁴] the chief of the people sought to destroy him, And could not find what they might do: for all the people were very attentive to hear him [hung, listening, upon him,⁵ ἐξεκρέματο αὐτοῦ ἀκούων].

¹ Vs. 42.—We consider ourselves as obliged to retain both καίγε and σου, held as doubtful by Lachmann.
² Vs. 45.—The longer reading of the *Recepta*: τοὺς πωλοῦντας ἐν αὐτῷ καὶ τοὺς ἀγοράζοντας, appears to be borrowed from the parallels. [The briefer reading found in D., C., Cod. Sin., L.; accepted by Tischendorf, Meyer, Tregelles, Alford.—C. C. S.]
³ Vs. 46.—See TISCHENDORF, *ad locum*. [The reading, καὶ ἔσται, κ.τ.λ., at the beginning of the citation, for ἐστιν, at the end, is found in D., L., Π. Cod. Sin. omits both the copulative and the verb. The reading of Van Oosterzee is that of Tischendorf, Meyer, Tregelles, Alford.—C. C. S.]
⁴ Vs. 47.—I have inserted "also" as the briefest way of conveying the force of the separation of the third nominative from the first two.—C. C. S.]
⁵ Vs. 48.—Revised Version of the American Bible Union.—C. C. S.]

EXEGETICAL AND CRITICAL.

Vs. 41. **And wept.**—Not only ἐδάκρυσεν, as in John xi. 35, but ἔκλαυσεν, with loud voice and words of lamentation. What the cause of these tears is, appears from ἐπ' αὐτήν and the immediately following words. Again, it is Luke alone who has preserved to us this affecting trait, and it scarcely needs to be mentioned how exactly such a trait fits into the gospel which teaches us in our Lord to know the true and holy Son of Man. And yet we cannot be surprised that precisely this genuinely and purely human trait, even from of old, has been to many a stumbling-block and scandal. In relation to this, it is noticeable (*see* GROTIUS, *ad loc.*) that the words ἔκλαυσεν ἐπ' αὐτ. in individual ancient manuscripts do not appear; ἐν τοῖς ἀδιορθώτοις ἀντιγράφοις, says, however, Epiphanius, the words are read. "*Mutarunt homines temerarii et delicati, quibus flere Christo indignum videbatur.*"

Vs. 42. **If thou also hadst known.**—"Pathetic aposiopesis, and thereby the expression of a fruitless wish." Meyer. The **thou also** places the unbelieving inhabitants of Jerusalem in opposition to the disciples of our Lord, who had really considered τὰ πρὸς εἰρήνην, perhaps a delicate allusion to what the name of Jerusalem as City of *Peace* (Salem) signifies. The here-designated ἡμέρα can be no other than what our Lord, vs. 44, calls τὸν καιρὸν τῆς ἐπισκοπῆς. Comp. ch. i. 68. The whole time of the public activity of our Lord in Jerusalem was a respite of two years, which had been prepared for more than twenty centuries, and now, as it were, concentrated itself in the one day on which the Lord entered as King into Jerusalem. This Jerusalem would have known (ἔγνως), if it had unanimously rendered homage to its Messiah; but although the Lord here also had found individual believing hearts, yet Jerusalem as a city rejected its King; the Ἰουδαῖοι recognized Him not. It was hidden from their eyes who He was, and what a salvation He would bestow. Ἐκρύβη according to the righteous counsel of God, Matt. xi. 25, 26, but not without their own personal guilt.

Vs. 43. **Days shall come.**—Vss. 43, 44 is the text of the powerful discourse respecting the destruction of Jerusalem which our Lord, ch. xxi. 5 *seq.*, two days afterwards delivered before His disciples. The ἡμέραι which are now threatened are the terrible consequences of the fact that the ἡμέρα, vs. 43, has hastened by in vain. Ὅτι does not depend on ἐκρύβη, so that thereby the thing that is hidden is indicated (Theophylact), neither is it any strengthening word, in the sense of *profecto utique* (Starke), but the common signification "for" must be here retained, in the sense that the wish, vs. 42, has thereby a reason given for it, as if the Saviour would say, "I might indeed wish that, &c., for now the things that belong to thy peace remain hidden from thine eyes. Now impends," &c.

An embankment, χάρακα, masculine.—It is remarkable how our Lord not only in general foretells the destruction of Jerusalem, but also in particular describes the way and method in which this judgment should be accomplished. He announces a formal siege, in which they should avail themselves of all the then usual auxiliaries and should permit themselves all the atrocities which victors have at any time exercised against the vanquished. First He mentions the χάραξ, a camp strengthened with palisades and line of circumvallation, in short, a wall such as we actually read in Josephus (*De Bell. Jud.* V. vi. 2; V. xii. 2) was thrown up around Jerusalem, but burned by the Jews. Afterwards, in consequence of this structure, περικυκλώσουσίν σε καὶ συνέξουσίν σε πάντοθεν. We may here understand the wall thirty stadia long, which Titus in three days caused to be erected around the city, in place of the burnt χάραξ. In consequence of this measure the desolation now breaking in upon her and upon her children (ἐδαφιοῦσι) becomes general. This word occurs in a twofold signification: "to level with the earth" and "to dash to the ground" (Ps. cxxxvii. 9); the first prophesies the fate of the city, the other that of her inhabitants, both being here zeugmatically connected. Finally, the conclusion of all this, no stone remains upon another, so that now, vs. 40, the stones begin to cry out. This last part of the prophecy was first completely fulfilled after the insurrection of Bar-Cochba in the days of the Emperor Adrian, and this is the terrible result, continuing unto the present day, of this one blinding, **because thou knewest not the time of thy visitation!** In this conclusion, and especially in this continually ascending καί, καί, καί, lies a δεινότης *orationis*, which can be better felt than described.

Vs. 45. **And He went into the temple.**—Comp. the parallels in Matthew and Mark. Luke, who entirely passes over the cursing of the fig-tree, relates also the temple-cleansing only briefly. In fact, he only states the beginning of this symbolical transaction (ἤρξατο), while Matthew also notices the successful end (ἐξέβαλεν). To him it is especially remarkable that the Saviour begins His last sojourn and converse in the sanctuary with so strong a measure. Respecting the manner of the expulsion also, and for the precise description of the persons expelled, compare Matthew and Mark. The citation from Isaiah lvi. 7, Luke has in common with them, while he with Matthew omits the πᾶσιν τοῖς ἔθνεσιν, apparently only for the sake of brevity. As to the question whether the temple-cleansing took place once or twice, comp. LANGE, *Matthew*, p. 376. We also decide for a repetition of the transaction, since the opposite opinion falls into far more difficulties, inasmuch as it must either impeach John or the Synoptics of the greatest inexactness. It agrees entirely with the typical and symbolical character of this transaction, that our Lord began as well as concluded His life therewith. Besides, the circumstances also are so very different that they make identity improbable. As respects now particularly this second temple-cleansing, those who find difficulty in supposing that our Lord, a few days before His death, should have repeated an act which might prepossess or embitter the secular power against Him, may for the same reason account the denunciatory discourse (Matt. xxiii.) as entirely fictitious. That our Saviour did not perform this act at the second Passover, too, is simply to be ascribed to the circumstance that at that Passover He was not at Jerusalem, John vi. 1–4. Who knows whether, perhaps, after the first temple-cleansing, the abuse thus animadverted upon did not diminish or entirely cease; and on the contrary, the priestly party, out of spite against our Lord and at the same time in order to elicit new opposition, restore it anew on the last feast? Then it would at the same time be explained why His words of rebuke at the second cleansing sound even sharper than at the first. In view of the brevity of the Synoptical relation, we cannot be surprised that neither in the language of our Lord nor in the conduct of those expelled, do we meet with a reminiscence of the previous temple-cleansing. Perhaps, however, the still recollection of the first contributed to weaken opposition at the second.

Vs. 47. **And He was teaching daily.**—Striking and vivid representation of the state of things in this critical point of time. On the side of our Lord, unshaken courage, composure, and energy of spirit, with which He every day shows Himself publicly, joined with beseeming care for His own security, which moves Him not to pass the night in Jerusalem so long as His hour has not yet come. On the side of His enemies, irreconcilable hatred and thoughts of murder, especially on the part of the worldly aristocracy, which counts itself mortally endangered by Him. On the side of the people, undiminished delight in hearing Him, on which account His enemies, with their base designs, can as yet obtain no handle against the Saviour. The people hang on His lips. The more they hear the more they wish to hear (ἐξεκρέματο, *cum gen.*). "As bees on the flowers on which they seek honey, or as young birds on the mouth of the old ones from whom they would have food." Meanwhile His enemies are visibly perplexed. They find not what they shall do to Him. The Saviour and the people alike are for the moment an obstacle to them. Thus is displayed on the one side the might of unarmed innocence, on the other the impotency of armed and resolved malice.

DOCTRINAL AND ETHICAL.

1. "Never man spake like this man" (John vii. 46). This word proved true not only in Jerusalem's temple, but also at Jerusalem's gate. The eloquence of the words of Jesus is great, that of His silence, perchance, yet greater, but that of His tears passes all description. The tears of the Lord at the grave of Lazarus and those at the entry into Jerusalem have so much analogy, and yet again so much diversity, that the consideration of these relations furnishes admirable contributions towards the knowledge of the person and the character of our Lord. The contrast between this jubilant multitude and the weeping Saviour, between the deepest blindness on the one and the most infallible knowledge on the other side, is so speaking, and moreover so taken from the life, that here also the declaration can be applied: "This trait could not have been invented." With right says Augustine, *Lacrymae Domini, gaudia mundi.*

2. Not without reason has there been found at all times in this prophecy of the destruction of Jerusalem, on the very place where afterwards the Romans pitched their first camp, one of the strongest proofs of the infallible and Divine foreknowledge of Jesus. The comparison of this declaration with the account of Josephus is the work of the apologist. Thereby, at the same time, must not be forgotten what an unhappy result the godless attempt for the rebuilding of Jerusalem under Julius the Apostate had. *See* CHRYSOST., *Oratio* 3 *adv. Judaeos.* [Chrysostom says, in substance, that under the impious emperor the Jews were permitted to attempt the rebuilding of the temple, that it might not be said

that they could have rebuilt it if they would; but that flames bursting out from the foundations drove them away; while yet the foundations which they had begun remained even in his day as witnesses at once of their purpose and of their impotency to accomplish it. The truth of this account of Chrysostom is, as we know, supported by the testimony of the impartial Ammianus Marcellinus; and all the sneers of Gibbon at this "specious and splendid miracle" do not render it less certain that Divine Providence, in a wonderful way, took care that the prophecy of the Son of God should not be frustrated. Whether this were a miracle in the sphere of nature or not is a matter of little moment; it is, at all events, an illustrious miracle of Providence.—C. C. S.]

3. "The holy tears of Jesus show how God's heart is disposed towards men when they fall into sin and destruction. Even in God we may conceive a compassionate sorrow, only that it is ever at the same time removed again by His eternal love, wisdom, and holiness. In Jesus, these tears over Jerusalem are at the same time tears of high-priestly intercession and mediation, and belong, in so far, to all men. Comp. Heb. v. 7." Von Gerlach.

4. Our admiration of the majesty of our Lord increases yet more when we see how He, who certainly knows that He must give up Jerusalem for lost, continues yet, even in the last days of His life, with unwearied and holy zeal to be active in Jerusalem. Even when He knows that the mass will not let itself be saved, He continues to have compassion on the individuals. Precisely for this reason is His love so adorable, that it becomes at no moment weak; and while it weeps the fate of sinners, vehemently burns against sin, but this wrath seeks not itself, but the Father's honor. At His entry Jesus weeps over the lot of Jerusalem. At His going out He says, Weep not, Luke xxiii. 28.

5. The temple-cleansing is one of the acts of our Lord which have sometimes been elevated too high, sometimes depreciated too low. The former has been the case when men have believed themselves to see here a miracle in the ordinary sense of the word, nay, esteemed it as even greater than, for instance, the miracle of Cana. See ORIGEN, *ad h. l.;* JEROME, *ad* Matt. xxi. 15; LAMPE *in Comment.* Against this we have to remember the moral predominance which a personality like that of the Saviour must have had over souls which were so mean and weak as these, and to remember the many examples of similar triumphs of truth and right over the servants of deceit and unrighteousness which we meet with even in profane history. On the other hand, some have in this act, without reason, found occasion to throw suspicion on the moral purity of our Lord, and as it were turned the scourge of small cords against Himself. We have here to call to mind not only the right of the Zealots, but very especially the right of the Son in the house of His Father, and especially to take note of the union of a holy wrath with compassionate love which beams through this act of the Saviour. Shortly after He has wielded the scourge, He stretches out the helping hand, which has but just expelled the rabble, towards cripples and wretched ones; these wretched ones, whom compassion had brought into the temple, the omnipotence of love has healed. Comp. Matt. xxi. 14, and in reference to the first temple-cleansing the interesting section: *The Banner on the Mountain,* in BAUMGARTEN'S *Geschichte Jesu,* Brunswick, 1859, pp. 99–111.

6. The temple-cleansing the symbol of the whole life of our Lord, as also of the purpose of His manifestation on earth. See CYRIL. ALEX. ii. 1; ORIGEN, tom. x. p. 16; AUGUSTINE, *Tract. in Evangel. Joh.,* and others. Comp. Mal. iii. 1, and Luke iii. 15. An admirable work of art representing the temple-cleansing by Jouvenet.

HOMILETICAL AND PRACTICAL.

"Behold thy King cometh to thee."—How the Lord at His entry into Jerusalem reveals His kingly character: 1. By His tears; 2. by His word; 3. by His deed in the temple.—Jesus' tears the most beautiful pearls in His crown of glory.—Jesus' love to an unthankful people and to a native country destined to destruction. — Anger at sin and compassion for the sinners united in the Saviour.—The King of Israel at the same time the compassionate High-priest.—The acceptable time, the day of salvation (2 Cor. vi. 2).—Whoever despises the one day of salvation has many evil days to expect.—The Romans at the siege of Jerusalem the witnesses for the truth of the word of Jesus.—Great grace, great blindness, great retribution.—The contrast between the last entry of our Lord into Jerusalem and His last departure.—The Son in the desecrated house of His Father: 1. How vehement is His wrath; 2. with what dignity He speaks; 3. how graciously He blesses.—The Scripture the rule according to which everything in Divine service also must be guided.— Yet again will the Lord clear His temple: 1. In the heart; 2. in the house; 3. in the church; 4. in the whole creation.—"My house is a house of prayer," how this word points us: 1. To inestimable privileges; 2. to holy obligations; 3. to high expectations. —The temple of the Lord: 1. Its original destination; 2. its later perversion; 3. its final perfection.— It is the best, which through human wickedness is most shamefully corrupted (Rom. vii. 13).— The Passion-week a striking proof of the faithfulness of our Lord to the once uttered principle (John ix. 4). —The remarkable drama which the temple after the entry and the cleansing presents: 1. A throng of hearers eager for salvation; 2. an impotent throng of enemies; 3. over against both the Lord, immaculate, unwearied, fearless.—Jesus already triumphant even before His apparent overthrow; His enemies already defeated even before their seeming triumph.

STARKE:—LANGII *Op.:*—The nearer and greater the grace is, the nearer and greater the judgments if it is not received. — ZEISIUS : — Consider, O man, what the tears of Jesus have in them, and let them melt thy heart to repentance. — There is nothing more to be wept over than the spiritual blindness of man.—HEDINGER:—Blindness comes before destruction.—CANSTEIN:—Even the time of grace has with God its limitation. — OSIANDER:— When the wrath of God blazes forth, it rages very terribly against the impenitent. — LUTHER : — The contemning of the gospel brings lands and cities to destruction.—Holiness is the ornament of the house of God (Ps. xciii. 5).—Against open abominations there suits a thorough earnestness. — *Nova Bibl. Tub.:*—How many in the temple who have murdered their souls by presumptuous sins.—QUESNEL: —The Church is not only a house of prayer, but also a house of instruction.—Hardened men will rather inflict mischief on pious preachers than amend themselves.—ZEISIUS:—Without God's will no harm can happen to His faithful servants.—Jesus has among the common people more friends than among the chief ones.—To hang on Jesus' lips and hear Him is good, but not enough.

HEUBNER:—The diverse value of many tears.— To every blinded sinner we can exclaim, If thou hadst known!—To every one is his time of grace allotted. —The sinner has a bandage before his eyes.—The fate of our posterity should urge us to repentance.— The invincibleness of love.—Guard thee against everything which can disturb devotion in others and destroy the soul.—The churches the asylums of the truth.—Some friends the truth finds ever.

On the Pericope.—The sorrow of Jesus at the last view of Jerusalem: 1. Sources; 2. effects.—How the tears of Jesus yet speak to us.—Great cities as the seat of great corruption.—The value of the tears of the Christian.—COUARD:— Jerusalem and the Jewish people: 1. Jerusalem's time of grace; 2. Jerusalem's hardening; 3. Jerusalem's fall.—The tears of Christians here below: 1. Tears of joy; 2. tears of repentance; 3. tears of sorrow.—SOUCHON: —The knowing of the time of visitation.—PALMER: —Jerusalem's blindness: 1. Near to it is destruction, but no one forebodes it; 2. near to it is salvation, but no one will recognize it.—The Saviour: 1. In His tears; 2. in His zeal of fire; 3. how He by both calls us to repentance.—RAUTENBERG:—Jesus' tears over Jerusalem, tears to awaken: 1. Compassion; 2. terror; 3. affection; 4. consolation.—THOLUCK:— 1. These tears a shame to our cold hearts; 2. a rebuke to our light-mindedness; 3. a shaking of our security.— VON KAPFF:— The judgments of the Lord: 1. The judgment of grace; 2. the judgment of wrath; 3. the judgment of cleansing; 4. the judgment of hardening; 5. the judgment of condemnation.— ARNDT:—Jesus the Friend of His country.—VAN OOSTERZEE:—Jesus' tears over Jerusalem: 1. Jerusalem's shame; 2. Jesus' honor; 3. our joy.—THE SAME:—The temple-cleansing a type of the Reformation of the sixteenth century; it reminds us: 1. Of the history of the Reformation; 2. of the glory of the Reformation; 3. of the admonitions of the Reformation.—On 1. The abuses which the Reformation assailed; the principle to which it did homage; the spirit which it revealed; the reception which it found. On 2. Like the temple-cleansing, so was also the Reformation a restoration of the spiritual worship of God, the revelation of the glory of Christ, the beginning of a new development in the kingdom of God on earth. On 3, the Reformation admonishes those who desecrate the temple to repentance, those who honor the temple to zeal, those who know the Lord of the temple to continual remembrance of His deeds. Comp. John ii. 22.

B. *Controversial Discourses against His Enemies.* CH. XX.

1. The Closing Controversy with the Pharisees and the Chief of the People concerning the Authority of Jesus (CH. XX. 1-19).

(In part parallel with Matt. xxi. 23-27; 33-46; Mark xi. 27-33; xii. 1-12.)

1 And it came to pass, *that* on one of those[1] days, as he taught the people in the
2 temple, and preached the gospel, the chief priests [the priests[2]] and the scribes came
3 upon *him* with the elders, And spake unto him, saying, Tell us, by what authority doest
4 thou these things? or who is he that gave thee this authority? And he answered and
said unto them, I will also ask you one[3] thing, and answer me: The baptism of John,
5 was it from heaven, or of men? And they reasoned with themselves, saying, If we
6 shall say, From heaven, he will say, Why then believed ye him not? But and [om.,
and] if we say, Of men; all the people will stone us: for they be persuaded [are con-
7 vinced] that John was a prophet. And they answered, that they could not tell whence
8 *it was.* And Jesus said unto them, Neither tell I you by what authority I do these
9 things. Then began he to speak to the people this parable; A certain [om., certain[4]]
man planted a vineyard, and let it forth to husbandmen, and went into a far country
10 [went abroad] for a long time. And at the season he sent a servant to the husbandmen, that they should give him of the fruit of the vineyard: but the husbandmen beat
11 him, and sent *him* away empty. And again he sent [lit., he added to send[5]] another
servant: and they beat him also, and entreated [treated] *him* shamefully, and sent *him*
12 away empty. And again he sent a third: and they wounded him also, and cast *him*
13 out. Then said the lord of the vineyard, What shall I do? I will send my beloved
14 son: it may be they will reverence *him* when they see him. But when the husbandmen saw him, they reasoned among themselves, saying, This is the heir: come [om.,
15 come[6]], let us kill him, that the inheritance may be ours. So they cast him out of the
vineyard, and killed *him*. What therefore shall the lord of the vineyard do unto them?
16 He shall come and destroy these husbandmen, and shall give the vineyard to others.
17 And when they heard *it*, they said, God forbid [Let it not be, μὴ γένοιτο]. And he beheld [looked upon] them, and said, What is this then that is written, The stone which

the builders rejected, the same [this] is become the head of the corner? (Ps. cxviii. 22.) 18 Whosoever shall fall upon that stone shall be broken [dashed to pieces]; but [and] on 19 whomsoever it shall fall, it will grind him to powder. And the chief priests and the scribes[7] the same hour sought to lay hands on him; and they feared the people: for they perceived that he had spoken this parable against them.

[1] Vs. 1.—'Εκείνων, which is wanting in B., D., [Cod. Sin.,] L., Q., and some Cursives, and has been rejected by Lachmann, Tischendorf, [Meyer, Tregelles, Alford,] is perhaps only a spurious addition for the sake of precision.
[2] Vs. 1.—Ἱερεῖς. The *Recepta*, ἀρχιερεῖς, appears to be from the parallel [in Mark].
[3] Vs. 3.—The ἵνα before λόγον of the *Recepta* is wanting in B., [Cod. Sin.,] L., [R.,] some Cursives, and is rejected by Griesbach, Lachmann, Tischendorf, [Meyer, Tregelles, Alford. The fact that in some MSS. it is found before and in some after λόγον, adds to the suspicion of its spuriousness.—C. C. S.]
[4] Vs. 9.—The τις of the *Recepta* after ἄνθρωπος is decidedly spurious.
[5] Vs. 11.—The Hebrew: לְרֹאשׁ פִּנָּה.—C. C. S.]
[6] Vs. 14.—*Rec.*: δεῦτε, ἀποκτ. from Matthew and Mark.
[7] Vs. 19.—More correctly: "the scribes and the chief priests." The *Recepta* has the ordinary arrangement, according to rank, which, however, has not sufficient manuscript support. *See* Lachmann and Tischendorf.

EXEGETICAL AND CRITICAL.

Vs. 1. **On one of those days.**—General designation of the point of time, as about the same at which the entry of Jesus into Jerusalem and the temple-cleansing had taken place. From the comparison with Matthew and Mark, it appears that we have particularly to understand the last Tuesday. The cursing of the fig-tree is passed over by Luke, but the image of the fig-tree of Israel itself, with beautiful leaves but without any fruit, and already in process of decay, is represented by him in a striking manner in the delineation of the last controversy of our Lord with the Israelitish fathers. Although Luke in this connection entirely passes over two chief elements: the parable of the Two Sons, Matt. xxi. 28–32, and that of the Royal Wedding, Matt. xxii. 1–14 (the last-named parable he apparently does not give, because he had already, ch. xiv. 16–24, noted down a similar one), yet we can with his help very easily sketch a vivid image of the history of this most remarkable day. Like Matthew and Mark, he also makes us acquainted with the external intercourse of our Lord with His enemies during the last days of His life, while John, who passes over the controversial discourses, relates the history of the inner life of the Master in the circle of His apostles in these last days. All which is related Luke xx. took place within the walls of the temple, while the Saviour was teaching the people there, and (a peculiar, genuinely Pauline addition of Luke) *was preaching the Gospel.*

Came upon Him, ἐπέστησαν, comp. ch. ii. 38; Acts iv. 1.—Not the suddenness and unexpectedness, but the deliberateness and greater or less solemnity, in the appearance of these men is hereby indicated. It is a well-organized deputation, and one chosen, undoubtedly not without reflection, from the Sanhedrim, whose different elements are therein carefully represented.—Although they do not say that they speak in the name of the whole council, yet in view of the well-known hostile disposition of the great majority of this towards our Lord, we may confidently presuppose this, and so far compare this embassy with a similar one which at the beginning of the public life of Jesus had been sent to John; John i. 19–28. Perhaps the observation of this agreement in form had even some influence on the answer of our Lord. The chief authority in Israel was undoubtedly fully entitled to institute a careful investigation respecting the authority of all teachers publicly appearing, and our Lord, inasmuch as He submits to be questioned, shows that He recognizes the theocratic dignity of the speakers, and is not disinclined to answer, at least under certain reasonable conditions, to the fulfilment of which, however, they, as soon appears, have not made up their minds. The very fact that now for the first time do they come with such a question to Jesus, after He had performed so many indubitable miracles, and after a truth-loving Nicodemus had already, two years earlier, in faith on our Lord's divine mission, come to Him,—even this testifies against them, and makes an almost comical impression.

Vs. 2. **Tell us.**—Therewith do they open the series of ensnaring questions which are laid before the Lord on this day. "These controversial discourses are very especially genuine portions, because they are held so entirely in the spirit and tone of the contemporaneous Rabbinical dialectics." (Strauss.) Already, previously to this, more than one attempt had been made to take our Lord in His own words; but now it takes place in an intensified degree, with yet more deliberation, in a more refined way, and with united force. The work of enmity was at the same time a trial, since it was expected of the Messiah that He should know all things (John iv. 25; xvi. 30). It was natural, therefore, that they should surround Him who appeared in this exalted character with a net of fine-spun questions. In the firm hope that they should leave the field victorious, the Pharisees do not lose an instant publicly to interpellate the Lord.

By what authority.—The two questions do not express the same thing in different words (De Wette), but are rather to be thus distinguished: that the first member of the interrogation is designed to elicit an explanation as to the heavenly mission; the other, ἢ τίς, κ.τ.λ., the statement what messenger of God has mediately consecrated Him to this activity. Ταῦτα refers here not only to a single transaction of the Lord, the temple-cleansing (Meyer), but to the whole unfolding of His superiority and authority in the temple during the days last preceding this, something which, according to their opinion, could in no wise be legitimate.

Vs. 4. **The baptism of John.**—Here specially set forth as the centre and summary of His whole activity. Our Lord by no means declines the strife, and this very fact, that He answers with a counter-question, testifies of His heavenly wisdom. It must now be made manifest whether they, with their competency for questioning, were also capable of hearing the right answer, and this He could only assume of them if they showed themselves in a truth-loving character. It is not arbitrary that He answers them precisely with *this* counter-question; He, who had never separated His activity from that of His forerunner, could not tell them who had bestowed on Him His authority so long as they, as representatives of the people, had not definitely declared their opinion respecting John. If they recognize the divine mission of the Baptist, who had not even done miracles, they will be obliged to esteem His own even much more. If they reject the first mission, they deserve the reproach of not being competent to judge respecting the authority of Jesus. If they keep silence, then the incontestable right will belong to Him to send them also away unsatisfied. At all events, He can now wait with the utmost composure to observe what position they will take.

Vs. 5. **And they reasoned.**—They retire an instant, and make the matter an object not of an individual but of a common deliberation (συνελογίσαντο). It is plainly to be seen in them that they have never made the question proposed an object of earnest consideration, and now, too, are only concerned about withdrawing themselves with honor from the strife. All the Synoptics direct our attention to their deliberation, which took place in the midst of the temple, amid visible suspense, and must inevitably have soon come to the ears of many. Noticeable with this is the testimony wrung from them, that among the people the belief in the prophetic character of the Baptist was spread abroad on all sides. According to Luke and Mark, they still speak of λαός, yet undoubtedly in the sense of ὄχλος, as Mark writes it. Comp. John vii. 49.—**Stone,** καταλιθάσει, peculiar to Luke. Perhaps a later form of the tradition (Meyer), but yet quite as probably the original pregnant form in which they express the fear of which Matthew and Mark speak. "*Non erat populi, sacerdotes et scribas, prophetam quamlibet verum rejicientes, lapidare: sed sæpe etiam perversum multitudinis studium per accidens subserveit bonæ causæ.*" Bengel.

Vs. 7. **That they could not tell whence.**—Doubly painful to them is this declaration, if we compare it with the endless οἴδαμεν, which they elsewhere, *e. g.,* John ix. 24–34, caused to be heard. Luke has only the indirect form of the answer, which they, without doubt, gave as briefly and indefinitely as was at all possible. But the most terrible for them is that the Lord has by this answer gained the *right* to the decided counter-declaration: **Neither tell I you,** &c.—Now, both are silent; but He, because He on good grounds will not speak; they, because they through their own fault cannot speak; and among the people present as witnesses, there is no one who could seriously doubt which of the two parties leaves the field victorious.

Vs. 9. **To the people.**—According to Matthew and Mark, this parable is addressed to the Pharisees and elders themselves, to whom, at all events, it maintains a very definite reference, while Luke makes the Saviour speak πρὸς τὸν λαόν. The two statements, however, do not contradict each other; for according to Luke, also, vs. 19, the scribes and Pharisees are chief persons among the hearers of our Saviour, and according to Matthew and Mark, also, He speaks in a place and in a circle which makes it *a priori* probable that He is heard not only by them, but also by the people. The μὴ γένοιτο, also, which Luke alone has, fits only in the mouth of the chief priests, who certainly perceived more quickly than many others the intention of the parable. The course of the facts appears to have been this: our Lord, after the answer, vs. 8, leaves the Pharisees to themselves, and turns Himself to the more receptive people, yet so that the first interrogators, who had not immediately departed, hear His instruction also, and are forced to make the application to themselves. It is not enough for our Lord to have repelled the attack. He pursues the retreating enemy, and will have them mark how it stands with all their pretended ignorance (Matt. xxi. 28–32). When He has in this way unmasked their hypocrisy, He now brings also their guilt to light; and after He has put them below the most despised of the Jews (Matt. xxi. 31), He now gives them to see how their rejection of the Messiah will lead to the bringing in of the *Gentiles.*

A vineyard.—A favorite figure for the Israelitish people. *See* Isaiah v. 1–6; Ps. lxxx., and elsewhere. Comp. LANGE on the parallels in Matthew and Mark, and the dissertation of RUPRECHT and STEPHENSEN in the *Stud. u. Krit.* 1847–1848.

Vs. 10. **At the season.**—Intimation of the period in which the proper prophetic activity began in Israel, which, as is known, was a considerable time after the founding of the Theocratic state, so that, using still the image of the parable, we may say that the fruits had had abundant time to come to maturity. The wine-press and the tower, Luke omits. That it is untenable by these two objects to understand the Mosaic law and the temple (Euthym., Theophylact, Calvin, Melanchthon, and others), appears from this: that afterwards the vineyard, undoubtedly *including* the wine-press and the tower, is given to the Gentiles.

A servant.—Here, also, the different Evangelists do not belie their peculiarity. Matthew speaks, according to his custom, of servants and other servants, Mark and Luke individualize; the former mentions, besides the three whom Luke also has, many others, ch. xii. 5; the second has none of the three servants, however severely otherwise they are maltreated, suffer death, apparently to preserve so much better the climax in the delineation of the wickedness which at last destroys the lawful heir. According to all three, the husbandmen began at once with evil, but end with acts of deeper wickedness, without our having, at the mention of any particular maltreatment, to think exclusively also of some one definite person.

Vs. 13. **What shall I do?**—Matthew and Mark relate the act of the supreme love; Luke brings before us the lord of the vineyard in soliloquy, in order to place the act of love in yet clearer light. His son, the beloved, will he send to the unthankful ones, not in the silent hope that they would perhaps yet reverence him, but in the well-warranted expectation that their wickedness at least would not go so far as to assail him also. "**Perchance,** with which, even in our language, one does not of necessity express a doubt, but may express his expectation." Meyer.

Vs. 14. **When the husbandmen saw him.**—An evident allusion to the τοῦτον ἰδόντες of the lord of the vineyard, vs. 13. The sight which according to his expectation was to fill them with reverence, is precisely that which awakens in their heart the most hideous plans of murder. The last touch, that the **inheritance may be ours,** is by no means added merely for ornament, but intimates that in the murder of the Messiah, the most shameless self-seeking revealed itself. Almost in the same way did it express itself through the mouth of Caiaphas, in the familiar *votum,* John xi. 50; moreover, the coincidence with Gen. xxxvii. 19, 20, is striking.

Vs. 15. **Out of the vineyard.**—A striking prophecy of the crucifixion outside of the city. Comp. Heb. xiii. 12, 13.

Vs. 16. **He shall come.**—According to Matthew, they are themselves forced to pronounce the judgment, which, according to Mark and Luke, is uttered by Jesus. Perhaps the matter may be thus reconciled: that some are in this way their own judges, while others, terrified at this utterance, which was viewed as a *malum omen*, let the μὴ γένοιτο escape their lips. Even if one should assume here a little variation in the tradition, the fact would not suffer in the least thereby. The common result of all the accounts is this: that the Pharisees were confounded, and comprehended very well the meaning of our Lord.

Vs. 17. 'Ἐμβλέψας.—Here also, as often, *e. g.*, ch. xxii. 61, an intimation of the piercing and eloquent look of our Lord.—**What is this, then?**—He will thereby give them to understand that if they were right in their deprecation, the prophecy of the Scripture would not be fulfilled, which yet is an absolute impossibility. Comp. Matt. xxvi. 54.

The stone.—Comp. Ps. cxviii. 22, 23. This psalm, which Luther esteemed so highly above many others, was probably composed in the later period of the Old Testament, when, after hinderances for long years, the temple-service in the purified sanctuary was again erected. To attribute to this jubilant hymn a *direct* Messianic signification is forbidden, as well by the connection as by the context; but the humiliation or exaltation, whether of Israel or of the sanctuary, which is celebrated in this passage, serves the Saviour for a type and symbol of His own. What was there originally said in another sense is fulfilled in its highest power* at the rejection of the Messiah.

Vs. 18. **Whosoever.**—Instead of the continuation of the citation, "This is the Lord's doing," Luke has this threatening warning of our Lord, which is omitted by Tischendorf, Matt. xxi. 44. Comp. Lange *ad loc.* "*Cadere super Christum dicuntur, qui ad eum opprimendum ruunt, non quod ipso altius conscendunt, sed quia eo usque abripit eos sua insania, ut Christum quasi e sublimi impetere conentur*." Calvin.

Vs. 19. **The chief priests and the scribes ... sought.**—Comp. Matt. xxi. 45, 46. A statement which is here the more remarkable since it serves as a proof that the increasing bitterness of His enemies did not proceed from misunderstanding in reference to the discourses of our Lord, but on the contrary from the fact that they understood them only too well, and felt themselves thereby mortally wounded and outraged. The more light there was before their eyes, so much the more hatred in their hearts. We see they are in the way which at last leads to the commission of the sin against the Holy Ghost. Fear associates itself with hatred (καί not oppositive, but purely copulative), but at the same time is the reason why they cannot yet immediately do all that they wish.—Πρὸς αὐτ. Comp. vs. 9. They see now themselves that the people were indeed the auditors, but not the chief characters of the parable. Their conscience admonishes them that "*mutato nomine, de te fabula narratur*."

DOCTRINAL AND ETHICAL.

1. Compare the parallel in Matthew and Mark.

[* An arithmetical reference to the powers of roots.— C. C. S.]

2. The hard-heartedness of the enemies of Jesus is quite as conspicuously visible from their own behavior as from the parable of our Lord. Even the holiness of the temple does not withhold them from laying for Him their fatal snares. And yet more hideous does their behavior become by assuming the disguise of a deep earnestness, while they have beforehand resolved not to allow themselves to be persuaded at any price. Yet there is something tragical in the terrible blindness with which they, in the same moment at which they prove that they understand only too well the parable of the Wicked Husbandmen, prepare themselves to fulfil this prophecy also, and reject the stone that shall soon crush them.

3. This whole hour in the last week of the public life of Jesus may be called a continuous temple-cleansing, in fact. What He had first done with the scourge of small cords, He now continues to do with the sword of His mouth; He sweeps the enemy away from before His face, thus also cleansing the sanctuary. The method in which He here constrains His enemies first to pass judgment on themselves and then to be dumb, is at the same time a prophecy of that which at the day of His coming shall be repeated in yet greater measure.

4. While in the parable Matt. xiii. the idea of the kingdom of God stands in the foreground, on the other hand, in this, with which our Lord closes His work as Prophet and Teacher, the image of the King Himself begins to come forward ever more clearly and plainly. The manner in which He here at the same time testifies of Himself as of the Only and Beloved Son of the Father, who is distinguished from all former messengers of God by descent and rank, draws our attention to one of the points of contact between the Synoptical and the Johannean Christology.

5. Only by an entire misunderstanding in reference to the design of our Lord, would it be possible from the words: "Perhaps they will reverence my son," to draw such a conclusion as that God sent His Son not with the distinct *purpose* that He should suffer and die, but that He on the contrary seriously expected that His Son would find a better reception than His former servants. Our Lord simply intimates what God might have been able and entitled to expect, if the Omniscient One had really been in everything like the human lord of the vineyard. Κατ' ἄνθρωπον therefore the terrible and almost inconceivable character of the rejection of the Messiah is yet more strongly thrown into the foreground. Calvin has already hit the mark in writing on this passage: "*Haec quidem cogitatio proprie in Deum non convenit, sciebat enim, quid futurum esset, nec spe melioris eventus deceptus fuit, sed usitatum est, praesertim in parabolis, ad cum transferri humanos affectus. Neque tamen hoc abs re additum est, quia voluit Christus tanquam in speculo repraesentare, quam deplorata esset illorum impietas, cujus hoc nimis certum fuit examen, contra Dei filium, qui ipsos ad sanam mentem revocaturus venerat, diabolico furore insurgere. Hic scelerum omnium cumulus fuit, filium interficere, ut regnarent quasi in orbata domo, etc. conf. Act.* 4, 27, 28."

6. The work of grace performed on Israel, the enmity shown by it, and the punishment threatened against it, that the kingdom of God should be given to other nations,—all this is repeated in continually greater measure again in the days of the New Covenant, since the Theocracy has become a Christocracy

We may call to mind, for instance, some of the churches of Asia Minor, whose light of old stood so high upon the candlestick.

7. "Whoever shall fall upon this stone," &c. The two members of this threatening sentence contain by no means, as might indeed appear at first glance, a weak tautology, but a portrayal of the different fates which the enemies of the Lord have to expect; first from the rejected and after that from the elevated corner-stone. Whoever falls upon this stone, that is the one who takes offence at the yet humiliated Saviour, to whom the rejected building-stone is a λίθος προσκόμματος. Thereupon falls the judgment of retribution: συνθλασθήσεται ; for instance, as with Judas, the impenitent thief on the cross, and others. In spite of the offence taken, the Lord is elevated aloft—lifted to be the corner-stone; but he now upon whom the elevated stone falls is crushed to pieces like chaff (Gr. λικμήσει αὐτόν). In other words, when the glorified Christ comes again to judgment, the most terrible judgment comes upon His enemies. In order to understand the pregnant saying in its whole force, we must compare not only Psalm cxviii. 22, 23, but also Isaiah viii. 14, 15; xxviii. 16; Daniel ii. 44, 45. From the visible predilection with which the same image is often brought up and carried out by the Apostle Peter, in his discourses and epistles, we may perhaps draw an inference as to the deep personal impression which this declaration of our Lord, in particular, made upon the faithful disciple.

8. The hatred, the intensifying of which we have become aware of among the Pharisees, after their having understood and known the truth, discovers to us one of the depths of Satan in sinful hearts, and is surely fitted to open the eyes even of such as in well-meaning Pelagian superficiality view sin only as a weakness, exaggerated sensuality, and the like. If it has ever become plain that no faith of the heart is conceivable without the will being bowed, and that at the same time for the bowing of this will a power from above is indispensable, if even the Lord's own word is to make its way to the soul; this was true with these first enemies of the truth, who are at once the type and forerunners of so many later ones.

HOMILETICAL AND PRACTICAL.

After the accomplishment of the temple-cleansing the Lord remained behind as Victor upon the field.—After He has administered the law, He continues with the preaching of the Gospel.—The apparently very necessary and yet, in truth, entirely superfluous question of the Pharisees.—The use and misuse of the tongue.—How in the enemies of David delineated Psalm xi. and elsewhere, the portrait of the enemies of our Lord is vividly drawn.—The ever-continuing disquiet of the wicked.—If the Lord's enemies cannot even answer one question, how will it be when He lays a thousand questions before them ? Job ix. 3.—The Divine mission of John is acknowledged and vindicated by our Lord, even to the end.—Even yet he who does not believe and understand John, is unauthorized and incompetent to judge fittingly concerning our Lord.—The untenableness of the position of those who will remain disciples of John brought to light by our Lord.—Where calculations come into play, no grounds of reason can help.—The insecurity of the position *a tutiori*.—The people not seldom nearer the truth than their spiritual guides.—The si-

lence of the Lord already a beginning of the judgment.—Right must after all remain right, and that will all pious hearts follow; Psalm xciv.—The enemies wish to have the people see Jesus defeated, our Lord makes them the witnesses of His victory and of His retribution.—The parable of the Unthankful Husbandmen an echo of the song of the vineyard, Isaiah v. 1–7.—The history of centuries told in a few minutes.—God's way and counsel with Israel misunderstood and contemned by Israel: 1. The gracious election, vs. 9 ; 2. the long work of grace, vss. 10–11 ; 3. the fulness of the time, vs. 13 ; 4. the most hideous crime, vss. 14, 15 ; 5. the righteous punishment, vss. 16–18 ; 6. the curse turned into blessing (the other husbandmen), vs. 15.—The manifoldness of form, in which hatred against Divine things has of old revealed itself, and even yet continually reveals itself.—The fearful climax of sin.—The riches of the compassion and long suffering of God despised; Rom. ii. 4.—The sending of the Son of God: 1. The highest; 2. the last revelation of His grace.—Only when grace has reached the highest degree, can sin reveal itself in its full strength.—God remits nothing of His requirements, even though His messengers are treated with augmenting unthankfulness.—The Son is to be revered! Psalm ii.—"God forbid!"—What is least expected often happens first.—False rest over against threatening judgments.—When the light is not heeded, then may the candlestick be pushed from its place ; Rev. ii. 5.—The greater the privilege, so much the heavier the responsibility ; the more defiant the madness, the deeper the fall.—From our Lord the church may learn with what eye she must view the prophetic Scriptures of the Old Testament.—The history of the Corner-stone : 1. A most ancient ; 2. an ever-young history.—The fully-conscious hatred against the truth.—How little unbelief understood the Lord, even where it understood the meaning of His words with perfect correctness.—Behold the goodness and severity of God; Rom. xi. 22.

STARKE :—*Nova Bibl. Tub.* :—The devil cannot endure the preaching of the Gospel.—How dangerous to be in offices, if one misuses them.—BRENTIUS :—The ungodly are snared at last, by the righteous appointment of God, in the works of their own hands.—Whoever opposes himself to the truth out of wickedness, falls from one lie into another.—Hypocrites suppress the truth by unrighteousness ; Rom. i. 18.—OSIANDER :—They who do not give place to the truth, but are only skilled to blaspheme, are not worth disputing with.—HEDINGER :—God uses many people and many means to correct men.—QUESNEL :—The world may be ever very ill-disposed to hear of the punishment of the ungodly ; but it comes for all that, and will be so much the more terrible.—It is a fearful thing to fall into the hands of the living God.—BRENTIUS :—Truth breeds hatred, it is true; but it has God for its protector.—HEUBNER :—The world is against abstract truth not so hostile and full of hatred as against the concrete witnesses of the same.—God's judgments grow ever heavier.—The Jewish people a monument of Divine goodness and of human unthankfulness.—Christ and His enemies : 1. Typified in the Old Testament ; 2. fulfilled in the New.—EYLERT :—God's goodness, long-suffering and severity, in the treatment of unthankful and disobedient men.—ZIMMERMANN :—God and Israel.—LISCO :—The relation in which sin and error stand to one another.—ARNDT :—The history of Israel the history of mankind in miniature.—AL. SCHWEIZER :

—The rebellious husbandmen more particularly considered: 1. In their outrageous conduct; 2. in the judgment which they suffer.—W. HOFACKER:—The institution of God's kingdom in the Old Testament a type worthy to be taken to heart by the children of the New Covenant.—We enter: 1. Upon the theatre of rich Divine blessings; 2. upon a theatre of vile perverseness and blindness; 3. upon the judgment-place of unsparingly punishing righteousness and holiness.

* * *

2. Controversy with the Pharisees and Herodians respecting the Tribute (Vss. 20–26).

(Parallels: Matt. xxii. 15–22; Mark xii. 13–17.)

20 And they watched *him*, and sent forth spies, which should feign themselves just men,[1] that they might take hold of his words [of *some* word of his[2]], that so they might
21 deliver him unto the power and authority[3] of the governor. And they asked him, saying, Master [Teacher], we know that thou sayest and teachest rightly, neither acceptest thou the person *of any* [or, showest no partiality], but teachest the way of God
22, 23 truly: Is it lawful for us to give tribute unto Cesar, or no [not]? But he perceived
24 their craftiness, and said unto them, Why tempt ye me?[4] Show me a penny [a denarius]. Whose image and superscription hath it? They answered and said, Cesar's.
25 And he said unto them, Render therefore [Then render] unto Cesar the things which
26 be [are] Cesar's, and unto God the things which be [are] God's. And they could not take hold of his words [saying] before the people: and they marvelled at his answer, and held their peace.

[1 Vs. 20.—Van Oosterzee translates δικαίους, *gesetzesstrenge Leute*, "strict observers of the law," which is doubtless its meaning in this place. They professed an anxious desire to know just how they could reconcile their duty to the law with their actual subjection to the Romans.—C. C. S.]
[2 Vs. 20.—According to the most approved reading: ἐπιλάβωνται αὐτοῦ λόγου. It appears better, with Bleek, to make the first genitive depend on the second, than to regard both as depending directly on the verb, although, it is true, De Wette, Meyer, Van Oosterzee, and Alford adopt the latter construction.—C. O. S.]
[3 Vs. 20.—Τῇ ἀρχῇ καὶ τῇ ἐξουσίᾳ τ. ἡ. Van Oosterzee translates: "to the authorities, and especially to the power of the procurator," taking the two nouns as indicating respectively the Jewish and the Roman power. In this Meyer agrees with him, but it seems to be straining a point. It is enough to regard it as a formula for Pilate's jurisdiction, rendered pleonastically full by the solemnity of the events which it introduces.—C. C. S.]
[4 Vs. 23.—In B., L., [Cod. Sin.,] and some Cursives, these words [Why tempt ye Me?] do not appear. Perhaps they have crept in here from the parallel passage in Matt. xxii. 18.

EXEGETICAL AND CRITICAL.

Vs. 20. **And they watched Him.**—After the defeat just suffered, nothing is more natural than that the Pharisees should look around partly for other confederates and partly for other weapons. While they before sought in vain to make their authority weigh, they now take refuge in craft, and after old combatants for the law have been put to shame and obliged to leave the field vanquished, now new and, in great part, vigorous picked troops are despatched. While, after what has just taken place, the Pharisees remain standing on the watch (παρατηρήσαντες), they send the Herodians to Jesus (*see* LANGE on Matt. xxii. 15), together with some of their disciples (Matt. xxii. 16). Even earlier we have met with a similar temporary coalition of heterogeneous forces (Mark ii. 18; Luke xxiii. 5–17); later on, we shall find the same in yet greater measure. Moreover, it is easily comprehensible that two enemies should give up their mutual hatred for a while, when the concern is to strive against a dangerous third. Equally explicable is the change in the choice of the weapons. After the open defeat they pass over to a more concealed manner of waging war. A new disappointment will then be less ignominious, the ardently desired triumph not less advantageous. They choose, therefore, ambassadors who, as people strict in the law, must put on the guise of being concerned with a personal question of conscience, as if they were by no means set on by others to come to Him, and who must seek to accomplish their object through flattering speeches.

To the power and authority of the governor.—A statement of the purpose peculiar to Luke, which, however, is probable on internal grounds also. They wish to bring matters to this pass, that the civil power shall lend them its hand to remove this man out of the way, against whom the spiritual authority has in vain armed itself. Upon this support they reckon definitely in case He gives to the question proposed, as is expected, a negative answer, in order to please the people, with whom He now appears to be making common cause against their own rulers, vs. 9. If He, on the other hand, espouses the party of the foreign oppressors, He would thereby lose all His credit with this same people. After such a mature deliberation they came forward, like Satan, as angels of light, 2 Cor. xi. 14.

Vs. 21. **Teacher, we know.**—There is something naive and at the same time a proof of the incorrigible self-conceit of the Pharisaical party in this, that they even now, after the elders of the people had just before, vs. 7, seen themselves constrained to a public confession of their ignorance, begin with a presumptuous "We know." The purpose of this eulogy is, as to the rest, intelligible enough. "In thee," do they mean, "we believe we meet with exactly that independent man, from whose position our question can be answered with entire impartiality." That they could scarcely have uttered sharper satire on themselves than by this eulogy on the Saviour does not even remotely occur to them. As to the rest, the question how far they themselves really believed anything of the favorable testimony which they here publicly depose in reference to our Lord, can only be answered conjecturally.—**Showest no partiality.**—Literally, "Acceptest not the person (the countenance)," οὐ λαμβάνεις πρόσωπον, comp. Gal. ii. 6, yet stronger than the οὐ βλέπεις εἰς πρόσωπον in the parallel, and a definite designation of *judicial* impartiality.

Vs. 22. **Is it lawful for us.**—For the emphatical and most categorical form of the question, *see* Mark. Luke uses the Greek word φόρον δοῦναι, while the others make use of the Latin κῆνσον: "Poll and ground taxes, to be distinguished from τέλος, the indirect taxes (on goods)." Meyer. The question has its peculiar difficulty. It appeared to be forbidden, Deut. xvii. 15, for a stranger to rule over Israel, as was now the case. The malcontents, with Judas Galilæus at their head, who would have no other taxes paid than the temple-taxes, stood, therefore, apparently upon the ground of the Scripture. But if Jesus declared their principle valid, He would oppose Himself to the order of things that had now been induced under higher guidance, and would come into personal conflict with the civil power, with that of the Procurator.

Vs. 23. **Perceived their craftiness**, κατανοήσας.—Still more strongly does Matthew say γνούς, and Mark εἰδώς, by which the immediateness of His knowledge is made prominent, which was by no means the result of a long deliberate reflection. Not to gain time, does He desire that a denarius should be shown Him. With the inquiry, **Whose image and superscription hath it?** the question is in effect already decided. A number of Rabbinical declarations, for more particular explanation of the immutable principle, "He whose coin is current is lord of the land," we find in LIGHTFOOT and WETSTEIN, *ad loc.*

Vs. 25. **Then render.**—The wisdom in the answer becomes first fairly visible if we give heed to the tacit presupposition from which the question had proceeded. "The silly question," as the *Wandsbecker Bote* names it not unjustly, could not have arisen in their heart if they had not proceeded from the principle that such a civil transaction was in conflict with a higher religious duty. Our Lord resolves this antagonism in a higher unity, and already distinguishes the political from the religious sphere, while they confound the two jurisdictions. By the receiving of the coin of the Emperor—not the name of *Tiberius*, but the official title *Cæsar*, is given, because it is here not a person but a principle that is in question—they had shown that they regarded themselves as his subjects, and they now, therefore, would be inconsistent with themselves if they refused to fulfil the first civil duty towards him. Without expressing the least preference for the Roman dominion, our Lord was yet too well acquainted with the condition and the views of the Jewish nation not to have at once regarded every external essay for the restoration of civil freedom, which as such could not at that time have proceeded from a purely Theocratical, but only from an earthly temper, as mischievous and superfluous. He combated at the same time the opinion that such an obedience was in conflict with religious duties. The denarii were not even received as temple-taxes; the shekel of the sanctuary could therefore, as ever, be paid in addition. Here, therefore, the *suum cuique* holds good in the higher sense of the word, and they had only to see to it that they fulfilled each part of their double obligation with equal conscientiousness. The admirableness of the answer of our Lord consists, therefore, in this, that He: 1. Shows how the whole alternative in the present condition of things was entirely untenable; that He, 2. puts to shame before the judgment-seat of their conscience those who had come forward with the pretence of knowledge, since this must have given them plainly enough to know that they had fulfilled befittingly neither the one nor the other half of His double requirement; while He, 3. utters a principle for all following centuries, by which, on the one hand, the independence, on the other hand, the practically social direction, of the religious life is sufficiently secured. *See* below.

Vs. 26. **And they could not take hold.**—All the Synoptics are careful to speak of the astonishment of the questioners, which, therefore, must have revealed itself in a very visible manner. Luke denotes particularly the completeness of their defeat by this, that they themselves οὐκ ῥῆμα ἐναντίον τοῦ λαοῦ ἐπιλαβέσθαι ἴσχυσαν. The critical character that this moment would have had for the reputation of our Lord with the people, if He had not succeeded in rending the snare laid, is brought by this intimation to light.—Ἐσίγησαν.—Not only these speakers, but also in and with them the Pharisees, who now venture no further attack. Before their departure they stand there for a moment holding their peace.— A well-known painting of the whole event by Dietrici.

DOCTRINAL AND ETHICAL.

1. *See* on the parallel passages in Matthew and Mark, as also above.

2. The principle uttered by our Lord on this occasion, is not in conflict with the way in which He previously expresses Himself to Peter respecting the payment of the temple-tax, Matt. xvii. 24–27. Here it is a civil, there it is a religious tax that is spoken of; here the rule is established according to which subjects have to conduct themselves with reference to earthly authority; there, on the other hand, the freedom vindicated which the Son may assert for Himself in reference to the house of His Royal Father.

3. The answer of the text has been on one hand judged with considerable disfavor (Gfrörer); on the other hand greeted with warm praise, *e. g.*, by the *Wandsbecker Bote:* "What a sense there is in all that comes out of His mouth! It seems to me therewith as it does with those boxes where there is one inside of another and another inside of that, &c." That this praise is not pitched too high, appears plain if we consider how our Lord has here said no word too much, nor yet a word too little, and how His utterance is peculiarly adapted not only to remove for Himself every perplexity and difficulty, but also to hurl back the arrow which they had directed upon Him into their own conscience. Had they at all times given to God the things that were God's, they would now have had no tribute to pay to a foreign ruler. Therefore, even assuming that there prevailed here a conflict of duties, this had arisen from their own folly. If they give truly to the emperor his own—τὰ τοῦ καίσ. denotes first the coin, but then also, *latiori sensu*, the civil faith-

fulness and submission which, as it were, concentrated themselves in the tribute—they would then not so eagerly long to withdraw themselves from the imperial yoke, nor yet to make common cause with its enemies. Thus does our Lord coördinate and subordinate the different duties which in their opinion stood in irreconcilable opposition.

4. *To Cæsar the things which are Cæsar's.* By the answer of our Lord the fulfilment of the civil duty actually imposed is partly allowed, partly commanded, partly restrained within sacred limits. It shows plainly that it was not His business to encroach arbitrarily upon social life, comp. ch. xii. 14; that even from reverence to God we are to honor the authority appointed by Him; that the duty to be earthly lawgiver may be refused only in the one case when it comes into irreconcilable conflict with the requirements of the heavenly one. The principle here expressed is developed fully in the spirit of our Lord, Acts iv. 20; v. 29; Rom. xiii. 1–7; Peter ii. 13, and elsewhere; comp. also the writings of the elder apologists, and Calvin's Preface to his Institutes, &c. The Divine right to govern is, therefore, taken by our Lord and His first witnesses under their protection as definitely as the freedom of conscience, and political absolutism is as far from finding a support in His word as radicalism or the diseased craving for revolution. The independence of the church and of the state within the sphere appointed to each, is assured by the principle here uttered, and every essay towards the untimely absorption of the one in the other condemned, as in conflict with the spirit of the gospel.

5. *To God the things which are God's.*—The general rule, of which the preceding is only the application to a particular sphere. To Cæsar what is his, so far as it is required, but to God thyself, since thou art created after His image. Only if we assume that this thought hovered before the soul of our Lord, do we learn to understand the depth and beauty of His answer. The soul of man is to Him the coin which originally bore God's image and superscription the new birth cannot come here into view), and for his reason belongs wholly to the Heavenly Owner. Not only repentance, therefore (Ebrard), but faith, obedience unconditionally rendered, and faithfulness to God, is here demanded by our Lord. Comp. Prov. xiii. 26. Whoever understands this, will even for God and conscience' sake render to Cæsar also his own, and be thoroughly free, to what earthly lord soever he may owe service and obedience. The τὰ τοῦ Θεοῦ τῷ Θεῷ may be called a short summary of all the commandments of the first table, and affords at the same time a new proof how the Son even to the end at every opportunity sought not His own but the Father's glory.

6. QUESNEL: — The image of princes that is stamped upon coins, signifies that temporal things belong to their province. The image of God that is stamped in our soul, teaches that our heart belongs to Him.

HOMILETICAL AND PRACTICAL.

The controversy of the lie against the truth; the triumph of the truth over the lie.—The unnatural coalitions of ecclesiastical and political parties which are in principle opposed.—Craft over against our Lord is as powerless as force.—The end sanctifies the means, a rule that was not first discovered by Ignatius de Loyola.—Even His enemies are constrained to proclaim the praise of our Lord.—The ideal of a perfect teacher, as the Pharisees portrayed it, is to be taken to heart by every servant of the Lord: 1. He teaches the way of God truly; 2. he takes account of no man's authority; 3. he is in himself true, without depending on any one.—The masters in Israel not the only ones who have remained far below their own ideal.—What in each sphere is permitted and what not, must be made out by Jesus.—The crafty heart lies naked and open in its depths before the Omniscient, Jer. xvii. 10, 11.—"Render to Cæsar," &c., the fundamental law of the kingdom of God, whereby: 1. On the one hand the relation of the Christian to the earth; 2. on the other hand his vocation for heaven, is defined.—Our obligation towards God the natural consequence of our relation to God.—Render to God what is God's: 1. A simple but very comprehensive requirement; 2. a natural but necessary requirement; 3. a difficult but blessed requirement.—How many are put to shame and condemned by this word of our Lord: 1. There are those who give neither to Cæsar nor to God; 2. to Cæsar indeed, but not to God; 3. to God indeed, but not to Cæsar; 4. as well to God as to Cæsar what is His own, but still too weakly, too slothfully, and too little.—How the impotency of sin is every time revealed anew.—The best tribute have His foes stubbornly refused the Messiah, and therefore with the fullest right paid forced tribute to Cæsar.

STARKE:—When an ungodly man makes himself devout, he is worse than bad.—*Bibl. Wirt.:*—The ungodly continually torment themselves.—BRENTIUS: —To be able to settle their position and unsettle it is a troublesome evil, but the righteous marks it and abominates it.—*Nova Bibl. Tub.:*—Even the ungodly can tell the truth, and God may use them as instruments for His glory.—The children of the devil have great likeness to their father.—Take time in everything, and answer considerately.—It is a singular wisdom to convict the enemies of the truth by their own words.—LUTHER:—Fear of God and honor due the king are two fundamental particulars of the Christian religion, which are inseparably united.—HEDINGER:—To every one his own, to God obedience, to our neighbor love, to the government its dues, to the devil sin (? rejection).—The spiritual and the secular realm must neither abrogate nor hinder one another.—BRENTIUS:—The Divine truth imposes at the last on all witlings an eternal silence. —HEUBNER:—The true Christian is to be lifted above political parties.—The true saint inspires a reverence even in his enemies.—The saints are not fools.—The best Christian the best subject.—Of the three systems, the hierarchical, the territorial, and the collegial system, the latter appears to admit best of agreement with this passage.—FUCHS:—Render to God what is God's: 1. A penitent; 2. believing; 3. patient; 4. obedient heart.—COUARD:—The confession of His enemies that Christ teaches the way of God aright obliges us: 1. To receive His doctrine believingly; 2. to follow His doctrine willingly; 3. to work for His doctrine with joyful courage.—WESTERMEYER:—The right hand of the Lord getteth the victory.

On the Pericope.—AHLFELD:—The world's craft shattered against the simplicity of the humble Christian.—GABLER:—What assures us best against the falsehood of the world?—STIER:—Why and how are we as Christians subject to every earthly authority?—SEUBERT:—The true Christian is also the freest citizen.—STEINMEYER:—In all uncertainties say only: Show me the coin! Look upon it carefully, whose its image and superscription is, and then render to every one his own. If you are wavering on the Lord's day, whether you should use it for earthly activity or for participation in the sweet services of the Lord's house, only look upon the coin; the image and superscription of this day is God's: He hath hallowed it; therefore must we give Him what is His own, &c.—ARNDT:—The repulse of the Pharisees: 1. The rich intelligence; 2. the widely comprehensive application of the pregnant answer of our Lord.—By this requirement to give every one not what we please, but what belongs to him, the might of selfishness is broken, from which the whole attack and coalition of the Pharisees and Herodians had proceeded.—The Lord addresses Himself with this His principle to the natural feeling of right, which even in fallen man is yet extant.

3. Controversy with the Sadducees concerning the Resurrection (Vss. 27–40).

(Parallels: Matt. xxii. 23–33; Mark xii. 18–27.)

27 Then came to *him* certain of the Sadducees, which deny that there is any resurrec-
28 tion; and they asked him, Saying, Master [Teacher], Moses wrote unto us, If any man's brother die, having a wife, and he die without children, that his brother should
29 take his wife, and raise up seed [posterity] unto his brother. There were therefore
30 seven brethren: and the first took a wife, and died without children. And the second[1]
31 took her to wife, and he died childless. And the third took her; and in like manner
32 the seven [omit 3 words following] also: and they left no children, and died. Last
33 [Finally] of all [om., of all] the woman died also. Therefore in the resurrection whose
34 wife of them is she?[2] for [the] seven had her to wife. And Jesus answering[3] said unto them, The children [υἱοί] of this world [αἰῶνος] marry, and are given in marriage:
35 But they which shall be [have been, καταξιωθέντες] accounted worthy to obtain that world, and the resurrection from the dead, neither marry, nor are given in marriage:
36 Neither [For neither] can they die any more: for they are equal unto the angels [ἰσάγγελοι]; and are the children [υἱοί] of God, being the children [υἱοί] of the resur-
37 rection. Now that the dead are raised, even Moses shewed [has disclosed] at the bush (Ex. iii. 6[4]), when [or, since, ὡς] he calleth the Lord the God of Abraham, and the
38 God of Isaac, and the God of Jacob. For [Now, δέ] he is not a God of the dead [of dead *men*[5]], but of the living [of living *ones*]: for all live unto him [or, for him all are
39 living]. Then [And] certain of the scribes answering said, Master [Teacher], thou
40 hast well said. And [For[6]] after that they durst not ask him any *question at all*.

[1] Vs. 30.—[Omit all after the figure,] according to the reading of B., [Cod. Sin.,] L., 157. The greater fulness of the *Recepta* appears to have arisen from old glosses and from a certain impulse of completion. *See* details in Tischendorf.
[2] Vs. 33.—The most exact arrangement of words appears to be that of B., L.: ἡ γυνὴ οὖν ἐν τῇ ἀναστάσει, κ.τ.λ., "The woman, therefore, in the resurrection, whose wife does she become of the seven?" [Cod. Sin. has simply: ε. τ. α. τίνος ἔσται γυνή.—C. C. S.]
[3] Vs. 34.—The ἀποκριθείς of the *Recepta* is apparently only an interpolation from the parallel.
[4] Vs. 37.—Ἐπὶ τῆς βάτου, *i. e.*, in the division of Exodus which takes its name from the account of the burning bush. As is known, the division of verses not being used anciently, the only way of referring to a particular passage was to designate it by the name of some remarkable person, or object, or circumstance mentioned in it. Comp. Rom. xi. 2.—C. C. S.]
[5] Vs. 38.—Θεὸς δὲ οὐκ ἔστιν νεκρῶν ἀλλὰ ζώντων. It is hard to translate this so as to make it both perspicuous and concise. "A God of *the* dead . . . of *the* living," implies that the dead and the living are regarded as two actually existing classes, in which sense it would be, of course, impious to affirm that God was not the God of both. The absence of the article before νεκρῶν and ζώντων of course indicates that they are conceived indefinitely, as two possible classes, of which it is denied that the former can have any covenant relations with God. As God affirms, nevertheless, that the departed patriarchs still stand in covenant relation to Him, the inference is necessary, that they cannot be νεκροί in any true sense. They (and all their spiritual posterity) are destined to immortal life.—C. C. S.]
[6] Vs. 40.—Van Oosterzee rightly reads γάρ, with Tischendorf, Meyer, Tregelles, Alford, on the authority of B., L., (Cod. Sin.,) 5 cursives, and the Coptic version. As Meyer remarks, γάρ was not understood. It was not perceived that the subsequent silence of the scribes was foretokened in the unwonted modesty into which they had been awed, and which appears in their concluding remark.—C. C. S.]

EXEGETICAL AND CRITICAL.

Vs. 27. **Then came to Him.**—The attempt to entice our Saviour within the sphere of the controversy between politics and religion, had entirely miscarried; now they seek to allure Him upon another not less dangerous territory, to entangle Him in the strife between the purely sensual and the strictly religious view of the world. In none of the Synoptics do we learn that the Sadducees came forward with their well-known interrogation πειράζοντες, on which account it is perhaps not absolutely necessary to assume that they really undertook to bring the Saviour, however He might answer, into some sort of personal inconvenience. But undoubtedly they mean, in the persuasion that He agreed with the Pharisees in believing the resurrection of the dead, to expose the unreasonableness of this faith, and secondly also of His doctrine, and in case they succeeded in snatching a word from Him which contradicted this hope, they would have viewed it and used it as an advantage obtained over their Pharisaic opponents, and one not to be despised. Perhaps also the position which our Saviour had taken in respect to the Pharisees, gave them occasion to ascertain for once whether He who had expressed Himself so anti-Pharisaically, would prove of an equally anti-Sadducean temper.

Sadducees.—In order to judge aright their conduct, as also to judge aright Jesus' way of acting with reference to it, we must first remark that they, when they speak of the resurrection, mean thereby not merely the continuance of the soul after death, but also the bodily revivification of the dead, which the popular faith expected at the παρουσία of the Messiah. They conceived the seven brothers, not as successively reanimated one after another subsequently to death, but as awakened contemporaneously with the last deceased woman ἐν ἐσχάτῃ ἡμέρᾳ, and cannot now imagine with whom she must then anew connect herself. Secondly, that they knew this doctrine only in the travestied, grossly sensuous form, in which the pride and the earthly-mindedness of their days had clothed it, and with this form reject therefore the idea that lies at its basis. The case feigned by them had been perhaps often used by themselves, or by those of their sentiments, in order vividly to set forth the unreasonableness of this popular faith. Finally, that they had hitherto appeared less publicly and less hostilely than the Pharisees against our Lord, on which account also He does not deal with them so severely as with the others. As frivolous friends of the world, they had hitherto moreover felt themselves less than the proud Pharisees offended and injured by our Lord. But before the end of His public life it was to appear, as it actually does in this interview, that unbelief and earthly-mindedness hate and assail the King of truth, not less than the hypocrisy of the Pharisees.

Vs. 28. **Moses wrote unto us.**—*See* Deut. xxv. 5-10. "Thus do they commence, purposing to prove irrefutably (although they, scarcely suppressing derisive laughter, only propose a question as to this), that this Moses in all his laws, cannot possibly have presupposed a resurrection." Stier. By the representation of the palpable unreasonableness of the belief in it, they wish to furnish an indirect apology for their own unbelief. Since the whole emphasis, in the case here presupposed, must be laid upon the fact that children are not left behind, we cannot be surprised that this, vs. 31, is mentioned even before the ἀπέθανον.

Vs. 34. **And Jesus answering.**—The very fact that our Lord accounts so unreasonable a question, and one proposed with so dubious an intent, yet worth the honor of an answer, may be regarded as a sign of His condescending grace; but in particular the contents and tone of His words are a striking revelation of His wisdom and love. He answers this time not as in the former case with a cutting stroke, but with a more extended development of thought. Matthew communicates it simply and definitely; Mark gives a livelier dramatic representation thereof (comp., *e. g.*, Mark xii. 24 with Matt. xxii. 29); Luke goes a freer way, and has here also some *singularia* of the utmost importance, vss. 34-36. Comp. with Matt. xxii. 30; Mark xii. 25. On the other hand he passes over the beautiful commencement of the discourse of our Lord: Matt. xxii. 29; Mark xii. 24, in which Jesus discloses the twofold source of their censurable error.

The children of this world.—Not an intimation of the moral character of the men who are here described (De Wette), as in ch. xvi. 8, but in general all who live in the pre-Messianic period of the world. —They **marry and are given in marriage.**—This is not here, as in ch. xvii. 27, stated as a proof of carelessness and worldly-mindedness, but on the other hand as a consequence of their present condition, which however shall cease with the beginning of the new period of the world.—Καταξιωθέντες.—Those who are accounted worthy to inherit the future world (comp. 2 Thess. i. 5) are those in whom the moral conditions for the attainment of future blessedness are found.

Vs. 35. **To obtain that world.**—The Messianic αἰών is conceived as coinciding with the resurrection of the *righteous*, ch. xiv. 14, which is here exclusively spoken of. It is a privilege which is not communicated to all, but only to the ἐκλεκτοῖς, while those who at the moment of the παρουσία have not died but are found yet living, are here not further spoken of. But of those who have become participants of the highest privilege and have been awakened to the new life, our Lord now declares that they then never marry nor are given in marriage. In other words, the whole question of the Sadducees rests upon an incorrect conception of the future life. Marriage is here represented simply by occasion of the case feigned as the summary of all merely sensual, sexual relations; essentially the same thing is taught which Paul announces, 1 Cor. xv. 50.

Vs. 36. **For neither can they die any more.**—The cause, why there is then no longer any need of any marriage or any need of sexual propagation, since death has now ceased to reign, nay, has become a physical impossibility, while previously it might have been called a law of nature.—**For they are equal unto the angels,** ἰσάγγελοι. In Matthew and Mark : ὡς ἄγγελοι οἱ ἐν τοῖς οὐραν. With masterly tact our Lord here, by the way, vindicates against the Sadducees the belief in the existence of angels as personal beings, Acts xxiii. 8. At the same time it appears from this that the holy angels are raised not only above the danger, but also above the possibility, of dying. Finally: They **are the children of God, being the children of the resurrection** (sharers in the resurrection). This last statement brings us here to the idea of a Divine sonship, not in the ethical, as in Matt. v. 9, but in the physical, sense, as in Luke iii. 38. God is the ground of a new life imparted to them, and they may therefore be called His children; other children and therefore other marriages have no longer a place. By a so purely spiritual representation of the life of the resurrection, Pharisaism is at the same time opposed, which continually loved most to dream of a feast in the bosom of the patriarchs: "Jesus shows that both parties, the Pharisaical and the Sadducean, were involved in like error, and that neither had grasped the higher sense of the Scripture nor a just idea of God." Von Ammon, *Leben Jesu*, iii. p. 216.

Vs. 37. Ἐγείρονται.—So firm stands this hope before the eye of our Lord, that He speaks not in the future but in the present, without this, however, entitling us to assume that He taught a resurrection ensuing *immediately* after death.

Even Moses has disclosed.—"Note the carefully chosen ἐμήνυσεν, which denotes the proclaiming of something hidden. Καὶ Μωϋσῆς. **Even Moses,** to whom ye appeal for the proof of the direct opposite." Meyer. As to the question how far this appeal of our Saviour to the Pentateuch affords a proof that the Sadducees acknowledged only this part of the Old Testament canon, see LANGE on Matt. xxii. 31; and as to the force of the argument which our Lord here uses for the doctrine of personal immortality, see STIER, ad loc. If here nothing but a dialectical dexterity and Rabbinical hermeneutics had been displayed, our Saviour's answer would then hardly have made so deep and mighty an impression. It is true, in the words: "The God of Abraham, Isaac, and Jacob," the primary sense is: "The God who during their life was the protecting God of these men," and it would of itself, from the fact that God had once protected them, not necessarily follow that this protection still endured centuries later. But the protecting God had been at the same time the covenant God; at the establishment of the Covenant, there had a personal communion between Creator and creature come into existence, and since He therein named Himself *their* God, He had therewith assured to them the full enjoyment of His favor and fellowship. And should this enjoyment restrict itself only to the limits of this life? Of a being that had lived in fellowship with God, should there soon be nothing more extant than a handful of dust and ashes? Would not God be ashamed to name Himself centuries after their decease a God of wasting corpses? Impossible! Then He would at all events have had to say: "I *have been* the God of Abraham, Isaac, and Jacob." God as the Personal One contracts a covenant with men, and calls Himself after them. They must therefore be eternal, because they are the children of the Covenant of the everlasting God.

Vs. 38. **For Him all are living.**—This sentence Luke adds to the declaration which he has in common with Matthew and Mark, "God is not a God of the dead, but of the living." A sublime declaration, especially if we do not limit the πάντες to the νεκροί alone, but refer it to all creatures, which we commonly distinguish into living and dead. This distinction is in the Divine view entirely removed: for Him, αὐτῷ, there are only living ones, whether they may have breathed out their breath or not. This is a proof, therefore, that even the death of Abraham, Isaac, and Jacob could be for God no hindrance to be called enduringly their God. The visible world of men and the invisible world of spirits both stand before God's eye as one communion of living ones. Into the question of the connection between the uninterrupted life of souls after death, and the future resurrection of the body, our Lord does not here particularly enter.

Vs. 39. **And certain of the Scribes.**—Perhaps some of the Sadducees belonged to these, and therefore gave utterance to a better feeling than the wonted one, but more probably we have here to understand them as being Pharisees, who it is likely had not all left the field, and who certainly could never have been more inclined to forget their recent defeat, and frankly and openly to praise our Lord, than just now, after He had *thus* publicly humbled their deadly enemies. Luke expressly points us (vs. 40) to the fact that this extorted praise came in the place of farther questions, which no one ventured longer to address to the Saviour. In order not to be entirely superfluous, they render homage to the Victor, while they do not venture any longer to challenge the enemy again. From Matt. xxii. 34–40 and Mark xii. 28–34, it appears however that after the Sadducees, there still came forward a scribe with the question respecting the chief commandment. See LANGE, ad loc.

DOCTRINAL AND ETHICAL.

1. *See* on the parallels in Matthew and Mark.
2. In order to do full justice to the argument here used by our Lord for the resurrection, we must recognize that this rests not upon the abstract grammatical signification of the words in themselves, but upon the rich sense of the whole declaration, and that our Saviour does not assert that in this utterance the resurrection is taught, but only that it is thereby silently presupposed. By a just deduction, He derives the hope of eternal life from a declaration in which certainly no one without this index would have discovered it. What He finds therein is, however, primarily nothing more than the germ of a faith against which they scoffingly come forward, but a germ which, for His celestially clear view, was perfectly and necessarily contained therein. He shows therefore here in a striking manner how, even in the oldest documents, declarations appear which, if they are maturely weighed, must have necessarily led to faith in immortality, although thereby it is not meant that He could not have cited any stronger and more unequivocal declarations concerning these from the Prophets and Psalms. No wonder that even in later Rabbins, the proof here brought by Jesus is often repeated in a different way, and therefore at the same time an indirect confirmation of its usefulness has been afforded. See SCHÖTTGEN, *Horæ hebr.* ad h. l.
3. A very special attention is deserved by the exceedingly peculiar manner in which our Lord here establishes the doctrine of the resurrection. Far removed from the position of philosophers, who seek to deduce their ideas of immortality from the nature of the human soul, and therefore will demonstrate the doubted by the unknown, He finds on the other hand the firmest ground of eternal life in the personal fellowship of man with God. But herewith He gives us also indirectly to know that man, for the full persuasion of His own immortality, must first have become assured of personal fellowship with God, and have become conscious of it. He thereby points the Sadducees to the inmost ground of their doubts, which lies nowhere else than in the sundering of their inner life from Him, and designates at the same time the true ground of hope for the future, and the sole way to perfect certainty thereof. The religious philosophy and apologetics of earlier and later times, would certainly have lost nothing if they had followed this example more faithfully, and had not adventured the attempt to demonstrate the immortality of the soul to those who do not as yet believe in the living God, and have not even a faint conception of personal fellowship with Him. The deepest experience of our own heart teaches us that without these premises the faith in immortality is partly uncertain, partly unrefreshing, and that man, so long as he has not found God, loses also himself. This way moreover all the believers of the Old, nay, even those of the New Testament have walked; only after they knew themselves assured of God and His favor, did they gain certainty also of eternal life. *See* Ps. xvi. 10, 11; lxxiii. 25, 26; lxxxiv. 12; Rom. viii. 38, 39. But this inmost ground of divine hope is absolutely impregnable, so long at least as all the nerves of the inward religious life are not destroyed.
4. The question whether and how far the immortality of the soul is taught in the Old Testament,

is by this utterance of our Saviour sufficiently answered. Certainly, as a dogma that could be dogmatically proved by a number of *loci classici*, this doctrine in the Old Testament is not present in a developed form. The reference to reward and punishment in the future life, would have been in the whole Mosaic economy no profitable, but rather a heterogeneous, disturbing element. Only through the gospel, and not through the law, could life and immortality be brought to light, 2 Tim. i. 10. Immortality was therefore no such dogma of the Old Testament as, for instance, the unity and holiness of Jehovah. Comp. HÄVERNICK, *Vorlesungen über die Theologie des A. T.* pp. 105-111. This however does not exclude the fact, that for the individual expectation of believers, there existed a firm ground and wide field. If any one was conscious that God was his God, then he knew also that He would everlastingly remain so, and that whoever had experienced His fellowship might fall asleep in the hope of hereafter beholding His face in righteousness, Ps. xvii. 15. Taking all together, we may say that the hope of a Jacob, a David, an Asaph, and others, was quite as firm but not quite as clear as that of the sons of the New Covenant is. "Moreover we have here to consider what doctrine of immortality is understood.—The rationalistic doctrine is nothing better than the doctrine of Sheol. Everything depends upon gaining the conception of *life* after death, not that of bare *existence*. The latter has no religious interest whatever."

5. The conception of God, from which our Saviour here proceeds: God, no dead unit but the living God, is not only that of the Old but also that of the New Covenant, and the metaphysical foundation of the Christian doctrine of the Trinity. A similar relation to that between God and the creature exists also between our Lord and His people, since His life in them is the inmost ground of their immortal life, *see* John xiv. 19.

6. From this didactic discourse of our Lord, it results that the Christian conception of angels has not only an æsthetical and ontological, but also a very decided practical significance. As the angels stand in personal relation to man (*see* ch. ii. 14; xv. 10), so are we also called hereafter to take part in their joy; and whoever now affirms that there are no angels whatever, converts thereby the prospect opened to us by our Lord, of becoming hereafter ἰσάγγελοι, into a vain illusion.

7. The declaration that those who have risen again do not marry, but are like the angels, has often been used as an indirect argument against the angelic hypothesis of Kurtz a. o. on Gen. vi. 2. On the other hand, we must not fail to note that our Saviour speaks undoubtedly of that which the angels do not do, but not of that which they never could do, and that the present purely spiritual life of the angels may very well have been preceded by a previous catastrophe or fall of some of them.

8. With utter injustice some have seen in that which our Lord says about marrying and giving in marriage, an indirect disparagement of marriage. The history of celibacy proves, in opposition to these, what consequences the anticipation of the angelic state here portrayed has for public and private morality. "Grace and the Holy Ghost do not remove the propensities of nature, nor destroy them, as the monks dreamed, but where nature is distorted the Holy Ghost heals it and puts it exultingly on its feet, brings it again to its true condition." Luther. It even appears indirectly from the *Levirate* law, that a second marriage cannot possibly have in itself anything immoral. But this doctrine does indeed imply an earnest warning against such matrimonial connections as establish no higher than a merely sensual fellowship. Not as man and wife, but ἰσάγγελοι, shall the redeemed see one another again, and only that in married love is eternal which in its ground is spiritual. From this position we learn to understand the counsel of the Apostle, 1 Cor. vii. 29-31.

9. In the example of our Lord an important intimation is given to Apologists, how they also may best vindicate against the Sadducees of our day the revealed truth; in such wise, that is, that they place themselves on the impregnable ground of the Scriptures; that they show how the imperfect form in which the truth is represented, does not of itself entitle us to reject its substance also as unreasonable; that they lay bare the innermost grounds of the ignorance which conceals itself behind the escutcheon of all so-called, highly vaunted science. In this way even the simplest Christian gains the right of exclaiming to the apostles of unbelief: πολὺ πλανᾶσθε!

HOMILETICAL AND PRACTICAL.

The leaven of the Sadducees not less destructive than the leaven of the Pharisees, Matt. xvi. 6.—The difference and agreement between the Jewish Sadducees and the heathen Epicureans.—The denial of the resurrection in its different forms: 1. Thorough materialism, 1 Cor. xv. 32; 2. one-sided spiritualism, 2 Tim. ii. 18.—The authority of the law even for those who occupy an unbelieving position.—The eternal substance in the temporal form of the Levirate law.—Childless marriage.—The long and repeated condition of widowhood.—The dangerousness of an excessively sensuous conception of the future life.—The future life: 1. A continuance of the present, but also; 2. an antithesis to the same.—Marriage should be counted honorable in all, Heb. xiii. 4.—The supreme inheritance: 1. Wherein it consists; 2. who becomes worthy of it.—In heaven there is no other marriage than the marriage of the Lamb, Rev. xix. 7.—Propagation and mortality in their inseparable connection.—In what respect the blessedness of the redeemed may even exceed that of the angels.—The angels: 1. Purely spiritual; 2. perfectly pure; 3. eternally immortal; 4. supremely blessed beings.—God's Son became a little less than the angels, that He might make His redeemed equal to the angels.—The children of the resurrection the brothers of the inhabitants of heaven.—The resurrection of the dead a mystery, beginning to be unfolded even by Moses.—The burning bush itself a proof that by God's omnipotence that may be preserved and renewed which by nature is destroyed.—The blessedness of a soul to which the Lord has said: I God am thy God.—God's covenant faithfulness the highest pledge for the everlasting life of His people.—God the God of the living: 1. The majesty which He as such reveals; 2. the blessedness which He as such bestows; 3. the glory which He as such should receive.—The absolute opposition of life and death, the natural fruit of our limited view of the world.—In God's eyes, death has no reality.—The great chasm between the position of the Sadducees and that of our Lord;—they see nothing but death; He sees nothing but life.—The involuntary homage which even hostility offered to the Saviour's Divine superiority.—

He that is reduced to silence, is not yet thereby by any means won for the truth.

STARKE:— CRAMER:— God's word becomes to many the savor of death unto death, 2 Cor. ii. 16.— BRENTIUS:—The posterity of the Pharisees and Sadducees have ever wrought great harm to Christendom, and there is in the last days even something worse to be feared, 2 Tim. iii. 1.—The devil is a singular enemy of marriage.—*Bibl. Wirt*:—Human reason searches out in matters of religion unreasonable things wherewith to subvert the truth of the Divine word.—Let men content themselves with what Christ has revealed to us of the future world.—QUESNEL:— The remembrance and recompense of the righteous cannot be lost.—When a man's ways please the Lord, He maketh even his enemies to be at peace with him.—The silence of enemies not always a sign of conversion.

HEUBNER:—Insipid as this objection of the Sadducees is, quite as insipid are all others against the facts in the life of Christ.—The darkening or suppression of the Scriptures has either despotism in the faith, or anarchy in the faith, as its result.— Belief in the angels pervades the most intimate and highest relations of man.—It is very comprehensible why the Scripture even here reveals to us many things concerning the angels.—Christ's argument no empty, delusive argument κατ' ἄνθρωπον, as the heroes of accommodation say.—ARNDT:—The repulse of the Sadducees: 1. The assault; 2. the defence; 3. the consequences resulting therefrom.—W. HOFACKER:— Christ over against the Sadducees of His and our day. We direct our eyes: 1. To the Sadducees; and 2. to the position which Christ has taken in reference to them.—C. PALMER:—God, a God not of the dead but of the living.—On this rests *a.* the hope of eternal life to those whose God He is, *b.* but whoever will have such hope must become spiritually living.— THOLUCK:—On the feast of the dead: Before God the dead live (*Pred.* ii. p. 264 *seq.*).—Another in the six sermons upon Religious Questions of the Time, 1845, 1846, p. 60 *seq.*, and at the feast of the dead: Whereby may a man become firm in his faith in an eternal life?—DR. B. TER HAAR, Theological Professor in Utrecht:—For Him all are living: 1. They live; 2. they live to God; 3. they all live to Him. Therefore an imperishable, a holy, a blessed, a social life.—VAN OOSTERZEE:—They are equal to the angels of God in heaven: 1. What there will fall away? What is incompatible with angelic perfection. Our Lord says the angels marry not, sin not, die not; we shall therefore cease to be *a.* sensuous, *b.* sinful, *c.* mortal, beings; 2. What will there remain? what is kindred to angelic perfection: *a.* the angelic purity that was here striven after, *b.* the angelic love that was here cherished, *c.* the angelic joy that was here tasted; 3. What will there begin? what arises from angelic perfection: *a.* higher development, *b.* more perfect communion, *c.* more unlimited complacency of God, than the soul here upon earth enjoys.—In conclusion, the momentousness of this teaching of our Saviour: 1. For the frivolous Sadducees; 2. the high-minded Pharisees; 3. the sincere but weak disciples even of the present day.

---

4. Direct Controversy with the Pharisees on the part of Jesus (Vss. 41–47).

(Parallel to Matt. xxii. 41–46; xxiii. 14; Mark xii. 35–40.)

41, 42 And he said unto them, How say they that [the] Christ is David's son? And [yet] David himself saith in the book of Psalms, The LORD said unto my Lord, Sit thou on
43 my right hand, Till I make thine enemies thy footstool [lit., Till I place thine enemies
44 as a footstool of thy feet]. David therefore calleth him Lord, how is he then [and how
45 is he] his son? Then in the audience of all the people [while all the people were lis-
46 tening] he said unto his disciples,[1] Beware of the scribes, which desire [or, like] to walk in long robes, and love greetings in the markets, and the highest seats in the syna-
47 gogues, and the chief rooms [places] at feasts; Which devour widows' houses, and for a shew make long prayers: the same shall receive greater damnation [condemnation].

[1] Vs. 45.—Πρὸς αὐτούς, to which Tischendorf gives the preference, [also Alford,] has no other authorities for it than Q. [As an ecclesiastical lection begins here, Alford explains the *Recepta* as having arisen very early from the wish to specify αὐτούς. But it is strange that only a single authority should have retained the true reading.—C. C. S.]

EXEGETICAL AND CRITICAL.

Vs. 41. **And He said unto them.**—The conflict between our Lord and His antagonists has here visibly reached a turning-point. Long enough has He answered their questions; now He on His part takes the initiative, in order that the continued silence which He also maintained might not wear the guise of perplexity. From Matthew we perceive that the question was addressed to the collective body of the Pharisees here present (Matt. xxii. 46); from Mark (Mark xii. 35), that He therewith answers *de facto* all their former invectives against Him; from Luke (comp. vs. 45), that our Lord handles the point in question with the greatest possible publicity. First did He put the enemy to flight: now He also on His part passes on to the pursuit.

How say they.—Not in the sense of "How is it possible that they so speak?" but, "In what sense is this name given to the Messiah?" There is a distinction between the question which, Matt. xvi. 13, is addressed to the disciples and that which is here addressed to the Pharisees. There our Lord inquires after their view as to His own person; here He speaks in general, entirely objectively, respecting the Christ, the object of their expectation. Luke, who gives the account with the utmost possible condensation, passes over the answer, "David's Son," in order to let the second question : καὶ αὐτός, &c., follow immediately upon the first.

Vs. 42. **And yet David himself saith.**—That the Messiah was to be David's Son was, it is true, not the universal (comp. John vii. 27), but yet the most current, conception. It would be an entire perversion, however, of our Saviour's intention in making the citation from David, to suppose (WEISSE, *Evang. Gesch.* i. p. 168) that He wished thereby to controvert the conception in itself as an ungrounded or indifferent one, and to point to the truth that the Christ was rather to be called David's *Lord*. No: He proceeds the rather with His enemies *e concessis:* the Messiah *is* David's Son, an homage which we know that He often received without gainsaying. But now He proposes to them for solution the enigma, how David could yet speak of his Son at the same time as his Lord. To a generally acknowledged truth He attaches the conception of a higher, almost forgotten one.

In the Book of Psalms.—We seek in vain also in Luke for the very pregnant hint found in Matthew and Mark, that David spoke ἐν πνεύματι. Yet even according to his statement the Lord designates the 110th Psalm as a Messianic and Davidic one. In reference to the last point, critical investigation need not, it is true, be bound by this form of the citation, since our Saviour was evidently here not concerned with rendering critical judgment; but, on the other hand, a considerate criticism will certainly only venture upon sure grounds to deny the Davidic originality of this Psalm. But as respects the first point, we willingly acknowledge that it requires more courage than we possess in order, after so decided a declaration, to dispute the Messianic import of this psalm, which, moreover, is sufficiently established by Stier, Hoffman, Hengstenberg, and others. The question of the conception which the poet himself connected with the *Schechlimini*, does not lie within the sphere of our investigation; but that the poet in the element of the Spirit has greeted *the Messiah* as his Lord, can only be disputed by such expositors as, like those of the Jews, would place their authority above that of our Lord.

Vs. 44. **How is He his Son?**—The question, how David in his Son—that is, one standing below himself—could at the same time honor his Lord, and therewith one who stood above him, is for us Christians scarcely a question any longer, since we have been initiated into the secret of the Divine nature of the Messiah. To the Jews, on the other hand, who expected a Messiah endowed with heavenly gifts and energies, and that as an earthly king, who was to be in a Theocratic and not in a metaphysical sense God's Son, the matter was not so evident. It appears that the dead monotheism to which they surrendered themselves, especially after the exile, closed the eyes of most to the pregnant intimations which even in the Old Testament were here and there given respecting the supernatural descent and Divine dignity of the Messiah. The Lord will therefore show them that their whole Christology is imperfect and contradicts itself, so long as this integral element is wanting to it. He brings them to silence by pointing them to a sanctuary whose key they had lost. He wishes to stir them up to profounder reflection upon the truth which they had either never yet understood or had looked upon as blasphemy against God, and greeted with stones. In this way He will cure them once for all of their carnal expectations, and show them that He is in no wise minded to direct Himself according to their egoistic wishes. Even to-day the Jews are not in condition to answer satisfactorily the enigma proposed to them by the Great Master. Comp. the Ebionitic conception of the Messiah as φιλὸς ἄνθρωπος, and the Christological confession which the Jew Trypho, in Justin Martyr, has given.

Vs. 45. **While all the people were listening.**—Matthew (xxii. 46) and Mark (xii. 37) communicate especially the impression which this last question of our Lord made; Luke visibly hurries on and communicates only a little of the extended warning which our Lord before leaving the temple uttered in reference to the Pharisees and scribes. Comp. Matt. xxiii. 1–36. In the little that he mentions of it he faithfully follows Mark, while he himself has already (ch. xi. 37–54), preserved many a terrific "Woe to you" of the Lord in another connection. Respecting the historical accuracy of this arrangement *see* above (on ch. xvii. 20–37). Yet even from his compendious account (ch. xx. 41–47), there appears so much as this: that our Lord, after He had proposed that question to the Pharisees upon which they are not even to this day clear, turns forever away from them, in order to address Himself to the more receptive people, and to warn them yet once again before His departure, against the blind leaders of the blind. Luke mentions particularly in addition (vs. 45) that our Lord addressed these warnings to His disciples (not exclusively the apostles, but a wider circle of His followers), yet *coram populo*.

Vs. 46. **Beware of the scribes.**—The scribes, as the worst corrupters of the people among all the Pharisees, are here particularly brought forward and drawn from life; yet not according to their inward character, but according to their external guise. The Lord depicts their behavior: 1. In social life—the self-complacency with which they go about, ἐν στολαῖς, by which we have especially to understand the wide Tallith reaching down even to the feet; the value which they lay upon being universally greeted in the market, as well as upon extended titles; 2. in the Synagogues, where they lay claim to the πρωτοκαθεδρίας, which are allotted according to office and law; 3. in the house, where they transfer the controversy of rank for the place of honor from the Synagogue to the feast, and seek to dispute with others the first place; 4. in the sphere of philanthropy, where they devour widows' houses while they pretend to advance their interests. Thus are hypocrisy, pride, and covetousness the three chief traits of which their portrait is composed. The last reproach " has reference primarily to the parasitism of the saints, who in long exercises of devotion sought to acquire influence with wealthy women and widows. The susceptibility of the weaker sex has been ever an object of the attention of devout friends of the world, and has never yet lost anything of its attractive power."

Vs. 47. **Greater damnation.**—This expression also appears to be an indirect proof that our Saviour on this occasion brought up more than only this little against the corrupters of the nation. It lay, however, in the character of the Hellenistic, Pauline Gospel of Luke, that He speaks with less particularity and detail than Matthew of the terrific judgment with which our Lord, on leaving the temple, shakes the dust from His feet. Here also holds good what has been observed of Mark: " For young Gentile Christians the great sermon of denunciation would have been in part unintelligible and in part too strong a food."

DOCTRINAL AND ETHICAL.

1. The last question which our Lord proposes to His enemies, is on His part the first step to an irrevocable farewell. He closes therewith for those His work as Teacher, by proposing to them yet once again to be pondered the great problem of His Theanthropic personality; what He will now hereafter address to them will no more be uttered to instruct them as Prophet, but in order to answer them as High-Priest and King.

2. The last question with which Jesus parts from His enemies affords the convincing proof that for true Christianity everything depends on a correct judgment of His glorious person. If *conceptions* of faith (*Glaubensbegriffe*) were really a matter of quite subordinate importance, and the assertion of rationalism were well founded—namely, that not the person but the doctrine and example of our Lord are the chief concern, He would scarcely have given Himself the trouble of encouraging the Pharisees to an investigation which in this case would have concerned a dry, exegetical, and abstract dogmatical question.

3. On this occasion it plainly appears that our Lord finds direct Messianic prophecies even in the book of Psalms; that He conceives David as with his vision into the future taken up into a region of the Spirit; that to Him the prophetic Scripture, as an inspired, was also a perfectly infallible, Scripture. So long as one regards the Old Testament with His eyes, neither the Nomistic over-valuation nor the Gnostic contempt for the first and largest half of the Scripture has a satisfactory prospect of finding great acceptance in His church.

4. There is no book in which our Lord in His last week has so lived as in the book of Psalms; an intimation which should not be neglected, particularly by suffering and striving Christians.

5. There exists a palpable similarity between the image which our Lord has here sketched of the Pharisees and scribes, and Clericalism, especially that of the middle ages. Altogether spontaneously, one in reading the expression, vs. 47, thinks of the presents which the church and the monkish orders knew how to get for themselves, of the traffic in masses for the dead, of the unhappy influence of the confessional. The value also which they laid upon sumptuous garments and places of honor, the predilection for circumstantial titles, and the system of reciprocal deification and homage has all revived in many a form, and even to-day has not yet died out. But it would betray a very short-sighted view, if one knew how to find the traces of these perversions nowhere else than merely within the jurisdiction of Rome.

6. Severe, yet not too severe, is the tone wherewith our Lord prepares Himself to leave the sanctuary. Perhaps we may even rather wonder that He has not said more, than that He has not said less. Nor may it be overlooked that He does not attack the persons of His enemies in themselves, but their principles, whose working was so utterly ruinous; that He by no means denies the existence of individuals of a better mind among the scribes, but directs His eye principally to the spirit ruling among them; that the salt of His speech must here often more than elsewhere bite, if it was as yet even in any measure to stay the corruption. And may we not add that our Lord felt even for Himself the necessity of holding up to Himself the whole wickedness of His enemies once more in an overwhelming picture (Matt. xxiii.); that He might be able to rise up with so much the more power and dignity, and take of the temple a leave which was to Him so indescribably melancholy?

7. Immeasurable is the contrast between the first and the last visit of our Lord to the temple. The less may we leave unnoticed that the boy Jesus, who once by His questions threw the teachers in Israel into astonishment, and by His answers often made them suddenly dumb, and the Messiah, who often on the final day, both with questions and with answers, nobly maintains the field, exhibit really one and the same character. The Divine Sonship then presaged is now distinctly known.

HOMILETICAL AND PRACTICAL.

Even on the last day of His sojourn in the temple our Lord, as once at the wedding in Cana, has kept the best wine until the last.—The mystery of the Divinely human dignity of our Lord: 1. Revealed to David; 2. concealed from the Pharisees; 3. confirmed by Jesus; 4. brought for us to light.—The apparent discrepancies in the Scripture can be resolved for us only by Jesus Himself.—Sit Thou at My right hand: 1. The power of this word; 2. the right of this word; 3. the fruit of this word.—The devil in the garment of a scribe. Comp. Is. v. 20.—*Esse quam videri*.—How hypocrisy poisons: 1. Social; 2. married; 3. church, life.—The danger of a spiritless formalism in the ministers of religion.—Hypocrisy the sin which is always punished the hardest.

STARKE:—Let him whom the people like to hear take note of the opportunity to do good.—QUESNEL: —Proud, ambitious, avaricious teachers are more dangerous than the greatest sinners among the people.—HEDINGER:—Pride a sign of hypocrisy, believe it certainly; if an angel came and were proud, believe he were a devil, Psalm cxxxi. 1.—Widows can very easily be talked over and misled: they should therefore take good heed to themselves; but woe to him that misleads them. 2 Tim. iii. 6.— BRENTIUS:—It is an abomination above all abominations to deceive people and deprive them of their property under the guise of godliness.

HEUBNER:—Jesus here proposes no school-question, but the highest, weightiest question in life.— It is a serious duty to become clear as to the person of Jesus.—Christ is Lord *absolutely* of the whole human race, even David's Lord; His Lordship is the highest and most blessed one; Christocracy would be the best constitution for us.—ARNDT, *Predigten über das Leben Jesu*, iv. p. 251:—The weightiest article of faith in the Gospel. The Pharisees, with their 'David's Son,' yet only expressed in substance that Jesus was a man like all other men, only of royal race. It was only the half, not the whole truth. Even as our contemporaries, who also will let Christ pass for a remarkably gifted and virtuous character, and yet for a man such as they and all are. If Jesus had been really only that and nothing higher, He would have had to praise the answer of the Pharisees, and to say something like this: Ye are right; and I see that ye are very much at home in Moses and in the prophets. But our Lord is in nowise content with the answer; He demands, when the discourse is about the Messiah, a deeper penetration into the declarations of the Scripture, and into the character of His person. Must He, therefore, if God already calls Him Lord, even before He was born, not be infinitely more than David's Son—than a mere man?—PALMER:—There is, according to this inquiry, only one truth for our faith; for a living faith in God, in a providence, immortality, &c., is impossible without a knowledge of Christ.—FYCNS: —What think ye of Christ? In that name there is implied that He is: 1. The greatest Prophet ; 2. the true High-Priest ; 3. the eternal King.—OTTO :— Christ, David's Lord and Son.—MOLL :—What think ye of Christ, whose Son is He? 1. A question of life, which stands in the centre of all moral problems ; 2. a question of conscience, which lays hold of the personal life in its deepest root; 3. a question of faith, which finds its solution only upon the soil of revelation.

C. *Revelations concerning the Parusia, and Leave-takings in the midst of His Friends.*

CHS. XXI.—XXII. 36.

The Leaving of the Temple. Prophecy of the Destruction of Jerusalem and the Fulness of the Time.

1. The Widow's Mite (CH. XXI. 1-4).

(Parallel to Mark xii. 41-44.)

1 And he looked up, and [Looking up, he], saw the [om., the] rich men casting their
2 gifts into the treasury. And he saw also a certain [some one and that a, τινα καί for
3 καὶ τινα¹] poor widow casting in thither two mites. And he said, Of a truth I say unto
4 you, that this poor widow hath cast in more than they all : For all these have of their abundance cast in unto the offerings of God :² but she of her penury hath cast in all the living that she had.

¹ Vs. 2.—Καί must not be expunged, nor with Lachmann bracketed, but with Tischendorf be placed after τινα, as a more particular description of the woman.
² Vs. 4.—Τοῦ Θεοῦ, suspicious, as an explicative addition, which is wanting in B., [Cod. Sin.,] L., X., Cursives, Coptic version, &c.

EXEGETICAL AND CRITICAL.

Vs. 1. **And looking up**, ἀναβλέψας.—Here also we must unite the accounts of Mark and Luke, in order to be able to form to ourselves a correct conception of the true course of this miniature but lovely narrative. Even this deserves to be noted, that we see our Lord sitting so tranquilly in the temple (καθίσας, Mark) shortly after His terrific "Woe to you!" had resounded. He will avoid even the slightest appearance of having gone away in any excitement, or from any sort of fear of further attacks. The place where we have to seek Him, over against God's chest, is known to us also from John viii. 20. We may understand the thirteen offering chests (Shofaroth) which were marked with letters of the Hebrew alphabet, and stood open there in order to receive gifts for different sacred and benevolent purposes, about whose destination and arrangement we find much that is interesting gathered in LIGHTFOOT, *Decas Chorograph. in Marcum*, ch. 3. Perhaps, however, a particular treasure-chest is meant, of which also Josephus speaks, *Ant. Jud.* xix. 6, 1. Comp. 2 Kings xii. 9. In view of the uncertainty of the matter, it is at least precipitate to be so ready with the imputation that the Evangelists have been inexact in their statement, like, for instance, De Wette.

Vs. 2. **Some one, and that a poor widow**, τινα καὶ χήραν.—See notes on the text. Perhaps one of those whose unhappy fate Jesus had just portrayed, ch. xx. 47. We need not, however, assert on this account that He designedly made such honorable mention of this particular widow in order to make the contrast yet stronger with the haughty and unloving Pharisees. He is now through with them. The contrast was not made, but born of the reality of life. —**Two mites**, δύο λεπτά.—As to the pecuniary value, *see* on the parallel in Mark. It is a question of little account whether the Rabbinic rule, *nemo ponat λεπτόν in cistam eleëmosynarum*, is really applicable here, which Meyer disputes, and whether, therefore, it was true that in no case could less than two mites be cast into the γαζοφυλάκιον. It certainly cannot be proved that this rule was applicable also to the δῶρα τοῦ Θεοῦ. At all events, necessity knows no law, and Bengel's remark, *quorum unum vidua retinere poterat*, remains therefore true.

Vs. 3. Πλεῖον πάντων.—It deserves to be noted that our Lord does not at all censure or lightly esteem the gifts of the rich. Not once again does there resound a "Woe to you, ye hypocrites!" In rebuke He will, after what has just been said in the temple, not again open His mouth. Only He extols far above the beneficence of these, the gift of the poor widow. For the rich have of their abundance cast in εἰς τὰ δῶρα, that is, not *ad monumenta preciosa, ibi in perpetuum dedicata* (Bengel), but *ad dona, in thesauro asservata*. The woman, on the other hand, gave of her poverty, ἅπαντα τὸν βίον ὃν εἶχε, comp. ch. viii. 43; xv. 12 (yet more strongly and briefly, Mark: πάντα ὅσα εἶχεν). The value of her gift is, therefore, reckoned not according to the pecuniary amount, but according to the sacrifice connected therewith. How our Lord became acquainted with the widow's necessity we do not know; perhaps she belonged to those known as poor; nothing hinders us, however, to refer it to the Divine knowledge which penetrated the life of Nathanael and the Samaritan woman. Enough, He shows that He has attentively observed the work of love, and praises it because He knows out of what source it flowed. He does not, it is true, directly compare the disposition, but only the ability, of the different givers with each other; but certainly He would not have so highly valued the material worth of the little gift, if He had not at the same time calculated also the moral worth. In no case would He have praised the widow if she had brought her offering, like most of the Pharisees, from ignoble impulses. Now, He will not withhold from her His approbation, since her heart in His eyes passes for richer than her gift. He does not ask whether this gift will be a vain one; whether it is well to support with such offerings the temple-chest and its misuse; whether a worship ought to be yet supported by widows, which a few years afterwards is to fall before the sword of the enemy. He looks alone at the ground, the character and purpose of her act, and the poor woman who has given up all in good faith, but has kept her faith, gains now with her two pieces of copper an income of imperishable honor.

How the judgment of our Lord respecting this widow finds at the same time an echo in every human heart, appears to us if we direct our look to particular parallel expressions from profane literature. According to the Jewish legend (*see* WETSTEIN on Mark xii. 43), a high-priest who had despised a handful of meal which a poor woman brought to a sacrifice, is said to have received a revelation not to contemn this small gift, because she had therewith, as it were, given her whole soul. According to SENECA, *De Benef.* i. 8, the poor Æschines, who, instead of an offering of money, dedicated himself to Socrates, brought a greater offering than Alcibiades and others with their rich gifts. An act similar to that of the poor widow we find stated in HOFMANN, *Missionsstunden*, i. 5. *Vorlesung.*

DOCTRINAL AND ETHICAL.

1. The narrative of the Widow's Mite makes in this connection a similar impression to that of a friendly sunbeam on a dark tempestuous heaven, or a single rose upon a heath full of thistles and thorns. Just in this appears the Divine in our Lord, that He, in a moment when the fate of Jerusalem, and with this the coming of the kingdom of God into the whole world, so completely fills His mind, has yet eyes and heart for the most insignificant individual, and is disposed to adorn even so lowly a head with the crown of honor. We need no other proof for the celestially pure temper in which He left the accursed temple after such words of wrath. It is as if He cannot so part, as if at least His last word must be a word of blessing and of peace, so that we scarcely know in what character in this hour of sundering we shall most admire the King of the kingdom of God, whether more as Punisher of hidden evil, or as Rewarder of hidden good.

2. In the judgment also which He passes, the Son is the image of the invisible Father. Comp. 1 Sam. xvi. 1–13. Men judge the heart according to the deeds; the Lord judges the deed according to the heart. Therewith is connected, moreover, the phenomenon that the sacred history relates very much which profane history gives over to oblivion, and the reverse. Heroic deeds and great events of the world are passed over here in silence, but not the cup of cold water, the widow's mite, the ointment of Mary, and the like.

3. The history of the two mites is a new proof of the power of little things, and of the gracious favor with which the Lord looks upon the least offering which only bears the stamp of a *sancta simplicitas*. With right, therefore, has this text been regarded as an admirable mission-text, since the mission-chest receives no insignificant increment from widows' mites, over which an "Increase and multiply" has been uttered. By the example of this woman the penny clubs for the mission cause, the *Ketten-vereine* of the Gustavus Adolphus Society, [the weekly penny offerings of our Sunday scholars,] &c., are sanctioned. Even in a material respect the word, 2 Cor. xii. 10, becomes true for the church of our Lord.

HOMILETICAL AND PRACTICAL.

The last look of the Lord at those surrounding Him in the temple.—The rich and the poor meet together; the Lord is the Maker of them all, Prov. xx. 2.—The beneficence of the rich and of the poor compared with one another.—How one can be beneficent even without giving much, Acts iii. 6.—The true art of reckoning: 1. For love no offering is too great; 2. in God's eyes no offering of love is too little.—The judgment of the Lord: 1. Other than the judgment of man; 2. better than the judgment of man.—How little really a rich man does when he does nothing but give.—The heart is the standard of the deeds.—The need of bringing something as a sacrifice, inseparable from the inwardly religious life, 2 Sam. xxiv. 24.—How the history of the poor widow teaches us: 1. Carefulness in our judgment upon others; 2. strictness in our judgment upon ourselves; 3. watchfulness in respect to the approaching judgment of the Lord.

STARKE:—The eyes of the Lord are directed upon God's chest; keepers of it, look well to what ye do!—CANSTEIN:—It is something comforting and refreshing to the poor, that they can give more than the rich.—CRAMER:—As God does not regard the person, so does He not regard the gifts and offerings, but the heart and the simplicity of faith.—Let no one despise true widows; there are heroines of faith among them, 1 Tim. v. 3.—HEUBNER:—All gifts should be a sacrifice.—What once was done too much, now is done too little.—Even small gifts are of importance for the general cause; the Lord can add His blessing thereto.—Religion raises the value of all gifts.—Liberality, honor and love to the temple, contempt of earthly things, trust in God, are the main traits in the portrait of the widow.—CARL BECK:—The measure of the Heavenly Judge for our good works: 1. A staff to support the lowly; 2. a staff to beat down the lofty.—W. HOFACKER:—Jesus' look of pleasure and acknowledgment which rested upon the gift of the widow; 1. A look full of strengthening, comforting favor; 2. a look full of the earnestness of lofty and holy inquiry upon us all.—KNAPP:—The standard with which the Lord our Saviour determines the worth or unworthiness of our benevolent gifts and works.—KAPFF:—The practice of beneficent compassion.—N. BEETS:—The work of love and its Witness.

2. The Secrets of the Future (Vss. 5–36).

First Part (Vss. 5–24).

(Parallel to Matt. xxiv. 1–21; Mark xiii. 1–19.)

5 And as some spake of the temple, how [or, that] it was adorned with goodly stones
6 and gifts [offerings, ἀναθέμασιν], he said, As for these things which ye behold, the days will come, in the which there shall not be left one stone upon another that shall not be
7 thrown down [καταλυθήσεται]. And they asked him, saying, Master [Teacher], but when shall these things be? and what sign will there be when these things shall [are
8 about to] come to pass? And he said, Take heed that ye be not deceived: for many shall come in my name, saying, I am Christ; and the time draweth near: go ye not
9 therefore [om., therefore[1]] after them. But when ye shall hear of wars and commotions, be not terrified: for these things must first come to pass; but the end is not by
10 and by [but not immediately is the end].—Then said he unto them, Nation shall rise
11 against nation, and kingdom against kingdom: And great earthquakes shall [there] be in divers places, and [put "and" after "be"[2]] famines, and pestilences; and fearful
12 sights and great signs shall there be from heaven. But before all these, they shall lay their hands on you, and persecute you, delivering you up to the synagogues, and into
13 prisons, being brought before kings and rulers for my name's sake. And it shall turn
14 [result] to you for a testimony. Settle it therefore in your hearts, not to meditate be-
15 fore what ye shall answer: For I will give you a mouth and wisdom, which all your
16 adversaries shall not be able to gainsay [oppose[3]] nor resist. And ye shall be betrayed [delivered up] both [or, even] by parents, and brethren, and kinsfolks, and friends; and some of you shall they cause to be put to death [shall they put to death, θανατώ-
17, 18 σουσιν]. And ye shall be hated of [by] all men for my name's sake. But [Καί]
19 there shall not a hair of [ἐκ] your head perish. In your patience possess ye your
20 souls [By your endurance shall ye gain your souls (or, lives, ψυχάς[4])]. And when ye shall see Jerusalem compassed with armies, then know that the desolation thereof is
21 nigh. Then let them which are in Judea flee to the mountains; and let them which are in the midst of it [i. e., Jerusalem] depart out; and let not them that are in the
22 countries [country parts] enter thereinto. For these be [are] the [om., the] days of
23 vengeance, that all things which are written may be fulfilled. But [om., But] woe unto them that are with child, and to them that give suck, in those days! for there shall
24 be great distress in the land [or, upon the earth], and wrath upon this people. And they shall fall by the edge of the sword, and shall be led away captive into all [the] nations: and Jerusalem shall be trodden down of the Gentiles [shall be a city trodden down by Gentiles], until the times [καιροί] of the Gentiles be [are] fulfilled.

[1] Vs. 8.—The οὖν of the Recepta should be expunged, as by Lachmann and Tischendorf, [Meyer, Tregelles, Alford.]
[2] Vs. 11.—According to the arrangement of Tischendorf, [Tregelles, Alford]: σεισμοὶ τε μεγάλοι καὶ κατὰ τόπους λοιμοί, κ.τ.λ.
[3] Vs. 15.—Tischendorf, Tregelles, Alford, Van Oosterzee put ἀντιστῆναι before ἀντειπεῖν.—C. C. S.]
[4] Vs. 19.—With Griesbach, Rinck, Lachmann, Tischendorf, [Meyer, Tregelles, Alford,] we give to the reading of A., D., &c., the preference. See Exegetical and Critical remarks. [Cod. Sin. here agrees with the Recepta.—C. C. S.]

EXEGETICAL AND CRITICAL.

The eschatological discourse with which our Saviour, according to all the Synoptics, closes His public work as Teacher, has been at all times and justly reckoned among the greatest of the cruces interpretum. It is easier to propose a greater or less number of objections against any explanation of it than ourselves to give an interpretation thereof which should leave no difficulties remaining. The principal literature on this question we find given in LANGE on Matthew and Mark, to which may yet be added an unquestionably interesting dissertation by E. SCHERER, upon Jesus' prophecies of the end, in the Beiträge zu den theologischen Wissenschaften von Reuss und Cunitz, ii. pp. 63–83, Jena, 1851. Comp. the critical Comm. on the Eschatological Discourse, Matt. xxiv. 25, by J. C. MEYER, Franf. a. d. O. 1857, and an exegetical exposition by H. CREMER, Ueber die Eschatol. Rede J. Chr., Matt. xxiv. 25, Stuttg. 1860. So much we may well assume, as indeed almost all are now agreed, that as well the view of those who here understand exclusively (Michaelis, Bahrdt, Eckermann, Henke, and others), as also the opinion of those who here will allow no reference to Jerusalem's destruction (BAUR, Kan. Ev., p. 605), is entirely untenable. It is therefore established that here the discourse is of the destruction of Jerusalem, and at the same time of the end of the world, and it can only be the question in what connection these two events stand to one another in the prophetic portraiture of our text. For the solution of this enigma it is, above all, necessary that we well understand the question which the disciples addressed to the Master, and which in its original form Matthew has most faithfully communicated to us. They ask when these things (ταῦτα) shall be, and can on psychological grounds be thinking of nothing else than of the destruction of the city and the temple, the prophecy of which had just before shaken them to their inmost soul. They inquire besides after the sign of the coming of the Lord and the end of the world. By no means have they here two different events, but only two sides of one and the same event in their mind. Yet mindful of the declaration, Matt. xxiii. 37-39, they coördinate the fall of the temple, His παρουσία, and the conclusion of the present world-period (αἰών). They had, that is, as genuine Jews, hitherto ever conceived that the temple would stand eternally, and Jerusalem be the centre whither all the nations should stream together, in order to enjoy with the Jews the blessings of the Messianic reign (the assertion of EBRARD, *Ev. Krit.*, p. 611, that the Jews had expected even in the Messianic time a severe conflict and with it the destruction of the temple, is at least unproved; better has De Wette, on Matt. xxiv. 3, elucidated the subject); but now they have in the days and hours immediately preceding heard something by which this conception of theirs has been disturbed. They had believed that the Christ would remain eternally here below, and that the temple would outlast time; but now they hear that the Christ shall die, and the temple become a heap of ruins. How could they, as born Israelites, after this last fact, imagine any further continuance of the earthly economy? And yet they still expect as ever a glorious παρουσία of the Messiah, which in everything shall be the opposite of His present humble manifestation. Naturally they conceived this as occurring not after, but contemporaneously with, the fall of the temple, and desire therefore to know by what previous tokens they might recognize the approach of the decisive catastrophe, in which the great *double* event shall break in.

What now shall our Lord do in order to speak to them according to their receptivity and their need? Shall He say to them that the one fact shall be separated from the other by an interval of so many centuries? Then He would have had to give entirely up His own principle, John xvi. 12. With deep wisdom He places Himself, therefore, upon the position of the inquirers, and starts, it is true, from the destruction of Jerusalem, but in order at the same time to attach to this a delineation of the συντέλεια τοῦ αἰῶνος. However, we must from our point of view hold the different attempts to indicate a definite point in this discourse, when our Lord leaves the first object and afterwards speaks exclusively of the second, as rather doubtful. It has, for instance, been believed that we find such in Matt. xxiv. 29, but vs. 34, impartially explained, gives us plainly to see that even after this He yet speaks of events which the generation then living should behold. If we, therefore, will not assume that our Lord Himself erred in so important a case, or that the Evangelists have not at all understood His eschatological discourse, or have inaccurately reported it—assumptions which, from a believing point of view, the Christian consciousness condemns in the strongest manner, —there then is nothing left for us but to assume that our Lord speaks indeed of the destruction of Jerusalem, but all this regarded as a type of the last judgment of the world. In other words, that He speaks prophetically of the earlier as a type of the later.

Jerusalem's destruction, but apprehended in its ideal significance, is and remains, therefore, the theme of the discourse, yet so that He from this point of view at the same time beholds and prophesies the destruction of the earthly economy in general that follows afterwards. Here also the peculiarity of prophetic vision is to be borne in mind, in which the conception of time recedes before that of space, and what is successive appears as coördinate. "*Prophetia est ut pictura regionis cujusdam, quæ in proximo tecta et colles et pontes notat distincte, procul valles et montes latissime patentes in angustum cogit: sic enim debet etiam esse eorum, qui prophetiam legunt, prospectus in futurum, cui se prophetia accommodat.*" Bengel. Both events flow in His representation so together, that the interval almost wholly recedes, and the tokens of His coming, which already begin to reveal themselves before the destruction of the City and of the Temple, are repeated in over-increasing measure, the nearer the last judgment draws on. Therefore the interpreter must content himself if he is able to point out that all the here-threatened tribulations have already had a *beginning* of fulfilment in the period which immediately preceded the destruction of Jerusalem,—a beginning which then again bears the germ of subsequent fulfilments in itself, even as the fruit lies hidden in the bud.

On this interpretation, therefore, the eschatological discourse contains the exact answer to the question of the disciples, and it is from this sufficiently explained why in the apostolic epistles the expectation of a speedy return of our Lord arose, so that, for instance, Paul could entertain the thought of a possibility of himself even living to see it (1 Thess. iv. 15; 2 Cor. v. 4, and elsewhere). They saw the signs foretokening the destruction of Jerusalem come nearer and nearer, and had not yet learned from the Lord that even after this event the present economy should endure, yea, for centuries. The attentive reader will, however, not overlook the intimations which are plainly given here and there in this discourse, that the coming of the Lord should, nevertheless, not take place so soon as many believed, and that with Jerusalem's destruction the last word of the world's history would not by any means be yet uttered (comp. Matt. xxiv. 48; xxv. 5, 19; Luke xxi. 24). As concerns, finally, the relation of the different Synoptics to one another, in reference to the setting forth of this discourse of Jesus, we cannot agree with the expositors who think that the praise of greater originality or exactness belongs to Mark or Luke. Unquestionably, in this respect, Matthew deserves the preference, while we, on the other hand, meet, especially in Luke, with a freer, more fragmentary redaction of the whole discourse. Many utterances of special importance are preserved more complete by Matthew and Mark; on the other hand, we meet in Luke with particular *singularia*, which in and of themselves deserve the highest attention, and assist the view over the great whole of this discourse in many relations. For the locality of the discourse, Matthew and Mark must be compared. An admirable picture by Begas seizes the moment when our Lord is sitting with His four friends at evening-time upon the Mount of Olives, and is disclosing to them the secrets of the future.

Vs. 5. **And as some spake of the temple.**— Manifestly these words were not uttered after but during the leaving of the temple. It is as though the disciples, most deeply moved by the farewell to the temple (Matt. xxiii. 37-39), now seek to become the intercessors for the heavily-doomed sanctuary. They show Him the building (Matthew), which yet, far from being completed, appears to promise to the sanctuary a longer duration; the masses of stone (Mark), which may yet defy many centuries; the votive offerings with which (Luke) munificence and ostentation had adorned the house of the Lord. These ἀναθήματα had been for the greatest part offered by heathens; for instance, the holy vessels by the Emperor Augustus, other vessels again by the Egyptian Philadelphus, especially the magnificent golden vine which Herod the Great had presented, as Josephus relates, *De Bell. Jud.* vi. 5, 2, *A. J.* xv. 11, 8. If we now consider that according to the prophetic declarations, for instance, Ps. lxxii.; Isaiah lx., the heathen also should bring their gifts and offerings to Zion, it is then doubly intelligible that the Apostles found in these very objects one ground the more for their hope of the continuance of the sanctuary.

Vs. 6. **As for these things which ye behold.** —Nominative absolute, to indicate the subject, which now in our Saviour's discourse is to be made sufficiently plain. By this very construction the antithesis becomes the stronger, which prevails between the light in which that which is seen there yet displays itself, and the fate that impended over it. " It is very remarkable that the Hellenic Gospel, which, according to the words of Christ, has especially kept in mind the relation between beauty of manifestation in its truth and beauty of manifestation in empty guise, has attached His prophecies of the destruction of Jerusalem and of the judgment of the world, immediately to an allusion to the beauty and rich splendor of the temple."

There shall not be left one stone upon another.—Comp. ch. xix. 43, 44. In order rightly to comprehend the full force of the antithesis, we must represent to ourselves the whole magnificence of the sanctuary, over which later Jewish scholars exclaimed with wonder, "He that has not seen the temple of Herod has never beheld anything glorious." *See* the notes on the parallels in Matthew and Mark.

Vs. 7. **When . . . and what sign.**—Their question is, therefore, a double one; they wish to know precisely the point of time, and to recognize the tokens of this approaching catastrophe. Our Lord answers only the last question, while He in reference to the first gives to them only general intimations (comp. Matt. xxiv. 34-36). The signs which He gives are at the same time of such a nature that they, in fact, are only to be seen precursorily at the destruction of Jerusalem, but will appear decisively and in their full force only at the end of the world. It is here as with the boxes containing one within the other [Chinese boxes].

Vs. 8. **Take heed.**—In Luke, as in Matthew and Mark, the warning against being seduced by false Messiahs stands first. It is not to be denied that before the destruction of Jerusalem, so far as we know, no deceivers appeared to play a strictly Messianic part; Bar Cochba, the first of these more than sixty deceivers, did not come up till afterwards. *See* Eusebius, *H. E.*, iv. 6. But, certainly, there already lay in the misleading influence of a Jonathan, Theudas, Dositheus, Simon, Menander, and others, the germs of the same delusion which afterwards appeared more decidedly in the form of a false Messiahship. Bear in mind how the Goëtæ, by promises of miracles, allured many thousands into the wilderness, and thereby into destruction. Comp. Acts v. 36, 37; xxi. 38; Homily 76 of Chrysostom on Matthew. Thus did the general signs of the world's end begin really to go into fulfilment with the destruction of Jerusalem.

Vs. 10. **Then said He unto them.**—According to the representation of Luke the warning against misleaders was only something preliminary, an introduction, as it were, after which our Lord goes on to handle the question proposed, particularly and regularly.

Nation shall rise against nation.—The insurrections, earthquakes, famines, and other plagues, which are here adduced, were before the destruction of Jerusalem by no means so insignificant as, for instance, De Wette asserts. Bear in mind the massacres at Cæsarea, between Syrians and Jews, in which 20,000 of the latter fell, while in Syria almost every city was divided into two armies, which stood opposed to one another as deadly enemies; the quick succession of the five emperors in Rome within a few years, Nero, Galba, Otho, Vitellius, Vespasian, and the tumults connected therewith in wider and narrower circles; the famine under Claudius, Acts xi. 30; the earthquakes at the time of Nero in Campania and Asia, in which whole cities perished; the singular and terrifying signs in Judæa of which Josephus and Tacitus speak, and we have historical cases enough for the explanation of this mysterious declaration of our Lord. Yet, above all, we should lay the emphasis on His declaration in Matthew and Mark, that all these things are only ἀρχαὶ ὠδίνων, so that we have by no means to understand *exclusively* the wars, &c., which were to take place in the interval of forty years; but all the calamities of this kind which in continually increasing measure should precede the end of the world, of which the destruction of Jerusalem was only the type. In another form the same thought is still more intimated than expressed in that which immediately follows, vs. 12.

Vs. 12. **But before all these.**—The assertion of Meyer, *ad loc.*, that this statement of time is, perhaps, a later modification of the tradition, *ex eventu*, rests upon the *dogmatic* preconception that our Lord could not have predicted to His disciples that their personal persecution should precede these last calamities. But the farther the last words of vs. 11 extend beyond the great catastrophe of Jerusalem's destruction, so much the more natural is it also that our Lord points His disciples to that which awaits them even before.—**Shall lay their hands on you,** ἐπιβάλλειν.—Of course, with a hostile intent. A noticeable climax is found in the here-indicated persecutions. The lightest form is in a certain sense the delivery over to the synagogues, namely, in order to be there scourged, comp. Matt. x. 17. A severe conflict impends over them when they are brought before kings and governors to give a testimony to the faith, comp. Matt. x. 18. The worst awaits them when they (vs. 16) shall be delivered up by their parents, relatives, and friends. However, they have in the midst of this distress a threefold consolation: 1. All this is done for the sake of the Lord's name (ἕνεκα), comp. Acts v. 41; 2. it shall turn to them for a testimony; ἀποβήσεται, here, as in Phil. i. 19, the intimation of a salutary result; the persecutions mentioned shall serve as opportunity to the apostles to give a witness concerning their Lord, which here, as in Acts xviii. 11, is represented as something great and glorious. Finally, they shall in such moments be least wanting in the sense of the nearness of their Lord.

Vs. 14. **Settle it therefore in your hearts.**—See on ch. xii. 11; Matt. x. 19, 20. A promise of so high significance might be fittingly repeated. What they, according to our Lord's will, are to settle in their hearts is, as it were, an antidote to the care which should afterwards fill their hearts. "*Id unum laborate, ne laboretis.*" Bengel. The ground of the encouragement is the *ἐγὼ δώσω* of our Lord, that involuntarily reminds us of the Divine word which Moses received at his calling at the burning bush, Ex. iv. 12.—**Mouth and wisdom.**—*Mouth*, concrete expression for the words themselves which they were to utter; *wisdom*, the gift of delivering these words befittingly, according to time, place, and the like. Thus is everything needful promised them as well for the material as for the formal part of their defence, so that continued opposition should become extremely hard for their antagonists. It is, of course, understood that here it is not an absolute but a relative impossibility that is spoken of, and that, therefore, not only Acts vi. 10, but also vii. 51; xiii. 8–10, and other passages, must be compared.

Vs. 16. **And ye shall be delivered up.**—The notices of the Acts and of the Epistles are too brief to admit of the mention of special examples of the fulfilment of this prophecy. This declaration, moreover, is not addressed to the Apostles as such, but so far as they were the representatives of the first believers generally.—**Some of you shall they put to death.**—More definitely expressed than the general *ἀποκτενοῦσιν ὑμᾶς* in Matthew. Among the four auditors of our Lord was found James, who was to be the first martyr [among the Apostles.—C. C. S.], and Peter, upon whom the subsequent prophecy (John xxi. 18, 19) was fulfilled. But these were to be only the first fruits of an incalculable harvest of martyrs, who in the course of the centuries should fall for the cause of the Saviour, and the Apocalypse gives us only a vague foreboding of what outbreaks of iniquity, even in this respect, are hidden in the bosom of the mysterious future.

Vs. 17. **Hated by all men.**—In the apostolic epistles, *e. g.*, Rom. viii. 35–37; 1 Cor. iv. 9, 10; 2 Cor. xi. 23–29; Heb. x. 32–34, we find a rich array of proofs for the exact fulfilment of this word, even in the first period of the church. Bear in mind also the dangers which the flight of the first Christians to the Trans-Jordanic Pella gave occasion to, and, above all, do not overlook how this hatred also in its different phases becomes more and more intense the more rapidly the history and development of God's kingdom hastens to its end.

Vs. 18. **But there shall not a hair.**—Comp. ch. xii. 7; Matt. x. 30. Of course no assurance that they should in no case be slain, but only that they should be inviolable upon earth so long as they were necessary for the service of the Lord, as also that even their death should redound *εἰς σωτηρίαν* and to the glory of Christ; Phil. i. 19. And with this promise of absolute security in a negative respect, they are at the same time also assured of their absolute security on the positive side: **By your endurance,** &c.

Vs. 19. **Gain your souls.** Κτήσεσθε.—Although the κτήσασθε of the *Recepta* is strongly supported by external authority, yet the internal arguments in favor of the reading of A., B. [not Cod. Sin.] are in our eyes of prevailing weight. "The *Recepta* is an *interpretamentum* of the future understood imperatively." Meyer. We have here, therefore, the obverse of the promise, vs. 18; so far from a hair of their head being hurt (comp. Acts xxvii. 34), they should on the other hand, by their perseverance in the midst of all these persecutions, preserve their souls, their life. By ὑπομονή we are not to understand patience, but, as in Romans v. 4; James i. 3, 4, endurance; and to explain κτᾶσθαι not (De Wette) in the sense of εὑρίσκειν, Matt. xvi. 25; but rather in that of "maintain, preserve." (1 Thess. iv. 4.) It is moreover of course understood, that we are by the preservation of the soul not to understand the natural life in itself, but the true life, whose loss or maintenance is for the disciple of the Saviour the greatest question of life. [It is difficult to indicate in English the double meaning of ψυχή, which denotes both soul and life.—C. C. S.] By endurance they were to preserve this true life, even if they for it should lose the life of the body. We find here therefore, in other words, the same promise which is given Matt. xxiv. 13; Rev. ii. 10, and elsewhere, while, on the other hand, the admonition which, according to the common explanation, is found in this verse: Maintain the soul in patience (comp. Heb. x. 36), rests upon an incorrect reading, and without doubt would have had to be otherwise expressed.

Vs. 20. **And when ye shall see Jerusalem.** —Comp. Lange on Matt. xxiv. 15. The mention of the armies stands in Luke in the place of the abomination of desolation mentioned by Matthew and Mark, and the prophecy of Daniel, which is very especially important for the Jewish Christians of Matthew, Luke leaves out in his representation. The very uncertainty of so many expositors in reference to the proper signification of the βδέλυγμα τῆς ἐρημώσεως, is a proof the more how much has been done for the desecration of the holy ground, so that we scarcely know any longer what we have principally to understand. According to the redaction of Luke, even the appearance of the hostile hosts before Jerusalem is an ominous sign, and the disciples are to know that even with the most valiant defence, there is no deliverance any longer to be hoped for.

Vs. 21. **Then let them which are in Judæa.** —Commendation of a hasty flight as the only means of deliverance. In Judæa one finds himself in the heart of the population, and therefore he must seek to reach the lonesome mountains; at any cost he must leave the city, and if he is happy enough to get out of it at the right time he shall under no pretext return.—Ἐν ταῖς χώραις, not *in regionibus* (Bretschneider, De Wette), but *in agris*, where the principal Jews often inhabited country houses. For more particular directions as to their flight, *see* Matthew.

Vs. 22. **Days of vengeance.**—That is, not days in which the one people takes vengeance on the disobedience and refractoriness of the other people, but in which God the Lord accomplishes His judgments upon His enemies. Here the declaration of Moses (Ps. xc. 11), finds its application.—**May be fulfilled.**—According to the express declaration of our Lord, therefore, the fall of the city and the temple also is already prophesied in the Old Testament. We may call to mind Deut. xxviii., which in a certain sense may be named the ground-theme which was afterwards further carried out in the prophetical Scriptures. Daniel also may be included, yet he is by no means especially and exclusively meant. Instead of a citation of the prophetic word, we find in Luke only a general statement, which however evidently shows that this whole prophesying of our Lord is nothing else than the prolongation and continuance of the line which had been drawn centuries before. It is moreover noticeable how recognizably the stamp of Divine retribution was impressed upon the fate of Jerusalem and the temple, even for heathen eyes. We may call to mind the expression even of a Titus: "That God was so angry with this people that even he feared His wrath if he should suffer grace to be shown to the Jews," and how he refused every mark of honor on account of the victory obtained, with the attestation that he had been only an instrument in God's hands to punish this stiffnecked nation. Comp. the well-known expressions of Josephus, as to the height which the wickedness of his contemporaries had reached.

Vs. 23. **Woe unto them that are with child.** —An oὐαί not of imprecation, but of bitter lament, in which the compassion and sympathy of the Saviour expresses itself. [Equivalent to: Alas, for them!—C. C. S.] Comp. ch. xxiii. 29. Such women would be less fitted for rapid flight, without, however, on account of their condition finding compassion. The ground of this fact is a double one: great distress upon earth (entirely general), and especially great *wrath* upon this people. Thus nowhere does a refuge present itself, neither in nor out of Judæa. Comp. Is. xxvi. 20; Rev. vi. 16, 17.

Vs. 24. **And they shall fall.**—A more particular setting forth of the fate of the Jews, which the result confirmed most terrifically. According to Josephus, the number of the slain amounted to 1,100,000; 97,000 were dragged as prisoners mostly to Egypt and the provinces. Comp. Deut. xxviii. 64. —Ἔσται πατουμένη, Jerusalem shall be a city trodden down by the heathen; not alone an intimation of her desecration by a heathen garrison (De Wette), but a designation of all the scornful outrages to which the capital should be given over. Comp. Lam. iv. Nor is there any more reason here by the entirely general mention of ἔθνη to understand the Romans *exclusively*. On the other hand, we may here find the announcement of the interval of centuries in which the most different nations, in almost uninterrupted succession, have trodden down Jerusalem:— Titus, Hadrian, Chosroes, the Mussulmen, the Crusaders, and the later dominion of Islam,—an interval that yet endures, and whose end shall be appointed only when the times of the Gentiles shall be fulfilled.

The times of the Gentiles, καιροὶ ἐθνῶν.— Not the times of the calling of the Gentiles (Stier), by which an entirely foreign thought would be interpolated; but the times which are predestined to the Gentiles for the fulfilment of these Divine judgments. That by καιροί a long interval is intimated (Dorner), appears, it is true, not from this plural in itself, but from the whole connection, according to which these καιροί shall endure even to the final term, and (comp. Matt. xxiv. 29) shall finally be cut short by the last act of the drama of the history of the world. Remarkable is this expression in the first place, because an evident intimation lies hidden therein, that, after the fall of Jerusalem, there is yet a period of indefinite duration to be awaited; and secondly, because a thought of the restoration of Jerusalem gleams through, which is elsewhere expressed even more plainly.

DOCTRINAL AND ETHICAL.

1. Without ground have some taken offence at the manner in which our Lord here speaks of His Parusia, and wished to discover therein an irreconcilable antagonism between the Synoptics and the fourth Gospel. John also knows an ἐσχάτη ἡμέρα and a personal παρουσία of the Lord, although this in His spiritual Gospel comes forward with less prominence into the foreground; on the other hand, the Synoptical representation has nothing that would favor a grossly sensuous conception in reference to the secrets of the future. We should have good right to wonder at the eschatological conceptions which are found, for instance, in Paul's Epistles to the Corinthians and Thessalonians, if they had not the least Christian historical foundation in just such sayings of our Lord as we meet with in this discourse. The narrative of the Synoptics must in the nature of the case be offensive to all those who from dogmatical grounds find it incredible that the Lord should so long beforehand have with entire exactness foreseen and foretold the destruction of Jerusalem; but never will a purely historical criticism allow itself to be guided or intimidated by such a purely arbitrary conclusion *a non posse ad non esse.* And whoever attentively compares the prophecy with the result, will soon discover that it is entirely impossible to think here of a *vaticinium post eventum.* A so intimate amalgamation of two so heterogeneous events as the destruction of Jerusalem and the end of the world, was in the nature of the case only possible before, but no longer after the former event had taken place; besides that it would have been psychologically impossible for the inventor who, after the fall of Jerusalem, had composed this discourse and put it in the mouth of our Lord, to give so simple, so general, so brief and incomplete, a portrayal of the destruction of Jerusalem, since certainly the result offered him abundant material, and therewith an irresistible temptation, to embellish his picture with richer colors, and to make his prophecy more exciting. Had the Synoptics not written until after the destruction of Jerusalem, it would have been easier for them, like John, to be entirely silent about the event, than to place it in such a light that the very event seemingly convicted the prophecy of falsehood.

2. It is by no means arbitrary that our Lord joins the destruction of the temple and the end of the world so intimately together. For on the one hand it is historically proved that the fall of the Jewish state was the indispensably necessary condition to free the youthful Christendom from the limits of a confined nationality, to elevate it into the religion of the world, and therefore mightily to prepare the revelation of the glory of the Lord, and the triumph of His kingdom over the heathen world. On the other hand, Jerusalem and the temple, even in the prophetic Scriptures of the Old Testament, bear a typical and symbolical character. Zion stands there not alone as the local seat, but also as the visible image of the whole theocracy in its settled strength and beauty, and the whole Christianized world may in a certain sense be called a new spiritual Jerusalem. Is it, therefore, a wonder if the judgment upon Jerusalem serves at the same time as a mirror for the last judgment of the world? The destruction of the city and the temple was the first of those great world-events which forwarded the brilliant, triumphant, continually more powerful coming of the Lord. Herewith the series of events is opened which in the course of centuries was destined to coöperate powerfully for the coming of God's kingdom on earth. Ever more glorious does Christ appear on the ruins of annihilated temples and thrones; in continually greater measure do the here-indicated tokens of His coming

appear; misleadings, persecutions, insurrections, &c. Finally, the kingdom of light celebrates its highest triumph, after the might of darkness has immediately before concentrated its highest energy, and the destruction of the whole earthly economy is only the continuance and completion of the fall of the original seat of the Israelitish Theocracy. Whoever shall hereafter at the end of the world look back as the Lord here looked forward, he will discover that the long course of time between the destruction of the Temple and the destruction of the World, was nothing else than a great interval of continually richer manifestations of grace, and of continually severer judgments.

3. "*Die Weltgeschichte, das Weltgericht.*" The history of the world is the world's judgment." Schiller. The eschatological discourse of our Lord is especially adapted to bring into view as well the relative truth as also the superficial one-sidedness of this famous word of the poet. That facts like the fall of Jerusalem are Divine judgments, and that, therefore, the history of the world may be called the striking revelation of an inexorable Nemesis, our Lord said centuries ago. But that all these Divine judgments are only preliminary, only typical, only prophecies of that which hereafter shall take place before the eyes of heaven and earth at the expiration of the earthly economy, must be just as little forgotten. The Johannean idea of κρίσις finds its complement precisely in the Synoptical delineation of the ἐσχάτη ἡμέρα, and it remains therefore true, that the poet's utterance of the *world-judgment* of history must be complemented in this manner: that it is not yet for that the *final* judgment.

4. The fall of Jerusalem and the destruction of the Jews stands forth here not only as a destiny tragical beyond compare, but as a Divine judgment, whose ultimate cause can be obscure to no believing Christian. The present condition of Israel is the grand argument for the authority of the Prophet who proclaimed all this eighteen centuries ago, and whom they therefore unthankfully rejected. For that very reason we clearly see the decided unchristianness of such an emancipation of the Jews as is wont to be urged in our days, under the motto of freedom and culture. The right of hospitality for the banished ones of Judah cannot be ardently enough enjoined, nor too large-heartedly practised; but it becomes an actual injustice when Christians suffer themselves to be by these very Jews, only temporarily abiding among them, in any way hindered in the enjoyment of their Christian privileges and in the practice of their Christian duties. But this modern denial of Christ, therefore, avenges itself not less than the Jewish rejection of the Messiah; when Christians bring the Jews their Christ as a sacrifice, the Jews begin with material and moral power to control the Christian state, and liberalism, which is especially upheld, moreover, by Jewish Deistic influence, prepares the way for indifferentism, which finally—of course always under the excellent motto of enlightenment and right—leads to Atheism. Here also holds good our Saviour's word: βλέπετε, μὴ πλανηθῆτε.

[Without pretending to concur unqualifiedly in all these remarks of our author, which in part rest upon Millenarian views that I do not share, it appears to me that there is great force, nevertheless, in his words: "When Christians bring the Jews their Christ as a sacrifice, the Jews begin with material and moral power to control the Christian state." Take, as an instance, the assumption of the Jews—an insignificant fraction of our population—to dictate the forms of the fast and thanksgiving proclamations issued by our civil authorities, and to insist on every distinctively Christian feature—except the date—being expunged from them. How long will the Christians of our country tolerate this studious omission of the name of Christ in documents inviting the people to a worship which, for nine-tenths of them, can only be a Christian worship?—C. C. S.]

HOMILETICAL AND PRACTICAL.

Appearances deceive.—The temple in the days of Jesus, a beautiful form without life.—Earthly pomp: 1. In its outward brilliancy; 2. in its inward perishableness.—With the disciple of the Lord the sensuous perception must become a viewing with the spiritual eye.—The Apocalyptical tendency in the Christian life of faith not condemned or opposed by our Lord, but satisfied and sanctified.—The peculiar dangers to which the disciple of the Lord is exposed by the view into the future.—The false Christs who precede the coming of the true: 1. The judgment that precedes them; 2. the brilliancy that accompanies them; 3. the shame that follows them.—*Diabolus simia Dei.*—How the disciple of the Lord: 1. Must tremble when every one goes carelessly along; 2. must not be terrified when every one is seized with horror.—The end is not yet: 1. A word of righteous joy; 2. a word of holy earnestness.—New periods of development in the kingdom of Christ joined with mighty convulsions in the kingdom of nature: 1. So was it ever; 2. so is it yet; 3. so will it hereafter be in the highest measure.—The persecution of the disciples a sign of the coming of the Lord which: 1. Will be given first of all; 2. longest of all.—How the loss of the servants of the Lord becomes a gain to His cause and to the kingdom of God.—"Persecuted but not forsaken," the fate of the disciple of Christ.—"I will give you a mouth and wisdom,"—how this word has been fulfilled: 1. In the apostles; 2. in the first apologists; 3. in the martyrs; 4. in the reformers; 5. in the heroes of faith and witnesses of every time, even the present.—The conflict between the ties of blood and the requirements of the Spirit.—The security of the Christian, even in the most threatening danger.—How endurance preserves the life of the soul.—No striving to preserve external things helps when God has resolved to destroy.—The destruction of Jerusalem: 1. The fulfilment of the Old Testament prophesying; 2. the touchstone of the New Testament prophesying.—Jerusalem considered in its different periods: 1. The city of Melchisedek; 2. the capital of David; 3. the dwelling-place of God; 4. the murderess of the prophets and of the Messiah; 5. the city defiled by the abomination of desolation; 6. the city trodden down by the heathen; 7. hereafter the Salem of another Melchisedek.—Jerusalem's past, present, and future.—The destruction of Jerusalem an event which proclaims: 1. The shame of Israel; 2. the greatness of our Lord; 3. the glory of the kingdom of God; 4. the vocation of the Christian; 5. the judgment of the future.

STARKE:—HEDINGER:—Great sin, great judgments.—Look not so much at the visible and perishable, as at the invisible and eternal.—*Nova Bibl. Tub.*:—To put Christ's name forward, to come in

Christ's name, to be called Christian, is not all. All this deceivers also can do.—Convulsions in church and state, but especially persecution of the truth, is an omen of destruction.—One ungodly man must ever punish another; how holy, righteous, and terrible are God's judgments.—It is, in truth, something terrible that when the judgments of God break in, men do not become better, but much worse.—If the righteous man has a righteous cause he need fear nothing.—OSIANDER:—Although in persecutions many a confessor of Jesus has left his life behind, yet the Gospel cannot be blotted out.—CRAMER:— Let no one be surprised that he must suffer innocently.—BRENTIUS:—A patient spirit is better than a lofty spirit.—Woe to the land, the people, the city, from which God hath departed,—there is nothing more left than: haste to deliver thy soul, Gen. xix. 22.—LUTHER:—Upon the days of grace follow the days of vengeance.—The married state also sometimes a state of woe.—*Bibl. Wirt.*:—So often as we behold the dispersed Jews, we should be terrified at God's wrath, sigh over them and pray; Rom. xi. 20.

HEUBNER:—God solemnly proclaimed the abrogation of the Mosaic institute when He destroyed the temple.—Let not the true Christ be taken from thee; there is only one.—God decrees gradually heavier and heavier trials; yet the time of suffering is defined by Him.—Perseverance and faith under all afflictions is the condition of the deliverance of the soul.—There is a holy vengeance of God, and Jerusalem's fall is a manifest monument of His retributive righteousness.—ARNDT:—The future of Jerusalem and the world,—the inquiry as to the future: 1. When is it permitted us? 2. How is it answered by the Lord? 3. Whereto should the answer serve us?— VINET:—*Etudes évangéliques*, p. 265. *Les pierres du temple.*—SCHLEIERMACHER:—Sermon, Jan. 24, 1808, upon Matt. xxiv. 1, 2. The right honoring of native greatness of an earlier time.—J. J. L. TEN KATE:— The Wandering Jew:—1. An unexampled wonder in the annals of the world; 2. a living testimony of the truth of Christianity; 3. a future revelation of the glory of God; 4. a legitimate creditor of every believer.

Second Part (Vss. 25-36).

(Parallel to Matt. xxiv. 29-41; Mark xiii. 24-37.)

25 And there shall be signs in the sun, and in the moon, and in the stars [in sun and moon and stars]; and upon the earth distress [anxiety] of nations, with perplexity;
the sea and the waves roaring [nations in perplexity concerning a roaring of sea and
26 waves[1]]; Men's hearts failing them for fear, and for looking after those things which are coming on the earth: for the powers of heaven [the heavens] shall be shaken.
27 And then shall they see the Son of man coming in a cloud with power and great glory
28 [great power and glory]. And when these things begin to come to pass, then look up,
29 and lift up your heads; for your redemption draweth nigh. And he spake to them a
30 parable; Behold the fig tree, and all the trees; When they now shoot forth [have put forth], ye see and know [seeing it ye know] of your own selves that summer is now
31 nigh at hand. So likewise ye, when ye see these things come [coming] to pass, know
32 ye that the kingdom of God is nigh at hand. Verily I say unto you, This generation
33 shall not pass away, till all be fulfilled. Heaven and earth shall pass away; but my
34 words shall not pass away. And take heed to yourselves, lest at any time your hearts be overcharged with surfeiting [or, revelling], and drunkenness, and cares of this life,
35 and *so* that day come upon you unawares. For as a snare shall it come on all them
36 that dwell on the face of the whole earth. Watch ye therefore,[2] and pray always [ἐν παντὶ καιρῷ], that ye may be accounted worthy to escape all these things that shall come to pass [are coming], and to stand before the Son of man.

[1] Vs. 25.—According to the reading of Tischendorf, [Lachmann, Meyer, Tregelles, Alford,] ἐν ἀπορίᾳ ἤχους [instead of ἠχούσης, *Recepta*], which is sufficiently supported by A., B., [Cod. Sin.,] C., L., M., [R.,] X., Cursives, [Vulgate, Syriac,] &c.
[2] Vs. 36.—With Lachmann, Tischendorf, [Tregelles, Alford,] we read δέ instead of the οὖν of the *Recepta*, according to B., D., [Cod. Sin.,] Itala.

EXEGETICAL AND CRITICAL.

Vs. 25. **And there shall be signs.**—The Saviour does not now turn back again to the point of time of the destruction of Jerusalem, but He states what shall take place after the καιροὶ ἐθνῶν shall have been fulfilled. The consecutiveness of this delineation is plainly enough indicated by the καί of Luke, and it is purely arbitrary to assert (De Wette) that the Evangelist avoids the εὐθέως of Matthew because he wrote after the destruction of Jerusalem. The variation is simply connected with the freer form of the redaction of this discourse of our Lord in Luke, to which it is at the same time to be ascribed that he, since he writes for the Gentile Christians, does not speak of the flight on the Sabbath, of the shortening of these days, and of the false Jewish prophets, while he also does not so particularly specialize further σημεῖα, as is done by Matthew and Mark. As respects, moreover, the signs themselves, there is as little reason (Starke) to understand by the sun Antichrist, by the moon and the stars antichristian teachers, as (Besser and others) without any proof to understand the stars metaphorically of mighty princes, and the roaring sea of the tumult of nations. Other views we find given by Lange on the parallel in Matthew. Why do we not rather simply believe our Lord at His word, that His παρουσία will be accompanied with cosmic revolutions, whose actual course can be as little calculated as their possibility can be denied *a priori?* It was known even from the Old Testament that fearful signs in the realm of nature would herald the day of the Lord, see, e. g., Jer. iv. 23; Joel ii. 30, &c. Commonly such delineations are ascribed to the poetry of prophecy, and certainly it would betray little taste and little intimacy with the style of the Holy Scriptures if one upon such *dicta* would build a definite theory as to the future destiny of the heavenly bodies. But, on the other hand, we learn even by the extension which natural science has gained in our days to recognize the limitation of human science even in this sphere, and the genuine cosmologian and theologian will be modest enough not here too rashly to take the word "impossible" upon his lips. We are wanting in any fixed hermeneutic rule to determine *proprio marte* what is here to be understood literally and what tropically; only the event will determine where in this case lie the boundaries between imagination and reality.

On the earth anxiety of nations.—This allusion to the profound anxiety which shall fill the human world, is peculiar to Luke. The same thought is further developed, Rev. vi. 12-15, and has in itself psychological probability, without here supposing believers to be entirely excluded. As in the animal world important alterations in the atmosphere are instinctively perceived, as often an inexplicable presentiment of a terrible calamity, whose breaking in is feared, makes even the most courageous pale with terror; so does our Lord give us to expect that an obscure presentiment of great events shortly before His Parusia will weigh like heavy Alps on many a heart. Luke speaks of ἀπορία ἤχους (see notes on the text) as an indication of that to which the anxiety and perplexity of the nations *has relation.* The roaring of the sea and waves, that is, reminds even those who do not live in expectation of the coming of the Son of Man, of terrible things, nevertheless, which are about to come upon the earth, while their evil conscience testifies to them that they have the worst to expect therefrom. The allegorical expositors of Scripture here only understand again the sea of nations, apparently because they find it a little apocryphal that the ocean, at the approach of the mortal hour of this visible creation, should roar somewhat more heavily than wont. We, for our part, find the physical signs in the sea not more improbable than those in the moon and the stars.

Vs. 26. **Men's hearts failing them for fear,** ἀποψύχειν, that is, not only grow rigid (De Wette) or fall into swooning, but, as Hesychius interprets — ἀποπνευματίζεσθαι, *spiritu destitui.* What even now not unfrequently happens by a very high degree of heat, anxiety, or sorrow, that the tension of the moment has the loss of life as a consequence, will then especially no longer be classed among the rare casualties; no wonder, since even the **powers of heaven shall be shaken**, "perhaps the sustaining and working forces of the heavenly system, with their influences for the earth, so that the Lord finally comprehending all together, means to say, 'Everything together shall give way and finally fall to pieces, 2 Peter iii. 10-12.'" Stier. According to De Wette, this phrase from Matthew, forsooth, *limps behind*, but an exegesis which does not feel that just by this terrible word the sufficient explanation of the just-portrayed anxiety is given, appears itself not to stand upon a wholly good footing.

Vs. 27. **And then.**—Here also, as in Matthew and Mark, the personal coming of the Messiah at the very time when the whole visible creation threatens to sink into a chaos. According to Matthew, there is finally seen first the sign of the coming of the Son of Man, afterwards Himself. According to Mark and Luke, on the other hand, the appearance of the Messiah upon the clouds—Mark in the plural, Luke in the singular—is immediately beheld, while these two are silent as to the σημεῖον. For the principal views as to the latter, *see* LANGE on Matt. xxiv. 30. It may be very well supposed that the cloud of light itself which bears Him and the glory which surrounds Him might be this σημεῖον. Compare the assurance of the angels at the Ascension, which Luke alone has preserved to us, Acts i. 11, that the Lord shall come again even so (οὕτως) as (ὃν τρόπον, i. e., ἐν νεφέλῃ, vs. 9) they had seen Him go towards heaven. The mention of the appearance and activity of the angels at the last day, we find only in Matthew and Mark *ad loc.* [and in almost all the passages in the first three Gospels in which our Lord refers to the day of judgment.—C. C. S.] On the other hand, Luke lays emphasis on the practical side of the matter, the expectation and joy with which the disciples of our Lord, who are conceived as then still living upon the earth, shall behold the approach of these things. This again is genuinely Pauline, comp. Rom. viii. 19-23.

Vs. 28. **And when these things begin to come to pass.**—There is not the least reason for understanding by τούτων exclusively what is last named, the coming of the Son of Man in His δόξα. This manifestation is in a certain sense the work of a moment, and when this shall have come to pass, then is the redemption of His own not only near (ἐγγίζει), but really present. Rather are we to understand thereby all previous tokens, which are named vss. 25, 26, and which must necessarily endure for some time (therefore also ἀρχομένων). These same events which the world shall gaze on with helpless terror, must be for believers an awakening voice to joyful hope and expectation, since these very ὠδῖνες prove that the birth-hour of their salvation comes with every moment nearer and nearer. The heads which hitherto had often been bowed under all manner of misery and persecution, must then be lifted up, comp. Rom. viii. 19; James v. 8.

Vs. 29. **And He spake to them a parable.**—Here also, as in vs. 10, Luke appears as narrator, while with Matthew and Mark the tone of discourse continues undisturbed. The latter is internally more probable. The former is a new proof of the greater freedom of Luke's redaction. Moreover, the mention of all the trees, with and beside the fig-tree, is peculiar to him. Perhaps our Lord speaks here especially of a fig-tree, because this had served Him so frequently as a type of the Israelitish people, Mark xi. 12-14; Luke xiii. 6-9. But that He here also speaks of *that* symbolical fig-tree, in other words, that He designates the reviving Israel as a prophet of His near approach (Stier), appears to us quite as unproved as that the Lord means to allude to the *amarum* and *renenatum quiddam* in the sap of the fig-leaves, and adduces the *incrementa malignitatis*, as presages of His coming (Ebrard). In both

CHAP. XXI. 25–36.   325

cases the mention at least of *all* the trees would be quite incongruous, and we therefore consider it as better to assume that He spoke so especially of *the* fig-tree because He wished to designate it as a special *kind* of tree, in distinction from the others.

Vs. 30. **When they now put forth.**—Designedly Luke expresses himself here somewhat less definitely than Matthew and Mark, because he does not intend to bring into prominence the specific peculiarity of the fig-tree, whose leaves develop themselves at the same time with the setting of the fruit, but only has in mind that which is common to all trees. With the various kinds of trees the putting forth of leaves is the token of approaching summer; whoever sees the one knows then of himself that the other is at hand.—'Ἀφ' ἑαυτῶν, "*etiamsi nemo vos doceat.*" Bengel.—**The kingdom of God.**—Here, of course, agreeably to the whole text, definitely apprehended as *regnum gloriae.*

Vs. 32. **This generation shall not pass away.**—For a statement of the different views with reference to the signification of ἡ γενεὰ αὕτη, see LANGE, *ad loc.* The explanation that our Lord had in mind the generation then living is certainly the least artificial, while every other gives immediate occasion to the conjecture that it has arisen from the perplexity as to how to bring the prophecy into agreement with the fulfilment. It may be asked, however, whether the words ἕως ἂν πάντα γένηται cannot be understood in such a sense that they make the explanation of γενεά as designation of that generation at all events possible. By πάντα we have no longer to understand the destruction of Jerusalem in itself, which now already lies behind our Lord's view, nor yet His παρουσία itself, for in the following verse there is again mention of a passing away of heaven and earth, but we have to understand the presages of His coming which He had just indicated symbolically, as, for instance, in the image of the putting forth of the leaves of the trees. These presages now occupy necessarily a certain period of time (ἀρχομένων, vs. 28, and γίνεσθαι, used of things of this sort, is an elastic idea, by which not only that which is momentary, but also that which is successive, is expressed). So must, therefore, the explanation be permitted, "until all things *shall have begun* to come to pass," all things, that is, which are to serve as the previous signs of His coming; and this was really the case during the life of the contemporaries of our Lord, who in the destruction of Jerusalem saw the type of the approaching end of the world. He will therefore say: This generation shall not pass away without the beginning of the end of the world here foretold you having come to pass in the actual destruction of Jerusalem. Our Lord by no means says that everything which was to take place before the τέλος will be *omnibus numeris absolutum atque ad finem perductum* before a generation of men will have passed. The question cannot be merely what γίνεσθαι signifies in itself, but what it is to signify in this connection. An explanation of this verse, it is true, in which no difficulty at all remains, and every appearance of arbitrariness is avoided, we, alas, even at this day, are not acquainted with.

Vs. 33. **Heaven and earth shall pass away.**—After the discourse has risen to this height, there would ensue a dreary anti-climax, if we would recognize in these words only a figurative designation of the destruction of the Jewish state. Our Lord points evidently to the destruction of the earthly economy, which shall be followed by the appearance of a new heaven and a new earth, 2 Peter iii. 8–14, and gives assurance therewith that even then, when an entirely new order of things shall have come in, His words, in particular the promises of His coming, then first fully understood and fulfilled, would not cease to remain words of life for all His own. "They will approve themselves as eternal in an eternal church, and that one of eschatological character." Lange.

Vs. 34. **And take heed to yourselves.**—The eschatological discourse in Matthew and Mark is concluded with a description of the unexpected coming of the Parusia, and a parabolic allusion to watchfulness, which we have already met with in Luke in a somewhat different form, chs. xii. and xvii. Instead of this he has another conclusion, which, indeed, entitles us to inquire whether the Evangelist, in a freer form, has condensed the main substance of the admonitions given Matt. xxiv. 43–51, or whether our Lord on this occasion used those very words. However this may be, his rendering has so much the more value, as it in some measure takes the place of the missing parable of the Ten Virgins, which, according to Matthew, was delivered this same evening by our Lord, but has been passed over by Luke. With deep wisdom our Lord ends His eschatological discourse by leading His disciples back into their own hearts, since their view had involuntarily lost itself in the far future, and in thinking upon the universal historical character of the events here foretold, they might very easily lose out of mind in how strict a connection this Parusia stood with their personal salvation. With a faithful and earnest προσέχετε, He begins to use the expectation of His coming for their sanctification, as He had just before, vs. 28, applied it to their consolation. He warns them that their hearts be not burdened as by a spirit of deep sleep. This might come to pass through three things: κραιπάλῃ, heaviness and dizziness, such as drunkenness of *yesterday* gives, μέθῃ, drunkenness, which makes them for *to-day* unfit to reflect maturely upon their highest interests, and μερίμναις βιωτικαῖς, which would plague them for *to-morrow*, and impel them too strongly to labor for the meat that perisheth. The one, as well as the other, would be able to rob them of the clearness and sobriety of mind with which they should await the coming of their Lord. Not only should that which is entirely unlawful be avoided, but also that which is relatively lawful used with wisdom, in the consciousness that they in no case could reckon upon it for a long time; for the great day was to be, even for them, the servants of the Lord, an unexpected one, αἰφνίδιος ἐπιστῇ, comp. 1 Thess. v. 3, while it would come upon other inhabitants of the earth, especially those who were living on in careless quiet, without fellowship with Christ, **as a snare.** The *tertium comparationis* lies as well in the unexpectedness as in the ruinousness of such snares as are commonly used for ravening beasts. Ἐπὶ πάντας τοὺς καθημένους, here emphatic for a designation of quiet and comfortable sitting, comp. Amos vi. 1–6, in which they, therefore, are taken at once, as soon as only the snare is thrown out upon them. *See* also Jer. xxv. 29; Rev. xviii. 7, 8.

Vs. 36. **Watch ye ... always.**—Comp. Mark xiii. 37: ἐν παντὶ καιρῷ may be referred quite as well to ἀγρυπνεῖτε as to δεόμενοι. The former is probable, on account of the antithesis, and the uncertainty of the Parusia in vs. 35, which requires an unremitting watch. Watching and praying are here also, as in Matt. xxvi. 41; 1 Peter iv. 7, 8, joined together. Δεόμενοι, ἵνα, κ.τ.λ. indicates the frame of mind in which they must be found watching and waiting; καταξιωθῆτε, comp. Luke xx. 35; 2 Thess. i. 5, not "become worthy," *sensu morali*, but to be accounted worthy, *sensu forensi, digni, habiti atque declarati, sc. a Deo*. The word appears in the same sense Acts v. 41.

To escape all these things, πάντα ταῦτα, here, as in vs. 32, especially of the premonitions of the Parusia considered exclusively on their terrifying side; for to escape the Parusia itself (which is first alluded to in the immediately following expression) is indeed for friend and foe impossible. He escapes τὰ μέλλοντα, who is not carried away by persecutions, brought to apostasy by misleaders, or robbed of courage by trial. (The genuineness of ταῦτα is doubtful; it is rejected by Tischendorf and accepted by De Wette; It has little influence on the sense, since, at all events, our Lord means no other future things than those of which He had just spoken.) On the other hand, they must desire above all things to appear before the Son of Man, σταθῆναι ἔμπροσθεν, κ.τ.λ. It may, indeed, signify, "to pass the trial," as in Rom. xiv. 4, but at the end of this discourse it is very probable that our Lord will designate therewith something higher: the fearless appearance, the composed standing before His throne, in order to view Him, to serve Him, and to glorify Him. "The ἐπισυναγωγή of believers is meant, and this, as it appears, of the living, because as a condition the escaping of all the tribulations is named, 1 Thess. iv. 17; 2 Thess. ii. 1; Matt. xxiv. 31." De Wette. This σταθῆναι is, therefore, not only the beginning, but also the substance, of the highest happiness, the opposite of which is portrayed, Ps. i. 5; Nahum i. 6; Rev. vi. 16, 17.

DOCTRINAL AND ETHICAL.

1. It is of high significance that our Lord ends His prophetical office, immediately before His last suffering, with such an eschatological discourse. The course which our Saviour's teaching has taken during His public life, shows the type of the natural course of development of Christian dogmatics. As He had appeared with the preaching of faith and conversion, so ought at all times the practical questions to come first. But as He did not leave the earth without having also disclosed the secrets of the future, so a Dogmatics which, in reference to the ἔσχατα, takes an indifferent or sceptical position, is in itself imperfect, and like a mutilated torso. It lies in the nature of the case that Christian eschatology, the more the course of time advances, must become less and less an unimportant appendix, and more and more a *locus primarius* of Christian doctrine.

2. Whoever asserts that the expectation of a personal, visible, glorious return, which shall put a decisive end to the present condition of things, belongs only to Jewish dreamings, which one from a Christian spiritualistic position may look down upon with a certain lofty disparagement, is here contradicted by our Lord in the most decided manner.

3. What our Lord here announces in reference to the termination of the history of the world is only drawn in strong and broad lines. It is no picture that already contains all the traits of the image of the future complete, but a sketch with which the more detailed painting is outlined, which afterwards could be elaborated by the hand of the apostles. He who believes in the unity of the Spirit in our Lord and His first witnesses, cannot be hindered from seeking in the Apostolic Epistles, or in the Revelation, for the answer to many questions which this eschatological discourse leaves yet remaining for us. Not easily will any one be able to show in this last a conception for which the fundamental thought is not more or less contained in this eschatological discourse, and which, therefore, might not be named, with entire justice, a further explanation and completion of the same. So is the Pauline doctrine of the restoration of Israel only the development of the germ which we find here, Luke xxi. 24; so is the Apocalyptical image of the convulsions of the realm of nature which shall accompany the coming of the Lord, only the development of the eschatological foundation thoughts already given here. The eschatology of the apostles is related to that of our Lord as the nobly unfolding plant to the bud swelling with sap; not as the subsequently clouded sun to its earlier brilliancy.

4. "The soul works on the body, and there is no member or part of the body that does not feel with the soul. So shall the Lord that shall come work upon all creatures, and they shall not be able to withdraw themselves from His working. Even before His visible appearance will the creatures become aware that the time of His coming is at hand. The lifeless creation, that bends itself without opposition to His almighty will, and men, who can oppose themselves with their impotent will to His almighty will, —both shall be seized with the terrors that hasten on before His appearance. The heaven and the sea, and on earth men, shall have forebodings of that which is to come. There rests upon the prophesyings of our Lord concerning the end,—threatening as they are, terrible as they sound,—nevertheless an obscurity by which their terrible impression is augmented. They wait for their literal and most striking interpretation, for their fulfilment. Before this comes, God's hand itself has veiled them in a twilight which yields to no human endeavor; but when the fulfilment comes, man shall not only clearly know how fully it fits the prophecy, but also how the prophecy fits the fulfilment,—how they shall, as it were, exactly cover one another." Löhe.

5. Although our Lord in this eschatological discourse does not speak expressly of His Divine nature and dignity, it contains so powerful and incomparable a self-testimony of Christ, that it is utterly impossible not to ascribe to Him who so speaks a superhuman character. Nothing is to be compared with the quiet majesty of that word: "Heaven and earth shall pass away, but My words shall not pass away." Scoffers think exactly the opposite—namely, that heaven and earth shall remain; the words of our Lord, on the other hand, be forgotten and exposed as lies, 2 Peter iii. 3 *seq.*—Yet our Lord, who apparently delays the promise, will not rest until it is all fulfilled. *Patiens quia aeternus.*

6. The eschatological discourse is also remarkable on this account, that it shows that a connection according to the intent of our Lord exists and must exist between πίστις and γνῶσις. The example of the apostles and the teaching of the Master show anew; there cannot possibly be any talk of γνῶσις so long as no πίστις precedes it. *Non intelligere ut credas, sed credere ut intelligas.* Where faith however is living, it feels to a certain extent the necessity of also knowing the secrets of the future. Our Lord

satisfies this need, so far as the receptivity of His people permits Him, and while the σημεῖα of His coming are only images of terror and riddles to the unbelieving, believers are at the same time the γνωστικοί, who know what these things denote, and whither they tend. Their faith has, therefore, become a knowing; but, on the other hand also, this knowing, which is still very limited and only in part, leads again to faith, and must end in ever firmer faith, hope, and waiting. *Per fidem ad intellectum, per intellectum ad firmiorem fidem.*

7. The eschatological discourse of our Lord may be considered as a type of a fitting and edifying treatment of future things for all preachers. Let us consider well how closely this doctrine of His coheres also with the prophetic words of Scripture; how the chief strokes of the picture are placed in a clear light, while points of a subordinate importance remain veiled in an unprejudicial obscurity; how He, above all, delivers this teaching not for the satisfaction of an idle curiosity, but uses it directly for the admonition, for the consolation, and for the sanctification of His own. It admits of no doubt that had the impending end of the history of the world been always written of and spoken of in this way, much less offence would have been taken, and also much less offence would have been given.

8. It is not impossible that our Lord on this occasion uttered the so-called unwritten expression of which Justin Martyr, in *Tryph.* ch. xlvii., makes mention with the simple words: διὸ καὶ ὁ ἡμέτερος Κύριος Ἰ. Χρ. εἶπεν, and which has all the internal traces of genuineness: "In that in which I shall find you, therein will I judge you."

9. Compare on this Pericope the *Dies iræ.*

HOMILETICAL AND PRACTICAL.

The visible creation must perish before the heaven and the new earth appear.—The joy of the world perishes often before the end of the world.—If the righteous scarcely be saved, where shall the ungodly and the sinner appear?—The day of Christ at once a day of terror and of glory.—The different temper in which men go towards and look towards this day: 1. While unbelief yet mocks, faith mourns; 2. while unbelief fears, faith hopes; 3. while unbelief despairs faith triumphs.—The ordinary laws of nature are abolished when the kingdom of Christ celebrates its highest triumphs.—The coming of the Son of Man: 1. Seen by all eyes; 2. surrounded by heavenly glory 3. greeted by the redeemed with joy.—Even nature prophesies of the approaching summer of the kingdom of God.—How much the Christian, by attentive observation of the kingdom of nature and of grace, can know of himself.—The knowledge of the hour which has struck in God's kingdom: 1. its ground; 2. its degree; 3. its limits.—The contemporaries of our Lord, even in their lifetime, witnesses: 1. Of the most glorious event; 2. of the most terrible event, that ever the earth has seen.—What is perishable and what remains.—Heaven and earth shall pass away, but My words shall not pass away: 1. The sublimity; 2. the truth; 3. the comfort; 4. the serious depth, of this utterance.—What the word of our Lord shall continue for His people, even after the end of the world.—What is the greatest danger to whic the disciple of the Lord is exposed at the approach of the day of His coming?—He that is full of wine cannot be full of the Holy Spirit, Eph. v. 18.

—The day of the Lord comes unawares;—woe to the man whom it finds wholly unprepared!—How the best preparation for the coming of the Lord consists: 1. in watchfulness; 2. in activity; 3. in thoughtfulness.—They who sit down in selfishness and carelessness, will be not less surprised by the end than they that pass the night at their wine.—Watching and praying must we await the Lord's coming.—Nothing higher can the praying Christian desire than: 1. To escape the destruction that lights upon others; and 2. to stand with all His people before the Son of Man.

STARKE:—They that have not feared God in their life, shall melt away for terror in the end.—Many weighty things have already come to pass on earth, but the weightiest is yet to be looked for.—QUESNEL: —Whoever has despised Jesus in His humility, will see Him against his will in His majesty.—There comes at last a time when we shall be redeemed from all that is a burden to us, 2 Tim. iv. 18.—The earthly-minded regard the spring as the most convenient time for their lust and desire, but true Christians as a type of the glory and resurrection of the children of God.—The summer a beautiful image of eternal blessedness.—God does not let the race of the ungodly perish till all is come to pass, which serves as the proof of His righteousness, and for their punishment.—True Christians who seek that which is above in heaven are as the birds of the heaven who, because they are not on earth, have nothing to fear from the nets of the fowler.—BRENTIUS:— Because man does not know his time, he must learn wisely to accommodate himself to the time.—It is God alone that can make us worthy and ready for the enjoyment of His everlasting glory.—Watching and praying men ever keep together.

On the Pericope:—FUCHS:—Concerning the return of Christ and the hour of death: 1. For the ungodly, terrible; 2. for believers, joyful.—Lift up your heads: 1. In good days, and thank the Lord; 2. in evil days, and trust the Lord; 3. in the last days, and be joyful in hope.—HERBERGER:—Concerning the last Advent of Jesus and the flower-buds of the last day.—OTHO:—The last judgment. —FRESENIUS:—The redemption of Jesus Christ in its different aspects: 1. The procuring of salvation; 2. the preparation of salvation; 3. the complete revelation of salvation.—AHLFELD:—Behold the King cometh to thee in night and glory.—COUARD:— Christian-mindedness in evil times.—SOUCHON:—The comfort and admonition of Christ's prophecy of His coming.—STIER:—The day of the Lord's return: 1. How; and 2. whereto it is placed before our eyes.— RANKE:—How we have to receive our Lord's prophecy of His coming again: 1. With deep reverence; 2. with great joy; 3. with holy seriousness.—RAUTENBERG:—The course of the gospel among the terrors of the time.—GAUPP:—The coming again of our Lord a strong incitement to a godly life, for: 1. It awakens the spirit to a living hope; 2. It inspires in all believing hearts sweet comfort even in the dreariest condition of the kingdom of God; 3. it admonishes most deeply to become worthy, by prayer and watchfulness, to stand before the Son of Man.—Ch. HARMS:—The setting forth of the coming of our Lord is seasonably done even in the Advent season: 1. It awakens sleepers; 2. shakes the presumptuous; 3. helps the wavering to a decision; 4. strengthens the weak in faith.—KRAUSSOLD:—The coming of our Lord at the end of days: 1. A coming to judgment, and moreover; 2. a terrible and glorious; 3. an undoubtedly certain, coming, and therefore; 4. a coming for which we should perseveringly wait in joyful faith.—STAUDT:—How believers demean themselves at the coming of Christ: 1. As attentive observers of the tokens of this coming; 2. as joyful spectators of these mutations in the world; 3. as those delivered out of all judgments.—Dr. A. BOMHARD:—The established heart of the believing Christian.—B. STEGER: —Of the joyful and blessed freedom of the perfectly righteous.

General Conclusion (Vss. 37, 38).

37 And in the daytime [τὰς ἡμέρας] he was teaching [or, was wont to teach] in the temple; and at night he went out, and abode [lodged] in the mount that is called *the* 38 *mount* of Olives. And all the people came early in the morning to him in the temple, for to hear him.[1]

[1] Vs. 38.—After vs. 38 some cursive manuscripts have the Pericope *de adultera*, John vii. 53—viii. 11. On internal grounds the reception of this event into this connection is vindicated by Lange (*Leben Jesu, ad locum*). Comp. LANGE on *Matthew*. In his work on the *Gospel of John, ad locum*, the author has modified this view.

EXEGETICAL AND CRITICAL.

Vs. 37. **And in the daytime He was wont to teach**.—Luke does not at all mean that our Saviour even after the eschatological discourse continued to teach in the temple, but he simply sums up what had been wont to take place in the days immediately preceding; looking back therewith to ch. xx. 1. This appears as well from the expression: ἦν διδάσκων, as from τὰς ἡμέρας, which in general refers to the Sunday, Monday, and Tuesday of the Passion-Week. The purpose is not therefore to state that our Lord delivered the eschatological discourse also in the temple, but only to indicate that so long as He continued in the temple He spoke there as a Teacher, and was listened to by the people with undiminished interest, so that He by no means saw Himself constrained to leave the sanctuary for want of hearers. However, the account of Luke must be complemented by that of the other Evangelists. In this way we know what Luke has already (vs. 5) caused us to conjecture, namely, that the prophecy of the destruction of Jerusalem was not delivered till after the leaving of the temple, while we become aware from John xii. 36 that He after the departure from the temple hid Himself from the Jews (ἐκρύβη), which undoubtedly appears to point to a seclusion of some hours, or very possibly of a whole day, before the beginning of the last conflict. If everything does not deceive us, then all took place in the Tuesday of the Passion-Week, which is stated Matt. xxi. 20; xxvi. 5; Mark xi. 20—xiv. 2; Luke xx. 1—xxi. 36; so that we find no other day in the whole public life of our Lord, of which the Synoptics give us so rich an historical survey. The occurrence with the Greeks in the temple, John xii. 20-36, may have taken place on the Monday. Over the Wednesday, the whole of which our Lord, as it appears, spent in Bethany, there is spread an impenetrable veil. We may suppose (with Lange) that He on this day made the wider circle of His followers acquainted with His approaching suffering. [The extreme difficulty which the apostles themselves, up to the very hour of our Lord's arrest, had in admitting the idea of any such thing befalling Him, appears to render it exceedingly improbable that the wider circle of His disciples had any intimation of it beforehand, or at least any but the most general intimation; there is certainly not the least hint in any of the Gospels that they had.—

C. C. S.] The conjecture (Wieseler) that John xii. 44-50, is also to be considered as a part of an address which our Lord at this very time delivered as a final address to the people, appears to us less probable. These concluding phrases after the general account, John xii. 37-43, appear rather to bear a chrestomathical character, and to contain a freely-condensed summary of that which at all times, and especially in the last days, had been the main substance of the preaching of our Lord.

Vs. 38. **And all the people came early in the morning**, ὤρριζε πρὸς αὐτόν. De Wette: "Sought Him out eagerly." According to LXX, Ps. lxxviii. 34 ; lxiii. 2 *et alib*. Better in the sense of *mane veniebat*, see Luther, Vulgate, Meyer, and Ewald. Designation of the undiminished desire of the people, who could scarcely wait for the day in order to go again to Him, and who therewith, so long as they had not yet been wholly misled and blinded by the Pharisees, continually proved that they knew how to appreciate their Prophet. A few days afterwards we see all changed, see ch. xxiii. 18. This statement of Luke is worthy of note on this account also, that it shows that the few last days which our Lord abode in the temple must have been very long days, on which therefore there could not have wanted time for so much as took place, for instance on the Tuesday. Tertullian's translation therefore holds good, *De luculo conveniebant;* although it was a not very happy thought of Grotius, when he from this early hastening of so many hearers, drew the conclusion: *apparet, non caruisse fructu meritum illud Christi:* ἀγρυπνεῖτε. This pregnant admonition was certainly not fulfilled merely by so inadequate a proof of interest; besides, it had not even been addressed to the people, but specially to the Twelve.

DOCTRINAL AND ETHICAL.

1. See on the *Exegetical* and *Critical*.
2. The imperturbable composure with which our Lord, so long as it pleased Him, held to the end the post assigned Him, and continued His daily usage of teaching, presents a striking contrast to the restlessness and perplexity of His enemies, which increases every moment. Here also the wisdom of the old word of Scripture, Prov. xxviii. 1 ; Is. lvii. 21, was revealed.
3. The undiminished result of the preaching of

our Lord, in which He was able to rejoice even to the very last day, is a new argument for the voluntariness and unconstrainedness of His surrender to the night of His foes.

4. The secret of the unbroken energy which our Lord revealed even unto the last hour of His public life, is to be sought in the holy hours upon the Mount of Olives.

5. It is worthy of note that our Lord, so far as we know, on the last Tuesday and Wednesday of His public life, performs no more miracles ; the time for that had already passed.

HOMILETICAL AND PRACTICAL.

"As long as I am in the world, I am the light of the world," John ix. 5.—Our Lord does not leave the temple till it has become plain before all men's eyes that He leaves it as Victor.—The hen does not become weary of calling her brood, even when she sees the eagles coming from afar.—The Mount of Olives, the sanctuary of the solitary prayer of our Lord.—The holy consecration to the agony of Gethsemane.—The high significance which the principal mountains of the Holy Land had in the history of the Life and Passion of the Lord. Behind Him there already lie the Mount of Temptation, where He overcame the Evil One ; the Mount of the Beatitudes, where He as Teacher proclaimed the constitution of His kingdom; the Mount of the Transfiguration, where He in the distance beheld His suffering and His glory. Before Him yet lies the Mount of the Cross, where the most agonizing strife was to be striven ; the Mount of the Manifestation (Matt. xxviii. 16), where the most glorious triumph was to be celebrated; the Mount of the Ascension, where the noblest crown was to be attained.—The final stillness before the final strife.—How remarkable, and yet how indecisive, the last undiminished interest of the people in the instruction of our Lord is.—The early and week-day preaching of the Lord.—*Ora et labora.*

STARKE :—When the end of their life draws manifestly near, then especially must servants of God faithfully administer their function, and seek thus to conclude it worthily, 2 Peter i. 13, 14.—Christ's servants must early and late serve the Lord, even to the end of their life, Acts xiii. 36 ; Is. xl. 31.—Labor for our neighbor's salvation must be joined with prayer. — QUESNEL : — Oh, how happy and blooming is the Church when a people hungering for God's word has a faithful minister, who is even as hungry and eager to feed them therewith, 1 Thess. iii. 6, 10 ; Rom. i. 11.—To neglect God's worship and preaching for the sake of comfort and convenience, is not capable of being answered before God, Ps. xlii. 4.—The love and the thronging of a people after God's word encourage the zeal of the pastor ; the zeal and diligence of the pastor encourage the people, 1 Thess. ii. 8-13 ; Prov. xxvii. 17.—ARNDT:—Jesus' threefold elevation : 1. The elevation of His body ; 2. of His soul ; 3. of His spirit. "If Jesus had need, in order to preserve to Himself freshness and vigor for His day's work, now and then to collect Himself in stillness and prayer, we need it yet much more, and the unhappy ones who know no still hours in their life, know not at all how much they lack. Not in vain does the old proverb join labor and praying, to intimate thereby that prayer, though it is a labor, is at the same time an enjoyment, yea, an enjoyment of all enjoyments and the chief refreshment from labor, the chief consecration for labor. Verily, they have done most in their life that have prayed most, and very rich matter is therefore contained in the little rhyme: "*Halt dich rein, acht dich klein, sei gern allein, mit Gott gemein!*" [Keep thyself pure ; esteem thyself of small account ; love to be alone, together with God].

The History of the Passion.

The more particular and intimate Leavetaking of the Saviour with His Disciples at the Approach of the Final Conflict.

1. The Last Conspiracy of His Enemies, assisted by Judas (CH. XXII. 1–6).

(Parallel to Matt. xxvi. 3–5 ; 14–16 ; Mark xiv. 1, 2, 10, 11.)

1   Now the feast of unleavened bread drew nigh, which is called the passover [πάσχα].
2   And the chief priests and scribes sought how they might kill him ; for they feared the
3   people. Then entered Satan into Judas surnamed Iscariot, being [or, who was] of the
4   number of the twelve. And he went his way, and communed [consulted¹] with the
    chief priests and captains, how he might betray him [deliver him up, παραδῷ²] unto
5, 6 them. And they were glad, and covenanted to give him money. And he promised,
    and sought opportunity to betray him [deliver him up] unto them in the absence of the
    multitude [or, without *attracting* a multitude *together*].

[¹ Vs. 4.—Revised Version of the American Bible Union.—C. C. S.]
[² Vs. 4.—Παραδίδωμι, which properly means "*to betray*," is only used in the Gospels once of Judas, in the form of its derivative προδότης, Luke vi. 16. Elsewhere the Evangelists speak of him as "delivering up" the Saviour, leaving the character of the act to speak for itself.—C. C. S.]

EXEGETICAL AND CRITICAL.

For the history of the Passion in general, and respecting the literature belonging to it, *see* LANGE on Matt. xxvi.

As respects the form of the relation of the history of the Passion in Luke, he has on the one hand much in common with the other Evangelists, but on the other hand, also, not a little peculiar to himself. Like Matthew and Mark and John, he also, in this part of the history of the life of Jesus, is unquestionably most detailed, and while he, in the beginning of his gospel, upon the events of many years gives only a few lines, he enables us at the end of it to accompany our Lord almost step by step upon His way of sorrow. Like his predecessors, he also brings into a strong light, on the one hand, the innocence and greatness of our Lord over against His enemies, on the other hand, the adorable providence of God over against the free acts of men. In the choice of that which he relates or passes over, he agrees much more with Matthew and Mark than with John, who, in the history of the Passion also, has taken a way peculiarly his own. And yet we find in Luke by no means a spiritless repetition and supplementing of that which the first two Synoptics have already communicated, much as in many respects his narrative is undeniably inferior to the narratives of these. The sequence of the events is with him less chronologically exact, as BYNÆUS, *De morte Jesu Christi*, ii. pp. 12, 13, has remarked, comp. *e. g.*, his account of the celebration in the passover-chamber with that of Matthew and Mark. How much less complete and well arranged is his narrative of the agony in Gethsemane than that of the others, and again how brief and general are his notices of that which took place in the judgment-house of Pilate! But, on the other hand, it is to no other than Luke that we owe a number of notices and intimations by which our historical knowledge of the last hours of our Lord is partly cleared up, partly enlarged. He alone gives the names of the disciples who prepared the Passover—Peter and John, ch. xxii. 8, and communicates to us, vs. 15, the affecting words with which our Lord opens the meal. Besides him, no one of the Synoptics mentions the disciples' dispute as to rank, vs. 24 *seq.*, which in all probability was the occasion for the foot-washing, as well as also the remarkable utterance, vss. 28–30. At the agony in Gethsemane he alone mentions the strengthening angel, as well as the sweat of blood, vss. 43, 44; he has also, at the same time, in this preserved for us some remarkable words of our Lord. All the Evangelists relate the denial of Peter: Luke alone speaks, vs. 61, of the look of the Lord. All relate the night-session: Luke alone gives account of the official session of the Sanhedrim, in the morning, vss. 66–71, which is not to be confounded with the former. Without him we should have remained in ignorance of the first special accusation which the Jews had preferred to Pilate against Jesus, ch. xxiii. 2, and also of what our Lord suffered before Herod, ch. xxiii. 5–16; of His address to the weeping women, vss. 27–31; of His first word on the cross, vs. 34; of the absolution of the Penitent Thief, vss. 39–43; of the last exclamation of the Dying One, vs. 46; of the part taken by Joseph of Arimathæa in the Jewish senate, vs. 51, and many other minor traits besides. The special mention of the women who came into relation to the suffering Saviour is peculiar to Luke, ch. xxiii. 27–31, and also vss. 55, 56, as indeed even previously, ch. viii. 2, 3, he had given a special statement of the service rendered by the Galilean female friends. Taking all together, we see that Luke, in the history of the Passion also, does not at all belie his character as physician, as Hellenist, as Paulinist; and for the very freshness and originality of his delineation he deserves that we, even after that which has been related respecting the history of the Passion by Matthew and Mark, should devote to his narrative a particular investigation. As respects general topics which he has in common with the two before named, in particular all that is of a chronological, archæological, and topographical character, as, for instance, Passover and Gethsemane, Golgotha, &c., we must, as a rule, in order to avoid too great a prolixity, refer the reader to the admirable expositions of LANGE in the *Gospel of Matthew*, at the passages in question.

Vs. 1. **Now . . . drew nigh.**—In the beginning of the history of the Passion, Luke agrees most with Mark, although he is chronologically less exact. The decisive transition, in Matt. ch. xxvi. 1, from the accomplished prophetical to the now beginning high-priestly work of the Lord, does not appear so conspicuously in Luke, although it is plain enough that he also now begins to give account of a new period.—**The feast of unleavened bread, which is called the Passover.**—An exact periphrastic designation of the approaching feast in its whole extent (not of the first evening alone), as was requisite for readers who were not acquainted from their own observation and experience with the Israelitish Passover.

Vs. 2. **Sought how they might kill Him.**—Here, especially, Luke must be complemented from Matt. xxvi. 3–5. It appears, then, that we have not to understand an indefinite and planless ζητεῖν, but a definite assembling of a part of the Sanhedrim, apparently the first one, *ad hoc*, after that which is mentioned John xi. 47–53. This gathering, held in the palace of the high-priest, had probably a more confidential character, and was, we may suppose, in chief part composed of those of like mind. The theme of their deliberation was in general πῶς ἀνέλωσιν αὐτόν. That their will is, at any cost, to remove Him out of the way, is already tacitly understood; but now they must yet further become agreed upon the manner in which to carry out their purpose, and that this costs deliberation as well as effort, Luke brings to view by: **for they feared the people.**—Comp. Mark xiv. 2; Matt. xxvi. 5. It is by no means their intention to remove our Lord out of the way, even *before* the feast (Neander), but they mean to let the time of the feast go by, in order immediately afterwards to seize the favorable opportunity. Yet unexpectedly the carrying out of the murderous plan is hastened, and the fulfilment of the prophecy of our Lord, Matt. xxvi. 1, 2, prepared by the base offer of Judas.

Vs. 3. **Then entered Satan.**—Not an expression for the completed, fully confirmed resolution of the traitor (De Wette), but for a preparatory influence of Satan upon him, whereby a later decisive possession (John xiii. 27) is by no means excluded. Not all at once does Satan possess himself of the soul of the unhappy traitor. Not till after several assaults does he fully succeed in this. His plan itself was devilish, but not less the carrying out. For more particular details upon this transaction, *see* Matt. xxvi. 14–16. The anointing at Bethany, which Matthew and Mark narrate previously, Luke passes

CHAP. XXII. 1-6.   331

over, because he had already, ch. vii. 36-50, related something similar. Apparently the offer of Judas was made on Wednesday, after the Jewish council had separated on Tuesday evening with the preliminary conclusion, "Not on the feast."

Of the number of the Twelve.—It is worthy of note that this particular circumstance is mentioned by all the Evangelists with so much emphasis. So much the more natural is the question how precisely one of the Twelve could have come to commit such a crime. That Judas was a man of peculiar talents, who, however, more than even the other disciples, had been filled with earthly-minded expectations, cannot be seriously doubted. Only he can become a devil, who has possessed the possibility of becoming an angel. In his expectations he now saw himself more and more deceived, when he became aware that our Lord did not at all make the desired use of the enthusiasm of the people; nay, that He suffered the Hosannas of the people to decline into a jubilee of children. This disappointed hope must have made him doubly receptive for the feeling of injured self-love, when he at Bethany was humbled before the eyes of all, and his covetousness unmasked. From a Nazarene, who would be no Messiah, who would be only a Rabbi, a Judas could naturally endure no hard words. Perhaps also the prediction of the σταυρωθῆναι, Matt. xxvi. 2, had given to his revengeful thoughts more form and fixedness, while his avarice had at the same time impelled him to indemnify himself by treachery for the damage which he believed himself to have suffered by Mary's unointing. On the consequences of his act he appears in truth scarcely to have thought, but, like a drunken man, to have stumbled along on the dark way of destruction, until afterwards his eyes were opened in the most terrible manner upon his guilt. By no means is the opinion well grounded that he wished to constrain the Lord to free Himself by force or by a miracle from the hands of His enemies, and so to reveal His majesty. "What a common comedian nature he must needs have been to let his holy Master pass unharmed, as profitable capital, through a danger as through a speculation. According to this opinion Judas does not become better, but instead of a devillishly revengeful man, we gain only a rascally soul, of which it is inconceivable how Jesus could have chosen it among His disciples." Ebrard. On the contrary, two of the Evangelists give us a very pregnant intimation that the treason towards Jesus, psychologically considered, cannot be fully comprehended unless we assume a direct Satanic influence, of course not without the guilt of the traitor, who had voluntarily and stubbornly opened his heart to this influence.

Vs. 4. **The captains.**—These had a very important part in the matter, since they constituted the clerical force of the temple, who, in any case, would have to appoint and despatch the necessary force for the arrest of the Saviour. They were the subordinate executive board for discharging the commands of the high-priest, a Levitical corps of officers that stood under the command of a στρατηγός, while by the name στρατηγοί commanders of the individual watches are denoted.

Vs. 5. **And they were glad.**—Not only because there now opens to them the prospect of the fulfilment of their intended wishes, but also (Euthymius) because among Jesus' disciples themselves a spirit of unfaithfulness and hatred begins to reveal itself. In this joy they assume the obligation (συνέθεντο) of giving him money, and Judas, who concludes the bargain with them (ἐξωμολόγησεν), seeks now, on his side, without delay, a good opportunity therefor. Like Mark, Luke also speaks only of money in general, without a more precise statement of the sum, which is mentioned by Matthew alone. It is entirely without ground (De Wette, Strauss, Scholten) to consider the number of the thirty pieces of silver as the fruit of a construction of the history according to the prophecy of Zechariah, least of all if we assume that this sum was only intended for a preliminary payment, which subsequently, perhaps, if the plan should have been carried out successfully, was to be followed by a more considerable one.

Vs. 6. **Without attracting a multitude**, ἄτερ ὄχλου, without having a popular tumult arise. The opposite, see in Acts xxiv. 18. The poetical word ἄτερ used only here and in vs. 35. Without doubt, a quiet execution of the plan appears quite as desirable to Judas for himself, as the chief-priests consider it necessary in the general interest. Wickedness is always cowardly.

DOCTRINAL AND ETHICAL.

1. With the last Passover the hatred of the principal Jews towards Jesus has reached its highest point. The reason of the augmentation of this hatred with every feast which the Lord celebrated at Jerusalem, becomes especially visible from the fourth gospel. His enemies destroy for themselves the joy in the Passover of the Old Covenant, and rise without knowing it to slaughter the Passover of the New Covenant. No fear before God, only fear before men, dwells in their hearts; withal their impotency is so great that they are not able to carry out their plans unless they find an accomplice from Jesus' own circle of disciples.

2. By the mention of the treachery of Judas the veil of the spiritual world is lifted, and the folly of those becomes manifest who will not believe in a personal influence of Satan. After the Evil One has vainly sought (Matt. iv. 1-11) to bring our Lord in person to apostatize, he now seeks to destroy His work, and to inflict upon Him through one of His own disciples a deadly wound. The manner in which he now possesses himself of Judas, after the latter had belonged for a while to the disciples of our Lord, serves as a new proof of the deeply earnest utterance, ch. xi. 24-27. " *Dicitur in reprobos intrare Satan, eum, reverso Dei metu, extincta rationis luce, pudore etiam excusso, sensus omnes occupat.*" Calvin.

HOMILETICAL AND PRACTICAL.

The approaching of the last Passover of the Old Covenant.—The very different manner in which our Lord and in which His enemies prepare themselves to celebrate the feast.—Spite and despondency united in the enemies of our Lord.—Two gatherings, that of our Lord with His disciples and that of the chief-priests and scribes: 1. Here the composure of innocence, there the suspense of wickedness; 2. here certainty as to that which is to be suffered, there uncertainty as to that which is to be done; 3. here courageous awaiting of danger, there unquiet fear of the people.—The Divine and the human plan of suffering.—The first steps in the way of treason: 1.

Their preparation; 2. their carrying out; 3. their aim.—The uncommonly deep significancy of a first step.—Satan in the way to cast down: 1. Judas; 2. our Lord; 3. himself.—The hellish joy of the confederates of sin.—The fearful might of money.—The evil covenant of Judas with the enemies over against the unsuspiciousness of the faithful disciples, a new proof for the truth of the saying, Luke xvi. 8b.—Craft and covetousness in covenant against the Redeemer of the world: 1. The terrific character of this covenant; 2. the impotency of this covenant; 3. the instructiveness of this covenant.—The greatest crime that was ever committed, the way to the greatest blessing of the world.—The might and the impotency of sin: 1. The might, *a.* it has mighty servants, *b.* strong weapons, *c.* ready confederates; 2. the impotency, it is not capable, *a.* of covering its own shame, *b.* of shaking the composure of Jesus, *c.* of frustrating the counsel of God.—Judas a warning example of the insufficiency of a merely outward fellowship with Christ.—Nothing is casualty, nothing without purpose.—Even the mode of death, like the time of death, predetermined.

STARKE:—*Nova Bibl. Tub.:*—One may from fear of men omit or postpone the sin, and yet have a plan of murder against Jesus in the heart.—Like and like join together.—Sin has its degrees.—Woe to covetous priests! — CRAMER: — Unfaithfulness is widely extended upon earth, and a man's foes are often they of his own house.—QUESNEL:—He that has once made room for Satan in his heart is capable of the greatest sins.—He that loves sin easily finds opportunity to commit it.—Whoever sins presumptuously seeks opportunity thereto, but who out of weakness, is overcome by the opportunity.—To promise evil is a great sin, but to keep the evil promise is even greater.—HEUBNER:—Christ addresses Himself to bring Himself as a sacrifice, and His enemies to sacrifice Him to their hate.—Judas a type of those who value all religion, Christianity, and the virtue of men according to their profitableness.—Jesus, for Judas, had His price.—Interrogate thyself whether thou wouldst not have been ready, had enough been offered thee for it, to give up Jesus, therefore whether thy faith, thy virtue have a price for which it may be bought.—F. R. ARNDT:—The sudden appearing of Judas in the great council: 1. His coming; 2. his going.—THOLUCK:—The Passion-Week makes plain in Judas to what degree even the human heart is capable of being hardened that has already known the way of righteousness, 2 Peter ii. 2, 21.

---

2. The Preparation of the Passover (Vss. 7-13).

(Parallel to Matt. xxvi. 17-19; Mark xiv. 12-16.)

7 Then came the day of unleavened bread, when the passover must be [had to be]
8 killed. And he sent Peter and John, saying, Go and prepare us the passover, that we
9, 10 may eat. And they said unto him, Where wilt thou that we prepare? And he
11 said unto them, Behold, when ye are entered into the city, there shall a man meet you, bearing a pitcher of water; follow him into the house where he entereth in. And ye shall say unto the goodman [master] of the house, The Master [Teacher] saith unto thee, Where is the guestchamber [κατάλυμα], where I shall [may] eat the passover
12 with my disciples? And he shall shew you a large upper room furnished: there make
13 ready [prepare *the passover*]. And they went, and found as he had said unto them: and they made ready the passover.

EXEGETICAL AND CRITICAL.

Vs. 7. When the Passover had to be killed, ἔδει θύεσθαι.—It is really an enigma how one could ever have found in this chronological datum of Luke, and in the words of our Lord, Matt. xxvi. 18, a ground for the entirely unprovable conjecture that our Savior ate the Passover a day earlier than other Israelites. Upon every impartial person the beginning of this Pericope makes far more the impression that Luke speaks here of the definite day on which, according to the appointment of the law, the Passover lamb had to be slaughtered. Only on this day was the question of the disciples, Matt. xxvi. 17, perfectly natural; moreover, the beginning of the discourse at table, preserved by Luke alone, vs. 15, shows that our Lord attributes to this very Passover an especially high significance. As to the rest, it is not here the place to enter into detailed discussion as to the actual day of our Lord's death. Be it only granted to us to express our conviction—the result of special and repeated investigation—that as well according to the Synoptics as according to John, our Lord, on the 14th Nisan, at the same time with the other Jews, and at the time appointed by the law, ate the Passover, and on the 15th suffered the death on the Cross. We believe that the grounds for this view in WIESELER'S *Chronolog. Synopse,* p. 339 *seq.,* have been, it is true, controverted by Bleek, Tischendorf, and others, but not refuted; and that, moreover, there is just as little reason for placing the meal, (John xiii., ou Wednesday evening (Wichelhaus), as (KNAPFT, *Chronologie und Harmonie der 4 Evangelien,* Erlangen, 1848, p. 125) to speak of two meals, and to transfer this evening to the 12th and 13th Nisan. The objections, which even after the powerful demonstration of Wieseler, may be raised from an entirely different stand-point against the view accepted by us, are not unknown to us; but we believe that these, at all events, are of infinitely less importance than the difficulties in which one involves himself if he assumes in this particular an irreconcilable discrepancy between John and the Synoptics. Respecting the Passover controversy of the ancient church, and its relation to the chronology of the Passion Week, comp. RIGGENBACH, *l. c.,* p. 635 *seq.,* where at the same time the most recent literature on this question is given. *See* also : *Der Tag des letzten Paschamahles Jesu Christi, ein harmonistischer Versuch,* by SERNO, Berlin, 1859.

Vs. 8. **And He sent Peter and John.**—According to the more detailed account of Matthew and Mark, the disciples themselves first began to speak to our Lord of the Passover meal, apparently on Thursday morning, at Bethany. Perhaps the Master was now more silent than of old ; of the feast, without doubt, He did not speak, and this mysterious fact, as well as also the sight of numerous pilgrims to the feast, very naturally occasioned the disciples to ask the question: ποῦ θέλεις, κ.τ.λ. That our Lord would eat the Passover on that day on which it *must* be slaughtered they tacitly presuppose, and perhaps had not spoken even earlier of it only because the prophecy of death, Matt. xxvi. 2, has filled their hearts more than the thoughts of the feast, or because they already have a dark presentiment that this Passover would be something entirely different for them from what any earlier one had ever been; or because they were expecting a direct intimation from Jesus Himself before they betook themselves to the capital, whither He Himself yesterday, for the first time, had no longer gone. If we compare Luke with the other Synoptics, we may then unite the accounts thus : that at a preliminary inquiry of the μαθηταί as to the ποῦ, our Lord gives Peter and John a definite command to go away to prepare the Passover ; whereupon then they now repeat with more definiteness the natural inquiry as to the ποῦ, and now receive the mysterious direction in reference to the man with the pitcher of water, which Matthew does not give account of. It is still simpler, if we, with Tischendorf, and others, read εἶπαν, and explain the fact thus : that, vs. 9, the question is really brought up afterwards, which, strictly speaking, ought to have been stated before the command, vs. 8.

Vs. 10. **There shall a man meet you.**—In Mark and Luke we have the more special account of the condition in which they would find the furnished upper room, without however their statement being in conflict with the general one of Matthew. Our Saviour gives His disciples a similar token to that which Samuel once gave Saul, 1 Sam. x. 2–5.—**A man.**—Although he is here represented as occupied in a menial service, comp. Deut. xxix. 11 ; Josh. ix. 21, we have not necessarily to understand a slave (Sepp even knows that it was a slave of Nicodemus), but in general only a person of the lower classes ; the pitcher, the carrying of water, point possibly to domestic preparation for the coming Passover, and would in this case in a certain measure concur as a proof that we have here to do with the ordinary Passover day. Luke has συναντήσει more exactly for the ἀπαντήσει of Mark ; He will so meet you, so come together with you, that you will go one way with him.

Vs. 11. **Ye shall say to the master of the house.**—Not a prophetic but an imperative future.—Οἰκοδεσπότης τῆς οἰκ. a pleonastic expression not unusual with the Greeks, especially in the more familiar style.—**The Teacher saith.**—The remarkable words, Matt. xxvi. 18 : " My time is at hand," are omitted in Mark and Luke, while they on the other hand render the address to the master of the house in the form of a question.—Tὸ κατάλυμα, *diversorium* (Luke ii. 7), then also *cœnaculum. See* the LXX, in 1 Sam. ix. 22. Mου is here, at all events, spurious, and might also be very well dispensed with in the parallel passage in Matthew.

Vs. 12. **And he,** ἐκεῖνος, according to Mark αὐτός. —The man with the pitcher of water has now accomplished his service, and the master of the house now comes in his place. The direction which the disciples receive is so precise that it does not leave them one uncertainty remaining. They will find an upper room, ἀνάγαιον (which reading appears to deserve the preference above that of the *Recepta,* ἀνώγεον, and even above that commended by Tischendorf after B., M., S., ἀνώγαιον)=ὑπερῷον, an upper chamber, used often as a place of prayer and assembling. Comp. Acts i. 18. This great hall (μέγα) is moreover ἐστρωμένον, furnished with pillows, *stratis tricliniis,* and so, according to Mark, already ἕτοιμον, so that there would need no further loss of time for the purpose of putting the hall in good order.

Vs. 13. **And they went.**—We may assume that the way of the apostles led through the water-gate (Nehemiah viii. 1), past the Pool of Siloam, which as is known furnished almost the whole city with water, and that they there also met the man with the pitcher of water. Yet there was a spring also in the neighborhood of Cedron ; therefore it is remarkable that our Lord does not give them the least specification as to the way which they had to take, but only tells them what should meet them on the way. From Mark xiv. 17, it seems to be the fact that the two, after having punctually fulfilled the duty enjoined on them, returned back to the Master, and that He entered the Passover hall with all the Twelve.

DOCTRINAL AND ETHICAL.

1. It belongs to the Divine decorum of the history of the Passion, that our Lord celebrates the Passover at Jerusalem, at the time appointed by the law. Had not to-day been the legally-appointed evening of the feast, on which every Israelite was under obligation to eat the Passover lamb, there would have been properly no ground for at this particular time entering the capital, in which, as was well known to Him, His enemies were watching for Him. But now literally the way of obedience has led Him to death, and the last Passover celebration of the Old Covenant coalesces with the institution of the Holy Communion. Inasmuch as He celebrates it in this way, He does away forever with the old Passover, as He did away with circumcision, when it was accomplished on Himself on the eighth day, ch. ii. 21.

2. *As to* the question, how we have to understand the prediction concerning the man who should meet them with the water-pitcher, we have the choice between five possible opinions :—Invention, accident, previous concert, revelation, supernatural knowledge. That it is an invention (De Wette, Strauss, Meyer), is wholly unproved. The analogy with Samuel proves nothing. It would, moreover, have been incomprehensible to what purpose a trait apparently so insignificant should have been invented for the history of the Passion. To understand accident is forbidden, as well by the precision of the prediction as by its exact accomplishment. Previous concert (not only Paulus, but also Olshausen, Kern, Krabbe, Neander, Braune, in a certain measure, also Lange) is certainly in itself not impossible. It is unquestionably conceivable that our Lord had already arranged this matter with a secret friend in the city. However, the

tone of the command, the analogy with 1 Sam. x. 2–5, and the similarity to what happened at His public entry with respect to the ass-colt, appear to indicate that we have here rather to understand something supernatural. With the ordinary prophet we should be able here to assume a momentary revelation, by means of which before his enlightened view the limits of time and space vanished; with the Lord, however, we can here see nothing less than the activity of the same Divinely human knowledge by which He was rendered capable of discovering all which He must fathom for the accomplishment of His holy intent. To find even in this case a manifestation of such knowledge can have nothing strange, if we bear in mind the entirely unique importance which just this Passover celebration had for our Lord as well as for His disciples. Without doubt, our Lord made the acquaintance of the designated host in a natural way, but by His Divine knowledge He is assured that this friend will be immediately ready and in a condition to receive Him, and that his servant has just now to-day gone out to the spring before the city in order to bring water. Thus, in the manner in which our Lord, as the Good Shepherd, prepares for His own a table in the presence of their enemies, there is displayed an admirable knowledge of the human heart, of a definite locality, of an apparently casual arrangement.

The view that our Saviour designedly gave this command in so mysterious a form, that the place of the celebration might remain unknown to Judas, and that He might therefore be able to spend the evening entirely unobserved with His own (Theophylact, Neander), cannot indeed be mathematically proved, but yet is by all means probable on internal grounds; the result, moreover, showed that in consequence of this arrangement the traitor was not able to carry out his plan until later in the night. At all events, this embassy was for John and Peter an exercise in faith and in obedience; they had to learn therefrom to follow our Lord even blindly, even when they did not see the purpose of His command, and in the future also to leave the care of their earthly interests unconditionally to Him, under whose high guidance they should never lack for anything, Luke xxii. 35. At the same time, such revelations of the hidden greatness of our Lord might be for them a counterpoise against the depth of humiliation into which He was soon to sink. Without doubt they, afterwards, in dark hours of life, may sometimes have still thought upon this mysterious errand, and looked back to its satisfactory issue.

3. This whole occurrence is a speaking proof of the greatness of our Lord, even in that which is small and seemingly insignificant. This preparatory measure shows us His immovable composure, which He preserved even in spite of the most certain prospect of death; His holy presence of mind over against the secret plotting of the traitors; but, above all, His wisdom, love, and faithfulness, with which He cares, even to the end, for the training of His disciples, and gives them, even in a slight command, a great lesson for the future. Thus does He remain even to the end in silence, and in speech, in temper, and action, perfectly consistent with Himself, and goes undaunted and quiet as a lamb to the slaughter, at about the same hour in which the Paschal lambs were bought and slaughtered.

4. Allegorical interpretation of this narrative among the ancients: The water-pitcher, an image of the insipid and burdensome law which the Jews bore; the roomy upper chamber, an image of the abundant room for all whom the Saviour has invited to His spiritual supper, Luke xiv. 21–23; Rev. iii. 20, &c. Juster is the remark of John Gerhard: *Christus hac sua prædictione fidem discipulorum confirmare et contra crucis scandalum eos munire voluit, ut magis ac magis intelligerent, nihil temere in urbe magistro eventurum.* Even because our Lord, like any common Israelite, observes the Passover and voluntarily humbles Himself, does He will that His glory shall shine out in the manner in which He makes ready for this meal.

HOMILETICAL AND PRACTICAL.

The worth of trifles in general and in sacred history, particularly in the history of the Passion.—We men are often little in great things, the Saviour is great in little things. Even by His greatness in little things, He shows Himself: 1. The image of the invisible God; 2. the perfect Redeemer of the world; 3. the best Guide of His people; 4. the noblest example for imitation.—Our Lord is, even on His last day of earth, faithful to the high principle which He uttered at His first appearance, Matt. iii. 15.—Peter and John here also, as often, united. John xx. 1; Acts iii. 1; iv. 19.—In every perplexity the disciple may turn to Jesus.—Even the man with a pitcher of water must have his place in the history of the Passion.—The significance of apparently insignificant and subordinate persons for the carrying out of the counsel of God, for example, 2 Kings v. 2; Acts xii. 13; xxiii. 16.—There exists more evil but also more good than shows itself to the superficial view.—Even in the most corrupted city, Jesus finds hidden friends and knows them.—"I will come unto him and sup with him."—The best in the house of His friends is for the Lord not too good.—The obedience of faith is never put to shame.—The true disciple of Jesus is faithful not only in the great, but also in the small.—He loved His own even to the end, John xiii. 1.

STARKE:—*Nova Bibl. Tub.:*—How shall we prepare and address ourselves to worthy enjoyment of the Paschal lamb of the New Covenant in His feast of love? 1 Cor. xi. 28.—Not our will but Thine, O Lord, be done. Acts xxi. 14.—God provides His own with habitation and shelter, even though they have nothing of their own in the world. 1 Kings xvii. 9.—That we find everything in the world as God's word has said, is an irrefutable proof of the truth and divinity of the Scriptures.—HEUBNER:—Notwithstanding His high vocation, Jesus thinks also on the little concerns of love.—The disciples obey willingly, without making objections that were very obvious.—BESSER:—In wonderfully beautiful simplicity they did as the Lord had commanded them; that was a true communion temper.—FR. ARNDT:—1. The signification of the Paschal lamb; 2. the preparation for the same.

3. The Passover and the Celebration of the Lord's Supper (Vss. 14–23).

(Parallel to Matt. xxvi. 20–29; Mark xiv. 17–25; John xiii. 21–35.)

14 And when the hour was come, he sat down [reclined at table], and the twelve
15 [om., twelve[1]] apostles with him. And he said unto them, With desire I have desired
16 to eat this passover with you before I suffer: For I say unto you, I will not any more
17 eat thereof,[2] until it be fulfilled in the kingdom of God. And he took the[3] cup, and
18 gave thanks, and said, Take this, and divide *it* among yourselves: For I say unto you,
     I will not drink of the fruit of the vine, until the kingdom of God shall [have] come.
19 And he took bread, and gave thanks, and brake *it*, and gave unto them, saying, This is
20 my body which is given for you: this do in remembrance of me. Likewise also the
     cup after supper, saying, This cup *is* the new testament in my blood, which is shed for
21 you. But, behold, the hand of him that betrayeth me [delivereth me up] *is* with me
22 on the table. And [For[4]] truly the Son of man goeth, as it was determined [κατὰ τὸ
23 ὡρισμένον]: but woe unto that man by whom he is betrayed [delivered up]! And
     they began to inquire among themselves, which of them it was [might be] that should
     [was about to] do this thing.

---

[1] Vs. 14.—The δώδεκα of the *Recepta* is, with Lachmann, Tischendorf, [Meyer, Tregelles, Alford,] omitted, according to B., D., [Cod. Sin.,] 157, Sahid, Itala, &c.
[2] Vs. 16.—Van Oosterzee translates: "eat *it*," reading αὐτό instead of the *Recepta*, ἐξ αὐτοῦ, with Lachmann, Tregelles, Alford, according to B., L., and various Cursives and Versions, including the Vulgate. Cod. Sin. also reads αὐτό. Van Oosterzee adduces Tischendorf's authority, but Tischendorf in his 7th ed. has reverted to the *Recepta*, which Meyer also defends.—C. C. S.
[3] Vs. 17.—The τό, which A., D., K., M., U., and some Cursives read, and which is also received by Lachmann, appears to have crept quite early into many manuscripts, from the liturgical form, but not to be genuine.
[4] Vs. 22.—The *Recepta* has καί; Tischendorf, according to B., D., [Cod. Sin.,] L., &c., ὅτι. [Meyer remarks that the OTI was overlooked on account of the following OYI, and then the lack of a connective being felt, καί was subsequently interpolated.—C. C. S.]

EXEGETICAL AND CRITICAL.

If we attentively compare the narrative of Luke respecting the Passover and the celebration of the Lord's Supper with the accounts of the other Evangelists, we shall on one hand be strengthened in the conviction that all give account of the same festal meal and the same discovery of the traitor, but we must, on the other hand, at the same time concede that Luke's chronological sequence is not wholly exact. Only when we complement his narrative by that of the others, does it become to us in any measure possible to place the whole course of facts vividly before our eyes. Not the arrangement of the different elements of the celebration, but the sharp contrast between the state of mind of the Apostles and the words of the Saviour, comes in his representation decidedly into the foreground, and Luke is here also, where he introduces us into the upper chamber, more a painter than a diplomatically exact historian.

Vs. 14. **The hour.**—The ὥρα of the law, Matthew and Mark ὀψίας. Respecting the manner of celebrating the Passover, *see* LANGE on Matt. xxvi. 20, and FRIEDLIEB, *Archäologie der Leidensgeschichte*, § 18 *seq*. Comp. LIGHTFOOT, WETSTEIN, SEPP, a. o., although it is yet very much a question whether all the usages and acts there adduced were already practised precisely in the same way in the time of Jesus; besides, we ought to consider that the Evangelical account by no means makes the impression as if our Lord had celebrated the Passover even to the minutest particulars according to the existing usages. We might rather suppose the opposite, if we consider how He, with all obedience towards the law, observed in respect to the ritual tradition a becoming freedom, and how He was here less concerned for a duly arranged celebration of the feast than for an hour of undisturbed society, composed farewell, and prayer with His own.

Reclined at table.—Although originally, Ex. xii. 11, a celebration of the Passover standing was prescribed, it afterwards became usual to recline at table during it as at any other meal, apparently a symbol of the freedom which Israel had obtained by the Exodus from Egypt, since only slaves were accustomed to stand during eating. In respect to the arrangement of the places for the company at the table, little can be determined with certainty. From John xiii. 23 it only appears that John has the first place, nearest the Saviour, while Peter must not be looked for immediately next to him, but only near him, since he does not speak to him, but only beckons to him (ch. xiii. 24), about that which he wished to inquire about of him. The place of the father of the house, who presided at the paschal celebration, our Lord here occupies, and by Luke the very moment is brought before us, vss. 15–18, in which He opens the celebration. Perhaps He uttered the words vss. 15, 16, instead of the customary thanksgiving to God, who had made this day for His people.

Vs. 15. **With desire I have desired.**—Hebraism: ἐπιθυμίᾳ ἐπεθύμησα, compare the LXX on Numbers xi. 4; Ps. cvi. 14. This very first word gives us to know our Lord's frame of mind, which in this whole evening remained the prevailing one. His suffering stands so clearly before His soul, that He no longer even expressly announces it, but presupposes the nearness of it as something sufficiently known. He has already, for a considerable time, desired to eat *this* Passover, and is thinking thereby not of the meal of the New Testament (Tertullian and other fathers), but of the Israelitish feast, which for one and twenty years had gained continually deeper significance and higher value for His heart. He has very peculiarly desired to eat it with His own, μεθ' ὑμῶν; He feels that He is not only Redeemer but also Friend of His disciples, and He has especially longed after such a reunion, on account of the institution of the Supper, which is even now to be entered upon. It is as if He forgot the presence of Judas, as if He knew Himself to be in a circle of none but sincere, faithful friends, out of whom He however was soon to depart. In the very beginning therefore He gives to the festal celebration the character of a feast of farewell, and therewith prepares His disciples for the institution of the Supper that commemorates His death.

Vs. 16. **For I say unto you.**—It is of course understood that our Lord, before or in the utterance of these words, must have eaten at least something of the meal, as He indeed Himself, vs. 15, indicates. He declares here only that after the present one, He will no longer celebrate the Israelitish Passover, ἕως ὅτου πληρωθῇ ἐν τῇ βασιλ. τοῦ θεοῦ; that is, "not until all be fulfilled which must be fulfilled in My kingdom of grace" (Starke); nor is ὁ καιρός or any such thing to be supplied, but simply τὸ πάσχα. To wish to conclude now from this that our Lord expects a literal Passover at the revelation of His Divine kingdom in glory, is purely arbitrary, since it is plain enough that He here, as often, describes the joy of the perfected Messianic kingdom under the *image* of a feast. The Passover is only fulfilled when the outer form, the Passover celebration, is entirely broken down, and the eternal idea, a perfect feast of deliverance, is fully realized. The Lord points "to the eternal coronation-feast of His glorified Church, the shining image of the eternal supper, the anticipatory celebration of which in the New Testament covenant meal, He is now about to establish." Lange.

In the kingdom of God — ἐν παρουσίᾳ μου. As our Saviour in the paschal lamb sees the type of His own immaculate sacrifice, so does He see in the paschal celebration a symbolical setting forth of the perfect joy of heaven.

Vs. 17. **The cup.**—There is no other meant by this than the first, with which the festal celebration *ex officio* had begun. The word εὐχαριστήσας appears to indicate that our Lord uttered the customary blessing: "Blessed be thou, O Lord our God, the King of the world, who hast created the fruit of the vine;" perhaps we hear the echo thereof in the words, vs. 18, ἀπὸ τοῦ γεννήματος τῆς ἀμπέλου. The address: **Take this and divide it among yourselves** (ἑαυτοῖς), appears, it is true, to indicate that our Lord puts from Himself the enjoyment of the paschal wine. However, we may yet conclude from the following words, vs. 18, that our Lord says this after He has previously drank, even as He had in vss. 15, 16 previously eaten, but in no case does there exist, even on the first interpretation, a ground for considering this expression of our Saviour, even at the first cup, as improbable (Meyer). The drinking of the paschal wine was at all events not prescribed by the law, like the eating of the paschal lamb, on which account our Lord might place Himself composedly above the common forms, without His act therefore having become illegal, irreligious, or offensive.—**Until the kingdom of God shall have come.**—That is, of course, in glory, as in vs. 16. That our Lord repeated the same expression in a somewhat altered form after the institution of the Supper, as is related in Matt. xxvi. 29 and Mark xiv. 25, cannot possibly in itself be incredible.

Vs. 19. **And He took bread.**—The institution of the Supper, to the description of which Luke now already passes over, was undoubtedly preceded by the dispute about rank, vs. 24–27, and the foot-washing, John xiii. Luke visibly makes not the Passover but the Lord's Supper the centre of his whole delineation, and communicates the dispute about rank, vs. 24, apparently only by occasion of the dispute which, vs. 23, had arisen through the uncertainty in reference to the person of the traitor. By attentive comparison of the Evangelical accounts, we can decide only for the following arrangement of the different events in the Passover-hall: 1. Opening of the meal (Luke xxii. 15–18). 2. Almost contemporaneously, or even before this, the dispute about rank, vss. 24–27 (comp. John xiii. 1–11). 3. Further remarks of the Saviour (John xiii. 18–20; Luke xxii. 28–30). Meanwhile the continuation of the celebration, undoubtedly more on the part of the disciples than on the part of our Lord, and participation of the second cup, which is not expressly mentioned in the gospels. 4. The discovery of the traitor (Matt. xxvi. 21–25; Mark xiv. 18–21; Luke xxii. 21–23; John xiii. 21–30). 5. After his going out, the institution of the Lord's Supper, in all probability to be inserted John xiii. 34, 35. Although in and of itself it may be concluded, from the account of Luke literally taken, that Judas was yet present at the institution of the Lord's Supper, yet from the comparison of all the other accounts, the opposite becomes evident, so that all dogmatic debates about the enjoyment of the communion by the unworthy Judas, together with all deductions therefrom, are without any firm historical basis.

Vs. 19. **This is My body.**—The institution of the Lord's Supper took place therefore just before the third cup, which in consequence of it was hallowed as the cup of the New Covenant. The Lord takes up one of the remaining cakes of bread, and now speaks the words of institution. As respects the form of the words themselves, it appears at once that Matthew here agrees most closely with Mark, Luke most closely with Paul, 1 Cor. ii. 23 *seq.*, so that the genuinely Pauline character of his gospel in this place, also, does not belie itself. Before we quite make up our minds to the opinion that our Lord repeated the words of institution several times, more or less modified, we prefer to consider, as being thoroughly authentic, those words which He according to all the narrators uses, while that which each Evangelist gives in particular can only be judged on grounds of internal probability. With the words, **This is My body,** Luke has τὸ ὑπὲρ ὑμῶν διδόμενον. These words are on internal grounds probable, even on account of the parallelism with the subsequent "which *is shed* for you," and are by no means in conflict with 1 Cor. xi. 24, since κλώμενον is decidedly spurious. Agreeably to the connection, διδόμενον can be understood only of a surrender to death, while ὑπέρ here does not of necessity express the idea of representation, but may be translated generally: *in commodum vestrum.*

This do in remembrance of Me.—These words, at the distribution of the bread, are also given by Luke and Paul alone, but they have internal probability, as well on account of what immediately follows at the giving of the cup, as also of the character of the celebration, which is to be a permanent memorial institution. If we could assume (Stier, Nitzsch, a. o.) that the Pauline words: ἐγὼ γὰρ παρέλαβον ἀπὸ τοῦ κυρίου point to a direct revelation, in which the glorified Saviour gave to a letter the formula of institution communicated by Him, then undoubtedly the exactness of the rendering of Luke with its Pauline coloring, would be raised above all doubt. There is however nothing in the words of the Apostle to necessitate us to understand such an extraordinary revelation, since he may have also meant thereby the evangelical tradition that had come to his knowledge.

Vs. 20. Μετὰ τὸ δειπνῆσαι.—The third cup commonly went round for the first time after the meal was finished, and we do not therefore need, from this expression of itself, to draw the inference that now the paschal celebration for this evening had been entirely ended; on the other hand, there belong thereto a fourth and fifth cup, as well as the singing of the hymn of praise, Matt. xxvi. 30. The institution of the Supper is therefore taken up as a special act into the course of the paschal celebration, although it is not probable that this last, at least as concerns the eating, was yet continued after the reception of the communion bread. Our Lord (Matthew and Mark) now names this cup τὸ αἷμά μου τῆς διαθήκης, while He according to Luke and Paul speaks of ἡ καινὴ διαθήκη ἐν τῷ αἵματί μου. But whichever expression may have been the most original, yet the signification of it is not hard to understand. As the Old Covenant was not established without blood (Exodus xxiv. 8, comp. Heb. ix. 16), so through the blood of Christ was the New Covenant, which God now concluded with man, Jer. xxxi. 31-34, confirmed and sealed. Of this blood it is said (Matthew and Mark), that it was shed ὑπὲρ or περὶ πολλῶν, according to Luke, τὸ ὑπὲρ ὑμῶν ἐκχυνόμενον. We might almost suppose that the latter was the original, the former, on the other hand, a later ecclesiastically established formula. But in no case is the application of the blood limited by the πολλῶν, as if it had taken place for many and not for all, but on the other hand the purpose is thereby as much as possible extended, as embracing not only the Apostles, but in addition *many with them*.

If we consider the whole formula of the distribution of the bread and wine, we believe that we must understand it so as to explain the τοῦτο as referring to the broken piece of bread, and to the wine poured into the cup which He reaches to His disciples. That our Lord did not in His language once use the much controverted ἐστίν, is as certain as that it must necessarily be understood to complete the sense. He means that the broken bread which He hands to them in this instant represents His body, and that that (τοῦτο ποιεῖτε) which they were just about to do,—the eating of the bread handed to them, namely,—they should do for the remembrance of Him. The same is the case with the cup, &c. From the statements of Luke and Paul it appears yet far more plainly than from those of Matthew and Mark, that our Lord here ordains a permanent meal of remembrance for those that confess Him, even in following ages. How fitting, finally, this whole symbolical act already was for the necessities of the disciples at that moment, appears at once so soon as we even in some measure transport ourselves into their state of mind, and consider what hard trials they were to experience even in the same night.

Vs. 21. But behold the hand.—"This allusion to the traitor (according to Luke, in distinction from the rest without any more particular specification), Luke has in the wrong place." Meyer. Evidently he is merely concerned to give a condensed reference to a particular which he will neither pass over entirely nor yet communicate in greater detail. That, in Matt. xxvi. 21-25, only a first preliminary designation of the traitor appears, which took place even before the institution of the Supper, supposed to have subsequently taken place in the presence of Judas, and which was finally succeeded by yet a second more particular designation, which Luke alone, vs. 22, communicates (Stier), we cannot possibly assume. The consternation and the whispering of the Eleven, vs. 23, is only comprehensible if they now for the first time hear anything of it. Least of all can we understand a double designation of the traitor uttered on two different evenings, or a repetition of the intimation on one and the same evening. There remains, therefore, no other choice than to assume that Luke has communicated our Lord's declaration concerning Judas more κατὰ διάνοιαν than κατὰ ῥητόν, as indeed appears even from the incomplete form in which he, vs. 22, has noted down the Woe uttered upon Judas (comp. Matt. xxvi. 24; Mark xiv. 21). It is especially the *beginning* of the discovery of the traitor, as previously the beginning of the paschal celebration, which Luke places in the foreground.

With Me on the table.—Very fine is the remark of BENGEL: "*mecum, non vobiscum ait. Proditorem igitur a reliquis discipulis segregans, sibi uni jam cum into, tanquam hoste quidem, rem esse docet.*" If, however, we assume that Luke relates merely the main fact, then it will hardly be necessary to paraphrase with Bengel a "*manus quæ sacram cænam sumpsit.*" Quite as well may we here insert in thought: The hand which but just now, as an instrument in the eating of the *Passover*, was stretched out upon the table. As well the deep affliction as the displeasure of our Lord exhibits itself in these words; but very peculiarly does His long-suffering reveal itself in this, that He yet endures in His presence the traitor whose shameful plan He penetrates. As to the rest, the formula of commencement that now follows: πλὴν ἰδού, which plainly shows that the discourse passes over to something else, of itself entitles us to give up any direct connection of vs. 21 with vs. 20. According to our view, this expression utters in a freer form the same thing which we read Matt. xxvi. 21; Mark xiv. 18; John xiii. 21, while vs. 22 (*see* parallel) appears again to have been spoken some moments after.

Vs. 22. For truly the Son of Man goeth.—"Ὅτι states the ground why the Lord could again, as already previously, Matt. xxvi. 2, speak of a παραδιδόναι. "The Son of Man," that is, "goes, it is true, κατὰ τὸ ὡρισμένον" (Matthew and Mark, καθὼς γέγραπται, and that περὶ αὐτοῦ). According to the counsel of God predicted in the prophetical Scriptures, the Son of Man must necessarily die, but by no means does this take away the responsibility of him who threatens voluntarily to become the instrument of His death (πλὴν οὐαί). A word of warning for Judas before he took the decisive step, in order even on the verge of the abyss to open his eyes. With a fearful mixture of compassion and intense displeasure, our Lord is absorbed in the fate which impends over the traitor. Perfectly conscious of His own dignity, He feels that no other crime can be placed by the side of this; fully acquainted with the secrets of eternity, He sees that no restoration from this terrible wretchedness is to be expected. Too strong would the expression have been which our Lord (according to Matthew and Mark alone) yet adds, "it had been better for that man if he had never been born," if He had seen glimmering even in the extremest distance one single ray of light, in the night of the eternal doom pronounced upon Judas. "It is the immeasurable fall and the immeasurable curse which He so designates; the Woe which He pronounces upon Judas is a deep Woe of His soul; He profoundly pities that man even back unto his birth. He is troubled so much about the time and eternity of this man, that thereat He can forget His own woe which that man is preparing for Him." Lange. [This declaration of our Lord: "Good were it for that man if he had never been born," is in reality the strongest argument in the whole Bible against the doctrine of a final restoration of all men, an argument which it appears to me that we have a right to regard as perfectly conclusive.*—C. C. S.]

Vs. 23. **And they began.**—Comp. Matt. xxvi. 22; Mark xiv. 19; John xiii. 22 *seq.* A vivid representation of the disputation which soon arose among them. That Luke does not bring the tragic scene completely to a close, is a new proof that he is by no means here concerned for the completeness of his account. Comp. further the Exegetical and Critical remarks on the parallel passages in Matthew and Mark.

DOCTRINAL AND ETHICAL.

1. See on the parallel passages in Matthew, Mark, and John. Worthy of consideration also are the representations of the Last Supper of our Lord given by Christian art, not only the world-renowned one of Leonardo da Vinci, but also of Giotto, Ghirlandajo, Signorelli, Gorgione, Raphael, Juan de Juanes, Carlo Dolce, Poussin, Thorwaldsen, and others.

2. Our Lord's longing for the eating of *this* Passover with His disciples, is one of the most affecting revelations of His all-surpassing love of sinners, which are preserved to us in the Gospel. It is as if He longs for the death which is to give life to the world. But, furthermore, the prospect given on this occasion of a perfect festal celebration in the kingdom of God, encourages us also to the assertion that His own blessedness, capable of infinite increase, will only then be fully perfected when the kingdom of God shall have fully come, and that He does not less long to see His people with Him than they can ever long to be with Him.

3. Not sufficiently can we admire our Lord's wisdom and greatness which become visible in the institution of the Lord's Supper. This is meant to assure the disciples, who had never been able to believe in His dying, of His impending death; it is to place before them this death, which was so offensive to them, in the most comforting light, εἰς ἄφεσιν ἁμαρτ. It is finally to oblige them to a continual remembrance of this death, and thus to bind them most intimately together with one another, as well as with the Lord, and with the believers of all following times. The institution of the Lord's Supper is no fruit of a momentary inspiration, or of a sudden excitement of feeling, but is evidently the result of a previously carefully developed plan. With the sure knowledge of His approaching suffering our Lord unites the clear consciousness of the blessed effect of His death; with His love for His disciples, which causes Him entirely to forget Himself, a wisdom which determines Him even during this meal, and at the right hour of the same, to prepare a strengthening cordial for their faith, their love and hope; with His care for them a salutary institution for the maintaining, uniting, and training of His Church for all following time. Never can His Church be thankful enough to Him for the rich treasures which He bequeathed to her in this institution.

4. That the Holy Communion, which is intended for the union of all believers in Jesus Christ, has been the very cause of the most intense controversy, is certainly one of the most mournful phenomena which the history of Christendom and the Reformation has to show. Nowhere does the apple of discord make a more mournful impression than when it is thrown upon the table of love. So much the more fortunate is it that the blessing of the celebration of the Lord's Supper is not necessarily dependent on the interpretation of the words of institution. In reference to this last we have only to place ourselves in the position of the disciples, and to inquire how they, it is likely, understood the Master, in order immediately to recognize the full preposterousness of the doctrine of Transubstantiation. Therewith, however, we do not mean that the strictly Lutheran or the old Reformed interpretation does not yet leave many difficulties unsettled. Strauss was not wrong when he, in this respect, more impartially than many a dogmatic author, wrote: "To the writers of our gospels the bread in the Lord's Supper *was* the body of Christ; but had any one, therefore, asked them whether the bread was changed, they would have denied it; had any one spoken to them of a receiving the body with and under the species of bread, they would not have understood this; had one concluded that therefrom the bread merely *signified* the body, they would not have found themselves satisfied with that." It could be wished that all Christians would unite in this proposition, that in the Lord's Supper there takes place not only a symbolical celebration of the death of Christ, but a real communication of Christ Himself to believers, so that He at this table gives Himself to them to be beheld and to be enjoyed in the whole fulness of His saving love. That in John vi. the idea of the Lord's Supper stands in the background, although the instruction there given does not refer immediately to the Communion, hardly admits of doubt, 1 Cor. x. 16, 17. If only the mystery of the real personal communion with Christ is believingly acknowledged as the mystery of the Holy Supper, then the subordinate question whether this self-communication of our Lord to His people takes place in a *corporeal* or exclusively in a *spiritual* way, need not really divide the members of the Evangelical Church forever from each other. [This statement, though very true, has little significance in this country, where the doctrine of Consubstantiation is hardly known.—C. C. S.] That the decidedly Zuinglian interpretation has *its* truth, but not the *full* truth, is recognized more and more generally by believing theology in the Reformed Church. Compare the admirable monograph of Ebrard, 1845, and on the Lutheran side that of Kahnis, 1851, to say nothing of the manifold observations on this subject in RUDELBACH and GUERIKE's *Zeitschrift für Lutherische Theologie*. In a critical way, the doctrine of the Supper has been in the most recent period investigated with a rather negative result by L. J. Rückert at Jena. A very weighty article has been furnished by JULIUS MÜLLER in *Herzog's Real-Encyclopädie*. As to the rest, we must refer the reader to the history of doctrines.

---

* [Dr. Schaff, in his book on the *Sin against the Holy Ghost*, considers this passage conclusive against the apokatastasis, since an *endless* happiness even after millions of years of pain "would be preferable to non-existence."]

5. That the discovery of the traitor belongs to the most affecting and extraordinary moments in the life of our Lord, we should believe even if this did not clearly appear in the Evangelical accounts, nay, even in the brief statement of Luke. So, much the more adorable is His composure, long-suffering, and self-control on the one hand, His grave earnestness, His displeasure, and His wrath on the other hand. The first separation which here goes on in this circle of the disciples between light and darkness, is the beginning of a continuous process of purification, and the prophecy of the κρίσις of the great day.

6. "He hath heartily desired to die for us—who would not heartily desire to live in Him? Christ is more eager to make us partakers of His benefits than we to receive them from Him." Tauler.

HOMILETICAL AND PRACTICAL.

The last assembling of the Lord with His disciples.—The longing of our Lord for the last Passover: 1. How it exhibits itself; 2. from what it springs; 3. to what it quickens.—The paschal cup the last bodily refreshment of our Lord before His suffering.—The feast of the redeemed in the perfected kingdom of God, the fulfilment and glorification of the Israelitish Passover.—We also have the Paschal Lamb, that is, Christ, sacrificed for us, 1 Cor. v. 7.—The coincidence and the diversity, the agreement and the difference between the Passover of the Old and the Supper of the New Covenant. Through both: 1. A perfect redemption is sealed; 2. a blessed fellowship founded; 3. a glorious prospect opened; the Passover points to the Communion, the Communion to the marriage-supper of the Lamb, Rev. xix. 9.—The noblest gifts of nature sanctified into symbols of grace.—The atonement of love.—The institution of the Lord's Supper in its high significance: 1. For our Lord; 2. for His Apostles; 3. for all following times.—The fellowship in the Communion: 1. Of our Lord with His people; 2. of believers with one another; 3. of earth with heaven.—"This do in remembrance of Me": 1. A pregnant command; 2. a holy command; 3. a salutary command.—The feast of the New Covenant: 1. The fulfilment of that which-is only intimated in the Old Covenant; 2. the prophecy of that which shall hereafter be enjoyed at the heavenly feast.—The institution of the Lord's Supper a revelation of the Prophetical, the Priestly, and the Kingly character of our Lord.—The high significance which our Lord, in distinction from every other stage of His earthly manifestation, attributes to His suffering and death.—The institution of the Lord's Supper essentially inexplicable to him who in the death of our Lord sees only a confirmation of His teaching, an exalted example, a striking revelation of the forgiving love of God, but no actual expiatory sacrifice.—The Lord's Supper: 1. A memorial supper; 2. a covenant supper; 3. a supper of love.—How our Lord in the Communion gives Himself to His own: 1. To be beheld; 2. to be enjoyed; 3. to be adored.—The devil among the disciples, John vi. 70.—Jesus over against Judas: 1. His immaculate purity over against the enormous guilt; 2. His infallible knowledge over against the deep blindness; 3. His unshakable composure over against the painful disquiet; 4. His measureless love over against the burning hatred of the traitor.—Jesus the Searcher of all hearts.—The discovery of the traitor; it shows us: 1. What our Lord once suffered here on earth; 2. what He now is in heaven; 3. what He shall hereafter do at the end of the world.—Jesus glorified by the way in which He discovers the traitor, comp. John xiii. 30, 31. He reveals in this way: 1. A knowledge deceived by no illusive guise; 2. an affliction marred by no petty weakness; 3. a love cooled by no wickedness; 4. an anger accompanied with no ignoble passion.—The night of the betrayal: 1. From its dark; 2. from its bright, side.—Even on the Communion-table, as on the Paschal board, our Lord sees the hand of His betrayer stretched out.—Here is more than David, Ps. xli. 10.—When our Lord utters a general warning, no one of His disciples may remain wholly indifferent, but each one is under obligation to enter into himself.

STARKE:—*Bibl. Würt.:*—Oh, how great a longing hath Jesus had for man's salvation!—(QUESNEL:—One communion prepares the way for another; they that have been celestially received Christ sacramentally shall there be celestially united with Him.—*Nova Bibl. Tub.:*—All our food we should, after Jesus' example, hallow by prayer and thanksgiving, 1 Cor. x. 31.—The foretaste of Divine goodness is even here so sweet and pleasant, what will the perfect enjoyment of blessedness be?—The Holy Communion must, in danger of life, and in the pains of death, be our best cordial and refreshment.—The Lord's Supper without the cup a maimed one.—Everything, it is true, takes place according to the providence of God, but not always according to the will of God.—Genuine test of a true Christian, to do his enemies good and let them eat with him, even at his table, out of his dish, Rom. xii. 20.—*Nova Bibl. Tub.:*—Nothing more necessary than self-examination.—We cannot answer for our own hearts without the grace of God.—Many a one thinks not that that shall come to pass with him which yet does come to pass.—HEUBNER:—When separated, let it be the spirit of Jesus that unites our hearts.—The hope of eternal communion in the presence of Jesus lightens separation to the Christian.—The righteous are ever concerned lest there should be anything evil hidden in them.—Christ Himself ascribes to His death atoning power.—Christ's love would gather His own around Him.—F. ARENS:—The Communion of our Lord: 1. The blessed mystery; 2. the rich springs of blessings; 3. the requisite condition of soul.—FLOREY:—The Holy Supper and feast of love: 1. Love has founded it; 2. of love does it remind us; 3. love celebrates it; 4. love blesses it.—The communion of our Lord the most admirable hour of solemnity in the house of God: 1. An hour of holy remembrance: 2. of blessed communion; 3. of loving brotherly union.—HARLESS:—The tree of the new creation of Christ.—ARNDT:—The discovery of the traitor a revelation: 1. Of Divine omniscience; 2. of holy love; 3. of fixed resolution.—KRUMMACHER:—*Passions-buch:* the denunciation of woe: 1. The awfulness of this denunciation; 2. the limits of its applicability.—J. SACHS, *Nouv. Serm.* i. p. 45:—*Sur la sentence de nôtre Seigneur contr. Judas.*—VAN DER PALM:—The greatness of our Lord visible in the institution of the Holy Communion.—W. HOFACKER:—Where does the holy meal of the Lord place us?—THOMASIUS:—(Judas); The steps to the abyss: 1. The evil lust in the heart; 2. the sin against the conscience; 3. the judgment of reprobacy.—BÖCKEL:—Jesus over against His betrayers.

4. Familiar and Farewell Discourses (Vss. 24–38).

(In part parallel with Matt. xxvi. 30–35; Mark xiv. 27–31; John xiii. 36–38.)

24 And there was also a strife [there arose also a contention¹] among them, which of
25 them should be accounted [appears to be, δοκεῖ²] the greatest. And he said unto them,
The kings of the Gentiles exercise lordship over them; and they that exercise authority
26 upon them are called benefactors. But ye *shall* not *be* so: but he that is greatest
among you, let him be as the younger; and he that is chief, as he that doth serve.
27 For whether [which] *is* greater, he that sitteth at meat [reclineth at table], or he that
serveth? *is* not he that sitteth at meat [reclineth at table]? but I am among you as he
28 that serveth. [But] Ye are they which have continued [*steadfastly*] with me in my
29 temptations. And I appoint unto you a kingdom, as my Father hath appointed unto
30 me; That ye may eat and drink at my table in my kingdom, and [ye shall] sit on
thrones judging the twelve tribes of Israel.
31 And the Lord said,³ Simon, Simon, behold, Satan hath desired *to have* you, that he
32 may sift *you* as wheat: But I have prayed for thee, that thy faith fail not: and when
thou art converted [or, hast hereafter returned to thyself], strengthen [στήρισον] thy
33 brethren. And he said unto him, Lord, I am ready to go with thee, both [or, even]
34 into prison and to death. And he said, I tell thee, Peter, the cock shall not crow this
day, before [until⁴] that thou shalt [have] thrice deny [denied] that thou knowest me.
35 And he said unto them, When I sent you without purse, and scrip [wallet], and shoes,
36 lacked ye any thing? And they said, Nothing. Then [Therefore] said he unto them,
But now, he that hath a purse, let him take *it*, and likewise *his* scrip [wallet]: and he
that hath no sword, let him sell his garment, and buy one [and he that hath not, let
37 him sell his garment, and buy a sword].⁵ For I say unto you, that this that is written
must yet⁶ be accomplished in me, And he was reckoned among the transgressors (Is.
38 liii. 12): for the things concerning me have an end [or, are fulfilling]. And they said,
Lord, behold, here *are* two swords. And he said unto them, It is enough.

[¹ Vs. 24.—Revised Version of the American Bible Union.—C. C. S.]
[² Vs. 24.—That is, as Bleek explains it, which of them was so conspicuous above the rest, that he appeared, could be recognized, as greatest—a question hardly consistent with Peter's supremacy.—C. C. S.]
³ Vs. 31.—This abruptly introduced formula of commencement appears, as in ch. vii. 31, somewhat suspicious. *See* Tischendorf. [B., L. omit it, but Cod. Sin., which so commonly agrees with B., here has it.—C. C. S.]
⁴ Vs. 34.—According to the reading of B., [Cod. Sin.,] L., Cursives, Lachmann, Tischendorf, [Meyer, Tregelles, Alford,] ἕως, which appears to deserve the preference above the *Recepta*, πρὶν ἤ.
[⁵ Vs. 36.—Ὁ μὴ ἔχων, πωλησάτω τὸ ἱμάτιον αὐτοῦ καὶ ἀγορασάτω μάχαιραν.—C. C. S.]
⁶ Vs. 37.—Ἔτι is omitted by Lachmann, [Tregelles,] according to A., B., D., [Cod. Sin.,] H., L., [Q.,] X., &c. Perhaps it was quite early interpolated for the purpose of giving this prophecy more prominence in reference to what precedes and follows. On the other hand, it may be conceived that it was quite early and unconsciously omitted on account of the immediately preceding ὅτι. [The latter appears much the more probable.—C. C. S.]

EXEGETICAL AND CRITICAL.

Vss. 24–30. Entirely peculiar to Luke.—Quite correctly explained by Ewald, p. 348. "Luke here puts together (vss. 21–38) a number of expressions of Jesus which, according to Matthew and Mark, are spoken partly earlier and partly later, as if this sublime point of the history were peculiarly adapted for attaching to the words of institution of the Holy Supper, similar thoughts respecting the faithfulness of the disciples towards Him." That the dispute with the disciples about rank took place even after the institution of the Communion, and discovery of the traitor, cannot be at all imagined. It must, therefore, together with the admonitions belonging to it, necessarily be placed before both events. Perhaps the thought on the impending departure of the Master brought the disciples entirely spontaneously to the inquiry, who then above all others was worthy to stand at the head of the company; or that some were ill content with their place at the feast-table.—This appears to us, at least, yet more probable than that the dispute arose about the question, who of them should discharge for their other brethren the business of foot-washing before the meal, not yet begun. For although this controversy, in all probability, had given occasion to the foot-washing,—before or at which the words, vss. 25–27, were probably spoken,—this act, and therefore also this discourse of our Lord, appears not to fall before the meal, but at the beginning of it. But however that may be, the dispute of the disciples gives our Lord not only occasion for a symbolical act, but also, moreover, for a special admonition.

Vs. 25. **The kings of the Gentiles.**—A commencement exactly adapted to make them at once feel that the temper which now came into view among them was essentially an ethnic one, and in this way deeply to shame them. It is known how often the name of Euergetes was given to Roman Emperors, and also to other princes, for instance, Ptolemæus Euergetes, and others. The Apostles give only too plain a note of being animated by the same spirit of pride with those who listen to such a flattery with complacency.

Vs. 26. **But ye shall not be so.**—Our Lord recognizes that His own disciples in a certain sense are kings, but he will have them in the establishment of their kingly rights distinguish themselves in a very important point from the princes of earth. To become more humble they should regard as an elevation, and serviceable love as the sum of their greatness. Only then would they submit themselves to the immutable constitution of the kingdom of God; only then would they bear the King's image. Whoever indeed was the greatest among them, he must become as the younger, νεώτερος, whose business it naturally was, as a rule, to serve the others (Acts v. 6–10), and even so the *dux gregis* must prove his superiority by showing himself the most zealous *diaconus*. Far from levelling down all distinction of rank and office in the circle of His disciples, our Lord here recognizes a real aristocracy in the Christian sphere, but an aristocracy of humility, which He, indeed, does not merely demand, but which He also in His own example sets forth.

Vs. 27. **For which is greater.**—Although it remains true that the reference to the foot-washing is not directly necessary, since our Lord, even besides this, might on account of what He does during the meal, as well as on account of the whole of His self-surrender, well call Himself the διάκονος of His people, yet it is true, on the other hand, that under the Johannean picture of the foot-washing, one could set no more congruous and beautiful motto than the utterance which Luke alone has here preserved to us: "I am among you as he that serveth." He appeals to the position which He at this moment occupies among them,—a position in which every guise of a superiority falls away. In words our Saviour had already previously expressed the same thought (Matt. xx. 25-28), but now He adds to the word the deed.

Vs. 28. **But ye are they.**—If we assume that vss. 28–30 were spoken *uno tenore* with vss. 25–27, then certainly the most natural connection of thought (Meyer) is this: that our Lord, upon this humiliation of His disciples, now also causes their true elevation to follow, by assuring them of their future glory in His Messianic kingdom. We know not, however, what should hinder us from assuming that these words were uttered somewhat later on this evening. Entirely arbitrary is the assertion (De Wette, Strauss), that these words here stand out of all historical connection, and contain only a modified repetition of the promise given Matt. xix. 28. It appears to us far more probable that they belong in the portion of the discourse after the foot-washing and before the discovery of the traitor, of which also John (ch. xiii. 12–20) has communicated to us some portion. Not incongruously may they be attached to John xiii. 20, and that in this way: that our Lord now praises and encourages His faithful disciples, after He had just thrown upon the traitor a look of warning, vs. 21 seq. It is with Him, in His increasing agitation of spirit, a necessity to turn His eyes from the unfaithful one to the faithful ones, and to show to them how dear to Him the Apostolic circle yet remains, in spite of the sorrow which the unfaithful apostle has caused Him.

Continued steadfastly . . . in My temptations, πειρασμοῖς μου.—Just the word for Luke, according to whom Satan, ch. iv. 13, even after the forty days' temptation in the wilderness, had only departed from the Lord ἄχρι καιροῦ, so that according to him, the whole earthly life of Jesus is represented as a continuous temptation. In the mouth of Jesus this word points decidedly to this painful and tempting experience of life, through which His obedience to the Father had to be exercised and perfected. In the midst of all these conditions, it redounded to the no small praise of His disciples that they had so faithfully continued with Him (διαμεμενηκότες). Without adding a word upon their manifold weaknesses, He does justice with manifest pleasure to their sincerity and their steadfastness,—the direct opposite, it is true, to the temper of mind which He expresses, ch. ix. 41, and yet the one utterance is as natural as the other,—each in its own peculiar connection.

Vs. 29. **And I appoint unto you a kingdom, as My Father hath appointed unto Me.**—To the mention of that which the disciples have been for Him, our Lord now adds an intimation of what He has purposed for them. Διατίθεμαι signifies not only a bestowal or assurance, but a disposition such as a dying man forms when he makes his will for those left behind. That our Lord bequeaths to them the kingdom by a particular institution— namely, by the Communion, is not directly said; even without such a reference to the Supper, the promise preserves its full truth and force. It is in this of course understood that the verb, when our Lord uses it of the Father, who can never see death, καθὼς διέθετό μοι, must be understood *cum grano salis*. The sublimity of such an expression can be better felt than described. The poor Nazarene, who bequeaths to His disciples not one penny, and whose garments after a few hours are to be parted under His eyes on the Cross, here bequeaths to His friends, as the reward of their immovable fidelity, a more than royal inheritance, and therewith even removes the disparity that yet lay between Him and them. There exists a noteworthy, as yet too little noted, coincidence between this utterance and that of the Intercessory Prayer (John xvii. 22), which serves for a new proof of the higher unity of the Synoptical and the Johannean Christ.

Vs. 30. **That ye may eat.**—An allusion to the purpose, and secondly, to the inestimable fruit of this bequest, by which there is prepared for them as well a rich enjoyment as also an imperishable honor. The *enjoyment* is this: that our Lord in the Messianic kingdom entertains them at His table; the familiar Biblical imagery is here also chosen with preference, not only in view of the already instituted Holy Supper, but also by occasion of the present Paschal celebration; the *honor* is, that they are appointed as judges over the twelve tribes of Israel. It is commonly believed that the mention in particular of the twelve thrones which appears Matt. xix. 28, was omitted here on account of the apostasy of Judas. It may, however, also be that this altered form is connected with the freer character of our Lord's discourse in Luke. Almost too refined is the question which Bengel adjoins to the mention of the φυλαί: "*Singuline singulas?* We know, moreover, how our glorified Lord opens this same prospect, only somewhat modified, for all His friends, Rev. ii. iii., and how also the Apostle Paul states the judging of the world at the Parusia of the Lord as a prerogative which is intended for all His saints, 1 Cor. vi. 2.

Vs. 31. **Simon, Simon.**—We agree with those who believe that a double intimation of Peter's denial took place; the one even in the Paschal hall, the other on the way to Gethsemane, which latter is exclusively mentioned by Matthew and Mark. Of the former John gives us an account (ch. xiii. 36–38); vss. 31, 32 of Luke appear to run parallel therewith. It took place, therefore, shortly after the institution of the Lord's Supper, immediately following the new commandment of brotherly love (John xiii. 34, 35). Very well may our Lord to the earnest warning (John xiii. 36–38) have yet added the words which Luke alone has preserved for us, and which as well by their form as by their character were fitted to make on the Apostle's heart the deepest impression. Even the double **Simon, Simon**, comp. Luke x. 41; Acts ix. 4, must have given him deeply to feel that he soon would not be like a rock, but like an unsteady reed. The Biblical mode of speech: "Satan hath desired you, ardently entreated for you," points back to the prologue of the book of **Job**. Note the distinction between the plural, ὑμᾶς (vs. 31), and the singular (vs. 32), περὶ σοῦ. Without any one having known it, there had to-day the most fearful danger threatened *all* the disciples; but no one more than Peter, who had least feared it, and yet had been the object of the very special personal intercession of his faithful Lord,—Τοῦ σινιάσαι. "The word has not been preserved to us elsewhere, but the signification is not doubtful. The *tertium comparationis* is the testing ταράσσειν: as the wheat is shaken in the sieve that the chaff may thereby separate itself from the wheat and fall out, so will Satan also disquiet and terrify you through persecutions, dangers, tribulations, in order to bring your faithfulness towards Me to apostasy." Meyer.

Vs. 32. **But I.**—In this discourse of our Lord also, His person forms the immovable centre. His majestic ἐγὼ δέ, on the one hand plants itself in the way of Satan's threatening, and on the other hand stands in opposition to the direct καὶ σύ, which immediately follows thereon. First has our Lord granted His disciple a look into the crafty plottings of hell; now does He grant him to look up into the heaven of his loving Saviour's heart. But for *whom* hath the Lord prayed? This time especially for Peter: "*Totus sane hic sermo Domini praesupponit, Petrum esse primum apostolorum, quo stante aut cadente ceteri aut minus aut magis periclitarentur.*" Bengel. *When?* After He had penetrated Satan's crafty plotting in all its depth. *For what?* Our Lord does not express Himself with many words thereabout. By no means that Peter might entirely escape the sifting, comp. John xvii. 15. *With what purpose?* In order that (ἵνα) his faith may not cease (ἐκλείπῃ), since, indeed, his whole energy for resistance would be lost if the faith which he had so often confessed should no longer remain in him, comp. 2 Tim. iv. 7. *With what result?* The prayer is heard; Peter will indeed fall, but he will also rise again: καὶ σύ ποτε ἐπιστρέψας. **When thou art converted.**—There is, therefore, predicted for Peter an ἐπιστροφή visible to others, which was to be the consequence of an inward μετάνοια. Through what depths of sorrow and contrition the way should lead to this height is as yet wisely concealed from him, but in this very night he experiences it.—**Strengthen thy brethren.**—"*My* brethren, our Lord does not here say, as in John xx. 17; nor yet "*ours*," but *thy* brethren, since He here conceives them as afflicted with the same weakness which should bring Peter to so deep a fall. Thus does the address return again obliquely to the ὑμᾶς, vs. 31. How Peter afterwards strengthened his fellow-apostles by his word and example, appears plainly from the Acts. How he strengthened his fellow-believers, is manifest in his Epistles; but how little he was as yet on the way to this conversion, and how little he was fitted for this strengthening of others, appears in the words with which he at the same instant answers this address.

Vs. 33. **Lord, I am ready to go with Thee.**—Μετὰ σοῦ he places emphatically first, to designate the source from which his exultant feeling of strength proceeds; he conceives the threatening danger in a twofold form, as death or imprisonment; but love will surely give him strength to defy both. It is as if he would thereby intimate that the Lord's intercession for him had not been so especially necessary.

Vs. 34. **I tell thee, Peter.**—Now not *Simon*, though he might have doubly deserved it, but, *Peter;* inasmuch as our Lord places Himself in the position of the man who, in his own eyes, stands there so rock-fast. In language free of all ambiguity, He now announces to him what He had just made known to him in Biblical allusions, in order that the possibility of a misunderstanding may no longer remain. Peter will even deny that he knows the Master, ἀπαρνήσῃ μὴ εἰδέναι με, properly a double pleonastic negation, as in ch. xx. 27, on which account also some MSS., although without sufficient critical grounds, have omitted μή. Respecting the prediction of Peter's denial itself, comp. moreover LANGE on Matt. xxvi. 34.

Vs. 35. **And He said unto them.**—From Peter the address of our Lord now turns, after a short pause, again to the whole circle of disciples. That our Lord uttered the words, vss. 35–38, when all were outside of the Paschal hall, immediately before the entrance into Gethsemane, we consider as less probable. For these words are not preceded by the second but the first announcement of Peter's denial; moreover, they bear so familiar a character, that they appear to belong as yet to the feast table. We believe that we ought to assign them a place even immediately after vss. 31–34—namely, so that our Lord now, to the description of the *inward* danger which threatens His disciples, joins the description of the *outward* distress that impends over them.—As friends in the parting hour like to while away yet a season with their thoughts in the sweet days of the past, so does our Lord now lead back the Eleven into the period which then perhaps appeared to them to be a very tiresome one, but which, in comparison with this night, might yet be called a peaceful and happy one. He points them back to the time when they first preached the Gospel in Galilee, and on the part of many had found open ears and hearts, ch. ix. 1–6. Then they had in no respect had want, no care had oppressed them; but now it was another time. So unacquainted are they as yet with that which to-night impends, that the Saviour can bring to them in no other way a presentiment of it than by holding up to them the sharp contrast of *then* and *now*. He enjoins on them the direct opposite of that which He had then commanded them. Once the least care was superfluous, now the most anxious care was not too much.

Vs. 36. **Therefore He said.**—Οὖν subjoins the opposite of their acknowledgment, that at that time they did not lack the least thing. **He that hath a purse, let him take it,** ἀράτω: Let him not leave it at home, but take it with him on the journey, in order by so careful a preparation to assure himself against any possibility of a lack. Even so let him who possesses a wallet, hasten to avail himself of it. **And he that hath not,** neither purse nor wallet, let him **sell his garment,** which he otherwise would at last expose to robbery, **and buy**—not a purse or a wallet, but what is now more indispensable than clothing and food—a **sword.** Self-defence is now not only an urgent necessity, but the first necessity of all. This last word we have to understand, not in an allegorical, but in a parabolical sense. If one understands (Olshausen) the spiritual sword (Eph. vi. 17), he is then also obliged to give to the garment, the wallet, and the shoes a spiritual signification. Our Lord will simply, in a concrete pictorial form, represent to His disciples the right and the duty of necessary defence, in order that they may, by the very opposition to the former command (vs. 35), finally come to the consciousness that an entirely peculiar danger shall break in upon them.

Vs. 37. **For I say unto you.**—The rendering of an immediate and sufficient reason for the previously apparently so enigmatical command. If matters go even so far with the Master that He is reckoned with the malefactors, then His disciples also may well have occasion to fear the worst. Here again we find an allusion to the truth, that the impending fulfilment of the prophecy is grounded in an irrevocable Must ; at the same time also a proof in what light our Lord regarded the well-known prophecy (Is. liii). He numbers it among the περὶ ἐμοῦ sc. γεγραμμένα (not "The circumstances surrounding Me," Meyer), in respect to which He gives the assurance that they τέλος ἔχει. Excessively feeble would this expression be, if He meant to say nothing else than: "With Me, as with that subject of Isaiah's prophecy, matters are coming to an end." Our Lord feels and knows that He is Himself truly the Subject of the prophecy of Isaiah, and, therefore, it cannot here be the *end*, in the common sense of the word, but only the *accomplishment*, in the sense of the τετέλεσται (John xix. 30), that is spoken of. Our Lord therewith undoubtedly states the ground (γάρ), why He expects for Himself nothing less than the fulfilment also of Isaiah liii. 12. Everything that is written of the Messiah must go into complete fulfilment, and that can only be done when this declaration also, in a certain sense the crown of the whole prophetic announcement of the Passion, is accomplished in and on Him. "If this τοῦτο yet comes to pass, because all must come to pass, then the fulfilment and coming to pass has with this undoubtedly an end." Stier.

Vs. 38. **Lord, behold here are two swords.** —It is unquestionably surprising that the disciples have come at once in possession of these swords, and not probable that they were found in the Passover hall itself. Bengel. It is, however, known that the Galileans were wont to travel armed; perhaps Peter and another disciple had taken their swords with them in the journey towards the capital, in the presentiment of a danger on this very evening. Certain it is that they have them at all events now lying ready, and at the word of our Lord, vs. 36, they think that they can use them very well. To understand large butcher-knives for the Paschal lamb (Chrysostom) sounds singular.

It is enough, ἱκανόν ἐστι.—If it were possible for us to imagine our Lord for a moment in the Paschal night with a melancholy smile on His heavenly countenance, it would be at the affair of the two swords. Two swords over against the whole might of the world, of hell, and of death, which were to engage in the assault upon Him! He accounts it impossible to make the whole preposterousness of this thought as visible to them as it is to Himself, and, therefore, breaks off the conversation on the subject, in the tone of one who is conscious that others would not yet understand Him, and who, therefore, holds all further speech unprofitable. A double sense (Olshausen, De Wette), we do not find here, but we may, a melancholy irony.

We apprehend that after this conversation : 1. The great Hallel was sung; 2. the farewell discourse (John, ch. xiv. 17) held; 3. the Paschal hall left; 4. that on the way to Gethsemane the second prediction of the unfaithfulness of Peter and of his fellow-disciples took place, which was with one voice repelled. All this Luke passes over in silence, in order to lead us without further detention immediately to Gethsemane. *See* LEX *Evang. Harm.* p. 93.

DOCTRINAL AND ETHICAL.

1. While on the one hand the renewed dispute among the disciples as to rank on this very evening is a mournful proof of how deeply pride and self-seeking remain rooted even in the soul that was the beginnings of faith and renewal; so, on the other hand, is the peculiar way in which our Lord at the Paschal table opposes this perversity, a new revelation of His wisdom, love, and faithfulness. The almost literal repetition of an earlier, yet already forgotten, admonition, must of itself have doubly shamed His discordant friends. Therewith He recalls to their memory an hour in which the same perverse disposition had become visible in them, and had been by Him combated powerfully, indeed, yet, as now appeared, in vain. It is the fundamental law of His kingdom, which He now will, as it were, in the style of a lapidary and in a stereotyped form, engrave anew in the fleshy tables of the hearts of His own; and in order to impress it on them the more deeply, He represents it to their sight by an act, which must have remained eternally unforgotten by them.

2. "But I am among you as he that serveth." This word is first of all the brief summary of the whole now almost completed earthly life of Jesus in humiliation. Comp. Matt. xx. 28; Phil. ii. 5–11; 2 Cor. viii. 9. It is, secondly, the worthy initiation of a Passion in which He was again to serve His own in a manner entirely different from hitherto, by this, that He humiliated Himself now more deeply than ever; and finally, it is even the watchword of His heavenly life, now that He is enthroned at the right hand of God; for even there upon the throne He rules by serving, and never reveals His glory more brilliantly than in His condescending love.

3. Not enough can we here in the antechamber of the Passion admire the sublime, entirely unique self-consciousness of our Lord. While He certainly knows that He is at the very point of being reckoned with the transgressors, He yet claims for His disciples no lesser rank than that which earthly potentates and kings possess (vss. 25, 26). Nowhere has He on earth to lay His head, and yet He bequeaths to them, as if by testament, the highest place of honor in the kingdom of God, and inaugurates them as future judges of the twelve tribes of Israel. With every moment He is going down deeper into the night of suffering, and yet He shows even now especially that the secrets of the heart, of the future, and of the spiritual world, lie naked and uncovered before Him. He feels that He is in the fullest sense of the word the Son in whom the Father is well pleased (vs. 29), the centre of the prophetic Scripture (vs. 37), yea, the Vanquisher of Satan (vss. 31,

32), and yet all this hinders Him not from walking in the midst of His own as their servant, and bearing their unreceptiveness with a patience which can never be sufficiently praised with human tongues.

4. From this utterance of our Lord it appears that the kingdom of darkness was in more than common activity and intense exertion when the night of the betrayal had fallen. Not Judas alone (vs. 32), the circle of the faithful disciples also was the target of the Satanic arrows. To understand such expressions only figuratively, and in view of them to deny the existence and the influence of Satan, is pure rationalistic caprice. On the contrary, there appears very evidently from this that the existence of a kingdom of darkness peopled by personal evil spirits is nothing less than a terrible reality. And it is certainly a permitted conclusion *a minori ad majus* that if Satan desired to sift the disciples as wheat, he can, least of all, have left our Lord untouched, either in Gethsemane or on Golgotha.

5. The assurance of our Lord that He had prayed for Peter, is the solid basis for the evangelical doctrine of the intercession of the Saviour for His people in heaven, Rom. viii. 34; Heb. vii. 25; ix. 24; 1 John ii. 1. Thereby He shows us at the same time the supreme and final goal which the Christian, in his prayer for himself, must also keep before his eyes, namely, that his faith fail not. Whoever suffers shipwreck of his faith (1 Tim. i. 19), suffers loss not only of his goods but also of his life.

6. The decided prediction of Peter's denial belongs to the sublimest self-revelations of the humiliated Saviour. Gloriously does there shine out from this His wisdom, His love, His faithfulness, but far more gloriously yet does there beam forth from these words upon us, His Divine knowledge. For He announces not only in a general way that Peter especially will succumb to the impending trial—to any one acquainted with men, that looked somewhat more deeply than common, that would not have been so very difficult—but He gives beforehand every particular; the *threefold* denial, the *cock-crowing*, the *form* of the denial—ἀπαρνήσῃ μὴ εἰδέναι με—not only as possible but as certainly occurring, and shows thereby that He views with perfectly clear vision not only the hidden but also the seemingly casual. The assertions that the expression "before the cock crow" is only meant to denote: "before the morning shall break;" moreover, that the "*three times*" (vs. 34) signifies only an indefinite round number, and that the prophecy only took this exactly definite form afterwards from the event (Strauss and others), rest upon presuppositions which are destitute of every exegetical proof, as well as of all historical ground. No example can be brought of THREE signifying anything else than what it expresses, and it is forgotten that the cock-crowing is so far from being anything unessential that, according to Mark, it must even take place twice. So far, however, from an unavoidable *fate* being here foretold to Peter, there is, on the other hand, at the basis of this admonition the intent of guarding him against the danger. Peter did not deny our Lord *because* it was previously foretold, but it was foretold to him that he might not do it. While Satan's design was so to sift the wheat that it should be found only as chaff, our Lord, on the other hand, will so sift it that it may be cleansed from the chaff, may come forth from the trial as good wheat. Had the disciple but comprehended the intimation of his Master, and reconciled himself to the thought that his Master was to endure the hard struggle without him! But, alas, the very one who fancies himself to be stronger than ten other men, very soon gives the proof that he is even weaker than a single woman.

7. The Lord would certainly have avoided the expression as to buying a sword for threatening danger, if He had willed that His disciples in no case should think of self-defence with outward weapons. Their error lies only in this, that they in this moment, and over against the more than earthly might which now threatens them, will have recourse to ordinary weapons. Judge then how thoroughly it must conflict with the spirit and mission of our Lord when the Roman Curia vaunts itself of the possession of the two swords of Peter, and a Boniface the VIIIth, for example, from this very passage, believed himself to be able to prove that the papal chair possesses as well the right of spiritual as of secular jurisdiction. By the ἱκανόν ἐστι of our Lord, this folly is condemned in its very principle. "It is a sigh of the God-man which breathes like a sound of complaint over the Roman swords and stakes, over the armed camps of the Paulicians and Hussites, over all the violent measures of the New Testament time that are meant to further His cause."

HOMILETICAL AND PRACTICAL.

How little the disciples, even in the Paschal hall, are yet in a condition to comprehend the gravity of the moment and the temper of the Lord.—How much the disciples yet contribute to embitter to their Master even the still enjoyment of the last quiet evening.—The old Adam is not so quick to die.—The royal dignity of the disciples of our Lord: 1. Its high rank; 2. its holy requirements.—The heavenwide distinction between the flattering titles and the ruling character of many an earthly monarch.—*Esse quam videri*.—The way of willing humiliation the way of true greatness in the kingdom of God: 1. The ancient way; 2. the difficult way; 3. the safe way; 4. the blessed way.—Christ in the midst of His people as one that serves: 1. The character which as such an one He reveals, *a.* condescending, *b.* active, *c.* persevering love; 2. the requirement which He as such repeats, *a.* adore in this very thing His greatness, *b.* let yourself be served by Him, *c.* serve now others also for His sake.—Immutable faithfulness in the midst of severe temptation, is by our Lord: 1. Well borne in mind; 2. graciously praised; 3. a thousandfold rewarded.—The bequest of the dying Testator to His chosen friends.—The judicial function which our Lord above in heaven commits to those that suffer with Him on earth, 2 Tim. ii. 12.—The heavenly feast in the yet future kingdom of God: 1. The blessed Host; 2. the completed number of guests; 3. the infinite refreshment.—Simon Peter: 1. Dangerously threatened; 2. invisibly defended; 3. thoroughly converted; 4. in rich measure active for the strengthening of his brethren.—Satan intent on the destruction, the Lord on the deliverance, of Peter, Simon alone careless.—Jesus the Intercessor for His weak but sincere disciples.—How many a danger is averted from us unnoticed, even before we ourselves become aware of its approach.—The holy vocation of the converted one to strengthen his brethren: 1. That only he can do who is himself converted; 2. but this one should, would, and will then do it.—Even over against our Lord, unbelief will still be in the right.—He that trusteth in his own heart is a fool.—The dangerousness of a superficial excitement of feeling, instead of a deeply-rooted life of faith.—Let him that thinketh he standeth take heed lest he fall, 1 Cor. x. 12.—Even in the guidance of His most intimate disciples, our Lord not seldom strikes into an entirely different way afterwards from that which He followed earlier.—Rest once enjoyed no pledge of future security.—" Did ye ever lack anything? Lord, never anything." Admirable text for New Year's Eve.—On superfluity the disciple of our Lord must never reckon, 1 Tim. vi. 6–8.—Against extraordinary dangers the Christian must arm himself in extraordinary wise.—The prophetic word the light of our Lord upon His gloomy way to death.—On the Christian also must all be accomplished that is written, both concerning his suffering and concerning his glory.—The persevering incapability of the disciples to comprehend our Lord, one of the deepest sources of His hidden suffering.—Patience with unteachable friends a difficult art, yet sanctified by our Lord's example.

STARKE:—CRAMER:—Great people also come short.—Intestine wars have done the kingdom of God more harm than foreign ones.—Nothing can move us more powerfully to humility than the example of Christ.—Where the mind of Christ is, there is also the following of Him.—*Nova Bibl. Tub.:*—The cross suits Christ's servants better than lordship.—Whoever will be Christ's property must make himself ready for temptation.—Whom the Lord praises, he is praiseworthy, 2 Cor. x. 18.—QUESNEL: —Who can comprehend the dignities and advantages of a genuine disciple of Jesus?—The Lord Jesus' faithful servants shall be in heaven His fellow-rulers and fellow-kings.—CANSTEIN:—Ignorance, security, and presumption prepare Satan a way for his temptations.—The devil can do nothing without Divine permission.—Without Jesus' intercession our little ship of faith must suffer shipwreck.—OSIANDER: —The flesh before danger comes is courageous, and is only thoroughly convinced by an afflictive experience of its impotency.—To mean well is not everything in religion.—*Nova Bibl. Tub.:*—The sins that we shall commit the Lord Jesus knows beforehand. —It is edifying often to call to mind how God has led us.—BRENTIUS:—Faithful servants of God have a rich and mighty Lord.—One must accommodate himself to the time, be it good or bad.—Servants of God have not ever sunshine in their office.—See well to it how thou understandest Christ's word.—To the magistrate the secular sword is entrusted, to the minister the spiritual, Rom. xiii. 4; Ephes. vi. 17.

HEUBNER:—The attacks of the wicked must turn out for the best good of the saints.—Interceding prayer availeth much.—How many a wandering son has been saved by a pious mother's prayers! (Augustine and Monica).—Sins are as dangerous as they are because they may bring about the loss of our faith.—Unanxious service of the Lord makes life glad.—God always helps through.—PALMER (vss. 35, 36):—What there in the life of the disciples appears as a succession, must with us exist as simultaneous, joined by faith: 1. The admirable child-like trust that supports itself on experience; 2. the manly valor that bears a sword, indeed, but the sword of the Holy Ghost.—ARNDT (vss. 31-38):—The words of the loving providence of Jesus: 1. The words of His warning providence to Peter; 2. the words of His upholding providence to the other disciples.—F. W. KRUMMACHER, *Passions-buch*, p. 173 *seq.*:—The night conversation, how it unfolds to us the Mediator's heart of the great Friend of sinners: 1. In His conversation with Simon Peter; 2. in His utterance to the disciples altogether.

A. *The Deepening of the Conflict.* (CHS. XXII. 39—XXIII. 45.)

1. Gethsemane.

a. THE CONFLICT OF PRAYER (CH. XXII. 39-46).

(Parallel with Matt. xxvi. 36-46; Mark xiv. 32-42.)

39 And he came out, and went, as he was wont, to the mount of Olives; and his
40 [the[1]] disciples also followed him. And when he was at the place, he said unto them,
41 Pray that ye enter not into temptation. And he [himself] was withdrawn [withdrew]
42 from them about a stone's cast, and kneeled down, and prayed, Saying, Father, if thou
 be willing, [to] remove this cup from me:—nevertheless, not my will, but thine, be
43 done. And there appeared an angel unto him from heaven, strengthening him.
44 And being in an agony he prayed more earnestly: and his sweat was as it were great
45 drops of blood falling down to the ground.[2] And when he rose up from prayer and
46 was come to his [the] disciples, he found them sleeping for sorrow, And said unto them,
 Why sleep ye? rise and pray, lest ye enter into temptation.

[1] Vs. 39.—Without adequate authority the *Recepta* has μαθηταὶ αὐτοῦ.
[2] Vs. 41.—Respecting the state of the case critically with respect to vss. 43, 44, see *Exegetical* and *Critical* remarks.

EXEGETICAL AND CRITICAL.

Vs. 39. **And He came out.**—Here also Luke does not fail of his peculiarity. The account of Matthew and Mark respecting the agony of our Lord in Gethsemane is much more detailed and complete than his, and only from the union of the three accounts does it become possible to represent to ourselves distinctly the course of the event. Evidently

Luke condenses all, neither mentions the selection which our Lord made from among the disciples, nor the threefold repetition of the prayer, and passes over also the warning words of our Lord to Peter. On the other hand, we owe to him the mention of the bloody sweat and of the strengthening angel, as well as also his delicate psychological intimation, vs. 45, that the disciples were sleeping ἀπὸ τῆς λύπης. He alone defines the distance between the praying Saviour and the disciples, ὡσεὶ λίθου βολήν, vs. 41, and communicates the remark that the Mount of Olives was the place in which our Lord was commonly wont to pray, vs. 39. From all this it becomes evident that his account is invaluable for the complementing of the representation of Matthew and Mark, which, it is true, is more detailed and also more perfectly arranged.

As He was wont.—Comp. ch. xxi. 37. That our Lord goes straight thither is a new proof that the time is now past when He still sought to go out of the way of His enemies, for according to John xviii. 2, this place is known also to Judas, who will, therefore, undoubtedly seek Him there with the band, if he no longer finds Him in the paschal hall. At the same time it is a proof of the heavenly composure and clearness of mind which our Lord continually maintained. Not in the city, in the midst of the joyful acclamations of the paschal night, but without it, in the bosom of open nature, after He had previously strengthened Himself in solitary prayer to His Father, will He surrender Himself over to the hands of His enemies.—**At the place.**—The before-mentioned place where He would be; perhaps Luke does not mention the name Gethsemane because this was already sufficiently known through the evangelical tradition.

Vs. 40. **He said unto them, Pray.**—According to Luke it appears as if our Lord said this to all His disciples. From Matthew and Mark, however, we know that He took three of them with Himself deeper into the garden, and addressed them in about this manner. As is to be recognized by the infinitive, the μὴ εἰσελθεῖν εἰς πειρασμόν is to be the substance of their prayer. The πειρασμός can here, agreeably to the connection, be no other than the threatening danger of suffering shipwreck of their most holy faith by all that they were soon to experience.

Vs. 41. **And He Himself withdrew,** ἀπεσπάσθη ἀπ' αὐτῶν, Vulgate: "He was withdrawn from them." Correctly Schöttgen: "*Eleganter dicuntur ἀποσπᾶσθαι vel ἀποσπασθῆναι, qui ab amicissimorum amplexu vix divelli possunt ac discedere.*" Of course we have not to understand the word as if our Lord almost against His will, as it were, impelled on by secret might, separated Himself from the circle of His disciples, but simply thus, that He, following the constraint of His agitation of soul, with visible intensity of feeling and rapid steps, sought the still solitude.—'Ωσεὶ λίθου βολήν, the accusative of distance: since our Lord was not further removed from a stone's throw from His three friends, He was still near enough to them to be seen and heard by them, especially in the bright moonlight.

Kneeled down.—Stronger yet in Matthew and Mark: He fell down on His face on the earth. He cannot now pray standing with head erect, as so lately in the paschal hall. Luke evidently condenses the substance of the three prayers into one, although he also (vs. 44) indicates that our Lord prayed at least more than once.—**If Thou be willing,** εἰ βούλει, equivalent to, "If it can consist with Thy counsel." Grotius: "*Si tua decreta ferunt, ut alio modo tuæ gloriæ atque hominum saluti æque consulatur.*" Παρενεγκεῖν not infinitive for imperative (Bengel), but an aposiopesis, by which is admirably expressed that the prayer is, as it were, already taken back before it is entirely uttered. Note the distinction between εἰ βούλει and τὸ θέλημά σου; respecting the sense and the purpose of the prayer, *see* below.

Vs. 43. **And there appeared unto Him an angel.**—There are many questions to be asked here: 1. Respecting the genuineness of this statement. As is known, the words (vss. 43, 44) are wanting in A., B., Sahid, and other authorities.* Some have indicated their doubts by asterisks and obelisks. Lachmann has bracketed the words. The most of modern critics and exegetes, however, declare themselves in favor of their genuineness. It is assumed that they were, in all probability, omitted by the Orthodox, who found in this account something dishonoring to Jesus. *See* EPIPH., *Ancor*. 31, and besides, WETSTEIN, *ad loc.* On the other hand, no tenable ground can be assigned why any one should have interpolated these verses into the text if they did not originally stand in the Gospel of Luke. 2. Respecting the manner and purpose of this strengthening through an angel, there have been at all times the most exceedingly diverse opinions. Here also Dogmatics has evidently controlled Exegesis. Without reason has Olshausen here assumed a merely internal appearance, and spoken of the afflux of spiritual energies which were bestowed upon the Redeemer wrestling in the extremity of abandonment, although, on the other side, it is not to be denied that the possibility of perceiving the angelic manifestation at this moment was conditioned by the suffering and praying Redeemer's state of inward agitation; the text says also ὤφθη αὐτῷ, not ὤφθη αὐτοῖς. To make the strengthening a merely bodily strengthening (Hoffmann), is certainly quite as arbitrary as (De Wette) to understand a strengthening to prayer. We know not what unreasonableness there could be in the conception that here the holy ψυχή of our Lord, which was now seized by the intensest feeling of suffering, was strengthened by the brightening prospect of future joy, which was symbolized to Him by the friendly angelic appearance. With Bengel, however, we are disposed to believe that the strengthening mentioned took place *non per cohortationem*. 3. As respects the inquiry as to the time in which this appearance occurred, we can hardly believe that it (Dettinger) took place between the second and the third prayer of our Lord. If we attentively compare the evangelical accounts, we then see that the strengthening through the angel came in immediately after the first prayer—the most fervent and agonizing one—so that in consequence of it the anguish of soul had already at the second prayer in some measure subsided. It is true, Luke appears, considered entirely by himself, to lead us to another conception, but he has here also not wished so much to describe the course of the event in its different stages as to give a general view of the whole. The words, vs. 44, **and being in an agony He prayed more earnestly,** are not meant to denote what followed after the angelic manifestation, but that by which this manifestation was called forth and made necessary. With Meyer we take καί in the sense of "namely," and find not the consequence but the motive of the manifestation thereby inti-

---

* [They are found in Cod. Sin.—C. C. S.]

CHAP. XXII. 39–46.

mated. 4. Finally, as respects the credibility of this account, this is not lessened by the silence of the other Evangelists, and the very brevity, mysteriousness, and apparently unsatisfactory character of the representation of Luke speaks for its credibility. Whoever upon dogmatic grounds denies the possibility of angelophanies, cannot possibly accept this one either, but whoever acknowledges our Lord as that which His believing church have at all times held Him to be, will soon feel that the light of an angelic manifestation can make scarcely anywhere a more beneficent impression than in the night of these sufferings.

More earnestly, ἐκτενέστερον.—No wonder; He is in a veritable death-struggle (ἀγωνία), and summons up, therefore, all His energies to an unremitting struggle of prayer. Comp. Hosea xii. 4, 5. The most striking commentary on this expression is given undoubtedly by the Epistle to the Hebrews, which also bears a thoroughly Pauline coloring (ch. v. 7–9), where strong crying and tears are spoken of with which our Lord offered up His prayers and supplications to Him who was able to save Him from death. It is noteworthy that this last passage is brought up as proof, as well for the view that our Lord would deprecate the whole suffering of death, as also for the opinion that He would deprecate only this momentary anguish of soul. For the former view appeal is made especially to the πρὸς τὸν δυνάμενον σώζειν αὐτόν ἐκ θανάτου; for the other to the εἰσακουσθεὶς ἀπὸ τῆς εὐλαβείας. [The former interpretation is better, as the prevailing usage of the conjugates of εὐλάβεια in the New Testament decidedly favors the translation: "heard on account of His reverent fear," which, moreover, according to Robinson, is supported by all the Greek commentators.—C. C. S.]

And His sweat.—The reading ὡσεί deserves the preference above ὡς, and expresses, even as ch. iii. 28, a relative similarity. The question, answered sometimes negatively, sometimes positively, whether our Lord in Gethsemane really sweat blood, is primarily connected with another, namely, whether the weight of the comparison must be laid upon θρόμβοι or upon αἵματος. The latter is unquestionably more probable, since otherwise it is hard to conceive why Luke speaks of αἷμα at all if it is not meant to refer to the nature of the sweat. To understand actual drops of blood is, it is true, forbidden by ὡσεί, but, at all events, we must conceive them as heavy thick drops, which, mingled and colored for the most part with portions of blood, looked altogether like drops of blood. Comp. hereupon, the passages adduced by EBRARD, *Evang. Kritik.*, *ad loc.*, as well as also what HUG, *Gutachten, ad loc.*, remarks on historical grounds upon this distinction between a thin and thick sweat, which latter appears also to show itself in the case of those in the agonies of death. If we add to these now the medically certified cases of actual blood-sweat, and if we keep in mind the complete peculiarity of the condition in which the suffering Saviour is here found, we shall account it as unnecessary to understand here poetical embellishment (Schleiermacher) as mythical invention (Strauss and others).

Vs. 45. **Sleeping for sorrow.**—Not an excuse of the disciples, but an explanation of their seemingly strange condition, nor is there any ground to reject this explanation as unsatisfactory. Sorrow, it is true, makes men sleepless sometimes, but when it is very great it may so weary down the whole outer and inner man that one, as it were, sinks into a condition of stupor; nor do the Evangelists tell us that it was a common sound sleep. There may, moreover, unknown to the disciples, an influence on the side of the might of darkness have been exerted, which, while it in Gethsemane assaulted the Shepherd, is certainly not to be supposed to have left the sheep unassailed.

Vs. 46. **Why sleep ye?**—The more exact statement of the words of our Lord to the sleepers we find in Matthew and Mark. The account of Luke is too brief for us to have been able to get from it alone a satisfactory explanation of the case. We must conceive that our Lord after the third prayer so entirely recovered His composure that the sight of the still sleeping disciples now no longer distressed and disquieted Him. He granted them, on the other hand, this refreshment, which on this whole terrible night was not again to fall to their lot, and Himself for some moments guards their last transient rest (Matt. xxvi. 45a). Only when Judas approaches with the band does He bid them rise, knowing well that now not a instant more is to be lost, and admonishes them not only to expect the enemy in a waking condition, but also to go courageously forward to meet them. Only the spirit, not the form, of this last utterance is communicated by Luke, vs. 46, who here repeats the main substance of vs. 40. "We put this, therefore, in Luke to the account of the inexactness of the more remote observer." Stier.

DOCTRINAL AND ETHICAL.

1. Arrived at the *sanctum sanctorum* of the history of the Passion, a similar feeling seizes us to that which seized Moses (Exod. iii. 5), or Elijah (1 Kings xix. 13). Only a few intimations have the Evangelists communicated to us respecting the nature of this Passion. Not unjustly has it been at all times designated a *suffering of the soul*, because the conflict was carried on in the sphere of the ψυχή. Formerly Jesus had been troubled ἐν τῷ πνεύματι (John xii. 21); but now His ψυχή was as never before shaken and agitated. This soul is troubled by the terrific image of approaching death, although the spirit was pervaded by the clear consciousness that this death was the way to glory. In the so called High-priestly prayer—[What we call more commonly the Intercessory Prayer.—C. C. S.]—(John xvii.), the spirit celebrates its triumph; in the first part of the prayer in Gethsemane the soul utters its lamentations. The suffering springing from the soul overmasters also the body of our Lord, and brings Him into a conflict that may most strictly be called a mortal conflict. Unexpectedly does the anguish of soul overwhelm Him; like the billows of the sea, it rises and it falls, and even lifts itself so high that the Lord of angels can be refreshed by the strengthening of His heavenly servant. Like fragments of clotted blood (θρόμβοι) His sweat flows in streams to the earth, and like a worm must the Lamb of God writhe, before He conquers as a lion. Certainly there is here a mystery, of whose complete solution we must almost despair, on which account, therefore, it does not disturb us that the most diverse explanations of this enigma have been sought in the course of the ages. *See* on the parallel passage in Matt. p. 481. We also cannot refrain from making an attempt to find a satisfactory answer to the question: Whence now so unexampled an anguish?

2. We cannot be surprised that often the anguish of our Lord in Gethsemane has been conceived as something entirely peculiar, and, therefore, it has been asserted that He by the ποτήριον, for the passing away of which He prayed, meant not the whole suffering of death, but especially this anguish, which, if it had not subsided, would have hindered Him from bearing the suffering of death worthily and courageously. (*See* LANGE on Matthew and Mark; among the Dutch theologians, Heringa, Bouman, Vinke). On the other side, however, it cannot be denied that the former interpretation of the prayer finds a very powerful support in the grammatical exegesis, and it therefore cannot surprise us to see it already defended by Calvin. By the cup (ποτήριον) and the hour (ἡ ὥρα) our Lord designates commonly not a part, but the whole of His impending suffering. It is true, He here speaks definitely of τὸ ποτήριον τοῦτο, but so had He also, John xii. 27, prayed for deliverance ἐκ τῆς ὥρας ταύτης, which, however, certainly refers to nothing less than to the whole mortal passion. According to Mark xiv. 35, He prays in an entirely general way that ἡ ὥρα might pass over, by which we can hardly suppose anything else to be meant than the same ὥρα as in xiv. 41; comp. Matt. xxvi. 45; John H. 4; vii. 30; viii. 20; xiii. 1; xviii. 11, not to speak of Matt. xx. 22, 23; Mark x. 38. On the basis of all these passages we can do nothing else than, while submitting ourselves to better judgment, to subscribe to Bengel's expression: *ubi solus calix memoratur, passio intelligitur universa*. We need not, however, forget that the key to the complete solution of the enigma cannot be sought in the sphere of grammar, and that in a certain sense, the whole distinction between the momentary and entire suffering of Jesus helps us little. For in that moment the terrifying image of His collective suffering already presented itself before the soul of our Lord, and this, therefore, already really begins in His consciousness; it fares with Him as at the first bitter draught of vinegar on the Cross, Matt. xxvii. 34. The question as to the possibility of such a condition, can only be answered by looking at the nature of the suffering, as well as, on the other hand, at the theanthropic personality of our Lord.

3. The suffering impending over our Lord was, on the one hand, the most terrible revelation of the might of sin, on the other hand, the great means to the *atonement* for sin. Jews and heathen, friends and foes, Judas and Peter, the whole might of the world with its prince unite against Him, and in this whole might He is at the same time to feel the whole curse of sin: as Representative of sinful mankind, He is to place Himself before the judgment of God: He is to be made sin that yet knew no sin. Must not this prospect fill the holy soul of our Lord with an inconceivable horror? He was the Word that was with God and was God, but this Word had become flesh, like to His brethren in all things, except sin, on which account also one would seek in vain to form a correct conception of that which for such a theanthropic personality the approach of such suffering and dying must have been! If even for the purely human sense, the thought of death has something fearful, for Him who had life in Himself, dying was in addition something entirely preternatural. If for us death is only the end of a life which may with right be called a daily dying; on the other hand, for the sinless and immaculate Saviour, the destruction of the bodily organism was as entirely in antagonism with His being as for us, for instance, the annihilation of our immortality would be. His delicately sensitive humanity shrinks from death; His holy humanity from the might of darkness; His loving humanity from the hatred that now is about to reach its most fearful culmination. Nay, if His humanity was of a finite nature, He might, standing over against the burden of the sin of millions, conceive, as we believe, even the possibility of sinking under His fearful burden; certainly even His utterance: ἡ δὲ σὰρξ ἀσθενής, was the fruit of His own agonizing experience; sin and death show themselves now to His eye in an entirely different light from before His Incarnation, when death stood already, it is true, before Him, without however having dared to essay any direct assault upon Himself. Now is the God-man to become the victim of powers which the Logos in His preëxistence had seen before Him as powerless rebels. Indeed we comprehend and subscribe to the remark: "We, for our part, speaking as fools, could at least, if psychological and Christological ideas formed on the plane of our conceptions are here of any value, easier doubt the elevation of consciousness which the Intercessory Prayer exhibits to us than the depression of the same in Gethsemane." Stier. Of a change of essential purpose respecting His suffering we find here no trace; but we do seem to find trace of an alternation of moods, in which the feeling of anguish first obtains the upper hand, and the thought rises in Him for a moment whether it might not be even possible for Him that the cup should pass by. Here also Luther has hit the right view when he in his sermon on this Passion-text says: "We men, conceived and born in sin, have an impure hard flesh, that is not quick to feel. The fresher, the sounder the man, the more he feels what is contrary to him. Because now, Christ's body was pure and without sin, and our body impure, therefore we scarcely feel the terrors of death in two degrees where Christ felt them in ten, since He is to be the greatest martyr and to feel the utmost terror of death." Comp. ULLMANN, *Sündlosigkeit Jesu*, 5th ed. p. 164. In this we are not to forget how to our Lord His certain and exact knowledge of all that which should come upon Him must have so much the more heightened His suffering, John xviii. 4. But that He was in Gethsemane itself abandoned by His Father, and that such a special mysterious suffering, even besides the suffering of death, was necessary for atonement for sins, is nowhere taught us in the New Testament. Nothing, however, hinders us from assuming that an indescribable *feeling* of abandonment here seized upon Him, which upon Calvary reached its culmination, as, indeed, the first rushing of this storm of sorrow of the soul had already previously been perceived, Luke xii. 49–51; John xii. 27, 28. Nor are we by any means to forget that the kingdom of darkness now least of all remained inactive (John xiv. 30); although no one will be able to decide how far this hostile might acted directly upon the body and upon the soul of our Lord.

4. Gethsemane, therefore, leads us spontaneously back to the wilderness of the Temptation; as there, so also here is our Lord tempted, yet this time also without sin. Unbelief, it is true, has here too, as it were, out of the dust of the garden raked up stones against Him; "He"—thus scoffed Vanini, when the sentence of death was executed upon him —"in the agony of death, sweat: I die without the least fear." But if it would have been sin to pray as He did, then it was already sin that He was a true and holy Man. Such an one cannot do otherwise

than shrink from such a death-agony. God's Incarnate Son might have a wish—the word *will* is almost too strong for a prayer which was uttered with so great a restriction—which, according to the Father's eternal purpose, could not be fulfilled; but difference is not of itself at all a strife, and in reality He also wills nothing else than the Father, although He naturally for Himself might wish that the Father's counsel could be fulfilled in another way. Moreover, His obedience and His holiness are as little obscured by this prayer as His love and His foreknowledge. There is no more incongruous comparison than with the courage of martyrs in death, who had only by beholding Him obtained the strength to endure a suffering of a wholly different kind. "No martyr has ever been in His position, least of all, Socrates." As well in His prayer to His Father as in His discourse with His disciples, our Lord shows Himself in adorable greatness, even in the midst of the deepest humiliation.

5. The momentousness of the suffering of Jesus in Gethsemane, can hardly be estimated high enough. As well over the Person as over the Work of our Lord, there is diffused from this point a satisfying light. He Himself stands here before us not only as the true and deeply-feeling Man, who through suffering must learn obedience and be perfected (Heb. ii. 10; v. 7–9), but also in His unspotted holiness and untroubled unity with the Father, which is raised above all doubt. At the same time it is here shown that the Monophysite, as well as the Monothelitic error has been condemned with reason by the Christian church, as also that it is possible to ascribe to the God-man a limited humanly susceptible nature, without in the least throwing His sinlessness into the shade. As respects the *severity* of His suffering, we can nowhere gain a juster conception of it than here; Gethsemane opens to us the understanding of Calvary; for we now know that the elevated nature of His person, instead of making the burden of His suffering less oppressive for Him, on the contrary increases this in terrible wise. The *necessity* of His sacrifice becomes clear to us if we give heed to this: that the Father, even after such a prayer, does not let the cup pass by for His beloved Son. The *completeness* of the redemption brought in by Him is convincingly established for us when we see to how high a degree His obedience and His love raised Him; and the *crown* which this combatant there gained in the strife is to us so dear, for the reason that we know that He through this suffering has become the merciful Highpriest, who can have compassion on our weakness. Heb. ii. 16–18; iv. 15.

6. It is known that the olive garden has also borne its fruits for the extension of the kingdom of God. The first Greenlander who was converted, Kajarnak, owed his conversion to the preaching upon our Lord's Passion in Gethsemane. See KRANZ, *Geschichte von Grönland*, p. 490. The representations of "Christ in Gethsemane," by RETOUT and ARY SCHEFFER, deserve attention.

HOMILETICAL AND PRACTICAL.

In a garden the disobedience of the first, in a garden, again, the obedience of the second Adam was manifested.—Comparison of the course of Jesus to Gethsemane with the course of Abraham to Moriah (Gen. xxii. 5), and with David's passage over the brook Cedron (2 Saml. xv. 23).—Our Lord also had His fixed customary place of prayer.—Prayer is for Jesus' disciples the best weapon against temptation. —Our Lord's prayer that the cup might pass away: 1. Heartrending; 2. intelligible; 3. unforgettable for all who confess Him.—To will what God wills, the essence of true religion.—The strengthening through the angel in Gethsemane: 1. What it reveals, *a.* the depth of the suffering, *b.* the greatness of our Lord, *c.* the love of the Father; 2. to what it awakens, *a.* to humble faith in the suffering Lord, *b.* to an unshaken trust when we ourselves are suffering, *c.* to the strengthening of other sufferers, to whom we appear as angels of consolation.—What it must have been for the angel during such a Passion to perform such a ministry.—The hotter the combat burns, the intenser must the prayer become.—The bloody sweat of the second Adam over against the sweat of labor of the first Adam and his posterity (Gen. iii. 19).— *Eo terra benedictionem accepit*. Bengel.—The touching contrast between the waking Lord and the sleeping disciples.—Whoever is richly strengthened of God, can at last do without the comforting of men. —Compassion on weak friends is brought home to us by the example of our Lord.—Gethsemane, the school of the prayer well-pleasing to God.—Our Lord, by His example, teaches us to pray: 1. In solitude, with fervent importunity; 2. with submission and unshaken perseverance, and with more fervent ardency the more our suffering augments; 3. with the fixed hope of being heard, which the angel of consolation instilled into His heart.—Gethsemane the sanctuary of the sorrow of Jesus' soul: 1. The Priest who kneels in the sanctuary; 2. the sacrifice that burns in the sanctuary; 3. the ray of light that falls into the sanctuary; 4. the awakening voice that issues from the sanctuary.—Gethsemane, the battle-field of supreme obedience: 1. The Combatant; 2. the Victory; 3. the Crown.—The one cup of our Lord, and the three cups which daily pass around among His people: 1. The foaming cup of temptation; 2. the bitter cup of trial; 3. the final cup of death.—Heb. v. 7–9. How our Lord: 1. Offers prayers and supplications with strong crying and tears; 2. learns obedience; 3. was also heard; 4. has thus become for all His people the Author of eternal salvation.

STARKE:—He that will talk with God does well to repair to solitude.—BRENTIUS:—Let us learn to pray the third prayer aright (Matt. vi. 10).—CRAMER:—So soon as man surrenders himself to God, he will find strength and refreshment therein.—QUESNEL:—God knows how at the right time to send an angel for our strengthening, should it be only an humble brother or sister.—J. HALL:—Even the comfort that comes from an humble hand we must not contemn.—*Litany:*—By Thine agony and bloody sweat, Good Lord, deliver us!—*Nova Bibl. Tub.:*— Let no one jest concerning death and devil; they have hunted from the Son of God bloody sweat.— Alas that we sleep, where we should watch!—HEUBNER:—A wonder it is how an angel—a creature, could strengthen the God-man; but it is a great consolation for us.—Near us also are there angels.—God will also strengthen us the more the heavier the temptations are.—Of certain formulas of prayer the saint never becomes weary.—His prayer hindered Jesus not from the exhibition of love, as it indeed should nowhere disturb a duty.—ARNDT:—Jesus' conflict in Gethsemane: 1. His anguish; 2. His prayer; 3. His strengthening.—KRUMMACHER:—Christ's conflict and victory in Gethsemane.—Significance and fruit of the suffering on the Mount of Olives.—(On vs. 44):

—The blood of the Lamb.—(*Sabb. Gl.* 1852):—1. Its nature and its significance; 2. its might and wonder-working.—STAUDT:—The threefold way of our Lord in Gethsemane: 1. What it brought upon our Lord; 2. what it brings upon us.—THOLUCK:—The heart of our Lord in Gethsemane.—We hear here: 1. A human Nay; 2. a Divine Yea; 3. a Divine decision.—LANGE:—The suffering of Jesus' soul in Gethsemane (*Langenberger Sammlung*, 1852): 1. The nature of this suffering of soul; 2. our suffering of soul in the light of it.—J. J. L. TEN KATE:—Jesus' Passion in Gethsemane: 1. The nature of this suffering; *a.* an unspeakable, *b.* a holy, *c.* an incomparable suffering; 2. the causes: I point you *a.* to the brooding treason, *b.* the impending suffering, *c.* the present temptation; 3. the value of the suffering; Gethsemane remains for us *a.* a joyful token of accomplished redemption, *b.* a holy school of Christian suffering and conflict, *c.* a consoling pledge of God's fatherly compassion.

---

b. THE ARREST (Vss. 47-53).

(Parallel with Matt. xxvi. 47-56; Mark xiv. 43-52; John xviii. 3-11.)

47 And [om., And] while he yet spake, behold a multitude [or, throng], and he that
  was called Judas, one of the twelve, went before them, and drew near unto Jesus to
48 kiss him. But Jesus said unto him, Judas, betrayest thou [deliverest thou up] the Son
49 of man with a kiss? When they which were about him saw what would follow, they
50 said unto him [om., unto him¹], Lord, shall we smite with the sword? And one of
51 them smote the servant of the high priest, and cut off his right ear. And Jesus an-
52 swered and said, Suffer ye thus far.² And he touched his ear, and healed him. Then
  Jesus said unto the chief priests, and captains of the temple, and the elders, which were
  come to him, Be [Are] ye come out [Ye are come out, V. O.], as against a thief [rob-
53 ber], with swords and staves? When I was daily with you in the temple, ye stretched
  [not] forth no [your] hands against me: but this is your hour, and the power of darkness.

---

¹ Vs. 49.—*Rec.:* αὐτῷ. Critically doubtful. [Om., B., Cod. Sin., L., X.—C. C. S.]
[² Vs. 51.—Van Oosterzee translates this: *Lasset mich so lange!* "Let me alone so long," *i. e.*, till Ho could heal the servant. Others take it to mean: "Suffer them (the soldiers) to go as far as they are doing." A good deal may be said for either interpretation, but, as Bleek remarks, ἀποκριθείς . . . εἶπεν, appears to designate our Lord's words as in reply to Peter's, which would establish the second interpretation as the right one. The weight of authority appears also to favor this, though De Wette and Alford support the former, and the mildness of the words, if considered as a rebuke to His disciples, are, as De Wette remarks, greater than we should expect.—C. C. S.]

EXEGETICAL AND CRITICAL.

Vs. 47. One of the Twelve.—With this name as with a branding-iron Judas is designated even unto the end. In painter's style Luke also brings forward the unexpectedness and rapidity of the coming forward of the enemy, although he only speaks in general of the ὄχλος, which is more specialized by Matthew and Mark. The question whether the treacherous kiss of Judas, which all the Synoptics mention, had preceded or followed the falling to the earth of the band, John xviii. 3–9, we believe (with Hess, Lücke, Olshausen, Tholuck, Ebrard, and others) that we must answer in the former sense. According to all the Synoptics, Judas presses forward while Jesus is yet speaking with His disciples, and gives the concerted sign too early, on which account the band, in advance of which he had hurried on, do not remark it, and therefore do not recognize our Lord. We should without ground magnify the guilt of the unhappy man if we assume that he had seen the falling of the band upon the earth, perhaps had been himself struck down, and even yet, as if nothing had come to pass, had himself given the token, which, moreover, had now become superfluous. The words, moreover, which D., E., H., X., &c., read after vs. 47, τοῦτο γὰρ σημεῖον δεδώκει, κ.τ.λ., are certainly borrowed from Mark.

To kiss Him.—If we consult Luke alone, it might appear to us as if Judas had indeed the intention of pressing the kiss of betrayal upon the lips of innocence, but had been hindered in the carrying out of his purpose by our Lord's address. From Matthew and Mark, however, it appears that the kiss was actually given. The accounts, however, make the impression that the answer of our Lord followed this shameful act as immediately as upon the burning lightning the stunning thunder-peal follows.

Vs. 48. With a kiss, φιλήματι, the hallowed token of friendship. This in Luke stands emphatically first. Mark omits this utterance of our Lord; Matthew, on the other hand, has: "Friend, wherefore art thou come?" (Matt. xxvi. 50.) If Judas had, perhaps, approached in the thought of being able wholly to escape rebuke while he did what could only be the work of a moment, he now at once experiences that even this last wretched consolation is torn from him. Brief as his last tarrying in the presence of the Saviour was, it appears, nevertheless, at once, that he is seen through, vanquished, and condemned. If we assume that the ἑταῖρε, κ.τ.λ., of Matthew was uttered when Judas was first hurrying to Him the moment before the kiss, the φιλήματι, κ.τ.λ., immediately after it, everything agrees admirably. It is as if our Lord would, in the last word with which He gives Judas over to his self-chosen destruction, with every syllable yet thrust a sword through his soul. Φιλήματι — τὸν υἱὸν ἀνθρώπου — παραδίδως; the emphasis may be laid on every word, and yet even then we have only imperfectly rendered the force of this crushing question, which loses by every paraphrase. But alas, our Lord could therewith only reveal His own forbearance, holiness, and majesty, but could not win the wretched man for heaven who was already consecrated to hell. Cold as his kiss, remained the heart of the betrayer; from now on, we see Judas no longer standing with the disciples, but with the enemies, John xviii. 5. Even the Mohammedans have marked the place at which this abomination has been conjectured to have been committed, with a heap of stones. *See* SEPP, *l. c.*, iii. p. 460.

Vs. 49. **When they which were about Him.**—Unconscious but strong contrast between the unfaithful disciple and the faithful ones. They see τὸ ἐσόμενον: what is now on the point of taking place. By the approach of the band and the insult of Judas, they are at once persuaded that they themselves are no longer a step distant from the dreaded hour. They believed themselves hitherto to have dreamed, and appear now all at once to awake. Whether they shall strike in with the sword, is the question which they, looking upon the weapons brought with them out of the paschal hall, addressed to the Master, and before He could answer approvingly or disapprovingly, already one of them has followed the ill-considered question with a hasty act. No one of the Synoptics has here mentioned the name of Peter; the occurrence did not redound to the Apostle's honor; the repeated narration of this occurrence with the statement of his name might have had the effect of bringing the Apostle into trouble; but for John, who did not write his gospel until after Peter's death, such a ground of silence no longer existed. If, on the other hand, John, with Matthew and Mark, leaves the healing of Malchus' ear unmentioned, this was not done because this miracle—the last miraculous benefit which Jesus bestows—was in itself compared with other miracles less remarkable, but because it was, of course, understood that the Master immediately made good the harm which the inconsiderate zeal of His disciple had occasioned. Luke, the physician, can not, however, omit to add: καὶ ἁψάμενος, κ.τ.λ. It is alike arbitrary to declare the ear to have been only wounded (Von Ammon), and to deny the whole reality of this miracle, as Neander, Theile, De Wette, Strauss, and others do.

Vs. 51. **Suffer ye thus far.**—Instead of the more detailed address to Peter, Matt. xxvi. 52-54, Luke has only a brief but most remarkable utterance of our Lord to His enemies, ἐᾶτε ἕως τούτου. For that our Lord here speaks to the disciples (Grotius, Bengel, Meyer, and others), in the sense of: "Leave them, the ὄχλος, alone," *nolite progredi*, is proved by nothing, not even by ἀποκριθείς. Much more probable is it that the interrupted sentence is more particularly explained by the immediately subsequent act of healing. Our Lord, namely, sees how the band are just addressing themselves to take Him prisoner, with the greater bitterness, perchance, because blood had already flowed, and He Himself is not minded to counterwork their designs. He only desires that they would leave His hands yet a moment free, that He might bestow yet one more benefit. "'Leave Me,' He says in other words, "still free for the moment that I need in order to be able to perform *this*." He does not even say, but only indicates by a sign, what He means. While He thus speaks, He attaches again the wounded member, and heals with one act two men, the one of a wound in the body, the other of a sickness in the soul. With this last friendly beam of light, the sun of His majestic works of wonder goes down in the mists of Gethsemane. [This interpretation of Ἐᾶτε ἕως τούτου, although opposed to the usual view, is accepted by Alford, and appears to me more natural and simple than any explanation of the words as addressed to the disciples.—C. C. S.]

Vs. 52. **Then Jesus said.**—Probably we can understand these words as spoken during the seizure and binding, or even after this. From the fact that our Lord's words in Gethsemane are comparatively many, we may in some measure conclude as to the great tension of His spirit and the great composure of soul in which He inwardly passes through the beginning of His suffering, of which particularly the character of what He says may most strongly convince us.

To the chief priests.—If we place ourselves fairly in the intense excitement of the moment, we shall not be able to find it at all incredible that, as appears from Luke in this passage, some chief priests were personally in Gethsemane, in order to convince themselves of the fact of the arrest, and, in case of need, to encourage their servants by their presence. The servants had been sent out, but their masters had come of their own accord, and, perhaps, had only just now entered the garden (Ebrard, Lange). Why might they not, in their impatience, have rushed after their dependents, when these, on account of the delay in Gethsemane, did not return so quickly as had probably been expected? It is worthy of note that they are mentioned only at the end but not at the beginning of the arrest. The words which our Lord addressed to them and the captains of the temple, with the elders, were well fitted to shame them, provided they had been yet capable of shame. Without doubt, we find in this address of our Lord a resemblance to the words which He, John xviii. 20, addresses to the high-priest. However, the distinction is still considerable enough to refute the conjecture (Strauss) of our having here no independent part of the history of the Passion, but only two variations upon one and the same theme. Better than to concede this is it to direct attention to the manner in which by this Synoptical sentence, the truth of the Johannean statement, John vii. 30, 44; viii. 20, 59, is confirmed, without the comparison with which the words of our Lord in the text cannot be even understood.

As against a robber.—Our Lord deeply feels in this moment as well the ignominy as the injustice that is inflicted upon Him, and therefore expresses his resentment that they should have come to take Him as they would a robber and murderer. Then first does He direct their view back to the memorable past: **I was daily with you,** &c. This utterance must remind them of many a fruitless plot which they had meditated, and many a word of rebuke which they had heard, although our Lord, who is not minded to eulogize Himself, is entirely silent as to the miracles which He has performed before their eyes, and as to the triumphs which He by word or deed has won over their perplexity and weakness. Finally, after He has upbraided them with their month-long cowardice, to which wretched presumption has now succeeded, He takes from them even the fancy of having really taken Him against His will and to His harm, by speaking (Matthew) of the Scriptures which are fulfilled in precisely this way, and at the same time (Luke) by saying to them that they are not serving the kingdom of light but that of darkness.

Vs. 53. **This is your hour, and the power of darkness.**—Our Lord alludes therewith to the just fallen hour of night, and gives the reason why they have taken Him now and not in open day, in the temple, when He there walked and taught, καθ' ἡμέραν. *Your* hour, not the favorable hour suited for you (De Wette), but the hour destined according to the Divine decree *for you* to the carrying out of your work (Meyer); καὶ αὕτη (so may we supply) ἡ ἐξουσία τοῦ σκότους, that is, the might which now reveals itself and works through you, is that which God, according to His own eternal purpose, had left to the kingdom of darkness. Without doubt, our Lord makes use of this figurative language in view of the nocturnal darkness which had been chosen for the carrying out of the wicked deed, and His words thereby become only the more striking; τὸ σκότος, however, of which He here speaks, can be nothing else than the kingdom of darkness, whose faithful accomplices in this moment Judas and the whole throng are. This whole address affords, at the same time, a proof of the clearness of mind with which our Lord, in the midst of the darkness surrounding Him, looked through the past, the present, and the future. Luke, who alone relates to us this last word of the Lord in Gethsemane, on the other hand, passes over the flight of the disciples and that of the naked young man, Mark xiv. 48–52.

DOCTRINAL AND ETHICAL.

1. If we yet needed a proof of the completeness of the strengthening which our Lord had gained from His prayer in Gethsemane, it would be afforded by the composed and yet so dignified demeanor in which He went forward to meet the traitor and the officers. Here there is, indeed, no word too much or too little; even now He yet speaks and acts altogether as the Mighty One, although He gives plainly to be observed that He will not avail Himself of His might for His own deliverance. The position which our Lord in Gethsemane occupies, between dismayed friends on the one hand and implacable enemies on the other, has, at the same time, a typical and symbolical character.

2. The manner in which our Lord deals with the traitor, is an act of the sublimest self-revelation in the midst of the deepest humiliation. Whoever could so speak and act, had also full freedom to speak even in prayer concerning the son of perdition, as our Lord had done, John xvii. 12. The whole scene, in which heaven and hell, as it were, looked in each other's eyes, endured not much longer than a moment; but now our Lord occupies Himself no longer with this adder, who has wound himself hissing through the garden, and whom He flings from Him with a single gesture, but He goes out towards the band come to arrest Him. Yet was His last word to Judas tremendous enough to thunder through his ears even to all eternity.

3. The wound which Peter inflicted with his sword on Malchus, is the first of innumerable wounds which perverted carnal zeal has inflicted on the cause of the Lord. The weapons of our warfare are not carnal but spiritual, 2 Cor. x. 4. Where this is forgotten, and men think themselves able to serve the truth not by dying but by killing (*non moriendo, sed interficiendo*), there it is no wonder if the Lord of the Church often utters in the ears of the combatants in very palpable wise, "*non tali auxilio.*" In this respect, therefore, there is perpetually an immense significance in the manifold misfortunes of the Crusaders, the defeat of the Reformed in the battle-field of Kappel, &c. What would have become of the kingdom of God if our Lord had not, as here, every time advanced anew into the midst, in order by His wisdom and might to make good again the consequences of human rashness? "Even as Peter here hews off the servant's ear, so have those who vaunt themselves to be his successors taken from the church the hearing and understanding of the word of God. But Christ touched the church and healed her." J. Gerhard.

4. How entirely different is the situation of our Lord in which He leaves Gethsemane, from that in which He had entered the garden! And yet now, when He is led away as prisoner, the crown is much nearer to Him than before, when He could as yet in perfect freedom speak to His disciples and to the Father.

HOMILETICAL AND PRACTICAL.

The sanctuary of prayer turned into a battle-ground of wickedness.—Judas, which was guide to them that took Jesus, Acts i. 16.—Our Lord between perplexed friends on the one hand and implacable enemies on the other.—Gethsemane in the hour of the arrest: 1. Scene, and; 2. school of a great alteration.—The kiss of betrayal, how it was: 1. Once given and answered; 2. is even yet continually given and answered.—The traitor over against the Lord: 1. His iniquity before; 2. his falsehood in; 3. his disappointment after his crime.—The Lord over against the traitor: 1. His still presence of mind; 2. His forbearing love; 3. His judicial severity.—In Gethsemane we may learn how the combat against the kingdom of darkness must not be carried on, and how it must be carried on: the one in Peter, the other in Jesus. How oft we are doing our own will although we appear to be consulting the Lord's will!—Inconsiderate zeal in the service of the Lord: 1. What it does; 2. what it destroys.—Peter is zealous with a Jehu zeal, 2 Kings x. 15, 16.—Peter's sword: 1. Rashly drawn; 2. peremptorily commanded back into the scabbard.—The disciple may forget himself, but the Lord forgets him and Himself not an instant.—The last movement of the unfettered hand of our Lord used for the accomplishment of a benefit.—The great-hearted love of our Lord for His enemies: 1. Warmly attested; 2. coldly requited.—How His enemies disgrace themselves by the way in which they seek to overmaster the Nazarene.—Jesus in bonds free, His enemies in their seeming freedom bound.—The cowardice of the armed ones, the courage of the Prisoner.—The hour of darkness: 1. How threateningly it fell; 2. how brief its duration; 3. what glorious light followed it.—Even darkness has its hour, yet its might is of just as short duration as its hour.—The might of darkness: 1. Permitted of God; 2. used by God; 3. vanquished by God.—God is there working most where He seems to be wholly inactive.—The Lamb bound in order to be led to the slaughter, Ps. xxii. 16.

STARKE:—BRENTIUS:—Government should not be against, but for Christ.—Hot-tempered people have special need to go to Christ to school.—*Nova*

Bibl. Tub.:—Even zeal for Christ is sinful when it is displayed unintelligently, Rom. x. 2.—Where power prevails over justice, there to be still and patient is the best counsel.—When the world acts against Christ, it has no scruple to give up its convenience and dignity for a while.—RAMBACH:—When one regards the hours as his own, he is thereby misled into many sins.—*Nova Bibl. Tub.:*—The bonds of Jesus our deliverance.—ARNDT:—The arrest: 1. Jesus' prevalence over His enemies; 2. His providence for His friends; 3. His sparing love towards Judas.—KRUMMACHER:—*Passions-buch:*—The Judas kiss: 1. The separation; 2. the farewell.—Simon's sword and Jesus' cup.—The Saviour, how He gives Himself as Gift and then as Sacrifice.—BRAUNIG:—The treason committed against the person and cause of Christ: 1. How we are to think of such treason; 2. how we are to combat such treason.—" *Gratia sit vinculis tuis, bone Jesu, quæ nostra tam potenter diruperunt.*" Bernard.

---

2. Caiaphas.

a. PETER'S DENIAL (Vss. 54–62).

(Parallel with Matt. xxvi. 69–75; Mark xiv. 66–72; John xviii. 15–18; and 25–27.)

54 Then took they him, and led *him*, and brought him into the high priest's house.
55 And Peter followed afar off. And when they had kindled a fire in the midst of the
56 hall, and were set down together, Peter sat down among them. But [And] a certain maid beheld him as he sat by the fire, and earnestly looked upon him, and said, This
57 man was also with him. And he denied him, saying, Woman,[1] I know him not.
58 And after a little while another saw him, and said, Thou art also of them. And Peter
59 said, Man, I am not. And about the space of one hour after another confidently
60 affirmed, saying, Of a truth this *fellow* also was with him; for he is a Galilean. And Peter said, Man, I know not what thou sayest. And immediately, while he yet spake,
61 the cock crew. And the Lord turned, and looked upon Peter. And Peter remembered the word of the Lord, how he had said unto him, Before the cock crow [to-day[2]],
62 thou shalt deny me thrice. And Peter went out, and wept bitterly.

[1] Vs. 57.—Γύναι must, according to Tischendorf, [Tregelles, Alford,] be placed last, instead of first.
[2] Vs. 61.—Σήμερον, which Tischendorf has received into the text, [also Meyer, Tregelles, Alford,] is supported by D., [Cod. Sin., K.,] M., L., X., and some Cursives.

EXEGETICAL AND CRITICAL.

Vs. 54. Into the high-priest's house.—As to the question which high-priest is here meant, we can give no other answer than "Caiaphas." We must, therefore, regard his palace as the theatre of Peter's denial. If our Lord, according to John xviii. 13, after His arrest appears to have spent a moment also in the house of Annas, it seems only to have been in order that this old man, who, although no longer active high-priest, yet still as ever possessed considerable influence, might enjoy the sight of the fettered Nazarene. That, according to Luke, the unnamed high-priest, this chief person in the history of the Passion, was no other than Annas himself (Meyer), we consider as incapable of proof. In Luke iii. 2; Acts iv. 6, he is undoubtedly placed first as ἀρχιερεύς, but this may be explained from his former rank, his more advanced years, his continuing influence,—even if not perchance also from his enjoying the supreme dignity alternately with Caiaphas. A disturbing element is without ground brought into the harmony of the narrative of the Passion when it is asserted that Luke here, entirely against the united Synoptical tradition, understood any other than Caiaphas. Besides, it at once appears that Luke passes over as well the particulars of the clerical trial, which Matthew and Mark give, as those also which John communicates; so that here also we can only learn the historical sequence of the facts by the comparison of the different accounts. We believe we may arrange these in the following manner: 1. The Leading Away first to Annas, then to Caiaphas. Inquiry in the house of this latter respecting Jesus' disciples and doctrine, John xviii. 12–14 and 19–24. 2. The beginning of Peter's Denial, Matt. xxvi. 69, 70; Mark xiv. 66–68; Luke xxii. 56, 57; John xviii. 15–18. 3. The False Witnesses, the Adjuration, the Preliminary Condemnation of our Lord by the night session, Matt. xxvi. 59–66; Mark xiv. 55–64. 4. Adjournment of this precipitate session, Mocking of our Lord by the servants, Matt. xxvi. 67, 68; Mark xiv. 65; Luke xxii. 63–65. During and partially before all this, 5. The second and third Denials of Peter take place. In the very moment when this third denial is made, at the second cock-crowing, our Lord is led across the inner court again to the hall of the high-priest, where the decisive final session is to be held, and finds thereby opportunity in passing to behold the fallen disciple with a look by which, 6. The repentance of Peter is effected. Finally follows, 7. The Morning Session, which Matthew and Mark only briefly touch on, but which Luke describes more at length, Matt. xxvii. 1; Mark xv. 1; Luke xxii. 66–71; xxiii. 1, comp. John xviii. 28, immediately on which follows the Leading Away to Pilate. Luke now passes over all which His enemies in this night in the high-priestly palace undertake against the Saviour, and directs almost exclusively our attention to Peter. Here also, in the way in which he describes his fall, his awakening and repentance, the penetrating view of the psychologist is not to be mistaken.

And Peter followed afar off.—It is scarcely

possible to form a distinct image of the mood in which the impetuous disciple, impelled by curiosity, disquiet, and affection, ventures to enter the high-priestly palace. From John xviii. 15 *seq.*, we see how he finds entrance into it. In explaining and pronouncing upon his thrice-repeated denial, Bengel's hint is to be borne in mind: "*Abnegatio ad plures plurium interrogationes, facta uno paroxysmo, pro una numeratur*," that we may not with Strauss and Paulus von Heidelberg, fall into the absurdity of assuming even eight denials.

Vs. 55. **And when they had kindled a fire.**—It is well known that the nights in Palestine, especially in the early year, are often very cold. [Particularly at Jerusalem, from its great elevation above the sea.—C. C. S.] We cannot, therefore, be surprised that the servants are warming themselves in the open court, while Peter, assuming as well as he can the appearance of an indifferent observer, takes his place in the midst of them, in order to be able to be eye and ear witness in the immediate vicinity. The expression of Luke: περιαψάντων (Tischendorf, following B. L.), gives us the very sight of the circle which is formed around the fire. According to the Synoptics, Peter sits; according to John alone, ch. xviii. 18, he stands by it. Without doubt, the account of the former is here the more exact, although at the same time we must bear in mind the restlessness and disquiet of Peter, which must have spontaneously impelled him not to sit still in one place, but now and then involuntarily to stand up. John xviii. 18, moreover, does not even speak of that which took place *during*, but what took place *after*, the first denial. This very disquiet of Peter's demeanor may have helped to direct attention yet more upon him.

Vs. 56. **This man was also with Him.**—According to Luke, the maid says this about Peter to others. According to Matthew and Mark, she speaks directly to him; according to John, she speaks in the form of a question, not positively affirming;—"Apparently with maliciously mocking caprice, ignorant of the facts, yet hostilely disposed." Lange. According to Luke, she directs her look fixedly upon Peter, ἀτενίσασα αὐτῷ (favorite word of our Evangelist), the more sharply because she, as θυρωρός, John xviii. 16, 17, well knows that he is a stranger, whom she has just admitted. The very unexpectedness of the assault demands an instantaneous repulse; and already Peter rejoices that he can preserve the guise of an external composure, and his answer is quick, cold, indefinite: **Woman, I know Him not!**—*See* the more original form of his words in Matthew and Mark.

Vs. 58. **Another.**—The first cock-crowing, which Mark, vs. 68, alone mentions, immediately after the first denial, is not even noticed by Peter. He appears, meanwhile, to have succeeded in assuming so indifferent a demeanor that he at first is not further disturbed. The disquiet of his conscience, however, now impels him towards the door (Matt. xxvi. 71); unluckily he finds this shut. He does not venture to seek to have it opened, that he may not elicit any unfavorable conjectures, and is therefore obliged to return to his former place. This very disquiet again excites suspicion; according to Luke, it is another servant, according to Mark, the same, according to Matthew, another maid who now puts the question. The last-named difference may, perhaps, be thus reconciled: that the door-keeper of the προαύλιον, into which Peter had entered, is meant.

The maid begins, the ἕτερος follows, nay, several others (John) join in and make merry with his terror, while they ask: "Art not thou one of His disciples?" "Man, I am not," says Peter, in the tone of a man who seeks as suddenly as possible to free himself of a troublesome questioner, and adds (Matthew) even an oath thereto. If we consider now that these accounts must have had Peter himself for their first source,—a man, that is, who, by his very bewilderment, was not in condition to relate the event with diplomatic faithfulness, and in a stereotyped form; if we consider further, that in a circle of servants one word very easily calls forth another, and that when many place themselves over against a single one, several may have spoken at the same time,—we shall then find in the minor diversities of the different accounts respecting matters of subordinate importance, rather an argument for than against the credibility of the Gospels.

Vs. 59. **And about the space of one hour after.**—So long, therefore, they now left the unhappy man in quiet. Attention had been diverted from the disciple and directed to the Master, whose process meanwhile had gone forward with terrific rapidity. The first denial should seem to have taken place almost at the same time at which Jesus appealed to the testimony of His disciples, John xviii. 19–23; the second while He was keeping silence before the false witnesses. Much of this may have been seen and heard by Peter, since from the court there was an unobstructed view into the open judgment-hall, separated only by a colonnade from the vestibule, but now he sees also how the Lord is adjured, how He is condemned. He sees Him at the conclusion of the sitting fall into the hands of the servants, who throng around Him, and begin the first united maltreatment. From afar Peter is eye-witness thereof, and sees that the Master takes all without opposition, and if now it fares thus with Him, what a fate will then come upon His disciples! This solitary hour has, therefore, yet more disheartened and bewildered Peter, instead of his having been able during it to come more to himself. Now they begin the third time to interrogate him, but find him less than ever prepared therefor. According to all the Synoptics, it is now Peter's Galilean dialect that excites suspicion against him. Respecting the peculiarities of this dialect, and the misunderstandings often arising from it, *see* FRIEDLIEB, § 25, and BUXTORF, in his *Lexicon Chald. et Talmud*, p. 435 *seq.* The discomfiture of the apostle becomes at the same moment complete through the attack of one of the relatives of Malchus, John xviii. 26; and Peter now denies the third time, hurling out, according to Matthew and Mark, terrible curses and self-imprecations.

Vs. 60. **The cock crew.**—As respects the possibility of a cock-crowing in the capital, audible to Peter, it is plainly evident that it could not have been demanded of the Romans to avoid the keeping of animals which the Mosaic law had declared unclean. According to the Talmud, Jews of later times also had the custom at wedding celebrations of offering a cock and a hen for a present, as a symbol of the matrimonial blessing. As to the exact hour in which ordinarily in the Orient the *gallicinium* is heard, we find in SEPP, iii. p. 477, interesting accounts. Interpretations of the cock-crowing, in a figurative sense, which have been attempted in different ways, we may with confidence regard as exegetical curiosities.

Vs. 61. **And the Lord turned and looked upon Peter.**—According to De Wette and Meyer, this touching feature is on local grounds hardly probable, but if our representation before given is applicable, this objection falls away. However, De Wette allows it as possible that our Lord cast this look upon Peter while He was led to the hearing, vs. 66. If we now succeed in demonstrating that Luke, vss. 66–71, actually relates *another* hearing than Matt. xxvi. 59–66, then there is no longer anything to object to the internal probability of a feature of the narrative which is one of the sublimest of the whole history of the Passion.

And Peter remembered.—According to Luke, therefore, Peter's repentance is the result of the concurrence of two different influences—the cock-crowing, and the look of Jesus. The πικρᾶς of Matthew and Luke explains, moreover, in some measure, the ἐπιβαλών of Mark, where we consider it as the simplest way to supply ἱμάτιον (Fritzsche). For other explanations *see* LANGE on Mark xiv. 72.—In his bitter sorrow Peter cannot bear the view of man. Veiled in the mantle cast around him, he suddenly precipitates himself out of doors and opens himself a way through the crowd, which no longer detains him. A testimony for the depth of his repentance and of his longing for solitude is found in the fact, that after this in the whole history of the Passion, we no longer discover the slightest trace of him.

DOCTRINAL AND ETHICAL.

1. The exactness and vividness with which all the Evangelists relate the deep fall and the heartfelt repentance of Peter, deserves to be named one of the most indubitable proofs of the credibility of the whole Evangelical history.

2. We cannot possibly be surprised at Peter's denial, if we direct our view to his individuality, and to the pressure of the circumstances and the unexpectedness of the attack, and consider that after the first momentous step it was almost impossible to refrain from the second. Quite as unreasonable is it, however, to excuse Peter, as has been essayed on the rationalistic side by Paulus von Heidelberg, and on the Roman Catholic side by Sepp, iii. p. 481. Even if we take into account the might of darkness (Olshausen), in order therefrom to explain his deep fall, yet the denial remains as ever a moral guilt, which, as well in and of itself as by its repetition, by the warning that had preceded it, and the perjury that attended it, was terrible and deep. Showing as it does a union of unthankfulness, cowardice, and falsehood, the sin is still increased by the circumstances in which our Lord at that very time found Himself, and, therefore, undoubtedly contributed not a little to the augmentation of His inexpressible sorrow. Whoever is too eager to vindicate Peter, makes his repentance an exaggerated melancholy, and thereby actually declares that our Lord dealt with him afterwards almost too severely; on the other side we may undoubtedly, in mitigation of his guilt, point to the fact that he denied the Lord only with his mouth, but not with his heart, and sought to make good the error of a single night by a whole life of unwearied faithfulness.

3. The fall and repentance of Peter was one of the most powerful means by which he was trained into one of the most eminent of the apostles. A character like his would never have mounted so high if it had not fallen so low. Thus does the Lord make even the sins of His people contribute to their higher training, and (as continually appears *a posteriori*, without anything thereby of the guilt and moral responsibility of the sinner being taken away) not only the hardest blows of fate which strike us, but also the evil deeds which we can least excuse, but have sincerely wept over and repented of, must afterwards subserve our best good. Rom. viii. 28–30.

4. When Dogmatics describes the nature of a sincere conversion, it can least of all neglect to cast a look into the heart and life of Peter—the David of the New Covenant. While he thus deeply humbles himself, Peter becomes great; while afterwards one of the others οἱ δοκοῦντες στύλοι εἶναι, who was the greatest of the apostles, becomes in his own eyes so little, that he calls himself the least of the brethren, yea, absolutely nothing. 1 Cor. xv. 9; 2 Cor. xii. 11.

HOMILETICAL AND PRACTICAL.

The union of courage and fear, energy and weakness, love and selfishness, in a Peter's variable character.—The heart is deceitful above all things, Jer. xvii. 9, 10.—The experience of Peter in this night a proof of the truth of the two parables, Luke xiv. 28–33.—Beware of the first step.—How dangerous a hostile female influence can be for the disciple of the Lord.—A ship without anchor or rudder is given a prey to the storms and waves.—How much he ventures who throws himself with an unguarded heart into the midst of the enemies of the Lord.—The precipitous path of sin the longer the worse.—The Christian also is betrayed by his speech.—The word of our Lord is literally fulfilled.—True repentance impels us to seek solitude.—Blessed are they that mourn, Matt. v. 4.

Peter's denial: 1. Remarkable in the Evangelical history; 2. in the history of the human heart; 3. in the history of the suffering and death of our Lord.— How have we to judge of Peter's conduct?—Let us consider his transgression: 1. In the light of his vocation, and his guilt is unquestionable; 2. in the light of his character, and his conduct is intelligible; 3. in the light of the circumstances, and his transgression is mitigated; 4. in the light of conscience, and the sentence dies upon our guilty lips.—Whoever thinks he stands, may well take heed that he does not fall, 1 Cor. x. 12. Comp. Rom. xi. 20.—The history of the Denial a part of the history of the Passion: 1. Peter's denial an aggravation; 2. Peter's repentance a mitigation of the suffering of our Lord.—The preaching of the unfaithful disciple.—Peter and Judas compared with one another in their repentance. Peter: 1. Sorrowful; 2. sorrowful with a godly sorrow; 3. sorrowful to salvation with repentance not to be repented of, 2 Cor. vii. 10; in Judas, the sorrow of the world, which worketh death.—The history of Peter's fall a revelation of the weakness of man; how weakness: 1. Brings man into danger; 2. hinders him from escaping from danger; 3. in the danger brings him to a fall.—It is a precious thing to have the heart established, which is done through Christ.—The look of our Lord, the expression: 1. Of an unforgettable reminder—What have I said to thee? 2. of a heartfelt sorrow—Is this thy compassion for thy friend? 3. of a blessed consolation—I have prayed for thee; 4. of a timely intimation—To go at once from hence.—The Lord turned and looked upon Peter. Hour of preparation for the Holy Communion in Passion Week.—Peter's tears: 1. Honorable for Jesus; 2. refreshing for Peter; 3. important for us.—The bitter tears of Peter render not less honor to the Saviour than the rejected silver pieces of Judas.—Peter our forerunner in the way of genuine penitence.—The history in the text shows us: 1. A sleeper who quickly awakens; 2. a sinner who is graciously regarded; 3. a sorrower who is divinely afflicted; 4. a fallen one who is enabled again to rise.— The noble harvest from the sowing of Peter's tears: 1. For himself; 2. for the church; 3. for heaven.— Striking expressions from Peter's Epistles confirmed by the history of his fall and of his repentance, *e. g.,* 1 Peter i. 13; ii. 1, 11; iii. 12, 15; v. 5, 8, *et alibi.* STARKE:—*Nova Bibl. Tub.*:—Forgetfulness of the word of God, insincerity, bad company, presumption, bring grief of heart.—QUESNEL:—The stronger trust one puts in himself and others, the more God's strength removes from him.—The least opportunity, a weak instrument may precipitate even a rock, if he without God will rest in security upon himself.— BRENTIUS:—The cock-crowing should be for us a daily summons to repentance.—J. HALL:—Where sin abounded, there, nevertheless, grace much more abounds, Rom. v. 20.—Learn rightly to apply and preserve the gracious regards of God.—No sin so great but may be blotted out.—ARNDT:—The denial of Christ: 1. Its sin; 2. the repenting of it.—F. W. KRUMMACHER:—Peter's fall: 1. As to its inner causes; 2. as to its outward course.—Peter's tears.—COUARD: —Simon Peter, the Apostle of our Lord. A look: 1. Upon the fallen; 2. upon the penitent Peter.— THOLUCK:—Passion Week brings to view in Peter how great the wavering may be, even in a human heart that has already confessed itself to have found the words of eternal life with Jesus. Comp. John vi. 67–69.—J. SAURIN:—*Nouv. Sermons,* i. p. 121; *Sur l'abnégation de St. Pierre.*—An admirable representation of Peter's denial, by the Dutch painter, Govert Schalken.

b. THE MOCKING AT THE LORD, AND HIS CONDEMNATION (Vss. 63–71).

(Parallel with Matt. xxvi. 67, 68; xxvii. 1a; Mark xiv. 65; xv. 1.)

63, 64 And the men that held Jesus mocked him, and smote *him.* And when they had blindfolded him, they struck him on the face,[1] and asked him, saying, Prophesy, who is 65 it that smote thee? And many other things blasphemously [or, contumeliously] spake 66 they against him. And as soon as it was day, the elders [lit., the eldership, πρεσβυτέριον] of the people and the chief priests and the scribes came together, and led him into 67 their council, saying, Art thou [or, If thou art] the Christ? tell us. And he said unto 68 them, If I tell you, ye will not believe: And if I also [om., also[2]] ask *you,*[3] ye will not 69 answer me, nor let *me* go.[4] [5]Hereafter [From henceforth] shall the Son of man sit [be 70 seated] on the right hand of the power of God. Then said they all, Art thou then the Son of God? And he said unto them, Ye say that I am [or, Ye say it, for (ὅτι) I am[6]]. 71 And they said, What need we any further witness [testimony]? for we ourselves have heard of his own mouth.

[1 Vs. 64.—What the *Recepta* has here, ἔτυπτον αὐτοῦ τὸ πρόσωπον, καί, appears to be a glossematic addition, which has gradually got the upper hand. See TISCHENDORF and MEYER, *ad locum.* [As Alford clearly explains it, αυτου το προσωπον was substituted for αυτον from the parallel in Mark, then united with the text, ετυπτον being then inserted to account for παιοας below. The variations confirm this explanation.—C. C. S.]
[2 Vs. 68.—Καί before ἐρωτήσω omitted by Lachmann, Tischendorf, [Meyer, Tregelles, Alford,] according to B., [Cod. Sin.,] L., Cursives.
[3 Vs. 68.—He means probably, as Bleek explains it, that if He should ask them questions as to the cause of His arrest, and the like, they would not answer him.—C. C. S.]
[4 Vs. 68.—Μοι ἢ ἀπολύσητε. These words also awaken at least the suspicion, that they are a somewhat incongruous expansion of the text. See Tischendorf and Meyer. [They are omitted by B., Cod. Sin., L., Coptic Version, Cyril. Numbers are for them, weight of testimony and internal evidence against them.—C. C. S.]
[5 Vs. 69.—After ἀπὸ τοῦ νῦν insert δέ on the authority of A., B., D., (Cod. Sin.,] L., X., and many other authorities.
[6 Vs. 70.—Van Oosterzee, agreeing with Luther, De Wette, Meyer, and others, translates ὅτι *denn,* "For," as it appears to be used in John xviii. 37. The sentence then means: "I acknowledge the title, for I am the Son of God." "Ye say," the well known idiom of assent to another's statement or question.—C. C. S.]

EXEGETICAL AND CRITICAL.

General Remarks.—The maltreatment of which Luke now gives account appears to have taken place immediately after the sentence had been uttered in the night-session, even before its legal confirmation in a morning-session. Meanwhile, part of the Sanhedrists left the hall, so that the Prisoner remained behind in the hands of the servants. Without ground, SEPP, *l. c.* iii. p. 480, supposes that Christ was in prison; it appears rather that He remained in the same hall in which He had stood before the council. Respecting this whole act of scoffing, comp. Matt. xxvi. 67. That the act can in no way be excused, does not even need mention. Among all civilized nations the condemned, so long as he yet lives, stands under the protection of the law. Nay, he finds in the pitiable fate that awaits him a security against new injuries. But here they cannot even wait till the injured law has its course, and so the council of blood is changed into a theatre of insult and cruelty. The servants who guard the Prisoner have noticed the hatred of their lords against Him, and although hitherto, perhaps, withheld by some fear of the might of the Prisoner, yet now when it becomes evident that He will make no use of this, their terror passes over into unrestrained insolence.

It is as if they would indemnify themselves for the discomfiture which they had suffered in Gethsemane. They mock Him especially in His prophetical and kingly character. First, He must with covered countenance make out which of them gave Him the hard blows of the fist, then He is mocked and spit upon, in token that He is much too contemptible for a king even of these meanest servants. But that even more than one maltreatment of the kind took place in the house of Caiaphas (Ebrard), we regard as a superfluous concession, in view of the comparatively little diversity of the different Synoptical accounts respecting this. Still less can we agree with Schleiermacher and Strauss in regarding it as in itself improbable that even counsellors took part in this maltreatment, when we consider how in Matt. xxvi. 67, those who maltreat the Lord are not definitely distinguished from those who condemn Him, xxvi. 66; and how according to Mark xiv. 65, the men who spit upon Jesus are especially distinguished from the servants, who, according to Mark as well as according to Luke, strike our Lord in the face. We are then rather led to the belief that their masters, in their hellish joy at the triumph achieved by them, made common cause with the servants, and themselves lent their hands to draw down their Victim into the mire of the deepest ignominy. If we unite the different features of the narrative which the individual Synoptics have preserved for us, with one another, we then obtain an image of outraged majesty which inspires us with terror, but at the same time also reminds us vividly of the prophecy, Isaiah l. 4–8.

Vs. 66. **And as soon as it was day.**—The view that the Jewish council was only assembled once for the condemnation of our Lord (Meyer and Von Hengel) has, superficially considered, much, it is true, to commend it, but comes, nevertheless, carefully considered, into too direct conflict with the contents of all the Synoptical gospels to make it possible to accept it. Even in and of itself it is rather arbitrary to wish to determine the sequence of the events according to Luke, who goes to work with so much less chronological strictness in the history of the Passion than Matthew and Mark, amalgamates similar events, and even by the account of the maltreatment, vss. 63–65, tacitly presupposes that this must have been preceded by a condemnation, without which such an outrage could not possibly have taken place. The answer which our Lord, according to Luke, vss. 67, 68, gives to the question of the Sanhedrim, would have been incongruous if He had now addressed His enemies for the first time, and if nothing at all had preceded which could justify so strong a tone. The narrative of Matthew, ch. xxvii. 1, and Mark, ch. xv. 1, would have been wholly purposeless, if the Sanhedrim had been only assembled once on this occasion, and although the account of Luke agrees in many points with the *night* session in Matthew and Mark, it has, however, on the other hand, its peculiar coloring, which sufficiently characterizes precisely this second official and decisive session of the council. It is this partial agreement itself that is the cause why Matthew and Mark speak only of the first, Luke only of the second sitting. The assembly which utters the first sentence of death bears all the marks of precipitation, incompleteness, and incompetence; the high-priest assists at it only in his common attire, as it was not permitted him to rend his magnificent official apparel. The bitterest enemies of our Lord have in the night quickly run together in order without delay to introduce the case; but now in order not to violate, at least, the form of law, they come together the second time, early in the morning at a legally permitted hour and in fuller numbers, not in order to deliberate further, but in order to ratify, so far as requisite, a resolution already taken. Without doubt, the chief managers in the night session have already instructed the other counsellors sufficiently upon the state of the case as already reached, before the Prisoner is again brought in. The transaction of Caiaphas receives the approbation of the others, so that the thread is simply taken up again where his hand has let it fall. If we can from ch. xxiii. 51, conclude that Joseph of Arimathæa also was present at this morning session, his voice then, it should seem, in connection with a few others, only hindered the unanimity, which indeed, according to all appearance, was not really obtained.

Vs. 67. **Art thou the Christ?**—Now we see no more of the perplexity which even a few hours before betrayed itself in every word. They have now found a fixed point of departure in the declaration which the Prisoner under oath had deposed concerning Himself, and only desire yet to hear the repetition of the same, in order to press upon the already uttered condemnation the formal seal. For these judges are not come together in order to investigate, but in order to pronounce sentence. Therefore, they desire an affirmative answer, which our Lord now also gives them, in the presupposition that His previous answer is known to them; "If thou art the Christ, tell us," so ask they all, because they *all* wish to hear it from His own mouth, comp. vs. 71, and therefore at the beginning, with prudent craft, do not place first the religious but the political side of the question. "They would have been only too glad to have extorted more from Him, but only succeed in hearing the same."

If I tell you.—That this answer "does not suit well" (De Wette) would only be true if we identified both sessions, and forgot all that had already preceded this. Our Lord says nothing directly, but only presupposes what, according to the experience He had already had, would take place if He thought good to speak. The highest purpose of such a testimony, namely, to produce faith, would here not have been at all accomplished, and if He now began to do as they had done to Him, and that which He was well conscious of having a right to do, namely, to propose to His antagonists some questions, they would yet never have been able to answer these satisfactorily to Him, and would, therefore, bring their perplexity only so much the more to light. Of the possibility of being released, which is mentioned according to the critically suspicious reading ἢ ἀπολύσητε, He now no longer thinks. It is true, "questioning belongs only to the examining judge, not to the defendant" (De Wette); but here is a Defendant of a very special character, and He who had already spoken so many incomparable words *hors de ligne* to His judges, might also have well allowed Himself this freedom in speaking, without modern criticism needing to shake its head thereat.

Vs. 69. **From henceforth.**—Our Lord will therewith simply say that the word previously uttered remains good, and places the future with all its glory over against the present with all its ignominy. Even the last time that He calls Himself the Son of Man He exhibits Himself in all the still magnificence of His majesty.

Vs. 70. **Art Thou then the Son of God?**—It

is known that the Jews also expected the Messiah as the Son of God, in the theocratical sense of the word. But that they now utter this name with a special emphasis is not because they would denote thereby anything essentially different from vs. 67, but because they can scarcely trust their ears that He, the one so deeply humiliated and already condemned to death, attributes to Himself the dignity that is supreme above all. They now take cognizance of the religious side of the case, and express themselves as strongly as possible, in order so to be the better able to give a reason for the sentence of blasphemy. To their question Jesus answers with a simple affirmative, while from vss. 68, 69, it sufficiently appears why He does not add even a word more. Herewith the session has now reached its end, with a similar result to the former one. If Caiaphas had formerly, in view of two false witnesses, exclaimed: "What need we any further witness?" now, in answer thereto, his adherents, who find his statement sufficiently confirmed by Jesus' own word, declare that they need no further testimony, since they have now heard it from Jesus' own mouth. Now there is not even an express sentence of death uttered; the one formerly passed simply continues in force, since the crime is now satisfactorily established. But thereby they testify at the same time against themselves, and rob themselves thus of the last excuse for their sin.

4. That in the condemnation of Jesus by the Sanhedrim shameful injustice was committed, and not even the form of law was respected, appears at once to any one who only takes the trouble to follow somewhat particularly the course of the process. The legal validity of the sentence, which especially Salvador defends, has been from a juridical point of view controverted with the best success by DUPIN, *L'aîné, Jésus devant Caïphe et Pilate*, Paris, 1829.

5. It is remarkable how once, almost with the same words, sentence was uttered upon the reformer Farel, when, in October, 1532, raging priests in Geneva exclaimed upon him: "He has blasphemed God; we need no more witnesses; he is worthy of death," so that Farel, exasperated, raised his voice with: "Speak the words of God, and not those of Caiaphas." (*Leben Farels und Virets*, by Dr. E. SCHMIDT, Elberfeld, 1860).

HOMILETICAL AND PRACTICAL.

The Holy One of God the football of unholy sinners.—Wickedness, in appearance, humiliates the Lord, but in truth only itself.—The Saviour with covered face: 1. How much He sees; 2. how sublimely He keeps silence; 3. how powerfully He preaches.—Who is it that smote Thee? I, I and my sins.—Who when He was reviled, reviled not again, 1 Peter ii. 22, 23.—The morning of the mortal day of Jesus illumined by the glory of His majesty: 1. He keeps silence where He could have spoken; 2. He speaks where He could have kept silence; 3. He spares where He could have punished.—Jesus' condemnation by the Sanhedrim preaches to us: 1. The might of sin; 2. the greater might of grace; 3. the greatest might of the Divine Providence.—The Sanhedrim that rejects Jesus is itself smitten by the judgment: 1. Of blindness; 2. of hardening; 3. of reprobacy.—The deep humiliation of the Lord over against His future glory.—The depths of Satan looked through by the Searcher of hearts.—Even against the scribes of His day our Lord is unqualifiedly right, because He even to the end remains upon the standing-point of the Scripture. Dan. vii. 12-14.—The Christian also, after the unequivocal declaration of Jesus, needs, in reference to His heavenly dignity, no further witness.

STARKE:—Be not angry when thou art injured in thy good name, for even the highest majesty has been blasphemed.—*Nova Bibl. Tub.*:—Jesus was brought before an unjust tribunal, that we might be able to stand before the righteous tribunal of God. —We must use modesty towards our rulers, how unjust soever they may be, Rom. xiii. 7.—The last degree of the humiliation of Christ is the one next to His exaltation, 2 Tim. ii. 11, 12.—BRENTIUS:— Sincerity is agreeable to God.—QUESNEL:—O, how different are Christ's auditors! Some rejoice at His words as words of life, but others grow fiercer thereat and make thereof words of death.—ARNDT:—Jesus before Caiaphas: 1. The confession; 2. the condemnation; 3. the maltreatment.—KRUMMACHER, *Passions-buch*, p. 336 *seq.*:—Prophesy to us, O Christ! C. PALMER:—How the world seeks to rid itself of the truth.

DOCTRINAL AND ETHICAL.

1. In the midst of the rudest maltreatment, as shortly before over against the false witnesses, we see our Lord observe an unmoved silence. Four times in the history of the Passion we have the mention of such a silence: before Caiaphas (Matt. xxvi. 63), before Herod (Luke xxiii. 9), and twice before Pilate (Matt. xxvii. 12; John xix. 9). It is one of the most admirable problems to interpret this silence in its full force, and not a little will it contribute to the augmentation of the knowledge of our Lord, if we consider when He has spoken and when He has kept silence.

2. As the Lord there keeps silence when He might have spoken, so does He also speak before the Jewish council when He might have kept silence. With the traces of the outrages received on His countenance, He might have counted them unworthy of any further answer, but with an indescribable dignity He once again deposes testimony; with Divine condescension which places itself in the position of His enemies, He unites infinite long-suffering; while He shows that He completely sees through His enemies, He yet, even to the last instant, leaves nothing unessayed which can serve for setting them right and convincing them. He spares where He could punish, He only warns where He could dash in pieces, and His very last word to the Jewish council justifies the eulogies of the officers, John vii. 46.

3. With His own hand, as it were, our Lord here, even before His resurrection, as subsequently, ch. xxiv. 26, after it, points to the inseparable connection between His suffering and His glory. "*Ἀπὸ τοῦ νῦν, ab hoc puncto, quum dimittere non vultis. Hoc ipsum erat iter ad gloriam.*" Bengel.

3. Pilate and Herod.

a. JESUS LED TO PILATE, INTERROGATED BY HIM, AND FOUND INNOCENT (Ch. XXIII. 1-4).

1, 2 And the whole multitude of them arose, and led him unto Pilate. And they began to accuse him, saying, We found this *fellow* perverting the[1] nation, and forbidding to
3 give tribute to Cesar, saying that he himself is Christ a king. And Pilate asked him, saying, Art thou the King of the Jews? And he answered him and said, Thou sayest
4 *it*. Then said Pilate to the chief priests and *to* the people [crowds, ὄχλους], I find no fault in this man.

[1] Vs. 2.—With Lachmann, Tischendorf, [Meyer, Tregelles,] we read on the authority of B., D., [Cod. Sin., H.,] K., L., M., [R.,] Cursives, &c., ἔθνος ἡμῶν. [Alford omits it, regarding it as a probable reminiscence of ch. vii. 5.—C. C. S.]

EXEGETICAL AND CRITICAL.

Vs. 1. And led Him.—The solemn leading away of our Lord to Pilate, and His delivery to him, is one of the particulars of the history of the Passion which all the Evangelists visibly emphasize. No wonder, for the process herewith enters upon an entirely new stadium, and passes now from the spiritual to the secular sphere. As to the time and manner of the leading away, as to the sequence of events and the character of the judge, *see* LANGE on Matt. xxvii. 1. As respects this whole trial, compare, moreover, besides the writers whom *inter alios*, HASE, *Leben Jesu*, § 3, gives, the *Dissertatio*, by the Dutch divine, P. J. J. MOUNIER, *De Pilati in causa servatoris agendi ratione*, L. B. 1825. As respects the source from which we draw our knowledge of what here took place, the gospel of Nicodemus, it is true, contains some traits, which, on internal grounds, appear credible, but, on the whole, it has only this value, that we know from it how, in the fifth and sixth century, they represented to themselves this process. In the Acts, and in the epistles also, there are not wanting descriptive allusions to that which took place under the Roman Procurator (Acts iii. 13, 14; iv. 27; 1 Tim. vi. 13). But here, also, the four gospels remain the chief source, belying here in no way their respective peculiarities. While the Synoptics, namely, delineate to us especially the public side of the trial, John alone makes known to us what passed between our Lord and the Procurator in private. Matthew, who more than the others, even in the beginning of his gospel, speaks of dreams and visions, is the only one who gives account of the remarkable dream of Pilate's wife, as well, too, as of the genuinely Israelitish ceremony of the washing of Pilate's hands. Mark describes, in his way, briefly, vigorously, rapidly, how the Lion of the tribe of Judah hurries over the field of conflict to His complete triumph. Luke has enriched the delineation of this trial with a new particular, with the appearance before Herod, but at the same time condenses the occurrences more closely, takes more account of arranging the facts than of the sequence of time, and even passes over in almost entire silence the scourging and mocking by the Roman soldiers. The actual commencement of the trial John alone describes, ch. xviii. 28-32. On the other hand, we owe to Luke, vs. 2, the very precise statement of the actual ground of accusation with which the chief priests open the series of their charges.

Unto Pilate.—The question whether we, by the πραιτώριον, have to understand the well-known tower Antonia, or the palace of Herod, we believe that we must answer in the former sense; for it was in the tower Antonia that the Roman garrison lay, and the Procurator, therefore, during his temporary abode in the capital, might best lodge there. Tradition does not permit us to identify the places named, and it is entirely arbitrary to consider the palace of Herod as the established and ordinary residence of the Procurators in their visits to Jerusalem. JOSEPHUS, *De Bell. Jud.* ii. 14, 8; PHILO, *De Legatione Judæorum*, p. 1034, to whom appeal is commonly made in favor of Herod's palace, leave it entirely undecided whether this palace was always, and also at the time of Jesus, the residence of the governor. The above tower Antonia we are to look for on the northeast side of the temple mountain, while the place "Gabbatha," according to Josephus, also lay between the tower Antonia and the western corner of the temple, immediately before the judgment-hall.

Vs. 2. And they began.—It is not easy for them so to introduce the case as to make from the very beginning a favorable impression upon Pilate. The substance as well as the tone of their address betrays plainly enough that they intend this. Τοῦτον, first, δεικτικῶς, without statement of name, with visible contempt; εὕρομεν, with affected gravity, with which the subsequent declaration of Pilate that he had found no fault in Him, he, as little as Herod, vs. 14, singularly contrasts; τὸ ἔθνος ἡμῶν, with the full warmth of genuine friends of the people, who cannot endure that their true interests should be set at stake. Comp. John vii. 49. The accusation itself is threefold. First, He perverts the people, διαστρέφοντα. Properly, He "gives them a false direction," He brings them from the good way on which they themselves and the Romans with them would be so glad to see them walk. Moreover, He forbids to give tribute to the Emperor, since He—and this is the ground as well of the one as of the other offence—finally declares concerning Himself that He is Christ a King. Not without ground do they as yet intentionally avoid speaking of a king of the *Jews*, although it at once appears that Pilate interprets their indefinite expression in no less significance. With noticeable tact they place first not the religious but the political side of their imputations, and then, before making the attempt to prove, at least in some measure, their false accusation, they wait until Pilate himself shall inquire for the grounds of their assertion. He, however, already knows the Jews well enough, and therefore appeals as quickly as possible from the accusers to the Accused.

Vs. 3. Art thou the King of the Jews?—Pilate, not unacquainted with the prevailing Messianic hope, formulates his question very precisely, and seeks to find out whether Jesus is really the promised and long-sighed-for King of Israel. To this question our Lord cannot possibly answer otherwise than, without delay and without the least equivocalness, with Yes. By denial or silence He would have come into contradiction with Himself. And if it is alleged that our Lord would have had to define more particularly the sense in which He called Himself so, since otherwise a misunderstanding on the part of the heathen ruler would have been possible, we may confidently assume that the tone as well as the manner in which He uttered His answer was fully calculated to excite the Procurator to a more particular investigation. And indeed He attains this purpose, inasmuch as Pilate takes Him apart with himself, that He may now more particularly explain and give the reason for His affirmative answer.

Vs. 4. **I find no fault in this man.**—According to Meyer, Pilate finds in the confession itself the token of innocence.—"It is, in his view, the expression of the fixed idea of an enthusiast." Possible, certainly, although for this opinion not a single proof can be given, but the question would still remain whether such an instantaneous and merely subjective impression would have entitled the Procurator, without further investigation, to declare the Accused at once innocent, and, secondly, if his declaration had been accepted, to relieve him immediately of any further prosecution. We are much more disposed to assume that Pilate, after the first public audience, which all the Synoptics give, ordered then the private hearing, which John alone has preserved, and only in consequence of this uttered the declaration of innocence which Luke, vs. 4; John xviii. 38, relate. In the private interview of Pilate with Jesus, the charge preferred Luke xxiii. 2, it is manifest, is tacitly presupposed. Here, also, Luke remains really unintelligible if he is not complemented from John.

DOCTRINAL AND ETHICAL.

1. The leading away of Jesus is one of the most remarkable turning points in the history of the Passion. It serves not only to fulfil our Lord's declaration that He should be delivered over to the Gentiles, ch. xviii. 32, but it also brings the Passion of our Lord into direct connection with the history of the world, the reins of which, at that time, God had, as it were, placed in the hands of the Romans. It becomes the means of bringing to Him, again according to His own declaration, the death on the cross, but previously prepares, through the declaration of Pilate which it elicits, the revelation of His innocence and majesty. The Jews' rejection of the Messiah is here already, in principle, decided, and with it, at the same time, also, the destruction of the City and of the Temple. While the Sanhedrim, therefore, is leading Him away, it declares therewith that it will not have this Messiah, and gives the promised salvation out of its own hands into the impure hands of heathens. From this hour Israel's Passover becomes an empty echo, and Israel itself, like an impure leaven, is purged out of the house of God, the church of Christ. But thus do they, at the same time, help to fulfil God's everlasting counsel, that all things should be comprehended under one head in Christ, Ephes. i. 10. From the moment when the Great Sufferer trod the threshold of the heathen dwelling, the wall of partition which was between is broken down, Ephes. ii. 14–16, and the heathen world invited in to a nobler feast of freedom than Israel was able to celebrate in the paschal night. As the night,

Acts xvi. 9, 10, was for the spiritual weal of Europe a decisive one, so was this morning for the salvation of the whole heathen world.

2. It is one of the most adorable ways of the providence of God, that at the very time at which Christ must die, a man stood at the head of the government in Judea, who in every respect was most peculiarly fitted to be, in his ignorance, a minister of the counsel of God for the salvation of the world,—on the one hand, receptive enough to recognize the truth, courageous enough to declare it and to confess several times the innocence of our Lord, conscientious enough to omit no effort to deliver Him; but, on the other hand, moreover, so weak that he loved honor among men rather than honor from God, and so selfish that his own honor lay more at heart with him than the cause of the innocent.—We feel that just such a man must the secular judge have been, under whom the Deliverer of the world should suffer death.

3. By the delivery of our Lord to Pilate, the heathen world now becomes partaker with the Jewish world in the greatest wickedness that has ever been committed. In this it appears that the true light is hated as well by those who are under the law as by those who are without the law, and the judgment Rom. iii. 19, 20, appears as a perfectly righteous one. But, at the same time, there is also revealed therein the grace of God, as having appeared to all who believe, without respect of persons, Rom. iii. 21–31.

4. The very manner in which the chief priests here introduce the secular process reveals from the very beginning the part which they are now resolved to play. No means, even slander, is too base for them; for we can only call it thoroughly conscious slander when they, after what had taken place three days before, ch. xx. 20–25, yet venture with bold brow to assert that our Lord had forbidden the payment of taxes. Sometimes they come creeping, sometimes they spitefully erect themselves, and prove therewith that they do homage to the principle: the end sanctifies the means. And scarcely have they failed in one attempt when they proceed immediately with desperate stubbornness to another. So much more gloriously beams over against this night of wickedness the glory of the immaculate innocence of the Lord, to which Pilate must repeatedly bear witness. In union with other voices which were audible in honor of the moral purity of Jesus in the last hours of His life, from different sides, the testimony of Pilate also serves to strengthen us in our most holy faith, that the Lamb of God is indeed an ἀμνὸς ἄμωμος καὶ ἄσπιλος. The connection in which this sinlessness of our Lord stands with the atoning virtue of His death, is something which it is the business of Dogmatics to bring to view.

HOMILETICAL AND PRACTICAL.

The early morning hour of the most remarkable day of the world's history.—The most terrible injustice practised under the forms of law.—The King of the Jews delivered into the hands of the Gentiles.— Christ the centre of the union of the Jewish and the heathen world: 1. The sins of both He, *a*. reveals, *b*. bears, *c*. covers; 2. both He reconciles in one body, *a*. with God, *b*. with one another, *c*. with heaven, Col. i. 19, 20.—Slander against our Lord and His people: 1. Inexhaustible in its weapons; 2. impotent for victory.—Jesus the Faithful Witness, Rev.

Vs. 5.—"Thou sayest it"; 1. The truth; 2. the dignity; 3. the requirement, of this utterance.—The first favorable impression which the Accused makes upon His yet impartial judge.—The immaculate innocence of the Suffering One: 1. Slandered; 2. vindicated; 3. crowned.—The praiseworthy manner in which Pilate opens the trial of Jesus, in contrast with the lamentable way in which he ends it.—Pilate the image of the natural man in his relation to Christ.

STARKE:—They who would otherwise have no communion with one another easily become one when one must help the other to carry out his evil schemes.—QUESNEL:—There is no course of life so righteous and innocent that it cannot be accused and persecuted.—BRENTIUS:—Judge not at once, but hear also the other side.—*Nova Bibl. Tub.*:—One finds often even more uprightness in a heathen than in a Christian judge.—OSIANDER:—Christ has suffered not for His sin but for ours, 2 Cor. v. 21.—HEUBNER:—The preacher of obedience is charged with insurrection.—Jesus, it is true, has caused the greatest imaginable commotions.—ARNDT:—The first hearing of Jesus before the Procurator; how Pilate has to do: 1. With the Jews; 2. with our Lord.—KRUMMACHER:—Christ before Pilate: 1. The leading away of Jesus to Pilate; 2. His entry into the judgment-hall; 3. the beginning of the judicial proceeding.—The accusations.—Christ a King.—The Lamb of God.—THOLUCK:—The history of the Passion makes evident in Pilate to what degree the human heart is capable of becoming shallow and frivolous.—J. B. HASEBROECK, Preacher in Amsterdam:—Pilate: 1. As man: 2. as judge; 3. as witness to us.

---

b. JESUS BEFORE HEROD (Vss. 5-12).

5 And they were the more fierce [insisted, ἐπίσχυον], saying, He stirreth up the people, teaching throughout all Jewry [Judea], beginning from Galilee to this place.
6 [And] When Pilate heard of Galilee, he asked whether the man were a Galilean.
7 And as soon as he knew that he belonged unto Herod's jurisdiction [or, was from Herod's jurisdiction], he sent him to Herod, who himself also was at Jerusalem at that
8 time [in those days]. And when Herod saw Jesus, he was exceeding glad: for he was desirous to see him of a long *season* [had been long desirous], because he had heard
9 many things[1] of him; and he hoped to have seen some miracle done by him. Then he
10 questioned with him in [him with] many words; but he answered him nothing. And
11 the chief priests and scribes stood [by] and vehemently accused him. And Herod with his men of war [or, guards; lit., armies] set him at nought [handled him ignominiously], and mocked *him*, and arrayed him in a gorgeous robe, and sent him again to Pilate.
12 And the same day Pilate and Herod were made friends together [became friends with each other]; for before they were at enmity between themselves.

[1] Vs. 8.—On the authority of B., D., [Cod. Sin.,] K., L., M., the πολλά of the *Recepta* is omitted by Griesbach and others [Meyer, Tregelles, Alford.] The conjecture that it has been interpolated *a scriore manu* to strengthen the text, is sufficiently plausible.

EXEGETICAL AND CRITICAL.

Vs. 5. **And they insisted,** ἐπίσχυον, in an intransitive sense = κατίσχυον, *invalescebant*, Vulgate.—The declaration of Pilate has not corresponded to their expectation. Since now they see that their last charge of the assumption of royal dignity finds no acceptance with the judge, they now come with so much the stronger emphasis back to the first—namely, that He is perverting the people. That the Procurator may still take note that there is nothing less at question here than the peace of the state, they again accuse Jesus of being incessantly occupied in stirring up the people (ἀνασείει, in the Present). The starting point of His tumultuary efforts, they say, is Galilee, ἀρξάμενος, Acts i. 22, but He has already made His way even hither to the centre of the land. According to Matt. xxvii. 12–14; Mark xv. 3-4, they add yet many other accusations, so insignificant, however, that the Evangelists do not even cite them, and our Lord answers them only with silence. Pilate, however, sinks deeper and deeper into perplexity, and so soon, therefore, as he hears the name of Galilee, he seizes on this as a welcome way out of the difficulty. Not without hostile intentions have the Jews named Galilee, since the hatred of the Procurator against the Galileans and against Herod was well known to them; they hope therewith to engage him the more against our Saviour, as a Galilean. But in this respect, at least, their wish is not fulfilled; Pilate hears Galilee spoken of without noticeable bitterness, and since Herod, the Tetrarch of this land, is, by reason of the Passover, just now at Jerusalem, he resolves, so soon as he has learned that Jesus (according to the superficial view of the people, who know nothing of His birth at Bethlehem), is of Galilean origin, to send Him immediately to the Tetrarch.

Vs. 7. **He sent Him to Herod.**—The question is: To what end? According to the common view, in order to relieve himself of the case. According to Meyer, "he seeks by the reference to the judgment of Herod, who could possibly have Him transported to Galilee, to draw himself out of the affair, and to get rid of the case." Unquestionably such a reference from the *forum apprehensionis* to the *forum domicilii* was in and of itself permitted, and also, according to the usages of the Romans, not unusual; comp. Acts xxvi. 3, 4. FRIEDLIEB, *ad loc.* It is, however, a question, whether this intention now really existed in the Procurator's mind. Pilate gives no sign of wishing to remove the case entirely from him; so troublesome and burdensome it was not yet even in this instant to him that he would have wished at any price to be relieved of it. Much more probable is the view (Ewald), that he hopes if possible to obtain a favorable opinion of Herod for the accused; or yet more probable, that he hopes to receive from Herod a further explanation in reference to a person and a case that becomes to him with every moment more obscure, and yet more interesting. Therewith he at the same time, out of policy, shows Herod a courtesy, while he, in case he had committed to Herod the decision of so important a matter without reservation, would thereby have conceded to him a right over himself. The former but not the latter agreed with the disposition of the Procurator, who, indeed, previously had not sent the Galileans, whose blood he had mingled with their sacrifices, Luke xiii. 1, to Herod for execution, but had had them hewn down by his own soldiers. Thus is also explained why our Lord could be silent before Herod, because He recognized in him no legal judge. Thus do we comprehend, moreover, why Pilate, after the return of Jesus from Herod, shows himself in no way disappointed in his expectations, but simply, vss. 13–16, communicates the impression which both he and the Tetrarch had received of the Accused, and thus finally does it become clear why only one Evangelist has considered it as necessary to speak of this occurrence, which, doubtless, even on account of its political consequences, had become generally known. We have here, not a decisive turning-point in the process before us, as was, for example, the case at the arrest, or at the leading away of our Lord to Pilate; but it is a simple endeavor of the Procurator to obtain clearer light about the mysterious element in the case before him, by a measure which was as prudently chosen as perfectly admissible. It was not, however, at all in his design to prepare for the Accused in this way new scorn and sorrow, although it is true the result showed that this, nevertheless, had befallen Him at the hands of Herod.

Vs. 8. **And when Herod saw Jesus, he was exceeding glad.**—Once, when the report of Jesus' miracles came to his ears he had trembled, but even this sting is now blunted: he can now only laugh and scoff. It is the wish of the frivolous Tetrarch now for once to see something right piquant, and to have his court take part in this pastime. For some time already he has had the wish to be able for once to see Jesus (ϑέλων), comp. ch. ix. 7–9, since he has continually heard much about Him, and hoped accordingly to be able to induce Him to the performance of some miracle or other. The possibility that his wish may remain unfulfilled he does not even forebode. Of what sort his questions, vs. 8, were, may be very well conjectured on the one hand from his well known character, and on the other hand from the unshaken silence of the Lord. As a thaumaturge, for whom, without doubt, he took our Lord, he could at most meet Him with childish curiosity, but could not possibly treat Him with even a trace of respect. "Jesus was to entertain him as a mighty magician, divert him, or perhaps foretell luck to his egoistic superstition; anything else he sought not of Him. It is an awful sign to see what a caricature this prince's conceptions were of this First among his subjects, although Jesus had moved his whole land with His spirit. And for so common a character would he take Him, notwithstanding that the Baptist had lived near him and made on him an impression of the spirit of the prophets." Lange.

Vs. 10. **And the chief priests.**—From vs. 15,
we learn that Pilate had commanded them also to appear before Herod, and how could they indeed have neglected this, leaving the prisoner to escape from their hands even for a moment? They see very well that their interest requires them to paint Him to Herod in colors as black as was any way possible, and accuse Him, therefore, with visible emphasis, comp. Acts xviii. 28, as if they feared that even Herod himself, perchance, might be too equitable towards their victim. It was, however, not so much in consequence of their imputations as rather on account of his own disappointed expectations that Herod does not send back our Lord without first overwhelming Him with new ignominy.

Vs. 11. **Mocked Him.**—The priests accuse the Saviour, the courtiers mock Him. With the first it is hatred, with the others contempt that strikes the key. Scoffing is here the vengeance of insulted pride, and reveals itself in a peculiar form. They hang round the shoulders of our Lord a brilliant vesture, ἐσϑῆτα λαμπράν, not exactly of purple, *coccineam vestem*, which is not implied in the word, but brilliantly white, in order to designate Him in the Roman manner as a candidate for some post of honor (Kuinoel, Lange, and others), or in order to characterize Him as King, by arraying Him in a similar garment to that in which generals went into battle (Friedlieb, De Wette, Meyer). In the latter case there was implied in this at the same time an unmistakable intimation for Pilate that such a pretended king did not deserve condemnation, but at the most, contempt.

Vs. 12. **Pilate and Herod became friends.** —The cause of the enmity is unknown. Perhaps it was the massacre of the Galileans, ch. xiii. 1. This result, however, appears at any rate remarkable enough to the delicate psychologist, Luke, not to be passed by unmentioned. In view of the general publicity of this unexpected reconciliation, this remark affords at the same time an indirect but yet a very strong proof of the truth of the event related. That John knew nothing of this intervening scene is indeed asserted by De Wette, but not proved; even if this were the case, however, it would not of itself by any means shake the truth of the fact, since such a thing might very well happen without having come to the knowledge of John, or without being retained in his memory at the writing of his Gospel. In view of the eclecticism of all the Evangelists, even in the history of the Passion, it is dangerous to lay too great weight on an argument *e silentio*. On the other hand, this narrative, in which Herod is depicted to us even as he is known from other accounts, bears altogether the internal character of truth, and may very fittingly be inserted immediately after John xviii. 38. Strauss' conjecture that this whole account has arisen "from an endeavor to bring Jesus before all the judgment-seats that could possibly be brought together at Jerusalem," is without any trace whatever of proof, and if Luke had been induced by an anti-Jewish interest to invent this narrative, in order, namely, to get as many witnesses as possible for the innocence of the Saviour, something of which Baur speaks (*Kanon. Evang.* p. 489), he would without doubt have put a more direct declaration of this innocence in Herod's mouth. Over against these unreasonable doubts it deserves note that as far back as Acts iv. 27, the names of Herod and Pontius Pilate are mentioned together in the prayers of the first believers, and that also Justin Martyr, *Dial. cum Tryph.* ch. 103, is acquainted with this event.

DOCTRINAL AND ETHICAL.

1. At the court of Herod there returns for the Lord once more that temptation, in its deepest ground Satanic, which He, ch. iv. 9–12, had triumphantly repelled. Once again before He is to be elevated on the Cross He sees the opportunity opened to win in the easiest way the favor of the mighty Tetrarch. The scornful courtiers on the one, the blaspheming priests on the other hand—could a more admirable opportunity well have offered itself in order to elicit on the one side astonishment, on the other confusion? But neither of the two the Saviour does; He remains faithful to His fundamental principle, and performs no miracle of display for His own advantage; He explains with His silence His sense of the precept of the Sermon on the Mount, Matt. vii. 6. The shade of John could have observed no more inviolable silence, if it had really appeared to his murderers.

2. If there was during the whole duration of the trial before Pilate an hour which for our Lord deserves to be named an hour of the most unparalleled anguish of soul, it was certainly that of His presentation before Herod. What the view into the depths of Herod's soul must have been for the holy Searcher of hearts, and how much it must have cost Him to see the hand defiled with the blood of the Baptist stretched out caressingly towards Himself, of this we can have only a faint conception. But in the midst of this deep humiliation, in which He is, as it were, tossed like a football from the one impure hand to the other, there shines forth so much the more gloriously the majesty of His eloquent silence. Even the silent Jesus before Herod, doing no miracle, is Himself a sign that is spoken against, but that also awakens wonder. Comp. Luke xi. 29, 30.

3. The silent Jesus over against the laughing court, expiates the sins of the tongue, of vanity and of scoffing contempt, and the white garment of His humiliation is, although Herod presages it not, the prophecy of the shining garments of His glory. Rev. i. 13; xix. 16.

4. The coalition between Herod and Pilate over against the suffering Lord is the prototype of many a shameful covenant which equally implacable enemies in former and later times have concluded, in order together to oppose the sect that is everywhere spoken against.* Acts xxviii. 22.—Unbelief and Superstition, Pharisaism and Sadduceeism, churchly Hierarchy and political Liberalism, Romanism and Republicanism, [Republicanism, in the meaning of this Continental divine, is doubtless synonymous with *red* Republicanism. Indeed, this is certain, as Dr. Van Oosterzee is a warm friend of our country.—C. C. S.] are by nature just such antipodes as Pilate and Herod, and yet, out of egoism, just as disposed to a temporary coalition, when the effort for self-preservation and the irreconcilable hatred towards living Christianity leads the way. In this respect also, the primitive history of the Passion remains a very fresh one, and the past the mirror of the present. [Seeing that, as far as there was any coalition at all between Pilate and Herod, its result was rather favorable to Jesus than the reverse, and certainly was not, on Pilate's part, intended against Him, I can hardly see the exegetical justice of these remarks, although we know that they are sustained by a common proverb. Of the truth of the remarks concerning later coalitions against Christ, there is, of course, no doubt.—C. C. S.]

[* The flourishing condition of living Christianity in our country, renders it difficult for us to apprehend the literalness with which this ancient designation of Christ's people can be used even now by one writing, like the author, in the midst of a kingdom deluged with Rationalism, in which those who are animated by a living faith are little more than a despised and disparaged *ecclesiola in ecclesia*.—C. C. S.]

HOMILETICAL AND PRACTICAL.

The false accusation against Jesus an involuntary eulogy upon Him.—The suffering of our Lord before Herod mentioned in the prayer of His first disciples, Acts iv. 27, 28.—The leading away of our Lord to Herod with its attendant circumstances a revelation of the adorable leading of God in reference to the suffering Saviour. In the beginning we see here: 1. Gloomy night, but soon; 2. a happy dawn, finally; 3. the breaking morning light.—The desire of Herod to see Jesus in contrast with the desire of other kings, ch. x. 23, 24; John viii. 56; xii. 21.—The Saviour in the palace of Herod: 1. Deeply humiliated; 2. severely tempted; 3. found entirely spotless.—The unbridled lust of wonders not nourished but repelled by our Lord.—The frivolity of the court in contrast with the solemnity of the Passion.—How Herod stands over against our Lord, and how our Lord stands over against Herod.—The many unprofitable questions with which even now our Lord and His gospel are besieged by so many who neglect the one question that is needful, Acts xvi. 30.—There comes a time in which our Lord at last gives no more answer at all to His adversaries.—There is a time to speak and a time to keep silence, Eccl. iii. 7.—The silence before Herod: 1. A wise; 2. a dignified; 3. an eloquent silence.—Jesus often keeps silence long, but—in order to speak yet once again.—"Answer not a fool according to his folly," Prov. xxvi. 4.—Spiritual pride is filled with yet deeper enmity towards our Lord than worldly frivolousness.—The High-priest of the New Covenant also in the white garment, even like the High-priest of the Old Testament on each recurring great day of atonement.—Now as ever, false politics knows how to draw much advantage from the name and the cause of our Lord.—[As, for instance, in the pretensions of the European despots to be in a peculiar sense protectors of Christianity, doing it thereby infinitely more damage than if they treated it with all the contempt of Herod.—C. C. S.]—The Lord brings the counsel of the heathen to nought, He maketh the devices of the people of none effect, Ps. xxxiii. 10, 11.—He that overcometh, the same shall be clothed in white raiment, Rev. iii. 5.

STARKE:—QUESNEL:—The high ones in the world always want to be having a new spectacle and a new sensation to feed their eyes and mind.—*Nova Bibl. Tub.*:—When people who have no religion want to inquire, talk, and dispute much about religion, it is best not to answer them, but to shame them with a humble silence.—To enter into talk with courtiers does more harm than good.—Ungodly teachers are Christ's most implacable foes.—Envy is intensely zealous, but without understanding.—The children of the world take Christ for a puppet and amuse themselves therewith.—Great people's friendship is like April weather,—no one can reckon upon it.—HEUBNER:—The history of Christ repeats itself in different periods of His church.—How many honest witnesses are charged with making uproars.—The great world often regard religious preaching as entertainment, as diversion.—Not a few clergymen at court have been even merrymakers.—Never use thy gifts, intellect, wit, skill, to make laughter.—The friend of God should, in company, and even in the power of scoffers, maintain his dignity (like Haller before Voltaire). — LUTHER : — Every true Christian, if he preaches Christ aright, has his Herod and Pilate.— RIEGER :—" Where the people have no ears to hear, there Jesus has no mouth to speak."—ARNDT :— Herod's behavior towards Jesus: 1. His false expectation; 2. his great disappointment; 3. his ineffectual vengeance.—KRUMMACHER :—Christ before Herod. This Passion Gospel shows us : 1. A mirror of the world ; 2. a glowing sacrificial flame; 3. a glorifying of Jesus against the will of those that render it.—BESSER :—A miracle had Herod expected to see of our Lord; he really saw one, but he comprehended it not. For a miracle of the love which traverses all the depths of shame for us, which suffers itself to be arrayed in a white robe, that we might appear before the throne of God in white garments of honor, a miracle of this love is it indeed that our Lord withholds the curse which otherwise might have fallen upon His mockers, as upon the mocking children at Bethel, 2 Kings ii. 24.—*A. des Amorie van der Hoeven.* Remonstrant, Professor at Amsterdam. † 1855.—Jesus before Herod the object: 1. Of indifference; 2. of idle curiosity; 3. of slander; 4. of scoffing; 5. of the policy of men.—SAURIN :—*Nouv. Serm.* i. p. 239 *seq.*:—He perverteth the people.— WOLF :—Worldly wisdom as judge in Jesus' case. —PALMER :—Three main forms of sin: 1. Ignominious servility in Pilate; 2. contemptible frivolity in Herod ; 3. lying malice in the chief priests.

c. FRUITLESS ENDEAVORS OF PILATE TO LIBERATE JESUS (Vss. 13-25).

(Parallel with Matt. xxvii. 15-26; Mark xv. 6-15; John xviii. 39, 40.)

13 And Pilate, when he had called together the chief priests and the rulers and the
14 people, Said unto them, Ye have brought this man unto me, as one that perverteth [turneth away] the people [*i. e.*, from Cesar]; and, behold, I, having examined *him* before you, have found no fault in this man touching those things whereof ye accuse
15 him : No, nor yet [even¹] Herod: for I sent you to him ; and, lo, nothing worthy of
16 death is [has been] done unto [by] him. I will therefore chastise him, and release
17, 18 *him*. (For of necessity he must release one unto them at the feast.²) And they cried out all at once [πανπληθεί], saying, Away³ with this *man*, and release unto us
19 Barabbas: (Who⁴ for a certain sedition made in the city, and for murder, was [had
20 been] cast into prison.) Pilate therefore, willing [wishing] to release Jesus, spake
21 again to them. But they cried [against it, ἐπεφώνουν], saying, Crucify *him*, crucify
22 him. And he said unto them the third time, Why, what evil hath he done ? I have
23 found no cause of death in him : I will therefore chastise him, and let *him* go. And they were instant [urgent, ἐπέκειντο] with loud voices, requiring [demanding] that he
24 might be crucified: and the voices of them and of the chief priests prevailed. And Pilate gave sentence that it should be as they required [their demand should go into
25 effect]. And he released unto them [om., unto them⁵] him [the one] that for sedition and murder was [had been] cast into prison, whom they had desired; but he delivered Jesus to their will.

[¹ Vs. 15.—The ἀλλ' οὐδέ implies that if even Herod, though well acquainted with the Jewish law, and, as the sovereign of the accused, especially solicitous that he might not be allowed to stir up the people against the Romans, Herod's patrons, if even he could find no matter of complaint, the case might be looked upon as decided. Herod, it is true, does not appear to have instituted any formal inquiry, but Pilate is willing so to represent it, to support his intended release of the prisoner by Herod's authority.—C. C. S.]
² Vs. 17.—Respecting the grounds on which the genuineness of this verse is doubtful, see *Exegetical* and *Critical* remarks. [Omitted by A., B., K., L.; retained by Cod. Sin. Omitted by Tischendorf, Meyer, Tregelles; bracketed by Lachmann; approved by Bleek; retained by Alford.—C. C. S.]
[³ Vs. 18.—Αἶρε. "Make away with," " *E medio tolle.*"—C. C. S.]
[⁴ Vs. 19.—Ὅστις ἦν, κ.τ.λ., *quippe qui*, as Meyer remarks, not equivalent to the simple *qui*, but, as ὅστις always denotes category, " a man of such a sort as to have been," &c.; the form of the relative reflecting unconsciously the indignation of the Evangelist at so hideous a preference.—C. C. S.]
⁵ Vs. 25.—The αὐτοῖς, which Griesbach adds to the ἀπέλυσε, is from Matthew and Mark.

EXEGETICAL AND CRITICAL.

Vs. 13. And Pilate, when he had called together . . . the people. — It is not enough for Pilate to communicate his peculiar views merely to the Sanhedrists. He calls also the people together, the number of whom has considerably increased during the sending of our Lord back and forth, and who take a lively interest in the matter. He assembles them in order to communicate to them also his mind and will, which he wished to be regarded as definitive. He introduces his communication now by a more or less official address, in which the motives of the sentence to be uttered are stated. The judge sums up the *acta* before he declares them concluded. He comes back to the first charge (vs. 2), that this man perverts the people (ὡς ἀποστρέφοντα). On this charge he had heard Him in their presence. *See* vs. 3 ; comp. Matt. xxvii. 12-14; Mark xv. 3-5, which is not in conflict with John xviii. 33 *seq.* (De Wette, Meyer), if only we distinguish between the private interview and the public audience, of which latter Pilate here speaks. They see, therefore, that he has taken up the matter in earnest, but in direct opposition to their εὕρομεν, vs. 2, he is obliged to declare himself, for his part, to have found nothing which could be maintained before the secular judge, as legal ground of an accusation. Respecting the peculiar construction of this passage, *see* Meyer. Nay, not even Herod, who, as Tetrarch of Galilee, would yet undoubtedly have known if there had existed ground for a serious accusation, not even he has been able to discover anything tenable in their charge. On the contrary, they are both convinced that, whatever reports may have been circulated abroad, this man has, in fact, neither committed anything (πεπραγμένον) nor brought about anything that could be called criminal. After this introduction, there appears to be scarcely any other final judgment possible than a simple release, but—"*hic capit nimium concedere Pilatus.*" Bengel.

Vs. 16. **Chastise Him and release Him.**—"Chastise." Although the word "scourge" is not yet uttered, Pilate can scarcely have had any other chastisement in mind. He makes this proposition that he may not, on the one hand, too heavily load his own conscience, on the other hand, because he must not let the Jews go wholly unsatisfied. A light punishment of the kind, at all events, the enthusiast probably deserves in his eyes, who, harmless as He is for the Roman authority, has yet given Himself out for a King. The alleged confusion with John xix. 1-4 (De Wette) is by no means real, but Luke in his summary notices, relates only a plan of the scourging, the execution of which the three other Evangelists relate. It is remarkable, moreover, how in the connection of the two words: CHASTISE and RELEASE, Pilate begins already evidently to show either that he is disposed to do too much or too little. Hitherto he has done three good things: he began a careful investigation, he has made a solemn declaration of Jesus' innocence, he has taken an admissible way to gain more particular information. The word "release" would set the crown on all this, if it were not that the illegal chastisement announced simultaneously with this prepared the way for three opposite measures, by which his weakness passes over into crime. A dishonoring comparison, a painful scourging, a mournful spectacle (Matt. xxvii. 24) are the steps which make way for that most unrighteous judgment. Luke has only described the first.

Vs. 17. **For of necessity he must release one.**—Although it is unquestionably possible that this verse was omitted quite early, because it appeared to be placed with more or less incorrectness, and interrupted the course of the narrative (De Wette), it is, however, more probable that it is not genuine. It is wanting in A., B., K., L., [retained by Cod. Sin., *see* notes on the text.—C. C. S.] Copt., Sahid., Vers., and is placed after vs. 19, by D., Æth., Cant., while, besides this, many variations appear in the details. It appears, therefore, after having seemed suspicious to Griesbach and Lachmann, to have been omitted with reason by Tischendorf, although the clause must be tolerably old, since it has found its way into by far the greatest number of manuscripts and versions. But, however this may be, the fact itself, namely, that the governor at the Passover was under obligation to release a prisoner, cannot be doubted, although the origin of this usage is veiled in obscurity. To us everything appears to favor the opinion that this had grown up rather on Jewish than on heathen soil. Even the expression of Pilate, ἔστι δὲ συνήθεια ὑμῖν, John xviii. 39, appears to point to the former; the connection of this custom with the Passover was far more likely to be a Jewish than a heathen idea. The coincidence with the Roman Lectisternia and [the Greek] Thesmophoria, which are referred to, is exceedingly slight, and it was much more in the spirit of the Roman policy to leave the inhabitants of a province in possession of a national privilege than to press on them a foreign benefit, especially when they had such an aversion to foreign manners as the Jews. They could the more easily assume to themselves the *jus gladii* if they still, at least one day of the year, did not bestow, but left yet with the nation, a seemingly free disposal over life and death. And although the Scripture, no more than the Talmud, brings this usage into connection with the signification of the Passover, yet with a people who, like the Jewish, were accustomed to symbolical actions, this connection struck the eye at once. In this manner it is, at the same time, intelligible why the people attached so great a value to this their prerogative, Mark xv. 6-8, that it was from them first that the demand proceeded, which gave Pilate occasion to the most dreadful comparison. *Finally, this voice of the people furnishes one convincing proof the more, that to-day was really already the first day of the Passover, since the prayer would have come very much out of season if the feast had not yet had a beginning.*

Vs. 18. **Away with this man.**—Here, also, we first gain a clear conception of the fact, when we complement Luke from the other gospels. The wild cry αἶρε presupposes that our Lord already stands before the eyes of the multitude, together with the hideous Barabbas. But how matters had gone so far is described especially by Mark, while Matthew, by the narrative of the dream of Pilate's wife, solves for the reader the difficulty how it had been possible that the people in so short a time could have been filled with so fanatical a fury. The short absence of the Procurator is used by the priests most energetically to work the people over to their mind, and very soon does the clue to this labyrinth slip out of Pilate's hands.

Vs. 19. **Who for a certain sedition.**—Respecting the character of Barabbas, *see* LANGE on the parallel in Matthew. In all the gospels, but especially in Luke, vss. 19, 25, there is expressed the deepest displeasure at the blindness and hardened temper of the Jews, who could make such a choice. An echo of this tone of righteous resentment we still hear in the declaration of Peter, Acts iii. 14.

Vs. 20. **Spake again to them,** προσεφώνησε, which is used, Acts xxi. 40, of a longer address, here, however, probably consisted only of a few words, and those not essentially different from the ones which are communicated to us a little before and a little later. In all this the good intention of Pilate cannot possibly be entirely lost sight of. His proposal had sprung from a laudable principle, had a laudable end in view, and appeared, at the same time, to offer for its accomplishment an exceedingly fitting means. In the persuasion that personal hatred impelled the chief priests, he seeks to win the voice of the people in favor of Jesus, and believes that he may expect nothing else than that the result will fully correspond to his wishes. But still his conduct remains worthy of reprobation, not only before the judgment-seat of strict righteousness, but even before that of wise considerateness. All the words with which he now, after this, seeks to conjure down the rising storm, signify little or nothing, because he does not yet come to the one act which he has already indicated as his purpose—ἀπολύσω!

Vs. 21. **Crucify Him, Crucify Him.**—For the first time the terrible cry is here heard, which, as the secret wish and thought of the chief priests, is now by these placed upon the people's lips, and with fanatical rage raised by these. According to John, ch. xviii. 40, they cry again, πάλιν: "Not this man but Barabbas" must be released, although the Evangelist has not mentioned a previous cry,—a new proof how admissible and necessary it is to complement the statements of the fourth Evangelist from the narratives of the Synoptics, which were familiar to him. This cry was the direct answer to the question which Matt. xxvii. 22, and Mark xv. 12, communicate.

Vs. 22. **The third time.**—To Luke alone we owe the remarkable, and of itself probable, account, that the governor at this point of the trial raises for the third time his voice in favor of our Lord. No wonder, he feels that if he here gives way, the death of Jesus is as good as decided, and that all further endeavors which he might, perhaps, yet make for the discharge of his official duty, would, after this great concession, be fruitless. He repeats, therefore, essentially what he has already said, vss. 14, 16, and assumes outwardly a demeanor so much the firmer the more he is inwardly beginning to waver.

Vs. 23. **And they.**—It is as if the one word, "Release," which he has once more ventured to utter, filled them with all the more furious rage. Now the chief priests also join in the impetuous cry of the raging people for blood. "*Etiam decori immemores cum plebe clamabant.*" Bengel. These voices obtain the upper hand, κατίσχυον. The same word which, Matt. xvi. 18, is used of the gates of hell over against the church.

Vs. 24. **And Pilate gave sentence,** ἐπέκρινεν, 2 Macc. iv. 47. In contrast with the provisional judgment which the Sanhedrim had already passed, the final judgment is here spoken of, without our, however, being required by Luke to understand a formally uttered sentence. On the contrary, the distinction in the demeanor of Pilate in reference to Barabbas and Jesus is not to be mistaken. The former—Luke, in righteous displeasure, does not even mention his name, but only discloses to us a view into the disgraceful history of Barabbas—he expressly releases: apparently the murderer is unfettered before his eyes, so that he after a few moments hastens free through the streets of Jerusalem. The other he delivers up, παρέδωκεν, not by a solemn *ibis ad crucem*, but by simply letting go the weak hand with which he had hitherto vainly sought to protect the victim of priestly hate. Not to the will of the judge or the requirement of the law, but to the judgment of the people, τῷ θελήματι αὐτῶν, is the Prisoner surrendered. On this account, also, it is not even necessary to inquire into the genuineness of the old record of the sentence: *Jesum Nazarenum, subversorem gentis*, &c., which ADRICHOMIUS, *Theatr. terræ sanctæ, Colon.* 1593, p. 163, has, it is said, taken from old annals, and which FRIEDLIEB, *ad loc.*, communicates in a note entire.

Since we here have to do, not with the history of the Passion in general, but with the narrative which Luke has given us of the same, we also pass over the particulars which he does not communicate expressly. As respects, however, the sequence of the different scenes in the trial before Pilate, we believe that a correct harmony requires the following arrangement: 1. The Leading Away to Pilate, which Luke relates with its particulars; 2. The First Public (Synoptics), and immediately after that the First Private (John), Examination of our Lord by the Procurator; 3. More Vehement Accusation by the Jews after Pilate's first declaration of innocence, followed then by the sending to Herod; 4. First Decision of Pilate, in which his wavering first becomes visible (Luke xxiii. 13–16); 5. His proposal to select Barabbas or Jesus (all the Evangelists); 6. Delay by the communication of the dream of Pilate's wife (Matthew), during which the people are persuaded over; 7. Decision of the question, "Barabbas or Jesus," in favor of the former (all the Evangelists); 8. The Scourging, as the customary, yet not indispensably necessary, preliminary of crucifixion, which, however, according to Luke, is used as a measure of compromise, as well as in order, by presentation of the pitiably maltreated Prisoner, to dispose the people to compassion (John); 9. In consequence of this, the Crucifixion decidedly refused, and a new accusation brought up by the disappointed priests (John xix. 6, 7); 10. Further, but fruitless, endeavors even yet to deliver Jesus (John xix. 6–12); 11. The Washing of Pilate's hands (Matt. xxvii. 24, 25), which Matthew, in view of his objective representation of the Scourging as the preparation for Crucifixion (which it, considered *a posteriori*, in fact became), places before this maltreatment, but which, as evidently appears, has only sense and significance if we conceive it as a concluding act; finally, 12. The scene described in John xix. 13–16, for which we may with more right assume a place after than before the washing of the hands (as is proposed by Sturm). Immediately after this, the Leading Away to Calvary, which Luke communicates most in detail. —It appears, therefore, that Luke xxiii. 24, 25 cannot be attached immediately to the choice of Barabbas, but is to be regarded as the concluding act of the trial before Pilate, some intervening scenes of which Luke has passed over. As to the actual point of time of our Lord's Delivery to Crucifixion, which Luke also leaves unmentioned, comp. also LANGE on Matt., *ad loc.*, and on Mark xv. 25. It is noticeable that Luke, with the exception of vs. 44, refrains in his account of the Passion from almost any attempt to give any particular notes of time.

DOCTRINAL AND ETHICAL.

1. By the unequivocal declaration of Pilate after our Lord's return from Herod, not only did His innocence appear in the most brilliant manner, but it thereby, at the same time, became evident also how unreasonable the opinion of Christians and theologians was, who, like the older Deists and Rationalists, ventured to invent for our Lord political views. Pilate and Herod do not yet know anything of that which in the last century was hatched out by the Wolfenbüttel Fragmentist concerning this. Even the Jews are not able to destroy Him by political charges. They must immediately, John xix. 7, proceed further to an accusation founded on religious grounds.

2. The sad observation how Pilate with every moment sinks deeper and deeper, gives us a powerful contribution to Anthropology and Hamartology; but, at the same time, there is implied therein, not less

than in the direct testimonies borne to the innocence of our Lord, a striking argument for the immaculate purity of Jesus. Soon, also, does it appear that weakness, as well as hatred, may mislead man to the most terrible crime. Pilate, who first only becomes Herod's friend, will at last also remain Tiberius' friend, and becomes therewith a confederate of the chief priests and of the people, nay, the accomplice of Caiaphas. Then how is the truth of the saying here proved: "He that is not with Me is against Me."

3. In the transaction respecting the choice between Jesus and Barabbas, it appears very plainly how dangerous it is to let the popular voice decide upon the highest questions of life, upon truth and right. The history of the Passion raises a terrible protest against the familiar maxim: *Vox populi, vox Dei;* while, on the other hand, it powerfully confirms the truth of the poet's sentence:—

*Was ist Mehrheit? Mehrheit ist ein Unsinn,
Verstand ist stets bei Wen'gen nur gewesen;
Der Staat muss untergehn, früh oder spät,
Wo Mehrheit siegt und Unverstand entscheidet.*

[What is majority? Majority is absurdity. Understanding has ever been with few only; the state must perish early or late, where majority prevails and folly decides.] In church history, also, we see how often ecclesiastical and political democracy have led to genuine Barabbas-choices. Compare the admirable dissertation by ULLMANN, *Die Geltung der Majoritäten in der Kirche,* Hamburg, 1850.*

4. For the typical significance of that which here took place with Barabbas, the Mosaic law, Lev. xvi. 5–10, must, in particular, be compared. The importance of this part of the history of the Passion is only comprehended perfectly when we find represented to the very sight therein, in historical symbols, the idea of representation, and behold in the released Barabbas the image of the sinner, who, in consequence of the death of this immaculately Holy One ὑπέρ αὐτοῦ, is acquitted of the guilt and punishment of sin. [The release of a murderer, without the slightest sign that he was changed for the better, is a rather equivocal type of the justification of the sinner.—C. C. S.] In this way, moreover, we learn also to understand the significance of the unshaken silence which our Lord in these awful moments of decision, during which He remains so entirely passive, maintains. It is here, in the full sense of the word, the silence of the Lamb of God, on whom the sins of the world were laid, Isaiah liii. 6.

5. The choice between Jesus and Barabbas is the striking type of the choice which, through all the centuries, is proposed to mankind, the choice, namely, between life and death, between blessing and cursing, Gen. ii. 16, 17; Deut. xxx. 18, 19; Josh. xxiv. 15, &c. The motives which here misled the people to so perverted a choice are the same as those which now, as ever, induce most of men to choose the appearance instead of the reality, and the curse instead of the blessing.

* [A crime which was forced on a populace that, left to itself, would not have committed it, by a corrupt and implacable aristocracy, is a curious text for this diatribe against popular government. However, this, like all similar expressions of our author, must be judged in view of the dislike which he has to a democracy so deeply infected with infidelity as the European democracy, even though that infidelity is in no small measure owing to the tyrannies and frauds of priests and Most Christian kings. Dr. Van Oosterzee, however, has expressed his most unqualified sympathy with our national cause.—C. C. S.]

6. The moment of the popular choice between Jesus and Barabbas is the decisive moment, not only in the history of the Passion, but also in the history of Israel and the world, Rom. ix. 30–33.

7. "It is something yet other and worse to reject the Lord after He was there rejected, and first became the foundation of our salvation. These Jews had, at all events, at that time not yet rejected Him who in infinite love had ascended the cross for our redemption. Woe to the betrayers of the Crucified!"

HOMILETICAL AND PRACTICAL.

In the mouth of two or three witnesses every word shall be established, 2 Cor. xiii. 1, even where our Lord's innocence is declared.—Whoever complains that Christ and the gospel pervert the world in a political respect, stands in principle even below Pilate and Herod.—Pilate the man who wishes to serve two masters.—The false lust of compromise condemned in the person of Pilate.—The mournful triumph of persistent wickedness over hesitating weakness.—Jesus over against Barabbas a picture of universal history.—The fatal choice of the Jews a primitive and yet eternally new history.—Whoever prefers sin to Christ, he chooses like them: 1. A robber instead of the wealthiest Distributor of grace; 2. a rebel instead of the King of peace; 3. a murderer instead of the Prince of life.—The choice of the service of the world instead of the service of Christ, how it: 1. Bears the same character; 2. betrays the same origin; 3. deserves the same judgment; 4. needs the same atonement, as the fatal choice of the Jews.—The fatal choice even yet, as then, a fruit: 1. Of heedlessness; 2. of misleading influence; 3. of weakness; 4. of the enmity of the flesh.—The inconstancy of popular favor and of human honor [There is no certainty that the masses who hung on Jesus' lips as He taught were the same that here demanded His blood. There were surely men enough in Jerusalem to furnish crowds for this purpose, without of necessity involving one of those who had so recently heard Him with delight.—C. C. S.].—The cry of Crucify Him! over against the Hosannas of the throngs.—The first cry for murder considered in reference: 1. To the judge who elicits it; 2. to the people that utter it; 3. to the Saviour who hears it; 4. to the Father who accepts it; 5. to the world which yet in all manner of forms repeats it.—" O, My people, what have I done unto thee? and wherein have I wearied thee?" Micah vi. 3.—The highest activity of the love of Christ in the midst of seemingly complete passivity.—The murder of Messiah the suicide of Israel.—Whither concessions and compromises may at last lead.—The blind policy of Pilate, who will: 1. Deliver our Lord by evil means; 2. give up our Lord to save himself.—Jesus: 1. Reckoned with the transgressors, Isaiah liii. 12; 2. humbled among the transgressors; 3. by that very means given up for transgressors, 2 Cor. v. 21.—Jesus most deeply humiliated: 1. By comparison with a malefactor; 2. with a malefactor like Barabbas; 3. with a malefactor that, moreover, is preferred to Him.—The diverse departure of the Prince of life and of the murderer from Gabbatha.—The fearful defeat of wickedness even in a seeming victory.—For every man there appears, as once for Pilate, an hour when he must decide for or against Christ.

STARKE:—BRENTIUS:—Christ had to pass from one unrighteous judge to another; be content, my brother, if without cause the like of this befalleth thee, 1 Peter ii. 21.—CRAMER:—The gospel of Christ must be true, for the heathen, His enemies, testify of His innocence.—Christ's innocence has given to the whole Passion the just weight before the judgment of God, Heb. vii. 26.—*Nova Bibl. Tub.*:—Innocence at last breaks through all imputations.—Sinful and evil usages must not be furthered by the magistrate, but disregarded, especially when they take place on Sundays and feast days.—A malefactor who, according to God's law, has deserved death, must be allowed right and judgment.—Unrighteous judgment of the world: the murderer shall live, the Prince of life die.—CANSTEIN:—The world loveth her own, it is a den of murderers.—Human wisdom goes with the tide and is partial.—*Nova Bibl. Tub.*:—Hatred and envy is something utterly devilish.—Of evil things, too, there are wont to be three, vs. 22 [an allusion to the German proverb, *Aller guten dinge sind drei*, "All good things go in threes."—C. C. S.]—"I will, I will," is indeed the speech of godless people too, but woe to them if they rest satisfied therewith.—Where the people have more power than the government, there is a dish spoiled and a most unhappy state.—The world judges not according to right, but according to favor.—OSIANDER:—It is nature's view of the world for the vicious to escape punishment and the innocent to be punished, Ps. lxxiii. 12.—

BRENTIUS:—The issue demonstrates ever how far human wisdom reaches, and what we can promise ourselves therefrom.—ARNDT:—The choice between Jesus and Barabbas; 1. What determines Pilate to this choice; 2. on what rock it splits; 3. how it turns out for the salvation of the world.—KRUMMACHER:—Pilate our advocate, who frees us from the threefold imputation of seditious tendencies, of senseless teachings, and exaggerated consolations.—Jesus and Barabbas, the great picture.—The release of Barabbas: 1. How this was effected; 2. how the joyful tidings was received on the part of Barabbas.—The conclusion of the process.—THOLUCK:—The dreadful illusion which unbelieving Israel is under, inasmuch as it, instead of Jesus the Son of God chooses Jesus Barabbas; 2. which the unbelieving world is under, inasmuch as it, instead of Jesus the Son of God and man, chooses Jesus the child of man (*Predigten*, i. p. 127 *seq.*, together with an appendix very well worth reading, p. 156). [Calmet has this statement: "Origen says that in many copies Barabbas is called JESUS likewise. The Armenian has the same reading: 'Whom ... will ye that I deliver unto you: JESUS Barabbas, or JESUS who is called Christ?' This gives additional spirit to the history, and well deserves notice."—C. C. S.]—In Barabbas Pilate released the murderer of *his* soul; in the Lord Jesus he rejected the deliverer of *his* soul.

---

4. Calvary (Vss. 26–43).

a. THE LEADING AWAY TO THE CROSS (Vss. 26–31).

(Parallel with Matt. xxvii. 31, 32; Mark xv. 20–22; John xix. 16, 17.)

26 And as they led him away, they laid hold upon one Simon, a Cyrenian, coming out
27 of the country, and on him they laid the cross, that he might bear *it* after Jesus. And there followed him a great company of people, and of women, which also bewailed and
28 lamented him. But Jesus turning unto them said, Daughters of Jerusalem, weep not
29 for me, but weep for yourselves, and for your children. For, behold, the days are coming [there come days], in the which they shall say, Blessed *are* the barren, and the wombs that never bare, and the paps [breasts] which never gave suck [nourishment[1]].
30 Then shall they begin to say to the mountains, Fall on us; and to the hills, Cover us.
31 For if they do these things in a [on, or to, the] green tree [or, wood], what shall be done in [happen to] the dry?

[1] Vs. 29.—*Rec.*: ἐθήλασαν, apparently an *interpretamentum* of the original ἔθρεψαν, which Lachmann and Tischendorf, [Meyer, Tregelles, Alford] read, on the ground of B., [Cod. Sin.,] C.¹ and ², D., L., [C.², D. having ἐξέθρ.] 4 Cursives, [Versions. It is almost needless to say that ἐθήλ. might very easily be substituted for ἔθρεψ., but ἔθρεψ. we may be sure was never substituted for ἐθήλασαν.—C. C. S.]

EXEGETICAL AND CRITICAL.

Vs. 26. **And as they led Him away.**—As respects the identity of the present *via dolorosa* (Haradell-Alahm) with the way of our Lord to the Cross, this is at least doubtful. It is about a league in length, starting from the *prætorium*, inside the walls of the city, in a northwesterly direction as far as Mount Calvary. The actual way to the Cross was hardly so long, and appears also to have tended more southerly. The spuriousness at least of the so-called Stations, as, for instance, of the place from whence the train set out, where Simon of Cyrene met the Lord, where Mary sank down speechless, and heard a "*Salve Mater*" from His mouth, where Veronica handed Him the handkerchief, upon which immediately, in a miraculous way, the features of His countenance impressed themselves, &c., can hardly need any further mention, although, for instance, even Chateaubriand has defended their identity. Even Sepp, iii. 536, no longer ventures to take these traditions under his protection, and Lamartine also allowed that he had found here stone-heaps of far later date. In reference to specialities of this sort, the admirable expression of Von Schubert holds good, *Reise durch das Morgenland*, ii. p. 505: "Although it may be that here the childlike devotion of the natives, when it describes to us the individual features of the great picture, sometimes appears similar to a countryman whose cottage stands in the neighborhood of a battle-field, when he, not with the words of an experienced soldier, still less with the certainty of an eye-witness, relates to us what here and there took place upon the greatly-altered spots: still the relation will ever move us to deepest sympathy; for it is at all events an echo of that which his ancestors here really saw and experienced. There is now passing the sixteenth century since Constantine and Helena's times, of those that have edified and spiritually refreshed themselves from the monuments of these mighty recollections." Respecting, however, the identity of Calvary and the Holy Sepulchre, see LANGE, *Matthew*, p. 520, and the there cited authors, with whose results we ou the whole can agree.

They laid hold of.—A more exact expression, ἀγγαρεύειν, is found in Matthew and Mark, a word which, with the exception of Matt. v. 41, is only found in this passage of the New Testament. That the idea of a military constraint is implied in it is certainly beyond question, wherein, it is true, in respect to the person of the one thus impressed, the form in which the impressment took place, and the occasion why precisely he was chosen in preference to all others, a wide field remains open to the fancy of exegetes for all manner of conjectures. The most important we find in Matthew, *ad loc*. Unless we assert that the notice of Mark, "father to Alexander and Rufus," was written down without any purpose, then the conjecture is obvious that this meeting with our Lord became for Simon and his house an event of great importance, and the occasion of his afterwards bearing the Cross after Christ in a yet higher sense. In this case then, the King of the kingdom of God has, even on His way to the Cross, won a subject, and the well-known fiction of the Basilidians (of whom EPIPHANIUS, *Hæres*. 24, 3, makes mention), that Simon died on the Cross instead of our Lord, acquires then a beautiful symbolical sense. Not in the place of our Lord, but in His fellowship, was, thus, not indeed his body, but his old sinful nature nailed with Jesus to the tree. Comp. Rom. vi. and Matt. xvi. 24.

Coming out of the country.—" Belongs to the Synoptical traces of a working day." Meyer. To this, however, the fact is opposed that we do not learn how distant this field [ἀπ' ἀγροῦ] was from the city, and as little whether he had been working in the country, in which case it must not at the same time be left out of sight that a feast day with the Jews was by no means observed more strictly than the Sabbath; but, on the contrary, less strictly. Very justly, therefore, does Wieseler remark : "We Christians [He means, of course : "We *Continental* Christians."—C. C. S.] easily mistake the true relation, by comparing the Jewish Sabbath with our Sunday, and then remembering that the feast days to us are holier, celebrated with more Sabbath rest than our common Sundays." The name of the *greatest Sabbath*, Levit. xvi. 31, [Shabbathon,] is among all the feast and memorial days only given to the great day of atonement; but on the remaining feasts this strict abstinence from all labor is not required as on every seventh day (comp. Lev. xxiii. 31 with vss. 7, 21, 25, 35, where there is a careful distinction made between labor and servile labor). Even among the present Jews the greater holiness which the weekly Sabbath and the great day of atonement have above all other feasts is among other circumstances visible from this fact, that during the two first-named days, but not during the latter, mourning for the dead is suspended; that on the former they bury no corpses, but they do so on the latter, &c. We do not, accordingly, even hold it necessary for an explanation of the compulsory service imposed upon Simon of Cyrene to assume (Lange) that they were disposed therewith, regarding him as somewhat of a Sabbathbreaker, to let him smart a little for it.

On him they laid the cross, ἐπέθηκαν ... φέρειν ὄπισθεν τοῦ Ἰησοῦ.—The general expression of Matthew and Mark, ἵνα ἄρῃ τὸν σταυρόν must be explained according to this more precise one of Luke. It is no φέρειν ὑπέρ τοῦ Ἰησοῦ, but ὄπισθεν, so that our Lord obtains, it is true, some lightening, but not a freeing from bearing the cross. The cross was bound with cords upon the shoulders, and it is hardly probable that they would have lost much time in unbinding it from our Saviour and laying it in His stead upon the back of Simon; it is, therefore, not an entire transfer of the cross that is spoken of, but only a bearing of it with Him, and particularly the hinder part; and if one should even assert that our Lord found His burden hereby much rather aggravated than relieved, since then the fore-part must have pressed so much the more heavily upon Him, it would only follow from this, as often, that the tender mercies of the wicked were cruel. As to the rest, we do not read in any of the Evangelists that our Saviour was about to sink under the load if just at the right time Simon had not supported Him. Here also the Saviour bears the heaviest part of the burden, while the (comparatively) lightest part rests on the shoulders of him who follows after Jesus.

Vs. 27. **Women, which also bewailed.**—A beautiful trait of genuine humanity, which in the third Gospel is exactly in its place. As customary at public executions, so here also, a great crowd have streamed together, among whom there are also women from Jerusalem. Luke, in whose Gospel the most of the women who stood in connection with Jesus are described, relates to us also how their compassion strewed yet one last flower for our Lord upon His path of thorns. This phenomenon was the more remarkable because it, at least according to a later Jewish tradition, was considered as entirely unlawful to bestow on a malefactor who was led to the place of punishment any proof whatever of compassion. These women have, however, been placed too high when they have been put on a level with the Galilean friends of our Lord, and again too low when it is asserted that they only showed traces of an entirely superficial sympathy, such as is brought up so easily at the view of any pitiable object. In the last case our Lord would assuredly never have deemed these women worthy of a particular address, and what, moreover, could there be against supposing that at least some were found among them who personally knew Jesus, who had been affected by His preaching, or who, by report, or by their own experience of His benefits, had become engaged in His favor ? We do not need, therefore, (Sepp,) to understand highminded matrons who had come to a work of love, and bore in their hands a wine drugged with myrrh (which was to be a composing draught for the Saviour). They have no myrrh wine, but tear-water, wherewith they moisten the way to the Cross; but the sincerity of their sympathy becomes for our Lord upon this sorrowful course a refreshment, and He who before a frivolous Herod has kept silence, gives now these sorrowing women to hear His powerful admonitions. It is the last connected discourse of our Lord of any length that is uttered on this occasion; afterwards we shall hear only single interrupted words before His death. Perhaps He uses thereto the moment of delay which the impression of Simon had occasioned; in this case the difficulty at once disappears, "that at this moment we are hardly to presume a witness as present who could have caught up and related any words uttered by Jesus." (Weisse). What our Lord had uttered with composed dignity and intelligibly enough, may very well have been related by a sufficient number of witnesses, and particularly by the women themselves to His disciples.

Vs. 28. **Daughters of Jerusalem.**—Our Lord undoubtedly does not overlook the fact that the compassion of these women had not the three condemned in equal measure, but Himself personally as its object. Therefore, also, He does not say: "Weep not for *us*,"—the terrible equalizing of Him with two murderers is only to be made some minutes later by the hands of His executioners,—but "Weep not for Me," and He directs their look from Himself to their own future by the touching words: "Weep for yourselves and your children." The latter certainly not without direct allusion to the imprecation of the Jews, Matt. xxvii. 25, whose fulfilment should come upon the children of these women also. Not to elicit new fruitless emotion, He now adds, not a Woe upon those with child, but a somewhat softer "Blessed" upon the unfruitful, not without a still retrospect, perhaps, to the "Blessed" which once a Galilean woman had uttered upon His mother, Luke xi. 27; yet this prophecy of evil is not, therefore, the less terrible. He foretells days in which the highest blessing of marriage should be regarded as a curse, and on the other hand a sudden, even though a terrible death, as a benefit. Comp. Hosea ix. 14; x. 8; Rev. vi. 16. The moment of the outbreak of this desperate condition of things (ἔρξονται), which is here drawn entirely after life, can be no other than the point of time at the destruction of Jerusalem, when all hope of deliverance is cut off. It is worthy of note that our Lord now, after His condemnation, no longer warns against this catastrophe, but foretells it as unavoidably impending, without adding even the faintest intimation of any way whatever in which it could be escaped. The day of visitation for Jerusalem is now already passed; nor will our Lord, so near His end, at all assume the guise of being any longer concerned to deliver Himself or the people so as in any way in this moment to excite them even yet to believe on Him as the promised Messiah. The preaching of repentance becomes by this very fact so much the more tremendous.

Vs. 31. **For if they do these things to the green wood.**—So long as the enemy at his incursion into a land spares the green wood, he will, perhaps, even refrain from destroying the dry; but if he does not even spare the fruitful, how should he not deny compassion to the unfruitful? The image, sufficiently intelligible of itself, is probably taken from Ezekiel xx. 47, and places the fate of the innocent Saviour as a prophecy of evil over against that of the guilty Israel. We have here not the contrast between young and old (Bengel), and as little the continuation of the exclamation of the despairing women themselves, vs. 30 (Baumgarten-Crusius), who, he supposes, from the fate which comes upon themselves as guiltless, now make inference as to the lot of the guilty; but, on the other hand, a pathetic allusion of our Lord Himself to that which even now is coming upon Him, in which this is given to the women as the standard according to which they were to measure the fate impending over themselves. Comp. Jer. xlix. 12; Prov. xi. 31; 1 Peter iv. 17, 18. Εἰ ταῦτα ποιοῦσιν, He does not even say *what*, in order not to agitate the souls of the women yet more deeply; they were themselves to see it in the moments next succeeding; ποιοῦσιν, Impersonally; it designates neither the Jews nor the Romans alone, but is an indefinite expression of what is here to be accomplished by human hands.

DOCTRINAL AND ETHICAL.

1. The meeting of Simon the Cyrenian with the suffering Saviour is again one of the most striking proofs of a *providentia specialissima*, in which the history of His life and suffering is so incomparably rich. It was not merely for Simon himself, but also for our Lord of importance, since it prepares for Him a relief, even though a brief one, on the way to the cross. Simon Peter is not at hand, although he had promised to follow his Master even to death. But from the distant Cyrene must there another Simon appear to lighten the burdened course of the Lamb of God, on the way to the slaughter. The willingness with which Simon takes the burden forced upon him, renders for his character, perhaps for his awakening courage of faith, a favorable testimony. In the women also there is manifested a feeling for our Lord, which we, after all that hitherto had come to pass, should expect least of all in this hour. "Now already the first breezes of another temper begin to breathe; the harbingers of the courage of the cross are coming into view." Lange.

2. The address of our Lord to the weeping women causes the light of His heavenly greatness to beam afar through the mists of the way to the cross in surprising wise. In an hour in which all presses in upon Him, and He might have had all occasion to think only of His own suffering, He wholly forgets this in order to occupy Himself only with the salvation of persons who yet really only exhibited for Him an inconsiderable sympathy. While the present with its whole weight rests upon Him, the future stands bright and clear before His unclouded spirit, and His eye already beholds the day that shall extort quite other tears. The feeling of His own innocence and dignity leaves Him not a moment. He knows and designates Himself as the green wood, in the same hour which He is about to end, nailed on the dry wood of shame. No word of bitterness against His murderers is mingled with the tones of love and compassion; even the fate of the children goes to His heart, upon whom their parents have recklessly called down the curse, and as if His own conflict were already endured, He will only have tears shed for Jerusalem's fate. Thus does His prophetic character reveal itself in the same hour in which He goes to perform His High-priestly work, and He yet, as the Good Shepherd, seeks that which is lost, while He is already on the way to give His life for the sheep.

3. The difference between this leading away of our Lord and the entry which had only taken place five days before. The place which Calvary occupies as a link in the chain of those mountain-tops which are remarkable in the life of our Lord. An admirable representation of the Cross-bearing Christ, by Ary Scheffer. Another, the Moment Before the Crucifixion, by Steuber.

4. "God's wrath is harder to bear than Christ's Cross." Rieger.

HOMILETICAL AND PRACTICAL.

Compare here and in the following divisions the homiletical hints on the parallels in Matthew and Mark.

The leading away to Calvary: 1. The Victim of wickedness led by the hands of men; 2. the atoning sacrifice of the world led by the hand of the Father to the slaughter.—The *Via Dolorosa:* 1. How far the Saviour alone treads it; 2. how far His disciples must continually tread the same in the following of Him.—The way of the cross: 1. Strown with the thorns of malice; 2. moistened with the tears of compassion; 3. illuminated by the light of the greatness of Jesus; 4. ended by the hill of death.—The Christian's cross-bearing in following Jesus, like that of Simon, a work which is performed: 1. Seldom voluntarily; 2. best with resignation; 3. never without reward.—How our Lord now, with His cross-bearing disciples, has taken upon Himself the work of Simon the Cyrenian. —Not a single woman in the whole Evangelical history is hostilely disposed towards our Lord.—The great contrast between superficial feeling for, and living faith in, the Saviour.—" Weep not for Me."—How much value is to be laid upon emotions such as are not seldom awakened in the hearers by a sermon on the Passion.—The view of the cross-bearing Christ calls us to weep for ourselves: 1. Such a suffering have human hands prepared for the most innocent and the holiest One; 2. such a sacrifice was requisite for the atonement of our sins also; 3. such a grace is even yet vainly proclaimed to many—and should we not weep over all this ?—The fearful punishment of the rejection of Christ: 1. Foreseen with infallible certainty; 2. fulfilled with terrible severity; 3. held up for an example for all Christian nations who do not honor God's Anointed.—Faith or despair; no other choice.—How shall we escape if we neglect so great salvation ! Heb. ii. 23.

STARKE:—God knows the cross-bearers most perfectly.—The greatest and most splendid cities have often the fewest to bear the Lord Jesus' cross after Him; small places are before them in it.—CANSTEIN :—It is to be reckoned among the hidden benefits when God, through others, against our own will causes the cross to be imposed on us which we do not like to bear, and which, yet, is so good for us.— Rather help thy neighbor to bear his burden than make it heavier, Gal. vi. 2.—All true Christians are cross-bearers.—At the Passion of Jesus the disciples, though men, become women, and the women become men.—CRAMER :—The right way to consider Christ's Passion begins thus: that we, with our children, bewail ourselves and our sins.—*Nova Bibl. Tub.:*— We commonly lament most what we should lament least, and least what we should lament most, Joel ii. 12 ; Ps. cxix. 36.—To have no children is in many circumstances happier than to have children.—The wrath of God, when it breaks out, is unendurable, Heb. x. 31.—The righteousness of God must be satisfied ; if He did not spare His own innocent Son, how much less will He spare an impenitent sinner.— HEUBNER:—Such lamentation, vs. 27, is itself a fulfiluent of the prophecy, Zech. xii. 10-14.—Christ restraining the weeping ones proved His own high dignity.—The Passion of Christ is the most solemn warning for the impenitent.—Paternal and maternal love—the thought of the future fate of their children should move parents to repentance.—For every blinded sinner there will come a day when he shall curse his life.—Vs. 31 by no means is in conflict with the Evangelical doctrine of Atonement.—ARNDT: —Jesus' death-journey to Calvary.—F. W. KRUMMACHER:—Simon the Cyrenian : 1. The Lord Jesus with the cross of the sinner; 2. the sinner with the cross of the Lord Jesus.—The daughters of Jerusalem. —BESSER :—And He bore His cross. The two thieves also bore their crosses, for such was the manner ; but He has borne a heavier one than they, outwardly and inwardly.—W. HOFACKER:—The solemn death-journey of Christ to Calvary: 1. As a mirror of wholesome doctrines; 2. as a mine of peaceful consolation ; 3. as a ground of obligation to willing following; 4. as a warning picture against guilt and its account.—HAGENBACH :—What temper of mind the celebration of the death of Jesus should awaken in us.

---

b. JESUS ON THE CROSS (Vss. 32-38).

(Parallel with Matt. xxvii. 33-44; Mark xv. 22-32; John xix. 18-24.)

32 And there were also two others, malefactors, led with him to be put to death.
33 And when they were come to the place, which is called Calvary [A skull], there they crucified him, and the malefactors, one on the right hand, and the other on the left.
34 Then said Jesus, Father, forgive them ; for they know not what they do.[1] And they
35 parted his raiment [clothing], and cast lots. And the people stood beholding. And the rulers also with them [om., with them[2]] derided [ἐξεμυκτήριζον] *him*, saying, He
36 saved others; let him save himself, if he [if this] be Christ, the chosen of God. And
37 the soldiers also mocked him, coming to him, and offering him vinegar, And saying, If
38 thou be the King of the Jews, save thyself. And a superscription also was written over him [And there was also a superscription over him[3]] in letters of Greek, and Latin, and Hebrew [om., in . . . Hebrew, V. O.[4]], THIS IS THE KING OF THE JEWS.

---

[1] Vs. 34.—*See Exegetical* and *Critical* remarks.
[2] Vs. 35.—The σὺν αὐτοῖς of the *Recepta* is wanting in B., C., D., [Cod. Sin.,] L., Q., X., &c., and is therefore rightly rejected by Tischendorf. [Received again in his 7th ed.—C. C. S.] It appears to have been added to avoid its seeming as

if the rulers alone had mocked, since, according to the parallels, the people mocked also. [Lachmann brackets the words. Meyer, Tregelles, Alford omit them.—C. C. S.]

[2] Vs. 38.—The γεγραμμένη of the *Recepta* is in all probability spurious, as well as superfluous. *See* TISCHENDORF, *ad locum*. [Om., B., L., Cod. Sin.—C. C. S.]

([3] Vs. 38.—Van. Oosterzee in omitting the clause, "in letters of Greek and Latin and Hebrew," follows Tischendorf, with whom Meyer, Tregelles also agree. Lachmann, followed by Alford, brackets it. The omission rests upon the authority of B., C.[1], L., some Versions. Cod. Sin. has it with the rest of the uncials, and apparently all the Cursives. Tischendorf and Meyer regard it as a very ancient interpolation from John xix. 20. But Alford pertinently asks why it should not have been equally interpolated into Matthew and Mark, and why the interpolation should vary so much in language from its source. There are some variations in the copies of Luke, but only such as can be naturally accounted for.—C. C. S.]

EXEGETICAL AND CRITICAL.

Calvary, κρανίον, Greek translation of the Hebrew Golgotha. Respecting the probable ground of this appellation, as well as respecting the whole locality, *see* LANGE, *Matthew*, p. 520, where, moreover, respecting the Crucifixion itself, the necessary information is found. As respects the question about the nailing of the feet, there is, without doubt, not a little to be brought forward for it as well as against it that is worthy of serious consideration; yet the grounds for it appear to us to be by far the stronger. The first rank here is taken by the testimony of JUSTIN MARTYR, *c. Tryph.*, ch. 97, and TERTULLIAN, *Adv. Marc.* iii. 19. As to the latter, especially, we can scarcely conceive how he, after the interpretation of the words, Ps. xxii. 16, as applying to our Lord's death on the cross, should have written: *qua propria atrocitas crucis*, if he had not found the peculiar cruelty of this capital punishment in this very particular, that both the hands and the feet were pierced. The well-known drama, Χριστὸς πάσχων, also, which is ascribed to Gregory of Nazianzen, represents it so, and retains its value as proof, even if its spuriousness were demonstrated. In the common Martyrologies, the nailing of the feet as well as the hands is always either presupposed or described, and is at the same time strongly supported by the testimony of Cyprian, Hilary, Eusebius, Athanasius, and others. That the familiar passage in PLAUTUS, *Mostellaria*, ii. 1, 13, concerning one condemned to crucifixion: *bis offigantur pedes, bis brachia*, indicates an unusual cruelty, has been indeed said, but not yet proved. That, moreover, the conception of feet nailed through lies at the basis of Luke xxiv. 39 can hardly be disputed. But especially the declaration of Thomas must also be brought into consideration, John xx. 25, "Except I shall see the print of the nails and put my finger into the print of the nails," &c. Unless we will assume that Thomas wished a *double* certainty in respect to the *same* marks of the nails, so that he wished first to see them, and then, besides that, to touch them, we shall, it seems, be obliged to explain his words thus; that he first wishes to see in the hands of our Lord the marks of the nails, and after that, bending himself to the earth, wishes to lay his finger in the nail-prints of the feet, and, finally, lay his whole hand in the side; so vanishes at the same time every appearance of a tautology and of an incorrigible unbelief, and it then appears that Thomas also may be reckoned among the witnesses *for* the nailing of the feet.

Vs. 34. **Father, forgive them.**—The first of the seven words on the cross, of which Luke alone has preserved three for us. The genuineness of this prayer is, it is true, not beyond all controversy, but yet it is above every reasonable doubt. It is lacking in B., D.[1], 38, Sahid., It., &c. [found in Cod. Sin.], while other manuscripts also have individual variations. Since, however, the words themselves bear an indelible stamp of genuineness and inward sublimity, it seems that the omission of them must be explained from an exaggerated craving to establish the harmony of the Synoptics at any cost. As respects the sense of the words, it is undoubtedly a question whom the Lord meant by the ἄφες αὐτοῖς, and in reply to this question, it is certainly not admissible to say (Gerlach): "This intercession Jesus made *not* for the soldiers who fastened Him to the cross," but yet more arbitrary is it to limit the reference of this prayer exclusively to the four men who carried out the sentence of death (Euthymius, Paulus, Kuinoel, and others), since our Lord may indeed primarily, but can by no means exclusively, have had these in mind. Without doubt He comprehends here both the executioners and the authors of His death, the heathen, with their Procurator, the Jews, with their High-priest, in one prayer together. Of all these, even of the most implacable among them, it could in a certain sense be said, as indeed the first witnesses of Jesus afterwards said (Acts iii. 17; 1 Cor. ii. 8), that with their wickedness there was united a high degree of blindness, but this blindness, which a strict righteousness might have been able to reckon to them as their own guilt, since it had by no means arisen without their concurrence (John xv. 22–25), the inventiveness of love makes the very ground of the intercession for grace to the guilty. Nay, inasmuch as our Lord, in the Jews who caused His death, beheld merely the representatives of the whole of sinful mankind, we may say that He with these words, by implication, commended this race of men itself, which was the author of His Passion on the cross, to the Father's compassion. To-day He does what He in His intercessory prayer had not expressly done, John xvii. 9. How such a prayer, which was probably uttered during the terrible act of the affixing to the cross (τί ποιοῦσιν), is most peculiarly in the spirit of the third, the Pauline, gospel scarcely needs remark.

And cast lots.—The partition of the garments Luke mentions only with a single word, as he also passes over, as well as Mark, the remarkable citation from Ps. xxii. which Matthew and John have added to their account. It is as though he, instead of this, wished to bring into view a feature which is also in the same Psalm so powerfully set forth (Ps. xxii. 17), namely, the unfeeling staring upon the incomparable Sufferer by an indifferent and hostile crowd.—**And the people stood beholding.**—A contrast to the just uttered prayer of the Lord, which is so great and terrible that it could only appear in the unexampled reality of the Passion; Luke therewith does not deny that the people scoffed (Meyer), but he only passes over this in order to direct attention to the scoffing of the rulers, who appear somewhat later, but in connection with the people. It appears that the standing and beholding must be limited to the moment of the affixing to the cross and the one immediately subsequent. It lies, however, in the nature of the case that such a *status quo* in so great a throng at such a moment could not possibly have lasted long. Perhaps it was the ἄρχοντες, whom

Luke specially mentions, that led on the crowd with evil example. Our gospel, however, here also takes less strict account of the sequence of the different stages than Matthew and Mark.

Vs. 35. **And the rulers also.**—If καί is genuine (see MEYER, *ad loc.*), then there is indirectly implied in this itself, that the rulers in this respect were by no means alone.—**Divided.**—Comp. ch. xvi. 14. In Luke also they speak of our Lord in the third person, while the passers-by (Matthew and Mark), calling out to Him with their mocking speeches, address Him directly in the second person. Here also they involuntarily proclaim the Saviour's eulogy, inasmuch as they acknowledge, "He saved others"; but, at the same time, tempt our Lord therewith, inasmuch as they will seduce Him to leave the ignominious tree. Might it be possible that even yet a trace of earthly-minded expectation expresses itself in their words? Could it be possible that even yet some one might have conceived the possibility that the Crucified One might even yet reveal His miraculous might for His own deliverance? After He is now gone so far, and has silently endured all, we can scarcely suppose that they wished and expected the realization of a condition, upon the fulfilment of which they pretend that even now they are willing to believe in Him. As little does it admit of proof that they here designedly took the words of the 22d Psalm into their mouths. That which awakens astonishment in this one great spectacle is precisely this, that they themselves, without wishing or willing it, must attest the greatness of Him whom they are most deeply outraging. The insolence of one sharpens the biting wit of others, and there arises a contest which of them can utter the most outrageous words of blasphemy. Luke is the only one who communicates to us the fact that the soldiers also took part in the mocking, which the example of the chief priests had excited. They leave their previous composed demeanor, drink to Him in soldier's style, and while they appropriate to themselves the words of the chief priests quite as eagerly and willingly as they had previously done the garments of the Condemned, they exclaim, not without bitterness towards despised Judaism: **If thou,** &c. This psychologically probable account could be called a misunderstanding of Matt. xxvii. 48 (De Wette) only if we read that they at the same time had refreshed our Lord, and, therefore, more or less mitigated His suffering. But of a reed, by means of which the draught would have been really brought to the lips of Jesus, the narrative says nothing, but we have rather to conceive the case thus: that they, holding forth to Him the vinegar at a certain distance (προσφέροντες), jestingly drink to Him, and, therefore, even by the exhibition of the scanty refreshment, increase His bodily suffering.

Vs. 38. **A superscription.**—That Luke reckons this also among the mockeries (De Wette) we could hardly assert. We are rather disposed to conjecture that this superscription, as to which he, perhaps, would otherwise have kept silence, is here given by him subsequently, in order therewith to give the reason for which the soldiers also, and that in such a way, took part in the scoffings. The superscription itself gave them occasion to throw now with ignominy before the feet of our Lord the royal name which they so pompously displayed above His head. Respecting the custom itself of putting such a superscription over crosses, see WETSTEIN and LANGE on Matt. xxvii. 37. The diversity in the statements of the superscription is sufficiently explained from the fact that in the original languages it had a somewhat different form. In the Latin, for instance, *Rex Judæorum*, which Mark renders literally for his readers in Rome. In Greek, ΟΥΤΟΣ ΕΣΤΙΝ Ο ΒΑΣΙΛ. ΤΩΝ ΙΟΥΔΑΙΩΝ, which is reported almost without alteration by Matthew and Luke. In John, finally, the literal translation of the original Hebrew superscription appears to be communicated to us. According to all, it contains no accusation, but simply a title, the purpose of which is not so much to insult the Crucified Himself, as in particular the Jewish nation, as is clear at the first glance.

DOCTRINAL AND ETHICAL.

1. The sublime simplicity with which all the Evangelists delineate the unexampled fact of the crucifixion of Jesus, without in any way mingling with it their subjective experiences and feelings, is one of the most striking proofs of the credibility of this part, also, of the sacred history; the farther we press into the sanctuary the more impossible does it become to us to utter the word "Invention" or "Myth" even in thought. From the very beginning of the statement of the coming to Calvary, everything is avoided that could have even the least appearance of the romantic or tragic. Much genius has been shown in endeavoring to fill up this seeming hiatus with legends of Veronica, of the Wandering Jew, &c.

2. The crucifixion of our Lord is the realization of that obscure presentiment of heathenism which Plato had already uttered, *De Republica*, ii., when he makes Glaucus say to Socrates that the perfectly righteous man, if he appeared among men, would certainly be beaten, scourged, tortured, and when he should have endured all this, would be crucified (ἀνασχινδυλευθήσεται). Also the end and the crown of the Typics of the Old Covenant, and of the prophecy of the Messianic Passion, Is. liii.; Ps. xxii., which last is no direct prophecy of that which went into fulfilment upon Calvary, but a typical symbolical picture, in which David describes his own sufferings, yet, under the guidance of the Holy Spirit, in exactly such forms and colors as, although to him entirely unconsciously, yet, *a posteriori*, became a perfectly exact description of that one whole unique and unexampled event, which took place upon and around Calvary.

3. Not without reason have the words of our Lord on the cross been reckoned among His most precious legacies. The first, preserved to us by Luke exclusively, is, at the same time, the most generally loved. In itself indescribably striking, it is so yet more through the circumstances of the time at which it was uttered, and through the contrast with the demeanor of the people who stood there beholding. It is, at the same time, the best commentary on the sublimest precept of the Evangelical ethics, and an unequivocal proof of the majesty of our Lord in the midst of His deepest humiliation; the worthy conclusion of His earthly, and the striking symbol of His heavenly, life ["There for sinners Thou art pleading," &c.] Even before Him there was no lack of saints who prayed for the wicked, nay, for their enemies (Abraham, Jeremiah, and others), and after Him His example has not seldom been followed in the most surprising degree (Stephen, James the Just, Huss, H. V. Zütphen, and others). Of His predecessors, however, no one has reached the ideal height to which His love has here raised itself, and it is only through His might that His followers have

learned so to pray and forgive. The enforcing of this prayer by reference to the ignorance of His enemies would only have arisen in His loving heart. But more strongly yet than through this pathetic "They know not what they do," was the prayer, without doubt, supported in the Father's view by the blood which in the utterance of this prayer was drunk by the earth on Calvary, a blood that spoke better things than the blood of Abel. And it was, moreover, heard, as is plainly attested by the renewed preaching of the gospel to the Jews at Jerusalem, the conversion of so many thousands, and the continuous work of grace on Israel. For us who read it, it is a new proof of His love and greatness, a proof of such kind as does not occur again, even in our Lord's own history, and, at the same time, a reminder of that feature of the prophetic portraiture of the Passion which we read, Is. liii. 12: "He made intercession for the transgressors." Compare, respecting this and the following words on the cross, Dr. G. J. VINKE, *Dissert. Theol. de Christi e cruce pendentis vocibus*, Traj. ad Rhen. 1846.

4. From a doctrinal point of view, the first word on the cross is peculiarly important, because it points us to the natural connection that exists between the pardonableness of a sin and the ignorance of the sinner. It is here plainly expressed that if one knows perfectly what he does, all hope of forgiveness falls away, since the capability of receiving it, remorse and repentance, is lacking. On the other hand, we are not to forget that in almost every sin there is a minimum of ignorance present, which may be accounted as a lessening of the guilt, nay, that the blindness, however self-caused, becomes the greater in the degree in which the bondage of sin increases in duration and obstinacy. However, here, before all, it must not be forgotten that all which must be weighed and brought up for the diminution of the guilt of others cannot, on that account, serve as a mantle with which we can cover and excuse our own sins. With entire justice, therefore, does J. MULLER, *Lehre von der Sünde*, i. p. 239, say, in reference to the sin of the first rejectors of our Lord: "If their not knowing removed their guilt, they did not need forgiveness; if it did not diminish their guilt, the prayer for forgiveness could not have used it as a motive for forgiveness."

5. The mocking on the cross by four different classes of men was not only a dreadful revelation of the might of darkness, but for our Lord, at the same time, the last return of the Temptation in the Wilderness, ch. iv. 9-11.

6. In the midst of the deepest humiliation, God provides that the royal dignity of His Son shall be proclaimed by the superscription over the cross. Notwithstanding the urgent entreaties of the Jews, not a jot nor a tittle may be altered therein; in three different languages—in the language of the empire, of culture, of nationality—there stands there on the cross for thousands to read, the shame of Israel and the glory of Jesus. In view of such a concurrence of circumstances, it is easy to comprehend that some fathers of the church were of the view that Pilate had ordered and maintained this superscription *divinitus inspiratus*, in order in this way to help fulfil the prophetic word, Ps. ii. 6. To us, at all events, this little trait of the history of the Passion remains a palpable proof of the truth of the other prophetic word, Is. xlvi. 10.

7. The sacred narrative in the account of the Partition of the Garments might well have deserved a better fate than to have given occasion for the most wretched superstition and priestcraft of later ages. The legends about the garments, especially about the seamless coat, of our Lord, cannot be here all given, but only be rejected with a word. Compare the writings of Dr. J. GILDEMEISTER and H. V. SEIBEL, "The holy coat of Treves and the twenty other holy seamless coats," Düsseldorf, 1844; and "The advocates of the coat of Treves brought to silence," 1845.

8. We can also indicate with only a word what the poetry and painting of the church have done for the glorifying of this bloody scene of the Passion. Compare the beautiful hymn: *Vexilla regis prodeunt*; the *Stabat Mater* [Exquisite in poetry, but so unhappily and deeply defiled by Mariolatry.—C. C. S.], the *Improperia*, the *Miserere* of Allegri, the famous paintings of Poussin, Gué, and innumerable others. Comp. STAUDENMEYER, *l. c.* p. 440 seq.

HOMILETICAL AND PRACTICAL.

Jesus has, as the true Sin-offering, suffered without the gate, Heb. xiii. 11, 12.—Jesus reckoned among the transgressors; this word considered in the light of the history of the Crucifixion of our Lord, points us: 1. To Israel's shame; 2. to Jesus' glory; 3. to the Father's counsel; 4. to the Christian's boast; 5. to the world's hope.—To whom do we in our own eyes belong—to the transgressor who deserved what He suffered, or to those justified through His blood and reconciled with God?—The Lord of glory upon the summit of shame, the Prince of life among the murderers.—The high value of our Lord's words on the cross for His dearly-purchased church.—How each single word of the first utterance on the cross is a new pearl in the shining crown of our Lord: 1. He prays in the hour of crucifixion; 2. He prays to God as to His Father; 3. He prays in this hour for others; 4. for enemies; 5. with most urgent importunity; 6. with the richest result.—Not the murder of the Messiah in itself, but the continued and obstinate rejection of the apostolical preaching, the ultimate cause why Israel has obtained not pardon but punishment.—Here is more than Elijah, 2 Kings i. 10.—*Oravit misericordia, ut oraret miseria*, Augustine.—The first prayer of our Lord on the cross an entirely unique prayer: 1. Unique in its sublimity, *a.* For whom prays He? *b.* When? *c.* What? 2. unique in its significance; this prayer is, *a.* the crown of His earthly life, *b.* the consecration of His cross, *c.* the image of His heavenly activity; 3. unique in its power, it serves, *a.* to our humiliation, *b.* to our consolation, *c.* to our sanctification.—Jesus on the cross the Intercessor for His enemies and the example for His friends.—The glorified Jesus the object: 1. Of frivolous covetousness (the lot-casting soldiers); 2. of cold indifference (the beholding people); 3. of cowardly mocking (the insulting rulers).—The mocking upon Calvary the crucifixion of the heart of Jesus.—How with the mocking at the cross everything reaches the highest culmination: 1. The sin; 2. the suffering; 3. the grace of God who surrenders His Son into the extreme of misery.—Jesus' foes, even when they curse, are involuntarily constrained to bless.—God's way in the sanctuary, Hab. ii. 20. We see upon Calvary a God: 1. Who keeps silence; 2. who rules; 3. who thus reconciles the world unto Himself.—Jesus on the cross tempted once again, yet without sin, Heb. iv. 15.—The Christian crucified with Christ must also often yet hear this tempting voice and repel it.—"The world loves to blacken that which shines" [*Es liebt die Welt, das Strahlende zu schwärzen*].—The different degrees of wickedness in those who mock alike.—The superscription on the cross a speaking proof of the adorable providence of God. It proclaims: 1. The innocence; 2. the dignity; 3. the destiny of the crucified Christ.—This superscription: 1. Written in three languages; 2. read by the Jews; 3. unchanged and unchangeable.—What does the superscription on the cross testify: 1. Concerning God; 2. concerning man; 3. concerning Christ; 4. concerning the way of redemption; 5. concerning the hope of the future.—This superscription: 1. Was read by all; thou surely wilt not go unheeding by? 2. it was offensive to many; thou surely wouldst for all that not alter anything therein? 3. one man has stubbornly maintained it (Pilate); thou surely wilt not let it be taken from thee?

STARKE:—OSIANDER:—Christ has been willing to be reckoned among the transgressors, that we might come into the number of the children of God.—This is, so to speak, the supreme masterpiece of the Mediator, that He knows how to make an intercession out of that of which others would have made an accusation.—The best we can entreat for ourselves and others is forgiveness of sins.—It is equitable to have more compassion on those that sin ignorantly than on those that sin maliciously.—*Nova Bibl. Tub.*:—The crucified Jesus to the Jews a stumbling-block, to the Greeks foolishness, but to us, &c., 1 Cor. i. 23, 24.—It is a terrible sin to give any occasion for the name of God and Jesus to be blasphemed among the heathen, Rom. ii. 24.—All languages and tongues have a share in Jesus the King.—HEUBNER:—Christ prays for all the authors of all His sufferings.—The most glorious hearing of the prayer of Jesus is yet reserved in the future conversion of Israel.—If Jesus then prayed for His enemies, He will now continue to pray also for penitents and believers.—ARNDT:—The superscription over the cross.—The partition of the garments:—KRUMMACHER:—The *Crucifixion*: 1. Jesus' arrival at His death-mount; 2. the act of crucifixion; 3. the erected cross. The *Partition*: 1. The Testator; 2. His bequest; 3. the heirs. The *Superscription*: Jesus on the cross a King: 1. His majesty; 2. His victory; 3. the founding of His kingdom; 4. His judgments; 5. His government.—"Father, forgive": 1. Contents of the prayer; 2. grounds justifying it; 3. limits within which it finds acceptance.—VAN OOSTERZEE:—The crucifixion a union without compare: 1. Of triumph and baseness; 2. of ignominy and majesty; 3. of caprice and providence; 4. of condemnation and acquittal; 5. of earth and heaven. In conclusion, the double question: Belongest thou to those who crucify Christ afresh, or to those who in truth are crucified with Christ?—VINET:—*Les complices de la crucification du Scigneur.*—J. SAURIN:—*Nouv. Disc.* i. p. 365, *sur la prière de Jésus Christ pour ses bourreaux.*—W. HOFACKER, *l. c.* p. 311:—The magnificent sunset of the life of Jesus Christ on Calvary.—The world-atoning death of Christ in its mighty working.—The words on the cross: *Septem folia semper viventia, quæ vitia nostra, cum in crucem elevata fuit, emisit.* Bernard. The first: *res miranda, Judæi clamant: crucifige, Christus clamat: ignosce. Magna illorum iniquitas, sed major tua, o Domine, pietas.* Idem.—SCHLEIERMACHER, *Pred.* ii. p. 436 *seq.*:—The mystery of redemption in connection with sin and ignorance: 1. The redeeming suffering of Jesus was a work of ignorance; 2. but the redemption which proceeds from Him, the farther it goes, abolishes so much more the excuse: "They know not what they do."—THOLUCK:—The intercession: 1. The thought of the Redeemer at this word; 2. the thoughts which it must call forth in us.—NITZSCH:—The execution of Jesus in its connection with other works of the world and of the temper of the world.—PALMER:—Christ between the malefactors.—For further citations, *see* LANGE on the parallels.

---

c. THE PENITENT THIEF (Vss. 39–43).

39 And one of the malefactors which were hanged railed on him, saying, If thou be
40 Christ [Art not thou the Christ?[1]], save thyself and us. But the other answering rebuked him, saying, Dost not [even[2]] thou fear God, seeing thou art in the same con-
41 demnation? And we indeed justly; for we receive [are receiving[3]] the due reward of
42 our deeds: but this man hath done nothing amiss. And he said unto Jesus, Lord, [he said, Jesus, remember, V. O.[4]] remember me when thou comest into [in] thy kingdom.
43 And Jesus said unto him, Verily I say unto thee, To-day shalt thou be with me in paradise.

[1] Vs. 39.—According to the reading of Tischendorf, [Meyer, Tregelles, Alford]: οὐχὶ σὺ εἶ; after B., [Cod. Sin.,] C.[1], L., Versions. The *Recepta* comes from vs. 37.
[2] Vs. 40.—That is, "any more than the mockers around, who at least have not a fellow-suffering to restrain them from impious cruelty towards a dying man."—C. C. S.]
[3] Vs. 41.—Revised Version of the American Bible Union.—C. C. S.]
[4] Vs. 42.—The κυριε of the *Recepta* is wanting in B., C.[1], D., [Cod. Sin.,] Curetves, &c. Ἰησοῦ is supported by the authority of B., C.[1], L., [Cod. Sin.,] Origen, and the Coptic and Sahidic Versions.

EXEGETICAL AND CRITICAL.

Vs. 39. **And one of the malefactors which were hanged.**—According to Matt. xxvii. 41, and Mark xv. 32, our Lord is mocked by both robbers; according to Luke, only by one. The different harmonistic attempts to remove here all appearance of contradiction are familiar. *See* LANGE, *Matthew*, p. 525. The view of Lange, that we must make a distinction between ὀνειδίζειν and βλασφημεῖν in the following manner, namely, that the latter could be said only of the impenitent, the former also, on the other hand, of the better-minded robber, who had begun as well as his fellow to urge our Lord to leave the cross, but had soon given up this earthly-minded expectation—this view diminishes the difficulty without doubt, but yet does not wholly remove it. For even in this way the psychological objection cannot be refuted as to how so sudden a conversion could all at once have arisen in the soul of the penitent thief, and as to whether it is not in contradiction to the nature of an unfeigned conversion, when the penitent begins his conversion with rebuking a fellow-sinner on account of an act which he himself had only a few moments before been committing. We rather assume (Ebrard), that Matthew and Mark express themselves indefinitely; that they meant only to give the *genus*, but not the number of the last class of the scoffers, and that it was reserved for Luke to instruct us more fully about a particular which, in the Pauline Gospel of justification by free grace, is so very peculiarly in its place.

Vs. 40. **Dost not even thou fear God?**—It is not, therefore, the blaspheming of Jesus itself which gives occasion for this outspoken rebuke, but the frivolous forgetfulness of God, the lack of the fear of God which manifests itself in the words of a man who is now suffering the same punishment with Jesus, whom he blasphemes, and who, therefore, now at least ought to have exhibited a more serious temper. But now the powerful antithesis with this word: ἐν τῷ αὐτῷ κρίματι, comes before his awakening consciousness of faith, and he expresses, as strongly as possible, the heaven-wide distinction which exists between the Saviour and the companions of His fate.

Vs. 41. **And we indeed justly**, sc. ἐν τῷ κρίματί ἐσμεν.—He knows himself to be before God a man as guilty as the companion of his fate, although he censures his blasphemy.

This man hath done nothing amiss, οὐδὲν ἄτοπον.—Nothing censurable, evil. Comp. 2 Thess. iii. 2. "The mild expression denotes innocence the more strongly." (Meyer). Even had the robber said nothing more than this, yet he would awaken our deepest astonishment, that God—in a moment wherein literally all voices are raised against Jesus, and not a friendly word is heard in His favor—causes a witness for the spotless innocence of the Saviour to appear on one of the crosses beside Him. This murderer is the last man who before Jesus' death deposes a testimony in honor of Him. But now he soon shows a yet clearer and firmer faith, while he directs his look upon the middle cross, and now begins to speak no longer *of*, but *to*, Him Himself.

Vs. 42. **Jesus, remember me.**—He desires no instantaneous liberation from the cross, on which he on the contrary is convinced that he must die, but he desires solely and singly that our Lord in grace may remember him, and receive him into His kingdom. Undoubtedly he is not wholly free from earthly Messianic expectations, and here is thinking not of the heaven in which our Lord after His death would be, but he represents to himself the moment when the Messiah comes in His kingly glory to erect His kingdom upon earth, and desires that he then, awakened from the grave, may enter in with Him into the joy of his Lord. Comp. Matt. xvi. 28. But even on this interpretation his prayer is assuredly one of the boldest and most surprising that has ever been uttered. A crucified malefactor, the first that has fully understood the deep sense of the superscription over the cross, and becomes the herald of the royal dignity of our Lord, in the same instant in which the Messianic hope of the apostles themselves was most vehemently shaken—of a truth this phenomenon may be called one of the brightest points of light in the history of the last hours in the life of our Lord! And even if we assume that he had previously heard and seen our Lord; that he, although a murderer, could not yet have been a hardened felon; that he attentively observes Jesus in the last hours, and that the approach of death had filled him with the deepest seriousness, yet all this clears up for us only a part of the riddle, which finds singly and solely its full solution in the faith of God's free grace, which has in this very moment in fullest abundance glorified itself in the robber, while it had, we may believe, even previously prepared him by all the circumstances of his life for this courageous faith and this sincere conversion, which comes to light here in him in so surprising wise. An examination of the history of the psychological development of his inner life, which commends itself by great originality, *see* in LANGE, *Leben Jesu*, ii. p. 1568. Only in this way does it become explicable how he in clearness of knowledge, in strength of faith, as well as in courageousness of confession, could be so far prominent above all others, and behold now a source of life and a royal throne in the cross, that even for the most advanced disciples was a stone of stumbling and a rock of offence. [Trench's conjecture appears to be a reasonable one, that this robber may have been a companion of Barabbas, and that both these λῃσταί may have belonged to that class of turbulent zealots for freedom who had already begun to appear in the Jewish land, and who, like the Greek Klephts in Turkish times, united audacious wickedness with a perverted but ardent feeling of devotion to their country. The fact that Barabbas had just about this time "made a sedition," which implies accomplices, who were not like himself released, but doubtless punished, lends weight both to the conjecture that some vague Messianic longings may have been mixed up with his crime, and that this man may have been a participant of it. A nature led through the very strength of noble impulses into crime, might well be more receptive of Divine grace in the hour of utter disenchantment and of mortal agony, than that of a common ruffian. Of course, this must remain only a conjecture, but I think we may be free to say, a not improbable conjecture.—C. C. S.]

Vs. 43. **And Jesus said unto him: To-day.**—We can but faintly guess what, for the suffering Saviour, a word like this must have been. Over against all the voices of blasphemy He has observed steadfast silence; but such a petitioner He permits not to wait a moment for an answer. He promises to him something much higher than he had desired—the highest that he could pray or conceive—Paradise, and that even to-day, and in fellowship with Him. Senseless is the combination **To-day** with λέγω σοι, of which Theophylact already speaks, and which is vindicated in particular by Roman Catholic exegetes, in order as much as possible to weaken the proof which has always been derived from this word on the cross against the doctrine of Purgatory. It is self-evident that our Lord spoke to-day, not yesterday; never has He so pleonastically expressed Himself; moreover, on this interpretation the so thoroughly definite promise would lose all precision. But now there is implied nothing less in it than first the assurance that the murderer should die even to-day, and that with the Saviour, while He had perhaps feared that he should have to languish slowly away, hanging yet one or several days upon the cross [as we know was frequently the case in crucifixion, before death ensued.—C. C. S.] ; a promise which was fulfilled a few hours later by the *crurifragium*. But at the same time our Lord promises him Paradise, a word whose whole sweetness in such a mouth, for such ears, could only be experienced if one had himself hung there with the Saviour upon the cross. We have, however, by this Paradise to understand not the heavenly Paradise, 2 Cor. xii. 4; Rev. ii. 7, but that part of Sheol which is opposed to Gehenna, and which was also named Paradise, and moreover, apparently, "Abraham's bosom." Nothing else could the forgiven one understand, who unquestionably had grown up entirely within the sphere of the Israelitish popular expectations ; nothing else could the Saviour have had in view, since He undoubtedly from His death-hour to the resurrection morning, must abide in the condition of separation. "*Dubium non est, quin Christus ita locutus sit, quomodo sciebat, a latrone intelligi.*" Grotius. In the assurance of a being with the Lord in this Paradise, there is at the same time included for the Penitent Thief the promise of the resurrection of the just, and of further participation in the blessings of the Messianic kingdom. Respecting the Jewish popular conception of the future state, comp. SEPP, iii. p. 557 *seq.*

DOCTRINAL AND ETHICAL.

1. The history of the Penitent Thief may in the fullest sense of the word be called an *Evangelium in Evangelio.* The inner truth and beauty of this account of Luke strikes the eye with special clearness, when we compare it with that which the Apocryphal Gospels have to relate about this man, whom tradition has named varyingly, Titus, Demas, Vicinus, and Matha. According to the Arabic *Evangelium Infantiæ,* ch. 23, see THILO, *Cod. Apocr.* l. p. 93, the man had already protected the child Jesus on the flight to Egypt, against the wickedness of the second robber, and our Lord then for a reward therefor, foretells to His mother with childish lips, what thirty years afterwards should take place on Calvary with these two. The Gospel of Nicodemus, ch. 26, even proceeds to tell us about the meeting of this man with Enoch and Elijah in Hades. Does there now exist between these narratives and the account of Luke no other distinction than between secondary and primary myth-formations?

2. The beatitude uttered upon the Penitent Thief appears to have preceded the commendation of Mary to the disciple John (John xix. 25–27), so that we have here before us in Luke, not the third, but the second word on the cross.—According to the course of the Synoptical representation, the mockery follows so quickly upon the crucifixion, and the scene between our Lord and the Penitent Thief so quickly upon the mockery, that it appears forced to insert the Johannean account between the one and the other event. On internal grounds, moreover, we consider it as much more probable that our Lord provided for His mother only after He had previously saved this sinner, than the reverse; the spiritual at every time with Him preceded the natural. The first word on the cross was for His enemies, the second for a penitent sinner, only the third for His sorrowing mother, while then finally the fourth reveals to us His own anguish of soul; thus does the circle draw ever closer together.

3. Brief as the utterance of the Penitent Thief was, yet there is nothing lacking to it that belongs to the unalterable requirements of a genuine conversion,—sense of guilt, confession of sin, simple faith, active love, supplicating hope,—all these fruits of the tree of the new life we see here ripen during a few moments. The address of our Lord, on the other hand, comprehends, as it were, in a short summary, the whole riches and the glory of redemption. The first word on the cross gives us a view into His High-priestly heart. His kingly character reveals itself in the second. Grace and majesty suddenly diffuse their bright beams through the night of the deepest humiliation. We wonder not that history gives us no account of an answer of the forgiven robber to the promise of the Saviour. On a cross there is not long or much speaking, and how, moreover, could he have found words for his thanks! But without doubt the consolation of this promise illumined his last hours, and he stands forth before our eyes as the first fruits of the millions of subjects whom the King of the kingdom of God has won even on His cross, and through the same.

4. The possibility of a conversion even in the last moments is undoubtedly established by the example of the Penitent Thief; the impenitent companion of his fate, however, proclaims quite as powerfully by his terrible end, how dangerous it is to postpone conversion so long.

5. The second word of our Lord on the cross contains a very significant intimation in respect to His *Descensus ad Inferos,* with which the yet further developed teaching of 1 Peter iii. 18 ; iv. 6, &c., is in no way in contradiction; but at the same time it renders not less than Philip. i. 23 ; Rev. xiv. 13, and many other passages of the New Testament, a powerful testimony against the Roman Catholic doctrine of Purgatory.

6. The two robbers on the cross, the representatives of the whole human race in its diverse behavior towards Jesus. The crucified Jesus also the fall and the rising of many, Luke ii. 34. The beatitude pronounced upon the Penitent Thief a type of the great judgment day.

HOMILETICAL AND PRACTICAL.

The three crosses.—The hill of death a place of triumph.—Calvary shows us: 1. The triumph of stubborn wickedness; 2. the triumph of penitent faith ; 3. the triumph of redeeming love.—The view of death cannot of itself break the froward heart.—The rebuke of the sin of our neighbor a difficult but holy duty.—The different ways in which two sinners proceed towards the terrors of eternity.—The desperate cry for help and the believing petition for redemption.—How the penitent looks upon the Saviour, how the Saviour looks upon the penitent : 1. The sincere penitent is *a.* humble in the acknowledgment of guilt, *b.* eager for salvation in coming to Christ, *c.* courageous in the confession of the Saviour ; 2. the Saviour, *a.* accepts the confession of guilt, *b.* hears the humble prayer, *c.* crowns the courageous hope.—The theatre of judgment changed into a working place of grace.—How penitent faith may expect after the hour of death : 1. the joy of Paradise ; 2. the joy of Paradise with Jesus ; 3. the joy of Paradise immediately after death.—As the

Father so also the Son does exceedingly, abundantly, above all that we can ask or think, Eph. iii. 20.—Conversion in the hour of death: 1. Possible, certainly; 2. but yet rare; and 3. only to be expected when one does not stubbornly and presumptuously strive against the drawings of the prevenient grace of God.—Wonderful guidance of God, which at the boundary of life: 1. Gives the sinner yet to find his deliverer; 2. gives the King of the kingdom of God even yet to find one of His subjects.—For God's grace no sinner too vile.—Salvation and damnation in a certain sense already decided before the hour of death.

STARKE:—Men are not of one kind, as not in life, so not in death.—BRENTIUS: It is an infallible token of a sound and true repentance when one acknowledges God's judgment upon himself as righteous, and publicly praises the same.—The Christian is under obligation to deliver the innocence of the innocent.—How profitable it is to talk with the suffering Jesus.—The eye of hope must look farther than upon the visible things of this world, 1 Cor. xv. 19.—It is not the "with Me," that comes first, but the "through Me."—God's acceptance of a fervent prayer is not delayed.—BRENTIUS:—Christ has again opened the closed Paradise.—Man will after death be either with Christ or with the devil.—Whoever remains in his suffering steadfastly united with Jesus, will also remain united with Him in His glory.—HEUBNER:—The suddenness of this conversion should excite no doubt, for: 1. It is bound to no conditions of time; 2. there was found in the thief everything that precedes conversion; 3. undoubtedly there was here a miracle of grace in order to reveal the power of the death of Christ, even to coming generations.—This is what every poor sinner should daily pray: Lord, remember me.

Compare the well-known inscription on the grave of Copernicus: "*Non parem Paulo veniam requiro, gratiam Petri neque posco, sed quam in crucis ligno dederis latroni, sedulus oro.*"—The sermon of Chrysostom, *De latrone*, and that of Melanchthon in Bretschneider, *Corpus Reform.* ii. pp. 478-487.—The Passion Week's sermons of RIEGER, p. 641-643.—SAURIN:—*Sur les deux brigands*, p. 403.—T. THEREMIN:—The Cross of Christ, the third sermon.—F. ARENS, Preacher in Osnaburg:—The value of the grace on Calvary set forth in one of the crucified thieves.—THOMASIUS:—Our own death-hour in the light of this history.—Dr. J. J. RAMBACH: 1. The prayer of the malefactor; 2. the answer of the Saviour.—PALMER:—Christ between the robbers.—KRUMMACHER:—The robber: 1. A look into the heart of both robbers; 2. into the great kingly word of Immanuel.

B. *The End of the Conflict.* CH. XXIII. 44-56.

1. The Repose of Death (VSS. 44-46).

(Parallel with Matt. xxvii. 45-50; Mark xv. 33-37; John xix. 28-30.)

44 And it was [now[1]] about the sixth hour, and there was [came, ἐγένετο] a darkness
45 over all the earth [land] until the ninth hour. And the sun was darkened, and the
46 vail of the temple was rent in the midst. And when Jesus had cried with a loud voice, he said, Father, into thy hands I commend [commit] my spirit: and having said thus, he gave up the ghost [expired, ἐξέπνευσεν].

[1] Vs. 44.—Ἤδη may here be confidently received into the text. [Found in B., C.[1], L. Cod. Sin. omits it. Tregelles brackets it. Lachmann, Tischendorf, Meyer, Alford adopt it. Has dropped out of the MSS. from its resemblance to the preceding ἦν δὲ which is found in nearly all the MSS. that omit ἤδη, instead of καὶ ἦν or ἦν, which those have that read ἤδη —C. C. S.]

EXEGETICAL AND CRITICAL.

Synoptical Remarks.—The more the history of the Passion hastens towards its end, the more evidently does it appear that Luke sums up his narrative in few words. The commendation of Mary to John, the lamentation of our Lord upon the cross, the last refreshment of the Dying One, he passes over. On the other hand, he gives account of the rending of the veil in the temple immediately before our Saviour's death, although from Matthew it appears that this took place simultaneously, or, indeed, even a moment later. In view of the rapid succession of events, it is, however, almost impossible to speak here of *former* and *latter*. We also owe to Luke alone the communication of the last, the seventh word on the cross, and the statement of the miracles during the dying of our Lord. He attaches himself, although he is very brief, more to Mark than to Matthew, and while he, like the other Synoptics, passes over in silence the breaking of the legs of the robbers and the piercing of our Saviour's side, he coincides again, in the rather detailed description of His burial, with the other Evangelists.

Vs. 44. **A darkness.**—Respecting the cause, the character, and the historical certainty of this darkness, comp. LANGE on Matt. xxvii. 46. Entirely without ground do the Jews, in the Gospel of Nicodemus, tell Pilate (ch. xi.) that an ordinary eclipse took place. *See* THILO, p. 592. The well-known testimony of Phlegon, to be sure, we also should not venture to use to prove therewith the credibility of this Evangelical account, since he speaks rather of a natural, although more than ordinarily deep darkening of the sun, as to which, moreover, it is still doubtful in which year of the 202d Olympiad it took place. Yet whoever holds our Lord for Him for whom He declared Himself, will, in this mourning of nature at the death of Jesus, be as far from finding anything incredible as anything insignificant. Unquestionably, there are mythical accounts of similar natural manifestations even at the death of Romulus, of Cæsar, and others; but what in the sphere of profane history is invention, may none the less in the sacred history be true. And if, in certain Rabbinical writings, the death of famous men is compared to the darkening of the mid-day sun, these expressions are, at all events, later than our Evangelical narratives, and may indeed, moreover, have very well originated from the analogy of the here-related fact. In a word, the idea so strikingly expressed in the familiar

Sol tibi signa dabit, solam quis dicere falsum audeat, &c.

has become reality. As respects, particularly, the account of Luke itself, it might, on a literal interpretation, seem as if he meant that the sun until the ninth hour, although there was already a deep darkness, yet had remained all the time visible, but that then, in the moment of Jesus' death, the sun itself also became invisible. But, even supposing that the genuineness of the words καὶ ἐσκοτίσθη ὁ ἥλ. were above all doubt (De Wette disputes this, and Griesbach is also for omitting them), there would yet be no essential difficulty in connecting the thought thus, that (vs. 45) with καί the proper cause of σκότος κ.τ.λ. is stated. It often occurs that two phenomena are coördinated or arranged together, of which the second constitutes the natural ground of the first. Precisely the same interpretation appears, moreover, to lie at the basis of the reading which appears in B., C., L., cursives, Origen [Cod. Sin. has τοῦ ἡλίου ἐκλιπόντος.—C. C. S.], τοῦ ἡλίου ἐκλείποντος. The participial clause indicates a causal connection, and on internal grounds it is not probable that Luke meant to give an account of a great darkness, during which the sun for three hours yet remained continually visible.

Vs. 45. **And the veil of the temple.**—Attempts have been made to explain these phenomena also naturally, as a mere result of the earthquake, of which Luke has given no particular account. But can we represent to ourselves an earthquake by which—not from below up but from above down— a curtain should be rent which was one finger thick, thirty ells long, woven of purple and scarlet, and, according to the testimony of Jewish scholars, renewed from time to time? How could anything of the kind take place without other buildings in the capital, and especially the temple, having suffered serious harm, and, indeed, without their having been converted by the convulsion into a heap of ruins? Quite as arbitrary is the conjecture that the curtain was old and worn out (Kuinoel), as well as the assumption that it was, perhaps, too tensely stretched and too tightly fastened both at the bottom and on the two sides (Paulus). Even in the last case, a rending through an earthquake would have been impossible without a simultaneous rending of the walls or roof of the temple. As to the rest, Luke is entirely silent as to the sleeping saints whose resurrection Matthew relates; but that John passes over all these miracles appears to be best explained from the character of his whole gospel, which has less reference to the outer revelation of the glory of the *Logos* than to the spiritual character of His whole manifestation and activity. Of Luke's account the same holds good, although in a lesser measure, which Lange has remarked in respect to that of Matthew: "The Evangelist has gathered the reminiscences of these traits, and comprehended them in words which, in effect, have the resonance of a hymn, without thereby losing their historical character, for here the history itself took on the character of a hymn."

Vs. 46. **Father, into Thy hands.**—It is involved in the nature of the case that this utterance must be placed after the τετέλεσται of John, since he also states the substance of it with a παρέδωκεν τὸ πν. According to Matthew and Mark also, the dying Christ cries out with a loud voice, but what He exclaims Luke alone relates to us. Here, too, we hear from His lips an utterance from the Psalms, Ps. xxxi. 5. (The reading of Tischendorf, παρατιθεμαι, deserves the preference above the *Recepta*, παραθήσομαι, which appears to be borrowed from the Septuagint, Ps. xxxi. 5.) Παρατίθεσθαι is to be understood here not in the weak sense of "commend," but in its proper sense of "commit," *tradere*. Into the Father's mighty hand our Lord now commits, as a precious deposit, the spirit which is ready to depart from the body, and departs, therefore, with composure and hope, to the condition of separation (Paradise, vs. 43), preceding the Penitent Thief and all his fellow-redeemed.

Expired, ἐξέπνευσεν.—So also Mark, stronger still Matthew, ἀφῆκεν τὸ πνεῦμα, *emisit spiritum*. Even then, when He, according to the nature of the case, finds Himself in deepest dependence, He yet exhibits and uses His true freedom (John x. 18), and does what now is commanded by the course of nature so entirely with free choice, that the dying becomes not only His present *lot*, but also the supreme *act* of love and obedience.

DOCTRINAL AND ETHICAL.

1. Comp. LANGE on the parallels, and, respecting the significance and the purpose of the death of our Lord itself, Christian Dogmatics.

2. The last word of our Lord on the cross impresses on all the rest, as also on His whole life, the seal. With composed, clear spirit, He proceeds, the immaculately Pure, into eternity. With childlike trust He gives His spirit into the Father's guardian hand; with joyful hope He looks towards the rest and joy of death. Only after He, in the sixth word on the cross, has rendered account of His completed work, does He give us, finally, in addition, knowledge of His personal expectation. A word of Scripture is the torch which lights Him down into the valley of the shadow of death; He dies with the Scriptures on His lips, in which He has ever lived. Therefore, also, it is not necessary to ascribe to the 31st Psalm a direct Messianic signification; our Lord simply takes a word of Scripture on His lips as an expression of His own inward state, while He, doubtless not casually, passes over in silence that which the poet immediately adds: "Thou hast redeemed me, O Lord God of truth." What David in a certain sense utters as his motto of life, that He uses as His dying device.

3. The darkening of the sun in the moment of the dying of Jesus, points us to a deep hidden connection between the realm of nature and that of grace, which has yet been but little investigated by theologians. Not only as "sorrowing, as it were, with her greatest Son" (Hase), does nature veil herself in a mourning garment, but where the Incarnate Lord, through Whom all things were made, grows pale in death, there does convulsed nature depose concerning His greatness an unequivocal testimony. And as respects the rending of the curtain, the Epistle

to the Hebrews (ch. ix. 8) refers us clearly enough to the symbolical significance of this fact. Apparently their terror at the occurrence occasions the first involuntary information on the side of the Jews, since otherwise they would have been glad to keep it hidden. Various Jewish traditions respecting the miracles which at this very time, about forty years before the destruction of Jerusalem, came to pass in the sanctuary, we find collected in SEPP, *l. c.* iii., p. 580; they permit the faint traces of the truth of a fact to be recognized, whose actual occurrence stands more exactly detailed in the gospels. As respects, finally, the objection that in the Holy Scriptures, besides here, there exist no further actual allusions to the miracles here mentioned at the death of our Lord, we can in part very well acknowledge this without deriving therefrom any unfavorable inference in reference to the Evangelical narratives, but must also refer to Rev. xi., where it speaks of the wakening of the two witnesses, a revelation connected therewith, the opening of the heavenly temple (=the rending of the veil), and other miracles, which involuntarily remind us of what is here related.

4. The dying of Stephen, Huss, Luther, and others, even in their last words, an echo of the last words of our Lord.

5. The last word on the cross an unequivocal argument for the personality of God, as well as for the personality of the human spirit and its individual immortality. "Whoever could think that Jesus, with these words, breathed out His life forever into the empty air, such an one certainly knows nothing of the true, living spirit, and, consequently, nothing of the living God, and of the living power of the Crucified One." Ullmann.

HOMILETICAL AND PRACTICAL.

"When even the creation is stirred, be not thou slumbering, O my heart."—Light and darkness in the dying hour of our Lord united upon Calvary: 1. Gloomy night in nature, and therein the light of Providence; 2. gloomy night of suffering, and therein the light of Jesus' greatness; 3. gloomy night of death, and therein the light of a living hope.—The rent veil; of what it gives testimony: 1. That, *a.* a new economy is begun, *b.* a perfect atonement effected, *c.* a blessed fellowship founded; 2. to what it incites: *a.* to believing beholding, *b.* to courageous approach (Heb. x. 19), *c.* to holy self-surrender.—Jesus' death: 1. The lowest depth of His humiliation; 2. the beginning of His exaltation.—"Let us go with Him, that we may die with Him," John xi. 16.—A pilgrimage to Calvary on the mortal day of our Lord: 1. What seest thou there? 2. what feelest thou there? 3. what confessest thou there? 4. what promisest thou there? —The ninth hour; the high significance of this moment: 1. For our Lord; 2. for His friends and foes; 3. for the world; 4. for the Father.—"Ye do show forth the Lord's death," 1 Cor. xi. 26.—Calvary a school for Christian life, suffering, and dying.—Christ has: 1. Died; 2. died for us; 3. died for us that we also might die with Him.

STARKE:—Darkness is finally punished with darkness; consider this, ye children of darkness.—Since Christ has died, we need no expiatory sacrifice more. —Christ from the deepest abandonment passing over into the highest composure.—No longer in the hands of His enemies, but in those of the Father.—The saint prays not only in the beginning and the continuance, but also at the end of his suffering.—CANSTEIN:—Jesus dies, like a true corn of wheat, to bring forth much fruit, John xii. 24.—Die willingly where God wills, for Jesus died not in a sumptuous canopied bed, but poor and naked on the cross.— BRENTIUS:—The souls of the righteous are in God's hands, and no torment touches them. What would we more?—HEUBNER:—As Jesus did all that He did for us, so also for us was this prayer; He has committed our souls also with His own to the Father.—STEINMEYER:—The last word on the cross proclaims: 1. The glory of a blessed death; 2. the glory of the dying Son of God; 3. the glory of His high-priestly sacrificial death.—DRASEKE:—The death of Jesus as culmination and completion of His life. He shows: 1. A supreme composure of soul; 2. supreme love to man; 3. supreme Mediatorial power; 4. supreme Filial glory.—THOLUCK:—How the Lord dies: 1. With inner freedom; 2. with clear consciousness; 3. with perfect trust.—ARNDT:—Vs. 46 as cap-stone of the last words. Taken together: 1. The first two, words of compassion; 2. the two following, words of comfort for those outwardly and inwardly forsaken; 3. the last three, words of strengthening for those wrestling with death.—KRUMMACHER: —Father, into Thy hands. The How and Why of the death of Jesus.—HARMS:—The word "for you" to be weighed: 1. The faith which the word demands; 2. the repentance which it effects; 3. the consolation which it brings with it.—SCHMIDT:—How holy and awful the dying of the Saviour is.—VAN DER PALM:—1. Jesus' death the fulfilment of all God's promises; 2. Jesus' death the main substance of the Apostolic preaching; 3. Jesus' death the completion of His teaching and the crown of His life; 4. Jesus' death our life.

---

2. The Mourning of Nature and of Mankind (Vss. 47–49).

(Parallel with Matt. xxvii. 51–56; Mark xv. 38–41.)

47 Now when the centurion saw what was done [took place], he glorified God, saying,
48 Certainly this was a righteous man. And all the people [throngs, ὄχλοι] that came together to that sight [this spectacle], beholding [having beheld] the things which were
49 done, smote their breasts, and returned. And all his acquaintance, and the women that followed him from Galilee, stood afar off, beholding these things.

EXEGETICAL AND CRITICAL.

Vs. 47. Now when.—The mourning of nature Luke has already mentioned, vss. 44, 45, with a word. Matthew and Mark connect this yet more closely than he with the signs of a great change, which at the moment of death began to reveal itself in the human world. The leader in the array of witnesses for the glory of the death of Jesus, is the heathen centurion who saw τὸ γενόμενον. Without our having thereby particularly to exclude the events of the previous hours, this, however, appears to point particularly to the moment of the death of Jesus, in connection with the wonderful phenomena of nature occurring at the same time. Τὸ γενόμενον, vs. 48 goes, it is true, somewhat farther back, and comprehends all that from the moment of the affixing to the cross had taken place upon and around Calvary.

The centurion.—Comp. LANGE on Matthew and Mark. The impression which what took place produced upon a noble soldier's soul like his, is psychologically very explicable. Such a death the proud Roman, who had beheld death and its victims in its most diverse forms, has never yet seen. In the midst of the gloom of the three hours' darkness, the day begins to break before the eye of his soul: the mighty voice with which the last word on the cross is uttered resounds in his ears like the voice of a God, and with Jesus' death-hour there strikes also for 'him the birth-hour of a higher life. He has, doubtless, heard that this Jesus has been condemned as a blasphemer of God, but he cannot possibly believe it. He remembers the testimony of Pilate, and concurs fully with that which the Penitent Thief but a short time before had said in Jesus' honor. The substance of his confession Luke communicates when he makes him call our Lord a δίκαιος. But the original form of this, Matthew and Mark appear to have preserved to us, although the possibility undoubtedly must be allowed that both the one and the other expression may be genuine. As to the supposed sense of his words, see LANGE. It must, above all, not be overlooked that they are less the expression of an exactly defined conception of the understanding than the outgush of a deeply-moved sensibility, and that it is as unreasonable to deny the echo of superstition as the voice of sincere faith in his manly words.

Vs. 48. And all the people.—Scarcely can we conceive the number of the witnesses of Jesus' death and of the events connected therewith as great enough. At the time of the Passover there were from two to three millions of Jews, gathered from all lands of the earth, in the capital, a multitude almost as great as that which had once come out of Egypt, and of these it may be presupposed that there was no stranger among them that had not heard of Jesus of Nazareth (Luke xxiv. 18). So far as the hills and plains around Calvary give room for it, all are covered with beholders, who now, however, are found in a wholly different mood from that which is described vs. 35. As the centurion, in fact, glorifies God by his confession (a doxological trait entirely in the spirit of the third gospel, ch. xiii. 17; xviii. 15), so do these beholders accuse themselves as sharers in the guilt of the death of Jesus, and as objects of the holy displeasure of God. Even in itself such a transition in the mood of a mixed throng is not at all uncommon, and the objection (Strauss) that here is related to us, not so much what the Jews felt and did, as rather what they, according to the Christian view, *should* have felt and done, proceeds from an unpsychological and, for that very reason, an exceedingly uncritical mistrust. The murder of the Messiah had been a deed of national intoxication and bewilderment, upon which an hour of awakening must follow. The extraordinary phenomena of nature spoke, therefore, so much the more loudly to their conscience, and the remembrance of everything great and good which our Lord had done bestowed on Him in their eyes a so much greater dignity after they had rejected Him by their own guilt. The terror of death upon so many countenances is also an involuntary homage which is brought to the dead Christ, and the mournfully earnest Passover mood of so many contrite hearts becomes the preparation for the earnest Pentecostal inquiry: *Men and brethren what shall we do?*

Vs. 40. All His acquaintance.—Luke mentions these in addition to the people and the women, of whom he also, as well as Matthew and Mark, speaks. "Only Luke has this notice, which is so mere a summary, that it does not even by the ἀπὸ μακρόθεν, contradict the account of John (ch. xix. 25)." Meyer. We may understand particularly the acquaintance in the wider sense of the word, at Jerusalem and of the region round about, to whom, for instance, the owner of the colt at Bethphage and the owner of the Passover-hall at Jerusalem belong. In respect to the women, comp. ch. viii. 2 and the parallels. In what mood they now stood there, after they were now no longer hindered by the scoffings of the people from coming near, may be better felt than described. With the deepest sorrow over this irrevocable loss, which was not yet softened by the joyful hope of the resurrection, there is united melancholy joy that now at last the agonizing conflict is ended, and the heartfelt longing to render now the last honors to the inanimate corpse. In infinite diversity of moods, according to the measure of their spiritual development, receptivity, and their peculiar relations to our Lord, they stand there in the neighborhood of the place which had heard His last sighs, while we even now do not yet read respecting the disciples that they were with the women. John has led Mary home. Peter wanders lonesomely about. The other scattered sheep have vanished, without leaving a trace, when the Shepherd was smitten. Only the faithfulness of female love holds its ground when all seems lost.

DOCTRINAL AND ETHICAL.

1. The death of our Lord was glorified, and at the same time confirmed, as never a death after it. Even though we only rightly understand and interpret the signs at His death in nature and the human world, we shall be conducted to a higher Christology than to the Nazareo-Ebionitic one of ancient and modern Rationalism.

2. The heathen centurion the first fruits of the believing heathen world which shall yet one day bow the knee before Jesus. His joining in the confession of the robber in honor of our Lord the first union of Jews and Gentiles, who hitherto had been separated from one another by the middle wall of partition, and the presage of the communion of saints, Ephes. ii. 14-16. If we may assume that he stood at the head of the *Legio Germanica*, which the Romans, as is known, had in service at this time in Palestine, then the Germanic Christendom of Europe

may consider him in a yet closer sense of the word as their representative and Prodromus.

3. The awakening remorse of the people a precursory fulfilment of Jesus' own word, John viii. 28, and, at the same time, a prophecy of the hour in which Israel as a nation shall acknowledge what it did when it rejected the Son of David, Zech. xii. 10–12; Rev. i. 7. Here also, however, wickedness remains consistent with itself even to the end. Only the people, and not the Pharisees and Scribes, return from Calvary smiting their breasts. With reason, however, may we regard these first penitents of Israel as a first fruits of the hearing of the prayer, ch. xxiii. 34.

4. Never has the might of love been more speakingly revealed than on the death-day of our Lord. It yet keeps its ground even there where faith has suffered shipwreck and hope is utterly frustrated. With right, might Paul extol it as the chief among the Three, 1 Cor. xiii. 13.

HOMILETICAL AND PRACTICAL.

The dead Jesus glorified: 1. By God; 2. by man.—What the miracles in the realm of nature declare to the honor of the dead Saviour: 1. Jesus the immaculate, innocent Sufferer; 2. Jesus the perfect Atoner of sin; 3. Jesus the Resurrection and the Life.—The new covenant considered in the light of these miracles: 1. A ministration of the Spirit, where that of the letter is done away; 2. a ministration of righteousness, which replaces that of condemnation; 3. a ministration that abides, in contrast with that which ceases, 2 Cor. iii. 6–11.—The centurion under the cross a presage of the calling of the Gentiles at the rejection of the Jews.—The impression which the view of the dying Jesus produces in the truth-loving soul.—The triumph of the enemies of Jesus ending in a complete defeat.—The impression of the death of Jesus on the female heart.—How the view of the dead Saviour calls us: 1. To a fuller confession than that of the heathen centurion; 2. to a deeper humility than that of the remorseful people; 3. to firmer faith than that of the Galilean women.—Heaven and earth united in doing homage to the dead Christ.—The first witness concerning the death of Jesus: 1. Wherein we must follow him; 2. wherein we must be distinguished from him; 3. wherein we must excel him.

STARKE:—Confess Jesus even when He is on the cross, and when it seems to fare worst with His church.—The first fruits of the power of the death of Christ are so remarkable, what great things shall not the full harvest bring?—BRENTIUS:—Miracles, as well in nature as in grace, have no other design than the conversion of men.—He must certainly have a hard heart whom the Passion of Christ cannot move to repentance.—CRAMER:—God can be mighty even in the weak (2 Cor. xii. 10).—There are witnesses enough of the cross of Christ; he that will not believe cannot be helped.—SCHULTZ:—Concerning the miracles at the death of Christ, they show us: 1. Wherein the benefit consists which He has purchased for us by His death; 2. what the dispositions are to which the benefit must excite us.—GEROK:—The holy evening stillness upon Calvary: 1. The still rest of the perfected Sufferer; 2. the still repentance of the shaken world; 3. the still labor of the loving friends; 4. the still rest of the holy grave.—AHLFELD:—What seest thou on the cross of Christ? 1. The love that sues for us; 2. the love that dies for us: 3. the love that never dies.—THYM:—The cross on Calvary: 1. A sign of grace for us; 2. a sign of judgment against us.—RAUTENBERG:—Christ's death, my sin's death (John xix. 1–30).—My Jesus dies, why should I live?—(On Vs. 47) BOBE:—How do believing Christians stand under the cross of the dying Redeemer?—ACKERMAN:—The death of the Redeemer of the world in its composing influence on our death.—ALT:—The death of Christ a strong incitement to conversion from sin.—SCHMID:—The preaching of the Crucified: 1. A preaching of repentance for sinners; 2. a preaching of joy for believers; 3. a preaching of glory for our Lord.—ARNDT:—The signs at Jesus' death: 1. The signs of God's almightiness in nature; 2. of the grace of God in the hearts of men.—KRUMMACHER:—The funeral: 1. How it is rung in from heaven: 2. how it is attended on earth.

---

3. The Sabbath of the Grave (Vss. 50–56).

(Parallel with Matt. xxvii. 57–66; Mark xv. 42–47; John xix. 38–42.)

50 And, behold, *there was* a man named Joseph, a counsellor; *and he was* a good man'
51 and a just: (The same had not consented to the counsel and deed of them:) *he was* of Arimathea, a city of the Jews; who also himself[1] waited for the kingdom of God'
52, 53 This *man* went unto Pilate, and begged the body of Jesus. And he took it down' and wrapped it in linen, and laid it in a sepulchre that was hewn in stone, wherein
54 never man before was laid [there was no one yet lying]. And that day was the prepa-
55 ration [And it was the day of preparation[2]], and the sabbath drew on. And the women also [om., also], which came with him from Galilee, followed after, and beheld the
56 sepulchre, and how his body was laid. And they returned, and prepared spices and ointments; and rested the sabbath day [indeed[3]] according to the commandment.

---

[1] Vs. 51.—The words καί ... καὶ αὐτός should be omitted from the *Recepta*, and we should with Lachmann, Tischendorf, [who has, however, restored them,] read simply ὃς προσεδέχετο [with Meyer, Tregelles, Alford also. The MSS. which have the suspected words show so many variations in writing them as to make it probable that they came from the parallel passages in Matthew and Mark.—C. C. S.]

[2] Vs. 54.—B., Cod. Sin., C.[1], L., have παρασκευῆς instead of the παρασκευή of the *Recepta*. The Genitive is adopted

by Lachmann, Meyer, and Tregelles. Tischendorf and Alford retain the *Recepta*, which, however, besides being opposed by the above-named MSS., is not supported by D., which has προσαββατου. As all the uncials which read the Nominative, omit the following και, while those which read the Genitive retain it, there seems little doubt that Meyer is right in supposing the final ς to have been dropped from παρασκευης in consequence of the following σαββατον, while και, where it remained, protected the Genitive ending.—C. C. S.]

[³ Vs. 56.—Καὶ τὸ μὲν σάββατον ἡσύχασαν . . . τῇ δὲ μιᾷ τῶν σαββάτων . . . ἦλθον. "And the sabbath day, indeed, they rested . . . but on the first of the week . . . they came."—C. C. S.]

EXEGETICAL AND CRITICAL.

Vs. 50. Joseph.—Comp. LANGE on Matt. xxvii. 57. In a peculiar way Luke portrays his character as that of a good and righteous man. The latter, of course, not in the juridical, but in the theocratical sense of the word. Bengel: "*Omnis homo ἀγαθός est etiam δίκαιος, non contra. Lucas totum laudat ante partem.*" Whether he was the only one who in the Jewish council had raised his voice against the sentence of death upon our Lord, cannot be with certainty stated. So much, however, is clear, that he by this account is indirectly distinguished from Nicodemus, who is named indeed ἄρχων, but not βουλευτής, and who, therefore, appears to have had no voice in this case. As respects Arimathæa, this city is by no means identical with Rama, in Benjamin, which appears also Matt. ii. 18, as Friedlieb, *ad loc.* asserts without stating his grounds. In all probability we must understand by it Ramathaim, in Ephraim, where Samuel was born, and which lay not far from Lydda or Diospolis. *See* WIESELER in HERZOG'S *Real-Encycl. ad vocem.* The additional trait, finally, that *he waited for the kingdom of God,* gives Joseph a claim to an honorable place in the spiritual family circle of those who are named in Luke ii. 38.

Vs. 52. Went unto Pilate.—For the more particular circumstances, *see* Mark. According to CICERO, *In Verrem,* v. 45–51, the Roman Procurators sometimes conferred such a favor for money. Moreover, the Roman laws also provided: *corpora eorum, qui capite damnantur, cognatis ipsorum denegandu non sunt. See* ULPIAN, *Digest.* 47, t. 24. That Pilate demanded no money of the rich Joseph, who did not belong to the relations of our Lord, may have had its ground in a secret joy at the speedy death of our Lord (Lange), or perhaps also in the wish to give at once a mark of his complacency to that member of the supreme council who displayed respect for Jesus, and thereby also in this way indirectly to mortify the priests, who had violently extorted the sentence of death. In this matter also, Pilate, even as in the refusal to alter the superscription over the cross, shows himself great in little things, while he, it is true, in the great matter had been, alas, only too little.

Vs. 53. In linen.—To be understood of fine sindon, a cotton stuff which was cut into strips, and is elsewhere called *clean* linen, because the priests were commonly clothed with this stuff. The head was wrapped separately in a σουδάριον of the same stuff, John xx. 7. The preliminary costly embalming Luke passes over, probably because soon, in place of it, the anointing by the women was to come. To speak of "enormous consumption of spices" (Strauss), would only be reasonable, if we did not know what a lavish expenditure in this respect often prevailed in the Orient, so that according to JOSEPHUS, *Ant. Jud.* xvii. 8. 3, at the funeral of Herod the Great, not less than five hundred servants were required to carry the spices.

A sepulchre that was hewn in stone.—If we must in general acknowledge the identity of the present and of the original Calvary, then the Holy Sepulchre is at all events to be sought in the immediate neighborhood of the place that even yet is shown as such, in the church of this name. Comp. hereupon the admirable words of VON SCHUBERT, *l. c.* iii. p. 509.

Vs. 54. It was the day of preparation, παρασκευή, preparation for the Sabbath, and particularly that part of the Friday which was regarded as the introduction to the Sabbath (προσάββατον, Mark xv. 42). When Meyer says *ad loc.* "Here also there betrays itself the absence of a festal character in the day of Jesus' death," it may be inquired whether, on the other side, the Jewish council on this whole day, and even at evening, would have exhibited such a restless activity if on this evening the Paschal Lamb had yet to be bought, slaughtered, and eaten. In all probability we have to understand the late Friday afternoon, between five and six o'clock. Ἐπέφωσκε signifies here the dawning, not of the natural, but of the legal Saturday.

Vs. 55. And the women... followed after.—Κατακολουθήσασαι. The strengthened expression appears in this connection to intimate a following down, κατά, even into the grave. *See* LANGE, *L. J.* iii. p. 521. They accompany the funeral of our Lord as far as possible ; that they, according to the common view, were also present at the taking down from the cross, and active in it, is not related to us by the history. According to all the Synoptics, they joined the little funeral train only after the corpse had been taken down and suitably wrapt around. In this work Joseph and Nicodemus had apparently the assistance of servants or friends, but not directly of the women. It is, therefore, very possible that they did not know precisely the quantity of the spices brought by Nicodemus, and even if this had been the case, love does not inquire how little will suffice, but how much it can perform. Even the view of the abundance of the manifestations of love on the part of these two men must also have disposed them to like zeal, and made the thought unendurable to them that they who yet had served the living Master with their possessions should now render no further service to the dead. The observation also that all was accomplished sumptuously, it is true, but with comparatively great haste, must have spontaneously brought up the thought to them, whether there might not be here something still to be cared for. Therefore, after the men had returned home, they remain alone, and still regard the grave for a while (vs. 55), going home then with the resolution as soon as possible to buy spices and ointment, but resting the Sabbath day, according to the commandment. According to the more exact statement of Mark, the spices were first bought and prepared after the Sabbath was already passed (ch. xvi. 1), that is, according to our reckoning, on Saturday evening, after six o'clock. This is also internally probable, since the Sabbath, we may suppose, had already begun when they had returned to Jerusalem from viewing the grave (vs. 55). That the purchase took place *directly* after their return, Luke does not at all say, although he does not deny it (ὑποστρέψασαι δὲ ἡτοίμασαν); he only intimates that they did not permit themselves to be kept back from their work of love by the strict observance of the Sabbath law.

Vs. 56 of his account is immediately connected with ch. xxiv. 1, and the antithesis between μέν and δέ would properly indicate that at the end of ch. xxiii. only a comma ought to have been placed. Sense: After they had viewed the grave, they bought (not stated when?) spices, and rested indeed on the Sabbath day, according to the law, but when this was over they went with the (just-purchased) spices as quickly as possible to the grave.

DOCTRINAL AND ETHICAL.

1. If it has ever plainly appeared that decisive events in the kingdom of God must serve to bring its hidden friends to light, and that a great sorrow is capable of uniting men of diverse rank, condition, and age, this then took place at the burial of our Lord. For the Eleven we here look round in vain; so scattered are the sheep that even the care for the corpse of the Shepherd is not capable of uniting them; but love to the Lord has turned women to heroines, and if even to this moment there has not yet a single voice from the Jewish council been lifted against the atrocity committed, yet it now appears that not all the members are animated by the spirit of Annas and Caiaphas.

2. The certainty of the death of Jesus before His burial is raised above every rational doubt, and partially attested even by the manner of His burial. Only the modern romance of unbelief, which in late years has sought in a magnificent manner to deceive a credulous public by the publishing of quasi-ancient manuscripts out of which the connection of Jesus with Essenism was to appear as clear as the sun, undertakes to assure us that Joseph of Arimathæa still discovered signs of life, and, therefore, attended the supposed corpse with the utmost care. See, *e. g.*, *Jesus der Essäer oder die Religion der Zukunft*, Leipzig, 1849; the *Buch Jesu*, Kassel, 1850. "The important discoveries about Jesus' manner of death," and the like, which a few years ago were circulated by thousands, now are in part already forgotten again, but in part serve even yet as weapons in the hands of the most stupid unbelief. 2 Thess. ii. 11.

3. The burial of our Lord constitutes the precise transition from the condition of His humiliation to that of His exaltation, and is therefore sometimes reckoned with the one, sometimes with the other. It is, with all that took place hitherto, the fulfilment of the prophetic word (Is. liii. 9; 1 Cor. xv. 3, 4), and in the more particular circumstances, remarkable in the extreme. A new grave receives our Lord, even as before an ass's colt bore Him, on which never yet a man had sat. A grave in the rock, so strong that only angels' power could open it; with only one entrance, so that the local circumstances themselves forbid the supposition that the corpse had been stolen; in a garden, so that thus, in a place like that in which sin was born, it is also borne to the grave. Thus does all concur to procure for our Lord an undisturbed repose, and to prepare for Him a glorious resurrection morning.

4. As respects the condition of our Lord during the interval which His corpse passed in the grave, we venture boldly to apply to it the word of John, that "that Sabbath day was a GREAT day." Ch. xix. 31. It was, without doubt, a condition of full consciousness, of refreshing rest, of the beginning of joy in company with the Penitent Thief, and of blessed hope of the approaching resurrection morning. How far we can now begin to speak of an activity of our Lord in the condition of separation, is connected with the question when the preaching to the spirits in prison (1 Peter iii. 19-21) took place. We believe that the apostle places it between our Lord's resurrection and His ascension.

5. The Sabbath which our Lord passes in the grave is the last Sabbath of the Old Covenant. Therefore, also, His friends spend it in the sadness of those who do not yet know that the day of the New Covenant has dawned, wherein life and immortality were brought to light. His enemies embitter to themselves this their Sabbath rest with the endeavors which they use to guard the corpse of our Lord, as related by Matthew alone. It is a poetical justice that they who have so often accused the Saviour of Sabbath-breaking, now themselves finally desecrate this day. Scarcely has the day after the Friday dawned (the legal Sabbath day, that is, which began on Friday evening after six o'clock), when they already come to Pilate and make their proposition to him, Matt. xxvii. 62. Not a single night will they leave the corpse unwatched, and do not rest until the guard is posted in the garden of Joseph. But by this very means they concur in the revelation of their shame, in the revelation of the resurrection of our Lord, and of the glory of God.

6. An admirable representation of the Taking Down from the Cross, by Rubens; of the viewing of the grave by the two women, by E. Veith; beautiful grave hymn: "*Nun schlummerst die, O meine Ruh,*" &c.

HOMILETICAL AND PRACTICAL.

See on the parallels in LANGE.—Joseph of Arimathæa the representative of an honorable minority. —Just when all appears to be lost, does the heroic courage of faith awake.—The dead Saviour the centre of union between His male and female friends.—Love stronger than death, Sol. Song, viii. 6.—"They beheld the sepulchre" (admirable text for Good Friday evening): 1. How far our beholding of the sepulchre may be distinguished from that of the first female friends; 2. how far, however, it must agree with theirs. —Jesus' sepulchre viewed in the light of faith: 1. The monument of the wickedness of His enemies; 2. the goal of the Passion of our Lord; 3. the working-place of the providence of God: 4. the grave of the sin of the world; 5. the pledge of the Christian's rest in the grave.—The great Sabbath: 1. A feast of delusive rest for Israel; 2. a day of refreshing rest for Jesus; 3. a time of active rest for the Father; 4. a pledge of restored rest for the sinner: 5. an image of the present rest of the Christian, Heb. iv. 9.— The great Sabbath: 1. The history; 2. the significance; 3. the admonitions of this very memorable day.—The Sabbath rest: 1. Of Christ; 2. of the Christian.

STARKE:—Say not, "If everything is thus corrupt, how can I alone live so devoutly?"—He that is inwardly concerned for right, must also make it known in seasonable time.—There is no fear in love, but, &c.—Before our rulers we must have befitting respect, Rom. xiii. 7.—Believers' best and dearest treasure is Jesus.—One may and should, even yet, clothe Jesus in His naked members.—HEDINGER:— Even to the dead must we show love, and Christianly commit them to the earth.—To lose one's money for Christ's sake is a great gain.—Through a blessed death there is a passage to the true rest, O beauteous Sabbath!—J. HALL:—The true Christian is not content with having others show love towards their neighbor, but he does it also himself.—*Nova Bibl.*

Tub.:—This is the way of pious souls, that they are God-fearing, loving, active.—ARNDT:—The burial of our Lord: 1. Its possibility; 2. its glory; 3. its importance; 4. its obligation.—J. C. STERN:—The confession of the Christian at the grave of the Saviour.

SECOND SECTION.

THE PERFECT TRIUMPH.

CHAPTER XXIV. 1–48.

A. *Over the Might of Sin and Death.* CH. XXIV. 1–12.

1 Now [But] upon the first *day* of the week, very early in the morning, they came
unto the sepulchre, bringing the spices which they had prepared [end verse with "pre-
2 pared"[1]], and certain *others* with them. And they found the stone rolled away from
3 the sepulchre. And they entered in, and [having entered in they] found not the body
4 of the Lord Jesus.[2] And it came to pass, as they were much perplexed thereabout,
5 behold, two men stood by them in shining [glittering] garments: And as they were
afraid, and bowed down *their* faces to the earth, they said unto them, Why seek ye the
6 living among the dead? He is not here, but is risen: remember how he spake unto
7 you when he was yet in Galilee, Saying, The Son of man must be delivered into the
8 hands of sinful men, and be crucified, and the third day rise again. And they remem-
9 bered [or, called to mind] his words, And returned from the sepulchre, and told [re-
10 ported[3]] all these things unto the eleven, and to all the rest. It was Mary Magdalene,
and Joanna, and Mary *the mother* of James, and other *women that were* with them,
11 which told these things unto the apostles. And their words seemed to them as idle
12 tales, and they believed them not. Then arose Peter, and ran unto the sepulchre; and
stooping down, he beheld the linen clothes laid by themselves, and departed, wondering
in himself at that which was come to pass.[4]

[1] Vs. 1.—The clause which follows in the *Recepta*, καί τινες σὺν αὐταῖς, is probably, as Kuinoel already conjectured, an interpolation from vs. 10. The words are wanting in B., C., [Cod. Sin.,] L., 33, Vulgate, Itala, and others, and are rejected by Lachmann, Tischendorf, [Meyer, Tregelles, Alford.]

[2] Vs. 3.—The words of the *Recepta*, τοῦ κυρίου Ἰησοῦ, are omitted in D. but appear in all the other uncials, and though rejected by Tischendorf and marked as doubtful by Van Oosterzee, are retained by Lachmann, Meyer, Alford. Tregelles omits τοῦ κυρίου, following one Cursive, and some Versions. The great weight of authority, therefore, is for the words in question. A concordance of the Acts will show that "The Lord Jesus" is a favorite appellation with Luke, as Alford remarks. But the concurrence of both appellations would, as he also remarks, be quite sure to provoke the erasure sometimes of one and sometimes of the other, thus leading to a doubt of the genuineness and the consequent omission of both.—C. C. S.]

[3] Vs. 9.—Revised Version of the American Bible Union.—C. C. S.]

[4] Vs. 12.—Although vs. 12 is wanting in Cod. D. and moreover in the Syriac, Itala, Jerome, &c., yet it appears to be original and genuine, and only to have been omitted, because it appeared to conflict with vs. 24. An interpolator would, in the interest of harmony with John xx. 1–10, not have neglected to mention also the ἄλλος μαθητής. The very incompleteness and fragmentariness of the report is an argument for its genuineness.

EXEGETICAL AND CRITICAL.

General Remarks.—In the history of the Resurrection and Ascension also, Luke preserves the same character which we have already more than once remarked in him. In that which he communicates in common with the two other Synoptics, he is less detailed and exact than they, so that he must rather be complemented from them, than they, on the contrary, from him. But, on the other hand, he furnishes us new contributions to the knowledge of the Risen and Glorified Lord, the contents and tendency of which are in the most beautiful agreement with the broad humanistic character of his gospel, as will appear from the expositions of the individual accounts. The appearance on the evening of the first resurrection day he relates, vs. 36 *seq.*, much more at length than John, and that our historical faith in a visible Ascension rests almost exclusively on his testimony, as well at the end of the gospel as at the beginning of the Acts, scarcely needs mention. Respecting the history of the Resurrection and its *Enantiophanies* in general, comp. LANGE on Matt., ch. xxviii. After that which is there so admirably remarked, we are at liberty to occupy ourselves exclusively with the account of Luke. " *In resurrectione et vita, quam ostendit quadraginta diebus, reficimur et delectabilibus pascimur argumentis.*" Bernard of Clairvaux.

Vs. 1. **Very early in the morning,** ὄρθρου βαθέος, or, according to the reading of A., C., D., [Cod. Sin.] with an unusual ancient genitive βαθέως, see Tischendorf, *ad loc.* The account is immediately connected with ch. xxiii. 56, and the women of whom Luke here makes mention can be no others than those of whom he has said, vs. 55, that they had come with Jesus from Galilee. Altogether arbitrary, therefore, is Bengel's remark: *aliæ, quæ non venerant e Galilæa.* Since Luke, vs. 10, mentions three of these women by name, and then adds, αἱ λοιπαὶ σὺν αὐταῖς, the company, according to his account, consisted at least of five. Mary Magdalene all the Evangelists mention. Matthew and Mark speak of the other Mary, the mother of James. Mark mentions as third only the name of Salome, while Luke, in her stead, places Joanna as third. It may be that this difference may be explained from their having gone in two divisions to the grave (Lange); although it is, on the other hand, a question whether a going out in company at so early a morning hour is not psychologically more probable. It is difficult to establish anything certain here, but at all events, unreasonable, where the account of the one Evangelist complements very well that of the other, but does not exclude it, to consider *difference* and *opposition,* without further inquiry, as words of like signification.

Vs. 2. **The stone rolled away,** τὸν λίθ.—By whom it had been rolled away appears from Matthew; with what unnecessary propositions and anxieties the women on the way to the grave had occupied themselves is related to us by Mark. After Mary Magdalene had viewed the stone that was rolled away, she hurries back to the city to bring this intelligence to Peter and John (John xx. 2 *seq.*); this Luke is silent about, but, on the other hand, he describes to us the terror and joy of the other women in a vivid manner.

Vs. 4. **Two men.**—"The angels are designated according to that form of manifestation which they had in the view of the women." Meyer. As respects the well-known controversy as to the number of the angels, we are satisfied, instead of occupying ourselves with all the harmonistic schemes that have been in earlier or modern times thought out, to remind the reader rather of the well-known word of Lessing in his *Duplik,* where he, with a liberality strange to most of the modern critics, wrote: "Cold discrepancy-mousers, do ye not then see that the Evangelists do not count the angels? The whole grave, the whole region round about the grave, was invisibly swarming with angels. There were not only two angels, like a pair of grenadiers who are left behind in front of the quarters of the departed general; there were millions of them; they appeared not always one and the same, not always the same two; sometimes this one appeared, sometimes that; sometimes on this place, sometimes on that; sometimes alone, sometimes in company; sometimes they said this, sometimes they said that."

Vs. 5. **Why seek ye.**—In the redaction of the angels' discourse in Luke, it is especially the groundlessness of the seeking of Him in the mansions of the dead who already is actually living, which especially comes into the foreground. The difference in the account of the angels' address is an internal argument for its truth, since the women, in the agitation of the moment, could not possibly have stated correctly, and with diplomatic exactness, the intelligence heard. Enough that all the Evangelists concur in the main matter. "Thus is the fact of the first announcement of the resurrection of Christ represented to us, not in the form of its abstractly objective course, but taken together with its living working in the living image of the first Easter harmonies which it called forth. But these harmonies now do not present themselves in the measured mood of a unisonous choral, but in the form of a four-voiced very agitated *fugue.*" Lange.

Vs. 6. **When He was yet in Galilee.**—The reminder of that which the Lord had uttered particularly in Galilee takes in Luke the place of the direction to go into Galilee, as the place where the Risen One should be seen again, as he, moreover, communicates afterwards no Galilean appearance whatever. The prophecies of the Passion, which the women had forgotten, were known to the angels. Why it is psychologically impossible that the women should now first remember again the predictions of our Lord's resurrection if He had really so definitely uttered them (Meyer), we do not comprehend.

Vs. 9. **Told all these things.**—Obediently to the express command of the angel, which Matthew and Mark state. The mood in which they return from the grave is also, in particular, not stated to us more particularly by Luke; on the other hand, we owe to him the account that they proclaimed the joyful message in a yet wider circle than merely to the Twelve, as we soon after shall learn, vss. 22–24, yet more particularly from the journeyers to Emmaus. Respecting the here-named women themselves, see on ch. viii. 2, 3.

Vs. 11. **As idle tales,** ὡσεὶ λῆρος, nonsense and superstitious gossip, crazy talk. Dutch: *ydel geklap.* That they also brought the intelligence with the same result to the ἀδελφοῖς of the Lord (Acts i. 14) is undoubtedly possible (De Wette), but by no means proved. The individual experience of the Magdalene, who is connected in vs. 10 also with the other women, and, according to John xx. 18, gives her individual account, is, for brevity's sake, passed over by Luke. It appears, however, from his condensed account, that she too found no better reception than the other messengers of the Resurrection.

Vs. 12. **Then arose Peter.**—Comp. John xx. 2–10. John is here unmentioned, but from vs. 24 it appears, at all events, that several of the disciples on this morning had gone to the grave. Had Luke, as Baur supposes, wished to place in the background the appearance vouchsafed to Peter by the narrative of the appearance which the journeyers to Emmaus experienced, then he might just as well have left this whole narrative of the apostles' visit to the grave entirely unmentioned. As to the rest, in view of the brevity of Luke's account, it cannot be a matter of surprise that he speaks of μόνα, but does not mention the σουδάριον (John xx. 7).

DOCTRINAL AND ETHICAL.

1. *See* Lange on the parallels in Matthew and Mark.

2. "The re-awakening of the dead Christ has, humanly apprehended, something so sublimely touching and beautiful, that if it were a fable, as it is not, the truth of history would be wished for it." Herder. To have comprehended the great miraculous fact on its purely human side especially, and to have described it, and thus to have brought it yet nearer to us on this side than was done by Matthew

and Mark, this belongs to the incontrovertible merits of Luke.

3. The announcement of the Resurrection by angels, like that of the Nativity, was in the highest degree worthy of God, and the receptivity of the women for the objectively present angelophany was conditioned by their subjective frame of mind. No inventor would have contented himself with one or two heavenly messengers, when in the Christmas night a whole throng of the heavenly host had come down to earth. A Resurrection without such extraordinary circumstances would have been a spring without flowers, a sun without rays, a triumph without triumphal crown.

4. A remarkable agreement exists between the awakening of the first and of the second life of our Lord upon earth. In both beginnings we see doubters and anxious ones quieted by a heavenly messenger. In both the attendant circumstances are related at length, but over the commencing point itself of the life and of the Resurrection of our Lord there remains a mysterious veil. He is awakened by the power of the Most High, as He by the same power had been conceived (Luke i. 35; Rom. vi. 4). By His Resurrection He becomes manifest as God's Son (Rom. i. 4), as He had been named even before His birth (Luke i. 32).

5. The Resurrection of our Lord is, first, the *Restoration* of the life which appeared to be quite ended, while the broken bond between soul and body is again knit together; secondly, a *Continuance* of the previous life, wherewith the consciousness of its identity again awakes (Luke xxiv. 39), the memory returns, and the objective fact acquires also subjective truth for the Risen One Himself; finally, the *Glorification* of the former existence, whose burdens now all fall away, so that the Risen One shows Himself entirely different from before, without being on that account another.

6. The Scripture testifies that Christ rose with a truly human body, from an actual sleep of death, in the literal sense of the word, out of the grave. Condemned, therefore, is the Docetic representation, by which either the reality or the identity of His body is doubted, or the manner of His resurrection so represented that it becomes entirely impossible to conceive a true corporeality (see, for instance, the essay of F. KRUX: *Wie ging Jesus durch des Grabes Thür?* Bonn, 1838). But not less is the coarser or more refined rationalistic interpretation, according to which the revivification of the Lord becomes only the awakening out of a seeming death, against the Scripture and the Christian consciousness. How would it be possible that the double expression of the self-consciousness of the Lord (Rev. i. 18), "I was dead, and behold I am alive again," should contain in its second part objective, in the first only subjective, truth? Finally, we reject the one-sided symbolical interpretation, according to which the Resurrection history is regarded only as an unessential involucrum of religious ideas, not as a fact in itself (Spinoza, Kant, Hegel, Strauss).

7. The possibility of the Resurrection of the Lord from the dead is *a priori* controverted by those who, in Pantheistic or Rationalistic wise, ignore every essential distinction between spirit and matter. Over against this we have simply to bring to mind that the justice of the fundamental anthropological views of unbelief is yet in no wise proved. To explain the possibility of the Resurrection so perfectly that one clearly sees that it, according to natural laws, not only can take place, but also must take place, is a preposterous requirement, since the fact precisely by such an explanation would lose the character of a miracle, and sink out of the class of the *Miracula* down into that of the *Mirabilia.* Enough that the possibility is grounded in the personality of the Lord, for whom death, not less than sin, as we have already previously reminded the reader, may be called something entirely and utterly preternatural. It is a folly to dispute about this possibility with such as deny the miraculous deeds of the earlier period of His history. Only when these latter are proved or allowed can we go farther, and find it also assumable and rational that He, although bodily in the grave, could not see corruption. Whether we have to conceive His Resurrection as the fruit of a quiet but regularly proceeding development in the grave, very much as in the dead *pupa* the arising life of the butterfly is, as in a closed laboratory, developed, or whether we have rather to assume a magnificent transition, in consequence of which the hitherto entirely senseless corpse in an instant was, as it were, streamed through with Divine life—this is a question to the decisive answer of which all fixed historical data are wanting to us. Enough that we have to conceive of the Lord's Resurrection as being both the proper work of the Son (John x. 18), and as also a miraculous act of the Father (Acts ii. 24). Whoever takes our Lord for that which He, according to His own word and according to that of His apostles, is, accounts the raising again of the God-man, wonderful as it is, as being in the highest sense of the word perfectly natural, since the presupposition becomes Christologically unreasonable that He should have remained in death. As to the conception of the miracle itself, there deserve here to be compared the weighty remarks of Schenkel, in GEZLER'S *Protestant. Monatsblatt*, 1833, and by Rothe in his *Abhandlung zur Dogmatik* in the *Theol. Stud. u. Krit.*, 1858, i.

8. For the Lord Himself the hour of the Resurrection was, without doubt, an hour of blessed joy and glorious triumph, and then also an hour of hopeful preparation for the different revelations which He on the very first day bestowed on different friends in different places. We stand here at the entrance of one of the most remarkable transition periods of His outer and inner life, of a character almost like the transitions in His twelfth or thirteenth year. From henceforth He enters into an entirely different relation to His foes and to His friends, to the world of spirits, to the kingdom of darkness, to death and the grave, yea, in a certain measure, even to the Father. Hitherto we have learned to know Him as the Son who must yet become perfect and learn obedience by that which He suffered (Heb. ii. 10; v. 8); now we find Him entirely perfected and purified, as it were, at the foot of His throne.* Au hour like this He had on earth never yet seen, and not less than at the Baptism (Luke iii. 21), may we suppose Him now also to have consecrated the new life in prayer to the Father. Nay, as His whole first life may be named a preparation for His suffering and death, so now did His second life become a preparation for the hour of ascension. Perverted as it is essentially to identify Resurrection and Ascension (Kinkel, Weisse), as

---

* [The author, of course, by the word "purified" has anything in mind but a purification of the Sinless One from sin. But He is now purified even from the sinless infirmities which appertain to humanity as yet unglorified.—C. C. S.]

little may we forget that the two are most intimately united. With every day which removed our Lord farther from the empty grave He drew nearer and nearer to His waiting crown, and the blessed celebration of His victory coalesced with the still preparation for His coronation in an admirable unity, so that He, even on the first day, might speak of an entry into His glory, vs. 26. Yet scarcely do we venture to enter more deeply into this sanctuary. If we cannot even express what a glory and blessing is reflected in the Lord's Resurrection, what must then the experience have been? In the appearances of the Risen One has His glory become most clearly visible for the finite eye, and to them we have, therefore, above all things, to give heed if we will learn to know Christ and the power of His Resurrection, Phil. iii. 10. The fulness of detail with which Luke communicates to us the fourth appearance compensates in rich measure his silence respecting the first and the second, while the third, vs. 34, is only intimated by him. Respecting the number and sequence of these appearances, *see* LANGE, *Matthew*, p. 540 *seq*.

9. In view of the supreme moment of this miraculous fact, we cannot be at all surprised that it has been in manifold ways glorified by Christian art. Painting owes to it masterpieces of Raphael, Tintoretto, Paul Veronese, Caracci, Rubens, and others. In the most of these pictures Christ appears surrounded with heavenly glory, as He breaks the bands of death and swings the banner of victory, while the watchers of the grave are trembling and fleeing. Yet, in view of the difficulties of representing the moment of the Resurrection itself, perhaps the efforts to paint what immediately preceded or followed it deserve the higher esteem. The journey of the holy women to the grave, and the second appearance to Mary Magdalene, both by Ary Scheffer, belong to his most admirable masterpieces. Hymnology has been enriched by the Resurrection with the exquisite lays of a Gregory the Great, Ambrose, Gellert, Klopstock, Claudius, Manzoni, and others, [and our own Hastings, whose "How calm and beautiful the morn," is scarcely equalled.—C. C. S.] The scene of the Easter bells in Faust has bestowed on Goethe a part of his own earthly immortality.

HOMILETICAL AND PRACTICAL.

General Points of view:—The Resurrection of the Lord—I. In relation to the *history of the world*. The vanquishing of the might of sin and death, which had revealed itself in all manner of forms, as well among Israelites as among the heathen nations; the implanting of a new principle of life in man and in mankind. The empty grave the boundary between the old and the new economy, 2 Cor. v. 17. The triumph of the might of light over the might of darkness in the course of the history of the world, typically expressed in the triumph of the second Adam over all the powers of darkness and death. II. In relation to *Israel*. The sublimest expectations of the Old Testament are fulfilled, Ps. xvi. 9, *et alibi*, and what there was typified in Joseph, David, Israel, that, namely, the way of humiliation led to the highest glory, was realized in unexampled measure. The triumph of the King of Israel, the beginning of the temporary overthrow, rejection, hardening of Israel, and yet also the pledge of its final re-establishment. The empty grave the dumb and yet eloquent accuser of the Messiah's murderers. III. In relation to the *Apostles and first friends of our Lord*. His Resurrection the foundation of their renewal to a life of faith, hope, and love, after that all with His death had appeared lost. The Easter morning the commencement of a new period for every one among them and for their whole body. The certainty that their Master lives, bestows on their spirit new life, on their heart new joy, on their feet new strength, on their future, new hope. Even unbelief has seen itself forced to the acknowledgment that a transformation such as becomes manifest in the circle of the disciples between Good Friday and Whitsunday, can only be explained by their having believed in the great fact which the Easter morning proclaims. But how this subjective certainty could have arisen, unless from the objectively present fact, no apostle of unbelief has been able to explain to us in a way which, psychologically, and, much less, historically, has even any degree of probability. IV. In relation to *Jesus Himself*. The Resurrection is: *a*. the satisfactory solution of the otherwise entirely inexplicable events of His life, whereby the otherwise disturbed harmony of His life is again restored; *b*. the crown of His miraculous deeds, especially of His raisings from the dead; *c*. the seal of His declarations in respect to His own person and to His condition after His death; *d*. the decisive step on the way to His glorification, after the *status exinanitionis* now lay forever behind Him. V. In relation to the foundation of the *Kingdom of God* in general, the Lord's Resurrection is the indispensably necessary condition, without which the coming forward of the apostles, the conversion of thousands of Jews, and the union of many thousand heathen with them in one spiritual body, must have remained something entirely inexplicable. VI. Nay, for the whole *Doctrine of Salvation*, Jesus' Resurrection is the *conditio sine qua non* of the personal redemption, renovation, and resurrection of all His people. The certainty of reconciliation is not perfectly assured so long as it has not become manifest that the sacrifice of the Son has been accepted by the Father; on this account, also, Paul lays yet more weight upon the Lord's Resurrection than even upon His death (Rom. v. 10; viii. 34). *a*. The type, *b*. the ground, *c*. the power, of our Lord, we find offered only in faith on the Christ who has personally arisen from the dead, and it is by this great fact of the Easter morning that, *a*. the possibility, *b*. the certainty, *c*. the glory of our own resurrection, so far as we believe on Him, is triumphantly confirmed. All this offers to the Christian homilete on the highest feast of the church a so infinite wealth of points of view and considerations, that we can scarcely conceive how any one who has experienced in himself, at least incipiently, the truth of the apostle's word, Gal. ii. 20, could ever be able on this feast to complain that he had entirely preached himself out.

On the Section.—The first Easter morning; the realm of nature a symbol of the realm of grace, *a*. the gloomy night, *b*. the much-promising dawn, *c*. the breaking day.—The first pilgrims to the Holy Sepulchre: *a*. how mournful they go thither, *b*. how joyful they return.—The experience of the first female friends of our Lord on the day of His Resurrection a proof of the truth of the declaration, Ps. xxx. 5. *Weeping may endure for a night, but joy cometh in the morning.*—The stone rolled away.— How on Easter morning it began to be bright: 1. In the garden; 2. in the human hearts; 3. over the cross; 4. for the world; 5. in the realm of the dead.—The first Easter gospel: 1. The hearers; 2. the preacher; 3. the message; 4. the fruit of the sermon.—How unbelief mourns precisely for that which was to give it the first ground of hope.—The empty grave viewed not joyfully, but doubtfully.—The Easter morn a festal day for the angels of heaven also.—The fruitless seeking of the living among the dead: 1. Of the living Christ in the grave; 2. of the living Christian in the dust of the earth.—"He is not here," for the first and only time the absence of Christ a source of inexpressible joy.—The coincidence and the diversity between the first Christmas night announcement and the first Easter morning announcement.—Jesus' Resurrection the confirmation of His earlier and the pledge for the fulfilment of His later words.—Of how many words of the Master does the Christian become mindful at the view of the empty grave!—No command was on the Resurrection morning so often given and carried out, as that to proclaim the joyful message to others also.—The distinction between the unbelief of the first apostles and friends of Jesus in His Resurrection, and that of modern criticism.—Only the Risen Saviour Himself was able to put an end to the doubt and sorrow of His first friends.—They doubted, that we might not need to doubt.—The empty grave viewed by a fallen apostle; he: 1. Longingly entered it; 2. carefully examined it: 3. found it empty; 4. left it thoughtful.—The lovely harmony of the Easter evening arising from the manifold sharp dissonances of the Easter morning.

STARKE:—QUESNEL:—What one will do for love to Christ he must accomplish very soon and carefully.—*Nova Bibl. Tub.*:—No stone is so great but the mighty Providence of God can lift it.—Believers often find Jesus not as they seek Him.—CANSTEIN:—The angels have ten times served the Son of God from His manifestation in the flesh to His Ascension.—God has many means and ways to comfort the terrified; if He does it not through the holy angels, yet it comes to pass through the angels of the church.—*Bibl. Wirt.*:—With God there is no respect of persons; to Him a woman is as good as a man, &c., Gal. iii. 28.—The holy angels abide by the word of Christ.—CANSTEIN:—To forget Christ's word brings trouble.—Sometimes weak women must be evangelists to men, that ought to be so strong.—*Nova Bibl. Tub.*:—The secret of the Resurrection passes all men's reason and thoughts.—Jesus, the Supreme Good, is worthy that we leave not off till we find Him.—OSIANDER:—Faith and unbelief wrestle sometimes in a man.

ARNDT:—The first rays of the glory of Christ in the dawn of the Easter morning: 1. The stone rolled away; 2. the glittering angels; 3. the hastening women.—KRUMMACHER:—In the miracle of the Resurrection we behold: *a*. the glory of the Father, *b*. the glory of the Son, *c*. the glory of the elect.—NITZSCH:—The happiness of the disciples of Jesus to be revivified by the resurrection of their Head.—FLATT:—The morning of the Resurrection of Jesus: 1. How it diffuses the brightest morning twilight over the earth, and in its light the morning of eternity beams kindly upon us.—W. HOFACKER:—The open grave of the Risen One: 1. An arch of His triumph; 2. a bow of peace denoting heavenly favor and grace; 3. a door of life for the resurrection of our spirit and our body.—RIEGER:—How God wills not that we should seek and anoint a dead Jesus in the grave.—AHLFELD:—The celebration of the first Easter.—SOUCHON:—The Easter preaching of the angel.—STIER:—The Resurrection of Christ the true comfort of all believers: 1. In tribulation; 2. in sin; 3. in death.—RAUTENBERG:—Easter among the graves: 1. The stone of the curse is rolled away therefrom; 2. there dwell angels therein; 3. the dead are gone out therefrom.—The great Easter consolation: 1. For sorrowing love; 2. for the troubled conscience.—SCHMID:—Easter the most glorious feast: 1. Of the most glorious joy; 2. of the most glorious victory; 3. of the most glorious faith; 4. of the most glorious hope.—JASPIS:—How we may celebrate Easter in the right spirit.

B. *Over the Despondency of Unbelief.* CH. XXIV. 13–45.

1. The Appearing to the Disciples of Emmaus (Vss. 13–35).

13 And, behold, two of them went [were journeying] that same day to a village called
14 Emmaus, which was from Jerusalem *about* threescore furlongs [stadia]. And they
15 talked together of all these things which had happened. And it came to pass, that, while they communed [were conversing] *together* and reasoned [or, were discussing],
16 Jesus himself drew near, and went [journeyed] with them. But their eyes were holden
17 that they should not know him. And he said unto them, What manner of communications *are* these that ye have [are interchanging] one to [with] another, as ye walk,
18 and¹ are [*why* are ye] sad? And the [om., the] one of them, whose name was Cleopas, answering said unto him, Art thou only a stranger in Jerusalem, and [the only stranger in Jerusalem who] hast not known the things which are come to pass there in
19 these days? And he said unto them, What things? And they said unto him, Concerning Jesus of Nazareth, which was a prophet mighty in deed and word before God
20 and all the people: And how the chief priests and our rulers delivered him to be con-
21 demned to death, and have crucified him. But we [*for our part*²] trusted that it had been he which should [was to] have redeemed Israel: and beside all this [or, yet even³

22 with all this⁴], to day is the third day since these things were done. Yea, and [But also, ἀλλὰ καί⁵] certain women also of our company made us astonished, which were
23 early at the sepulchre; And when they found not his body, they came, saying, that
24 they had also seen a vision of angels, which said that he was alive. And certain of them which were with us went to the sepulchre, and found *it* even so as the women
25 had said: but him they saw not. Then he said unto them, O fools [ye without understanding, ἀνόητοι], and slow of heart to believe all that the prophets have spoken:
26 Ought not Christ to have suffered [Was it not needful that the Christ should suffer⁶]
27 these things, and [so] to [om., to] enter into his glory? And beginning at [from] Moses and [from] all the prophets, he expounded unto them in all the Scriptures the
28 things [*written*] concerning himself [him⁷]. And they drew nigh unto the village,
29 whither they went: and he made as though he would have gone further. But they constrained him, saying, Abide with us; for it is toward evening, and the day [now⁸]
30 is far spent. And he went in to tarry [stop] with them. And it came to pass, as he sat at meat [reclined at table] with them, he took [the] bread, and blessed *it*, and
31 brake, and gave to them. And their eyes were opened, and they knew him; and he
32 vanished out of their sight [ἄφαντος ἐγένετο ἀπ' αὐτῶν]. And they said one to another, Did not our heart burn [Was not our heart burning] within us, while he talked with
33 us by the way, and [om., and⁹] while he opened to us the Scriptures? And they rose up the same hour, and returned to Jerusalem, and found the eleven gathered together,
34 and them that were with them, Saying, The Lord is risen indeed, and hath appeared to
35 Simon. And they told what things *were done* [took place] in the way, and how he was known of [recognized by] them in [the] breaking of [the] bread.

[¹ Vs. 17.—Cod. Sin. has here a singular variation; instead of ἐστε σκυθρωποί, it has ἐσταθησαν σκυθρωποι. If this be genuine, it would depict the displeased silence in which the disciples stood for a moment on being interrupted, as they supposed, by an unsympathizing stranger, broken at last by the reply of Cleopas.—C. C. S.]
[² Vs. 21.—Expressed by the ἡμεῖς ἠλπίζομεν instead of the simple ἠλπίζομεν.—C. C. S.]
[³ Vs. 21.—That is, as Bleek explains it, "notwithstanding these hopes which His prophetic works and words justified, it is already the third day after His crucifixion."—C. C. S.]
⁴ Vs. 21.—Καί after ἀλλά γε is with good reason received into the text by Lachmann and Tischendorf, [Meyer, Tregelles, Alford,] according to B., D., [Cod. Sin.,] L.
[⁵ Vs. 22.—The ἀλλά in vs. 21 and this in vs. 22 appear to indicate how the mind of the speaker was repelled from one conjecture to another, finding none tenable—C. C. S.]
[⁶ Vs. 26.—"Παθεῖν καὶ εἰσελ. = παθόντα εἰσελ. It was not the *entering into His glory*, but the *suffering*, about which they wanted persuading." Alford.—C. C. S.]
[⁷ Vs. 27.—Αὐτοῦ, not αὐτοῦ.—C. C. S.]
⁸ Vs. 29.—Ἤδη. Reading of B., [Cod. Sin.,] L., Cursives, Vulgate, Coptic, Slavonic, &c. Bracketed by Lachmann. [Omitted by Tischendorf; accepted by Meyer, Tregelles, Alford.—C. C. S.]
⁹ Vs. 32.—The καί of the *Recepta* appears to have been interpolated to connect the clauses. B., D., [Cod. Sin.,] L., 33, Cant., Origen do not have it. *See* Lachmann, Tischendorf, [Meyer, Tregelles, Alford].

EXEGETICAL AND CRITICAL.

Vs. 13. **Two of them.**—Not of the Eleven, from whom, vs. 33, they are definitely distinguished; nor even necessarily of the Seventy, who must not be conceived as a definitely established college; but of the wider circle of disciples who were now together at Jerusalem. Cleopas, vs. 18, accidentally named, because he appears speaking, is not the same with Clopas, John xix. 25, but = Cleopatrus. In respect to the other, the conjectures are legion; some have understood Nathanael (Epiphanius), Simon (Origen), Luke (Theophyl. Lange), Peter, on the ground of vs. 34, and many others. The last conjecture rests upon a misunderstanding,—the next to the last has something for it, on account of the fulness of detail and the visible predilection with which this whole occurrence is delineated by Luke. Perfect certainty herein is, however, impossible, and also unnecessary.

Emmaus.—Mentioned also by JOSEPHUS, *De Bell. Jud.* 7, 6, 6. Comp. 4, 1, 3. Not to be confounded with the city Emmaus, in the plain of Judæa, which lay 170 stadia from Jerusalem, was called in the third century Nicopolis, and by a misunderstanding of some ancient expositors was taken for the birth-place of Cleopas. The fathers Eusebius and Jerome already confounded the last-named city with our place, whose situation has been long uncertain. It appears that we have to seek the here-mentioned Emmaus nowhere else than in the present Kulonieh, which lies two full leagues from Jerusalem. Comp. among others, SEPP, *l. c.* iii. p. 653; and ROBINSON, *Bib. Res.*— Sixty stadia = 1½ German miles, 7¼ Italian miles, [= 6¾ English miles]. It lay west from the capital, and the way, therefore, went past the graves of the Judges, by the old Mizpah, the dwelling place of Samuel, through a beautiful, charming district. But if it was ever manifest that nature alone cannot possibly satisfy the heart that has lost its Christ, it was on this day the case. Even into the sanctuary of creation do these wanderers take the recollection of the scenes of blood and murder, whose witnesses they had been in the last days. What they are conversing on together, we hear them themselves (vs. 18 *seq.*) make known more in detail. Apparently we may conceive that our Lord, in the form of a common traveller, came behind them and soon overtook them.

Vs. 16. **But their eyes.**—According to Mark xvi. 12, the Lord appeared to them ἐν ἑτέρᾳ μορφῇ, and this, too, would of itself have sufficiently explained why they did not know Him at once. In no other form did He stand so ineffaceably deep before their souls as precisely in the form of His Passion and death. They are, moreover, not thinking of His resurrection, and least of all of His being immediately near, and how could they in this quiet, vigorous, dignified traveller, be able to recognize the Crucified One, languid in death. It is, however, not to be doubted that, with this natural, a supernatural cause must have concurred, or rather that our Lord used this ἑτέρα μορφή ás a means to manifest Himself so to them that they should not at once recognize Him. The expression ἐκρατοῦντο τοῦ, points to a definite design of His love; He will remain yet some moments concealed before He at once makes their joy perfect. Comp. vs. 31. Had He wished at once to be recognized, He could at once have so revealed Himself that no doubt would have been possible.

Vs. 17. **And why are ye sad?**—If we expunge with Tischendorf, on the authority of D., Syr., Cant. (B., L. have variations), the words καί ἐστε, we then get instead of a double only a simple question: What manner of discourses are they which ye, walking along mournfully, interchange with one another? At all events it appears clearly that He who interrupts their conversation wishes to induce them to grant Him a participation in their sadness. What He already knows He wishes to hear from their own mouth, and begins, therefore, with a question of the kind with which shortly before He had already introduced His revelation of Himself to Mary; while He then for a while is significantly silent, until Cleopas, sometimes speaking alone, sometimes relieved by his companion, has told everything which lies so heavily upon the heart of both. Without doubt, He not only became silently displeased at their unbelief, but also rejoiced over their love, although Cleopas, in the beginning of his reply, makes sufficiently manifest his dissatisfaction at being suddenly disturbed by a troublesome third party.

Vs. 18. **Art thou the only stranger in Jerusalem.**—He takes the questioner for a παροικῶν, not exactly on account of the somewhat peculiar dialect (De Wette), but because he in a settled inhabitant of the capital would not have been able at all to conceive such an ignorance, and perhaps, also, because this traveller now, like themselves, after the Passover lamb had been eaten, seemed to be about to leave the capital. That, moreover, as a rule, every stranger must also have heard what now fills the whole capital and their own hearts, that they suppose is anything but doubtful.

Vs. 19. **Concerning Jesus of Nazareth.**—Now the stream of their lamentations over their disappointed expectations breaks loose. From οἱ δὲ εἶπον it appears that both spoke, without its being possible precisely to distinguish their words, as some (Paulus, Kuinoel,) have attempted to do. Their anguish of heart is especially remarkable, since it showed what the Lord was in their eyes and remained, even in the moment when they had seen their dearest hope vanish. The official name CHRIST, they do not now take upon their lips, but respecting the name Jesus of Nazareth, they presuppose that it is sufficiently familiar to every one, in and out of Jerusalem. That He, although He had been reckoned among the transgressors, was a prophet and extraordinary messenger of God, such as, with the exception of John, had not appeared in Israel for centuries before, this admitted of no doubt. As such He had attested Himself by word and deed, not only in the eyes of the people, but also before the face of God—(ἐναντίον), and even after His death, it is impossible for them to mention the name of this ἀνήρ otherwise than with reverence and love. They are not afraid to declare that in respect to Him an irreconcilable difference of opinion exists between them and the chiefs of the people. While these latter had delivered Him over to the punishment of death, they on the other side hoped that it had been He that should have redeemed Israel (ἠλπίζομεν, in the Imperf.) Of what nature their hope and the redemption expected through Him was, they do not more particularly make known. But enough, whether their expectation had had a more political or more religious direction, the grave was the rock on which it had suffered shipwreck. Perhaps after a short pause they continue almost rather to think aloud than to instruct the stranger, to whom their discourse, supposing that He was entirely a stranger, must have been almost unintelligible: "But it is true (ἀλλά γε, although we had cherished such hope, even hitherto had not wholly given up hope) it is also," &c. This comes *besides all this* to make their feeling of disappointment yet greater. The first and second day, therefore, they had still had a weak hope, but now that also the third day is already half elapsed without the enigma having been solved, they do not venture longer to surrender themselves to this hope.

Vs. 22. **But also.**—Thus they begin in the same moment when they are complaining over lost hope yet still to speak of that which to-day had somewhat fanned up again the already almost extinguished spark, in order finally to end with the acknowledgment of utter uncertainty and discouragement. Some women of the company of the friends of the Nazarene (ἐξ ἡμῶν) had astounded them, ἐξέστησαν (comp. Acts ii. 12), so that they had entirely lost possession of themselves, and no longer knew what they had to think about the whole matter. Early in the morning, they said, these had gone to the grave, and had in all haste come back with the account that they had seen an appearance of angels, which had said to them that He was alive. (Καὶ ὄπτ., besides that they had not found there what they sought, they had, moreover, seen what they did not seek, and had heard what they could not believe.) It is worthy of note, how the Emmaus disciples in an artless manner confirm the narrative of the visit to the grave, and the experience of the Galilean women. At the same time it appears from the immediately following: καὶ ἀπῆλθόν τινες τῶν σὺν ἡμῖν, that according to Luke also, not Peter alone (vs. 12), went to the grave, but also others, so that by this plural the visit to the grave among others by John (ch. xx. 2-10), is tacitly confirmed. According to Stier, we should not by τινὲς ἐξ ἡμῶν even understand apostles at all, but members of the more extended circle of disciples, to which these two also belong, who on the other hand had also instituted the requisite investigation, so that on this day there had been thorough confusion and distraction. Possible undoubtedly. But, however this may be, this investigation had led to no happy result. It is true, they had found it, sc. τὸ μνημεῖον, as the women had said, that is κενόν, and so far, they could make no objection to the credibility of their account. But further than this the deputed disciples had been as far from discovering anything about the angels as about the Lord, and if He had really risen, could it be then that no one had seen Him Himself?
—**But Him they saw not.**—The last word is a sufficient excuse for their believing themselves obliged to bid farewell to all hope.

Vs. 25. **Then He said unto them.**—In the demeanor of the supposed stranger there must have been something that irresistibly impelled them to speak continually more confidentially to him, as he on his side suffered them without disturbance to pour out their hearts. Nothing would have been easier than just as with Mary, to turn their sorrow into joy by the utterance of a single word; but the Lord designs to bestow on them something higher than a transient, overwhelming impression. Now His turn came to speak, and when they think He will now begin deeply to commiserate them, He begins, on the other hand, in all severity to rebuke them. He assumes the tone of an experienced Rabbi, and gives them to understand that the cause of their whole inward suffering lies entirely within themselves. He calls them ἀνόητοι, unreceptive on the intellectual side, καὶ βραδεῖς τῇ καρδίᾳ, τοῦ πιστεύειν ἐπὶ πᾶσιν, κ.τ.λ.; upon this last here the emphasis visibly falls. That they had believed something He does not dispute, but their faith had been one-sided, and had, therefore, been able to kindle no light in the dark night of their soul. Here also, want of understanding and sluggishness, discouragement of heart and will, stand simply alongside of one another, but so that we have to understand the second as the deepest ground of the first. It was so dark before their eyes for the reason that they had been so slow of heart to the belief of the whole truth. Not so much from the head to the heart, as rather from the heart to the head, does divine truth find its way, and no one can here understand what he has not inwardly felt and experienced.

Vs. 26. **Was it not needful?**—The Lord speaks of a necessity that was grounded in this truth— namely, that all these things had been foretold. That which had been a matter of offence to them had been for this very reason, according to a higher order of things, inevitable, and they could not possibly have been so driven hither● and thither if they had given such heed as they ought to the prophetic annunciations respecting the suffering Messiah.—**And (thus) enter into His glory.**—What had seemed to them incompatible with the glory of the Messiah was precisely the appointed way thereto. The Lord does not mean that He is already entered into His glory (Kinkel, a. o.), but speaks as one who has now come so near to His glory as that He sees the suffering already behind Him. (Supply δεῖ, Meyer); εἰσελθεῖν, designation of the glory as a heavenly state.

Vs. 27. **And beginning,** ἀρξάμενος.—Emphatic indication of the consecutive character of His discourse, so that He began with Moses, and afterwards went on to all the prophets, in order to demonstrate to them therefrom what in these related to His person or His work. It is true, "it is much to be wished that we knew what prophecies of Jesus' death and glory are here meant," (De Wette), but when the critic continues: "There are not many to be found which admit of application to this," then above all things the inquiry would be authorized, whether his Hermeneutics stand in full accord with those of the Lord Jesus, and if not, whether the former might not submit to a revision according to the principles of the latter. Whoever consults the manifold expressions of Jesus and the apostles in reference to the prophecies of the Messiah, needs not to grope around here in entire uncertainty, if only he does not forget that our Lord here probably directed the attention of His disciples less to isolated passages of Scripture than to the great whole of the Old Testament in its typical and symbolical character. Truly an hour spent in the school of this Master is better than a thousand elsewhere.

Vs. 28. **He made as though,** προσεποιεῖτο—ἅπαξ λεγόμενον in the New Testament (except in the clause John viii. 6). On a dissimulation which would make a more or less set defence of our Lord's sincerity requisite, we have here, of course, no right to think. He *could* not act otherwise if He would still retain the character hitherto assumed; He *will* not act otherwise, because He will not only enlighten their understanding, but also make trial of their heart; He *would* actually have gone farther had they not held Him back with all the might of love. Apparently He now shows Himself ready to say farewell to them with the usual formula of benediction, but already they feel themselves united to Him by such holy bonds that the thought of separation is entirely unendurable. Entreating with the utmost urgency, they invite Him in (παρεβιάσαντο, comp. Luke xiv. 23; Acts xvi. 15), and point Him to the sun hurrying to its setting, in the living feeling that their spiritual light also will set if He should leave their company. They wish to remind Him that He cannot possibly continue His journey in the night (comp. Gen. xix. 2, 3; Judges xix. 9), and desire that He should therefore turn in with them; since probably one of them possessed a dwelling at Emmaus, where a simple supper was awaiting them.

Vs. 30. **He took the bread.**—It will scarcely need any intimation that here it is only a common δεῖπνον, not the Holy Communion that is spoken of, and still less a *communio sub una specie*, which Romish expositors undertake to prove, *e. g.,* SEPP, iii. p. 656, with an appeal to this passage. On the other hand, we might find a proof here that the κλάσις τοῦ ἄρτου (vs. 35), in the New Testament, is not as a rule the same thing as the Lord's Supper. The guest simply assumes, on the ground of a tacitly acknowledged superiority, the place of the father of the house, and utters the usual thanksgiving, to which, according to the Jewish rite, three who eat together are expressly obliged. *See* BERAC. f. 45, 1. But whether He has anything peculiar in the manner of breaking the bread and uttering the blessing that reminds them of their association with the Master in earlier days, or whether they now discover in His opened hands the marks of the wounds, or whether He Himself refers them back to a word uttered before His death,—enough: their eyes are now opened. Διηνοίχθησαν, according to the antithesis with vs. 16, intimation of a sudden opening of their eyes, effected by the Lord Himself, and for which He has used as a means, vs. 35, the breaking of bread. In consequence of this they now recognize Him, who up to this moment had been wholly unknown, so that they are not only fully persuaded of the identity of this person with Jesus of Nazareth, but at the same time also inwardly know Him in His full dignity and greatness.—**And He vanished out of their sight,** ἄφαντος ἐγένετο, *ex ipsorum oculis evanuit.*—Not in and of itself, perhaps (*see* MEYER, *ad loc.*), but in connection with all that which we learn further respecting the bodily nature of the Risen Redeemer, the expression appears undoubtedly to give us to understand a sudden vanishing of the Lord, a becoming invisible in an extraordinary way, not αὐτοῖς, but ἀπ' αὐτῶν (Beza), in which, of course, we need not exclude the thought that the Lord used therefor the confusion and joy of the first moment after the discovery. *See* below, in the Doctrinal and Ethical remarks.

Vs. 32. **Was not our heart burning within us,** καιομένη.—Expression of extraordinary emotion of soul. Ps. xxxix. 3; Jer. xx. 9. If one could have asked the disciples of Emmaus whether they had meant an *affectus gaudii*, *spei*, *desiderii* or *amoris*, upon which the expositors dispute, they would have failed, perhaps, to give a satisfactory answer. Enough—they will express an indefinable overpowering feeling on the way during the Lord's instruction (*loquebatur nobis, id plus est quam nobiscum*, Bengel), and even by that ought to have recognized the Lord, so that to them it is now even incomprehensible that their eyes were not earlier opened. It is a good sign for their inner growth that at this moment it is not the breaking of bread, but the opening of the Scripture which now stands before the eye of their memory.

Vs. 33. **The same hour.**—The day has indeed yet further declined than in vs. 29, but if it were even already midnight, they must now hastily return to Jerusalem, in order to announce the joyful message. What the women do at the express command of the angel, and Magdalene, at the command of the Lord, this the two disciples carry out at the impulse of their heart. The meal, also, they leave apparently untouched (comp. John iv. 31-34), and know no higher need than together to make the event known. As commonly, so here also the labor of love is rewarded with new blessings; since they come to give, they receive for their faith an unexpected and longed-for strengthening. Here we have indeed one of the few cases in which it might in good earnest have been questioned, whether it was more blessed to give or to receive.

The Eleven gathered together.—As appears from John xx. 19, with closed doors, which, however, were soon opened to the brethren who even as late as this, desired admission. Then are they for a greeting received with a jubilant choral: "The Lord is risen indeed, and hath appeared unto Simon!" "One of the most glorious moments in the Easter history, an antiphony which God has made." Lange. They answer then, on their side, with the narrative of that which happened to them in the way (vs. 35), and how the Lord had been recognized by them in the (ἐν), not exactly *at* the breaking of bread (which would not suit so well to the miraculous representation, vs. 31). Thus do they spend an hour of blessed celebration, which, without their knowing it, becomes again the preparation for an evening appearance.

Vs. 34. **Hath appeared unto Simon.**—There is no ground for understanding this ὤφθη of a merely transient, momentary seeing, as Stier, *ad loc.* will have it. Without doubt we must here understand an appearance, which not less than that, *e. g.*, bestowed on the women deserves this name. He was, therefore, the first of all the [male] disciples on whom the privilege was bestowed, according to Chrysostom: ἐν ἀνδράσι τούτῳ πρώτῳ, τῷ μάλιστα αὐτὸν ποθοῦντι ἰδεῖν, ὅτι μάλιστα χρῄζοντι. Unquestionably this appearance was that which had preceded that to the Emmaus disciples, after Peter had already heard the friendly καὶ τῷ Πέτρῳ (Mark xvi. 7). Chased hither and thither by fear and hope, he had probably wandered around the city in solitude. Perhaps he had just come back from the visit to the grave, which Luke has described, vs. 12, (John xx. 2–10), and is asking himself whether, even if the Master is again in life, there is also hope that he shall see Him; when this supreme privilege becomes his portion. What there took place between him and the Master has remained a holy secret between both, which even his fellow-apostles have not sought to inquire into, but have rather respected. However, even by this, the later appearance by the sea of Tiberias and the reinstatement in his apostolic function did not become superfluous for Peter, and we must, therefore, so far regard the comfort and the refreshment which was given him in this hour as a preliminary, although already a rich and blessed one.

DOCTRINAL AND ETHICAL.

1. The appearances of the Risen Lord were for His first disciples of altogether inestimable value. Their understanding was thereby healed, partly of doubt, partly of injurious prejudices; their heart was thereby comforted when it was burdened by sadness, the sense of guilt and anxiety for the future; their life was thereby sanctified to a life of spiritual communion with Him, of united love among themselves, of vigorous activity, and immovable hope. The period of forty days after the Resurrection of the Lord was at the same time the second period in the history of the training and developing of His apostles, one which was noticeably diverse from the first.

2. The appearances of the Risen One present on the one hand a remarkable coincidence, on the other hand a remarkable diversity. All agree in this, that they fall within the sphere of the senses, beginning or ending in a more or less mysterious manner, and for the purpose of showing that the Lord was really alive, and that He was for His friends ever the same as before His death. They may, therefore, all be named in the fullest sense of the word revelations of His glory, sometimes of His love, sometimes of His wisdom, then again of His knowledge and of His faithfulness; yet, at the same time, each appearance has something which characterizes it above others, even as the colors of the rainbow are different from one another and yet melt into one another. Before Magdalene the Risen One uses no food; she recognized Him at a single word. The instruction respecting the Scriptures which was bestowed upon the Emmaus disciples, Thomas does not also receive. His unbelief sprang from another source, and was revealed in another way than theirs. Only one appearance (John xxi. 1–14) is accompanied by a miracle. In the others the First Fruits from the dead stands Himself as the Miracle of miracles before us. At one time He instructs the erring ones before, at another time after, the hour of meeting again; here His appearance flashes by like a lightning stroke, there it is like the soft, lovely shining of the morning sun. Before Mary we see Him appear especially in His High-priestly, before the Emmaus disciples in His prophetic character, while He reveals Himself in the evening appearances as the King of the kingdom of God, who legitimates and despatches His ambassadors. The form also in which He comes to His disciples is different (Mark xvi. 12), even so the way in which He persuades them that He is alive. All are prepared for His appearance in different ways, but each one again finds in the meeting an individual necessity satisfied. With the Emmaus disciples He proceeds a way sixty stadia long. Past the women He slowly hovers as an appearance from the higher world. The appearance before Mary and the women bears on the side of the Lord the tenderest, that before the disciples, without and with Thomas, the most composed, that before James, before Peter, at the sea of Tiberias, the most mysterious; that on the mountain in Galilee, that before the five

hundred brethren (1 Cor. xv. 6) the most sublime, that before the Emmaus disciples the most human, character. No wonder that John comprehends the appearances of the Lord under the general conception of His σημεῖα (John xx. 30), and that the history of all these different revelations has been at every age considered as one of the mightiest supports of our faith in the historical reality of the Resurrection.

3. The appearance before the Emmaus disciples bears in the whole narrative an inner stamp of truth which can be better felt than described. It is unreasonable to wish to correct, word by word, the brief notice (Mark xvi. 12, 13), by the detailed account of Luke; but this is evident enough, that both relate the same thing, and as respects the discrepancy between Luke xxiv. 34, and Mark xvi. 13, one must be utterly out of his place in the psychological sphere if he could not see how in a circle like this in a few moments faith and unbelief might dispute the mastery with one another. If we assume either (Bengel) that they at the beginning (Luke) believed and afterwards (Mark) doubted, or the reverse (Calvin), there will in neither case be anything hard to understand in the representation that the Eleven and those with them at the beginning received the journeyers to Emmaus with believing joy, but yet so long as they had themselves not seen the Master, were agitated by so many difficulties and doubts that the Lord, in a certain sense, might reproach them with their ἀπιστία, Mark xvi. 14. Whoever barely strains words, without trying the spirits, will never understand the deep harmonies of the Easter history. If we take pains to do the latter, we find in the fulness of detail with which Cleopas speaks of his hopes and fears, and the only half-intelligible mention of the third day, in the outspoken condemnation of their chief priests and leaders before an utter stranger, in the word about the burning heart, such a truth, freshness, and naturalness that we can scarcely refrain from writing the apostle's words, 2 Peter i. 16, upon this leaf of the Resurrection history also. The same may be said of the appearance to Peter; there is, alas, wanting to us a more particular account in reference to this entirely unique scene, worthy of the pencil of a Raphael, but some compensation for this lack is offered us by the recollection that the frugality of the Evangelists on this very point, the embellishment of which must have been for the inventor an irresistible temptation, affords a new proof for its faithfulness and credibility. The same inner character is displayed by every appearance in greater or less measure, if closely considered; and so far from the force of this proof admitting of weakening by the oft-repeated objection: Why did not the Lord show Himself to His enemies? (see as far back as ORIGEN, *Contra Celsum*, ii. ch. lxiii., and elsewhere) this very thing is a new proof of His holiness, wisdom, and love. His holiness could not do otherwise than account those who had resisted the Light of the world, even to death, unworthy of this honor. His wisdom forbade Him by an outward appearance to constrain them to a faith which at best would have filled them with new earthly expectations, while He besides this foresaw plainly enough that no appearance before Caiaphas, before the chief priests, or before the leaders, would accomplish the desired purpose. Comp. Luke xvi. 31; John xii. 10; Matt. xxviii. 11–15. Nay, His love reveals itself in this also, that He veils the full glory of the Resurrection from hostile eyes. That the Son of God had not been accepted in His servant's form might yet be forgiven, but if He had been viewed in the glory of His new life, and even yet stubbornly rejected, this would have admitted no other retribution than an irrevocable judgment. Our Lord would thus, if He had appeared without success before His enemies, have made the preaching of the Gospel among them entirely impossible, for how could He have yet sent His ambassadors without prejudice to His dignity, with the hope of any fruit, to those who, after mature consideration, had again despised Him and thrust Him from them? Would not rather an appearance to them have been in direct conflict with the peculiar nature and the special purpose of His new life? Would the testimony of the Sanhedrim have really been then more likely to have been acceptable to any one than that of His disciples, whose persevering unbelief in the fact of His Resurrection was only overcome after much difficulty, and therefore, at all events, forbids us to consider them in this point as superstitious? If we take all this together, there is indeed not a single ground why in the Church of the Lord the jubilant tone of " The Lord is risen indeed," should resound in the least more weakly than on the first Easter evening.

4. The appearance before the Emmaus disciples is one of the strongest proofs of the high value which the Lord places upon the prophetic Scriptures, and upon the predictions of His suffering and of His glory. Whoever denies either the existence or the importance of these *Vaticinia*, finds himself not only in decided conflict with the believing church of all centuries, but also with the Lord Himself.

5. The whole conversation of our Lord with these disciples has a strong symbolical character, which Christian Ascetæ and Homiletes have ever brought to light with visible predilection. (*See below*.)

6. "When Jesus in temptation holds our eyes, so that the soul neither can nor may recognize, that is good, for soon will joy, light, and comfort follow; but when the sinner holds his own eyes, and will not recognize Jesus, that is evil, for he incurs danger of eternal blindness and darkness." (Starke.)

HOMILETICAL AND PRACTICAL.

Behold how good and pleasant it is for brethren to dwell together in unity. Ps. cxxxiii. 1.—The way from Jerusalem to Emmaus a devious way, whereupon the Great Shepherd of the sheep who is risen from the dead (Heb. xiii. 20), seeks the wanderers.—About what do disciples love best to speak when they are intimately together?—The living Christ the Third in every Christian friendship.—Jesus is already near to us, even when we believe Him yet distant.—The invisible Witness of our hidden communings with our friends.—"Why are ye so sad?" this is the question with which the Risen One, on the feast of His Resurrection, comes to all the weary and heavyladen.—The publicity of our Lord's history a palpable proof of its truth.—Our Lord demands the full confidence of His disciples, not for His sake, but for their sake.—Jesus' prophetic mission carried out by His words not less than by His deeds.—The complaint of disappointed hope: 1. How sorrowful it sounds when the Lord abides in death; 2. how quickly it is silenced when it becomes plain that He is risen indeed.—Love to the Lord stronger than shaken faith and frustrated hope.—Him they saw not: 1. The deepest sorrow of the Easter morning;

2. the source of the highest Easter joy.—How good it is, with our unbelieving difficulties and complaints not to go away from Jesus, but directly to Him.—The rebukings of the risen Lord not less sweet than His most pleasant visitations.—Want of understanding in the spiritual sphere born of sluggishness of heart.—One-sidedness in faith.—The Scripture cannot be broken, John x. 34.—The connection between suffering and glory for Christ and the Christian: 1. Suffering prepares the way for glory; 2. suffering is transformed into glory; 2. suffering endured heightens the enjoyment and the worth of glory.—Word and spirit: 1. One must already know the Scripture if the Lord is to explain it to us; 2. the Lord must explain it to us, if one is to understand the Scripture well.—The heaviest trials of faith often immediately precede the most glorious visitation of grace.—" When only No appears, only Yea is meant." [*Wenn lauter Nein erscheinet, ist lauter Ja gemeinet.*] —WOLTERSDORF:—" Abide with us," &c., admirable text for New Year's Eve, at the last communion of the year, and when not? What this prayer: 1. Presupposes; 2. desires; 3. obtains.—The prayer in the evening hours: 1. Of the day; 2. of the kingdom of God; 3. of life.—The Lord allows Himself not to be called on in vain.—Even yet must our eyes be open if we are to become rightly acquainted with the Prince of life.—Even yet the Lord reveals Himself to His people in surprising, unmistakable manner, but even yet for only brief fleeting moments.—How our Lord yet reveals Himself to His disciples in the breaking of bread (Communion at Easter). In this we may show how the risen Lord at the Communion: 1. Still seeks like disciples; 2. still satisfies like necessities; 3. still requires like dispositions; 4. still prepares a like surprise, as at and after His appearance to the disciples at Emmaus. The burning heart of the genuine disciple of the Lord.—The communion of saints: 1. Most ardently sought; 2. blessedly enjoyed; 3. richly rewarded.—The appearance to Peter: 1. A proof of the love of Jesus, *a*. Jesus appears to the fallen Peter, *b*. to Peter first, *c*. to Peter alone; 2. an inestimable benefit for Peter; it bestowed on him, *a*. light instead of darkness, *b*. grace instead of the feeling of guilt, *c*. hope instead of fear; 3. a welcome message of joy for the disciples of Emmaus; it served, *a*. to strengthen their faith, *b*. to determine the demeanor of all in reference to Peter, *c*. to prepare them for new revelations at hand; 4. a school for us, *a*. of faith, *b*. of love, *c*. of hope.—Christ our life: 1. What life would be without Christ, vss. 13-24; 2. what it may become through Christ, vss. 25-31; 3. what it must be for Christ, vss. 32-35.—The living Christ the best guide; come and see how He: 1. Kindly seeks out His own; 2. lovingly listens to them; 3. graciously instructs and rebukes them; 4. wisely proves them; 4. ineffably surprises and rejoices them.—The manner in which our Lord reveals Himself to the disciples at Emmaus a prophecy of the surprise which He reserves in heaven for His people.—The returning Emmaus disciples teach us: 1. To look back thankfully; 2. to look around lovingly; 3. to look upward and forward hopefully.

STARKE:—*Nova Bibl. Tub.*:—When one speaks of Jesus and remembers His death, yea, His Resurrection, then does he live.—CANSTEIN:—Out of the abundance of the heart the mouth speaketh.—In sadness and temptation Christ appears not to be present, but He is there, only we know Him not.—With melancholy people we must always go to the bottom if we will heal and make them sound.—Oh! that Christ among so many Christians were not a stranger! John i. 26.—An intimate conversation of teachers and hearers remains not without blessing.—If great people will not have evil said of them, neither must they do evil.—BRENTIUS:—Faith and unbelief have, especially in the hour of temptation, a hard battle.—The soul will have Jesus Himself.—Comfort belongs not to the erring until they have come to thorough knowledge of their faults.—*Nova Bibl. Tub.*:—Nothing is harder than faith.—The grounds of our faith are the prophetic Scriptures, 2 Peter i. 19.—HEDINGER:—The sun is bright, indeed, but not to a blind man.—Christ is the best Expositor of the Holy Scriptures.—Let the course of this life be burdensome as it will, we come yet at last to the goal.—LANGII *Opera*:—O how rare are examples of those who receive a rebuke so that they for that love a teacher better.—Prayer is a firm cord which holds the Almighty, who also is glad to be held.—Opened eyes of the understanding distinguish spiritual men from natural.—Where Jesus hides Himself, there it is time to rise and neither to hope for rest nor joy till we have found Him again.—Even unbelievers may yet become believers,—despise not that which is weak.—Every Christian for whom God has done great things is bound to relate the same.—LUTHER:—Only see how God with special providence guides His people.

HEUBNER:—Love to the Risen One is a true bond of friendship.—Jesus is often not among us because we speak not of Him.—Oft is God long hidden to us and His ways a riddle.—Jesus knows very well what oppresses thee.—Jesus wins from His disciples the confession of their faith.—Who only lives in earthly hopes, cheats himself.—The hearts of men hope where there is nothing at all to be hoped for, and despond where hope shows itself near by.—The glory of the Risen One is the prize of His suffering.—The saints are never more zealous, never keep faster hold of God, than when they fear to lose Him.—Christ the best comfort in the evening of life, better than Cicero *de Senectute*.—The more unbelief spreads itself abroad, the more should we pray that the Lord may abide with us.—Every enjoyment is sanctified through Christ.—At last there comes after trials and gloom the blessed hour of revelation.—There comes a time when Jesus never vanishes again.—Jesus' words inflame the heart; the words of Christless men are cold and powerless.—The journey of the disciples to Emmaus an image of our journey of life.—The new life of the disciples of Jesus after His Resurrection as a presage of the future blessed life.—The progress from weak to strong faith.

On *the Pericope*.—ARNDT:—The twofold Easter celebration: 1. Of those whose eyes are holden; 2. of those whose eyes are opened.—RUDELBACH:—The soul-winning art of Jesus.—CHR. PALMER:—By what do we know the nature of the living Saviour, although we do not see Him?—BRASTBERGER:—The blessed condition of a soul that knows and believes: The Lord Jesus is risen indeed.—FRESENIUS:—True Christians as spiritual pilgrims who are sometimes weak, sometimes become strong.—AHLFELD:—The pilgrims of Easter evening.—PALMER:—The leadings of Providence which the Risen Saviour causes His disciples to experience.—SOUCHON:—Jesus scares away sadness.—STIER:—When must and oughtest thou to believe that the Risen Saviour is peculiarly near to thee?—Dr. W. HOFFMANN (vs. 26):—The

Divine Must.—RIEGER:—The Risen Saviour a companion in journeying who certainly is glad to company with us, and in what way He companies with us.—DIETZ:—The gradual rising of the Easter light in the soul of man: 1. How mournful life is without Easter light; 2. What bars the way to our hearts against the Easter light; 3. how in the soul of man the Easter begins to dawn; 4. how the full Easter light rises in his soul.—BODE:—The intercourse of the Risen One with the disciples of Emmaus as an intimation where we are to seek and find the Lord. —BURK:—The wished-for abiding of the Lord with His people.—The holy employment of the living Jesus.—VON HARLESS:—The way to faith on the Risen One.—RAUTENBERG:—Easter in our way through the world; it here becomes Easter when the Risen One: 1. Shows Himself to us; 2. instructs us; 3. gives us strength to return home.— Shall we also constrain the Risen One to abide with us?

---

2. The Appearing at Evening (Vss. 36–45).

(Parallel with Mark xvi. 14–18; John xx. 19–23.)

36 And as they thus spake, Jesus [he¹] himself stood in the midst of them, and saith
37 unto them, Peace be unto you.² But they were terrified and affrighted, and supposed
38 that they had seen a spirit. And he said unto them, Why are ye troubled? and why
39 do thoughts arise in your hearts [heart³]? Behold my hands and my feet, that it is I
   myself: handle me, and see; for a spirit hath not flesh and bones, as ye see me have.
40, 41 And when he had thus spoken, he shewed them *his* hands and *his* feet.⁴ And
   while they yet believed not for joy, and wondered, he said unto them, Have ye here
42 any meat [anything to eat, βρώσιμον]? And they gave him a piece of a broiled fish,
43, 44 and of a honeycomb. And he took *it*, and did eat before them. And he said unto
   them, These are the [my⁵] words which I spake unto you, while I was yet with you,
   that all things must be fulfilled, which were written in the law of Moses, and *in* the
45 prophets, and *in* the psalms, concerning me. Then opened he their understanding,
   that they might understand the Scriptures.

¹ Vs. 36.—The 'Ιησοῦς of the *Recepta*, accepted even by Scholz, is omitted by some authorities, by others placed after ἔστη. An explicative addition, occasioned by the beginning of a lesson.
² Vs. 36.—There is no ground for regarding this Easter greeting of the Lord, with Tischendorf, as not genuine. What Lachmann, however, has bracketed, ἐγώ εἰμι, μὴ φοβεῖσθε, a reading of G., P., &c., appears to have been taken from John vi. 20.
³ Vs. 38.—'Εν τῇ καρδίᾳ. Internally more probable reading of Lachmann and Tischendorf, [Meyer, Tregelles, Alford,] after R., D., Italh. [Cod. Sin. agrees with the *Recepta*.—C. C. S.]
⁴ Vs. 40.—Tischendorf omits this verse, on the authority of D. and some Versions. Tregelles brackets it. Meyer suspects it of being, as well as κ. Λ. α. Εἰρ. ὑμ. in vs. 36, an interpolation from John xx. 19, 20. Alford retains it, remarking with force, that if it were interpolated from John we should certainly have in some MSS. πλευρὰν instead of πόδας, either here only or in vs. 39 also.—C. C. S.]
⁵ Vs. 44.—Οἱ λόγοι μου. Tischendorf, according to A., D., K., L., U., [X.,] 33, Coptic, Cant., &c.

EXEGETICAL AND CRITICAL.

Vs. 36. **He Himself stood.**—As appears from John xx. 19, though the doors were closed. Suddenly He stands there, without any one knowing how He has come in, *ἐν μέσῳ*, *id significantius quam in medium*, Bengel. They hear the voice which they would have known again from thousands, and which repeats the wonted salutation of peace, which, however, from these lips and in this moment had an infinitely higher significance, which involuntarily reminds the disciples of the farewell benediction, John xiv. 27. With this word begins the evening appearance, which we unhesitatingly venture to name the crown of all His appearances on the Resurrection day. Till now He has satisfied individual needs, but now He comes into the united circle, into the first church of His own. No appearance had been so long and so carefully prepared for as precisely this; all that had been seen or heard besides on this day, were so many single beams which were to be concentrated into this focus. In no appearance, moreover, did our Lord reveal Himself with so many infallible signs (Acts i. 5), and so victoriously overcome the unbelief of His first witnesses, as here. For their whole inner life, yea, for the founding of the kingdom of God upon the empty sepulchre as its foundation and corner-stone, was this evening of the highest significance and greatest worth. Nor can we wonder, then, that not less than three Evangelists give testimony to what here took place, each in His peculiar way. Mark, who visibly hurries rapidly to the end, does this only briefly in vs. 14, and proceeds, vs. 15 *seq*., to the general concluding account. John places before our eyes what here took place, on its most inward spiritual side, and relates, moreover, that Thomas to-day was not in the company. Luke, on the other hand, maintains his character as Historiographer, by communicating the external course of what here took place, and with special detail, as physician, gives the visible and sensible proofs of the new life and corporeality of the Lord. Without making any further distinction between hours and days, he lets this evening appearance, with which for the true and inner life of the apostles everything was decided, coalesce with the last commands of the departure of the Lord as He blessed them. Modern criticism which would prove that our Lord, according to Luke, went to heaven on the very day of His Resurrection, and that, according to Mark, from a closed chamber, had here, therefore, in view of the fragmentary character of these last lines of the Evangelical history, an exceedingly easy work, but has unequivocally shown its lack of good will to connect these fragments into a well-ordered whole. We believe ourselves fully in the right when we consider Luke's account respecting the evening appearance as ended in vs. 43, and see in vs. 44 the beginning of the last promised precepts which the Lord, according to all the Synoptics, imparted to His disciples shortly before His departure from the earth.

Vs. 37. **Terrified and affrighted.**—From John xx. 20, also, it appears that the disciples only became joyful after the Lord had shown them His hands and side, and that they, therefore, even a moment before, were terrified and affrighted. Even the manner of His entrance must have contributed to this, and however much they had begun to be prepared by all the events of the day for this meeting, yet this surprise must have come upon them the more strongly as the message of the angels had directed them to Galilee, and they, therefore, could by no means reckon on an appearance of the Master in the midst of them this very evening at Jerusalem. In their heart now prevails, as at evening in nature, a mixture of light and darkness. There is no longer the hopelessness of spirit, the bewilderment and uneasiness of early morning. The need of speaking together about the many enigmatical, nay, self-contradictory experiences of this day, has united them. In the hearts of some a spark of faith has arisen at Simon's account; it is these who with joy greet the Emmaus disciples (vs. 34). With others, however, even after the account given by these latter, the understanding yet reluctates to yield adherence to that which the heart above everything desires. To these doubts is now added fear of the Jews, anxious care for the future; grounds enough for the Lord in His appearance to rebuke them in His peculiar way (Mark xvi.).

Vs. 38. **Why are ye troubled.**—With this question begins the rebuke of unbelief. They believe that they see a departed spirit which has returned from Hades, φάντασμα, an *umbra* veiled in the semblance of a body, and, therefore, in a certain sense, a dead man; He will show them that it is He Himself who stands living before them, and this not in a seeming but in a real body, although one in the commencement of its glorification. We must represent to ourselves the immeasurable contrast between the mood of our Lord, who has peace and gives peace, and over against that the feelings of those who, as it were, will with trembling hands, scare back the supposed spectre into the spiritual world, and through their unbelief disturb our Lord's enjoyment of the noblest evening of His life—this must we do in order to comprehend the whole value of the condescending goodness with which He in this address stoops to those of little faith. He asks them why thoughts, that is, scruples of a discouraging nature, doubting and gainsaying thoughts, arise in their hearts, since they without such wretched misgivings ought at once to have recognized Him as their living Master, and now He even encourages them to do what He had not even permitted to Mary. In order to convince them not only of the reality but also of the identity of His appearance, He will have them feel His hands and feet, nay, Himself, His body, and, moreover, especially the exposed places which bear the traces of the wounds of the cross. "But not merely as the signs of His crucifixion for the identification of His body did the Saviour show His wounds, but manifestly as *signs of victory*, proofs of His triumph over death. Moreover, therefore—and this is properly the deepest sense of His entering salutation—as the *signs of peace*, the peace of the sacrificial death, of the completed atonement." Stier.

Vs. 40. **He showed them.**—To the word He added, therefore, the deed of His love. Apparently they now actually touched with reverence the places indicated. Therefore John could afterwards justly speak of that which their hands had handled (1 John i. 3), and it becomes doubly explicable why Thomas so decidedly demanded just this sign. He will in no respect be inferior to the others.

Vs. 41. **While they yet believed not for joy.**—A profoundly psychological expression, which betrays the hand of the Evangelist-physician, and makes palpable to us the overwhelmingness of the joy which John (vs. 20), not without indirect retrospect to the promise of the Lord (ch. xvi. 22), so strikingly describes. First, the fact in their eyes was too terrible for them to be willing to believe. Now, it is too glorious for them to be able to believe. The anxiety as to yet possible illusion is the last dam which yet checks the stream of joy. In a similar temper of mind Jacob, perhaps, was, Gen. xlv. 26.—But now that matters have come so far, our Lord rests not until He has completely accomplished His work on His disciples.

Vs. 42. **Broiled fish . . . honey-comb,** ἀπὸ μελισσ.—Honey of bees, such as in Palestine is frequently found in clefts of the rock and in hollow trees, so that it may literally be said of the land: "a land flowing with milk and honey;" to be distinguished from the honey of grapes and dates, which even at the present time is everywhere there prepared and exported in various forms, and which appears to be spoken of in Gen. xliii. 11. The here-named viands constituted, perhaps, the remains of the already ended supper of the disciples, who, perhaps, during the last days had, in the upper chamber of the unknown house in which our Lord celebrated His last Passover and elsewhere in the capital, a definite place of meeting. The objection that in the Old Testament angels also had eaten without possessing a true human body, could now no longer arise in the hearts of the disciples, since they had previously touched Him. Without further delay our Lord takes the food and eats it before their eyes, and they—drank with full draughts from the cup of the most blessed delight.

In this word and in this sign consisted, according to our opinion, the rebuke of the unbelief which Mark, in his summary statement (vs. 14), designates as the characteristic feature of this particular appearance. We account this, at least, as much more probable, than that our Lord, even after and besides that related by Luke, should have embittered the joy of this evening to His disciples by the holding of a severe preaching of repentance after they had recognized and believed Him. Then we should also have to assume that they had brought up something in their own excuse, as indeed, according to JEROME, *Advers. Pelagium* ii. *in quibusdam exemplaribus et maxime in Graecis codicibus*, they did, where we read respecting the apostles: "*Et illi satisfaciebant, dicentes: saeculum istud iniquitatis et incredulitatis substantia est, quae non sinit per immundos spiritus veram Dei apprehendi virtutem, idcirco, jam nunc revela justi-*

tiam tuam." The internal improbability of this addition, however, strikes the eye at once, but it deserves note how precisely that part of the evening appearance, which John exclusively relates, reveals again entirely the spirit of this apostle, visibly alludes back to a part of the farewell discourse, and is related also with the contents of the Synoptical gospels, comp. John xx. 21 with Matt. x. 40; vs. 22 with Matt. x. 21, 22; and vs. 33 with Matt. xxviii. 18. The second greeting of peace which he mentions, vs. 21, we are to place after all related by Luke, and to regard as the beginning of the farewell which our Lord actually takes, with His command and His promise, vss. 21–23. Peace is, therefore, here in the fullest sense of the word the first, and peace the last tone of the harmonious Resurrection-bell.

Vs. 44. **And He said unto them.**—So far to be parallelized with Mark xvi. 15–18 as this, that Luke, on his part also, adds immediately to the evening appearance some commands and promises of our Lord, which He uttered shortly before His departure, although it is undoubtedly possible that vss. 44, 45, still belong to the history of the evening. Yet it is, in view of the intimate connection of the different elements of discourse, vss. 44–49, more probable that Luke here also already relates by anticipation what took place immediately before the farewell, comp. Acts i. 4–8. Not that the whole didactic activity of the Risen One is, therefore, here described in general (Ebrard), but out of the rich treasure of the bequest of his Lord's word, the third Evangelist also, on his part, communicates various things, without its being possible, in vss. 44–49, to show the place where a mention of the forty days, Acts i. 3, had to be inserted. Whether Luke, however, in the Acts, followed another tradition than the gospel in respect to the conclusion of the history of Jesus' life, we believe that we must doubt. At least we find in the two narratives of the Ascension not a single feature contradictory to other features. For the Evangelist certainly gives by no means assurance at the end of his first book that our Saviour went on the very day of His Resurrection to Heaven. He here leaves the time entirely *unmentioned*, while he in the second work gives more particular explanations thereupon.

These are My words.—A somewhat abrupt beginning, which, however, does not by any means allude back to what immediately precedes. Our Lord, on the other hand, holds here, before He parts from His disciples, a grand retrospective review of His now almost accomplished earthly career. Even in the last meeting He holds up before their eyes the mirror of the Scriptures, to which He had so often directed them, and speaks of the days when He *was* yet with them, as of a period forever closed, which should now no more be continued through bodily manifestations.

In the law of Moses, and in the prophets, and in the Psalms.—As our Lord previously also had not satisfied Himself with bringing up several times, out of different parts of the Scripture, particular prophecies, and even before His death had given testimony to the Old Testament as a whole, Matt. xxiii. 35, so does He here also bring up the three chief portions of the canon, in order to indicate therewith that He points to the Scripture in its unity. The Psalms are here named as the beginning of the Hagiographa, and, at the same time, as the portion which in this contains the directest Messianic elements, even as the prophets do, and these two are therefore joined together as one by the omission of an article between.

Vs. 45. **Then opened He.**—As elsewhere in the Scriptures, so also in Luke, it is emphatically placed first, that not only the Scripture must be opened for the understanding, but also the understanding and the heart for the Scripture, in order to understand the truth aright. *See* vs. 32; Acts xvi. 14; and comp. Ephes. i. 18. Whether the Evangelist means the mediate or immediate opening of the understanding cannot, in view of the brevity of the expression, possibly be decided; but, unquestionably, it was such an one as was brought into effect directly by the Risen One Himself. How necessary this was even to the apostles of the Lord had been sufficiently shown by their scandal at His death, and their unbelief as to His Resurrection. What fruits it bore is to be seen on the first Whit-sunday, and afterwards in their epistles. Had it been indubitably certain that Luke was relating something that belongs to the first evening, we should then, perhaps, be able to suppose that he has in mind the same symbolical act of our Lord which is described John xx. 22. In view of the brevity and the fragmentariness of the sacred narrative, it is, however, difficult to state here anything trustworthy.

DOCTRINAL AND ETHICAL.

1. *See* on the parallels in Mark and in John.

2. The evening appearance gives us weighty information as to the corporeality of the Risen Redeemer. As is known, there has sometimes been ascribed to the Risen One a common human body, and everything which the sacred narratives contain that is mysterious surrounding His coming and going has been placed to the subjectivity of the Evangelists, and sometimes it has been asserted that He only showed Himself in a seeming body to His people (Kuhn, Marheinecke, Zelbig, and others). In opposition to both, this appearance especially gives us ground to assume that He bore a true but not common, a glorified, but not a merely seeming human investment; in a word, the same body, but with entirely different properties. In order to become acquainted with the nature of this His body, we are not, as so often is done, to apply our own conceptions of such a *vehiculum* as the standard of judging the evangelical narratives, but directly the reverse, to form our conception of a matter to us emphically entirely unknown, from and according to the evangelical narratives. The whole polemics of unbelief (*e.g.*, STRAUSS, ii. p. 674) proceeds from the unprovable proposition that what holds good of a man not yet dead must also hold good of one risen. Precisely because here every analogy is wanting, it is also entirely inadmissible to borrow from our daily experience an argument against an account of an entirely unique condition. With greater right may we from the seeming contradictions of their statements, which we may well believe did not remain concealed from the Evangelists, thus derive an indirect argument for its strict objectivity. If we inquire, therefore, what conception we, according to their historically credible account, have to form of a glorified body, and especially of that of the Lord, we obtain about the following answer: It is palpable, not only as a whole, but also in its different parts; raised above space, so that it can in much shorter time than we transport itself from one

locality to another; gifted with the capability, in subjection to a mightier will, of being sometimes visible, sometimes invisible. It bears the unmistakable traces of its former condition, but is at the same time raised above the confining limitations of this. It is, in a word, a spiritual body, no longer subject to the flesh, but filled, guided, borne by the spirit, and yet none the less a body. It can eat, but it no longer needs to eat (" *Aliter absorbet terra aquam sitiens, aliter solis radiis cundens,*" AUGUSTINE, Ep. 49. " *Cibo minime utebatur ad necessitatem, sed ut veritatem humanæ suæ naturæ suis comprobaret ;* " ZWINGLI, *in Hist. Dom. Resurr.* p. 60); it can reveal itself in one place, but is not bound to this one place; it can show itself within the sphere of this world, but is not limited to this sphere. Thus does the Resurrection of the body appear before us adorned with a threefold character of true freedom and beauty, and we are not surprised that with all the attractiveness of our Lord's appearance to His people, yet, nevertheless, something mysterious respecting His personality hovered before their eyes, of which they were scarcely able to give an account to themselves, *see*, for instance, John xxi. 12.

3. Even so does the evening appearance deserve to be named a brilliant revelation of the inner life of the Risen One. There is a reflection of heavenly peace diffused over His whole being, and the comparison between the forty days of His second life and those of His temptation in the wilderness furnishes matter for a continuous antithesis. His whole previous life lies as a completed whole before His eyes, and the marks of the nails which He bears have become the honorable insignia of His love, and yet it is plainly shown that His word, "It is I Myself," is, in the most extended sense of the word, true, and that death has indeed changed His condition, but not His heart. As the appearance at the Sea of Tiberias, John xxi. 1-14, shows a noticeable coincidence with the miraculous draft of fishes, Luke v. 1-11, so also does this evening appearance with the walking of our Lord at night upon the water of the sea, John vi. 15-21. There also He finds His disciples terrified, but rejoices and composes them by lovingly assuring them of His nearness, and stills with a single word the storm which had risen in their heart. Just such appearances as this could afterwards give His witnesses the right to utter themselves in so decided a tone as Peter, *e. g.*, Acts x. 40-42.

4. Christian Anthropology has to thank this appearance of the Lord for declarations which confirm the specific distinction between spirit and body, define the conception of spirit, and raise above all doubt not only the objective, but also the subjective, identity of the man before and after his death.

5. In the Lord we behold the image of that perfection prepared beyond the grave for all His people, a peace subject to no disturbance, a glorified body that no longer checks the spirit, but serves it; a clear, yet no longer painful, recollection of the previous life, with its now accomplished conflict; a blessed fellowship and reunion with all who are here connected with us by bonds of the Spirit; an unimpeded continuation, for the glory of God, of the activity interrupted by death. This, and yet far more, which no eye hath seen and no ear hath heard, will the life of the Resurrection be for the subject and for the King of the Divine kingdom.

HOMILETICAL AND PRACTICAL.

And at evening time it shall be light, Zech. xiv. 7.—The King of peace in the midst of unquiet subjects.—The Easter feast a feast of Peace.—How faith on the Risen One bestows peace: 1. In the doubting understanding; 2. in the disquiet of conscience; 3. in the sorrows of life; 4. in the fear of the future; 5. in the view of death.—Unbelief embitters to itself even the most exquisite hours of life. —How the Lord gradually lifts His people to the participation of His peace.—" It is I Myself: " 1. The Lord feels that He is the same; 2. He shows that He is the same; 3. He will as the same be recognized and honored by His own.—When the disciple of the Lord is doubtful, the Risen One still shows him His hands and His feet, nailed through for His everlasting salvation.—Not all unbelief is equally guilty.—" When I was yet with you," the looking back out of the future into the present life.—The prophetic Scripture the best key : 1. To the enigma of the manifestation of Christ; 2. to the enigma of the life of the Christian.—As a WHOLE will the Scripture be regarded and esteemed.—Not to isolate, but to combine, the way to the knowledge of the truth.—Our Lord : 1. Kindles the light for the eye ; 2. opens the eye to the light.

HEUBNER :— Jesus Himself seeks out His disciples to strengthen them.—In reference to the realm of spirits, unbelief, superstition, and faith are to be carefully distinguished.—The Christian should be unterrified even amid the presentiments of a higher world.—The Lord will hereafter be yet recognizable even as Man.—The marks of Jesus' wounds are fearful to His enemies, precious to His friends.—The difficulty of faith in Christ exalts its value and its power.— Christ's love is not altered by His exaltation.—He received from them bodily food, and they receive spiritual food.—The Resurrection of Christ impresses on His words the seal of truth.—The understanding of Scripture is indispensable to religion.

On the Pericope.—HEUBNER :—The first evening which the Risen One spent in the midst of His disciples.—The blessed consequences of the Resurrection of Jesus to His disciples.—The certainty of the testimony of the disciples for the Resurrection of Jesus.—ARNDT :—The Easter evening, what did it bring to the apostles? what did it bring to us all ? 1. Full certainty; 2. deep peace; 3. apostolic power.— PALMER :—Our Lord's: 1. Greeting; 2. commission; 3. promise (John xx. 19-23).—DIETZ :—What is the way in which one arrives at Easter peace?—ALBRECHT : — What the glorious gift of Christ has brought us with His Resurrection: 1. Peace before us ; 2. within us; 3. among us; 4. around us.—KRAUSSOLD :—Where do we find the peace of God which the world cannot give?—AHLFELD:—What the Lord has brought to His people from the grave: 1. Himself; 2. His peace; 3. the last seal of His Resurrection (comp. John xx. 22).—COUARD :—The blessed activity of the Risen One in the circle of His disciples.—BOBE :—Whereby do we attain to a blessed faith ?—*See* further on John xx. 19-23.

C. Over the Opposition of Israel and the Heathen World. (Intimated Ch. XXIV. 46–48.)

46 And [*He*] said unto them, Thus it is written, and thus it behooved Christ to suffer,
and to [written that the Christ should suffer and should[1]] rise from the dead the third
47 day: And that repentance and remission of sins should be preached in his name among
48 [or, for] all nations, beginning at [from] Jerusalem. And [om., And] ye are witnesses
of these things.

[1] Vs. 46.—According to the reading of Tischendorf, οὕτως γέγραπται παθεῖν, κ.τ.λ., [Meyer, Tregelles, Alford. Lachmann brackets the suspected words.—C. S.] The addition of the *Recepta*: καὶ οὕτως ἔδει, appears to have been interpolated for the sake of perspicuity, and is wanting in B., C.[1], D., [Cod. Sin.;] L., Coptic, Æthiopian, Itala, &c.

EXEGETICAL AND CRITICAL.

Vs. 46. And He said unto them.—In the organic articulation of this last chapter of Luke there is found a noteworthy climax. After he, in the narrative of the first Easter Message, has pointed us to the victory which the Risen One had accomplished over the might of sin and death, he has in a triad of appearances delineated the triumph which He celebrated over the doubt and unbelief of His first disciples. But the nearer the Lord comes to the final goal of His earthly manifestation, so much the more strongly does it come into view that the conquering Lion of the tribe of Judah is continually pressing forward *ad altiora*. It is true, His words only testify by intimations as to the victorious hope with which He casts a parting look upon the whole Jewish and heathen world before He bids His disciples the last farewell. Here also He begins with the mention of the word, in order then with a promise of the Spirit to conclude His meeting with His own and His instructions to them.

Thus it is written.—Yet once again a γέγραπται, as at the beginning of His first life. We might assume (Meyer) that ὅτι was meant to indicate the cause why He had opened their understanding (vs. 45), if here the thread joining the different elements were not so slack that it perhaps appears better not to undertake the stating of any connection. The mention of the Resurrection on the third day is perhaps an indirect proof that at least these words of our Lord were not uttered on the day of His Resurrection. Here also, as to the rest, as in vs. 26, and throughout the Apostolic writings, suffering and glory are inseparably joined together.

Vs. 47. And that . . . should be preached, κηρυχθῆναι also depends upon γέγραπται and sets forth to us the preaching of the Gospel among the Gentiles and Jews, as the fruit of the Divine predetermination and of the fulfilment of the prophecies. According to Matthew and Mark also, the Lord, upon His departure from the earth, gives a commission for a general preaching of the Gospel, but in Luke again it bears a peculiar character. It is, first of all, a κήρυγμα ἐπ' ὀνόματι Ἰησ., that is, a preaching which takes place on the basis of this name, and therefore borrows the significance and authority from Him in whose name and in whose commission it takes place. Withal it must proceed from Jerusalem, and from there spread itself over all the nations. Comp. Acts i. 8. A proof of our Lord's great love of sinners on the one hand, and of the world-vanquishing destiny of the Gospel on the other hand, and which in the broad Pauline Gospel of Luke stands surely in its just place. Finally, while elsewhere there is only mention of the Gospel in general, here in particular μετάνοια and ἄφεσις τῶν ἁμαρτ. are spoken of. Even as was the case with John the Baptist, and afterwards with the apostles, *see* Acts ii. 38; iii. 19; xxvi. 18.

Vs. 48. Witnesses of these things.—Meyer, who here perhaps binds himself almost too strictly to the letter, insists on referring this τούτων not only to our Lord's death and Resurrection, but also to the just-mentioned commission for the proclamation of the Gospel. But precisely because they were to carry out this latter they could not at the same time be witnesses thereof, and, strictly speaking, the Ascension of the Lord, which at this moment had not yet taken place, would have had then to remain excluded from their testimony. Nowhere are the apostles represented as witnesses of that which they themselves accomplished, but everywhere as witnesses of that which the Lord had done. Therefore, we think it is better to refer τούτων to all the here-named facts of the life of the Lord, which was concluded by His departure to the Father, the great centre of which was, however, the Resurrection, comp. Acts i. 8, and 22.

DOCTRINAL AND ETHICAL.

1. The preaching of the Gospel proceeding from Jerusalem directed to all nations, the fulfilment of the prophetic word, Ps. cx. 2; Is. ii. 2–4; Micah, iv. 2–4.

2. The preaching of Repentance and Forgiveness most intimately connected together. The μετάνοια is an alteration of the inward disposition, which precedes πίστις, upon which latter the ἄφεσις τῶν ἁμαρτ. follows. The faith, however, in this latter, which is granted and received freely, must of itself lead to ἁγιασμός, the continuation of μετάνοια.

3. Christian missions here appear before our eyes as an institution of the Lord Himself, and as a holy vocation of the church. The apostles have not to remain at Jerusalem until the last Jew shall receive their testimony, but, on the other hand, after having there made the beginning, they must then as soon as possible extend as widely as possible the circle of their activity, and found the kingdom of God by means of their testimony. All which in the activity of supposed or real successors to the apostolic commission does not coincide with the actual witnessing function is here indirectly, but plainly enough excluded. Precisely, then, when the messengers of the Gospel are nothing more and nothing less than witnesses, do they walk in the footsteps of Him who Himself has been The Faithful Witness upon earth, John xx. 22; 1 Tim. vi. 13; Rev. i. 5.

HOMILETICAL AND PRACTICAL.

The institution of the preaching of the Gospel the last and noblest command of our Lord.—The command to begin the preaching of the Gospel at Jerusalem: 1. Surprising to the enemies; 2. beneficent for the friends of the Lord; 3. honorable for Himself.—This command a proof of: 1. The historical truth; 2. the heavenly origin; 3. the blessed goal of the Gospel.—As the Gospel proceeded from Jerusalem so will it return to Jerusalem.—Even yet the inner renewal must begin nowhere else than from the sinful Jerusalem in the heart.—The Commission for the preaching of the Gospel: 1. What must be preached? 2. in what name? 3. from whence? 4. how far abroad?—What the world owes to the last commandment of the Lord.—The preaching of the Lord a testimony: 1. Of Whom? 2. through Whom? 3. for Whom?

STARKE:—Christ directs His disciples to the Scripture not less than His enemies.—*Nova Bibl. Tub.*:—Repentance, forgiveness, &c., the blessed fruits of Christ's Resurrection.—Without repentance no forgiveness.—OSIANDER:—The apostles' writings concerning Jesus are a genuine testimony, for they have testified to what they saw and heard, and, moreover, have received from heaven. Who, then, would not believe them?—HEUBNER:—The main substance of the Christian preaching is Repentance, and Forgiveness of sins.—The Risen One is Lord of the earth.—Whoever gainsays the apostles gainsays Jesus.

THIRD SECTION.

THE GLEAMING CROWN.

CHAPTER XXIV. 49–53.

The Prophetic Promise; the Priestly Benediction; the Kingly Glory.

(Parallel with Mark xvi. 19; Acts i. 3–9.)

49 And, behold, I send the promise of my Father upon you: but tarry ye in the city
50 of Jerusalem [om., of Jerusalem[1]], until ye be endued with power from on high. And he led them out as far as to Bethany, and he lifted up his hands, and blessed them.
51 And it came to pass, while he blessed them, he was parted from them, and carried up
52 into heaven.[2] And they worshipped him,[3] and returned to Jerusalem with great joy:
53 And were continually in the temple, praising and blessing God.[4] Amen.

[1] Vs. 49.—The Ἱερουσαλήμ of the *Recepta* is decidedly spurious. [Omitted by B., C.[1], D., Cod. Sin., L, Itala, Vulgate, &c.—C. C. S.]

[2] and [3] Vss. 51, 52.—The words: ἀνεφέρετο εἰς τὸν οὐρανόν and προσκυνήσαντες αὐτόν are, remarkably enough, omitted by the same authorities—D., several copies of the Itala, &c., see Tischendorf. Apparently the eye of the copyist slipped from καὶ α(νεφέρετο) to καὶ α(υτοι), and he overlooked προσκυνησαντες, while he confounded αυτοι with αυτου. We thus comprehend better (against De Wette), how this was omitted, than how it should have been interpolated if not original. [Cod. Sin. omits the words; a much more important fact than their omission in D.—C. C. S.]

[4] Vs. 53.—In some MSS. αινουντες και, in others και ευλογουντες are wanting. Perhaps errors of a wearied hand at the end of the Gospel. At all events, the number and the weight of the authorities, [B., C.[1], Cod. Sin., L. omit α. κ., D. omits κ. ε.,] is not so great as to make it needful with Griesbach to suspect the former or with Tischendorf to omit the latter.

EXEGETICAL AND CRITICAL.

Vs. 49. **I send the promise of My Father.**—Here the Lord speaks of the Holy Ghost, comp. Acts i. 4–8, whom He had often before His death repeatedly promised, and He calls Him an ἐπαγγελία πατρός, not *quia sibi promissum* (Grotius), nor merely inasmuch as God has promised the bestowment of the gifts of the Spirit by prophetic oracles (Meyer), but with retrospective reference to utterances like John xiv. 16, *et alibi*, and to the symbolical act, John xx. 22. That this first actual, but yet preliminary and prophetical, communication of the Spirit did not, therefore, exclude a later but abundant communication on the day of Pentecost lies in the nature of the case. The meaning of our Lord is given more fully by Luke when he, Acts i. 4, makes Him speak of the promise of the Father, ἣν ἠκούσατέ μου.

Καθίσατε.—The command which Luke gives to remain in the Capital is in conflict with Matthew (De Wette) only if we consider the silence of the former respecting the Galilean appearance as a denial, and forget that this last command was only given after this and immediately before the Ascension of the Lord. The remaining at Jerusalem was to be not only a μένειν, but a retired, although temporary and not long continued καθίζειν, because they must there wait till the promise of the Spirit was fulfilled, and they were not to wait in vain, but to be clothed with δύναμις ἐξ ὕψους, in consequence of the fulfilment of the promise of the Father. It is noticeable how Luke, at the end, as also at the beginning of his gospel, ch. i. 35, unites most intimately the conceptions of Spirit and power, without, however, entirely identifying them. As to the rest, we must compare Acts i. with this whole concluding address and with the account of the Ascension, and in the treatment of this first chapter of Acts there will be occasion to discuss both more at length.

Vs. 50. **He led them out.**—Out of Jerusalem,

where He was, together with His disciples, on the fortieth, as well as on the first day.—**As far as Bethany** (ἕως εἰς, as far as to the neighborhood of Bethany. The reading of Lachmann, who has πρός Β., does not appear to us worthy of acceptance.) The statement of the Acts that the disciples returned from the Mount of Olives is only apparently in conflict with this, if we consider that it was over this mountain that the way to the beloved Bethany passed, which lay on its eastern declivity; then the proceeding to this mountain, from whose summit our Lord appears to have ascended, may be called a leading out to the neighborhood of Bethany, although our Lord no longer entered into the last-named place. Perhaps, also, the name Bethany was given, not only to the particular village, but also to the whole region round about, to which also the Mount of Olives belongs. Thus, also, is the tradition justified which designates as the actual place of the Ascension, not the plain, but the middle of the three summits of the Mount of Olives, while, according to it, the angelic appearance shortly after the Ascension took place upon the highest summit. *See* SCHUBERT, *l. c.* ii. p. 519.

He lifted up His hands.—Comp. Lev. ix. 22. After the prophetical promise, there follows the high-priestly benediction, as it were from the threshold of the heavenly sanctuary into which He is about to enter. "*Jam non imposuit manus.*" The Epistle to the Hebrews, with its Pauline coloring contains the more particular elaboration of this beautiful image, in which the nature and destiny of the whole earthly and heavenly life of the Lord are, as it were, completely symbolized. In the midst of (ἐν), not after (μετά), thus blessing is He parted from them. Διέστη ἀπ' αὐτῶν, He goes back a few steps from them, and immediately after that He is taken up. The passive ἀνεφέρ. does not require us to understand angels or other means by which He was lifted up from the earth, but it leaves room, at all events, for the cloud of which Luke, in His more particular account, Acts i. 9, speaks.

Vs. 52. **With great joy.**—Even in such little additions the fresh Pauline character of Luke does not belie itself. That they could now rejoice, in spite of the separation, nay, even over the departure of the Lord, because He was thereby exalted unto glory, and they should now soon receive the promise of the Father, is a speaking proof of the great progress which they in this forty days had made in this school of the best of Masters.

Vs. 53. **In the temple.**—More particularly defined "in the upper chamber," which probably belonged to the buildings of the temple, Acts i. 12; ii. 1. In the Doxological conclusion of his gospel also, Luke shows himself a genuine Paulinist, comp. Rom. xi. 36.

DOCTRINAL AND ETHICAL.

1. Although the account of the Ascension at the end of the Gospel of Luke, considered entirely by itself, and from a strictly historical point of view, does not perfectly satisfy us, yet the course of his representation offers us an advantage not to be rejected, that we from it learn so much the better to understand the near connection of the Resurrection and the Ascension. Over against the historical arbitrariness which almost identifies the Resurrection and the Ascension, as though the forty days had produced no essential alteration in the condition of our Lord, stands the shallow external interpretation, as though He after His Resurrection had continued to live yet forty days *on earth* in a wider or nearer circle, indeed, in separation from other men, and now, on the fortieth, is to be supposed to have exchanged converse with men for the society of angels. The one opinion, as little as the other, does full justice to the miracle of the Ascension. Without doubt, it must be apprehended as a special, and that as the last, stage in the history of the earthly manifestation of our Lord, but, at the same time, as a necessary consequence and as the most excellent crown of His Resurrection. "The Ascension of the Lord was the completion of the Resurrection and the perfect expression of the exaltation." Martensen. Or to use Tholuck's language (*Stund. Christl. Andacht*, p. 524): "His Resurrection is a Glorification, yet not a full Glorification." From this position it causes comparatively little difficulty that Luke does not so sharply distinguish the appearance at the end of which the Ascension took place, from the other. Had the last appearance of our Lord not ended with the Ascension, then we should have had decidedly to assume that the one before the last had ended with such a miracle, whether with a visible or invisible one. "The opponents of the history of the Resurrection could, therefore, not have got the least advantage, even if they had succeeded in setting aside the actual history of the Ascension. The whole history of the Resurrection has an Ascensional character; the whole history of the Resurrection is to be regarded as a giant tree of His Ascension in the wider sense, as the crown of which the actual Ascension stands forth. Our opponents, therefore, with the setting aside of it, would only have cracked the summit of the tree, or rather, only have broken off a branch of the same. For the apostles, the Ascension was self-evidently understood from the Resurrection." LANGE, *L. J.*, ii. p. 1766.

2. By this, however, it is by no means meant that the actual fact of a bodily visible Ascension of our Lord on the fortieth day is doubtful, or of subordinate importance. It has been asserted, among others, by Meyer, that quite early a twofold tradition grew up in this respect. According to the former, our Lord ascended to heaven on the very evening of the Resurrection (Mark, Gospel of Luke), according to the other, not till the fortieth day (Acts). But the indefinite statement in Mark, ch. xvi. 19: μετὰ τὸ λαλῆσαι αὐτοῖς, surely does not constrain us to assume that our Lord, according to this gospel, ascended immediately after the preceding utterances; just as well might it be deduced from vs. 20 that the disciples, on the very same night or the following morning, had begun to preach and to do miracles. And, as it respects Luke, is it conceivable that he in his gospel should represent our Lord as leaving the earth in the night-time, when He had already at evening revealed Himself at Emmaus, and had appeared at least three hours after to the Eleven? In truth, unless we will invent absurdities for the Evangelist, it seems that we are constrained to assume that he, by the statement of a more exact chronology in the Acts, has not contradicted his gospel, but decidedly complemented it; how, moreover, assuming that his earlier account contained an actual incorrectness, could he have omitted to recall this, at least, with a brief word? Were his more detailed narrative to be put to the account of a later more or less mythical tradition, the pious invention would certainly not

have contented itself with a final act of our Lord's life so little pompous and brilliant, and if Luke, at the conclusion of his first work, had already the design of writing afterwards the history of the apostles also, he might, even in the interest of his historical pragmatism, consider it as desirable to touch here on our Lord's Ascension only with a brief mention, and at the beginning of the history of the kingdom of God to come back more particularly to it. In no case can the course of the event itself offer convincing ground for doubt and contradiction. It may be called laughable, when some, in reference to the body of our Lord in the beginning of its glorified condition, will be talking about the laws of gravitation and the force of attraction. Heaven, it is true, is everywhere where God reveals His glory, but nothing hinders us, on the position of the Scripture, from supposing a locality of the creation where God permits His glory to be seen more immediately than anywhere else, and to conceive our Lord as repairing directly thither. Though it has been said a thousand times and repeated that we are not to understand heaven as a *place*, but as a *condition*, and must not here speak of a *ποῦ*, but only of a *πῶς*, yet we confess that we can only conceive the enjoyment of this condition as experienced in a locality where one is separated from this visible world. An exaggerated spiritualism might here easily mislead to Acosmism and Pantheism. And finally, as respects the often advanced objection, derived from the partial silence of the sacred authors, this silence appears to us neither so general nor so inexplicable as has been already countless times asserted. Respecting that of Matthew, *see* LANGE on Matthew, p. 561. John evidently knows a visible Ascension, ch. iii. 13; vi. 62; xx. 17, and must have assumed it, unless we are to suppose that he doubted of the fulfilment of such words uttered by his Master Himself. With Peter it is, 1 Peter iii. 22, also distinguished as a separate statement from His Resurrection, even as the descent into hell. Even so with Paul, Ephes. i. 19, 20; ii. 5, 6; iv. 8-10; Rom. viii. 34; Col. iii. 1, and in the Epistle to the Hebrews there is even almost more weight laid upon the Ascension of our Lord than upon His Resurrection. In short, in reference to most of the epistles we must agree with the opinion: "Even though the outward fact is not here found, yet so much the more is the dogmatically important consequence of the thus effected exaltation, the sitting at the right hand of God, found throughout the whole New Testament, and that in expressions which also indicate the event itself" (SCHMIDT, *Bibl. Theol. d. N. S.* i. p. 189). And as respects the gospels, all of them have set forth the Risen One in His glory, although two of them are silent as to the moment in which He has ascended this highest degree. Nay, this Ascension itself, the final goal of the earthly manifestation of the Lord, what is it itself in its turn but a transition to a new, but by no means to a last, period of His miraculous history? Here, according to our opinion, lies the deepest ground of the seemingly enigmatical phenomenon, that the miracle on the Mount of Olives is not placed more strongly in the foreground. No final point, but a point of rest, is it. The Lord is indeed gone away, but in order to return again, and the whole heavenly life into which the Ascension introduced Him is only a great interval, comprehending centuries, between His first and His second appearance. The angels themselves declare it: the history of the Lord in relation to the earth is with the Ascension not accomplished, but is only momentarily interrupted, in order afterwards to be continued. If a John and a Matthew in this hope saw the Lord ascend, why should they then feel themselves peremptorily obliged to fix the last moment of their being with Him with such diplomatic conscientiousness, as though thereby between the Master and the earth all connection were now and forever done away?

3. Respecting the idea of the Ascension in connection with the corporeality of our Lord, and respecting the distinction of the Lutheran and the Reformed conception, Dogmatics and the History of Doctrines must speak. "Oh, that we might yet learn to stop at the right place!" R. Stier.

4. Our Lord's bodily and visible Ascension is the worthy crown of the history of His earthly life. Many a word that He uttered is thereby most strikingly confirmed (John vi. 62; xx. 17; Matt. xxviii. 18, *et alibi*), and the harmony of the events of His life becomes only through this miracle perfected. A second death, even had it been ever so soft, would have taken away the whole significance of His Resurrection, and the poetical expression (Πάσχ.): "Even as Moses' grave, so was His never seen," can only elicit an exclamation of astonishment and displeasure. "He a grave, He, who swallowed up death eternally!" (Olshausen). Whoever contents himself with saying that He went to the Father, although one does not know *how, where*, or *when*, such a one lets his history end with an unsatisfactory note of interrogation, and unthankfully repels the satisfactory solution which His first witnesses have given. Now, His manifestation displays itself to our eye as a ring whose ending is lost again in its beginning, while both Bethlehem and the Mount of Olives bear the stamp of a still and hidden, but even thereby heavenly greatness. And as the Ascension of the Lord thus first diffuses over His person a perfectly satisfying light (John vi. 62; xvi. 28), so does this event stand as well with the incipient perfection as with the happy continuation of His work in direct connection. Never would the apostles without this miracle have been freed from the last remains of their earthly-minded expectations; nor did they, on the other hand, become by this very means capable of receiving the Spirit of truth, of love, and of power. Never, so long as the visible presence of the Lord on a spot of earth had remained, could a kingdom have been founded that embraced all nations, and as little would, in this case, the Church have been able to maintain herself without an incessant intervention of continually increasing miracles. Now, raised above all finite limits, the Lord reigns everywhere where His word is preached in the power of the Holy Spirit, and, far from bringing any harm, it is His departure which for His people has become a source of incalculable gain (John xvi. 7). This whole event reveals the full glory of the kingdom of God, is surety for the highest blessing of the kingdom of God (vs. 49), and prophesies the final perfection of the kingdom of God. No wonder that the Ascension also has been painted and sung by the Christian art of all ages. We have only to mention the names in the first sphere, of Raphael, Peter Perugino, Titian, Paul Veronese, Ricci, Raphael Mengs, and others, and in the other the venerable Bede, Tersteegen, Lavater, Knapp, Luis de Leon, not to mention many others.

5. Superficially considered, the homage which the apostles bring to the glorified Saviour appears to be more or less on a level with the reverence which

often was rendered to the kings of the Orient, especially to the King of kings, the Messiah. *See* Matt. ii. 2; xx. 20. But if we consider that this homage was now offered by the disciples of the Lord at the moment when they see Him crowned with superhuman glory, and honor in Him more than ever the bearer of the Divine nature and majesty, then we shall hardly be content with the assertion that our Lord was here worshipped in His Messianic dignity, but must, on the contrary, acknowledge that He here, not only on account of His kingly rank, but also and above all, for His Divine nature, deserves the honor of adoration. Thus do we find in Luke xxiv. 52 an intimation how the command, John v. 23, must be understood and followed.

6. The command of our Lord, before His departure, that His disciples should remain at Jerusalem, testifies as well to His wisdom as the final promise of the Holy Spirit gives witness of His love and might. But, at the same time, there lies in the manner in which His first friends fulfilled this command (Acts i. 12–14), an apologetic element that must not be overlooked. *With one accord* do the disciples remain together; this is the first blessing of the exaltation of our Lord; now that their visible centre is wanting, the young church feels the necessity of an inward union more intimate than ever. *Undisturbed* and publicly are they ten days continually together; a proof that they had not stolen the corpse, and that the Jewish council itself does not believe its own charge. *Composed* and quietly do they wait; this is what no excited enthusiasts do. *Praying* do they expect the fulfilment of the promise of the Lord; the miracle of Pentecost was thereby a direct hearing of prayer, of whose inestimable blessing the consideration of the history of the apostles will now give further testimony.

HOMILETICAL AND PRACTICAL.

The friends of the Lord are brought unto the school of waiting; therewith is their inner training perfected; so then; so previously (Jacob, Moses, David, &c.); so even yet.—"I will send upon you the promise of My Father." Thus can only the Son of the Father, none of the servants, speak; how altogether differently Elijah, 2 Kings ii. 10.—The Benediction of the departing Lord: 1. The crown of His earthly manifestation; 2. the symbol of His heavenly life; 3. the prophecy of His coming in glory.—The Lord departs in order to remain.—The exalted King of the kingdom of God, the worthy object of the most reverential homage.—How can the disciples return with great joy to Jerusalem? 1. Faith sees in this farewell the highest glorifying of Jesus; 2. Love thinks of His gain, not of its own loss; 3. Hope waits unshaken for the fulfilment of all His promises.—Jerusalem the grave of the Old, the cradle of the New, Covenant.—The inward connection of the young Church with the old Israelitish temple.—God's glory the last word of our narrative, at the same time the concluding word of our whole gospel, and the final accord of the whole history of the world.

The Ascension of our Lord in its high significance: 1. For Himself, *a.* the confirmation of His words, *b.* the clearing up of the events of His life, *c.* the beginning of His most powerful and blessed activity; 2. for His apostles, *a.* the perfection of their training, *b.* the energy of their labor, *c.* the prophecy of their future; 3. for His people all, *a.* the Ascension the honor of mankind (Heb. ii. 5–9), *b.* the way of the renewal of the sinner (the Holy Spirit), *c.* the source of the joy, rest, and hope of Christians.—The Ascension a hearing of the Lord's own prayer, John xvii. 5.—The feast of the Ascension the feast of the coronation of the Lord. This coronation: 1. The end of the Saviour's strife; 2. the beginning of the highest honor; 3. the source of the richest blessing; 4. the pledge of the most blessed hope.—What sees the Christian when He on the Ascension morn directs his look believingly towards heaven? (comp. Acts vii. 56): 1. A glorified Son of Man; 2. an Almighty King; 3. an ever near Friend; 4. an open place of refuge; 5. an approaching triumph. But to see all this, we must (vs. 55), even as the first Christian martyr, be: *a.* a disciple of the Lord, *b.* filled with the Holy Spirit, and *c.* have our eyes directed towards heaven.—Heaven and earth considered in the light of the Ascension morn.—The Ascension the last palpable revelation of our Lord on earth: 1. His majesty; 2. His wisdom, *a.* time, *b.* place, *c.* witnesses, *d.* circumstances, *e.* consequences, of the Ascension; 3. His beneficent faithfulness to His own, comp. Matt. xxviii. 20.

STARKE:—OSIANDER:—Whom God sends into the holy ministry, them does He also equip with the necessary gifts.—To the receiving of the Holy Spirit there belongs a patient waiting in prayer and consideration of the word.—Whom Jesus blesses, he is and remains blessed.—Beautiful and edifying is it when parents depart from the world, for they even thus bless their children.—BRENTIUS:—Christ has at His Ascension bequeathed us the blessing, why do we longer fear the curse?—*Bibl. Wirt.:*—Jesus departed to prepare the place.—HEDINGER:—Thus have we then a sure and open entrance to the sanctuary that is within the heavens, Heb. x. 19, 20.—J. HALL:—Rejoice, oh thou holy soul, for thy last conflict also shall be crowned with triumph.—The fellowship of the Spirit makes a fellowship in the worship of God.—Servants of God labor, pray, suffer, and praise God in fellowship.—OSIANDER:—Jesus is ours also, with all His treasures, therefore let us praise and glorify Him with the Father and the Holy Spirit.

HEUBNER:—The place of the Passion of Christ also the place of His glorification.—With blessing did He come, with blessing did He part.—How different this blessed parting from that on the cross!—The apostles showed after the Resurrection far more reverence for Jesus; they had a sense of His Godhead, therefore we read here for the first time: they worshipped Him.—Worship befits Christ, else would He not have received it.—The disciples return back, in prayer unseparated from Christ, no longer alone. —ARNDT:—The Ascension of Christ the perfection: 1. Of His prophetical; 2. of His high-priestly; 3. of His kingly, office. — SCHLEIERMACHER: — The promises of the departing Redeemer.—PALMER:—The lovely position in which the departing Redeemer hath left us behind in this world: *a.* above our heads we have an opened heaven, *b.* above our eyes a blessed home, and *c.* under our feet the way which the feet of the Lord have smoothed and hallowed.— RUPERTI:—Why do we stand after the Saviour has ascended and look towards heaven?—SCHMID:— What the earth is to them who look after the Risen Saviour towards heaven.—Why does the Saviour point us at His Ascension to the Holy Spirit?—ARLFELD:—The last will of our Lord Jesus Christ.— STEINMEYER:—The separation through the Ascension is the source of true union.—SOUCHON:—The comfort which the Ascension of Jesus Christ assures to us.—THOLUCK:—The refreshing thoughts to which the history of the Ascension leads us: 1. The place of His suffering the place of His parting; 2. veiled is His beginning, veiled is His exit; 3. the conclusion of His ways is blessing for His people; 4. He has departed from us and yet has remained to us; 5. He remains veiled from His people till He shall appear in brightness.—W. HOFACKER:—The significance of the Ascension-day: 1. As a day of the richest and most glorious blessing; 2. as a day of the grandest homage; 3. as a day of the most joyful encouragement.—HARLESS:—The way to the blessed understanding of the Ascension of Christ.—VON KAPFF:—The Ascension of Christ as: 1. The glorification of Jesus; 2. of our human nature; 3. of our whole earth. —SCHUUR:—Heart and soul towards heaven! 1. Here is darkness, there is light; 2. here is strangeness, there is home; 3. here is combat, there is victorious palm; 4. here is sorrow, there is bliss.— FLOREY:—The Ascension of our Lord the crown of His glory.

Compare further on this whole section the welldigested essay of Dr. H. G. HASSE: *Das Leben des verklärten Erlösers im Himmel, nach den eigenen Aussprüchen des Herrn, ein Beitrag zur Bibl. Theol.* Leipsic, 1854, and *Die Christl. Glaubenslehre, herausgegeben von dem Calwer Verein,* 2 *Theil,* 2 *Abthlg.* pp. 266-286, Stuttgart, 1857.

www.ingramcontent.com/pod-product-compliance
Lightning Source LLC
Chambersburg PA
CBHW031934290426
44108CB00011B/546